Beginning Writer's Answer Book

Beginning Writer's Answer Book

Edited by
Kirk Polking
and Rose Adkins

Writer's
Digest
Books

Cincinnati, Ohio

Newly revised edition, 1984

Copyright 1984, 1971, 1968 by Writer's Digest. Title of First Edition: *The Beginning Writer's Handbook*. Printed in the United States of America. All rights reserved. No part of this book may be reproduced in any form or by any electronic or mechanical means including information storage and retrieval systems without permission in writing from the publisher, except by a reviewer who may quote brief passages in a review. Writer's Digest Books, 9933 Alliance Road, Cincinnati OH 45242.

Library of Congress Cataloging in Publication Data
Main entry under title:
Beginning writer's answer book.
  Bibliography: p.
  Includes index.
  1. Authorship—Handbooks, manuals, etc. I. Polking, Kirk. II. Adkins, Rose.
PN147.B42   1984   808'.02   84-3599
ISBN 0-89879-131-6

Design by Charleen Catt Lyon

Acknowledgments

Contributing and Consulting Editors: Joan Bloss, John Brady, Jane Budd, Leslie Cannon, Kay Cassill, Theodore Cheney, Jean Chimsky, Nancy Dibble, Connie Emerson, Vera Henry, Melissa Hoel, Lois Horowitz, Judson Jerome, Barb Kuroff, Michael Larsen, Victor Marton, Jack McKee, Leonard Meranus, Hugh Rawson, Ellen Roberts, David Rosenthal, Evelyn Stenbock, Michael Straczynski, George Wagner, the editorial associates of Writer's Digest School and Writer's Digest Criticism Service, and the authors and friends of Writer's Digest Books.

Contents

Preface

Magazine writer Frank Thomas says, "I've been guided by the maxim that if you ask a question you may seem ignorant for the moment; but if you do not ask questions you may be ignorant forever." This newly revised and expanded edition of *The Beginning Writer's Answer Book* anticipates all the questions a writer has about writing and selling his work.

Included in this completely revised edition are questions writers most often ask the editors of *Writer's Digest* arranged under subject categories for the reader's convenience. An in-depth cross index provides additional aid in locating topics.

Whether you are just starting out and need to know the specifics of manuscript preparation and submission, or you are a more seasoned writer looking for details about book proposals and contracts, you'll find the answers in these pages. You'll find explanations of the new copyright law and how it affects the writer, how to avoid suits for libel and invasion of privacy and how to use a pen name.

You'll learn what editors mean by certain terms they use and the pros and cons of collaboration with another writer or a photographer. You'll learn whether the IRS considers you a "business" or a "hobby" writer and what kind of deductions you can take. Individual chapters discuss the specific problems of newspaper and magazine writers, fiction and nonfiction writers, poets and screenwriters.

Included in the appendix are sample manuscript pages and a query letter; a chart of the average length in words or pages of short stories, novels, TV and radio scripts, speeches and children's books; and details on how to submit various types of manuscripts.

For more in-depth information on writing subjects, the reader is referred in the text to books and reference volumes that are included in the Bibliography. *Writer's Digest*, the monthly magazine containing market information and professional advice for writers, has been indexed in the *Readers' Guide to Periodical Literature* from January 1968 through December 1977; and in *Access: The Supplementary Index to Periodicals* from January 1978 to the present.

Keep in mind that information included here is meant to serve as a general guideline and is not intended to substitute for legal advice. If you have a question about a specific clause in your book contract or are unsure about current tax laws, consult an appropriate attorney or accountant.

If you have a writing-related question that is not included in this book, by all means drop the editors a note. But be sure to include an SASE. What's an SASE? A self-addressed, stamped envelope. For similar terms, see chapter 5!

The Editors

Beginning Writer's Answer Book

1 How Do I Know if I Have What It Takes?

Novelist Willa Cather insisted "most of the basic material a writer works with is acquired before the age of fifteen." And yet, the person who only starts thinking about becoming a writer at middle age has a lifetime of living and learning to bring to the task. Whether you are fifteen or fifty, here are some questions and answers that may erase some of your own self-doubts.

Writer Qualifications

Q. What does it take to become a writer?
A. Curiosity, energy, persistence in learning, a willingness to research, and an awareness of human behavior all are needed in the writing field. Curiosity generates ideas and sustains interest to carry a writer through the process of writing articles, stories, or books. A higher-than-average energy level helps, since a writer must sometimes work long and irregular hours to meet deadlines or to accomplish the writing while the words are flowing smoothly. Persistence in learning is important. For any writer, a liberal arts education, while not absolutely necessary, is certainly an asset. There are, however, many self-taught writers who have become successful through determination, dedication to the craft, discipline, and hard work.

A nonfiction writer directly encounters people when conducting interviews, while a fiction writer observes people and perceives the motivations of human behavior. Research, often the key to regular sales, broadens general knowledge, sharpens the mind, and uncovers new territory for a writer.

Finally, you'll definitely need a knowledge of the markets and their needs if you hope to have your work published.

Writers Made or Born?

Q. I am interested in writing, but am not sure I have the aptitude for it. Are all good writers born with writing talent?
A. Certain writers may be born with more innate talent than others, but many factors help to build a successful writing career. The chief "aptitude" a writer needs to be successful is determination to learn and to write well. Anyone with normal intelligence and the energy and willingness to develop as a writer can learn the craft and become successful at it. It is possible

for a talented and gifted writer to lack the energy and persistence necessary to publish with any degree of success. A less talented writer with ambition can produce an impressionable amount of publishable material.

Can an Unknown Sell?

Q. I am a beginner trying to sell stories and articles. Five months have passed and no sale. Would personal letterheads and envelopes help me make my first sale? Does it go against my chances to sell because I have never sold?

A. Personal letterhead is not going to influence the sale of a story or article. A manuscript has to sell itself. You mentioned that you've been trying for five months, but you didn't mention how many submissions that represented. Have you really analyzed your work in light of the type of material these magazine editors are publishing? Five months is not long enough to test your writing skills. If you think your work is good and is marketable—don't give up. Editors to whom you submit your work don't know you've never sold before, so the fact that you haven't sold doesn't diminish your chances to make your first sale.

Too Old to Start Writing?

Q. I recently retired and for the first time in my life I've found the time to write. Am I too old to begin?

A. You're never too old to start writing. Physicians, gerontologists, and other scientists agree that thinking processes, imaginative powers, and facilities for expressing oneself need not diminish with age. In fact, after sixty-five, the combination of leisure time and development of new interests tends to spark creativity. Editors never ask to see your birth certificate. Don't tell editors that you are fifteen or ninety; just write the best piece you possibly can and submit it to suitable markets.

Am I a Writer?

Q. How can I be sure I really have creative writing ability?

A. Many creative writers admit to a compulsive drive to put their thoughts on paper, while others grasp every opportunity to do volunteer writing, just to see their words or bylines in print. Good writers often find knowledgeable people who insist their work is "good enough to be published." Take a correspondence course and have your manuscripts professionally evaluated by an instructor. Join a writers' club, sign up for an evening class in creative writing, or attend a writers' conference. Find ways to get objective feedback from successful writers and editors. Submit manuscripts to appropriate magazines you've studied and see what your acceptance rate is.

Young Author

Q. I have a boxful of short stories, ranging in length from 8 to 110 handwritten pages. Since I'm only fourteen, I wonder if there's any market you could suggest for my work, or am I too young?

A. You are never too young to submit your work to markets, but before you do, read and become familiar with magazines that publish stories similar to yours. There are many young people's publications, and you'll find them listed in *Writer's Market*. Try to decide what age group would be most interested in your stories, then write for sample copies of magazines that are geared to this readership group.

Specialize?

Q. I've been a full-time article writer for the past two years. My articles, on various topics, have appeared in newspapers and magazines. I eventually would like to become a specialist, writing only about business subjects. How can I accomplish my goal? Are there any advantages or disadvantages of being a specialist writer?

A. You have made a wise choice by beginning with a variety of subjects because your name and the quality of your work are already known to some editors. Writing on several topics gives you the opportunity to sample different fields before deciding on your one field of specialization. Establishing yourself as a specialist in business subjects can help bring you assignments from editors who come to rely on your expertise. However, many specialist writers, even after they have established themselves in one field, continue to write on other topics in which they are interested. If a specialist limits his writing to one field, he runs the risk of being so closely associated with it that his credibility in other fields is weakened, thereby making it difficult for him to sell to markets other than those in his special field.

How Much Practice?

Q. I may have to write regularly for a long time before my work becomes publishable. As a part-time writer, how much time each day should I spend writing?

A. You should be spending at least one hour a day on your freelance writing efforts if you expect to accomplish very much. A piano teacher, for example, asks her students to spend at least that much time practicing. Should a freelance writer expect less of himself?

Training Period

Q. How long must I work at writing to become a competent, professional freelancer?

A. Writers—even established ones—are continuously developing their skills, improving their style, and learning more about their writing, their markets, and the world. In that sense, you will never stop striving to better yourself. A good test of your competence is whether your work is being accepted by publications or book publishers that you respect. Being unpublished doesn't necessarily mean that you don't have *writing skills,* but sales will probably make you feel more like a professional writer.

Self-editing

Q. After I've finished the first draft of an article or story I am never quite sure how to edit. What should I look for when revising my manuscript? Is it possible to edit too much?

A. The process of editing is one which each writer develops on his own, with experience, trial and error. There are no definite number of drafts you should write before the piece is finished. Too many writers submit the first draft, with minor revisions, as the final copy. Most successful authors find it useful to set aside the first draft for a day or more before reading and revising it. Some read their work aloud, using the sound of the spoken word to help them find weak points in the work. Still others correct the first draft a page at a time, as it is written. Retyping seems to bring weak areas to light, allowing the writer to strengthen them. The best writers keep editing until they feel they have their best effort.

Your method will develop as you gain experience and may vary from piece to piece, depending on the topic and schedule. Nevertheless, there are some things you should look for in each work you produce. First, read through the rough draft to eliminate redundancies, irrelevancies, statements that are too obvious, unnecessary words, and circumlocutions.

Assess the logical order of the remaining elements. Some writers use highlighters or felt-tip pens to color-code the work's major elements to make sure the structure best suits the point the writer is trying to make. Next, add any necessary new information, and check your word choices. Look for imprecise verbs and weak nouns that require too many modifiers. Finally, check for consistency of verb tense, verb agreement, other grammatical points, punctuation errors, and misspellings. Remember, some changes you will make in editing can be avoided by completing all your necessary research and organizing before you start the actual writing. Also, some retyping can be avoided by using scissors and tape to reorganize earlier drafts.

As important as self-editing is, you must be careful that it isn't overdone by the urge for perfection. If this happens, self-editing can be self-defeating.

Professional Advice

Q. I need some comments and advice on a manuscript that I just finished. I'd like to consult a well-known magazine writer whose work I admire. What's the best way to approach her? Should I send her a copy of the manuscript?
A. Sending your manuscript to a writer for a critique would be an intrusion into the writer's own workday unless you know that writer provides such professional advice for a set fee. You can write and ask, but don't send the manuscript unless you've clarified this first.

Many well-known writers who speak at writers' conferences set aside time for writers' individual questions and informal criticism, so it may be better to ask your questions in those situations.

Writers' Locale

Q. Do writers who live in New York have more successful careers than those who live in other cities?
A. Not necessarily. New York writers are closer to some major publishing houses but most cities have libraries and other resources of high caliber. No matter where you live and write, you must be able to turn out quality work, and external environment is only part of what enables you to do so. Top-quality writing attracts the attention of editors everywhere, no matter where it originates.

Professional Writer?

Q. Exactly what is a professional writer? Can this term be defined?
A. Though not all professional writers have achieved wide recognition and six-figure incomes, they all have common working methods that have contributed to successful, profitable careers. First, of course, a professional writer has a firm grasp of the skills of his craft, both in the basics of grammar and composition and the techniques required for writing successful fiction or nonfiction. In these areas, as well as in the development of his writing style, the professional constantly strives to improve. Daily writing is a work habit of the professional, as is the setting of specific writing goals. Professionals study the markets before submitting their work so that they know their audiences, and the needs of specific editors, making their acceptance rate higher. When professionals receive rejection slips, they realize that their manuscripts are simply products being sold, and that there was not a need for the product in that particular market at that time. Therefore, they proceed by querying another suitable market.

Since fiction writers, poets, playwrights, and filmmakers usually must deliver complete manuscripts rather than queries on their ideas, they face an even more demanding and time-consuming task of matching their manuscripts to suitable markets. Persistence, then, is another personal quality all professionals must have.

Professional writing is also defined as writing done on assignment, on the job, or on demand. This might range from beginning staff writers to freelance authors whose work brings top dollar in the marketplace. Most importantly, professional writing is an attitude. For the beginning writer, it means professional presentation of queries and manuscripts and a thorough study of the markets.

Writers' Production

Q. How are professional writers able to write so much?
A. Most writers are attracted almost obsessively to their work; that is, they have an inner urge to write. Professional writers find that the satisfaction their writing brings is enough to outweigh the deadlines, rejection, and other problems they face. On a more practical level, self-employed writers know that if they don't write, they don't eat, so they structure their work as though they had a regular job working for an employer. For example, they begin at the same time every day (but not necessarily in the morning), produce the same number of words or pages each day, and establish a place—at home or away from home—to be used exclusively for writing. In addition, they make their working hours known to friends and family to minimize distractions.

Writing Quotas

Q. I sometimes wonder if I write fast enough. Are there any standards I can measure my writing against, such as daily quotas for the fast, the average, and the slow writer?
A. It is said that Marcel Proust would spend three and four days working on a single paragraph. On the other hand, John Jakes worked seven days a week, ten and twelve hours a day to turn out eight novels in the bicentennial series he produced for a major paperback house. It is best for each writer to set his own goal, since writing speed seems to vary with the individual. When setting your daily quota of number of pages or number of words, you should make it a little higher than you think you might be able to reach, so that you can have something to shoot for. Above all, when the words begin to flow—keep writing!

Fiction vs Nonfiction

Q. I am only interested in writing nonfiction, so is there any reason why I should read fiction?
A. Nonfiction writers should be familiar with fiction techniques, as these are often incorporated into nonfiction. Dialogue, suspense, characterization, description, and emotion are parts of the fiction writer's craft that the most successful nonfiction writers also use in their work.

Writing as a Career

Q. I have always loved to write, but I'm not sure that's what I want to do as a profession. How do I know if writing is my best career choice?
A. Since the required skills and personal characteristics vary widely depending on the type of writing career, you'll have to learn as much about the various job opportunities as you can before making a decision. For example, can you write quickly under a tight deadline as required of a newspaper reporter? Can you generate the kind of clever copy required by some

advertising clients? Do you have the educational background to be a writer for a corporation? Two government publications which provide some helpful background information are: *Toward Matching Personal and Job Characteristics* and *Occupational Outlook Handbook*, available in most libraries. The library's card catalog can also point you to vocational guidance books whose titles are frequently *Your Career in. . . .* or *Your Future in. . . .* publishing, or public relations, or broadcasting, or advertising.

Freelancing Full Time

Q. Can you point out any special advantages or disadvantages that I might face as a full-time freelance writer?
A. You would be your own boss. You would control your working hours and, in a sense, the amount of money you would make. You would practice as a profession the thing you enjoy most. You might have much more opportunity to be creative than if you worked as a staff writer. You could choose what you want to write about and get paid for learning something new through research. You could work at home. Therefore, you wouldn't need many business clothes and could probably save in that area of your budget. If you are a parent, you could save on childcare expenses, since you would be available when your children needed you. In addition, the research involved in writing could bring you into contact with interesting, stimulating people.

On the other hand, most writers face innumerable rejections—and no income—before making their first sale. To avoid losing faith in yourself and your career at this stage, it would help if you were thick-skinned, self-confident, and persistent. Unlike a job in a company, freelance work does not bring regular paychecks in regular amounts. Further, you would be responsible for collecting your own payments. Similarly, you would receive no fringe benefits, such as insurance or retirement benefits that company employees receive. Being self-employed, you would have to spend part of your working time on administrative tasks, such as bookkeeping, filing income tax, and social security forms.

Writers usually work alone, and this could be a disadvantage (depending on your personality), especially after a number of days without contact with your colleagues. If you are married it would be best to have a spouse who approves of your career and all it entails, since he or she might be affected by your irregular working hours and irregular income.

Prison Writer

Q. I am interested in learning more about writing. Unfortunately, I am in prison and not permitted to purchase any services. What writing opportunities are there for someone in my position?
A. PEN American Center, a writers' organization, operates a Prison Writing Program. The Center sponsors an annual writing competition for writers who are in prison, and sends prisoners information on writing, ranging from answers to frequently-asked questions and referrals to other programs for prisoners, to listings of magazines which will accept manuscripts from prisoners. PEN also distributes free publications, as well as books and magazines writers have donated to the prison program. (Writers wishing to donate such material to prisoners—it's tax deductible—should contact PEN for further information.)

Every year, the Center's Writing Awards for Prisoners competition presents nine awards: first-, second-, and third-place prizes in fiction, nonfiction and poetry categories. The Center accepts entries between September 1 and March 1, and presents the awards in late spring. The winning entries are published in *The Fortune News*. For contest requirements and other information, write to PEN American Center, 47 Fifth Ave., New York NY 10003.

Good writing is bought and published regardless of where the author lives. Practice to improve your skills and your work will be judged solely on its own merits.

Perfect Grammar?

Q. How important to an editor are spelling, punctuation, and sentence structure? I believe I'm weak in these areas, and no matter how much I read grammar books, I just can't remember the rules. Does my writing have to contain perfect grammar, punctuation, and construction, or will an editor make corrections before publishing a manuscript?

A. These elements are worth a great deal of your attention. Some famous writers have published without a perfect command of grammar or spelling (and have had their manuscripts corrected by editors), but they succeeded because they possessed genius in other areas. Unknown writers, on the other hand, *must* make a favorable impression on every editor they submit to, and knowledge of writing mechanics is part of this impression.

It might help to remember that punctuation can be learned without rules: observing punctuation in others' work can help you become familiar with how to use punctuation, and reading your finished pieces aloud can point out errors or omissions in the punctuation you have used.

Sentence structure is flexible. For example, an editor may change the structure of one of your sentences, to change the emphasis or for some other reason, but that doesn't necessarily mean that your original structure was incorrect. A book you might find useful is Harry Shaw's *Punctuate It Right!*.

Manuscript Criticism

Q. Where can I get constructive criticism of my manuscript?
A. Local writers' clubs can provide critiques from other writers. Teachers of writing courses and sometimes fellow students are potential critics. Or, you can use one of the commercial criticism services advertised in writers' magazines.

Commercial Critique

Q. What are the advantages and disadvantages of using a commercial criticism service?
A. One advantage is that the critique is done on a one-to-one basis instead of in front of a group. A writing critic employed by a criticism service would be more objective than a teacher, writers' club member, friend, or spouse. To avoid any disadvantages, check the track record of criticism services advertised in writers' magazines. The professional critic should have a background in the particular field of your manuscript (novels, plays, etc.), and should have produced salable works for clients.

To Write or Not to Write

Q. In an issue of Writer's Digest, *one famous writer's advice to young writers was: "Don't write." In the same issue, another writer said, "To be a writer you must write." What's your reaction?*
A. These two statements, taken out of context, are not as contradictory as they may appear. Instead of spending all his time writing, the young writer should expose himself to experience, involving himself in life so that he will, in time, have something to write about. On the other hand, the writer should discipline himself in order to avoid all the trite excuses to put off

writing, for example, sharpening pencils and changing typewriter ribbons. The assumption is, of course, that he has something to say and just needs to get started.

Use Rewrite Specialists?

Q. Is it a good idea to send my manuscript to those advertisers in writers magazines who offer rewriting services?

A. If you're just starting out as a writer and you don't have criticism advice available from professional writers through a local writers club, or from a writing teacher who has published widely, then yes, it might be a good idea to get a professional evaluation of your script, or a rewrite, to see what you could learn from it. But don't use those services as an excuse to avoid sending your manuscripts to markets. Editors don't have time to tell you what's wrong with a story or article, but studying the individual markets and getting rejections or acceptances is an important part of writing to publish. Keep in mind, too, that a rewrite specialist can't guarantee that your rewritten manuscript will be salable.

2 What Education Do I Need?

Nora Ephron says her mother often told her the best way to learn to write is to write a letter to your mother and tear off the salutation. "I don't think she made up that maxim herself," says Ephron, "but I know that in writing to my mother, with whom I felt completely confident, I began to become a writer." Ephron's letters undoubtedly were written after a formal education and many informal learning experiences—similar to those that every writer undergoes. Training for writing can come about in diverse ways, and at any age.

Education and Experience

Q. I've heard some experts say that a college education is the best training for a writer, and others say that a variety of experiences is better. Can you clarify this issue?
A. A college education is most beneficial for young writers who want to become professionals in today's market. You will have to set your own career goals, for example, to pursue a career in science and write poetry as a hobby, to work at different jobs in several fields in order to gather impressions as material for fictional places and characters, or to work at a writing-related job so that you can practice your craft and freelance in your spare time. For the older beginner, refresher college courses and self-education enhance writing skills.

One quality necessary to all writers, however, is the ability to sort out those impressions or experiences that are significant enough to be rearranged into fiction or nonfiction. Experience and insight can be gained from your immediate environment: Emily Dickinson, for example, created fine poetry without ever leaving her home.

As a freelance writer, you will have to modify the writing style you learned in college, because the style of newspaper and magazine articles is different (in general, it's more direct) from that used in scholarly term papers.

Continuing Education

Q. I have a college degree and have sold some articles. I still think I need to learn more about the writing craft and the writing business. What are some ways I could get more education?
A. You could attend the national and regional workshops sponsored by professional organizations such as the American Society of Journalists and Authors, Women in Communications, Inc., and the Society of Professional Journalists, Sigma Delta Chi. The

trade journals *Quill* and *Editor & Publisher* can keep you abreast of news in the newspaper field, as can *Folio* for the magazine business and *Publishers Weekly* for the book publishing industry.

In addition, you can read books about writing. For specific titles, check *Subject Guide to Books In Print* under "Authors and Publishers," "Authorship—Handbooks, Manuals, etc.," "Authorship—Juvenile Literature," "Authorship—Study and Teaching," "Copyright," "Detective and Mystery Stories—Technique," "Fiction—Technique," "Literary Agents," "Plots," "Psychological Fiction," "Poetry—Authorship" and "Writing"; and under headings describing areas of writing, such as "Medical Writing," "Playwriting," and "Technical Writing."

You can learn about other useful books by perusing the ads in writers' magazines or obtaining book catalogs directly from publishers. The two major publishers of books about writing are Writer's Digest Books and The Writer, Inc.

No matter how much formal education you have had, it's best to read as many of the literary classics as possible and keep abreast of today's popular reading, especially in the area to which you hope to contribute. *The Elements of Style,* a classic in the nonfiction field, concisely instructs and advises on usage, composition, and writing style.

Journalism Education

Q. I'm a high school student who's interested in a career in journalism. What are some subjects I should take in high school and college to prepare for work in this field?
A. Formal education and experience in the field can help you begin a journalism career. Most media organizations look for a college degree in job applicants, though they don't insist that it be in journalism or English. Some fields of study recommended by professionals are history, political science, psychology, and economics; knowing a foreign language also can give job applicants an advantage. Of course, whatever subject you choose to study, you must have a broad knowledge of literature and a command of English grammar, usage, and composition skills. If possible, work on your high school and college papers or literary magazines for hands-on experience. If you plan to be a freelance writer, you'll benefit from the discipline instilled by taking writing courses. Since newspaper experience and a background in printing are both valuable, look for part-time jobs in that field.

Many college students participate in internship programs, which provide work experience before graduation. Internship opportunities in the fields of newspapers, magazine and book publishing, radio, television, advertising, and public relations are outlined in the annual directory, *Internships*.

Journalism Departments

Q. Could you tell me the rank or list of the top ten or fifteen journalism departments in our universities?
A. There is no definitive list concerning the academic standing in journalism. However, your public library undoubtedly has the booklet, "Accredited Programs in Journalism" (Accrediting Council on Education in Journalism and Mass Communications). It lists, in alphabetical order, all the accredited schools and departments of journalism on the college level. For additional information, address your inquiry to: Secretary-Treasurer, Accrediting Council on Education in Journalism and Mass Communications, School of Journalism, University of Missouri, Columbia MO 65205. Columbia University in New York (graduate), Northwestern University in Chicago, University of Missouri, and Stanford University in California have good journalism departments.

Grammar Refreshers

Q. What books would you recommend for improving my grammar and punctuation?
A. You might want to spend some time in the public library or a college bookstore to see what's available and what fits your needs. *Harbrace College Handbook* and *Random House Handbook* are examples of instructional grammar books. *The Elements of Style* is a compact refresher on composition, usage, and writing style. *Make Every Word Count* is a general instructional guide to fiction and nonfiction and includes exercises in writing technique. You might also want to become a regular reader of the monthly Grammar Grappler column in *Writer's Digest.*

Creative Writing Courses

Q. Can workshops or courses in creative writing help me become a better writer?
A. Courses in creative writing can help by giving you motivation and discipline to write consistently, but after the class is over you must be self-motivated enough to apply what you have learned.

Scholarships and Loans

Q. I am a high school senior planning to enter college next fall. The field I am interested in is journalism. Where can I find information on journalism scholarships and loans?
A. *Journalism Career and Scholarship Guide* is published by the Dow Jones Newspaper Fund, Box 300, Princeton NJ 08540. Write for a free copy. No SASE required.

Creative Writing Schools

Q. Where can I find a list of the best creative writing schools for would-be novelists?
A. The best creative writing school for you would depend on what you expect from it, how much you can afford to pay, your own talents, the school faculty, and many other factors. A list of colleges throughout the U.S. and Canada with degree programs in creative writing, or at least offering some creative writing courses, can be obtained from Associated Writing Programs, c/o Old Dominion University, Norfolk VA 23508.

Photojournalism Departments

Q. Can you recommend any journalism school that also has a good photography curriculum?
A. Check your local library for the *Editor & Publisher Year Book,* which contains a list of journalism schools and describes the areas of study available in each, such as "newspapers, magazines, advertising, public relations and photography." Local community colleges may also have evening classes in photography. Local high school continuing education programs also offer courses in photography, and would be a good place for you to begin.

Books about Writing

Q. I am interested in learning how to write. But I don't have the money for a correspondence course, and most of the college texts I've seen say nothing about how to write books or magazine articles. What should I do?
A. There are a number of books designed to take you step-by-step through the writing process, many of which are published by Writer's Digest Books and The Writer, Inc. One, which gives a

basic overview of writing, is Evelyn Stenbock's *Teach Yourself to Write*. This is a step-by-step guide to writing for publication, with a series of assignments to complete at the end of each chapter. You can work at your own pace and master each skill before moving along to the next.

Fellowships, Grants

Q. Can you direct me to a list of known literary fellowships and grants connected with publishers and colleges? Also, is there a directory of foundation grants?
A. Lists of private and government foundations of interest to writers are: *Grants and Awards Available to American Writers,* 12th revised edition, published by PEN American Center, 47 Fifth Avenue, New York NY 10003; *National Directory of Grants and Aid to Individuals in the Arts,* 4th edition, and the *National Directory of Arts Support by Private Foundations,* Vol. 4 published by the Washington International Arts Letter, Box 9005, Washington DC 20003; and *Study Abroad.*

Technical Writing

Q. I'm interested in the field of technical writing. Where can I learn more about it?
A. Southern Illinois University offers a two-day seminar on technical writing. Several accomplished professionals in the field are featured each year, and give advice and instruction in the form. The fall seminar generally costs under $50, including housing and meals. For further information contact Joe Lynch of the Division of Continuing Education, Southern Illinois University, Carbondale IL 62901.

If you desire to read about technical writing, *Subject Guide to Books in Print* lists many titles under that heading. Check for recent titles in your local library or ask to obtain them on inter-library loan.

Technical writing is often learned on the job. In addition to pursuing education, consider an internship where you could work with and learn from professionals in the field.

For more information on technical writing, contact the Society of Technical Communications, 815 15th Street NW, Suite 506, Washington DC 20005. The Society produces several publications of help to a budding technical writer; you could also find the address of a local chapter of the organization through the Washington office.

Classics vs Contemporary

Q. I read a lot in my spare time, for pleasure as well as for improving my writing. Some writing instructors have told me to concentrate on the classics, and others have suggested reading different magazines, especially those I hope to write for. Which kind of reading is better?
A. You need both. If you hope to write magazine articles, you should be reading magazines, especially those you consider future markets for your work. By reading magazines, you grasp their style and editorial needs. On the other hand, if you are a fiction writer, your reading also will consist of popular novels and stories, or literary fiction, whichever you hope to publish. Reading literary classics is basic to all good writing.

Learning about Writing

Q. What advice would you give a young writer who wants to learn more about the craft of writing?

A. Join or start a writers' club in your community. Attend writing workshops at your local community college or university. Read many books on the craft of writing, and write, write, and rewrite, until you have something to submit to the marketplace. Writers' magazines such as *Writer's Digest* and *The Writer* provide monthly inspiration as well as valuable, current information on markets and writing techniques.

Correspondence Courses

Q. What kinds of correspondence courses in writing are available, and what do they offer a writer?
A. Correspondence courses are available through private organizations and through universities. A writer can choose the form of writing he wishes to study (for example, short stories or poetry). Some schools offer courses in special fields, such as writing for children, screenwriting, or religious writing. University courses can be taken for credit or audited. Correspondence courses provide one-to-one contact with and critique from an instructor, as well as provide a stimulus for writing. However, students generally need more self-motivation for correspondence courses than for traditional courses, since they don't actually meet with their instructors, and therefore can procrastinate more easily.

For information on which colleges offer home study courses in specific types of writing, contact the National University Continuing Education Association, One Dupont Circle, Washington DC 20036. For information on private organizations offering home study courses, see advertisements in writers' magazines.

College Credit?

Q. Can I obtain college credit for a course I take from a private correspondence school?
A. Just as some colleges will accept transfer credits from other institutions and some will not, this is an individual college's decision. The private school will furnish whatever data (e.g. transcript of grades, summary of assignments completed) to the college registrar on behalf of the student, but the decision about offering credit is up to the college.

Evaluation of Correspondence Schools

Q. How can a writer evaluate correspondence courses across the nation? I would like to look into all the writing correspondence courses that are offered, and I want to be sure when I do enroll, that I've chosen a good one. What about Writer's Digest School?
A. There is no national rating service for correspondence schools. Most reputable ones, however, are registered and licensed in their own state, as Writer's Digest School is in Ohio. By writing to the state board of school and college registration you can get an honest evaluation of the school in which you are interested. (Writer's Digest School's number is #73-10-0409H.) If you wish to write to the State of Ohio, address your letter to Executive Secretary, State Board of School & College Registration, 88 E. Broad St., Columbus OH 43215. Writer's Digest School offers courses in magazine article writing, short story writing, and the elements of effective writing; and an advanced writer's workshop. Instructors for the school are professional writers or editors who have expertise in the specific field in which they instruct. Each student keeps the same instructor for the length of the course. For more information, write Director, Writer's Digest School, 9933 Alliance Rd., Cincinnati OH 45242.

3 How Do I Get Started?

"Some writers like to think about what they are going to write, others like best holding their finished book in their hands," says Isaac Asimov, "but neither is too fond of writing itself. But for me, it's the in-between part—the writing itself—that I like best." For writers who have been doing more thinking about writing than writing, the questions and answers in this chapter may provide a pertinent prod.

Making Your Debut

Q. How do authors usually write and publish their first article?
A. It normally happens one of two ways. The author chooses a topic—one that greatly interests him and one he feels he can write well—writes the piece, then tries to find a magazine to publish it. Or he studies a magazine he's personally interested in, to discover ideas for articles that would interest the editor of that magazine. He then queries that editor asking for an expression of interest in the article idea, or he prepares the article manuscript and submits it without querying first.

Getting Started, Getting a "Name"

Q. I've been writing for my local newspaper, without pay, for several years. When I try to query a national magazine, I have no published credits to list. I've run into the problem of people not granting me an interview because I have no credits, and they feel it's wasting their time to let me interview them. Even when I get a go-ahead from an editor I've queried, I find people hesitant to give me their time for an interview. How do you suggest I get started in the national market, and how can I get my name before readers other than those who read the local newspaper?
A. You *do* have published credits—in your local newspaper. Sometimes being published in the newspaper helps, even if you don't get paid, because it gives you valuable experience. You can tell editors and potential interviewees you've been published for several years in your local newspaper and they will be impressed. And so will those people you want to interview. If they are hesitant to grant the interview tell them you've done some research on them and you want to be sure your facts are accurate. If you show confidence, they will have faith in you. Landing your first interview may be tough, but the experience you gain will make interviews that follow much easier.

Newspaper Training Ground

Q. Is newspaper reporting accepted as good training ground for creative writers in the short story and novel fields?
A. Yes. Newspaper work teaches proper organization, the skill of condensing, the discipline of following a required style and the importance of meeting deadlines. Many successful writers, such as Jimmy Breslin and Paul Gallico, have worked in the newspaper field. Though the style of news reporting is different from that of fiction, reporting offers the opportunity to observe human behavior in various situations. In reporting, writers develop the ability to generate ideas, which is necessary to any category of freelance writing. Newspaper editors who are seasoned journalists are among the best writing teachers available.

Shortcuts to Writing Success?

Q. I am in great distress over the marketing of articles and short stories. Apparently, my four years of liberal arts plus three national writers' conventions is not enough. I just don't publish. Even my prize-winning short story has received six rejection slips. Are there shortcuts writers must know in order to publish? How does one sell more writing? How do you get a "yes" from editors? What are the markets for short stories?
A. There really are no shortcuts to getting published—other than strictly adhering to editorial and submission requirements of various markets. Some people think a shortcut might be to "know someone on the inside," but that usually doesn't help. The only way to sell more writing is to do more writing, to circulate more of your material and to be persistent. How do you get a "yes" from editors? By sending them the kind of material they're looking for, or by sending them something so fresh, so new, so exciting that they can't wait to share it with their readers. What are the markets for short stories? Check through the Consumer Magazines section of *Writer's Market* and the market columns in *Writer's Digest* for specific names, addresses and editorial requirements. The market for short stories is not dead—it's very much alive. To sell, you need to write short stories for individual audiences, for specific magazines. To know the audiences you must study magazines' back issues, including editorial matter and advertisements (which reveal plenty of information about the readers who buy the magazines).

Writing Locale

Q. Where's the best place to write?
A. Ideally, a place that is quiet and conducive to thinking and writing. You can write at a desk in a home office, in a rented office away from home, on the kitchen table, or even in the garage. The most important thing about where you write is that you write there consistently, and that others in your household respect your writing place. Using the same place every time you write helps you establish a routine so that you will write regularly.

Developing Discipline

Q. Are there any secrets or formulas for disciplining yourself to write regularly? Some days I just don't feel like writing.
A. Discipline separates the would-be writer from the published writer. You should think of yourself as a professional and regard your writing as any other job. Techniques that make the writing task seem easier are finding the best time of day for your individual thinking processes and writing during those hours, and dividing a project into easily accomplished parts, so that the entire job doesn't loom above you as insurmountable.

Value of a Journal

Q. Is it a good idea to keep a journal?
A. A journal can be invaluable to a writer, since it records ideas, impressions and anecdotes that can be of future use. For example, describing a person you observed on a city street may have no relevance to any of your current writing projects, but you might be able to retrieve that description later to fit conveniently into a short story. The same principle applies to the nonfiction writer regarding ideas, anecdotes that are observed or overheard and recorded in a journal. Even if your journal entries never get into print, the journal-writing itself can help your career by instilling in you the habit of writing regularly. To learn about keeping a journal, read *One to One*, by Christina Baldwin; *At a Journal Workshop*, by Ira Progoff; and *The New Diary*, by Tristine Rainer.

That First Submission

Q. How can I get up enough courage to send out a manuscript?
A. One way is to put distance between yourself and your work. You can do this by creating a pen name for yourself (thereby separating your self-image as a writer from your self-image in other areas of life), or by pretending the manuscript belongs to a friend who asked you to submit it as a favor. Alternatively, you can impose consequences on yourself for sending out a manuscript or for neglecting to. When you send a manuscript or query, reward yourself with something you enjoy; when you fail to, deny yourself something pleasant or do some unpleasant task.

It's important to remember that the overnight successes in the writing field are exceptions: most writers have to send out a lengthy succession of manuscripts before having one accepted.

Finally, you can adopt the insurance agent's rule of thumb: of every twenty cold calls, expect to get two lukewarm prospects and possibly one sale.

Self-Promotion

Q. As a beginner, I would like to know some ways I can make my name and services known. I write nonfiction, proofread, and edit copy.
A. You can have brochures printed that describe your services and mail them to businesses or organizations who might need editorial work done. Or you can post business cards in public places. Don't overlook university or library bulletin boards. Run classified ads in your local papers and writers' magazines (where organizations look to find qualified writers). List yourself in the Yellow Pages. You could inquire to see if you qualify for a listing in a directory such as *Literary Market Place* or *Working Press of the Nation*. Although you might not be directly promoting your editorial business, you can make yourself and your name familiar to the public by becoming involved with organizations, as a volunteer, or accepting public speaking engagements for businesses and organizations.

What to Write?

Q. How can I get started as a writer?
A. The first step is to decide whether your first submission will be fiction or nonfiction. One way to determine this is to note where your reading interests lie. Next, you'll need to learn all you can about your chosen field by taking courses and/or reading instructional books. Choose your subject and get a first draft on paper. Then revise and rewrite it to the best of your ability. Before submitting your work, find out which markets it is best suited to by reading *Writer's*

Market or *Writer's Handbook*. Also, be sure your manuscript conforms to the standard manuscript format (see Chapter 13). Many editors prefer to receive a query before a complete manuscript; *Writer's Market* listings indicate individual policies.

If your manuscript is not accepted, make a note of the editor's reason for rejecting. Some editors make specific comments about pieces; you should interpret these as constructive criticism that can help you improve in the future. You may be able to find areas of weakness common to several of your pieces by studying a group of rejected manuscripts. If you believe you've submitted material for too long without an acceptance, you might consider consulting a professional criticism service. (For information on research, see Chapter 7 and Chapter 8.)

Writing Job vs Freelancing

Q. I have a full-time job, and I write in my spare time. My job is in the communications field and I often have opportunities to develop my skills by editing and writing. I sometimes think I'd have more energy to devote to freelancing if I worked in a field unrelated to writing—it seems like I do the same thing twelve to fourteen hours a day. Which kind of job is better?
A. That question has to be answered by each individual writer, primarily because success in getting published depends a great deal on the writer's determination. Perhaps you lack energy to write for reasons unrelated to your job. On the other hand, you may find a completely different kind of work to be a refreshing break from writing, so that you would be more eager to write during your off-hours. If you're serious about becoming a full-time freelancer in the future, and not interested in a career with one company, you might try changing jobs or fields periodically to see what kind of work best complements writing for you.

Full-Time Freelance Gamble

Q. I'm seriously considering quitting my full-time job to become a full-time freelance writer. I've already sold some articles and my name is known to those editors. I have a home office and have saved some money for future business expenses. Would I be taking too big a risk?
A. Leaving a steady job is risky if your freelance work doesn't bring in the amount equivalent to a salary plus an additional 25 percent to allow you to pay for insurance, retirement, and other fringe benefits given by corporations. Setting aside funds for personal and business emergencies is a good idea. When you have built up your sideline writing business, you might consider taking a part-time job before becoming completely independent.

Writer's Digest periodically carries articles on this subject. Check the editorial index in the December issue each year and read the latest advice.

Full-time Freelance

Q. For many years, I've had a deep-seated desire to write, but I guess I've been too lazy to sit down and get started. How do you break into the field and make enough to support a family? The dull routine of the business world is beginning to irritate me. There isn't even very much money in it.
A. I'm afraid if you think there isn't much money in the business world, you will be disappointed, too, in how little remuneration there is for the beginning freelancer *until* he develops his talent and marketing ability. There are hundreds of full-time freelancers, however, who started small and did freelance writing on the side while holding a regular job until they reached the point where they could support themselves and a family on their writing. The best place to start is with articles, since the market for them is much greater than for short stories, and there is article material all around every person in every town. Trade journals are one place to start.

Getting Started in the Morning

Q. I work alone in my home office and sometimes have trouble starting to work at the beginning of the day. How can I overcome this problem?
A. A writer can begin a day's work in various ways that are related to, but not directly connected with, the piece he is working on. One good way to begin is to edit or revise work that has already been written. Another way is to write *about* the piece, for example, as though in a letter to a friend or simply in a group of random thoughts. Some writers deliberately stop at the end of one writing session, in the middle of a thought, section, or sentence, so that they will know exactly where to resume the next day and will be less likely to procrastinate. Browsing through the *Writer's Market* or writers' magazines, or reading a chapter from a how-to book on writing can also put you in the mood and is an important part of your workday. But know when to stop reading and start writing!

Writing Career

Q. How do new writers get started in the business world? I want a career in writing but I find it difficult to get started.
A. First, read about the different fields in which writers are employed. Books published by Writer's Digest Books and the magazine *Writer's Digest* are good sources of information on all aspects of freelance writing. *Jobs for Writers* describes more than forty kinds of writing and writing-related jobs for freelancers. National Textbook Company has published the "opportunities in" series—a group of books that profile various career fields, including journalism, book publishing, magazine publishing, writing, freelance writing, advertising, broadcasting, and public relations. The U.S. Department of Labor publishes periodicals that can keep you abreast of career trends. You could consult *Occupational Outlook Handbook* and *Occupational Outlook Quarterly*. To locate pamphlets about writing and related fields, check *The Vertical File Index* in your local public or university library.

For students and newcomers to the field, an internship—a temporary job that serves to introduce the potential employee to a profession—can be a learning experience as well as a head start into the working world at job-search time. The annual directory, *Internships,* lists sixteen thousand internship opportunities.

4 What Equipment Do I Need?

"The ideal view for daily writing, hour on hour," said Edna Ferber, "is the blank brick wall of a cold-storage warehouse. Failing this, a stretch of sky will do, cloudless if possible." No avocation in the world has as little start-up expense as that of freelance writing. Ideas, energy, a scrap of paper, and a pencil are all that a beginner requires. As skill develops, a few more tools are necessary for a professional presentation of your work. But your inventory is as inexpensive as some notebooks and a memory; and other entrepreneurs cast envious eyes on your one-man labor force.

Starter Supplies

Q. What equipment or supplies will I need to get started? At this stage, I'm trying to keep expenses to a minimum.
A. All you need as a beginning writer is zeal, an idea, paper, pens, and a good typewriter. Your equipment needs will expand with your success. Eventually, you'll want a sturdy table or desk on which to lay out your current project. It need not be anything elaborate; a hollow-core door across two two-drawer filing cabinets is one idea. The chair and lighting for your work area are essential to your health and well-being, so make sure any bargains you find are of good quality. The chair should give your back good support and leave your feet flat on the floor. Most doctors find fluorescent lighting less desirable over long periods of time than incandescent light. The light you need, of course, will depend on how much natural light is available in your work area.

The telephone should also be near your work area. It is your arm to clients as well as research resources, and should be readily available. You'll save money by turning your present home phone into a business phone, rather than having a separate business line installed.

A good, sturdy office file will also become necessary. Many writers have tried to do without a file cabinet, but sooner or later have realized the need for organizing correspondence, old manuscripts, financial records, etc. You'll also need an accounting ledger to keep track of your finances.

Your final basic need is a bookcase for your reference library. This will keep your most-used books nearby for handy reference.

As you build your list of contacts, you may wish to purchase a Rolodex phone file. A telephone answering device is another possible addition as your workload increases.

Writing Space

Q. Is it possible to be successful as a writer without having my own writing room?
A. It's not impossible—just a little harder. You don't need a room that is used only for writing, but most writers find they need space, a quiet spot, where they do most of their writing—a place used consistently and regularly to write. It's easier to concentrate on work when you are in the same area every day, with your typewriter, books, and files nearby. Kay Cassill, author of *The Complete Handbook for Freelance Writers,* says that once she set up her own work space at home, her productivity and assignments increased considerably. You don't need a plush, elaborate office—just some small place where you can go to do your work every day.

Typewriters for Beginning Writers

Q. What kind of typewriters are available and what kind is best for a beginning freelancer?
A. Each writer chooses a typewriter to fit his particular needs. Typewriters are available with a variety of special options, including self-correcting features. Carbon ribbon gives sharper images when copy is to be reproduced, than is possible with the less expensive cloth or nylon ribbons.

It isn't necessary to have a fancy typewriter. Choose a typewriter with which you feel comfortable, and within your budget. Most writers and editors prefer electric models because they allow the user to type more words per minute and turn out cleaner, better-looking copy than manuals. But for those writers who work at the beach or hideaways without electricity, a manual typewriter is their choice for first drafts. (Unfortunately, the last American portable machines were produced in 1983, so writers without electricity will have to depend on foreign imports.) A round-up of portable typewriters appeared in the June 1983 issue of *Writer's Digest* and electric models were surveyed in the April 1982 issue.

Prices vary according to brand name and special features, so a writer should do some comparison shopping. In 1983 manual portables ranged from $100 to $235; electric portables from $300 to $650. Standard electric typewriters ranged from $800 to $2,600. Beginning writers might consider used or rebuilt models.

Basic Reference Books

Q. What books should I buy first for my home reference shelf?
A. At the top of the list is a good, desk-size dictionary, such as *Webster's Collegiate, American Heritage,* or *Random House.* Writer and editor Art Spikol prefers the *Shorter Oxford English Dictionary* ("shorter" since the larger edition contains thirteen volumes) because of the word histories of each entry and quotes in which the word is used.

Writer's Market, published annually, tells you everything you need to know about magazines and book publishers—the markets to which you want to submit your work.

Roget's Thesaurus can be of help when you're looking for just the right word to describe something. Some writers feel the alphabetical arrangement edition is easier to use than the original subject-classified edition, and it's available in paperback.

The Elements of Style, by William Strunk and E.B. White, is a helpful aid to writing more clearly and concisely. The book covers grammatical points and principles of writing style in such a way that even the novice writer can learn to communicate well.

A good almanac can save you time you might spend looking up facts in other sources. Either *World Almanac and Book of Facts* or *Information Please Almanac* will provide you with information about events in the previous year, statistics, and other information about other years, facts about famous people and foreign countries, and much more. A one-volume reference such as *The Concise Columbia Encyclopedia* can also save you time between visits to the library to consult the multi-volumed *Britannica* or *Americana* encyclopedias.

These are general references, of course, and both fiction and nonfiction writers will want to have their own basic references, depending on their interests in certain historical periods or contemporary settings, or specialities such as medicine, science, etc.

Photographer-Writer

Q. Should I consider taking my own photographs to accompany my articles? What equipment will I need?
A. A selection of good photographs can increase the salability of an article because editors like having the complete visual and verbal package in one piece. You can either work out an arrangement with a freelance photographer, or (if you plan to use photos frequently) it will be an advantage to invest in some photographic equipment

You don't need much to take effective pictures. You should buy a good 35mm camera from one of the major companies: Nikon, Leica, Pentax, Olympus, Canon, etc. These brands all have established reputations and service records. A bargain-basement camera could leave you high and dry when it comes to needed service and extra equipment.

You will also want to buy a flash unit, a collapsible tripod, and an equipment bag to carry it all. Depending on your taste and the equipment you choose, as well as the rate of inflation, you should plan on investing between $300 and $700 in your basic camera system. Eventually, you may wish to add wide-angle and telephoto lenses to increase the variety of your pictures.

Learning to take effective pictures is a matter of time and practice. Universities and colleges often offer courses in photography, as do continuing education programs in local school districts. The salespersons at your local camera shop can direct you to the best places to learn how to use your camera, as well as providing excellent "hands-on" advice and instruction after you've bought your equipment.

Tape Recorders

Q. Is it necessary to have a tape recorder? What kind should I get?
A. Whether or not to purchase a tape recorder is a personal decision, but many writers find recorders useful in a variety of situations. Tape recording an interview allows you to concentrate on your subject, the surroundings and other questions you want to ask. Using a recorder is a good way to verify quotes and can help establish credibility with editors. You can also use it to take down information at the library, and to record your impressions and ideas when driving home from an interview.

The ideal tape recorder should not be too large or it might intimidate the interview subject. Neither should it be too small. Some "microcorders" currently available only use certain brands of tape, and may produce poor-quality recordings. They only record thirty minutes per side. The pocket-size models that use regular cassettes are best.

The model you choose should have a built-in microphone, since the remote mikes are too visible and might make the interview subject feel ill at ease. You should also try to get a recorder with a tape counter, so you can note points in the tape where the interviewee makes important comments. An adapter capability will allow you to run the recorder with electrical current, saving the batteries.

The recorder you buy should be reliable—a standard brand with a good guarantee. In 1983, prices for tape recorders ranged from $100 to $500.

Stationery

Q. Are stationery and business cards necessary for a freelance writer? How elaborate do they have to be and how can I obtain them? What will they cost?
A. Printed stationery is not necessary for a beginner, but as you develop as a freelancer, you may want to accompany your professional manuscripts with a professional-looking letterhead. It need not be elaborate or expensively designed. Most office supply stores and "quick print" shops offer standard imprinted letterheads in a variety of typestyles, ink colors, and quality of paper. You can also order rubber stamps, invoices, and other supplies from these stores.

In 1983 the cost of a ream of five hundred imprinted letterheads on 25 percent rag bond paper averaged about $35 while matching No. 10 envelopes averaged about $45. If the imprinted letterheads ran on a twenty-pound bond without rag content, a ream would cost about $15 with $25 for envelopes.

Business cards enhance your image as a professional writer. They can be ordered at the same place that prints your stationery. A box of 500 costs about $15 to $20. Give them to people you interview and post them on bulletin boards at locations where writers' services are advertised.

More References

Q. After I accumulate some basic reference books, what are other useful and enjoyable extras I can get?
A. Once you've acquired the necessary "tools of the trade," the number of extra reference books you can obtain is limited only by your interests and your bank account. There is almost no end to the books you will find useful or interesting.

First of all, you might want to invest in a good book of quotations. *Bartlett's Familiar Quotations* has been the favorite for many years; it contains many of the memorable words of history's greatest public and literary figures. Other quotation collections worth considering are *Peter's Quotations* (more contemporary thoughts divided by subject) and *The Quotable Woman* (since the vast majority of authors quoted in *Bartlett's* are male).

For reference purposes, depending on your interests, there are a number of specialized works that can give you the information you need. Books such as the *Bantam Medical Dictionary, Harvard Brief Dictionary of Music* and H.G. Wells's *Outline of History* are good, basic works about specific topics. Other areas in which you might want to have books include science, industry, psychology, and the arts.

You might also want books to help you with your writing. William Zinsser's *On Writing Well* and Gary Provost's *Make Every Word Count* can help you write more clearly, while John Brady's *The Craft of Interviewing* is a good guide for handling every type of personal contact with a source.

For help in locating additional reference sources, try *Reference Books: A Brief Guide.* This handy book will lead you to most of the references you will need in many subject areas. It's updated every few years. For other sources, check *Writer's Resource Guide*, which lists corporations, associations, museums, and libraries in thirty subject areas.

Good Reading: A Guide for the Serious Reader and *Books That Changed the World* can help familiarize you with many of the great books that you may have not yet read. *The Reader's Encyclopedia* is a guide to literature and myth.

Finally, some reference books don't fit into a particular category; they are simply useful and fun to read. The best known of these is perhaps the *Guinness Book of World Records*, listing the biggest, smallest, fastest, highest and other "-ests" of everything you can think of—and some you can't. *The People's Almanac* and its two sequels are billed as reference works made to be read for fun—and they live up to their billing. They feature thousands of articles on specific aspects of every topic from American history to Zoology.

Mailing Carton

Q. Will you give me the address of a supplier of carton containers for the purpose of mailing book manuscripts?
A. Some of these firms advertise in the classified pages of *Writer's Digest*. See the latest issue for current names and addresses.

Buy a Word Processor?

Q. What are the advantages of having a word processor and should I invest in one?
A. A word processor, a specialized computer designed for writing, editing, and proofreading, can help a writer in many ways. It can increase productivity and help make editing easier. A word processor consists of three components. The keyboard is composed of letter keys (like those on a typewriter) and special keys which give the word processor its operating instructions. The display is a television-like screen on which is displayed the material the writer has just typed on the keyboard or retrieved from the machine's memory. The printer does just what the name implies—takes material from the word processor and prints it on paper. Speed and quality of printing vary from printer to printer.

Word processors have a number of advantages over typewriters. If you are a poor speller, for example, most word processors have available a supplementary dictionary program to correct your misspellings and typographical errors. Most display a page or more of type, making editing easy. You won't have to retype an entire page to make a small correction; simply make the change on the word processor before you print. Even if you do reprint a page, it can be done in a fraction of the time it would take the fastest typist to retype. *Writer's Digest* columnist Art Spikol claims that a word processor will not only increase the quantity of the work you are able to do, but also the actual *quality* of your writing. Since you don't have to worry about constantly retyping drafts of your work, Spikol says you will be able to edit your work more thoroughly before submitting it to a publisher. In addition, if you need to retype a submission that is showing signs of wear from going to market or you need several originals for multiple submissions, a word processor saves time and energy.

Despite all the advantages, a writer should ask himself whether he is productive enough to merit investing in a word processor. Prices start at almost $2,000 and can go as high as ten times that much. If you decide the expenditure is worth the results it can bring, be sure to examine the various brands and models of word processors available. Check the monthly Word Processing column in *Writer's Digest* for updating information. Another helpful source is *The Word Processing Book*, by Peter A McWilliams. Besides being a good introduction to word processors and providing a helpful brand-name buying guide, the book is written in an entertaining style.

5 What Do They Mean When They Say. . . .?

To the beginning writer it sometimes seems as though editors and established writers are from another planet, using a language he has never heard before. The jargon, a handy shortcut for the initiated, is a confusing stumbling block for the beginner struggling to enter the inner circle. Here are some down-to-earth explanations for terms you read in editorial listings, writers' magazines, and books on writing.

Anecdotes

Q. What are anecdotes and how can a writer use them?
A. An anecdote is a short narrative of a curious, amusing, or insightful incident that illustrates a point or idea. An anecdote can contain dialogue, explicit detail, plays on words, and/or a humorous ending. Anecdotes can be biographical, or can result from a writer's observations.

Anecdotes can be used to enliven an article and help to make it more personal, and therefore more readable. They provide a "glimpse of life" to humanize a topic. All types of articles use anecdotes in one form or another. Articles about large groups or trends use them to give specific examples or add a human-interest dimension. Profiles of public figures use anecdotes from people acquainted with the subject to show a side of him that the writer might not get from a direct interview.

In addition to being useful within the boundaries of an article, anecdotes can be sold on their own as fillers to various publications. The best-known examples of this are the various departments in *Reader's Digest* specializing in anecdotes: "Life in These United States," "All in a Day's Work," "Humor in Uniform," etc. (For more about how to write fillers, see Chapter 20.)

Belles Lettres

Q. What does the category "belles lettres" cover? I've seen it in several of the market listings and would like an explanation.
A. The dictionary definition of "belles lettres" is literally "fine letters"—literature that is an end in itself and not practical or purely informative. This would seem to include all fiction, but in practice it includes only writers' finer works which literary critics have acclaimed as superior.

"Clips"

Q. What are "clips" and how are they used by professionals?
A. A clip, or clipping, is a sample of a writer's published work, usually taken from a newspaper or magazine. Editors often indicate that clips should be mailed or presented in person when sending a query letter or applying for a job. Clippings show an editor how a writer handles a variety of topics, as well as serving as proof of a writer's published credits. When sending clips, a writer should make sure they are neat and readable; a high-quality photocopy is preferable to the original, especially in the case of newspaper articles, since newspapers tend to age and deteriorate quickly. If the story is an unusual size or shape, *Writer's Digest* columnist Art Spikol recommends a reduced photocopy. Be sure you have sufficient postage on the return envelope if you want your clips returned. Some writers send photocopies of their clips to sources they have used in researching an article, to show how the piece turned out and to thank the source for his help.

Writers also use the term "clips" to refer to newspaper or magazine articles written by other writers. They file the clips for research purposes, for reference, and for possible future article ideas.

"Fam Trip"

Q. In a travel writer's newsletter I saw a reference to a "fam trip." What does this term mean?
A. It's an abbreviation for "familiarization trip," in which the public relations agency for a country, hotel, or airline invites travel agents, travel editors, and travel writers to visit and become familiar with the amenities offered by the host country or firm in expectation of subsequent business and travel articles. Transportation and lodging costs might be paid for travel agents and/or offered at a considerably reduced rate for editors and writers.

Who Is a Freelancer?

Q. What is meant by the term "freelancer" and how much work and pay is involved in this classification?
A. The term "freelancer" is used to describe an editor, writer, or other fully or part-time self-employed person who works for a variety of clients on a temporary or per-assignment basis. The term originated in medieval times when a knight or soldier who was paid for fighting and who offered his services—his lance—to any available employer, was called a "free lance."

How much work a freelancer does depends on how much time a writer wishes to devote to the job. Freelancers perform their work with varying degrees of frequency. There are the occasional freelancers, who make a few scattered sales over the course of several years. Most freelancers begin their careers part-time, writing in the evenings and on weekends while simultaneously holding down a full-time job. Many writers remain part-time freelancers, moving in and out of the field as their lives and careers change. Full-time freelancers are writers who have achieved the track record and reputation to make freelance writing a permanent career. These writers include those whose names are listed in *Publishers Weekly* as the authors of new books, or whose articles appear in issue after issue of national magazines.

Freelance writing as a full-time occupation is not easy. While it is possible to earn a living wage as a freelancer, it requires a great deal of time, skill, discipline, and dedication. Art Spikol, author of *Magazine Writing: The Inside Angle,* says that considering the hours a freelancer works and the amount of money he earns, most freelancers don't even make minimum wage. "A freelance writer who miraculously sold to the top-paying dozen markets in the country in as many months—and who also managed to sell one shorter piece each month for $250—might not earn $25,000 a year," he writes. "All that work . . . and you still might end up making less than somebody in a semi-skilled trade, even though your performance would make you a superstar among writers." In 1981, the Authors Guild Foundation surveyed 2,239 book authors and learned that their *average* annual income from writing was $4,775. If you wish to make writing your full-time occupation, you will have to build up experience and reputation over the course of several years. (For more information on how much a freelance writer can expect to earn, see Chapter 41.)

Kill Fee

Q. What is a "kill fee" and when is it used?
A. Kill fee is a fee paid to a writer who has worked on an assignment which, for one reason or another, was not published. The writer, for example, is asked (assigned) to write a 3,000-word article, but after he does the research and writes the 3,000 words, the editor decides that the piece will not be published after all. The writer is then given a percentage (usually 20 percent of the purchase price offered for the full manuscript—or a percentage of the expected income from a discontinued project other than an article) as a kill fee. The 20 percent kill fee is flexible, depending on the publication's policy. It may range from ten percent to fifty percent. Kill fees are usually offered only to professional writers. It's rare for an editor to offer a kill fee, for example, to a writer whose work is not familiar to him, or to a writer who hasn't previously worked for him. The writer is, after receiving the kill fee, permitted to submit the manuscript to other markets for possible sale. A writer does not ordinarily receive a kill fee unless it is mentioned in the original assignment.

Amateur vs Professional

Q. When editors say they want professionally written or sophisticated material, what do they mean?
A. They mean they want the type of writing that represents a polished use of the language plus skillfully developed treatment of the subject. Flaws in grammar and word choice, lacklustre style, sloppy plotting or research, poor organization, absence of a point, are all signs of the amateur rather than the professional. The demand for sophisticated material rules out anything trite or corny but suggests a desire for a certain degree of wit and subtlety that would appeal to readers who are intellectually sharp about the significance of the world around them.

Literary Magazines/Journals

Q. How do "little" and "literary" magazines differ from general publications? Are they the same thing as literary journals?
A. Little or literary magazines are publications with limited circulation—generally 5,000 or less—which offer writers a vehicle of expression not found in commercial magazines. They are usually literary in nature, stressing the unorthodox or experimental in approaches to poetry and prose. Little magazines aim for an audience of writers, editors, and students of literature. Their contributors are usually writers striving for literary excellence. T.S. Eliot, Flannery O'Connor, and John Gardner all received their early attention by having their work published in little magazines.

Editors of the literaries do not rely on general public support; hence, they do not have to compromise the ideals of their publications with popular taste. A little magazine can be centered on a specific theme or can be "eclectic"—open to work on any idea. Pay is usually low or non-existent; contributing authors are often paid with copies or subscriptions to the magazine. Writers submitting work to the literaries should know that some of them are not copyrighted, so all work should carry the author's copyright. Check *Writer's Market* and *Fiction Writer's Market* for details on specific publications.

Where literary magazines rely on creative prose and poetry, literary journals rely more on criticism. These literary journals, most often connected with and financed by a foundation or university, tend to include a small proportion of imaginative literature. Such journals as the *Antioch Review* or *Yale Review* publish articles on national issues, politics, art, music, international relations, and scholarly research, in addition to some fiction and poetry. Unlike the little magazines, literary journals may offer some payment, but accept little work from freelance writers. Instead, they rely on academic contributors and writers sought out by the journal's editor. Publication in a literary journal carries prestige, but the competition is heavy.

Magazine vs Journal

Q. What's the difference between a journal and a magazine?
A. Although a journal and a magazine are similar in format, a magazine is intended for the general public, while a journal is usually published by and for a professional group, such as orthopedic surgeons, microbiologists, or history professors. "Trade journals" are magazines published for workers in various industries; these include publications such as *American Printer and Lithographer, Broadcast Engineering,* and *American Drycleaner.* Journals usually contain articles written by members of the profession that makes up their readership; manuscripts are not usually sought from writers outside the profession. Magazines, on the other hand, appeal to a general-interest audience, or to consumers and businesspeople with special interests. Most magazines actively seek manuscripts from freelance writers.

Mailing Services

Q. What does "mailing and remailing" or "drop-off mailing" mean in the classified ads in Writer's Digest?
A. A mailing service agency mails an author's work from its own locality when the author travels frequently or prefers a postmark that does not reveal his place of residence.

Market

Q. What is meant by a "market"—and what does the phrase "marketing your material" mean? I've often seen both referred to in Writer's Digest.
A. A "market" is a magazine, publishing firm, or company to which you sell what you write. "Marketing your material" means selling what you write. "Study the market" means just that—read back issues of the magazine, or in the case of a book publisher, study the company's catalog, and visit bookstores to view the books firsthand. Also study the magazine or book firm's editorial requirements in the market listings in writers' publications, so you will understand what type of material the market is purchasing.

Objectivity

Q. What does an editor mean by "objectivity?"
A. Objectivity is the journalistic ethic requiring a reporter to present a complete, accurate, and

undistorted account of any news event he covers, keeping his writing as free as possible of personal opinion or prejudice. In recent years, various critics have called objectivity an unattainable ideal. Journalist Bill Moyers called it the greatest myth of journalism. Since a reporter influences each account with his personal powers of observation and consciousness, and chooses the facts to include in a story, critics say that complete objectivity is an impossible goal.

Nevertheless, objectivity is an ideal for which every writer should aim. In *Newsgathering,* Daniel Williamson outlines the five basic elements of objectivity. To be objective, an article should be impartial, containing all viewpoints with equal balance. The writer should avoid conflict of interest—involvement with causes or organizations which may make him vulnerable to suspicion of partiality. If he is making a damaging allegation, he should give the individual or firm a chance to make a denial, or to refute the allegation. The writer should not allow personal relationships, such as those between him and his news sources, to influence his coverage of a news story. Finally, a reporter should not use his access to the media to gain vengeance, by reporting unfairly on individuals he personally dislikes. Although these are primarily the goals of newspaper and broadcast journalists, the ethic of objectivity is an effective guideline for all nonfiction writing, including that of freelancers.

"On Spec"

Q. What does it mean when a publisher listed in Writer's Market *says he will accept a writer's work "on spec?"*
A. When an editor responds to a query letter by offering to look at the proposed work "on speculation" ("on spec" for short), he means he is interested in the article idea and will consider the finished article for publication. In his response, the editor will usually indicate a deadline due date, the desired word count for the article and the terms of payment if it is accepted. However, agreeing to look at the work on spec in no way obligates an editor to buy the finished manuscript. Since an agreement on spec does not assure a sale, some leading freelancers will only write an article on assignment, with the editor giving a firm commitment to purchase the finished product, but beginning writers should celebrate an invitation to submit an article on spec. Often the editor will buy the finished manuscript, if it meets editorial specifications and is submitted within the time specified.

"Over the Transom"

Q. What is meant by "over the transom?"
A. "Over the transom" is a collective term for unsolicited manuscripts received by a publisher; the phrase implies that the works were not requested, but were slipped "over the transom" into the publisher's office through the small window above old office doors which were left open for air circulation. The actual origin of the phrase is unknown.

Paperback Types

Q. What is the difference between mass-market paperbacks and trade paperbacks?
A. The difference can be defined in terms of size, distribution, and the amount of royalties the author receives. Mass-market books are sold in drugstores, airports, and supermarkets, as well as in bookstores; they are published in a single size, designed to fit paperback book racks and to be conveniently carried. Trade paperbacks are larger, cost more, and are distributed mainly in bookstores and department stores. Publishers are turning to trade paperbacks as a way of

reaching the book-buying public at a lower cost than hardcover trade books. Royalties for original mass-market titles are usually based on a percentage—such as 6 percent—of the retail price on net copies sold. For example, a publisher may distribute 100,000 copies, but only 50 percent might be sold and the rest destroyed. For trade paperbacks, the author usually receives an escalating royalty such as 6 percent of the retail price on the first 10,000-20,000 copies, 7 percent on the next 10,000-20,000 copies, and 8 percent on any copies sold after that.

Photocopied Submissions

Q. When an editor says he will accept photocopied submissions, what does he mean?
A. Many editors who once insisted on seeing the original, good-bond copy of a manuscript will now accept a photocopy of the original. This change in attitude on the part of editors and publishers is largely due to the improvements in the quality of photocopies available. Photocopying a manuscript is a convenience to the author; it is also a good precaution against having a manuscript lost or damaged in the mails, or misplaced at an editor's office. If such a mishap should occur, the writer will still have the original copy on file, eliminating the time, expense, and bother of retyping the manuscript. Also, when a well-traveled copy of a manuscript becomes dog-eared, a fresh copy can be made.

A writer who submits a photocopied manuscript should make sure the editor knows whether or not the manuscript is a simultaneous submission being considered by several editors at the same time. Photocopied manuscripts should also be as clean, neat, and legible as the original.

"Potboiler"

Q. What is a "potboiler?"
A. A potboiler is a piece of writing created for the express purpose of making money quickly—in other words, to "keep the pot boiling," or to eat—while the writer works on major articles, stories, or books. Depending on a writer's facility and knowledge of the marketplace, a potboiler may run anywhere from a six-line filler to a 1,500-word short story, to a 65,000-word novel. In other words, a potboiler can be any writing project designed to bring a quick paycheck with a minimum of trouble and effort on the part of the writer. Writing potboilers is a practice that can be slanted to nearly any market the writer knows well. The secret to success lies in quantity and quick production. If the project eats up more time than it's worth, it isn't practical. Because potboilers are usually written in the shortest span of time possible, they rarely are of superior literary quality. However, potboilers should appear as clean and professional as any other material. Wise beginners learn to turn out potboilers as a part of their learning process. They always have something simmering "in the pot" and something in the mail.

Reader Identification

Q. What is reader identification and how do I achieve it in my writing?
A. Reader identification is the process by which a reader projects himself into a work of fiction, associating himself with the adventures, conflicts, desires, feelings, and responses of the characters in a story. The writer's ability to create strong, believable characters involved in a significant conflict in pursuit of a goal is a crucial element in achieving reader identification. Many commercial magazines that publish short fiction *require* that the protagonist and setting of a short story are such that the magazine's readers can easily identify with them. Reader identification is also important in nonfiction writing. Through choice of market and treatment

of subject matter, a writer projects himself into the reader's mind to better hold the reader's interest and increase his chances of making a sale.

SASE

Q. What does SASE mean? And why is SASE in almost every market listing in Writer's Digest *and* Writer's Market*?*
A. SASE means self-addressed, stamped envelope. It should be enclosed in every query, every manuscript submission, to every editor. When requesting information from an editor or from a magazine's subscription or service departments, it's always best to enclose SASE to cover return postage and reply from that market. Make sure the envelope is at least a #10 envelope—nothing like the tiny personal-size stationery envelopes, which are useless when sending reprints of articles, flyers or publications, or literature which is requested. And when submitting a manuscript, always enclose the proper size envelope (usually the same size as the one the manuscript was mailed in), with adequate postage for return. Always *glue* the stamps to the envelope, rather than using a paper clip. If you only clip them, there's a chance that they might get separated from the manuscript. Remember: some editors will not return material submitted without SASE.

Simultaneous Submissions

Q. What are "simultaneous submissions," as listed by some publishers in Writer's Market*?*
A. A simultaneous, or multiple, submission is a manuscript submitted for consideration to more than one publishing company at the same time. Once taboo, multiple submission has become a moderately common practice for certain types of articles, book proposals, and finished manuscripts. Some editors, however, want to be sure that their competitors are not considering the same material at the same time they are. When a major magazine pays top prices, its editors expect to get an exclusive look at the ideas writers present to them. Therefore, writers should not send multiple submissions to major magazine markets. Smaller magazines, such as religious and company publications, pay lower rates and have readerships which are not likely to overlap with other magazines in the same field; these factors make them more willing to look at simultaneous submissions. A writer may be able to sell one-time rights to the same story or article to a dozen of these publications which buy other than first rights.

Obviously the quality of the writing must be just as good with simultaneous submissions as with those submitted individually. Amateur material submitted to several publications stands small chance of serious consideration by anyone, while an editor sympathetic to beginners may give valuable advice on a piece if he knows he is the only one who has received it.

It is usually acceptable for a writer to make multiple queries—especially if his article idea is timely. The outline and sample chapters of a book proposal can also be submitted simultaneously to several publishers, provided an original cover letter is included with each, addressed to the appropriate editor. Should you inform the editor in the cover letter that the manuscript is being considered by other publishers? Opinions vary. About half of the book publishers listed in *Writer's Market* indicate they will accept multiple submissions. However, many prefer that the author tell them that a multiple submission has been made. Some also require that the writer tell them the names of other publishers to whom the material has been sent.

"Slushpile"

Q. What is meant by the term "slushpile?"
A. "Slushpile" is a collective term for unsolicited material received by magazine editors and book publishers. This refers to any manuscripts not specifically assigned by an editor or submitted by an agent.

Story or Article?

Q. When a story is based on an actual happening, but changed to a degree, should it be called a story or an article?
A. If a story is told only from the narrator's viewpoint and the incidents are factually accurate and based on a true personal experience, it would probably be considered an article. Fiction contains a degree of imagination, does not attempt to get in all the facts, and usually strays from the true account to add color and drama.

Subheads

Q. What do editors call the small descriptive phrase or sentence that usually appears under the main title of an article?
A. Most editors call it a "subhead." A subhead is usually designed to pique the reader's interest in reading the article or story by telling just a little bit about the subject matter.

Synopsis

Q. What is a synopsis?
A. A synopsis is a brief condensation of a topic or subject. It is most frequently used to summarize the plot of a story, novel, or play. A synopsis also forms part of a book proposal that an author submits to a publisher. A nonfiction book proposal generally consists of a comprehensive summary of the contents of the proposed book (the synopsis), along with two or three sample chapters and an outline detailing chapter by-chapter highlights of the book. Some publishers require a synopsis for fiction and nonfiction works; others require a full manuscript for fiction.

Publishers of novels require a synopsis and usually want a chapter-by-chapter summary of the book, including all the characters, subplots as well as the main plot, and any other pertinent details. Such a synopsis could run from ten to thirty pages depending on the complexity and length of the novel.

Some editors use the words "synopsis" and "outline" to mean the same thing, but in general, a synopsis is a brief review of the proposed manuscript, while an outline is an organized plan.

Tearsheet

Q. What is a "tearsheet?"
A. "Tearsheet" is another term for "clipping," a sample of writing in its published form which has been cut—or "torn"—from the newspaper or magazine in which it appeared. Tearsheets can be a writer's own work or another writer's articles used for research purposes.

Trade Book vs Library Edition

Q. What is a trade book and how does it differ from a library edition?
A. A trade book is a hardcover title distributed mainly through retail bookstores. Trade books can be novels, works of nonfiction or children's books. The author's royalties, based on the retail list price, are usually escalating, for example: 10 percent of the retail price on the first 5,000 copies, 12½ percent on the next 5,000, and 15 percent on any additional copies sold. A library edition is a trade book with a binding stronger than that used for books to be sold to the general public. The library binding is designed to withstand the heavy use a library book will receive.

Unsolicited Manuscript

Q. What is an unsolicited manuscript?
A. When a writer submits a book, article, story, or poem without the publisher requesting it, the manuscript is *unsolicited*. In such a case, the editor or publisher has not given any indication he will read the work; he and the writer have not communicated, either by mail or through the writer's agent. Some publishers will not read unsolicited manuscripts. Since publishers have no legal responsibility for unsolicited manuscripts, the author should always consult *Writer's Market* to make sure a specific publisher accepts them. The writer must always include SASE when submitting unsolicited manuscripts.

Penetrating Barriers

Q. What can a writer do when a magazine or book publisher won't look at unsolicited manuscripts?
A. Over the past several years, some book and magazine publishers have discontinued accepting unsolicited manuscripts and have announced in *Writer's Market* and *Fiction Writer's Market* that they only accept manuscripts submitted by an author's agent. Most writers don't have agents and some circumvent this policy by directing an advance query to a specific editor. When the idea has sufficient appeal they obtain a go-ahead to submit the manuscript to the editor's personal attention. However, most publishers accept unsolicited submissions. Check *Writer's Market* for specific magazine and book publishers' policies.

6 How Do I Get Ideas?

Sir William Osler, physician and medical historian, reminded us that "In science, the credit goes to the man who convinces the world, not to the man to whom the idea first occurs." The freelance writer faces the same challenge. Ideas are only as good as what you do with them. Small comfort that you're thinking salable material if you are scooped in your own backyard on an idea you, too, had for a local feature; or if a magazine carries an article you were going to query about but never got around to. Or maybe getting ideas to start with is your problem? Read on!

Local to National

Q. I've written several articles for local newspapers and magazines, but I'm not sure I can write a national-interest article. How can I write something that will sell to a national publication?
A. Many local and regional articles can be expanded in scope to fit the needs of national publications. By examining how a local story relates to a national trend, or by using it as an example of that trend, a writer can create an article that will be attractive to a national magazine. Of course, you'll have to supplement your local information with related examples from national sources, which you have gleaned from research. You should also contact persons involved in the subject on a national level, obtain their viewpoints and comments, and add their quotes to your story. For a year-round calendar of ideas for either local or national markets, see Frank Dickson's *1001 Article Ideas*.

Idea Sources

Q. Is there some way, other than through the local newspaper, I can find out about community and corporate happenings as possible subjects for freelance articles?
A. Most public relations departments of large organizations maintain mailing lists and notify interested persons of upcoming events on their calendars. Large companies, universities and nonprofit groups schedule a variety of events that can be grist for the freelancer's mill. Convention and Visitors Bureaus of large cities can also inform you when special-interest groups and professional organizations will be holding conventions in your area. All you have to do to start receiving information is write to the organization and ask—as a professional freelance writer—to be placed on their mailing list.

Sell Ideas?

Q. I've come up with several ideas for articles, but I don't know enough about the topics to write the actual pieces. Do magazine editors purchase story ideas, or will writers more knowledgeable in the specific areas buy the rights to use my ideas?
A. Magazine editors usually will only purchase completed manuscripts, not ideas. A few exceptions, such as the "Talk of the Town" section of the *New Yorker,* tabloids like the *National Enquirer,* the "The Better Way" section of *Good Housekeeping,* are listed in *Writer's Market.* Writers who specialize in specific fields of information usually have so many ideas of their own that they do not purchase from others. However, it may surprise you how little the average writer knows about a given topic before he begins to write about it. With some research and interviews with knowledgeable sources, you probably can learn enough about your subject to write the article yourself. (For more advice on finding "experts" and doing research, see Chapter 7 and Chapter 8.)

Fresh Ideas

Q. I'm having trouble coming up with fresh ideas for my fiction. What are some ways I can jog my imagination into action?
A. The number of ways to find story ideas is almost limitless. First of all, you should read widely—not just novels and short stories, but magazines and newspapers. Something in a factual article might jog your imagination. If something makes you think, "I wonder what kind of person would do something like that," chances are you could use it as a starting point for your next story.

An interesting person you've met or something that happened to you at work, or even a daydream or nightmare can be a catalyst. Listen to what people say on the street, and jot in your notebook any interesting pieces of dialogue.

New settings might also spark your imagination. Add these descriptions to your notes. You don't have to take an expensive vacation; a trip to a neighboring town or a detour through another area of your city on your way home can show you something that could catch your imagination. Your own life experiences can also be the foundation for a short story or novel, but do not become entrapped in facts.

History and the classics of literature can be retold in modern surroundings; Othello as chairman of a corporation or a Napoleon figure as President of the U.S. are only two of the many possible twists on old stories.

Above all, remember that inspiration doesn't always strike like a flash of lightning. Ideas generally ripen slowly, starting from a single impression or bit of information. The more opportunities you give your imagination, the greater the chance ideas will come to you.

Plot Problems

Q. I have in mind a story involving several character types, but I'm having trouble coming up with a strong plot. What can I do about this?
A. Most fiction is based on what the characters do. Interesting, believable characters create the atmosphere and conflict necessary to the success of a short story or novel. But no matter how good a writer's characters are, if he hasn't outlined the plot, his story won't go anywhere. Every story has a basic conflict. By carefully examining your characters—their backgrounds, likes, dislikes, beliefs—you can gain ideas about how to set up that conflict. Ask yourself questions. What does the main character want? What obstacles might interfere with his goals?

How do the characters relate to one another? Once you've set up the basic conflict, you can begin to outline the action of the story.

According to Maxine Rock's *Fiction Writer's Help Book,* there is no "right" way to outline; each writer develops a method that best suits him. But by understanding your characters, their motivations, and the conflicts they face, you lay the groundwork for your story, and make it easier to figure out "what happens next."

Slanting

Q. It seems that every topic I want to write about has already been covered by a magazine currently on the newsstands. How can I use my idea without duplicating another writer's work?

A. There are many different slants to the same subject. The creative part of marketing is the work the writer does in finding a different approach to a subject in order to interest readers of a specific magazine that has not already covered that subject. Check the specific topic that interests you in *Reader's Guide to Periodical Literature.* Read the articles and see what angle of your topic they covered. Then see what alternative approach you might use for a different magazine, using *Writer's Market* as a guide. For example, an article on the postwar generation of "baby boomers" published in *Money* magazine set out to answer the question, "Can they ever live as well as *their* parents?" An article for an education administration magazine might talk about the number of children this generation plans to have and how that affects the need for schools, classroom space, and teachers in the coming years. By varying your approach, you can sell articles on the same idea to a wide variety of publications.

Saving Ideas

Q. Sometimes when I'm working on a particular story, I come across a bit of information that sparks an idea for another story. But when the current work is finished, I can never seem to recall the second story idea. How do other writers handle this?

A. One of the most valuable tools a writer has is his notebook. The notebook is a kind of "surrogate memory," in which a writer can jot thoughts, impressions and story ideas *when they occur.* Character descriptions, bits of dialogue, facts from research—all can be recorded in the notebook for easy retrieval.

Another valuable method of keeping ideas is a clipping file. When you find a piece of information or newspaper article that gives you an idea, you may want to clip it (or copy it, if it's library property) and file it for later use. Your clipping file can be divided into whatever categories best suit your purposes. This method is useful because it not only preserves your idea, but also the information that caused it to occur to you.

People As Research

Q. I know many people who have had unusual experiences or are themselves unusual in some way. I think their lives would make interesting stories or articles. But I don't want to interview all of them and write only personality sketches. Is there a way to turn these unusual experiences and people into marketable stories and articles?

A. You are on the right track. Personality sketches give the beginning writer excellent experience in interviewing, organizing the highlights of a person's life or experience, and writing colorful, concise articles about interesting people. They also sell widely, thus providing opportunity to get your work in print. But this material can be used other ways, too.

Instead of seeing the person and his or her whole life, think about using brief references as anecdotes or illustrations to strengthen an argument in another article. Quotations or clever remarks can become strong leads for both fiction and nonfiction, sometimes sparking an entire article idea. And real people and their motivations form the characters used in many stories that sell.

Keep recording all the impressions you can as your path crosses the fascinating lives of strangers and acquaintances. Consider this information as money in the bank. You will draw on it for years to come.

7 How Can I Get in Touch with Information Sources?

Someone once said that a good nonfiction writer doesn't have to know much, he just has to know the right people. Learning who the right people are, where they are, and what to ask them are some of the earliest tasks of the freelance writer. Fiction writers, too, need to verify medical or legal situations in their stories, maintain historical accuracy in their novels or discuss a character personality problem with a psychologist. No matter what the subject of your article, story, or book, there is someone who can help you add insight and authority to your manuscript.

Finding Addresses

Q. How can I find the addresses of authors and/or well-known persons or "experts" for requesting interviews by mail, telephone or in-person?
A. Book authors can generally be reached by writing to them in care of their publishers; the publishers' addresses can be found in *Books in Print*. You might also check the directories: *Contemporary Authors* or one of the several *Who's Who* directories to find their home addresses.

Other directories contain the addresses of specialists in various fields; such as *American Men and Women of Science* and *Who's Who in American Art*. These directories can be found at most libraries.

If you cannot locate a performer's or famous person's address through the biographical directories, Celebrity Service, Inc. may be able to provide the name and telephone number of the celebrity's manager, agent, or press agent for a fee of ten dollars. Contact them at 171 W. 57th St., New York NY 10019.

Government Sources

Q. I need information from several U.S. Government agencies for an article I am writing. Is there a central news and information bureau in Washington, and will they give me information by phone? How can I find the addresses of government agencies?
A. There is no central information bureau, but you can call the government operator at 202/655-4000 for the number of a specific department or agency's Public Information Officer, or P.I.O. The P.I.O. is the person you should contact in reference to any story which deals with a government agency, since most federal officials won't give out information for publication

without clearing it with their P.I.O.s. You may be able to get the answer you need by telephoning the government agency specialist the P.I.O. refers you to. Addresses of government departments, bureaus and agencies, can be found in *United States Government Manual*, available at your local library. Another valuable source is Matthew Lesko's *Information U.S.A.*

Primary and Secondary Sources

Q. What's the difference between a primary source and a secondary source?
A. A primary source—or primary research—provides the writer with original, firsthand information. It is based on the writer's own experience and observation, direct contact with other people (usually in an interview), or information gleaned from personal papers, correspondence, diaries, or manuscripts written at the time or on the scene of the person or subject being studied. Primary research is closer to the subject, and therefore preferable to secondary research, which is based entirely on subsequently published newspapers, books, or magazines. If a writer uses only secondary sources, he runs the risk of his research being inaccurate, since his sources may contain misquotations or other errors. Secondary sources are used to gain supporting information and background material for an article.

Thank-You Notes?

Q. Many sources across the country have answered my written requests for information with long letters giving me detailed information I might not have gotten anywhere else. Is it customary to acknowledge each of these replies with a thank-you note? I owe these people a great deal for providing me with so much information, but sending individual thank-you notes can become costly and time consuming.
A. Although notes of thanks are not obligatory in this case, they certainly would be welcomed and appreciated, and could help ensure that these persons will be equally helpful if you need to use their resources again. Individual notes are probably not necessary; a photocopied form letter and copy of your published article should suffice to thank them for their trouble.

Permission to Include

Q. In doing a "round-up" article in which I publish the opinions and comments of several different people, should I have the consent of the individuals I include, if the information is gathered by other than personal interview? What I have in mind are actors with some background trait in common.
A. Yes, it is best to have the consent of individuals you include in a "round-up" article.

Locating Magazine Writers

Q. How can I contact the author of a magazine article I recently read?
A. Write to the author in care of the magazine in which the article appeared. The magazine's editorial office address will appear somewhere on its masthead or contents page. Since some publications have their subscriptions fulfilled at a different address, be sure you write to the editorial address, not to the circulation or advertising addresses. Most editors will forward mail addressed to contributing writers. However, most magazines will not give the home addresses of their contributors.

Conflicting Information

Q. I'm researching an article and some of my sources disagree on several points. What can I do about this?
A. One of the most difficult tasks of writing a nonfiction article or book is reconciling information received from different sources. In some cases, the writer's own prior research has given him enough knowledge about the subject or the backgrounds of his sources to judge who is right. But at other times, it becomes necessary for the writer to communicate conflicting information to the conflicting sources, letting each answer the questions raised by the other. For example, if you were writing about the effects of cigarette smoke on nonsmokers, and two researchers had given you contradictory statements, you could call or write each and say, "Dr. So-and-So of Such-and-Such University disagrees with your position [and quote the other expert]. Could you comment on that?" This way, by the comment in your finished piece, readers of your article can decide for themselves which source is credible, and you will have covered the topic fairly. In some cases, both sources will be equally credible and readers will come to the conclusion that enough research has not yet been done on the subject to affirm or deny contradictory conclusions.

Magazine Back Issues

Q. How can I obtain a copy of an old back issue of a magazine?
A. Write to the magazine first; many publications operate a back-issue service. If the magazine in question is no longer being published or does not have the issue you need, check the New York City (Manhattan) Yellow Pages for advertisers under "Magazines—Back Number," or check with any used book stores in your area. A large city or college library may have back issues you could photocopy.

Magazine Research

Q. How can I find out which issues of a special-interest magazine contain articles on a specific topic I'm researching?
A. Indexes to periodicals catalogue information published in magazine, newspaper, or journal articles by title, subject and author. Most indexes are available in large public libraries or college libraries. Indexes to publications in specialized fields include directories such as *Education Index, Business Periodicals Index, Abstracts and Indexes in Science and Technology, Film Literature Index, Abstracts on Criminology and Penology, Religion Index One: Periodicals* and *Index to Legal Periodicals.* Another good resource is *Ulrich's International Periodicals Directory,* which lists publications by subject matter and tells where each is indexed or whether it publishes its own index. If, for example, you were researching an article on interior design, and *House Beautiful* was the only publication in that area with which you were familiar, finding that title in *Ulrich's* would lead you to more than 125 other periodicals on the subject and show you where each is indexed.

For general-interest magazines, some indexes to consult are *Reader's Guide to Periodical Literature, The Magazine Index* and *Access: The Supplementary Index to Periodicals.*

Newspaper Addresses

Q. How can I find addresses of daily and weekly newspapers to submit articles of regional interest?
A. *Editor & Publisher* magazine produces a yearbook which contains a directory of all

newspapers. The yearbook is available in most large libraries and newspaper offices. If you wish to purchase a copy, call the magazine's Manhattan office, 212/752-7050, for the current price. Two other sources for addresses are the Newspaper Directory (volume 1) of *Working Press of the Nation* and *Ayer Directory of Publications,* also available at the library. Both directories are set up geographically by state, then city, which will help you locate regional prospects.

Sample Copies

Q. I would like to obtain sample copies of a number of magazines not sold locally. To whom do I address such a request and is payment expected?
A. Send your request to Sample Copy Dept., along with SASE, and offer to pay for the sample copy and mailing costs if necessary. Some magazines charge; others don't.

8 What's the Best Way to Do Research?

American playwright Wilson Mizner said; "When you take stuff from one writer, it's plagiarism; but when you take it from many writers, it's research." Today's writer-researcher has at his fingertips not only the traditional resources of books, magazine articles and directories of experts' names and addresses, but a host of new computer data bases which can save him hours of tedious manual searching. Don't forget to ask your librarian "What's new?" in relation to your current project. A librarian may have some new resource you didn't know about.

Planning Your Research

Q. I'm writing a piece that requires a lot of research and I don't know what to do first. Where do I start?
A. Every writer develops his own system of organization, so there is no "right way" to prepare your research. But it is important to develop *some* system to keep you from wasting time.

Kay Cassill, author of *The Complete Handbook for Freelance Writers,* recommends some general guidelines for planning your research: Think through your article outline from beginning to end and decide what you need to know and what *kind* of information you'll need such as statistics, advice from experts and illustrative anecdotes. Make a list of pertinent questions that must be answered in the course of the article, as well as secondary questions that are beneficial but not crucial. Decide what your probable sources are and list them in the order in which you should consult them. Adjust your research plans to fit your schedule (how much time can you spend on this article?), budget (is the publisher covering any of your costs?) and the scope of the topic. Cassill urges you to do your homework early and keep to a well laid-out schedule. As you gain experience, your system of research will develop and you'll gain confidence, increasing your ability to cut your research down to size.

Organizing Your Research

Q. When I'm finished researching an article, I have so much raw material that I'm overwhelmed by the sheer bulk of it and don't know where to begin. How can I distill all my research material into a manageable size?
A. There are probably as many ways to organize article material as there are writers who do it. Each writer has a system, ranging from complex arrangements of classified index cards to casual groupings of related notes.

The first thing to do is reduce the bulk of material you've gathered. Get rid of books you aren't going to use anymore and remove the clippings you need from the publications you've gathered, rather than keeping whole magazines and newspapers. Next, you must decide what information is essential to your article and what is only tangentially related to your topic, filing the latter for future use. Hayes Jacobs, author of *Writing and Selling Non-Fiction* and New York market columnist for *Writer's Digest,* recommends that as you handle every piece of information you've gathered, you notice how the material looks—whether it's in a *green* envelope or written on *yellow* paper or in a small notebook—each will provide you with a mental trigger to help you find the material immediately when you need it.

Divide your material into subject categories. Some writers use colored pencils to code the information, others use card files and file folders to classify their material. In distilling the research into written copy, many writers cut and paste bits of information onto a single page.

It's important to have everything you need close to you to write your article, but don't over-emphasize the importance of organization. Over-organization can be used to avoid getting started with the actual writing.

Note-Taking vs Tape Recorder

Q. I'm not sure whether to take written notes or use a tape recorder when researching an article. What are the pros and cons of each?
A. Both methods have their good and bad points. Tape recorders allow an interviewer to concentrate on conducting the interview and making other observations of the interviewee and the surroundings, rather than writing the conversation. They also provide a solid proof of what someone said if the subject later claims he was misquoted. Taping can also be useful in the library, allowing you to record lengthy bits of research more quickly than if you wrote them longhand when a photocopy machine was not available. You can also use a recorder to note thoughts and observations in the car.

However, there is always the possibility that the tape recorder will go on the blink when you need it most. Also, some interview subjects are uncomfortable with tape recorders and will not talk as freely as with someone who unobtrusively takes notes. You could also mistakenly erase important material.

Unless you take shorthand or develop your own speedwriting system, note-taking can be difficult. Even the best set of notes may seem incomprehensible once cold and the best memories may fail. Some authors recommend using a tape recorder to be sure they have accurate information, supplementing the tape with notes. That way, not even accidental erasure can foul up a story, and written notes will provide an easy way to check the content of the interview without listening to the entire tape.

Research for Historical Fiction

Q. I am currently working on a novel set in the eighteenth century. How do I go about researching it?
A. Everything in your fiction must be accurate and realistic. It isn't enough to create background details in your imagination, because a knowledgeable reader might recognize a factual error and you'd lose credibility. Start your historical research with a relatively simple book on that period of world history or a general history of the country in which you've decided to set your novel. This will give you information about the time and the names of the period's important people.

Even if you're not writing about an actual historical figure, biographies can be a valuable source of information on the manners and mores of the time. From a biography's historical framework, you can create everyday people upon whose actions there are fewer restrictions than if you were dealing with real people.

To check on the customs, foods, clothing and technology of the time, novelist Roberta Gellis recommends *The Everyday Life* series. The series covers every historic period through the nineteenth century and every culture from ancient Egypt to the Vikings. More detailed books on certain areas, such as clothing and transportation, can be found at most libraries. Check the titles volume of *Books in Print* under *Everyday Life In . . .* (the specific country/time you're interested in). Also check *Subject Guide to Books in Print* under the country or historical figure around which your research is centered. Remember, however, that books might contain inaccurate information, so be sure to cross-check your research with other sources.

Data Bases

Q. What are data bases and how can they be useful to a writer?
A. A data base is a collection of specialized information stored in a computer. Numeric data bases direct a researcher to numbers and statistics; bibliographic data bases lead the way to citations and summaries of textual material.

Data bases are generally housed in libraries, corporations, and government agencies, although only libraries usually grant a freelance writer access. Government and industry data bases usually contain classified and proprietary information and are closed to the public.

To use a data base, a writer can request that a librarian do a computer search, which will result in a printout containing references to books, or periodicals, or other information sources pertaining to his topic. The library will generally charge the researcher fifteen to forty dollars for the computer search; the fee can be lower or higher, depending on the library and how much computer time is used and how many sources are found.

The Foundation Directory gives annual information on private foundations, while *Foundation Grants Index* categorizes foundations which have assets of one million dollars or more and have granted awards of over five thousand dollars. You can search these books manually, but computer searching is faster and can research a topic more specifically. For instance, if a writer wanted to know only those foundations which made awards to writers on scientific topics, the data base computer search would be able to narrow the topic and eliminate all foundations not relevant to the writer's specific needs. Also, some data base material is unavailable in printed form and may only be obtained through computer search.

If you aren't sure where to start your search, there are directories which list the data bases themselves, such as *Computer Readable Data Bases: A Directory and Sourcebook* and *Online Database Search Services Directory*. Subject indexes in these directories will help you find the data base you might want to search.

Writers who live in isolated areas without libraries having computer access terminals can avail themselves through the telephone of commercial data base search firms which, for a fee, will provide the same kind of service obtainable through libraries. A list of such companies appears in the chapter "Information on Demand" in the *Encyclopedia of Information Systems and Services*.

Data bases which are currently available either through libraries or commercial search firms include such varied sources as *The New York Times Information Bank, The Magazine Index, Legal Resources Index, Trade and Industry Index, Dow Jones News/Retrieval Service*, and many others.

Shy Authors

Q. What are the opportunities for the writer who does not like to interview people and wishes to write magazine articles?
A. There are several kinds of magazine articles that do not require interviewing to make them salable. Each of these can be completed with other types of research. The how-to article, for example, demonstrates or explains to the reader how to accomplish something, such as woodworking projects or sewing different types of clothing. Illustrations are often an integral part of how-to articles. The service article gives the reader information regarding the use or purchase of items, services or facilities. A guide to low-cost vacation spots or pointers on buying a used car would fit this category.

A writer can also base an article on his personal experiences. Such an article is designed to inspire, educate or entertain the reader. Writing about the experience of returning to college at age forty-five or making a career change are examples of this type of article. Your account of a personal struggle to get through a life-threatening experience or other human conflict can become a salable magazine article, for example, the "Drama in Real Life" series in *Reader's Digest*.

The think article analyzes facts, events or trends as the writer perceives them. The writer presents informed opinions, drawing conclusions intended to persuade the reader. Think articles appear in newspapers on the op-ed page and in the "quality" magazines, such as *The Atlantic* and *Harper's,* where, of course, your opinions would have to be buttressed by those of experts you had researched in periodicals, books, and perhaps through personal correspondence.

Different aspects of historical events can be covered in a light manner for popular magazines, or through in-depth research for scholarly publications. Many editors indicate their lack of interest in "routine historical pieces," but a well-written historical piece related to a magazine's content can sell almost any editor, providing the slant is right and the approach is fresh and lively.

The travel article has two objectives: to inform the reader by way of facts and to enlighten him by way of impressions. This type of article requires a certain amount of preliminary research and the writer must be perceptive enough to see the less conspicuous elements of his trip, such as the people, customs, and atmosphere of the place he visits. Photos are an essential part of most travel pieces.

The humorous article, although one of the most difficult forms to write, can be one of the most financially rewarding. Most writers of humor attain success only after years of experience.

Conducting interviews by mail is an alternative to the in-person interview, and can glean enough information from an expert or celebrity to develop a salable article.

Other Research Sources

Q. What resources, other than books and libraries, are useful in researching an article?
A. There are many ways of finding out what you need to know other than using the library. Professional and special interest associations exist for a variety of common goals and interests. An association can give you information or steer you to an expert in the topic about which you're writing. Check the key word index in the *Encyclopedia of Associations* or call the American Society of Association Executives at 202/626-2723 and ask for the Information Center to find the organization that can help you.

In addition to the government experts mentioned in Chapter 7, there are also many government reports on specialized topics. Check in your library for the Subject Indexes to material issued by the U.S. Government Printing Office. There is a *Cumulative Subject Index to the Monthly Catalog of U.S. Government Publications, 1900-1971* and annual indexes after that time. The Government Printing Office also issues a monthly bulletin of government publications.

The Library of Congress maintains a National Referral Center which can direct the writer to any of thirteen thousand information sources in almost any subject area. A freelancer can write for information to the National Referral Center, U.S. Library of Congress, 10 First St., Washington DC 20540 or phone 202/287-5670.

To find information sources on practically any subject, check *Writer's Resource Guide* which lists many organizations, companies, libraries and museums under thirty subject headings. It might be the quickest place to find what you need.

Poetry Sources

Q. In my novel, I'm quoting from a poem I learned years ago. How do I locate the source or author?
A. *Granger's Index to Poetry* indexes poetry by title and first line, and by subject. *Bartlett's Familiar Quotations* also contains many well-known passages, arranged by author and indexed by the key word in the passage.

Photocopy?

Q. Most books now carry the legend: "No part of this book may be reproduced or utilized in any form or by any means, electronic or mechanical, including photocopying, recording, or by any information storage and retrieval system." Copying material longhand when researching is tedious and time-consuming. Does the warning mean I can't copy material for my private research without first contacting the publisher?
A. If the photocopy is for your research only, and you do not intend to reproduce the copied page in your article, then using the copy machine is as legal as taking notes longhand. However, if you intend to quote the material verbatim in your manuscript, you will need permission.

Specialized Books

Q. How would an author build a reference library of books about a field in which he wants to specialize? I have chosen an area of interest, but I don't know what books are available.
A. *Subject Guide to Books in Print* lists every book currently being published in the U.S. Listings are alphabetical by subject and field of interest the books cover. For instance, a book on President Truman's Korean War policy might be listed under Truman's name, "Korean War 1950-1953" and "Military History." Go to your library and see what material they have on your topic and check the *Subject Guide* to see if the books you want are still available from the publishers.

Inter-Library Loan

Q. My local library doesn't have a book I need for my research. How can I get a copy of the book without buying it?
A. Most libraries participate in a service called inter-library loan. Through this service, a library can obtain a book from another library—a university library in the same or another city,

a public library in another town or the Library of Congress. Charges for the service vary according to the requirements of the library providing the book. Ask your local librarian about this plan.

Library Searching

Q. Is there any way a library can find out if another library has a book I need?
A. If your library has access to OCLC, yes. OCLC stands for Online Computer Library Center, a service which links the information centers of 3,500 businesses and institutions and 6,000 public, private and special libraries in all of the fifty states, Australia, Canada, Finland, Mexico, England and West Germany. OCLC provides libraries with catalog card index files, helps them exchange information and lend books to member libraries. OCLC's central office, in Dublin, Ohio, keeps record of more than 110 million location listings of library material. Its data base contains material in 244 languages and dialects. It adds more than 25,000 titles to its file every week.

To find a book, a librarian feeds a title into the OCLC terminal at the member library. The central computer gives the author's name, publication date, name of publisher, location of publisher, price and subject headings under which the title could be listed. The libraries having copies of the book are listed by codes. The librarian selects those libraries from which he desires borrowing privileges and makes arrangements to obtain the book for the patron. It can take a little time to get the book—four weeks or longer. If you need a book and don't mind waiting, as long as you know it's on the way, OCLC could be beneficial to your research.

Research Survey by Mail

Q. How do I go about conducting a research survey by mail?
A. The first step in conducting your survey is to thoroughly research the topic and develop a questionnaire. The questions should be typed so as to give your respondent the opportunity and space to answer directly on your questionnaire. Be sure to include a final question such as "Any further comments you wish to make?" so that people inclined to give you more than brief answers can do so. In addition, they may include information that you didn't think to ask for. Write a form letter to accompany the questionnaire, stating the purpose of the survey and how you intend to use the information in your article—either as general results or direct quotations from their answers. Indicate that if they don't wish to be quoted directly, you'll respect that. Your questionnaire should conclude with a place for the respondent's signature along with one of two statements the respondent can choose to check: Permission granted to quote directly from this questionnaire ( ), or Please do not quote me by name directly from this questionnaire ( ). Include SASE for the respondents to return the questionnaires.

Controversial Article

Q. Among several articles I hope to write is one of a very controversial nature. Even if an editor thinks the piece is interesting, he will likely want to be very sure of the authenticity of the source material—especially since I'm an unknown writer. How do I proceed?
A. Most writers of controversial articles maintain a detailed list of their sources of information and have this ready for presentation to an editor who questions the author on any specific point. Send your article or query and advise the editor you'll be glad to provide verification on any points.

Legal-Free Research?

Q. I'm doing some research using old, turn-of-the-century books and material from state archives, including some family papers. Can I use this material in my own manuscript? Would it be covered by copyright?
A. Under the old (pre-1978) copyright law, copyright lasted for twenty-eight years and could be renewed for an additional twenty-eight. The new copyright law lengthened by nineteen years the renewal term of copyright on works which were in their renewed term when the law took effect. Thus, works already copyrighted and renewed as of January 1, 1978, are protected for a total of seventy-five years from the year of first publication. If that time has passed, the material would now be in the public domain and you could use it as you pleased, without first obtaining permission.

The state archives should pose no problem for you, if they aren't copyrighted. However, the family papers could possibly raise the question of invasion of privacy, if any members of the family or families survive. It would be a good idea for you to verify with any descendants whether they would object to your use of the material.

Too Much Research?

Q. Is there such a thing as over-researching an article?
A. Yes, but it can be useful. Sometimes a writer will end up with a stack of material several inches thick and realize he can never use it all. That's when he has to begin the long process of "weeding out" his information, choosing only the material most pertinent to his topic. Material he cannot use in the main article might shed some light on another angle of the subject, or provide human interest. That material might be developed as a "sidebar"—a short feature accompanying an article to provide more depth or additional factual information that would not fit well into the body of the article. A writer could also use the material to write another article on the same subject, using a different approach and slanting it to another non-competing magazine. It's usually better to have too much information than not enough, but a writer should make sure he is not simply using further research as an excuse to put off beginning the actual writing of his article or book.

Getting Quotes from Experts

Q. How can I get quotes from experts? Also how can I find incidents and examples to add substance to magazine articles I'm writing?
A. After you've decided which experts you'd like to get quotes from, write them individual letters in care of their business addresses. Explain the subject matter of your article and the magazine for which you're writing and ask your appropriate questions. Be sure to enclose SASE for the reply. As for finding incidents and examples—read a lot of other reference material on the same subject. Talk to people in your area who may have had experiences in the specific field you're writing about. Ask them and the experts you write to suggest other people in other parts of the country who may be able to help you in your research.

Hire Researchers?

Q. I have an idea for a book that is going to require a lot of research and interviews with people from all over the country. Is there a way I can find someone who will do some of my research for pay, and are there persons in other cities I could contact for help?
A. Established book authors who can afford it hire paid researchers to help them gather the

raw information they need before they start to write. Newspaper editors can tell you if their policies permit any of their reporters to do extra off-hour freelance research. Editors and specialist reporters' names are listed in *Editor and Publisher Yearbook* geographically by newspaper. Most reporters are approachable—if they aren't facing a tight deadline. For persons who specialize in doing research, check ads in such publications as *Editor & Publisher, Literary Market Place* (under "Research & Information Services" and "Editorial Services"), and the classifieds in *Publishers Weekly,* and *Writer's Digest.* Rates of pay will vary according to experience, geographical area and the nature of the work. Another possibility is to hire university students and library assistants. They can be knowledgeable in their field of specialization and will work for less money than full-time researchers. You can contact head librarians at public or college libraries either locally or in other cities where necessary, and ask if they can recommend some researchers to you.

Research Retention

Q. Is there any reason to keep interview notes and other research material after an article is finished?
A. Many writers keep old research material for several reasons. They may need to answer questions from editors, readers, or other writers who request information on the sources of the research. They may want to use the research for future articles. Depending on the type of research it is and how much further use the writer may have for it, most magazine writers save material for at least three to six years. Some newspaper reporters who are involved in investigative journalism have developed the practice of destroying their notes once they have served their purpose. This prevents the notes from being subpoenaed if the reporter is being questioned about his sources in an investigative piece.

9 How Much Can I Quote from Others' Work?

The rare occasion when one author sues another for plagiarism usually makes the headlines. The fact is, most writers—especially beginners—are scrupulous about getting permission and fairly attributing their sources when they borrow from another's copyrighted work. Here are some answers to questions about when, how much, and under what circumstances you can quote from others' work.

Quote How Much?

Q. In several articles I have written I quoted briefly from several hardcover books written by doctors. In most cases I referred to the doctor by name, the title of his book, and the publisher. How much can I quote without asking for special permission?
A. There are no hard and fast rules on fair use. The guidelines in the copyright law considered by the courts when deciding whether there is "fair use" or copyright infringement include: how much is quoted in relation to the length of the copyrighted work, whether it's for commercial or nonprofit educational purposes and whether it impairs the potential market for, or value of, the original work.

Quote Types

Q. What's the difference between a direct and an indirect quote?
A. A direct quote is information presented in a source's exact words, enclosed in quotation marks. An indirect quote is information paraphrased by the writer. In other words, direct quotes present information verbatim, while indirect quotes present the *substance* of the information, rewritten to shorten it or make it more precise. When using indirect quotation, the writer must be careful that his paraphrase doesn't distort or misrepresent the original intent of the remarks. For example, if you were to quote a source directly, the form would be as follows: In answer to a question about U.S. monetary policy, the President said, "Well, you'd have to check with Paul Volcker about that." But an indirect quote would read: In answer to a question about U.S. monetary policy, the president referred reporters to the chairman of the Federal Reserve System, Paul Volcker.

Getting Permissions

Q. Is it the responsibility of the author or the book publisher to obtain releases for the use of published material? How does a writer go about doing this?
A. Although some book publishers obtain releases, most feel it's the job of the writer to do so after the final manuscript has been accepted. Releases are usually obtained from the author of a work by writing him in care of his publisher. Letters of request to reprint material are sent to the publisher, who either acts in behalf of the author or forwards the request to him for his action. The author, of course, should make copies of the letters asking for permission and forward those to his publisher, along with copies of the letters of permission received.

If permissions fees are required, the author should not pay them until the work is published—in case some items are cut in the editing process and not used.

Permission Fees

Q. How much do publishers usually charge for reprint permissions and to quote from their copyrighted material?
A. If the use of the material is incidental, obtaining permission usually does not entail a fee and is sometimes unnecessary. For instance, if a novelist introduces a chapter with a few lines from another book or if a nonfiction writer quotes a paragraph from a work by an authority in the field, this would usually be considered "fair use" for which permission is not required.

If a writer is editing an anthology of fiction or a collection of articles, however, he may be required to pay permission fees to various copyright holders. These fees could run about $10 per page for magazine and journal articles and vary considerably for other material. An anthology of poetry or plays could run over $15,000 in permission fees. The matter of who is to accept responsibility for paying permission fees must be settled before beginning work on a book, and is generally included in the contract. Costs may be shared with the author up to an agreed upon maximum on the publisher's part—or charged to the author completely—by deducting those costs before royalties are paid. (For further information on editing anthologies, see Chapter 31.)

Unexpected Permission Fee

Q. I completed an article on assignment for a magazine. When they offered to buy it, a letter accompanying the "author contract" stated that I needed to obtain permission from the publisher of a book I quoted from. I contacted the book publisher and learned that a fee is required for using the quotes. How do I pass along this fee to the editor who is buying the article, knowing that the contract was already drawn up requesting me to obtain permission from the publisher?
A. Phone the editor. Discuss who pays such expenses *before* you sign the contract, if possible. If the contract has been returned already, send the editor a copy of the fee request and ask if he can reimburse you on this unanticipated expense. If he says no, you can still use the material. Rephrase it, not using direct quotes, giving credit to the publisher—including title and author of the book from which the information was taken. If the quotes are extensive and vital to your article, though, it's best to pay the permission fee if the editor refuses to.

Stealing from Yourself

Q. Would you please discuss the ethics involved in an author's taking from one of his own published stories a sentence, a phrase, a simile—or anything for that matter—for use in another story.

A. The use of only a sentence, a phrase, or a simile from your original story shouldn't present any ethical problems. The only prohibition would be the risk of having some alert readers tag you as belonging to that *New Yorker* category known as the "Infatuation with sound of own words" department!

Reuse Material in New Book?

Q. Is it okay for me to take a couple hundred words from a previous book of mine and use it in a new one?

A. No, unless the necessary permission has been obtained from the first publisher. Also, editors generally do not like the idea of authors using old material in a new book.

Using People's Names and Quotes

Q. I've finished writing a novel of truth in fictional form centered around the life of a doctor, and the book includes lots of facts and quotes. Names are mentioned in actual quotes. But I cannot give proper credit for some other items because my clippings were destroyed. How should I handle the use of people's names and quotes?

A. If you're using actual names in your novel, you'd better make sure you have permission, in case one of those persons decides to sue you for invasion of privacy, even if whatever you are quoting is not libelous. Otherwise, change the names, as well as the appearance and locale of the characters so they are not readily identifiable as real persons.

Government Publications

Q. Is it permissible to quote directly from a document issued by the United States Government Printing Office? I have never been able to discover whether that material is copyrighted or how credit should be given. Many of the leaflets would be very useful incorporated in articles or books or as research for an article. Do our taxes, which pay for printing these items, give us the right to appropriate the words?

A. Yes, materials published by the government are in the public domain. There are a few minor exceptions—some connected with the post office and some exceptions in which copyrighted material is inserted in an uncopyrighted public domain government publication. Such material would be accompanied by the printed copyright notice. If you have any doubts about whether a specific leaflet you want to use is copyrighted or not, the presence or absence of the copyright notice is your guideline. Even though you are legally free to use materials from government publications, you should cite the source so that both your publisher and the reader will know where your information came from.

Exposé Problems

Q. I am in the process of writing an exposé-type book. Since the materials I plan to expose are copyrighted, obviously I cannot quote from them without permission of the authors. I doubt that any author would consent to my using his material to prove a point against himself. How do I go about doing this legally?

A. Remember that copyright protects only the exact wording of a passage. One way of accomplishing your goal without needing permission might be to paraphrase those authors' remarks, using footnotes to indicate their source.

Show Manuscript to Sources?

Q. *Should I submit copies of my manuscript to each source I quote in an article?*
A. Unless you want to verify some technical material for accuracy before submitting it to your publisher, it's not a good idea. People often want to change their quotes when they see them—even though you accurately reported what they said. Unless such clearance was one of the conditions of your getting the interview with the source or you feel the need to check for accuracy, you can send them a copy of the published article with a thank-you note.

Quotes in Context

Q. *If I quote from a copyrighted source, should I get permission from the publisher and explain to him what material I'm using and how I'm using it?*
A. If you intend to quote at length from a copyrighted source, writing the publisher for permission is necessary, and, of course, when writing the publisher, you should specify exactly what words on which pages the permission is being requested for. If you use a *great deal* of copy from the source, then an explanation of how you plan to use the material is important. Most sources who are being quoted at length want to see the context in which their words appear, and while it probably won't be necessary to send each person you quote a copy of your entire article, you should send them, for example, a copy of the page before and the page after the quote, and mention in your cover letter the thrust of your article. Most writers will want to see how you intend to use their words. The context, length, and purpose of your material will also determine any fee that might be required.

Quote the Primary Source

Q. *I'm writing an article in which I quote from a newspaper article about a university study. Is it permissible to quote or paraphrase the general findings of such a study, as well as a statement about the findings from the researcher, who was also interviewed in the newspaper article?*
A. Quoting the general findings of the study should pose no problem; however, if you go into any detail, it would be advisable to obtain a copy of the study and quote directly from that. As far as quoting the researcher, you should check the quotes with the source. Newspaper stories produced on a tight deadline will sometimes include errors in quoting people, so it would be a good idea for you to go back to the source and make sure you quote him correctly.

Quote vs Paraphrase

Q. *For an article I'm writing, I want to use some statistics I found in a recent issue of Reader's Digest. If I quote from the article directly, should I write the Digest for permission, or can I paraphrase the material without obtaining permission?*
A. You should not need written permission to use brief statistical material from *Reader's Digest*—or any other publication—as long as you cite the source of your information in the article. Whether you quote the source verbatim or paraphrase, you should always acknowledge the original source of the material. If you intend to use the *Digest* article extensively when you write your article, then you must obtain written permission.

Uncopyrighted Brochures

Q. I have access to a number of brochures and pamphlets about a topic I want to use as the subject of a syndicated weekly newspaper column. Is it all right to use these pamphlets as my resource material—I will use other material too—and should I write the publisher of the brochures for permission? The brochures do not carry a copyright notice.

A. If you intend to use the pamphlets as your major resource, then a credit to the publisher—as a matter of ethics, not copyright—is certainly in order. But it usually is not necessary to request permission to use uncopyrighted material.

Guidelines for Quoting

Q. For an article I'm working on, I need to quote several authors on the subject. Each quote need only be long enough to establish the author's particular view, but should also convince the reader that I have not misrepresented the author. What are the guidelines for this kind of use of previously published material?

A. As long as your quotes are brief and you credit your sources, you won't have any problem using the quotes and therefore won't have to write for permission. If you will be referring to one particular source extensively, then it will be necessary for you to obtain permission in advance, to avoid violating the principle of fair use. (For more information about fair use and other legal problems, see Chapter 36.)

Paraphrase Credit

Q. If material is paraphrased from a published source (for example, a magazine or a book), is it enough to mention the source in the bibliography or must written permission be obtained from the publisher of the original material?

A. It depends on how extensive the material is that you are paraphrasing from the original published source. If the material is presented in only a paragraph or two, you need only to refer to the source with the standard "According to (the book *Title* by *Author*) . . ." or "in the (month, year) issue of (magazine), So-and-So states. . . ." If, however, what you are writing, in substance, deals exclusively with material quoted or taken from the original source, you must obtain written permission in addition to mentioning the source in the bibliography.

Magazine Reprint

Q. Some friends and I want to publish a magazine for students. How can we obtain permission to reprint an article which has previously appeared in another magazine?

A. In order to reprint the article you will have to write to the editor of the publication in which it first appeared. Depending on whether or not that magazine purchased only first rights or all rights to the article the editor may or may not be able to grant you permission to reprint. If he only bought first rights, he will give you the address of the author or forward your letter requesting reprint permission. In most cases, you can expect to pay the author for the use of the material you are reprinting. If the editor purchased all rights, you may have to pay a reprint fee to the magazine, but this is negotiable.

Footlights vs Footnotes

Q. I'm writing a play in which I want to use about half a page of material from a book published several years ago on the same topic. Do I have to obtain the publisher's permission

for this? I can't have footnotes mixed in with the dialogue, so how should I give credit?
A. The amount of material you are using is probably small enough that you should not need to write in advance to get the author or publisher's permision to use it. However, you should give attribution to the source. Make sure the program for any production of the play gives credit to the original source, and of course, if the play is published, credit should appear in the published version also.

Using Titles/Brand Names

Q. Can I use titles of television shows, books, and movies in a general way? How about brand names?
A. Yes, since titles are not copyrightable, you are free to refer to them in your writing. Brand names may also be used, as long as they are not used in a derogatory manner. Some companies, such as Coca-Cola and Xerox, object to their brand names being used generically since that jeopardizes their trademark. Writers should not refer to a cola drink as "coke" or refer to photocopying as "xeroxing."

New Magazine Title

Q. I'm starting a magazine and have decided on a title. How do I check to make sure the title isn't already in use?
A. Titles cannot be copyrighted, so you should have no trouble using the title of your choice. However, some magazines have had their titles registered as trademarks by their owners who have well-established use of the title. Obviously, you should avoid such imitative use of currently successful magazine titles.

Quoting Which Bible?

Q. Can I quote from the Bible without being concerned with copyright infringement?
A. Yes, you can quote anything from the King James Version, which is in public domain. However, most modern translations such as *The Living Bible, The Holy Bible: New International Version, A Reader's Guide to The Holy Bible: Revised Standard Version, Jerusalem Bible,* and *Reader's Digest Bible* are under copyright and permission is needed. To quote from these later versions in articles you write for the general market, treat them as you would any book: Write for the original publisher's requirements, request permission to use the material, and give a proper credit line. Many religious magazine and book publishers have standard arrangements with the Bible copyright owners, and already have permission, in which case you, as a writer, might wish to check with the editor you hope to sell to before requesting permission on your own.

Song Permission?

Q. A cartoon I have recently completed has a line from a popular song as the caption. Do I need to obtain permission for the line?
A. Such use of a line from a popular song could be dangerous. Songwriters and poets are often fiercely protective of their copyrights, so when using their material it is always safest to query the copyright owners for permission.

Fair Use

Q. If I lift paragraphs or short quotations from published, copyrighted sources and duplicate and sell these for a profit, would that be a violation of copyright laws? I plan to start a service in the field of religion, which consists of short-length abstracts, extracts, quotations, mini-bibliographies, and how-to-do-it ideas taken from other published sources.
A. As long as you credit the source and pick up only "short-length" copy, it probably will come under the fair use provision of the copyright law. A rule of thumb in deciding how much copy you can use without permission from a copyrighted publication is this: "Am I impairing the fair market value of the original by the amount of copy I'm using?" Past writers in the field of religious writing were once very lenient in giving permission. Today's religious writers protect their copyrighted work and expect the same treatment as other writers.

Quoting Lyrics

Q. In my story it would help add realism to use the titles of a few currently popular songs, and some snatches of the lyrics being played by a band or coming from the juke box. Would it be necessary to get permission or give credit for this use?
A. If you're going to quote directly from the lyrics, you will definitely need the music publisher's permission. A list of publishers of current popular songs appears in the charts of best selling records in music magazines such as *Billboard* and *Cashbox.*

Pay Sources?

Q. If I quote someone, from a personal interview with him, do I have to pay him?
A. In the case of a personal interview, the subject is rarely reimbursed for his participation. The subject usually is pleased to receive the "payment" of publicity and a copy of the article about himself.

Borrowing Characters

Q. I have written a poem utilizing characters and themes from a novel that was published a few years ago. Do I need permission from the author or publisher of the original novel to do this?
A. You may feel free to use the *themes* from the novel, since they are uncopyrightable. Characters, however, are a different matter. If a character—and especially a character's name—is associated with a particular work in the public mind, then the question arises of infringement of the author's right to adapt his own work to other forms. Recently, Warner Brothers, producers of the *Superman* movies, sued ABC-TV, claiming that its *The Greatest American Hero* series infringed on the Superman copyright because the series featured a flying hero with a red cape and x-ray vision who used the same arms-extended flying position as the Superman character. In a similar case, a Los Angeles woman sued *E.T.* director Steven Spielberg for $750 million of the film's profits, claiming she originated the idea in a copyrighted one-act play. Although a Manhattan federal judge rejected Warner Brothers' claims, the studio is appealing the decision; the *E.T.* case is still being argued, as of this writing. Even if you successfully fought an allegation that you had stolen a character, the legal fees could be astronomical. It's always safer to write for permission before you begin a work based on characters from already published sources.

Cookbook Recipe Permissions

Q. In compiling a cookbook, I am taking recipes from newspapers and magazines, as well as from pamphlets put out by companies that manufacture the various ingredients. What procedure should I follow to get permission to use this material? Some of the older recipes I've saved don't show where they appeared originally.

A. Generally, the list of ingredients in a recipe cannot be copyrighted, but the written directions can. If you take a recipe from a food company pamphlet, and it's not copyrighted, that should pose no difficulty. But if the recipe comes from a copyrighted magazine, then the material is protected by copyright law. Successful cookbooks are generally compiled by excellent cooks who have tried intriguing recipes, adapted them to their own style of cooking, and in the process developed a new recipe. Ingredients are altered and the directions completely rewritten. When original sources of recipes are unknown to you, alter the ingredients and completely rewrite the directions.

TV Broadcast Quote

Q. Will you please explain the rules governing the use by writers of quotes and information gained from TV broadcasts? As a feature writer with an extensive clipping file, I have taken notes on some programs and speakers covering topics on which I am collecting information and leads into further research.

A. Generally speaking, if you accurately attribute your information to the proper source, you shouldn't run into any legal difficulty. In the case of direct quotations of *any length*, it might be best to write to the network or to the speaker, requesting permission to use the particular quotes.

Ownership of Letters

Q. I'm writing a book and half of my research is done by writing letters. The interchange of thoughts and ideas between people has developed into an interesting aspect of the work. Is it absolutely necessary to get permission to reprint personal letters? Letters are from universities and hospitals, members of certain associations, and state representatives, among others.

A. Thoughts and ideas in personal letters are the property of the *sender*, not the receiver, so you must get permission for their publication. Personal letters may seem to belong to the person to whom they are sent, but to publish the letters, it is imperative to seek the letter-writer's permission in all cases. This can be accomplished by enclosing a permission release form with your original letter to the person you are interviewing by mail. A statement such as "I give permission for the publication of my letter to (So-and-So)," and an underscore with "Signature" typed under it usually will bring you a return of the letter-information and the written permission to use that information.

Request Permission

Q. I write articles for various dental trade journals and sometimes I write to people in the field for opinions regarding methods. I explain my intentions of writing an article concerning the subject of the information I'm seeking. Is it okay to use their correspondence in my article or must I ask for their permission to do so?

A. Since the opinions in the letters are the property of the sender, not the receiver, you do need permission. Request that permission when you write them with your question, so that their reply would give you the information you want and their permission to have you quote them in your article.

Poem Rights

Q. I have been sending an article each week to a newspaper in which I use a poem (not composed by me) along with Scripture and a few words of my own. Am I allowed to use these poems?

A. If these poems come from books, for example, whose copyright is still in effect, you will definitely need permission to quote them. You need no permission if the poems are from uncopyrighted sources.

Well-Known Quote

Q. In an original poem, I have written, "Good will upon earth, peace among men," which is based on the well-quoted phrase, "Peace on earth, good will to men." Is this legal?

A. The line you're paraphrasing is already in public domain, so you don't have to worry on *that* score. For more current phrases that might have copyright or trademark protection, it would be advisable to reword the basic idea in your own way.

Quoting Songs

Q. If I only mention the title, do I have to have permission from the song publisher? And what about old songs I quote from memory, like ballads or nursery rhymes? Must I locate the publisher and ask his permission? I plan to use quotes from some old lumberjack ballads and a few songs popular ten or fifteen years ago. I don't think a music store could help much on songs that old, could it?

A. Since titles are not copyrightable, you may mention a song title without having to get the song publisher's permission. As for old familiar folk ballads and nursery rhymes, if they are all older than seventy-five years they are in the public domain and can be used by anyone, without obtaining permission. In the case of songs popular about fifteen years ago, however, their copyright will not have run out yet so you probably need permission. Check for the publisher of older popular songs by title in a directory called the *Variety Music Cavalcade*, available in most public libraries.

Quoting from Newspapers

Q. Can I quote personalities whose statements are included in daily newspaper columns? Where can I obtain permission to quote? From the author? From the newspaper? Or from the columnist? I collect inspirational sayings and want to publish this material in a book.

A. Since news cannot be copyrighted, if you are using quotations that are in *news* stories about personalities, you would not have to request permission, assuming that the quotations were accurately recorded by reporters and not of a nature that the personality would subsequently sue for inaccuracy. Many newspaper features and columns, however, are covered by copyright and you would not be able to use quotations from these without requesting permission from the newspaper or the syndicate.

Brief Quotes for Reviews Without Permission

Q. Many books have statements similar to the following: All rights reserved. No part of this book may be reproduced in any form without written permission from the publisher, except for brief passages included in a review appearing in a newspaper or magazine. May brief passages be quoted by reviewers in their reviews from books that do not bear similar statements?

A. Yes, even though books do not make this statement, reviewers may quote briefly from them under the "fair use" provision of the copyright law.

Paraphrasing

Q. Must I write for permission from the copyright holder in order to paraphrase material, as with quoted material? When quoting from another book, may I omit surplus words such as "the," abbreviate or engage in other editing without using distracting dots to indicate such minor deletions?
A. No permission is needed for paraphrased passages, though sources should be acknowledged. The fact that a verbatim quote has been edited should, in all fairness, be indicated primarily to show readers that this is not exactly the way the original author wrote it. The use of the ellipsis (three dots) is the accepted practice, and not usually considered distracting.

Permission to Quote?

Q. In writing an article, is it legal to quote from sources occasionally and give credit in a footnote or is it necessary to get permission from each author or publisher quoted?
A. If the quotes are short, they would come under the copyright principles of fair use and no permission is needed. You should, of course, acknowledge your sources within the text since popular magazines don't use footnotes.

Uncopyrighted Magazine

Q. Can I quote from work that appears in an uncopyrighted magazine without obtaining the author's or the publisher's permission?
A. Although legally this material is in the public domain and permission is not necessary, it would be a courtesy to the original author to request permission to use any sizable amount of the material.

10 What's the Secret of a Good Interview?

Television has shown us in microcosm the wide range of technique and effectiveness possible in the interview—the long, relaxed discussion, the sharply pointed investigative inquiry, the sudden, unexpected question. Depending on what the writer is trying to accomplish, he'll use all these methods, and others, to get facts and opinions, and to break through the surface facades people build up to conceal their real personalities.

Learning to Interview

Q. I am interested in writing magazine articles, but the thought of interviewing someone scares me. I know I have to interview to write successfully. How can I teach myself this method of gathering information?
A. It is common for many beginning writers to feel uneasy about interviewing. One way to combat this feeling is to begin writing about topics that will permit you to interview people you already know and with whom you feel comfortable talking. For instance, an article about how parents handle their children's problems would permit you to interview a variety of friends, neighbors, and relatives. If you live in a small town, talking to the local shopkeepers can give you information on how changes in economic conditions affect the small businessman. Working on these types of articles will give you the experience of interviewing and help build your confidence to handle tougher subjects. Writing résumés requires interviewing and is also a source of income. Since the interviewee is asking you to question him, the job becomes easier and can provide valuable interviewing experience. (Remember that every person you interview for any reason is providing information you may be able to use in future writing.)

Interviewing is a skill that grows with time and practice. Remember that your job is to *listen* to the conversation and keep it flowing without monopolizing it. Prepare your questions before you interview and try to design them so that your interviewee will do most of the talking, and you will soon begin to feel more confident in your abilities.

Research Before the Interview

Q. How much research do I need to do for an interview?
A. The late historian Cornelius Ryan claimed that one of the rules of writing was, "Never interview anyone without knowing 60 percent of the answers." He said that the person being

interviewed has done *his* homework, so the writer should be equally prepared. Research is the best way to know what you need to find out from an interview and the best way to get it. Some interviewers recommend ten minutes of research for every minute of the planned interview. That may sound like a lot of work, but it's always better to be over-prepared than to run out of questions before you run out of time.

The main purpose of research is to enable yourself to talk and ask questions intelligently on any topic the interviewee raises. In addition, doing your homework often makes your subject more receptive. If you've obviously taken the time to do your research, the interviewee will expect an intelligent discussion of the subject, which is always more interesting for an interviewee than talking to someone about a topic on which he is uninformed.

To research an interview, you will use many of the same techniques discussed in Chapters 7 and 8. You should research the interviewee's background and any topics you think might be discussed. For a profile, interview *around* the subject, talking to friends, family, and co-workers to learn more about the person before you actually meet him.

Researching for an interview takes time and you may not make use of even half the information you gather. But a thorough knowledge of the subject can help you ask good, specific questions and get the quotes that will make your article more lively and salable.

Need a List?

Q. After I finish research for an interview, is it necessary to write a list of questions before the interview takes place? How many questions?
A. By deciding on a particular list of "must-ask" questions, the interviewer makes sure he doesn't conclude the interview without obtaining all the necessary information for the article. However, the interviewer should pursue any interesting path down which his subject wanders; the list of prepared questions is a set of boundaries, rather than a hard-and-fast road map. In John Brady's *The Craft of Interviewing,* freelancer Edward Linn says, "The list of questions and the logical sequence invariably disappear very quickly. If they don't, you're in trouble."

To decide on a list of questions, first choose your angle—or let your editor tell you what he has in mind. Then look at your research and decide what you need to know from the interviewee. The number of questions you need will vary, depending on the topic of the article, the interviewee, and in some cases, the amount of time an interviewee allows. The more questions you prepare, though, the better chance of leaving the interview with the essential answers plus additional interesting information.

Structure the outline of the interview to follow a logical course. You might open with easy, mechanical questions, such as those that would establish the interviewee's relation to or view of the topic; then moving on to knottier, more thoughtful probes, such as asking what he thinks about someone else's particular criticism of his actions or point of view; then moving back to the mechanical, and ending with a query such as, "Is there anything else we've not talked about that you'd like to comment on?" This process gives the interview, and your article, a sense of direction and structure, and keeps you in charge.

Interview Techniques

Q. What are some good techniques to remember when I'm conducting an interview? How can I make sure the interview is productive and interesting for both myself and the subject?
A. First, try to build rapport with the interviewee. This serves two purposes: It not only makes your subject feel more at ease and more receptive to questions, but it can help relax *you* and keep the interview flowing smoothly. Be a little formal at the start, rather than jumping into

familiarity right away. Don't take liberties you wouldn't want a guest of yours to take; this includes smoking and handling objects in the interviewee's office or home. First impressions count, so dress in such a way that you don't draw attention to yourself.

Don't talk too much at the outset. Encourage the interviewee to do as much of the talking as possible. Be flexible and follow the subject's lead. If an answer is very general, don't interrupt, but follow it up. Follow-up questions not only secure specific details and anecdotes, they reveal a lot about the interviewee's personality and bolster rapport by demonstrating your genuine interest in what he has to say. Reciting an anecdote you have previously heard about the subject will often nudge the interviewee into providing further human interest comments; this can often provide you with a good anecdote to open or close your article.

Playing dumb can provide depth to your interview. When a subject rambles or is unclear, place the onus on yourself by saying, "I'm sorry, but I don't quite understand that last point. Could you explain it for me?"

Interview: Tape or Notes?

Q. When conducting an interview, which is better—a tape recorder or written notes?
A. Some writers decry the tape recorder as the tool of a lazy journalist who doesn't like to take notes, but an increasing number of authors are finding them useful, especially when interviewing. Taping your interviews can allow you to ask more questions in less time and concentrate more on the replies you receive, looking for possible follow-ups. If the subject matter is at all controversial, a tape-recorded interview is your proof that an interviewee said what he said in the context being quoted. If you must interview a subject in a situation where it would be difficult for you to take notes, such as over lunch, a tape recorder can be a real lifesaver. Most sources, however, caution against relying *too* much on the tape recorder and suggest augmenting it with some note-taking. This can help you note where in the interview a subject says something particularly provocative or relevant. Taking highlight notes is also insurance in case the recorder or tape breaks down. Keep your interview tapes and notes in a safe place after an article has been published. An editor may need them after publication if an interviewee claims, "I've been misquoted."

(For more information on use of tape recorders, see Chapter 8. Chapter 4 contains information on choosing a good tape recorder.)

Interviews by Phone

Q. I can't afford to travel to conduct all my interviews in person. Can't I get the same information just as easily by phone? What are the advantages and disadvantages of this method?
A. Telephone interviewing prevents the writer from observing his subject's mannerisms and surroundings; for this reason, in-person interviews are usually best. Nevertheless, interviewing someone by telephone can be useful in various situations. When you need only one key source and the subject is too far away for you to meet in person before your deadline, telephoning can get the quote you need in the least amount of time. Interviewing by phone can also be helpful when many sources are scattered far and wide. The practice even has a couple of advantages over face-to-face questioning. Many times, a subject will be willing to talk more freely if he can't watch you taking notes. Also, even the difficult subject who won't answer the door when he hears you knock will answer the telephone's insistent ring.

When interviewing by phone, always have your note-taking apparatus and your reference material nearby. If you use a tape recorder, advise the subject in advance. Remember the value of good telephone manners; be prepared to identify yourself and the publication for which you are writing, and also to answer some preliminary questions from a secretary or assistant to gain access to your subject. Keep track of differences in time zones when calling long distance, since a call made at 9 a.m. EST would rouse a Californian at 6 a.m. Remember, too, to handle names, titles and numbers with special care, to avoid errors that might result from the sound distortion inherent in talking over the telephone. Double-check this information by mail immediately.

At the end of the phone conversation, thank the subject and advise him that you might need to call again for follow-up questions, or to fill in any gaps you find after you've transcribed your notes. Be sure to give the interviewee your phone number so he can reach you with any additional information or afterthoughts about your article.

Interviews can be conducted by mail, too, as explained elsewhere in this chapter.

Touchy Topics

Q. How do I interview someone about information he might be reluctant to discuss?
A. Making the cross into sensitive territory can be a delicate process. You know you need the information, but find it difficult to broach the subject without losing the interviewee's confidence. The tenuous path to sensitive information can only be traveled with patience and subtlety.

Each writer will find his own methods of dealing with each reluctant interviewee, but there are a few tried-and-true methods that will work in many situations. You could blame the question on someone else, such as asking an allegedly corrupt politician, "There are those who claim you do some 'creative accounting' with the budget. Since you've heard these allegations, would you like to respond to your critics?" A playful approach—"Let me play devil's advocate . . ."—can often place the question in a framework that makes it easier for your subject to answer. Prefacing a sensitive question with some praise for your interviewee can cushion the blow and make him more responsive.

Imply that you know more about a situation than you do; the interviewee may discuss the topic with you as if you know all about it and he's only filling you in on details. For example, if you wanted a government employee to admit he had awarded a contract to a company in which he owned 25 percent interest, you might ask, "When did you obtain one fourth of the Q.E.D. Corporation?" Merely asking if he actually owned the share of the business could result in his denial.

Asking a question in a straightforward, matter-of-fact way, no matter how sensitive the area, may elicit a response when all else fails. If the interviewee *still* does not respond, point out the gap in information and tell him that, in the eyes of the reader, silence can be more damaging, since it can lead to speculation on the answer.

The manner in which you cover sensitive material can influence how much information the interviewee will give you, says veteran writer Hayes Jacobs, author of *Writing and Selling Non-Fiction*. "If you manage to extract a gem that has been under lock and key, don't pounce at your notes and act as if you'd just captured the enemy's general; such lack of restraint can cause your subject to say something like, 'Oh, but—uh—maybe you'd better not print that.' Just show normal interest, not wild delight that would distract, worry, or even frighten your subject."

Pay the Interviewee?

Q. If I write a profile, must I pay the subject?
A. Not usually. The question will rarely arise if you're interviewing a local businessman for a

trade publication, or a friend or neighbor for a crafts magazine. If it does, you should tell the subject that publications don't pay interviewees, other than perhaps providing complimentary copies of the article when it is published.

However, some writers and editors—including the television program *60 Minutes*—have paid for certain interviews in the past and consider the practice a good investment. Sometimes, interviewees request a fee because they are reluctant to talk, and feel that charging for an interview will discourage writers. Others ask for payment because they know that some publications and syndicates will spend a lot of money to obtain exclusive rights.

When a freelancer receives a request for payment to an interview subject, he should tell the editor who gave the go-ahead for the piece. One time *Playboy* interview editor Murray Fischer told writer John Brady that, while his magazine's answer to such requests is usually "no," that isn't always the case. If the magazine wants the subject badly enough, it will pay.

Tape Recorder Etiquette

Q. I would like to use a tape recorder when I interview. Should I ask the interviewee beforehand if he minds, or should I simply plop it down without a word, turn it on, and proceed with the interview as if it didn't exist?
A. It's more courteous to ask him first if he minds your using the tape recorder to make sure his statements are recorded as accurately as possible. Few interviewees will object. With experience you'll learn how to approach each interviewee with the idea. To learn how professional magazine writers have used the tape recorder in interviews, you might want to see their comments in *The Craft of Interviewing*, by John Brady.

Surreptitious Taping?

Q. I have a small gadget that records telephone conversations. When I conduct a phone interview, do I have to inform the person that he's being taped?
A. Yes, unless the reporting is clearly investigative. Then, some writers do not, feeling that the real crux of the matter is what is done with the information gained in this manner. However, phone company regulations prohibit taping unless there is a recorder connector with a beeptone. If the phone company discovers a violation of this rule, it can disconnect your phone. The FCC is currently considering rescinding this regulation. Advising an interviewee that the conversation is being tape-recorded for the sake of accuracy and recording his agreement on tape at the beginning of the conversation is the best defense against later problems. Some states, such as Pennsylvania and Maryland, have laws *requiring* that both parties consent to the tape-recording of a conversation which takes place within the state. No federal law prohibits taping of telephone conversations by either party as long as the taping is not being done for an illegal purpose, but some national publications, such as *Newsweek*, have written policies prohibiting surreptitious taping of interviews.

Contacting a Celebrity

Q. I'm a beginning writer and haven't sold anything yet. A well-known singer is going to be in town in another month. Is it possible to arrange an interview with him? If so, how do I do it?
A. Contact the entertainment editor of your local newspaper to find out the name and address of the singer's manager. Write or call the manager and explain that you're a freelance writer and would like to interview the singer when he's in town. You'll have a better chance of getting the interview if you can tell the manager you have a specific magazine in mind for the interview (and if at all possible, get an expression of interest from its editor before you write the manager).

Interviewing

Q. I am interested in learning how to interview people—not just celebrities, but ordinary people, too. I need their opinions and answers to questions for several articles I am working on. Do you just walk up to people and ask them? Do you have to have some sort of credentials? Do you need a release on the material they give you? Do you have to name them in an article, or are you not supposed to name them?

A. Yes, many freelance writers just walk up to people at a shopping mall or other public place and ask if they can interview them briefly for some research material they are seeking. No, you don't need any credentials, although it sometimes helps if you open the conversation by saying something like "I'm a freelance writer researching an article on [topic] for [name of magazine]. May I ask you a few questions?" No release is necessary unless what you're asking them is controversial. Whether you name them in the article or not depends on how you write the article. For example, if you write, "Sally Jones, a 20-year veteran teacher in inner-city schools had this to say about merit pay increases in teacher salaries . . .," it might have more credibility than if you just referred to "One Chicago veteran teacher. . . ." If Sally Jones had some comment to make that was critical of school administrators, you'd probably want to get a release from her to include her comment in your article. The second example—in which the teacher was not named—wouldn't require a release.

Reluctant Interviewees

Q. Sometimes when I'm setting up interviews for an article I encounter people who are reluctant to talk about even the most innocuous of topics. The material isn't particularly controversial; they just aren't used to being interviewed and don't know what to do. How do I handle these shy interviewees?

A. Celebrities are quite used to the questions put to them by interviewers, but businessmen, scholars, doctors, and other people who are not often interviewed may be fearful of being misinterpreted. Sympathy to the subject's quandary, friendly understanding, and professional performance on your part can overcome barriers. Your best response to an executive's reluctance is to point out positive effects of the article, such as complimenting the firm's managerial style and introducing its products and services to other customers. The article might also be reprinted for distribution to colleagues, stockholders and salesmen. It is sometimes helpful—if you can accomplish it—to avoid the public relations department of a large corporation and direct your request to the top. The executive may get back to you quickly or ask his PR department to do so.

Scholars and physicians can also be reluctant subjects, since many of them view publicity as unprofessional. When faced with this attitude, point out the need for public information in the subject's area of expertise. Your interest and sincere enthusiasm can be the catalyst that will spark the interviewee into sharing his knowledge.

Persistence pays off. If you become a more or less ubiquitous presence around a busy subject, you may find that he will make time for the interview in his packed schedule. John Brady tells of tracking down author Jessica Mitford at a university seminar. By "hanging around a lot," he found the right time to get the interview; although her schedule was filled each minute of the seminar, he drove her to the airport and got the interview on the way. Recommendations from friends and co-workers of reluctant interviewees can also be an aid to getting the time with them.

If none of these techniques work and the interview is necessary to the story, tell the subject that his comments are crucial to the story and he probably will appear in the article anyway, but you'd rather get his opinions first-hand.

Limited-Time Interview

Q. If I only have a few minutes of an interviewee's time, how can I get the information I need?
A. The tightly scheduled interview makes the job more difficult in a couple of ways. Not only do you have a time limit on getting the information, you must dispense with much of the preliminary conversation that can build rapport and good will with the interviewee. Cutting the chitchat must be done carefully, however; you don't want to seem abrupt or rude, which could affect the interviewee's receptiveness to questioning.

When you're interviewing "under the gun" you should have your questions arranged in descending order of importance when the interview begins. This practice will ensure your getting as much pertinent information as you can in the time allotted. Take a gamble with your last few questions, making them more thought-provoking so that the subject is interested and permits the interview time to run longer.

To supplement your brief notes, you can, at the end of the conversation, request a more detailed interview by mail. The way to conduct a mail interview is discussed elsewhere in this chapter.

Mention Everybody?

Q. When I've interviewed thirty or forty people for an article, shouldn't I try to quote all of them, or at least as many as I can? Won't they expect to be quoted in the article?
A. Not all the people you interview will appear in the finished manuscript. Some will be poor spokespersons, some will be misinformed and therefore useless, others will not be able to shed any new light on the subject whatsoever. Unless you are interviewing someone you *know* will be a key figure in the finished piece, you should make clear to each interviewee that you are interviewing a lot of people in order to obtain background information, as well as for quotation in the article, and that not all sources will be mentioned. If an interviewee later objects to not being quoted in the finished article, you can always say there was a problem with limited space or the article was heavily edited. If you anticipate this response from an interviewee, it's professionally polite to phone the subject in advance of the article's publication.

Interview by Mail?

Q. I've heard that some writers conduct interviews by mail. How good is this practice and how do I go about it?
A. Although a limited substitute for the in-person interview, mail interviewing can be beneficial to the freelance writer. It can save time, especially if you need to ask many people the same questions. For example, if you were doing an article on defense spending and how it affects social programs and wanted to ask the members of the U.S. Senate for their views, mail interviewing would be one way to get a lot of their opinions in a very brief time. This would also save you money, eliminating the need for travel and long-distance telephoning.

To conduct a mail interview, query your subjects in a covering letter, rather than only sending them the questionnaire and requesting their response. Your query should be personal, explaining the nature of your project, and the name of the publication interested in your article. Your correspondence should be neatly typed. Since your letter is your only communication with your subject and serves to represent you, it could influence his willingness to answer your questions. If you are sending a number of people the same questionnaire, make good-quality photocopies and always include a personal cover letter. Make sure your questions are thoughtful and succinct and leave ample space for replies. Give your phone number and tell interviewees to feel free to call you collect if a question needs clarification or talking to you is more convenient. Tell your subjects that you have a deadline, requesting that they reply within two weeks, if possible. Always include SASE for their replies.

Examine the replies for any possible follow-up questions that are necessary or that might provide additional, provocative answers, then write the subject(s) at once. If a subject does not return the questionnaire within two weeks, send a photocopy of the original letter and list of questions, along with a note suggesting that perhaps your original request was lost in the mails or misplaced in the shuffle of paperwork. Give a gentle prod that will not offend the interviewee, reminding him you still have a few days to meet your deadline and would appreciate any help he could give you.

Research Release?

Q. What is meant by needing a release *on the material I get from an interview? What can happen if I don't have one? Are releases used with all interviews, or with only extensive conversations central to the purpose of the article?*
A. A release, or publication consent agreement, gives an author the right to use information about someone or quotes from someone. It gives a writer permission to edit the manuscript and sell it to an editor, and waives any right of inspection or approval the person might otherwise have requested. A release is generally obtained by asking the person to fill out a small standard form and sign it in front of a witness. The form's text may be as simple as this:

_____ has reviewed "_____" by _____, and affirms that he is accurately quoted in the manuscript.

Or, the form may be more all-inclusive, such as the sample Publication Consent Agreement in the Appendix to the *Writer's Encyclopedia*.

The main use of the release is to protect the author against a subject who may subsequently change his mind about revealing information he gave the writer, take exception to the way the reader may perceive what the source said, or to protect the publication from a source who may wish to sue. If you don't have a release, you must be absolutely certain of your facts and confident that your subject could not sue you for libel or invasion of privacy. Releases are usually obtained on research that you think may be the cause of one or more of the problems described above.

Off the Record

Q. When a subject wants to talk "off the record," should I accept or turn him down? Do anonymous sources lessen the quality of an article?
A. Within certain limits, using "off the record" sources can be helpful to a writer, but the writer should make sure he and his source understand the ground rules for their interview. (Some writers refuse to take "off the record" information, since they may already have it from another source and it might seem they violated the ground rules.) There are two ways a source can talk off the record. He can request total anonymity, talking only to give the reporter background information; in such cases, the source is never to be quoted in the article. A source can also agree to talk "not for attribution." This means he is willing to give information for use in the article, but doesn't want his name mentioned; he can be quoted or paraphrased, but the material is attributed to "a source close to the scene," "a high-ranking official," "a veteran observer," or some other such tag.

Anonymous sources can provide the writer of an article with incisive, revealing information which he otherwise might not have been able to obtain. But there are dangers inherent in using off-the-record sources. You could conceivably hide the names of sources that should be identified to make your article complete and credible. Also, sometimes anonymity can become an excuse for a subject to grind his particular ax without fear of retribution. Check what your anonymous sources tell you, and if a source gives you information, makes charges, or provides descriptions that he cannot document, ask him to go on the record.

You can go back to him after you check out his statements, point out that another source disputed his charges and ask him to clarify his position for the record.

Query Editor Before Interview?

Q. Should I query an editor before or after I ask the interviewee for his or her permission to be interviewed? And what should I do if I can't deliver an article because my interviewee wouldn't grant me an interview?

A. It is best to first get an editor's okay on an interview assignment before asking the subject for an interview. A subject is more willing to give you the time for an interview if he knows an editor is seeking the interview for his pages. But it can be done either way—if a subject is willing to be interviewed without a commitment from an editor, you can also work that way. If a subject refuses to give you the interview, just drop a note to the editor and say that the interview was refused. Editors understand this. If a subject refuses the interview because you *don't* have an editor interested yet, then tell the editor this, also. He may then give you a firm assignment for the interview.

Interviewer Credentials

Q. Since I haven't had any articles published as yet, what do I do when an interviewee wants to know about my background?

A. One thing you should *not* do is try to pass yourself off as a seasoned professional who is certain of publication. Try to get an expression of interest from a specific magazine before approaching your subject to set up an interview. If you've done enough preliminary research to query an editor successfully, you can tell your subject that although you have never published before in this particular magazine, the editor has asked to see the article you proposed. By revealing your status as a beginner, it is possible that you won't get as much time with a source as he might give a full-time magazine staffer or a well-known freelance writer with a firm assignment. You might come up short in terms of time spent with a subject, but you may hit the jackpot when it comes to how *much* information you get. Some public officials, for example, tend to be more relaxed when dealing with the beginning writer; hence, they are freer with information. Some interviewees may even take *extra* time and effort to help a beginner.

Press Agent Problems

Q. I recently tried to interview a celebrity, but his press agent insisted on ground rules, telling me that there were only certain topics his client would discuss. What do I do when this happens?

A. If you need the interview, you have little recourse but to accept ground rules suggested by subjects who are "gun shy" about being interviewed. The rules are often self-serving and confine the interviewer, making it difficult to get the knowledge he needs from his subject. However, while it may be necessary to agree to ground rules in order to get someone to grant an interview, it may not limit you in the final result. Your subject may simply be wary of discussing certain topics because of the way he has been handled by writers in the past. Once you begin the conversation, he may loosen up and discuss almost anything you wish. Agree to ground rules and you may be surprised. Once your foot is in the door, the ground rules may go out the window!

Advance Approval?

Q. I called to set up an interview for an article on which I am currently working, but the subject told me he'd only agree to see me if he could see his quotes before the article went to press. What should I do in a situation like this?

A. Unless the particular interviewee is essential to your article, it is best to tell him sorry, professional writers don't do that. There are a few times when it becomes necessary for a writer to allow his interviewee to see the manuscript before it is printed. When dealing with scientific, technical, or medical topics, the writer may need the subject to check the facts and figures to make sure they are accurate. If the interviewee is your key source, then it may be necessary to agree to his review of the manuscript to get the interview. But the writer should make clear to any subject with whom he has such an agreement that the article is submitted for the interviewee's correction of factual material, not for his approval. It should be made clear to him that he is only proofreading the quotes and any alteration of the manuscript may be done only by the editor.

News Source

Q. Do newspaper reporters need releases from the people they quote in straight news stories?

A. When a news event is happening, a reporter has the right to cover it. If an interviewee is informed that he is talking to a reporter from the *Daily Herald* and agrees to answer questions, a release is not needed. News is generally excepted from many statutes regarding invasion of privacy, since the dissemination of ideas and information is vital to First Amendment concepts.

11 Should I Work with Another Writer, Photographer, or Artist?

"I've always believed in writing without a collaborator," wrote Agatha Christie, "because where two people are writing the same book, each believes he gets all the worries and only half the royalties." Some other writers believe that using a collaborator can divide the work and increase the income for both partners. What if your collaborator has certain skills you don't have or don't want to acquire, such as photography? The following information can help you decide the best working method for you.

Writer Collaborators

Q. A friend wants to collaborate with me on a writing project. Is this a good idea?
A. Helene Schellenberg Barnhart, author of numerous articles, novels, and *Writing Romance Fiction*, says, "Collaboration is like a marriage. It can help make a dream come true through putting two heads together. It can also turn into a nightmare when differing temperaments clash, or when communication breaks down."

Collaboration has obvious advantages. Two writers can pool the resources, contacts, and efforts. But two writers can also have differing opinions at any point in the development of an article, book, or story. One way to help insure the success of a collaborative arrangement is to discuss each aspect of the partnership before work begins. Two writers should agree beforehand on exactly what contribution each will make to the project, and what work each will do. In the case of a book collaboration it would be a good idea to have this in writing to protect all concerned—including the heirs, should one partner die before the other.

The secrets of successful collaboration are congeniality, respect for the other writer's abilities and opinions, and a willingness to compromise. Collaboration means dividing any fees you receive, but if you've carefully considered the projects you do, and plan accordingly, you can decrease the number of hours invested by dividing the work, and possibly increase the number of sales.

Locating a Collaborator

Q. I'm writing a book for which I'd like to find a writing partner—especially someone with experience in the field I've chosen. How do I find a collaborator?
A. There is no foolproof method of choosing a writing partner, but here are a few suggestions

for locating a coauthor. Talk to other writers at writers' workshops and conferences, meetings of writers' groups, and writing classes. Review the work of newspaper and magazine freelancers and staff writers. If they've written on a topic that interests you, they might be willing to collaborate. The more writers you meet, no matter what their field, the better the chance you'll find a writer who'd like to work with you. You could also place an ad in the "Writers Wanted" classifieds of *Writer's Digest* or other trade magazines.

Friendly Arrangements

Q. I have been offered the opportunity of collaborating on some stories. A friend of mine went on safari to Africa and took some excellent photographs of his hunting trips. He wants me to write his experiences and he will furnish the photos. If the stories are sold, what percentage do I pay him? Of course, all money received for photos would be his, but I have no idea how much I should share with him of the money received for a story.

A. If you act as the marketer and are successful in selling some articles to sport and outdoor magazines, for example, there is no set rule for collaboration fees between writers and photographers. They have to decide when the item is sold how much each person contributed to the sale (in your case, both the writing *and* the selling) and make their share of the check reflect that. If the magazine pays the photographer and writer separately, you are relieved of making this decision yourself, since the magazine editor is deciding what proportion of the total check he feels is due each partner.

Rewrite Collaborator

Q. I've recently been asked to collaborate on a book with a man who is interested in self publishing his autobiography. He has already completed a first draft of the manuscript and wants me to finish the book. How much pay should I request for a job like this?

A. It sounds as if you are being asked to do a rewrite of the man's completed manuscript. In such a case, the amount of pay you receive would depend on how much work is to be done on the book before it can be submitted to the printer. If the draft is *very* rough and needs a substantial amount of rearranging and rewriting, you probably should charge an hourly rate. If the manuscript is in fairly good shape and you only have to do a little copyediting and proofreading to polish and refine it, you might charge a set fee per page. (For more information on copyediting jobs, see Chapter 31.)

Artist Collaborator

Q. I'm collaborating with an artist on a picture book for children. When we study the markets and make our selection, do we send color transparencies of the artwork?

A. When marketing a picture book, send the text and good photocopies of some of the artwork you have available, but in a cover note accompanying the text, advise the editor that you can provide full-color illustrations upon request. (For further discussions of picture book submissions, see Chapter 28.)

Locating Photographer Collaborator

Q. How can I find a photographer to work with me on books and articles?

A. Getting good, high-quality photographs can increase the salability of any book or article. You could hire a professional photographer, but some charge as much as $200 per day for their services, so unless you had worked out an agreement with an editor beforehand, this could be an unwise expense for you. The American Society of Magazine Photographers can recommend member photographers in your area if you or your editor want to hire an experienced professional. Contact ASMP at 205 Lexington Ave., New York NY 10016.

College art departments that teach photography might be able to recommend talented students; putting notices on the department bulletin board can also help. Local camera clubs and the classified ads of your local newspaper are other good sources. Any of these methods can help you find a photographer to take the photos you need at a fraction of the top professional's fee.

When selecting a photographer, examine his portfolio, checking subject matter, quality and style, and the relation of his work to the type of writing you do. After you've found your collaborator, the two of you will have to work together to find ways to enhance your writing with his pictures. Prints chosen for publication should be accompanied by a brief, signed statement in which the photographer grants permission for his work to be used in conjunction with your manuscript.

(For more information on how photography and illustration can be used with your writing, see Chapter 23.)

Photographer Collaborator

Q. What arrangements should I make to pay a photographer for any of his pictures I use to illustrate my article?
A. There are a number of ways to pay photographers. The writer and photographer can agree beforehand on a flat fee to cover the photographer's labor and the cost of prints. The writer can pay the photographer a percentage of the total article price. If the photographer belongs to a professional organization, the writer may have to agree to a fixed price. In all of these cases, the actual amount of payment will depend on several factors, including the nature of the work, the amount of the photographer's time involved, and the quality of the photographs. The price should always be negotiated before work begins. In some cases a writer can recommend a qualified photographer to the magazine editor who assigned the article, or an editor might accept responsibility for selecting a photographer.

Illustrator Collaborator

Q. What are the opportunities for writer/artist collaboration on magazine articles or stories?
A. There are very few opportunities for this type of collaboration. Acceptability of a manuscript with accompanying artwork is limited because an editor has to like both the writing and the artwork. Most editors prefer to assign illustrations to artists whose work they know. Illustrations have to fit the format of the magazine and the style of the article.

Critic Collaborator?

Q. How useful is it to have your manuscripts read by friends or relatives before you submit them?
A. It depends on how qualified and how honest they are. Most friends and spouses only offer compliments, not criticism. A better way to get feedback on your work would be to join a writers' club—one that offers members manuscript readings and criticism. Another way is to attend a writers' conference or workshop where manuscript criticism is offered.

As-Told-To Writer

Q. What is an "as-told-to" book or article? What types of subjects lend themselves to this kind of writing? What financial arrangements are made between the people who collaborate on the work?

A. An "as-told-to" work is a first-person narrative for which the actual writing is done by someone other than the person allegedly telling the story—in other words, the work is "ghostwritten." The resulting book or article may have a joint byline, giving the author credit by saying the work is written "as told to Frank Jones" or "with Joe Smith." In some works, credit is given only on the acknowledgment page.

The "as-told-to" format is most often used in three kinds of material: a story of a dramatic personal experience, an authority's opinion on a matter of public interest, and the commentary or autobiographical narrative of a celebrity. Magazine and newspaper articles can give a writer leads on prospective clients he might approach for this type of writing. The writer develops the concept for the work, "sells" the subject and the publisher on the idea, and works out the financial arrangements with both. These arrangements vary. In the case of articles, the writer usually gets the check while the subject gets the publicity; other times they split all monies fifty/fifty. If a book is being written, the author negotiates the division of advance money and royalties depending on the relative contributions of the two parties to the book's salability. Sometimes the author enlists the help of an agent or lawyer to do this. Professional writers often prefer to cover their work on a book "up front," by negotiating to receive 75 percent of the advance and a lesser percentage of the royalties, in case the book doesn't sell as well as they expected. When the manuscript is completed, the subject gives the writer permission to publish the material by signing a release form. (For advice on how to locate the home addresses of experts and celebrities, see Chapter 7.)

Ghostwriter for Celebrity

Q. If I agree to ghostwrite a book for a celebrity, do I get a cover credit? How about a percentage of the royalties? Are ghostwriters looked down on by other writers?

A. Unless the work is specifically intended to be an "as-told-to" book, ghostwriters generally don't get a byline, and rarely receive any sort of public acknowledgment, even if they are established professionals. But because a ghostwriter must subdue his own voice, write entirely in the style of another person, and satisfy both subject and editor, he is recognized and respected in the publishing community.

While public acclaim is rare for ghostwriters, there are considerable monetary rewards. Ghostwriters usually receive a flat fee, rather than a percentage of the royalties. What that fee will be depends on the book publisher, the celebrity, the reputation of the ghostwriter and the book's salability, but it could be $10,000 or more.

Expert Collaborator

Q. I've become friendly with a professional who would like to collaborate with me on magazine articles in his field of expertise. There is also the possibility of later doing a book. Would his contribution of expertise and the status of his title help make a sale?

A. In certain markets, it would be a help for you to collaborate with a professional. For example, if you were writing about the problems of executive stress, a joint byline with a clinical psychologist specializing in that area could increase your chances of a sale to *Psychology Today*. Teaming with a practicing attorney for a book on avoiding lawsuits might make a book more attractive to a publisher than if a layman had written it alone. However, it isn't wise to expend a lot of time and energy on a book until you get some expression of interest from a publisher based on your ability as a writer to assemble a provocative, practical book proposal, the value of which is bolstered by your co-author's credentials as an expert in the field.

Take-Over Writer/Collaborator

Q. A writer I know has recently abandoned a book project (for which he had obtained a book contract) due to unforeseen circumstances. He has already amassed and organized a great deal of research material; all that remains to be done is the actual writing, which he has asked me to do. How should we handle the division of money for this project?
A. Assuming that the first writer is not expecting you to act as a ghostwriter, the book publisher should be notified first (send samples of your writing), to find out if he is agreeable and if the original contract can be changed to reflect your participation as co-author. As to the separate working agreement between you and the first writer, you should agree to no less than 50 percent of the advance and royalties for the work, including any subsidiary rights for film or other media. Negotiating a flat fee paid to the original author so that you can take over the entire project is another possibility. All such transactions must be in writing.

Ghostwriter for Individual

Q. A person with a unique background has asked me to write his life story. Do I sign a contract with him, and what should the financial arrangements be?
A. In any situation where a writer is working with someone else and there is no publisher lined up, the writer should not begin work on the project until there is an agreement on paper, spelling out exactly how much the writer will be earning while he's doing the writing, and how he'll be credited and paid on publication. The agreement should be as detailed as possible, covering not only the book itself, but any further money the book might earn, including subsidiary rights such as serialization, paperback and foreign reprints, dramatic, film, radio, and television adaptations. It's advisable to have a lawyer draw up the agreement, which should also cover the exact amount of work each party is to contribute.

You don't mention whether the subject intends to self publish the book or wants you to market it as well as write it for him. If the latter, it might be wise to query a few publishers to see if there is any interest in the book idea before you—and the subject—invest time and money in the project.

In matters of money, the big question is always "how much?" Writer Hayes Jacobs recommends that you "ask for as much as you can get," but never settle for less than 50 percent of the royalties. If you are doing all the writing, 75 percent is reasonable. The money you are paid by the subject while writing the book will apply as an advance against your future percentages of royalties. This reduces your risk of putting in a lot of hard work and receiving no money if the book isn't successful in terms of sales.

Pay for Life Story?

Q. A friend has offered to relate to me the very unusual story of her life, for use in a novel. The entire writing project will be mine, as well as marketing the work. I feel she is entitled to some percentage of any profit from the novel. What is the usual percentage in such cases? Am I within my rights to request exclusive use of the material at any later date to use other than for the novel in question?

A. In cases of this type, as well as in biographies, the subject whose life is being used is not usually given any payment except the satisfaction of seeing his life story in print. If you feel a personal obligation, why not simply offer a flat sum (whatever is agreeable to both parties) for use of this material, dependent, of course, on its sale to a publisher. If at all possible, you should secure legal help with any financial arrangement that is made. Since there are others who are probably familiar with the events of your subject's life, you cannot reasonably expect to have exclusive control over this material. Remember that "facts" themselves cannot be copyrighted, although your presentation of them in books and articles can be copyrighted.

12 What Is a Query? How Should I Write It?

Nonfiction writers have one great advantage over fiction writers: the query letter. Before completing research for a manuscript, the article writer or nonfiction book writer can elicit, through a query letter, the interest of an editor and sometimes even the particular slant an editor prefers. Since the editor has participated in this dialogue before seeing the finished manuscript he has a greater investment in its success. The form the query takes, however, differs on the type of manuscript offered. The questions and answers in this chapter will fully explain the query letter and its advantages.

Content of a Query

Q. What information should the query contain?
A. The information in a query letter serves two purposes. It should convince the editor that your idea is a good one for his publication's readership, and it should sell you as the best writer to turn out a good article on the subject. The query letter should contain an alluring, but concise summary of the article's central idea, and the angle or point of view from which you intend to approach it. You can, if you wish, begin the letter with a double-spaced paragraph which approximates the lead of the article; this will give your potential editor a sample of your writing style. Outline the structure of the article, giving facts, observations, and anecdotes that support the premise of the article. Don't give *too many* facts; the idea is to leave the editor wanting more. The letter should tell the editor why the article would be important and timely and give a convincing argument of why it would fit into this particular magazine.

You should also give the editor some indication of why you think *you* could write a good article on this particular subject. Share some sources of information and describe any special qualifications you may have for developing the idea. For example, if you were proposing an article on a topic in which you have some professional expertise or of which you have been an interested observer for some time, you should mention that. Samples of your published work will also help the editor see what you can do. The close of the query can be a straightforward request to write the article. Also specify an estimated length and delivery date. If photographs are available, mention that, too. Don't discuss fees or request advice.

These are guidelines, of course, not a hard-and-fast pattern for a query letter. Good query letters are as individual as the writers who send them and as unique as the ideas that are proposed.

Length of the Query

Q. Is it okay for a query letter (on a nonfiction feature) to run as long as two to three typewritten pages (single-spaced) so as to give the editor the gist of the story?
A. There should be a better way to present your subject—most successful query letters are only one page. Two or three pages of single-spaced typewritten copy facing a busy editor is more than he or she wants to read. If that much copy is needed to give an editor the gist of the article, you probably have failed to focus on a specific angle. If the subject warrants it, you can accompany a one-page query with a synopsis. The letter tantalizes the editor and helps him decide whether the article is right for his readers. The synopsis—double-spaced—shows the treatment of the subject.

Fiction Query?

Q. What should the short-story writer put in his query? Should the smaller, less well-known publications be queried at all? What should be the length?
A. Because of the nature of fiction, editors rarely expect to be queried about it. Good fiction usually defies the type of summarization or highlighting used in query letters because so many of the integral elements, for example, style, mood, and characterization, would be lost. Therefore, most editors prefer to receive the complete manuscript. A few magazines that are short-staffed may ask for queries, in which case you'll want to give a brief statement of the main theme and story line, including the conflict within the story and the resolution. (For more information on short stories, see Chapter 25.)

Mailing Query Letters

Q. What do you suggest for mailing queries: a ten-inch envelope with a six-incher for the return, or an eleven-inch envelope with a ten-incher for the return?
A. The eleven-inch envelope with a ten-incher return would probably have a neater appearance, especially since the editor may return other material such as writers' guidelines along with his answer.

Multiple Query

Q. Is it permissible to submit a query covering the same article to two different editors at the same time? Sometimes the time element is important and if one editor delays answering, it could be too late to query another.
A. It is permissible, but not always practical, to submit the same article idea to several magazines simultaneously. Most writers abhor the long delay it takes to get an answer from a magazine editor, but realize that if they do make simultaneous submissions to editors they are going to face the possible situation of more than one editor asking to see the article and having to be told that someone else is considering it. An editor who is told that he will have to wait in line is not going to look very kindly on the next query from that particular writer. In the case of timely article ideas, many freelance writers use this technique: they either point out in the letter to the editor that it is an extremely timely query and request a reply in a certain number of days, or tell the editor the idea is being sent to several editors. Most editors respect this, and in fact, some editors listed in *Writer's Market* indicate that they are open to multiple submissions.

Query First?

Q. I would like to ask about the "query first," which is always stressed in market listings. It seems so presumptuous for a beginning and unpublished writer to query first. How much attention would be paid to a beginner?
A. A busy editor would much rather read a query to decide whether he's interested in a certain property than plow through a lengthy manuscript for the same purpose. From the writer's standpoint, think of the savings in postage and wear and tear on the manuscript. What *is* presumptuous is the writer who disregards an editor's stated request to "query first" and deluges him with completed manuscripts. Editors pay as much attention to beginners as they do to professionals, as long as the query letters are professionally written and the ideas are suitable to the magazine's readership and the editor's needs.

Query Follow-Up

Q. How soon can I follow up a query letter if I don't get a response? Should I phone?
A. If you've not heard from the editor in three to four weeks (unless the market listing in *Writer's Market* specifies a longer report time), don't hesitate to write the editor a *brief* follow-up. The note should describe the query fully so the editor can readily identify it, and should simply ask whether he's had time to consider your proposal. Be sure to include the date of the original query, since some magazine offices file unsolicited queries and manuscripts by date of arrival. In case the original query never reached the editor, you may want to enclose a carbon of the original query to save time and correspondence searching for it. Some writers include a self-addressed postcard for a quick reply. This usually elicits a response; if not, you may then want to try a phone call. A follow-up letter, however, rarely fails to get a reply.

Manuscript Delivery Time?

Q. After receiving a favorable reply to a query, how soon will the editor expect the manuscript?
A. When an editor gives you a favorable response on an article idea and doesn't specify a deadline, it's up to you to decide how quickly you can get it finished. Acknowledge his letter with a note telling when you will deliver the article. If the editor has a specific issue in mind for your article, it's up to him to suggest a deadline for you.

Query by Phone?

Q. Is there any situation in which I can query by telephone?
A. Most established writers query by mail. A written query allows the editor to examine the proposal at his convenience, and to show it to his associates for their opinions. An editor is better able to judge the merits of an idea if it's in tangible, written form than if it's related to him over the telephone.
      To the writer, time and energy required to develop a carefully written proposal without an editor's interest seems a large investment, when a telephone call might sell the editor on an idea, with far less effort. However, a phone call interrupts the editor's workday and he is forced to answer without proper time to think the matter through. Except in rare instances (for example, when the writer may only have access to a subject for a limited time and needs a fast answer), an unexpected phone query usually receives either a no (which allows you to eliminate his publication and gives you a sense of what other similar markets might think), or a response which puts you back in square one: "We're willing to look at it if you send a detailed

query by mail." If you receive a negative response by phone, you have closed the door to a query that might have been considered, had it come by mail.

Published Samples with Query

Q. Is it better to send two or three samples of my work when sending a query letter, or should I send only the article proposal in order to save time for the editor and eliminate my extra postage expense?

A. It's always a good idea to include a few tearsheets of your previously published articles. If an editor is not familiar with your work, looking at other pieces you've written is one way he can familiarize himself with your abilities and the quality of your work. The articles you send with your query ideally should be of the same category as the article you are proposing; if you wanted to profile Liza Minelli, for example, a copy of a previously published article on Burt Reynolds would show the editor your skills in this field. A suggestion for an article on making house painting easier could be bolstered by your published article on how to reupholster furniture. Even if the tearsheets you send differ from the type of article you're proposing, send only your best published articles. Showing the editor of a major publication insignificant tearsheets could defeat your purpose. If you are dissatisfied with something you wrote, chances are the editor will not be too impressed with it either.

Letterheads with Publication Credits?

Q. One of my friends who freelances uses letterheads that list all the magazines for which he has written. Do you think that's a good idea?

A. Elaborate letterheads are distracting. The real focus of a query letter should be the article it proposes, not a list of magazines the writer has sold in the past. If the writer wishes, he can mention in the body of the letter significant or similar publications in which his articles have previously appeared, or include a résumé with a more complete listing. If the idea is good, the editor will buy it; the ornateness of the stationery will not influence his decision, and is sometimes taken to be a sign that the writer is an amateur infatuated with small success. (For a discussion of writers' letterheads, see Chapter 4.)

Query or Not?

Q. Do I always have to query before sending a manuscript or are there times when it isn't necessary?

A. For certain types of articles, editors prefer to see the finished manuscript rather than a query. For example, personal experience articles, humor, nostalgia and editorial opinion pieces rely so much on the writer's personal style that reading the finished product is the best way an editor can assess their acceptability for his publication. Articles requiring extensive research, however, are best attempted after an editor has responded favorably to a query. That saves the writer time since the editor may prefer a different approach to the subject than the one the writer originally had. If you have any doubts, check *Writer's Market* for the specific magazine's policy on various types of articles.

Query Credentials

Q. I have very little writing experience, but I don't want to hurt my chances of having my article accepted by admitting that to a editor. How much must my query letter tell about my background?

A. If you've never been published before, it's best to ignore the subject of past credits and discuss instead your qualifications to write the article at hand. Discuss only those aspects of your background which relate to your subject. If you're proposing an article about how small businesses use computers, for example, mentioning your computer knowledge through education or employment would be a plus. What's important to an editor is not how many articles you've had published, but how much promise is shown by your query letter. Even if you've never published anything, a thorough and professional approach to the query letter will allow you the same chance to sell an article as someone who has a few articles in print.

Multiple Queries and Submissions

Q. I have written chapters for two nonfiction books. I have sent the sample chapters and a query letter to publishers for consideration. As you well know, it can take three to four months for a publisher to analyze the market and reply to the query. Both these potential books, however, are topical. If each publisher takes that long to reply, the material I have researched and collected will become outdated. In such a case, can I send sample chapters and queries for a book to more than one editor for consideration? If not, do you have any suggestions to speed up the process?

A. In some cases, and especially when the topic of the book is timely, it is necessary to query several firms at one time. When sending multiple queries, some writers feel each editor should know that others are considering the idea. Other writers feel it is best not to inform the editors of multiple queries, but to work out the best deal if more than one editor expresses an interest.

One matter to consider, however, is whether such dated material is suited to books. Except in rare instances, book publishers work on a schedule involving two or more years. Topical material is better suited to magazines, while books on extremely timely subjects cannot usually withstand the normal delays at various levels of scheduling.

Query a Book Publisher?

Q. Is it permissible to write a book publisher regarding the status of my book manuscript? I sent the manuscript a month ago, and so far have heard nothing.

A. It's permissible, but it sometimes takes over three months for a publisher to report on a book-length manuscript. Unless the *Writer's Market* listing for a specific publisher specifies sending the entire manuscript, you'd get faster service on a synopsis, two or three sample chapters, and a short cover letter asking if the publisher is interested in seeing more.

Book Submissions

Q. Would you explain about sample chapters, outlines and synopses?

A. Many book publishers request sample chapters, outlines and synopses for nonfiction book proposals. The outline gives a brief summary of the entire content of the proposed book, followed by a chapter-by-chapter synopsis showing the organization of the book and what angle of the subject each chapter will contain; the sample chapters show the writer's style and writing ability. It is a good idea to include the first chapter, a chapter from the center of the book showing some highlight or climax, and the concluding chapter, unless the publisher's listing in *Writer's Market* indicates he wishes to see consecutive chapters. Authors who send only the first chapter or two (since the latter chapters have not been written) are sometimes disappointed by rejection, since they had not planned the book sufficiently to bring it to a well-rounded conclusion.

Although contracts may be issued on a book proposal, sometimes called "selling the partial," some publishers accepting general books from freelance writers who are unknown to them issue the contract only after the completed manuscript has been read and accepted.

Nonfiction Book

Q. I have written a self-help psychology book. It is written like a test in order to pique the reader's mind; but is also in regular manuscript form in some places. I would like to know whether I should send the complete manuscript to a publisher, send a query, or submit it through an agent? Should I get it notarized? Should a manuscript be sent by registered mail? Could you suggest some suitable publishers?

A. Query the publisher first and if he expresses interest, you can submit the completed manuscript. In your query, you might include excerpts from one of the tests and from the standard prose passages, too, so the publisher can get an idea of your style and treatment. Notarization is not necessary. If you keep a copy of your manuscript, you don't really need to send it by costly registered mail. Consult *Writer's Market* for the names and addresses of book publishers who indicate they are interested in self-help books.

13 How Should the Manuscript Look? How Should It Be Presented?

"Many writers who have earned their reputations through hard work agree," says David Madden, "that one writes at first just to have something to rewrite." Once you have achieved that final draft you think is your best, what is the format in which it should be submitted to a publisher? Here are some guidelines to help you properly submit your matchless manuscripts.

Writing Mechanics

Q. I have often read the term "manuscript mechanics." Would you please tell me what this means?
A. "Manuscript mechanics" refers to the business of making a manuscript as attractive as possible from the standpoint of overall appearance, which includes neatness of typing, punctuation, width of margins, and centering of titles.

Manuscript Paper

Q. What kind of paper should I use to type the final manuscript?
A. Editors are immovable on two points: the manuscript must be on white paper, and it must measure 8½x11 inches. Colored typewriter paper does not photocopy easily and is difficult for an editor to read or edit. Cheaper paper is all wood content, but is absorbent, giving a fuzzy texture and causing the type to blur. This paper also tears easily; sometimes the typewriter keys will punch right through it. Also do not use airmail stationery which is difficult for editing. The more expensive types of paper are 100 percent rag content, nice, but astronomically priced. For best results at lowest cost, use a good 25 percent cotton fiber content paper, no less than sixteen-pound bond—twenty-pound is preferred. This paper holds up well when erasing mistakes, shows type neatly, and is excellent for editing.

Erasable Bond

Q. Please set me straight once and for all. Half the time I read that manuscripts should be prepared on non-Corrasable paper because it smudges less, and the other half of the time they say that liquid erase should be avoided, and that a good eraser is best. This leads me to believe that neither is a steadfast rule. I would, however, appreciate knowing what the general consensus is.

A. It's general knowledge that Corrasable bond is an editing nuisance. Most editors prefer good quality bond paper, and the use of either liquid erase, or strike-over erase. If you have more than three corrections on a manuscript page, it's best to retype that page to avoid the first-draft look that editors dislike.

If you have a book manuscript ready for final typing—a horrendous job for most writers—and plan to type it yourself, consider owning or renting a self-correcting typewriter to do a professional job in much less time.

How Many Drafts?

Q. How many rough drafts should precede the final copy?
A. The number differs from writer to writer. Very few writers are able to submit the first draft with minor revisions as the final copy; most must edit, reedit, and re-reedit before they are satisfied. You'll have to find by trial and error the method that's best for you, and it may vary from piece to piece. (For a detailed description of what to look for in the editing process, see the question on revising the first draft in Chapter 1.)

Cover Letter?

Q. Is it necessary to include a cover letter with my manuscript?
A. If you have already queried an editor and received an affirmative response, a brief cover note would be a good idea. All it need say is something like, "Here is the article you asked to see in your letter of July 17. I have also included a selection of photographs that I mentioned are available." If you are sending an unsolicited manuscript, no cover letter is necessary, unless it buttresses your sales effort by describing some credentials you have relating to the topic of your manuscript.

First Class or Special Fourth Class?

Q. Can I send a manuscript at the cheaper fourth-class mail rate, or does it have to go first class?
A. First class and fourth class each have their advantages. Fourth class, with its special low rate for heavier manuscripts, costs less. Make sure, however, that your name, address, and the phrase "Return postage guaranteed" appear on any fourth-class package, since the post office isn't obligated to return the package (if for some reason the addressee can't be located) unless you guarantee the return postage.

First-class mail is assured of speedier delivery. However, if your book manuscript weighs more than twelve ounces, first class doesn't apply. You would have to send it "priority" mail, which costs and is handled the same as first class. Whether you send your manuscript first or fourth class, it can be insured for a small fee against loss or damage. Editors are not concerned with the type of mail service you use.

Standard Submission Format

Q. Are there different manuscript submission formats for short stories, magazine articles, and book-length projects?
A. No. There is only one standard manuscript submission format: double-spaced on 8½x11-inch white paper.

Which Type?

Q. I have only one typewriter and it has elite type. I know when manuscripts are submitted that pica is preferred. But does it make that much difference?
A. Both pica and elite are acceptable. The more "exotic" types, such as fancy script or all capitals, are what editors find objectionable.

Pen Name Placement

Q. How should I indicate on my manuscript that I am writing under a pseudonym?
A. Type your real name, followed by your pen name in parentheses, then your address in the upper left corner of the first page of your manuscript; type your pen name as the byline under the title of your manuscript. Type your real name, followed by your pen name in parentheses, then a dash and the page number in the upper left corner of each page after page one; e.g., Jones (Smith)—page 2. Of course, if you don't want even your editor or publisher to know your real name, then you'll have to be a little trickier and use the pseudonym in the byline, in the upper left corner, *and* on the return envelope. If this is your wish, you'll have to notify your local post office and bank that you are using a pen name in your work. (For further information on using a pen name, see Chapter 16.)

Include Dedication?

Q. When submitting a book manuscript, should I include the dedication page?
A. No. Including the dedication page on the manuscript could seem presumptuous. It is best to wait until publication is assured before sending the dedication.

Carbon Copy?

Q. Is it necessary to make a carbon copy of my final manuscript while typing it?
A. Making a copy is absolutely necessary, and a carbon copy is cheaper than having your manuscript photocopied. The extra copy of your work is insurance against your story or article getting lost in the mails or misplaced in the enormous shuffle of manuscripts at the publisher's office. You may want extra copies of a manuscript for discussing revisions with your editor and possibly sending to reprint magazines. At least one good carbon copy should be made, two or more if you think you'll need them. Use a medium-weight carbon paper. Copy sheets can be of a lower quality paper than your original manuscript, or even of a different color. Very thin duplicate copy paper can also be used to save expense and filing space. Make sure, however, that the carbon copy is dark enough to be photocopied in the event the original manuscript gets lost and you need another clear photocopy to submit to market.

Style on Foreign Words?

Q. When using foreign words or phrases in my writing, what are the typing guidelines?
A. When a foreign word or phrase with which the English-speaking reader would be unfamiliar appears for the first time in the text, it should be underlined, which tells the typesetter that you want it italicized. Some publishers have a style in which, after the first use, such repeated words remain in Roman type, and therefore would not be underlined. For help with specific problems involving the use of foreign words and phrases, consult an unabridged dictionary or *A Manual of Style*. Most libraries have copies.

Word Processor Printer

Q. I'm interested in buying a word processor, but would prefer to buy a dot-matrix printer, since it's less expensive than the letter-quality type. Is it okay to send in manuscripts printed in dot-matrix?

A. A dot-matrix printer uses many tiny dots to form each letter of every word, like the "personalized" mass mailings of direct mail so popular a few years back. Art Spikol, *Writer's Digest* columnist, says a dot-matrix format makes your manuscript *look* as if a computer wrote it. Some editors object to the dot-matrix type style, finding it hard to read. The letter-quality printers are more expensive, but provide a more professional appearance to your work. Some editors, however, have expressed in their listings in *Writer's Market* willingness to accept dot-matrix printer submissions.

Word Processor Printout Paper

Q. I recently bought a word processor with a letter-quality printer. It came with a sheaf of computer-style "tractor paper," joined with half-inch perforated strips at the sides, and perforations at top and bottom of each sheet. Is it possible to submit a manuscript without separating the 8½x11-inch sheets of paper?

A. It would probably be a good idea to stick to separate sheets of paper when printing your manuscript on a word processor. It is better to have it look as if it were typed on a regular typewriter using manuscript paper.

Handwritten/Typewritten Manuscripts

Q. I don't have a typewriter, but my longhand is very legible. Does my manuscript have to be typed?

A. All manuscripts must be typed. However, that does not mean the writer must do the typing. Some writers pay to have their final drafts typed by professional typists. You can find available typists and current fees in the classified ads in *Writer's Digest;* you can also place your own classifieds in local newspapers. College campuses often have advertisements for typing services posted on various department bulletin boards. When using a typing service, make sure you and the typist agree on the payment, type of paper to be used, format, typestyle, and any other considerations. If you are sending your manuscript to the typist via the U.S. Postal Service, you should enclose SASE with three times the amount of postage you needed to send the copy to the typist; this covers the amount needed to mail you the original, the final typed copy and a carbon copy. Remember to keep itemized bills and receipts for all transactions with the typist, because typing costs are tax-deductible expenses for a writer.

Quotes in Manuscripts

Q. How should I handle quoted material in the final typed manuscript?

A. Use quotation marks to open and close all use of quoted material. When quoting within a quotation, use single marks. If the quoted material runs eight lines or more, it generally is set off from the text, double-spaced, and indented. No quotation marks are used in block quotations of this type. These are, of course, general guidelines. If you're submitting to a specific magazine or book publisher, follow their format. For other specific questions, you should consult *A Manual of Style,* a comprehensive style and editing manual. It contains detailed information on the use of quotation marks in many situations, as well as other mechanical questions about putting your manuscript into its final, typewritten form.

Cover Page?

Q. Should I use a cover page, even on a short manuscript?
A. Cover pages aren't usually necessary unless the manuscript is one being submitted after a go-ahead from an editor. All relevant information is included on the first page of the manuscript. Your name, street address, city, state, and zip code should be typed on three single-spaced lines in the upper left corner. Type the approximate number of words in the upper right corner; single-spaced beneath that, type the rights you are offering to sell the publisher. The title of the story or article and your byline should appear in two double-spaced, centered lines above the beginning of the copy, which starts halfway down the page.

Manuscript Pages

Q. Do the rest of a manuscript's pages differ from the first in format and appearance?
A. Yes. For all subsequent pages, type your name and the page number at the upper left (Jones, pg. 2 or Jones—2) and the title single-spaced beneath it, with nothing at the center or right. If the title is too long, use a keyword to serve as "shorthand" for the full title. A keyword for this chapter, for instance, might be Manuscript. See the sample manuscript page in the Appendix.

Multiple Stories to One Editor

Q. Can you send more than one story at a time in the same envelope?
A. There's no reason why you can't send more than one story in the same envelope. However, it might be a good idea to include individual SASE for *each* story in case they are reviewed by different editors. Providing SASE for each story will make it easier for editors to reply to you.

Book Manuscript Details

Q. Do I have to use a lot of footnotes, or is a comprehensive bibliography at the end of my book manuscript sufficient?
A. It will depend on the individual preference of the publisher or editor. General-interest trade book publishers usually prefer a bibliography, while textbooks and scholarly efforts usually include footnotes as a way of identifying source material. It would be a good idea to use a bibliography with your sample chapter but ask in your covering letter about the publisher's preference. Many publishers produce style guides covering such details for their authors.

Social Security Number?

Q. A writer friend of mine recently advised me that when submitting a manuscript I should include my social security number. Is this necessary? What's the reason for such a requirement?
A. Book publishers and major magazine publishers require social security numbers on all manuscripts since publishers who pay at least $600 to nonemployees must report such payments to the Internal Revenue Service.

While you may include your social security number on a book manuscript, such matters are usually handled by the business offices of publishers who will request the number when the contract is signed or when they ask you for other personal and promotional details.

Unless a magazine publisher is one of the few specifying this request in *Writer's Market,* it isn't required. Social security numbers are optional information; you may include yours if you wish in the upper left corner of page one, underneath your name and address.

Sidebar Format

Q. How do you type a sidebar in manuscript form?

A. Sidebars should be typed in the standard manuscript format. Begin the sidebar on a separate sheet of paper and clearly mark it "Sidebar." Type in an identifying caption after the word "Sidebar" to indicate what main article it accompanies. Place the sidebar at the end of the feature or main article manuscript. When the sidebar is typed separately from the featured manuscript, it's easier for the editor to mark it for the typesetter, since most sidebars are printed in widths that differ from the widths used for feature material. (For a discussion of sidebars, see Chapter 22.)

Two-Sided Manuscript?

Q. With the new photocopy machines accepting and reproducing copies on two sides of paper (page), is it acceptable to print on both sides of paper, then submit my book manuscript to a publisher? Such a practice could certainly save tons of paper and postage, especially when submitting lengthy manuscripts.

A. Manuscripts copied on both sides of a page are not acceptable because they are not *workable* in that format. Editors often photocopy and cut up a page of the manuscript, rearrange paragraphs or pages, and send sections of the manuscript to another editor for input. Yes, it would save paper and postage costs for writers, but the standard manuscript format developed to what it is today because it is efficient and extremely workable for editors.

Underline for Italics

Q. I am working on a short story in which short paragraphs in italics are interspersed throughout the narrative, and I would like to know whether there is any way to indicate italics without underlining. This amounts to quite extensive underlining, which in my opinion, is not only bothersome and time consuming but is distracting to the reader. I don't want to distract an editor who reads the manuscript.

A. Underlining *is* the standard way to denote italics; editors would not be any more distracted by it than readers would be by the actual italics.

Thoughts in Quotes?

Q. I have been told that thoughts should not be enclosed in quotation marks. This works very well in some cases, but there are instances in which I do not know how to handle the punctuation, as in the following: Jim said, "Walter is a wonderful fellow." Alice agreed and thought, "You are wonderful too." Should quotation marks be used in this case, and if not, should "You" begin with a capital letter?

A. Quotation marks need not be used here, but the capital letter for "You" should be retained. Or, if the use of a capital in the middle of a sentence disturbs you, you might handle it this way: Alice agreed. You are wonderful too, she thought. If you like, you may underscore her thought to indicate italics, which would differentiate it nicely from the direct quotations.

When to Hyphenate

Q. What is the fundamental rule, if there is one, about hyphenated words?

A. If you consult the introductory pages of most standard unabridged dictionaries, you will find rules pertaining to the use of hyphens. Rules *can* be rather complicated. But a few simple ones to bear in mind are that the hyphen can be used (1) to clarify meaning, e.g., honey-child . . . not a child made of honey; (2) to avoid having a double vowel or a triple consonant, e.g. wall-like is preferable to walllike; (3) to aid proper pronunciation, e.g., all-embracing is less likely to be mispronounced than allembracing. In general, just remember that if the hyphen helps to make your meaning clearer, use it. Take note of compound words as you read top magazines and newspapers, since they are the trendsetters in the spelling of new words entering the printed language.

Dot or Dashes

Q. Is there any current guide with editorial sanction for the use of the three dots (. . .) and the dash (—)? If so I would appreciate knowing about it.
A. There is no strict editorial policy governing the use of the three dots (. . .) and the dash (—). In popular magazines such as *McCall's, Esquire, Argosy, New Yorker,* and *Redbook* the dash seems to be more prevalent than the dots, though most of the magazines do use both, sometimes in the same story. The dots are used mainly to indicate that the speaker's voice trails off . . .; the dash is used sometimes in place of parentheses or sometimes to indicate an abrupt interruption in speech or thought or to suggest a pause longer than a comma but not as final as a period. The dots are also used to show omission of words from a quote (in which case they are called an ellipsis); e.g., *Senator John L. McGee said, "We must examine closely . . . the effect of postal rate increases on the magazine industry."* This statement could have appeared in a magazine industry newsletter where the omitted words, *"agriculture grants, education proposals, and,"* would have been of little interest to the readers of the newsletter. It's a good idea to follow the format of the particular magazine or book publisher to which you're submitting.

Retype Again?

Q. Is it essential that a manuscript be typed perfectly? I have a 480-page manuscript that I've retyped three times and it's still a mess. Every time I retype it, I reread it, which is disastrous because my pen flies with revisions (usually of words, not sentences). If I retype it again, I'll be wasting weeks that could be used in creating. Or should I send it out with the word substitutes neatly penned?
A. Since you can't resist revising every time you retype, you would probably find a professional manuscript typist the answer to your problem. The cost of this service would be worth the considerable saving in time and effort. Under no circumstances should you send out a manuscript that has more than three corrections per page marked on it. Also to save wear and tear on the finished product, send the publisher a query letter first instead of submitting the complete manuscript. A *clean* photocopy can cover "a multitude of sins." Certain pages or the entire manuscript can be corrected and photocopied to appear professionally typed.

Word Count

Q. Does it make a difference in what I'm paid if I don't include the word count on a manuscript when I submit it? Might I get paid more if I add it?
A. Most editors prefer to have the approximate word count noted on the upper right corner of page one of the manuscript. If the magazine pays by the word, they'll pay for the number of words in the final accepted version of your manuscript.

Novel Manuscript

Q. I have just finished a novel. What should the margins be on a manuscript?
A. The margins on the left and right sides and the top and bottom should be at least one and one fourth inch.

The End or 30

Q. I have a question pertaining to novels and short stories. On the last page of the manuscript should I type "The End"? I've seen "30" in some places, indicating the ending of the manuscript (both for fiction and nonfiction). Which is correct?
A. You can type "The End" at the end of a short story or novel, although you don't have to. The number 30 is usually written at the end of the copy for nonfiction, most often used in newspaper stories and reports. It is a legacy from old newspaper telegraphers who used the Roman numeral XXX as a symbol to indicate the end of the message. Some writers also use the symbol # to indicate the end.

Subtitles Included?

Q. In many magazine articles there are subheads placed between paragraphs to attract the reader's attention to a change in thought. Should a writer put these in the manuscript or is this an editorial procedure?
A. This is usually an editorial procedure. The editor may want them placed in certain locations for editorial emphasis and/or to help a layout paste-up problem. Writers need not include subheads (also called subtitles) in the original manuscript submitted; however, some articles lend themselves to this treatment, and appropriate subheads could enhance the possibility of a sale.

Credits for Quotes

Q. Where should quotation credits be given in a manuscript—at the bottom of the page where the quotation appears or at the end of the manuscript?
A. Credits may be given in a short manuscript by placing an asterisk next to the quote and a corresponding asterisk and notation of the source at the bottom of the page. Long articles and book manuscripts should follow the style suggested by *A Manual of Style:* number each quotation within the text, and on a separate sheet write the corresponding number, followed by a period and the credit line. Footnotes or end notes (at the end of the chapter or the end of the book) are set in a different size type. The publisher decides on the basis of his own style preference whether to put the notes at the bottom of the page or elsewhere.

Date Style

Q. In my writing, I often need to refer to the days and months of the year, omitting the year. Is it correct to use ordinal numerals to designate the days (for example, January 12th, May 1st, March 5th)?
A. The accepted practice is as follows: January 12, May 1, March 5.

Get Quotes for Book Jacket?

Q. I've seen quotes from well-known people on the jackets of books, commenting on the book's excellence. I'm sure comments like these improve sales. Would you advise me to type extra

copies of the book I'm writing and send them to various people to solicit similar letters for my book?
A. The garnering of letters of praise (testimonials) from famous people is usually the job of the publisher's publicity department. Remember that you haven't yet obtained a contract for the book you're working on, so wait until the publisher accepts your manuscript before discussing testimonials with him. After acceptance, if you have in mind people you think would respond favorably to your book, suggest them to the publisher.

Triple-Space?

Q. I triple-space on manuscripts rather than double-space because my typewriter has elite (small) type. Is this acceptable to magazine editors or do they always prefer double-spacing?
A. Double-spacing is preferable but triple-spacing would probably be acceptable to magazine editors. Elite type is commonly used and needs no special treatment.

Quotation Credits

Q. I am writing a textbook. In places, for a line or so, I quote from Webster's Dictionary *or an encyclopedia; in other places I use published material but reword it to make it simple for a child to understand. Will it be sufficient, at the end of the book, to give references used without listing each single place in which they are used?*
A. You may safely reword the reference book material to make it understandable to children. And although it is usually necessary to request permission to quote from copyrighted material, in your case the length of quotations would undoubtedly come under the principles of "fair use" which legally allow *brief* quotations. Correct acknowledgment of the source material as you propose should be acceptable.

Word Count

Q. I have never learned how writers arrive at the total number of words in a manuscript. Can you tell me?
A. Count every word on five representative pages; divide by five to get an average number of words per page, then multiply that average by the total number of pages in the manuscript. When counting words, abbreviated words count as one word as do the words "a," "the," etc. Type approximate number of words in round figures, such as 2,700 words (not 2,693) in the upper right corner of page one.

Estimating Word Count

Q. Is there a fast method of estimating the number of words in a manuscript?
A. Many production editors at book and magazine publishing companies consider the "average" word length to be six typed characters, when taking into account the number of short words, such as articles and prepositions, balanced against the longer words present, even in children's books. To estimate the number of words in your manuscript, count the number of characters in a full line of type; multiply by the number of lines on the page; multiply again by the number of pages in the manuscript; and divide by the magic number, six. The result will be a fairly accurate count of the words in your story or article.

14 Are There Any Editorial Taboos?

A writer's challenge is to send an editor what he wants. But it's also to avoid sending him manuscripts he doesn't want, or engaging in practices which cause him extra work. A thorough study of market listings, editorial guidelines, and publishers' products will help you hit your target more precisely.

Magazine Taboos

Q. What subjects are taboo in magazines?
A. Some magazines have no taboos, and state this in their editorial requirements in *Writer's Market*. Others state what their particular taboos are. For instance, you wouldn't submit an article about a plane wreck to an airlines magazine. Car magazines sometimes specify no accidents. Many men's magazines use sexy stories; others are not markets for this type. The confession magazines are now accepting stories about racial and religious conflicts which were formerly taboo. Religious magazines have taboos which vary from magazine to magazine. Church school papers use stories which follow the precepts of their particular religion. Some state flatly, "No smoking, drinking, dancing, etc." Some police trade journals object to the use of the word "cops." When writing for the youngest of the juvenile set, keep the ending happy. You should write for sample copies of the magazines you plan to submit to, and study them to see just what they use.

Insufficient Market Analysis

Q. I've got an article that I've submitted to several different magazines, all without success. McCall's, Vogue, Cosmopolitan, Woman's Day—it's made the rounds of all the women's magazines. I've researched and written my article carefully, and I think I ended up with a good manuscript. Why isn't it selling?
A. Although it's true that all the magazines you've mentioned come under the general category of "women's" publications, each one has a slightly different audience from the others; each magazine's readers have interests and characteristics that attract them to that particular publication, instead of to the others. The fact that you have submitted the same article to four very different publications might reveal that you have not *slanted* the article to one specific publication. Each magazine has different needs to satisfy its readership.

Cosmopolitan, for example, caters to the sophisticated single woman; *Woman's Day* concentrates on family-oriented topics. It's clear that an article written for the needs of one would clearly not meet the needs of the other. *Woman's Day* would be the place to market an article on problems of child-rearing; *Cosmopolitan* would not be interested. Check *Writer's Market* for the needs of any publication, and read several issues of the magazine to learn the kinds of material it publishes.

Changes for Article

Q. I have two minor changes I'd like to make in an article I mailed to a publisher last week. Would it be all right to send the editor a note specifying the changes I'd like made in my manuscript?
A. No. For better or worse, the manuscript you mailed is the one the editor now has. Any changes will have to be made after the article is accepted. To send in the corrections now would only serve to exasperate the editor. If your manuscript is accepted, you will probably have an opportunity later to suggest the changes.

(For further tips on dealing with editors, see Chapter 35.)

Multiple Purpose Letter?

Q. I have several questions for various departments of a magazine, dealing with a query, my subscription, and other facets of their business. Is it okay to write just one letter?
A. Such a practice can save you postage, but can also try an editor's patience. *The Basics of Selling Your Writing* includes an article by Meg Hill—"How to Drive an Editor Nuts (And Assure That Your Words Never See Print)"—in which she describes a letter to a women's magazine which contains a query, points out that last issue's recipe for banana fritters didn't work, proposes a cookbook idea, informs the publisher of an address change (to be routed to the subscription department), and encloses a letter to be forwarded to the author of an article. Honoring all those requests takes a lot of time (making photocopies, routing to various departments). It's best to write separate letters. Not only will it ensure that your requests get to the right people, it will make the editor look more kindly on you in the future.

Follow-Up Phone Call?

Q. I submitted a manuscript to a publisher a few weeks ago, and have heard nothing since. Is it okay to phone the editor to ask about the status of my manuscript?
A. No. Most publishers and magazines receive so many manuscripts that it is impossible for the average staff member to know the status of a particular article at any given time. Most publishers have a reporting time listed in *Writer's Market,* so don't expect to hear anything from them for at least that long. If that time passes and you still have heard nothing, don't call—*write* a note requesting a report on your manuscript. Editors don't like phone calls from writers requesting immediate reports.

Content vs Appearance

Q. Why is it so important to buy expensive paper and new typewriter ribbons? Isn't the quality of the article what will make the sale?
A. Look at the physical appearance of a manuscript as being similar to your first meeting with a prospective employer. Since *you* wouldn't show up looking less than your best, why should

your manuscript? The small and careless factors in your manuscript can aggravate the most tolerant editors. A faded typewriter ribbon makes a manuscript hard to read and harder to photocopy. Heavily edited manuscripts leave no room for the editor to do *his* editing. Cut-and-paste, or cellophane tape, also annoy an editor. The ancient, dog-eared manuscript which has obviously been seen by too many other editors makes an editor think there must be a reason no one has bought it before him. If you want a manuscript to sell, make sure it has no counts against it *before* it's even read by an editor. Neatness counts when making a positive impression with your manuscript.

Teenage Book

Q. Do you think a publisher of teenage books would reject a story if it includes several violent but common incidents related to high school football? I need to know if these incidents could be objectionable.
A. It is highly doubtful that these incidents alone could be responsible for the rejection of your book manuscript. Other factors, such as style, plotting, and credibility, should be considered.

Hand Deliver Your Manuscript?

Q. I'm going to New York with my husband to a convention just about the time I'll have my short story finished. Would it be to my advantage to hand deliver the manuscript?
A. No, it would be a disservice to the editor who can't really tell you anything about your manuscript until she reads it, which she can't do right on the spot, and it will interrupt her day.

Knowing an Insider

Q. I have a cousin who is in sales with a leading book publisher and I sent him my manuscript asking him to pass it along to the right editor. After weeks of waiting, I sent a follow-up note inquiring. Shortly after that I got a form rejection letter from the editorial department. Am I wrong to have expected a more personal response?
A. If the manuscript had interested the editorial department for possible publication, you would have gotten the personal response. Some beginning writers think that "knowing someone at the publishing company" will be an advantage. It isn't. Your manuscript has to sell itself.

Same Book, New Title?

Q. I submitted a book proposal about a year ago which was rejected. I've now come up with a better title that I think is a natural for one of the houses that rejected it. Should I resubmit it?
A. As long as the same editor is at that publishing house, changing the title isn't likely to make the book *idea* any more appealing to this particular publisher than it was the first time. As one editor put it, "Think up new ideas, not just new strategies to sell your old one." That doesn't prevent you from submitting your new title/book idea to another publisher.

Current Market Information

Q. I sent an article to a magazine and it came back without a rejection slip. Somebody had just crossed out the editor's name in my covering letter and just scrawled "Read the magazine!" across the letter. Isn't this a rather insulting reply?
A. Apparently not, if you hadn't looked at a recent issue and learned that the editor you were

addressing the submission to no longer worked there. By the same token, the editorial slant of the magazine may have changed and the type of article you were submitting was no longer appropriate. It's very important to also look at recent sample issues of a magazine in addition to reading the *latest* market requirements for a magazine. Don't depend on an old edition of *Writer's Market* for your information.

15 What Is Style?

The headmaster of an English elementary school commented, "I see four kinds of writing: 1) Just plain bad. 2) Correct but dead. 3) Incorrect but good. 4) Correct and good." The beginner's search for that last ideal is often a struggle. Editor and writer Theodore Bernstein reminds us: "Everyone who has made it at least through high school uses two languages—both of them English. They are not vastly different, yet they are distinct. One is spoken English, often colorful, clear in its intended emphasis and assisted by facial expression, tone, and gestures. The other is written English."

Writing Style

Q. When an editor or teacher talks about my style, what does he mean?
A. Style refers to the way an author expresses his ideas. It's *how* he says something in his work, rather than *what* he says; style is form rather than content. Each writer's work has an individual style, as unique as a fingerprint; this is true whether he writes novels, magazine articles, poetry, or plays. Good style need not be characterized by complex constructions and polysyllabic words; it *is* marked by a clear presentation and apt expression of ideas. A writer's personal style doesn't appear overnight. It takes time and practice to develop your own method of putting thoughts into words.

Writing in "Depth"

Q. Would you explain the term "depth" in the field of writing?
A. "Depth" means many things to many editors. But perhaps the one interpretation they would all agree on is that a piece of writing that has depth has something important to say to readers. It would avoid frivolity or top-of-the-head superficiality about the ideas presented; it would require thought on the part of the writer *and* the reader. Nonfiction of depth would be based on well-researched data. Fiction of depth would arise from thoughtful sensitivity to and perception of human behavior.

Pedestrian Writing

Q. Several times I have come across literary criticism using the phrase "pedestrian writing." The phrase has been used in discussing published material without stating whether it is

considered good writing. Exactly what is "pedestrian writing?"
A. The term "pedestrian," when applied to writing, is definitely unflattering. It means the work is prosaic or dull. The Latin root "ped-" refers to the foot, and the usual definition of the noun "pedestrian" is one who travels on foot . . . such as the common man (who presumably doesn't have a better way to travel). In connection with writing, the adjective means common or ordinary.

Style for Young Readers

Q. I want to write books and stories for children, but I don't want my style to be too involved or mature for them to read. How can I make sure I'm writing for the proper age group?
A. One way is to spend time with children and their relatives; teachers, librarians, and other people who are familiar with the way children think. Family members who have children can be a good resource. Read literature aimed at the age group for whom you intend to write. One helpful reference is *Best Books for Children,* which lists 13,000 books for children preschool through the sixth grade, and the age group for which each is written. The titles are arranged by subject, so you can easily find what has been written on your chosen topic.

The He/She Question

Q. Has grammar been updated to compensate for the use of the generic pronoun "he?"
A. Although the phrase "Everyone does what *he* likes" would once have been read without second thought, it now raises the question of whether automatic use of the masculine pronoun in generic situations is an acceptable practice. As Casey Miller and Kate Swift write in *The Handbook of Nonsexist Writing For Writers, Editors and Speakers,* "Like 'generic' *man,* 'generic' *he* fosters the misconception that the standard human being is male."

There are several alternatives for the writer who wishes to avoid "he" as a generic pronoun. The word *they* can be used. For instance, in the above sentence, "Everybody does what they like." A double pronoun construction could be used: "Everybody does what he or she likes." Used extensively, however, this technique can become awkward. It has been shortened with the use of the slash, resulting in an equally distracting "he/she" or "s/he."

Rewriting the sentence can eliminate the need for the pronoun in many cases.

Publishers in general are sticking to the masculine pronoun, understood as including everyone, but study individual publisher's guidelines and read the publication to learn the preferences of editors you're aiming toward.

Style vs Content

Q. I seem to spend so much time on style that it takes forever to finish a manuscript. Is there such a thing as worrying too much about style?
A. If you spend all your time worrying about *how* to say something, you may never get it said. While it is important to write clearly and with appealing style, too much concentration on the technique of writing can create a roadblock that prevents you from finishing a piece. It's more important and helpful to get finished pieces out into the marketplace for the perusal of professional editors than it is to spend endless time refining the same manuscript over and over again. If the content is good, an editor will probably iron out stylistic problems.

If a particular section of your article or story bothers you, it's best to leave it alone for a couple of days. If you look at one piece for an extended period of time, you can lose all perspective and find fault with even your best work.

Improve Writing Style

Q. How can I improve my style?
A. Each writer has his own personal style, his own way of expressing his ideas, so there are no set rules or guidelines for improving style. Style should be natural for the writer, acceptable to the reader and appropriate to the content of the piece. Good style can only evolve and be refined through the practice of writing and the study of good writing.

To improve style, the writer should read widely and determine what is good about a particular piece of writing. He should not parrot the style of another writer; rather, he should evaluate his own writing by comparing flaws and strong points in what others have written. Evaluation by either a writing teacher or a professional criticism service is also helpful.

Helpful books on style include Strunk and White's *The Elements of Style,* Ted Cheney's *Getting the Words Right* and Gary Provost's *Make Every Word Count. American Usage and Style: The Consensus* is Roy Copperud's comparison of differing opinions on usage and style from several well-known sources.

Short Title Value?

Q. Is a short title considered a virtue for a magazine article or short story?
A. A good, short title can help catch the attention of the editor. Connie Emerson, author of *Write on Target,* says that most magazine article titles have no more than six words. Always study previous issues of the magazine to which you are submitting your work to learn the kind of titles it uses. Short stories also benefit from short titles designed to pique the curiosity of readers and editors. The title should be succinct and closely related to the characters and the action. While the length of title an author chooses is part of his style, he's also subject to the editor's preferences, which are sometimes determined by the short story's placement within the magazine.

Loosened Style?

Q. What does my writing teacher mean when he suggests that I "loosen up" my writing style?
A. The statement implies that you should try to lessen the formality of your writing and strive for a style that is more casual and easier to comprehend. Conventional idioms, slang, contractions ("he's" instead of "he is"), common words, and shorter sentences can achieve an informal style. "Loosening up" your style gives your manuscript a more conversational tone and makes it easier to read.

Personal Style

Q. I recently read an article by a well-known fiction writer who said it isn't good to read other fiction writers. He stated it confuses a writer's style and makes his work seem inferior. Is this true?
A. The narrow view of that particular writer is not generally shared by most writers who have one love in common—the love of reading. If reading the work of others confuses a writer's style, then such a style was probably not individual enough or rooted deeply enough to begin with. The novice writer may go through several phases of stylistic expression before he establishes the one that is his own. Remember that a writer who reads only his own work may find that he is writing only for himself.

First Person Always True?

Q. How can a humorous book written in the first person (such as those by Erma Bombeck) be thought of as fiction, even allowing for exaggerated anecdotes?
A. Essentially these books are more imagination than reality, even though they are probably inspired by factual bits and pieces in the writer's life. Writing in first person doesn't necessarily guarantee that the material is true.

Manual of Style

Q. I've often seen the Chicago Manual of Style *referred to by editors. Just what is it and where can I find a copy?*
A. *A Manual of Style* is a book which refers to the manner of preparing a manuscript according to the style guidelines developed by the University of Chicago, published in an extensive volume by The University of Chicago Press. It gives guidelines for capitalization, punctuation, italicization, and much, much more. It is not designed to help you develop your own "writing style." Style in this case refers to the way a manuscript is set up for typesetting. You can probably see a copy at the reference department in your local library, or order a copy directly from The University of Chicago Press, 5801 Ellis Ave., Chicago 60637.

Magazine Style

Q. Can you please tell me why all the articles and stories in some magazines appear to have been written by the same author? The articles are the same style as the fiction. Can any of these magazines that seem to be written by one person be considered freelance markets?
A. The stories and articles in certain magazines may seem to be the product of one prolific writer, but usually they're not. Individual magazines have specific formats and preferred styles, and in the hope of selling to them, many writers are careful to slant to their known preferences. Editors do some rewriting where material warrants it, and this tends to give an additional familiar touch to the work. These magazines are freelance markets, with strong style preferences.

Write Naturally

Q. At the bottom of a form rejection slip I received for an article, an editor had written, "Write more naturally!" What does that mean?
A. It could mean that instead of using words and phrases that an average person would, you use the longer rather than the simpler word, the convoluted rather than the straightforward sentence. "Write as you talk" is a good guideline when writing for popular magazines.

Lively Writing

Q. How can I make my writing more vigorous—something a writing teacher said my writing lacked?
A. Make good use of the active voice (Not, "the car was stolen by Bob," but "Bob stole the car.") Write with strong, specific nouns and verbs instead of depending on adjectives and adverbs. ("The Volkswagen skidded through the blockade.") Avoid too many qualifiers like the words "very," "little," "rather." Read aloud what you've written to check for rhythm, pace, and clarity.

16 What Do I Need to Do to Use a Pen Name?

Writers use pen names for a variety of reasons—anonymity from their families and friends, to foil sexist editors, to establish audiences for different types of work. How do you select a pen name and let your mailman and banker in on the secret so you can receive mail and cash checks? The following information will smooth the way for you.

Selecting a Pen Name

Q. How do I go about choosing a pen name?
A. There are no guidelines for deciding on a pen name. It can be a combination of first and last names the writer finds attractive. A baby-name book is a good source of first names; last names can be names the writer has heard or imagined, or names taken from the newspaper or phone book. Choosing a pen name is similar to naming a fictional character. The writer might wish to consider the name's appropriateness to the material carrying the byline. "Letitia Beauregarde," for example, would be more likely to write the saga of a southern family than a first-person account of a hunting trip in the Amazon jungles.

Name Influence Editor?

Q. What is in a name? Would an editor be more likely to accept an article by an author with a more distinctive sounding name than a plain name? My name is very ordinary, but I don't want to use a pen name. What would you suggest?
A. Use your real name. Editors don't care a John Doe about a name for the byline. It's always the quality of writing and the interest of subject matter that sell a manuscript. Names are incidental.

Copyright Under Pen Name?

Q. If an article or book is written under a pseudonym must I copyright it under my pen name, or can I use my real name in the copyright form to protect my rights to the work?
A. On the copyright registration form, you can list your pseudonym under "Name of Author" and your real name under "Copyright Claimant," with a brief explanation of the name difference. This guarantees proof of your authorship of the work in the event your heirs need to establish that the work is yours.

Anonymous Author?

Q. Can a writer use a pen name, become successful or famous, and still remain anonymous? Suppose a writer dislikes publicity, and is very shy with persons outside her family and friends' circle. What in your opinion would be the advantages and disadvantages of anonymity in such a case?

A. With the publisher's help, a writer could achieve both success and anonymity. The chief advantage of this would be the fulfillment of the author's desire to remain unidentified. The disadvantages would include lack of public acclaim and the thrill of seeing one's own name on successful books. Other disadvantages would include the necessity to reject all interviews, and worst of all, the burden of having to keep a secret.

Adopt a Real Name?

Q. I want to use as a pen name a lovely name which happens to belong to a little girl in England, an occasional pen pal of my daughter. Must I ask permission? What if I were to pick a name out of a telephone directory?

A. Yes, it would be best to ask permission of the little girl in England (or her parents) if you plan to use her name as a pen name in America. It's not a good idea to pick a complete name out of a telephone directory. The person with that real name may sue you for libel or invasion of privacy—depending on what you wrote and how well it sold. A better idea is to choose a combination of two different names. The spelling of a nice-sounding name can also be changed.

Pen Name Value?

Q. What is the real value of using a pen name? Are pen names customarily used by professional writers today?

A. A pen name is used to protect the identity of the writer employing it. There are any number of reasons why a writer wouldn't want his name associated with the material he writes.

Sometimes an author will use a pen name if he writes a different kind of book than he has written before, such as when mainstream novelist Evan Hunter writes mysteries under the pseudonym "Ed McBain." This practice keeps an Evan Hunter fan from picking up a book that is radically different from what he expects from the author.

Prolific writers often have to adopt pen names, since most hardcover publishers will frequently ask for exclusive rights to the name of a successful author. In the words of novelist Dean Koontz, "He [the publisher] doesn't want *his* new Sam Hepplefinger novel to be in competition with some other publisher's new Sam Hepplefinger novel." Writer Victoria Holt publishes under two other names because of this.

There might be a college professor of mathematics who secretly authors who-done-its and doesn't want the word to get around to his students and colleagues. Or, a writer's family might object to her career and, to disassociate herself from them, she changes her name. Or a writer might simply dislike her real name—it may be hard to pronounce or look unwieldy in print—so she adopts a more suitable one. For most writers, though, there is sufficient satisfaction in seeing one's real name in a byline.

Check Cashing

Q. Sometimes an author writes under a pen name because he doesn't want his real name known. How does the writer cash a check made out to his pen name—especially if he's well known in a small town?

A. When the manuscript is submitted under a pen name, the author usually includes his real name and address on the title page, so that the check will be made out to him and he can cash it without letting anyone know what the check is for. If the check is made out to the pen name, the author can simply endorse it with the pen name, then endorse it over to his real name and cash it that way. In any case, it's always best to notify both your bank and the local postmaster that you'll be using a pen name. Letting them know that you're "d.b.a. (doing business as)" your pseudonym will ensure that your mail will be delivered and that you'll be able to cash checks, should they be made out to your pen name. In some communities, a writer must register that he is doing business under another name.

Already in Use?

Q. I would like to use a pen name, but how can I be sure the name I select isn't one that is already being used by someone else?

A. Except in cases where extremely well-known names, such as Ann Landers, might be registered as a trademark, most writers simply go the Library of Congress Catalog card directories in their public library, look up the last name they want to use, and see if anybody else has already copyrighted books in that name. Your librarian can assist you in locating the directories of Library of Congress Catalog authors.

Pen Name Protection

Q. Please tell me how I can write an article under a pen name and yet be able to prove in event of a court case that I wrote it. I know that I can register it in the copyright office under my real name and the pen name, but I prefer to copyright it and register it under my pen name. The article is not going to be published by a magazine—it's a private effort—but I don't want to lose my rights when it's printed and circulated. This leaves me with the problem of having to prove that the pen name is really me. Could I mail a copy of the article to myself with both names on it and keep it unopened in a safe place—as proof? Could I send a copy to a banker or lawyer or someone? I think some plays in England are handled in this way. What would you suggest?

A. Writing an article under a pen name and mailing one copy of it to yourself with both your pen name and real name included might work. Or you could get the copy notarized with both names on it. Most writers who are going to use pen names usually notify their postmaster and banker that they will be receiving mail and checks in that business name. Keep in mind that in the United States, if you privately print an article and distribute it, you must be sure to print the copyright notice on it before distribution. Otherwise you are placing your article in the public domain.

Pen Name Disadvantages

Q. Are there any disadvantages in using a pen name?

A. When an editor notices the same byline several times in other publications, he's more apt to buy the work of that writer who has a track record of delivering publishable material. The use of pen names dilutes the impact of your repeated sales for the editor and for the reader who looks for more material by a writer he likes.

Male/Female Pen Names

Q. Although I am a woman writer, I am chiefly interested in the type of material that would sell to those magazines traditionally classified as "men's publications," such as Esquire *or* Field & Stream. *Can I use a male pseudonym or my initials, rather than a feminine name, and will it increase my chances of sales?*

A. In general, your writing will be judged on the basis of your authority on the subject, not your sex. It's possible that some editors might have second thoughts about running a men's article written by a woman. Although discrimination against women has decreased, it still exists; a male editor *might* assume that a woman could not write a traditionally "male" article. If using a male pen name will help make a sale, use one.

On the other hand, since women writers outnumber men in religious and small circulation periodicals, a male pen name could appear to an editor as possibly having a new slant to well-worn subjects, thus enhancing chances of a sale.

The pen name situation would apply also when men are writing female-oriented material. A number of authors of romance novels, for example, are men using female pseudonyms.

Danger!

Q. Because I hope to begin my political writing where George Orwell (Eric Blair) concluded his career, I would like to adopt the pen name, George Orwell II. Will I need permission from his heirs?

A. Yes, you will need permission, but I doubt that Mr. Orwell's heirs would allow you to cash in on his reputation. Try to make it on your own!

17 How Can I Protect My Work?

Beginning writers seem to be divided into two large groups—paranoids who are afraid someone will steal all their ideas, and innocents who don't take the time to learn enough about what they should worry about: holding on to as many rights to their work as possible. A careful reading of these questions and answers can help you protect your work.

Definition

Q. What is meant by "rights?" What rights are you supposed to sell?

A. A writer owns all rights to his literary creation. He is entitled to decide who shall own the right to print his story for the first time or reprint it or make it into a movie or adapt it to any other print or electronic format. Such rights are his protection against those who would come along and freely use his work for their own purposes. The rights most commonly offered for sale to publications are first North American serial rights, which mean the writer is selling the right to be first to print this particular work the first time in a magazine or newspaper. All other rights still belong to the writer. On the manuscript, in the upper right corner of the title page, indicate the rights you are offering for sale. And make sure that any check you cash for an accepted work does not carry an endorsement for rights other than those you want to sell.

Editor Stole My Idea

Q. I had an idea for an article, which was rejected by an editor, and a similar article appeared in that magazine a few months later. This has also happened when an entire manuscript was rejected. How can I protect myself from editors who steal my ideas?

A. A writer will often suspect piracy when he sees his idea published in a magazine shortly after his query or manuscript was rejected by the same publication, but this assumption is usually false. Freelancer Gary Provost has coined what he calls his first law of plagiarism: "The better your understanding of the market, the greater the chance of your thinking you were plagiarized." In other words, similarities between your idea or manuscript and the published article are the result of both you and the author of the published piece knowing what the magazine is looking for. Since a magazine has between three months and one year "lead time" between an issue's creation and its publication, the published piece was probably written or assigned before you even wrote your query letter.

Unless the published article uses word-for-word the same paragraphs and sentences as the rejected work, there is no proof of editorial piracy.

There are, however, steps you can take to ensure that your completed manuscript will not be stolen. First of all, be sure that your manuscript carries your copyright notice. Also, you should *always* keep a carbon or photocopy of your manuscript. If you ever have reason to believe an editor has stolen from you, consult an attorney.

Rights Question

Q. What is the difference between first North American rights and first serial rights when submitting to a major magazine?
A. Both phrases mean almost the same thing, the right to publish the material once for the first time. The word "serial" refers to newspapers, magazines, and publications that are published on a continuing basis. First North American serial rights covers first publication rights in both the United States and Canada, and American magazines that distribute in Canada usually want this extra protection.

Newspaper Column Rights

Q. A local copyrighted newspaper is interested in my column. Does the paper have all rights to my column until the rights are reassigned to me; and do I put the copyright symbol on copies submitted to other publications as copyrighted by me or by the paper?
A. Most newspapers are *not* copyrighted, but your column will be protected initially by your newspaper because it is copyrighted. Under the new copyright law it is assumed you are only selling one-time rights to this newspaper unless you both agree to something else in writing. Verify this with your newspaper editor and get a letter in reply from him which spells out exactly what rights his paper is using. Hold the letter on file. Tell the editor that you plan to resubmit some of the column material to other publications. Sell one-time rights and hold the copyright for yourself.

All Rights

Q. What does "buys all rights" mean? Does it mean they buy first and subsequent rights? Or that they buy any rights offered?
A. "Buys all rights" means they buy the rights to *all* possible avenues of sale on that manuscript—such as book, movie, TV, and other rights. Some publications that buy all rights will reassign rights to the author after publication. Check this point with the editor.

Book on Government Agency

Q. I've based my book on extensive research of government information from government publications and files. Can I copyright my book since most of the information is in the public domain?
A. While government material is in itself uncopyrightable, your particular rewritten presentation of it is. However, any work that consists in any large part of verbatim government material must carry in the copyright notice a statement which identifies those parts of the work which are yours and those parts which are government-produced. For specific guidelines on your work, it would be best to check with the Information and Publications Section, LM-455, Copyright Office, Library of Congress, Washington DC 20559.

Publication Doesn't Stop You

Q. An article recently appeared in a magazine, strikingly similar to one I have been trying to sell to the same magazine for some time. Because of this I am now forced to forget about selling my article, since the subject's already been covered. What can I do about this?

A. One frustrating fact of a freelance writer's life is to find that an idea he has, someone else also has had and beaten him to publication with it—sometimes even using the same words. You're not forced to forget about submitting your manuscript elsewhere, because many articles are published on the same subject in a variety of publications within a two- or three-year period. If your article is well written, and hits the right magazine at the right time, publication of the other article will not be a deterrent to publication of yours.

Friend Stole Idea?

Q. A writer friend of mine recently sold an article about a topic on which I've been working for some time. I believe he stole my idea. Is there any way I can keep this from happening?

A. Sometimes, when fellow writers gather and "talk shop," a writer will casually mention a piece he's working on. Months or years may go by and another writer may end up doing an article on the same idea. Once your idea is discussed, you've put it out where others can get at it—consciously or unconsciously. A good rule is this: Don't discuss a work in progress with other writers. They don't intentionally steal, and may not remember that you were working on the same idea, since most writers get ideas from many different sources—newspapers, magazines, books, television, films, neighbors, and fellow workers.

Right of Approval?

Q. An article I recently sold was heavily edited, distorting the meaning of some of the opinions and quotes contained in it. Can I ask for the right of article approval on any future sales?

A. It might not be a good idea to propose such a request in your query letter, since such preconditions might turn off the editor. The question can be raised after correspondence has passed between author and editor, and after the article has been finished and submitted. Include a paragraph in your cover letter asking that if the article is changed from your original manuscript—in terms of content, not just copyediting revisions—you would like the opportunity to see the final edited copy before publication.

Title Rights?

Q. Nine years ago I sent a manuscript to a publishing firm. They rejected it (as did others) after keeping it so long it was necessary to write them about it. Now I read they are publishing a book by that exact title. The title is extremely important to my book. Do they have all the rights in this case?

A. A title cannot be copyrighted, so there's nothing stopping you from using your title. As long as your story is completely different from the published one with the same title, that publisher can't claim unfair competition by the publisher who accepts your book.

Tapes from Book

Q. Some years ago, I wrote a children's book about the whaling era. It included several stories of foreign lands, each having a special song. The book was published in 1956 and copyrighted in my name. The book is now out of print. As the stories and songs are my own

material, I would like to know if I have the right to make tape recordings of them for sale to a publisher who produces visual aids and programs for school use. If there are restrictions to such usage, will you please tell me how I can meet them?
A. Unless the book contract you signed with the original publisher of your children's book about the whaling era reserved to the publisher the right to make tape recordings of your book, you have the right to use the book in that way. These special rights for the use of material contained in books are usually the subject of a special clause in the contract and you should review the contract to see whether you, or the publisher, or both, share in these rights.

"Best" Rights?

Q. What are usually the best rights and/or most profitable rights offered by writers of short stories and books?
A. The "most profitable" or "best" rights can't be predicted in advance. Some short stories may turn out to be optioned by movie companies; others may only appear in a magazine. The main thing for the writer to do is to hold as many rights to his work as he can, selling the rights individually, not ever granting "all rights" to his work to any one buyer. For example, a short story writer should only sell "first serial rights" or "one-time rights" to his story to a magazine.

A book contract spells out in detail what rights the author is granting to the publisher and which rights the author retains. For recommendations in this area see Chapter 38 on book publishing.

Erroneous Phrase

Q. Some periodicals indicate "Buys all rights. Publication not copyrighted." If a periodical is not copyrighted, it seems the only rights it can claim are the rights to first publication. Am I correct?
A. The publisher of an uncopyrighted publication may say "all rights" on his check, but the lack of copyright will permit anyone to make whatever further use of the material he wishes. So the original publisher could reprint it if he wanted to—and so could anyone else.

Who Owns What?

Q. Suppose Smith wrote a manuscript, in first draft, and gave it to Jones to read? Jones, a professional writer, keeps the manuscript, and in due time writes a book based on Smith's manuscript. If the book sells, and/or a movie is made from it, or paperbacks are published, or any other form of benefit derives from the sale of this book, does Smith have any rights in this book or the benefits from it?
A. Much would depend on the agreement Smith made with Jones when he gave him his manuscript. Why, for instance, did Smith allow Jones to keep the manuscript? Smith might be able to take this matter to court as an infringement of his copyright, which protected his unpublished manuscript. In doing so, though, he'd have to prove that Jones actually copied his exact language or the development, treatment, arrangement or sequence of ideas in the work. And he would have to take legal action within the period of the applicable statute of limitations. It would, of course, be more desirable if Smith and Jones could work out some financial arrangement agreeable to both, rather than go to the expense of court action.

What Rights?

Q. While most "how to" books about freelancing advocate specifying rights for sale on manuscripts, one popular seller claims this is a mark of amateurs and that editors who buy rights other than what are offered might reject the manuscript rather than dicker over rights. What is the accepted practice?
A. It is customary and businesslike to offer first serial rights unless the magazine's editorial listing in *Writer's Market* states it buys all rights. Then the writer has to decide whether he wants to sell under those terms.

Reassign Rights

Q. Can rights be reassigned to me from a magazine that is now defunct?
A. If the magazine was owned and published by a still-operating corporation or association, the author's material would still be their property. You might contact the rights and permissions department of the organization that published the now-defunct magazine. If you can't locate any present owners, then indicate that fact to the editor to whom you're trying to sell reprint rights.

Reprint Rights

Q. I sold first and reprint rights for an article to a magazine. Can I sell reprint rights to another publication, or must I wait until the first magazine has used its reprint rights?
A. It is permissible to sell reprint rights to the second publication. The only exception would be if you sold the first magazine exclusive reprint rights for a certain period of time. Then you would have to wait until the article was reprinted before reselling.

Second vs Reprint Rights

Q. Are second and reprint rights the same? Can they be sold more than once?
A. Second serial rights is the term used by publishers to refer to the right to publish a book excerpt in a magazine or newspaper *after* book publication. But some magazine editors use the term to also mean rights granted by a work's copyright owner or author to a magazine, giving permission to reprint an article, poem, or story after it has already appeared in another publication. These reprint rights may be sold as many times as the author or copyright owner wishes, to any number of publications.

Revised vs Original?

Q. About five years ago, I sold a children's story to a magazine that greatly altered and shortened it. It was published with a credit line that said, "adapted from a story by Jospeh P. Ritz." There is no question the magazine owns the publication rights to the story as it was published. But does it also own the rights to the original manuscript, to date unpublished?
A. It depends on what rights you sold to the original story which they paid for and revised. If they only bought first rights, then you can resubmit your unpublished original elsewhere.

Fire/Theft Protection

Q. How can I protect myself from losing my manuscripts and writing equipment in a house fire or burglary?

A. One way is to make sure your writing operation is covered by your homeowner's or personal property insurance policy. Since freelancing is a business, it's possible that your files, reference books, typewriter, word processor, or other equipment may not be covered by your current policy, and you may need a rider to add to your present coverage. You may even need a separate policy for your business. If you live in an apartment, or don't have such an insurance policy for some other reason, the Federal Crime Insurance program can insure your equipment against burglary or theft; for a premium (in 1983) of $120 per year, you receive $10,000 protection. Contact the program at Box 41033, Bethesda MD 20814-0436; toll-free telephone number is 800/638-8780. To protect against loss by fire, fireproof strongboxes are available for your papers.

Watch the Check Too!

Q. If I sell a novelette to a publisher, and some movie producer reads it in the magazine and wants to buy the movie rights, does he buy from me or the publisher? Must I reserve some kind of rights? Will the publisher be entitled to part of the money paid for the movie rights?
A. Reserving movie rights to a novelette depends on what rights you sell to the magazine in which it initially appears. Most magazines buy only "first serial rights." Some magazines, however, buy "all rights," which would give them complete return of money on any subsidiary sale of the story to movies, TV, etc. If you want to reserve these other rights to yourself, when you submit your novelette to a magazine publisher, you must type in the upper right corner "First North American Serial Rights Only." The magazine editor will know these are the only rights you want to sell. You should also notice carefully the check from the magazine publisher, since sometimes the endorsement on the check indicates the magazine is buying all rights. Often the accounting department of a magazine does not know what rights your manuscript indicated and if their normal procedure would be to buy all rights, the check will so indicate. By endorsing the check, you would be giving away all rights, even though your manuscript had indicated you were interested in selling first rights only. If you receive such a check, return it to the editor requesting a check without the "all rights" endorsement.

Infringement Action

Q. A recently published book contains verbatim, unattributed quotes from an article I wrote on the same subject for a magazine some time ago. What action, if any, should I take? Do I have the right of monetary compensation from the book's publisher for this unauthorized use of my work?
A. How much material from your article was used? Would it be allowable under the fair use provision of the copyright act? (See details on that in Chapter 18 of this book.) If there is substantial quoting from your piece, the next question is what rights did you sell to the magazine publisher? If you sold more than first serial rights to the piece, he could have given permission to the book's author to use portions of your work. If that is the case, then it's just a question of non-attribution.

If you sold only first rights, you may have been the victim of copyright infringement, and you should have an attorney write to the book's publisher, attach to the letter a copy of your article, and inform the publisher that you may sue for copyright infringement.

Whether you were able to collect monetary compensation from the book publisher would depend on whether you could prove you sustained actual damages as a result and/or whether the publisher was aware he was infringing your copyright.

18 What Do I Need to Know About Copyright?

The advent of the new copyright law in 1978 is a boon for every writer. Copyright is now effective as soon as a writer creates a work. The new law puts the burden on the publisher to notify the author in writing if he wants to buy other than one-time rights to the author's work. The law contains termination provisions that allow an author to regain rights he assigned to others, after a specific period. But since copyrights which were obtained under the old law must still operate under *its* regulations, it's important for the writer to know what his rights are, whether copyright was secured before 1978 or after.

New Copyright Law

Q. When writers talk about the "new" copyright law, what do they mean?
A. They mean the latest revision of the copyright law which was passed by Congress in 1976 and which took effect on January 1, 1978. Some of the details of the new law are covered in other questions in this chapter.

How Much Can I Quote?

Q. How much can I quote from copyrighted materials without infringing on copyright?
A. There aren't any set number of lines you can quote without getting permission. In determining whether an author has made "fair use" of, or infringed, another's copyrighted work, the copyright law says the factors to be considered shall include: 1) the purpose and character of the use, including whether such use is of a commercial nature or is for nonprofit educational purposes; 2) the nature of the copyrighted work; 3) the amount and substantiality of the portion used in relation to the copyrighted work as a whole; and 4) the effect of the use upon the potential market for or value of the copyrighted work. As current and future legal cases illustrate these points, writers will have a better idea of how these guidelines will be interpreted.

Public Domain

Q. What is public domain?
A. Any published or distributed material without a copyright notice or on which a copyright

has expired is considered to be in the public domain—that is, available for use by any member of the general public without payment to, or permission from, the original author.

Copyright Procedure

Q. How do I copyright my articles and stories?
A. Under the copyright law which became effective January 1978, your work is protected by statutory copyright as soon as it is created in tangible form. All you need to do is display the copyright symbol (©), the year, and your name on the first page of your manuscript. It need not be published to be protected.

Only if you think you might have to go to court and fight to prove your ownership of the work, is it necessary to register the material with the U.S. Copyright Office. For the proper forms and more information, write to U.S. Copyright Office, Library of Congress, Washington DC 20559.

Omission of Copyright Notice

Q. If a publisher inadvertently omits the writer's copyright notice is the work then placed in the public domain?
A. Not if the writer had given express direction in writing to the editor that his copyright notice was to appear. Two other circumstances under which the omission of the notice would not invalidate the copyright would be: 1) if the notice had been omitted from only a relatively small number of copies or 2) if registration for the work had been made before or within five years after the publication without notice, and a reasonable effort is made to add notice to all copies distributed after the omission was discovered.

Lose Your Copyright

Q. Under the new copyright law, how does one lose copyright protection?
A. Since under the new law your copyright exists as soon as you create a work, for your life plus fifty years, the primary ways to lose your copyright would be: 1. By publishing your work in an uncopyrighted publication and failing to have your own copyright credit line appear with your contribution—whether it's a story, article, or poem. 2. By publishing a book without your copyright notice. 3. By distributing unpublished or unproduced copies of other forms of your work—play, movie script, teleplay—which do not carry your copyright credit line.

Let Publisher Have Copyright?

Q. A publisher for whom I am writing an article offers the option of either giving the writer copyright for the piece or keeping it himself. Is it possible that the publisher could do a better job of handling copyright and legal matters stemming from an article? In other words, wouldn't it be a great load off my back if the copyright was in the publisher's name?
A. No! A writer should never give up his copyright to another party when it is possible to keep it in his name. To give up copyright means that you give up all legal rights to the work. Therefore, you could not benefit from any use of the article after the initial publication.

Rights vs Copyright

Q. When I sell various rights to my work, doesn't that affect my ownership of the copyright?
A. No. Various rights are all part of your copyright, but selling them in no way diminishes

your ownership of the actual work. William Strong, in *The Copyright Book*, likens copyright to ownership of land. "If you own a parcel of land, you can sell mineral rights to *A*, water rights to *B*, and a right-of-way to *C*, and still be considered the owner of the underlying property," he writes. In the case of written work, you may sell paperback reprint rights to one company, film and television rights to another, and book club rights to still another without impairing your ownership of the original work.

Register for Copyright

Q. How necessary is the effort and expense of having a work registered at the copyright office?
A. Since your work is now copyrighted from the moment you create it, the existence or validity of your copyright will not be affected if you don't register the work. But registration can be important to the protection of your work. It can offer proof of copyright if, for any reason, notice is omitted from distributed copies of your work. Registration is also a requirement if you want to bring a law suit to enforce your copyright. And if registration was made before, or within five years after first publication, the courts consider it undeniable evidence of a valid copyright.

Nevertheless, there are some writers who feel that copyright registration isn't worth the bother. "It's an awful lot of trouble, a bit of an expense, and for my money, a waste of time," writes freelancer Brian Vachon. He adds that he has never registered his work, "and in twenty years as a professional writer, never worried about that oversight." The necessity of registration is something the individual writer must decide for himself. It may be bothersome, but it is the most foolproof method of protecting your work.

Copyrighted Newspaper Material

Q. Although news cannot be copyrighted, can bylined newspaper articles and feature stories be?
A. What is not copyrightable is an actual news *event*—the facts of a news happening. For example, one newspaper could not copyright the facts about a fatal airplane crash and thereby prevent other publications from writing about the story. However, the newspaper's *presentation* of the facts, the style and manner in which the facts are given to the reader, is copyrightable. One criterion for the copyrightability of newspaper articles is the concept of "authorship"—editorial comment, conjecture, deductions, or descriptions separate from the specific facts of a story. If any of these factors is present in an article, then it may be copyrighted. For this reason, many newspaper features and analytical articles can be copyrighted.

Edited Manuscript Still Mine?

Q. When an editor tightens up my article, correcting a weak ending and other flaws, is the resultant article still under my copyright?
A. Yes. Usually, an editor's changes in your manuscript will not be extensive enough to qualify as a new work derived from your own. However, if your work is going to be heavily revised, you should clarify with the editor that the article is still yours, not his.

Book Contract

Q. Does the royalty publisher's clause (on copyright) state that the publisher shall obtain the copyright but that copyright shall be in the name of the author and shall be that author's property? Where might I obtain an agreement contract from a royalty publisher for observation?
A. Most royalty contracts do set up an agreement whereby the publisher takes out the copyright in the name of the author. The publisher merely handles the paperwork on behalf of the author and the copyright is the author's property. If you glance through a sampling of current bestsellers, you'll find that it is the author's name that usually follows the copyright symbol. Publishers don't make a practice of sending out sample contracts for study, but you could always verify this point on any contract offered to you before you sign it. A sample book contract is available for 75¢ and a No. 10 self-addressed stamped envelope from the Society of Authors' Representatives, Box 650, Old Chelsea Station, New York 10113.

Joint Copyright

Q. I made an agreement with a fellow writer for him to revise the first draft of my short novel. He's done some good work on the book, but a lot remains to be done. However, he went ahead and had the version he finished copyrighted in both our names. Can I still use my original draft? To what extent am I bound by the existing copyright?
A. You certainly may use your original draft and apply for registration of your own copyright. Although the Copyright Office accepted the other version in good faith, that would not affect the validity of your own version being copyrighted separately.

Old Songs

Q. I have read children's plays in which poems were sung to the tunes of old-fashioned songs. Where do the authors write to get permission to such old airs as "Flow Gently Sweet Afton" and "Jingle Bells?"
A. Anyone may use old airs without getting permission because these songs are in the public domain. Well-known and more recent songs, however, might still be under copyright. You can check the copyright dates on older popular songs in a directory—*Variety Music Cavalcade*—available at the library.

Humor Collection

Q. For the last fifteen years I have been collecting jokes, riddles, funny sign slogans, and humorous writings. I've gathered these from friends, acquaintances, and therapists. I don't have a clue as to their origins, and I don't know if they are copyrighted or in the public domain. My problem is this: I am attempting to write a book (probably paperback length) incorporating the idea that a little humor in one's life will make the rough road of rehabilitation a little easier. Since I can't identify the author of some of these masterpieces of humor, how can I protect myself against possible plagiarism suits?
A. Short gags and jokes cannot be copyrighted, so you wouldn't have any difficulty in assembling those in a book. Two hundred- to three hundred-word short prose humor pieces, however, might present a problem. If they did appear originally in copyrighted publications, you would have to rewrite them substantially to avoid plagiarism.

Book on Copyright

Q. I'm a young writer with work I'd like to send to magazines, but I don't understand copyrights. I'd like to know the name of a good book explaining copyrights in layman terms.
A. The new copyright law and its ramifications for writers are detailed in books like *Law and the Writer,* edited by Kirk Polking and Leonard S. Meranus; *The Writer's Legal Guide,* by Tad Crawford; and *The Copyright Book,* by William S. Strong.

Copyright Unknown

Q. Does it cost anything to have the copyright office check to see if a certain old book is still copyrighted or is now in the public domain?
A. The Library of Congress has a search fee of ten dollars per hour to search for copyright. Most searches take at least an hour or two. For further information on the book in question, you might write the Register of Copyrights, Library of Congress, Washington DC 20559.

Translation Rights

Q. A few months ago, while in Vienna, I read in an Austrian magazine a short article that I found impressive. I asked the doctor-author for the translation rights into English which he gladly gave me. Under whose name should one ask for the copyright—in the name of the author or translator?
A. You had best make sure the doctor *had* the rights to give you. Query the Austrian magazine to verify that he had the translation rights. Then, yes, you would get a U.S. copyright in your name as the author of the translation. The original author's name, of course, would appear with any published version of your translation.

Rights Infringement

Q. Since ideas can't be copyrighted, would it be necessary to obtain permission from the author of a short story before expanding the material to book length?
A. You are not at liberty to base a book on another author's short story without the consent of that author, since he has the exclusive right of adaptation of his own work. If you're only using the theme (the point the author makes in the story, such as perseverance pays off or crime does not) and not the actual characters and other aspects of the story, then you're only using the idea and you can proceed without permission.

Getting Permission

Q. I would like to use some material in a book for my own research. Even though the copyright date is as recent as 1970, the publisher is no longer in business and the author is deceased. The book was copyrighted by the publishing house. How do I get permission to use the material?
A. Even though the publisher is not currently in business, he still owns the copyright, which has to run its course of 28 years under the old copyright law. You would need his permission to use the material. Contact the local chamber of commerce of the city in which the publisher was located for the most recent address on its records for the publisher. If that search fails, then keep your correspondence showing your attempt to locate the publisher, and acknowledge your source either in the text or on an acknowledgment page.

Copyrighting a Book

Q. What is the approximate cost to register a copyright for a book?
A. The fee for registering a copyright claim is ten dollars. Make your check or money order payable to the Register of Copyrights, Copyright Office, Library of Congress, Washington DC 20559. Send the fee and the filled-out application form TX previously obtained from the copyright office, with one copy of the unpublished manuscript or two copies of the published book carrying the copyright notice.

Facts in Public Domain?

Q. Are "facts," such as those found in medical journals and reports, in the public domain? Scientific literature, the way I understand it, is in the public domain and can be used by other writers. Is this true?
A. Most medical journals are copyrighted, so material in them would not be in the public domain. "Facts" as such cannot be copyrighted, however, so if there are well-established findings quoted in a number of medical journals that could therefore be called "facts," you could work them into your articles without the original writers' or researchers' consent. You can't lift written copy verbatim but the information—the "facts"—can be included in your writing.

What is "Publication?"

Q. Each year our writers' club holds contests in several divisions: short story, article, and various types of poetry. First-, second-, and third-place winners, as well as honorable mentions, are announced in the published and unpublished divisions. As the procedure now stands, no method exists for exposing the winners' entries to the view of the league membership. We would like to start a creative magazine with subscription limited to club members, or a yearbook with the same type of limited subscription. Objections concern copyright. Some members fear that such exposure of material would place the material in the public domain; or that a first rights sale to a paying magazine would be jeopardized.
A. To make your contest entries available to members all you need to do is copyright the magazine in which they appear. Whether circulation only to league members would jeopardize the sale to a paying magazine would have to be checked with some magazine editors. However, unless you *do* show a copyright on this material, printing it even by mimeograph or multilith with a subscription method of distribution could put it in the public domain.

Copyright

Q. How important is it for a writer to secure a copyright for his book manuscript before submitting it to trade houses? Isn't it safe to entrust this somewhat bothersome detail to the publisher if and when the book is published?
A. The publisher who buys the manuscript usually copyrights the book in the author's name. The publisher's contract usually discusses the copyright procedure.

Magazine Article Rights

Q. I've been out of the freelancing field for several years and I need to update my understanding of the copyright laws. Does the new copyright law have any different effects on the selling of magazine articles?

A. Yes. Formerly, when a writer sold a magazine article, the assumption was that he was selling all rights to his material, unless an agreement between him and the editor stipulated otherwise. Now the assumption is that, unless otherwise specified, the writer is selling one-time rights only.

Performance vs Publication

Q. I have written an original play which has been produced only once. I would like to protect it from being videotaped. Can I copyright it?
A. Yes. "Performance" is not the same as "publication," so the production of your play did not place it in the public domain. The procedure for registration of copyright is the same for dramatic scripts as it is for books and other printed matter, except you use application form PA (performing arts) rather than form TX which is for non-dramatic literary works.

Copyright Titles?

Q. Does the new copyright law give copyright protection to titles? Is it legal for me to use an article title that is already the title of a published book?
A. It is not possible to copyright titles, so you can use the title of a book for an article title. It may quickly capture an editor's attention, even if the magazine decides to change it before publication in case there is a concern about a challenge of unfair competition.

Photocopying without Permission

Q. I am a teacher and would like advice about photocopying articles from magazines for class distribution and use. Do I need to request permission to do this copying?
A. The copyright law sets out certain criteria for "fair use" of copyrighted materials and states that "reproduction in copies . . . for purposes such as . . . teaching (including multiple copies for classroom use) . . . is not an infringement of copyright." Obviously, the amount of copying is a consideration when judging fair use. A recent copyright infringement suit, for example, established some guidelines which state "Not more than one short poem, article, story, essay, or two excerpts may be copied from the same author; nor more than three from the same collective work or periodical volume during one class term." The Copyright Office publishes a free circular R21 "Reproduction of Copyrighted Works by Educators and Librarians" which you can obtain by writing the Copyright Office, Library of Congress, Washington DC 20559. (For more information, see *Law and the Writer.*)

English Translation

Q. I want to write a story in which I would use three verses from The Rubaiyat of Omar Khayyam. *Are his verses, rendered into English by Edward Fitzgerald, in the public domain?*
A. Whether the English translation of *The Rubaiyat* that you have, which was copyrighted originally in 1938, has been renewed should be investigated before using that particular English version. A letter to the Register of Copyrights, Library of Congress, Washington DC 20559 could probably determine whether that copyright is still in effect.

Reuse Old Newspaper Columns?

Q. While cleaning out an old writing desk, I happened across several examples of a very funny old newspaper column from about fifty years ago. The columns would make amusing reading

for the modern reader, and I'd like to submit them for sale. Can I do this?
A. If the columns were copyrighted, as many syndicated and local columns are today, then you wouldn't be free to use the material. Since under old copyright laws, the copyright was good for twenty-eight years and could be renewed for another twenty-eight, you would have to take that fifty-six-year total into consideration. If the work had been renewed at the time the new copyright law took effect in 1978, the law extended the term forty-seven years for a seventy-five-year total rather than fifty-six-year total. If the columns were not copyrighted, you would be free to use the material.

Republish Public Domain Poems?

Q. I have a book of poems which have no copyright and therefore are in the public domain. Can I include some of these in an anthology and publish it under my copyright?
A. If the anthology contained only the public domain poems, you could not. It isn't possible to copyright anything that's already in the public domain. If you added other poems that were copyrighted, or wrote a commentary or other original material, then you could publish the anthology with your copyright.

Copyright Game Idea?

Q. How do I copyright a game idea that I have? How long would it be protected?
A. Ideas cannot be copyrighted, so you'd have to have an actual printed game board and set of rules before your game idea could be copyrighted. To register the copyright for an unpublished game, you should include a photograph of your game board and the set of rules, rather than the actual game board itself, to see if that would satisfy the "Deposit" rules. If accepted for copyright, the term of copyright would be the same as for any other literary property—life of the author plus fifty years. If the game is published, the Copyright Office wants a complete copy of the game if it is not larger than 12x24x6-inches. For more information, write the Copyright Office, Library of Congress, Washington DC 20559 for a free copy of Circular R40b "Deposit Requirements for Registration of Claims to Copyright in Visual Arts Material."

Reusing Articles in a Book

Q. The book on which I'm working relies heavily on information from articles I've written over the years. Only a handful of editors have given me permission; others have not replied. None of the checks I received in payment for the works indicated I signed away all rights. Can I use the material without infringing on the copyrights of the various publications involved?
A. Since you never signed a check with a statement that you were selling all rights to your articles, and assuming the editors had not publicized in writers' magazines or *Writer's Market* a policy of buying all rights, you should be able to use material from them without being sued for copyright infringement.

Defunct Magazine

Q. A magazine to which I had sold articles recently stopped publishing. I have an opportunity to resell some of these published pieces elsewhere. Can I do this without infringing on the copyright of the defunct magazine?
A. That would depend on what rights you sold to the first publisher. If you sold first rights only, then you can resubmit an article without any trouble. If you sold more than first rights,

then you must try to locate the publisher and obtain his permission. Although the magazine is defunct, the publisher still owns the copyright. Keep a record of all correspondence in this effort; that way, if you're unsuccessful in finding the publisher, and you don't know what rights you sold, you can resell the piece, and if he raises any objections you will have proof that you tried to contact him. Then, it's up to the judge.

Reuse Uncopyrighted Article?

Q. In researching a magazine article I came across an article in a magazine that I would like to use. The magazine was not copyrighted. Can I use this material?
A. If the item you found is in an uncopyrighted publication and the author's personal copyright notice did not appear with the article, it is in the public domain. This means that no one has placed a copyright on it to protect it. Public domain material may be used by anyone. It cannot, however, be copyrighted by someone else once it has been placed in public domain, unless you considerably revise it and add to it.

Foreign Protection?

Q. How well does my U.S. copyright protect my work if it's distributed or published in a foreign country?
A. It depends on which country. If it is one of the seventy nations belonging to the Universal Copyright Convention, the work will be protected in the same way that nation would protect the writings of any of its own citizens. But, unlike U.S. copyright requirements, the U.C.C. requires the use of the © symbol to designate copyright; the phrase "Copyright 1984 by Jon Edwards" is not adequate notice. The international notice would be printed "© 1984 Jon Edwards."

The U.S. also belongs to the Buenos Aires Convention, which includes several Latin American nations. Protection in these countries is extended to the holder of a copyright in any member country; the only other requirement is an indication that property rights have been reserved, by use of the phrase *Derechos Reservados* or "All Rights Reserved."

Canadian Copyright

Q. If my work is published in Canada, will I need to register it there, too? How does Canadian copyright differ from U.S. copyright?
A. Since Canada and the United States both belong to the Universal Copyright Convention, your Canadian-published work is protected just as if it were published in the U.S. Registration, as in the U.S., is optional, but advisable to prove ownership in the event of legal action. The fee for Canadian copyright registration is $35. In general, U.S. and Canadian copyright laws are similar; the author having specific questions should contact the Copyright and Industrial Design Branch, Bureau of Corporate Affairs, Consumer and Corporate Affairs Canada, Ottawa, Ontario K1A 0C9.

Copyrighted Story in Uncopyrighted Publication?

Q. If a copyrighted story is reprinted in an uncopyrighted publication, does this in any way affect the copyright?
A. If the publication prints your personal copyright notice with the story, your protection will remain the same. If the copyright notice is eliminated, through the editor's error—not yours—there could be problems. They won't be as severe as losing your copyright, which was

what would have happened under the old law. A copyright registered with the Library of Congress will remain in effect if the piece is published without copyright notice. If the work had not been registered, it will be protected by copyright as long as it is registered within five years of publication. In both cases, the law specifies that the writer must make a "reasonable effort" to add his copyright notice to any copies distributed after the omission is discovered.

Magazines Copyrighted?

Q. How does a writer know which magazines are not copyrighted? Is there a way I can state on my poems, fillers, and manuscripts that I want my work copyrighted? How can an author obtain a separate copyright?

A. Before you submit a manuscript to a magazine, you should ascertain whether that magazine is copyrighted. Look for the copyright notice which usually appears at the bottom of the Table of Contents page or on the masthead page listing the staff. To copyright your material that may appear in an uncopyrighted publication, at the bottom left corner of your manuscript's first page, type your own copyright notice: © Your Name, Year. When submitting to an uncopyrighted publication, ask the editor to be sure to show your copyright credit line with your poem. Since your copyright exists from the moment you create a work, it's not necessary to formally register it unless you wish to. In that case, as soon as the work is published with your copyright notice and made available to the public, register your claim by mailing to the Copyright Office the application form plus two complete copies of the publication containing your work, and the registration fee of ten dollars.

Copyright Symbol

Q. When submitting a manuscript, should the writer place the symbol © "copyright by . . . author's name and the year" on the manuscript copy? Or is this unnecessary? What is the procedure regarding copyright when submitting a manuscript?

A. It's always a good idea to show your copyright notice on the first page of your manuscript. A copyrighted magazine's copyright notice covers your individual contribution to that magazine; if you should happen to be submitting to an uncopyrighted publication it would be important to make sure your copyright notice appeared on the first page of your article, story, or poem.

Copyright Duration

Q. Once my work is copyrighted, for how long is it protected?

A. For works copyrighted on or after January 1, 1978, copyright protection lasts for the rest of the author's life and for fifty years after his death. If the work is collaborative, the death of the last surviving collaborator determines the starting point for the fifty years. If the work was produced under a pen name or anonymously, or if it is a work make for hire, copyright expires seventy-five years after first publication, or one hundred years after its first creation, whichever is earlier.

Copyright Expiration

Q. I've obtained a book of photographs taken and copyrighted in 1905. Can I use them as illustrations in my book without infringing on copyright?

A. Under the new copyright law, any work registered for renewal or already in the renewal term before January 1, 1978, had its copyright duration extended to a total of seventy-five years from the date of original copyright. Copyright protection for your photographs would have expired December 1980. They are now in the public domain and you are free to use them.

"Publication" and Public Domain

Q. What's the difference under the new copyright law as opposed to the old law regarding "published" and "unpublished" manuscripts and the public domain?
A. Under the old law, if you distributed reproduced copies of your unpublished manuscript to the public—either through typed copies or mimeographed or other reproductions—you were considered to have "published" it. If you had not registered it for copyright and it did not contain a copyright notice, it fell into the public domain. Under the new law, your work is copyrighted as soon as you create it—whether you formally register it for copyright or not—but you must show your copyright notice on your original manuscript and any reproduced copies.

Get Rights Back?

Q. If I transfer certain rights to my manuscript to another party, are those rights relinquished forever, or can I get them back at some point in the future?
A. If an otherwise specific time period is not written into the rights you grant someone—for example, such as an option on your book by a motion picture producer for a period of one year—then you still have the right to terminate the grant of those rights. This can be done thirty-five years after you granted the right. Or, if the grant covered the right of publication, the period begins at the end of thirty-five years from the date of publication or forty years from when you made the grant, whichever term ends earlier. But you must execute this right of termination within a period of five years at the end of the thirty-five years or forty-year period.

Foreign Copyright

Q. I am curious to know if a word-for-word translation of any foreign language book without the publisher's consent is considered plagiarism?
A. If the foreign language book is copyrighted and copyright has not expired, it may *not* be translated without the consent of the copyright owner.

19 Do I Need an Agent?

"If I could only spend my time writing and have somebody else do the marketing, I'd like freelancing a lot better." How many times have you said that or heard another writer say it? The trouble is, most agents usually won't represent unpublished authors, so many writers become published through the learning process of marketing itself. Once you have established some creditable sales on your own—especially one or more books—agents will be easier to find. Here's how to find them, get them to work with you, and fire them if you feel you and your agent are no longer compatible.

Locating an Agent

Q. How can I find an agent?
A. There are several ways to locate an agent. *Literary Market Place* lists agents, indicates whether they represent authors of books, scripts, etc. and have foreign representation. *Poets & Writers, Inc.*, (201 W. 54th St., New York, NY 10019) publishes *Literary Agents: A Complete Guide,* a booklet on how to deal with agents; current price on request. Some editions of *Writer's Market* and *Writer's Yearbook* contain lists of agents, with details on those who will work with beginners.

Another paperback directory is *Literary Agents of North America 1984-85 Marketplace,* published by Author Aid/Research Associates International, 340 E. 52nd St., New York NY 10022. Check with them on current price.

Submitting your own book to publishers can sometimes lead to finding an agent. When the publisher makes an offer, ask him to recommend an agent; sometimes editors like a manuscript, but for some reason cannot buy it and will recommend an agent to the author. If you contribute regularly to a magazine, or have some rapport with an editor, he may be able to recommend an agent. Writers' conferences sometimes have agents as guest speakers, and you can at least meet them before sending a query letter. Check with other writers and writers' groups to see if they can guide you to an agent.

The agencies which are members of the Society of Author's Representatives, (Box 650, Old Chelsea Station, New York NY 10113) and Independent Literary Agents Association (21 W. 26th Street, New York NY 10010) usually only work with already established authors.

Securing the Agent's Services

Q. Once I locate a prospective agent, how do I get him to represent me?
A. Write the agent a query letter, describing your book and your reasons for writing it; a brief outline is also helpful. Never send an entire manuscript. Include SASE, of course, for the reply. Sometimes the agent will ask to see the first few chapters of your manuscript.

"It's easier to get some agents to take on your book properties than others," writes veteran agent Bill Adler in *Inside Publishing*. "Obviously, some of the superagents are difficult to get to. But most of the young agents and even some of the better-known and established agents will be willing to look at your material. Whether they will take it on depends, of course, on the material."

Recommended List?

Q. How will I know whether an agent is reputable or not? Is there a printed list I can obtain of recommended agents? I am uncertain as to the qualifications of the company who is representing my interests and I would like to check on its qualifications. The comparative group I have in mind is the Better Business Bureau for companies. Would they also handle literary agents?
A. Yes, the Better Business Bureau in the city in which your prospective literary agent is located could let you know whether it has had any complaints about that agency's business operation. Other ways you could check on the reputation of an agent are to contact publishers with whom he has dealt, or to ask the agent for the names of some of his clients whom you could write to in care of their publishers, to ask about his work with them.

Types of Agents

Q. Are there different types of literary agents?
A. Yes. There are two ways in which agents differ. First, some literary agents have an established clientele of published authors, and will not take on any new clients; other agents are willing to work with previously unpublished writers, and some of those charge reading fees.

The second way to categorize agents is in terms of the material they handle. There are agents who deal only in trade books—fiction and nonfiction—and others who deal in scripts. Dramatic agents who handle plays are usually located in New York, whereas those handling scripts for films and television are on the West Coast.

Reading Fees

Q. Is it routine for agents to charge a fee for reading a manuscript? What does this fee entail?
A. Some don't; others do—claiming that the fee is compensation for time spent reading unsalable new material which might otherwise be time used in selling books. Some agents also give extensive criticism as compensation for the fee.

When dealing with an agent that charges a reading fee, you should always check his background—what books he has sold recently, who he represents, and if his clients are satisfied. Find out if the agent offers criticism on manuscripts. Find out if the agent will refund the fee if he agrees to represent you and sells your book. Make sure you know what you're getting for the fee you pay.

If an agent is interested, either from your letter of inquiry or sample chapters, he will read, and often comment on, your manuscript free of charge.

Beginner Need Agent?

Q. Is it a good idea for a beginning writer to get an agent?
A. An agent is not necessary or even desirable for a beginner, and in most cases it isn't even possible for a beginner to get one. Generally, agents are only interested in representing writers who have written salable books, and unless you have a book in manuscript or outline and sample chapters, finding an agent will be tough.

The best way for a beginner to sell a book is to market it himself. "My first three novels were sold without benefit of an agent," says novelist Dean Koontz. "I believe I gained valuable marketing experience by handling my own books in those early days. You will not be able to get a first-rate agent or even a second-rate agent until you have sold at least one novel on your own."

Research suitable publishers for your book through *Writer's Market,* and check in bookstores and libraries to see which publishers are publishing books similar to yours. Then send your manuscript to a likely publisher, including SASE for its return. If the first publisher rejects the work, contact the next prospect. Remember, some very successful books were marketed by their authors, and rejected by several publishers before they saw print. Dr. Seuss's first book was rejected by twenty-eight publishers before the twenty-ninth bought it!

Agent's Commission

Q. What is the standard percentage an agent receives as his commission?
A. Generally, agents receive 10 percent of the writer's income on manuscripts as their fee. Some agents are raising their price to 15 percent, because of increasing overhead and costs for mail, messenger services, and telephone bills. They feel that 15 percent enables them to do a better job of selling their client's work, since they can afford to have a more efficient staff and better facilities.

Agent for Short Manuscripts?

Q. Can I get an agent to sell my short stories or magazine articles?
A. Probably not. Unless the agent is also making a lot of money on an author's book sales, he won't handle magazine pieces or short stories because such sales aren't economically feasible for the agent. Editors of magazines and journals buy shorter pieces directly from writers on a regular basis, so an agent isn't needed on these sales. "Literary agents cannot make enough profit on 10 percent or 15 percent of a $500 or $1,000 magazine article sale to expend the effort," says agent Diane Cleaver. However, if you've done a series of articles on a specific topic that might be made into a book proposal, an agent might be interested in that.

Agent Contract?

Q. Do agents sign contracts with clients?
A. Some agents require a contract before they'll do business with a writer. They feel that written agreements offer the agent protection, since the author doesn't pay him any money until a contract is drawn up by the publisher containing a clause which provides for payment to the agent. The agreement should cover several areas to benefit both author and agent. The scope of representation should be spelled out; will the agent be handling all your work or just this particular book? Also, specify if you wish to be informed of every offer the agent gets for your work. Money matters, the length of the agreement (one or two years seems to be the

average), and a clause spelling out how the agreement may be terminated if there is no specific time limit mentioned, should be included in any agreement.

There are, however, agents who prefer not to have a written agreement with authors. "Bill Adler Books does not require a contract with an author, which may not be the best business judgment in the world, but we prefer it that way," says Adler, a veteran agent and author. "If the author doesn't want to do any more business with us (or if we don't want to do any more business with the author) then we would rather sever the relationship. Life is too short to try to make bad relationships work."

Agent Report?

Q. Although I've not been published before, I was able to secure an agent through a friend who recommended me to him. The agent has had my novel for three months and I've heard nothing. Doesn't he at least owe me a report on which publishers he's shown the manuscript to?

A. Just because you've heard nothing doesn't mean the agent isn't trying to sell your book. Remember, if he doesn't sell the book, he won't get his commission; a book sale would be to his benefit as well as yours. It takes time for the agent to find the right publisher for your book, and the agent represents other authors, so there isn't always time to report every move of a manuscript. Also, the agent can serve as a buffer between you and the rejecting publishers.

Nevertheless, it is your manuscript and you want to know how it's doing. If you haven't heard anything in another month or so, call or drop the agent a short letter of inquiry, and he should get back to you.

A writer can avoid this problem by establishing at the outset when he can expect to hear from the agent.

Agent for Poetry?

Q. I am a poet who needs a literary agent. I wonder if you could help me find a reputable one who would work with me on agreeable terms.

A. There is such a small market for poetry that almost no agent will handle someone whose sole output is poetry. Most poets attempt to sell their poems individually to magazines, hoping eventually to be able to present enough published credits to a book publisher to interest him in publishing an anthology of their work. If by "literary agent," you really meant literary critic, and would like to have an evaluation of your poetry by a professional, several firms offer this service for a fee, and advertise in magazines for writers.

Agent vs Direct Submission

Q. If an agent decides he isn't going to handle a particular manuscript of mine, is it okay for me to start submitting it to publishers on my own?

A. Yes. The agent has decided he no longer has any prospects for your work, or cannot sell it for some other reason. Therefore, it would be perfectly acceptable for you to submit it yourself to any publisher you think might buy it, or to contact another agent who might handle it.

Once and For All

Q. If a writer authorizes an agent to sell one or more of his works, is the author committed to pay a fee to the agent for other work he subsequently sells himself?

A. Normally, if an author acquires an agent, he is committed to pay the agent a fee for any of his work which is sold after that date, unless there is an agreement between them specifically exempting from commission certain work sold by the author himself—such as poetry. This may seem unfair, but writer Hayes Jacobs offers a good explanation: "That makes up for the hard work the agent devotes to material that never sells."

Two Agents?

Q. Can you tell me whether it is ethical to have two agents, in this case one in Los Angeles and one in New York? Each handles the same type of material, but in his own locale. Do agents frown on this procedure even though the material submitted to each is not the same?
A. The first agent will expect to handle all of a writer's work. If the agent rejects a project, the writer should be free to go elsewhere with it. Agents use co-agents for rights they don't sell themselves.

Agent for Religious Material?

Q. I write religious material and would like to market my books on my own. What about agents in the religious publishing field?
A. Unlike the secular book market, publishers in the religious field deal directly with the author. Agents aren't usually familiar with the religious markets, and as a result can be of little help to the religious writer. The exceptions might be agents who have dealt with major trade publishers which happen to have a special department for religious books. The writer who takes care to learn about the religious publishing business and marketing process can act as his own agent. For information on religious markets, refer to *Writing to Inspire*, and *Writer's Market* which contains a listing of religious markets.

Agency Problem

Q. I paid a literary agency for criticism analysis of two children's stories. They notified me of the opinions of various publishers; but when I asked to whom they showed these stories, they didn't answer my letter. Did I have a right to ask the names of the publishers?
A. You did indeed. Any reputable agency would not hesitate to reveal the publishers to whom they had submitted material.

When Agents Collect

Q. Do agents offer client manuscripts to publishers on speculation and receive their money only after they make a sale?
A. Yes. The only way agents can earn their money is by selling a writer's manuscript and deducting commissions from the sales. In essence, they are similar to writers who do magazine articles "on spec," in that when they accept a manuscript from a writer they don't know whether or not a publisher will buy it.

Return of Manuscript

Q. When an agency ignores a request to return a book manuscript sent for possible representation, what recourse does a writer have other than continuing to write letters? Is there some organization set up for the protection of writers to whom a writer might appeal?
A. The best procedure is to write a registered letter to the agency stating that you are

withdrawing the manuscript from their consideration and resubmitting it elsewhere. You should always keep a copy of the manuscript in your files; that way, in the event something like this occurs, you are free to begin resubmitting the manuscript immediately. By keeping a copy you will save time and frustration.

If the agency is a member of the Society of Authors' Representatives or the Independent Literary Agents Association, you can contact that organization.

Agents for Screenplays?

Q. Most movie producers state that they look at original scripts only if submitted by an accredited agent. They list no agent's name, so how do I go about finding their agents? Also, I have several children's stories, two of which would make excellent cartoon movies. Would the same agent handle both types of stories? What is his fee?
A. A list of agents who deal with movie producers is available from the Writers Guild of America West, 8955 Beverly Blvd., Los Angeles CA 90048. The price is $1. The agent tries to market your work and handles the business arrangement. You have to provide him with scripts, however, not stories, he can sell. An agent who sells to movie producers could handle both regular scripts and scripts for animated films. The agent's fee is a commission on sales—usually 10 percent or 15 percent.

Becoming an Agent

Q. Can you tell me what the requirements are for becoming a literary agent or tell me where I may obtain such information?
A. The main requirement for becoming a literary agent is knowing the publishing market so well that you can prove to prospective clients that you are able to successfully place the work of professional writers with magazine and book editors. Many literary agents came to their jobs after successfully marketing their own work or after being editors in the field and knowing what publishers want to buy.

Agent Auctions

Q. I've read in Publishers Weekly about agents establishing a "floor price" for a book they intend to auction, and getting "escalation clauses" if the book hits the New York Times bestseller list. Can I get my agent to make such deals for me and my book?
A. It's not likely. Auctions take place when an agent has what he thinks is a really "hot" property. He establishes a floor price—the minimum for which he will sell the book—and makes multiple submissions to prospective publishers, giving a deadline for responses. If one publisher's bid is topped by another, the first publisher is given the opportunity to top his competitor's offer. Escalation clauses provide that an author's royalty percentage will increase if the book sells particularly well; this provision is determined by various sales reports, including the number of weeks the book is on the *New York Times* or other bestseller lists.

Obviously, these contract provisions all hinge on one factor: the book must be one everybody believed was going to be a big seller. That's why these deals can be obtained by established authors whose books the publishers *know* will be promotable and salable. "I must be sure that I have something everyone will want—because of the stature of the author, the brilliance of the manuscript, the timeliness of the subject, and the commercial value of the book—before I conduct an auction," says agent Diane Cleaver. "Nothing is more embarrassing than holding an auction that no one wants to participate in."

One Agent at a Time

Q. If a book or story is in the hands of an agent, is it possible to make such arrangements that a copy may be submitted to another agent or to a publisher while it is still in the hands of the first agent?
A. Once a manuscript has been turned over to one agent, it is not ethical to submit copies either to another agent or to a publisher. If you feel the agent is not handling your work to your satisfaction, terminate your arrangement with him, ask for the return of your manuscript and you shall then be free to try marketing it yourself or to place it with another agent.

Agents for Puzzles?

Q. Are there agencies that handle crosswords, crostics and double crostics?
A. Most agents are interested only in handling authors of books, television scripts and other more profitable-length manuscripts. The financial return on items such as crosswords, filler material and poetry is so small, no agency can afford to handle just those. There are a great many magazines which use crossword puzzles other than crossword puzzle magazines themselves. They are listed throughout *Writer's Market*. (For more on filler items, see Chapter 20.)

Handle on Speculation?

Q. I have many manuscripts and they all need to be revised, but I'm on a pension and haven't money to pay for professional revision. Is there an agent who will revise and sell, take out his share of the money and send me the rest?
A. No agent is willing or financially able to do revisions on speculation, in the hope that he will be paid eventually out of the sale of the work. Perhaps by studying *Writer's Digest* and the magazines to which you would like to submit, you will be able to learn to revise your own manuscripts and resubmit them for sale. *Writer's Digest* and several other advertisers in writers magazines offer professional criticism services.

By joining an organization such as The National Writers Club (1450 S. Havana, Suite 620, Aurora CO 80012) you can obtain low cost manuscript evaluations from volunteers or from staff personnel. You might want to write them about membership and manuscript evaluation fees. Then you can do your own revisions based on suggestions from these professional writers and editors.

Changing Agents

Q. Is there a way to dissolve your relationship with one agent and go with another?
A. Sometimes a writer feels that his agent is not spending enough time on his projects and is no longer the person he wants representing his interests. But the agent will have remaining ties to the author, in terms of any works the agent sold for him, so the relationship should be kept as friendly as possible. If a writer has a problem with an agent, the writer should call the agent, discuss it, and try to settle it. When the time comes to sever ties with an agent, send a simple letter suggesting that parting company would be better for both of you.

Payments to Former Agent

Q. If you discontinue your relationship with an agent, do you still pay him his royalties on works he sold, including royalties for subsequent years after the break?

A. Yes. Your former agent remains the agent of record in contracts for all works he sold before you left his representation. Therefore, the publisher will continue to send your royalties in care of that agent whether or not he continues to represent you. He sold it, so he gets the royalty checks from which he deducts his commission. If the book should go out of print, and your new agent negotiates a reprint edition or you do so yourself, whether your former agent would receive any royalties would depend on the terms of the initial sale.

20 What Are Some Easy Things I Could Get Started With?

Beginning writers who have never published have several opportunities to build their writing skills and confidence before tackling the full-length article or short story. Creating short filler material, needed by consumer and trade magazine editors, helps teach economy of style and is a first step in analyzing market needs. Working with local organizations on newsletters or publicity is good practice that later can be translated into paying markets. Even writing letters to the local newspaper editor—and getting them published—can provide assurance that people are interested in what you have to say.

New Writer

Q. I'm really intrigued by the idea of being a writer, but since I've had no experience, I'm a bit afraid to get my feet wet. Can you give me any ideas for some basic, but challenging writing I could do to get some practice?
A. As Peggy Teeters says in her guide, *How to Get Started in Writing,* "the only way to learn to write is to write." One overlooked but excellent way to get practice is by writing letters to the editor. Everyone has ideas and opinions, and getting them down on paper in an organized and concise manner is a key starting point in good writing. Although you won't receive a response from the editor, you can compare what you wrote to what was printed in his paper to see how your copy might have been edited to exclude repetition, awkward sentences, and excessive wording. Most clubs and various local organizations use volunteer writers to publish or contribute to newsletters and to handle publicity. Any such writing is excellent training and bolsters your confidence as well as giving you published work for your portfolio.

Idea Sources

Q. Where do writers get their ideas? Every time I consider trying to write a piece of fiction, I find my mind empty of ideas. Do I really lack imagination or am I trying too hard?
A. Nobody lacks imagination! You may be expecting too much inspiration, though. Maxine Rock advises in the *Fiction Writer's Help Book* that "developing ideas can be a painful process . . . don't lock yourself into preset notions of how or when you should produce ideas . . . ideas usually don't flash before you like bursts of divine light. They ripen slowly. Be patient." The only way to get ideas is to actively seek them all the time. Look at your experiences, your

family, your work place, your home, your reading, the newspaper, the television, places you've been. Things you're familiar with can provide a gold mine of ideas and make more viable stories than things you know little about. For instance, suppose a responsible woman in your office just didn't show up for work for an entire week. Would you wonder during that week what had happened to her? Where did she go? Would she come back? Many different plot lines can come from this very simple start. Constantly ask yourself questions. If an idea comes to you, write it down immediately, no matter where you are or what you're doing. It may never pass through your mind again. Most ideas need to gestate for a while before developing. Get in the habit of keeping a journal, writing every day about *anything*. Go through it periodically organize the good ideas, and set aside those you see as less valuable. You can't expect to sit down at a typewriter and always have a new idea. You must *work* to develop a store of ideas and you must always be updating that store.

Fiction or Nonfiction

Q. People with whom I've corresponded for years have told me I have a gift for writing. I'd like to make some money as a writer, but I don't know whether to try writing fiction or nonfiction. How can I determine which I would be better at?
A. If you're solely interested in making money, you'd probably do better writing articles, as the magazine market is better for them right now than for short stories. If you're interested in finding your "niche" as a writer, there are a few things you can think about that may help you decide whether to try fiction or nonfiction. For instance, the writer of nonfiction must be willing to do research and conduct interviews, always working to ferret out facts. His writing may cover a variety of topics ranging from a how-to article for a juvenile publication to an inspirational article to an in-depth article exposing fraud in certain businesses. Nonfiction writers rely on a variety of reading interests, an awareness of the world around them and an ability to organize thoughts and ideas. Although many of these characteristics are also aids to writers of fiction, *these* writers need other elements, among them an active imagination and an ability to tell stories. Probably one of the most important traits of a fiction writer is his interest in what goes on inside other people: their emotions, personalities, and reactions to various situations. Take a good look at yourself, your interests, and your skills and you may be able to decide whether you should write fiction or nonfiction. Either way, writing will take some time and isn't easy, so don't lock yourself into one form of writing too quickly.

Clippings

Q. In the Writer's Market *listings under "Fillers" some editors say they buy clippings. What do they mean?*
A. Clippings are short news items that can be submitted as interesting, humorous, or odd material for filler space or as material pertinent to a particular trade magazine. *Writer's Market* lists magazines that buy clippings, and includes an indication of the kinds of clippings an editor will be interested in. The average filler length is 300 to 500 words, but some magazines will accept clippings as long as 1,000 words. While you can earn small payments for clippings, don't expect this to be a sizable monthly income, unless you have access to a great many different newspapers and magazines from which you can obtain clippings at no cost to you. It is important to remember that you should only send to an editor the specific kinds of clippings he requests. General mass mailings of clippings to editors will be a waste of your time and postage.
      Submit clippings on an 8½x11-inch sheet of white paper, one to a page, with your name,

address, and telephone number in the upper left corner. The source and date of the item should be acknowledged underneath it. Don't include SASE, as most editors receive too many clippings to be able to acknowledge or return them.

Book Reviews

Q. I would like to write book reviews, but I'm only a beginning writer. What chances do I have?
A. If you live in a small town or in the suburban area surrounding a city, you may be able to interest the local newspaper editor in publishing your book reviews. To start, you'd have to buy or get new books from the library and review them to show the editor what you can do. If you have selected books he thinks will interest his readers and he likes your writing style, he may make you his regular Book Review Editor, so that you could write (on the newspaper's letterhead) to major book publishers, asking them to send you review copies of their latest books. Your only payment would probably be the copies of the books and your newspaper byline, but the experience could help you go on later to write book reviews for national magazines.

Using Quips

Q. If a filler writer publishes a one- or two-line quip, is it okay for another writer to copy it verbatim, change only one word, and pass it off as being his own?
A. No. He should indicate the original source when resubmitting elsewhere. Jokes, however, cannot be copyrighted, so they're in the public domain.

Fillers to Resell

Q. I recently bought some bound volumes of old magazines dating from 1897 through 1908 in which there are many perfectly delightful human interest fillers. How can I use them, if I can use them at all? Can I rewrite and bring them up to date to fit our more "modern" humor?
A. Since these fillers are now in the public domain, you may indeed use them however you wish. You can modernize them and try to sell them individually or as part of a collective article. They are also a possible source for unusual human interest anecdotes to incorporate into your own articles.

Fillers

Q. Is it okay to submit identical fillers to the 150-200-word filler markets that pay $2 to $3 per filler?
A. As long as the markets are noncompetitive in subject matter or geography, you can submit fillers to more than one market at a time.

Beginning Christian Writer

Q. I would like to write for the Christian markets, but I have no experience. Where is a good place for me to start?
A. Good advice from Sue Nichols Spencer in the book *Writing to Inspire* is to write for your own church, where you won't be competing with scores of professionals. You could be a reporter or columnist for your church if it has a regularly published newsletter. If it doesn't, you could volunteer to develop one and be its first editor. You could write poems, prayers and

meditations for Bible study groups. You could write a history of the church and bring it up to date with current church projects. Most of this will be volunteer work without pay, but you will develop your writing skills and confidence to submit short articles to national magazines.

Epigrams and Proverbs

Q. I have written several hundred original epigrams and poetical proverbs which I believe are good. Would it be more profitable for me to submit them in manuscript form for book publication or in small lots to magazines?
A. Since it is usually easier for a beginner to sell to a magazine rather than to a book publisher, it might be to your advantage to send these fillers to magazine markets. If possible, try to retain book rights so that eventually you can publish them as a collection in book form.

Submitting Cartoon Gags

Q. I am interested in writing gags for cartoonists. How do I submit these?
A. Find a cartoonist who seems best to suit the style and mood of the gags you write. Then type individual gags single-spaced on 3x5-inch cards, assigning a number to the corner of each one and including your name and address on the opposite corner. You can send packets of ten to twenty gags at the same time to the cartoonist in care of the magazine in which his work regularly appears. If the cartoonist buys the gag, the writer usually receives between 25 percent and 40 percent of the sale price of the finished cartoon.

Pay for Clippings?

Q. How much do editors usually pay for clippings?
A. The amount of money editors pay for clippings usually ranges from two to ten dollars or more, depending on length and use of the clipping. For example, *Writer's Digest* uses clippings that pertain to the writing life—clips about authors, new books, current news about writing and publishing. The magazine can't return or acknowledge unused clippings because of the number it receives. WD pays five to twenty dollars or more for each clipping used, depending on its use. The magazine sometimes uses clips as a source for a more developed piece for its Writing Life section, or it may use only a quote from the clipping.

Clipping Markets

Q. How can I send clippings to editors in such a way that they know I'm not sending them gratis, but to receive payment?
A. Policies are established; either editors pay for clippings they use or they don't. Only submit to those publications which indicate in *Writer's Market* that they buy clippings. If you like, you can type "at your usual rates" in the upper right corner of each clipping you submit.

Recipes

Q. I want to sell information by mail and plan to start with something simple like recipes. Are recipes copyrighted? How do writers go about getting recipes?
A. Recipes that appear in copyrighted magazines are covered by that copyright. Writers of cookbooks either create their own recipes or read about others in newspapers, magazines, and books, then alter the recipes, test them, and create their own versions for their cookbooks. Simple lists of ingredients cannot be copyrighted, but the directions for how to make

something from those ingredients can be copyrighted.

Writers who like to cook are naturals for developing new, popular recipes that will sell. Look for recipes in newspapers and on food containers which you might adapt and promote. Be alert to comments at restaurants and pot-luck dinners and listen to your guests and family members. Once you have developed an easy, delicious recipe, write the directions and have friends test it to see if it works as well for them.

Fillers

Q. Some authors rewrite unusual news stories to submit to other markets. Are there laws against using and reusing ideas culled from newspapers? Does this apply to bylined features as well?
A. News items are facts open to anyone's interpretation, but feature articles usually have a specific angle or slant, involve the research, selectivity, and interpretations of the individual writer and are protected by the overall copyright on the paper, if there is one; or by the syndicate if it is a syndicated feature.

Newsbreak

Q. What is a newsbreak?
A. A newsbreak is a newsworthy event or item. For example, an opening of a new retail shoe store in a town might be a newsbreak for a shoe trade journal that publishes news items of new openings. Some publications (such as *The New Yorker*) use newsbreaks in a different sense—that is, to indicate a typo or an error in reporting that appears in a printed news story. Such newsbreaks—followed by tongue-in-cheek editorial commentary—are bought from contributors and used in *The New Yorker* and other publications as filler items. Newsbreaks solicited by editors usually appear under "Fillers" in the editorial listings in *Writer's Market*.

Newspaper Writer

Q. I'm interested in writing for a newspaper, but I have no idea how to get started. What advice do you have for an aspiring journalist?
A. If you are young and interested in a career in newspapers, you should secure a good liberal arts college education or go to journalism school. If you are older submit feature articles to the editor of your local newspaper. Good articles will show that you know what a feature is and how to write one well, and may be a plus for you if there is a staff opening. If you want to be a stringer, find and submit news items not well covered in that newspaper's circulation area. Study the newspaper you are interested in working for and try to submit articles similar in style and subject to what they publish. For more information on newspaper writing, see Chapter 21 in this book and *Stalking the Feature Story,* by William Ruehlmann.

Puzzle Markets

Q. I would like information regarding the marketing of crossword puzzles. I have created a few which are now in varying stages of completion. All mine are 15x15, though I do have a few 21x21. I have written four syndicates concerning crossword puzzles; one syndicate said they were well stocked, thanks anyway; another said they did not use crossword puzzles; and the other two didn't even have the courtesy to answer my letter.
A. Magazines buying puzzles are listed in *Writer's Market*. Magazines usually want puzzles

aimed toward their specific audience, so it's a matter of creating a puzzle to fit a specific magazine rather than creating some puzzles, then trying to sell them. There are crossword puzzle magazines also listed in *Writer's Market*. To find out which syndicates are currently handling puzzles, check *Editor and Publisher Syndicate Directory*, available in most libraries.

Filler Material

Q. What is meant by "filler material?" What is it used for?
A. A filler is any of a variety of short pieces of writing, such as jokes, anecdotes, short humor, recipes, proverbs, household hints, unusual trivia, brain teasers, puzzles, insightful quotes, and news clippings. Although editors originally used them to fill empty spaces at the ends of columns, fillers are now often used as regular magazine features. Because they are short and focus on one point, fillers are good practice for beginning writers and give novices a greater chance of being published. The trick to writing a filler lies in grabbing the reader, causing him to laugh or nod in agreement, or sparking his interest to learn more. One can find ideas for fillers anywhere from strange road signs or bumper stickers to old books of poetry that might contain sage sayings. Everyday experiences often provide humor—but you may have to look hard at what's going on around you to see it, then develop it into a humorous anecdote. If you think you might like to write fillers, study the fillers in several magazines to get an idea of what editors are looking for . . . and go to it!

Children's Sayings

Q. I am just getting started as a writer and have submitted some children's sayings and anecdotes to bring in a little extra income. Some of the material in them would fit well in a couple of larger pieces I am working on. Is it okay for me to incorporate these fillers into my other work?
A. Whether or not you may continue to use your filler material as originally written will depend on what rights you sell to magazines publishing it. Under the 1978 copyright law, sale of first rights only is understood unless otherwise indicated in writing. This means that the magazine has claim only to the first publishing of your work and you are free to reuse it at any time. If they buy all rights, you would have to request the editor's permission to reuse the material. An alternative is to rewrite the material so it is different from the version originally published.

Craft Magazines

Q. A friend of mine says craft magazines are a good place to start. What do you suggest?
A. If you have ever designed a pattern for an embroidery project, or made your own Christmas tree ornaments, or built a home darkroom, there are craft, hobby, and handyman magazines waiting to hear how you did it, step-by-step. Since these how-to articles are relatively simple to write, many beginners find them an easy way to get started writing. Then you can move on to articles which require more research, organization, and writing skills. Another area open to beginners is that described by the title of Lois Duncan's book: *How to Write and Sell Your Personal Experiences*.

Simultaneous Submissions

Q. Can I send the same filler items to more than one publication at a time?
A. There's no reason why you can't, as long as you don't submit identical fillers to markets

with common audiences. Editors of magazines with similar readerships don't want to see a filler they just bought from you published in a competitive magazine. You may want to type in the upper right corner of a manuscript that is going to more than one publication at the same time: "Simultaneous submission to publications not in your same readership area."

Pay for Fillers

Q. How much money can I hope to get for my published fillers?
A. Depending on the magazine, the filler, and how it is used, the average payment is anywhere from two to one-hundred dollars. *Saturday Evening Post* pays ten to one-hundred dollars for jokes, gags, anecdotes, cartoons, and short humor of 500 to 1,000 words. *Homeowners How To* regularly features a Problem Solvers column that pays twenty-five dollars per published idea. Magazines that place a lot of emphasis on filler items, such as *Reader's Digest,* pay as much as three-hundred dollars for a published item. See *Writer's Market* for payment rates of other magazines.

Filler Format

Q. What is the proper format for submitting fillers to an editor?
A. Each item should be centered and typed on a separate sheet of 8½x11-inch white paper in standard manuscript form; your name, address, and telephone number in the upper left corner of the page, and the approximate number of words in the upper right corner. A cover letter isn't necessary unless you are submitting a longer item such as a short article or a review, which needs comment such as your credentials in some specific area. Sending SASE is a must if you wish to have the material returned to you, though some publications will not return fillers in any case.

Marketing Fillers

Q. I have written several anecdotes and other fillers taken from my own personal experience. How can I find magazines that might be interested in buying these fillers?
A. Successful marketing is a combination of writing what you want to write and what magazine editors want to print. Read *Writer's Market* to find magazines that publish what you'd like to sell (anecdotes, for example) and then look at copies of those magazines to help you get a feeling for the style, content, and audience they cater to. Knowing what an editor is looking for before you send in your work will save you from quick rejection you'd get if, for example, you sent your personal anecdotes to a political magazine that only publishes bureaucratic bloopers as fillers. Your chances of making a sale will be greatly enhanced if you are careful about deciding where to send your work.

No Response to Fillers

Q. Several months ago I sent a few jokes and a puzzle to a magazine. I have heard nothing from the editor so far. What kind of reply can I expect from the editor and how long should I have to wait before inquiring?
A. Although some editors may hold a filler for six months before using it, if you have not received any sort of acknowledgment within two months, you should not inquire, but rather retype your piece and send it elsewhere. Due to the large volume of fillers that many editors receive, reply to individual contributors is often impossible. If you do receive a rejection slip, it may be very dry and to the point, or it may encourage you to keep trying. Look closely at the

reasons given for rejection and consider them seriously before submitting other items to that magazine.

Clippings Permission?

Q. Do I need to get permission from the original publisher to submit clippings to another magazine?
A. You do not need permission to submit clippings. However, you should always acknowledge the original source of the items so that the editor to whom you submit can decide whether or not permission is needed to publish them. If so, he will make the necessary inquiries.

Permission Procedure

Q. I am in the process of starting a magazine for the elderly. If I use clippings as fillers, do I need to get permission to publish them?
A. If a particular clipping is simply a news item, you won't need to get permission, since news cannot be copyrighted. However, if copy is of some length and comes from a copyrighted magazine or syndicated newspaper column, you will need to secure permission to use it. Write to the original publication. In the case of a syndicated newspaper column, the editor will inform you where further correspondence should be sent to get permission from the syndicate.

Tag Line

Q. What is a tag line? Is it necessary to include one every time I submit a clipping?
A. Author Connie Emerson says in *How to Make Money Writing Fillers,* "The tag or twist, when it's added to a news clip, is actually a kind of quip—a phrase that reverses what has been said or makes a humorous comment on it." Here is an example from *The New Yorker,* one of the best known users of taglines:

> Ptarmigan Mountain Properties, one of the largest condominium rental/management firms in Mt. Crested Butte, may be sold in the present future—*Gunnison* (Colo.) *Country Times.*
> Somebody's in an awful hurry.

Some magazines require tag lines while others don't use them at all. However, payment for a clipping with a tag line often will be better than that without one. See *Writer's Market* for information on any particular magazine's requirement.

Greeting Card Idea

Q. I understand that greeting card companies purchase "ideas" as well as original verse. Would a suggestion that they use a poem by a well-known author come under the classification of an "idea"? The poem I have in mind was written in the sixteenth century so there would be no copyright problem.
A. Yes, your suggestion could be considered an "idea." Check *Writer's Market,* since various greeting card publishers have different requirements for submissions. Some will not accept ideas, preferring instead to see a mock-up or rough sketch of the complete card. Payment ranges from $10 to $75 for greeting cards.

Greeting Card Research

Q. I'd like to write for the greeting card market. Other than going to greeting card shops and stores with greeting card display racks, how can I learn what cards are being marketed today?
A. See *A Guide to Greeting Card Writing,* edited by Larry Sandman, which contains how-to information on writing every kind of greeting card. Greeting card market information is updated annually through market listings which can be found in *Writer's Market.* Another helpful publication is *Greetings Magazine,* the business magazine for retailers and manufacturers of greeting cards, stationery, gifts, and allied products. Write *Greetings Magazine,* 309 Fifth Avenue, New York NY 10016, for additional information.

An artist's and writer's market list is also available for a No. 10 SASE from the National Association of Greeting Card Publishers, 600 Park Ave. SE #300, Washington DC 20003.

Greeting Card Writer

Q. What qualifications do I need to write greeting card verse?
A. Nothing more than the ability to study existing greeting card material and to provide appropriate copy to those editors. Greeting card verse sells best if your ideas are original and they imply a "me-to-you" message in a conversational tone. Enthusiasm is important, since writing verse for greeting card publishers is not as easy as it might seem. Companies that publish greeting cards are listed in *Writer's Market.*

Greeting Card Formats

Q. What is the proper format for submitting manuscripts to greeting card publishers?
A. There are three basic formats. You can type the idea or verse on a 3x5-inch or 4x6-inch card, including your name and address on the back. Another method is to type the card's message on a folded sheet of paper, putting the material intended for the front and inside of the card in their proper locations. This format is especially good for humorous cards, since the punchline is hidden from view as it would be on the finished card. However, some editors insist on 3x5-inch cards for all ideas. Check individual companies writers' guidelines and follow their preferences. The third and most elaborate form of submission is to make a complete "dummy" that is close to what the finished product should look like. Mainly used for humorous, "studio," and juvenile cards, this format includes every element of the finished card, such as color, rough sketches, and any mechanical action.

Submitting Greeting Card Verse

Q. What is meant by "identifying marks" on poems sent to greeting card firms?
A. Since such poems often do not have titles, it's a good idea to number them (one poem to a page), and keep carbon copies with the corresponding numbers for your own records. When the editor sends payment for one poem from a group, he can refer to it by number.

Anecdotes

Q. Some magazine editors say they buy anecdotes. What is an anecdote?
A. An anecdote is a short narrative "slice of life," a description of a particular incident, usually biographical, autobiographical, or stemming from something the author has observed. Anecdotes may employ humor, dialogue, plays on words, or unexpected endings to make an insightful comment or illustrate a point. Successful anecdotes will evoke laughter, surprise,

sympathy, or some other emotional reaction on the part of the reader. Due to their brevity, they work quite well as fillers. Here is one of many good examples that can be found in *Reader's Digest:*

"A woman who works for the state of Louisiana got a call from a man who paused when she told him the name of her agency. He then asked her to repeat it again. 'It's the Governor's Office for Elderly Affairs,' she told him again. There was another pause. 'For gosh sakes, sign me up,' he said. 'I didn't do too well when I was young.' "

Smiley Anders in the Baton Rouge Morning Advocate

When writing an anecdote, make sure that your narration is uncomplicated and free from extraneous detail. Since description has to be short, every word used should be essential to the picture. The impact of the anecdote comes with a good punchy ending.

Word Games

Q. I have made up several word games. Should I copyright them before I try to sell them? If so, how do I go about it?

A. Sorry, but game ideas, titles, and methods for play cannot be copyrighted. Although you can obtain a copyright for the rules of instruction, you cannot protect your game *ideas* from public use. Artwork and text found on a game board, container, or label can be copyrighted. For more information, write the Copyright Office, Library of Congress, Washington DC 20559.

21 Do Newspapers Use Freelancers?

Newspaper readers, often the first audience for many freelance writers, want news and human interest material directly related to their local community and they want it accurate and easy to read. Filling those needs are first lessons in writing for the market. Writers who have developed the techniques for newspaper reporting and writing have laid important groundwork toward future work in the magazine field.

Rejected Newspaper Articles

Q. I've submitted several factual articles to my local newspaper, but all of them have been rejected. Having read the paper for years, I know the kinds of things they publish. Could it be my writing? If so, what kinds of things should I consider when writing features for a newspaper?

A. Your editor might want more than just facts in the features he prints. As I.E. Clark says in the *Writer's Digest Handbook of Article Writing*, "Newspapers use features to intersperse life and emotion among factual news; to interpret the news; to inform readers on subjects that are not 'news' in the sense they do not rise out of current climactic events." Feature writing style is not a slave to the strict formula required for straight news articles and can be as varied as styles of fiction are. A good basic structure for the feature article starts with an attention-getting lead which sets the mood and theme of the article, a narrative body sprinkled with anecdotes and direct quotes, and a quick conclusion. Features are human interest stories, so a good article will cover something or someone unusual or worthy of note. Often, it's the slant in the article that *makes* something unusual. For instance, a dry listing of facts about the opening of a museum of Indian artifacts will hold readers' interest a lot more easily if it is slanted toward the crazy adventure one of the curators had while he was searching for artifacts for one of the displays. Your editor may be looking for articles that are short, to the point and lively.

Editorial Market?

Q. I am interested in writing editorials. Is there a market for them?

A. Unfortunately, there isn't much of a market for editorials, since most newspapers have their own staff writers who prepare the editorial page. You could send a few sample editorials to newspaper editors in your immediate area. "Op-Ed" (Opinion-Editorial) markets are published in *Writer's Digest* from time to time in the Markets column. Other markets for Op-Ed pieces can be found in *Writer's Market*, in listings that indicate "opinion pieces" and essays are needed. Some broadcasting stations are prospective markets for editorials. See the chapters on "Radio Editorials" and "TV Editorials" in *Jobs for Writers*.

Stringer Job

Q. I understand that a stringer is one who relates local news to a newspaper—a correspondent of sorts. Is obtaining a job like this a good way to break into newspaper writing? How does one become a stringer?

A. Yes, if you are interested in obtaining a staff reporter's job, it could be a plus for you to be a stringer because you will get practice in being on top of the news, digging for facts and writing as a journalist, and your editor will know your abilities. If your town does not already have a stringer corresponding with a particular newspaper, you may be able to get the job by noting eight or ten local news stories that the paper missed over the last month; writing up three of them and submitting them with a cover letter to the editor of the local paper or to the state editor of the nearest large city daily. If an editor needs stringers, he will be most impressed by those who show the enterprise to approach him. Freelance writers pursuing other writing interests will also find that being a stringer keeps them out in the real world, in touch with ideas and up to date on information of value to the creative mind. Stringers are usually paid by the column inch, though some earn a flat monthly fee.

Write Headlines?

Q. I've heard that newspaper stories written by staff reporters have their headlines written by another person, such as a copyeditor. Is this true also for material written by stringers, or are stringers expected to create and submit headlines with their work?

A. Whether news articles are written by a staff reporter or sent in by a stringer, the headlines are always written at the time of publication by one of the copyeditors at the paper. The importance placed on the story at the time it goes to press and the column width allowed for it are factors in determining the wording of headlines written by an experienced newspaper staffer.

Wire Service Stringer

Q. Are there any freelance opportunities as a stringer with the wire services like AP and UPI?

A. Most of the wire service stringers are full-time news reporters with daily papers, but occasionally the state bureau chiefs for wire services will contract for certain columns or features from freelancers. To find out the name, address and phone number of the bureau chief in your state, contact the Associated Press, 50 Rockefeller Plaza, New York NY 10020 and United Press International, 1400 I Street NW, Washington DC 20005.

Tabloid Markets

Q. Are tabloids a lucrative market? How do I break in?

A. Like any other freelance work, writing for a tabloid involves careful examination of particular newspapers to determine the writing style and subject matter they're interested in. Stories found in tabloids include those on celebrities, strange phenomena, consumer issues, unusual human interest, self-help, and developments in medicine. Access to the kinds of facts you need to create a sensational article is a help in breaking into the market. The money you make will depend on the size of the publication—payment may be less than $50 or more than $1,000. Editorial requirements for tabloids that buy freelance material are given in *Writer's Market*.

Rights Bought

Q. What rights are usually bought by a copyrighted newspaper?
A. Under the new copyright law of 1978, a newspaper or magazine buys only one-time publishing rights unless otherwise indicated in writing to the author. Thus, if a copyrighted newspaper prints an article of yours, you are free to use it again. However, if the newspaper is not copyrighted, anyone may use your printed article, since it would then be in the public domain.

Uncopyrighted Newspaper

Q. When submitting feature articles to a newspaper that is not copyrighted, should I include my own copyright notice? Will the editor honor my notice and print it?
A. Yes, unless you want your article to fall into the public domain, be sure to show your copyright notice on your manuscript's first page. Ask the editor in your covering letter to publish your copyright notice if he is interested in publishing your article. Most editors will honor that request if they publish your piece.

Copyright Protection

Q. Are my articles protected if at least one of the papers in which they appear is copyrighted? Do I have to get permission from all copyrighted papers that my column appears in to reuse the material?
A. If your article appears in an uncopyrighted paper, it enters the public domain and cannot be protected by the fact that it also appears in a copyrighted paper. This also means that you don't have to request permission to reuse the material. In fact, anyone can reuse it if it's in the public domain. If your work was published only in copyrighted newspapers, you wouldn't have to request permission unless you had agreed in writing to sell other than one-time rights to those papers. (For additional information on copyrights, see Chapter 18.)

Newspaper Reprint

Q. If another newspaper lifts my article and prints it, are they obligated to pay me for it?
A. If the newspaper in which your original article appeared was not copyrighted (and some newspapers aren't) then your article became public property as soon as it was published and any reprinting paper was not obligated to pay you. If the original newspaper in which your article appeared was a member of the Associated Press, the AP is permitted to pick up local news stories and reprint them in member papers without permission or payment. If your article was a copyrighted feature, then yes, a reprinter would be obligated to pay you.

Multiple Submissions

Q. Is it ethical for me to submit a freelance feature article to more than one newspaper at a time?
A. Yes, as long as they are in non-competing circulation areas. Some writers, when making multiple submissions of this kind, type in the upper right corner, "Exclusive in your circulation area."

Factual Columns

Q. I want to syndicate a factual column. How much material will I need to present to newspaper editors? The idea only? A sample? A month's or year's worth?
A. It depends on whether you're suggesting a daily or weekly column. If a daily, then it would be best to have a month's columns ready to show; for a weekly column, have two months' supply written. In both cases, have ideas written for another three to six months' columns.

National vs Local

Q. I am interested in syndicating my own newspaper column. Will it be necessary for me to copyright the column in my name in order to send it to several different markets? If I must copyright the column in my name, how do I go about doing this?
A. Yes, it will be necessary for you to copyright the columns in your own name to protect your rights. A practice that has been followed by many national syndicates and persons syndicating their own columns has been to copyright a collection of columns. The author then puts the copyright symbol, year and name in the column "reprints" sent to newspapers. This is less expensive than taking out an individual copyright on each column, since there is a ten dollar fee per column, or collection. Applications for either can be obtained by writing to the Register of Copyrights, Library of Congress, Washington DC 20559.

Newspaper Column Markets

Q. Where can I find a list of newspaper markets for my column?
A. The worldwide *Editor & Publisher Yearbook* lists daily, weekly, and minority papers along with feature agencies. It's published by *Editor & Publisher*, 575 Lexington Ave., New York NY 10022. *Ayer Directory of Publications* lists newspapers, magazines, and business, trade and professional journals. These directories, both set up geographically by state, then by city, are available at most large public library reference departments. *Writer's Market* includes some newspapers and weekly magazine sections in its "Regional" category, giving editorial requirements for active newspaper markets for freelance material.

Marketing a Syndicated Column

Q. How do I market my column to a national syndicate?
A. To find out what competition might already exist for your idea, check the *Syndicate Directory* published by the trade magazine *Editor & Publisher*. (If a copy of this isn't in your local library, write for information on the current price to *Editor & Publisher*, 575 Lexington Ave., New York NY 10022.) This *Syndicate Directory* lists by title, author, and subject matter, all of the syndicated columns, features, and cartoon strips currently published. It also tells which syndicate currently distributes them and gives the name and address of the editorial director of the syndicate. If your syndicated column idea, for example, was a "Tips for Consumers" idea, you could see which syndicates already have similar continuing features. After you find a syndicate that best suits your needs, query the editorial director. Enclose at least six sample columns and, as always, SASE. Sample columns should only be sent to one syndicate at a time. You should hear from the editor in one week to three months.

Protect Column Title?

Q. Is there any way I can protect the title of my column and the symbol I plan to use both as a business letterhead and at the top of my column?
A. Titles are not copyrightable, but you may be able to get your title and symbol registered as a trademark. For information, write the Commissioner of Patents and Trademarks, Patent and Trademark Office, Washington DC 20231. To obtain a trademark, of course, you would have to personally search or hire a patent attorney to search the Trademark Office records to see if the symbol you wanted to use was not already in use.

Column Pay?

Q. How much can I expect to be paid for my self-syndicated weekly column? Is payment something that I should specify or do newspapers have a standard?
A. Pay rate is for the most part what the paper is willing to pay and what your column is worth to them. You may only get five dollars from a small paper, but larger circulation dailies may pay as much as fifteen to twenty-five dollars per column. Of course, well-known columnists will make much more than that for their columns—but they started small too! In the beginning, offer your column to newspapers "at your usual rate." If they haven't bought any your material before and ask *you* to name your price, you could ask for five dollars or more depending on the circulation of the paper. In some cases, especially if you're trying to break into suburban and small-town papers, you might want to offer the column on a trial basis, free of charge. If the column receives good reader response, then you can ask for payment after a few columns have been printed.

Selling Newspaper Column

Q. After twenty-five years as an Air Force wife, I think I have enough experience under my belt to be able to write a humorous column that many might enjoy. I'd like to try selling my column to a newspaper—or even to several. How do I know if my style is one that will sell? How do I go about marketing my column?
A. About the only way to find out whether or not your column will sell is to try selling it! Writer Kay Cassill suggests some questions an editor might ask himself as he looks over your work: Will it make complete strangers laugh? How diverse is the age group to which this would appeal? Is it easy to read? Does the writer know what she's talking about? Is my paper lacking something because it doesn't carry this column? If you've shown him something lively and original, you just might be able to make a sale. In marketing your column, be sure you know your markets well enough so that you don't send them something they already have—and don't try to sell the same column to papers with competing circulation areas. Personal contact with each editor is a step in the right direction. Send a sincere, concise letter explaining what you feel are the merits of your column and enclose SASE. Start out looking for local markets from which to build a base. If your column catches on, you may want to try to increase your sales. If so, be prepared to work hard as a business person and as a salesperson. You might be surprised at how well it can pay off!

Protect Your Column?

Q. How would my column be protected if it were published through a syndicate?
A. A syndicate will obtain copyright protection for your column by obtaining a copyright on a

collection of your columns and requiring the copyright symbol to appear in newspaper reprints. *Your* rights may be different if you publish though a syndicate rather than doing it yourself. Syndicates usually buy all rights to a columnist's work, copyrighting the work in the name of the syndicate, and rendering him unable to reuse the material without their permission.

Self-Syndication vs National Syndication

Q. Can you give me a basic definition of a syndicate? Exactly what is the difference between self-syndication and national syndication? What are the advantages of each?
A. A syndicate is a business that will simultaneously sell a piece of writing to many different publications. A writer can sell his column or feature to one hundred or more daily or weekly newspapers through a syndicate. Self-syndication involves a writer himself marketing his work to many newspapers. The major advantage of self-syndication is that the writer can collect full payment directly from the publications to which he sells his work, whereas he only gets 40-60 percent of the gross receipts when operating through a syndicate. However, the self-syndicator must do all of his own promoting and selling, which costs time and money. Syndicates, on the other hand, provide this service for the writer.

Syndicate Payment

Q. When a syndicate is said to pay $25, what does this cover?
A. Such a flat rate usually refers to the payment for a single feature—a one-shot item rather than a continuing column.

Waiting Time

Q. When I submit a feature to a syndicate, how soon can I expect a decision? How can I make sure I get my percentage of sales?
A. Most of the syndicates report on submissions in one week to three months. Unless the sum is large enough to warrant sending an auditor to check the accounts, most writers accept the syndicate's statements in good faith, since publishers and syndicates couldn't stay in business long if they weren't honest with their writers.

Newspaper vs Other Writing

Q. How is newspaper writing different from other kinds of writing?
A. Since newspaper writing has to fit specific space on a page, writers will often find their stories have been cut. The most important parts of a newspaper story are in the first few paragraphs, so the ending is what is deleted if space is limited. Newspaper editors also tend to cut adjectives, images and other "nonessential" additions to a sentence, when space restrictions force tighter editing. Magazine article writers and book authors have more freedom to write more imaginatively and still include all the facts.

22 How Do I Write and Sell a Magazine Article?

Webster's Dictionary reminds us that the original definition of the word magazine was that of a storehouse, and today's magazines literally are storehouses of information and entertainment. To provide their readers with exciting articles and stories, editors depend heavily on freelance contributors. The listings in *Writer's Market* usually tell you the number of manuscripts each magazine buys a year, so you have a good idea what your competition will be. For a listing of the top 100 magazine markets see the annual: *Writer's Yearbook.*

Manuscript or Market First?

Q. Is it better to have a specific market in mind when writing an article, or to write the article first, then look for a market for it?
A. It is usually better to write with a specific market in mind so that your writing will have a certain direction. Writers trying to earn a living as freelancers study potential markets before starting to write; this increases potential sales. However, you can write an article and then look for a suitable market. Make sure you carefully research the market before you submit anything. Editors do not appreciate writers who bombard them with material that is obviously not aimed toward their audience.

Beginners' Markets

Q. Where can I find a listing of secondary markets where a neophyte can break in?
A. Secondary markets are magazines with smaller circulations and lower payment rates, but their editors are quite demanding about the kind and quality of material they accept from freelancers. Hundreds of secondary markets are listed in *Writer's Market.*

Types of Articles

Q. How many different kinds of articles are there?
A. Articles most commonly published today include how-to, personal experience, interview, inspirational, humorous, exposé, historical, personal opinion, success story, travel, technical, new product, and merchandising technique articles. Article format depends on the magazine it's written for and the writer's individual style.

Quality/Little Magazines

Q. What are "quality" magazines and "little" magazines?
A. Quality magazines such as *The New Yorker, Harper's, The Atlantic,* and *Saturday Review* aim toward the educated, intellectual sectors of the population, concentrating on articles that analyze current events or trends and present informed opinions, thereby encouraging thoughtful analysis on the part of the reader. Humor found in these magazines is sophisticated and often satirical. Although payment for articles published in quality magazines is usually less than from larger general interest magazines, writers whose work appears in a quality magazine have the respect and attention of other editors—an advantage when looking for further freelance work.

Little magazines are limited-circulation, often short-lived publications that print political, literary, often unorthodox material that might not otherwise be published. They represent creative writers interested in fine literary quality and are read by writers, editors, and students of literature. Since these publications make little or no profit, payment for published work is usually no more than a contributor's copy or a subscription to the magazine. Writers should be warned that many little magazines are usually uncopyrighted, and if an article appears without a copyright byline, it becomes part of the public domain.

Trade Terms

Q. What is a "think piece"? Does it mean a controversial article? Or does it mean all kinds of nonfiction? For example, even historical pieces, noncontroversial, will cause me to think—and doubtless most other readers.
A. A "think piece" is usually any article that has an intellectual, philosophical, provocative approach to its subject.

Contributor's Copies

Q. Isn't the phrase, "Payment in contributor's copies" ambiguous? Does it not mean "payment in copies to contributors"?
A. "Contributor's copies" is a term that is generally taken to mean copies of the issue in which the contributor's work appears.

Anecdotal Style?

Q. An editor rejected my article, saying he uses a more anecdotal style in his magazine. What does that mean?
A. Used in article writing, an anecdote is a brief human interest story illustrating a point. Although each anecdote is complete in itself, it should be relevant to the purpose of the article. Anecdotes can serve to hold reader interest by breaking up a lot of factual material. They can be used to add insight to the personality of someone discussed or featured in an article, to act as a transition from one topic to another, or to provide a "grabber" of a lead in a news or feature article.

Good interview technique will easily yield anecdotes. Ask your subject questions like "What person influenced you most in life and how?" or "What was your greatest opportunity?" or "What do you consider the most important decision in your life?" Through such inquiries, you will learn much about the forces that guide and shape the person. If you are writing about someone not available for interview, talk to people who know him and get them to relate incidents and personal characteristics of your subject. Often writers use anecdotes stemming from personal experience, so be alert to what's going on around you. Using anecdotes in your writing, without overdoing it, will add the spice your article may need for you to make the sale.

Essay vs Article

Q. In college we wrote what teachers referred to as essays, but I don't see many markets for essays in Writer's Market. *What's the difference between an essay and a magazine article?*
A. An article is usually based on fact uncovered in research and/or interview and manifests itself in forms like the personality sketch, the exposé, or the how-to. It will have a particular slant, but any opinion will be backed up with quotes, anecdotes, and statistics. While they are often entertaining, articles are usually meant to educate and inform.

In its original sense, the essay was meant to express opinion, to be persuasive, or to be interpretive. It is marked by a more personal treatment of the subject matter, which may or may not interest a wide audience. Although an essay may require research, the information is used along with subjective ideas in an essay, whereas an article remains fairly objective. More recently, newspapers have printed interpretive essays. These pieces are really extensions of the news story, analyzing the background of a political event. Editorials, humor pieces, and inspirational articles could all be considered essays.

Which Editor?

Q. If a magazine masthead lists an editor and a managing editor but no articles editor, who should get my unsolicited manuscript?
A. Since it is the editor's job in most cases to determine what stories are assigned and to whom, and what will be printed in a particular issue, you should send your manuscript to him. At most magazines, the managing editor is concerned more with the actual production of the magazine.

Travel Expenses

Q. I want to do an article that will involve some travel expense to a near-by state. Will an editor reimburse me for these expenses in addition to payment for the article?
A. If you are fairly new to the business of freelancing and have not built up many writing credits, you will probably be expected to cover extra expenses yourself—but it never hurts to ask! Expenses may include travel, extensive research, photography, photocopying, and the like. An established writer can often get an advance from the editor to cover expenses, and when writing on assignment may even get a flat-out expense-paid trip to wherever he needs to go. If you *do* have to cover your own travel expenses, keep receipts, and remember that travel expenses can be written off with your other business expenses as a tax deduction. Take full advantage of every trip by making notes, being observant, taking photographs, and following leads that will open and enhance other writing projects, too.

Ordinary People

Q. I have known some very ordinary people who have done some very unusual things in their lives. Is there a market for articles about these people? It seems I only read stories about famous *people.*
A. Your stories may not interest editors of major magazines, but they may very well sell to local newspapers and possibly to a specialized consumer magazine or trade publication. The

only way to find out is to look through *Writer's Market* until you find some magazines interested in buying the human interest nonfiction you want to write. Make sure you study a magazine thoroughly before you decide to query or send a manuscript to its editor.

Lead Time for Sunday Magazine

Q. I have written a human interest article that I think would be perfect in the Sunday supplement magazine in our local newspaper. How many weeks in advance should I make my submission since I have a particular Sunday in mind?
A. It would be wise to submit your piece three to four months before the date you would like to see it published. This gives the editor plenty of time to make a decision concerning your article, and, if it is accepted, to decide upon the format and prepare accompanying artwork.

Recipe Sales

Q. During a spring trip to the Pacific Northwest, I developed a form of "oven" camp cooking along with some special recipes. One recipe involves the use of six nationally known food products. I have two objectives: 1) the presentation of the six-product recipe to the individual companies involved; 2) an illustrated article describing the "oven" cooking including all the recipes. How might I offer the recipes six separate times to the six companies? Could I then, if any one of them used the recipe, retain the rights to incorporate this six-product recipe in the article to be presented early next year to a magazine devoted to outdoor living and camping?
A. You might be putting the dessert before the main dish here. You would do better *first* to write the article featuring the recipe. If and when it appears in that camping magazine, you could then send six copies of this published article to the six companies. These companies will no doubt be pleased to learn of this original use of their product, but do not expect any remuneration from them.

Magazine Rights

Q. What is the difference between selling "one-time rights" and "first North American rights"?
A. If you sell first North American rights to a magazine, you are guaranteeing that they will be the first publisher of your article in the United States and Canada, without restricting yourself from selling it elsewhere at a later time. One-time rights can be sold to any publication regardless of whether or not they are the first to print it. In this case, you would be prohibiting the magazine from running your story more than once.

Column Rate

Q. What's the going rate for a magazine column?
A. What a magazine will pay a columnist varies greatly with the size of its circulation and the eminence and expertise of the writer. A popular magazine with a large audience, like *McCall's*, might pay anywhere from $750 to $1,500 and up per column, depending on how well-known the author is. Smaller secondary publications pay up to $75 to $200 per column. The pay is much less enticing in this case, but chances of securing a regular columnist's position are much greater with these smaller magazines than with the larger ones. Although payment is usually on a per column basis rather than per word, the editor will usually specify desired column length. If you have an idea for a column for a small magazine, send a query along with half a dozen sample columns to the editor, telling why you think the column would benefit his readers.

Contributing Editor

Q. To what does the title of "contributing editor" entitle a writer?
A. Contributing editors are writers who have written and sold several articles or items to a magazine, which then lists the writer as "contributing editor." It usually gains the writer no additional money or special favors, but it is prestigious in that it indicates that the writer knows how to successfully (and repeatedly) write for, and sell to, that magazine. It also gives him more visibility in that his queries and suggestions and manuscripts are given red-carpet treatment (they are read sooner and acted upon more quickly than unsolicited mail). It also gives the writer more clout when arranging interviews for articles for the magazine to which he contributes. It may also give the writer more credibility when he wants to break into other markets.

Article Slant

Q. What is meant by the "slant" of a magazine article? How does one go about putting slant in an article?
A. A writer *slants* his article when he specifically gears it to a particular reading public. Finding the proper slant demands in-depth market study to determine the subject matter and style an editor is interested in, and the kind of audience his magazine is intended for. Carefully read several issues of a magazine you wish to write for, analyzing the articles. Are there mostly opinion pieces? Factual features? Personality profiles? How about the average article length? Close observation of the advertisements will give you an idea of the average age and socioeconomic status of the readers, as well as some of their hobbies and interests. By studying the market, you will be able to present an editor with the kind of article he wants, thereby greatly increasing your chances of making a sale.

Magazine Correspondent

Q. What exactly does a magazine correspondent do? How can I get a job as a correspondent?
A. Magazine correspondents usually work on assignment, conducting interviews, making phone calls, and doing all sorts of other research for articles that are sometimes initiated by the magazine and written by staff writers. The results of this "legwork" are usually submitted as a research report and are incorporated into articles of larger scope. The correspondent may also be able to initiate, research, and write articles of his own for the magazine. He's in a better position than the regular freelancer here, because his editors know the quality of his work and are more willing to consider it for publication.

To get a job as a correspondent, you must usually have a substantial track record as a writer and be able to demonstrate a wide knowledge and interest in the subjects you write about. These jobs are normally obtained with a particular magazine after the writer has had several pieces published in that magazine.

Editorial Changes

Q. When a magazine published my article it was completely changed from my version although they used my facts. Does this mean they didn't like my writing and only wanted to use my research? I know they needed to shorten it, but I was surprised to see it changed so much from the way I submitted it.
A. An editor will often change syntax, clean up grammar, and rearrange ideas in order to make an article clearer and more easily read. If the article is longer than the specified number of

words, it will be cut. Editorial space is limited. The editor may be forced to do a lot of rewriting, even though the article may contain valuable information, because he knows that it does not conform to reader expectations and/or the personality of the magazine. As *Writer's Digest* editor William Brohaugh says, "Editors edit to make you sound better *relative to the rest of the magazine.*" You can avoid severe editing of your work by studying and knowing the slant and style of the magazine to which you are submitting. Look closely at the printed version of your article and analyze the reasons for changes. And it wouldn't hurt to drop the editor a note and ask *him* why the changes were made. He will probably be frank with you, and you may learn something from the experience.

Resubmit Same Subject?

Q. I have an idea for an article that would be perfect for Better Homes and Gardens. *However, I found that the magazine published a similar article several years ago. Does this mean they won't be interested? Should I try other magazines instead?*

A. You can query *Better Homes and Gardens,* but emphasize your piece as an update of their previous article and suggest new ideas and angles. If you are rejected, query other home-oriented magazines.

Types of Nonfiction

Q. Some terms appear in magazine market listings that I'm not sure I understand. One reason may be that I have never seen a list of comparative definitions for them. I would appreciate such definitions and comparison—showing, if possible, any clear cut differences between the following terms: articles, essays, features, "new journalism."

A. Articles are always nonfiction—accounts of real things that have happened. They can be informational, how-to, personal experience, interviews, profiles, inspirational, humor, historical, think articles, exposé, nostalgia, personal opinion, photo articles, travel, successful business operations articles, new product articles, merchandising technique articles, and technical articles. Essays are written compositions, usually personal in tone, giving one's personal opinion or ideas on a given topic. Features are human interest articles giving the reader background information on the news. The term "feature" is sometimes used by magazine editors to indicate a lead article or distinctive department in their publication. In other words, a feature article may be the article given most importance in a particular issue of the magazine. "New journalism" is article writing using many fiction techniques; it's a form of journalism that also involves the writer's own feelings about his subject as opposed to "objective" journalism. For additional definitions of writing terms see *Writer's Encyclopedia.*

Skimpy Research?

Q. I've done very little writing, but I'd like to write an article about working mothers—especially those with small children. I know several in my neighborhood and am impressed by what they manage to accomplish in a day's time. But whenever I begin to write, I quickly run out of things to say—after only a page or two. What's my problem?

A. It seems that you have a fairly solid interest in your subject, so your problem might be a lack of ample research. Have you really *talked* to these women about their trials, the advantages and disadvantages of their two-career situation? Another problem may be that you do not have a clearly developed angle for your article. Instead of merely making random comments on how working mothers cope, you could perhaps better interest your readers by including specific tips on how they could manage their *own* time better, secure cooperation of other family members, etc. A writer who knows enough about her subject will never be at a loss for words: ideas, anecdotes, facts, and angles will come easily. Begin by formulating a solid outline and strive for smooth transition between ideas. And take plenty of time to plan, research, and write your piece; rushing things will result in disorganized and unclear writing.

Resubmit?

Q. I have written some articles that I would like to see in more than one magazine. I take several religious magazines and would like to send the articles to each of them. Would this be legal? If these were paid for, would it be legal then to send to another editor?
A. On future submissions, you might want to type in the upper right corner of page one of your manuscript: "Submitted on a nonexclusive basis at your regular rates." This tells the editor that he or she is not the only editor offered the manuscript. Many editors of religious magazines know that their readers are not likely to see the same article in another denomination's publication and are willing to accept these "simultaneous submissions."

Free Articles

Q. Do editors accept free contributions from an author? I have written a moralistic essay that carries a message and do not feel that I should accept money to have it reach the public. What do you think?
A. Some magazines do not offer payment for contributions. If it is a magazine's policy to pay for material it uses, you should not offer your contribution free. Don't be misled into thinking that just because it's free, an editor will use it. If, in the editor's estimation, it's worthy of being printed, he will automatically pay for it (and you can send the check to your favorite charity). If it doesn't seem publishable to him, then the fact that it's free will not persuade him to use it.

More Than One Idea?

Q. Is it okay for me to submit more than one idea at a time to the same magazine?
A. Submitting one idea at a time is preferred. Due to space limitations in a good query letter, it is difficult to fully develop more than one idea at a time. Since ideas may be considered by several editors at a particular magazine, it is easier for them to contend with only one idea per letter. They can get back to you sooner. However, you might develop each of your ideas into a separate query and send them all in the same envelope to an editor. It would show him that you spent some time analyzing the magazine's readership and could lead to more than one "go ahead on spec." (See Chapter 5 about this term.) Magazines like *National Geographic* request writers to send a letter containing several one-paragraph ideas. If the editors find any idea to be promising, they request a more detailed two-page outline. However, you should look in *Writer's Market* to find out what a particular editor prefers.

Query vs Manuscript?

Q. Do magazine editors prefer queries rather than unsolicited manuscripts?
A. Close study of market listings will often reveal an editor's preference on this. It's usually a good idea to query, especially when you're planning to invest a lot of time and effort in researching and writing a major article. Unless he knows your writing, an editor is not likely to give you a firm assignment after reading your query. But if he likes your idea and you are told to go ahead and write the article on speculation, your chances of making a sale are much greater

than those of most of your competitors. Certain types of articles, such as humor, opinion and commentary, and book reviews, cannot be adequately described in a query, so are best submitted as a finished manuscript.

Advance Assignments?

Q. I'm planning a trip into the Middle East this next fall and am interested in doing some magazine article writing while I'm there. Is there any way I could get some assignments before I leave?

A. Unless you've written many articles in the past and editors know your name and your abilities, you probably won't be able to get any definite assignments. However, if you are able to suggest *in detail* some of your ideas in a query letter, you may find a couple of interested editors who will consider your work on speculation. General suggestions—for example, "I'd like to do an article about life in modern Arabia,"—will only serve to label you as a novice and will yield few interested editors.

Article Peg

Q. I sent an article to a magazine, and jotted on the rejection slip was the comment, "Too general—no peg." What does that mean?

A. It means that you did not concentrate on one specific aspect of your topic, rendering the article too general for the audience of that magazine. Most article ideas lend themselves to several pegs, each one of which could be developed into a separate article. For instance, an article on buying a computer could be geared toward the needs of a college student, a household, a self-employed businessperson, a teacher, or a corporation . . . five different article possibilities (or "pegs") that could end up in five different magazines, each with a different audience.

Photos with Article?

Q. Will including photographs with my article help sell it? What size photographs should be submitted with a manuscript?

A. A look through *Writer's Market* will confirm the fact that many magazines request or require photographs with article manuscript submissions. When you submit photographs, you certainly are increasing your chances of making a sale. If you are not confident in your abilities as a photographer, you may have to hire someone to take the pictures for you. However, if you are intent on being a full-time freelance writer, it will save you time, energy and money if you learn to do the photography yourself. Photographs submitted should be sharp and clear and should give the editors a good variety to choose from. Study the publications to which you want to submit your package to get an idea of the kinds of photographs they like to print with their articles. When submitting black-and-white photographs, 8x10-inch glossy prints are preferred. For color, don't send color prints—send transparencies. Mark each print or slide with your name and address and include caption material if it is appropriate. Don't overlook the possible free sources of photographs available to you from government agencies, professional organizations, corporations and others listed in directories such as the *Writer's Resource Guide*. (For more information on illustrating your work, see Chapter 23.)

Creating Anecdotes

Q. I need advice on the use of anecdotes in articles. Do they have to be true to be ethical? How about making up anecdotes to suit the need?
A. If you're going to mention people's names, then you'd better stick to real-life facts; but if you want to make up an anecdote to illustrate a point, then you might preface it with something like: "It's the sort of town where something like the following could easily happen:—" or "There's a rumor going around that—" or "I wouldn't be surprised if—." The point can be made, but without giving the erroneous idea that the incident actually did take place. A true-life story may be fictionalized, or could use a little "fixing" to give it the right charm, and small changes in time span and dialogue are acceptable. But as Connie Emerson says in *How to Make Money Writing Fillers*, "However much you alter what really happened, you must succeed in making the story 'read true.' " The secret of good anecdote-telling is the ability to spot a small true-life happening and describe it in such a way that your interpretation gives it new dimension and significance.

Articles from Abroad

Q. I am planning to take an extensive trip through the British Isles this fall and will be writing several articles for some newspapers that I have served for years as a correspondent and feature writer. I also plan to write some freelance travel features which I hope to sell to one or more magazines or wire services. How does a traveling freelance writer handle work like this from abroad?
A. It is customary for freelance writers submitting to markets from abroad to send a self-addressed envelope addressed to them at the point they next expect to be. Usually enclosed is an International Reply Coupon which can be bought in European Post Offices to cover return postage from anywhere in the world. If you'll only be dealing with American markets, of course, you can take U.S. postage with you to affix to your self-addressed envelope. You might want to consider submitting queries on your features rather than complete manuscripts since the publications may want a different slant than what you have in mind.

Sidebar

Q. An editor said part of my article would work better as a sidebar. What does he mean?
A. Editors print sidebars with articles to enhance or clarify a certain point. They are boxed off and titled separately from the rest of the article and may even be set in different type. Your editor may feel that a particular point in your article fits awkwardly and would be more clearly presented as a separate "mini-article." Sidebars are also used to add information to or to take an in-depth look at something mentioned in the article. For example, included with a *Time* magazine article on a papal visit to the United States might be a sidebar recounting the city-by-city heavy security precautions. Other kinds of sidebars include historical notes, tables of statistics, and how-to's.

Publish Too Much?

Q. Is there any danger a writer might get too many articles going at the same time?
A. Planning your production time—whether you are a part-time or full-time freelance writer—is important. If deadlines are too close together, you may be inclined to rush through

an article without sufficient research, eliminate some important interviews, or turn out a draft that really needs better organizing and rewriting. You will be judged by your readers and editors on what appears under your byline, so give only your best effort to each assignment.

SASE or Not?

Q. Unsolicited manuscripts and SASE go together like kids and colds, but what about solicited manuscripts? To SASE or not to SASE?
A. Editors should pay the freight for their own solicitations—that is, for an article *on assignment.* If you query and an editor says, "OK, let me see," better include SASE, though. That's not a solicited manuscript.

Reprint Submissions

Q. How do I indicate on my manuscript that my article submission has been previously published?
A. In the upper right corner of your first page, indicate "Reprint Rights" and the name and date of the publication in which the material first appeared.

Reprint Buyers

Q. In such magazines as Reader's Digest, *do the editors select the articles from perusal of various magazines or do authors submit printed articles they believe are suitable for reprint?*
A. Editors usually select the articles for reprinting, but an author may submit tearsheets to bring his material to their attention. *Reader's Digest* buys original articles as well as reprints. For their editorial requirements, see *Writer's Market.*

Article/Photo Package

Q. I've written a magazine article for which I've taken some photographs as possible illustration. How do I submit a manuscript-photo package?
A. Choose a couple of your best shots, and send eight by ten-inch enlargements to the editor with your manuscript. Let him know in your letter that you have other pictures available. Mail the manuscript and photos flat, with some sort of fiberboard reinforcement so the photos don't get bent in the mail. Identify your photos with your name and address, since they may be separated from the manuscript temporarily at the publisher's. Don't write on the back of the photo—use address labels or a rubber stamp with your name and address, and attach your typed caption with tape to the back of the photos.

Filler Credits?

Q. When sending a query letter, can jokes and fillers that carry my byline be used as credits along with other published material?
A. Jokes and fillers, if published in national magazines under your byline, can be used as examples of your published works. You should only mention these credits if the article you are querying about is somehow related to this short, humorous material.

Writing Sample

Q. When an editor requests samples of my writing, is it sufficient to send a copy of the first

page of a six-page published article, or must I send the complete article?
A. A photocopy of the complete published article is preferable so the editor can see how you handle examples, transitions and the conclusion as well as the opening. The same applies to a story so the editor can see how you handle character development, plot progression, and climax. If you have a very long article or story you might mention its length and send only the first few pages, indicating the complete copy is available on request.

Consistent Contributor

Q. A trade publication bought and published seven articles I submitted to the magazine over the last several months. Each check was accompanied by a letter encouraging me to submit more of my work. Should I continue to enclose SASE? Would it be out of line to ask to write a regular column for the magazine?
A. Continue to enclose SASE unless the editor specifically tells you it's no longer necessary. However, you needn't enclose SASE if you are sending an article that you have written *on assignment,* after having queried the editor. Asking to write a regular column for the magazine would not be out of line, since you obviously write according to the magazine's style and are providing subjects of interest to the readers.

Travel Writing

Q. I just discovered the travel-writing field and am very excited about it. How can I get started in this field? How much money can I expect to earn, and would the money used for traveling be paid by my publisher or out of my own pocket? I have a fairly good paying job; would you advise me to leave it to become a travel writer?
A. One way to get started in travel writing is to do some short travel features aimed at local newspaper and regional magazine markets. It helps if you have a general knowledge of newspaper and magazine article writing and some experience in freelance writing. If you're new to the writing field, you can prepare yourself by reading many books on writing and taking a writing course at a local university or community college, or through a correspondence school. You can begin by reading Louise Purwin Zobel's *The Travel Writer's Handbook.*

At the beginning of your career, you will have to finance your trips out of your own funds. Later, when your name becomes known in this specialty, the publications you write for will often pay your travel expenses.

It wouldn't be advisable for you to quit your job to become a travel writer. You should work as a freelancer in that field until you have established enough credit with magazine and book editors to enable you to support yourself entirely from your writing income.

23 Do I Need to Provide My Own Illustrations?

For freelance writers, "Double your talents, double your checks" might be an appropriate parody of a popular advertising jingle. Article writers find the investment in a camera will easily pay for itself in increased sales, since many editors want a manuscript/photo package and some may even require it. The same theory doesn't hold true for writer/artist collaborators since editors have their own preferences and contacts for artwork.

Photo Cost

Q. Who covers the fees involved in securing photographs for magazine articles—writer or editor?
A. It depends on individual magazine policy. At most magazines, it is usually the writer's responsibility to either supply the photographs or make arrangements to work with a local freelance photographer. The procedure at some magazines is to pay the writer a flat fee for an article/picture "package." If this is the case, the writer must arrange a fair split of the proceeds with his photographer. Check *Writer's Market* for the policies of individual magazines.

Submitting Photos

Q. What is the best way to send photographs with a manuscript so that they aren't mangled by the postal system?
A. Black-and-white prints should be placed between pieces of stiff cardboard and secured with a rubber band. Paper clips can mar photos, so don't use them. Mark your mailing envelope "PHOTOGRAPHS—DO NOT BEND." This will alert postal workers and your pictures should make it through without being damaged. Color photos should be submitted as slides, not prints. They are best submitted in the page-size plastic sleeves that hold twenty 35mm slides. If you number them, the caption material can be typed on a separate sheet of paper with numbers to match.

Permissions on Photos?

Q. I have been asked to put together for publication a scrapbook on a world champion track star who has a collection of photos that tells his story quite well. Some of the photos are snapshots, but most are excellent, some having been published before, and many, published and unpublished, of nationally known personalities. Do I need the permission of the numerous photographers or individuals appearing in the photos? What about previously published photos?

A. Since the photographs are all of "public figures" and you don't plan to use the photographs in any kind of advertising, you probably don't need any model releases signed by the subjects in the pictures. However, your publisher may want you to obtain releases anyway, in case some of these photos appear in advertising or promotion materials for the book. Unpublished photographs belong to the photographer, so you will have to obtain permission to use them. In the case of previously published photographs, who gives the permission depends on the rights the photographer sold to the original publisher. You'd have to write him to find out, then obtain permission where necessary.

Model Releases?

Q. I want to submit some photographs with my fishing article, but my two partners are in most of the shots. Do I need model releases from them? When is a model release necessary?

A. A signed model release is necessary if the photograph in question, whether it be of a person, someone's pet, or a recognizable building or piece of property, is to be used for any commercial purpose: advertising, endorsement, or promotion. Normally, you do not need to obtain releases for pictures used in the editorial sections of newspapers, magazines and books. If you think, however, that the photograph might be used on the cover and be construed by some as "advertising," it might be a good idea to have your two fishing partners sign forms permitting you to sell their photographs for editorial or commercial use. That way you will have the forms on file if your editor decides he needs them, or if you ever want to sell the photographs as advertising material. You can easily obtain release forms at most photography stores, or you can get your own printed. A sample form appears in *Photographer's Market* and in *Writer's Encyclopedia*.

Basically, the model release is a signed and witnessed statement from the subject of a photograph (the model) giving the photographer the right to use the photograph for sale or reproduction, in consideration for value received. The "value received" is usually a copy print of the photograph.

Children's Book Illustrations

Q. How do I arrange to get an illustrator for my children's book?

A. You don't need an illustrator, as most editors prefer manuscripts without illustrations. Publishers have their own preferences in illustrators, sometimes on staff. An editor is usually good at visualizing artwork to accompany a story, and if his ideas are radically different from yours, you run the risk of losing a sale. The final decision as to who will do the illustration lies with the editor, who has a group of reliable illustrators for the books his company publishes. If you have ideas that you feel are necessary to the success of your story, you might submit a dummy copy along with a copy of the straight text. Include sketches only though—don't bother with finished artwork until the editor has agreed that you will illustrate the book. (For more on collaboration with an artist, see Chapter 11).

Photo Sources

Q. In writing articles I often need pictures for illustrations and do not know where to get them.

(I am not a photographer.) Of course, I should like them at a reasonable price, or better still, free.

A. There is a wealth of stock photos to be had, and many of them for free. See the subject sections of *Writer's Resource Guide*. For a comprehensive list of picture sources, see also *World Photography Sources*, edited by David N. Bradshaw and Catherine Hahn. In addition to listing general stock photo agencies and freelance photographers, it lists sources located all over the world in areas such as agriculture, geography and history, industry, military, visual and performing arts, plants and animals, science and the social sciences, and sports. Each listing gives names and addresses of contact people, procedure for obtaining photos, and what fees, if any, will be charged. You should be able to find the book in the reference section of your public library. Pictures from any of these sources can be used by themselves or to supplement pictures shot specifically for your article, either by a professional photographer you engaged for the purpose, or by a photographer who has agreed to work with you on speculation for an agreed-upon fee if and when you sell your article.

Rights to Photos

Q. What rights should I sell with photographs when they are submitted with a manuscript?
A. Photographs are often bought in a "package" with the manuscript they accompany. Thus, editors will usually buy the same rights to the pictures that they buy to the manuscript. If they buy photographs independently, they will normally buy the same rights they buy for articles and stories printed in their publications. Ideally, you should only sell one-time rights to photographs, the same as you would to an article, story, or poem.

Photo Rights

Q. When an editor says that "rights remain with the photographer," what does he mean?
A. In the case of a copyrighted magazine, this means that the editor is buying one-time rights only. In the case of an uncopyrighted magazine, the photographer would have to secure copyright protection for the photograph by requiring the editor to carry the copyright notice, year, and the photographer's name under the published picture.

Article/Photo Package?

Q. I submitted an article and fifteen photographs to a magazine and the article was printed with three of the pictures. However, I was not paid anything extra for the photographs. Is this common practice, or was it an oversight on the part of the editor?
A. Your situation is most likely one in which the magazine buys article and photographs as a package, implying one payment for the two items. Some editors buy pictures separately. Make sure you understand a particular editor's policy before you agree to sell him your work.

Photo Return

Q. Can I expect to have photos returned to me that are not used with an article? How can I indicate that I would like to have the unused ones returned?
A. The unused photos belong to you and you are justified in requesting their return. Enclose SASE with your submission and ask in your cover letter that unused photos be returned.

Slides and Transparencies

Q. I'm confused by the term "transparencies," which most editors use when discussing their requriements for color photos. Does it mean one thing to all editors, or does it mean slides to one editor and negatives to another?

A. "Slides" and "transparencies" are terms used synonymously by most editors when referring to positive color film. "Negatives" usually refers to black-and-white (b&w) film only. Most editors will not work with color prints, developed from color negatives. They prefer the reproduction quality of color slides.

Photos with Query?

Q. How many photos should I send with my article query?

A. You are trying to sell your *idea* in a query, and photos aren't usually included, but if a couple of good photos buttress that sales effort, include them. When it gets down to submitting a completed manuscript with photos included, some writers send contact sheets of their black-and-white photographs along with a couple of their best choices as 8x10 glossies. Rohn Engh, author of *Sell & Re-Sell Your Photos* doesn't recommend this—"don't display your less-than-perfect pictures by sending contact sheets," he says—and suggests rather that you submit only those 8x10s that you think best illustrate your article. If you have color shots, make sure they're transparencies, not color prints, and include up to twenty in one of the 8½x11-inch plastic sheets designed for submitting color to editors.

Photos—Who Pays?

Q. Are photos that have not been shot by the author, such as government or stock photos, paid for by the editor when included with a manuscript? If photos are considered part of the purchase price, does the editor have to pay for them? If so, who receives payment—the agency where you obtained the photos, the photographer who took the pictures, or the writer who submitted them?

A. If photographs are to be included in the purchase price of an article, then the writer will not be reimbursed for any extra costs involved in securing photos from the government or purchasing them from a stock agency. This is a good reminder for the author not to invest in stock photographs unless he is sure he'll make a sale and that the money he receives will cover those costs and allow him a profit.

Picture Problems

Q. I might have the chance to interview some celebrities this summer. I cannot take the pictures, but there is a good professional photographer in this city who can. He is a complete stranger to me. Should I contact him before I query an editor or should I get the writing assignment first? If the editor does not purchase the story and pictures separately, what percentage does the photographer usually get?

A. Before you query the editor, explain your project to the photographer and ask if he would be willing and available to furnish his services this summer. Reach an agreement with him regarding payment. (Being a professional, he will let *you* know his usual fees.) Then in your query to the editor, you can have the added advantage of informing him that you will be able to furnish professional photos of the interviewees. It is up to you to make sure you are paid enough to cover your expenses as well as your photographer's.

Artist/Writer

Q. As an artist and writer, I think I would do well as an illustrator for children's books or magazines, but how should I market my work?
A. Check the Book Publishers and Magazines sections of *Artist's Market* for publishers of children's literature. Then find copies of some of the works for children published by these companies, either in your local library or bookstore, or by writing to the magazine publishers for sample copies. As you study them to learn their styles and audiences, isolate two or three that you think might be interested in your work. Most magazine editors prefer artists to mail in a few samples and book publishers usually request an artist to mail them a portfolio or to arrange an interview in which he can present it himself. Editorial preferences are listed in *Artist's Market*. Also included in that guide are articles describing good market technique, portfolio preparation, tips on business practices, and your rights as an artist.

One-Time Permission

Q. If I used a Miami Seaquarium photo in a magazine article and it was given the appropriate credit line, could another author lift the photo and use it in his article as long as he transfers the credit line, giving the source proper recognition?
A. Since the photograph is the property of the Miami Seaquarium, each individual author must write for permission to use it. A credit line in one article does not imply permission is given to anyone else who wants to use it.

Illustration Permissions

Q. I hope to write a book on teaching high school art (I've had thirty-three years of experience in the field). Such a book would include the works of famous artists and sculptors, past and present. How do authors go about using reproductions of these works? Can I just cut pictures from books and magazines and include a byline of the creator, or would that be illegal?
A. You may use the clippings only to indicate your ideas in the manuscript you send to an editor. If the book is accepted, you will have to request permission and photographs of the works from the museums where they're housed. In addition to owning the pieces of art, museums also usually own the reproduction rights.

Reproduction Rights

Q. I bought two oil paintings done by an Arizona Indian a number of years ago and think they would make good illustrations for a children's book I'm doing. Since I own the paintings, would a credit line be sufficient?
A. No. Even though you own the paintings, reproduction rights still belong to the artist. You would have to contact the artist (or his heirs if he is dead) to obtain permission to reproduce the paintings as illustrations in your book.

Copyright

Q. A magazine is using a photo of mine (along with an article) which I would like to copyright separately. Never before have I used a photo which I thought I wanted to protect, so I'm not sure how to go about this.

A. If you wanted to copyright a photograph of yours you would have to advise the editor in advance so he could publish the copyright symbol alongside the photo with your name as the copyright owner. You would also have to write for the necessary copyright forms from the Register of Copyrights, Library of Congress, Washington DC 20559, fill them out and return them with the $10 copyright fee, and two copies of the published photo.

Photo Alterations?

Q. In a case where one of the branches of the military's promotional and public relations department sends a news release with illustrating photo to the news media, is it okay for newspapers to use one section of that photo (masking part of the persons) to illustrate a different news item?
A. It would be advisable for the newspaper to check with the military PR department on the use of that photo for a purpose other than was originally intended.

Limitations on Permission?

Q. I had an idea for a humorous piece in which I used several photographs. I obtained permission to use the photos, but I was not successful in selling my idea. Do I now lose the right to use these pictures?
A. Unless you had a detailed written agreement putting some limitation on the purpose or time period in which you could use the photographs, it seems that you would retain your right to them until you sell them with an article.

Reprint Permission?

Q. A nonfiction book I am writing would be greatly improved if I could use the charts and drawings from another book I found on the same subject. How can I do this? Who do I contact and how would the artwork be reproduced?
A. The usual procedure would be for the publisher to decide whether to write the original publisher for loan of the camera-ready art and reprint permission charges; or to write for permission and have his own art department redo the art. It's best for an author to only include photocopies of the art he wishes to obtain reprint permission on, when trying to find a publisher who is interested in the book.

Photography Training

Q. I've written and sold some articles and would like to offer photos with my future submissions. Where and how can I get training in photography?
A. Courses, seminars, and workshops offered through universities and other organizations can teach you the skill of taking photographs. *Photographer's Market* lists various workshops, and *A Survey of Motion Picture, Still Photography, and Graphic Arts Instruction* lists courses and degree programs in the three fields noted in its title. Both directories present listings from the U.S. and Canada. (Also see Chapter 2.)

Submitting Maps

Q. I am preparing a travel article for which I will need maps as part of the illustrations. I don't know what kind of maps to submit. Do I need permission to reproduce maps?

A. Maps are copyrightable, so permission would be necessary to reproduce previously published, copyrighted ones. Submit the maps you think best for your article along with the copyright owner's address so that the editor can write for reprint permission if he decides to use them.

Travel Book

Q. I have written a nonfiction travel book. Should I send photographs with my manuscript when I submit it?
A. First of all, editors rarely want to see unsolicited manuscripts for book-length work. Query your editor first and include several representative photos to show him what your illustration ideas are. Let him know that you can provide all photos needed for the book. After an editor has agreed to consider your manuscript for publication, send it to him with photos included.

Although some travel books, cookbooks, and books on photography are printed with color photographs, many other nonfiction books aren't. Using color illustrations greatly increases the cost of production, automatically leading to a higher cost for the consumer. So unless color photos are indispensable to your book idea, your chances of finding an interested editor are greater if you propose black-and-white photos, or don't use photos if they aren't absolutely necessary. And the editor may decide on his own that your manuscript should be illustrated with art rather than photos.

Illustrations for Poems?

Q. As a poet and artist could I submit illustrations to accompany my poems?
A. Some little magazines and small presses that have limited budgets for hiring illustrators might welcome illustrated manuscripts. Check the individual listings in *Writer's Market* to see if the editors mention any such preferences, or include an illustration with your poetry submission and get the editor's reaction. Most smaller publications use black-and-white sketches only.

24 How Do I Sell My Nonfiction Book?

The overwhelming majority—often 80 percent or more—of the 30,000 to 40,000 new titles published each year are nonfiction books. Freelancers who read the spring and fall announcement issues of *Publishers Weekly* can't help but mutter when reading some of the titles, "Now, why didn't I think of that?" Serious freelancers read announcements of new titles, then find what personal interests of theirs are translatable into a salable nonfiction book. What could be more appealing than to be able to research a subject you're interested in and have a publisher pay you to do it!

Book Proposal

Q. I'd like to write a book on vegetable gardening. I've had a lot of experience and have many resources at my disposal. I understand that to market my idea, I should come up with a book proposal. What is a book proposal?
A. A book proposal consists of a hard-sell cover letter, a sample of your writing—two or three finished chapters to allow the publisher to see your writing style—and an outline of the rest of the book, so the publisher can see where you plan to take your idea.

Your letter should convince the editor that there is a big market for your book and that you are most capable of writing it. Your outline can be a lettered and numbered topical breakdown, or it can be, as writers Barbara Toohey and June Bierman recommend, "small descriptive paragraphs that not only tell what will be covered in each chapter, but give the flavor of how it will be covered." They also suggest sending your proposal to several likely markets at the same time because editors are often slow about replying. Writing a book proposal will make you think your book all the way through, ultimately helping when it comes time to do the actual writing.

Travel Book

Q. I'm almost sure I have enough material gathered to be able to write travel books about England and Norway, but I don't know where to begin. I don't want to produce guidebooks, but would rather write descriptive books that could include some of my personal experiences. Ultimately, I'd hope that my memories would interest others in seeing these places. Can you help with my first step? Do I write a query letter?

A. As a first step, you must search for possible markets for your idea. Look (in the book publishers subject index section) of *Writer's Market* for publishers of travel books. Then go to your library, look up books of the type you'd like to sell, and match their publishers with your list from *Writer's Market*. Then send a query letter to the nonfiction editor at one of the publishing houses. In the letter, enclose an outline of your book and ask if the editor would like to see a sample chapter. If your idea is rejected, send the query to other publishers until you get an acceptance. If you can't find an interested publisher, it is possibly because the execution of your idea just isn't what the publishers think will sell. They may feel a guidebook for travelers is more practical, therefore more salable.

Your alternative would be to try to sell individual articles to travel magazines and other markets, although the preference here is largely for the practical rather than personal experience type of information.

Columns into Book

Q. I have copyrighted some printed material that I am trying to sell as columns to newspapers. If it is published in the papers and I then want to put the same material into book form, would I have any copyright problems?
A. As long as you are selling only simultaneous serial rights to the newspaper columns you have copyrighted, book rights belong to you. The best thing to do when submitting the printed column to the newspapers is to print in the upper right corner of the column, "North American Serial Rights Only." Be sure to request that newspaper editors print the copyright symbol, the year and your name, because if your column appears in an uncopyrighted newspaper without this notice, the column falls into the public domain. Your book must acknowledge the original copyright date of the columns.

Cookbook Market?

Q. Is there any market for cookbooks from unknowns, on such subjects as menu planning and preparing easy meals or full-fledged dinner parties? How does a writer go about breaking into this field?
A. It all depends on how appealing your ideas and writing style are, and your ability to find the right editor at the right time. Cookbooks have been bought from previously unknown writers. Send a query and brief outline to book publishers listed in *Writer's Market* who are interested in cookbooks.

Articles before Book?

Q. In writing a nonfiction book, is it advisable first to try to publish single chapters as magazine articles?
A. It isn't necessary to publish individual chapters because if your book idea is a good one, and your query convincing, you should be able to interest an editor. However, previously published articles can certainly be used to sell a book idea. They show the editor your abilities and that your idea is a marketable one. If you do sell your book chapters as articles first, make sure you don't sell all rights to the material. Some book manuscripts are rejected because they are simply a collection of articles. A successful nonfiction book has a definite focus and thread of continuity which runs from beginning to end.

Articles vs Books

Q. I've written a lot of articles but I don't know if I have what it takes to write a book. Do you have to be an expert on something to get a nonfiction book published?
A. A lot of what it takes to write magazine articles also applies to writing nonfiction books. In both cases, expertise is usually necessary to produce a successful how-to book or a work for a specialized or decidedly academic audience. However, other types of nonfiction, such as exposés, informational, or historical pieces can be written by anyone who has good research skills plus organizational and writing abilities. For instance, author Harry Neal has published 32 books on subjects as diverse as *Chicken, The Secret Service in Action Saga,* and *The Story of Offshore Oil.* The ideas for articles and books all come from the same cache; that is, from what the writer sees, hears, thinks, reads and knows. The book author must consider broad topic coverage and a diverse audience.

Bibliography

Q. I am writing a book which, though not an authoritative document, uses material from about twenty references. In all except one or two instances, I have taken no quotations from these sources. I don't wish to clutter up the book with a lot of reference symbols to indicate where I have drawn from sources. I would like to acknowledge all such unquoted references in an appendix. Can you advise me?
A. Why not simply prepare a bibliography to accompany your manuscript and precede it with a statement such as, "The author acknowledges the following references used in preparation of this text: . . ." If your publisher prefers a different method, you can work that out between you. Where you have quoted directly, you should footnote within the text the appropriate books quoted.

Humor Book

Q. I have a book-length manuscript on wit and humor which is in the form of quips, jokes, doggerel, etc. What first step do you advise me to take?
A. In your local library or bookshop, find some humor books and then query those publishers. Also consult the subject index list of book publishers in *Writer's Market.* If you cannot sell this material in book form, you may want to sell small batches to magazines as fillers, or to cartoonists who buy gags. Write the cartoonist in care of the magazine that publishes his work.

Obtaining Permission

Q. I am writing a how-to book. Do I need permission to use names and addresses of sources of equipment and supplies necessary to execute the project I explain in the book? What about obtaining permission for titles, authors, and publishers of books I recommend for supplementary reading?
A. It is not necessary to request permission for use of book titles in your bibliography, but you should check with suppliers for permission to include their names and addresses in your reference list to make sure their equipment and supplies will be available as long as your book is in print. General suggestions, such as what heading to consult in the Yellow Pages or what type of store would carry the products, are very helpful to the reader.

Unauthorized Biography

Q. What is the difference between an authorized and an unauthorized biography?
A. An authorized biography is written with the cooperation of the person it's about—or his estate, if he's deceased. This means the writer has access to in-depth interviews with the subject and his family and friends, and to private records and correspondence. In some cases the writer shares byline, advance, and royalties with the subject. Authorized biographies are sometimes rejected by the critics for their lack of objectivity. An unauthorized biography, on the other hand, is written without the cooperation of the subject or his estate. Publication of these works is strongly based in current public interest and they cover such people as television personalities, rock stars, sports heroes and political figures. Although there have been claims that a celebrity has the right to write and/or authorize his own biography, the courts have not upheld them.

True Biography?

Q. In writing a biography about a deceased person, do you have to be careful about what you tell, or can you tell the truth?
A. Most state laws prevent the heirs of a person from suing for either libel or invasion of privacy. Usually these suits only can be brought by a living person who feels he has been defamed or his privacy invaded. In writing about a deceased person, if you also discuss others who are living, be sure of your facts, since the truth (if you can prove it) is the best defense against libel. Truth is not a defense, however, against invasion of privacy, so if you have any qualms about possible suits from living persons on that score, you had best either get releases or eliminate those references.

Marketable Biography?

Q. Through my experience as a freelancer, I have had contact with someone who would make a good biography subject. If I write the book, I think it will have national appeal. Any suggestions on how I can get started?
A. Depending on the situation, it might be wise to discuss the possibility of a biography with your subject before you approach any publishers. Whatever you decide, look in *Writer's Market* and find publishers interested in biographies, and query one of them, indicating your contact with the proposed subject and why he or she would make a salable biography. If you fail to find an interested publisher, it may be because the publishers don't think your idea would sell well. You will have to rethink it and either change the emphasis or abandon the idea. Once you *do* receive a positive response, your research is cut out for you. If you've already interviewed and written an article on your subject, you've got a head start. However, you should read all other material written about the person as well. Then approach the subject, family members, and close acquaintances for interviews. In planning the book, you will need to know about outstanding events and conflicts that your subject has encountered so that you can show how he became the person he is now. Earlier biographies were usually done in strict chronological order, but now they often open with some dramatic episode attesting to the subject's character and/or fame, and later recapitulate the formative years. A sound knowledge of your subject and of the other people strongly influencing him is necessary to write a strong and viable biography. But avoid tedious detail and references to relatively unimportant people. Focus on highlights and the impact such events had on the subject's life.

For a list of comprehensive guides to writing biography, check *Subject Guide to Books in*

Print under "Biography as a Literary Form." Reading plenty of contemporary biography will give you a good idea of what publishers are interested in these days. Titles of single and collective biographies currently in print can be found under the heading "Biography" in *Subject Guide to Books in Print.*

Not Authoritative

Q. My nonfiction book was rejected by a publisher who said it wasn't "authoritative" enough. What does that mean, and how can I solve the problem?
A. If the book wasn't authoritative enough, you are not adequately qualified to write about the subject, which is reflected by a lack of quotes from "experts" or authorities. Such knowledge shows the publisher that a writer has done his homework, and gives the manuscript that air of expertise that makes it salable. Even if you are an accomplished person in the field, talking to other authorities makes a better-rounded book.

To find experts in a specific field, look in *The Directory of Directories,* found in the reference section of most libraries. This book lists guides to specialized directories in many subject areas which can lead you to the authorities you need.

(For more information on finding experts, see Chapter 7.)

Textbook Idea

Q. I've taught high school English for almost twenty-five years, and in that time have come across some common major weaknesses in the grammar texts I have had to use. I'd like to write a text of my own, but I don't know how to approach a publisher with my idea. Can you help?
A. Look in *Writer's Market* for publishers specializing in the subject and level of your proposed text. Unless a publisher's listing states a letter of inquiry is necessary, you should send a prospectus that includes your experience and qualifications, a brief statement of title, contents and purpose of your text, a description of your competition (and a statement of why your approach is better), and samples of material you've written and tested in the classroom. Thus, short of sending a complete manuscript, you will be presenting as comprehensive a picture of your proposal as possible. A publisher should respond within four to six weeks with either a polite rejection, a request for more material, suggestions for reworking your idea, or, in the rarest of cases, a contract.

Textbook Royalties

Q. I would like to know if textbook publishers have a standard royalty schedule. Does the same standard royalty apply to textbooks as well as to books in the trade division?
A. No, textbook publishers do not have a standard royalty or the same royalty schedule as trade book publishers. College textbooks may vary from 8 percent to 19 percent of the *net* price the publisher receives, while elementary and secondary texts may be only 3 percent to 5 percent based on the amount of illustration costs and staff work by the publisher.

Paperback vs Hardcover Book

Q. I have an idea for a paperback pocket reference book, but I'm getting nothing but rejections from paperback publishers. Should I give up and try a hardcover publisher?
A. Mass market paperback publishers can only afford to produce books that will appeal to *millions* of readers. If your nonfiction book idea is specialized, appealing only to a limited

market, no paperback publisher is likely to be interested. Study the book publishers' listings in *Writer's Market*, plus the appropriate subject bookshelves in the library and bookstores in your town, then make up your list of hardcover publisher prospects.

Mailing Book Manuscripts

Q. Please let us know what you think of sending book-length manuscripts in "jiffy bags," and enclosing correct return postage.
A. They're all right as long as you protect your manuscript with cardboard cut to just above the 8½x11-inch manuscript size to prevent page corners from bending.

How-To Book Manuscript

Q. How do I prepare a manuscript for a how-to book? About half of the published page will be pictures and diagrams.
A. The manuscript should be typed in the same way as other book manuscripts, with appropriate illustration references such as (See Figure 1) or (See photo, page 12). All diagrams and photographs should be numbered so that they correlate with both the text and a separate sheet listing captions. Standard photos are 8x10-inch black-and-white glossy prints and 35mm color transparencies. Diagrams are usually drawn on 8x10-inch sheets. Individual preferences will vary, so check with your publisher on this.

Photos for How-To Book

Q. Is it okay to include snapshots with my how-to book manuscript?
A. No. Most publishers want 8x10-inch black-and-white glossy photos or 35mm color transparencies (slides). Check *Photographer's Market* to see what individual publishers prefer. It's a good idea, when sending photos with your manuscript, to send a mixture of horizontal and vertical shots, so the editor has a better idea of how he might arrange the material on the pages of the book.

Submitting a Book

Q. What advice do you have for a writer submitting his first finished book to a publisher?
A. Keep a copy. If your manuscript is lost, the publisher will not pay for retyping. Do *not* bind or staple the pages. Many writers use empty stationery boxes to ship book-length manuscripts to publishers. Manuscript box suppliers advertise in *Writer's Digest*. The post office also sells mailing cartons. Check your local postmaster for sizes and prices. The least expensive mailing cost would be the Special Fourth Class—Manuscript rate. Be sure to mark "Return Postage Guaranteed" under your name and return address on the package. Enclose a self-addressed label with correct return postage. Type your name and address on the title page and your name and page number on each succeeding page in the upper left corner. Information in your covering letter should be specifically important. In a covering letter belongs a list of your previously published works only if of some importance and issued by a respected publisher, as well as information regarding documentary evidence to support any facts in the book that might be questioned.

25 Why Don't My Short Stories Sell?

When queried by a reader about how he worked, Somerset Maugham replied, "Madame, all the words I use in my stories can be found in the dictionary—it's just a matter of arranging them into the right sentences." All writers know that it isn't that easy. Once a beginning writer learns the necessary ingredients for a short story he is challenged not only to write it effectively but to get it to the right editor, at the right time.

What Is a Short Story?

Q. I like to write short stories, but my teachers have said that the things I write are not exactly stories. How can I find out what a short story is?
A. The basic elements of a short story include plot, setting, characters, and theme. What is it that turns these items into an appealing manuscript and a salable story? A story involves a logical connection of incidents. A story needs a character who, while participating in these incidents, meets conflict, either within himself, with another character, or with some other force outside of himself. Encountering the conflict and finding a resolution should leave the character changed in a way that he might not have been otherwise. It is this change, for better or worse, that makes a story. Consider for example the idea of two young boys on a Saturday afternoon fishing trip. If the author tells us about the nice time they had looking for the right spot along the bank to cast their lines and the large number of fish they caught before they trotted happily home, would it be a story? Not unless one of the boys, who always thought of himself as a coward, had to muster up his courage to save the other boy who fell into the rushing river and couldn't swim. Here a character is in conflict with what he sees as his own limitations and learns that he can go beyond them—and a series of incidents has become a story.

Look closely at what you've written. Does it contain character conflict, change and growth, or are you just relating a series of events that involve one or more characters? That may be the difference between what you've written and what a story is. Two good reference books written for the beginning short story writer are *How to Write Short Stories that Sell,* by Louise Boggess (1980), and the *Writer's Digest Handbook of Short Story Writing.*

Getting Started

Q. I have trouble translating thoughts to paper. I have stories in my head, but when I try to

write them, it becomes difficult. Do you have any suggestions?
A. Maybe you're worrying and concentrating too much in the beginning on *how* you put your thoughts to paper. Write in fragments, and don't be concerned about the style of writing or if the notes you are jotting make sense or are structured in any way. Or try dictating into a tape recorder—writers sometimes feel more comfortable "telling their stories," then transcribing them. Some writers write a synopsis of their story which makes it easier to organize their notes into a unified whole. Once they have decided what's going to happen in the story, and to whom, the words begin to flow. Then they do the final editing and polishing of the story.

Short-Short Story Length

Q. How long is a short-short story compared to a short story?
A. The average short-short story is from 500 to 2,000 words and the short story runs 2,500 to 5,000 words. Individual publishers may have varying requirements which would be listed in *Fiction Writer's Market*. For average word lengths on a variety of manuscripts—novel, play, juvenile book, etc.—see "How Long is a . . .?" in the Appendix.

Short vs Short-Short Story

Q. Besides the obvious one of length, are there any other differences between short stories and short-short stories?
A. Plot in a short story is limited to a small chain of events. It is confined in a short-short, however, to a single power-packed incident that gives the story its thematic value. There is no room for extensive character development; rather, it is the change of attitude of the central character in the incident which gives the story its depth. The writer doesn't try to do more than focus intensely on one truth of life that may or may not be new to the reader. Good subjects for short-shorts include changes in parent/child or husband/wife relationships, a child's awakening to some facet of life, or an individual's re-evaluation of his role in society.

Crisis vs Climax

Q. What is the difference between crisis and climax in a short story?
A. The crisis in a short story arises from conflict that leads to a turning point. After a series of obstacles, the major character experiences a dark moment in which he or she sees no way to solve the problem. Then there is a moment of revelation as the character figures out everything. The climax normally follows the crisis and represents the most intense point in the story line. Here the character finds the solution to his problem and often regains what he thought he lost. The story should end shortly thereafter.

Need a Message?

Q. Does my short story have to contain a message?
A. If you want to call it a short story rather than a sketch, an incident, or an anecdote, it should contain a message, or theme, that can be summarized in a single sentence. This gives your writing added purpose. It is not always advisable to start writing with a specific theme in mind, as you may try to elaborate on it in such a way that the story becomes mechanical and the characters unnatural. If you have the emotional involvement and present your character with an obstacle, your theme will most likely generate itself from your characters, setting, situation, and emotion. Some magazines, such as juvenile and confession publications, stress the

importance of the theme being stated directly somewhere in the story. It might be incorporated into the narrative after the moment of revelation, for instance, or into the main character's thoughts or speech as she reflects on what she has learned. Other magazines, such as science fiction and quality publications, prefer an implied theme, allowing the reader to relate to the theme in his own way.

Story Plants

Q. What is the difference between a plant and a false plant in a story?
A. A writer *plants* any information such as people, places, objects, or facts to be used later in the story so as to eliminate any possibility of coincidence. For example, in a short story, if an adventurer whose horse has died, and who is sun-parched and dying of thirst himself, is traversing the desert of the American Southwest and suddenly comes to an old deserted homestead that has a spring close by, the reader will be bewildered. Where did that house and spring come from? A good writer will find a way to plant them earlier in his story, thus getting rid of contrived coincidence.

The *false plant* is deliberately placed by the author although it has no connection with the conclusion or resolution of conflict in a short story. Introducing innocent suspects with viable motives in a mystery story is a common use of this device. False plants differ from *dangling plants* in that they are always adequately explained somewhere in the story. If the writer of that short story mentioned an old homestead with a spring close by, and didn't put it to some use later in the story, he would have placed a dangling plant. These can be annoying to editor and reader and should be avoided.

Weak Ending

Q. Looking at the short story I've written, I can see that the conclusion is weak and unconvincing. How can I fix it?
A. There are a couple of possible reasons for your disappointment in the ending. For one, is it too obvious? Is the outcome exactly what a reader would expect from your characters and plot? Your problem may be that you failed to plan for your ending before you started writing the story. If you were hoping something would come to you as the story progressed, and nothing did, your ending undoubtedly seems irrelevent or illogical. In either case, your solution will involve going back to the beginning of the story and doing some replotting. Make your major character's decision a difficult one rather than an obvious one. Or use the conflict structure to misdirect your reader, leading him to expect a different ending than what you finally give him. Changes like these must be incorporated into the whole story, for if you merely tack on an ending, it will remain inappropriate and weak because it is not justified by the rest of the story.

Story Outline

Q. Must I outline my story? What are the advantages? Outlining takes so much time.
A. Although it is not always necessary to construct a detailed outline before you begin to write, you will end up saving yourself a lot of time if you do some planning. As author Damon Knight says in *Creating Short Fiction,* "It is inefficient, certainly, to leap into a story without any idea where you will end up." It is inefficient because the less you know about your characters, setting, situation, and emotions you wish to convey, the harder it will be to decide what can and will happen in a story. Every author has his own method of planning and writing stories, and only trial and error will tell you what you need to know before you start to write.

It's a good idea to write your plan. Knight suggests that before you start writing you should at least know *who* the story is about, *why* they're doing what they're doing, *what* the story is about, *where* the story takes place and *when* it takes place.

Story Theme

Q. What is a story theme? Is it any different than a story problem?
A. A theme is the message an author imparts to his readers through the plot and characters in his story. The writer starts with an idea and as his story develops, it is influenced by his own philosophy or observation of the human condition. This is his theme. A story problem is the vehicle by which an author presents his theme. For instance, the problem facing Dorothy in *The Wizard of Oz* is getting home to Kansas from the Land of Oz. It is through her trials and adventures there that she learns of her folly in wanting to run away from home earlier in the film, finally deciding "there's no place like home," the overall theme of the story. Thomas Wolfe chose an opposing theme for his book, *You Can't Go Home Again.*

Transitions

Q. The transitions in my stories never seem to work. How can I handle them without being abrupt or taking too much time?
A. Scene transitions involve changes in time, place, and emotion. As Louise Boggess says in *How to Write Short Stories that Sell,* the key to smooth transition is to "link the old with the new." Boggess suggests that in the last paragraph of a scene, preferably the last sentence, the writer should indicate the present place and time period, and if possible, imply the new ones. Then the first sentence in the new scene can establish the time lapse and change of place. Note these points in the following example:

Natalee halfway hoped the Crandalls wouldn't like her antiques, but that must wait until tomorrow, she reminded herself, and tried to get some sleep.
The next morning worry about the Crandalls completely left her mind when . . .

Single Viewpoint

Q. An editor told me I should strive to present a single viewpoint in my short story. Why should I? How do I decide whether third person or first person is better?
A. In a short story, strong reader identification with one of the characters is very important and is easily lost when the author employs a multiple viewpoint. Suspense and continuity are often lost in the transition from one viewpoint to another. For these reasons, short stories told from more than one viewpoint are rarely successful. The choice between first and third person should be made with the plot, characters, and desired market in mind. Usually first person only can be subjective, lending itself well to strong emotion and fast reader identification. Third person, on the other hand, is useful if your plot and characters demand an objective treatment. Study your potential markets to determine what viewpoints are prevalent in the stories they publish.

Too Complicated Story

Q. One of the editors who rejected my story told me he liked the basic idea very much but the whole story was much too complicated. How can I simplify it?
A. If you have too much going on in your story, it may be because you've tried to incorporate

too many characters or incidents into it. You have to decide who the story is about and focus your narrative on that character and his problem. All other characters should be a part of the story you build around the major character. You may have to reduce arbitrarily the number of characters (to three or four at the most) and restructure your plot from there. The result should be greater simplicity and unity.

Implied Theme

Q. How does a writer get his point across in a story without repeating it?
A. It is through the change occurring in the major character as a result of his experiences that a writer often makes his point. In the course of the story, the major character must experience a moment of revelation and/or make a decision and, just as in real life, he changes as a result of these experiences. He wouldn't have to change from all-bad to all-good, but he should gain insight into a negative aspect of his personality and either decide to change it or accept that it cannot be changed. It is through these revelations and decisions that the writer sends his message, not through overtly stating it.

Who Buys Stories Today?

Q. There are very few magazines on the newsstands that contain stories. Magazines print mostly articles. Who buys stories today?
A. While a few major magazines—*The New Yorker, Esquire, Atlantic* and others—are still active fiction markets, the majority of markets for short stories are magazines that you won't find on the newsstand. Religious, juvenile and specialized consumer magazines all buy stories aimed toward their specific readerships and you'll find their requirements in *Fiction Writer's Market.*

True Confession?

Q. Should a confession story be completely true, or can it be fictional? Should the byline be a pen name?
A. The important thing about a confession story is that it *could* happen, not that it did. However, recently there has been a much greater emphasis on the reality of confession stories, or at least their basis in reality. Magazines are even requesting *readers* to send in their true life experiences. Readers go to the confessions for answers to their own problems, and what better way to write about alcoholism, divorce and unemployment than to draw upon real life? Of course, the incidents may be altered to dramatize or condense them, but most stories are based on true happenings. Most confessions do not give bylines, so it is unnecessary to be concerned about pen names. Only the editors know who the authors are . . . and they don't tell the readers! For more information, see the *Confession Writer's Handbook,* by Florence K. Palmer.

Male Confession Writer?

Q. Does a male writer, writing as a female, have a chance in the confession markets? Is it true that some of these publications require an affidavit attesting to the truth of the story?
A. Since confessions do not carry bylines, men have just as good a chance as women in this field, provided they can write convincingly. Most confession publications today require the writer to sign a release form that is not notarized, but attests to the originality of the story and the fact that it is based on true happenings you've experienced, heard about or know about.

Slow Motion Story

Q. I submitted my story to an editor and he returned it saying it was "too slow-paced." What is he talking about?
A. If your story is too slow-paced, you are giving too little attention to action and dialogue that moves the story toward the problem and its resolution. Editors often complain that stories written by beginners don't even start until page five of the manuscript. If the reader must watch the main character wake up, light a cigarette, make coffee and start breakfast before he learns what the problem in the story is, the story is too slow-paced. Since word space is so limited in short stories, the opening scene, as well as every other scene, should be short on exposition and quick to provide action and dialogue that engages the reader and is pertinent to the story's end.

Loose Ends

Q. When an editor says my story has loose ends, what does he mean?
A. Your story needs tightening up—inconsistencies need to be resolved. This may mean adding or omitting incidents or merely adding a phrase that refers to an earlier part of the story. Your story needs to be unified in time and action and the course of events must be logical. For instance, don't introduce some line of plot action for which the reader expects some meaning in the story and then arbitrarily drop it. It only confuses and annoys editor and reader.

Story Rambles?

Q. How do I detect rambling in my story? A teacher told me I was rambling at some places where I thought description was necessary.
A. Examine the passages your teacher marked and evaluate them for their relevancy to the story. Be able to define the purpose of each episode and descriptive passage. If you can't determine a function for each part, either discard it or rewrite it. If you determine that the information really is necessary, your teacher's assessment that it rambles is a sign that it should be incorporated into the story more subtly. For instance, can your spelled-out characterization be compressed into the character's actions or his dialogue? In *Creating Short Fiction*, Damon Knight says that "every passage must perform three or four functions at the same time—advance the plot, add to the characterizations, introduce background information, and so on . . ." Being able to write this concisely takes practice, but in the long run, your stories will be better and more salable.

Real Names?

Q. In a juvenile fiction story based on true historical incidents, may I use authentic names of teachers, mayors, ministers, businessmen, etc.?
A. If the people you mention were part of that historical event and were public figures at that time, there should be no problem with your use of their names.

Textbook Readers

Q. I would like to query textbook publishers with my ideas for textbook reader stories. Where can I find names of current publishers of textbook readers?
A. Check listings for book publishers in *Writer's Market*. The librarian in your local school system may also be able to provide you with names.

Role Playing

Q. I have often wondered whether a man can write effectively about a woman, or vice versa. If he is writing from the viewpoint of a woman or girl, could he possibly portray her problem and her various reactions to situations? Would he be better advised to choose a man as protagonist, or does it matter? What is the practice among successful writers?
A. There is enough proof in literature of the world that a writer can successfully portray a member of the opposite sex. Look at what Flaubert did with Madame Bovary, what Margaret Mitchell did with Rhett Butler, and Tennessee Williams did with Blanche Dubois, to name just a few. The ease with which a male writer can slip into the consciousness of a female character and vice versa depends ultimately on the individual writer and how much insight he has into the workings of human nature, regardless of sex.

Lead Time

Q. Can you give me information about the lead time required for submitting stories to quarterly publications? At the moment I am interested in submitting a Christmas story to a quarterly religious magazine.
A. A Christmas story for a quarterly publication should be submitted nine months to a year in advance. Lead times for monthly magazines vary from four months to a year, and for weekly publications, three to six months. Check with each editor for his preference. This information is often contained in the writer's guidelines which are available to potential contributors of a publication. Some listings in *Writer's Market* offer such guidelines to writers on request with accompanying SASE. (A business-size envelope will suffice unless otherwise specified.)

Downbeat Story Market?

Q. I have written a story about a woman's emotional disintegration as various pressures upon her reach the point where she can no longer cope with them. It does not end happily. A recent rejection comment was, ". . . it's a little too grim to be entirely satisfactory to us." I believe this attitude toward an unhappy ending is shared by all women's magazines. And this is definitely a woman's story; it is not a confession. I am discouraged, not by rejections per se, but by the apparent lack of markets for this kind of story. Do you have any suggestions?
A. If the caliber of your writing is high, you could try the quality markets, such as *Atlantic, Harper's* or some of the university literary magazines. Bear in mind, though, that your story must have something to say to readers above and beyond the mere chronicling of one woman's misfortunes. It must in some way deepen readers' insight through its larger view of life.

Rule Breakers

Q. Maugham and Hemingway were considered great writers, but most of their short stories did not have plots—that is, "conflict." If either writer were alive today, would his stories sell?
A. Works that have become classics have the ability to go beyond the narrow time in which they were produced because of the universal truths and insights they offer. The stories of these writers do sell today because of their authors' inherent skill in bringing characters to life and making their problems interesting. Their work deals with the conflicts of man's relation to man and to himself.

Story Titles

Q. In submitting short fiction to general slick magazines, what is the best procedure to follow when a good title does not come to mind? Is it better to submit an untitled story or to submit a title that does not satisfy the author? In these circumstances, should a letter accompany the piece explaining that a title is lacking and the author would like the story titled by the magazine, or that the author feels the title submitted is unsatisfactory?
A. Titles are often changed by the magazines, but a good title is more than a label; it's often an enticement to read the story. For purposes of identification, it *is* advisable for a manuscript to have a title, so choose the best one you can rather than none at all. Do not enclose any explanatory letters.

Confession Rights

Q. I am writing a true confession story. If I sell it to a magazine, can I retain the rights to expand it into a novel?
A. If you sell only first serial rights to your story, it is yours to use as you wish. Often, if you have sold all rights to your story, you will be able to get them back on request. Some confession publishers, however, publish reprints and may insist on purchasing all rights to a story. If you aren't sure about a publisher's policy, send a polite letter of inquiry.

Short Story Character

Q. How can I effectively create a character in the limited space of a short story?
A. Think of your character and examine him closely in your mind. Try to determine what is so unique about him that warrants a story. Try to find a single fact which sets him apart and gives him a recognizable trait. Then portray him in *one* sentence. Though difficult to write, one-line character descriptions can be extremely incisive and are definitely space-saving. For example, note this passage from Damon Knight's short story "Semper Fi": "Price came forward with his heron's gait, folded himself into a chair, twitched, knotted his thin fingers together." In one sentence we have a clue to Price's appearance and to his nervous emotional state. Character traits should not be thrown at the reader, but rather should be woven gradually into the story. Consider the difference between the above passage and "Price was a long, thin, nervous man." A writer should let words, actions and reactions be the defining features of a particular character.

More True-Life Problems

Q. My short story embraces a true event in a nineteenth century man's life which is recorded in newspapers and books. Can I properly call it fiction since two-thirds of the story contains my own dialogue and events?
A. Yes, it is permissible to fictionalize a historical event. Since you are creating the dialogue and much of the dramatic action, it can properly be called fiction.

Problem with Heirs?

Q. I know of no living relatives of the real-life character I am basing my short story on. Am I free to continue my short fiction without thought of his living heirs?
A. Go ahead and write your story, since most state laws say heirs can't sue—only the live person who is libeled or has had his privacy invaded. Many writers feel safer changing names, dates, and places in their stories.

Definitions, Please

Q. Fiction requirements of many magazines specify either "no contrived" or "no slick" stories. So far as I can determine, "contrived" means planned (what story isn't planned?) and "slick" means a slick paper (many types of stories are on slick paper). Please give me your definition of these terms.
A. By "contrived," editors usually mean plots whose action is constructed in an artificial, implausible way. For example, if a character purposely sets fire to a barn to kill the man inside, that's a credible, well-motivated act. But if a fire happens to break out in the barn for no reason other than the obvious one of helping the author dispose of the man inside, that's contrived. "Slick" *did* originally refer only the type of paper used in a magazine, but it has come to mean the familiar, formula-type story; for example, boy meets girl, loses girl, gets girl, which has a neat, pat (and usually happy) ending.

True Stories?

Q. Why aren't true-life experiences the best way of planning a story? How could I possibly improve on the way it really happened?
A. True-life experiences often make a good skeleton for a short story, but they usually need to be dramatized before they will interest others. If the basic action of your story needs a lot of exposition, which it invariably does, you may need to invent action and dialogue to get it across more effectively. Readers will be bored by a straight narrative explanation. If your characters are based upon people you are acquainted with, chances are you don't know them as well as a writer of fiction must know his characters. In order to provide them with sufficient motivation, you may have to provide traits that make them unique and worthy of the reader's sympathies. Plot may need changes in time span and in order of events so that it effectively moves the story along.

Book of Short Stories

Q. Do book publishers put out collections of short novels and stories that haven't previously been published?
A. Yes, but rarely. More often in the case of established writers, they prefer collections to be a combination of both published and new stories. In the case of an unknown writer, however, the publisher is usually reluctant to bring out a collection of work that has not stood the test of print. It is easier for the beginning writer to establish his reputation through periodicals, then try to get a book publisher interested in a collection.

Settings are Scenes

Q. How does a writer go about isolating a scene, in dissecting a short story? To me the scenes seem somewhat continuous. I fail to see any sharp dividing line in a taut story.
A. Whenever the action moves to a different setting, that's automatically a new scene. If, for example, a story opens in a young couple's kitchen, then moves to an incident in the husband's office, these two different settings constitute two different scenes. But suppose the story is a taut short-short in which all the action takes place in the kitchen. Then we look for a division that is not geographical but a time change. This could develop if your first scene shows the husband and wife in the kitchen at breakfast time. Then after setting this stage, you may want to have a time break to five o'clock when the wife is preparing dinner. This is a device used often.

For example, "Jim stomped out during breakfast without finishing his coffee. As Ellen prepared dinner, she thought of the silly argument they had had early that day."

Short Story/Novelette?

Q. It's hard to draw the line between short stories and novels, now that there are also novelettes and novellas. Just what are the differences in length, subject matter, and form in all of these types of fiction?
A. Although there are no set rules of length, the short story usually runs 2,000 to 5,000 words. The novelette and novella (editors use the terms interchangeably) can both be viewed as long short stories or short novels and will range anywhere from 7,000 to 40,000 words. Herman Melville's *Billy Budd* and Ernest Hemingway's *The Old Man and the Sea* are examples of this genre. Novels are the longest types of fiction. The structure is similar to that of a short story in that it presents a series of conflicts and temporary obstacles leading to a climax where the major conflict is resolved or accepted as unsolvable. The difference lies in the fact that the novelist has more time and word space to develop his plot and characters and can more easily change the viewpoint of the narrator.

Italicize Thoughts?

Q. When writing a short story, are you supposed to underline everything that is spoken or thought?
A. As a general rule, use quotation marks for dialogue spoken by story characters. Magazine styles vary for punctuating a character's thoughts: some use quotation marks, others put a character's thoughts in italics (meaning you should underline them in your manuscript), and others merely set them off with a comma and capitalize the first letter. Check out the magazine you're submitting your story to, so that you can match their form. If you are submitting to multiple markets, you most likely won't have the right style for every publication. If your story is purchased, it will undoubtedly be edited to conform to the magazine's style; but an effort to match the style shows your professional skill.

Formula/Nonformula Story

Q. What is the difference between a formula story and a nonformula story?
A. When editors speak of the formula story, they usually mean a familiar theme treated in a predictable or familiar plot structure, such as the formula plot of boy meets girl . . . etc. mentioned earlier. The editor who is looking for a nonformula story wants to get away from such plot situations and development. He wants an unusual central problem treated in an original manner. Very likely characterization and/or symbolism in the story will be more important than the situation, as can be seen in stories like Ernest Hemingway's "Big Two-Hearted River." You might find examples of other nonformula stories in magazines such as *Atlantic* or *The New Yorker,* and in some women's magazines as well.

Overstated Stories

Q. I'm taking a course in short story writing and my teacher keeps noting "overstatement" in my stories. But she's never given me a solid definition of the problem. Can you help?
A. Your teacher may be referring to what others call "overwriting" or "purple prose." Redundancies, an excess of adjectives and adverbs in descriptive passages, or an overplay of

emotion can all be considered overstatement. Passages that seem contrived or just don't fit the tenor of the story may be overwritten. While it's most easily spotted by someone other than the writer, you should develop the skill of recognizing and correcting this flaw which will obviously hinder sales.

Gimmicks

Q. I've read that some publishers accept "gimmicks" for publication. What does this term mean?

A. A gimmick is a short, mystery-type story giving clues to help the reader solve a puzzle or uncover a secret before checking the solution on another page. Gimmick stories are usually 500 to 1,000 words, and appear in crossword puzzle and game books, such as Dell's various puzzle publications. They are written in short story form up to the point of the climax, when the reader is asked an all-important question, the answer to which is intrinsic in solving the puzzle or "mystery."

There are at least three types of gimmick stories. One kind, the fact gimmick, involves some verifiable common knowledge needed to unravel the story, such as knowing the legal meaning of *hubeas corpus* Seasonal gimmicks are based on a fact tying in with a holiday or special season; they should be submitted to editors six to eight months before the tie-in date. The detective story gimmick is based on skillfully concealed clues that require no special knowledge to understand.

Successful gimmicks must be carefully constructed. Clues should not be unbelievable or contrived. Both content and "gimmick" must be believable if a writer wants to make a sale.

Fiction Techniques

Q. For the past ten years I have been active in religious work in a rural county. I want to write these experiences in book form. Each chapter will represent a short story with a unifying overall story thread and quite a bit of local color. What effects can I use to heighten story interest?

A. Use plenty of dialogue, including vivid human-interest details, build a mood (through weather, landscape, etc.), try to create suspense by suggesting your characters' emotional reactions to a situation and humorous observations about life in general as a result of some specific experience. Above all, keep your style lively and colorful so that readers will enjoy your narrator. Fictionalize the events and make enough changes in the characters so that they become *your* literary creations, even though originally based on real people.

Vignettes

Q. One rejection I received from a magazine editor stated, "We don't use vignettes or slice-of-life pieces." What does that mean?

A. A "slice of life" story or vignette is usually one that depends less on plot for its interest than on mood and atmosphere and the detail with which the setting and/or environment and their effects on the characters are described. *Writer's Encyclopedia* describes it as "a seemingly unselective presentation of life as it is; a brief, illuminating look at a realistic rather than a constructed situation, revealed to the reader without comment or interpretation by the author." This form does have a plan, however, and the viewpoint character experiences at least a slight change. Since it is not strongly based in plot, this form is most often published in the literary and little magazines, rather than in the larger commercial magazines.

Pays on Publication

Q. When a story is accepted with "payment on publication," is payment to the writer assured?
A. Payment on publication is risky, though it is sometimes necessary to the beginning writer trying to get established. No, there is never a guarantee that an article will be published or paid for when it's accepted by the "pays on publication" market. Sometimes an article is accepted, with payment promised on publication, but editors change their minds and the piece is eventually returned to the author neither used nor paid for. Most publications, though they may take a long time to actually publish the piece, will pay after publication. It doesn't happen too often that you don't get paid, so it's worth the risk, if you want to get published. In the case of new markets that pay on publication, you have the risk that they may fold (discontinue publication) after one or two issues are published, and you'll never be paid. If a magazine folds, you will not be paid, but you are free to submit that material to other markets.

Fiction Research

Q. I would like to set my story in the city of Detroit. Do I have to use real names of streets and places, or can I mix fiction with fact?
A. If you're going to use a real city as the setting of your story, you had better use names of real streets and places. It will give your story authenticity. Make sure all facts in your story are correct. Just because your story is fiction doesn't give you the right to present any factual inaccuracies. Fiction writers must spend time researching so that they can write with a sure knowledge of their subjects.

Do Credits Help?

Q. I have finally made a short story sale. Should I indicate this sale on the first page of future manuscripts to insure more careful consideration?
A. Since most editors prefer to judge a fiction manuscript solely on its own merit, it is better not to try to impress them with a list of credits. A record of past sales won't increase the chances of selling a good story or make a poor story any better. A list of insignificant sales is a sure sign of amateur status.

Downbeat Story Market?

Q. I have written a story about a woman's emotional disintegration as various pressures upon her reach the point where she can no longer cope with them. It does not end happily. A recent rejection comment was, ". . . it's a little too grim to be entirely satisfactory to us." I believe this attitude toward an unhappy ending is shared by all women's magazines. And this is definitely a woman's story; it is not a confession. I am discouraged, not by rejections per se, but by the apparent lack of markets for this kind of story. Do you have any suggestions?
A. If the caliber of your writing is high, you could try the quality markets, such as *Atlantic,*

Harper's, or some of the university literary magazines. Bear in mind, though, that your story must have something to say to readers above and beyond the mere chronicling of one woman's misfortunes. It must in some way deepen readers' insight through its larger view of life.

26 Can a New Writer Sell a Novel?

Susan Scarnecchia, an editorial assistant at G.P. Putnam's, had just finished reading a host of novel manuscripts, and wrote: "What makes a good novelist is not total recall, nor the ability to articulate 'the way it really happened.' It is the author's own peculiar vision—the world view that he has distilled from experience that makes what he writes worth reading." That challenge to separate reportage from representation, "to recollect experience, sift it down, spread it out in a new light and restructure it—not all of it, but select parts, not the whole truth as it happened to one man, but that element of his personal truth that may have meaning for many men,"—that's what drives the writer to the novel form, again and again.

Types of Fiction

Q. Explain what you mean by "genre" fiction. An editor said that's the kind of fiction he buys, but I've never seen any reference to it before now.
A. Genre fiction, sometimes called category fiction, includes stories that can be easily labeled, such as science fiction, fantasy, mystery, suspense, Gothic, Western, and erotica.

Mainstream/Experimental

Q. What are "experimental" and "mainstream" fiction and the differences between them?
A. Mainstream—the type of fiction that most often becomes a bestseller—employs conventional techniques to tell the story, while experimental fiction is unconventional Experimental novelists such as John Barth and William Burroughs share a common interest in form—style, structure, symbol, narrative technique—over and above the development of the "story." Beginning writers usually are urged to follow the traditional route for their first attempts, since markets for experimental fiction are limited.

Mystery Novel

Q. I've got a couple of good ideas for mystery stories, but I'm not quite sure how to go about getting them into the form of a novel. What are some of the basics one should be aware of before attempting to write a mystery?
A. One of the problems facing mystery writers today is a need for new ideas to revitalize the

genre. Be careful of imitating other popular writers too closely, although it's important to notice the format, style, techniques of the genre itself. Mystery writers often get so wrapped up in the intricacies of the puzzle that must be presented to the reader, that the novel ends up lacking any strong theme or well-rounded characters. Try to step back from your writing enough to be able to add some human elements to it. You can be sure you'll have a better chance of selling your manuscript. Some basic elements of mystery stories are described in Lawrence Treat's preface to the *Mystery Writer's Handbook*. He says that necessary components include a crime dastardly enough that the readers care about it (which usually means murder), a criminal that appears early in the story, though the reader doesn't have to know he's the bad guy, an honest author who, subtly or obviously, presents all of the clues to his reader, and a detective who *tries* to solve the mystery, meaning coincidences aren't allowed. For some other good novel-writing basics, see Lawrence Block's *Writing the Novel from Plot to Print*.

Unsolicited Mss Read?

Q. Do all large publishers read unsolicited manuscripts?
A. No. Publishers who won't accept unsolicited manuscripts usually indicate that in their listings in *Writer's Market* or *Fiction Writer's Market*. Others only accept agented manuscripts. Some publishers, however, will read queries only, then ask to see those manuscripts they want to consider.

Dialogue Revelations

Q. My writing teacher says dialogue has to do more than just let characters talk. What does she mean?
A. Besides the fact that good dialogue makes a novel easier to read by relieving the reader from long descriptive passages, it also effectively characterizes and adds to the reality of the speakers. It can take the place of long, tedious character descriptions. What and how a character speaks about herself, other characters and events should give messages as to her personality, emotions, attitudes, opinions, and desires. Good dialogue is also structured to convey a character's meaning, since voice inflection is not easily reproduced in print. Good dialogue must also advance the plot.

Dialogue Length

Q. Editors tell me my dialogue passages are too long, but I'm only telling it the way it is in real life. What's wrong?
A. You're probably doing too much in the way of "telling it the way it is in real life." You need to refine your dialogue so that you present the reader with only the *essence* of that reality. Conversation in real life is never as pointed as writers present it in fictional dialogue. Readers will be bored by dialogue that merely recounts the polite rituals and trite conversations that are a part of everyday life. Compress and focus your dialogue so that your characters get right to the point when they talk. All dialogue should either advance the plot, characterize the people, or both. If it doesn't do these things, it's not effective or necessary.

Query on a Novel?

Q. When a novel publisher wants a query first, what should go in the query letter?
A. As novelist Jean Hager says, "Query letters should be brief, but complete and persuasive. If at all possible, try to keep the letter to one page." Address the letter to a specific editor at the

publishing house, as listed in *Writer's Market* or *Fiction Writer's Market*. The first paragraph should state what kind of novel it is (for example, historical or contemporary romance), the approximate number of words in the manuscript and its title. In the second paragraph, describe in fifty to one-hundred words the general storyline of the book. Try to write this as though it were the selling "blurb" that might appear on the jacket. In the third paragraph, give quick sketches of your hero and heroine. In the next paragraph, include details about books you've previously published or any specialized expertise that qualifies you for writing this book. In a final paragraph, ask if the editor would like to see a synopsis and sample chapters, or the complete manuscript. In any case, ask for a copy of the publisher's editorial guidelines.

Chapters and Synopsis?

Q. Is it a good procedure to send the first few chapters of a novel to a publisher, with a synopsis of the rest of the novel?
A. Many publishers suggest a synopsis, sample chapters and cover letter rather than the complete novel manuscript. (This saves postage and wear and tear on the manuscript.) But if a publisher lists in *Writer's Market* that he prefers to receive the entire manuscript, then that's what you should send.

Mystery Length

Q. A close friend insists an editor will not accept a mystery novel if it exceeds 50,000 words. My novel will exceed this amount by 10,000 to 20,000 words. Will an editor insist I cut my words to reach his required length?
A. Publishers generally look for quality, not specific length. If any publisher were producing a series of mysteries with word limits, those requirements would be listed in *Writer's Market*.

Non-Sex Novel

Q. Must a novel include sex in order to sell to a publisher these days?
A. No. Many novels are published each year which have little or no sexual activity in the plot. A glance at the bookshelves and any of the major bestseller lists reveals many books which rely on plotting, characterization, and style rather than sex. The novels of Michael Crichton, for example, are diverse in setting and style; they contain little, if any, sex. If you don't feel comfortable putting sex into your novel and if you don't feel it advances the plot or deepens the characters, there's no reason to include it.

Novel Plan

Q. What kind of planning should I do before I start to write a novel? How detailed should my plan be?
A. Planning methods vary greatly among writers and writers will modify their systems as they gain experience and maturity. Some are satisfied with a general outline summary of the plot, the characters' problems and the resolution. Others may put together as much as fifty pages of detailed charts of action, character, and environment sketches. You might want to start by thinking the novel through and writing a skeleton plot. Novelist Tom Cook advocates exploring and outlining characters before doing any other writing, because if you know your characters well enough, a logical plot will be much easier to produce. However you do your planning, be sure to ask yourself plenty of exploratory questions and be flexible enough to anticipate needed changes in the plot. Most likely, as a beginning writer, the more detailed your

plan the better. It will save you from encountering dead ends and having to do endless writing.

Research

Q. How important is research in the novel?
A. Many beginning writers know a novel is a work of imagination, but seem unaware that the factual material in a novel must be as accurate as that in a nonfiction work. The fiction writer uses the same research tools as the nonfiction writer—sources on the period he is writing about, whether it's a Regency Romance or a novel set in the 1930s in the U.S. And the research must be carefully woven into the story, not dropped in awkwardly to interrupt the flow of the story. Study good novels to see how professional authors handle research.

Viewpoint/Person

Q. I'm writing a novel about two central characters. How do I decide which to use as my viewpoint character? What are the various advantages for writing in first and third person?
A. In using third person omniscient viewpoint, where both of your characters as well as other minor characters can become viewpoint characters, you can more easily develop subplots, develop suspense by allowing the reader to know more than the characters, and be freer to delve into the personalities of more than one character. Care must be taken to switch viewpoints only at scene changes—never within a scene. In the case of third person limited viewpoint, the author portrays only those events which involve one particular character. By showing the way the hero perceives and reacts to events throughout an entire novel, the author is able to make him very well-rounded and demanding of reader sympathy. First person viewpoint, which must also involve only one character, allows closer reader identification. However, all other characters must be developed only through their actions and dialogue as observed by the hero, which is difficult and limiting. To choose the best point of view for your story, you might try writing several different passages, each with a different point of view and central character. Play around with it a bit to see which you (and your characters) are most comfortable with. And once you've decided on a particular viewpoint, stick with it throughout the *entire novel*. Inconsistencies in viewpoint destroy the reality in your novel and will render it unsalable.

Synopsis/Outline

Q. I've read that many book publishers want a synopsis along with an outline for a fiction book proposal. How do I go about writing a synopsis? How is it different from an outline?
A. By synopsis most editors mean a comprehensive description of the basic plot of your novel. An outline, on the other hand, is a chapter-by-chapter summary of your plot. In it you should introduce all of the characters, include subplots as well as the major plot, and you should reveal the ending. Your outline may be as long as twenty or thirty pages, depending on the length and complexity of your novel.

Reader Identification

Q. I am writing a novel about a fourteen-year-old ballerina. She is telling the story. I am concerned about reader identification. Will adult readers "identify" with a leading character of this age?
A. It's rare, but adult readers *have* been known to identify with younger heroes and heroines.

Shakespeare's Juliet was only about fourteen. Since there is presently a strong need for books geared to teenage interests, you might be wise to develop your story as juvenile fiction. With teenage girls making up most of your readers, you should have no worries about their identification with your young ballerina. Some editors report that young readers identify best with a central character who is a little older—not younger than themselves—so perhaps you'll want to make your ballerina fifteen or sixteen.

Technical Accuracy?

Q. In writing a novel concerning the life of a professional person, such as a laboratory technician, would the author need official verification of the accuracy of technical matter in it before a book publisher would publish it, assuming the rest of the book was of publishable quality?
A. In a cover letter, it might be helpful to state the sources on which the technical information is based. If the publisher is interested and requires further substantiation, he will let you know.

The Rules?

Q. I am doing research for a proposed biographical novel. The famous people on whom I am basing my novel lived in the early 1800s. I am not always able to get to an original letter or document written by the subject, so I am taking material from factual books by other authors in which they quote from these originals. Can you tell me the rules about biographical novels? Must I get permission from all the authors I have read in order to provide character dialogue? Must I get permission from the people who have the original letters, manuscripts or documents, if I can find them? And how about a book that was written in this 1800 period by the famed person himself? May I use his material to build my character? Could living descendents of these famed people object?
A. In a novel of this type, you could acknowledge, in an introduction or preface, the sources on which the factual material is based. Write to the book publishers, describing your project and asking their permission to use information in the letters they published. To be on the safe side, you might also write to the publisher of the book written by the famous character himself, requesting permission to make use of that material. As for the descendants, there is the delicate question of the "right of privacy." Since each state has its own laws about this right, consult a lawyer who could advise you how much latitude you have under law. Incidentally, a fact worth remembering is that playwright-producer Dore Schary paid $18,615 to Franklin D. Roosevelt, Jr. to compensate for "loss of privacy" brought about by *Sunrise at Campobello*.

Time in the Novel

Q. I have had a novel in mind for almost ten years. My insurmountable problem is one of skillfully covering too many years without taking the reader's mind like a kangaroo on a long journey. Please advise whether to 1) cut down on the number of years covered in the novel; 2) cut down on the detail during those years; 3) cut down on both of the above; 4) lengthen the novel to include both, then return later with a more skillful knife.
A. First you'll have to decide exactly how many years the story needs. If the same basic story can be told in either five or fifteen years, by all means choose the shorter period. Remember that for dramatic purposes, you can telescope events that might, in real life, be spread over several years. Regardless of how much time the story spans, you must be discriminating in your choice of detail. Don't include anything that does not keep the action moving forward

toward the climax. Avoid all irrelevancies and descriptions for description's sake. Important incidents will be developed in full scenes. But information of minor significance can sometimes be handled by brief transitional summaries that link the highlights together. Flashback can help a story make a time leap, but this technique should be used sparingly because too much hopping back and forth between the past and the present can create havoc with readers' time sense. For additional tips on novel writing, see *Writing the Novel: From Plot to Print,* by Lawrence Block.

Posthumous Work

Q. My husband, a freelance writer, died two years ago, leaving numerous stories, several novels and other material which has not been published. I would like to submit the novels to publishers. How do I go about doing this? Must I mention the circumstances when submitting the novel?
A. If the book is accepted by a publisher, you could then explain the situation, since the book contract would have to take into account that you are his legal heir. Submit the manuscripts for judgment on their own merits, and don't mention the circumstances.

Opening Chapter

Q. I've found a publisher who's interested in my novel, although he wants me to revise parts of it. One of his complaints is that the exposition in the first chapter is too long. Can you tell me how much exposition I should have?
A. Everything in your exposition should have a purpose, whether it is to give tone or mood, describe the setting and time, for characterization, or to provide necessary background. One thing beginning writers often forget is that background information doesn't have to come in the first paragraphs of the novel. The reader doesn't need to know what you're telling him, and you're likely to lose him quickly if you start with a long uninteresting history. However, if you start off with an interesting situation that grabs the reader's attention, he will *demand* explanation. Then breaking into the flow of the plot is more easily justified. Author Nancy Ann Dibble puts it this way: "Make everybody fall out of the plane first, and *then* explain who they were and why they were in the plane to begin with."

Epistolary Novel

Q. What is an epistolary novel?
A. An epistolary novel is written completely throughout in the form of letters, usually letters to and from the protagonist. Both plot and characterization are achieved through the letters. Because it is a very demanding form for a writer, epistolary novels are not very prevalent today. However, it is an old form: the nineteenth century thriller *Dracula,* written by Bram Stoker, is in the form of letters and diary entries. Two more recent examples include Bob Randall's *The Fan* and Elizabeth F. Hailey's *A Woman of Independent Means,* both published in 1978.

Well-Rounded Character

Q. I've heard editors say how important it is for a character to be well-rounded. What makes a character well-rounded?
A. Well-rounded characters are distinctly individual because the writer allows the reader to see not only the physical aspects of a character but also the character's motivation, flaws,

emotional traits, and other distinctive qualities. These can be related through a character's actions, his reactions to situations and other characters, dialogue, and also through narrative. A flat character, in contrast, usually carries only one distinguishing trait. With the limitation of space, short story protagonists and minor characters in novels are often flat, whereas the protagonist in a good novel is invariably well-rounded.

Faction

Q. What does the word "faction" mean?
A. A work of faction is one that is written and sold as fiction, even though it's about real people and events. One form of faction, called the *roman à clef*, or "novel with a key," thinly disguises the famous people and events it portrays. An example is Robert Penn Warren's *All the King's Men,* whose central character most readers took to be the politician Huey Long. Some publishers use the word faction to describe novels in which a great deal of fact about a particular industry is woven into the story. Arthur Hailey's *Hotel* and *Wheels* are typical of this form of faction, because Hailey did extensive research into the factual operations of the industries he wrote about in his novels.

Organizing the Novel

Q. What makes up a chapter in a novel? How do I separate scenes within a chapter?
A. Exactly what and how much goes into a chapter is up to the individual author. Chapter divisions are an author's means of organizing the major events and developments in his novel. In planning the novel, a writer should have a general idea of the length of the chapters and what will go into each one so that he will be able to keep them balanced. Chapter breaks can provide easy transitions in time, place, or point of view. Changing scenes within a chapter can be accomplished by a simple paragraph change, starting the new one with a transitional phrase like, "The next morning, she promptly. . . ." Or it can be accomplished by leaving several blank lines between paragraphs, especially when the scene change also involves a change in viewpoint.

Timely Publication

Q. I've written a novel strongly based in football, and I know it would sell best if it came out during the fall season. What is the lead time required when submitting novels for seasonal publication?
A. There is at least a one year—sometimes two year—delay between the arrival of the finished manuscript at a book publishing company and the date the book appears in bookstores. And since you may have to allow a number of months for your query to find an interested publisher you can take that time into consideration as well. An established and reputable book publisher will time the release according to guidance from experts in the marketing department, so the seasonal aspect of publication date will probably be their responsibility rather than yours.

Novel Market Research

Q. I am completing a novel and am very interested in having it published. However, I've had no experience in getting a novel accepted. Where do I start?
A. Check the Book Publisher's section of *Writer's Market* for companies likely to be interested in your book. Then check the library or bookstores to see first-hand the kinds of novels the companies on your prospect list publish. The listings in *Writer's Market* will tell you

whether to send a query letter or several sample chapters and an outline/synopsis, to send the completed manuscript, or whether to submit through an agent. Send SASE with every submission.

Personal Style

Q. Is it permissible to have one scene in an outline or synopsis of a novel in your usual style of writing? It seems difficult to write in a straight narrative and give it the color of your own style.
A. Writers usually let editors see their writing style by submitting two or three sample chapters along with the novel outline and synopsis. This way, the synopsis can be as brief and pointed as possible, allowing the editor to see just what the story is about, and the outline can be a chapter-by-chapter summary of what occurs in the novel.

First Novel Publishers

Q. How can I find out which publishers are most likely to be interested in a new novelist?
A. The American Library Association publishes *Booklist Magazine,* which periodically lists profiles of first novelists and information about their books. This is a handy indicator of these publishers which consistently produce first novels, and a guide to their subject matter.

Switching Viewpoints

Q. I keep reading warnings not to switch viewpoints in the middle of a scene, but I can't seem to find out how to detect accidental shifts. What's wrong with switching viewpoints, anyway?
A. The reader needs time to shift gears as the viewpoint of the story changes. Switching viewpoint also destroys the reality of a scene. Through how many viewpoints do *you* see the world? Only one, of course. You cannot see into any mind other than your own, so you cannot perceive things any other way. You can only know as much about other people as is indicated by their actions and what they tell you. You can detect an accidental shift in viewpoint in a scene by noticing how many characters' minds you have entered as the writer. It should only be one.

The effectiveness of a single viewpoint per scene is apparent in Colleen McCullough's novel, *An Indecent Obsession.* In an early scene, Honour Langtry encounters Michael Wilson, and we learn of her growing love for him. But all we know about Michael is that Honour thinks he is aloof and therefore must not have similar feelings. His *true* feelings are not revealed. It is later, in a scene written from Michael's point of view that we learn of his deep love for Honour, even at that early encounter. The result? The reader can identify with and become more deeply involved with each character individually and the scenes can develop with more intensity.

Novel Money

Q. What kind of advance and royalties can I expect on my novel?
A. It depends on the publisher. Some companies produce only books sold to libraries, pay only a few hundred dollars advance and have a limited pressrun. Others will pay a larger advance and royalties based on the terms listed in *Writer's Market.* In general, hardcover books will pay 10 percent of either the retail price or the net moneys received by the publisher on the first five thousand copies and a sliding scale upward on subsequent sales. Mass market paperback publishers of original novels will usually pay an advance and royalties of 6 percent of the cover price on those copies sold. For more information on book contracts, see Chapter 38 on book publishing.

Series of Novels

Q. Is it proper to indicate in a cover letter that my novel is the first of a series? Also, may the publisher who accepted a portion of a series turn down any succeeding books in that series? Would it be ethical to submit these to another publisher?

A. Indicate the proposed series, but do it in an initial query, rather than in a cover letter sent with your manuscript. Don't send the complete manuscript unless the publisher asks for it. Check *Writer's Market* for submission requirements. It is possible that a publisher could accept one or two books in a series, then turn down succeeding books in a series. It is doubtful that the series could be divided among different publishers, but if you change the characters' names and make no references to events in previous books, there's no reason why these books couldn't be marketed on a separate basis without any tie-in with the series.

27 Does Anyone Buy Poetry?

The composer of *The Poet and Peasant Overture* must have known some freelance writers. Robert Graves remarked, "There's no money in poetry, but then there's no poetry in money either," and writers continue their pursuit of the perfect poem even though the rewards often are only psychic. For the beginner, the ability to write about intense personal experiences is eagerly sought but often denied. "The poet still has to find the verbal and technical means," says James Dickey. "You have to rely on form—the right words in the right order." Then the poem can be the Emersonian ideal: "as new as foam and as old as the rock."

Prose vs Poetry

Q. I find myself with many thoughts and emotions that I'd like to be able to express as poems. I've kept a journal for many years, but I can't seem to get from the prose to poetry. Any suggestions?
A. If you've never really studied the techniques of writing poetry, you should read some books on the subject, to get an idea of where to start. Poetry differs from prose in that it utilizes metaphors, similes, allusion, imagery, and sound patterns such as rhyme and alliteration. As is stated in *Writer's Encyclopedia*, "The emphasis in poetry is on economy of language—as the poet compresses as much meaning as possible into the fewest possible words, the language is elevated to a unique artistic expression." This may be something you should think about as you learn more about converting your journal into poetry. A good book to refer to is *The Poet's Handbook*, by Judson Jerome.

Poetry Markets

Q. Where can I find a list of current and new magazines that use poetry?
A. In Judson Jerome's monthly Poetry column in *Writer's Digest*. "Poetry Notes" lists poetry publications. While not all of the publications pay for poetry, they are excellent markets for beginning poets.

Publishing Poems

Q. Is it wise to let a "little magazine" use my poetry to get it into print or should I hold out for

better markets?
A. "Holding out" can be a frustrating game. There is prestige and satisfaction in being published by the "little magazines," so don't be afraid to try them—if they are copyrighted. "Little magazines" are the main avenue of publication, even for the best-known poets. If an uncopyrighted magazine accepts your poetry, make sure the editor runs your own copyright notice with the published poem.

Contest Poems

Q. If my poem wins a contest prize, will I retain the right to sell the poem to magazines?
A. Check carefully the contest rules for each contest you wish to enter. Some contests permit you to retain rights to your work; others do not.

Poetry not Selling?

Q. I have yet to sell one poem. What are some of the reasons poetry doesn't sell today?
A. It isn't original enough. Poets want to write about the everyday human emotions that stir us all—the birth of a baby, impending death, the strange quality that we call charisma—but unless the poet brings imaginative insight or language to the reader on the subject, editors won't buy it. In some cases, poetry has faulty construction or uneven meter. You've probably read many books on the principles of poetry, but it doesn't hurt to review them again and read the poetry in the magazines you want to sell to, to analyze what it is about those poems that made the editor buy them. Are there any magazines that print the kinds of poetry you like to read? If so, they're the magazines you should aim for.

Poetry "Batches"

Q. Why do some poetry markets ask that batches of ten to fifteen poems be submitted at one time? Surely, any one *poem speaks for itself.*
A. A single poem certainly does speak for itself, but a batch of poems gives the editor an idea of the style, versatility, and scope of your work, and a selection from which to choose.

Imagistic Poetry

Q. Please explain unimagistic *and* imagistic *in relation to poetry.*
A. Words that describe with some clarity the physical appearance of something are referred to as *images*. Thus, a poem that is *imagistic* is one that creates sensory impressions, or sense-pictures of the events or objects in the poem. Most images are visual, creating a focused photographic mental picture. But a good many images touch the other senses and permit us to participate in the aroma, spice and heft of the poem's subject. *Unimagistic* words are words which have no physical presence. Ideas, philosophical abstractions (for example, eternity, soul) are unimagistic words. Most dictionaries of literary terms give a more thorough definition (see *Imagery,*) and one that is especially useful for poets is *A Handbook to Literature,* ed. by W.F. Thrall and A. Hibbard, available at most public libraries.

Traditional Poetry

Q. When editorial listings in Writer's Market *say they'll accept "traditional forms" of poetry, what do they mean?*
A. The editor wants to make it clear that he will accept forms other than contemporary free

verse. He will accept poetry that rhymes and has a definite and consistent meter. There are some fixed forms of poetry that are considered traditional, like the Japanese haiku (sometimes mentioned specifically by editors in *Writer's Market*) and the five-line cinquain. The sonnet, which originated in the thirteenth century is almost always fourteen lines of iambic pentameter and follows one of several rhyme schemes. Much of what is considered traditional poetry (in terms of form rather than subject matter or theme) can be found in the works of many pre-twentieth century poets. "Traditional" may mean different things to different editors, so it's always best to study a particular publication before submitting any work to them.

Manuscript Style

Q. How should I prepare my manuscript when I'm submitting a poem? Should the byline be just beneath the title or in the upper right corner?
A. Type your name and address in the upper left corner of a plain white sheet of 8½x11-inch bond paper. The title of your poem should be centered above the body of the poem. Center the poem on the page, with equal distances above and below, and approximately the same margins to the left and right. You should double-space short poems, but you can use double- or single-spacing on long poems. If your poem is longer than one page, be sure to put your last name and the page number on all succeeding pages. As a last line, your byline should be typed off to the right so that it ends about where your average line ends.

Type only one poem per page. Include SASE with each submission.

Cover Letter?

Q. Do I need a cover letter when submitting poems?
A. No.

Light Verse

Q. What is light verse? What are some markets for it?
A. Light verse is a form of poetry (usually less than ten lines) intended only to amuse and entertain the reader, rather than to impart any deep literary message. It is marked by its wit and subtlety and conventional rhyme and meter schemes. Subject matter is varied, and light verse often deals with ordinary topics common to the experience of many, such as nature, personal and family relationships. Markets include most magazines, since light verse is universally appealing. In addition to listing markets for light verse, *Writer's Market* includes editorial requirements and pay rates for the individual magazines.

Poetry Definitions

Q. What is the difference between free verse and blank verse? Is rhyming in either necessary or optional?
A. Blank verse is unrhymed five foot iambic verse. Free verse does not follow any of the patterns of alternating accents and unaccents of metric verse. It sets up a music all its own which is neither a measured beat nor haphazard prose. As a general rule, lines that are not metric verse, accent verse, or prose are probably free verse. Free verse can be rhymed (as in some of Ogden Nash's work), but most frequently it isn't. Blank verse is not rhymed. For additional help with versification, consult *The Poet's Manual and Rhyming Dictionary* by Stillman and Whitfield.

No Sale

Q. I study the markets and I'm sure the poetry I submit is appropriate, but I haven't had an acceptance yet. What could be wrong with my poetry?
A. Your problem may lie in the technical form of your poetry. The diction, meter, line and stanza divisions, and sound patterns should all be an integral part of what you want your poem to say. Editors tend to reject poems in which the sound patterns (such as rhyme and alliteration) seem forced or overdone. Imagery that is trite and over-used, such as "the golden dawn" and "twinkling stars" is also a problem for many beginning poets. Make sure the rhythm, or meter, in your poetry is smooth and fits in with the other elements. Look for original word arrangements and relationships. Your poetry should involve the reader, showing, rather than telling him how you feel. There really is no definite answer to your question, since "good poetry is such a relative term." Spend some time studying the various techniques that go into writing poetry—and do a lot of practicing and revising. Study and analyze existing poetry, both traditional and contemporary. Study especially the poetry appearing in magazines you have submitted to. You might learn from seeing how the published work is different from your own. Above all, don't give up—keep submitting your poetry to editors.

Modern Poetry

Q. I don't understand most modern poetry. Is there some book which has taken these kinds of poems apart, analyzed them and discussed what the poet is saying?
A. Yes. *The Poet and the Poem* and *The Poet's Handbook,* both by Judson Jerome, have chapters on this subject along with discussions of other matters of interest to poets attempting to become professional poets.

Offbeat Poetry

Q. I write a poetry column for a local journal. Some of my recent poetry is unrhymed and has no regular rhythm. Readers constantly hound me with the comments, "That's a poem?" or "It doesn't rhyme!" or "It has no set rhythm!" The truth of the matter is, I have sold more so-called "offbeat" poetry than the "perfect" poem. What can I say to my readers?
A. Tell them you are writing free verse because that *is* the kind of poetry you're writing. Point out to those readers that this is an accepted literary tradition, followed by Walt Whitman and T.S. Eliot, to name just two.

Prize-Winning Poem Marketable?

Q. May a poem be offered for sale to a magazine if it was entered in a prize contest and read over the radio, or if it received a prize, or if it was circulated in a mimeographed brochure that carried notice that the author retains all rights?
A. Yes, such a poem may be submitted to professional markets, but some indication of its previous exposure should be included in a covering letter.

How to Submit Poetry

Q. Must poetry always be double-spaced? Length requirements are given in numbers of lines. Does the number of lines, then, replace the usual word count? Or should both be given? How should I arrange the manuscript for a book of verse? One poem to a page? If illustrations are offered, how should the page for which they are intended be indicated? What are the

established minimum or maximum length requirements for a book of verse? Is it wise to combine humorous and inspirational verse in a single volume?
A. Preferably all manuscripts should be double-spaced. It is not necessary to include a word count—only a line count. Prepare the manuscript with one poem to a page, in the order you prefer, and insert the illustrations, also one to a page, where you would like them in the printed version. In view of your two different themes, it might be helpful to divide the volume into two sections, with appropriate headings for the inspirational and humorous segments. There are no strict rules about length, but have at least twenty poems.

Resell Poems

Q. A few years ago, I had a volume of poetry published at my own expense. Fortunately, the books sold well. Now I would like to submit some of these poems to magazines, but have hesitated to do so as I'm not sure if this is permissible.
A. As long as the volume of poetry you had published at your own expense was copyrighted, then all rights to the poems still belong to you. It would be advisable to let the magazine editors know that your submissions originally appeared in book form.

Resubmit?

Q. My great-grandfather was a poet and published a book of poems. He had only three hundred books printed and distributed them to friends. The book went out of copyright years ago. There are some wonderful poems in this book and I would like to see them reprinted. Would it be legal to take these poems and have them reprinted in magazines? If this would be legal, would I still use his name on them or my own?
A. You could try to bring these poems to the attention of current magazines, but under no condition would it be ethical to sign your name to them. They are the original work of your great-grandfather and should remain so. If magazines decided to publish some of them, they would make payment to you, since you would, in effect, be acting as his agent. In such a case, assuming his other heirs were agreeable to your attempt to market the poems, the profits would be yours or yours and theirs as you agreed.

Idea Borrowing

Q. I have written and sold a poem based on an idea which I do not believe was original. Is such borrowing considered unethical?
A. Set your mind at ease. Ideas cannot be copyrighted, so you have done nothing unethical.

Poem in an Uncopyrighted Magazine

Q. Does having a poem published in an uncopyrighted magazine entitle it to be reprinted without author's knowledge or consent?
A. Unfortuntely, once the material appears without copyright notice, it falls into the public domain and anyone may make whatever use of it he wishes. This would include reprinting it without notifying the author.

Song Lyrics

Q. I write some poetry that I think would make good song lyrics, but I can't write music. How can I get some of my poems put to music?

A. Your best route is to collaborate with a musician. If you don't have contact with anyone who can write publishable music, you may have to seek musicians in your area and approach one of them about collaborating. Make sure that you are aware of a particular person's talent with melody before you approach him. Beware of "song sharks" that advertise in certain publications that, for a fee, will set your lyrics to music. Many are interested only in profit for themselves and will accept lyrics that have no chance of ever earning any money for the writer. Don't pay anyone for setting your words to music. It is better to collaborate with a song writer/musician and have a reputable publisher decide whether or not your work is good. (Also see Chapter 30.)

Adapted Poetry

Q. When my poetry is adapted to other forms—such as greeting cards and plaques—is my work being placed in the public domain, or do I retain my copyright?
A. Most companies that manufacture plaques, posters, and greeting cards purchase all rights to the copy they use. Copyright notices printed on the products are usually there to protect the company or, in the case of a syndicated cartoon feature, to protect the syndicate. Thus, in having your poetry adapted to these other forms, you don't necessarily put them in the public domain, but you do give up all of your rights to the material.

Poetry Markets

Q. I don't see much in the way of poetry collections on the bestseller lists. Is there a demand for it at all? I'd like to see mine published, but how do I decide where to send it?
A. The market for books of poetry is very small today, because only poets and a few readers with a serious interest are willing buyers of poetry. Most poets cannot make a living on the monetary returns, and a serious poet usually writes for his own pleasure, concentrating on the quality rather than the mass distribution of his work. Your best chance for publication is through the magazine markets. Read poetry published in the literary and quality magazines and find those magazines that publish poetry similar to yours in taste, skill, and values. If you think the editor would be interested, follow his submission guidelines (often listed on the same page as the magazine's masthead) and send him some of your work to consider.

If you don't feel your poems would suit this type of publication, you might want to explore the popular women's magazines, religious and inspirational magazines as well as general interest publications as possible markets. You can find many poetry markets listed in *Writer's Market* and in the *International Directory of Little Magazines and Small Presses*.

Reprint Rights

Q. If my poems have been sold to a magazine that buys all rights, how do I go about getting permission to publish them in a book? What if I only sold first North American serial rights? Is there any fee involved for getting permission to use my already published poems?
A. Write the original publishers to see if you can get all but first serial rights released to you for the purpose you mention. They may not release the rights to you, but they may grant permission to a book publisher to use them as long as the magazine's original copyright line appears on the acknowledgment page. If you only sold first North American serial rights, then all other rights belong to you and you need not get permission from the first publisher. Some magazine publishers who bought all rights may expect you or the book publisher to pay a permission fee. Those who bought only first rights should not expect a permissions fee.

Poetry Anthology

Q. Does being published in a poetry anthology count as a published credit in the same way publication in a magazine does?
A. If your poems appear in a published anthology, they can be listed as credits. On the other hand, if the anthology were the type requiring you to pay a fee or buy a copy to have your poems included, editors and your peers would not hold this in as high regard as publication in a magazine that paid *you* for the privilege.

Rewrite Tennyson?

Q. I recently rewrote a poem of Alfred Lord Tennyson's, using only a few of his original stanzas, and took the viewpoint of the woman rather than the man he had written about. Can this poem be published? If so, what type market would consider it?
A. Lord Tennyson's work is in the public domain, so you are free to write your own version of that poem. Since you do not indicate which poem it is, or whether your version is an amusing parody or a serious poem, it is difficult to suggest markets. But since appreciation of your poem would probably depend on the reader's familiarity with the original, some of the quality literary or quarterly magazines would be possible markets.

Poems in Newspapers

Q. Our weekly newspaper recently started a poetry corner and invited contributions of poems. I've contributed several and enjoyed seeing them in print. A friend tells me I've lost all rights to the poems I've sent in to the newspaper. Would I be able to sell them to a magazine? I hate to lose the poems, as someday I might want to put them in a book.
A. If the newspaper in which your poems appeared is not coyrighted (and some of them aren't) then your poems are now in the public domain and can be used by anyone, including you—if you want to submit them to other markets. You might be able to sell them to a magazine but the copyright of the magazine would not cover your particular poems since they are still in the public domain. And you must notify the magazine that your poems are in the public domain. If you assembled them later into a book, those particular poems are not covered by the copyright on the book. The only way this material can be coyrighted in the future is if you revise it, and submit it as original poetry.

Books of Poetry

Q. I have what I consider a worthwhile manuscript of poetry. Are there any publishers who would consider publishing it on a straight royalty basis?
A. Yes, there are publishers who have a regular royalty contract for poetry books (see the *Writer's Market* list of Book Publishers). However, most of them hesitate to gamble on an unknown poet and would prefer to publish poets with established reputations. To lay the groundwork for the possible future publication of your book, it would be helpful for you to get your poems published in magazines first, while retaining book publishing rights.

Missing Authors

Q. I am writing a small book of poems, and I wish to include a few poems given to me by a friend. She told me the lady who wrote the poems never published them. Both my friend and the writer are dead. I tried to contact the writer's sister but the postmaster did not know her.

Probably she is dead also. Should I use these poems in my book?
A. It is not advisable to use the poems given to you by a friend, since their publication with the author's byline might turn up some heirs who would frown on the use of this work. You seem to have made an effort to locate the author's sister, but you might open yourself to a legal problem here if you include these few poems.

Poetry Collection

Q. I have a collection of favorite poems by other writers which I've clipped from newspapers and magazines over the years. Can I publish them in book form? How do I go about it?
A. Yes, you could try to get your collection published as an anthology. However, in order to find an interested editor, you will have to be able to suggest to him something more than just a book of poems. Try to find a central theme that could unify them into a book. This may mean dropping some of them from your collection and searching for others. Query one or two publishers that you think might be interested. In your letter you'll have to argue your case to the editor—explaining why you think your book would be worth his risk, and include half a dozen or so of the poems you'd like to see in the book. If you find an interested publisher, you'll have to secure permission from the original publishers or authors for reprint.

Anthology Question

Q. Some of the poems I would like to include in my anthology come from uncopyrighted publications. Does this in any way affect my copyrighting the anthology as a whole?
A. If your anthology contains original and/or other copyrighted poems, you could copyright the collection. The acknowledgments page, however, would have to indicate those poems in the book which were previously copyrighted. You will have to get permission to use copyrighted material from either the poets or the magazines in which the poems were printed.

Rejections

Q. I keep getting form rejection notes. Does that mean my poetry's no good?
A. Although editors usually don't have the time to write comments on the rejection slips they send, rejection doesn't automatically mean your poetry is bad. It may mean that you're submitting your work to markets that don't publish the kind of poetry you write, or that the editors' files are overstocked. Always explore your markets carefully. You might also have better luck with some of the small literary magazines where poets can get a start. And if you keep reading and analyzing published contemporary poetry in the magazines you want to appear in, you will better prepare yourself to write salable poems.

Performance Is Not "Publication"

Q. I intend to give nonprofit readings of poetry that is under contract for future book publication. Would such reading in any way endanger my future copyright? Is there any good, practical reason to first copyright such poetry as a lecture, then later change its category to book?
A. Under the copyright law, your readings of poetry would not jeopardize your statutory copyright on your book—as long as you make sure no recordings are being made of your readings. If copies of such recordings were distributed with your authorization, these could jeopardize your future book copyright.

Group Poetry Submissions

Q. I'm sending my poetry to several magazines listed in Writer's Market. *Some magazines specify that the writer should send "4-6" or "3-5" poems. Since I will sell one, at the most, to each publication, I don't want to have the others tied up for a couple of months while an editor makes his decision. Couldn't I just send one poem and save time for everyone concerned?*
A. It would probably be all right to send only one poem, but it might be to your advantage to send three or four. Most poetry publishers specify the minimum limit because they want to see a fair representation of your work. If they like one of your poems, they'll probably like others just because they like your style. Go ahead and send in a group of poems. It can't hurt, and may help your publication record.

Simultaneous Poetry Submissions

Q. Is it okay to submit my poetry to more than one magazine or journal at the same time?
A. Major magazines usually expect to get an exclusive look at manuscripts they receive. But many of the small poetry magazines and journals are used to receiving multiple submissions, so sending your poetry to several of those publications is quite acceptable. Some, however, specify that they will *not* look at simultaneous submissions, so first check the listings in *Writer's Market.*

28 Is Writing for Children Easier than Writing for Adults?

In his National Book Award speech, Isaac Bashevis Singer gave a number of reasons why he began to write for children, and one of them was, "Children read books, not reviews. They don't give a hoot about critics." If a book is boring, children won't read it just because an adult says they "ought to." If a book is interesting and enjoyable, they can't wait to tell their friends to read it. Beginners who want to write for young readers must know what children are like to-day—not write only from their own remembrances. But when they successfully capture those emotions, dreams, and curiosities of childhood and adolescence, they'll find young readers eager for their stories, articles, and books.

Writing for Children

Q. I've written stories for adults for many years and would like to try writing for children. Can you give me some general advice concerning the differences between writing for children and writing for adults?

A. When it comes to the basics of producing a good story, there isn't much difference between writing for children and adults. As Lee Wyndham points out in *Writing for Children and Teenagers,* "The truly appealing [central] character is not wholly good or wholly bad, but possesses a balance of positive (good) and negative (bad) qualities." For instance, you must work in the same way to create believable characters with plausible motivations; strong plot is still important in stories for all age groups. Conflict and emotion must be integrated into the story. The difference is that all of these things must be accomplished with the simplicity and subject matter geared to young readers. Remember that a story that pleases an eight-year-old such as Beverly Cleary's *Ramona the Pest,* will not be very entertaining to a twelve-year-old who would be more interested in books by Paul Zindel and M. E. Kerr, so you must gear your stories accordingly.

You must be well aware of the problems and attitudes of children so that you can incorporate them realistically into your stories. Extent of characterization increases with the age of the reader, to the point that stories written for young people twelve-to-fifteen-years-old are different from stories written for adults only in the kinds of situations the characters face. Try to put yourself on the level of your reader so that you don't inadvertently "talk down" to or patronize him. The best way to get a feeling for how stories for children are written is to read lots and lots of them.

Research on Children's Books

Q. I'm trying to write books for children. I've been all through the library and bookstore in my town to see what's on the market right now. However, my town is very small, so I don't get the full picture. Are there any other resources available that would give me a good idea of the popular children's books presently in print?
A. The Children's Book Council (CBC), 67 Irving Place, New York NY 10003, offers several annotated bibliographies, free with a 6½x9½-inch SAE with first class postage for one ounce. "Children's Choices" is a list compiled annually from schoolchildren's votes on books selected by member publishers of the CBC. Write "Attn: Children's Choices" on the outside of the envelope when you request this list. Other lists available are "Outstanding Science Trade Books for Children" (write "Attn: NTSA" on the outside of the envelope), and "Notable Children's Trade Books in the Field of Social Studies" ("Attn: NCSS"). If you request all three lists, you must include first-class postage for two ounces. The CBC is an association of children's book publishers that works with groups in other fields through joint committees to create children's book programs.

Biographical Articles

Q. I've tried to write biographical pieces for children's magazines, but I can't seem to get the total picture of the subject's life into a short article that children would understand. Any suggestions?
A. One of the hardest things about writing biographies for juveniles is deciding what to leave out. This is especially true when the writer is confined to a piece the length of a magazine article. When researching your subject, pick out one important event and focus the entire article on it. You might concentrate on some childhood experience, if you are lucky enough to find information on it. (Read juvenile biographies by Jean Fritz to see how this author uses period detail to bring the *setting* of a subject's childhood to life in lieu of bonafide historical detail.) Then your ending can state what this child grew up to do that made him famous. Lacking any good information on your subject's childhood, it's still a good idea to open the article with a reference to his early years in order to let young readers know that these famous people were children once, too. Then focus the article on an incident important in your subject's adulthood— probably the one that made him famous—but keep it simple. Force yourself to delete anything extraneous, remembering that children don't have the conceptual framework to remember historical details. Keep your story to the editor's prescribed length. Most children's magazines will send editorial guidelines for a self-addressed stamped envelope.

The subject of a biography for juvenile magazines can be anyone with courage and determination whether it's the Revolution's Paul Revere or Gwendolyn Brooks, the American black poet.

Vocabulary Lists

Q. I am interested in writing children's stories for elementary school-aged children. Where can I obtain a suitable word list for these stories?
A. Publishers of trade books for leisure reading by children do not use formal vocabulary lists, but publishers of textbook readers for the primary grades often have formal restrictions on vocabulary (based on studies made in elementary schools). Consult individual publishers, enclosing SASE, for vocabulary requirements. Also, check your local library for books on readability that contain word lists.

Children's Magazines

Q. I've written a few short stories for children and would like to get them published. The problem is, I don't know how or where to sell them. I thought of sending them to magazines like Jack and Jill *or* Humpty Dumpty, *but I'm not sure if my stories would be suitable for those magazines. What would you advise?*
A. The magazines you mention would be primary places for you to sell your short stories. However, since these and other children's magazines are carefully geared to specific age levels of readers, you should get some sample copies of magazines you think might be prospects for your stories and read them before you submit your manuscripts to the editors. Other possible markets for your work are listed in the Juvenile section of *Writer's Market*.

Handicapped Children Stories

Q. I've written some stories aimed to help handicapped children deal with their problems. Do you think I could get them published?
A. You could look through the Juvenile section of *Writer's Market* for magazines that might be interested in your stories. Since the market for which your stories are written is very limited, you could try rewriting them to help the normally healthy child understand the handicapped person. You might want to write for sample copies of the juvenile magazines listed in *Writer's Market* that you think would be interested in your subject matter and study their styles to see how to prepare your manuscript.

Children's Stories

Q. I would like to specialize in writing for children, but I need some basic instruction in how to go about this. What do you suggest?
A. Two good basic references are *Writing for Children and Teenagers* by Lee Wyndham and *How to Write for Children and Young Adults: A Handbook* by Jane Fitz-Randolph. If you're interested in writing for very young children, *The Children's Picture Book: How to Write It, How to Sell It* by Ellen Roberts would be a good reference book.

Juveniles Seasonal?

Q. Is there a special time of year that material is read and accepted by publishers of children's books? If not, how far ahead should seasonal material be sent?
A. Most publishers read manuscripts year-round. Seasonal material should be submitted at least one year in advance, but book publishers work so far in advance that you probably will not see the finished product until the second season. One might expect a Christmas book submitted after Christmas and accepted in July to go into Christmas advertising the following summer.

Children's Books

Q. I'm interested in writing children's books, but I don't know how to prepare the manuscript. Should I include illustrations with my story?
A. Children's books are typed in standard manuscript format just like short stories and novels. It's usually best not to submit illustrations with the manuscript. An editor may like the story, but not the illustrations. He may think you're offering the text and illustrations as a package and would be unwilling to sell the text without illustrations. If you feel picture ideas are essential to the story, prepare a "dummy" book with pictures or picture ideas included. Make a

two-column text with illustration ideas facing the text of the story or cut up a copy of the manuscript and paste it into place with your rough sketches. Don't send this with your initial story manuscript, but mention in your covering letter that you have artwork ideas available if the editor would like to see them. Most editors of children's books have their own preferences for artists they like to work with, whose styles they like and who can work according to the firm's production specifications.

Juvenile Novels

Q. At what age do children start to enjoy juvenile novels? What kinds of subject matter are most popular?
A. Children eight- to twelve-years-old enjoy books of 20,000 to 40,000 words, and their interests are limitless. Detective stories are especially popular as first novel reading, but trends in subject matter for children's books often reflect trends in public interest. Realistic treatment of current themes, such as dealing with divorce and other problems of growing up in today's society, interest readers in the eight- to twelve- as well as the twelve- to fifteen-year age group. Books written for children in these groups are usually geared either for boys or girls, and the protagonist is always older by a year or two than the reader. Also, it is best to keep adult involvement in these stories to a minimum.

Age Level Is Important

Q. I have written a book (about children in Mexico) that I think could be the beginning of a great series (for children) about youngsters in foreign cultures. So far, publishers have rejected it, some saying that they like the idea, but that it isn't geared closely enough to any particular age group. I thought it would reach a larger audience that way. Any suggestions?
A. Two or three years' age difference in children can mean a vast difference in reading ability and topics of interest. For this reason, children's books, both fiction and nonfiction, must be geared to a specific age group. Your best bet is probably the eight- to twelve-year-old group, since these children are interested in a wide variety of topics. A good way for you to gear your book to a certain age group would be to make your central characters one or two children in Mexico in that age group, rather than presenting it in straight narrative form. In this way, readers have someone they can identify with and the reading is made all the more enjoyable. Remember to make your characters one or two years older than the age group for which your book is intended.

To see what other kinds of books about children in foreign cultures have been successful, see *Best Books for Children*, in your public library. It categorizes recommended books selected by librarians and other critics, both by subject matter and age level.

For a specific example of a novel for eight- to twelve-year-olds, set in Mexico, Elizabeth Borton De Trevino would be a good author to study.

Juvenile Readers

Q. What are the most common age-level groups for which juvenile publishers produce books?
A. Publishers differ, but Lee Wyndham, author of *Writing for Children and Teenagers*, describes five common groups: 1. Picture books for children ages two to five. 2. Picture story books to be read by adults to children ages six to nine. 3. Easy-to-read books for children ages six to nine to read themselves with their first- to third-grade skills. 4. Fiction and nonfiction for children ages eight to twelve. 5. Fiction and nonfiction for teenagers, ten to fifteen. Study each publisher's requirements in *Writer's Market* and write for editorial guidelines if available.

Fictional Dialogue in a Biography

Q. In the writing of biographies for children, is it possible to make the reading more interesting through use of fictional dialogue and setting? If so, to what extent can liberties be taken in order to assure a relatively accurate account of the nonfictional material while providing "readability" for youngsters?
A. Working with the basic facts, you may create conversations and incidents that will best dramatize them, but don't devise anything that would not be in keeping with the character of the subject or his times.

High/Low Books

Q. I've been hearing about "high interest, low level" readers and the market for books catering to this group. What age reader does this concern? Do you have any tips for writing these kinds of books?
A. Short stories and books for "high interest, low level" readers are written for high school students with about a third grade reading vocabulary, either because they are reluctant or slow readers, or they haven't yet learned to speak fluent English. These stories combine a high interest subject with a lower-level vocabulary. The writing must be direct and involve plenty of action, through dialogue rather than exposition. The plot must move quickly into the action so that the reluctant reader is immediately hooked. Subject matter should concern the problems of contemporary teens, such as drugs, dating, prejudice, family relations, etc.

If you plan to write for this group, you might investigate the readability formulas, such as those by Frye and Dale-Chall, that some publishers use when choosing and editing easy-reading manuscripts. Write the publishers for their individual guidelines.

It is best to write your story first, then check its readability. If readability is a concern as you write, a stiffness in your story could arise that might actually make it more difficult to read. If, after it's written, you determine the readability to be too high, you can lower it by simplifying the words and breaking up sentences.

Scholastic Scope magazine is published just for this group of readers and includes both short stories and nonfiction articles. Book publishers catering to these readers include E. P. Dutton, with their Skinny Book Series, and Franklin Watts. For other major publishers of "high/lo" books, check *Writer's Market*.

Audiovisual Markets

Q. Since so many schools these days have "media centers" instead of libraries, and teachers use films and filmstrips as teaching aids, how can I break into this audiovisual market?
A. Few film producers will accept scripts from any source other than a recognized agent, and few agents will accept work from a writer who isn't established, so you may have to break into the business through the back door, so to speak. Often adaptation of a successful book or story for use as a film or filmstrip will bring an author into the realm of audiovisual writing. Author Jane Fitz-Randolph suggests you set two goals for yourself: to get your work published in the print media and to learn as much as you can about film writing and production. Once you have achieved these goals, you will have a good grip on the techniques of writing a good story, and you will be ready to take on the additional, very exacting demands of the audiovisual media. Courses in television and film production offer practical help, as well as a possible route to contacts in various production companies. Producers listed in *Writer's Market* under "Scriptwriting/Business and Educational Writing" and "Scriptwriting/Screenwriting" will indicate their preferences for queries, unsolicited scripts, or scripts submitted through an

agent, as well as their specific needs in terms of films, filmstrips, and cable and regular television programs for adults and/or children.

Illustrations for Books

Q. What is the standard format for preparing illustrations for juvenile books? Also, is material considered more salable to juvenile publishers if accompanied by illustrations?
A. Publishers of juvenile books prefer manuscripts without illustrations, since they prefer to work directly with freelance or staff artists who know their requirements.

Film Market for Animal Stories?

Q. I am a professional storyteller via radio. I write children's stories and songs. My animal stories would lend themselves to film cartoons. Will you please advise me if there is an open market for this?
A. Most film companies work through agents or on the basis of assignment. Write to a West Coast agent (send $1.00 to the Writers' Guild of America, West, 8955 Beverly Blvd., Los Angeles CA 90048 for a copy of their list of agents). Tell him about your radio credits, asking for his representation for your stories with an animated film company.

Book Award

Q. Could you give me information on the Newbery and Caldecott awards? How do you get a book nominated?
A. These awards are given annually through the American Library Association by a member committee of children's and school librarians. Usually in November, members of the Association for Library Service to Children receive blanks for nominating their choices of published books for the awards. The Newbery Medal is awarded for fine writing, while the Caldecott Medal is awarded for excellence in illustration.

Children's Series

Q. I have an idea for a series of children's books. How would I sell this series to a publisher? What are my rights? What are the usual rates?
A. Query the publisher with an outline of the proposed series and sample chapters. The question of rights (such as book club, reprints, etc.) and rates, including the advance, would usually be negotiated by the writer or his agent with the publisher upon acceptance of the work and receipt of his contract terms. The usual royalties on a juvenile book are 5 percent to 15 percent, often split fifty/fifty with the illustrator. In some cases, where there are only a few illustrations, the illustrator is paid a flat fee and the author receives full royalty, which could vary from 5 to 10 percent, depending on the type of book, publisher, and author.

Fantasy Market?

Q. I've been trying to sell a children's fantasy with no luck at all. What could be wrong with my book?
A. Fantasy is difficult to write well because it demands from the writer the ability to make real the unreal, believable the unbelievable. If you are just starting out as a children's writer, you need practice writing here-and-now stories before you attempt to write fantasy. A solid

understanding of the techniques of plot, character, scene-building, and viewpoint are necessary because a fantasy story must be as logical as any other story. It must give the illusion of reality.

You don't say what kind of fantasy your story is, and it may be the kind that just isn't selling right now. The market for stories like the classical fairy tales of Andersen and the Brothers Grimm is nearly nonexistent. Editors are looking for stories that are totally different from anything published in the past or present. Popular fantasy books are those in which animals are personified—either as having human traits and participating in human activities, or merely as talking animals in a human world. Joseph Slate's *How Little Porcupine Played Christmas,* published in 1982, is an example of an animal fantasy. Dr. Seuss-type imaginary animals are much harder to sell. Few fantasies today feature inanimate objects, like the old favorite, *The Little Engine That Could.* Also popular with children of all ages are trips taken through time and/or space such as *The Tunnel to Yesterday,* by Jerome Beatty. Study the market carefully and strive for originality in your stories. Then you may find yourself making sales!

Juvenile Mysteries

Q. It seems like a lot of what makes up adult mystery novels, such as the severe crime, violence, and fearful suspense, just doesn't belong in juvenile mysteries. But what can be put into juvenile stories?
A. You are right in assuming juvenile mystery editors shy away from descriptive violence—especially murder. Most juvenile mysteries contain elements of humor along with hair-raising suspense that make the story effective. One key to success is knowing children well. Anything of interest to children in the age bracket you want to write for can be used as the subject of a mystery. Tight plotting and a fantastic climax are important, as is a main character who is actively involved in solving the problem of the story. To learn of current subject matter and techniques used in writing juvenile mysteries, spend some time reading and analyzing books from that section of your public library. To further study this genre, you might want to read books by Richard Peck, Jean Lowery Nixon and Mary Blount Christian.

Markets for Children's Own Writing

Q. I think my eleven-year-old niece has the potential to become a very good fiction writer. Her imagination seems boundless and she has a knack for developing good stories. Is there any way she could get some of her stories published?
A. Publications such as *Alive! for Young Teens, Christian Science Monitor, Highlights for Children* and *Scholastic Scope* all have sections for stories, poems, articles, and drawings by children. Furthermore, *Tigers and Lambs* and *Stone Soup* are magazines entirely written by children. *Seventeen, Straight, Teen Age* and *Tigerbeat* will sometimes accept material written by teenagers. Of course, each of these publications has its own editorial needs and submission formats, so you should study sample copies and look through *Writer's Market* before submitting. In some cases, your niece may have to include a letter from her teacher or a parent confirming the originality of the work.

Advance/Royalty on Children's Books

Q. A friend sold all rights to her children's book to a small publisher and only received a flat fee for the book. Is that common practice?
A. No, but whether a publisher pays an advance and royalties or buys outright varies with each company. Terms are presented in a contract which a writer can accept or decline.

Multiple Query

Q. My partner and I have collaborated on a children's book. She is doing the text and I am doing the illustrating. We sent several query letters to different publishers to see if they were interested in the material. We received a letter from a publisher who said he would like to see the material immediately, so we sent it to him. In the meantime, we have received answers to all our letters, all saying they are interested and would like to see the material. Can you tell us the best way to answer these letters? Also, can you tell us approximately what the going rate is on a book of this type? What can the writer and illustrator expect to receive?

A. You have two choices. You can write to the other publishers saying that your book is currently being considered by another company and enclose a copy of the manuscript. This might either heighten their interest or turn them off completely, depending on the editor. The other possibility is to write the other publishers saying you had decided to revise your manuscript before submitting it to them and that as soon as you have done that you'll send it to them. This will buy you a little time while waiting for the first publisher's decision. As for royalties on heavily illustrated books, they range from 10 to 15 percent with splits between author and illustrator depending on the amount of work by each.

29 How Do I Market My Script?

Some of the pitfalls of scriptwriting were pinpointed by Herbert Selby, Jr. in a *New York Times* article. "A couple of years ago a network was going to do a series on the Ten Commandments," he recalled, "and I wrote one of the two-hour segments. The entire project was ultimately cancelled, probably because it was too radical. But the thing that really amused me was the fact that the network only took five of the Commandments with an option on the other five. That, my friend, is television."

While most other manuscripts can be successfully marketed directly by the writer, scripts usually require the intermediary of an agent to make it to the producer. This chapter details this and other concerns of the playwright, TV or screenwriter.

Play Agent?

Q. I have been writing one- and two-act plays for little theaters. Is there a writer's guild? Is it necessary to submit play manuscripts through an agent?
A. Yes, there is a Writer's Guild of America but it is for radio, TV and film writers. For playwrights there is the Dramatists Guild of the Authors League of America (234 W. 44th St., New York NY 10036). There are some producers who do not require submissions through an agent. For a list of these as well as producers who work only through agents, see the Scriptwriting section of *Writer's Market*.

How to Submit

Q. How does a writer go about submitting his book or short story to a production studio for possible televising as a series?
A. Although you may occasionally see credits on the television screen such as "From a story by . . .," if you are an unknown writer, you would probably first have to rewrite your short story into an actual script. Producers won't look at ideas from unproduced writers. Most TV producers work through agents who know the markets for various story themes. You can obtain a list of TV agents by writing the Writers' Guild of America West, 8955 Beverly Blvd., Los Angeles CA 90048. The price is $1. For more details on how to approach an agent, and other information on where and how to sell TV scripts, see *The TV Scriptwriter's Handbook* by Alfred Brenner.

Movie Scripts

Q. I am writing a screenplay for the movie industry and need to learn more about the camera shots. I want someone familiar with movie writing to take parts of my screenplay and set them to the proper shots.
A. Your best bet would be to study some actual movie scripts to get a feel for how this is done. Several publishers have produced books that contain the complete scripts of both classic and contemporary movies. These include Ballantine Books, Viking Compass Books, and The University of Wisconsin Press. Also, companies which sell television and movie scripts advertise in the classified pages of *Writer's Digest.*

Dissolve/Fadeout

Q. When writing a screenplay format, what is the difference between "fadeout" and "dissolve," or are they synonymous?
A. The term "fade-out" is used only once, at the very end of the script, signalling its conclusion. "Dissolve" is used as a transition between scenes or short lapse of time within a scene. It is accomplished by having the first scene gradually disappear as the second scene appears.

Documentary

Q. What is a "documentary" and to what extent may a writer fictionalize and still maintain a "factual" format?
A. A documentary is a dramatically structured piece of work (writing, film, etc.) of an actual event. A movie or television documentary may combine elements of real people "playing" themselves and events recreated based on research and factual information about the subject. You can be flexible in fictionalizing these recreations, but don't stray from the actual facts, or you'll lose the credibility of the work.

Beginning Scriptwriter

Q. Can a beginner break into scriptwriting for TV or movies?
A. Yes. Articles about beginners breaking into scriptwriting have appeared in *Writer's Digest.* They were not overnight successes. They studied existing TV series, for example, and prepared complete scripts based on the characters in the series, whose personalities they're familiar with. They obtained names of agents from the Writers' Guild of America West, (Cost $1.) 8955 Beverly Blvd., Los Angeles CA 90048. They queried a few agents to see if they worked with previously unproduced writers, and included a description of the complete script they had to offer. Since writers for movies also need agents to represent them with producers, the same system would apply: a query to an agent with a description of the script available.

TV Script Length?

Q. Could you please tell me how many typewritten pages are in an average half-hour TV script and an hour-long teleplay?
A. There are about thirty pages in a half-hour script and sixty pages in an hour-long script.

Children's Plays

Q. My problem concerns a children's play I have written in which some of the characters are dolls or cartoon characters that have been made into dolls. Do I have to obtain permission from these doll manufacturers and the cartoon originators before I can use them? I would also appreciate any information you might give me concerning markets for children's plays.
A. Yes, you'll need to obtain permission. Write the doll manufacturers (any large shop can provide their names and addresses) and the cartoon originators in care of the movie studios or newspapers that present their work. Explain your project and request permission to use the characters' names in the way you have described. Be sure to enclose SASE. Some markets for children's plays are listed in *Writer's Market* under the playwriting, juvenile magazine, and education trade journals sections.

Playing Time

Q. What is the actual performing time per page of dialogue?
A. Since actors are not constantly in dialogue in a play (each manuscript page has a mix of dialogue and action in which dialogue is not present) the following figures are given for performing time per manuscript page rather than page of dialogue. The average playing time of a twenty- to thirty-minute one-act play is twenty to thirty typewritten double-spaced pages. A ninety minute to two-hour full-length play usually runs ninety to one-hundred-twenty double-spaced typewritten pages.

TV Series Idea

Q. I have a great idea for a television series. Can you sell ideas like this to other writers or to television networks or producers?
A. You can't sell ideas for either existing television programs or for a new series. Your idea must be presented in the form of a television script. And, since television producers usually will not look at scripts from writers directly, you'd best present your pilot script to a television agent. You can obtain a list of accredited agents for $1 from the Writers' Guild, 8955 Beverly Blvd., Los Angeles CA 90048.

Copyright before Production?

Q. Is it necessary to have copyrights on all scripts before they are used for production purposes?
A. Although "production" does not imply "publication," your play will be protected if it is copyrighted before it is used for production purposes. Show your copyright notice on all copies of the script. To register your scripts, write to the Register of Copyrights, Library of Congress, Washington DC 20559. Request application forms PA (Performing Arts). Then mail the filled-out form, two copies of the script and ten dollars to the copyright office.

Play into Film

Q. I have written a short religious play that has already been successfully produced. I think it would also work as a film. How do I find an interested producer? Who is responsible for adapting the play to a film script? How is my copyright affected by this adaption?
A. As creator of your play, you hold all rights to it, including the right to adapt it to film production. For a possible producer, check the Scriptwriting/Screenwriting chapter in *Writer's*

Market. If you find an interested film producer, he may want to assign another writer to do the adaptation. In that case, you and the producer can negotiate for film rights to your play.

Scriptwriting Information

Q. Where can I find information about scriptwriting?
A. Good sources are *The Complete Book of Scriptwriting,* by J. Michael Straczynski, and *The TV Scriptwriter's Handbook,* by Alfred Brenner. Also see the bimonthly Scripts column in *Writer's Digest,* which discusses writing scripts for plays, films, or TV and radio dramas.

Songs in Plays

Q. I'm planning to write a play based on a song. Is it necessary for me to get permission from the songwriter before publication of the play? What about songs that are used as incidental music in the play?
A. Yes, in either case, you must secure permission in advance from the copyright holders of a published song or record.

Movie Musical

Q. When writing a screenplay musical, is it necessary to collaborate with a composer or songwriter, or should the writer simply make insertions in the play where a song should enter?
A. Since motion picture producers have their own ideas about who should write the songs for musicals, your best bet would be to simply make insertions in the play where the song should enter, describing the type of song you have in mind, comparing it, perhaps, to a currently popular one. Remember—most motion picture producers will only look at scripts submitted through literary agents.

Selling Plays

Q. I need information concerning requirements for play submissions—whether sales are made on a cash or royalty basis, information about rights, and a list of reputable agents. I also need information on the Dramatists Guild contract that says the author can demand his living expense away from home on tour while participating in production. Does this pertain to previously unproduced authors or just members of the Guild?
A. Plays for the legitimate theater are handled through a dramatic agent. A list of dramatic agents appears in *The Literary Market Place,* available in most libraries. Payments are made on a royalty basis usually with an advance payment to the author before the play opens. For complete details on the Dramatists Guild contracts, write Dramatists Guild, 234 W. 44th St., New York NY 10036. Plays are copyrighted by sending a filled-out copyright application form PA (Performing Arts), two copies of the play and ten dollars to the Register of Copyrights, Library of Congress, Washington DC 20559.

Comparative Dialogue

Q. I am writing a play on a historical character. How would I incorporate exact quotations of his and other characters into my own dialogue? For example, in a papal brief I think I would have to use the exact words of the Pope and also the exact words of the reply, of personal letters, etc., that are in the public record. How would I do this and also use dialogue of my own creation?

A. Steep yourself in the life and speech of that historical period to the point where there would not be any noticeable difference between the verbatim quotes and the dialogue you invent, as Arthur Miller has done in *The Crucible*. Or, impose your own style of speech on the period, paraphrasing the sources to make them sound compatible with your characters' dialogue as in Robert Bolt's *A Man For All Seasons*.

TV Scripts

Q. On completion of an hour-long TV script adapted for a program that is filmed in California, would it be wiser to contact an agent in New York or California, or would it make any difference?
A. If the film producer is located in California, it would be better to work with an agent who is in that area.

Books on Playwriting

Q. I'd like to write a play. Can you recommend books for writers just starting in the field? I'm interested in basic books on how to write a play.
A. Books you might find useful are *The Art of Dramatic Writing*, by Lajos Egri and *How To Write a Play*, by Raymond Hull.

Script Protection

Q. How can a writer protect a TV script he has submitted to an agent?
A. Nonmembers of the Writers' Guild of America can mail their scripts to that Guild with a check for ten dollars and have the script's completion date registered. Registering simply verifies that you were the author of that particular script on that particular date should a similar story be subsequently produced and you wished to challenge the other author, the producer, or the agent. The address of the Writers' Guild West is 8955 Beverly Blvd., Los Angeles CA 90048. The price for registration is subject to change, so you might want to verify it before you send your script.

Permission to Adapt

Q. Several years ago I read a story that I felt would make a good TV play. If I adapt the story, whose permission do I have to get? Do I write the play first, or ask permission to adapt the story first?
A. You'd have to get permission from the original author to do a TV adaptation of the story. Write the author, in care of the magazine in which you saw the story before writing the adaptation, since there is the possibility permission may not be granted.

Radio Material

Q. What is the copyright status of radio broadcast material—helpful hints, short features, poetry, recipes, etc.? Can this material be reused verbatim or are there restrictions?
A. Radio scripts *can* be copyrighted, so your use of brief items should be governed by fair use guidelines. In considering fair use, decide: 1) whether use is for profit or nonprofit; 2) the nature of the copyrighted works; 3) how much you're using; 4) how it could affect the market value of the work you're quoting from. For an explanation of copyright and its application to radio and TV, see *Law & The Writer*.

Film Scripts

Q. In writing for industrial film production companies, are scripts prepared like TV scripts?
A. Industrial scripts are prepared like TV scripts. These film production companies are not preparing films for exhibition in regular movie theaters as you probably know. Their films are "nontheatrical" and specifically designed for industrial public relations use, for free loan to schools, libraries, community groups, and others.

Autobiography—Film

Q. I am writing a story about myself and my early life. I believe my story would make an interesting movie. How can I get it into the hands of the right producer? I am writing it in play form. Is this acceptable and where would I send it upon completion?
A. The play form is acceptable, but motion picture producers and studios will look at original scripts only if they are submitted through recognized agents. A list of these can be obtained (for $1) from the Writers' Guild West, 8955 Beverly Blvd., Los Angeles CA 90048.

TV "Treatment" and "Synopsis"

Q. What is the difference between "synopsis" and "treatment"?
A. A synopsis is a short, concise summary of the story. A "treatment" is a scene-by-scene explanation, indicating the specific action, motivation, possible special effects, etc. It provides a fuller interpretation of the script's potential. Established writers can sell a script on the basis of a treatment, but beginners must have a complete script if they wish to make that important first sale.

Submit Directly to Producer?

Q. Are there any conditions under which television producers will look at a script submitted directly by the writer rather than through an agent?
A. If you submit your script with a signed release form, similar to the one found in the Appendix of *Writer's Encyclopedia,* you *may* be able to get a producer to look at it. Among other things, the release form makes it clear that you understand your idea may not be new to the producer, and the company is under no obligation to you if, although your script is rejected, a similar idea appears later on television. To avoid having the script returned unopened, be sure to type "Release Form Enclosed" on the outside of the envelope.

More TV Markets?

Q. With the growth of the cable industry, it appears that there are a lot more opportunities for writers in broadcasting today. Is this true?
A. Yes. The increase in basic cable services has meant an increase in locally- and minority-oriented programming. The opportunities for beginning telescript writers are excellent, for these new stations provide an outlet and a place to gain experience for those who haven't had enough credits to sell to the big networks. Pay cable program producers, who started out sending viewers a wide selection of movies and variety specials, are beginning to see a need for more original programming in the form of soap operas, mini-series, weekly series, documentaries, and the like. Thus, these stations also open up many new avenues for the telescript writer.

Script Format

Q. I'm trying to break into movie and television writing. What's the proper way to type a script?
A. The basic difference between writing straight prose and writing scripts is that scripts also contain instructions regarding action, sound, light, and camera usage. These directions are typed single-spaced on a full-width line of type at the points in the script where they occur. Dialogue is typed single-spaced in a column in the page's center, indented ten spaces from the margin both left and right. Characters' names are typed in caps and centered over their dialogue. Acts and scenes are numbered. Double-space between scene directions and dialogue. The manuscript should be submitted in a softcover binder which can be purchased in a stationery store.

Play Format

Q. I'm writing plays for local productions. How do I type the dramatic form?
A. Center the character names over their lines, and type in capital letters. Single-space the dialogue directly under character names, indenting the first line of each speech. All stage directions are to be indented five spaces, enclosed in parentheses and underlined. Dialogue and stage directions are typed in caps and lower case. You might want to get some published plays from the library to help you get the usual pattern established in your mind. Like film scripts, plays should be submitted in a flexible binder; the exceptions are short one-act plays, which can be paper-clipped.

Radio Copy

Q. How many words will make an average radio story of sixty minutes?
A. Radio feature copy usually runs fifteen full-width double-spaced lines to equal one minute, so a sixty-minute radio story would run about thirty-six typed, double-spaced pages, twenty-five lines to the page, or nine thousand words.

Submitting Plays

Q. Do all plays—one-act or full-length plays—have to be bound before they are submitted to a play publisher, producer or little theater? Some contest rules state they consider only "bound" plays.
A. Very short plays can be submitted as loose pages held only by a paperclip. The request for "bound" plays means only that they should be submitted in a flexible binder, available in a stationery store.

30 How Can I Sell My Songs?

Unless a lyricist is also a musician, he must collaborate with a composer who can help him put his ideas and words into acceptable format; then find a music publisher or record company or recording artist, or advertising jingle buyer. The specialized field of songwriting has specific requirements that must be followed for success. Here are some guidelines.

Songwriting

Q. How can I learn to write songs? Is it easy to break into that area of writing?
A. Just as with any other type of writing, songwriting success comes with concentrated study of the existing market, practice, trial, and error. There are several ways you can get information and training. Many songwriters' organizations will send information on memberships, workshops, and other services they offer to both beginning and established songwriters. Helpful organizations include the American Guild of Authors and Composers/The Songwriter's Guild, 40 W. 57th St. New York NY 10019, Los Angeles Songwriter's Showcase, and Songwriter's Resources and Services, both at 6772 Hollywood Blvd., Hollywood CA 90028, and Nashville Songwriter's Association, International, 803 18th Ave. S., Nashville TN 37203.

There are also many helpful publications available: *If They Ask You, You Can Write a Song,* a book by Al Kasha & Joel Hirschorn, and *Songwriter's Market* (containing how-to articles on songwriting and listings of song buyers). A new magazine, with a column on song markets, is *Songwriter Connection,* 6640 Sunset Blvd., Suite 201, Hollywood CA 90028. Available workshops and classes listed in *Songwriter's Market* would also be beneficial. And be sure to check local colleges and universities for their course offerings in this area.

Song Published

Q. How do I go about getting my song published? I have music and lyrics.
A. There are two ways you can try to get your songs published. Song publishing companies look for new songs and peddle them to the artist and recording directors of record companies, or directly to artists who are looking for songs to record. These companies also handle the business end of music publishing, for example, demo-making, lead sheet preparation, and royalty payment agreements. Read carefully the listings of song publishers in *Songwriter's*

Market to determine what type of music they publish, what songs they've had recorded and by whom. Individual listings will specify whether to send a query first, or to send a demo tape and lyric sheet.

Although record companies usually depend on the publishing companies for songs to record, many will accept demo tapes directly from songwriters. Record companies listen to new songs with specific artists and projects in mind, so study their listings, too. Some indicate that first contact should be made through a publishing company. Whatever direction you take, it won't be easy, but if you stick with it and listen to any advice a knowledgeable person might give, you may be able to sell your songs.

Song Collaborator

Q. I can write lyrics and a sketchy melody for a song, but I need a co-writer to write the music. How much will I have to pay that person if a particular song makes it?
A. If a co-writer uses your melody, he is entitled to between 25 percent and 40 percent of the rights and resultant royalties. If you allow him to discard your original melody and write his own, he becomes an equal co-writer in terms of rights and royalties.

Advertising Jingles

Q. I would like to be a songwriter, but I haven't made any sales yet. Is there any other way I can make money with my abilities?
A. As you continue to practice and refine your songwriting talent, you might consider writing advertising jingles. You can try to get assignments from an advertising agency or sell directly to local businesses that don't employ advertising agencies. Advertising agencies don't look for a finished product in the demo tapes they listen to, they look for versatility and an ability to create a mood. Agencies listed in *Songwriter's Market* specify what types of clients they sell to and how they want samples to be submitted. Demo tapes submitted directly to businesses should cater to the needs of that particular company. Writer James Dearing has some advice for would-be jingle writers: "Before you begin recording, spend some time watching and listening to commercials. What do they say? How do the lyrics sell the product? Is the appeal 'hard' or 'soft' in its approach? Your jingles should closely approximate the ads now running. This isn't to say that originality isn't important. Advertisers are always looking for that special 'twist' that will make consumers notice and remember their advertisement. The twist can be your song—the way you meld lyrics and music into an identifiable, repetitive, even haunting, theme. A good jingle is really very much like a top forty song: It has to be catchy and have a strong hook that listeners will walk about humming or singing."

Contacting Popular Singer

Q. I just finished writing a song I know would be perfect for one of my favorite popular singers. How do I go about bringing my song to her attention?
A. Approach the person who produces your artist's albums, since he has the most say in the choice of material for the artist. Locating him may take some detective work. Start by finding out all you can in the way of names and addresses of your artist's record company, publishing company, producer and manager. Names can be found on album covers and record labels. Check *Songwriter's Market* for addresses and phone numbers. You may have to do further digging through phone directories. If you can't find an address or phone number for the producer, try calling the recording or publishing company that appeared on the album cover. They may be able to direct you to him so that you can call or write about submitting your work.

Song Played Locally?

Q. I've written a couple of songs that I'm sure would be acceptable to a couple of the radio stations around here. How can I get my songs played on the air by a disc jockey?
A. As a rule, disc jockeys play songs that are chosen by the program director of the radio station. These songs are almost always songs by major artists, recorded on major labels with thousands of dollars spent in promotion. The exception to this might be very small local stations, or a public broadcasting station, if your material is unique enough to merit air time. Submit your record to the Program Director, and keep in mind that songs will usually only be aired if the records are available for sale.

Song Title Protection

Q. I have several proposed titles to songs, and suggested lyrics for them, but I fear if they are sent to songwriting people, I'll have no protection. If I get a song copyrighted, can the title be stolen?
A. Titles are not subject to copyright, even though you copyright your lyrics. If you established prior use of the title, you might be able to prevent re-use of it by others through the challenge of unfair competition, rather than copyright infringement.

Songwriting

Q. I have a talent for songwriting and have composed many songs in my spare time, just for the fun of it. Now I would like to get serious about it. How can I inexpensively protect my material until I find out if it's any good?
A. Protect your songs by registering them for copyright. The price is ten dollars per song or "collection" of songs by the same writer(s). Write for application forms to the Register of Copyrights, Library of Congress, Washington DC 20559.

Music Markets?

Q. Where can I get a list of music markets?
A. Detailed editorial requirements of music publishers, record companies, and record producers appear in *Songwriter's Market*.

31 What Other Freelance Writing-Related Skills Can I Sell?

Freelance writers who think only in terms of articles, stories, poems, or books, often overlook hundreds of other opportunities awaiting the use of their writing skills, many of them in their own backyard. If you've been walking too narrow a path as a writer, broaden your horizons with some of the other ideas suggested in this chapter.

Local Writing Jobs

Q. I'm not making as much money as I had hoped I would as a freelance writer. Can you suggest other sources of extra income that might utilize my skills as a writer?
A. There are many part-time, seasonal, or "one-shot" opportunities that will help you during the lean periods of your writing career. For example, there might be a local advertising agency that needs someone to write an annual report or do other types of staff-related work for clients. Do you know of a national, regional, or local association that might need a newsletter, public relations help, or any other kind of writing help? You might also contact manufacturers about their need for technical writers. Local politicians and others of authority may be able to use your abilities as a speech writer. If your town is large enough to attract a convention, you might find out if any groups need someone to man the press office and act as a liaison with the local media. Are there any local printers in need of competent writing, copyediting, or proofreading for themselves or their customers? If you've had enough experience, you might consider teaching journalism at the high school or community college level. Use your Yellow Pages as a job finder and put on your sales hat! *Jobs for Writers* is a good book that describes many options open to writers.

Business Writer

Q. How can I, as a freelancer, get work writing brochures and other copy for businesses?
A. Many large corporations have full-time staffs to produce speeches, new-product literature, annual reports, articles, catalogs, brochures, and the like. However, a lot of this copy is purchased from advertising agencies, public relations firms, and freelance writers. The market is quite lucrative for the writer who has the patience and persistence to know and understand the market. Locate potential buyers in your area by studying *Million Dollar Directory* published by Dun & Bradstreet and probably available in your local library. This directory lists

alphabetically and by location companies that claim a certain amount in yearly sales. Talk to a local printer, who might have contact with both the local companies and the freelancers, to find out which companies might be in need of your work. Selling yourself to those companies is more difficult. Business writer Robert E. Heinemann recommends in-person queries. Having a referral always helps, too. Sometimes when dealing with small companies, you may have to ferret out the right person to approach for an interview. It may be the advertising manager, the public relations director, the vice-president of marketing, or a number of other people. When you do get in to talk to someone, don't suggest assignments. Rather, explain what you do and offer your services. If you've had no previous experience as a business writer, suggest that you'll work on speculation. Remember that this is not a hard-sell business. Buyers take their time when hiring for this kind of work, and the best thing you can do to get yourself some of those big assignments is to do a quality job on the little ones that come along first.

Technical Writing

Q. I have Bachelor's Degrees in both Engineering and English, so I think I would do well as a technical writer. What steps should I take to break into the field?
A. If there are no nearby large manufacturing or industrial plants where you can apply directly, your best bet would be to go through a "body shop"— an agency that provides technical writers and other services to manufacturers and research firms that need them. Look in the Yellow Pages under "Employment Contracts—Temporary Help" for the names of some of these organizations. This work is usually secured on a per-job basis. You might also look under "Technical Manual Preparation Service and Engineers—Consulting" for potential tech-writing jobs. If prospects in your area don't look good, you can find out about possibilities in near-by communities by writing C.E. Publications, Inc., Box A, Kenmore, WA 98028 for the current price of their *Directory of Contract Service Firms,* which lists 750 technical service firms throughout the world.

Speechwriting Ghost

Q. I have a talent for writing prose meant to be spoken. Is there any way I could find a speaker who needs a ghostwriter—that is, someone to write his material for him?
A. Politicians, business executives, educators, and community leaders often lack the time and skill to write a speech they've been asked to deliver. Chambers of commerce, large corporations, and community service and nonprofit organizations can sometimes let you know who needs a speechwriter; you can find the names of town leaders and local businessmen in the newspapers. Also advertise your services in the Yellow Pages under "Writers."

Once you've found a likely customer, submit a query, including samples of your writing and evidence of your knowledge and interest in the subject; deliver it in person whenever possible. Establish a price for the assignment, including a cash advance, and a first-draft deadline, at which time you and the speaker will smooth out any rough spots in the speech. The final draft is delivered to the speaker in some pre-arranged form, such as a typed manuscript accompanied by an outline on three by five index cards. The speech then becomes the permanent property of the speaker, who may use it as frequently as he wishes.

Fees for ghostwriting a speech could range from $100 for writing a six-minute talk for a local businessman, to $1,000 or more if you write for a national political figure. If you can find enough busy people with limited spare time and writing talent, you can make a writing career of putting your words in someone else's mouth!

Speech Length

Q. I'm writing a speech for a local businessperson. How do you measure the length of a speech in terms of how many words equal how many minutes?
A. Usually a speech can be measured in this way: two hundred fifty words equal about two minutes; or twelve to fifteen manuscript pages (typed, double-spaced) equal a one-half hour speech.

Research for Writers

Q. I once saw a request for someone to do research for other writers. How can I locate and obtain such a job?
A. Writers who need researchers advertise in writers' magazines, so watch the classified ads there.

Reviews

Q. I'd like to get started in theater and movie criticism, but don't know where to begin. Are there any shortcuts to the field?
A. One way beginners get started in theater and movie criticism or review is by writing sample reviews and sending them to local newspapers that don't have a staff critic. The newspapers sometimes can be persuaded to take the beginner on as a stringer—a part-time correspondent.

Book Reviews

Q. Do I need special training to write book reviews?
A. You don't need special training, but you should know how to write interesting, brief book reviews that editors will want to publish. Most local newspapers don't pay for reviews—although the reviewer gets to keep the book. See *Writer's Market* for magazines that pay for reviews. When contacting book review editors to see if they can use your work, enclose a sample review you've written of a relatively new book.

Payment for Reviews?

Q. As a freelance book reviewer, I have published work in several newspapers. From submission to publication, I have waited from two weeks to two months and have always been paid after publication. With my last three reviews, however, I have been waiting for three to six months without publication or payment. In each case, I asked to review a specific book, and the book editor sent the book. I read the books, researched, and wrote the reviews. I expected, from payment I'd received before, to receive a total of $130 for the reviews. Are these newspapers obligated to pay me for the reviews which they assigned to me and which I did as competently as any other reviews I've done?
A. Since so few newspapers pay for book reviews—other than the book and the byline—you were lucky to have collected cash for the previous reviews. Newspaper editors are not geared to working with freelancers, and under daily pressures rarely respond to letters of inquiry. The fact that you asked to review a certain book and the editor sent you the book doesn't necessarily mean he "assigned" the review to you nor is he legally obligated to use or pay for it. He sends out many books on request, and depending on space and the reviews, decides what to publish.

Advertising Copywriter

Q. What qualifications does a person need to write advertising copy? There must be hundreds of businesses that need copy, but how do I reach them?
A. To land freelance assignments with an advertising agency, you must have hard experience writing advertising copy. However, a willingness to study what's already been produced and for whom, and to hit the streets asking for business, could get you copywriting jobs in a number of different areas. Small businesses and industries which don't have advertising agencies usually rely on outside help for their advertising, and although they pay less than the big ad agencies, they are more willing to work with an inexperienced person. Retail department stores put out volumes of advertising copy in the media and in their direct mail catalogs. Newspapers, radio, and television stations often need people to write copy for their smaller advertisers who have no agency. Check *Standard Directory of Advertisers* in your local library. In a geographical supplement you should be able to find out which companies in your community use advertising agencies to write their copy. Companies which aren't listed either write their own advertising copy or hire freelancers to do it.

Advertising Slogans

Q. Can you offer suggestions for selling original mottoes and slogans for advertising?
A. Selling original mottoes and slogans for advertising is difficult since many national advertisers automatically reject any idea submissions of this type from individuals because they are afraid of plagiarism suits. A few freelancers have been successful in placing advertising slogans with local advertising agencies handling local clients' work. For your slogan ideas for nationally-distributed products, consult *Standard Directory of Advertisers*. Companies are grouped in this book by products. Select a company, then find from the listing which advertising agency is currently handling their account. Then write the advertising agency to find out whether they would be willing to look at your ideas and, if usable, pay you for them.

Copyright Advertising Art?

Q. Is advertising art and lettering published in national magazines copyrighted? I plan to use text, photos, and drawings from parts of different ads and combine them in a paste-up to be photocopied and printed as an original work.
A. Such work is copyrighted, so you will have to get permission to use it in any way.

Commercials

Q. Where can I find advertising agencies and companies that might use material I'm writing for commericals?
A. Very few advertising agencies will buy freelance material for commercials. You might try breaking into the business by approaching advertisers in your area. Ask for an appointment with the creative director. If you want to contact national companies, see *Standard Directory of Advertising Agencies* (available at large libraries), which lists names and addresses of manufacturers and their advertising agencies.

Family Histories

Q. Is there a market for freelancers interested in researching and writing other people's family histories? I'd like to try that kind of writing, but where do I find potential customers? How much will I get paid?

A. Most of the market for writing family histories comes from the elderly, so you could try placing ads in local newsletters to senior citizens, or on bulletin boards in places you know they gather. Direct mailing is often effective. You can get names and addresses of elderly in your area through senior citizen centers, church newsletters, and sometimes company pension rosters and labor union lists of retired personnel. If you make yourself known to area museums, librarians, and historians, they can refer inquiries to you.

Payment will vary according to the extent of research involved. One writer received one hundred dollars for editing research data that a family had already gathered, and one thousand dollars for a project that involved extensive research on his own. Depending on the client and the writer, research fees could range from five to thirty dollars per hour plus expenses. Your fee for writing would be added to this.

Comic Strip Idea

Q. How can I get my comic strip published? Can I get it copyrighted?

A. You can submit to newspaper markets yourself, or you can market your work to various national syndicates. (For more on syndication, see Chapter 21.) It would probably be best to try to sell your strip to noncompeting local markets first. When submitting to a newspaper or syndicate, you should have finished art samples to submit and a backlog of perhaps six months of ideas to carry on the strip.

You can copyright your strip, but it is expensive to copyright each one individually. Many nationally syndicates and persons syndicating their own material have a collection of strips copyrighted. For more information, contact the Register of Copyrights, Library of Congress, Washington DC 20559. Ask for Circular R44 on Cartoons and Comic Strips.

Comic Books

Q. Do the publishers of comic books buy freelance material? Is the story sent in standard manuscript form or is there a special form? Are there any books on the subject?

A. Comic book publishers have different policies concerning the purchase of freelance material. Usually the editorial staff determines current needs, then assigns a story to a writer and designates its length. There are no how-to books on the subject, but Marvel Comics Group Editor-in-Chief Jim Shooter recommends that beginners in the field start by writing for fanzines—small, often amateur productions devoted to study of the field. A "Fanzine Index" of such publications with their addresses appears in *The Fandom Directory* distributed by Bud Plant, Inc., Box 1886, Grass Valley CA 95945. For the budding comics writer, Shooter also recommends diverse reading "from classics to mythology to modern literature. Anything to lend inspiration to the imagination that is so essential to the writing of comics." When you're ready to submit ideas, most publishers prefer *brief* plot sypnoses of two pages maximum; since comics are a visual medium, only essentials are necessary to judge a story.

Freelance Indexes

Q. Do publishers use freelancers to index the books they put out? Do you have to be an expert in a subject before you can index a book on it? How can I get started in work like this?

A. Ideally, a book should be indexed by an expert, preferably the author himself, but many authors are not interested in learning this specific and tedious skill. A professional indexer must be prepared to do some research while putting together an index. Basic sources such as biographical, geographical, and historical dictionaries, a good set of encyclopedias, and an almanac, atlas, and thesaurus are usually adequate, though specialized sources would be needed for work of any technical nature.

In order to get indexing assignments you must have experience. To have been an editor or librarian helps. You might also look for an index you consider inadequate, work up a sample of how you would handle it, and submit it to a publisher along with your request for work.

Contact the American Society of Indexers at 235 Park Ave. S., 8th Floor, New York NY 10003 for information on how to get started in indexing. They will also be able to direct you to some of their workshops and seminars.

Copyediting/Proofreading

Q. What's the difference between copyediting and proofreading? Does anyone hire freelancers to do this type of work?
A. A copyeditor deals with a manuscript before it goes to the typesetter. He checks for proper syntax and spelling and makes sure the manuscript makes sense and reads well. Names and facts are verified, which means that a copyeditor must have some background in the subject his editing assignment covers. He looks for consistency in spelling, abbreviations and numbers, making sure they comply with the publishing house standards.

A proofreader compares typeset galley proofs with the original manuscript to make sure that nothing is omitted, added or changed. He also makes sure that the typesetter has followed specifications for typeface, style and margins. The proofreader must be on the lookout for mistakes in the original manuscript. This is very good training for copyediting. Some colleges offer courses in copyediting and proofreading. To locate firms that often need copyeditors and proofreaders on short notice and are willing to work with beginners, look under "Typesetting" in the Yellow Pages. If you live in a rural area, there may be no listings under this heading, so look under "Printing" for firms that advertise typesetting services. Whenever you apply for this type of work specify the fields in which you have enough background to be able to edit someone else's writing. As you build up credits and experience, you can approach some of the larger publishing houses.

Publisher's Proofreaders

Q. Are there book publishers who hire freelancers to do copyediting and proofreading work?
A. Larger publishers have more of this kind of freelance work available, but a small publishers may not have enough full-time work for regular employees, so they'd be prospects, too. Check listings in *Writer's Market* or *Literary Market Place* to locate publishers who produce one hundred or more books per year. These houses are probably your best prospects for work.

Cartoon Gags

Q. Can cartoonists be trusted not to steal my ideas if I send them batches of gag ideas for cartoons?
A. Cartoonists who are good illustrators, but who lack the original gaglines (cartoon captions) and ideas to create salable cartoons, are eager for good writers to work with them. Your concern that someone might steal your ideas is shared by others—article and short story writers. But it happens so rarely that it should in no way prevent you from sending work out for consideration.

Selling Gags

Q. I have gathered about 75,000 jokes and anecdotes covering American life from 1870 through today. Many of the sources were books and items which are out of print. I have also written my own gags. I would like to start a service furnishing gags or jokes to cartoonists at five dollars each—they select the topic they desire and I come up with the number of items they want under the topic. I have the gags under all headings. A separate file would be maintained for each customer. How can I start this service to help cartoonists with good material and to help me with part-time work?

A. Write to individual cartoonists in care of the magazine in which their work regularly appears. Also write to Gag Re-Cap Publications, Box 86, East Meadow NY 11554, which offers newsletters of interest to gagwriters.

Jokes for Sale

Q. Where can I find markets for jokes?

A. Markets for jokes include magazines, disc jockeys on radio stations, and comedians who work in nightclubs and on television. The magazine joke markets are listed in *Writer's Market*. Gags for disc jockeys can be submitted to them directly with SASE for return. Jokes submitted to nightclub comics are usually submitted to them in care of the club where they are performing. TV comedians depend almost entirely on staff writers, so there is not much of a freelance market for jokes for them.

Comedy Skits

Q. I've written several short comedy skits. Where and how can I submit them?

A. Much would depend on the subject matter and the level of humor that is employed. There are various possible markets such as TV, school productions, etc. If your skits could be used on TV, for example, you would have to submit them through an agent to specific TV entertainers. If the skits are one-act plays suitable for school productions, send them to play publishers who specialize in this area. Check *Writer's Market's* scriptwriting chapter.

Locating Entertainers

Q. Big-name entertainers have big-name writers, but I think my material would be welcome to some lesser-known comedian. Where can I find names and addresses of entertainers needing comedy routines?

A. Several avenues are open to you. Since it's helpful to know a comedian's style of delivery, watch for rising young entertainers on TV shows emceed by Merv Griffin and Johnny Carson, and contact these newcomers in care of those programs. You might also subscribe to *Variety*, the show business newspaper that mentions the names and places where lesser-known comedians appear. In fact, you might get this information from city newspapers. Write the performers in care of the clubs where they appear.

Humor for Sale

Q. I have written material I think is humorous. I'm interested in finding a market for this material, which is written in the form of comic dialogue. I'm also interested in finding an agent who could market it for me.

A. No agent will represent a client who writes humorous material unless the writer has already attained a certain amount of success on his own. Most beginning comedy writers write specific comedy material for nightclub comedians in their area or speakers at club gatherings, etc. If there are no such prospects in your community, see other questions in this chapter about contacting comedians who appear on TV or at resorts or big city nightclubs.

Humorous Monologues

Q. Who buys humorous monologues?
A. It depends on what the subject matter is and who the potential audience is. If, for example, your material is the type a nightclub comedian could use in his routine—he's your market. If it's material of the type that would appeal to a women's club—they're your market. A monologue implies a spoken delivery so there aren't many published markets for this type of material. If by humorous monologue you really mean short prose humor—these markets are scattered throughout *Writer's Market*.

New Agent

Q. I have been thrust into the position of "agent" and I need help! The book I've been asked to market is a good one (it's an exposé) and I have confidence in its salability. I know that since it is nonfiction, I need only send to prospective publishers two or three chapters, a table of contents, and the author's credentials. What I don't know is how to present myself as an agent. I am not familiar with book contracts or with agents' shop talk. Just what do I say in my covering letter?
A. Simply write a covering letter to the prospective publisher, indicating what you're enclosing on behalf of your client and why you think it's a good prospect for that firm, its market potential, and so on. If you're eligible to join the Authors Guild—because you've published a book or written for national magazines—do so, so that you can get and study their sample book contract. The Society of Author's Representatives (P.O. Box 650, Old Chelsea Station, New York NY 10113) publishes a pamphlet entitled *The Literary Agent*, which may be helpful. When requesting a copy, enclose SASE. Keep in mind that contracts will vary from publisher to publisher. The amount of advance and terms of subsidiary rights will also vary depending on whether the book author is a first-time writer or a well-established professional with a "name." Read *Publishers Weekly* to see what books are being published by whom and what kind of sales can be expected.

Company Book Author

Q. A computer company is willing to hire me to write a book on the uses of personal computers, with promotion of their products emphasized, of course. How much should I charge for my services?
A. Payments for this kind of work are usually in the form of a flat fee, and will vary with the size and importance of the company, your reputation as a writer, your evaluation of the extent and difficulty of the work involved, and what you think your time is worth. A booklet of twelve to sixteen pages might bring $750 to $2,000, while a hard-cover book of two hundred pages might bring $10,000 to $25,000 or more.

List of Translators?

Q. Is there a listing of translators with details on which languages they're proficient in? I'd

like to find out if my qualifications are acceptable to be included in such a listing.
A. There is a listing of translators in the directory, *Literary Market Place*. Send your qualifications to the editor of that directory, published by R.R. Bowker Co., 205 E. 42nd Street, New York NY 10017. If you qualify, there is no charge for your editorial listing.

Translator Job

Q. How can I get a job as a translator? I speak German and English equally well and am also an aspiring writer. Could I start by translating technical articles or books? If so, how?
A. Translation jobs are available primarily with companies that have technical reports and correspondence to translate, although a few book publishers might be prospects. A professional association of translators can supply additional information. Contact the American Translators Association, 109 Croton Ave., Ossining NY 10562. If there are companies in your city with foreign subsidiaries or foreign export markets, they also might be prospects.

Translation Markets

Q. What are the markets for translations of foreign stories, articles, and books?
A. Few magazines are interested in translation material, but you can contact any magazine whose subject matter is similar to what you propose. A few book publishers have published translations of previously-published foreign works. To find these publishers, see *Subject Guide to Books in Print* under the appropriate categories such as "French Fiction—Translations Into English." Other languages are similarly listed.

Resell Foreign Story

Q. I speak and read French and found a marvelous short story in a foreign magazine. I'd like to translate and sell the story to an American magazine. How do I do it?
A. If you have a facility with another language and would like to submit a translation of a foreign short story, you must write to the publication in which the foreign story appeared and get permission from the author and the publisher to do your translation. Whether you would be required to share payment from the American publisher with the original author and/or publisher depends on what arrangements you make with them. It's always best to clarify this point before you approach any American editor so there is no delay if he is interested in your idea.

32 How Do I Submit My Manuscript?

Can the manuscript be folded, or must it be flat? Should it be loose or in a binder? Typed on 8½x11-inch paper? When a freelancer has reached his final draft, he doesn't want his good idea jeopardized by poor submission technique, or a deadline missed because of slow mail delivery. Double-check the answers in this chapter—or in the chapters on poetry, novels, etc.—before putting your next submission in the mail.

How Much Personal Background?

Q. I'm a beginning writer, but I don't think I have to scream that fact to an editor. How much information should I include with a manuscript? Also, what do editors think of short manuscripts sent folded in half in 6½x9½-inch envelopes?
A. The only personal information necessary is your name and address in the upper left corner of your manuscript. A manuscript folded in half in a 6½x9½-inch envelope is satisfactory, but be sure to include SASE for the editor's reply or for the return of your manuscript if the editor can't use it.

Which Editor?

Q. I submitted a manuscript to a magazine, addressed to the top editor. The assistant to the editor replied: "Although we can't use this piece, we'd like to see more of your work." Now I have an idea for that magazine. Do I correspond with the assistant, or with the top editor, as I've done in the past?
A. Direct all future ideas or manuscripts to the person from whom you received the last correspondence. If it's the "assistant to the top editor," chances are your previous correspondence will be remembered and pulled from the files, and your current correspondence will go in to the top editor with a recommendation by this assistant, who no doubt handles the incoming mail.

Tearsheet Copy

Q. When an editor asks to see my work, can I send him a photocopy of my tearsheets instead of the original?

A. Several years ago, when photocopies faded and disintegrated easily, they were considered undesirable. New machines make copies on regular paper, so you can send an editor a photocopied clipping.

Tracing Lost Manuscripts

Q. I sent a manuscript to a magazine listed in Writer's Market. *I waited for a reply for three months, then sent a letter asking about the status of my manuscript. I received a card saying that they had no record of such a manuscript, that it most likely got lost in the mail. Fortunately, I do have a carbon copy of the manuscript. Is there any way of tracing a lost manuscript?*

A. If your manuscript was sent at the special fourth class rate and it did not carry the phrase "Return Postage Guaranteed" on the front of the mailing envelope, it can't be traced because the post office is not obligated to return it to the sender if for some reason it was misaddressed or undeliverable. If your manuscript was sent first class, you can ask the post office where you mailed it to put a tracer on it. Magazines are not responsible for unsolicited manuscripts. Keep a clean photocopy to save retyping time and cost in a situation like this.

Certified and Registered

Q. Can you explain the difference between "certified mail" and "registered mail"? And when is it necessary to use special types of mail when submitting manuscripts to various markets?

A. Certified mail is used when you just want a record of receipt of mail at a certain address. It's handled like regular mail, but a signed receipt is mailed to you. Registered mail is used to send valuables such as stock certificates and jewelry, because the post office signs a receipt when *they* get it and they know where the package is at all times. Certified mail is the less expensive way to requery a publisher, to follow up on a manuscript that's been held too long by an editor or to withdraw a manuscript. A receipt is mailed to you, so you have a record that the editor received your correspondence. That record should be kept in your files. For more information, ask for the booklet, *A Consumer's Guide to Postal Services and Products* at your post office, or write for a copy to the Consumer Advocate, U.S. Postal Service, Washington DC 20260.

What Mailing Method?

Q. Many times when I mailed stories or articles with photos by the special fourth class manuscript rate, with postage for that rate, my manuscripts were returned to me by first class, with the added postage applied and my own directions crossed out. Does editorial policy frown on the cheaper rate and am I obligated to reimburse the editor? If a writer is regularly sending out manuscripts, the fourth class rate certainly saves postage. Do I downgrade my material by using the fourth class rate?

A. The fact that some of your manuscripts are returned by magazines first class instead of special fourth class rate is to your advantage. It is probably the magazine's policy and you certainly aren't under any obligation to reimburse the editor. The special fourth class rate is an advantage for the writer who is making a great many submissions, especially of packages containing photos, and you do not downgrade your material by sending it at that rate. Editors understand the financial concerns of freelance writers and realize it is professional to mail material the least expensive way.

Tearsheets

Q. If it is necessary to submit a tearsheet or sample of previously published work, how are these usually obtained?
A. Publishers frequently furnish free tearsheets on request. If these are not available, you may offer to buy copies of the issue from the publisher. If you only have one copy of your published article, story, or poem, photocopies may be made on machines in most large libraries.

Canadian Writers

Q. Do Canadian writers stand an equal chance in the American market with writers who live in the United States? How can a Canadian writer manage return postage?
A. Yes, Canadians stand an equal chance in the American market, if they send material that is competitive with what American writers supply. Many Canadians solve the return postage problem by sending a check for the correct amount, plus or minus the Canadian exchange, to the postmaster of the nearest large American city, requesting that he send them a number of American stamps, which they can then paste on their return envelopes. International Reply Coupons (available at your post office) for the amount of postage may also be enclosed rather than stamps.

Chain Publishers

Q. There are cases where a publisher will issue several magazines, all of the same type, editorial style and content, from the same address. (They have different titles, though.) In such cases, when a writer is submitting material for use in these magazines, is the material considered for all magazines published by that company, even though it is addressed to one particular magazine? Or should a writer resubmit it for consideration to another magazine, even though it is published by the same company?
A. That depends on the company, but in this day when every editor is inundated with manuscripts, many firms reply only for the magazine to which the item is submitted, or to the group of periodicals which the editor works with closely. Editorial libraries in some companies serve as a clearinghouse, circulating the manuscripts to those magazines the item seems to fit. It would be to your advantage to send your manuscripts to other magazines published by a firm that has rejected it, if you have done your homework and know that the editor is not the same one who has already said no. Chances are no one else has seen it.

Cover Letter

Q. What is a cover letter and when should it be used?
A. A cover letter accompanies a completed manuscript that an editor has asked to see. They are usually not used on unsolicited manuscripts where there has been no previous correspondence between writer and editor, especially when the work must be judged exclusively on the writing style, as with fiction or humor. But cover letters are useful when you are submitting finished material at an editor's request; they can serve to remind the editor, "You asked me to send this." A cover letter should be short and to the point, and should not mention rates or fees; no biographical information about the writer should be given unless such information would help demonstrate the writer's credentials to write a given work. If the material is timely, the writer may request that the editor reply within a certain time period.

Mail Delivery

Q. Ordinarily, I send my manuscripts to publishers first class mail. Are there any other ways to deliver my work?
A. Writers who are submitting heavy manuscripts such as article/photo packages or book-length works often use the Special Fourth Class Rate—Manuscripts which is cheaper than first class. In 1983, for example, it was sixty-three cents for the first pound. It's a little slower in delivery, but much less expensive. (Be sure to write "Return Postage Guaranteed" on the address side of your package because if for some reason it's incorrectly addressed, the post office is not obligated to return it to you unless you have guaranteeed postage for its return.)

Another alternative to regular mail service is United Parcel Service, which sometimes can save a day over the postal service on coast to coast delivery. Packages of up to a pound in 1983 cost $1.59 for delivery from Los Angeles to New York, and since the recipient must sign a receipt, there is a record of a publisher receiving your manuscript. If you're delivering against a deadline, you have several choices for one day delivery. The U.S. Postal Service has an Express Mail service which, depending on your location to the nearest airport, guarantees overnight delivery, but the minimum cost (in 1983) was $9.35 for the first two pounds. That's still cheaper than the commercially owned companies. United Parcel Service "blue label" shipping provides two day air service which is not quite as expensive as Express Mail. Priority mail (air mail) is often adequate if you don't need guaranteed one or two day delivery.

Seasonal Rejection

Q. I submitted a seasonal article too late and received a rejection slip. Should I resubmit it again to that same market in about four months?
A. Seasonal material should be submitted at least six months ahead of schedule. Some editors prefer material at least one year ahead of season. So, if you receive a rejection for seasonal material with a note stating "received too late," resubmit it again in plenty of time for the editor to consider it for next season. See *Writer's Market* for individual publishers' policies. Be sure to reevaluate the material before resubmitting. "Received too late" may also mean that it is not good enough to keep on file for the following season.

Foreign Markets

Q. What are the mechanics of submitting manuscripts to foreign markets?
A. They should be typed double-spaced on 8½x11-inch white paper, and in many other ways the submission techniques are the same as those for submitting to American publishers. The main difference is that the manuscript must be accompanied by International Postal Reply Coupons in sufficient number to cover the cost of return postage. One of these coupons (current price in U.S. is sixty-four cents) can be exchanged in any other country for the number of stamps necessary to mail a single-rate, surface-mailed letter of the first unit of weight (usually 7/10 oz). (For an airmail letter reply, postmasters would usually suggest two coupons be enclosed with your letter.) The number of coupons required for a manuscript is determined by the weight of the manuscript at the post office, which is where the coupons are purchased.

If you will be dealing regularly with a particular foreign market, you may find it easier and less expensive to arrange to purchase foreign postage stamps from the country's postal service. The specific nation's embassy office in Washington DC, whose address can be obtained from your local public library, can provide information to any writer wishing to purchase postage.

Some foreign markets are interspersed throughout the various chapters of *Writer's Market*. For more information on foreign markets, consult *International Writers' & Artists' Yearbook*. This annual reference gives information on book, magazine, and newspaper publishers in English language countries abroad, as well as TV, radio, and theatrical producers, agents, literary prizes, clubs, and music and art markets. There is also a section on copyright and tax information pertaining to foreign sales.

Foreign Special Manuscript Rates?

Q. What procedure should I follow for submitting manuscripts to publishers abroad? The difficulty seems to be in getting them back again at a reasonable rate of postage. Is there a cheaper method than the International Reply Coupon which I understand is limited to first class?
A. The International Reply Coupon is the most convenient method of handling the return postage, but some countries also have special rates for manuscripts. Inquire about specific countries' postal rates at their embassies in Washington. Your local library can give you addresses or phone numbers of the embassies.

Folded Manuscripts

Q. Can I mail my manuscript folded instead of flat?
A. Yes. Short stories, articles, and poems of fewer than six pages may be folded in thirds and mailed in a regular number ten business envelope. However, any manuscripts *longer* than six pages should always be mailed flat. Never staple a manuscript, use new (non-rusty) paper clips; and be sure to include a self-addressed, stamped envelope of the proper size with any submission.

Enclose Previous Editorial Comments?

Q. Is it an advantage to send along to an editor photocopies of one or two "friendly rejections" I've received on a project from previous editors?
A. If an editor rejects a manuscript because it isn't quite right for that publisher at that time, but says something like "Good luck in placing it elsewhere," you can take that as a sincere comment. While some editors to whom you resubmit your manuscript might view enclosing such letters as a pressure tactic; in general, since your idea has to be appealing to the new publisher you're submitting to, the idea is going to be the deciding factor, not whether you enclsoed some "near misses" with other editors.

33 How Many Times Can I Sell the Same Idea/Manuscript?

Freelancers who discover that the research they do or the manuscripts they write can be sold to multiple markets feel like they've found the new miracle of the loaves and fishes. They feed hungry markets and still have leftovers to save for future use. It takes time and creative marketing to search for extra sales, but it's a way to get maximum return on writers' investments in their original efforts.

Using Basic Research

Q. Can I use the basic research for one article I sold to a magazine and rewrite it, reslant it, add a few mini-interviews and quotes to it, and sell it as original material to another magazine? Is it true that the research a freelance writer does is always his property, even though he sells an article written from that original research?

A. Yes, research always belongs to the writer, and you can rewrite and reslant that same basic research many different ways and sell several articles to various magazines. Many writers find this a lucrative and professionally sound way to do business. You shouldn't submit rewritten articles to magazines that are closely competitive with the buyer of your original article.

Reprint Rights?

Q. As a newcomer to the writing profession, I find the procedure for reselling an article or story confusing. Having used Writer's Market *as a guide, I find many publishers listed as buying first and second rights. After a story has been sold once, does the term "second rights" apply to each consecutive sale? Much of my writing has been to small religious magazines. I have been told the possibilities of selling a story numerous times are good because of the nonconflicting audiences. If a story has already sold three times, should I signify this by printing "Reprint Rights" in the upper right corner, followed by names of the three publishing companies and the dates purchased, or is this unnecessary?*

A. When a publisher buys first and second rights it usually means he will consider material which has not been published before or which has been previously published. To some editors, however, it might mean they're buying the rights to publish first and then reprint either in an anthology or another publication they own, or in a future issue of the same periodical three or four years later when the age-group audience is new. Second rights means the editor buys (usually for a lower price) the right to publish again an article, story, or poem that has already appeared in another publication. In the upper right corner of your manuscript, type "Reprint Rights Offered" and then perhaps as a last page to the manuscript, list magazines in which the story has previously appeared or where it has been purchased.

Reprint Fee

Q. What will I get paid if my article is reprinted in another publication?
A. Assuming you only sold first rights to the original publisher, the reprint publisher will either make an offer or ask the writer to suggest a fee. This payment will be a per-word rate or a flat fee, which could be, for example, 50 percent of what the publication would pay for an original article.

Copyright Owner Not Located

Q. If I am unable to trace the copyright owner of my story, can I resell it?
A. If you don't own the copyright and have made an honest and reasonable attempt to contact the original publisher—and you didn't sell all rights to the story—you can resell the story. Keep records of correspondence in your attempt to locate the copyright owner.

Time Limit on Resale?

Q. If I sell first rights to a magazine article, does a certain amount of time have to pass before I sell reprint rights to a second publication?
A. The piece you sold may be resold immediately after the first publication publishes it. Actually, you can *sell* reprint rights any time after you sell first rights; but the second magazine may not publish the article until the owner of the first rights has done so.

No Replies on Submissions

Q. I've submitted manuscripts to small publications that never returned them or notified me if the pieces were published. How can I find out if they were ever printed so I can sell them to larger markets without infringing on other publications' rights?
A. If you have requeried the small publications about your work and failed to get a reply, you can resubmit them to larger markets. Be sure to keep a record of your correspondence showing your attempt to clarify any previous publication.

Free Newspaper Reprint?

Q. Several times in the course of my writing career, newspapers have written me for permission to reprint my articles. I've always given my permission, but I've never been paid for this use of my material. Should I request pay when this happens, or should I just be content with the publicity?
A. If you've never brought up the subject of payment, then that's why the newspapers haven't paid you! As long as you give permission without asking for payment, the newspapers aren't going to volunteer to pay you. "I used to allow newspapers to reprint my work for nothing, thinking I was lucky to have additional readers and the publicity," says writer Hayes Jacobs. "Now, nobody prints or reprints any of my work without paying me . . . Sometimes it's only token sums, but one can have a lot of fun with token sums."

No Resale

Q. Under what conditions may I not resell a work?
A. You may not sell a published work to another publication if you sold all rights to the piece to the first publication. If the first rights purchaser has not yet published your manuscript, then you can only sell second rights to a publisher if he agrees to hold off his publication until the holder of first rights has printed the work. You can't blantly resell a work if it belongs to somebody else. Some people find old pieces of writing and try to have them published under their own name. Even if the piece of writing in question is not covered by copyright and is in the public domain, this practice would be ethically wrong.

Adapt Your Story

Q. Can I use my published story as the basis for writing another piece to sell elsewhere?
A. Unless you sold your right to create derivative works when the publisher bought the story, you can. The author of a work owns the right to adapt his work to another form, or create a derivative work. If you sold the first publisher all rights to the work, then you no longer have the right to use the piece. If you sold first rights only, then you can go ahead with your project.

Reuse Characters?

Q. Can I use characters from my short stories in other works, if different publishers buy them?
A. Yes. The writer of an original story owns exclusive rights to his specifically created and named characters, so they may be used in future stories. The only characters which are uncopyrightable are historical characters or otherwise well-known types of individuals.

Defunct Magazine

Q. A local magazine had several editorial shake-ups, finally leading to its "folding"—going out of business and discontinuing publication permanently. Several poems and one short story of mine had been accepted but not published before the magazine folded. Can I now send that material to other markets for consideration?
A. If the material was not purchased, you are free to market it elsewhere. If, however, the magazine paid for the poetry and short story, the company that owned the magazine may choose to sell the rights to publish to another investor who may resurrect the magazine under its own or another name. The deciding factor, then, is whether or not the material was *purchased*. If it was, contact the magazine owner and request that the rights be reassigned, in writing, to you.

Manuscript or Published Copy?

Q. Several of my articles have been published in magazines which bought one-time rights. I'd like to offer these to other magazines for reprint. Should I send typed manuscript copy or clean photocopies of the published articles to other markets?
A. Sending a clean retype *and* a photocopy of the originally printed article is preferable. Include the issue date of original publication and the title of the magazine in which the article appeared. Typesetters prefer to set type from original typed manuscript copy, but editors also like to see the published form.

Reslant to Sell

Q. A magazine article a publication rejected was slanted so specifically that I can't find another market. How can I make the article marketable elsewhere?
A. Change the slant. Although your particular arrangement of the facts in your article isn't salable to other magazines, revision and rewriting could make it suit the slant of another publication. *Writer's Digest* columnist Art Spikol points out for example, that an article about stress tests could be sold to an airline magazine, with a slant toward executives; with the same research, another article could be written for a sports magazine, slanting the piece toward how stress tests can improve sports performance. In any rewritten article open the piece with the specific tie-in to that magazine's readership. Amplify the point with some extra quotes and information you've gathered through additional research. (For more on writing and slanting magazine articles, see Chapter 22.)

Reuse Earlier Work

Q. I wrote and sold a series of short biographical pieces several years ago. I now have the opportunity to expand them into full-length books on the subjects. Do I have to contact the original publisher and get permission?
A. You should be able to expand the shorter pieces into more comprehensive biographies, since the facts and specifics of each person's life are not copyrightable. You won't have to contact the publisher for permission unless you intend to use verbatim a large portion of the earlier works and you sold more than first rights.

Juvenile Book Reprint?

Q. Would it be possible for me to have my juvenile book, now out of print, published as a reprint edition? If so, which publishers could I contact?
A. You might query publishers of reprints in the juvenile field, such as Harper and Row Junior Books, 10 E. 53rd St., New York NY 10022 or Scholastic-Tab Publications, 123 Newkirk Rd., Richmond Hill, Ontario, Canada L4C 3G5.

Newspaper Column

Q. A public service newspaper column I write in connection with my job has the potential to become a regular syndicated feature. After it has been printed for the purpose of my job, can I sell it elsewhere?
A. Companies generally feel that the writing produced as a part of a person's job falls under the category "work for hire" and belongs to the company rather than to the writer. However, it's possible that you might be able to work out an agreement with your employer allowing you to have outside use of the material. If that happens, you might have to rewrite columns which appeared in any uncopyrighted newspapers since they would be in the public domain if they ran without copyright notice.

Foreign Sales

Q. How can I sell my work to foreign markets?
A. Many factors affect the sale of foreign rights, but magazine articles and short stories can be sold in foreign countries, either as original manuscripts or in reprint sales. (Some American magazines which have foreign editions often buy worldwide periodical rights from the author,

and in such a case would have the right to reprint articles from their American editions without further payment to the author.) Magazine markets abroad are scattered throughout *Writer's Market*, and *International Writers' & Artists' Yearbook* lists some English language foreign magazine and book publishers. For book reprints, the contract between author and publisher should specify which party has the authority to contract with foreign publishers. If the publisher handles foreign sales, the author will usually receive 75 percent of the royalties. An agent negotiating a foreign sale will usually work with a foreign counterpart, and each of them will receive a ten percent commission. If the author owns and sells all foreign rights independently, he receives all royalties.

Wait Before Resubmitting?

Q. When a magazine specifies "contributions cannot be acknowledged or returned," how long must a contributor wait before submitting the item to another magazine for consideration?
A. Submit articles or items to other publications after a "reasonable" length of time—about four to six weeks.

Published but Unpaid

Q. I submitted an article to a magazine which ceased publication with the issue in which that article appeared. I was never paid for the article. Can I submit it to other publications?
A. Since the publication never paid for your article, although it was published, you would be legally free to use it elsewhere. Be sure to inform the editor who buys the article the circumstances under which it was originally published.

Resubmit Subsidy Published Work?

Q. I paid to have a collection of short pieces published by a subsidy publisher some time ago. Can I now submit them individually to magazine publishers? Can I submit the entire book to regular publishers?
A. Since rights to a subsidy-published book remain with the author, the contents of your book are yours to use as you please.

Publisher Defaults on Payment

Q. An unscrupulous book publisher accepted my novels, heavily edited them, changing both style and content drastically, and although the contract I signed promised payment, I was not paid. Nobody I've contacted—collection agencies, attorneys, even the post office—is able to help me. Can I resubmit my novels (as originally written) to another—and more reputable—publisher?
A. Since you were never paid, the manuscripts are yours, and you are free to use them.

New Version

Q. I've had work published in an uncopyrighted magazine, so it's now in the public domain. But I'd like to get it copyrighted. How much do I need to change and revise in order to create a "new work" that I can copyright?
A. The law doesn't say how much—it just says that the revisions would have to be substantial.

Copyright of a new version, whether the original was copyrighted or in the public domain, only covers the additions or changes which appear for the first time in the new work. Unless you extensively rewrite your work and change it considerably from the way it appeared in the uncopyrighted magazine, it must remain in the public domain.

Sell Article Twice?

Q. Is it unethical to write material in different ways for different types of magazines or does an editor automatically assume that information in an article is offered to him exclusively?
A. It is common practice among nonfiction writers to get the most out of their research by slanting various aspects of their subject toward different noncompeting markets. There has to be enough distinction between treatments, though, so the writer cannot be accused of selling the same story to two magazines.

Reselling Your Story

Q. What rights to my story should I sell to a magazine so that I also may sell it to a number of other magazines?
A. The first time you sell a story, specify first serial rights only, then all secondary rights will belong to you and you can try to resell this story to other magazines that use previously published material. You should inform subsequent magazines where and when the story originally appeared.

Resubmitting Articles

Q. I have contributed a great deal of material, free, to our local natural history group's mimeographed magazine. Is it permissible to sell some of these articles? If so, is it necessary to tell the prospective buyer the details about how it has been used?
A. Since the mimeographed magazine presumably is not copyrighted, all the material it contains is in the public domain, which leaves you (or anyone else) free to make whatever use of it you wish. It would be ethical to advise prospective buyers where and when the articles first appeared. You would have to significantly rewrite these articles to obtain copyright protection in magazines.

Selling Your Story Twice

Q. I have sold a Christmas story to a juvenile publication. Can I legally sell this same story to other publications that accept simultaneous submissions, or does this apply only to articles? How do I notify the editors that it is a simultaneous submission?
A. Simultaneous submissions can be made for fiction as well as nonfiction. Let each editor know it is a simultaneous submission by noting the previous sale in the upper right corner of the first page of your manuscript.

Weekly Articles

Q. I wrote several articles for a semimonthly rural newspaper and received no payment. Must I get a release from the publisher to submit revised versions to national magazines?
A. Since you weren't paid and there was no written statement by the publisher that he wanted further rights to any of the material he obtained from you, you can submit the articles elsewhere. Keep in mind that if the newspaper was not copyrighted, the original articles are in

the public domain. You'll have to substantially rewrite them to make them copyrightable for resubmission to national magazines.

Poetry Resubmitted

Q. About twenty years ago, I had a book of poetry published. Can I now submit these poems to markets and should I mention the book? I also write two columns for free. Should these be copyrighted?
A. If you own the serial rights to your book of poems, you are free to sell them to magazines that use reprints; but you should mention the book in which they originally appeared. If your columns appear in an uncopyrighted publication, and you don't want them to fall into public domain, then you should see to it that they are printed with a notice of copyright in your name.

Book Reprints

Q. My hardcover book exhausted its sales potential and the publisher is taking it off the market. The publisher has not made any plans to sell it to a paperback house. Can I sell it to a paperback publisher myself?
A. If your hardcover book sales have run their course and you think the book has potential sale in paperback, write a query to a reprint publisher describing your book, providing details on the date and publisher of the original version, number of copies sold and asking if he'd like to see the book for possible reprinting.

Revise and Sell Publicity Features?

Q. As a publicist I write and send feature stories to newspapers which frequently use the material verbatim. If I select one of these stories, delete the commercial overtones and send it to a magazine, where do I stand legally and ethically?
A. Many companies and institutions feel that what you write as their employee belongs to them and it isn't ethical to resell it for your own gain. Discuss this with your employer and clarify his attitude. He may feel that what you're writing—while it doesn't mention the company specifically—does benefit it in general from the national coverage, and will give you permission.

Resell Idea?

Q. I recently came across an old story of mine published in an uncopyrighted senior high magazine. I think with a little updating and a slightly different ending it would be suitable for a young person's magazine. Can I market this?
A. Since you intend to revise the published story it can be marketed as a new work for current magazines.

Story into Book

Q. If a children's story has been published in a magazine, is it possible to gain permission to offer it to a book publisher for publication as a picture book? If so, what procedure should be followed?
A. Yes, a published story can be turned into book form provided the author has retained the book rights. You will need to check with the magazine to ascertain which rights were originally purchased. If the magazine bought *all* rights, then you'll have to try to make some special

arrangements concerning the book rights. If you own these rights, submit your story to the book publisher and inform him of its previous publication.

Multiple Sales?

Q. A photographer recently asked me to write copy to go with his pictures. To date we have sold two Sunday pictorial articles. Now he wants to resell these articles to subsequent markets. Can we keep reselling them to different newspapers and magazines?
A. You will have to check what rights were bought by the original Sunday pictorial. Resales should be to noncompeting magazines and newspapers.

American Resale?

Q. I have sold some verses and articles to a British magazine and would like to sell them to American publications also. Can I still offer first North American rights? Should I mention that they have already been printed in Britain?
A. You should advise the American publications of the British sales record of your material. You will also need to check with the British magazine to find out what rights, if any, they still retain to this material.

Story Rewrite

Q. Two years ago a short story of mine appeared in my high school's annual literary magazine. I have recently added more to the story and changed the beginning, but some of what appeared in the magazine is still the same. I would like to know if this work is considered a published manuscript. I would like to try to sell it, but most magazines want short stories not previously published.
A. Yes, your work has been "published"; but since the school magazine probably wasn't copyrighted, and since you have revised the story, thereby technically producing a new work, you are free to market the *new* version as an unpublished manuscript. ("Publication" in an uncopyrighted magazine places that version of your work in the public domain.)

Reuse Without Permission?

Q. For several years I have edited a monthly bulletin for a club (I am a member). I may want to gather all my bulletin material and publish it in a small book. Each issue of the bulletin is published with the notice, "Permission to reprint material from this bulletin is granted provided proper credit is given." May I legally gather and print my material without permission from the club? I intend to make it clear that the material came from the bulletin.
A. You should notify the club that you plan to reprint material which you originally edited for its monthly bulletin. Tell the club that the bulletin will be credited.

Resell Same Article?

Q. If I sell an article with pictures to a magazine, can I sell the same article again to another magazine?
A. If the first magazine bought first rights only, you can resell. If you attempt to resell the piece after the first magazine buys it and *before* they print it—you will have to be sure you're completely reslanting the piece so the editor who bought first rights will have no cause for complaint if the articles are published simultaneously. Advise the second editor that another aspect of this subject was treated by you in an article bought by another magazine.

Resell Another Way?

Q. An original party plan which I recently sold to a leading children's magazine included a novel idea for a party invitation. Do the rights purchased by the magazine prohibit me from selling the invitation to a greeting card company?
A. If the children's magazine lists in *Writer's Market* which rights it buys, or if it indicated which rights it buys on the check you received for the plan, you'll know if those rights prohibit your further use of the material. If you don't know what rights the magazine bought, drop them a note and clarify this point before you resubmit your idea to a greeting card company. If they only bought first, or one-time serial rights, you can resubmit. Although ideas themselves cannot be copyrighted, the particular presentation of the idea—in this case, a party invitation—might be covered by copyright.

Serial Rights

Q. I sold a story to Modern Romances. *There was no mention of serial rights but the check I endorsed stated they were buying all serial rights. Can I sell second serial rights to another publication?*
A. Since the magazine bought all rights, the second serial rights are no longer yours to sell. You might try writing the editor to see if she will reassign the rights to you.

"Rights" Problems

Q. Is it necessary to write for permission from each publication that has published my poems, in order to compile a book of poetry from my published work? Some indicated they bought first rights only. Does this automatically give me permission to sell or publish again? And if some poems were published under pen names, must they be republished under the same name or can they be published under my own name?
A. If you sold only first rights, then you own book rights. If the poems were published before 1978, your book rights are held in trust for you by the original publisher and he must be contacted. If there are some instances where you're not sure what rights were purchased, you'd better check with the publisher. Though written originally under pen names, the poems may now be presented under your own name. Your projected book should contain a list of acknowledgments, indicating where the poems first appeared.

Reprint Sales

Q. Would you explain how "digest" magazines pay for articles they reprint from other magazines? What percentage does the original publisher get, and what percentage goes to the author? If the author has sold first serial rights only to the original publisher, does the author receive the entire reprint amount? Should he try to sell a reprint of his article to a digest magazine, or do digest editors read most publications and make their own selections?
A. In the digest reprint market, payments vary. Some pay 50 percent to the original publisher and 50 percent to the author. Others pay the publisher or the author—depending on who owns reprint rights. Digest editors *do* make many of their own selections, but don't let that stop you from submitting. When you sell reprint rights to publications on articles you own, you are entitled to the entire reprint fee. But before 1978 when the new copyright law went into effect, the original publisher held other rights in trust for you, even if he bought first rights only. So you must write and ask that the rights be returned to you.

Resubmitting

Q. One of my stories was published in a non-paying magazine. Can I sell it to a paying magazine?
A. Yes, but there are several things to keep in mind. First, if the magazine was not copyrighed, your material is now in the public domain and anyone could have reused it as is. To submit it now to a copyrighted magazine and get it copyrighted as part of the magazine, it would have to be revised sufficiently to be considered a new work by the Copyright Office. If the magazine in which it originally appeared *was* copyrighted, you'll have to clear with the editor whether they acquired only first rights or all rights to the material.

Book Rights to Stories

Q. Does a writer retain subsequent rights to his own stories published in a magazine? I have had seven confession stories purchased and printed by one company. Now I want to market these pieces as a collection in one book. Do I need permission from the original publisher? Suppose I rewrite these stories and have them registered as a book manuscript with the Copyright Office? Would I then be able to offer it for sale?
A. You will have to check with the publisher who purchased your confession stories to determine who owns book rights. To register the rewrittten stories with the Copyright Office in book form, the published book must carry your copyright notice.

Magazine and Book Marketing

Q. While my nonfiction book is circulating among publishers, may I sell parts of it as magazine articles? If so, what rights should I sell to the article? How should the manuscript be noted? If I sell first rights, what happens if the book is published before the article is printed?
A. You can sell parts of your book as magazine articles. Type in the upper right corner of the manuscript's first page, First Serial Rights Only while your nonfiction book is circulating among publishers. If you do subsequently sell the book, and it is published before an article you have also sold, then you should write the magazine editor and explain the circumstances. Since he would, in effect, only be buying second serial rights at that point, he may ask that a portion of the payment be returned.

Poetry Book

Q. I'm arranging to publish a volume of my poems. What is the proper and simplest procedure for securing release of copyright from publishers of magazines where the poems first appeared? Must individual letters be written to each editor giving the titles and dates of publication of the various verses, or could I make a mimeographed form in sets of three and a very simple request note? What if a magazine has ceased publication and the original publisher or editor is deceased?
A. The basic letter can be the same; all you have to do is change the poem titles and publication dates for each. So a mimeographed form will save you time. Even though a magazine is no longer being published, or the publisher or editor is deceased, the copyright still continues to run the course of its term and would be owned either by the publisher or his heirs so you will still need a release. You may have to write to the Chamber of Commerce or Postmasters in the cities where the magazines were published for the most recent address for the copyright owner.

Defunct Magazine

Q. I sold a short story to a magazine which is now defunct. Who owns the story now? Can I submit it to a reprint magazine?

A. The publisher who bought the story owns it for as long as his copyright is valid. Your right to submit it to a reprint magazine depends on what rights you originally sold.

Offer to Buy

Q. After submitting a two-thousand-word article to a magazine, I received a letter of acceptance saying they were buying five hundred words of the article at five cents a word, with a check for twenty-five dollars enclosed. Is this a usual procedure, or should a publisher pay for the whole article even if he only wants five hundred words? And what about the remaining fifteen hundred words? Are they still my property to sell?

A. A publisher who is not able to use a full article may offer to buy a part of it from the writer. If the writer accepts, then he agrees to the terms. The balance of the article can be sold by the writer to a *noncompetitive* market since he still owns the rights to that material.

Free to Use?

Q. My husband and I bought at an antique shop a notebook of original poetry by an author who died in 1942. Are we required to locate his descendants before publishing any of the poetry? His most prolific year of poetry was 1931 and much of it has historical value. How can we find his descendants if we need to?

A. You would be required to locate his descendants. The best place to start would be with the owner of the antique shop who probably bought the notebook along with other items from the executor of the author's estate.

34 How Do I Cope with Rejections and Writer's Block?

Reminding a freelancer that Beethoven wrote some of his greatest symphonies after he became totally deaf is small comfort to a writer facing an uncompromising blank page or a stack of rejection slips. The best thing to do is remember that every writer—pro and beginner alike—faces these problems from time to time. "Success begins," aphorizes one editor, "where most people quit."

Resubmitting after Rejection

Q. Is it advisable to submit a story more than once to a magazine that has rejected it?
A. If the editor tells you he's rejecting it because he's overbought at the time, or he's recently bought something similar, it isn't at all impossible to sell that piece to the same market at a later date. If you wait one year before resubmitting, you may have a chance. But that's only if the rejection letter was hopeful and gave sound reasons for rejection. Also, editors change jobs and a new editor may buy what a previous editor rejected.

Nineteen Markets for the Same Idea?

Q. I am puzzled by writers who claim that after mailing a piece nineteen times and having it rejected, they mail it once more and sell it. Are they telling the truth? It seems that if a piece is slanted to a given magazine and it's rejected, there can't be nineteen other magazines with similar editorial needs.
A. These writers *are* telling the truth, because they have carefully explored all possible allied market areas. For instance, a piece about Washington State fishing may not sell to other specialized sports magazines, but it might find a place in one of that state's Sunday supplements or in general men's magazines, fraternal order publications, etc. The number of markets a writer finds depends on his own resourcefulness and ability to revise, where necessary, to suit the new market.

Special Meaning?

Q. A children's story of mine was recently rejected. Instead of the usual rejection slip in the return envelope with the manuscript, I received a letter saying my manuscript was sent under

separate cover. When I received it, it was insured. Does this have any special meaning that my manuscript has any merit that would interest another publisher?
A. Some publishers just have a company policy of returning manuscripts insured. If the original company had any special comments to make on the merits of your manuscript, they would have said so in their rejection letter. Do not hesitate, however, to send it to another publisher right away.

Controversy Rejected?

Q. Because magazines are dependent on advertising for revenue, would they reject articles because of controversial subject matter which might offend some advertisers?
A. Magazines are businesses so they are sometimes forced to think long and hard about running controversial material. Any such article receives extra-close scrutiny, and if it will offend an advertiser who purchases a large percentage of the publication's ad space, then there is a chance an editor would reject it. Some editors have been courageous enough to run controversial material—for example, material leading the way to needed improvements in some industries, but most magazines are careful about the articles they publish.

Reaction to Rejection

Q. What should I do after an article is returned with a rejection slip?
A. Freelancer Kay Cassill recommends sending a rejected query or manuscript to another appropriate publisher the day it is returned to you. "You'll have it off your desk and on its way to another possible sale," she says. "You won't sit around feeling dejected, and the current project won't have suffered from the interruption."

Sincere Rejection

Q. If an editor writes "Sorry. Try us again" on a rejection slip, what does that mean?
A. When an editor indicates some interest in future submissions, it means he thinks enough of your work to offer the encouragement of a personal note. It means your writing style and approach are suitable for his readers, and he wants to see more ideas from you.

Comments on Rejection Slips

Q. On recent rejection slips from greeting card companies were handwritten messages, "Terrific possibilities but more punch" and "Ideas good but lack sales appeal." I don't know what comprises "punch" and "sales appeal." Should I take these handwritten remarks to be encouraging?
A. These handwritten criticisms certainly should be regarded as encouraging. By referring to "punch" and "sales appeal," these editors probably meant that your work lacked the impact necessary to make the prospective card buyer immediately react favorably to the cards. It would seem, then, that your underlying ideas are good, but you need to present them in a more colorful, entertaining, or dramatic way that will catch the customer's attention and make him buy. If, after studying published cards and revising your own work, you feel your ideas now have the right sales appeal, don't hesitate to resubmit them.

Rejected?

Q. My first story was recently returned. It did not have the usual printed rejection slip attached. I received instead a short personal note telling me the publication was overstocked and I should not submit material until late August. Was my story rejected completely or should I feel it was adequate for that magazine?

A. It is possible that your story wasn't read, but was automatically returned because the market is overstocked at present. You should resubmit the story in late August, as suggested, since the note seems noncommittal about rejecting or accepting it.

Give Up—When?

Q. How many rejection slips do you consider the cutoff point—where you give up on that particular article?

A. If the idea for the article was good enough at the onset for you to take time and work to produce the finished manuscript, you should not abandon it too soon. Look at the rejection slips as bits of advice for improving the original manuscript. Glean whatever an editor jots as the reason for rejecting the article or story—and improve, revise, take from or add to, until the piece is sold. Rejections, if used properly, can be learning lessons to improve your writing. Be sure to send your work to the appropriate market. Sending an article to a market that is completely unsuitable is a mistake that many beginners make, but marketing—just as writing—is a skill that one learns from experience and study. Some ideas and manuscripts have to be set aside after a dozen or so submissions because either the market isn't ready for them—or they're not ready for today's market.

Editor Holding Manuscript

Q. If an editor keeps my manuscript a long time, does that mean he likes it? Or am I setting myself up for disappointment?

A. It takes magazine editors two weeks to two months to report on manuscripts; book publishers take as long as four months. Some publishers take longer than others, so you should always check *Writer's Market* to see an individual publisher's reporting time. If that time passes without any report, then it is possible that the editors like your manuscript and are considering accepting it. However, it could also mean that the editor hasn't had time to look at it, or is on vacation, or broke a leg skiing and is in the hospital. Or, your manuscript could have been lost in the mail, so it's best not to get your hopes *too* high. If four to six weeks pass and you don't receive any word from the publisher, write and ask about the status of your submission. Be sure to include SASE for a reply.

Writer's Block

Q. I'm having trouble completing an article. What causes writer's block and how can I combat it?

A. Ask twenty writers what causes writer's block, and you'll probably get twenty different answers. The causes of writer's block usually don't have anything to do with writing, but rather are connected to factors which serve to distract the writer, keeping him from concentrating on his craft. Overwork is one such factor. A writer who is fatigued from overwork should stop writing for a couple of days. Financial worries, personal problems, and illnesses all could keep a writer from his work.

Look at your article and see if you're actually ready to begin writing; it may be that you haven't done all your preliminary work yet. If you haven't gathered enough information or haven't outlined the piece clearly enough, you might not have a firm idea of what you want to write. Step away from the work and try to look at it objectively. You may be trying to write it without having a clear understanding of how you want it to turn out. You may be writing it one way, when you know subconsciously that it would be better if it were treated some other way.

Freelancer Brian Vachon says that a writer should make sure he *wants* to write about his current subject; if you're trying to make yourself write about something you just don't like, your mind could be rebelling.

Anxiety about the quality of writing is a frequently cited cause of writer's block. Novelist Dean Koontz claims this is easily solved: "Read a novel by a really bad writer whose work you despise, and tell yourself, 'If this junk can get into print, publishers will fight one another for the rights to *my* book'."

The important thing to remember is that worrying too much about writer's block will only make it worse. If the block persists, take some time off from writing. Read, or do some correspondence. Buy a new piece of equipment or a reference book. The best way to fight writer's block is to remember that the harder you push against it, the harder it struggles to remain.

Time to Write

Q. I have never suffered from an extended period of writer's block, but I do find it difficult to put enough time together in one segment to get any writing accomplished. What can I do about this problem?

A. Your problem seems to be one of time management rather than writer's block. In other words, the work seems to be so enormous that you don't know where to start. Here are a few suggestions. Get up at least forty-five minutes earlier than you normally would, and spend at least thirty minutes of that time on writing and related work; if you're not a "morning person," do this at the end of the day. "Brown bag" your lunch at least once a week and work during your lunch break. You can also do research reading or review your notes on the bus or other public transportation on the way to work. If you work at home during set hours, let friends know you prefer not to be called at those times. Plan your time for outside "leg work," such as interviewing, research, library visits, and other calls so you can do them all on one day. Save your home office time to write. Take writing-related work with you to the doctor's office; if you have a long wait you can get some work done. Above all, never say you don't have enough time to do the work. Even if you only have an hour on a given day, that can really add up over the course of a year.

Certain Authors "Losers"?

Q. If I'm aiming at a specific type of market, should I continue to submit my manuscripts to publications which have rejected my past work? Do editors begin to recognize certain authors as "losers" and push their work aside because of past rejections?

A. Just because a market has rejected your manuscripts in the past doesn't mean that will always be the case. Editors reject manuscripts for many reasons that have nothing to do with your manuscript's value. For example, the editor could have recently bought or assigned an article on a topic similar to yours. Don't assume that the sight of your name on a manuscript will cause an editor to automatically reach for a rejection slip. Assuming your manuscripts are neat, appealing, and suited to the publication, the next manuscript you send may be the happy combination of the right idea in the right place at the right time, while your earlier pieces weren't.

Jealous Writer

Q. I've been writing for a couple of years and have had some small success with magazine sales, but a writer who started about the same time I did has managed to sell a couple of novels, along with getting an advance for a third. I'm jealous. Why can't my career take off like his?
A. Novelist Dean Koontz says, "Writers should be supportive of one another and should take pleasure in one another's successes. Don't waste time stewing in envy . . . just work harder than before and put in longer hours than ever, until you finally get your own huge advance." You are your only competitor; your only goal is to make each of your works better than your last.

Form Rejections

Q. After four years of freelance writing and not selling a word, I would like a personal remark from an editor about why my manuscript didn't qualify, instead of the usual cold-blooded rejection slip. Is there a special approach you can recommend?
A. An editor's job is to find publishable material, not explain rejections. Most editors have too much work and too little time, so personal analysis of the thousands of manuscripts that cross their desks is impossible. For constructive criticism, take a writing course, join a writer's club, or use a criticism service such as those advertised in writer's magazines.

Marks on Rejected Manuscripts

Q. I've received manuscripts from reputable publishers which have had very encouraging remarks scrawled across the first page in red ink. Is this acceptable editorial practice?
A. It is considered improper for an editor to mark on a rejected manuscript, but there are many writers who would be delighted to have such personal attention from an editor, even if it did mean typing the first page over again.

Not Quite Right for Us

Q. I receive letters from editors saying my manuscripts are interesting, but "not quite right for us." What does this mean? If it's so interesting, why isn't it right?
A. These letters expressing interest are meant to encourage you and show you your work does have a degree of promise. The material's style or content, however, may not be in keeping with the magazine's editorial requirements, or something similar may have recently been published or bought for future use. Get to know the markets better by studying what these publishers are buying. Pages of current magazines give writers valuable clues as to what kinds of articles editors are looking for. *Writer's Market* can also help you determine editorial needs of magazines.

35 What Do Editor and Writer Owe Each Other?

In his book, *Max Perkins: Editor of Genius*, A. Scott Berg comments, "Two qualities . . distinguish the professional editor: the vision to see beyond the faults of a good book, no matter how dismaying; and the tenacity to keep working, through all discouragements, toward the book's potential." Magazine editors are equally eager to help the promising writers they deal with achieve their best efforts. If along the way there are occasional misunderstandings, the writer should not overlook the editor's essential goodwill toward his work.

Editor's First Name?

Q. If an editor addresses me by my first name, do I address her, for example, as "Clarissa" or "Ms. Jones"?
A. Until the correspondence reaches a friendship stage in a long editorial procedure, the safest salutation is probably "Dear Clarissa Jones."

Forgotten Author?

Q. Once in awhile I sell a story that the magazine pays for, yet I never see it in print—even though the editor says he will send copies of the issue containing it. Can you give me some advice explaining this situation, as I'm typically egotistical enough to want to see my "brainchildren" in published form.
A. Sometimes magazine editors forget to send copies of stories they published to the original authors. Write a note to each of the editors asking for a copy of your story, if it has been published. In some cases, editors leave a magazine or editors' policies change, and although stories are bought, they are not used.

Editor Stole My Idea?

Q. In December, I submitted an article to a new magazine. The following February, I received a rejection slip with the note: "We are quite taken with your style and would appreciate receiving material from you in the future." Then, this magazine's August issue appeared on the newsstand, bearing an article with the same title as mine. Though the printed article is admittedly better than my submission, longer and more thoroughly researched, it is similar.

The title, style, and content are almost identical. It is hard for me to accept this as coincidence. Do I have any right to question this similarity? Can I copyright my manuscripts in the future so editors can't steal my ideas?
A. Many writers get the same idea at the same time and often use the same language in writing, so *your* idea may not have been "stolen". Someone else may get a similar idea to yours at the same time you do (as often happens in science), and execute the article better than you did so that the editor chooses to use their story. Ideas cannot be copyrighted; you can only copyright the *presentation* of an idea. Under the new copyright law, a manuscript is copyrighted automatically at the moment of creation. The law says if you created it and can prove it's yours, you're protected. Protect your presentation by showing the copyright notice (the copyright symbol, the year, and your name) on the first page of your manuscript. Keep carbon copies and research that show you created the work. Put dates on these and on the manuscript.

Get Editor to Pay?

Q. My magazine article was published four months ago and I haven't received payment for it. What recourse do I have? How can I get the editor to pay me?
A. If the magazine's policy is "pay on publication," you might expect to receive payment within thirty or sixty days after publication. You should *never* be expected to wait longer than ninety days. If you still haven't received a check, send a follow-up letter requesting the specific amount of payment. Give the editor all the details—whether the manuscript was submitted on speculation or assignment, date of original submission, date and title of the published piece.

If you are still unable to get a response, write the state's attorney general, the Better Business Bureau and the post office in the city where the magazine is located. Its Postal Inspection Service sometimes investigates such claims. Also send a letter with all the above mentioned information to *Writer's Digest* which will notify its readers to be wary of dealings with this publication. Other than that, there is no recourse but to sue—which can cause you financial loss because of legal fees, unless you can take your case to a nearby Small Claims Court.

Negotiate Rate?

Q. Can I set the price on my articles or must I accept what the magazines offer? Can I negotiate payment?
A. Most magazines have a certain rate they pay writers and make an offer based on those standard rates. If you're a new writer and have never sold anything to the publication before, you can't expect to get more than that. Remember that sometimes, especially early in your career, a byline is more important than a check, since it bolsters your confidence, builds your reputation, and may lead to other sales. Your value increases as you prove yourself to an editor, so keep a file of all the work you've done for him to substantiate your future requests for a raise. If you're a well-established writer and think you might be able to negotiate a better rate because of your experience and the value to them of the particular article you're offering, go ahead and suggest a higher rate than their standard. All they can do is say no, or offer a compromise figure and in either case you've lost nothing.

Collecting an Advance

Q. The publishing contract I signed promised me a six hundred dollar advance when my book was published. I now have copies of the book, but no advance. The contract was signed two

years ago. Do I have any chance of getting the advance? I've written to the publisher several times, but have received no answer.
A. If you have sent a registered letter to the publisher and still received no reply, it might be advisable to take the publisher to Small Claims Court. If the six hundred dollars is promised in the contract, you should receive that money. You would be wise to contact a lawyer and let him look over the contract and suggest a course of action you might take. You may also want to tell the U.S. Postmaster in the publisher's city about your grievance, and notify *Writer's Market* as well. They operate a complaint service which solves 50 percent of the conflicts writers have with listed publishers. The Authors Guild, which you are eligible to join once you have signed a book contract, can give you advice as well. Their address is 234 W. 44th St., New York NY 10036.

Work-For-Hire Contract

Q. What is a "work-for-hire" contract?
A. A "work-for-hire" contract is one which permanently gives all the rights of a work to the person who assigns it, for example, to the periodical or to the publisher. A freelance writer who signs a "work-for-hire" clause gives up his copyright and also his right to any further income from that material. As Kay Cassill says about these contracts in *The Complete Handbook For Freelance Writers*, "Don't sign them."

Why Revise?

Q. Why do I have to revise according to an editor's suggestions? My story is written exactly how I want it. How do I know an editor's criticism is valid?
A. Writers who are new to the business sometimes consider an editor's requests for revision a personal affront, when in reality the editor is only trying to get the best possible manuscript for his market. "I don't believe a writer exists today who can't occasionally profit from that editorial blue pencil," says author Kay Cassill. Editors know what works for their audience, and have the experience and expertise necessary to objectively criticize work. Author Stuart Woods says, "Sensible suggestions come from editors," and this is generally true. If you don't want to revise your work to the editor's style or suggestions—and you could be right—you can always withdraw it. But there's a good chance you will never get your work published if you don't learn to take constructive criticism from editors.

Editorial Changes

Q. I sold a piece to a specific magazine, and it took a year before it was published. When it was published they spelled my name right, but that was about all. The style was hacked apart until there was no style. What's more, facts were altered, so the reader was bound to get an impression different from what I had intended. How much can my story be edited or changed without my permission?
A. Ethically, an editor should discuss any significant changes with you, especially if they affect the intent of your piece. Some editors will show galley proofs to authors; others will not. If you see galleys and don't like what is there, you can ask to have your original meaning restored or the manuscript returned to you for submission elsewhere. But be sure you aren't mistaking tight editing for changes in meaning, as beginning writers sometimes do. Most of the editor's changes are to make the story more readable—not different.

Title Change

Q. Can a magazine change the title of my story?
A. Just as the editor has the right to make editorial changes, so too does he have the right to change your title. Some editors might consult you first, but titles are changed routinely for a variety of reasons. If the editor should change your title in a way which distorts your meaning, you certainly have cause to complain.

Hold Your Query?

Q. What should I do if a magazine tells me they would like to keep my query letter for future consideration? I had planned several other slants to the story which might interest other publications.
A. Write to the editor, acknowledging your interest in his future consideration but indicating your intentions to query elsewhere with different versions of the story in the meantime.

How Long to Wait for Publication?

Q. What reasonable amount of time should I wait for a purchased article to be published? I sold an article to a monthly publication a year ago, was paid for it, but it has not yet appeared in print. The material could be slightly dated by now. If a magazine purchased a piece and then decided not to use it, would they return it to me? Would I then be obligated to return the money?
A. If a magazine has not published material it has bought within twelve months, the writer should ask the magazine to return it for resubmitting elsewhere and be permitted to retain the original fee paid for it. This guideline is used by the American Society of Journalists & Authors, Inc. and you might mention this to the publisher of the magazine that bought your material.

No Name, No Pay!

Q. When a magazine lists in Writer's Market payment of a set sum per word, shouldn't they be expected to pay it? It was only a six-line verse filler, but they used it! I received no letter of acceptance or rejection. To add insult to injury, they didn't even give me a byline. How can I be sure this won't happen again with a longer, more important piece?
A. You should write to that editor, asking why you received neither byline nor the payment listed in *Writer's Market*. Don't submit future material to this publication. Before you submit to other magazines, you might ask about filler payment if there's no rate given in *Writer's Market*.

Waiting Time

Q. How long should I wait for an editor's decision on my manuscript? How do I follow up on an article that's being held by an editor an unusually long time?
A. Depending on a magazine's staff and the amount of mail it receives an editor may take from three weeks to two months to report on submissions. A book editor may require three months or longer. Check *Writer's Market* for specific reporting times. Remember that when an editor says he reports in six weeks, that means six weeks from the time he receives your manuscript. If you live on one coast and he's on the other, it may take a week to reach him. If you've had no report from an editor by the maximum reporting time, send a brief inquiry asking if your manuscript or query is still being considered. Include the story title, date of original submission and brief

description of the piece as well as an SASE. In the rare case where a publisher fails to report even after your inquiry, send a certified letter to the editor, advising that you are withdrawing your manuscript from his consideration so you may submit it elsewhere. Be sure to notify *Writer's Market* editors of the problem.

Acknowledge Acceptance?

Q. When a manuscript is accepted for publication, should a writer acknowledge that acceptance? If so, should it be on acceptance, on receiving the check, or on publication?
A. A response isn't mandatory, but if a writer's overwhelming joy, gratitude, or surprise needs an outlet, by all means he should acknowledge the acceptance.

Story Acceptance

Q. What happens when a story is accepted by a magazine? Does the writer get a check in the mail or are there preliminaries to go through, such as signing something regarding rights or originality?
A. The writer is customarily notified of acceptance by mail. The check may be included or may follow later, depending on the policy of the publisher. Check *Writer's Market* for information on what rights the magazine buys, or ask the editor. The editor assumes the writer is the story's originator, so there is rarely any paper to sign to this effect. While acceptance by mail is the usual policy, some small magazines use the story or article, assuming that the writer is selling whatever rights the magazine usually buys at whatever price the editor pays. Be sure you know what rights you're selling for what price by checking the *Writer's Market* listings before you submit.

Withdraw Material?

Q. Three months ago, I sent some of my best poems to a publisher who never acknowledged receiving them. Eager to put them back in circulation, I requested their return. My letter was not acknowledged, nor have the poems been returned. SASE was enclosed with correspondence. May I legitimately write the editor stating that I withdraw my offer of the poems, then send them to other editors?
A. The procedure is to send the editor a certified letter indicating that you are withdrawing the poems from his consideration. Be sure to list the titles of the poems and date of submission. Then resubmit this material elsewhere. Hold on file the return receipt and a copy of your certified letter.

One Editor Replaces Another

Q. Is one editor liable for another editor's commitment? When an editor assigns something to a writer or offers payment for a manuscript, then leaves the magazine staff, is the replacement editor liable for that assignment or payment?
A. There are no rules on this one. Often it depends on the terms of departure for the editor. If he is fired, chances are his replacement or his former manager wants to disregard his editorial thinking—perhaps that was the reason for his dismissal. If he was promoted, transferred, or if he departed on good terms, there is likely to be more transitional grace, and old projects and commitments may be honored. The writer should summarize the situation in a letter to the new editor, including copies of all correspondence. The new editor then will be in a position to judge whether he wants to keep the writer on assignment or kill the idea. Whether this is

accompanied by a kill fee (usually a minimum of 20 percent of the anticipated payment for the piece) depends on whether a kill fee was part of the original agreement and how far the writer has gone with the idea. If an article has been written on assignment for a previous editor and a kill fee was agreed upon, this may have to be discussed with the magazine's publisher or owner. Most editors will be fair with the writer. But when a magazine staff changes, it is often because the publisher is unhappy with earlier staffers—and it can signal a new editorial direction for the publication.

Lost Manuscript

Q. Is a magazine publisher responsible for stories he received but apparently lost in his office? My story was lost by a major magazine. I have a letter from the editor stating he cannot find it. Should I ask him to pay for it, since I cannot send it elsewhere?
A. You could try, but many magazines go on record as indicating they are not responsible for unsolicited manuscripts, so legally they cannot be charged. If you have kept for your file a clean photocopy of the story, make another copy and submit it. Or retype another original from your carbon.

Legal Recourse?

Q. After reading the outline of my proposed historical novel, a leading publisher asked me to mail a synopsis and four chapters. The manuscript was mailed with first class postage enclosed for return. The publisher acknowledged receipt, but I did not hear from the publisher again. After three months I wrote a letter inquiring as to their decision. The editorial department replied that my manuscript had been misfiled; they did not know it had arrived until receipt of my letter. Within a few weeks the senior editor wrote a vague letter saying the chapters had not lived up to the outline; that the manuscript was being returned fourth class. More than two and one-half months have passed and the manuscript has not arrived. The publisher says they have asked the post office to trace it. If the post office is unable to locate it, as now seems possible, do I have recourse against the publisher? There's something illogical about the publisher's explanation.
A. Although this is an unfortunate experience, you are probably unduly suspicious of the publisher. As a professional author you undoubtedly kept a carbon of the manuscript, so you might as well forget this experience and start retyping the manuscript for submission to other publishers. It wouldn't hurt, however, to ask the publisher if he would be willing to pay for the retyping.

Nudge Editor?

Q. To an unestablished writer, marketing becomes as difficult as the creative effort. My particular problem is trying to place timely or seasonal material. The classic example was a Christmas poem I mailed in August to a top publication which returned the poem the following February. Would sending seasonal material by registered mail help, or would this antagonize an editor?
A. When sending seasonal or timely material, include in a covering letter a brief request that since the material is timely, you would appreciate a reply by a specific date. This won't help in every case, but it may reduce your frustrations with a few editors.

Can't Meet Deadline?

Q. I've queried an editor about an article that will require extensive research. The editor gave me the assignment, but the deadline he gave me is one that I find impossible to meet. What can I do that won't alienate the editor? I want to be honest.

A. Write the editor a short but courteous note explaining that you will need more time than he has suggested for the deadline, and let him know the approximate date you will have the article to him. Most editors will understand this and appreciate the honesty.

Weak Idea?

Q. A magazine editor assigned an article to me, based on a variation of an idea I queried him about. When I got into the actual research I found the article wasn't going to produce what the editor was looking for. There just wasn't enough solid information available to support the editor's thesis. What's the best way to handle this?

A. Let the editor know right away what the problem is. The editor will either abandon the idea and pay you a kill fee based on the amount of work you put into the research or suggest some contact persons who may be able to supply you with what the editor is searching for. Editors, as well as writers, sometimes have to admit that a certain idea has to be temporarily abandoned.

36 How Can I Avoid Legal Problems?

"Ignorance of the law excuses no man" is an often quoted adage of English jurist and scholar John Selden, and one that writers especially should keep in mind. While in recent years a few book publishers have offered libel insurance to their authors, the burden of legal awareness still lies with the writer on any work of his that appears in newspapers, magazines, and books. Truth is a defense against libel, but not against invasion of privacy. The 1976/1978 copyright law gives authors new rights, but work-for-hire contracts take them away. Writers must know not only their own rights, but the rights of the persons they write about and quote in their manuscripts. Here are some basic reminders for beginning writers.

Use Real City?

Q. I want to use a real city in my fiction. Must I use the names of actual streets and places, or can I mix facts and fiction?
A. You'd better stick to the facts. The entire point of setting a fictitious work in a real city is to lend credence to the story, so use of made-up places and streets would detract from that realism. Readers in the city where the work is set would see the factual errors immediately and the author would lose credibility. William Kienzle's *The Rosary Murders* gains an air of truth from the author's detailed knowledge of the Detroit area, as do the rest of his Father Koesler mysteries. Similarly, Jonathan Valin's Harry Stoner novels utilize blueprint-perfect Cincinnati locations. If you're using an actual city for your setting, stick as close to the truth as possible.

Test Method Copyrightable?

Q. I have been writing a vocabulary column which I would like to sell to small newspapers. Without realizing it, my column is much like the monthly word power column by Peter Funk, printed in Reader's Digest. *In fact, although I am not using the words in his two books,* Thirty Days to a More Powerful Vocabulary *and* Six Weeks to Words of Power, *my daily vocabulary tests in my written columns resemble the vocabulary tests used in his books. Is there a copyright on Funk's column? If I sold my newspaper column, would I have to get permission from Peter Funk? I stress this point: I am not using his words, but my test methods resemble his.*

A. Although Funk's column title, "It Pays To Enrich Your Word Power," is a registered trademark, his actual test method is a simple multiple choice format: the word, followed by the possible definitions a, b, c, and d from which the person chooses the correct answer. The individual words and choices of definition could be copyrighted, but the test format itself could not; many textbooks and universities use the multiple-choice format.

Off-the-Record Information

Q. Is it unethical to print information that a source has labeled off-the-record or not-for-attribution?

A. If you have taken information off-the-record or not-for-attribution, then you are obligated to keep it that way. Failure to do so can damage your reputation as a trustworthy writer and harm your chances of getting information from that source in the future. Some writers have the practice of telling sources who want to speak off-the-record that they don't want such information. These writers reason that they may already have the information from another source, or that the present source might be convinced to reveal the facts on-the-record later.

Use My Air Force Photos?

Q. I want to write a memoir of my World War II experiences. Do I have rights to photos I took while on Air Force assignment?

A. In situations where you produced photos or other work in connection with your regular duties, you'd have to contact the Air Force to see what their regulations are regarding this. You may need permission from them before you can use the photos.

Similar Concept

Q. A recently published book of cartoons around a single idea has given me the idea for a similar book based on a related concept. Can I use this idea?

A. The only possible problem would be if the publisher felt you were taking advantage of the book's success and trying to cash in on it by modifying their idea. In that case, they might be able to challenge you on the basis of unfair competition and try to get an injunction preventing you from selling your book. Your best plan of action would be to submit the idea, along with a couple of sample cartoons, to a potential publisher and see what their reaction would be. They would be your best guideline on what is legally permissible in this situation.

Fiction or Nonfiction?

Q. If I write a true story, but change the names, is it fiction or nonfiction?

A. If the story is a factual account, with only the names changed, then it would be nonfiction. One example of this type of writing is *Cold Storage* by Wendall Rawls Jr. The book is an exposé of the horrible conditions at a hospital for the criminally insane. Most of the patients' names were changed, as were the names of hospital personnel.

Can Third Person Sue?

Q. Can a person I interview for an article be sued by a third party he mentions in the interview? Can the writer be sued for what the interviewee said?

A. The interviewee can be sued for libel or defamation by the third person. The writer and publisher of the interviewee's statements can also be sued. A writer, therefore, should not include such possibly libelous statements unless he can prove their truth if challenged.

Sue Book's Writer of Introduction?

Q. If I write the introduction to a book and later there is legal trouble involving the book's contents, am I liable?
A. If the plaintiff felt that your introduction lent credence to the book's contents, then you could possibly be named in the lawsuit. Before writing an introduction, become familiar with the book's contents and be sure you are in agreement with the author's viewpoint, since anyone who sues the author may also sue you.

Corporation Permission?

Q. Do I need the permission of a corporation to publish an article or book about it?
A. No, and if the company has been treated fairly, you should have no legal problems. However, if the company takes exceptions to any part of your work, you may have a lawsuit for libel on your hands. Even if what you write is true, the company might sue simply as a way of denying what you have written. Books about corporations written without their consent include: *CBS: Reflections in a Bloodshot Eye,* by Robert Metz; *Big Mac: the Unauthorized Story of McDonald's,* by Max Boas and Steve Chain; and *The Condensed World of The Reader's Digest,* by Samuel A. Schreiner Jr. Writers should exercise extreme caution when writing such material, and make sure that all facts are verified.

Invasion of Privacy?

Q. I am writing the life story of a remarkable woman I knew a couple of years ago who has since died. I'm sure she would have given permission, but I'm not sure her husband would be so willing. Do I need permission to write about someone who isn't in the public eye?
A. The husband may interpret your work as invading his privacy and institute a lawsuit. It is possible to use the woman's story as the basis for fiction, but you'd have to substantially change the names and situations so that there were no obvious, direct connections between your story and the real people or happenings.

No Extra Pay?

Q. I work for a trade publication which also owns a consumer magazine. I recently found my work for the trade magazine appearing in the consumer publication. I was not notified or paid extra. My fellow employees and I want to know if this practice is legal. What should we do?
A. Work produced by salaried and work-for-hire employees is usually the property of the employer. Therefore, the magazine probably has every right to reprint your work in its sister publication. You might wish to take the matter up with your employer, however, if you and your fellow employees feel that you deserve some compensation. Work-for-hire writing belongs to the company, but publishers have been known to make concessions when workers present a reasonable argument.

Famous Names

Q. Can I use the names of famous people in my fiction?

A. Using the famous as characters in your fiction causes no problems as long as they are depicted in a favorable light. However, if your work makes negative allegations about the people involved, you could be asking for a lawsuit. Famous authors have used celebrities in their stories, but beginners should play it safe and use fictitious characters.

Photos from TV?

Q. I'm working on a photo essay which necessitates my taking photos from the television screen. Is there any legal problem involved in my doing this?
A. The problem you might encounter would involve copyright infringement. Videotapes of programs are usually copyrighted. Check with the program's producers just to be sure. They may grant permission and may or may not charge a fee.

Out-of-State Publisher

Q. I'm having trouble getting paid by a magazine. Can I sue a publisher in another state?
A. Many states have adopted a "long arm law" which provides that business transactions are subject to the jurisdiction of courts in the state where some part of the transaction occurred. Check with a lawyer to see if you can use this law to sue an out-of-state publisher.

Plagiarism

Q. I recently found a pre-1850 magazine which has a piece I would like to publish. The magazine's so old it's in the public domain. Can I retype the piece and submit it to a magazine?
A. Not under your name. While such use is possible without copyright infringement, it violates all standards of ethics for a writer. Such an act is called plagiarism. You would in essence be a thief, having stolen someone else's work and passed it off as your own. If you plagiarize another's work and people find out about it, you will have ruined your reputation as a writer. "You'll usually get caught," says freelancer Brian Vachon, "but that's not the worst part about using someone else's words and calling them your own. The worst part is that it just doesn't feel good. It's hard to call yourself a writer when you really aren't, and plagiarists really aren't."

Legal Help

Q. Where can I get legal assistance?
A. Volunteer Lawyers for the Arts is a nationwide organization of lawyers offering free legal services to persons in the creative arts, including writers. The lawyers advise artists on matters related to their individual art form. Eligibility for the service is based on the writer's income, with the writer in some cases paying court costs even if legal service is free. Contact the organization at 36 W. 44th St., New York NY 10036, 212/575-1150. Other helpful contacts are: Bay Area Lawyers for the Arts, Fort Mason Center Bldg. 310, San Francisco CA 94123, 415/775-7200; and Lawyers for the Creative Arts, 111 N. Wabash Ave., Chicago IL 60602, 312/987-0198. You could also contact the Lawyer's Referral Service of your local Bar Association. This service is not free but you could obtain an initial consultation for a nominal fee ($10 and up).

Use Real People

Q. Can I base my fictional characters on real people, only change their names?

A. Even if you change their names, real people might think readers would recognize them, and consider your work an invasion of their privacy. If these people believe they are shown in an unfavorable light, they might sue for libel. It's safer to make a composite character with traits and characteristics culled from several people. It's more creative to alter the events and characters of real life, since they are rarely suitable for use in fiction without some authorial control.

Composite Character

Q. I've used a man I knew as the central character of a personal account which I plan to use to start my article. I refer to him as "Bill S." and I'm using made-up quotes and other details to illustrate the situation. Can I do this?
A. What you might do instead is use a composite character—the creation of a fictitious person who symbolizes several people by combining their experiences, attitudes and/or quotes. This technique is useful when the writer needs to protect individual identities or to avoid having numerous people make similar comments. The writer using this technique shoud always advise the editor of the fact, so the editor can in turn inform the readers. Newspaper writer Janet Cooke lost a Pulitzer Prize because she didn't let her *Washington Post* editor know that her young drug user "Jimmy" was a composite.

Company Names

Q. Can a writer legally use the name of a business firm in fiction if the story doesn't reflect uncomplimentarily on the business?
A. Well-known companies such as Macy's or Marshall Field & Co. do not look unfavorably on a little free advertising inbedded in a nationally distributed piece of fiction, provided such usage is strictly for purposes of atmosphere and realism. To be completely safe, however, you could check first with the firm. Nothing even remotely illegal or distasteful should be connected with the company name. For example, if your story deals with a criminal who dupes a department store, you'd be on safer ground if you used a fictitious company name, to avoid the possible impression that the real store is not smart enough to escape being duped. As a rule, when in doubt, fictionalize.

They're Yours for the Taking

Q. I recently wrote a short story as an assignment for a correspondence course. When the assignment was returned, a number of specific word changes were suggested. When I sell the story, can I legally use the wording suggested by the instructor?
A. It is okay to appropriate revisions of correspondence course instructors. They lay no claim to any word changes made as part of the teaching process.

Will the Real JB Stand Up?

Q. How careful must a fiction writer be with names he contrives but which could turn out to be names of living persons? For example, if I name the villain in a story Jack Bowlton, could a real Jack Bowlton sue me for defamation of character for characterizing him as a villain? Also, what became of the old disclaimer, "Any similarity to persons, etc., is strictly coincidental"?
A. Unless the real Jack Bowlton happened to be circumstantially similar in personality and actions to the fictional character you gave that name, there probably wouldn't be any cause for

legal recourse. The old disclaimer probably doesn't appear anymore because a person who can prove that a real person was used in a fictional account and can also prove defamation or invasion of privacy may still have legal recourse in spite of the disclaimer.

More Cookbook Problems

Q. I am writing a cookbook in which I am going to use old family recipes adapted to present-day materials. Do I need a release form from people from whom I secured recipes? There will be no payment made, other than a copy of the cookbook.
A. Yes, you need a release from the people from whom you are assembling recipes for your cookbook. Ask them to sign a form similar to the following: "For value received, I assign the rights to my recipe for _____ to _____ for use in her cookbook, _____." The "value received" is the copy of the cookbook you're going to give each of the contributors.

Fact into Fiction

Q. What rules pertain to fictionalizing an actual event about which there was considerable mystery and secrecy? The event was a semiscientific experiment which was unique and which received nationwide publicity when it occurred. Since it was unique and widely publicized, the event and all its participants would be easily recognized. Because military security is still in effect about the experiment, I am sure there is no possibility of doing a factual piece on the subject. Where and how is the line drawn between fact and fiction in such a case? To what degree would the event and characters have to be changed to make them fictitious?
A. Since the event received such widespread publicity, you may use a similar idea in a fiction plot, but you would be wise to surround it with a new, invented set of characters (e.g., one character could be made considerably younger than the real-life one and given different personal traits and appearance), and sufficiently altered circumstances (perhaps in a different locale) so that the resultant story will be the product of your own creativity rather than straight reporting.

Is It Plagiarism?

Q. I read a story in which the main character had many suppositions as to how his adventure would end. None was right. I want to write a short story using one of these suppositions for my ending, but my story would have to be very close to the original. Is this plagiarism?
A. It is unlikely that an author would allow you to use *his* character in *his* story with a solution written by you. You'll find that originality is the best way of avoiding plagiarism.

Rewriting Songs

Q. I have written a song based on another writer's poem. Some words are different, but others are words of the original author. Is this legal? If not, how can I get permission from the original author? Could I use the music from another original song or do I need the consent of the composer? I have written "answers" to several hit songs. The words are different, but they fit the original music.
A. You cannot use music or a number of words from another writer's song if the copyright is still in effect on that song. If you want to use older songs, check the directory, *Variety Music Cavalcade*, to determine if the copyright is still in effect on the songs in question. This book lists songs by title and tells when the copyright was originally issued. It also gives the name of the publishing company to whom you should write to inquire about permission to use parts of

the song. Check *Billboard's International Buyer's Guide* for publishers of current songs.

Using Real Names

Q. In a book of personal experiences, is it permissible to use real names and to relate real episodes without obtaining written permission from the persons mentioned? Or should characters and events be fictionalized?
A. It's advisable to change the names of real persons and the locale of real episodes to avoid suits for invasion of privacy by the parties concerned. Even if your copy is complimentary, the individual sometimes resents being placed in the public spotlight and goes to court to prove his point.

Permission to Quote

Q. If I want to include in an article a remark about a magazine or article I have read, or comment on something I saw on TV, am I free to, or do I have to obtain permission from the writer? I'm not going to quote directly, but will mention actual names.
A. You may make the comments you wish concerning actual names and places without getting permission from the people involved, but be sure your statements are accurate and not libelous.

Ownership After Death

Q. My brother and I worked together on his manuscripts. He asked me to help rewrite, edit, and type his work. When he passed away, all the manuscripts he had were packed into a box and given to me. I have found some I am sure will sell with some rewriting and corrections. I would like to submit these for publication using both our names. What are my legal rights? Will it be necessary to ask permission from his other heirs, and would I have to share any profits with them?
A. If these manuscripts were transferred to you by your brother's written will or some other valid form of transfer, then they are your possession and you may get them published without asking permission of the other heirs. If there is any doubt about the legality of ownership, it would be best to consult an attorney.

Invasion of Privacy?

Q. A neighbor of mine who is disfigured from the hips down is a recluse. I have built an interesting story around such a woman, saying she became this way because of an auto accident, at which time her lover was killed. I slander her in no way, yet my husband feels I will have a lawsuit on my hands if the story gets published. I would appreciate any advice.
A. It would be best to change as many of the obvious true-to-life facts as possible to avoid an invasion of privacy suit. Give your heroine a different age, size, hair coloring, nationality, etc. Add new mannerisms, idiosyncrasies and other aspects of personality. Use a totally different setting if you can. After all, the only basic idea you need is that of a disfigured recluse. It is not necessary to make the type of disfigurement identical to that of your neighbor. Use your creative imagination to produce a completely new character based on the general idea but not the exact details of your neighbor's life. In fact, you might even experiment with the idea of making the leading character a man instead of a woman.

Where Research Ends

Q. I haven't written nonfiction articles because I don't know where "research" ends and plagiarism begins. Where do you draw the line?
A. If long passages are lifted verbatim, the writer must get permission from the copyright owner. Ideas can't be copyrighted, so after you've researched the facts, simply relate them in your own words. Make certain you use only *facts* from a work, rather than the author's conclusions or observations. Facts belong to everybody, but an author's conclusions and opinions are his alone.

Libel Insurance for Writers?

Q. Will a magazine's libel insurance protect me from libel suits for articles I write?
A. It depends on the publisher. Many major magazine publishers have libel insurance that *can* be applied to a freelancer at the discretion of the publisher, and in most cases the publisher will extend coverage to protect the writer. But if the publisher feels the writer has been negligent in preparing the material, he may decide to let the writer get himself out of the situation. Many publishers have no coverage for freelance writers.

If an article involves investigative reporting and/or a potential lawsuit, a freelancer should consider asking the magazine about freelance insurance when negotiations are underway for such an assignment. The writer should ask the publisher the circumstances under which he would be covered if his article caused any libel action. But don't count on publishers' insurance bailing you out of hot water if you haven't properly researched and written your article. Accuracy is still the best insurance against libel.

Same Names

Q. Could a person actually named William Faulkner, or Ray Bradbury, or Ann Landers publish work under that famous name?
A. No. Ann Landers, William Faulkner and Ray Bradbury have already established the reputation of those names; anyone who tried to publish his work using the names would be guilty of infringing on the reputation those writers have already built. This holds true even if the writer's real name is the same as that of an already-published author. The second writer would have to take a pen name. Remember, actor Stewart Granger had to adopt a stage name at the beginning of his career, because somebody else was already using his real name: Jimmy Stewart! (For more information on pen names, see Chapter 16.)

Time Limit in Contract

Q. I sold an original story and screenplay almost a year ago. Since the time the contract was signed and my work was taken, the producer has not been in touch with me. He hasn't paid me. According to the contract, he has to pay only when they start the principal photography, or when the production money is banked. Since there is no time limit in the contract, I wonder if there is any law that protects me? What can I do if the producer is unable to raise sufficient money for the production?
A. Unless you had a time limit written into the contract you signed (which is always advisable), you do not have much choice except to wait for him to obtain production money. On the other hand, if he has abandoned the project, he may be obligated to return the material to you depending on the terms of your contract. It is up to you to contact him to see what can be worked out.

37 Are There Any Business Tips I Need to Know?

Freelance writers are envious when bestselling authors refer to "my accountant" or "my tax man" because the beginner has to not only create his work, but market it, and keep accurate records to get all his appropriate tax deductions. If you are picked at random by the IRS for an audit of your tax form, you'll want to know you're on firm ground because you know what's allowed and you have the receipts to show for it.

Bookkeeping

Q. I'm just starting out as a freelancer. How do I handle my bookkeeping?
A. First, set up a separate checking account for your writing business; this will make it easy for you to keep track of income and expenses related to writing, and keep them separate from your other income and expenses. For the beginner, a single-entry account book is adequate. This method has one column each for you to record expenses and income. Each entry should be verified at the end of the month with your canceled checks. Avoid paying cash for writing expenses; if you must establish a petty cash fund, putting money in the fund each month and keeping receipts for cash outlays.

You'll need to keep a filing system for all your receipts so you can verify expenses at the end of the month. A budget sheet for each month can help you keep track of any problems arising in your writing business—what expenses are exceeding expectations, which markets aren't buying as much as you had planned, etc. A file for submissions helps you keep tabs on your marketing track record, what you submitted where, how long ago, what you were paid, etc.

These are only a few basic suggestions to get you started. If your business becomes very successful, you might wish to advance to a more sophisticated record-keeping process. For more detailed information on keeping books, see Kay Cassill's *The Complete Handbook for Freelance Writers*.

Business or Hobby?

Q. I've been writing for years, but I don't make a lot of sales. Can I still take business deductions for writing-related expenses?
A. If you've been pursuing a writing career for years without much success, the IRS may

challenge your deductions on the basis that you did not have any profit motive in writing, and therefore you were writing only as a hobby, not as a business. In that case, you would only be able to deduct expenses up to the amount of income you made from writing, whereas if the IRS regarded your writing as a business, you could deduct any business expenses, even if they exceeded any profit from writing. One guideline used by the IRS is that you must make a profit in two out of five consecutive years, or you cannot deduct losses as a "business." You'd be considered a hobbyist.

Deductions

Q. When can I begin taking my writing expenses as deductions on my income tax return? What kinds of things can I deduct?
A. If you have made any amount of profit from your writing—in other words, if your earnings are greater than your writing-related expenses—you must pay income tax. However, you cannot claim deductions unless you make a profit in two of five consecutive years. If you don't meet this test, the government considers your writing as a hobby, not as a business. Keeping detailed records is important when claiming deductions. Writing supplies, including paper, carbons, pens, ribbons, and mailing and copying costs are deductible. Typewriters, word processors, and other equipment can be depreciated. Courses and conferences can also be deducted, as long as they were to enhance or refresh writing skills; you can also deduct transportation, lodging and meal expenses when traveling for business purposes. Be sure to keep accurate records when traveling for business purposes. Write down the mileage before starting out and when arriving home or at new point of outset and indicate the writing job covered by those miles. Dues to writers' organizations are also deductible. Check *Law & the Writer, The Writer's Legal Guide,* and "The Business of Writing" in *Writer's Market* for more information on taxes.

Home Office Deduction?

Q. I don't have an office outside my home, but I write in my home and have sold a few freelance articles. Is there any way I can deduct my home work space on my tax return?
A. A home office can be deducted, but only if it is an entire room set aside for writing alone, and is used on a regular basis. For example, if you rent a five-room apartment, and use one room only for research and writing, you can deduct one-fifth of your rent, heat and electric bills. If you own a seven-room house, and have a writing room which represents one-seventh of the total space, your deductions can include one-seventh of your total interest on your mortgage, real estate taxes, repairs to the house, utilities, home insurance premiums, and depreciation on the room. In either case, any long-distance phone calls and similar home expenses directly related to your writing are deductible. If you have a second phone in your home office used just for your business, then, of course, the entire cost of that phone is deductible.

Vacation/Business Trip

Q. If I take a vacation and pick up information on that trip which I later use in my writing, can I deduct the trip as a business expenditure?
A. If the trip is a mixture of business and pleasure, then the author must keep accurate records of how much time he spent on business during the trip, and only deduct that percentage of the costs. For example, if you took a trip to California for three weeks, and spent a week of the time researching an article about the movie business, while the remaining two weeks were spent

visiting relatives, you could only deduct one-third of your expenses for food, travel, and lodging. If the entire trip were spent on business, then all such expenses could be deducted if you can produce receipts and records to that effect. You must also be able to prove to IRS that you're a business, not a hobby writer.

Equipment Deductions

Q. I write for outdoor, travel, recreation, and other such magazines. Can I deduct any costs related to my recreational vehicle or boat as business expenses?
A. Much like the stipulations for travel expenses, the amount you can deduct on these vehicles would depend on what percentage of their use is related to your writing. If you spend one-fourth of your time on each in the pursuit of freelancing, then that amount of the maintenance and repair costs for each could be deducted. However, the IRS would probably assume that you use the vehicles for your own pleasure and recreation too, so it's doubtful you could deduct these expenses in full. Keep a "ship's log" of your travels with these vehicles, along with receipts and documentation that they were being used for business.

Fees Plus Expenses

Q. The magazines for which I've worked have paid me the fee and expense money in one check. Since business expenses aren't real earnings, how do I treat this on my tax forms?
A. Since publishers don't have a convenient method for separating business expenses from payment for manuscripts they usually send one check to cover both. You can, however, deduct your expenses on your IRS tax form. Even though reimbursed expenses are shown as gross income on your tax form, they would be deducted before figuring the net income on which your tax is paid.

Press Cards?

Q. Last week, I visited a company to research some information I need in order to finish a project. Their behavior was very harsh. They said they would not give any information to anybody unless he had credentials proving he is a writer. The same thing happened when I did research work at a museum and at a medical research laboratory. Reporters, telephone operators, merchant seamen, detectives, private investigators, and even photographers have identification cards. Why not writers? Our job is just as important as theirs! I am sure that the rest of my colleagues feel as I do. Why don't we have a writers' association to bring together all those interested in the writing field and provide them with the backing, support and benefits of a powerful, nonprofit, internationally-recognized organization?
A. There are many freelance writers' organizations already in existence designed to meet the needs of specific groups of writers—National Association of Science Writers, Inc., American Society of Journalists & Authors, Inc., Society of American Travel Writers, etc. A list of such organizations, with addresses, appears in the *Encyclopedia of Associations* in your public library. If you're not already a member of such groups you might consider it. Otherwise try to get letters from individual publishers while you're working on a project to present as your credentials. Perhaps your approach needs polishing. Many writers never show press cards and are welcomed courteously.

Starting a Literary Paper

Q. I'd like information about how to start a literary paper or magazine. Where can I learn more about this project?
A. Two organizations which might offer you some specific suggestions are the Coordinating Council of Literary Magazines, 1133 Broadway, Room 1324, New York NY 10010 and the Committee of Small Magazine Editors and Publishers (COSMEP), Box 703, San Francisco CA 94101.

Movie and TV Rights

Q. How does an author keep movie and TV rights when a book is published?
A. Read carefully the clause in your book contract that pertains to those rights. A first-time book author usually can't keep *all* such rights. The Authors Guild recommends that book contracts should give the author 90 percent and the publisher ten percent of movie and TV sales. Read the contract carefully before signing it and ask questions by phone of the editor who sent it to you about anything you don't understand.

Writer's Guidelines

Q. Are there any rules concerning which editor or department should receive requests for writer's guidelines?
A. Type on the outside envelope, in the lower left corner, "Request for Writer's Guidelines," and address the envelope and the letter to the editor of the publication. If you don't know the editor's name, just address the request to "The Editor." Your request will be routed quicker and get faster response with the corner notation.

Get a Lawyer?

Q. Should I get a lawyer to look over my book contract?
A. If you aren't being represented by an experienced agent, it is a good idea to have a lawyer familiar with literary contracts to look over yours. Be sure the lawyer knows something about laws that pertain to publishing. "Publishing law is not particularly arcane," says publishing veteran Carol Meyer, "but is based on accepted ways of doing business, and a lawyer inexperienced with these customs and procedures can create a lot of confusion and unnecessary fuss." To find a lawyer versed in publishing and copyright law, contact the local lawyers' referral service of your state or city bar association.

Who's the Author?

Q. If a writer buys a plot from an advertised source, or if a writer pays for extensive help in plotting his story or novel, is the finished product legally and ethically his own?
A. In both cases, the finished product belongs to the purchaser who has actually produced the written manuscript, even though he has used the help of others and paid them for it. When you've received extensive help on your novel, you could include an acknowledgment in the foreword.

Dictating a Novel

Q. I am going to tape record the second draft of a novel. What is the fastest talking pace for a

good typist to get everything down on paper and the exact wording to indicate punctuation, parentheses, italics, spacing, etc.
A. Record at your own pace. The typist will adjust her speed accordingly. A good typist should be able to punctuate correctly from the way in which the lines are spoken. Indicate parentheses by saying, "Open parentheses" and "Close parentheses." Say "Underline" when you want italics, and say "Paragraph" when you want to start a new paragraph. Before you begin, you can explain that you want double-spacing except where you indicate otherwise, and indicate margin width, etc. Remember that all instructions throughout the tape should precede the dictation.

Ghost Credit?

Q. I did some ghostwriting for a friend who wanted to self-publish a book. I'm breaking into other fields of writing now, but have few published credits except for this book. Can I use this as a sample of my writing to show an editor?
A. The nature of ghostwriting is exactly what the name implies: work by an unseen hand. Ghostwriters receive money for their work, but the "author" receives all credit. Therefore, you must receive permission from your friend before revealing to anyone that his book is your work.

Find Freelance Editor

Q. How can I find a freelance editor to help me with my manuscripts?
A. Check the "Editorial Services" listings in *Literary Market Place*. You'll find many editorial services and freelance editors who might help you with your work. There's also a cross-reference listing each by field of activity. Write to several and compare their fees.

Starting a Magazine

Q. I am trying to start a small magazine and I need advice. Do I have to register with any state office? How do I handle having it printed? What about advertising? Can I have it distributed on newsstands or would I have to sell subscriptions? As owner and publisher, could I be sued for what is printed?
A. The first thing to do when starting a new magazine is to determine if an audience exists for your idea. Are there lists available of potential subscribers? Are potential advertisers a likely source of revenue?

Make up an editorial "dummy"—a facsimile of the finished magazine—and get bids from printers, based on the number of copies you want to print. Then you'll have to decide whether your costs will be covered by income from subscriptions and newsstand sales or from circulation *and* advertising revenues. Your local post office can give you information on obtaining a second-class mailing permit.

If you elect to use advertising, check the *Standard Directory of Advertisers* to find out which agencies handle ads for companies you would like to advertise in your magazine. Figure out an advertising page rate based on your planned circulation. Develop a list of prospective subscribers and work with an advertising letter shop on how to find subscribers through direct mail. You'll have to notify the department of taxation in your state of your decision to start publication; if you'll have a number of employees, you'll also have to pay workmen's compensation and work out any other legal requirements. Your city may also require you to obtain a vendor's license or file notice of your venture.

As owner and publisher, you could be involved in any lawsuits for libel, invasion of privacy, or copyright infringement which might arise from an article you publish. You could also be sued for nonpayment of debts, should you neglect to pay any bills. A magazine requires much hard work and investment, so you should examine your plan carefully before starting to work.

Self-Promotion

Q. How can I promote my work and myself?
A. For a freelancer, one of the best techniques to help boost sales is to keep his name in front of the public and editors. There are a number of ways to do this. Lecture dates can help keep interested parties aware of what you're writing, and get them to buy your book or the magazine in which your series of articles appears. The small response of a lecture audience can grow by word of mouth, leading to successful sales. Send published material to editors you've known who might be interested in a particular work; doing this can lead to reprint rights sales or assignments on related topics. Sending "For Your Information" clips of your work to editors and former interview subjects can keep your name fresh in their minds. You can send out news releases to appropriate newspapers and magazines for any of your writing-related activities, whether lecture appearances, a new book, or a series of magazine articles on a given topic that might be of interest. TV and radio stations can receive this information too; a media interview can let readers know about your work. If you've published a book, work with your publisher's Publicity Department to suggest any avenues of promotion related to your special expertise.

Retirement Plans

Q. How can a full-time freelancer provide for retirement?
A. Since the full-time freelance writer has no employer to provide a pension plan, if he wishes to provide for retirement benefits he must set aside funds himself. The federal government has provided two ways for the freelancer to do this. In 1962, Congress passed the Keogh Act, which allows a self-employed individual to establish a retirement fund—contributions to which are deductible and the income of which is tax-free—until he begins to make withdrawals when he retires and his tax bracket is lower. The law allows the person to deposit up to 15 percent of his net annual income, subject to a 1983 maximum of $30,000 per year, in an Internal Revenue Service approved account. He may then deduct this payment on his income tax for that year. He may not make withdrawals until he is 59½ years old; he must have begun withdrawals by the time he reaches 70½ years. The owner of the account isn't required to deposit money every year. If he makes a withdrawal prior to reaching age 59½ he will be subject to a 10 percent penalty on the amount withdrawn.

Another way for a writer to provide for retirement is to start an Individual Retirement Account (IRA). Even if a freelancer has another employer-funded retirement program, he may establish an IRA account. The contribution limits for IRAs in 1983 are $2,000 per year for single persons, and $2,250 for married persons, where the wife does not work outside the home.

Information about Keogh and IRA accounts is available from banks, savings and loan associations and your local Internal Revenue Service office.

Writer's Will

Q. Are there any special provisions an author should make when drawing up a will?
A. When a writer dies, his literary works remain for someone to look after. In the will, the

writer may specify who is to inherit the copyrights to his works and who is to receive any royalties after his death. He may also appoint a person to make artistic decisions about his work after his death, such as whether and under what circumstances unpublished works may be published posthumously. Additional information on a writer's estate can be found in *The Writer's Legal Guide,* by Tad Crawford.

38 What Do I Need to Know About Book Publishing?

The majority of freelance writers don't have agents, so when they have a book project and want to approach a publisher, they're pretty much on their own. They read reports in *The New York Times* or *Publishers Weekly* about million-dollar advances and escalator clauses in bestselling authors' contracts, and try to equate that with the modest terms of their own first book contract. They want the best deal possible without jeopardizing the sale. Here are some basics about book publishing to help beginners.

Getting Book Published

Q. What are the steps to getting my book published?
A. First, read the listings for book publishers in *Writer's Market* to find which companies would be most likely to have an interest in your manuscript. Check libraries and bookstores to see which publishers have published books that are compatible with your interests. Make a list of several suitable publishers. Settle on your most likely publisher and send him a query letter outlining a proposal for your book, with at least a few sentences on each chapter's contents and an offer of a sample chapter. If your book is nonfiction, it would also be helpful to explain why you think the book you're proposing is different from, and better than, any others that have been published in the same field. The editor also wants to know the market for your book and how many prospective buyers there are.

Be sure to enclose SASE for reply, so the publisher can let you know whether he would be interested in seeing more. After that, it's up to the publisher to decide whether he is interested in your book. If the publisher says "No," go on to the next publisher on your list. Sometimes finding the right company to publish your book can take a while. But don't give up. Dr. Seuss's first book was turned down by twenty-eight publishers before the twenty-ninth took a chance on this now bestselling children's book author.

Rights Offered?

Q. When submitting a book manuscript to a publisher, what data concerning rights should be attached?
A. It's not necessary to discuss the matter of rights when submitting a book manuscript to a publisher. If they decide to publish the book, the contract they draw up and present to you will

have all the rights provisions spelled out. If you agree with them, you can sign the contract; if you don't, you can discuss it further with them before coming to terms.

Book Synopsis and Outline

Q. When submitting a proposal to a book publisher, should a synopsis be overall or abbreviated chapter-by-chapter content? How extensive should an outline be?
A. A synopsis should provide a comprehensive summary of the contents in about two typewritten pages. An outline could cover chapter-by-chapter highlights.

How Many Readers?

Q. How does a book publisher handle an unsolicited manuscript? If the first person to read the manuscript doesn't like it, does it go any further or is it rejected then and there? If he thinks it has possibilities, does it then go to a second and third reader? Also, does a standard rejection slip without any comment usually indicate that the manuscript did not arouse any interest at all with that particular publishing house?
A. The first reader is as eager to find a bestseller as you are to write one. Through his experience and training he is able to spot those unsolicited manuscripts that show promise and those that do not. If he feels the manuscript has no market potential, he will reject it then and there. If it has possibilities, it may be given to another reader or to an editor. By a process of consultation and elimination the marketable manuscripts are decided upon. A standard rejection slip can mean several different things: they may have just bought a similar novel, or they've already asked one of their other authors to do a similar book, or they don't think they could make money with that particular book, even though some member of the staff may have found some degree of merit in the work.

Book Contract Terms

Q. What are the elements of a standard book contract and what terms should the author agree to?
A. There is no standard book contract—terms vary depending on the type of book, how it is sold, the track record of the author and other factors. The Authors Guild recommends that authors negotiate for royalty percentages on hardcover trade books of 10 percent of the retail price on the first five thousand copies, 12½ percent on the next five thousand and 15 percent thereafter. Publishers of textbooks and other specialized nonfiction books, however, often base their royalty percentages not on the retail price but on the publisher's net receipts—that is, the retail price less the bookstore discount, and often it is a flat percentage, not a sliding scale. Royalty contracts offered on paperbacks vary widely, but some common ones on trade paperbacks are: 6 percent on the first twenty thousand copies and 7½ percent thereafter. Mass market original paperback royalties are often 6 percent on net copies sold—the number of copies distributed minus the number of returns. And, of course, since paperback reprint rights are usually split 50 percent between author and original hardcover publisher, that means the author's royalty would only be 3 percent on a paperback reprint. Heavily illustrated children's books may split a 10 percent royalty (based on either retail price or net receipts) between author and artist.

Copyright should be in the author's name and the author may or may not grant "all rights" exclusively to the publisher or may share the rights to foreign editions, recordings or movie contracts on a non-exclusive basis.

A summary of other contract terms appears in the Appendix to the *Writer's Encyclopedia* and recommends ideals the established author should negotiate. Obviously the beginner with no previous publishing credits will probably have to settle for less.

A sample book contract can be purchased from the Society of Authors Representatives, Box 650, Old Chelsea Station, New York NY 10113 for seventy-five cents (send stamps or coins, no check) and a self addressed, stamped business envelope.

Book Advance

Q. What is an advance, and when does the author receive it? If it is indeed an advance on royalties, what happens if the book doesn't sell well? Does the author have to give the advance back?
A. An advance is an amount of money a publisher pays a writer before the book is published, in partial consideration for the time and effort the writer expends in producing the work. Often, the advance is a gauge of how well the publisher thinks the book will sell; advances are usually computed as a percentage of a book's estimated first year sales. When sales begin, the amount of the advance is deducted from the author's royalties before any payment is made to the author.

Ideally, the author's contract with the publisher should state that the advance is nonreturnable in the event that it exceeds the amount of royalties actually collected. A contract would also ideally provide that the publisher may not make any attempt to recoup the advance if he decides not to issue the book, or that the advance will be repaid only after the book is placed with another publisher.

Advances are usually paid in installments; for example, one-half of the advance might be paid when the author signs the contract, and one-half when he delivers a complete manuscript. The amount of advance will vary with the type of book, the author's writing ability and reputation, the type of publisher, and the specific book idea. There may be no advance at all in some cases, and the beginner can receive as little as $500. But as he writes book after book, and his audience and sales increase, he will usually receive increasingly larger advances.

Subsidiary Rights

Q. What are subsidiary rights and how should they be handled in my contracts?
A. "Subsidiary" is the classification for all rights to a book other than actual book publication. These rights include paperback reprint, book club, dramatic, radio, television, movie, foreign reprint, foreign language translation, audiovisual production, novelty and serial rights. The author and publisher divide profits from subsidiary rights, with the terms of percentages and who has the right to make subsidiary sales specified in the contract. Authors Guild guidelines suggest that the established author negotiate for at least 80 percent of the earnings on British editions of a book, 75 percent on other foreign reprints, 50 percent on paperback and book club sales, and 90 percent on sales to movie and television production companies. These terms should be discussed and agreed upon by author and publisher and included in any book contract. Actual earnings will, of course, depend on the success of the publisher or author's agent in selling the rights to the book.

Contract Negotiation

Q. If a publisher sends me a contract and I don't agree with certain parts of it but I do want that publisher to handle the book, what is the proper procedure? Should I cross out the questionable sections, sign it and return it? Or should I return the contract unsigned, with explanatory notes on the parts I don't like in the hope that the publisher will make the changes I want and send it back?

A. Handling the problem clauses by phone or mail is the usual practice. Contact the editor who issued the contract by phone and discuss the changes you want. If you handle negotiation by mail, you don't have to return the contract, since the publisher knows the contents. Just send a letter outlining your objections and the publisher will look it over and make his decision. Crossing out objectionable portions and signing the contract can be a good, aggressive way to get your point across, but this practice usually doesn't work for a beginner with no published books. If you've already had three or four books published, this tactic might work. But make sure you have a little clout before trying it.

Postponed Publication

Q. After a contract has been signed and the publication date set for my book, what do I do if the book isn't released on that date?

A. Whether publication postponements occur due to factors outside of or within a publisher's control, they *do* happen. Production schedules are often juggled when unexpected manuscripts and potential bestsellers bump from the publisher's list other, lower-priority books or "problem manuscripts" which need much work. There should be a specific time of publication inserted in your contract (usually a certain number of months after receipt of an acceptable manuscript). After you've delivered your manuscript, keep in touch with your editor by correspondence. Don't hestitate to ask, "What is the schedule for my book? When should I expect to receive the copyedited manuscript?" If the answers are vague and the time of publication as stated in the contract passes without production of your book, remind the editor with a prodding letter. Follow with a phone call, if necessary. If you still receive no word on when your book will be published, contact your editor's superior, the president of the company. When the delay reaches the point where you feel it's unreasonable, you can legally reclaim the rights to your book and try to sell it to another publisher.

Option Clause

Q. I sold a novel about fifteen years ago and the contract gave the publisher a sixty-day option on each of my next two novels. He has rejected my second novel since that time, and I'm almost finished with my third. Do I still have to submit it to him first, after all this time? What if he puts the same clause into the new contract?

A. Although fifteen years have passed, you are still required to submit the third book to the publisher to satisfy the terms of the contract. You may want to check with a lawyer about the wording of your option clause.

In answer to your second question, *don't sign* a contract with such a clause in it. Option clauses bind the author, not the publisher; this is why the Authors Guild recommends deletion of the clause from a book contract. Also, some option clauses state that the publisher can buy your book at the same price he bought the first; obviously, if the first book is a surprise bestseller, the writer would be able to sell the second book for a lot more money; so would come up the loser in a deal like this.

Until a publisher makes a decision on their option, you cannot submit the book to other publishers. If you must agree to some sort of option clause, novelist Dean Koontz advises limiting it to thirty days. That's long enough for a publisher to make up his mind. And the option clause should indicate that the terms are negotiable at that time.

Some other option items to remember: The option clause time period should not be keyed to publication of the first book, since this may hold up the author for a year on his next book. The author should be free to submit a new proposal any time after the first book has been accepted by the publisher. Also, the author should not have to submit a complete work under the option clause, but merely an outline and sample chapters.

Book Printer/Subsidy Publishers

Q. Two kinds of ads in writers' magazines confuse me. One is for "book printers"; the other is for a company which you pay to publish your book and which calls itself a "publisher" or "press." What's the difference?

A. The companies calling themselves "publishers" are usually subsidy presses, which produce your book for a fee. They do some advertising and send out review copies. They are discussed elsewhere in this chapter. Book printers print and bind a writer's book, leaving marketing and promotion to him. Local printers are often used by a writer who self-publishes his book, and are listed in the Yellow Pages.

Book Distribution

Q. I have recently self-published my book. Where can I find book sellers and distributors to handle it?

A. *The American Book Trade Directory* (published by R. R. Bowker Co. and available in most libraries) contains a list of names and addresses of major paperback distributors and book wholesalers, as well as bookstores. The work is divided into states and cities for easier reference.

Free Listings?

Q. I am in the process of publishing my own book. How can I notify libraries and advertise at an inexpensive rate?

A. To call your book to the attention of librarians, send a publicity release or similar newsworthy article to the various library magazines. Ask your librarian to show you some of these publications, such as *Library Journal*, the *ALA Booklist*, etc. Write advertising managers of these publications to learn their less expensive classified advertising rates. Another way to bring your book to the attention of librarians would be to send a mailing to the list of libraries in the *American Library Directory*.

Publishing Your Own Book

Q. If I have a book published, have it copyrighted, and advertise and sell a few copies, will I later be able to offer it to a larger publisher, or do you think this would ruin my chances of selling it to a larger firm?

A. Before printing this book on your own, first see if any "larger publisher" would be interested in it. If you couldn't interest a larger publisher in it before self-publishing, you might still find a buyer later, depending on your own success with the book.

Book Packager

Q. What is a "book packager?"

A. A "book packager" is a middleman supplying books to publishers. He may supply the books in any form, from raw manuscript to mechanicals (pasted-up camera-ready type), films for platemaking, or bound copies. The packager usually signs a contract with a publisher, then signs a different one with the writer based on what he thinks he can get the writer to do the work for, and what the writer thinks he's worth for that particular job. Some packagers pay the writer a flat fee, others split the advance and royalty with the author on a basis that may be fifty/fifty or some other terms. In either case, the author may not make as much money as he could if he sold his own book idea directly to a publisher. On the other hand, if the book packager has sold a set number of books to the publisher, the packager will be paid upon publication. This means that the author usually gets paid right away; whereas in the case of a regularly published book, the author has to wait another nine months or so for that first royalty statement and check. Also, depending on the packager's contract with the publisher, if the packager sells fifteen thousand copies, the author gets paid for fifteen thousand, not fifteen thousand minus, say, six thousand books that eventually are returned.

Self-Publishing

Q. What is "self-publishing" a book?
A. If an author submits his book and it is published by Random House, Doubleday, or another commercial publisher, the sales, promotion, production, and other facets of publishing are handled by them. If you self-publish your book, you in essence become your own Random House or Doubleday, and all the steps in publishing and marketing a book become your responsibility. You pay for the manufacturing, production, and marketing of your book, but you also keep all the profits. The basic steps in self-publishing are: having the manuscript typewritten or typeset in camera-ready form, planning or hiring the artwork, getting it printed and bound, advertising and distributing the book on consignment to bookstores or selling by direct mail order, keeping records and overseeing the entire publishing process. Each step involves considerable effort and some expense. Before self-publishing, you must decide whether sales of the book will earn enough money to pay back your investment. For more information on how to self-publish, see *The Publish-It-Yourself Handbook* and *How to Get Happily Published.*

Mimeographed Book?

Q. I am writing my first book manuscript and I plan to publish my own book. It will be eighty to one hundred pages. I will use letter-size paper folded, making pages about 5 1/2x8 1/2 inches. Has anyone ever produced a mimeographed paperback book? Can I copyright the mimeographed book? If, after offering it as a mimeographed work, I later wish to have it done by the printer I might choose, would there have to be another copyright?
A. Mimeographed paperback books have been produced, usually for local sales only. As far as the Copyright Office is concerned, a mimeographed manuscript is a "published work" and can be copyrighted. If you wish to have the mimeographed version redone later by a printer you would simply show on your copyright page, after your original copyright notice, "Second Printing" and the year.

Reprint Book

Q. I paid for the printing of a small how-to booklet (thirty-four pages), but don't know how to promote it. Could I send it to a publisher and expect it to be accepted, or because I printed it myself, would he refuse it?
A. A publisher would not necessarily refuse your booklet just because you printed it yourself,

but rather because book publishers don't buy such short books. You could sell copies of it to a how-to-do-it magazine which might use it for a subscription premium or for resale to their readers. Or, you might sell copies of it to some manufacturer of how-to tools or materials that might resell it or give it away to customers. An author has to be constantly searching for promotional ideas when promoting a book he's published himself. Paid classified ads in newspapers and magazines bring results, but you must be prepared to mail the books and keep accurate records, including state sales tax, if applicable.

Pay Publisher?

Q. Is it okay to pay a publisher to handle my book?
A. Subsidy publishers will issue your book only if you pay for the printing. That's the difference between subsidy and commercial publishers. Commercial publishers are willing to take a chance on the books they publish, but subsidy publishers make all their profits on the actual printing of books. Subsidy publishers provide minimal promotional effort. They usually agree to distribute copies of the book to reviewers and reprint rights buyers at other publishing companies, but these people usually ignore subsidy publishers' books. Consequently, publicity and sales prospects are not very encouraging. Since there is not a promising market for subsidy-published books, the publisher usually will not bind many copies of the first printing. When the contract expires, the author usually is offered all remaining stock of his title for purchase if he wishes—and that stock is usually in unbound sheets.

True, subsidy publishing *does* permit you to see your work in print, and some 10 percent of those writers who use subsidy presses recoup their losses. But a writer shouldn't subsidy publish unless he has tried without success to sell his book to a commercial publisher and is willing to make the investment for an unsure return.

For more information on subsidy publishing, send SASE to *Writer's Digest*, 9933 Alliance Rd., Cincinnati OH 45242. Ask for the free reprint, "Does it pay to have it published?"

Hardback vs Paperback

Q. Why are some books published in hardback and others in paperback? Does it make any difference in royalties?
A. Until recent years, most paperbacks were reprints of hardcover books. But now, many publishers of paperbacks are buying original fiction and nonfiction—especially of the types that can be sold to large mass market buyers. Hundreds of thousands of people will pay $3.95 for a romance novel, but won't pay $15.95 for a hardcover book. Other kinds of book buyers will buy the latest nonfiction book or mainstream novel by a bestselling author and pay the hardcover price. Royalties on hardback and paperback books are covered in another question in this chapter.

One or More Publishers?

Q. Some authors have more than one publisher, others seem to stay with the same one. Why is this?
A. Some authors produce books that are not handled by their original publisher—for example, science fiction novels and specialized books on golf. Other authors have publishers that produce a wide range of fiction and nonfiction in both hardcover and paperback. They are satisfied with the way their books are published and promoted, so they stay with one company.

License to Sell?

Q. I have written a book and am considering having it printed, taking out my own copyright and distributing the book myself until it realizes a market or dies. What kind of license, if any, will I need to sell and distribute my book? Can you recommend a reputable and economical printer in the Los Angeles area to handle a paperback edition?
A. If you are going to sell copies of your book to consumers in your state you will need a vendor's license and must collect sales tax. Contact the tax department of your state. If there are any local licenses required, you had best clarify this with local city officials. A list of book manufacturers appears in the directory, *Literary Market Place*, c/o R. R. Bowker, 205 E. 42nd Street, New York NY 10017 (also available at most main branch public library reference departments). You may also wish to contact companies listed under "Printers" in the Yellow Pages.

Second Edition

Q. I published my own book. I'd like to query commercial publishers about a second edition, but how can I approach them about this idea?
A. Submit a copy of your book to several publishers along with a concise description of it, and indicate what you consider the market potential for the book, details on the sales record you achieved on your own, and any other pertinent information likely to convince them to invest in your project. Include copies of notable reviews and special promotional contacts you may have. You should mention that you are making a simultaneous submission of this book to a number of publishers and would appreciate a response from them as to whether or not they would be interested in publishing a second edition.

Commercial vs Subsidy

Q. I have a collection of short pieces, many of which have been purchased and published by periodicals. I plan to offer these for publication in book form and have received letters of release from the periodicals. If I self-publish, will I own the copyright? If I sell the collection to a standard publisher, will he own the copyright?
A. All books published by standard royalty book publishers are copyrighted in the name of the author. Even if the author pays to have the book published by a subsidy publisher, he should require that the book be copyrighted in his name.

Book Publishing Costs

Q. Is an author required to furnish a large sum of money before his book is published? If photos are in the book, will these cost extra?
A. Only if his book is published by a subsidy publisher will the author have to pay. Trade publishers assume all regular production costs and usually pay the author an advance against potential royalty earnings. Photos increase the cost of publishing a book, and the publisher involved will determine who absorbs this extra expense. Black-and-white photographs are less expensive than color photographs.

Book Introductions

Q. I can write a good introduction for my book, but wouldn't it be better if a specialist in the field wrote the introduction?

A. An introduction by a specialist lends more authority to a book. This is usually handled by the publisher. In your covering letter, indicate that you know of several prominent persons in the field who might be willing to write an introduction if the publisher is interested in the book.

Pay for Foreword?

Q. Are book forewords paid for or are most of them complimentary? A well-known author knew the subject of a biography I am about to publish and I'd like to ask him to write the foreword for my book. Will he expect payment, and if so, how much should I offer him?
A. Most are complimentary, but people who write forewords are sometimes offered an honorarium. If offered, rate depends on several things: length required, the "name" of the person who is asked to write the foreword, the complexity of the material to be written. Rates range from one hundred to five hundred dollars and up. It depends on how much work is involved—if the author knows the subject of a biography you are about to publish and if that author is a good friend of the subject, he may be willing to write the foreword as a compliment and may not require payment for it. Suggest to your publisher that this person do the foreword, giving details about why you think he might be the best one to provide a meaningful foreword. In some cases, the publisher will pay the person who writes the foreword, or costs may be split between publisher and author.

Best Book to Write?

Q. What's the best book I could write to make sure I'd be published?
A. *Writer's Digest* editor Bill Brohaugh says it best: "The best book you can write to be published is *your* best book." In other words, your best shot at selling a book to a publisher is to write about what you want to write about, and write it as well as you can. It doesn't necessarily matter what's currently selling; the book business is full of unknowns and unexpecteds. Who would have ever thought that a philosophical novel about a bird, or the story of a Mafia family could have become bestsellers? It happened with Richard Bach's *Jonathan Livingston Seagull* and Mario Puzo's *The Godfather.* If anybody doubted the observations of a harried housewife, the life story of a Yorkshire veterinarian, or an eccentric English lady's tips on dog training would be successful, Erma Bombeck, James Herriot, and Barbara Woodhouse proved them wrong.

If you're writing a genre book such as a romance novel, you will have to follow some rather specific guidelines. Beyond that, however, choose whatever interests *you* and query a publisher with a good letter and a solid proposal, including sample chapters, to convince him that others will be informed, inspired, or entertained by what you've written.

Design Input?

Q. Will I have any input on the cover design for my novel?
A. When a publisher accepts a book he reserves the right to decide on such selling points as title and cover design, but you can make suggestions after the book is accepted. Most publishers usually prefer to work with their own graphic designers.

Reprint Your Book

Q. My book is now out of print, with all rights reassigned to me. I have the opportunity to self-publish it. Can I use the old plates purchased from the original publisher for this purpose?
A. As long as you have purchased the plates and have the rights from the original publisher,

you can self-publish a reprint of your book using the original plates. You will need to find a printer who is able to use the plates on his press.

Library of Congress Catalog Card Number

Q. How can I get a Library of Congress catalog card number for my book?
A. Your publisher's production or editorial department will usually do this for you. If you've self-published your book, apply for the number by contacting the Cataloging in Publication Program, Library of Congress, Washington DC 20540. They'll send you an application to complete. When your book is published, you must then send the Library of Congress a complimentary copy, and they'll determine whether or not to keep the book for their collections and prepare suitable catalog cards.

Textbook Royalties

Q. Do textbook publishers have a standard royalty schedule? Does the same royalty apply to textbooks as well as books in the trade division?
A. Textbook publishers do not have a standard royalty or the same royalty schedule as trade book publishers. College textbooks may vary from 6 percent to 19 percent of the *net* price the publisher receives, while elementary and secondary texts may be only 3 percent to 5 percent, depending on illustration costs and the amount of staff work that must be done by the publisher.

"Acceptable" Manuscript

Q. My friend says his book contract has a clause which states the manuscript "must be acceptable to the publisher in form and content," and that if it isn't, he must return the advance he was paid. Do most contracts have this clause?
A. Yes, although there are variations in the wording. Some clauses require the return of the advance only if the manuscript is sold to another publisher; others require it whether the manuscript resells or not. In attempting to avoid the burden to the author when his manuscript is subjectively pronounced unacceptable by his publisher, the Authors Guild recommends a rewording of the clause: "The Author shall deliver a manuscript which in style and content is professional, competent, and fit for publication." Publishers may find manuscripts unacceptable for several reasons. The author didn't deliver what his outline promised, and despite editorial suggestions refuses to revise. The market may have changed and the publisher is dissatisfied more with the terms of the bargain than the manuscript itself. The publisher's lawyers may have concluded that publishing a controversial book would put the house in danger of many lawsuits. All of these reasons help courts decide the good faith of the author or publisher when the unacceptable clause is invoked.

After Acceptance

Q. Once a writer submits his final manuscript to the publisher and it is accepted, what part does he play in the production process?
A. First of all, you'll have to read the copyedited manuscript and respond to any challenges of fact or clarify any vague statements. Then you'll have to read either galley proofs (the typeset copy prior to actual page makeup) or page proofs, if the publisher works with word processors and does not use galley proofs. These must be checked for errors on the part of the typesetter, or last minute corrections you may have previously overlooked. In special cases, such as illustrated books, the publisher may wish you to review a photocopy of the pasteup to

proofread the captions for illustrations. If your book is nonfiction, you may be responsible for providing an index. Usually the publisher will hire the indexer at the author's expense (this could cost five hundred dollars) and this appears as a deduction on the first royalty statement. You'll have to proofread the contents page, the glossary, and the bibliography if there are any, plus the acknowledgments page where any copyright permissions appear, along with any thanks for research help or access to special documents, etc. You'll be asked to review the jacket copy and your biographical information, along with the photograph if you provided one.

Simultaneous Submission

Q. A playwright I know sends seven copies of his plays simultaneously to various producers. He claims it is all right to do the same with book manuscripts. If two editors make offers, then you can take the best offer, or even bargain, he says. Is it all right to do this without telling editors it is a simultaneous submission?
A. Many writers who have tired of the long wait for replies from publishers have adopted this technique. Some writers advise the editor it's a multiple submission. Others say no, they'll worry about that if they get more than one acceptance.

Anthology Editing

Q. Over the years I've collected many articles on a particular topic that interests me. If they were compiled into an anthology, they would make very interesting reading. Putting together an anthology doesn't sound too difficult, but I don't know where to start. Any suggestions?
A. Rather than jumping into the preparation of a full manuscript, send some queries first, to find an interested publisher. With your query, include photocopies of the first pages of a few selections to be included. You may have trouble selling your idea because many editors feel that a book written by a single author stands a better chance for big sales. In your query, establish your authority in the subject area to be covered. You should know your subject well, or you'll have trouble compiling enough material for a book in a reasonable amount of time. You will have to work hard to convince an editor that your topic is important and warrants his risk in publication. For more on obtaining the proper reprint permissions and preparing the actual manuscript, see the chapter on Anthology Editing in *Jobs for Writers*.

Essay Anthology

Q. I want to compile an anthology of essays. Should I secure copyright releases before submitting it? Can I copyright the anthology?
A. You shouldn't get copyright releases before submitting to a publisher since a publisher may not want some selections and may want others not included in the original manuscript. After the manuscript is accepted, you should write the requests for permission, citing chapter and page, and preferably, also including a copy of the passage. Any reprint fees are usually paid for by the publisher, but deducted from the anthologist's royalties before he gets paid.

Anthologies may be copyrighted in the name of the author/editor or the publisher, depending on the type of book and the terms of the contract. The use of essays in your anthology does not inhibit their future use in some other anthology.

39 Where Can I Find Out About Writers' Groups, Conferences and Colonies?

Writing is a lonely art. Often a freelancer is the only one in his community pursuing the craft and trade magazines like *The Writer* and *Writer's Digest* are his only link with professional colleagues. That's why joining a national writers organization and attending local or regional workshops and writers conferences can add so much to the professional outlook of the isolated writer.

Finding a Writers Club

Q. Should I join a local writers club? How can I find one in my area?
A. There are many different opinions on the value of writers clubs, basically because there are many different types of clubs. A good club can provide the opportunity for you to establish friendships and contacts while gaining valuable tips from professionals who are currently writing and selling. Clubs which criticize manuscripts honestly, discuss only writing-related topics and invite prominent local writers to speak, instill motivation and zest in their members and are an essential lifeline to what's going on in the publishing world today. If you find a club in your area with these qualities, it would be a good idea to join. Writers need camaraderie.

Writers dislike some groups because they have a non-professional atmosphere where the emphasis is more on socializing than criticizing manuscripts or studying the markets and learning from each others' experiences. Others don't like clubs that allow their members to read their own work in a self-glorifying manner. Avoid clubs which have these amateurish characteristics, as well as those which seem to do nothing other than sit around and gripe about lack of sales.

Your local librarian or newspaper book critic may have names and addresses of clubs in your area. Or, if there is no local club in your area and you'd like to start one, send fifty cents and a business-size SASE for a copy of "How to Start/Run a Writer's Club" to Writer's Digest Books, 9933 Alliance Rd., Cincinnati OH 45242.

Writers Organizations

Q. Should I join a national writers organization? Are there specific organizations for

different types of writers?
A. Membership in a national professional writing group can help you establish a professional image, as it increases your visibility and may help you land assignments. Some of these organizations can also help you by acting as your representative in certain legal cases or disputes, as well as giving you access to specialized information and publications. Most national organizations require that you qualify for membership as a "professional," which may mean having sold to various reputable publications or publishers.

There are organizations for just about every type of writer, from the Mystery Writers of America to the Poetry Society of America. These are described in the *Encyclopedia of Associations* which can be found at most libraries. You should join the organization which is aimed at your field of writing. Membership fees are usually under fifty to one hundred dollars. A helpful organization for beginners is the National Writers Club, 1450 S. Havana, Aurora CO 80012.

Magazine Writers

Q. Is there a professional organization of magazine writers?
A. The Society of Magazine Writers is now called the American Society of Journalists and Authors, and is located at 1501 Broadway, Suite 1907, New York NY 10036.

Writers/Authors Guild

Q. What's the difference between the Authors Guild and the Writers Guild?
A. The Authors Guild is a national professional organization of over six thousand book and magazine writers. The membership of the Writers Guild consists of movie, TV, and radio script writers. Prospective Authors Guild members are required to have published a book at an established American publishing house within seven years prior to application for membership, or three fiction or nonfiction pieces in a general circulation magazine within the previous eighteen months. The Guild is involved in such issues as free speech, copyright, and taxes, and has represented the interests of writers both in Congress and in the courts. The organization also provides writers with information on contract provisions. If you are eligible for membership, contact the Authors Guild, 234 W. 44th St., New York NY 10036.

The Writers Guild of America (WGA) has two branches, East and West (divided by the Mississippi River for administrative purposes), each of which publishes its own monthly newsletter and operates a manuscript registration service for the purposes of verifying the date of script authorship. You must have sold to or been employed to write a TV, radio, or movie script within two years prior to your application. WGA West has an initiation fee of $1,500 with membership dues of $25 per quarter plus 1 percent of your gross earnings in the field. Fees for WGA East are $500 initiation, annual dues of $50 and 1½ percent of gross earnings. WGA West is located at 8955 Beverly Blvd., Los Angeles CA 90048. WGA East is located at 555 West 57th Street, New York NY 10019.

Trade Magazine Writers

Q. Is there a national association of trade magazine writers?
A. Yes. It's Associated Business Writers of America, and the mailing address is 1450 S. Havana, Suite 620, Aurora CO 80012.

Writers Workshops

Q. I have heard about writers workshops and conferences. Do I have to be a published author to attend one? What will I gain by going to a workshop?
A. Writers workshops and conferences are considered a great source of information and inspiration for all writers, beginning or experienced. They allow you to establish friendships with other writers and editors and escape the loneliness of writing. They offer not only encouragement but practical advice and information on market trends and needs, and writing techniques. At a conference, you may hear lectures from published authors, get to talk with an editor or publisher, or even acquire an agent—it all depends on the type of conference you attend. Conferences are varied—some have a focused theme while others are very general; some last one day or a weekend while others may run for two weeks. You don't have to be a published author to attend; in fact, beginners have the chance to gain the most by meeting other writers and establishing contacts with editors—fueling their enthusiasm for writing. You can get more information on conferences and workshops by consulting the annual May issue of *Writer's Digest* or the annual *Literary Market Place* and writing to individual conference directors for information.

Conference Locales

Q. When and where are writers conferences usually held?
A. Writers conferences are held throughout the year, but mostly in the summer months. Locations vary. Many are held on college campuses or in large hotels, but some meet at state parks or libraries. Consult the annual May issue of *Writer's Digest* for a state-by-state listing of conferences and when and where they are held.

Conference Checklist

Q. I'm about to attend my first conference and want to be sure to get the most out of it I possibly can. What should I do to ensure I get my money's worth?
A. Take advantage of *everything* the conference has to offer. Come on time to each session. Attend all the informal events as well as the structured ones. You may learn as much at lunch as you do in a lecture room, because the best "shop talk" always occurs at luncheons or banquets. Even if you don't get to talk to a staff member, you'll learn a lot just by staying in the circle and listening. Always ask good questions, but don't overstep your bounds by stopping speakers on their way to the lecture hall or monopolizing the question period. And if you find yourself in a group more concerned with casual chitchat than "writing" talk, move to another group. You'll get more out of your time that way.

Conference Preparation

Q. What should I do to get ready for my conference? What should I bring with me?
A. The most important thing you can bring with you to a writers conference is an open and alert mind, ready and willing to listen and learn. You should be filled with ideas and questions, and a desire to get out and meet and talk with the writers and editors who will be there. You will probably want to take along a specific manuscript to work on as new ideas are presented to you, as well as copies of some work you submitted for criticism, if that service will be available. And before going, inquire as to what clothes you'll need, as it may be totally casual or there may be one or two formal affairs.

Choosing a Workshop

Q. How do I select the right workshop for me?
A. The key word to remember when selecting a workshop or conference is *research*. "Select a conference as carefully as you would a publisher," the editor of *Writer's Market* advises. First, decide which type of conference will be most helpful to you—make sure the focus of the conference matches your writing interests and goals. Next, write for details about the conference's staff, location, accommodations, fees, length, and dates. Study the conference program: Will there be a chance for personal consultations with members of the staff? Are there opportunities for manuscript criticism? Research the staff carefully—check *Contemporary Authors* and *Books in Print* to see what they've wrtten and, preferably, read some of the staff's works. That way you'll know what they are qualified to speak about, and you'll be able to ask pertinent questions. You might also ask the conference director for the name and address of someone who has attended the conference in the past who might be willing to give you his opinion of it. If you take the time to do this basic research, you should feel confident that the conference you select is one which is well-tailored to suit your needs and will give you your money's worth.

Revisit Same Conference?

Q. Is it worth going to the same writer's conference you may have attended a year or two before?
A. Since the writers who are brought in to act as workshop leaders, panelists, and luncheon speakers are usually different each year, yes, most writers find it worthwhile to attend a conference more than once. Some writers who live within commuting distance of more than one conference, however, like to try new conferences from time to time, especially when a particular writer or editor they want to meet will be featured.

Where Writers Meet?

Q. I have read about the days in Paris when writers gathered at certain addresses. Are there such places where writers are known to gather informally today . . . Paris, London, New York City, or other cities in the world? How can I find the addresses of such places?
A. No, there aren't. But there are various writers colonies located throughout the United States, such as Yaddo in Saratoga Springs, New York and the MacDowell colony in Peterborough, New Hampshire, where hundreds of professional writers may come throughout the year to write in a peaceful environment and, if they wish, discuss their writing with others. Other places you may find writers gathered are writers conferences, many of which are held throughout the year on university campuses nationwide. A list of these appears annually in the May issue of *Writer's Digest*.

Writers Colony

Q. I have heard of special places where writers go to write on a daily schedule and where meals and facilities are included. Is this what one can expect at a writers colony?
A. If you are looking for a peaceful place away from the hustle and bustle of the everyday world, where you can write, uninterrupted, for hours each day, a writers colony is the place for you. Though each colony is slightly different from the others (some accept beginners, others do not, for example), all provide a comfortable and private atmosphere which seems to encourage writing, and the opportunity for interaction and discussion with other writers, if you

desire it. The cost of a stay at a writers colony varies greatly—some are free, while others offer scholarships or charge a weekly or seasonal rate. The cost may or may not include meals, again depending upon the colony. Some require you to submit an application, which may ask for writing samples and recommendations from former residents or other notable people. Information about writers colonies is sometimes available from Poets & Writers, Inc., 201 W. 54th St., New York NY 10019 and from The Center For Arts Information, 625 Broadway, New York NY 10012. The August 1983 issue of *Writer's Digest* featured a comprehensive article about sixteen colonies. Although back issues of that issue are not available, you could refer to it at a public library.

Prisoner Writers

Q. I have heard there are some organizations which provide services for writers in prison. How can I get in touch with these groups?
A. Art Without Walls is a group which mails free books to prisoners upon request, in addition to sponsoring writing workshops and lecture series in New York state prisons and promoting education programs in prisons nationwide. Its address is 72 Fifth Avenue, New York NY 10011. COSMEP Prison Project donates books and literary magazines to prisons and prisoners, as well as publishing a newsletter written by and for prisoners twice a year. You can write COSMEP % *The Greenfield Review*, Greenfield Center NY 12833.

40 What Full-Time Jobs Are Available to a Writer?

People who seek full-time writing or editing jobs usually traverse one of two routes. They attend journalism school or they acquire a good general liberal arts background. There are exceptions, of course; some start out in science and wind up in scientific or technical publishing; others turn from teaching to corporate communications. Being a full-time freelance writer is a challenging goal and many writers opt for a regular salary for their writing skill.

Getting a Newspaper Job

Q. What can a beginning writer do to get a job on a small newspaper staff?
A. Try to place some freelance features with the newspaper you'd like to work for, so the editor can see that 1) you know what a good feature is, and 2) you write well. Also supply them with news items from a section of their newspaper circulation area that is not well covered. Show them samples of your work that are similar to what they publish. For information on newspaper writing, see *Stalking the Feature Story,* by William Ruehlmann.

Newspapers vs Magazines

Q. What are the advantages of working for a magazine versus working for a newspaper?
A. One of the major differences is that newspapers work against much shorter deadlines than magazines, often a matter of hours for a newspaper as opposed to weeks or months for a magazine. A writer who doesn't like or doesn't work well under this kind of pressure is better off working for a magazine. Another difference is that due to the longer deadlines magazine writers have a chance to develop their ideas into more in-depth articles, and newspaper writers must be concerned with quick, up-to-the-minute reporting.

According to 1983 figures from The Newspaper Fund, starting salaries for newspapers were $191 to $200 for weeklies and $221 to $230 for dailies. Magazine starting salaries ranged from $231 to $240. Salaries for experienced writers vary depending on the circulation of the publication, whether a union is involved and the qualifications of the individual.

Journalism Internships

Q. How can I find out about internships in journalism?

A. Writer's Digest Books publishes an annual directory entitled *Internships,* which contains descriptions of and facts about available positions as well as a section on how to apply. Besides listing about sixteen thousand available positions, it offers articles on creating your own internship, applying for those listed and help for foreign applicants. *The Student Guide to Mass Media Internships* describes internship positions in several areas of both print and electronic media.

Book Publishing Jobs

Q. What kinds of writing jobs are available in the book publishing industry?
A. Although duties vary with the size and scope of each publishing house, here are some of the jobs that might be available: copyediting and proofreading, if the work is not usually sent out to freelancers; editorial assistants who screen unsolicited manuscripts; publicity writers for the promotion department, who do a variety of writing, including advertising copy, brochures, letters of policy and product introduction, press releases, and dust jacket copy.

A good direction for the novice to take when looking for work in a publishing house is to read the classified ads in *Publishers Weekly,* which carry job openings in publishing companies, as well as the names of employment agencies which specialize in hiring for publishers. Another thing to consider is the Radcliffe (College) Course in Publishing Procedures which is offered each year and whose graduates usually go on to jobs in the industry. A helpful book listing the Radcliffe and other specialized courses is *Peterson's Guide to Book Publishing Courses/Academic and Professional Programs.* This book is updated quarterly by the Association of American Publishers, One Park Ave., New York NY 10016, in the *Publishing Education Newsletter.*

Advertising Copywriter

Q. How can I get into the advertising field and put my skill to work writing copy for ads?
A. You have several options. Try to get freelance assignments from a local advertising agency. Send a letter of introduction to the creative director, possibly offering to write an ad on speculation for one of their clients. "Be honest about your inexperience," says writer Jean M. Stone. (For more on freelance ad copywriting, see Chapter 31.) If you want to work for an advertising agency as a staff copywriter, you might have to start out learning the trade in journeyman fashion. Small agencies occasionally have openings for new writers. These positions are usually low-paying and often involve mechanical, routine chores. However, they provide an excellent opportunity to learn the business, and to work up to a copywriting job. Also, some large corporations offer formal training programs for employees in their creative departments.

Broadcasting Jobs

Q. Where can I find out more about writing-related jobs in the broadcasting industry?
A. For books describing the different kinds of jobs available, check the *Subject Guide to Books in Print* under the categories of "Broadcasting" and "Broadcasting as a Profession." Read trade magazines for the field such as *Broadcasting,* available in most libraries, and contact professional organizations such as the National Association of Broadcasters, 1771 N St., NW, Washington DC 20036. A wide variety of internships available at both radio and television stations are listed in *1984 Internships.*

Public Relations

Q. I'd like to own my own public relations agency some day, but before I can do that, I have to break into the field. How can I go about this?
A. To start, it's a good idea to obtain training in the theory and techniques of public relations, whether it be through courses taken in college, or, if you aren't attending college, through workshops presented by professional groups such as the Public Relations Society or Women In Communications. However, the best training comes when theory and experience are combined in an internship. You don't need experience to get one of these entry-level (but usually short-term) jobs, and they are available with public relations firms, advertising agencies, business firms, newspapers, television, and radio stations. From this kind of work, you can gain valuable knowledge of the mechanics and operations involved in public relations. Furthermore, you will have a decided advantage over others with little or no experience when you apply for a job. If you don't want to deal with work as an apprentice, you could begin by applying directly to public relations firms or departments for a beginner's job. When making personal calls upon prospective business employers, ask to see the director of public relations, the personnel manager, or the office manager. At a newspaper or broadcasting station ask to see the Advertising and Promotion Manager. It may take a lot of calls and letters to land a job, but the stronger your efforts, the better your chances are of breaking into the field of public relations. For more information on the subject check *Subject Guide to Books in Print* under "Public Relations" and "Public Relations—Vocational Guidance." Then see if any of the listed books are in your local, public, or college library or bookstore.

Staff Writing Job

Q. Where can I look for a writing job in the publishing field? Are there any magazines with classified sections I can refer to?
A. You might wish to consult the trade magazine, *Publishers Weekly,* which has a large classified ad section that lists job openings with book publishers. *Folio,* a trade magazine for the magazine field, has a smaller classified section. *Editor and Publisher,* a trade magazine for the newspaper industry, has a large classified section which separates newspapers by region. Advertising in the "Positions Wanted" column of these publications may bring you results. These magazines are available at public libraries. Finally, consult the Yellow Pages for private commercial employment agencies which may also help you find newspaper, magazine, or book publishing positions.

Clipping Services

Q. What is a clipping service and how profitable is it to work for one?
A. Clipping services hire people to read thousands of newspapers and magazines and clip out items on various subjects that writers or publishers request. Authors often engage clipping services to collect information on a subject they are researching that is currently in the news, and publishers generally employ them to clip reviews of books they've published. Costs for a clipping service vary, but usually cover a set monthly fee and an additional amount for each clip provided. These firms are sometimes listed in the Yellow Pages under "Clipping Bureaus." Most services require their employees to work out of the company office, so it's not something you could do as a freelancer.

Other Writing Jobs

Q. I'd like to work on a newspaper but am having trouble finding any openings. What other similiar career choices do I have?

A. There is a wealth of related careers which you can pursue if you're having no luck finding a job on a newspaper. Businesses and industries are always looking for people to edit and write their company publications, just as unions need people to perform the same tasks for their newsletters and various labor press items. Charitable and health organizations also need freelancers and provide excellent contacts for future job opportunities. Trade magazines of industries where scientific or engineering work is reported need writers and editors. If none of these interests you, consider writing or editing for a city or town. These need people to work on their Chamber of Commerce magazines, write historical booklets on the city, or write tourist brochures. Doing this kind of work entails becoming as closely involved with the goings-on of a city as you would if you were a reporter with a certain local beat. If you want a job almost identical to that of a newspaper staffer, you could work as a wire service reporter or write columns and articles for the syndicated news feature services. Don't rule out writing for TV or radio even if your primary interest isn't on-air broadcasting; the reporters who work behind the scenes for these media do the same work newspapermen do. Finally, you can consider contacting the Office of Personnel Management about possible openings the U.S. government may have in one of the several thousand media-related jobs it has from time to time. In a government writing job you may find yourself doing work for the press, TV or other public information media, or creating pamphlets which describe public services and government projects. Any one of the above-mentioned careers may pay close to or more than a newspaper job pays, and if you land a job in an area that really interests you, you may find it even more rewarding than a newspaper career could have been for you.

41 How Much Can I Expect to Earn?

How much a writer can earn working as a staff person with a newspaper, magazine, book publishing, or broadcasting company is pretty well determined by already established rates in the industry and the writer's experience. How much he can earn as a freelancer depends on his ideas, energy, research and writing skills, and the marketplace. Before he can realize a profit, a freelancer needs to cover his overhead plus an additional 25 percent to cover the fringe benefits of insurance and hospitalization normally provided by an employer. But that doesn't stop a dedicated freelancer working to fulfill the dream of full-time self-employment as a writer.

Writers' Average Income

Q. Every so often I read something about the average salary of writers in America. The income mentioned is so low that I cannot see how the supposedly high-priced TV and movie writers can be included in this average. Is the average writer someone like me who works full-time at another job and has never sold anything for more than $15?

A. The "average salary" is arrived at by a study of the incomes of all types of writers. Since there are so many more part-time and low-earning writers (like yourself) than there are top TV and screen writers, it is not hard to see why the resultant average income is not very high.

Starting Salaries

Q. I will soon graduate from an accredited school of journalism. Can you give me any information on the starting salaries for entry level positions at newspapers and/or broadcasting stations?

A. The 1983 *Journalism Career and Scholarship Guide,* prepared by the Dow Jones Newspaper Fund, Inc., reports that the beginning weekly salary at large daily newspapers ranges from $221 to $230. Weekly newspapers and radio broadcasters pay $191 to $200 for starters, and television stations pay $201 to $210.

Newspaper Features

Q. Should I set a price for my feature article, or does the newspaper editor set the rate of pay? How do I determine my own pay scale?

A. If you are just getting started as a freelance writer, don't try to do too much bargaining with an editor. Take what he offers and give him the best piece of writing you can. If he wants you to rewrite, do it. It is important that you get quality work published. When you feel you have made enough sales to warrant it, you might begin to set your own rates. Before you quote a price to an editor, do some thorough researching of the going rate in your area and have a general idea how much work is involved and how long it will take you to complete the assignment. What payment you finally receive will depend on your previous record, the locale, and your ability to negotiate.

Magazine Rates

Q. How much money can I expect to earn from a typical magazine article sale?
A. What magazines pay freelancers depends largely on what they *can* pay (in terms of circulation and advertising revenue), the length of the article in question, and the reputation of the writer. With some publications, the fee paid is standard, and with others it is negotiable. For example, a small journal, like *Northeast Horseman,* with a circulation of only five thousand, pays $5 to $35 for pieces of 500 to 3,500 words. *Sports Illustrated,* on the other hand, will pay $1,000 for a story of national scope. Check the market listings in *Writer's Market* for specific rates various magazines will pay for freelance material.

Copy vs Charts

Q. I want to submit a how-to article to a magazine listed in Writer's Market *that pays by the word. The problem is that I spend much more time on the charts and diagrams that accompany the article than I spend on the actual writing. In fact, my articles often contain very little copy. What should I do?*
A. The magazine will most likely consider payment for artwork separately from that for the article itself depending on its quality. Often an editor must have his staff redo the artwork. You might write and ask this particular editor for an answer to your question.

Ghost Fees

Q. What is the average rate charged by ghostwriters for articles and books?
A. A ghostwriter's fees will vary from $15 to $40 an hour or $5 to $10 a page. When writing an "as-told-to" book in which he gets a byline, the writer receives at least the full author's advance and 50 percent of the royalties. The subject gets the other 50 percent.

Rates for Jokes

Q. I have an opportunity to sell some of my work to a well-known humorist for one of his books of collected jokes. He asked me to send my material and quote a price per joke. What is a reasonable price? I don't want to risk losing the sale by charging too much, but I also want to get as much as I can from the deal.
A. Gene Perret, who has written for Carol Burnett, Tim Conway and the television show *Three's Company,* as well as authored *How to Write and Sell Your Sense of Humor,* says single gags can bring from $2 to $10. It's hard to know what would be acceptable to this particular humorist, so you might consider putting yourself in his position and try to estimate how much he could afford to pay for a sizable number of jokes without taking too much out of the advance he's getting against royalties. And when you send your jokes to him, you can always quote a price and make it clear that you are open for negotiation.

Comedy Fees?

Q. An entertainer asked me to show him a few of my skits, which run from five to fifteen minutes. How much should I charge for permitting him to use the material?
A. What you should charge for your material depends largely on how much you can get. Minor entertainers obviously cannot pay large fees, while big-name entertainers pay their writers large salaries. A new comedian may try to get a five-minute routine for $150, but a leading entertainer might pay $1,500 for a five-minute skit from a top writer.

Fair Price?

Q. What is a fair price for writing historical articles to be published in a commemorative book marking the hundredth anniversary of a village?
A. Remuneration will have to be based on two factors: what you think the job is worth and what the customer will pay. You will have to calculate approximately how much time and effort will be spent on researching and writing these articles, try to find out the budget of your client, then charge accordingly.

Royalties—When?

Q. A book I've written has been accepted for publication. How soon will it be before I can expect to receive any of my royalties?
A. For starters, it probably will be at least a year before your book is published. After your book goes on sale, your first royalty statement will probably arrive six to eight months later. Publishers usually send royalty statements every six months.

Typesetting Writer

Q. I am trying to get started in the typesetting business. How do I decide what to charge for final page, camera-ready copy?
A. First, decide what your fixed costs are and the profit margin you need to successfully operate your business. Then make some phone calls around town as though you were a prospective customer, to find out what the going rate is among your competitors. Base your final price on a balance between what you think the current traffic will bear and the profit you need for successful operation of your business.

Research and Writing Fees

Q. I have a friend who wants me to help him write a book. My job would include manuscript rewriting, research work and editing. What should I charge for these services?
A. In the section entitled "How Much Should I Charge?" in *Writer's Market,* fees for book rewriting are listed at $7.50 to $12 per hour and up, sometimes $5 per page. Doing research for another writer can bring $10 to $30 an hour and up. Book copyediting runs $7.50 to $9 per hour and up; sometimes it's one dollar per page. To find out what the going rate is in your area, seek out other writers or friends in related businesses or agencies that hire freelancers and find out what has been paid for these specific jobs in the past. You might also try to get your friend to quote you his budget before you name your price.

Easiest? Best? It Depends

Q. What is the best market for freelance writers? What sells most easily?
A. There is no such thing as one best market since so much depends on the type of writing each individual writer does. A market is good for a particular writer if he writes the kind of material that market needs. In general there are many more markets for articles than short stories.

What's a Fiction Bestseller Worth?

Q. How much would a book on the fiction bestseller list bring an author if it were number one for a period of a week or a month? Assume the book sells at average price and a standard royalty is paid.
A. The minimum royalty payment paid on trade books by many publishers is 10 percent of the retail price of the book on the first 5,000 copies sold; 12½ percent on the next 5,000 and 15 percent thereafter. Prices paid for movie, paperback and book club rights vary, but a novel that sells 45,000 hardcover copies and is bought by movies, book clubs, and paperback houses could earn the author more than $300,000.

Royalty Audit

Q. Is there an agency whose service might be to investigate the actual number of books sold by a publisher? My royalties to date have been very low and I'd like to know just how many copies of my book have been sold.
A. Your royalty statement should show the actual number of copies sold. The only way to verify the actual number of books sold by a publisher would be to have access to the publisher's accounting records. Some book contracts have a clause which says the author has the right to bring his Certified Public Accountant to the publisher's office to check the sales records and accounting procedures. Even if your contract does not have such a clause, you still have the legal right to request such a review, provided you are willing to go to the expense of hiring a CPA. Fees for these services range from fifty dollars per hour and up and royalty examinations could cost several thousand dollars, so only an author with sales sufficient to warrant such an audit should engage a CPA.

Safe to Freelance Full-Time?

Q. How much should I earn as a writer before I can feel secure enough to quit my job and become a full-time freelancer? Can writers really make a living freelancing?
A. It's safe to start thinking about becoming a full-time freelance writer when your freelancing income over a period of several months equals or is greater than the salary earned on your regular job in that same time period. Plenty of writers have succeeded after breaking away from regular full-time employment, but the road to success isn't easy. You'll be better off if you enter into the venture with your eyes wide open to the disadvantages that you'll face. If you quit your job, you'll lose your steady income and all fringe benefits, like health and life insurance, retirement security, and paid vacations. You must also be prepared to discipline yourself to eight or more hours at the typewriter every day. As Clair Rees, author of *Profitable Full-time/Part-time Freelancing* says, "It's not poor writing skills that defeat so many full-time freelancers, but a lack of economic preparedness." It's best to start planning your switch to self-employment about a year in advance. Begin to cut down on your spending, try to accrue about six months' income for your savings account, and, several months before the break, begin to step up your editorial contacts and magazine sales. A clear view of the

difficulties to be encountered in the first months, some penny-pinching and a lot of hard work are the keys to succeeding in the field of full-time freelance writing.

Which Pays Better?

Q. Does fiction or nonfiction writing pay better?
A. It depends. There are many more markets for articles than short stories, so at this level, nonfiction probably pays the energetic writer more. In the area of books, however, a novel that has the potential for subsidiary paperback, book club, movie, and TV sales probably offers a greater return than the average nonfiction book. On the other hand, a textbook that obtains wide adoption among schools or colleges could be a very lucrative nonfiction book project.

Appendix

Note: Notice how the author makes the idea of a ranch vacation seem appealing no matter what your age, budget or preferred location. Although Mrs. Jones queried *Modern Maturity Magazine* (and her fourth paragraph showed the perspective she would bring to its readers), the editor chose to run the article in its sister publication for the National Association of Retired Teachers. Her original letter, of course, included both a date and her home address.

Mr. Hubert C. Pryor, Editor-in-Chief
Modern Maturity Magazine
215 Long Beach Blvd.
Long Beach, CA 90801

Dear Mr. Pryor:

Few people are aware of the advantages of some very special fun and relaxation places, where all ages can enjoy being together, yet each doing his or her own thing. Our dude and guest ranches stretch from the Everglades to the Pacific, from Canada to one in Arizona where we rode along a fence that separates the USA from old Mexico.

Singles, families and groups are looking for a special place where guests of all ages may individually join or watch activities or just soak in tranquility. Newcomers to areas as well as natives are totally unaware of the ranches within a few miles.

Ranches have expanded their activities beyond horses, food and hospitality. Some include all types of resort activities. Others specialize in unusual or educational interests.

My husband and I are 72 and 68 and began going to ranches 10 years ago. We have been to more than 60 ranches in 13 states and found a variety to fit every pocketbook. Some have excellent camping or house-keeping facilities. We have had our meals with the family and we have been assigned a table with a uniformed waiter. Guests were singles, teen-agers, retirees, several 3, and one 4, generation family reunions—all pursuing their own interests and enjoying the activities and each other.

Ranches attract interesting people. Age, social status and financial prestige are forgotten in the fun together, blue jeans (yes, even great-grandma) atmosphere. Participation in the action is the label by which a guest is known.

Would you be interested in an article enlightening your readers about delightful experiences that combine comfort, indoor and outdoor activities from which to choose or relax in away-from-it-all surroundings?

I am a freelance writer and have credits in the *Dude Rancher* Magazine, organization publications and newspapers.

Sincerely yours,

Mrs. E. Aliene Jones

Manuscript Preparation Guidelines

Jones--2

Begin the second page, and all following pages, in this

manner--with a page-number line (as above) that includes your

name, in case loose manuscript pages get shuffled by mistake.

Joe Jones
1234 My Street
Anytown, U. S. A.
Tel 123/456-7890

About 3,000 words
First Serial Rights
© 1983 Joe Jones

YOUR STORY OR NOVEL TITLE HERE

by

Joe Jones

The manuscript begins here--about halfway down the first page.
It should be cleanly typed, double-spaced, using either elite or
pica type. Use one side of the paper only, and leave a margin of
about 1-1/2 inches on all four sides.

If the author uses a pseudonym, it should be placed on the title page only in the byline position; the author's real name must always appear in the top left corner of the title page—for manuscript mailing and payment purposes.

Reprinted from *Writer's Market '83*. Copyright 1982. Published by Writer's Digest Books.

HOW TO SUBMIT MSS.:

Short articles, poems, stories of fewer than five pages may be folded in thirds and submitted in a #10 envelope to most magazines: everything should be typed double-spaced on 8 ½x11 white paper. Type poems one to a page. Always enclose a self-addressed envelope and return postage.

Longer articles, stories of more than five pages should be submitted flat in a 9x12 or 10x13 envelope with a self-addressed envelope enclosed, and return postage.

Book length manuscripts should be submitted loose in a manuscript paper box. Although a few book publishers prefer to receive manuscripts held together in a binder of some sort, most editors feel it is too heavy to hold to read comfortably. Always enclose sufficient postage for the manuscript's return.

Photographs and other illustrative materials should always be submitted flat, of course, with cardboard protectors and sufficient return postage. In the case of small filler items, a few trade journals and hobby books will accept (although they do not prefer) Polaroid shots of the item in question.

Play manuscripts should be submitted bound in a flexible binder of some sort, along with sufficient return postage. A few publishers of one-act plays have indicated that for the very *short* lengths they have no objection to the materials submitted flat, held only by a paperclip.

Television and motion picture scripts should be submitted in a softcover binder with sufficient return postage. Unagented scripts are rarely accepted.

Greeting card ideas and gag ideas for cartoonists should be submitted on 3x5 white slips of paper, flat, with sufficient return postage. The writer's name and address should appear in the upper left corner and the gag idea or verse centered on the page. A code number, for convenience in identifying the gag idea or verse in correspondence, should appear in the upper right corner. Studio and humorous card ideas may also be accompanied by a rough drawing on a separate folded sheet of paper similar to the published card. Always enclose a stamped, self-addressed envelope.

MANUSCRIPT LENGTH, AVERAGE

The following table provides average word counts for each of the basic forms of writing; it gives the beginning writer the usual expected length of most manuscripts. When submitting work to magazines, though, the writer should adhere to the editor's requirements, which may be more specific than the average word count. *Writer's Market* lists individual editors' preferences as to word length. (Note: The average full double-spaced typewritten page contains 250 words of pica typewriter type.)

How Long Is a . . .?

	Average Words
Short-short story	500-2,000
Short story	2,500-5,000
Novella	7,500-40,000
Novelette	7,000-25,000
Novel—hardcover	25,000-150,000
Novel—paperback	35,000-80,000

Children's picture book	500-2,500
Juvenile book	15,000-80,000
Nonfiction book	20,000-200,000
TV script: ½-hour	25-40 double-spaced typewritten pages
TV script: 1-hour	55-70 double-spaced typewritten pages
Play: one-act	20-30 minutes playing time
	20-30 double-spaced typewritten pages
Play: three-act	1½-2 hours playing time
	90-120 double-spaced typewritten pages
Movie scenario	1½-2 hours playing time
	120-250 double-spaced typewritten pages
Radio feature copy	1 minute = 15 double-spaced lines
	3 minutes = 2 pages
Poem	2-100 lines (most mags prefer 4-16 lines)
Query letter	1 full-page, single-spaced
Speech	250 words = 2 minutes
	12-15 pages = ½ hour

Bibliography

This list includes all the reference books and books on writing mentioned in *The Beginning Writer's Answer Book* with the exception of library references like the *Encyclopaedia Britannica, Subject Guide to Books in Print* and the various periodical indexes.

American Usage and Style: The Consensus, Roy Copperud. New York: Van Nostrand Reinhold, 1979.

American Library Directory. New York: R.R. Bowker Company, 1983

The Art of Dramatic Writing, Lajos Egri. New York: Touchstone Books, Simon and Schuster, 1960.

Artist's Market 1984, edited by Sally Ann Davis. Cincinnati: Writer's Digest, 1983.

At a Journal Workshop: The Basic Text & Guide for Using the Intensive Journal, Ira Progoff. New York: Dialogue House, 1977.

Ayer Directory of Publications. Fort Washington, Pa.: IMS Press, 1981.

Bantam Medical Dictionary, edited by Lawrence Ordang. New York: Bantam Books, 1982.

Bartlett's Familiar Quotations. Boston: Little, Brown & Co., 1980.

Best Books for Children, 2nd edition, edited by John T. Gillespie and Christine B. Gilbert, New York: R.R. Bowker Co., 1981.

Billboard's International Buyer's Guide. New York.

Books That Changed the World, 2nd edition, edited by Robert B. Downs. Chicago: American Library Association, 1978.

The Chicago Manual of Style, thirteenth edition. Chicago: U. of Chicago Press, 1982.

The Children's Picture Book: How to Write It, How to Sell It, Ellen E.M. Roberts. Cincinnati: Writer's Digest Books: 1981.

The Complete Book of Scriptwriting, J. Michael Straczynski. Cincinnati: Writer's Digest Books, 1982.

The Complete Handbook for Freelance Writers, Kay Cassill. Cincinnati: Writer's Digest Books, 1981.

Computer-Readable Databases: A Directory and Data Sourcebook, edited by Martha E. Williams. White Plains, N.Y.: Knowledge Industry Publications, 1982.

Concise Columbia Encyclopedia. New York: Columbia University Press, Avon Books, 1983.

Confession Writer's Handbook, Florence K. Palmer. Cincinnati: Writer's Digest Books, 1980.

Contemporary Authors, vol. 106, edited by Frances Locher. Detroit: Gale Research Company, 1982.

The Copyright Book: A Practical Guide, Wm. S. Strong. Cambridge: MIT Press, 1981.

Cumulative Subject Index to the Monthly Catalog of U.S. Government Publications, 1900-1971, 15 vols. Woodbridge, Conn.: Resource Publications, Inc., 1975.

The Craft of Interviewing, John Brady. Cincinnati: Writer's Digest Books, 1975.

Creating Short Fiction, Damon Knight. Cincinnati: Writer's Digest Books, 1981.

The Directory of Directories 1983, edited by James Ethridge. Detroit: Gale Research Company, 1983.

Directory of Online Databases, Carlos Cuadra et al. New York: Zeotrope, 1983.

Editor and Publisher Syndicate Directory. New York.

Editor and Publisher Yearbook. New York.

The Elements of Style: With Index, William Strunk, Jr., and E.B. White. New York: Macmillan, 1979.

Encyclopedia of Associations, Detroit: Gale Research Company, 1981. *Also E of A: Geographic & Executive Index 1984. E of A: New Associations & Projects 1983.*

Fiction Writer's Help Book, Maxine Rock. Cincinnati: Writer's Digest Books, 1982.

Fiction Writer's Market 1983-84, edited by Jean Fredette. Cincinnati: Writer's Digest Books, 1983.

The Foundation Directory, 8th ed. New York: The Foundation Center, 1981.

The Foundation Grants Index, New York: The Foundation Center, 1982.

Good Reading: Guide for the Serious Reader, edited by J. Sherwood Weber. New York: New American Library, 1980.

A Guide to Greeting Card Writing, edited by Larry Sandman. Cincinnati: Writer's Digest Books, 1980.

Guinness Book of World Records 1984, edited by Norris McWhirter. New York: Sterling Publishing Co., Inc., 1983.

The Handbook of Nonsexist Writing for Writers, Editors and Speakers, Casey Miller and Kate Swift. New York: Harper and Row, 1981.

A Handbook to Literature, edited by W.F. Thrall and A. Hibbard. Darby, Pa. Darby Books, 1980.

Harbrace College Handbook, edited by John C. Hodges and Mary E. Whitten. New York: Harcourt Brace Jovanovich, Inc., 1982.

Harvard Brief Dictionary of Music, edited by Nilli Apel and Ralph Daniel. New York: Pocket Books, Washington Square Press, 1968.

The Holy Bible: New International Version. New York: New York International Bible Society.

How to Get Happily Published: A Complete & Candid Guide, Judith Applebaum and Nancy Evans. New York: New American Library, 1982.

How to Get Started in Writing, Peggy Teeters. Cincinnati: Writer's Digest Books, 1980.

How to Make Money Writing Little Articles, Anecdotes, Hints, Recipes, Light Verse and other Fillers, Connie Emerson. Cincinnati: Writer's Digest Books, 1983.

How to Write a Play, Raymond Hull. Cincinnati: Writer's Digest Books, 1983.

How to Write and Sell (Your Sense of) Humor, Gene Perret. Cincinnati: Writer's Digest Books, 1982.

How to Write for Children and Young Adults: A Handbook, James Fitz-Randolph. New York: Barnes and Noble, 1980.

How to Write Short Stories That Sell, Louise Boggess. Cincinnati: Writer's Digest Books, 1980.

If They Ask You, You Can Write a Song, Al Kasha and Joel Hirschhorn. New York: Simon and Schuster, 1979.

Information Please Almanac. New York: Simon and Schuster, 1979.

Information U.S.A., Matthew Lesko. New York: Penguin Books, 1983.

Inside Publishing, Bill Adler. Indianapolis: Bobbs-Merrill, 1982.

International Directory of Little Magazines and Small Presses, edited by Len Fulton and Ellen Ferber. Paradise, Calif.: Dustbooks, 1983.

International Writers' and Artists' Yearbook (distributed by Writer's Digest Books). Pub. by A & C Black, England, 1983.

Internships 1984, edited by Joan Bloss. Cincinnati: Writer's Digest Books, 1983.

Jerusalem Bible, edited by Alexander Jones. New York: Doubleday, 1975.

Jobs for Writers, edited by Kirk Polking. Cincinnati: Writer's Digest Books, 1980.

Journalism Career and Scholarship Guide. Princeton: Dow Jones Newspaper Fund, Inc.

Law and the Writer, edited by Kirk Polking and Leonard S. Meranus. Cincinnati: Writer's Digest Books, 1981.

Literary Agents: A Writer's Guide. New York: Poets and Writers, Inc., 1983.

Literary Market Place 1984. New York: R.R. Bowker Company, 1983.

The Living Bible: A Topical Approach to the Jewish Scriptures, by Sylvan D. Schwartzman and Jack D. Spiro. New York: Union of American Hebrew Congregations, 1962.

Magazine Writing: The Inside Angle, Art Spikol. Cincinnati: Writer's Digest Books, 1979.

Make Every Word Count, Gary Provost. Cincinnati: Writer's Digest Books, 1980.

Max Perkins: Editor of Genius, A. Scott Berg. New York: Pocket Books, 1979.

Mystery Writer's Handbook, edited by Lawrence Treat. Cincinnati: Writer's Digest Books, 1982.

The New Diary: How to Use a Journal for Self-Guidance and Expanded Creativity, Tristine Rainer. Los Angeles: J.P. Tarcher, Inc., 1979.

Newsgathering, Daniel Williamson. New York: Hastings House Publishers, Inc., 1979.

Occupational Outlook Handbook 1984-85. Washington, DC: U.S. Government Printing Office.

On Writing Well: An Informal Guide to Writing Nonfiction, William Zinsser. New York: Harper and Row, 1980.

One to One: Self Understanding Through Journal Writing, Christina Baldwin. New York: M. Evans & Company, Inc., 1977.

Online Database Search Services Directory. Detroit: Gale Research Company, 1983.

Opportunities in various writing-related careers, such as broadcasting, publishing, etc. Lincolnwood, Ill.: National Textbook Company.

Outline of History: A Plain History of Life and Mankind, H.G. Wells. New York: Doubleday, 1971.

The People's Almanac Two, David Wallechinsky and Irving Wallace. New York: Bantam Books, 1978.

Peter's Quotations: Ideas for Our Times, Laurence Peter. New York: Bantam Books, 1979.

Peterson's Guide to Book Publishing Courses/Academic and Professional Programs. Princeton: Peterson's Guides.

Photographer's Market 1984, edited by Robert D. Lutz. Cincinnati: Writer's Digest Books, 1983.

The Poet and the Poem, Judson Jerome. Cincinnati: Writer's Digest Books, 1979.

The Poet's Handbook, Judson Jerome. Cincinnati: Writer's Digest Books, 1980.

The Poet's Manual and Rhyming Dictionary, Frances Stillman and Jane S. Whitfield. New York: T.Y. Crowell, 1965.

Profitable Part-Time/Full-Time Freelancing, Clair F. Rees. Cincinnati: Writer's Digest Books, 1980.

The Publish It Yourself Handbook: Literary Tradition and How to, edited by Bill Henderson. Wainscott, N.Y.: Pushcart Press, 1979.

Punctuate It Right!, Harry Shaw. New York: Barnes and Noble, 1963.

The Quotable Woman, 2 vols. New York: Pinnacle Books, 1980.

Random House Handbook, edited by Frederick Crews. New York: Random House, 1983.

The Reader's Digest Bible. Pleasantville, N.Y.: Reader's Digest.

The Reader's Encyclopedia, edited by William R. Benet. New York: T.Y. Crowell, 1965.

A Reader's Guide to the Holy Bible: Revised Standard Edition, Nashville, Tenn.: Thomas Nelson, Inc., 1978.

Reference Books: a Brief Guide, edited by Marion V. Bell and Eleanor A. Swidan. Baltimore: Enoch Pratt Free Library, 1978.

Roget's International Thesaurus. New York: T.Y. Crowell Company, 1977.

Sell and Resell Your Photos, Rohn Engh. Cincinnati: Writer's Digest Books, 1981.

Songwriter's Market 1984, edited by Barbara N. Kuroff. Cincinnati: Writer's Digest Books, 1983.

Stalking the Feature Story, William Ruehlmann. Cincinnati: Writer's Digest Books, 1977.

Standard Directory of Advertisers. Skokie, Ill.: National Register Publishing Company, 1983.

Standard Directory of Advertising Agencies. Skokie, Ill.: National Register Publishing Company, 1983.

The Student Guide to Mass Media Internships, Boulder: Intern Research Group, University of Colorado.

A Survey of Motion Picture, Still Photography, and Graphic Arts Instruction. Rochester: Eastman Kodak Company, 1981.

Teach Yourself to Write, Evelyn A. Stenbock. Cincinnati: Writer's Digest Books, 1982.

Toward Matching Personal and Job Characteristics. Washington, DC,: U.S. Government Printing Office.

The Travel Writer's Handbook, Louise P. Zobel. Cincinnati: Writer's Digest Books, 1980.

The TV Scriptwriter's Handbook, Alfred Brenner. Cincinnati: Writer's Digest Books, 1980.

Ulrich's International Periodicals Directory 1983. New York: R.R. Bowker Company, 1983.

United States Government Manual 1983-84. Washington, DC: U.S. Government Printing Office, July 1983.

Variety Music Cavalcade. Englewood Cliffs, N.J.: Prentice-Hall.

Who's Who in America 1982-83. Chicago: Marquis Who's Who, Inc., 1981.

Who's Who in American Art 1982. New York: R.R. Bowker Company, 1981.

The Word Processing Book: A Short Course in Computer Literacy, Peter A. McWilliams. Los Angeles: Prelude Press, 1982.

Working Press of the Nation, 5 vols. Chicago: Automated Marketing Systems, Inc., 1982.

World Almanac and Book of Facts 1984. New York: World Almanac, 1983.

World Photography Sources, edited by David N. Bradshaw and Catherine Hahn. New York: Directories Publishing.

Writer's Digest Handbook of Article Writing, edited by Frank A. Dickson. New York: Holt, Rinehart and Winston, 1968.

Writer's Digest Handbook of Short Story Writing, edited by Frank Dickson/Sandra Smythe. Cincinnati: Writer's Digest Books, 1981.

Writer's Encyclopedia, edited by Kirk Polking. Cincinnati: Writer's Digest Books, 1983.

Writer's Handbook, edited by Sylvia K. Burack. Boston: The Writer, Inc., 1983.

The Writer's Legal Guide, Tad Crawford, New York: E.P. Dutton, 1978.

Writer's Market 1984, edited by Bernadine Clark. Cincinnati: Writer's Digest Books, 1983.

Writer's Resource Guide, edited by Bernadine Clark. Cincinnati: Writer's Digest Books, 1983.

Writing and Selling Nonfiction, Hayes B. Jacobs. Cincinnati: Writer's Digest Books, 1975.

Writing for Children and Teenagers, Lee Wyndham, edited by Arnold Madison. Cincinnati: Writer's Digest Books, 1980.

Writing the Novel: From Plot to Print, Lawrence Block. Cincinnati: Writer's Digest Books, 1979.

Writing Romance Fiction for Love & Money, Helene S. Barnhart. Cincinnati: Writer's Digest Books, 1983.

Index

Other Books of Interest

General Writing Books
    Beginning Writer's Answer Book, edited by Polking and Bloss, $14.95
    Getting the Words Right: How to Revise, Edit and Rewrite, by Theodore A. Rees Cheney $13.95
    How to Become a Bestselling Author, by Stan Corwin, $14.95
    How to Get Started in Writing, by Peggy Teeters $10.95
    International Writers' & Artists' Yearbook, (paper) $10.95
    Law and the Writer, edited by Polking and Meranus (paper) $7.95
    Make Every Word Count, by Gary Provost (paper) $7.95
    Teach Yourself to Write, by Evelyn A. Stenbock $12.95
    Treasury of Tips for Writers, edited by Marvin Weisbord (paper) $6.95
    Writer's Encyclopedia, edited by Kirk Polking $19.95
    Writer's Market, edited by Bernadine Clark $18.95
    Writer's Resource Guide, edited by Bernadine Clark $16.95
    Writing for the Joy of It, by Leonard Knott $11.95
    Writing From the Inside Out, by Charlotte Edwards (paper) $9.95

Magazine/News Writing
    Complete Guide to Marketing Magazine Articles, by Duane Newcomb $9.95
    Complete Guide to Writing Nonfiction, by the American Society of Journalists & Authors, edited by Glen Evans $24.95
    Craft of Interviewing, by John Brady $9.95
    Magazine Writing: The Inside Angle, by Art Spikol $12.95
    Magazine Writing Today, by Jerome E. Kelley $10.95
    Newsthinking: The Secret of Great Newswriting, by Bob Baker $11.95
    1001 Article Ideas, by Frank A. Dickson $10.95
    Stalking the Feature Story, by William Ruehlmann $9.95
    Write On Target, by Connie Emerson $12.95
    Writing and Selling Non-Fiction, by Hayes B. Jacobs $12.95

Fiction Writing
    Creating Short Fiction, by Damon Knight $11.95
    Fiction Is Folks: How to Create Unforgettable Characters, by Robert Newton Peck $11.95
    Fiction Writer's Help Book, by Maxine Rock $12.95
    Fiction Writer's Market, edited by Jean Fredette $17.95
    Handbook of Short Story Writing, by Dickson and Smythe (paper) $6.95
    How to Write Best-Selling Fiction, by Dean R. Koontz $13.95
    How to Write Short Stories that Sell, by Louise Boggess (paper) $7.95
    One Way to Write Your Novel, by Dick Perry (paper) $6.95
    Secrets of Successful Fiction, by Robert Newton Peck $8.95
    Writing Romance Fiction—For Love And Money, by Helene Schellenberg Barnhart $14.95
    Writing the Novel: From Plot to Print, by Lawrence Block $10.95

Special Interest Writing Books
    Cartoonist's & Gag Writer's Handbook, by Jack Markow (paper) $9.95
    The Children's Picture Book: How to Write It, How to Sell It, by Ellen E. M. Roberts $17.95
    Complete Book of Scriptwriting, by J. Michael Straczynski $14.95
    Complete Guide to Greeting Card Writing, edited by Larry Sandman (paper) $7.95
    Complete Guide to Writing Software User Manuals, by Brad McGehee (paper) $14.95
    Confession Writer's Handbook, by Florence K. Palmer. Revised by Marguerite McClain $9.95
    Guide to Greeting Card Writing, edited by Larry Sandman $10.95
    How to Make Money Writing . . . Fillers, by Connie Emerson $12.95
    How to Write a Cookbook and Get It Published, by Sara Pitzer, $15.95
    How to Write a Play, by Raymond Hull $13.95
    How to Write and Sell Your Personal Experiences, by Lois Duncan $10.95
    How to Write and Sell (Your Sense of) Humor, by Gene Perret $12.95

How to Write "How-To" Books and Articles, by Raymond Hull (paper) $8.95
Mystery Writer's Handbook, edited by Lawrence Treat (paper) $8.95
Poet and the Poem, revised edition by Judson Jerome $13.95
Poet's Handbook, by Judson Jerome $11.95
Programmer's Market, edited by Brad McGehee (paper) $16.95
Sell Copy, by Webster Kuswa $11.95
Successful Outdoor Writing, by Jack Samson $11.95
Travel Writer's Handbook, by Louise Zobel (paper) $8.95
TV Scriptwriter's Handbook, by Alfred Brenner $12.95
Writing and Selling Science Fiction, by Science Fiction Writers of America (paper) $7.95
Writing for Children & Teenagers, by Lee Wyndham. Revised by Arnold Madison $11.95
Writing for Regional Publications, by Brian Vachon $11.95
Writing to Inspire, by Gentz, Roddy, et al $14.95

The Writing Business

Complete Handbook for Freelance Writers, by Kay Cassill $14.95
Freelance Jobs for Writers, edited by Kirk Polking (paper) $7.95
How to Be a Successful Housewife/Writer, by Elaine Fantle Shimberg $10.95
How You Can Make $20,000 a Year Writing, by Nancy Hanson (paper) $6.95
Profitable Part-time/Full-time Freelancing, by Clair Rees $10.95
The Writer's Survival Guide: How to Cope with Rejection, Success and 99 Other Hang-Ups of the Writing Life, by Jean and Veryl Rosenbaum $12.95

To order directly from the publisher, include $1.50 postage and handling for 1 book and 50¢ for each additional book. Allow 30 days for delivery.

Writer's Digest Books, Department B
9933 Alliance Road, Cincinnati OH 45242
Prices subject to change without notice.

Books by *Francis Steegmuller*

APOLLINAIRE: POET AMONG THE PAINTERS

LE HIBOU ET LA POUSSIQUETTE

THE CHRISTENING PARTY

THE GRAND MADEMOISELLE

THE TWO LIVES OF JAMES JACKSON JARVES

MAUPASSANT, A LION IN THE PATH

FLAUBERT AND MADAME BOVARY: A DOUBLE PORTRAIT

STATES OF GRACE

FRENCH FOLLIES AND OTHER FOLLIES

THE MUSICALE

THE SELECTED LETTERS OF GUSTAVE FLAUBERT (*translator and editor*)

MADAME BOVARY (*translator*)

GUSTAVE FLAUBERT: INTIMATE NOTEBOOK 1840–1841 (*translator and editor*)

PAPILLOT, CLIGNOT ET DODO (*with Norbert Guterman*)

SAINTE-BEUVE, SELECTED ESSAYS (*translator and editor,
with Norbert Guterman*)

Under the name BYRON STEEL

O RARE BEN JONSON

JAVA-JAVA

SIR FRANCIS BACON

Under the name DAVID KEITH

A MATTER OF IODINE

A MATTER OF ACCENT

BLUE HARPSICHORD (*hard cover; later, as a paperback under the name
Francis Steegmuller*)

COCTEAU

COCTEAU

A BIOGRAPHY

by Francis Steegmuller

An Atlantic Monthly Press Book

LITTLE, BROWN AND COMPANY · BOSTON · TORONTO

ATLANTIC–LITTLE, BROWN BOOKS
ARE PUBLISHED BY
LITTLE, BROWN AND COMPANY
IN ASSOCIATION WITH
THE ATLANTIC MONTHLY PRESS

Published simultaneously in Canada
by Little, Brown & Company (Canada) Limited

PRINTED IN THE UNITED STATES OF AMERICA

To Shirley

Author's Note

INVALUABLE assistance has been rendered to this work, since its inception, by the following persons, to whom I offer particular thanks: William Abrahams, Comte Henri de Beaumont, Douglas Cooper, Pierre Georgel, Mme. Albert Gleizes, M. and Mme. Maurice Goudeket, Norbert Guterman, Jean Hugo, the late Mme. Valentine Hugo, the late M. and Mme. André Maurois, Igor Stravinsky, Mme. Olivier Ziegel.

My thanks are due to Edouard Dermit for his permission to quote from Cocteau's letters and other documents.

I wish to express my gratitude also to the following persons: Miss Berenice Abbott, Harold Acton, Mme. Pierre Albert-Birot, Louis Aragon, Robert M. Asselineau, W. H. Auden, Georges Auric, Vander Barbette, Miss Natalie Barney, Jean-Louis Barrault, Jacques Barzun, Cecil Beaton, Yvon Belaval, Claude Bénédick, Ingrid Bergman, Emmanuel Berl, Sir Isaiah and Lady Berlin, Dr. Charles Berlioz, Eugene Berman, Leonid Berman, Princesse Marthe Bibesco, Mme. Madeleine Bourret, Mrs. Erse Breunig, Reginald Bridgeman, Dr. Henry Brill, Richard Buckle, Wesson Bull, Roger Caillaud, M. and Mme. Julien Cain, Mlle. Gabrielle Chanel, Miss Geraldine Chaplin, François Chapon, Morton N. Cohen, Leo Coleman, Lady Diana Cooper, Robert Craft, William Crawford, Mrs. Mina Curtiss, Colonel Deloste, Jean Denoël, the late Marcel Duchamp, Jean-Claude Eger, John H. Field, the late Don Antonio de Gandarillas, Signora Liliana delli Ponti Garuti, Georges Geffroy, Mrs. Romaine Brooks Goddard, Vladimir Golschmann, Miss Peggy Guggenheim, Philippe Halsman, Jacques Hébertot, Miss Mary Hoeck, Georges Hugnet, François Hugo, Herbert Jacoby, Philippe Jullian, Miss Pauline Kael, Mme. Jeannette Kandaouroff, Jean-Jacques Kihm, Lincoln Kirstein, Boris Kochno, Philip Kolb, Pierre de Lacretelle, Vincent Laloy, Richard Lane, Paul Leake, Henri

Lefèbvre, Raoul Leven, Harry Levin, William Lieberman, Serge
Lifar, James Lord, G. Magistry, Jean Marais, Miss Sylvia Marlowe,
Léonide Massine, the late Pierre de Massot, Robert Medley, André
Meyer, Bernard Minoret, Paul Morand, Raymond Mortimer, Dr.
Werner Muensterberger, Comte Anne-Jules de Noailles, Vicomte
Charles de Noailles and the late Vicomtesse de Noailles, Miss
Georgia O'Keefe, Alain Ollivier, George D. Painter, Francis Pal-
méro, Henry Pearlman, Lady Penrose (Lee Miller), Jacques Perry,
Saint-John Perse, Jean Petithory, Roger Peyrefitte, Mme. François
Porché (Mme. Simone), Jacques Porel, René Radiguet, Miss Vicky
Rippere, Mme. Denise Roché, Ned Rorem, Sir Robert and Lady
Sainsbury, Mme. Raphaël Salem, Michel Sanouillet, Vanni Schei-
willer, Mme. Elsa Schiaparelli, Mme. Robert Singer, the late Sir
Osbert Sitwell, Mlle. Suzy Solidor, Mlle. Nicole Stéphane, Roger
Stéphane, Miss Enid Starkie, Donald Ogden Stewart, Marchese
Uberto Strozzi, Daniel Talbot, Richard Thoma, Jean Vallier, René
Varin, the late Denise Van Moppès, Seymour de Vaulchier, Duca
Fulco di Verdura, the late Louise de Vilmorin, Paolo Vivante,
Baronne Wasmer (Marie Delle Donne), Mme. Alec Weisweiller,
Glenway Wescott, Monroe Wheeler, Henry Wibbels, Jean Wiener,
Edmund Wilson, the late Leonard Woolf, Princess X, Mrs. Marie
Shabelska Yakofleff.

And to the following institutions: Bibliothèque de l'Arsenal,
Bibliothèque Nationale, Bibliothèque Littéraire Jacques Doucet de
l'Université de Paris (Comité André Gide), Musée National d'Art
Moderne, Cinémathèque Française (Mme. Mary Meerson), Biblio-
thèque Royale de Belgique. New York Public Library (especially
its Library and Museum of the Performing Arts), the New York
Society Library, George Eastman House, Museum of Modern Art
(especially its Department of Film), American Museum of Natural
History, University of Florida Libraries, the Library of Congress.
Also: Manuscript Division, Syracuse University Library; Beinecke
Rare Book and Manuscript Library, Yale University; The Houghton Library, Harvard University.

And to Janus Films, Inc. (for a private screening of *Orphée*) and
Universal Education and Visual Arts (for a private screening of
Égypte Ô Égypte).

In addition, my thanks go to the many others who have kindly
responded to my requests for information or other assistance.

Except where otherwise specified, translations from the French
and the Italian are my own.   F.S.

Contents

Illustrations

COCTEAU

You who enjoy representing the highest
truths by a dazzling symbol that contains
them all . . .

— *Marcel Proust to Jean Cocteau.*

1
The Poet as Fregoli

SPEAKING of her visits, before the First World War, to the country house of her friend the painter Jacques-Emile Blanche at Offranville in Normandy, Edith Wharton wrote: "The first time I went, I met a young man of nineteen or twenty, who at that time vibrated with all the youth of the world. This was Jean Cocteau, then a passionately imaginative youth to whom every great line of poetry was a sunrise, every sunset the foundation of the Heavenly City. . . . I have known no other young man who so recalled Wordsworth's 'Bliss was it in that dawn to be alive.' Every subject touched on — and in his company they were countless — was lit up by his young enthusiasm. . . ."

Cocteau's enchanting diversity was a source of wonderment to another early friend, Maurice Rostand, who wrote in his memoirs that for him he would always remain the Jean Cocteau he had known in his youth, despite his subsequent *"transformations de Fregoli."* That phrase, as applied to Cocteau, is delightfully, if only partially, appropriate. One of the lighter entries in the French dictionary-encyclopedia, the *Larousse de XXe Siècle*, reads:

> FREGOLI (Leopoldo), Italian quick-change artist, born in Rome in 1867. Apprentice watchmaker, soldier, prisoner of war in Abyssinia. He was so successful at entertaining his fellow-prisoners and the Negus himself that the latter granted him his freedom. He was endowed with an uncommon talent for assuming different roles — in turn singer, dancer, imitator, mime, conjuror. He wrote scenarios in which he enacted up to sixty different parts, both male and female. Fregoli traveled with 370 trunks, 800 costumes, 1200 wigs and 300 tons of stage properties. His engagements took him several times around the world. . . . After more than thirty years of unbroken success he retired to Italy.

In the Parisian world of the arts Jean Cocteau was a Fregoli, and more than a Fregoli, for over half a century. Poet, novelist, dramatist, portraitist, designer of posters, pottery, tapestries, mosaics, neckties, costume jewelry, and objects executed in glass, pipe cleaners and other media — the list of his *transformations* could go on indefinitely. Throughout his career (he was born in 1889, died in 1963, and once said "since the age of fifteen I haven't stopped for a minute") he kept changing his guise, his views, his activities; to use a word he liked, his life was a series of *"mues"* — moultings. But between Fregoli and Jean Cocteau there was the great difference that Cocteau was seldom only an actor. Usually he actually *was* each person whose role he was playing. Cocteau had no need of Fregoli's mountain of baggage. As he moved from stage to stage displaying his *transformations,* his only properties were his selves.

About the multiplicity of his own activities, Cocteau once said "I have been accused of jumping from branch to branch. Well, I have — but always in the same tree." He was referring to the tree of poetry. Of all the titles to which he had a claim, he consented to use only one — poet — and that he insisted upon. He was the most self-proclaimed of poets, to the extent that he rigorously classified all his great variety of work, his poems, novels, plays, essays, drawings, and films, under the headings of *"poésie, poésie de roman, poésie de théâtre, poésie critique, poésie graphique* and *poésie cinématographique."* Even his sculpture he dubbed *"poésie plastique."* The insistence could be irritating, and sometimes it brought ill-natured charges of being a "counterfeit" poet. But that slur flies wide of the mark: Cocteau certainly never meant his work to pass as anyone else's, and even when it is imitative it bears a maker's mark that would disqualify any forger.

As a poet, Cocteau declared that he must be essentially "invisible." "Invisibility seems to me a *sine qua non* of elegance. Elegance ceases to exist once it is noticed. . . . My visibility, made up of ridiculous legends, protects my invisibility." In discussing the abstract themes that increasingly appealed to him in his later years — "visibility and invisibility," "criminal innocence," "a justification of injustice" — Cocteau often loses himself in a not too expertly contrived maze of paradox; but his discussion of "invisibility" arouses one's understanding and sympathy, as well as one's amusement. One portion of his meaning is that a poet's poetry must speak for itself: the poet must disappear. That is, the poet's *inner* life must disappear into the myth and image of the verse; and, given the conditions of existence in this world, the invisible inner life must be protected by an outer life, a "visibility," "a heavy coat of armor, flashing-bright and able to withstand all kinds of blows." That image is not without its appeal; but it is nonetheless difficult not to smile at Cocteau's application of the word "invisible" to himself in any connection. Difficult for a reason that reveals, perhaps, the coarser side of those who smile, and which Cocteau himself would certainly consider, or pretend to consider, unworthy and vulgar: the fact that Jean Cocteau — he would say that it was only the *outer* Jean Cocteau — was the most publicized, the most photographed, of men.

Photographs of Jean Cocteau, usually accompanied by interviews, or rather monologues, filled French newspapers and magazines for half a century. As a slim young pre-1914 aesthete; close to the front in his wartime ambulance-attendant's uniform, said to have been designed for him by the dressmaker Paul Poiret; posed by Man Ray in Dadaist settings that featured his beautiful hands; speaking into a megaphone during a performance of his spectacle *Les Mariés de la Tour Eiffel;* surrounded by the composers known as "Les Six"; standing with Jean Marais, with the casts of his plays, with Stravinsky, with Picasso, with Edith Piaf, with Colette, with Charlie Chaplin, with the Queen of the Belgians; perched on a ladder painting his murals; wearing his French Academician's sword or his Oxford gown: Cocteau was always photographed. André Maurois, president of a Cannes Film Festival jury that included Cocteau, lamented "I could never preside! Cocteau was always in the center!" and a photographer once remarked to Maurois "If I were to take a picture of a village wedding, Jean Cocteau would appear between the bride and groom." Cecil Beaton has photographed Cocteau smoking an opium pipe, and kissing, in shadow play, his friend Marcel Khill; there were documentary films and there was television; in the files of the Bibliothèque Nationale there is a press snapshot — one of the few unposed photographs — that shows him at the Palais de Justice along with other men picked up in a narcotics raid; and in his last film, *Le Testament d'Orphée,* he plays himself, "Le Poète."

All that, he would say, was in the cause of essential "invisibility," and he might well say the same for the several volumes of self-declared autobiography, or memoirs, which he wrote at various times during his life.* There is no dearth of either fact or anecdote in Cocteau's memoirs, but his manipulation of both those elements, which at various times he claims to despise, and his omission of so much information that is pertinent, result in his maintaining a certain degree of invisibility-by-autobiography, as he claimed to have achieved it by photograph and publicity. The memoirs are not "confessions." Cocteau never "confessed" — that is, not directly. Indeed, something in the tone of the memoirs, so brilliant with epigram and allusion, so unswervingly histrionic, makes one suspect that such total aversion to the humdrum may sometimes cloak motives that could more appropriately bear other names — snobbishness, prudence, perhaps even fear. Cocteau would probably be the first to insist that his allegedly autobiographical writings are the materials not of personal history but of personal myth. He might remind us that in Aristotelian language myth is "poetically true," and indeed he has said of himself "I am a lie that always tells the truth." But a lie, even one that tells the truth, implies a truth that is not told. In Cocteau's case the lie, the myth, and the two kinds of truth, the one that is told and the one that is not, make a fascinating amalgam.

Cocteau tends to be most factual in autobiography when he doesn't realize that he is writing it, or when he presents it as fiction (as in his revelations concerning his homosexuality in his "novel" *Le Livre Blanc,* although in this connection his drawings for another novel, Jean Genet's *Querelle de Brest,* are even more explicit), or when his memoirs carry over a tone *from* fiction. The latter is the case, for example, in a paragraph about the town of Maisons-Laffitte, the Paris suburb where the Cocteau family spent its summers and where Jean was born on July 5, 1889† — a passage he wrote shortly after completing his fairy-tale film *Beauty and the Beast,* and which retains the magic-wood, enchantment-for-children mood of the film:

* *Opium,* 1930; *Portraits-Souvenir,* 1934; *La Difficulté d'Etre,* 1947; *Journal d'un Inconnu,* 1952; *Le Cordon Ombilical,* 1962.

† On the birth announcement sent out by his parents his names are given as Jean-Maurice; on his military dossier as Clément, Eugène, Jean, Maurice. In later life he enjoyed having the initials J.C.

Maisons-Laffitte is a kind of training-ground for race horses, dotted with houses, gardens, lime-tree avenues, lawns, flower borders, and little squares each with its fountain. Here the race horse and the bicycle are kings. We played tennis on each other's courts: it was a bourgeois world, at that time sundered by the Dreyfus case. The river Seine, the track, the boundary wall of the St.-Germain forest with its little entrance gate, the hidden corners ideal for playing cops and robbers, the military camp below, the outdoor cafés with their arbors, the village fair, fireworks, the exploits of the local fire brigade, the Mansard chateau with its overgrown lawns and its busts of Roman emperors — it was all made to encourage the illusion enjoyed by all children, that they are living in a very special corner of the world.

Maisons-Laffitte *was* somewhat special, with its pretty green surroundings so close to Paris, and the great number of its four-footed aristocrats; the human inhabitants were chiefly stable or racecourse employees, or prosperous bourgeois who commuted to their offices in the city less than half an hour away by train. Cocteau's birthplace, like so many houses in the town, was large, comfortable, rich in bourgeois ornamentation. His family, at least his mother's family, the Lecomtes, were well-to-do, with connections on the stock exchange, in the navy and in the diplomatic service; Cocteau's father abandoned a vague law practice early and lived without working; none of his connections belonged to the horsy set that frequented the town but seldom lived there. Seymour de Vaulchier, whose grandfather, the Duc de Fitz-James, for a time kept his horses at Maisons, knew Cocteau there as a rail-like bourgeois boy who rode only his bicycle and was fearful of the horses. Most of the year the family lived in the heart of Paris, at 45 rue La Bruyère. Here and there, among his memories of the 1890's, Cocteau mentions a grandmother pleased to have known Rossini, an amateur-violinist grandfather permitted to play his Stradivarius in a Sunday quartet with professionals, a father who was a Sunday painter. His mother was "perfect," the family was "simple and charming": nevertheless, the impression conveyed is that of an atmosphere far from philistine but in which "love of the arts" was evidenced in a bourgeois way, unblessed by creativity. That picture, sketched in the earliest memoirs, is made explicit in lines written only after his mother's death: "My family was of no help to me. Success was its measuring stick. It was dilettantish and dabbling." And: "I came from a family that liked perfection. They were too artistic for me to be able to rebel against them, and too dilettantish to teach me anything. For example, my family loved Wagner, but also Massenet; Goethe, but also Rostand; and my grandfather collected paintings by Delacroix and Ingres, but also by Ziem. I lived in a great mélange. Let me say again: my family was too artistic for me to be able to rebel against them, and not artistic enough to give me useful advice. Now advice is an excellent thing — not to follow, but to disregard. I lost time because I thought that the Muses were like kindly fairies around my cradle: it was not until much later that I learned that they are praying mantises, who devour whomever they marry."

In his memoirs of his childhood Cocteau chats on in a charming period-piece way about skating at the Palais de Glace, watching the films of the Lumière brothers in a basement near the shop "Old England" where his mother bought his sailor suits, laughing at the clowns Footit and Chocolat (immortalized by Toulouse-Lautrec) at the Nouveau Cirque; he reminds us that Debussy's *Pelléas* and the paintings of Renoir and Cézanne were being produced in the shadow of *valses lentes*, Delmet's *romances*, and the Salon, where every year were to be seen the same pictures of cardinals sitting at tables playing with cats, the same military allegories by Detaille, the same marble busts of ministers with metal eyeglasses.

But the memoirs invite to no early intimacy. They barely mention his favorite cousin, his closest childhood companion, Marianne Lecomte (Madame Singer) two years his senior; they say little of his older sister and brother, Marthe and Paul, and little of his parents, beyond "My mother and sister were 'At Home' Tuesdays," and "My father died when I was ten." One has to search outside the memoirs for most of the rest. It is other people who tell how pretty his mother was, how graceful, how well acquainted she was through her brother the diplomatist Raymond Lecomte with the official world of ministers and other higher functionaries — a useful world to know. Raymond Lecomte, who served at the Holy See, in Berlin, in Cairo, in Athens, in Teheran, at the Quai d'Orsay, who was a

Chevalier and later an Officier of the Legion of Honor, was the most
nearly "famous" member of the family; the cosmopolitan, unmar-
ried brother of the pretty mother was far more attractive a model
for an impressionable boy than the dim father, Georges Cocteau.

It was a few lines in Jean Marais' autobiography, *Mes Quatre
Vérités,* published in 1957, during Cocteau's lifetime, that first
told of Cocteau's father having died by his own hand: "One night,
at the Boeuf sur le Toit, I sensed that Jean was in such despair that
I was afraid for him; I remembered that his father had committed
suicide. . . ." Cocteau himself spoke publicly of the event only in
1963, the last year of his own life, and then not very clearly: "We
were a family close to ruin; my father committed suicide in circumstances that would not cause anyone to commit suicide today."
Madame Singer has said a little more: "Jean and I came home
from a walk one day and were told that his father was dead. The
news made little impression on us at the time — I remember that
we were soon laughing and playing as usual. The word 'suicide'
was never used in the family, but later I was told that my uncle had
shot himself in the head with a pistol, in bed, and was found in a
pool of blood. I never heard why he did it. I have often wondered
whether Jean heard those details, and whether they have anything
to do with the blood and the suicides he put into his novels and
plays."

Official records say merely that Georges Cocteau, born at Melun
(Seine et Oise), July 8, 1842, aged 56, died April 5, 1898 at his
home in Paris, 45 rue La Bruyère, at 9:30 A.M. *Le Figaro* for
Thursday, April 7, announces: "M. Georges Cocteau . . . suddenly, aged 55. He was brother of the notary Cocteau and son-in-
law of M. Eugène Lecomte, stockbroker." He was buried in the
vault of his wife's family — not his own — in the Cimetière de
Montmartre on April 8.

Cocteau's work holds echoes of the events: "One day when I was
on my way to the rue Henner, passing through the rue La Bruyère
where I lived as a boy at No. 45, in a house in which the first floor
was occupied by my grandparents and the entresol by us . . . I
decided to conquer the fear that usually made me run through that
street hearing and seeing nothing."

And he wrote: "I should like some Freudian to tell me the meaning of a dream I had several times a week beginning when I was

ten. The dream stopped in 1912. My father, who was dead, was not dead. He had turned into a parrot in the Pré Catelan, one of those parrots whose squawking is always associated in my mind with the taste of foamy milk. In this dream my mother and I were about to sit down at a table in the farm of the Pré Catelan, which seemed to combine several farms and the cockatoo terrace of the Jardin d'Acclimatation. I knew that my mother knew, and that she didn't know that I knew, and it was clear to me that she was trying to discover which of the birds it was that my father had turned into, and why he had turned into that bird. I awoke in tears because of the expression on her face: she was trying to smile."

Fathers make few appearances in the works of Cocteau, and when they do appear they appear ingloriously. The attractive young people in two of the novels, *Thomas l'Imposteur* and *Les Enfants Terribles*, are strangely and completely fatherless; and of the father in another, *Le Grand Ecart,* the author says: "If we efface M. Forestier, it is because he effaced himself." Georges Cocteau, too, effaced himself — to such an extent that his son's memoirs barely mention him except in that dream. There he returns, a year after his death, a mere phallic bird, a poor parrot that is divined to be he, a cockatoo whose name is almost his own. At the Pré Catelan, that fashionable restaurant and tearoom with a farm attached, in the Bois de Boulogne, where up until almost yesterday a herd of cows was pastured to provide fresh milk for Parisian mothers and babies and wet nurses, his uncomfortable presence disturbs his wife and his son at their milky tête-à-tête. It is the son's fantasy — however true it may have been in life — that for his mother the bird was discordant, unwelcome, not even completely identifiable among other birds,* and the cause of a sorrow through which she

---

* The fact that Madame Georges Cocteau's two other children were already twelve and eight years old when Jean was born, and the rumor that her husband was secretly homosexual, have raised, in France, doubts about Jean's paternity.

One doesn't wish to echo Mark Twain, with his " 'Tis a wise Frenchman that knows his own father," but a biographer of French literary men cannot help being struck by the frequency with which paternity is questioned even when grounds for doubt have to be invented. The persistent legend that Flaubert was Maupassant's father is chronologically absurd, and the various listings of Maupassant's illegitimate children are vague and unconvincing. Apollinaire's paternity really *is* in doubt: no one can be sure that his father was the Italian army officer with the sonorous name, Francesco Flugi d'Aspermont. Between Jean Cocteau and his mother's husband there is a distinct physiological resemblance, and yet there are several illegitimacy stories. Madame Singer thinks that Jean was Georges's son — "They have the same sharp profile, and Georges loved Jean"; nevertheless she tells of rumors linking Madame Cocteau with

tried to smile for the sake of her son. Her son whom she had always pampered: "Jean was always charming, a droll little boy, very frail," Madame Singer has said. "Much of the time his mother kept him in bed and fussed over him. He loved to dress up in girl's clothes. . . ." The dream was to stop, as Cocteau said, in 1912, and for that the reason will become clear.

Cocteau reacted to his fatherlessness in a classic way, after passing through a confused period of transition. Before his father's suicide he had been overindulged and thought himself the center of the universe; with the shot came the onset of an uncertainty that was never to leave him. During the years preceding his adolescence he displayed considerable open antagonism to his mother, illustrated by a strange episode that took place in a train bringing mother, son and governess back to Paris after a holiday in Switzerland. Jean had insisted that Madame Cocteau buy a box of cigars as a present for their Paris manservant, Auguste, and once in the train he threatened to go into a tantrum if his mother didn't grant a whim he had conceived — that she hide the box under her dress, to cheat the customs. It is an indication of how fearsome the child's tantrums must have been, and how great his mother's indulgence, that she hid the box as he wished. At the border the customs inspector came to the door of the compartment, made polite inquiries, saluted, and was about to leave when Jean spoke up: "This lady is hiding a box of cigars under her dress." Consternation, stammered excuses, surrender of the box, and immediate recognition that a fine must be paid did not satisfy the customs: Madame Cocteau was ordered outside, made to undress, and searched. Throughout his life Cocteau referred to the moral quarantine into which his treachery put him:

---

the Salon painter Joseph Wencker, a family friend who several times painted her portrait, and of other, vaguer rumors about "a Russian, or some other foreigner." Another candidate sometimes mentioned is Marcel Dieulafoy, an archaeologist who excavated in Persia, sent back sculpture to the Louvre, and was well known in Paris society. (Gossip in this case has it that Dieulafoy enjoyed Madame Cocteau's pretty femininity as a relief from the aspect of his cropped-haired wife, who affected strictly male attire — collar, tie, jacket and trousers. In those days a lady so garbed had to be licensed by the police. As a card-carrying trousers-wearer, Madame Dieulafoy was a favorite subject of songs in the *cafés chantants*.) And just the other day, at a lunch in Paris, a Sorbonne professor showed that the Cocteau illegitimacy theory was still alive by expressing his own rather bizarre certainty: "You have only to look at a photograph of Cocteau to know that his father was a Hindu or an Arab — probably someone his mother met through her brother, Raymond Lecomte, who had been with our embassy in Cairo"! In all this there is something of the eternal reluctance to believe that genius can spring from "ordinary" background.

after arrival in Paris there was horrified family whispering, and consultation of doctors. The episode remained forever unmentionable between him and his mother, and he never lost the sense of having shown himself a monster.

What had happened — to put it one way — was that Auguste, Madame Cocteau's valet, had become, at least for the time being in the boy's mind, the head of the household: the train game invented by the boy, with Auguste as beneficiary, the customs inspector as agent, and his mother as victim, is rampant with blatant imagery and suggestion. So very blatant and unpleasant that even Cocteau, who was later, in the midst of sophistication, to write now and then of revelatory dreams and games with a staggering display of naïveté — whether genuine or feigned it is not always easy to determine — did not include it among his memoirs, though he did not keep it to himself. And he retained a lifelong tendency to indulge from time to time in similar procedures that smacked of what others would call duplicity — leading people on to a fall as he led on his mother that day in the train, or playing them off against one another, as in the train he played off the three members of his little cast.

The memoirs mention Cocteau's German governess several times — taking her young charge to the circus, sewing costumes for his toy theatre, helping him win school prizes in German, drawing and gymnastics — but her most noteworthy appearance is at table: "Children take in what goes on around them in a kind of half-sleep. My German governess, Josephine, used to let me lie in her lap, and I would curl up under her napkin, digesting my soup. As Fräulein Josephine ate, what fun it was to follow the course of her dinner, in my babyish doze. The sound of chewing, the stomach sounds, falling bits of bread, the heartbreaking sighs of a governess 'weighed down by responsibilities' — the whole comedy of an upper servant at dinner, eyes raised to heaven and little finger daintily uplifted, would reach me muffled by table linen and as though in a dream." A noteworthy passage, because that drowsy fusion between child and mother's-helper is one of the few physical contacts between a male and a female, and perhaps the most intimate of them, described in Cocteau's works.

Among French writers, only André Gide has made his adolescent hours in the classroom sound quite so autoerotic as Cocteau.

Gide, in *Si le Grain Ne Meurt,* tells of being sent away from his Ecole Alsatienne for masturbating (absentmindedly, "while eating pralines") at his desk; and Cocteau, preferring to share the crime with others, shows whole classes in a constant state of explosion: "I began the Lycée Condorcet in the third form. There the awakening senses of the boys were uncontrolled, flourishing like weeds. There was a hole in every pocket, every handkerchief was soiled. In drawing class the pupils were especially bold, screened by their drawing boards. Sometimes, in one of the other classes, an ironic professor would abruptly call on a pupil who was on the verge of orgasm. The pupil would stand up, his cheeks burning, mumbling anything that came into his head as he tried to make a dictionary serve as fig leaf. Our laughter would embarrass him still further. The classroom smelled of gas, chalk, and sperm."

That scene is found in *Le Livre Blanc,* an early example of the "Confessions of a Homosexual" type of book, decidedly minor from the artistic standpoint, written in the first person and published anonymously in 1928, with illustrations by Cocteau. There was widespread assumption that Cocteau was the book's author as well as its illustrator, and twenty years later he replied to this in a magazine, *Sexual Digest:* "No matter how highly I might think of this book — if it did happen to be by me — I should prefer not to sign it because it would then assume the form of autobiography, and I have not yet written my autobiography, which will be much stranger still." But Cocteau often inscribed *Le Livre Blanc* for friends — Roger Peyrefitte's copy bears the inscription *"Ce salut amical de ma jeunesse lointaine"* — and he entered no denial when it was included in his bibliography. Thus he did give it his signature and let it take "the form of autobiography"; and though it masquerades as a novel, comparison with any of Cocteau's true novels and with his volumes of avowed memoirs reveals *Le Livre Blanc* to be far closer to the latter category. Manipulated, of course, like all of them, even more manipulated than the rest (it was the first written), but essentially a work of nonfiction.

In *Le Livre Blanc* the pederast narrator seeks for the right man, a strong man — not so much to become his favorite as to identify with him, to *become* him. As a day student at the lycée he shadows the school bully, a large, handsome brute full of malicious animal magnetism, easily dominant over his smaller, meeker, physically less mature classmates. Cocteau calls him Dargelos, a name he found attractive and always used thereafter when a bully type entered his work. (The name was actually borne by a member of Cocteau's class, who was otherwise no Dargelos.) Cocteau's poetry, too, celebrates the handsome, magnetic ones, *"les forts de la classe,"* the "school vamps," the boys who looked down on the rest, the "college aristocrats," and Jean-Paul Sartre, analyzing the homosexuality of Jean Genet, finds a parallel in a passage from Cocteau's novel *Le Grand Ecart:* "Ever since childhood he had felt the wish to *be* the beautiful people whom he saw — not to make himself loved by them." But in Cocteau's case the one was not to exclude the other. The longing to *be* people whom he found marvelous, or at least to be like them, usually led to attempts to gain their affections or their approval: their favor could ease the way to the fulfillment of his deeper desires.

His sensibility to the extraordinary, the outstanding, was fostered by home and doting mother. He would see her leave for the theatre, "bristling with aigrettes and swathed in red velvet. She would bring home programs covered with mysterious, important-sounding names. Sometimes I was sick — I had scarlet fever, I had measles like all children. She would give me the programs to read in bed, and I had toy theatres and would cut out scenery, and finally I caught an illness much more serious than scarlet fever or measles — what I call the red-and-gold disease: theatre-itis." That particular kind of scarlet fever became virulent. Simply by looking out his bedroom window, each night, he could see the actress Réjane's famous pair of mules (given her by the King and Queen of Portugal), hitched to her carriage that awaited her outside the stage door of the nearby Théâtre du Vaudeville, and he would dream of the scenes being played within; when he was taken to see *Around the World in Eighty Days* at the Théâtre du Châtelet he ran a temperature. Summer vacations on the Swiss lakes with his family made him "weep out of an overwhelming sense of emptiness, a despair seemingly without cause." In Venice, one evening, sent to bed by his mother in the hotel while the city was still lively, he had his "first bitter taste of being alone amidst crowds, of the feeling of not belonging in the places one loves the best, of being powerless to be many-in-one, a prisoner inside one's own narrow self, of being unable to obtain immediate response in one's search for love, without first going through the usual stages." At the Lycée Condorcet his attention was too exclusively devoted to the only glamour it afforded, the "vamps"; his teachers knew he was bright, but application was lacking; "I was a very bad pupil, I was expelled from one school after another." Actually he seems to have been expelled only from the Condorcet. (One of his fellow pupils there, Maurice Goudeket, has said: "If we had known that he was going to become Jean Cocteau, we might have paid more attention to him then and would now remember more of what he was in those days.") Then he attended another school, the Ecole Fénelon; failed to pass his baccalaureate, and failed a second time despite a year of private tutoring. (During that year there was much matinée-going with his fellow tutees: he became a particular fan of Mistinguett, covered the walls of his room with her photographs, and took flowers to her dressing room.) All that was between the ages of fourteen and seventeen. At some time during that period he climbed the wall.

He says that *Around the World in Eighty Days* and the books of Pierre Loti had given him the longing to be "a sailor-boy before the mast," and that at fifteen he ran away to Marseilles. The French word used by Cocteau that emerges in English translation as "sailor-boy" is *"mousse,"* and in connection with the navy and commercial shipping *"mousse"* has a precise meaning: it refers to the youngest category of seamen, apprentices between the ages of ten and sixteen. Cocteau says that when he reached Marseilles he discovered that *"mousses* and sailing ships no longer existed." Actually *mousses* are working even today on French commercial vessels: it was only in the navy that the practice of training such young boys on actual voyages had been abandoned (in favor of courses on school ships). Did the fifteen-year-old Cocteau really try to join the navy? That would probably have been at Toulon, the chief French naval base on the Mediterranean, near Marseilles. It was in Marseilles itself that he went into hiding — he says for a year.

Before 1943, when the Germans systematically blew up the old quayside quarter of Marseilles, the "Vieux Port," it was one of the most labyrinthine casbahs on the Mediterranean. "An old Annamite woman found me, absolutely lost on the docks, and took me to the rue de la Rose, in the old quarter. I explained to her that I didn't want to go home, I lied to her, telling her that my family was monstrous, which it wasn't at all . . . And for a year I lived with *voy-*

ous. . . . I lived under a false name: a boy had drowned and I
had his papers. . . .The police would never have dared come into
the Old Town, where we were."

The Vieux Port is known to English readers who were never
there from the passage in Evelyn Waugh's *Decline and Fall* in
which Paul Pennyfeather, penetrating the lurid rue Reynarde in
search of *"les jeunes filles de Madame Beste-Chetwinde,"* is accosted by a Negro sailor and a swarm of prostitutes; Cocteau's rue
de la Rose was in the Chinese-Annamite subquarter of this priapic
casbah in which most of the houses were brothels and where prostitutes of both sexes, their pimps and their customers, swarmed by
day and by night. The *"milieu,"* as the French call the world of
organized vice and crime, had never been known to Cocteau in
Paris: in the rue de la Rose he would have lived in the midst of it.
What did he do, during his "year" there? He told a friend, in later
life, that in Marseilles he had worked in a Chinese restaurant,
where he first saw opium-smoking. "In Marseilles, among the An-
namites, where one smokes with implements calculated to confuse
the police (a gas pipe, a sample Benedictine bottle with a hole in it,
hatpins), cockroaches and spiders form a circle in ecstasy." Did
his family really not know where he was? Did they really send him
no money? "My mother wept, but my brother, who was much older
than I, was terribly severe, and told her, 'We mustn't try to find
him, this will teach him to stand on his own feet.' " Years later, in
1946, when Cocteau made a selection of his writings for an edition
of his so-called "Complete Works," to be issued by a Swiss publisher, he omitted much of his work, both poetry and prose, but he
included the only two pieces of his writing laid in Marseilles. They
both bear the same title, *Le Fantôme de Marseille,* the second of
them, a monologue composed for Edith Piaf probably in the
1940's, being a revision of the first, a short story published in the
Nouvelle Revue Française in 1933. The short story begins as follows:

"For four days Achille had been living [in the brothel] . . .
disguised as a woman. But we are not speaking of the legendary
Achilles: you are not beginning a Greek myth. The Achille I speak
of was an Arab, with a Marseillaise mother: he was twenty and
looked fifteen. He was beautiful in a feminine way without being
effeminate. I mean that his face was beardless and hard, his body

slender, his feet and hands small — all of which made it possible for him to wear marvelously well the fashions made for today's women, who try to look like young boys. On him, this type of dress became more feminine by contrast, and gave him a charm that is hard to put into words, fabulous (in the proper sense of the term) and ambiguous. Why was it that our Achille was wearing a dress, a necklace, women's stockings? . . .''

In both the short story and the monologue, a young thief, having disguised himself as a female prostitute to escape the police, allows himself to be courted by an elderly man ignorant of the transvestism — with fatal consequences. The short story is slight, little more than a bit of local color, and the monologue never became one of Piaf's popular numbers. But in both of them, and in retaining them forty years after his Marseilles adventure, Cocteau was revealing the importance of the associations which, for him, clustered around the name of the city — however long or short was his stay there — flight, disguise, pursuit, the exotic, the erotic.

Le Livre Blanc, the book that Cocteau characterized as belonging to his *"jeunesse lointaine,"* contains some scenes that sound young and *marseillais.* Cocteau lays these particular scenes in Toulon, which had its own bars and brothels and, in those days, like Marseilles, large numbers of *fumeries,* opium dens, supplied with drugs brought in from Indo-China on French ships. Cocteau knew Toulon — on his mother's side he was related to Admiral Darlan and other officers of the French fleet, and after writing *Le Livre Blanc* he spent more than one heavily opiumed summer there — but the adventures recounted in *Le Livre Blanc* befall an all but penniless adolescent, like the Cocteau of Marseilles. There is a description of a public bath that is also a male brothel:

"It made one think of the *Satyricon,* this place with its cubicles, its low-ceilinged room furnished with Turkish divans where young men sat playing cards. At a sign from the owner they would get up and stand against the wall. The owner would feel their biceps, stroke their thighs, exhibit their more intimate charms, and show them off as any dealer displays his merchandise."

And there is the peep show of the "transparent mirror":

"You enter a dark booth and open a shutter. This reveals a metallic cloth, through which you find yourself looking into a small bathroom. On the other side, the cloth is a mirror, so completely reflecting and so highly polished that it is impossible to guess that it is being stared through. When I had the money I sometimes went there on Sunday. Of the twelve mirrors in the bathrooms, this was the only one of that kind. The owner had bought it in Germany for a high price. His own employees knew nothing of the observation post. Working-class boys provided the show. They all did the same thing. They would undress and hang up their new clothes very carefully. . . ."

Such references cluster thickly around Cocteau's writings about adolescence. What was the teen-age dweller in the rue de la Rose up to, in Marseilles — the same youth who so recently, in the Lycée Condorcet, had shadowed the *princes du collège*? At fifteen, Cocteau was a good-looking *éphèbe;* his charm, which was to become so famous, must already have been considerable; the nature of his homosexuality was always well known to be passive. How did he live, in Marseilles? He himself, except for the mention of the Chinese restaurant, never told. He did say that the year in Marseilles was a glorious one: "It was the best time of my life. It taught me to stand on my own feet." "Marseilles," he said, "was my real school." Eventually, he says, his uncle — apparently Raymond Lecomte the diplomat, who at that moment was being transferred from Cairo to Berlin — "shocked when he learned of my running away, told the police to find me, and I was brought back from Marseilles by two gendarmes." The fact and the fiction of the Marseilles story will probably never be disentangled. When Roger Stéphane interviewed Cocteau on television in 1963, he asked him, among other questions concerning his youth: "You were happy in Marseilles?" And Cocteau replied, with a kind of ecstasy (he was seventy-three at the time) : "Ah yes! It set me free!"

However long he was away, his family can only have been impressed by the strength of the defiance he had shown. After his return from Marseilles few sustained attempts were made to tame him. France certainly contained thousands of talented young bourgeois who felt themselves "outside," were restless in and out of school, filled with aesthetic and homosexual longings and the urge to revolt. Only Jean Cocteau fled to the rue de la Rose. His reputation made him a kind of pro, a veteran, gave him very early an aura which, added to his literary and artistic glamour, would all his life attract around him young sexual rebels or would-be rebels, of varying degrees of talent, many of them destined to sink back to being timid, resentful *fils-à-papa* or *à-maman,* others to realize themselves, often encouraged by him. His stay in Marseilles was like Oscar Wilde's resolution to see things through, to "get to the bottom of the page."

Whatever the length of his stay in the casbah, it was probably long enough. Probably the *milieu,* fascinating when novel, had quickly revealed its sordidness; certainly he would eventually have been depressed by the underlying despair, by the monotony and the nullity. "In general, Cocteau was *bien entouré,*" a friend has said of him. "He loved a pretty twenty-year-old body, yes, but with a pretty twenty-year-old intelligence." Through most of his life, Cocteau continued to prefer those close to him to be intelligent, though in middle age he began at times to dream up intelligence for his companions and confer it on them. He always particularly enjoyed a young literary intelligence. One such, of whom he would later speak, was Harold Nicolson, the British diplomat and author of the delightful volume of sketches *Some People,* whom he knew when Nicolson was in Paris studying for the Foreign Office examination before 1909.*

Like many another homosexual, Cocteau was given to mentioning the names of women with whom he claimed to have had "affairs," chiefly during his very early years, and in his case once during his middle age. Here and there he mentions a thirty-year-old actress named Madeleine Carlier, with whom he was "madly in love," a vaudeville singer named Jeanne Reynette, and a music student, Christiane Mancini. Before he was twenty, however, his bent was so apparent that his friends (among them some now elderly gentlemen who remember) either hid or did not hide their smiles when he spoke of his infatuation for Madeleine Carlier, especially when he proclaimed himself an expectant father. Both she and Jeanne Reynette signed photographs for him with theatrically extravagant messages of affection, and Jeanne Reynette and Christiane Mancini wrote him notes "compromising" themselves so very

* That the two young men knew each other and that Cocteau was perfectly familiar with Nicolson's tastes at this time is confirmed in the last installment of Nicolson's own column, "Marginal Comment," in *The Spectator* for December 26, 1952. "I remember," Nicolson wrote there, "that when, long ago [it was 1913], I was engaged to be married, I wrote to my friend M. Jean Cocteau informing him of that most auspicious event. '*Evidemment,*' he telegraphed in reply, '*il faut quitter le Louvre avant qu'on crie "On ferme!"*' "

emphatically that one suspects the missives were designed chiefly to be shown to Cocteau's friends and that they may even have been of Cocteau's own composition. Carefully preserved by Cocteau, and recently printed in the catalogue of an exhibition of Cocteau documents (they belong to Cocteau's heir), they have a false ring. Perhaps if the ladies who wrote them were to speak frankly from the afterlife their stories would resemble, at least in part, the recent, more believable "confession" of another, still living *chanteuse*, for many years a familiar of Cocteau and his repertory company of male companions: "I have *slept* with Jean (and with him and his boyfriends, sometimes several at a time); I have never 'been to bed' with him." Mistinguett, who all her life claimed to have accomplished some kind of *déniaisement* on him during one of his adolescent visits to her dressing room, caused him undisguised but noncommittal delight whenever he heard that she had told the story yet once again. One woman who knew Cocteau well in all his guises and who was involved in his one middle-aged heterosexual "affair," has said: "Cocteau was all *esprit* — and later, of course, drugs. Even from the beginning almost everything was in his head, and later there was too much opium for sex anyway. Certainly he was no Oscar Wilde of bisexual capabilities. You will not find that women speak very well of Cocteau — they do not have very good memories of him."

Cocteau later particularly deplored what he considered the greatest defect of his own early revolt: "I was a very bad pupil, I was always a very bad pupil, I was expelled from one school after another, and to be a bad pupil was enough to gratify my rebellious spirit. But I should also have been a bad pupil in the realm of art. That I was not. I was simply an idiot." In that, he was doubtless contrasting himself with Baudelaire, Rimbaud and Radiguet, three French artists whose phenomenal artistic precocity he always envied and extolled. In his opinion, his own artistic maturity came only in 1917, when he was twenty-seven — "very late." Until then he was, in artistic matters, a "good pupil" — the wrong thing for an artist to be. But his public career as an artist began at eighteen, in 1908.

One of the most popular, if not the most sublime, actors in the history of the Comédie Française, that shrine of classical French

declamation and gesture, was one who never lost his native Rumanian accent and who, when he played his most famous role, that of
Nero in Racine's tragedy *Brittanicus,* turned the emperor into what
Cocteau called a "comic-opera Nero" by his special kind of outrageous flamboyance. This was Edouard de Max. His parents — their
name was simply Max — had brought him to France as a child,
and for many years he was a peculiarly Parisian theatrical orna-
ment. He was talented both in comedy and tragedy, and came close
to succeeding to the lofty place long occupied at the Comédie Française by the great Mounet-Sully, who was, by the time of Cocteau's
adolescence, "a blind old lion dozing in a corner of the menagerie."
In the opinion of Madame Simone, who played with De Max, there
were two reasons for his failure to attain supremacy: short stature
and pederastic exaggeration.

In those just post-Wildean days, when even in France pederasty
was hidden by most of its practitioners, De Max's offstage eye-
shadow and jewels told their story, and onstage a swishiness tended
to creep into his comportment in roles where it was inappropriate.
Paul Léautaud, for many years drama critic of the *Mercure de
France* under the name Maurice Boissard, praised him for his
comic gifts, but scourged him for never being able to achieve simplicity, for being "irritating in his mannerisms and his way of
declaiming" and "utterly ridiculous" at the wrong times. (He had
the interior of his sedan chair electrically lit when he was carried
onstage as Xerxes in Aeschylus's *The Persians.*) He was also famous for the overexuberance of his claque. The air of innocence he
assumed while the claque shouted "Bravo!" Léautaud says, was so
very innocent that nobody was taken in.

De Max, in short, was something of a ham. To his flat in the rue
Caumartin the sixteen-year-old Cocteau was taken, as a worshipper,
by a friend — apparently shortly after his return from Marseilles.
"With his blue-green chin, his grandiose gestures and his roaring
voice, De Max was like the ocean, and like the ocean he was
dreaded by mothers," Cocteau says, quoting a line from Victor
Hugo's *Oceano Nox* about terrified mothers praying for the safety
of their sailor sons — *"Flots profonds, redoutés des mères à gen-
oux!"* "I except my own mother," he says, "who was always trusting and perfect. But the others! 'Your son knows De Max! That's
the end of him!' Such was the leitmotiv, and it was completely

false. No black masses or flesh-colored masses. No boy-traps. From my first visit I still have a photograph, inscribed 'To your sixteen years in bloom from my forty years in tears.' "

All who ever knew Madame Cocteau are in agreement that the confidence she placed — or misplaced — in her younger son was enormous, and that it was facilitated by her talent for disregarding. It was impossible for her not to have known many things about Jean that were distasteful to her, but much of the time she declined to recognize them. Especially to those outside her family she only occasionally displayed awareness that from her point of view there was anything amiss: "I am not listened to, and I suppose that is more or less as it should be," she once wrote to Valentine Hugo. For the most part she was a mother concerning whom the word "permissive" is an understatement, but throughout Jean's life she punctuated indulgence with reproaches that sometimes showed incomprehension of his gifts, and despite Jean's description of her as "always trusting and perfect" his "adoration" of her was interspersed with fits of resentment. Their relations always remained emotional and immature. To the world, she was a rather old-fashioned, gracious lady, pious — she attended Mass almost every day. "Very nice, oh, very nice," Madame Simone has said of her, "but *évanescente*." *"Une brave femme,"* is the verdict of Mademoiselle Chanel, *"mais affrrreusement bourrrgeoise."* She lived until 1943, and during much of her life Cocteau lived with her or kept a room in her apartment. In her last days, he says, she was like "an elderly little girl, questioning an elderly little boy about his school, and urging him to behave. It is possible that my long childhood, which wears the mask of adulthood, comes to me from my mother, whom I resemble."

In his memoirs Cocteau provides a glimpse of De Max's "innocent" antics with his favored youths:

"I will tell you about the incident at the ball given by Robert d'Humières in the Théâtre des Arts, where he was manager. De Max, the most naïf man in the world, dreamed up the idea of arriving with an escort, consisting of [René] Rocher [a former classmate of Cocteau's], Chiro Vesperto (a model), and me. Our naïveté surpassed his. We thought of the expedition only as an excuse for dressing up. Imagine De Max's pearl-gray electric automobile disgorging, at the entrance on the Boulevard des Batignolles, under the dismayed glance of d'Humières, the following: De Max, wearing an eagle headdress and an Arabian veil, Rocher and Vesperto costumed as Arcadian shepherds, and myself as Heliogabalus, with red curls, a tremendous tiara, a pearl-embroidered train, anklets, and painted nails. We soon realized our mistake. Robert d'Humières hastily parked us in a stage-box, and everybody around us was laughing in our faces. Sarah Bernhardt despatched her maid, Mlle. Seylor, with a message for me: 'If I were your mother, I'd send you to bed.' I sniffled up my tears. The mascara ran down my face in stinging black streaks. De Max realized his blunder. He took us away, relieved us of our wigs and rouge, and dropped us at our respective doors."

And then, abruptly, comes another aspect of De Max. He "organized, and paid for out of his own pocket, an afternoon at the Théâtre Femina, devoted to my poems. The most celebrated actresses participated, at his request. Laurent Tailhade combed his gray crest, screwed in his glass eye and his monocle, and read a preliminary lecture, a veritable massacre of the poets of the day. Only me did he let live." It is the brief, first announcement that Cocteau had been writing poems, and that De Max launched him on the career that was to continue for fifty-five years.

The Théâtre Femina was an elegant little playhouse on the Champs-Elysées, decorated in tones of lemon and pearl-gray, so diminutive that the audience could feel itself on terms of intimacy with the performers: it was fashionable, that spring, to attend a recital or concert there on Saturday afternoon before going on to tea at the Pré Catelan. It was De Max who chose that theatre for Cocteau's debut, De Max's name that headed the elegant invitations, De Max's prestige that brought the actresses and singers to perform the works of the eighteen-year-old poet, and the dressy audience to listen and applaud. Apparently there was much applause. Cocteau has described himself as feeling, that Saturday afternoon — it was April 4, 1908 — that he was being "wafted on the wings of fame."

Everything he read that afternoon had been written since his return from Marseilles. Yet of Marseilles there is not the slightest echo. All is fashionable, Parisian, delicate. Freed from school, he had clearly been writing voluminously and going everywhere in Paris: his first book of verse, *La Lampe d'Aladin*, which would be published the next year, would contain about a hundred poems, and most of them bear dedications to well-known literary Parisians, whom he was meeting in great numbers — stars of the moment like Alfred Vallette (director of the *Mercure de France*), Lucie Delarue-Mardrus, Henri de Régnier, Jean Richepin, Catulle Mendès. One, "Les Façades," is dedicated to M. Pierre Lafitte, owner of the smart magazine *Je Sais Tout,* in which the poem appeared, Cocteau's first poem to be printed, in the issue of July 15, 1908. (It was accompanied — setting a precedent almost always to be followed — by the eighteen-year-old poet's photograph.) From *La Lampe d'Aladin,* from the poems' dates and some of their dedications, a few details of the matinée in the Théâtre Femina emerge. Certain poems are dedicated to the *artistes* who recited or sang that afternoon. To "Madame Lucie Bréval of the Opéra" is dedicated "Adoration": she doubtless sang someone's arrangement of the young poet's words:

> Dans le pavot amer s'endort le scarabée,
> Le parfum se répand des roses qui se fanent.
> En l'air, le ciel a des nuages diaphanes . . .

"Les Orgues" must have been recited by "Mademoiselle Provost of the Comédie Française":

> Pleurez, pleurez! Voici tourner la manivelle!
> Orgues naïfs qui ne savez que trois refrains,
> Sanglotez une valse avec sa ritournelle . . .

To the great tragedienne Madame Segond-Weber was allotted a sequence of four poems entitled "Les Salomé"; and one can imagine De Max himself intoning both "L'Aumône," a dramatic monologue:

> Un conseil, s'il vous plaît! Voyez, je tends mon âme . . .
> Remplissez-la des mots qui réconforteront,
> N'ayez pas de colère et n'ayez pas de blâme,
> Posez votre fraîcheur aux fièvres de mon front . . .

and especially "Les Bruits":

Avez-vous entendu l'appel hurlant et long,
L'appel, dans le fracas d'une mer glauque et flasque,
Et les volets mal clos claqués par la bourrasque,
L'appel désespéré du bateau moribond?

Avez-vous entendu le silence des nuits? . . .
Avez-vous entendu le long sifflet qui grince
D'un train fuyant la gare où trainaient les adieux . . . ?

Eh bien! tous ces bruits-là . . .
— Tous ces bruits désolés, je les ai dans mon coeur!

If one has attended French poetry recitals, one can see and hear it all — the gestures, the risings and fallings of the great voices, the appreciative murmurs, the applause.*

In *La Lampe d'Aladin,* when it was published, those poems were accompanied by pastel verses about Versailles and Watteau, by an inevitable "Nocturne," a "Troisième Ballade de Chopin," and other period pieces, many of them not at all lacking in charm and deftness. The Salomé sequence brings the first echo, in Cocteau's life and work, of Wilde and Beardsley; and the volume ends with a

---

* English versions of those samples might be:

> In bitter poppy sleeps the scarab,
> The fading roses spread their fragrance.
> Far above, the clouds are diaphanous . . .
>
> Weep, weep! See, the handle turns!
> Artless organs, with your three refrains,
> Sob out a waltz and then its *ritournelle* . . .
>
> Please counsel me! Here, take my soul . . .
> Fill it with comfort-bringing words,
> Be not angry, speak no blame,
> Touch your coolness to my fevered brow. . . .
>
> and
>
> Have you heard the long and howling call,
> The call amid the glaucous ocean's roar
> And the banging of the shutters in the gale,
> The desperate call of the dying ship?
>
> Have you heard the silence of the nights?
> Have you heard the whistle, long and sharp,
> Of the train, the station and the farewells left behind?
>
> Well! All those sounds . . .
> Those desolate sounds, are in my heart!

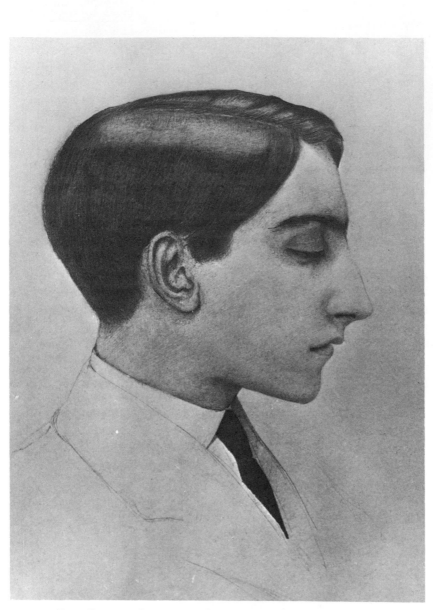

Jean Cocteau about 1910. Drawing by Lucien Daudet.

"one-act fantasy in verse," "Bric-à-Brac," in which porcelain fig-
urines converse archly inside a curio cabinet. Cocteau prefaced the
book with a few wistful words "in explanation of the title": "I have
wandered amid the gloom of life, with the marvelous lamp. Young
like Aladdin, walking with fearful step, I have seen fruits, jewels,
gleams and shadows. And, my heart filled with illusions, I have
wept at the difficulty of giving them to the unbelieving world."

It was De Max who had solved that difficulty. Writing gratefully
in later life about De Max's role in his debut, Cocteau said:
"Among his other lapses of taste, this generous man was guilty of
admiring my first poems and of helping to promote them . . . He
saw beyond my follies, and sensed that I had some hidden
strength." By the time he wrote that, De Max was dead, and Cocteau
had long come to consider not only the poems read and sung at the
Théâtre Femina and printed in *La Lampe d'Aladin,* but also those
printed in his next two books, *Le Prince Frivole* and *La Danse de
Sophocle,* as "stupid" verses that it would have been much better
not to give to the world. On another occasion he called those first
three books of poems "three silly performances." He never allowed
them to be reprinted. "Nevertheless my start does date from that
séance in the Théâtre Femina," he says, "and the efforts I had to
make later, to cause it to be forgotten, were enough to make it unforgettable to me."

Far from forgetting the matinée in the Théâtre Femina,
throughout his life Cocteau increasingly overremembered it. In an
autobiographical talk recorded in 1958 but never publicly released, Cocteau said about it: "What ennobled that period of my
life in my eyes, what made it possible for me not to be ashamed of
it, is the fact that when Edouard de Max and Laurent Tailhade
introduced me to the Parisian public at the Théâtre Femina with a
recitation of my detestable poems by great actors and actresses of
the day, the audience happened to include Roger Martin du Gard. I
was a young man, he was still young, and of so exquisite a character that he did not see me as ridiculous — he saw only an enthusiastic youth whom some older men had put up there on the stage and
who obviously felt that he had been wafted there on the wings of
fame. And instead of making fun of me, he made that person who
appeared on the stage of the Théâtre Femina the central figure of
his first novel, the novel that significantly enough is entitled *De-*

venir [Becoming]. From that afternoon at the Théâtre Femina,
which he describes in *Devenir,* he imagined what my existence
might be."

Now *Devenir,* Roger Martin du Gard's first novel, written long
before he gained fame with his many volumed *Les Thibault,* is not
a book that is nowadays often read; but it provides interesting
glimpses of life among young artists beginning their careers in
Paris in the first decade of the century, and added interest comes
from Cocteau's remembering that he himself was Martin du Gard's
model for the "central figure." *Devenir* does recount the debut of a
poet, but in a way rather different from Cocteau's indication.

Its "central" figure is a failed literary man named André
Mazerelles, not at all reminiscent of the debutant Cocteau. The
figure Cocteau had in mind can only be one, or the fusion, of a pair
of incidental characters. These are a collaborating poet and musician, who, in the novel, resemble Cocteau in their triumph on the
stage of the Théâtre Femina. The two young men are inseparable;
their names, Jemmequin and Coczani, are interestingly initialed,
and in fact are combined by their friends into a joint "English"
nickname, "Jemm and Co." They are taken up by a famous actor,
"le beau Cyprian," who organizes a Jemm and Co. matinée. "All the
newspapers carried announcements that there would be a matinée
of poetry and music at the Théâtre Femina on the last Saturday of
the month. The occasion was to be the 'introduction, to the world of
literature and the arts, of a pair of twin geniuses, M. Raoul Jemm
and Maté Coczani, who had been discovered by the divine Cyprian,
the masterly interpreter of French poetry. He himself would offici-
ate at their Parisian debut.' "

For his novelistic purposes, Martin du Gard has Jemm's poetry,
"that poetry that was so light, so indolent, so full of nuances," read,
at the Théâtre Femina, not only by De Max-Cyprian but also by
Sarah Bernhardt, who, in life, is not known to have been present.
(She is called "Rebecca Bechdolt" in the novel.) Amid the applause, the cries of *"Bravo! Auteur! Poète!"* the Co. half of the
team keeps cool — "he behaved as though he had been the public's
idol for years" — whereas Jemm, led forward by Rebecca,
"seemed so young, so slender, so touching, with his eyes bright with
tears, his tangled blond hair, his trembling lips, that the public was

completely won over and clapped and clapped. . . ." That evening, one of the Paris newspapers prints a rave review, headlined *"Un triomphe."*

Following the success, Jemm put together a volume of verse, "a sheaf of short poems garnered at Versailles"; there was nothing winged about it: "One felt that Jemm had had to take the train at the Gare St. Lazare and set off in search of impressions." The pair looks about "to see who might like" the volume, and they dedicate the separate poems. The dedications, Roger Martin du Gard says, "lengthily considered and discussed," were "actually a shrewd bit of business."

Those details from *Devenir* cast an amusing light on Cocteau's saying about Roger Martin du Gard that "He did not see me as ridiculous . . . he made that person who appeared on the stage of the Théâtre Femina the central figure of his first novel." And in fact by the last year of his life, in 1963, when Cocteau was asked to talk about "The Art of Fiction" for the *Paris Review,* he was saying confidently to his interviewer: ". . . in 1908 De Max and Sarah Bernhardt hired the Femina Theatre in the Champs-Elysées for an evening of my poems." Cocteau's mismemory had produced for the interviewer, although the latter was unaware of it, an example of the very "art of fiction" the two men had come together to discuss.

Long before the disc and the interview, Cocteau had written in *Opium:* "I wonder how people can write the lives of poets, since poets themselves are quite unable to write their own lives. There are too many mysteries, too many true lies, too much of a tangle." And in a sonnet:

> Le destin il est vrai m'a donné une apparence humaine
> Mais un étrange étranger habite en moi
> Je le connais mal et il m'arrive à l'improviste
> D'y penser comme on se réveille en sursaut*

As time went on Cocteau claimed to recognize himself less and less in what he called *"légendes ridicules"* (i.e., almost anything

---

* Though fate has given me a human look / A strange stranger dwells within me. / I barely know him; and now and then I think of him / Suddenly, as one wakes abruptly from a sleep.

ever said about him by anybody else), and he offered as his true portrait, as his "autobiography," chiefly myths, sometimes incorporating into them parts of those very *"légendes ridicules"* that he pretended to deplore. He adored acting the will-o'-the-wisp. It was one of his best *"transformations de Fregoli."*

The Announcement of the *Matinée Poétique*
at the Théâtre Femina, April 4, 1908.

2

The Poet of the Salons

When he had stretched himself on the sofa, he looked at the title-page of the book. It was Gautier's *Émaux et Camées*. . . . He came to those lovely stanzas upon Venice. . . . How exquisite they were! As one read them, one seemed to be floating down the green water-ways of the pink and pearl city, seated in a black gondola with a silver prow and trailing curtains. The mere lines looked to him like those straight lines of turquoise-blue that follow one as one pushes out to the Lido. The sudden flashes of color reminded him of the gleam of the opal-and-iris-throated birds that flutter round the tall honeycombed Campanile, or stalk, with such stately grace, through the dim, dust-stained arcades. Leaning back with half-closed eyes, he kept saying over and over to himself:

> *"Devant une façade rose,*
> *Sur le marbre d'un escalier."*

The whole of Venice was in those two lines. He remembered the autumn that he had passed there, and a wonderful love that had stirred him to mad, delightful follies. There was romance in every place. . . . Basil had been with him part of the time, and had gone wild over Tintoret. Poor Basil! what a horrible way for a man to die!

— Oscar Wilde, *The Picture of Dorian Gray* (1890)

COCTEAU's life and work took on a Wildean and Beardsleyan tinge for a time, during the years that followed his debut at the Théâtre Femina. His readings in Wilde had included not only the *Salomé* that was echoed in his own Salomé sequence recited by Madame Segond-Weber at the matinée, but also *The Picture of Dorian Gray* and *The Ballad of Reading Gaol*; and during a visit he paid to Venice in September of 1908 (his great debut year, when he turned eighteen) he had an adventure that recalls those words from *Dorian Gray* and he met a Wilde. Vyvyan, Oscar Wilde's son, whose name had been changed to Vyvyan Holland during his boyhood, was in Venice that September with a friend, "staying at the Grand Hotel . . . and lazing through the days in gondolas or roaming about the outer islands in a motorboat." At his friend's suggestion Holland called himself, at the beginning of the Venetian visit, Vyvyan Wilde, "as an experiment," but too many Italian journalists kept asking for interviews, and he reverted to "Holland." It was during his brief experiment that Cocteau met him. "Do you remember me, dear Vyvyan Wilde," he wrote later, "in Venice, in St. Mark's Square? I was *Prince du Ridicule*, very proud of my profile, amid a flock of pigeons that I think of today as being like so many slaps in the face, whereas they seemed to me at that time like a foretaste of a thousand clapping hands." He was still in the great flush of his Femina success.

André Germain, a Parisian of approximately Cocteau's age whose father had founded a great bank, the Crédit Lyonnais, but who preferred, himself, to found small literary magazines, has written of Cocteau's visit to Venice that year as being "a concession to a certain kind of indiscretion that was just beginning to be smart." He meant that in Venice Cocteau was with fashionably scandalous homosexual friends. "The trip quickly turned tragic," André Germain says. "One of Cocteau's companions, a young writer named Raymond Laurent, excessively romantic, shot himself on the steps of the Salute. Cocteau was not the cause: the other man involved was an American." The Venetian daily, *La Gazzetta di Venezia*, reported the incident on September 25, 1908:

> About two o'clock this morning the two policemen on night patrol in the area of the church of the Salute heard a pistol shot. Running to the scene, they discovered the body of a dying man lying on the edge of the embankment in front of the church. A small revolver was found nearby. At the hospital it was ascertained that the bullet had entered the left side of the chest and penetrated the heart, causing death to be almost instantaneous. On the body were found only thirty-seven lire and a receipt from the Hotel Europa which enabled the police to identify the suicide. He was Sig. Raymond Laurent, 23, brown hair, small brown moustache, who had occupied Room 81 of the hotel since the eighth of this month. A resident of Paris, he had been in Venice for some time, living at the Al-

bergo Luna before moving to the Europa. In his room, which Sig. Laurent had left at one o'clock and to which he had not returned, the bed had not been slept in, and four letters were found on the writing table. One was directed to the manager of the hotel, with the request that the young man's papers be forwarded to his mother; one was to Lady Layard, a request for permission to visit the famous Layard collection; a third was to the mother of the deceased, Mme. C. Laurent; and the last to Mr. L. A. Wister [*sic*], a guest at the Hotel Monaco. The reasons for the suicide remain a mystery.

André Germain speaks of Cocteau as having been "frightened at first"; but if the date he gave to one of his poems is genuine, terror did not prevent him from versifying the very day of the tragedy. There is a sonnet, "En manière d'Epitaphe," dedicated to Laurent's memory and dated September 25, 1908, and there is a ballad, "Souvenir d'un soir d'automne au jardin Eaden," also dated September, dedicated to "L.-H. Whister" (*sic*) — the "other man," actually Langhorn Whistler. Cocteau may not have been present at the shooting — in the ballad he chooses to place it in the Eden Gardens (then open to the public) on the Giudecca, rather far from the "area of the church of the Salute" — but since he knew both Laurent and Whistler he may well have been questioned by the police — the reason, perhaps, for the fright. One stanza can only be described as jaunty:

> Et ce fut tout! . . . Quelques effrois,
> Quelques amicales paroles,
> Et dans les joyeuses gondoles,
> L'ennui de n'être plus que trois!
> Et ce fut tout! . . . Quelques effrois,
> Quelques amicales paroles . . .*

"The bore of being now but three": who was the third, and are the words deliberately languid to hide the fright? André Germain ends his note on the Venetian visit by saying that Cocteau "later came to accept the rather bloody notoriety that was already attach-

---

* "And that was all! A bit of fright, / A few words spoken among friends, / And in the merry gondolas / The bore of being now but three! / And that was all! A bit of fright, / A few words spoken among friends . . .

ing itself to his name." That refers to the reputation he was gradually to acquire for being a dangerous friend to have. Cocteau himself was to say, some years later, "I have lost my seven best
friends" — he was never averse to accepting the role of *homme
fatal* — and throughout his life quite an astonishing number of
deaths were to cluster around his name.

One poem written about the time of the Venetian suicide bears a
Shakespearean-Wildean title, "Mr. W.H.," and another carries a
motto in English from Lord Alfred Douglas — "I am the Love that
dare not speak his name." Apparently a good deal of "smart indiscretion" was going on before, during and after the Venetian visit,
and this is one of the occasions when Madame Cocteau, learning
whatever she learned, spoke her mind. "I am really in a terrible
state," her son wrote to a friend, Maurice Duplay. "Maman has just
made a very serious and painful scene on the subject of my 'excessive freedom, that I put to such bad use,' the 'appalling people I
see,' my idleness, not earning my living, etc. etc. If she knew how
stormy these recent months have been . . . the way I have been
getting rid of so much unconscious filth . . . how I hate everything that is low and unsavory. . . . But such explanations are
difficult and useless. I promised her to write to you at once, since
you have always been so good to me, to ask whether you could still
find me something to do at *Les Paroles,* for instance. I'd jump at the
most minor job. Excuse this scribble, but I'm a rag and my eyes are
full of tears. Help me!" He wrote to another friend; "There was a
maternal scene awaiting me when I reached home, a very, very serious one — terrible, in fact. . . . I am being kept in prison here,
can't go out! . . ." And to still another friend, apparently
François Bernouard, a former classmate, there is a third "Letter,"
this one a sonnet:

Letter

François, you know the story, so unfair . . . I write you
From a kind of prison, like our dear Verlaine;
I am drained of sobs, of defiance, of cries,
I hold my pen in fingers weak as wool.

Here I am, limp, mute, a ridiculous wreck
After four days of full and open fun,

Victim of the eternal and stupid "misunderstood"
And of something I can scarcely guess.

Ridiculous, mute, limp debris — I am here
For having been too much the friend who gives what he has
And whom one caresses like a young and winning child . . .*

And a sonnet to his mother seems to refer to the same episode:

My Mother

These days of injustice and bitter revolt,
When I am the tortured one who bends his head,
And, weary of contending, longs for the coup de grace,
What admirable faith in my mother's eyes!

She knows childish indiscretion and its cost,
The absurdity of the words "police," "magistrate," and "mayor."
She gives her saintly pardon to the ephemeral mistake
And binds and closes the open wound. . . .

Her look and her heart go beyond appearances;
Far from hypocrisy and rancid moralizings
She covers my head with her long hands.

Oh! amid the swirls of future storms,
Delicious balm of sombre morning-after:
Beloved memory of her hands on my head.†

What "childish indiscretion" had Madame Cocteau discovered?
Cocteau rightly says himself that the "imprisonment" in his
mother's house following confrontation with "police, magistrate,
and mayor" resembled only slightly the fate of Verlaine, who in

---

* François, tu sais l'histoire injuste . . . Je t'écris / Un peu d'une prison comme le
doux Verlaine; / Je n'ai plus de sanglots, de révolte, de cris, / Je tiens mon porte-plume
avec des doigts de laine. / Je suis là, mou, muet, ridicule débris / Après ces quatre
jours de gaieté franche et pleine, / Victime d'éternel et bête "mal compris" / Et de je
ne sais quoi que je dévine à peine. / Ridicule, muet, mou débris . . . Je suis là / Pour
être trop l'ami qui donne ce qu'il a / Et qu'on berce en enfant si câlin et si jeune. . . .

† Par ces jours d'injustice et de révolte amère / Où je suis le supplicié qui tend le
cou / Et, las de se débattre, espère un dernier coup, / Quelle admirable foi dans les
yeux de ma mère! / Elle sait l'imprudence enfantine et son coût, / Le drôle dans les
mots gendarme, juge et maire / Et, sainte pardonneuse à l'erreur éphémère, / Elle
panse la plaie ouverte et la recoud. / Son regard et son coeur passent les apparences;
Loin de l'hypocrisie et des morales rances, / Elle couvre ma tête avec ses longues mains.
/ Oh! parmi les remous des futures tempêtes, / Baume délicieux des sombres lende-
mains: / Le souvenir aimé de ses mains sur ma tête.

1873 had been locked up in a real prison in Brussels after shooting Rimbaud. But something had occurred — something that made Cocteau willing, at eighteen, to obey his mother, stay at home, and write her a placating sonnet — which nevertheless contains confident prophesy of "future storms." Details are vague, but one thing is known that may be related to the "childish indiscretion": according to Cocteau, his mother had found that he was "maintaining a separate establishment," a *garçonnière* in the then-crumbling old Hôtel Biron, in the rue de Varenne.

"Playing truant one day," — Cocteau doesn't say from where: he was certainly no longer in school, and the moment seems to have been sometime after his return from Venice — "wandering along the rue de Varenne, I turned into the huge courtyard of the mansion on the corner of that street and the Boulevard des Invalides, and asked the concierge if I might look around. I learned that the house was called the Hôtel Biron, that it had last been the Convent [and Academy] of the Sacred Heart, that since the 'separation' a liquidator of government property had been in charge, that Rodin lived in the central part, that the rest was rented out, and that if I wished the concierge would show me what rooms were free. If I wanted one of them, I should make an offer to M. Ménage, the liquidator. That same afternoon I was the tenant of the former dance and music classroom of the nuns. I paid, by the year, what would be a single month's rent for a room in a disreputable hotel." *

What Cocteau had wandered into (if he really discovered the place by chance — he may have been on his way to visit his friends the Daudets, who lived nearby) was one of the most splendid mansions of the Faubourg Saint-Germain, designed in the eighteenth century by Jacques-Ange Gabriel, architect of the Petit Trianon and the palaces on the Place de la Concorde. One of Rodin's biographers, revering the Hôtel Biron as his hero's shrine, has written savagely of its condition after the government had taken it over and opened it up for rent piecemeal: "An uproarious horde rushed in, and soon every chink and corner was crawling with their lice. . . .

* At this time, and probably all her life until her death in 1943 when Cocteau was in his fifties, Madame Cocteau apparently made him an allowance, which varied with his age and seems to have been his steadiest source of income. In later years he was occasionally flush when a play, a film or a book was popular, but though he was usually comfortable he was never rich nor particularly financially minded. "Don't think me rich, whatever M. —— may say," Cocteau wrote to Max Jacob in 1918. "My mother spends what she has, and I have nothing. I should be glad to earn some money."

The liquidator was delighted . . . painters and sculptors, mostly, so wretchedly mediocre that even now, sometimes, long after they have been got rid of, the Hôtel Biron stinks of their putrid filth." The "lousy horde" included, at various times, Matisse, De Max, Isadora Duncan, who rented a gallery for her dancing courses, "several American women writers," and Rainer Maria Rilke, who in September, 1908 moved into quarters formerly occupied by his wife, the sculptress Clara Westhoff, once a pupil of Rodin's. Rilke led a solitary life in the Hôtel Biron: he was writing his *Requiems* and his half-memoir, half-novel, *The Notebooks of Malte Laurids Brigge;* and when he emerged it was chiefly to wander about Paris or to take the train to suburban Meudon to visit Rodin, whose secretary he had formerly been. Rodin's studio space in Meudon was becoming cramped, and when Rilke brought him to the rue de Varenne and showed him the vast, empty ground-floor rotunda of the Hôtel Biron the sculptor rented it and took to commuting daily from the suburbs to his new studio. Apparently both Rilke and Rodin were newly installed when Cocteau rented his room, but neither Rilke nor Cocteau then knew of the other's existence.

"After passing through a little empty chapel," Cocteau has written of his quarters, "painted with lilies and doves, you came into a room with several high window-doors. A stove, a piano, a sofa, a packing case draped with a cloth, a few chairs and some kerosene lamps quickly made the ex-classroom habitable, and after only a day or two I was inviting my astonished friends to my fairy-tale hideaway, bordered on one side by the gardens of the rue Barbet-de-Jouy, and on the right by the Boulevard des Invalides, down as far as the disaffected church where Comte d'Osnowitchine gave Russian parties." It was here that Cocteau later said his "companion" was Christiane Mancini. The garden was perfect for *fêtes champêtres* or *fêtes galantes.* Catulle Mendès came and declaimed his verses, the composer Reynaldo Hahn sang "disturbing Venetian songs," and with Cocteau the dramatist Francis de Croisset strolled around the "fabulous mound of rubbish, covered by a tangle of fragrant wild roses, that stood in the middle of a sandy circular space overgrown with weeds. This was the only place not encumbered by brambles and bushes. All the rest was a miniature virgin forest, an inextricable confusion of plant life. The moss-grown steps, the greenish windowpanes of the facade, the sundial on the wall of the house — these stood out amid the shambles." The tall windows of his room, Cocteau said, were hard to open because of the thick carpet of forget-me-nots just outside; once opened, they led to "veritable tunnels of greenery that ended in mystery."

Did Cocteau remember that, perhaps, when in 1945 he asked the technicians of the Joinville studio to construct the magic wood for his fairy-tale film *La Belle et la Bête?* The Hôtel Biron made Cocteau and his friends think of another old Paris mansion, the hôtel Pimodan on the Ile-Saint-Louis, where Baudelaire once lived. "It made us ape Baudelaire's receptions," he said.

The only non-coctelian account we have of Cocteau in his *garçonnière* is one by Robert Rey, a contemporary of Cocteau's who later became a professor in the Ecole du Louvre. Just out of the lycée, Rey was asked by his guardian, who happened to be Madame Segond-Weber of the Comédie Française, to deliver a roll of manuscripts to Cocteau at the Hôtel Biron. Cocteau's first volume had just been published; somewhere there was to be a recitation of his poems; he needed recent manuscript verses that had been lent to the actress. The concierge showed the young errand-boy the way, and the following are a few of his recollections:

> I found myself in a room whose stone floor gave off a poetically pastoral odor. Two sofas, a few rattan armchairs with soft-colored cushions, and, on the sofas and armchairs, on the floor, everywhere, goatskins. . . .
>
> Another visitor was present, whose appearance startled me at first, he looked so like an animated fashion drawing. The cut of his very light-colored suit went beyond the merely impeccable, his collar was fashionably, incredibly high, and his tie, a tiny silk bow, was tied about halfway up this giraffe choker. I knew him slightly. He was an actor at the Comédie Française, come to choose, with Jean Cocteau, some poems to be recited at a gala soon to take place.
>
> Jean Cocteau's welcome was perfectly affable, but not excessively warm. I couldn't have wished him to be more amiable — it was simply that he did not encourage familiarity. Listening to him, I was astonished and captivated. He wasn't showing off in the slightest, but it was incredible, how much

he knew, how much he had read, the freshness of his ideas, the pithiness of his expressions. He kept rumpling his hair with his long fingers, and every once in a while he would interrupt himself, clutch a goatskin, crush it, shake it out, and say "I adore the smell of furs." I had the uneasy, uncomfortable sensation of being in the presence of a monster: the extent, the power, and the scintillating variety of his mind, and the clarity of his thinking, contrasted so strongly with his physique — the nervous, slender body that seemed almost fragile. What we knew wasn't negligible, either, but we had learned it at school, whereas with Cocteau I sensed that he had grown up without tutors, following his curiosity wherever it led him.

Cocteau's tenancy at the Hôtel Biron was brought to an end by an accident, he says. Madame Cocteau belonged to the Société des Amis du Louvre, whose membership dues are used for the enrichment of the museum's collections; in turn the members are invited to attend lectures at the Louvre and elsewhere, visit private collections, historic buildings, and so on. The Hôtel Biron was a historic building, and a campaign for its restoration by the state was under way. "The Society" — such is Cocteau's tale "decided to organize a visit to the Hôtel Biron, and asked my mother to see whether her son would allow Les Amis du Louvre to use his porch. My mother answered that there must be some mistake, that her two sons both lived at . . . etc. Letter followed letter, I was called onto the carpet and my secret was out. My mother made the best of it and graciously set out cakes and orangeade on my packing cases the day of the visit. But I, alas, was obliged to renounce the luxury of having any domicile apart from my bedroom on the court in the Avenue Malakoff."

That can scarcely have been the whole story. Madame Cocteau may or may not have been shocked and angered by the discovery that part of her son's allowance was being spent on a *garçonnière* (a *garçonnière* is never without its implications); and the discovery may have been the immediate cause of the particularly "serious and painful" maternal scene and of the "imprisonment." But more than that had been going on — something involving "police, magistrate, and mayor": discovery of the *garçonnière* must have been the climax. One of Rilke's biographers says that all the tenants of the Hôtel Biron were eventually evicted following a series of "Roman" parties given by De Max, who had installed an exotic bathroom in the nuns' former chapel and its sacristy; but De Max seems to have lived in the mansion only after Cocteau's departure.

In most histories of the Hôtel Biron, Rodin is credited with the major role in the salvaging of the mansion and its garden (it is now the Musée Rodin), but Cocteau has made his claim: "Fate decreed that this poetic place be saved by a poet. One morning I heard the liquidator talking in the concierge's loge about a plan to divide the garden into building lots and extend the rue de Bourgogne to the Hôtel Rohan. I alerted the press. Journalists visited me and learned both of the existence of the treasure and its scheduled disappearance. Cabinet ministers came and were conquered. In short, I saved the gardens of the Hôtel Biron and I am proud of it."

Some years afterwards, Cocteau says, he was introduced to Rilke's poetry by Blaise Cendrars; but even later, in 1925, when Rilke was in Paris being lionized (*Les Cahiers de Malte Laurids Brigge*, written in the Hôtel Biron, had only then been published in French), he and Cocteau did not meet. In 1926 Rilke sent, from Switzerland where he was living, a telegram to his friend Madame Klossowska, in Paris. She had recently seen Cocteau's play *Orphée*, and had written Rilke of the pleasure it had given her and of an appointment she had with Cocteau. "Make Cocteau feel how warmly I admire him," Rilke telegraphed her. "He is the only one whom poetry admits to the realm of myth, and he returns from its radiance aglow, as from a seashore." Cocteau writes of Rilke as follows in one of his volumes of memoirs: "Rilke knew my play *Orphée*, produced in Berlin by Reinhardt, and . . . he sent Mme. K. this moving telegram: 'Tell Jean Cocteau that I love him . . . etc.' When Rilke died, he was beginning to undertake the translation of *Orphée*. You can imagine what good fortune that would have been for me, and how much I lost by his death." The substitution of "love" for "admire" in the telegram; the implication that Rilke knew Reinhardt's Berlin production of *Orphée*, which actually took place only in 1927, after Rilke's death; the fact that when Rilke died in December, 1926, he was translating Valéry, not Cocteau: they are minor details, perhaps, but eloquent, again, — especially given the unqualified admiration of Rilke's real message —

of some of Cocteau's emotional needs and stresses when writing "autobiography."

Now there enter the scene Maurice Rostand — for a time Cocteau's close friend but soon his model for much that he did not wish to be — and *Schéhérazade*.

Maurice, whose father Edmond Rostand was in the early 1900's at the height of his fame as the author of *Cyrano de Bergerac* and *L'Aiglon*, tells in his memoirs that his life pattern was set one afternoon when he was five. Sarah Bernhardt had acted in an early play by Edmond Rostand called *La Princesse Lointaine;* she had sometimes come to the Rostands' house, where Maurice had watched her arrive in her carriage, "a fairy coach drawn by two chestnut horses that suggested two prince charmings transformed into animals — a strange, delightful turn-out that caused passersby to stop and look, and from which she alighted with the airiness of a sprite, muffled to her nose in chinchilla, even in mid-July"; and in his parents' drawing room she would bestow an offhand, absentminded kiss on the little boy's hair — the hair which the father of one of his playmates, a gentleman who was "fond of hair," had likened to chrysanthemums. Then one day Maurice's parents "rashly" allowed him to be taken to call on Madame Sarah in her dressing room (where she fed him cream puffs and champagne), and then to attend her matinée of *La Dame aux Camélias:*

"It was a strange play indeed for a child to begin with. I watched the performance from the house box, which was almost on a level with the stage, and so close to it that I felt I was sitting in an extension of the stage itself. Suddenly, in the last act, when the dying Marguerite Gautier looks out the window and catches sight of something beyond, Sarah pretended suddenly to see *me*, and changing her lines she began to talk about '*le petit Maurice*' whom she had just recognized, there in the box. I don't know why I burst into tears. Was Sarah sending me the message that she had been acting, that day, just for me? . . . I left the performance feeling as though I had had a sunstroke. . . . I had entered the theatre a little boy dressed in black velvet, taken by his nurse to see his first play; I left it a child poet, who wanted to write plays for Sarah Bernhardt and wear his hair as she did."

Both those childhood wishes came true. Maurice Rostand did

write plays for Sarah Bernhardt. (How many actresses have appeared in plays by playwright father and playwright son? After starring for years in *L'Aiglon,* Sarah Bernhardt made some of her last appearances in Maurice's *La Gloire,* in 1922.) And he did wear his hair like Sarah's, in a "bleached tigress's mane," as he strangely calls it. (One day he saw Sarah pour champagne over hers, to prove that its frizz was natural.) Maurice kept his hair in its "chrysanthemum" state all his life by frizzing and bleaching; and eye shadow and face rouge did what they could to make him look even more like Sarah.

Maurice read *The Picture of Dorian Gray* at fifteen, and in and out of school he constantly wrote verse, "very much inspired by Beardsley." (He was never entirely to emerge from the shade of the Beardsleyan cypresses that he found so congenial in his teens.) He recited his verses at a very early age in the literary salon of his parents' friend the Baronne de Pierrebourg, at 1-bis Avenue du Bois, "standing in front of the fireplace where all the young poets of the day read their verses to the Baronne and her guests." Everyone found them and him charming, and Madame de Pierrebourg introduced him to Catulle Mendès, Anna de Noailles, and other literary lions. Perhaps it was chez Madame de Pierrebourg that Maurice made his celebrated reply to Paul Claudel, already a Catholic puritan man of letters, who was in Paris between diplomatic missions. Staring at the conspicuous Maurice, Claudel expressed, not in a whisper, the opinion that "such people should be ostracized." Maurice heard, and spoke up: "But Excellency! If they were, the salons would be empty!"

Toward the end of 1908 Maurice was at Cambo-les-Bains, near Biarritz, where his family had a country house, about to leave with them to spend the rest of the winter in the Hotel Meurice in Paris. "A few days before we left Cambo, two young writers, Jean Cocteau and François Bernouard, had written to me to ask for a poem to be printed in their magazine *Schéhérazade,* the first number of which was about to appear with a cover by Iribe. They came to see me at the Meurice."

Although Maurice Rostand and Cocteau had not previously met, they must have heard much of each other if only from De Max, who had acted in *L'Aiglon.* (De Max's dark beard grew so fast, Maurice says, that in the last act he always died with a blue chin.) Cocteau and Bernouard came to call on Maurice at the Meurice in January, 1909. "Already he possessed that fascinating, restless mind of his," says Maurice, "always active, always changing. We became friends at once. . . . Ah! I shall never forget those first conversations, full of our dreams and our strivings — those days when we thought ourselves Byron and Shelley because we wrote poetry and wore a gardenia in the buttonhole of our evening clothes." Cocteau wrote similarly of the friendship: "Maurice and I were 'the young' of those days. The true 'age of the young' had not yet opened — it was to be initiated only by Radiguet. We thought we were Byron and Shelley, considering ourselves fully justified in such a belief because we talked about Oxford and drove down the Champs-Elysées in an open carriage in the April sun."

The name "Schéhérazade" had already appeared once or twice among Cocteau's earlier poems, perhaps carrying with it a memory of the music of Rimsky-Korsakov, who had conducted it during Serge de Diaghilev's first musical season in Paris in 1907. (The famous ballet called *Schéhérazade,* to be danced by Ida Rubinstein, Nijinsky and Bulgakov, was still more than a year away.) Now, in 1909, working for the new magazine, Maurice Rostand finished, as a title poem, a very personal "Schéhérazade" of his own, part of which can be given simply in translation:

> Queen of the Orient where magic abounds,
> Bearing Bagdad in her sumptuous name,
> The sky is more beautiful in her eyes than over the world,
> And I have two heavens because her eyes are two.
> > She dazzles my entire life,
> > And in kissing my mother's hair
> > I laugh and kiss hers. . . .
> > Ah! How can one love her more
> > Than in that hair one loves the most?

That neatly combines Maurice's two fixations — hair, and his mother. Madame Rostand (Rosemonde Gérard) was a well-known poet herself. Maurice was seldom seen in public without her; the inseparable pair became one of the sights of Paris; and devotion to her bleached and painted son went hand in hand with Rosemonde's estrangement from her famous husband.

Schéhérazade is a beautiful little magazine. Printed on fine paper by François Bernouard, who was to become celebrated as a publisher of handsome books, with the artist Paul Iribe's lovely naked Sultana (a gallicized Beardsley vamp) reclining on each cover, the five issues (or six, depending on how one interprets a rather confused system of numbering: the magazine died what Maurice Rostand called "a beautiful death" with the number dated March 15, 1911) contain some of Dunoyer de Segonzac's sketches of Isadora Duncan, drawings by Bonnard, Marie Laurencin, André Mare and Luc-Albert Moreau, poems by Natalie Barney, Maurice and Edmond Rostand, as well as by Cocteau, and Cocteau's first printed story, an amusing Venetian trifle called "Comment mourut Monsieur de Trèves." (Monsieur de Trèves, fatally wounded fighting a duel to defend the honor of his three mistresses, enjoys seeing *them* fight, among themselves, as he fades away in a palace on the Grand Canal.) There are musical scores by Massenet and Reynaldo Hahn, articles on Van Dongen and on Paul Poiret. What has come to be known as the Poiret style — late Belle Epoque-Art Nouveau — permeates the magazine. Some of its numbers give its place of publication as "A la Belle Edition, 77 rue de Varenne" — the address of the Hôtel Biron.

Both Cocteau and Maurice Rostand later made fanciful claims for *Schéhérazade*. Cocteau called it "quite the first deluxe magazine ever devoted to poets." It was scarcely that, for *The Yellow Book*, which both he and Maurice knew, had lived from 1894 to 1897; and Maurice's memories are equally wide of the mark: "Anatole France gave us prose. . . . We had drawings by Picasso, poems by the Duc de Pimodan, verses by Guillaume Apollinaire and sonnets by Emilienne d'Alençon." The great Anatole France in *Schéhérazade?* The Duc de Pimodan, one of the few French poets who belonged to the Jockey Club? Emilienne d'Alençon, the poetess-courtesan? One searches for them in vain, even for Emilienne d'Alençon under her baptismal name, Emilienne André. Drawings by Picasso? During the lifetime of *Schéhérazade* Picasso and Braque were beginning to paint in the style that came to be called Cubism; there is no question of Cubism in *Schéhérazade*, nor is there any trace of Picasso in his earlier styles — he is not there. The magazine did print a single poem by Apollinaire, "Stances," one of his more Symbolist, least "modern" works (retitled "Signe" when it was included in his volume *Alcools* in 1913). Almost a decade was to elapse before Apollinaire would become known to a considerable body of readers as the spokesman of *"l'esprit nouveau,"* but already he had written many of the poems that were to make him so, and in 1909, the year *Schéhérazade* began, he published the famous "Chanson du mal aimé" in the *Mercure de France*. The surprise one experiences at finding Apollinaire's very modern name in *Schéhérazade* serves to identify the artistic world in which Cocteau was now beginning to move, his first artistic world. It was the one in which Braque, Vlaminck, Matisse and Derain had been dubbed "Les Fauves" — the "Wild Beasts"; in which the word "Cubist," as yet scarcely heard, would soon be uttered in a similar tone of outrage; the world of the Nabis, chief among them Vuillard, of Jacques-Emile Blanche, of Romaine Brooks. It was an artistic world that was still genteel.

It was in 1910, the year of his second book of poetry, *Le Prince Frivole*, that Cocteau, according to his later self-accusations, reached the highest point as "Prince du Ridicule." Maurice Rostand, his constant companion, whose own poems were now beginning to appear in *Figaro*, has written of this time: "That spring of 1910 we thought of ourselves as really the gods of the moment. Cocteau and I were setting out to make a conquest of life. A few scattered lines of poetry were enough to make the duchesses of those days cry 'Genius!' I loved that ridiculous life, that false excitement. Where had I read that Byron ruined himself through his tailor? I couldn't keep away from the haberdashers in the rue de la Paix, and Cocteau and I weren't ashamed to use for a rhyme the then magic name of Charvet."

Duchesses and their like have always been overready to cry "genius," and they still are, but it was more modish at the turn of the century than at present to insert the names of fashionable establishments into one's verse. In 1884 Comte Robert de Montesquiou, in London, was already praising Liberty's, the aesthetic silk shop in Regent Street:

Liberty, foulard bleu, vert, lilas, rose, écru

and in verses some of them so Parisian in their clever froth as to
mock a translator, Cocteau celebrated not only Charvet but other
smart shops in or near the Place Vendôme:

> Adorions nous assez l'orchidée ou la rose
> Sur la dame du Ritz ou de Rumpel-Mayer,
> Concurrence implacable au créateur d'hier
> Que Lespiaut* met au monde et que Guerlain* arrose. . . .

> Je ne fais pas de bile
> Je dors, je bridge et je bois
> Le matin, je vais au Bois
> Rouler en automobile . . .

And he wrote what might be put into English as:

> When I die of grief, do bring, please,
> Your huge chapeau to my last home.
> The graveyard's far from the Place Vendôme,
> But by auto it's easy — between two teas!
> Live flowers are ruinous chez Lachaume . . .†
> Do bring your huge hat to my last home.

There is a good deal of that sort of thing in *Le Prince Frivole*:

> To be young, and to loudly proclaim that you are,
> To laugh off reproofs you are offered
> For loving the adorable trickery of rhymes
> If your verse is young too and the game's to your taste. . . .

"Game" is the important word. Cocteau spoke later of "the days
when I first understood that art and poetry aren't a game, but a
descent into a mine, down toward the firedamp and danger. . . .
It was the shock of my life when I realized what poetry is — a
great solitude, a struggle against extraneous temptations and
charms."

One aspect of *Le Prince Frivole* is the rather dutiful-sounding

---

* Lespiaut sold artificial flowers, often sprayed with fashionable perfumes. In 1912,
when Jacques Guerlain baptized his new perfume "L'Heure bleue," had he read Cocteau's poem of the same name, dated 1906 in *La Lampe d'Aladin?* "*C'est l'heure bleue
où tout s'assoupit et s'endort . . . C'est l'heure où se font les aveux dans l'oreille . . .*"
† Still in the rue Royale.

insistence that beneath the frivolity there is anguish: the prince of the title has "a vague longing"; there is a motto "Dread nerve-sickness as you would the plague" and a satirical poem about a "calm young man"; a "neurasthenic little Lord" suffers from "an undefinable sickness." It all resembles the letters he was writing to young friends at the time: "I am so worried, what with my book and my wretched neurasthenia, that I haven't been able to come to see you." "Am still very sick. My agony is unbearable." "I am writing you from bed, with a fever of 104." Such lamentations were scarcely to cease for fifty years.

His ailments did not keep him from the salons. Maurice Rostand mentions some of the hostesses: ". . . Madame de Pierrebourg . . . the Duchesse de Rohan . . . the Marquis and Marquise d'Argenson . . . Madame Vacaresco . . . Madame Mühlefeld . . . the Duchesse de la Mothe-Houdancourt . . . the Comtesse de la Roche-Cantin . . . the Princesse de la Tour d'Auvergne. . . . how many others I forget! Charming times, now no more, when Le Bargy [the actor] could without fear of ridicule give a lecture on the art of carrying a cane in society, for you still entered a salon with your hat in one hand and your cane in the other, and there were all manners of doing it, from Robert de Montesquiou's way of brandishing his pommel-headed malacca that would have aroused the envy of Barbey d'Aurevilly, to the Duc de Montmorency's tucking his stick under his arm like a country umbrella. Faded, dead old days of Charvet vests and glacé kid gloves. . . ." Cocteau later charted as one high point of his youthful "imbecility" his appearance at the wedding of his friend Tiarko Richepin, son of the poet Jean Richepin: "I was *garçon d'honneur* with Maurice Rostand. I wore a frock coat, a top hat, a purple carnation (*sic*). I was the laughing stock of the haberdashers, and my mother, watching from a window in our apartment in the Avenue Malakoff, wept at the sight." In *La Lampe d'Aladin*, Tiarko Richepin's wife was, in her lifetime, the recipient of a rather extreme example of the kind of tribute a wife can always expect from some of her husband's homosexual friends, "devoted" to her though they may be: the poem dedicated to her is entitled "On the Death of a Beautiful Lady."

But others would find the apex of Cocteau's early "imbecility" (since he uses the word about himself) in his sycophancy before Comte Robert de Montesquiou, the poison-tongued, poison-penned, eunuchoid, essentially pathetic aristocrat dandy, poetaster, aesthete and party giver, some of whose aspects Proust was to put into his Baron de Charlus, endowing his invented character with more flesh and blood than the original. Following the death of his favorite and secretary, Gabriel de Yturri, Montesquiou had recently moved out of his palace in Neuilly, "Le Pavillon des Muses," into a pink palace in Le Vésinet, "Le Palais Rose," and in one of the several "Sonnets de l'Hôtel Biron" which close the volume *Le Prince Frivole* Cocteau associates himself with the aging strutter. Like the count, he too, he says, is leaving a place of happy memories. He indicates that he is abandoning the Hôtel Biron because of someone:

> Je quitte pour quelqu'un mon parc aux doux tapages,
> Votre amical exemple a fait agir mon coeur . . .
> C'est pourquoi j'ai voulu votre nom sur ces pages.*

Before printing his sonnet in *Le Prince Frivole*, Cocteau had inscribed it on a presentation copy of *La Lampe d'Aladin* that he sent to Montesquiou. There is no indication that the present was acknowledged. If, as seems to be the case, Cocteau was never invited to the count's famous fêtes in either of his palaces, it was not for lack of trying. He sent him an inscribed copy of *Le Prince Frivole* — "To Comte Robert de Montesquiou, whom I admire for the beauty of his style, for the virulence of his wit and for his unforgettable silhouette" — and, in 1912, a copy of his third volume, *La Danse de Sophocle*, which at present lies, uncut, among the count's papers in the Bibliothèque Nationale. He sent the count flattering, self-deprecating letters, couched in a preposterous style that apes the count's own; but the genuflections got him nowhere. The older dandy was jealous of his eager young understudy, and as an aristocrat (he was really only half an aristocrat, his mother being a stockbroker's daughter) he pretended to see in the twenty-year-old bourgeois a pretentious upstart who was, alas, being petted by many, including some listed in the Almanach de Gotha, who should have known better. Montesquiou's biographer, Philippe Jullian, relates the ludicrous sequel:

* "I am leaving, for someone's sake, my garden with its sweet sounds, / It was what you did out of friendship that moved me to do it . . . / That is why I wanted your name on these pages.

"Henceforth when Montesquiou met at the theatre, at Mme. Daudet's or at Romaine Brooks', a thin young man with sharp features, beautiful eyes and very expressive hands, he pretended always to confuse him with Anna Pavlova and affirmed 'I know her well' as soon as anyone wanted to introduce Jean Cocteau to him." And Monsieur Jullian continues: "It is, however, thanks to Cocteau that we have been able to hear some echo of Montesquiou himself: the absurdities and the exquisite quotations, the fabulous or grotesque anecdotes, the wild laughter behind a raised hand. Unfortunately Cocteau wished to please and spoke familiarly to anyone and everyone. His superficial kindness, pierced with flashes of malice, was never comparable to the insolence of Montesquiou."

Some of the lions whom Cocteau did meet in the Paris literary dens were rather jaded, and in his youth and grace and charm and good looks and facility they recognized the highly prized qualities that they themselves had once possessed, or thought they had; and soon he was on visiting terms with many of them and perhaps closer than that to some. Catulle Mendès, the aging chief of the Parnassian school of poets, shared with Cocteau his fading memories of Baudelaire, Nerval, Rimbaud and Verlaine; and of Mendès Cocteau remarked (according to André Germain), "He seemed so old and venerable that I had the impression that I was going to bed with ideas." (Was it Mendès, perhaps, by whom Cocteau had allowed himself to be caressed "like a young and winning child," as he put it in his letter-sonnet to "François"?) The venerable critic Jules Lemaître, who as a young man had had the benediction of Flaubert himself, called Cocteau his "Ariel" and invited him to inspect his library, full of rarities: Cocteau said that Lemaître's pink face, with its fluffy hair and silvery beard, resembled a "superb strawberry, delicately placed on cotton wool in January." He had met Lemaître through Lucien Daudet, the more effeminate and amusing, the less industrious and harmful, of the novelist Alphonse Daudet's two sons (the other was Léon Daudet of the *Action Française*): Lucien knew everyone, but his most serious occupation was acting as *cavalier servant* to the elderly ex-Empress Eugénie, whom he adored and whose letters he treasured and eventually published in a book whose title, everyone noticed, described his own situation exactly: *A l'Ombre de l'Impératrice Eugénie*. Through Daudet, Cocteau met the Empress once or twice, at her

villa on Cap Martin, and in Paris in the Hotel Continental, where
she looked out over the empty space once filled by her palace of the
Tuileries, burned in the Commune. It was through Lucien Daudet
that he would soon meet Marcel Proust.

About this time Cocteau moved with his mother out of the Avenue Malakoff, where they had gone from the rue Bruyère on the
death of Madame Cocteau's father, into an apartment at 10 rue
d'Anjou, just off the rue du Faubourg St. Honoré. The old-fashioned air of 10 rue d'Anjou inspired him to one of his remarks that
everybody likes: "Our elevator dates from before the age of eleva-
tors." Sacha Guitry lived next door, at number eight, and into an
apartment beneath Madame Cocteau's at number ten there moved,
in 1911, after the death of her husband, who had been gentleman-in-
waiting to the Comte de Chambord, the pretender to the French
throne, a lady who, especially through her daughter and granddaughter, was to count for a good deal in Cocteau's life. This was
the Comtesse Adhéaume de Chevigné, born Laure de Sade. Years
before, the young Marcel Proust had met her in a salon, had been
smitten by her beauty and distinction, observed her, followed her,
one day accosted her in the Avenue Gabriel and received for his
pains the proustian snub: "Fitz-James is expecting me! Fitz-James
is expecting me!"* Soon he had begun to write of her as "all that
was best" in the character whom he would call Oriane, Duchesse de
Guermantes. Cocteau knew nothing of that in 1911 — few people
did — but he knew other things about the countess. Not rich herself, she had, in 1902, married off her daughter, Marie-Thérèse, to
a wealthy banker's son named Maurice Bischoffsheim, and there
was gossip about the personal price she had paid the banker for the
match. Bischoffsheim had died two years later, leaving his widow
with a daughter, Marie-Laure; and in 1910, when Marie-Laure was
eight, the widow had taken as her second husband the popular,
witty playwright Francis de Croisset (born, in Belgium, Edgar-
Franz Wiener). The countess herself, Marie-Laure's grandmother,
was known for her hoarse, commanding voice (Proust's housekeeper Céleste said it sounded "like a train going through a tunnel"), for her sharp wit, and for the circle of distinguished men who

---

* The Fitz-James expecting her was Comte Robert de Fitz-James, younger brother
of the duke whose horses had frightened the boy Cocteau at Maisons-Laffitte.

gathered around her. Cocteau was determined to know her, and everyone has heard the story, first told by the Princess Bibesco, of his surprise attack on her one day when he met her on the stairs of 10 rue d'Anjou, leading her white Pomeranian, Kiss. As though impulsively, he prostrated himself and kissed Kiss. It was the countess who barked: "Careful — I don't want him covered with face powder!" But the ruse worked, and soon the bossy old lady was allowing Cocteau to address her as "Corporal Petrarch" and to entertain her with his badinage.

But Cocteau's most immediately important meeting at this time was with the reigning poetic spirit of the age that was post-Symbolist but not yet Apollinairian, post-Post-Impressionist but not yet Fauve or Cubist — the age of Vuillard and his fellow Nabis as the "moderns" among the painters: the Comtesse Anna de Noailles, herself painted by Vuillard, whose poems, as published in magazines and in the volumes *Le Coeur Innombrable* (1901), *L'Ombre des Jours* (1902) and especially *Les Eblouissements* (1907) won her universal acclaim. Proust, her great friend, said of her poem "Prière devant le Soleil" that it was "the most beautiful thing written since *Antigone*." Cocteau met her through the actress Simone,* apparently just after the publication of *Le Prince Frivole*, in 1910 or 1911.

She was thirteen years his senior, fascinating, dark-haired, oriental-looking (Harold Nicolson said she looked like "a hawk from some hieroglyphs in a temple at Luxor"), daughter of a Rumanian Prince de Brancovan and a Greek mother, but born and educated in Paris, and married to Comte Mathieu de Noailles, of an old French aristocratic line. *Le Coeur Innombrable* (The Multitudinous Heart) had won her a French Academy prize, and from then on she was queen of the literary salons. Tiny, intense, insis-

* Madame Simone (whose characterization of Madame Cocteau has already been quoted on page 22), one of the great ladies of the stage and of le Tout-Paris, was born Pauline Benda in 1877. She was a friend of Charles Péguy and was engaged to Alain Fournier, author of *Le Grand Meaulnes,* who was killed soon after the outbreak of war in 1914. Married to the actor Charles Le Bargy (whose lecture on the art of carrying a cane has already been mentioned), and to Claude Casimir-Périer, she is now Madame François Porché. A remarkable actress, able to play in both French and English, she was for a time with the Comédie Française, and has starred in a long series of plays by Edmond Rostand, Porto-Riche, Henri Bernstein and others. She has written novels and memoirs, is a member of the jury of the Prix Femina, and in 1960 was awarded the Grand Prix de Littérature de l'Académie Française.

The Poet of the Salons.

Jean Cocteau in 1912.
Portrait by Jacques-Emile Blanche.

Comtesse Anna de Noailles.
Portrait by
Paulet Thévenaz.

Cover of the
magazine *Schéhérazade*,
by Iribe.

tently voluble (Cocteau said that he had seen her "at table, holding her glass in her right hand and waving her left as a warning that no one should take over the 'conversation' while she drank"), for today's tastes often intolerably sublime, drunk on words like *azur, astre, langueur, éther, volupté,* she was nevertheless a strongly gifted poet, perhaps too content to be "enthusiastic" rather than devote herself to the concentrated "fabrication" that Paul Valéry said was "the more proper state of mind for a writer." She is said to have made the philosopher Bergson blush, when they first met, by advancing toward him in three stages, halting three times, each time with a greeting: *"Monsieur! . . . Maître! . . . Acropole de la pensée!"*

At her worst, in her poetry, she can sound like the sentiments printed on French lovers' postcards; but there are eloquent passages of passion and pantheism in all her books. She often wrote of death, anguished yet defiant in her inability to believe in a hereafter; her health was "delicate," and she would spend much of her day in her cretonne-covered bed, scrawling poetry, novels, memoirs and letters in her large hand, assuring friends that she was dying, reviving at dusk to make her appearance in a salon where everyone hung — perforce — on her words; at night, haunted by the thought of death, she would telephone her doctor at any hour, pour out her fears, resist his reassurances, and fall asleep toward dawn. After she and Cocteau met he became almost her *cavalier servant,* writing letters of breathless homage in a handwriting resembling her own, dining at a little table beside her bed (they called this *"un coup de guéridon"*), taking over her gestures of head and hands, her effusive speech, the *"Mon chéri"* that was her usual mode of address to friends and sometimes mere acquaintances. Her laments about fatigue and nerves and the insensitivity of the uncomprehending world, her constant cry "I'm dying!", fed his verbal neurasthenia. Her son has said of her and Cocteau that "each was the only one voluble enough to make the other keep quiet and listen." Robert Rey's picture of Cocteau in the Hôtel Biron shows him as already logorrheic even before meeting Madame de Noailles, but the brilliant, torrential monologues that were one of his lifelong trademarks always reminded the countess's friends of her own. If Maurice Rostand patterned his bleached tigress-mane coiffure on Sarah Bernhardt's, it is not too much to say that Cocteau patterned much of his high style and his breathless deportment on the countess's. People noticed this and laughed, calling him an *"Anna-mâle."*

"Madame," he would write her "(horrible word, since in you I see Ronsard, Montaigne, Pascal, Michelet, Racine, etc) . . . your face alone has all the *élan* of the Victory of Samothrace, and if poets were asked to model a face for her it would be yours." "I have been silent, Madame, because for nine nights exactly you have been filling my dreams. They were not at all incoherent — long walks in quite possible landscapes that were however a little vague, since you yourself absorbed all the precision and all the magnificence. . . ." "Simone has just been reading me your poems, from nine o'clock until one in the morning. I no longer had 'Mes vers,' the last poem in *Les Eblouissements*, word for word in my mind. It is, perhaps, along with 'Tu vis, je bois l'azur,' the most noble masterpiece of our modern tongue. How very proud I am to know you!" His poetry had reflected hers even before they met, and now it began to re-echo even more strongly her own echoes — French ears detect them all — echoes of Ronsard, Hugo, Verlaine and Rostand, sometimes more strongly the one, sometimes the other. *La Danse de Sophocle*, Cocteau's third volume of verse, published in 1912 (his first after meeting Madame de Noailles), contains a quotation from one of her poems, many a title reminiscent of hers — "Le Délire matinal," "Le Coeur éternel" — poems on insomnia, on death, on Greece, and one called "Le Dernier Chant du Prince Frivole": he is turning away from Maurice Rostand. Cocteau later deplored the "sublime" aspect of the countess's influence on his work. He reproached himself for his ignorance of the poetry in the modern mode, the *"esprit nouveau,"* that Apollinaire, Max Jacob and André Salmon were writing at the time, and he included *La Danse de Sophocle* among his three early *"niaiseries."* But if one compares the book with its predecessors one rejoices that such a closeness sprang up between Cocteau and Madame de Noailles. She was a noble soul; her personality and her writing led Cocteau deeper into poetry, encouraged him to greater seriousness. Later the character of his work greatly changed, but the affection and respect he always retained for her were his acknowledgment that, in her way, she had helped him grow.

The countess's influence bore a resemblance to his mother's

speaking out and "imprisoning" him, at the moment of "police, magistrate, and mayor"; for just when Madame Cocteau did that, the doors of the salons were opening for him, and Madame Cocteau made him see that certain compromises were necessary since he wanted to enter them. It was then, one might say, that he chose the way of life that he was always, with certain variations, to follow — and the choice seems to have been only momentarily difficult: independence of private behavior, but sufficient conformity with any society above the pettiest bourgeoisie to assure the privileges — and among the privileges was independence itself — that come from being accepted. Avoidance of personal scandal, of the outré or ridiculous. The Comtesse de Noailles accomplished something similar. He had been falling into "imbecility," and within the world of the salons — her world and his — she raised his tone. He soon grew impatient with the turn-of-the-century air that she always breathed, but she counted for something in his always retaining a hold on the great traditions of French poetry. If, later, he avoided the trashier aspects of Dada, for example, yet recognizing what there was in Dada of poetry, she is one of those to be thanked. She was sufficiently large-spirited, sufficiently dramatic, sufficient of a "sacred monster" to fascinate him and deflect him away from "police, magistrate, and mayor" sensationalism into an art that was a more absorbing game than the one he had been playing. Whether Cocteau's perpetual straddling, in both life and work, of two worlds — the libertarian and the conformist — was his great virtue, or, as many think, his great disaster, it was those two older women, Madame Cocteau and the countess, who number, among their other responsibilities, that for the right-hand side of the stance. It was the side that was to lead him eventually into the Académie Française.

La Danse de Sophocle had the "distinction" of being reviewed in the September, 1912 issue of the recently founded *Nouvelle Revue Française*, over the signature of Henri Ghéon. Ghéon was André Gide's companion at the time, and it has been guessed that Gide had a hand in the piece. Thus it is a review by one or two Jansenist literary homosexuals of the work of a fellow homosexual of a different brand — a circumstance that in the literary world rarely fails to color content. Outwardly respectful, feline, the review is the first mild sally in what was later to become Gide's full-fledged

campaign against Cocteau — a campaign designed to convince Cocteau, or at least to convince others, that he was overestimating his
own capacities.

As to whether or not young Cocteau has "genius," the review
says, "he may well believe it: everything has been done to make
him believe it." And it goes on: "M. Cocteau's previous book of
poetry, smart and light, was called *Le Prince Frivole*. That was his
excuse: the avowal, the display, of his frivolity. It was possible to
believe that he was judging himself at his true measure and making
fun of his admirers. But on this point the very title of the new book
. . . now casts a doubt. For anyone who fails to understand the
allusion, M. Cocteau quotes the following explanatory epigram
from Atheneus: 'In his early youth, Sophocles was chosen by Athens to dance at the games of Salamis.' That makes it quite clear:
just as the young Sophocles danced, so M. Jean Cocteau composes a
few rhythmic stanzas: the tragedies will come later. It is all very
well for M. Cocteau to have blind confidence in his secret potential
resources, and to aspire to something higher than a career of frivolity, but why does he proclaim this so loudly? And what does he
know of his still distant maturity? No more than did Sophocles,
who danced in all modesty. Will he write tragedies? No one would
rejoice more than I. But he must not be surprised if in the meantime we are embarrassed by the pose that he affects, and if we try to
consider his poems apart from his fame, past, present and future,
and taking into account his youth, which is extreme. [Cocteau was
then twenty-three.]

"M. Jean Cocteau seems to me extraordinarily gifted. But in
order to discern, among his gifts, which are his own and which are
borrowed, a very patient analysis would be required."

What the reviewer likes, he says, is "Jean Cocteau's Parisianism,
what remains in him of the *prince frivole*, of the prince who would
doubtless be less *frivole* if he were more modest, and whom one
wishes more modest nonetheless." As contrasted with Cocteau's
more "ambitious" pieces, "in *small* pieces M. Cocteau achieves a
graceful perfection that he does not surpass in the present volume;
and for the time being he must be judged on this basis. . . . M.
Cocteau is unquestionably gifted, but he must now devote himself
to his gift."

In other words, "You have a long way to go." For the moment, it was merely patronizing. Later, as Cocteau became more of a threat, there would be a tightening of the screw.

After *La Danse de Sophocle*, Cocteau published no further volume of poetry for seven years. But we have been getting a little ahead of his story. Even before that September, 1912 review by Ghéon or Ghéon-Gide, probably by the previous spring, someone else had expressed dissatisfaction with what Cocteau had been up to. This other complaint — it took the form of a command — was delivered in a strong Russian accent. For a year or two Cocteau had been frequenting, in addition to the people already mentioned, a fast-stepping and exotic company, among whom his personality was to achieve a brighter flowering.

3

A Kind of Fireworks

D URING the past hundred years or so, the history of the ballet in France has more than once been touched with paradox. It was given its greatest glorification by a French artist, Degas, but at a time when it was in its doldrums; and when next it flowered brilliantly, the splendor was due not to French dancers but to Russians — whose preceding generation in the dance, however, had been the creation of a choreographer who was French but living in St. Petersburg.

After half a century of delightful Romantic dancing, French ballet had fallen into a decline following the Franco-Prussian War, and many of the ballerinas who inspired Degas to his masterpieces were performing in mere interludes inserted into operas — spectacles which in the words of Alexandre Benois were "not *le dernier mot,* but rather *du dernier ridicule.*" Such, at least, was a Russian opinion. Benois, who along with Léon Bakst was to design stage sets for Diaghilev, was a St. Petersburg painter and balletomane who in the early years of the century preferred to live in Paris, the home of his Huguenot ancestors. In his memoirs he says that even in Russia ballet had lately been in a state of "dreamy lassitude," with most of its repertory the work of Marius Petipa, the great choreographer from Marseilles, long resident in Russia and now grown elderly and repetitious. Then in 1905 Isadora Duncan descended on St. Petersburg and with her ideals of freedom and fluidity gave the dancing world there what Boris Kochno calls "a shock it never recovered from." In Isadora's own words, "It was from that epoch that the Russian ballet began to annex the music of Chopin and Schumann and wear Greek costumes; some ballet dancers even going so far as to take off their shoes and stockings."

Among the St. Petersburgers who profited from the shock administered by Isadora were one of Petipa's youngest pupils named Michael Fokine and a balletomane named Serge de Diaghilev, a heavy, handsome young man of strong personality. Diaghilev came from a family of the provincial gentry and was endowed with acute artistic sensibility and immense energy and ambition. He had not found it easy to make his way in the world. He had longed for glory as a singer, but his baritone voice, although strong, was displeasing; his pride was greatly injured when he was told by Rimsky-Korsakov that he had no talent as a composer; and his difficult temperament quickly put an end to a budding administrative career with the Russian Imperial Theatres. What he became, after those setbacks, was an independent impresario. And on a grand scale. Later it was said of him that he had wanted to accomplish, and did accomplish, three things: reveal Russia to itself, reveal Russia to the world, and reveal the world, the new world, to itself.

The last part of that after-the-fact statement refers to Diaghilev's greatest career — his twenty seasons as impresario of the Russian Ballet, from 1909 to 1929; the earlier references are to his public beginnings: his exhibition of Russian historical portraits at St. Petersburg in 1905, which amazed the Russians, hitherto ignorant of their own riches in that domain; his exhibition of Russian art at the Salon d'Automne in Paris in 1906, which amazed the West, ignorant of artistic Russia; and to his seasons of Russian music in Paris in 1907 and 1908, when Glazunov, Rachmaninoff and Rimsky-Korsakov conducted their own works and revealed to Paris the music of Moussorgsky, Borodin and Scriabin. The high point was Chaliapin's sensational singing in *Boris Godunov* at the Opéra.

The shakiest side of Diaghilev's enterprises was, and was always to be, the financial. Subsidies from the Russian government were irregular, and one year Diaghilev earned a badly needed hundred thousand gold rubles by persuading a grand duke to get a patent of nobility for a galoshes manufacturer. In Paris he began by using more orthodox methods. He had himself introduced to the beautiful Comtesse Greffulhe, another of Proust's models for his Duchesse (and Princesse) de Guermantes.* In the world of the arts Comtesse Greffulhe was a Lady Bountiful and an indefatigable committee woman, active particularly in the French branch of the Comité International de Patronage Artistique that had been founded by the Parisian impresario Gabriel Astruc. Astruc had been bringing to Paris various foreign attractions and entire "seasons," such as

---

* The countess's husband once said of Cocteau and his youthful poems: "He's not a cock and he's crowing too early" — the French syllable *"teau"* being identical in sound with *tôt* — "early." The countess was a cousin of Comte Robert de Montesquiou.

Wanda Landowska and Artur Rubinstein from Poland, a troupe of American blacks who sang spirituals and taught Paris to cakewalk, an "Italian season" with Caruso, Lina Cavalieri, Bassi and Titta Ruffo, and the Metropolitan Opera Company with Caruso, Slezak, Yadlowker, Amato, Scotti, Destinn, Alda, Fremstad, Lucrezia Bori and Toscanini. So active and important was the countess in Astruc's enterprises, so constantly were he and she in correspondence, that his firm, the Société Musicale, was equipped with special memo stationery headed (with what is said to be an incorrect particle) *"Note pour Madame la Comtesse de Greffulhe."*

Through the countess, Diaghilev met Astruc. The impresario who had now enchanted the élite of Paris by his importations of Russian painting and music over three successive seasons was a person of the greatest interest to his experienced and astute French counterpart, and after one of the performances of *Boris Godunov,* when Astruc told him how beautiful he had found the production, especially the dancing in the Polish scene (designed by Benois), Diaghilev found it opportune to describe in seductive terms the "new" ballet in St. Petersburg, and especially the art of three superb dancers, Fokine, Nijinsky and Pavlova, all of them unknown in Paris. He could bring the Imperial Theatres dancers to Paris during the period of their summer vacation, he indicated, if properly induced. According to Astruc, who is sometimes thought to take too much credit to himself in the matter, the upshot was an immediate contract; and in any case the following spring every corner of Paris displayed a poster showing Pavlova on her points, painted by the Russian artist Serov, and announcing THEATRE DU CHATELET / SAISON RUSSE / MAI JUIN.

Opening night was May 19, 1909, a date that has remained famous in ballet annals. The ballets danced were *Le Pavillon d'Armide* (score by N. Tcherepnin, libretto and décor by Benois, danced by Nijinsky, Fokine and Coralli, Pavlova having been delayed en route to Paris); the Polovtsian dances from Borodin's opera *Prince Igor,* with décor by Nicholas Roerich; and *Le Festin,* a suite of dances to the music of several Russian composers, with costumes by Benois, Bakst and others. All these were spectacles that had been prepared especially for Paris. They were more stunning than anything that had been seen in Russia itself, and they caused a sensation.

Experience had taught both Astruc and Diaghilev that, were such enterprises as theirs to succeed with a large public, it was essential first to capture the patronage of the arrogant world of artistic fashion — "*Mes chers snobs*," Astruc called them, "without whom no new artistic venture could ever prosper"; and the first-night program of the ballet had been presented the night before at a gala dress rehearsal or "*répétition générale*," attended by friends of the management and of the principal performers and by society folk, journalists, writers, musicians and painters, "le Tout-Paris." Rodin, Ravel and Montesquiou were among the representatives of the various worlds. Diaghilev had insisted on a complete renovation of the Théâtre du Châtelet, a ramshackle house usually given over to scenic spectaculars like the *Around the World in Eighty Days* that had shaken Cocteau as a boy; and for the preview Astruc had prepared a particular surprise:

"It was always my principle to devote as much thought to my preview audiences as though they were themselves part of the production. In May 1909, the night the Russian Ballet was first revealed to the public, I offered the prettiest actresses in Paris front row seats in the balcony. Fifty-two were asked, fifty-two accepted. In the seating, I was careful to alternate blondes and brunettes; they all arrived on time, they were all very pleased; and the sight of this row of smiling beauties caused the rest of the house to burst into applause. That most serious of newspapers, *Le Temps*, devoted a front-page article to this innovation, referring to it as my *corbeille* — my 'flower basket.' Since then the first balconies of all new French theatres have been called not balconies, but *corbeilles*."

That gala revelation of the Russian Ballet to the artistic snobs of Paris terminates what might be called the regular-audience life of Jean Cocteau — terminates it in that he was not invited to that preview, and in that it was, speaking generally, the last Paris gala for fifty years to which he was not bidden. It was the last such occasion on which the publicity value of Jean Cocteau was not recognized.

"The first time I attended one of Diaghilev's productions — they were dancing *Le Pavillon d'Armide* — I went with my family. Everything took place far away, behind the footlights, in the midst of that great burning bush that the theatre is for people who are not of its world. Then I met Serge de Diaghilev at Madame Sert's. And from then on I was a member of the troupe."

Nijinsky, Armide's slave that night when Cocteau attended the ballet *en famille,* sprang from the wings in Benois' costume of white, silver and yellow; later in the evening he danced his Caucasian dance in *Festin;* perhaps (depending on the program) he and Pavlova leapt and floated through *Les Sylphides,* or Ida Rubinstein, in *Cleopatra,* emerging from her coffin, was unwound from yards of bandages before Mark Antony and stood there, as Cocteau wrote later, "like an ibis of the Nile." And when the performance was over Cocteau left the seat he had occupied beside his family as a mere member of the theatre-going public and never returned to it. "From then on I never saw Nijinsky except from the wings or from the box where Madame Sert sat wearing her Persian aigrette and Diaghilev stood behind her, watching his dancers through a tiny mother-of-pearl opera glass." The young man — he was now twenty — who had always suffered from the "red-and-gold disease" was transported by the Russian Ballet from one side of the curtain to the other.

Misia Sert, called by Cocteau "the queen of the Russian Ballet," was a fascinating, ruthless, quarrelsome lover of artists and the arts — "very Slav," according to Valentine Gross Hugo, one of the many artists who painted her portrait, "a fairy godmother one moment and a witch the next, frightfully malicious, adorably generous, out to destroy everything in the arts that hadn't been hatched or at least nurtured within her own four walls." She had been born Misia Godebska, in Belgium, of partly Polish ancestry, and studied the piano under Fauré. At fifteen she married, in Paris, Thadée Natanson, one of the three Natanson brothers who founded the *Revue Blanche.* Here she was at the heart of a circle that included Ravel, Debussy, Jules Renard, Mallarmé, Tristan Bernard, Renoir, Toulouse-Lautrec, Vuillard, Bonnard and the other Nabi painters; but she divorced Natanson to become the fifth wife of the rich and adipose Alfred Edwards, owner of *Le Matin,* the most widely circulated newspaper in Europe. (The story of Edwards' pursuit of Misia, encouraged both by Misia's husband and by Edwards' fourth wife, and of Edwards' subsequent infatuation for the actress Lanthelme, who in turn wooed Misia, is told in Misia's autobiography.) Proust, who found Misia and her entourage distasteful, endowed one or two of his less appealing women characters with certain of her attributes. When the Russian Ballet came to Paris, Misia was already separated from Edwards and living with the Spanish painter José-Maria Sert, whom she was later to marry, and examples of whose titanic style of mural painting can be seen in New York in the Waldorf-Astoria Hotel and in Radio City. She is most commonly known as Misia Sert. *Boris Godunov,* as produced by Diaghilev, was a revelation to her, she has written. Then one evening at Prunier's restaurant she met Diaghilev himself, and they remained friends until his death.

During the years that followed their meeting, the years of the Paris Russian Ballet seasons (after 1910 the company was no longer that of the Russian Imperial Theatres, but Diaghilev's own, including many of the same dancers, however, whom he had "stolen"), Misia Sert was recognized by all as a power behind Diaghilev's throne, the closest woman friend of that great woman-hater.* They telephoned each other every day, discussing details of the ballets, concocting and countering intrigues, deciding who among Astruc's *"chers snobs"* should be awarded the coveted *"carte de circulation"* that permitted attendance at every performance, deciding whom to flatter and whom to cut. It might be said that it was the Princesse Edmond de Polignac, the formidable rich American with the Dantesque profile, born Winaretta Singer, daughter of the inventor of the sewing machine, who became the greatest patroness of Diaghilev and the ballet; beneath her hatchet-like exterior and her nasal voice she had a considerable musical culture; her drawing room was the scene of frequent concerts both classical and avant-garde; she was financially generous; and a number of Diaghilev's ballets, as well as many other musical compositions, were dedicated to her. But it was Misia Sert who was Diaghilev's intimate. Serge Lifar describes their "twenty-year stormy friendship" as being shrill with recriminations and disputes, rich in accusations by Misia that Diaghilev cultivated her only to "use" her, and by Diaghilev that she was "indifferent" to him; but also rich in Slavic declarations of affection — "You are my sister, the

* Diaghilev's misogyny was notorious. The late Sir Osbert Sitwell has told of his brother Sacheverell's having several times to leave evening rehearsals of his ballet *The Triumph of Neptune,* in London, explaining to Diaghilev that he had to return to Aldershot. Diaghilev finally asked testily, *"Qu'est-ce que c'est que cette Aldershot? C'est une femme?"*

only woman I love" — and filled especially with the endless telephone conversations about the ballet company and its problems, many of them financial.

Diaghilev and Cocteau were both frequently at Misia's flat on the Quai Voltaire (she seems mysteriously to have moved back and forth between it and an apartment in the Hotel Meurice), with its screens and panels by Bonnard and Vuillard, "its crystal, its lacquer, its general air of exquisite rococo," as Paul Morand describes it. There Cocteau was seen for the first time by Jacques Porel, son of the actress Réjane, the sight of whose mule-drawn carriage, glimpsed from his bedroom window as it waited at her stage door, had aggravated Cocteau's red-and-gold disease as a boy. Porel tells of Cocteau's amusing everybody at Misia's with impersonations of Edmond Rostand and Madame de Noailles; "Jean was frail and sharp-featured," he says, "not what you would call a handsome man; but it would have been hard to improve on his youthful good looks. Along with his charm he had a great wish to charm, and he was the most entertaining talker conceivable. His conversation was like fireworks. He had a rare distinction, and his manners were delightful. In a word, he was irresistible."

Misia herself says, "Heaven knows that Jean was irresistible when he was twenty." "He walked," says Princesse Marthe Bibesco, "with the pride of a wild bird that had dropped by chance into a poultry yard." And there is the impression of Edith Wharton, already quoted: "I have known no other young man who so recalled Wordsworth's 'Bliss was it in that dawn to be alive.'" Then and always, until the end of his life, people spoke of Cocteau's personal charm and the brilliance of his conversation; and there were, and still are, some — usually either insensitive to the arts or desiring for one reason or another to belittle Cocteau's artistic gifts — who say "his life was his masterpiece" or "his talk was the best part of him." In this he has often been likened to Oscar Wilde; and despite their differences of personality they do resemble each other in that they share a dazzling conversational gift, which is the most difficult of accomplishments to recapture. More than mere eloquence, it is, at its best, one of the performing arts, a harmony of intellect, fancy, control and timing — evanescent, however, and not always to be re-evoked by the simple recording of words. Beyond Cocteau's conversation and charm, people sensed something phenomenal, something of particular promise, in his originality and the diversity of his talents.

Launched into the ballet world by Misia, Cocteau soon had his *carte de circulation,* and Diaghilev was calling him "Jeanchik." All the principal aspects of the ballet appealed to him, including the snob side, so well exploited by Diaghilev, Astruc and Madame Greffulhe, and the brilliance of the spectacles themselves. "The ballet splashed all Paris with colors," Cocteau wrote; he saw its full spectrum and bold designs influence dressmakers and decorators and transform the smart shop windows. Even the great "modern" couturier of the day, Paul Poiret, jealous of the rage for Bakst and his costumes, grudgingly admits in his memoirs that the ballet may have had "a certain influence" on him. For Cocteau it must have been as though his magazine *Schéhérazade* were suddenly come to life in color, as though Iribe's Beardsleyan sultana on the cover were herself one of the dancers: both Diaghilev and Bakst were Beardsley fans, and the spirit of Beardsley is one of the perfumes pervading the early Paris ballets. As to the dancers themselves, especially the male dancers . . . Ballet as a great attraction for homosexuals was something new. Paris had been accustomed to the men in its ballets playing minor roles, acting chiefly as assistants to the women, being lifters rather than dancers; now, with Diaghilev, things were different, and chief among his male mimes and leapers was the nineteen-year-old Nijinsky.

Throughout his life Cocteau never ceased writing about Nijinsky: "I have often spoken . . . of the contrast between the Nijinsky of *Le Spectre de la Rose,* bowing and smiling to thunderous cheers as he took his fifty curtain calls, and the poor athlete backstage between bows, gasping and leaning against any support he could find, half fainting, clutching his side, being given his shower and massage and rubdown by his attendant and the rest of us. On one side of the curtain he was a marvel of grace; on the other, an extraordinary example of strength and weakness. . . ."

Cocteau drew that picture of a great dancer's hidden aspects in 1945, as an illustration of a theme that had become his favorite — the invisibility of poets. Actually, Nijinsky personified a more radical contrast than Cocteau chose to mention. Offstage he was all too often an oaf, an overmuscled mujik; onstage he was a godlike dancer and mime, transformed with each change of costume and role, and seeming to achieve feats of suspension in mid-air. Stravinsky has said, "Nijinsky was a weak man, as weak as his muscles were strong." Misia Sert called him "an idiot of genius"; others, a Trilby to Diaghilev's Svengali. Up until the day when, separated for once from the impresario by thousands of miles of ocean, he allowed himself (displaying a greater degree of offstage passivity even than usual) to be married, he was Diaghilev's personal property, kept as much as possible out of contact with others unless Diaghilev too was present. "Of course Nijinsky made love only to the nymph's scarf," Stravinsky has said of the famous climax of *The Afternoon of a Faun* — "what more would Diaghilev have allowed?"

Diaghilev, celebrated and powerful, but portly and thirty-seven,* was well aware that Jeanchik was not alone in longing to fondle his fascinating young private leopard; but Jeanchik's reputation for being irresistible made him more dangerous than most, and although he was allowed to mingle with the dancers — his publicity value was well recognized — the impresario saw to it that his pretexts for hovering near Nijinsky, his opportunities for participating in the showers, massages and rubdowns, were kept to a minimum. Cocteau took care to let Diaghilev know that he was at his service, and stood ready to supplement Nijinsky in the role in which he was competent. Not all his signals were subtle — they included rouge and lipstick — and anything can be imagined as taking place in the tumble-sheet offstage atmosphere of the ballet. But when Cocteau made overt declaration of his feelings for Nijinsky, he was clever enough to give it a form that Diaghilev could only welcome as publicity. He wrote and published a poem to Nijinsky six lines long, each line illustrated with a drawing by Iribe. The handsome, very thin volume, *Vaslav Nijinsky, Six Vers de Jean Cocteau, Six Dessins de Paul Iribe* (1910), is one of Cocteau's earliest and rarest works. Three of Iribe's Beardsleyan woodcuts show Nijinsky in his role as the sultana's black slave in *Schéhérazade*, his massive columnar neck rising above the jeweled and embroidered brassiere designed by Bakst, bangles on arms and ankles, fingers heavily be-ringed, the androgynous figure posing and leap-

---

* Diaghilev was sometimes called "Chinchilla," from a streak of white in his dark hair — a streak that he was to retain all his life, even when he had to dye the rest of his hair to keep the streak a streak.

ing against Bakst's peacock-like décor. Cocteau's six-line love-letter
portrays Nijinsky as a divine puppet:

> Apollon tient le fil au bout duquel il pend.
> Nègre de la Sultane, il vole en s'échappant,
> Et le décor a l'air de la traîne d'un paon.
>
> Il lance, Hermès rempli de mystérieux zèles,
> Des fleurs qu'on ne voit pas pour courir après elles
> Et charge tous les coeurs sur d'invisibles ailes! *

That was discreet enough, with its message from "all hearts" rather
than from the poet's own; nevertheless, Diaghilev never abandoned
his uneasy watch on the poet.

It was with the Russian Ballet that Cocteau began his considerable career as painter and draughtsman, a career that was one of
his most engaging aspects until, in his last decade, it became pretentious. He was given his first professional encouragement by
Léon Bakst, who was one of the earliest admirers of Cocteau's talents in this sphere and who was chiefly responsible, along with
Misia, for the extent to which Cocteau was gradually allowed to
participate in the affairs of the company. Bakst became, in a way,
Cocteau's protector. He was no pederast, but Stravinsky remembers
him defending Cocteau at a moment when Cocteau was being nee-
dled in some way during one of the pederastic intrigues so frequent
in the Diaghilev court. Bakst drew one of the earliest portraits of
Cocteau. And when publicity posters were needed for the 1911 season he recommended Cocteau to Astruc. Cocteau painted not only
a pink and mauve poster of Nijinsky, clad in the rose-covered tunic
he would wear in *Le Spectre de la Rose,* but also a poster of Karsavina, who danced the role of the young girl visited and kissed in her
dreams by Nijinsky in that ballet. One wonders whether Diaghilev
noticed that the artist gave Karsavina, in the poster, a profile remarkably like the artist's own.

For the same season, Astruc commissioned Cocteau to write a
publicity text, announcing the glories of the forthcoming ballets

---

* Apollo holds the string he dangles from. / The Sultana's blackamoor, he flies as he
breaks his bonds, / And the décor suggests a peacock's tail. / A Hermes, eager to perform his mysterious errands, / He tosses flowers we do not see, only to pursue them, /
and carries off all hearts on his invisible wings.

and their stars. It was printed as an article in the magazine *Comoedia Illustré*:

> . . . . And now — Vaslav Nijinsky. In him is reincarnated the mysterious child Septentrion, who died dancing on the shore at Antibes. Young, erect, supple, he walks only on the ball of the foot, taking rapid, firm little steps, compact as a clenched fist, his neck long and massive as a Donatello, his slender torso contrasting with his overdeveloped thighs, he is like some young Florentine, vigorous beyond anything human, and feline to a disquieting degree. He upsets all the laws of equilibrium, and seems constantly to be a figure painted on the ceiling; he reclines nonchalantly in midair, defies heaven in a thousand different ways, and his dancing is like some lovely poem written all in capitals.*

Bakst was the designer of *Schéhérazade*, the most sumptuously oriental of all the ballets, about which more than one aesthete has written in rapturous memory — Harold Acton, for example: ". . . the heavy calm before the storm in the harem: the thunder and lightning of negroes in rose and amber; the fierce orgy of clamorous caresses; the final panic and bloody retributions: death in long-drawn spasms to piercing violins. Rimsky-Korsakoff painted the tragedy; Bakst hung it with emerald curtains and silver lamps and carpeted it with rugs from Bokhara and silken cushions; Nijinsky and Karsavina made it live. For many a young artist *Schéhérazade* was an inspiration equivalent to Gothic architecture for the Romantics or Quattrocento frescoes for the Pre-Raphaelites." The popularity of *Schéhérazade* induced Diaghilev to try another oriental ballet. Cocteau was commissioned to write the libretto — Fokine, who was to be the choreographer, apparently expressed a preference for a Siamese background, having once seen Siamese dancers in St. Petersburg — and Reynaldo Hahn the score. "Diaghilev needed Hahn," Stravinsky has said. ". . . He was the

---

* Cocteau's bill for this several-page article has been preserved: "Dear Astruc, Horrible to talk about money! Can the Société Musicale give me the 100 f. that a newspaper would give me for the article? I have to earn my bread, alas, and 100 f. means only 2000 breakfast rolls — not a great deal for someone with a good stomach! Let me have a telephonic yes or no (before ten-thirty) and I'll come running with the piece."

salon idol of Paris, and salon support was very useful to Diaghilev at that time."

Cocteau's libretto for *Le Dieu Bleu* concerns a pair of vaguely Siamese or Indian lovers crossed by wicked priests and rescued by a Lotus Goddess and by the Blue God who gives the ballet its name. It was well suited to the luxurious décor that Bakst proceeded to design, complete with temple, jungle, snakes, golden stairs and a wardrobe of dazzling eastern costumes, studded with pearls and jewels. Hahn took his piano score to be auditioned in St. Petersburg, where Diaghilev and the company were spending the winter, and Diaghilev sent to Astruc in Paris, in the name of advance publicity, one of the countless telegrams with which it was his habit to bombard him: "YESTERDAY GREAT BANQUET GIVEN BY DIAGHILEV IN HONOR HAHN PRESENT COMPOSERS GLAZUNOV CONSERVATORY DIRECTOR LIADOV TCHEREPNINE DAVIDOV PAINTERS SEROV BAKST GOLOVINE ROERICH DANCERS KARSAVINA NIJINSKY BOTH FOKINES SCHOLLAR BOLM BARONS BENKENDORFF AND DMITRY GUNZBOURG OTHER PROMINENT ARTISTIC AND SOCIETY FIGURES AND IMPORTANT JOURNALISTS AUDITION TWO PIANOS DIEU BLEU BY COMPOSER AND BARON MEDEM PROFESSOR CONSERVATORY UNANIMOUS APPLAUSE EVENING ENDED SONGS KAHN AND PIANO GLAZUNOV PLEASE CIRCULATE." Despite that telegraphic mention of "unanimous applause," Benois reports that although Hahn's singing and playing at the St. Petersburg auditions were delightful, the Russians were disappointed in his "pleasant, drawing-room music, characteristic of the post-Massenet generation of composers"; and Prince Lieven describes the score as "India seen through the eyes of Massenet, sweet and insipid."

During rehearsals in Paris, Cocteau was in an ecstasy of intimate association with the company, breaking appointments with non-ballet friends because he was "exhausted," or "frantic," or "covered with ceruse and blue" from the dancers' makeup. Hahn, too, was in high spirits, evident in a note that he sent to Astruc shortly before the Paris premiere on May 13, 1912, from the West Cliff Hotel, Folkestone, where he was apparently enjoying some kind of *bonne fortune:* "Don't write me here, as I'll be leaving almost at once, and besides, I'm here under the name William Shakespeare." But despite all that, and despite Bakst's brilliant set of orange rocks against a peacock sky, and the dancing of Nijinsky and Karsavina, *Le Dieu Bleu* was not a success. Perhaps Nijinsky's blue makeup seemed absurd and the whole thing a bit overdone. The public showed no liking for it, and it was soon dropped from the repertory. Cocteau himself later described the ballet as "not very good." It is the high-water mark of his uncritical acceptance of the early aesthetic of the Russian Ballet — an aesthetic of exoticism and luxury which Diaghilev, with his flair for changes of taste, was soon to abandon.*

In the history of the Diaghilev company, the chief importance of *Le Dieu Bleu* was the part it played in touching off the famous *"scandale"* of *The Afternoon of a Faun*, which had its premiere two weeks later. *Le Dieu Bleu* had given the season a dull start, and Diaghilev was determined that Fokine's *"tableau chorégraphique,"* to Debussy's music inspired by Mallarmé's sonnet, would remedy matters. The spotted, skin-tight leotard that Bakst had designed for Nijinsky to make him look *"plus nu que nu,"* the swaying bunch of grapes attached over his genitals, and especially his copulatory movements, on opening night, as he lowered himself over the nymph's scarf, brought down the house and the wrath of virtuous editors. Gaston Calmette, of *Le Figaro*, delighted Paris with the elegantly suggestive wording of his censure: what he deplored, he said, was "the too obvious pantomime of a body deliberately contrived to be bestial — hideous when seen from the front, and still

* *Le Dieu Bleu* seems to have been originally planned to be given in London in 1911, as part of the celebrations surrounding the coronation of King George V and Queen Mary. Lydia Sokolova, who danced in the ballet, conveys some of its opulence in her memoirs: "In *Le Dieu Bleu* there were two dances that struck me particularly. One was performed by our three tall beauties, each carrying a stuffed peacock — tails falling over their shoulders or floating in the air — the peacocks had a special container to be carried in when we traveled. . . . The other was the dance of the dervishes. Their costumes were made entirely of white ropes, about a thumb's thickness. Besides the ropes which formed the skirts, there were more attached to their caps, which hung down to about knee-length. The ropes were dead white, and the men's bodies were dark grayish brown. As the dancers spun faster and faster at the end of their dance, they presented an extraordinary picture of whizzing white discs. It is amazing to think that Cocteau was responsible for this scenario as far back as 1911."

When a quantity of Bakst's splendid costumes for *Le Dieu Bleu* were removed in 1967, along with other costumes and scenery of the Diaghilev ballets, from dusty storage in a warehouse in the Parisian suburb of Montrouge, for sale at auction in London, Richard Buckle was inspired to write, with some of the élan of the old days: "How many triumphant evenings, what miracles of artistry, what gasps of admiration, what beating hearts and clapping hands, what Arabian nights do these scenes and dresses represent, which are now to be sold to the highest bidder! And what a happy conclusion it would be if whole groups of costumes could find their way to museums, where, displayed on models, flattered by theatrical lighting, standing before their appropriate scenery, they could bear witness for a few more centuries to the genius of Diaghilev and incite further ceaseless revolutions in the world of art!"

more hideous in profile." Various more or less sincere apologies were offered by Astruc and his resourceful aides for this "offense against good taste" (including the straight-faced explanation that the grape genitals were of glass, and had broken at the crucial moment, causing Nijinsky to "writhe in agony"), but it was generally assumed that Diaghilev had known what he was about. The *"scandale"* of the first night of the *Faun* saved the season. Stravinsky, Rodin and others who were present thought the so-called "offense against good taste" one of the most beautiful moments in ballet. Cocteau analyzed Nijinsky's concept of the role of the Faun in his "Notes on the Ballets," the text for a luxurious volume of colorplates, *L'Art Décoratif de Léon Bakst*, by Arsène Alexandre, published in 1912: "Keep in mind that this is neither audacity nor archaeology nor any of the things that attackers or enthusiasts have been pleased to discover. It is a purely plastic attempt by a young barbarian of genius, stirred by his recent visits to museums, and eager to be of his own time and to reduce dance to the schematic expression of a state of mind."

By the time those lines were published, Nijinsky had been permitted by Diaghilev to sail to South America without him, for Diaghilev, superstitious, had been told that he would die "on the water." (He was to die in Venice.) And in South America Nijinsky had been captured as a husband by a minor Hungarian ballerina. Stravinsky, who was with Diaghilev in Switzerland just after the news came, watched the impresario "turn into a madman who begged me and my wife not to leave him alone." In none of the many passages that Cocteau wrote about Nijinsky throughout his life is there any reference to his marriage, or to his subsequent career, or to his years of madness, or to his death. Cocteau's silence is in its way the equivalent of Diaghilev's hysterics. The only Nijinsky for both of them was the Nijinsky of the troupe.

Cocteau once said of the Diaghilev company that "For me they were a family — not at all the miraculous beings one saw dancing." Disciplined though the Russians were in their roles, informality reigned elsewhere. "Cocteau tells us," Paul Morand records in his diary, "that one day he went to the Chabannais [a Paris brothel] with Astruc, Bakst, Diaghilev and Nijinsky. Bakst thought the women were superb. The women fought over Nijinsky, screaming 'I want the one that's never done it!' They were shown a room with blue lighting. 'I can't see a thing,' said Astruc. 'But it's the Moonlight Room, M. Astruc,' replied the manageress. 'Oh, I see,' said Astruc, always ready to accept the latest bit of daring from the avant-garde."

Cocteau delighted in the dancers' professional asides to each other: "*Le gratte-foutre m'a donné mal au ventre,*" he overheard one day. Nijinsky was always the greatest attraction. Cocteau watched him perfect his technique: "He came to realize that half the leap that ends *Le Spectre de la Rose* was wasted, being unseen by the audience. He invented the 'double leap,' which required him to twist himself in the air when out of sight, then crash straight down. They caught him like a boxer; he was wrapped in hot towels, slapped, and his valet Dmitri spat water in his face." Before the premiere of *The Afternoon of a Faun,* "he puzzled us several nights when we were having supper at Larue by moving his head as though he had a stiff neck. Diaghilev and Bakst were worried, asked him what was wrong, and could get no answer. We learned later that he was training himself to perform when wearing horns. It was this perpetual preoccupation with his work — I could give a thousand examples — that made him glum and moody."

The intense, deliberately orientalized artistic personality invented for herself by another of the Diaghilev dancers, Ida Rubinstein, inspired a phrase of Cocteau's that has been applied to the Russian Ballet as a whole: "Too beautiful, overpowering, like an oriental perfume." "To see Madame Rubinstein stand on the stage before the curtain goes up and be wrapped in yards of mummy bandage for her role in *Cleopatra* is an incomparable sight," he wrote. "A respectful, silent circle of stagehands and extras forms around her, diminishing as she disappears beneath her veils. One night I had the honor of helping Madame Rubinstein onstage for her bandaging — she is unable to walk alone because of the height of her clogs — and as I felt the tremulous pressure of her palm on my shoulder I thought of the Cleopatra of Flaubert. . . ."

Backstage and at after-theatre suppers at Larue (where Misia tells of his sometimes dancing on the tables), Cocteau drew caricatures of the company. A portly, bespectacled Bakst, with an exaggeration of his large nose (Stravinsky describes Bakst's nose as resembling that of a Venetian-comedy mask), dancing in *Le Spectre de la Rose,* "substituting for Nijinsky, who was in bad humor"; a bonneted, double-chinned Diaghilev as the young girl in the same ballet; Nijinsky being revived in the wings; Stravinsky at the piano: these early drawings by Cocteau are excellent linear wit.

The internal dramas of his new, exotic family were much to Cocteau's taste. Nijinsky's little exhibitions of his power over his impresario-lover, for instance; "I can still see Nijinsky ready to go on in his role of the black slave in *Schéhérazade*, saying to Diaghilev, 'I won't go on unless you promise to go to the hockshop tomorrow and get my Kodak.' Diaghilev flared back, 'Certainly not.' But he knew that Nijinsky meant what he said, that he really would not go on; and Diaghilev gave in." Stravinsky gives other details of the family mores: "It is almost impossible to describe the perversity of Diaghilev's entourage — a kind of homosexual Swiss Guard — and the incidents and stories concerning it. I remember a rehearsal for the revival of *Renard*, in Monaco . . . at which our pianist, a handsome *fificus* of Diaghilev's — suddenly began looking very intently beyond the music rack. I followed his gaze to a Monegasque soldier in a tricorne, and then asked what the matter was. He answered, 'I long to surrender myself to him.' Another of Diaghilev's protégés was discovered nude by the police beneath a bridge near Nice, and when one of the policemen said '*Ou vous êtes un vicieux ou vous êtes un fou,*' he is supposed to have replied, '*Je suis sûrement vicieux.*' And so on."

"For me they were a family. . . ." Diaghilev's troupe of sacred monsters was the most satisfactory substitute Cocteau had yet found for the cultured, artistic-minded bourgeois among whom he had grown up — richer than the fauna of the Marseilles casbah, more interesting than De Max, more authentic and exotic than Maurice Rostand and the salons. Diaghilev, the father of the troupe, was a formidable despot, whimsical, sarcastic, vindictive, practicing outrageous favoritisms and endowed with extraordinary artistic flair. Young Cocteau's charm and talents, and a toughness and resilience of which people were becoming aware, enabled him to hold his own with this ruthless autocrat: once having insinuated himself into the company, he managed to keep himself tolerated by the dictator who was also the lover of his fascinating male star.

Diaghilev had always welcomed and sought novelty. He had appreciated the revived ballet in Russia, and had revised it for exportation to the West; he welcomed the strangeness of *The Firebird* and *Petrushka,* and he had refreshed the repertoire with new ballets that were non-Russian — *Le Spectre de la Rose, The Afternoon of a Faun.* Now he was moving further afield, commissioning a ballet about the Old Testament Joseph with score by Richard Strauss, libretto by Hugo von Hofmannsthal, and costumes by José-Maria Sert, and, in addition, a ballet of a totally new kind, about a tennis match. (The latter, to be called *Jeux,* was to be set to a score commissioned from Debussy, and its cast of one man and two girls is said by its choreographer, Nijinsky, in his autobiography, to represent, in noncensurable terms, a wish that Diaghilev had often expressed to him — to make love to two men simultaneously.)

As for Cocteau, his originality still lay in his personality and his wit. He was, at this moment in 1912, coasting along with the company — coasting along in keeping to the windward of Diaghilev's temper gusts, coasting along in writing so traditional a libretto as *Le Dieu Bleu.* He himself was aware that he was on a path that seemed to be leading nowhere. In the spring, before the premiere of *Le Dieu Bleu,* he and Lucien Daudet had visited North Africa, which André Gide had already made his own territory in *L'Immoraliste*; and on their return Cocteau wrote to Gide, whom he had not yet met. He had taken with him on his trip, he says, all Gide's books except *Les Cahiers d'André Walter,* which was hard to find, and he recommends himself to Gide's attention:

> . . . A too-short and restless boyhood, chance encounters with dubious mentors, one dreadful turning after another — and all the while a kind of mental torture because my atavistic impulses were good ones — that is what makes me thrust myself so abruptly upon you, seeing how noble and pure you really are. You will find me a Nathanael who happens to be 'a born prodigal son.' . . . Your light beckons to me.

That letter was probably not pure homage to a yearned-for mentor, but rather the offspring of mixed motives: *La Danse de Sophocle* had just been published or was about to be, and there was the possibility of a review in the *Nouvelle Revue Française,* where Cocteau had sent the book to Gide. When after a time no review had appeared, Cocteau wrote to Gide again: "So you loathe my book so much you don't speak? Yet illuminating disapproval is surely as good as praise, and frankness coming from those we admire can dispel the most intolerable apprehension."

After the September, 1912 review by Ghéon or Ghéon-Gide, with its conclusion — "M. Cocteau is unquestionably gifted, but he must now devote himself to his gift" — Cocteau and Gide met. Cocteau was greeted with reserve: he once said that Gide's most personal remark to him in those early days was a petulant "Change your handwriting!" (Cocteau was writing a large, florid, Noailles script and sometimes using De Max purple ink. He was also already displaying a handwriting peculiarity that was to persist, though not consistently, all his life: he was writing the feminine article "la" as though it were the masculine "le" — an idiosyncrasy that Gide was scarely the one to object to.)

Meanwhile, it was shortly after the first letter to Gide that Diaghilev showed open exasperation with Cocteau. It was not, as might have been expected, a personal matter, but rather an artistic ultimatum — two words that were to affect Cocteau considerably. Cocteau has told the story many times, with minor variations: "One night in 1912, I see us in the Place de la Concorde. Diaghilev is walking home after a performance, his thick underlip sagging, his eyes bleary as Portuguese oysters, his tiny hat perched on his enormous head. Ahead, Nijinsky is sulking, his evening clothes bulging over his muscles. I was at the absurd age when one thinks oneself a poet, and I sensed in Diaghilev a polite resistance. I questioned him about this, and he answered, 'Astound me! I'll wait for you to astound me.' That phrase saved me from a flashy career. I was quick to realize that one doesn't astound a Diaghilev in a week or two. From that moment I decided to die and be born again. The labor was long and agonizing. That break with spiritual frivolity . . . I owe, as do so many others, to that ogre, that sacred monster, to the desire to astound that Russian prince to whom life was tolerable only to the extent to which he could summon up marvels."

"Astound me!" Cocteau had finally received a command that he felt he should and could obey. Coming from the "ogre, the sacred monster, the Russian prince," the father of the troupe, it carried with it an authority that had been lacking in his life since April 5, 1898, or probably since even well before that day of the revolver shot at 45 rue Bruyère, the street through which he could thereafter pass only in "fear," and by making himself "hear and see nothing." "I should like some Freudian to tell me the meaning of a dream that I dreamed several times a week beginning when I was ten. The dream stopped in 1912. . . ." Was it after that night in the Place de la Concorde, perhaps, when Diaghilev's command had been received and the grateful decision made to obey it, that he stopped dreaming the recurrent dream?

Although there were to be times when Cocteau avoided Diaghilev, and spoke of him as a monster none too sacred, he never recalled the impresario's "Astound me!" without gratitude. And he wrote: "Finally, in 1917, the opening night of *Parade*, I did astound him." Five years were thus to intervene between order and delivery; and during the interval, André Gide having shown himself so cool in response to the young man's advances, still another slightly older artist was to surge up on the scene and become the object of homage and attempted alliance.

Igor Stravinsky has said, "I believe that I first was introduced to Cocteau at a rehearsal of the *Firebird*, but it might have been sometime after the *Firebird*, in the street; I remember someone calling my name in the street — 'C'est vous, Igor?' — and turning around to see Cocteau introducing himself."

That was the spring of 1910, and a great deal was happening to Stravinsky. He was twenty-eight, just arrived in Paris for the first time, hearing Diaghilev announce to the orchestra at one of the *Firebird* rehearsals, "Take a good look at him — he's about to be famous," receiving an ovation at the premiere on June 25, and becoming an international figure overnight. One has the impression that although it may have been Cocteau who called to him in the street, quite possibly it was someone else. After all, the newly arrived young Russian had within the past few weeks been meeting — to quote the list drawn up by his latest biographer — Debussy, Ravel, Florent Schmitt, Maurice Delage, Erik Satie, Giacomo Puccini, Alfredo Casella, Manuel de Falla, Sarah Bernhardt, Marcel Proust, Jean Giraudoux, Paul Morand, Saint-John Perse and Paul Claudel.

Cocteau's memory of their first meeting is different. It is less *in*different, and it is made interesting by an error of date. "Stravin-

sky," Cocteau said late in life, speaking of the earliest Paris Stravinsky, the Stravinsky of *The Firebird* and *Petrushka,* "had already struck me as the very image of artistic rebellion, rebellion
against the habitual, even though he had so far written only ballets
of a pleasing kind; he had not yet written *The Rite of Spring.*"
Such was the subsequent impact of the *Rite* on Cocteau, that whenever he wrote of the pre-*Rite* Stravinsky (all his writings about
Stravinsky date from after the *Rite*), he either overendowed him
with revolutionary tendencies, as in that passage just quoted, or, as
in his account of their meeting, he associated him with a godlike,
supernatural figure. Here is the account. The scene is Monte Carlo,
where Nijinsky was dancing *Le Spectre de la Rose* and Stravinsky
working on *Petrushka.* This can only have been the spring of 1911.
Cocteau pushes the date back to 1910, the same year casually
guessed at by Stravinsky:

"It was in 1910. Nijinsky was dancing *Le Spectre de la Rose.*
Instead of watching the performance from out front, I went to wait
for him in the wings. There everything was quite fascinating. After
kissing the young girl, the ghost of the rose leaps out the window
. . . and drops down among the attendants, who spit water in his
face and rub him down with Turkish towels, like a boxer. What a
combination of grace and brutality! I will always hear the thunder
of the applause; I will always see that young man smeared with
rouge, gasping, sweating, pressing one hand to his heart and holding onto a prop with the other, or even collapsed in a chair. Then,
after being slapped, sprayed and shaken, he went back before the
curtain to bow and smile. It was in that semi-darkness, among the
great lamps that supplied the moonlight, that I met Stravinsky.
. . . Stravinsky was then finishing *Petrushka.* He told me about it
in the gaming room at Monte Carlo."

A few weeks later, in June, 1911, Cocteau attended the dress
rehearsal of *Petrushka* at the Théâtre du Châtelet, and from then
on, as he puts it, "I saw very little of Stravinsky until the famous
premiere of the *Rite.*" The reason was that during the next two years
Stravinsky was chiefly in Russia and Switzerland, composing the
new work. Its premiere was announced for May 29, 1913, at the
new Théâtre des Champs-Elysées in the Avenue Montaigne, just
built at great expense by Astruc, with decorations by Bourdelle,
Maurice Denis and Vuillard. Astruc had paid Diaghilev hand-

somely to bring the 1913 ballets there rather than to the *Châtelet* or the Opéra as in the past.

Thus the premiere of *The Rite of Spring* came about a year after the failure of *Le Dieu Bleu,* after Cocteau's letter to Gide about wrong turns, after Diaghilev's "Astound me!" and after the Ghéon or Ghéon-Gide ironic counsel: "Devote yourself to your gift."

"The idea of *The Rite of Spring,*" Stravinsky has said, "came to me while I was still composing *The Firebird.* I had dreamed a scene of pagan ritual in which a chosen sacrificial virgin dances herself to death." And: "The violent Russian spring that seemed to begin in an hour and was like the whole earth cracking . . . was the most wonderful event of every year of my childhood." Probably "the whole earth cracking" is as close as one can come in nonmusical terms to describing the tremendous score that he wrote for this "prehistoric ballet." For plot and décor he turned to his friend the Russian painter Nicholas Roerich, who was also a student of ancient Slav rites. Diaghilev entrusted the choreography to Nijinsky. On opening night this musical and choreographic realization of Stravinsky's dream was less a spectacle than a provocation to riot. Very soon, when danced in London and when repeated in Paris in concert form, the *Rite* achieved the recognition as a supreme work that it has retained. But Cocteau, perhaps more than most people, realized that the riot-provoking aspect of its career, though brief, was of considerable significance; and his accounts of the wild hour in the Théâtre des Champs-Elysées rank in vividness with Stravinsky's own both spoken and written. They surpass that of Misia Sert, who tells in her memoirs of Debussy's sadness at being unable to "take in" this new music, and that of Astruc, who recounts his fury at those who interrupted the performance: "Leaning from my box, clenching my fist, I cried with the full force of my lungs, 'First listen! *Then* boo!' "

The French call a tempestuous reception of a new work a *"scandale,"* and for Cocteau the premiere of the *Rite* was "the first *scandale* I ever witnessed." *"The Rite of Spring,"* he says, "was performed in May 1913, in a brash, brand-new theatre, too comfortable and too lacking in atmosphere for a Paris audience accustomed to experiencing its theatrical emotions while packed like sardines amidst the warmth of much red plush and gold. I have no thought that the *Rite* would have been more properly received in less pretentious surroundings; but this deluxe theatre symbolized very strikingly the mistake of pitting a strong, youthful work against a decadent public. An enervated public that spent its life lolling amid Louis XVI garlands and in Venetian gondolas, and on soft divans — and on pillows of an orientalism for which one can only say the Russian Ballet itself was responsible. Such an existence is like digesting one's lunch in a hammock; lying in a doze, you brush away anything really new as if it were a fly. It's troublesome."

Part of the confusion took place onstage and backstage. From the earliest rehearsals Nijinsky had had great difficulty in adapting a choreography to Stravinsky's novel rhythms, and "I myself," Cocteau says, "heard this historic work amid such a tumult that the dancers could no longer hear the orchestra, and had to follow the rhythm as Nijinsky, stamping and shouting, beat it out for them from the wings."

He returns to the audience:

"Now come with me through the little metal door leading to the auditorium. Every seat is taken. The experienced eye perceives that every possible ingredient of a *scandale* is here: a society audience, decolleté, festooned with pearls, aigrettes, ostrich plumes; and, along with the tail-coats and the tulle, daytime jackets and women's hair that never saw a hairdresser — the ostentatiously drab trappings of that race of aesthetes who invariably acclaim the new out of mere hatred for the people in the boxes. (The ignorant applause of such aesthetes is more intolerable than the sincere boos of the society folk.) Then there were the feverish musicians, like so many Panurge's sheep, torn between the opinion expressed by the smart set and the respect due the Russian Ballet. No more of this: were I to continue, I would have to describe a thousand shades of snobbism, super-snobbism, counter-snobbism, which would fill a chapter by themselves . . .

"The house played its appointed role: it rebelled, instantly. It laughed, booed, whistled, imitated the cries of animals; perhaps it would have tired more quickly if the crowd of aesthetes and some of the musicians, carried away by excessive enthusiasm, hadn't taken to insulting and even physically threatening the people in the boxes. What had begun as an uproar turned into a veritable battle.

"Standing in her box, red in the face, her coronet askew, the old Comtesse de Pourtalès brandished her fan and shouted: 'This is the first time in sixty years that anyone has dared make fun of me.' The good lady was sincere: she thought the whole thing was a practical joke. . . . Practical requirements," Cocteau sums up, "had obliged Diaghilev to present, in the form of a gala, a premiere that should have been for artists alone."

And in two phrases he presents the two principal aspects of *The Rite of Spring* as he heard it that night at its premiere: *"Quelle bombe! Quel chef d'oeuvre!"*

It was only when he heard *The Rite of Spring*, Cocteau has said, that he fully understood the "state of surprise" that Diaghilev must have had in mind when he gave his command, "Astound me!" "The idea of astounding had never entered my head. I came from a family in which no one had ever dreamed of astounding anyone. They thought that art was something peaceful, quiet, that there were many very different kinds of it, none preferable to another . . . *The Rite of Spring* was for me the revelation of a form of art that broke with the habitual, was anti-conformist . . . It was when I knew Stravinsky, and later, when I knew Picasso, that I understood that rebellion is indispensable in art, and that the creator always rebels against something if only instinctively — in other words, that the spirit of creation is the highest form of the spirit of contradiction."

What Cocteau did not consciously comprehend as he listened to the *Rite* — and his failure in this respect was to mark much of his minor work —was how little the creation of masterpieces and the desire to astound have to do with each other. Stravinsky, composing the *Rite*, was struggling not to astound Diaghilev or anyone else, but to express his own vision; and whereas Diaghilev, in his role of impresario, needed to be astounded so that he in turn might astound audiences as numerous as possible, the works that made up his programs were not necessarily the products of persons devoted to astounding. Diaghilev's command in the Place de la Concorde fell on ground which, superficially at least, was all too receptive, and Cocteau's acceptance of it colored his career. His many gifts, held

back until now by youth and the distractions of society, seemed
very close to flowering; but the insecurity that made Diaghilev's
command important to him permeated his achievement with the
compulsion to astound and to associate himself with astounders.
The slow fruition of a masterpiece in seclusion and solitude, like
Stravinsky's composition of the *Rite* or Proust's creation of his
great novel, and the obscurity that is the condition, initial or lifelong, of many an artist, would have been excruciating to him. A
kind of humility — a strange word to find oneself using in connection with Cocteau — made impossible for him any consistent realization that the true surprise of his genius might manifest itself
differently, that his greatest influence would be cumulative. Art
may "astound" instantaneously, or along a delayed fuse — sometimes in one night like the *Rite;* sometimes over a generation; and
sometimes posthumously: there are artists who have surprised the
world only after their own deaths.

So important was the *Rite* to Cocteau that he has twice associated
himself with the hours immediately following its premiere in accounts which a person who should know — the composer himself
— declares fallacious. In the second, better-known version, written
five years after the event, Cocteau says:

"At two in the morning, Stravinsky, Nijinsky, Diaghilev and I
piled into a cab and had ourselves driven to the Bois de Boulogne.
All of us were silent, the night was cool and delicious. The scent of
acacia told us that we had reached the first trees. When we came to
the lakes, Diaghilev, muffled in his opossum coat, began to mutter to
himself in Russian. I sensed that Stravinsky and Nijinsky were paying close attention, and when the coachman lit his lantern I saw
tears on the impresario's face. He kept muttering, slowly and per-
sistently.

" 'What is it?' I asked.

" 'It's Pushkin.'

"There was another long silence, then Diaghilev murmured another short phrase, and the emotion of the two men next to me
seemed so great that I couldn't resist interrupting to learn the cause.

" 'It's difficult to translate,' said Stravinsky, 'really difficult; too
Russian . . . too Russian. It is something like "Would you care to
sail to the islands?" Yes, that's it; it's very Russian, because you
see at home we go to the islands the way we've come to the Bois de

Boulogne tonight, and it was while we were sailing to the islands that we first imagined *The Rite of Spring.*'

"For the first time, we alluded to the *scandale.* We returned at dawn. You cannot imagine the sweetness and nostalgia of those men, and whatever Diaghilev may have done since then, I will never forget there in that cab, his huge face, wet with tears, reciting Pushkin in the Bois de Boulogne.

"It is from that cab drive that dates my real friendship with Stravinsky. He returned to Switzerland. We corresponded. I had the idea of *David,* and went to join him at Leysin."

The anecdote is so charming that one should perhaps let it stand unquestioned. But Stravinsky, although he has written genially of Cocteau's company in Paris earlier, at the time of *The Firebird,* although he admires much of Cocteau's work, especially the early drawings, and although he later asked Cocteau to provide him with a libretto for *Oedipus Rex,* does not find the Bois de Boulogne story delightful. "It is in bad taste," he has said — meaning that it should not have been written, because it is false. His own memory of what happened is quite different: "After the performance we were excited, angry, disgusted, and . . . happy. I went with Diaghilev and Nijinsky to a restaurant. So far from weeping and reciting Pushkin in the Bois de Boulogne as the legend is, Diaghilev's only comment was: 'Exactly what I wanted.' He certainly looked contented. No one could have been quicker to understand the publicity value, and he immediately understood the good thing that had happened in that respect. Quite probably he had already thought about the possibility of such a scandal when I first played him the score, months before, in the east corner ground [floor] room of the Grand Hotel in Venice." And he has written: "Diaghilev didn't like Cocteau, and Cocteau's story was only intended to make himself important. We weren't that intimate with him in 1913 to take him with us after such an event as the *Rite* scandal."

There is possible confirmation of that lack of intimacy in Nijinsky's memoirs, a strange and touching document in which the names of many persons close to the ballet are recited in a kind of general recall — Diaghilev, Stravinsky, Benois, Bakst, Chaliapin, Astruc, Rodin, Calmette, Debussy, Karsavina — but not Cocteau. The mention of Stravinsky's first imagining *The Rite of Spring* while "sailing to the islands" is certainly somewhat dubious. In his

writings Stravinsky has mentioned various circumstances connected
with the conception of the *Rite*, but has never spoken of "sailing to
the islands." They would have had to be islands off the mouth of the
Neva, not far from Stravinsky's St. Petersburg, in the gulf of Finland, would they not? The accuracy of Cocteau's account seems
questionable when, remembering that, one reads the lesser-known,
earlier version, published barely two years after the event:

"Two hours after the premiere I was walking in the Bois de Boulogne with the leaders of the Russian troupe. It was just before
dawn. They said nothing about the audience's reception of the
work: they recited Pushkin to one another. . . . They recalled
boat trips they had made on the Volga [sic] . . ."

After the unsettling experience of the *Rite*, Cocteau felt that now
he must and could "astound," and he worked feverishly, differently
from ever before. Convinced that hitherto he had been living and
writing "externally," he now began to "practice dreaming." "I had
read that sugar induced dreams; I ate whole boxes of it. I lay down
fully dressed twice a day. I stopped my ears with wax in order that
my dreams might be rooted more deeply than in external
sounds."

During a summer visit to the painter Jacques-Emile Blanche* at
his country house at Offranville in Normandy, where he had gone
expecting to work on a play, an "unplayable modern tragedy,"
about which nothing more has been heard, he began, instead, a
work that he always claimed was directly though inexplicably inspired by the *Rite*, or by the shock of the *Rite* — a book that is
strange in form and content and in its title, *Le Potomak*. No translation of *Le Potomak* has ever been made or is likely to be made, and

---

* Jacques-Emile Blanche, an excellent painter, son of the celebrated Dr. Esprit
Blanche in whose sanatorium at Passy Guy de Maupassant ended his days, painted several portraits of Cocteau about this time. Jacques-Emile Blanche was intelligent, knew
everyone, and has left several volumes of memoirs. Sharp-tongued and reportedly
eunuchoid, he was dubbed *"le vipère sans queue."* During these years Cocteau's portrait was also painted in oil by Frédéric ("Coco") de Madrazo (Proust's friend and
Reynaldo Hahn's nephew), drawn in languorous profile by Lucien Daudet, and painted
in oil again by Romaine Brooks. Mrs. Brooks has described Cocteau as "a delicate
sitter," having to rest a good deal and fearing draughts from the window against which
she posed him, with a view of the Eiffel Tower. He "posed beautifully," however, when
she met his conditions, which included being fed with frequent slices of her American-
style chocolate cake.

nonreaders of French can only be asked to believe the assurance
that it marks a stage in Cocteau's development. The "Potomak" of
the title is a *"megoptera coelenterous"* (*sic*) — a poet's combination of scientific terms that might indicate a fictitious kind of large,
winged jellyfish; this monster inhabits a subterranean aquarium
in the Place de la Madeleine and thrives on a diet that includes
olive oil, gloves, and rich items fed it by "an American gentleman" — such as spelling mistakes, a music box that plays Wagner, and a program of the Russian Ballet. The creature's structure
is such as perhaps to include a "tubular protrusion," thus hinting at
the nature of one kind of dream (if dream there was) induced by
Cocteau's sugar diet. In his text Cocteau insists in the final "k" of
"Potomak" (after spelling it with a "c" in his earlier drafts), and
pretends that to it "the river that flows, if I am not mistaken, into
Chesapeake Bay," owes its name. The book began with a game, Cocteau says. "Jacques-Emile Blanche had a young nephew or cousin
whom I used to keep amused — scaring him sometimes, for children dearly love to be scared. And I had found this word 'Potomak,' to stand for a kind of formless monster. And gradually this
formless monster took on a certain importance for me."

In addition to narrating a series of visits to the Potomak by Cocteau and his friends, the book is the chronicle, both drawn and written, of two clans — one, cruel and monstrous, called the "Eugènes" (Eugène was one of Cocteau's own baptismal names), the
other deadly dull, the "Mortimers." Cocteau says it all began as
drawings alone, drawings of these strange personages, who, he says,
"surged up from the score of the *Rite*." Around the drawings he
imagined the text: it seems to have been, in part at least, almost a
case of automatic writing, beginning with automatic drawing.

Cocteau has described its genesis:

1. First I met the Eugènes.
2. I drew, without a text, the album of the Eugènes.
3. Through them I felt the need to write.
4. I thought that I was going to write a book.
5. I had a great number of scattered notes.
6. I dictated these notes.
7. I saw that it was not a book, but a preface. A preface
   to what?

Certain aspects of the monstrousness of the Eugènes seem to have been suggested by details from Flaubert's *La Tentation de Saint-Antoine*, and the drawings themselves have a comic-strip air, a tinge of Breughel and what would now be called Surrealism, with occasional fellational details, not unrelated to the "tubular protuberance" of the Potomak itself. Some are masterly little sketches, remarkably sure in their outline, not unlike drawings by Thurber. In general the relations between the Eugènes, the Mortimers, and the Potomak, and between the text and the drawings that "illustrate" it, are far from clear — Cocteau says that the Eugènes are not "in" the text, but "pervade" it — and certain characters in the narrative bear names taken from the names on jars that Cocteau saw in a Norman pharmacy and that he pretended to think resembled the names of characters in books by Gide. (There is a general Gidean influence in *Le Potomak*.) Cocteau once described the book as one in which "occult characters represent the graph of the deep confusions that accompany the moultings of the intelligence," and he always spoke of it as the result of his first great artistic "moulting" brought about by the *Rite*. It marked a break away from conformity to the taste of the salons and of standard ballet. Before *Le Potomak*, he always said, he had been "awake" — a crippling condition for an artist. *Le Potomak* was the first product of his "sleep." "My work begins with *Le Potomak*," he later wrote. "It is a kind of preface."

Elsewhere he says that *Le Potomak* was set off by a phrase of Gertrude Stein's: "One night I heard friends laughing over a poem by an American woman. But her telegram went straight to my heart. 'Dining is west,' Gertrude Stein decides, quite simply, in the middle of a blank page. A single epithet should be enough to set off a dream — a light touch on the shoulder, the arrow on a road sign. What offended my friends — the American joke — seemed to me, on the contrary, a proof of confidence." Cocteau was not to meet Gertrude Stein until Picasso brought them together in 1917, and he had apparently not heard of her before that moment in 1913 when friends read her aloud. Her *Tender Buttons*, which contains the phrase "Dining is west" in its section "Food," was not to be published until the next year, by Donald Evans at his publishing house in Paris called "Claire Marie"; but somehow the manuscript — it must have been the manuscript, for only there can the words "Dining is west" be described as being "in the middle of a blank page"

— found its way to a group of Cocteau's friends and "pointed the way" to freedom, indeed to the responsibility to write what others might consider a "joke" — as Stravinsky, in the *Rite*, had "made fun of" the old Comtesse de Pourtalès. *Le Potomak* has its amusing moments, though it never hits quite so delightful a bull's-eye as Gertrude Stein's three words.

Cocteau dedicated the manuscript of *Le Potomak* to Stravinsky. It was accepted, apparently without much enthusiasm, for publication by the Mercure de France, which had published *Le Prince Frivole* and *La Danse de Sophocle,* but the war intervened, and for several years it remained in proof. During those years Cocteau occasionally dropped in at the offices of the Mercure. There his brilliance impressed the gifted and crotchety Paul Léautaud, dramatic critic, under the pseudonym Maurice Boissard, for the magazine that had given the firm its name. "Cocteau's talk when he visited the Mercure," Léautaud has written, "was marvelously funny and witty. Such originality, even in his choice of words — amazing! He had something of the acrobat about him. When he described certain people in official positions he had a way all his own; no one else would have dreamed it was possible to paint a portrait with such words as he used." Cocteau circulated sets of proof among his friends, and most of them recognized the book's significance for him; but in 1919, when it was finally published (not by the Mercure, but by the Société Littéraire de France), critics were understandably puzzled. The most intelligent and sympathetic of them, Fernand Vanderem, likened the drawings to those done by Alfred Jarry for *Ubu Roi,* saw the Potomak itself as "an apocalyptic monster in the manner of Odilon Redon," and enjoyed chiefly the epigrams with which Cocteau had peppered the book to express the spirit of his break with the past:

> The future belongs to no one. There are no precursors — only laggards.
>
> Whatever the public blames you for, cultivate it: it is yourself.
>
> Watch out: that man is no revolutionary. He's just a diehard anarchist of the old guard.
>
> A sensitive man with a tendency to adaptation is harmed by exposure to too many different surroundings.

> Once upon a time there was a chameleon. Its owner, to
> keep it warm, placed it on a piece of Scotch plaid. It died
> of exhaustion.

Le Potomak is the earliest book of Cocteau's that he was ever
willing to have reprinted — the senior of all his printed *Oeuvres
Complètes.*

Simultaneous with the composition of *Le Potomak* was the episode of Cocteau's never-completed ballet, to have been called *David*
and to have had — such was Cocteau's hope — a Stravinsky score.
Like *Le Potomak,* it was conceived in the great flush of excitement
following the premiere of the *Rite.* It sprang superficially from *Petrushka*: the scene was to be a fairground. Cocteau himself later
described it: "On stage, in front of a booth at a fair, an acrobat
would be doing a come-on for *David,* a spectacle intended to be
given inside the booth. A clown, who is later transformed into a box
(theatrical pastiche of the phonograph played at fairs — modern
form of the ancient mask), was to celebrate David's exploits
through a loudspeaker and urge the public to enter the booth and
see the show. In a way it was the first sketch for *Parade,* but unnecessarily complicated by biblical references and a text." During
the months while he worked in his "sleep" on *Le Potomak,* Cocteau
consulted, on the possible choreography for *David,* with his particular friend of the moment, the young Swiss painter and dancer
Paul Thévenaz,* who earned his living by teaching at the recently
founded Paris School of Dalcroze Eurhythmics.

Stravinsky was then living in Switzerland, at Clarens on Lake
Geneva, with his first wife, who was pregnant, and their three small
children, completing his opera *The Nightingale,* with its libretto
taken from Hans Christian Andersen's Chinese fairy tale of that
name. He came to Paris for a few days in January, 1914 to play the
score, as far as he had composed it, to a group of friends that included Ravel and Jacques Rivière, the chief editor of the *N.R.F.*

---

* Thévenaz later came to the United States, where he died in 1921. The February,
1922 issue of *Vanity Fair* contains a page of reproductions of his paintings, with a
legend: "The untimely death of Paul Thévenaz has left an empty niche in our Hall of
Arts. Thévenaz brought to New York from Paris the experimental tendency which is
all too rare among American artists. During his several years' residence in this country
he was a happy playboy among the arts, bringing to them a spirit full of whimsicality,
mondanité and inventive zest."

Before or during Stravinsky's Paris visit, or perhaps both, Cocteau told him something about *David*, and Stravinsky agreed, apparently rather casually and incautiously, that Cocteau might come to Switzerland to discuss it. Cocteau attended the audition of *The Nightingale*, which took place in a pretentiously furnished apartment on or off the Avenue Kléber, and after Stravinsky's return to Switzerland he wrote him a letter.

Cocteau to Stravinsky
February 4, 1914

Mon cher Igor,

I found it all but impossible, among those dreary Kléber orientalisms, to tell you of my deep pleasure. I had tears in my eyes, like the emperor of China, and I was proud of living in the same forest as you.

I am delighted with our project.

Dance must *express nothing*. The body moves, then is still, just as an instrument in the orchestra flares up and subsides. Along with the sound-curves there must be a visual curve that is an integral part of the ensemble. Thévenaz is thrilled to accept his very humble role.

I'm to arrange things with Copeau* at six tonight.

Je t'embrasse.

Jean

This letter, addressed to Stravinsky at the Hotel-Pension du Château, Clarens, was forwarded to him at the Clinique Mont Riant, Lausanne. Madame Stravinsky, who had been in poor health, had given birth to a daughter at the clinic on January 15. Her illness was diagnosed as tuberculosis, and as soon as mother and daughter could be moved the entire family went to Leysin, at a higher altitude. There Madame Stravinsky entered a sanatorium, and her husband and children lived at the Grand Hotel. Stravinsky had a piano installed in the apartment, and continued to work on *The Nightingale*. In addition to those distractions, something else occurred to make Stravinsky hesitate to discuss *David* further. The Free Art Theatre of Moscow, which had commissioned *The Nightingale*, went bankrupt, and Diaghilev stepped into the breach,

---

* Jacques Copeau, a member of the editorial board of the *N.R.F.*, was just founding his Théâtre du Vieux-Colombier in Paris. Perhaps through Gide Cocteau had heard that Copeau was interested in Stravinsky.

agreeing to produce the opera during his forthcoming seasons in Paris and London. Stravinsky well knew Diaghilev's jealous feeling that except in very special cases none of "his" artists should work with anyone else, and he knew of Diaghilev's particular distrust of Cocteau. The impresario was an expert at making trouble for recalcitrant or "disloyal" artists, and to do the job more thoroughly he had the habit of enlisting the very considerable troublemaking expertise of Misia Sert. With that team in action against him, the artist-victim was likely to find himself enmeshed in webs of intrigue, his project — whatever it might have been — mysteriously evaporated. Stravinsky wrote Cocteau about the need for discretion, even at so early and tentative a stage, and apparently questioned the wisdom of his coming to Leysin. The exchange of letters is revealing on both sides, and for that reason is given here as fully as possible.

Cocteau to Stravinsky
[n.d.]

Mon cher petit,

I have spoken to no one, except of course to Gide, and to Copeau and Delage* (Delage would probably be with us at Leysin). Nothing is known about the matter. It is known about only the way you want it to be known about — that is, I give evasive replies to the very few people around the *N.R.F.* who ask me about it. Outright denial seems to me even better. As far as Leysin is concerned, it is a way to escape from the telephone and all the rest. Therefore, not a word.

Precise answers, please:

1. Is it cold?
2. What date should I come with the work?
3. Do you want the text immediately, or shall I bring it with me and explain it to you?
4. Snow?
5. Could you write me — roughly — for Copeau, the size of the orchestra and chorus you plan to use.
6. Latest news of your wife.
7. *Suppose Serge were to question me?*

I have a sore throat, and keep gargling — this in imitation

---

* Maurice Delage, the composer. His role here is unexplained.

(charming coquetry, no?) of the Emperor of Japan.* I am finishing my (your) book and look forward to a healthy rest in Switzerland.

Je t'embrasse.

Jean

Whether or not as the result of indiscretion on Cocteau's part (he later acquired the reputation of being the proper person to tell a secret to if one wanted it broadcast), it took Diaghilev less than a fortnight, after Cocteau's first writing to Stravinsky from Paris, to learn that a group of Frenchmen, including Cocteau, had designs on "his" composer. At such a moment, his first step with an artist whom he respected and needed as much as Stravinsky was to show himself protective. He knew that Stravinsky's present circumstances had put him in need of money, and it is easy to imagine him, in this instance, saying to Stravinsky something like "I hope those Frenchmen are paying you well." Apparently everything about *David* was so extremely tentative that fees had not yet been discussed. Now Stravinsky wrote Cocteau stating his terms, or his needs, and Cocteau replied.

Cocteau to Stravinsky
[postmark Paris, February 17, 1914]

Mon cher petit,

All my hope of escaping from my depression and poor health lay in our meeting at Leysin. Your letter tortures me. I cannot answer you properly because I am in tears. The V. Colombier is the theatre of the young, and of the new movement: it carries on with high spirits and hard work like the *N. Revue Française,* on a shoestring. What it hoped for from you and me was some old thing to be revived, or three very short dances that you would write like three melodies for a concert. There was no question of a "work," but of a few measures, and your name connected with their theatre.

Mon cher petit, I will not even try to read them your letter — I would be too afraid of doing you a disservice in the eyes of a group of the young people who are responsible for your present fame.

---

* The "Emperor of Japan," like the "Emperor of China" in the earlier letter character in *The Nightingale.*

Mon cher petit — if I had the 6000 francs I would send it to you at once and we would tell them nothing about it or about my longing for these two weeks or a month that would help me to live. I was already picturing the hotel, the skating rink, the snow, *The Nightingale* on the piano. . . . I can't even speak of it — it breaks my heart.

Mon cher petit, I beg you to write me whether you don't see some way to arrange things — to write something very short for this enthusiastic and disinterested group — or, if not, to persuade Serge not to stand in the way of this project and my marvelous trip.

Je t'embrasse avec confiance et tristesse.

Jean

Stravinsky consented that Cocteau come, and Cocteau wrote again.

Cocteau to Stravinsky
[postmark Paris, February 21, 1914]

Mon cher Igor,

So I'll come March 2. What a joy! I will bring the notes for *David,* and probably Thévenaz if he isn't detained by Dalcroze — I'd like to do some winter sports with him if there is still enough snow.

A woman theosophist has described to me one of David's dances according to the Magi — it is terrific. He danced around the *Sacred Ark: The Dance of the Planets*!!!! Can you imagine the music!!!!! — what a noble thing we can make of it — strong and rugged like those times when Jehova was the ogre, when the church sacrificed two thousand *sheep* in order to *please* the good shepherd.

Je t'embrasse.

Jean

P.S. I hear that your wife is better.
P.S. 2. Write me the lowest prices in the hotels and which would be best.

On February 23 Stravinsky received a telegram saying in part M WARNED ABOUT EPIDEMIC SCARLET FEVER IS IT TRUE, and he lied the same day on a special delivery postcard: "No scarlet fever, and no Black Death either! Shall not finish *The Nightingale* for a month. Prefer to see you before that. Why not come now? There is still snow and you would find it splendid. In this villa there are rooms vacant (pension I think from 10–15 francs)." The next day brought another telegram from Cocteau: REPLY QUICKLY DEAR IGOR AM IMPATIENT TO SEE YOU SOON IS SECOND STILL ALL RIGHT. And two days later came a letter:

Cocteau to Stravinsky
[postmark Paris, February 25, 1914]

Cher petit,

What good luck! So I'll leave Monday. Dalcroze is lending me Thévenaz, as it is still impossible for me to travel alone. I'll be glad of the opportunity to acquaint you with this rough, ingenuous, fresh mind. I leave Paris a fugitive from the telephone, people, the newspapers, migraine, fever, the tango, the Sarah Bernhardt jubilees and a woman who is beginning to be a nuisance. Even the threat of scarlet fever won't stop me. It's a mania with me to prefer hotels. Telegraph if you can to a hotel near you to reserve two very simple rooms.

Je t'embrasse.

Jean

Stravinsky, having encouraged Cocteau to come, apparently began to have second thoughts about the guest who continued to fear scarlet fever, couldn't travel alone, inquired so incessantly about rooms, showed little awareness of the composer's busy life and its complications and referred to his sick wife only in postscripts or asides. He clearly thought well to reply immediately, in a tone still jocular and welcoming, but suggesting a postponement, and making clear to Cocteau what kind of a place Leysin was and that he himself would not be completely free.

Stravinsky to Cocteau
[special delivery postcard, postmark Leysin, February 26, 1914]

Petit Jean,

There are no hotels, properly speaking, in Leysin — t͐ are only sanatoria, with medical attendance, etc. That

keep you from coming to see me and getting away from the
pestiferous women, the migraines, the telephone, and God
knows what else (perhaps even 606) that may be plaguing
you in Paris. Nevertheless I am going to ask at the hotel if
there are two rooms vacant . . . I repeat, it is not really a
hotel, but a sanatorium: you understand that?

Go on Sunday and hear the Pierre Monteux concert at the
Casino de Paris — *Petrushka* — he thinks it will be interesting — first time in concert.

T'embrasse.

Igor

[As a postscript] Have just received two telegrams. They are
putting pressure on me to finish *The Nightingale*. It would be
more sensible, I think, to postpone our meeting a little — perhaps for three weeks. I am afraid you don't realize, *mon petit*,
how little time I have and that I work all day on *The Nightingale*. There would be a real *scandale* if I didn't finish it on
time.

Back came a telegram:

Cocteau to Stravinsky
[Paris, February 27, 1914]

COMING ANYWAY TOO TIRED WILL GO TO AIGLE IF YOU PREFER
AND RETURN LEYSIN LATER WILL BRING DAVID AFTER ALL IDEA
TOO EXCITING NOT TO SHARE WIRE ME IF PENSION DE FAMILLE
HAS COMFORTABLE BATH AND ROOMS FOR MANIAC LIKE ME
ARRIVE TUESDAY RESERVE DEFINITELY TWO ROOMS AFFECTION-
ATELY

It was, in truth, beginning to sound a bit maniacally insistent,
and it called for another special delivery postcard:

Stravinsky to Cocteau
Leysin, February 27, 1914

Vieux maniaque! What a strange idea, to go to Aigle! Go instead to Villeneuve (ten minutes from Aigle, the first station
after Territet), to the Hotel Byron. There you'll be comfor-
ble, and for relatively modest rates will find everything you
— rooms, baths, hot and cold water, lukewarm women,

boys from 8 to 13, etc. etc. Follow my advice and you'll be happy . . .

Cocteau to Stravinsky
Paris, February 28, 1914

I take the 9:30 train Monday night with Thévenaz. I absolutely must get away. Reserve two rooms for us at your pension to begin with — there will always be time to change. For I imagine you must be better treated than people making short stays. Wire the name of your *pension*. What a pleasure it will be to see you and to hear *The Nightingale* again! I am seeing a lot of the theosophical Magi and old Fabre, who know everything about David.

Je t'embrasse.

Jean

P.S. If I arrive too early in the morning, don't worry. I'll come back.

But Stravinsky was suddenly called away — perhaps to his relief:

Stravinsky to Cocteau
[special delivery postcard]

Leysin, February 28, 1914

Vieux, I leave tomorrow for Berlin and will be back Thursday or Friday. So put off coming until the end of the week. You won't be the loser, for just now we are having frightful weather, with fogs so thick that it's impossible to tell a goat from the housekeeper of our sanatorium. Be fair, and don't maltreat that poor woman you mention in each of your letters.*

After his return from Berlin, Stravinsky apparently tried to persuade Cocteau to postpone the visit still further, or to cancel it entirely as being physically too strenuous. But to no avail.

Cocteau to Stravinsky
[telegram, Paris, March 6, 1914]

I NEVER TAKE DECISIONS WITHOUT SERIOUS THOUGHT HAVE
BOUGHT TARTARIN COSTUMES AND FEAR MELTING SNOW [. . .]

* Perhaps Stravinsky had heard from Paris that Cocteau was pretending in certain circles that the current object of his affections (Thévenaz) was a woman.

ALPS BENEFICIAL MY EXHAUSTION TICKETS BOUGHT WILL NOT
INTERRUPT NIGHTINGALE AT ALL BECAUSE BRINGING SKIS AND
BOOK TO FINISH WILL SEE YOU WHEN YOU NOT WORKING TAKE
TEMPORARY ROOMS SO I KNOW WHERE GO ON ARRIVAL WILL
MOVE LATER IF TOO BOTHERSOME TO YOU WILL BE THERE SAT-
URDAY MORNING AFFECTIONATE GREETINGS

JEAN

The unenthusiastically awaited visitor arrived the morning of
the next day, March 7, and what immediately followed can be in-
ferred from a note he wrote to Stravinsky, before there had been
more than the briefest conversation between them. It is written on
the stationery of the Grand Hotel, Leysin, in whose annex Stravinsky was living, and where Stravinsky had obviously not taken
rooms for Cocteau.

Cocteau to Stravinsky

[March 7, 1914]

Forgive my coming in, but I saw only you in the room — a
thousand apologies to your wife.

I came with Thévenaz as far as Leysin hoping that there
might still be enough snow for skiing, but I will probably go
to Villeneuve. I'll be so glad to see you and talk about *The
Nightingale*! Let me know at the hotel, where I have taken
rooms, when I can come and embrace you.

Don't hold it against me that I came. With this rain, that
would be too much, and I was sick of Paris. Saw Serge day
before yesterday — he asked me to tell you "that he existed,"
and said that you are working like a black.

See you shortly —

Jean

The visit, begun so inauspiciously, continued as anything but a
success. Cocteau wrote a depressed letter to a recently made friend
of whom more will be heard.

Cocteau to Comte Etienne de Beaumont

Grand Hotel de Leysin
[n.d.]

. . . . Igor is composing prolifically. Is there much snow in
your garden? Here, a meter, and the result is the most utter

silence. . . . It snows and snows and snows. The lights keep
going out. One overeats . . . and a consumptive lady is expressing herself (badly) by playing Chopin. Ah *David!* . . .
The *Rite* sounds marvelous in the hotel lobby, played by a
lady patient and Thévenaz.

Writing to André Gide, he put on a bold front: "Intensive work.
Igor Stravinsky is a dynamo. Thévenaz is amazing. I think that
David is going to become something extraordinary (it is like nothing else), and if Copeau puts it on I assure you he will have full
houses."

But when he returned to Paris in April he brought with him
nothing for Copeau, and he telegraphed back to Stravinsky on the
twenty-seventh: COULD HARDLY SAY GOODBYE WAS SO SAD ABOUT
YOUR TROUBLES AND SO WORRIED ABOUT OUR DEAR DAVID.

The fact was that Stravinsky had not only had little time for Cocteau in Leysin, but never developed any real interest in *David*. "I
never did know exactly what Cocteau had in mind about *David*," he
has said. ". . . . I think *David* was biblical, and at that time I
avoided anything biblical." (Cocteau's autograph scenario for
David shows that it was indeed biblical.) He disliked Cocteau's letters, with their assumption, unshared by him, that they were colleagues, and he found his attitude toward the composition of music
insufficiently serious. Cocteau's suggestion that Stravinsky would
have been willing to give the Théâtre du Vieux-Colombier merely
his name and "some old thing," or scribble "a few measures" on
request, must have seemed particularly insensitive. The sense of
Cocteau's persistence in coming to Leysin increased with the years.
"Cocteau pestered me," Stravinsky has said. "He pestered me
about *David* and had to be driven away. He was an embarrassing
young man at that time, utterly persistent. One soon had enough of
his wheedling and his flattery."

For Stravinsky has always considered Cocteau's long, three-part
dedication to him of *Le Potomak* mere flattery, poured on to secure
his cooperation on *David*. He thinks that Cocteau may never have
had any serious intention of allowing Copeau and the Vieux-
Colombier to produce *David* had it been completed, or at least of
giving them the first option: "What he really wanted was my participation and on the strength of that to sell the idea to Diaghilev." In

Karsavina in
Le Spectre de la Rose.
Poster by Cocteau.

Cocteau with Diaghilev.

Nijinsky in the ballet *Schéhérazade*.

Stravinsky playing *The Rite of Spring*.
Drawing by Cocteau.

Picasso and Stravinsky.
Drawing by Cocteau.

Cocteau, Self-Portrait.

other words, a Cocteau-Stravinsky *David* was to have been Cocteau's means of astounding the impresario. (However, it seems equally possible that Cocteau, eager — as he was always to be — to penetrate the group of the *N.R.F.*, hoped to improve his position there by bringing them Stravinsky.)

Diaghilev visited Stravinsky in Leysin shortly after Cocteau's departure. His greeting to the composer was characteristic in its dry sarcasm: "Bonjour, Monsieur David."

With that, *David* became a thing of the past for Stravinsky and Diaghilev. Stravinsky finished *The Nightingale,* and its premiere in Paris was scheduled for May 26.

Back in Paris, it took Cocteau some time to assimilate the death of *David.* On May 4 he wrote another depressed letter to Etienne de Beaumont: ". . . my apologies for the strange card and the red ink, but nothing else is available in the disorder in which I live. . . . I need someone to help me live. When one's hair, eyes and heart are all in a mess, one doesn't get along very well in a city that deflects the brightest enthusiasm into debauchery, sets traps for the ambitious, and has its nets ready if one stumbles." For a while he continued to hope, and continued to work on the ballet with Thévenaz, but gradually he became aware of the full force of the Diaghilev-Misia cabal that had been working against him. When Stravinsky arrived in Paris for the premiere of *The Nightingale,* he wrote him two letters, one on opening night and the other just before or just after.

Cocteau to Stravinsky

[May 26, 1914]

Mon cher Igor,

I did not join you tonight because audiences disgust me and I find Serge intolerable. Misia, too, completely under his thumb, is becoming offensive. I was at the back of a box, overcome by your dear music and all the memories of Leysin that accompanied it. The further I go, the more I detach myself in my work from the Russian Ballet and all its parasites. Poor divine little Nightingale in its oversize cage!

Je t'embrasse, je t'admire et je t'aime.

Jean

P.S. I am told — too late, alas — that Madame Stravinsky was in the theatre. I am heartbroken not to have seen her — but she knows my affection for her and for you.

Cocteau to Stravinsky

Sunday

Mon vieux,

Stupid misunderstanding between us.

You are a long way from the work on *David*, and so am I because of the proofs of my book. It's as simple as that.

We should have said so to each other. Silence always complicates things. Misia has told me about your conversation of yesterday. But as my book has been dedicated to you since its birth I did not want it to appear while there was a cloud between us. Therefore I will come and embrace you tomorrow morning about eleven among the tennis courts, the roses and the cockatoos.*

Jean

With that letter — it shows Misia being her most witchlike to both Cocteau and Stravinsky — correspondence between them on the immediate matter of *David* ceased.

Later, when Cocteau had fully reconciled himself to the fact that *David* was never to be, and later still, when he was beginning work on *Parade*, *David*'s better-omened successor, he twice again wrote Stravinsky about the abandoned ballet.

Cocteau to Stravinsky

10 rue d'Anjou
October 4, 1915

Mon cher Igor,

I have seen Madame Edwards [Misia] — there is just one thing that you have not fully understood and that she has not fully understood — it is important that I emphasize it: I do not care about *David*. Never speak to me of *David* — *David* is

---

* Stravinsky does not recall this meeting. He suggests (1966) that it all sounds like "a *truc* of Cocteau's" — a rather uncanny thought, considering the resemblance between this place of supposed rendezvous and the cockatoo terrace of the Jardin d'Acclimatation in the Bois de Boulogne, so featured in Cocteau's recurrent dream about his father.

already transposed in my head, *David* is you, *The Rite, The Wedding* — *David* is a stage in our relationship. It was probably essential for our getting really to know each other. What must be retained from *David* is a pact of long, fraternal friendship.

Jean Cocteau

Cocteau to Stravinsky
[probably July or August, 1916]

Mon cher Igor,

Just a few words that must be said to dispel something troublesome. It has come to my ears that you consider me hostile. I am even more grieved than stunned, for I love you, and I love you in such a way that I must tell you so once and for all.

I will not speak of *David*. It was a work I was probably not ready for, conceived in a burst of youthful overconfidence, and spoiled by that plus the miasma of Paris and a series of unfavorable circumstances.

I can now appreciate as a spectator that period when it was impossible for me to understand your attitude. Today, a bit more mature and detached, I consider that you were right, that perhaps without fully realizing what you were doing, with the instinct of your genius, you rescued an idea. My devotion to you is well known, and will become better known through my work. It expresses my gratitude to you on two scores: first, for having sensed what was really happening underneath, despite surface appearances; and second, for having accelerated my "moulting" with your tremendous dynamo.

You are what I admire and respect above all. I think of Nietzsche's words: "I would let all my other human relationships go for a low price. At no price would I part with the days spent at Triebschen — days of confidence, of gaiety, of sublime happenings — moments of *deep* insight. I do not know what experience others have had with Wagner: *our* sky has never been clouded."

I do not remember ever approaching the annex of the hotel at Leysin without experiencing Nietzsche's emotion at the gate of Triesbschen — and you see that I retain a proper measure of pride. Leysin remains for me everything concentrated, right, divine, fecund, inevitable, invincible. It was in its warm snow that I shed an old skin, that I began afresh. It seems to me that it would cure anyone.

My somnambulism increases with my work, but as I descend toward the firedamp, as I rise toward the unbreatheable — the only dangers, the only solitudes that are worth the struggle — it is you whom I encounter. At such moments human misunderstandings are left behind. Everything is reborn. I listen to you, and you love me.

Mon cher Igor, I had to write you. Whenever I have spoken of you it has been as your disciple. Alas! Misunderstandings! No one is really worth the trouble involved in unraveling them. But you! That we should no longer be at one, even though distant in space, spoils the beginning of each day for me, and my work besides.

Je t'embrasse.

Jean

Cocteau, who was in the habit of speaking of his "breaks" and "reconciliations" with others, and who even published an essay about breaks (*De la Brouille*), often wrote of his "break" with Stravinsky (meaning the fiasco of *David* and some unfavorable words he was to write about Stravinsky in *Le Coq et l'Arlequin*) and of their subsequent "reconciliation" (meaning particularly their collaboration in 1925 on *Oedipus Rex*). Like others with whom Cocteau described himself as having "broken" and then having become "reconciled," Stravinsky finds those terms inappropriate to describe aspects of a relation which, in his eyes, had not been at all close, even though Cocteau's letters to him might on occasion be dithyrambic. After the "reconciliation" of 1925, Cocteau was always to give the impression in his writings that relations between himself and the composer had been intimate and easy, although he was not invariably to speak that way privately.

Cocteau's mishandling of the matter of *David* and Leysin, and his great disappointment, were due to both inexperience and experience. Inexperience, in his previous lack of close association with a great creative artist and in his unfamiliarity with intrigue; experience, in his having been so spoiled by De Max and the salons, so privileged in his participation in the ballets. He had come to take his irresistibility for granted. Cocteau had charmed birds off many a tree, but he had not charmed the Nightingale.

Cocteau was now seeing less of Maurice Rostand. "He began to avoid us, finding us too academic for his new ambitions," Rostand later wrote; and he tells of how he found in Cocteau's room, one day, a letter from Marcel Proust that Cocteau had not shown him, and how he read it, and saw in it that Proust said he had caught sight of the Rostand brothers at the Opéra one night, and would like to meet Maurice. Thus it was that Maurice learned of Cocteau's having met Proust (through Lucien Daudet), and of his unwillingness to share the acquaintance with him. One of Proust's early encounters with Cocteau, at an after-the-ballet supper in the restaurant Larue, with its painted ceiling and red and gold décor, was recorded by Proust himself in a bit of doggerel in which he compares Cocteau to one of the sylphs on the ceiling or to a skier, rhymes "ski" with "Nijinsky," and shows Cocteau leaping up onto the white tablecloth as the band plays "Indiana." Those autograph verses by Proust were stolen from Cocteau, along with "a hundred letters" that Proust had written him, and Cocteau wrote down the lines from memory.*

The theft and dispersal of most of Proust's letters to Cocteau, and the dispersal by sale of Cocteau's to Proust, make possible only a fragmentary narrative of their relations, which underwent various vicissitudes over the years. One of Proust's early letters, perhaps written even before the evening at Larue's, expresses affectionate concern regarding the possible dangers inherent in the younger man's state of complete freedom.

Marcel Proust to Cocteau

[1908?]

. . . . I have been thinking about you from time to time, and with the presumption characteristic of friends and philosophers have formulated certain futile wishes: such as, for something to happen that would isolate you and wean you from the pleasures of the mind, so that after a sufficiently long period of fasting you might again really hunger after those

* See Appendix XIII.

beautiful books, beautiful pictures, beautiful countries that
you now skim over with the lack of appetite of someone who
has spent all New Year's Day making a round of visits, each
complete with *marrons glacés*. This, according to my progno-
sis — I am sometimes right concerning others, though powerless to help myself — is the stumbling block that you, with
your marvelous and sterilized gifts, must be wary of. But the
life that I should wish for you would scarcely be pleasant to
you, at least in so far as at present your desires may be shaped
by a life of a very different kind. And so my wishes will fortunately prove to be futile, and nothing will be changed, thus
assuring the continuation of everything that pleases you most
— and perhaps without causing you any harm. For, intellectually as well as physiologically, any diet we may follow counts
for less than our temperament: some people walk ten hours a
day without losing weight and others eat five meals without
gaining a pound. . . . I am sending you some mistletoe for
Christmas.

If Cocteau answered that letter, his reply has not been discovered. He wrote later that he had seen Proust most frequently at a
time when he was too immature to appreciate him, but that Proust
(like De Max) had foreseen a brilliant future for him: "I often
visited Marcel Proust when I was scarcely older than he had been
when he wrote *Les Plaisirs et les Jours*, and I noticed something
that I then found perfectly normal — that he treated me as though I
had skipped that stage, and was already on the arduous path that
one day I really would take, and that he himself was already following. Doubtless Proust, unmatched in the art of reading the blue-
print of a man's life, knew more than I about my future, still completely hidden from me particularly because I found nothing
wrong with what I was then, whereas later I was to look back on it
as a sequence of serious errors. The explanation of his indulgence
toward me is found on page 122 of *A l'Ombre des Jeunes Filles en
Fleurs*." *

* The passage which Cocteau says is relevant is one in which the Narrator tells of
his feeling of freedom when in the presence of the writer Bergotte, who enjoys the
younger man's sincerity and intelligence. "Just as priests," Proust says, "having the
widest experience of the human heart, are best able to pardon the sins which they
do not themselves commit, so genius, having the widest experience of the human in-

Cocteau wrote also of finding it "difficult to read Proust's work rather than listen to it," because he had been so accustomed to hearing Proust read aloud from the manuscript of his novel; and he said that he and his friends had always thought of Proust as a great man, long before the first volume of the novel was published. When the proofs of *Swann's Way* were ready, in September or October, 1913, Proust sent a set to Cocteau, and Cocteau was one of the book's first reviewers, in *Excelsior* for November 23, 1913. *"Du Côté de Chez Swann* resembles nothing that I know of, and reminds me of everything that I admire," Cocteau wrote. "All masterpieces are akin. Mme. Swann's hat, with its single iris, is unforgettable in the same way as the red cap that Steerforth,* in *David Copperfield,* brandishes from the waves."

But although Cocteau and Proust continued to see each other and to correspond, Cocteau seems never to have become *involved* with Proust, as he was, at least in his own mind, with Diaghilev and Stravinsky, and later with Gide and Picasso. Cocteau liked to attach himself to heroes, usually artists, whom he admired and thought great and strong, and he liked to display the attachments. His artist heroes had to be in the limelight, a limelight that he could share. Proust was aloof, withdrawn, and entering his phase of dedicated solitude. Unlike Diaghilev, he never gave Cocteau a command; unlike Stravinsky, he was never conceivably accessible for collaboration. Unlike Gide, he had nothing of the patriarchal about him; he was far from being a brilliant class bully like Picasso. Compared with all of them, he was a slender insect of the greatest finesse, all antennae and introspection — too quivering (in that respect too like Cocteau himself) to make attachment profitable, even possible. Beyond all this, he was, unlike those others, interested in Cocteau's artistic and private essence; his province was human nature, that of the artist particularly. His letter shows an early penetration of the promise and risk that the future held for Cocteau. This very penetration may well have made Cocteau warier of Proust than of other great men.

---

telligence, can best understand the ideas which form the foundation of its own writings." (*Within a Budding Grove,* I, 201. Translated by C. K. Scott Moncrieff. New York, Albert and Charles Boni, 1928.)

   * Cocteau was "in love" with Steerforth at this time: he wrote of him rapturously in *Le Potomak.* In Cocteau's character Dargelos, especially in *Les Enfants Terribles,* some have found Steerforth's cruel beauty, his charm and brutality.

Later, when Cocteau had attained his own plateau of eminence, achieved his own limelight, he would change his pattern of attachments, choosing no longer older men more celebrated than himself, but promising youths (quite often named Jean), whom he would treat as he had wished to be treated by the heroes of his own early years. Sometimes he would take them as lovers, sometimes he would call them his "adopted sons," or he would do both; and usually he would go to considerable lengths to help them achieve fame. Sometimes he would play the game he had played with his mother and the customs inspector in the train, leading an unfortunate on only to let him fall, or he would play off one protégé against another. In several cases, affection took root, and these form interesting chapters in Cocteau's own life and work. In all cases, one understands why Cocteau sometimes signed himself "Narcisse."

Paul Thévenaz, the young Swiss artist who accompanied Cocteau to Leysin, painted while there a portrait of Stravinsky. On other occasions he painted Cocteau and Anna de Noailles. A Thévenaz portrait is not a Cubist picture, but it might be called "cubified" — a conventionally painted likeness overlaid with a cubistic treatment of planes. Since a large exhibition by the group of Cubists calling themselves the Section d'Or, at the Galerie de la Boétie in October, 1912, Cubism had been increasingly in the air in Paris. By now there were Cubists of all kinds, and about the time of the *Rite* Cubism became another of Cocteau's revelations.

Among the people he had "always" known, through his family, was a young woman named Juliette Roche, daughter of Jules Roche, who had been a deputy, a minister, and a member of the Conseil Supérieur des Beaux-Arts; she was handsome and intelligent enough to do honor to her godmother, the Comtesse Greffulhe, and she had a considerable gift for painting. At first she frequented, with her father, academic art circles; then, perhaps through her friend Misia Sert, who knew all the Nabis, she saw much of them, especially at the home of Misia's brother, Cipa Godebski, in the rue d'Athènes, where Paul Valéry, Léon Paul Fargue, Valéry Larbaud, André Gide, Ravel, Roussel, and Florent Schmitt often visited. In 1913 she was taken by her friend Ricciotto Canudo, founder of the avant-garde magazine *Montjoie!*, to see the

Cubist pictures at the Exposition des Indépendants. There she met one of the Cubist painters, Albert Gleizes.

In her unpublished memoirs, Juliette Roche Gleizes — she and Gleizes were to be married in 1915, with Cocteau one of their witnesses — tells of Cocteau's first meeting with a Cubist, in the spring of 1914:

> I had been rash enough to begin a portrait of Cocteau. He posed very badly, and his talk was so amusing* that it distracted me from the work. With his fresh features and tousled hair he looked at that time — at least so Ravel said — like a fawn, he was so light, graceful, elusive. It was impossible to capture him.
>
> Like so many who came to the rue d'Athènes, he jeered at the Cubists, at *Montjoie!*, at Canudo. Around *Montjoie!* he was considered a hanger-on of Madame de Noailles, Edmond Rostand, Jacques Blanche and Reynaldo Hahn — which was not absolutely true but not absolutely false either.
>
> However, he was made much of in the rue d'Athènes because his charm and wit were irresistible. Ravel — whom he was to treat so roughly a few years later — was especially fond of him.
>
> While I was struggling with Cocteau's profile, the doorbell rang. It was Albert Gleizes — I had not expected him.
>
> This unforeseen meeting between Cocteau and a Cubist made me nervous. I pronounced their names as indistinctly as I could, hoping that neither of them would hear, and then, preferring not to be present at the perhaps unavoidable clash, I disappeared behind a screen to make tea. When I returned a few minutes later with the teapot, the "Prince frivole" and the Cubist were exchanging visiting cards and telephone numbers and making an appointment.
>
> A few days later, Cocteau was talking of nothing except Duchamp-Villon, Jacques Villon and Albert Gleizes; and Misia Godebska reproached me sharply: "Why did you put Jean in touch with the Cubists? He is a man of the Right, not the Left. . . . He'll be ruined among such people as that. . . ."

* Madame Gleizes has said of Cocteau: *"Il était adorable — sauf aux moments quand vous vouliez l'étrangler."*

A few years later, Cocteau and Cubism were to coincide artistically, in *Parade*. But Madame Gleizes has confessed that as she introduced Cocteau to his first Cubist she felt, like Misia, that she was exposing him to danger. It was not without some regret and discomfort, she says, that she watched him align himself with the "moderns." He was so dapper and clever, socially so elegant; the company of the genteel Noailles, Rostands, Blanches and Hahns, and of the sublime monsters of the ballet, did indeed seem more appropriate for him in 1914 than that of the avant-garde painters of Montmartre and Puteaux, successors to those other painters, the "Wild Beasts," who had been strangers to Cocteau and his circle.

Madame Gleizes' memoirs contain another scene in which Cocteau plays a role, this one laid in the School of Dalcroze Eurhythmics where Paul Thévenaz was a teacher. In early 1914, Dalcroze Eurhythmics were much the mode in Paris, smarter even than the tango. Madame Gleizes captures the spirit of the moment:

> That winter, quite apart from an ever-increasing ferment in artistic circles, one could feel in the atmosphere of Paris, so responsive to every slightest change, a sort of instability, a malaise, something like the restlessness displayed by animals before an earthquake. It crystallized now and again in a few words, a few sentences, then dissolved. But the unusual symptoms kept manifesting themselves in various ways.
>
> One evening, in the large bare room of the Eurhythmics school that had just opened in the rue de Vaugirard, Jean Cocteau and I were watching some of our friends, airy and svelte, clad in black bathing trunks, capering around the room and moving their arms in time to complicated rhythms. There were no chairs in the room, and we were sitting one at each end of a board resting on a kind of block. The music accompanying the dancing was soothing, and I was full of pleasant daydreams.
>
> Suddenly Cocteau turned to me and said: "You see those shrimp-pickers there on the linoleum? That means it's all over." And in the style of his Sphinx in *La Machine Infernale* he began to improvise a sort of poem-sermon, an apocalyptic prophecy — a very eloquent one. Why had we been so shaken, the previous summer, by the rumblings of the *Rite*? Because

unconsciously we felt the need to rediscover what we had lost — the call of great elemental forces, savage rites, bloody sacrifices. That Cocteau should feel such a need came as a surprise.

Writers on Stravinsky have often spoken of the prophetic character of the *Rite*, its seeming forecast of the "dramatic irruption of the pent-up forces of dark, primeval barbarity" that were to be let loose in the First World War. It was a time when the world was hungering for new experiences in art, and it was beginning to have its hunger appeased during those months just preceding the catastrophe. Cocteau was one of the first to connect the impact of the *Rite* with the prevalent feeling of malaise described by Madame Gleizes, and it was the search for artistic innovation to which he was now beginning to devote himself — a never-ending search that was to lead him into varied companies — that had led him to the Cubists.

It was of course his own malaise that he was expressing to Madame Gleizes in his "poem-sermon" at the Dalcroze school. As he put it in the dedication of *Le Potomak*, ever since hearing the *Rite* he had been "keeping a fever chart." It is scarcely surprising that Cocteau, as war approached, should have been in a mood of frustration and pessimism. For one thing, Paul Thévenaz was withdrawing his affection.* *Le Potomak*, his great declaration of independence, was in proof, but was being held by the publisher, who obviously cared little about it. *David*, which was to have astounded Diaghilev, and perhaps opened the gates of the *N.R.F.*, had come to nothing. Diaghilev and Misia had played with him. Stravinsky, who in reality had simply gone his own way, was an enigma. Bakst, Benois and the other artists of the decorative tribe had begun to seem to him passé and superficial. It was doubtless such thoughts as those that made Cocteau say "It's all over." Later he was to say that the Russian Ballet was really "a kind of fireworks," and had counted for

---

* Cocteau had already hinted at this in his second depressed letter of that spring to Etienne de Beaumont. When he took his broken heart to the Abbé Mugnier, the wordly, witty confessor of le Tout-Paris, he received as perhaps not very great consolation a comparison between a love affair and the trick staircase in the château of Chambord: *"Vous connaissez l'escalier de Chambord? On monte ensemble, mais on ne se rencontre pas."*

little in his true development. It is evident from this distance that precocious though he was, he had not yet found his métier, and that he had sometimes been handling himself badly with artists who had.

It was now the summer of 1914.

4
The First World War of Jean Cocteau

War, *Misia's ambulances*, Le Mot, *Garros*, A Midsummer Night's Dream, *Enter Valentine Gross, Satie, Picasso* (1914–1915)

"**E**VERY institution, almost, in the world was strained," Winston Churchill wrote, after the First World War. "Great empires have been overthrown. The whole map of Europe has been changed. The position of countries has been violently altered. The mode and thought of men, the whole outlook on affairs, the grouping of parties, all have encountered violent and tremendous changes in the deluge of the world." The proposition that that nightmare, which slaughtered ten million people, mutilated twenty million others, and transformed the lives of billions forever after, might have been averted had one of Jean Cocteau's uncles been a bit more effectively charming, has been put forward — how seriously, one scarcely dares think — by André Germain.

His story is that Raymond Lecomte, Madame Cocteau's diplomat brother, was sent by the Quai d'Orsay as counselor to the French Embassy in Berlin to insinuate himself into the circle of aesthetic German aristocrats who during a certain period were the Kaiser's intimates: Lecomte's role was to instill in them, and thus in the Kaiser himself (known among those cronies as "Petit Chéri"), a love of France and a distaste for bellicose designs against her. Apparently he was making some headway when in 1907 a group of indignant "good Germans," led by the chauvinistic journalist Maximilian Harden, began to cry scandal, and the little band around the Kaiser was disgraced. "Wilhelm II, deprived of his friends and his playthings, found relief in travels and speeches that disquieted Europe, and, finally, in the war. . . . Lecomte was abruptly promoted from counselor to the rank of minister plenipotentiary, and, with thoughtful consideration, was sent to Persia, where he found things much to his taste."

So close (according to Germain) had francophilia come to being the official line in Germany before 1914. As it was, the war that broke out was to provide the minister plenipotentiary's nephew with new stages on which to perform his *"transformations de Fregoli"* — at times very different indeed from the tabletops in the Restaurant Larue, but at other times, in his case, not too different. We have seen how a single revolver shot in Venice inspired a rather jaunty poem: now, to the accompaniment of the artillery of the western front, Cocteau, although never a soldier, was to lead, during two periods of several months each, a life that was physically as well as spiritually adventurous. He claims to have felt guilty because his experiences in the military zones were so fascinating. "I left the war," he wrote later, "when I realized, one night in Nieuport, that I was enjoying myself. That disgusted me. As soon as I made that discovery I took steps to leave, taking advantage of being sick." If he was lucky in being able to "leave the war" when he chose, he displayed a certain gallantry in choosing to participate in it at all, for he could almost certainly have been completely exempted. He himself, in later years, attributed his participation to "curiosity." His principal public writings about the war are a novel and two long poems, which the artist Cocteau constructed as *montages* of wartime experiences and fantasies; for *reportage* one must look chiefly elsewhere among Cocteau's utterances, and some of these, too, are characteristically mythical. The chronicle of Cocteau's years 1914–1918 affords a rather special glimpse of a life in wartime.

In 1910 he had been exempted from the two years of military service then compulsory for all but certain categories of twenty-year-old Frenchmen.* Was that another privilege obtained for him by his mother, sister to a diplomat and friendly with cabinet ministers? (Madame Cocteau is said to have been able to ask favors of Louis Barthou.) But perhaps a mere doctor's certificate was enough to convince the army of the nonsuitability of the frail poet, who had been constantly sickly as a boy and was now obviously nervous and high-strung. Had they drafted him in 1910 he would have missed some of his Diaghilev years: no one can regret the army's decision.

---

* Those portions of Cocteau's military dossier which the Ministère des Armées has been willing to communicate will be found in Appendix I.

But now, in August, 1914, his artistic frustration, war fever, and the national alarm as the German army quickly drove to within a few miles of Paris, made him eager to participate in the monstrous novelty. "If possible," he wrote to a friend, "I would opt for another planet, where the ridiculous doesn't sour into drama. I hope — my breakneck side hopes — to be sent as correspondent for *La République*. Either you do your share for your country, or you commit suicide. I love life, and prefer to die for her if necessary." "Neither Cocteau nor Albert Flament nor Boni de Castellane was mobilized," says Madame Gleizes in her memoirs, "but all three could think about nothing but 'going,' and told everyone that they couldn't stand the feel of civilian trousers." It was Misia — now Edwards' widow and soon to become Madame Sert — who was to find for Cocteau a particularly well-cut pair of non-civilian trousers.

Classified as unfit for army duty, he had quickly gone to work for the Red Cross. On August 20 he had tea with André Gide, who has written a celebrated account of the meeting:

> Jean Cocteau had arranged to meet me in an English tearoom on the corner of the rue de Ponthieu and the Avenue d'Antin. I did not enjoy seeing him again, even though he made himself extremely agreeable; he simply cannot be serious, and to me all his aphorisms, his witticisms, his reactions, all the extraordinary dash of his customary way of talking, were as shocking as a luxury article on display in a period of famine and mourning. Dressed almost like a soldier, he looks much healthier thanks to the present excitements. He has given up nothing of his old self, but now what makes him bubble is the war. When speaking of the butchery at Mulhouse he goes in for funny adjectives and mimicking; he imitates bugle calls and the whistling of shrapnel. Realizing that I am not amused, he changes the subject and says he is sad . . . all of a sudden he feels with you and explains your own feelings to you. Then he talks about [Jacques-Emile] Blanche, apes Mme. R[umilly], and tells about a lady at the Red Cross screaming on the stairs: "I was promised fifty wounded for this morning; I want my fifty wounded." Meanwhile he is crumbling a piece of cake on

his plate and nibbling it; his voice rises and falls; he laughs,
leans forward, bends toward you and touches you. The odd
thing is that I think he would make a good soldier. He says
that he would, and that he would be brave. He is as carefree as
a street urchin; it is when I am with him that more than ever I
feel myself clumsy, dull, morose.

The last sentence is a crucial one, succinctly telling us a great
deal about Gide himself, about Cocteau, and about the effect of the
one on the other. It explains much of what Gide's attitude to Cocteau was always to be. Cocteau, even after periods of ambulance
duty behind the front lines, never disparaged Gide's own "war activity" — part-time paper work in a Paris reception center for
Belgian refugees. Nor did Cocteau's shortcomings ever include
Gide's intermittent forms of material and spiritual stinginess.

It was about then, still very early in the war, even before the
German advance was checked in the first battle of the Marne (September 6–12), that Cocteau joined forces with Misia Sert: apparently he had decided to forgive, under the stress of war, her
treacheries concerning *David*. Her energy diverted from ballet to
patriotism, she had obtained authorization from General Gallieni,
the military governor of Paris, to form a convoy of ambulances to
administer first aid as close to the front as possible; she persuaded
the *grands couturiers* to contribute their idle delivery vans, had
their interiors refitted, and formed a team of volunteers that included Sert, Cocteau, Iribe, and a professional nurse, apparently
the Madame Rumilly mentioned by Gide. Headed by Misia's own
Mercedes, which contained Misia herself, Iribe at the wheel, and
Cocteau beside him "dressed by Poiret as a volunteer male nurse,"
the convoy set off toward the firing line. The horrifying sights they
soon met up with are described by Misia in her memoirs — the
bodies of dead horses littering the roads, the fragments of men and
animals thrown into the air by explosions still hanging on the
branches of trees; eventually they reached Rheims, during one of
its many bombardments.

Eight years later, in *Thomas l'Imposteur*, one of his first two
novels, a book that remains remarkably fresh after almost half a
century, Cocteau was to write powerful scenes laid in the streets
and hospitals of shell-shattered Rheims:

The cathedral was a mountain of old lace.

The army doctors, kept from their work by the heavy shelling, were waiting for a let-up in the cellar of the Lion d'Or. There were three hundred wounded in the home for the aged and the hospital. Rheims, being expendable in wartime, given scarcely a thought by Paris, lacked facilities for evacuating wounded or feeding them. They were dying of their wounds, of hunger, thirst, tetanus, shelling. The night before, an artilleryman was told that his leg had to be amputated without chloroform — that this was his only chance; and he was lying there, pale, and smoking a last cigarette before the ordeal, when a shell pulverized the surgical apparatus and killed two medical assistants. No one dared face the artilleryman to tell him, and he was left with his gangrene, which would soon spread like ivy on a statue.

Such things happened ten times a day. The 150 wounded being cared for by the nuns had a cup of rancid milk apiece and half a salami for all. In a long, narrow ward gaping with shell-holes, a priest went from pallet to pallet administering the sacraments; sometimes it was necessary to pry mouths open with a knife blade in order to insert the host. . . .

We lived under the canopy of our own shells, roaring overhead like express trains, and German shells punctuating their sinuous course with a sudden black ink-blot of death. At this time Rheims was at the peak of its confusion, its nerves at the breaking-point.

That agony of the unevacuated wounded in Rheims inspired Cocteau in 1914 to immediate action. Back in Paris, he called on the novelist Maurice Barrès, who was also one of the most influential and chauvinistic journalists in France, writing for the newspaper *L'Echo de Paris,* and begged him to publicize the human tragedy taking place at that very moment in the city concerning whose stricken cathedral so much sentiment had been expended. But although Cocteau called on him a second time, Barrès did nothing, and Cocteau later said that the famous man's failure to act taught him forever to suspect "theories" — i.e., any proclaimed ideology: "To give yourself wholly to each particular case, even if this involves you in a series of seeming contradictions, puts you on a

straighter course and gives you deeper insights than abstract principles, which so often force you to be untrue to what is best in yourself." And he tried to enlist, writing on September 22 to the Abbé
Mugnier: "Monsieur l'Abbé, I wanted to see you and obtain your
precious blessing before leaving, and your card anticipates me. I
was happy about enlisting, but things are held up by the doctors,
who are being very strict. I am jittery waiting, but still hope for a
favorable verdict." On November 22, however, he was definitively
rejected as physically unfit, and *"classé Service Auxiliaire."* He
continued to serve with Misia's ambulances until they were rendered obsolete by services organized by the Red Cross itself. Cocteau's "gaiety, his tenderness and wit" were precious to Misia at
the time, she has written. "His vitality and good humor were indispensable to compensate for the fatigue, the irritations and the sleep-
less nights."

Princess Marthe Bibesco tells of evenings in that December,
1914, at the Hotel Meurice, when Cocteau, "just back from Rheims
with Misia Sert's ambulances," joined her and her aviator husband, Prince Emmanuel Bibesco, and friends: "We discuss *the*
subject — the death of our youth. Colonel Repington, military correspondent of *The Times,* just arrived from London, likens it to
grouse shooting: the young are killed and the old spared. Emmanuel sees that Jean is drawing for me an illustration of what he has
just said — that what we are witnessing is the Earth feasting on her
children. On a sheet of my notepaper he traces a globe, a horrible
old woman; she is at table, knife and fork upraised, napkin tied
under her chin, and is saying with the gluttonish smile of the ogress
in *Tom Thumb,* 'A bit more *Chasseur Alpin,* please.' " Cocteau was
now making a number of striking drawings, putting his horrible
"Eugènes" of *Le Potomak* into German uniform, and printing
some of them in a weekly newspaper, *Le Mot,* that he had started
with Paul Iribe. But he was seeing more physical action as well. By
December 3, 1914, Jacques-Emile Blanche was noting: "Although
he has not yet quite got over the shock he suffered when collecting
the wounded at Rheims, Jean is going on flights over Paris with
Garros." And in January, 1915, Princess Bibesco was writing in
her journal: "Jean has been given a new assignment, as he likes to
put it. As poet, he chose a star as his emblem, and now he has be-

come a companion of the stars in heaven: he is observer with Roland Garros on his reconnaissance flights above enemy lines."

The celebrated young aviator, Roland Garros, was about Cocteau's age and had been a pioneer flyer and developer of airplanes since 1909. After enlisting on the outbreak of war, he had been assigned to Paris, for experiment with monoplane armament. He was convinced that aiming could be effective only from a fixed gun pointed straight ahead, with the axis and nose of the plane itself giving the direction. The difficulty was to determine how to synchronize firing with the revolutions of the propeller blades, and the solution of this problem was Garros' assignment. Working with him was his friend the airplane builder Raymond Saulnier, and their experiments took place at Villacoublay, near Versailles, where Saulnier and his partner Morane had their own airfield. Garros was a dark, attractive, intelligent daredevil, who loved to share his flying with his friends. At the request of Misia Sert, through whom he met Cocteau or whom he met through Cocteau, he once took her on a flight complete with "loopings" that frightened her half to death and from which she emerged *"verte et décomposée."* He had been "charmed by Cocteau's brilliance," says the editor of his memoirs, Jacques Quellennec, "and Cocteau in turn admired the calm courage of the aviator, who was then at the height of his career." Soon Garros was inviting Cocteau to join him on air excursions. Cocteau's alacrity in accepting, perhaps even in requesting, was probably not unconnected with the fact that his older brother Paul had enlisted in the air corps, a fact of obvious importance to Jean and mentioned several times in the war poems and letters. "Jean tells us what it is like in the land of eternal morning," the ineffable Princess Bibesco records. "At a thousand meters altitude, above the dark clouds that hang, gleaming with deadly flashes, over France and Germany, it is springtime in the Alps: the sky is blue, the sun hot. Jean de l'Etoile asked his friend Garros for permission to leave the cockpit and gather some anemones. He brought them to me, and put them on the lunch table in the Restaurant Larue — Persephone's bouquet. The next day Roland Garros comes with him — they are on leave, and lunch with us. Jean tells us of something that had happened to them a moment before. On one of the pedestrian safety-islands in the Champs-Elysées a little old lady who was terrified as she felt the wings of death come a little too close, shook her umbrella at Garros and the automobile he was driving, and shouted *'Assassin!'* Garros said to Jean with a smile: 'Little does she know how true she speaks!' ''

Garros became an actual *assassin* on April 1, when, his firing problem solved, he downed a German plane near Dunkirk after a brief air battle witnessed by thousands of allied and enemy soldiers in their trenches below. "I finally got a Taube," he wrote Cocteau. "It was horribly tragic. The duel lasted ten minutes and my plane was hit by a bullet that went through one of the wings. The Taube was riddled, caught fire at about a thousand meters, and went into a flaming spin. Their drop — there were two men — lasted half a minute — a century. I went to see the debris: fragments, and two nude bodies, not charred, but grilled, and all their stiffened, twisted flesh still bleeding. What a ghastly nightmare!"

Two more victories followed, on April 15 and 18, 1915. It was perhaps on one of the days between those two flights — Cocteau says it was "the day before my friend's last takeoff" — that Cocteau made a portrait sketch of Garros, which Garros signed. Then, on the very day of the third victory, April 18, 1915, Garros flew again, this time on a mission to bomb the railway station at Courtrai. His plane was hit, and his motor failed. He made a landing behind the German lines, set fire to his plane in an attempt to destroy the device he had perfected, and hid under some branches in a ditch. But he was discovered and taken prisoner, and was to spend the next two years in various German prison camps.

It must have been on experimental flights only, not in combat, that Garros took Cocteau as passenger, and it is not known how often they flew together. Cocteau, who as time went on tended to resemble Misia in seeing himself as prime mover, was to write in 1925: "My friend Garros had discovered, in my house and helped by a photograph that was standing behind an electric fan, the principle of shooting through the propeller" — a claim that he twice expanded, twenty-five and thirty-seven years later: "I was living in the rue d'Anjou, in my mother's flat. One day Garros and Morane were there. Morane was on a sofa, watching an electric fan. Behind the fan was a photograph of Verlaine, the famous photograph that Montesquiou had had made, in which Verlaine is wearing a magnificent scarf. Suddenly Garros said to Morane: 'Look — now you see one of the eyes through the fan and now you don't. Why shouldn't we shoot through the propeller?' Morane answered: 'Because we'd destroy the propeller.' Garros said: 'No — we'll armor the propeller, triangularly, leaving an opening, and some bullets will go through and others won't. We won't have to take machine-gunners up with us — we'll do the shooting ourselves.' " And Cocteau goes on to tell how the Germans found the armored propeller in the wreckage of Garros' plane, and employed the principle in the arming of their Fokkers. "I think," Cocteau says, "that this story may interest aviators."

Cocteau's principal tribute to Garros is his volume of poems, *Le Cap de Bonne-Espérance,* which he was to write during the war and publish in 1919.

Meanwhile, Cocteau and Iribe continued to publish *Le Mot,* which appeared irregularly, supposedly fortnightly, from November 28, 1914 to July 1, 1915. The first number had carried on its front page a striking posterlike drawing by Iribe in blue and black, captioned in red "David and Goliath" and showing a French artilleryman beside his little '75, confidently smoking his pipe in the face of an immense German juggernaut fieldpiece disgorging from its underparts a horde of unwilling slave privates, one of whom is being kicked by his helmeted officer. Contents, too, were chiefly jingoistic, and mostly written by Cocteau over his own name or various pseudonyms. One article proclaimed the non-Germanism or anti-Germanism of the greatest German artists — Beethoven, Hauptmann, Nietzsche, Schopenhauer, Goethe — and sneered at "the rich poverty of *Der Rosenkavalier*"; another, unsigned, spoke against "*le graf von Kessler, le boche Strauss and l'autrichien Hofmannsthal,*" their ballet *Joseph,* and Wagner. The second number of *Le Mot,* dated December 7, 1914, contained a long unsigned stretch of wartime doggerel, "Au Kronprinz," sarcastically regretting the German crown prince's inability to visit Paris, his favorite city: Cocteau gave Princess Bibesco a copy of this written in his own hand, saying that it was his.* *Le Mot* was a wartime sequel to

---

* Since the princess was rumored to have been the crown prince's mistress, friends prophesied a break between her and Cocteau; but she denied the rumor and recognized his prerogatives as Frenchman and poet. On January 30, 1960, sending her, at her request, another copy of "Au Kronprinz," her earlier copy having been lost, Cocteau

Schéhérazade, printed on poorer paper (although a few "deluxe" copies of each number were announced), but just as faithfully echoing a tone prevalent in Paris at a given moment — chauvinism, this time, instead of late Art Nouveau and late Symbolist aestheticism. Although *Le Mot* warned its readers against contracting the war disease it called *"espionnite"* ("spy-itis"), and against trying to console a wounded soldier by calling him a hero to his face ("I'll be a hero for a year," they quote one doubly amputated veteran as retorting to a sentimental lady, "and after that just a legless cripple"), reading the magazine today induces the queasiness that is the common effect of old propaganda. Woodcuts by Dufy, Gleizes, Lhote and Bakst afford a certain relief, and there is Cocteau's portrait sketch of Garros; but Cocteau's drawings, some of them now taking on Gleizes-like forms, are chiefly scenes of German atrocity: one entire numbered series is called *"Atrocités."* Beginning now to display what was to be a lifelong obsession with hands, he concentrated on what is almost the only kind of wartime atrocity laid to the German armies in Belgium that has *not* been proved — the amputation of the hands of children; nor is it surprising to see him go further in one of the atrocity series and show the prospective victim of an amputation to be a young Highlander in a kilt. In one issue alone of *Le Mot* there are four atrocity drawings by Cocteau. He also contributed anecdotes about life with the ambulances.

Contrasting with that journalism are a few poems of great beauty, which seem never to have been reprinted. One of them, "Quand Nous Serons 'Ceux de la Guerre,' " prefigures in an extraordinary way another poem, the equally beautiful "Les Lilas et les Roses," by Louis Aragon, which became perhaps the most celebrated poem to come out of France during the Second World War.*

Especially in its later issues, *Le Mot* made many pronouncements on artists and aesthetics. It poured scorn on the old-fashioned refinement of the eighty-year-old composer Camille Saint-Saëns, master and friend of Reynaldo Hahn: "Monsieur Saint-Saëns is well. The wars of the intellect, as Rimbaud calls them, do not disturb him. In this great, confused period he continues to lisp and smirk while all the arts are being utterly recast." Cocteau was al-

wrote her: "Since it amuses you, here is that stupid poem, evidence of one's idiocy at twenty. Picasso is right in saying 'It takes a long time to grow young.' "
* See Appendix II.

ways to speak of Reynaldo Hahn as his friend, but he has clearly "gone beyond" the music of his former colleague. "What position should the artist choose," Cocteau seems to be asking himself in some of those late articles in *Le Mot,* "between excessive refinement and its opposite?" The answer appeared in the issue of April 3, 1915: "Between 'good taste' and vulgarity, both of them boring, there is a way that is both moderate and spirited — the tact to understand *how* far to go *too* far." *

Albert Gleizes, a number of whose drawings and articles appeared in the last numbers of *Le Mot,*† and whose influence was strong on Cocteau at that time, had been mobilized in August, 1914 and sent to barracks at Toul, in the Vosges. There, indulgent officers allowed him a room of his own, and he painted pictures that were increasingly abstract. Among Gleizes' paintings of this period are a full-length oil portrait of Cocteau that he apparently finished later in Barcelona without his model, and an earlier sketch for it in gouache: painted in bright colors and filled with tilted planes, both pictures show the abstracted pattern of a graceful attitude assumed by a slender, trim, youthful figure, its tightly belted waist suggesting Cocteau's ambulance uniform. The contrast between these "portraits" and the earlier likenesses of Cocteau by Blanche, Daudet, Madrazo, Romaine Brooks and Bakst is eloquent of the Cubist revolution and of Cocteau's changing tastes. Between their meeting in the spring of 1914 and the outbreak of war Cocteau and Gleizes had seen much of each other and had hatched a project — an ultramodern production of *A Midsummer Night's Dream*, which they hoped might be given in the famous Paris circus, the Cirque Médrano. Cocteau wrote a version of the play adapted for performance in the circus ring, Gleizes made designs for sets and costumes,

---

* This formula, and one somewhat similar — "A little too much is just enough for me" — are found repeated here and there in Cocteau's works. The latter was supplied him by Walter Berry, president of the American Chamber of Commerce in Paris and close friend of Edith Wharton. Cocteau, apparently quoting Berry, says it was first uttered by "an Indian chief dining at the White House."

† Cocteau said later, rather vaguely, about the last issues: "Suddenly Iribe let me cope with the newspaper alone, and we did the work in a little courtyard with a tree in the middle, in the rue des Saints-Pères." That "alone" followed immediately by "we" is a pleasant example of Cocteau's exactitude in factual matters. One has the impression that in Iribe's absence, Gleizes, who had recently been demobilized, was partly responsible for the content of the paper's final issues. Certainly the difference between the art of Iribe and that of Gleizes illustrates Cocteau's "progress." Cocteau was by now a resolute partisan of "modernism" in art and letters.

and they decided that the accompanying music, too, should be French and modern. The first public hint of it was given in *Le Mot* for March 27, 1915, in an article quoting and countering a bit of German publicity for Max Reinhardt's wartime productions of Shakespeare in Berlin: "England unworthy; Shakespeare deserts to Germany," the Germans had said. "A new production, with French music, around *A Midsummer Night's Dream*, by our ally Shakespeare," *Le Mot* declares, "would be a splendid benefit for the wounded — and for the non-wounded as well!" A second mention, in the issue of June 1, contains another gibe at Saint-Saëns: "Maître Saint-Saëns, eager to displease everybody, and never missing a chance to drop a brick, now thinks it clever to scold Firmin Gémier, who has the idea of producing *A Midsummer Night's Dream* with new music. '*A Midsummer Night's Dream* must *always* be done with Mendelssohn's music, etc.' "

Not only had the eminent Firmin Gémier been secured as director of the new *Midsummer Night's Dream*, but the great Astruc had consented to be its impresario. In his memoirs Astruc tells of rehearsals beginning during the summer: "About the middle of 1915, Jean Cocteau, Gémier and I met at the Cirque Médrano to put on a production of *A Midsummer Night's Dream* for the benefit of the Theatre Managers' Fund for the Wounded . . . The music was taken from Erik Satie's *Gymnopédies*.* It was Cocteau's brilliant idea to have the parts of Bottom, Flute and Starveling played by Paul, François and Albert Fratellini (the well-known circus clowns). The first rehearsals were exciting. Everybody felt that it was a wonderful project."

The *Dream* was still in abeyance when Albert Gleizes and Juliette Roche were married on September 8 † and set sail for New York on the tenth. Since Satie's musical collaboration was wanted, whether alone or together with that of other musicians, Cocteau now felt that he should meet and make a good impression on this com-

---

* Not entirely, perhaps. Cocteau said that the music was to be a "potpourri of everything we like." (Cf. p. 135.)

† Along with the Comtesse Greffulhe, the bride's godmother, Cocteau was a witness at the wedding, held in the church of St. Honoré d'Eylau in Paris. The ceremony was simple, but the officiating priest was the fashionable, witty Abbé Mugnier. After the ceremony, the telephone in the sacristy rang, provoking, before it was answered, the following bit of dialogue:

    Cocteau: "Monsieur l'Abbé, God is calling."
    L'Abbé Mugnier: "Tell him I'm coming."

poser, who was known for his crotchetiness.* Satie had had an unusual career as a known composer who returned to school at the age of forty (dissatisfied with his early work, he spent three years studying counterpoint, analysis and orchestration at the Schola Cantorum under teachers younger than himself). He had been "rediscovered" during the years preceding the war, and now, almost fifty, he was enjoying a new celebrity.

Cocteau knew where it would be most advantageous for him to meet Satie.

In May, 1914, at a rehearsal of the ballet *La Légende de Joseph* at the Opéra, he had met a striking beauty in a lovely green dress, Mademoiselle Valentine Gross, well known in artistic society as a delightfully talented painter, designer and illustrator. Her father was an Alsatian who after the Franco-Prussian War had opted for France and settled in Boulogne-sur-Mer, where he was a composer and professor of music. Tall, with a superb carriage, famous for her long and lovely neck (Cocteau was to call her his swan), in her early twenties, intelligent, Valentine Gross was one of the ornaments of le Tout-Paris. She was already well launched on her career. As part of the opening festivities of the Théâtre des Champs-Elysées in 1913 Astruc had exhibited some of her drawings and paintings of Diaghilev's dancers in the theatre, and during the preview of the *Rite of Spring* she had sketched a number of the poses assumed by the Chosen Virgin in the Sacrificial Dance, later noting, under the drawing of each pose, the musical theme accompanying it — thus creating a document that has become celebrated in the annals of ballet. Count Harry Kessler, the francophile German-

---

* Many people have written characterizations of Satie. Some of Cocteau's are among the best, for example:

"His deadpan eccentricity was a trait inherited from Scottish ancestors. He looked like a minor civil servant, with a little pointed beard, glasses, umbrella, bowler.

"Selfish, cruel, maniacal, he would listen to nothing that didn't accord with his own dogma, and he would fly into a violent rage against anything that went counter to it. Selfish, because he was interested only in his music. Cruel, because he defended his music. Maniacal, because he kept refining his music. His music was tender — and this means that so was he, in his way.

"Over the space of several years Erik Satie came every morning to 10 rue d'Anjou and sat in my room. He kept on his overcoat (always perfectly spotless), his gloves, his hat which he wore pulled down almost to his monocle; his umbrella never left his hand. With his free hand he would cover his mouth, which curled when he spoke and laughed. He came from Arcueil on foot. There he lived in a small room, in which, after his death, under a mountain of dust, were found all the letters his friends had ever written him. He had not opened one. . . ."

Irish art patron and diplomat, said to be the son of Kaiser Wilhelm
I, had collaborated with Hugo von Hofmannsthal on the libretto of
La Légende de Joseph (later so excoriated in *Le Mot*), and it was
he who introduced Cocteau to Valentine Gross at the Opéra. She
had been none too eager for the meeting. She presided over a modest literary and artistic salon on Wednesday afternoons at her flat
on the Quai de Bourbon, Ile-St. Louis, a salon with a strong
N.R.F.* tinge, and the lack of regard expressed there for Cocteau
by such men as Gaston Gallimard, Léon-Paul Fargue, Valéry Larbaud and Jacques Copeau had predisposed her against him. However, as they met now and again at gatherings during the months
that followed he interested her; and on Saturday, March 13, 1915
he wrote her a note, asking whether he might call. He had lost the
address of Edgar Varèse, he said, whom he badly needed to see
(Varèse had been asked to conduct the projected *Midsummer
Night's Dream*), and he counted on her "friendly magic." Not too
surprisingly, he suggested a Wednesday. He came to the flat, and he
was to come again many times — "But never on Wednesday," Valentine said later, "the day I was at home to my friends, none of
whom wanted to meet Jean Cocteau."

The beautiful young woman and Cocteau increasingly enjoyed
each other's company, and after she had met Cocteau's mother she
was invited to dinner at 10 rue d'Anjou, where she quickly became
a favorite. Before long Madame Cocteau was urging the young people to marry — they were both so clever and good looking and well
mannered (Valentine even hinted at having noble blood — that of
the great family of Mailly-Nesle; one of her grandmothers, she had
always been told, had been seduced by a Monsieur de Mailly, lord
of the manor in her village on the borders of Artois and Picardy);
Valentine would be "so good for Jean"; and one evening, when
Valentine, who often preferred to set off her statuesque beauty by
dressing exotically rather than fashionably, appeared wearing a
long white veil, Madame Cocteau astounded the guests: "This is an
engagement party" — or, as another version has it, "Just like an
engagement party." But any "engagement" ended with the party
itself.

---

* With the issue of August, 1914, the magazine had suspended publication (it was to
resume in June, 1919), but there were frequent reunions of those of its collaborators
not mobilized, or on leave.

Among Valentine's admirers was Erik Satie. Despite his present celebrity, Satie was poor; he had always been poor; and Valentine, whose drawings were much in demand with magazine editors, had been able, during the winter of 1914–15, to have him commissioned to write three songs to be published in *La Gazette du Bon Ton*. For these he received three thousand francs (the equivalent of about six hundred pre-First World War dollars), the largest sum of money he had ever seen. Gratitude was thus added to the other ingredients of Satie's affection for the beautiful Valentine, and when she wrote him in October, 1915, that Cocteau had some ideas for ballets and would like to meet him, he replied: "Of course! I shall be delighted to see Cocteau — and you, needless to say. Your idea is charming, as your ideas always are. You are one of the good ones." "I did not tell him," Valentine has written, "that Cocteau had been unable to come to an agreement with Stravinsky about *David;* and they and Gabriel Astruc came to my house on Monday, October eighteenth." The three men talked, Valentine says, about *A Midsummer Night's Dream* and the clowns who were to act in it.

A little later Cocteau was writing to Gleizes in New York:

Cocteau to Albert Gleizes

[n.d.]

. . . The *Dream* can and must be a marvel — Médrano — orchestra — potpourri of everything we like, directed by Varèse — clowns, etc. I accepted the friendly offer from Lhote* out of sheer fatigue — everyone had gone (Picasso very sick), and your reply was so delayed. A kind of cinema, sublime — Hippolytus in a Phrygian cap and Theseus like a nightmare General French.

Apparently the circus *Midsummer Night's Dream* was still alive when that letter was written, but Cocteau's letter sounds ominous. "Can and must be": the tone is reminiscent of the letters to Stravinsky about *David*.† And indeed, when Cocteau and Satie met for

---

* André Lhote had made designs for costumes and sets, now in the collection of M. Henri Lefèbvre. Gleizes' costume designs are in the Musée de Beaux-Arts of Lyons. On Satie's death his papers were found to include the score of *Five Grimaces for A Midsummer Night's Dream*, which was published in 1929 by Universal Edition, Wien-Leipzig. The whereabouts of Cocteau's version of the play are unknown.

† It was shortly before this, as though in early preparation for seeking to interest

the second time at Valentine's, on November 29, Cocteau spoke to
the composer not of *A Midsummer Night's Dream*, but of another
project — one that Valentine recognized as being a possible revival, much transformed, of *David* itself. What had happened to *A
Midsummer Night's Dream*? For some reason it had begun to die;
and sometime after that letter to Gleizes it did die — a death so
quiet that it has seldom been talked about, and then only vaguely,
as having been due to "wartime conditions." Even Astruc lets it
fade away: "For what reason I don't know, the project came to
nothing." Madame Cocteau wrote later to Valentine that "Jean
suffered with Gémier-Médrano": perhaps there was the kind of
brutal cancellation that is not unusual in the theatre. In any case, *A
Midsummer Night's Dream* was a casualty. But in the letter to
Gleizes Cocteau had mentioned the name — a name that here appears for the first time in Cocteau's writing — of someone who was
to be associated with him and Satie in something more original,
more "modern," than the *Dream* could ever have been.

When Cocteau had written to Valentine Gross in March, 1915,
that he needed the address of Edgar Varèse, and again when he
wrote her on November 26 to ask whether she would invite him
together with André Salmon, he was probably seeking an introduction to the artist whom he really wanted to meet — Pablo Picasso,
who was a friend of both Varèse and Salmon. (Salmon was one of
the group of so-called "Cubist poets," close to Picasso, Apollinaire
and Max Jacob.) Valentine did not know Salmon well enough to
invite him, and it was Varèse who eventually did introduce Cocteau
to Picasso, either at Cocteau's house or at Picasso's — Varèse's account and Cocteau's differ. Picasso was living at 5 rue Schoelcher,
where his windows looked out onto the Montparnasse cemetery.
Many of his friends, among them Braque, Derain, Léger and Apollinaire, were at the front; another, his dealer Kahnweiler, was a
refugee in Bern because of his German nationality; and shortly
after effecting the meeting with Cocteau Varèse himself set sail, on
December 18, for New York. Picasso had recently lost Marcelle
Humbert, the mistress with whom he had lived since 1912 (the
"Eva" of a number of his paintings). She had died of tuberculosis

---

Diaghilev in a Satie-Cocteau project, that Cocteau had approached Misia and written
Stravinsky the letter printed in Chapter 3, pages 108–109. Perhaps he was trying to
forestall the kind of intrigues that had helped kill *David*.

in a Paris hospital, and with Juan Gris, Max Jacob and a few others, Picasso had accompanied her body to the cemetery. For Picasso it was a period of loneliness and depression, and mental and spiritual exhaustion after the melancholy hospital visits to the dying girl, and her pathetic end. Cocteau's words in the letter to Gleizes — "Picasso very sick" — are readily comprehensible. But during the next few weeks Picasso invited Cocteau several times to the studio in the rue Schoelcher. Apparently the moment of depression was a propitious time for a change, and Cocteau *was* a change. His elegance and dandyism and his fountain of Gallic wit and observation contrasted with the international bohemia of Montmartre and Montparnasse. Despite increasing success, Picasso had as yet never lived a worldly life, and Cocteau's sparkle brought welcome distraction.

For Cocteau, it was nothing less than a *coup de foudre*, his meeting with this lithe little Spaniard, with his enormous dark eyes, the famous *mèche* of dark hair, the sensual face, the presence that exuded, along with so much else, an animal charm that was almost palpable. He fell under Picasso's spell and remained there for the rest of his days. It was the capital human encounter of his life, and, along with Stravinsky and the *Rite of Spring*, one of the two or three great artistic revelations. "I have said that Stravinsky was one of my great encounters," he once declared. "Picasso was *the* great encounter for me." "The staircase of the building where I first met Picasso, in the rue Schoelcher, had as its decoration the frieze from the Parthenon,"* he wrote. "How my heart would beat as I hurried up those stairs, never glancing at that bas-relief. Up in Picasso's studio I liked the pieces of Negro sculpture almost as little, but I did like, very much, the use to which their strangeness was put by that least strange of civilized beings. Lying around on the floor were lowly bits of scrap which Picasso was gradually rehabilitating by incorporating them in his works. Picasso has much more admiration for what he can make use of than for the finished product. From him I learned to waste less time gaping open-mouthed at things that are of no use to me, and to understand that a ditty sung by a street-singer, if listened to for what one can get out of it, may

---

* "This atrocious frieze climbs all the way up Picasso's staircase," Cocteau wrote to Valentine Gross on a postcard showing the frieze. "It brings home the sad fate of official sculpture."

prove more rewarding than *Götterdämmerung*." To fortify friendship with this most sacred of all monsters — so he immediately
recognized him to be — Cocteau staged a bizarre charade. On his
second visit, when he doffed his trench coat he revealed that he had
come wearing a harlequin costume — a tribute to Picasso's harlequin pictures. Picasso was pleased, and Cocteau left the costume
behind. (It appears in harlequin pictures painted in 1923.)

Picasso had never designed theatre sets or costumes, nor had any
of the artists who were his friends. Diaghilev, although constantly
modernizing his repertory, either knew nothing of the Cubists or
cared nothing for them. Montmartre and Montparnasse stayed
away from the Diaghilev productions. Cocteau, at *The Rite of
Spring*, had noticed "a particular feature of the audience — the
absence, with one or two exceptions, of young painters and the
painters they studied with. I learned much later that some of them
stayed away because they were ignorant of the Diaghilev pageants
(Diaghilev had never made any effort to attract them), and others
out of reverse snobbery and disapproval of anything deluxe."
Thoughts of that kind, perhaps nothing more definite as yet, must
have accompanied Cocteau on his visits to Picasso. Probably it was
quickly apparent to him that if there was ever to be collaboration
between him and this man who for some reason he had chosen to
seek out — later he spoke of their meeting as having been "inevitable, written in the stars" — it would necessitate the absence of all
other painters. (Perhaps he had come to the same realization about
Satie and other composers.) This would exclude Gleizes and Lhote,
whom Picasso chose to consider mere followers and imitators of
himself and Braque. Cocteau was to continue to correspond with
Gleizes throughout the latter's wartime sojourns in New York, Barcelona and New York again, and later he was to ask Lhote to illustrate one of his books; but from now on there is never a mention of
A Midsummer Night's Dream and their collaboration.

Gradually Cocteau was coming to a realization. He "understood
that there existed in Paris an artistic right and an artistic left,
which were ignorant or disdainful of each other for no valid reason
and which it was perfectly possible to bring together. It was a question of converting Diaghilev to modern painting, and to convert the
modern painters, especially Picasso, to the sumptuous, decorative
aesthetic of the ballet; of coaxing the Cubists out of their isolation,

persuading them to abandon their hermetic Montmartre folklore of pipes, packages of tobacco, guitars and old newspapers; of not giving the impression of wanting them to return to the easy cheapness of Fauvism, which already had a very bad reputation and would eventually turn into Vlaminck's 'strong' painting of the twenties. . . . The discovery of a middle-of-the-road solution attuned to the taste for luxury and pleasure, to the revived cult of 'French clarity' that was springing up in Paris even before the end of the war — such was the history of *Parade*."

Since *A Midsummer Night's Dream* wouldn't do, it was necessary to look elsewhere. By the end of 1915, Cocteau did not yet know what would turn up. Might *David* be somehow revived, in new form? But there had to be a delay. His military situation demanded it. In March, 1915 he had been called up for active duty, after all, with an artillery regiment, only to be plucked out, two weeks later, and made a clerk in the Quartermaster Corps — a post he apparently occupied in a purely nominal way while editing the last numbers of *Le Mot*. (Perhaps the authorities considered the editing of such a journal a sufficient form of war service, even if Cocteau himself did not.) Now, on November 13, 1915, undoubtedly at his own instigation, he was released from the Quartermaster Corps "at the request of the Société Française de Secours aux Blessés," and he prepared to begin another stint of ambulance service.

Etienne de Beaumont, Flanders, The Beginnings of Parade *(1915–1916)*

To see photographs of Comte Etienne de Beaumont and to inquire into his personality and behavior lead one to the conclusion that for Cocteau this friend served in many ways as a model, a model in life, as he was later to serve the young Raymond Radiguet as his model for a character in a novel, *Le Bal du Comte d'Orgel*. A model, for Cocteau, of aquiline, aristocratic appearance (especially later in Cocteau's life, when silvery or bluish hair was appropriate); of exquisite manners, of taste and flair and frivolity; of *bien-pensant* but very French Catholicism; of obsession with perpetual youth; of homosexuality at once overt and discreet, much of it sublimated in benevolent artistic activity with attractive artists. If Cocteau frequently failed to live up to one or another aspect of his model, it was because Cocteau was himself an artist, genuine and compulsive: creativity drove him. Physically, Beaumont was taller, more imposing than Cocteau, but he was no creator.

He was a balletomane, and Cocteau had met him before the war, probably at Misia's or at the ballet. Five years older than Cocteau, he belonged to an old family from Touraine, the Bonnin de la Bonninière de Beaumont, and had married a woman more cultivated, more serious, wealthier and older than himself, Edith de Taisne, of a noble family originally Flemish but whose Brittany branch, to which she belonged, had never taken steps to have its title to nobility recognized in France. An affection that many found strangely touching united the Beaumonts; the countess had several unsuccessful pregnancies; they were always thought of as a united couple. They entertained lavishly and delightfully in their palatial eighteenth-century house with a large garden in the rue Duroc, inherited from the count's mother, born Boisgelin; there was usually music, both ancient and modern, and the guests were of the artistic and social *gratin* — vulgarians and other bores being excluded. People said that the count in his mansion thought of himself as Louis XIV at Versailles; he liked to dress up and give splendid balls; the countess consented to lead a worldly life out of affection for him, but left to herself she read and translated Greek poetry. (In 1950 she published a translation of Sappho, with illustrations by Marie Laurencin, who lived for a time in an annex to the Beaumonts' *hôtel*.) The countess was witty and elegant and pleasing to look at, but reserved — "pure, untouchable," people have said of her.

Very early in the war, only a little later than Misia's expeditions, Etienne de Beaumont, exempted, like Cocteau, from military service, bothered his friends in high places until he had permission to organize, under the auspices of the French Red Cross, an ambulance service of a kind that was made particularly necessary by the lightness of French artillery. At that time "the French army shelled its enemies at close quarters and cared for its wounded far from the battlefield," says Bernard Faÿ, who was one of Beaumont's early volunteers, "for having no heavy artillery it could use only the '75, and there being no well-equipped mobile hospitals, the wounded were forced to travel twenty, thirty, sometimes forty kilometers to find a surgeon. . . . The 'Auxiliary Convoys' sought to transform the divisionary mobile first-aid stations into surgical centers, with antiseptic, electrically lit operating rooms and X-ray equipment. Such was Etienne de Beaumont's plan."

Edith de Beaumont accompanied her husband on some of his earliest ambulance expeditions, which took them into Belgium, to the region of Furnes-Coxyde-Nieuport, beyond the point where the Franco-Belgian border reaches the sea. In October, 1914, this was the scene of the ferocious battle of the Yser river; the sector continued active; and under the date of January 9, 1915, Jacques-Emile Blanche writes in his *Cahiers d'un Artiste* of the Beaumonts before, during and after the battle:

E. de B. and his wife have completed another month of duty at Furnes. Now the countess longs for some rest, and to forget the hell she has just left. An hour after her departure, the small inn where she had been staying was demolished by shells. A month of short rations, cold, lack of light, close to the Channel, Tauben, zeppelins and shrapnel constantly overhead; impassable roads, impossible ambulance work. The B's automobile had to pass over the bodies of two artillery horses, a mass of red flesh, still steaming after being hit by a shell. . . .

The B's learned of Joffre's famous proclamation, which was not released to the public. This was to be *the* great offensive. Our friends were ordered to expect wounded at six in the morning. They retired early, and were wakened by a sound like that of a tidal wave or a mountain torrent. It was automobile engines and wheels on cobblestones. B. rose. A string of Paris buses, lights out and curtains drawn, were carrying into battle hundreds of sleeping children. . . .

B. bared his head as the buses passed — blacker than so many hearses. He knew the road so well! They would continue straight ahead, then turn right, to the nearby point where the sleepers would get out, stretching and yawning. B. counted the seconds.

Scarcely was B. at his post, with his stretchers and his aides, when a few remnants of that youth began to return. The hecatomb had been in vain. No way of taking the offensive. The

boys who had just had their baptism of fire said that they had
been sleeping peacefully in the buses, thinking they were going to some depot. Their fate was to be shoveled into the furnace like so much coke.

The B's and two other members of the expedition came yesterday to Marie M's, and they were unanimous in their testimony. It is difficult to know what to think of these gay young
people, once again in their civilian clothes, as one listens to
them around the tea table: they devour little cakes, and they
describe hell. Just as with the wounded, an expression will
now and then come over their faces that is like a cloud in a
clear sky. They will suddenly break off speaking, as though
they were afraid of what they were about to say. The most
marvelous thing is the way they take it for granted that after
leaving the banks of the Yser for their house in Paris they
should return once again to the battlefield with no loss of good
spirits.

Et. de B. is courageous, even reckless, the life and soul of
the group: he is one of those in whom gallantry is a part of
good breeding. He remains the same under shrapnel as under
the chandelier of a ballroom. He will leave Paris the day after
tomorrow just as effortlessly as he arrived yesterday. From the
moment he organized his service, it has been a model for other
volunteer groups. His team has been mentioned in dispatches.

Toward the end of 1915 Beaumont organized his "Convoi Automobiles No. 2," and it was with that second unit that Cocteau, interrupting his series of visits to Satie and Picasso, set out from Paris.
Because the Beaumont ambulance units included shower baths,
people have laughed at Beaumont and Cocteau for spending part of
the war "giving baths to soldiers": some have likened it to Cocteau's participation in Nijinsky's rubdowns. There was a certain
amount of photographing of naked soldiers in the mobile showers;
and in Cocteau's poem "La Douche," in the series *Discours du
Grand Sommeil,* he celebrates both black and white bathers and
does not hide what was ever to be one of his chief preoccupations.
(*"Je ne crois guère aux hommes de petite verge,"* he wrote to Ned
Rorem in 1950.) Nevertheless — and apart from the fact that the

spectacle of soldiers bathing has over centuries had a recurring appeal to artists (one thinks of pictures by Michelangelo, by Pollaiuolo, by Sidney Nolan, and of the Second World War poem by F. T. Prince) — the ambulances went as close to the front as possible and alleviated the lot of the entrenched troops. By Christmas Cocteau and his teammates were living in a partially destroyed villa in Coxyde, near the extreme western end of the Allied trenches — "that city that wound, just below the surface, from one edge of France to the other," Cocteau called them. Close by were the North Sea dunes and the mouth of the Yser. The sector (Secteur Postal 131) was held by a patchwork of Allied troops: regular French, a battalion of French Marines, a British division, North African Zouaves, Senegalese sharpshooters. By now the region had quieted down. The Allies desisted from shelling German-held Ostend in return for the German courtesy of not shelling La Panne, where the Belgian royal family was still living; but there was occasional bombardment from gunboats offshore, and night shelling kept the air noisy and the sky bright. Short-range firing from trench to trench made it perilous to show oneself above the frontline parapet. On Christmas Eve there was a brief truce, and the Germans could be heard singing *"O Tannenbaum."*

After Christmas, Cocteau wrote letters (all of them seen by the censor) to several friends, hinting at where he was and telling what he liked and what he disliked about his new life.

Cocteau to Valentine Gross
[postmark January 12, 1916]

Ma chère Valentine,
Your letter is *good* ("He saw that it was good") — all intuition. At Nieuport, Dostoevsky and Whitman fill the periods of respite, which are a great strain, wound-up as we are. The Red + group is abject . . . They hate me and gang up on me because I refuse to laugh, to horse around and joke. Faithful to my system, I "coincide"; and coincidence with what is taking place is not conducive to fun — their kind of fun — my kind is over their heads. A different planet — Uranus . . . The Zouaves, the Arabs, are something else — they love me, welcome me, give me brass rings, feel vaguely that I

would "bear witness." Trenches in the dunes — Venice —
catacombs — sand, silence — what silence! A blue silence,
full of traps and of safety — the silence of an aquarium or a
balloon. Dugouts full of Arabs — showers of stars. (Sea-
coast.) Did you get the letter in which I told you about my
Christmas Eve ten meters from "the other city of trenches,"
aluminum stars, sharpshooters standing erect like the Magi,
the cease-fire? Dear Valentine, I am sorry that you scorn poetry: but it is true that the most beautiful roses may lack
scent, and that no pearl is perfectly round. Write soon . . .

It was a novelty for him to be disliked: "This is the first time that
I have had people hate me, despise me, ignore me," he wrote to
Madeleine LeChevrel, "— a real martyrdom for someone who is
lavish with his affection and weeps because the very seals in the zoo
aren't crazy about him." To Edith de Beaumont, in a long letter
listing the other members of his unit by name and characterizing
them in savage detail — he calls them *"papous"* — "Papuans" —
and says that he and a certain Pierre Bouvet whom he likes are "on
a little island in the midst of unbearable people such as I never
imagined existed" — he adds: "I will *tell* you, *viva voce*, about my
Christmas Eve. Too beautiful to spoil — never will I forget any of
it, but especially at one in the morning, eight meters from the
Boches, when I made an imperceptible sound stepping in water, the
gesture and expression on the face of the Senegalese sharpshooter
turning and watching me, a finger to his lips. It was marvelous, I
can't say why — that watchdog — one of the Magi — at the edge
of a silence peopled with men and cannon."

To the Abbé Mugnier and to André Gide he wrote Christmas
letters that are like "personalized gifts," calculated to suit the
tastes of each recipient. To the Abbé Mugnier: "I thought of you
all Christmas Eve, in the front lines. Silence of Bethlehem, smell of
the manger." To André Gide: "You would like it here — trenches
Arabian Venice at Luna Park — Senegalese sharpshooters do the
belly dance and Zouaves give me prehistoric rings. Peace of mind
is not to be sought in the neutral countries, but 'in the game,' as
Whitman sings."

Soon he was writing to Astruc on behalf of the Zouaves:

Cocteau to Gabriel Astruc

[n.d.]

Mon cher Astruc,

Do me and the Zouaves a great favor. Here's what it's about: the Zouave-Senegalese sharpshooter sector is organizing a mobile theatre for the rest periods between shifts. Our Astruc is a man named Bossuet! We have a few actors, but need stars. It would be a very good deed to get the cooperation of Dranem or other stars (ask Gémier — he will like the idea) and the authorization for them to come here to the front. Marvelous trip, marvelous audience. A woman — like Flory (or Mistinguett) — would have a triumph, but it seems that women would be forbidden these volcanic regions of ours. I ask your active help. This letter is being written in an Algerian *guitoune** among the "tribe of Zouaves," who send you their greetings.†

But amid the belly dancing and other merrymaking of the troops so close to the dance of death, Cocteau's chief thoughts were on a different ballet — the one for whose sake he had been courting Satie and Picasso even before he himself was clear as to what its precise nature would be. In a letter of February 2 to Valentine, in which he speaks of "deadly cold — snow that doesn't fall — huge rats that sit up and beg and that we train like little dogs," he says "Not a word from Picasso — he has forgotten how to write since he has taken to *collage.*" (The reference may be either to new pictures by Picasso or to the new friend with whom he was *"collé."*) Etienne de Beaumont had apparently expressed some understanding of Cocteau's aspirations, and Cocteau wrote him on February 21, referring in Zarathustran terms to his past "mistakes" and present goals.

Cocteau to Etienne de Beaumont

[postmark February 21, 1916]

Mon cher Etienne,

Thank you — you are as always — your eye is touched, and your heart *sees.* . . . "You have made danger your

---

* *"Guitoune"*: in Algeria, a hut; at the front, a dugout.

† For an anecdote concerning Cocteau and the African troops, see Appendix III.

trade," says Zarathustra to the tightrope dancer, and the mob
cares nothing for the tightrope dancer or for Zarathustra —
but the dancer is in mortal agony, and Zarathustra cares nothing for the mob . . . I am not mistaken *now:* I was mistaken
then. Just so, the *Rite of Spring*, the very peak of the ballet,
was regarded by the audience as a decline. I shouldn't have
tried to inveigle tourists up my mountain, nor asthmatics
either — I should have climbed up *alone* to join those who
live on the mountain. Today the tourists gasp and turn away
from me, and those who live on the mountain take me for a
tourist, with lungs a little better than the rest. Nevertheless, the
work progresses. . . .

To Valentine he wrote on March 18, glorying in his participation
in the war and telling of approaching leave: "How bored Gleizes
must be, far away from the *show* — on some 58th floor, while *life*,
the deep wellspring of modernity, is here, in a hole in the ground. I
shall be 'among thee' at the sign of the Fish . . ." By that he meant
about April 1. Sometime early in April he did arrive in Paris, and
it was during this leave that he began to conceive the "work" more
fully. He himself later wrote "The idea came to me during a leave
in April, 1915 [*sic*, for 1916] (I was at that time with the army),
while listening to Satie play his "Morceaux en forme de poire"
(four hands with Ricardo Viñes). A sort of telepathy inspired the
two of us with a wish to collaborate." It was on that occasion, he
said, that he "told Satie what he should write" — an arrogant way
of speaking that Satie was later to return a thousandfold. But it was
also during this leave that Cocteau began to speak of the "work" as
"Parade," and wrote on the cover of one of his notebooks a definition of the word *"parade"* from the Dictionnaire Larousse: "a burlesque scene played outside a sideshow booth to entice spectators
inside." Thus it is clear that the "work" was indeed conceived as
being a transformation of *David,** as Valentine Gross had heard it
discussed between Cocteau and Satie the previous autumn; so that
Cocteau's saying that the idea had come to him during his 1916

---

* In a letter that Cocteau had drafted, but perhaps not sent, to Misia Sert about
David in 1914 he had actually used the word *"parade"* and made *David* sound much
like what *Parade* was to be: "It is not a dance, but an act performed by an acrobat in
a traveling circus. It is a short piece, not a play, just a *parade. . . . C'est du music-hall.*
Three acrobatic numbers."

leave is but one aspect of the truth. On April 25, Satie indicated to
Valentine Gross that he did not know what Cocteau had in mind —
"I hope that the admirable Cocteau will not use my old pieces.
Let's do something new, no?" — but on the same day he sent Coc-
teau an enthusiastic postcard:

Erik Satie to Cocteau

Tuesday. *Cher ami,*
    Forgive me — sick — grippe. Impossible send word
    except by telepathy. All right for tomorrow. Valentine
    Gross tells me marvelous things. You are the *idea* man.
    Bravo! . . .

Before rejoining his ambulances, Cocteau sent to Satie in his
suburb of Arcueil "a big batch of work," a sheaf of notes and rough
drafts. These consisted in part of free-association jottings inspired
by three characters whom he had invented to play the "burlesque
scene outside the sideshow booth" — "the Chinese magician," "the
American girl," and "the Acrobat." He intended that the dancing
of those characters would be accompanied not only by Satie's score
but also by words and phrases or mere sounds, which were to blend
with the music or stand out against it, and his ideas for these words
and sounds, too, Cocteau jotted down. "Save these pages," he wrote
on one of them to Satie. "I have no copy."
    During his leave he saw Picasso several times, and began to be
acquainted with Montparnasse, a territory hitherto unknown to
him. "This morning, pose for Picasso in his studio," he wrote on
May 1 to Valentine Gross, who was visiting her mother at Boulogne-
sur-Mer. "He is beginning an 'Ingres' head of me — very suitable
for portrait of young author to accompany posthumous works after
premature death." That 1916 portrait drawing of Cocteau by Picasso is a famous one, showing him in an army-type uniform: it
is a new uniform, he tells Valentine — whether by Poiret, whom
Misia credited with being the designer of its predecessor, is not
known. From now on Cocteau was to say a great deal about modern
art, and some of it wittily and pithily, though his vision was not of
the surest. In 1916 he was repeating a cliché that called — and
still calls — Picasso's naturalistic line drawings "Ingres-like";
and in 1923, when in an essay on Picasso he said that they were *not*

Ingres-like, one suspects that it was from Picasso himself that he got
the new direction. In his promotion of modern artists he was to resemble his fellow poet Guillaume Apollinaire, almost ten years his
senior, who, with equally unsure eye, but with considerable flair
and enthusiasm, had written his *Cubist Painters* in 1913.

That spring of 1916, Apollinaire was in hospital in Paris, being
treated for a head wound suffered in the trenches on March 17. (He
had been exempt from military service, being non-French, but had
enlisted and insisted on being sent to the front lines.) Cocteau, in
his first recorded mention of the author of *Alcools*, speaks
strangely. "Picasso urged me to go with him to the Italian Hospital
to see Apollinaire," he wrote Valentine Gross. "I like his taste for
bringing people together — proof of richness of heart — but I feel
that the misunderstanding between Apollinaire and me, and the
difference between what we think of each other, are too great for me
to be willing to rush into a meeting." That might mean that Cocteau
had not yet met Apollinaire, that he admired him by reputation (he
had been a subscriber to Apollinaire's magazine, *Les Soirées de
Paris*), but hesitated out of self-esteem to meet him because he had
been told that he himself had been unfavorably spoken of by Apollinaire, or suspected that he had been. If such is the case, his
refusal is understandable, and in fact it is quite possible that for
Apollinaire — the poet who had had the genius to take *"la belle
dame Poésie"* out of her outmoded Symbolist trappings and "put
her in an automobile," as Pierre de Massot phrased it, the friend
for years of Picasso, Braque, Vlaminck, Derain, Max Jacob, André
Salmon and other artists of the Butte — Cocteau was still the
prince frivole that he was seen to be, from another angle, by Valentine Gross's serious Wednesday visitors from the *Nouvelle Revue
Française*.*

Now, in Montparnasse, Picasso introduced Cocteau to other artists. Modigliani drew and painted his portrait; after initial suspi-

---

* A clue to Apollinaire's feelings about Cocteau may be contained in a letter written
by Apollinaire to Bakst in Rome, April 17, 1917. In it Apollinaire says: "I will . . .
look after Cocteau's book [*Le Potomak*] at the same publishers [Mercure de France].
I am sure that I will have it . . . published this year. I will write him one of these
days about what steps to take." But Apollinaire, who was decidedly *persona grata* at
the Mercure, made either no moves or ineffectual ones, for the Mercure did not publish
Le Potomak.

cion he won, and was always to keep, the friendship of Max Jacob,
poet, painter, formerly dealer in modern pictures, who had been
converted from Judaism to Christianity after seeing visions of
Christ on the wall of his room in Montmartre. Picasso's company
during that leave of April–May 1916 was crucial for Cocteau in
facilitating his further emergence from the exotic, *Dieu Bleu* atmosphere of the Ballets Russes. He himself discusses it *viva voce*,
with some of his characteristic exaggerations, in a recording:

> There were two fronts: there was the war front, and then in
> Paris there was what might be called the Montparnasse front
> — the scene of what is now called *l'époque héroïque*. There
> was continual coming and going between the war front and the
> art-war front in Montparnasse, which was where I met all the
> men who helped me emerge from the famous Right in which I
> had been living. When Mauriac writes "You left us without
> looking back," I reply: "I left you without looking back be-
> cause I loved you, and if I had looked back I shouldn't have
> left you — had I looked back I'd have been turned into a pil-
> lar of SUGAR." I was on the way to what seemed to me the in-
> tense life — toward Picasso, toward Modigliani, toward Satie,
> a little later toward the young men who were to become "Les
> Six." Nevertheless, I was a "rookie." All those men had given
> proof of their Leftism, and I had to do the same: I was like
> Tiresias [*sic*] in *Troilus and Cressida,* suspect on the Right,
> which I was leaving, and suspect on the Left, where I was ar-
> riving. This new solitude was very painful for me, but I held
> on, and the man who made it possible for me to stick at the
> controls was Picasso. Picasso at once considered me a friend,
> and he took me around to all the groups. He introduced me to
> the painters and the poets, and new as I was in those surround-
> ings his authority was such that I could quickly make contact
> with people who might have been slow to accept me if it had
> not been for him. There was no politics at that time, no politi-
> cal Left or Right; there was only a Left and Right in art, and
> what we were full of was the patriotism of art. To such a point
> was this the case that when a journalist asked me who were the
> great French artists, I answered, without thinking that I was

mentioning a Spaniard, an Italian, and Russians, "Why, Picasso, Modigliani, Lipchitz, Stravinsky." *

That "heroic epoque" of Montparnasse, with its artists of many nationalities, had come into existence shortly before the war, and Apollinaire, who had moved from Montmartre to St. Germain-des-Prés (halfway to Montparnasse) in 1913, had celebrated its earlier aspect in his *Cubist Painters;* but Cocteau, as one of the most prominent bridgers of the gap between Left and Right, in revealing to the fashionable Right Bank world the artists who came to be known as the School of Paris, is a presence that hovers over many of today's great collections of modern art, over the fortune of many an art dealer — and even of an occasional artist. In 1916 he was just beginning to play that role. "Do you know Léonce (!) Rosenberg, who buys Cubist pictures?" he wrote in his letter of May 1 to Valentine Gross. "A dealer, who actually praises 'style' and 'the new freedom of the modern painter.' I like him, as I like everything that is good. . . . In brief, a man, a Jew who buys paintings for high prices and isn't a fashion designer or a dilettante. It's the

---

* On the record, Cocteau goes on to say, about Modigliani: "Modigliani did my portrait, which is now owned by Mr. Pearlman. Modigliani wanted to give it to me, but I did not want him to. 'Won't you sell it to me?' I asked him. So he sold it to me for *cent sous* — five francs. But to take away so large a picture an open cab was needed, and I didn't have the wherewithal to hire one. So it remained a long time in Kisling's studio. Kisling owed eleven francs to the owner of the Café Rotonde; he asked him whether he would take the portrait instead of the eleven francs, and he did. For a long time it hung above the banquette in the Rotonde, and then began that astonishing voyage that took it to England, where it was sold for seven million francs, and then to America, where it was sold for seventeen million. It is in America now."

Modigliani was painting at that time in Kisling's studio. A pencil sketch for his portrait of Cocteau, bearing the inscription, "I, the undersigned, author of this drawing, swear never to get drunk again for the duration of the war: Modigliani," is the property of Monsieur Edouard Dermit. Other pencil sketches of Cocteau by Modigliani also exist. There is also an oil portrait of Cocteau by Kisling, done about the same time, showing him in the same chair as in the portrait by Modigliani; and the collection of Madame Alec Weisweiller contains a portrait drawing of Cocteau by Kisling. Cocteau is said to have once spoken of the portrait as being "diabolical," and said he considered it proof that Modigliani had "detested" him.

It was with Modigliani that Cocteau first met the poet Pierre Reverdy, who later allowed himself to be paraphrased as follows: "Modigliani was the only true portraitist of the group, serious and gifted. He flattered no one, including P. R. He painted the portrait of Cocteau in 1916, in Kisling's studio in Montparnasse above the Rotonde, on the top floor. It was on that occasion that P. R. first met Cocteau. Cocteau talked without stopping — it was the same sound as the rain, which was all the while beating on the skylight. Nobody paid much attention to what he was saying. For P. R. and [Blaise] Cendrars, who was also present, Cocteau was merely the youngest of the Rostands. He was also LaGandara, Jacques-Emile Blanche, the Ballets Russes . . ."

kind of folly one likes. Picasso wonders whether the man may be putting on an act, pretending to be an utter idiot. But he is a shy man, a lover of Chinese and Japanese art, and I think rather that he must have the homing pigeon's (and the dealer's!) unfailing sense of direction, which is making him follow in Max Jacob's footsteps." Valentine knew quite well that Léonce Rosenberg (brother of Paul Rosenberg, who later became one of Picasso's dealers) had been buying Cubist pictures since 1912: despite his acquaintance with Gleizes, Cocteau was new to all this, undergoing a new "moulting." His dual frequenting of the salons of the Right and the milieux of the Left at this time is amusingly illustrated in a letter to Valentine of May 3 — one of the last letters of his leave. "Yesterday, at Edith Wharton's, run-in between Anna de Noailles and me. Sharp exchange and near blows about Claudel. . . . Dear Valentine — a letter from Satie. 'Very marvelous,' he says. Does that mean enthusiasm, in his faun's language? Try to find out."

His leave ended on May 6. Valentine, still on a visit to her mother, learned when his train to Flanders would pass through Boulogne-sur-Mer, and was on the station platform, but he was not allowed to leave his car, and could only make signs to her — apparently not even speak to her — through the window until the train moved on. "Your dear face, seen from the train!" he wrote her on May 9. "I keep you with me as a talisman." He found that he was now assigned to a new sector (Secteur Postal 129): it was in the same region as the last, but there were no Zouaves or Senegalese or Marines, only regular French troops — provincial bourgeois and peasants in uniform. His morale promptly slumped. "Gone to pieces overnight. I suppose *Parade* is just a dream — impossible to imagine that I'm anything but a frozen wretch jogging here and there. I'm swallowing my tears." On the twelfth he sent her a Gleizes-like Cubist drawing, but was still depressed: "Worried about *Parade.* — Drying up? Lack of verve." "Horribly sick," he wrote on the fifteenth. The regular French troops were a bore after the "delicious mixture of daydreaming and slapstick" he had so enjoyed in his earlier "contact Zouave-Montmartre-Islam": "Where are the Zouaves and the Marines, so careless with their money and so prodigal with their hearts?" Besides, these "men in blue," the "poilus," hated Parisians and even spat on the ambulances. Cocteau's explanation was that for peasants an automobile symbolized a tourist speeding along country roads annihilating chickens and other farmyard assets, but Valentine held Cocteau and some of his colleagues responsible for the soldiers' hostility: "Jean scandalized the regular military," she once said, "what with his lovely clean uniform — navy blue, with brass buttons, like a naval officer's." "Dear Valentine," he went on, "encourage me — I no longer dare have any faith in *Le Cap*,* in Satie — I'm back in a state of dreary low spirits — impossible to work — I stagger along these cold roads sneezing and discouraged." In the next letter he reports good news: "An admirable letter from Satie. Long live Cocteau, he says. Nothing could touch me more." But his spirits continued to fluctuate.

Cocteau to Valentine Gross

May 28, 1916
5 h.

Ma chère Valentine,
Dune dune dune cave cave cave cano cano canon
   Ratodromes
   Your letter — miraculous. You should come yourself, like the true angel you are, long-throated, great-winged, flying to me among the Tauben and the seraphim of the '75's. You *are* my angel, my good angel, watching over me, stimulating me. I am wandering bewildered on a planet of iconoclasts, where nothing, no one but you, ever speaks of *building* — everyone is destroying, smashing, wasting — sowing bile and death.

7 h.

   Back from dinner at the battery. Watched Boches through telescope — sea H. Heine — phosphorescent waves — purring searchlights — stars — secret machines — Terrific beauty — horrible but irresistible, like gypsies. Impossible to live anywhere else. I kiss your hands. . . .

---

* "*Le Cap*," thus mentioned for the first time, is a long poem, *Le Cap de Bonne-Espérance*, that he had conceived about Roland Garros and his aerial exploits and on which he was to work for several years: it would be published only in 1919. In his next letter to Valentine there is another first mention — that of a second long war poem, or series of poems, *Secteur 131* (a nostalgic memory of his old sector, chiefly concerned with the Marines, the Senegalese and the Zouaves), which was to take him even longer: it would be published in full only in 1924, under the title *Discours du Grand Sommeil*.

P.S. I long to follow a coastal trench that would come out at Boulogne in your house — hold your hands, tell you how grateful I am. I picture you in your long hall — sirens — wax in your ears like Ulysses, bound to the mast. May Satie have the same idea!

And on the thirty-first Valentine received a telegram marked (as a wartime security device) *"sans origine"*:

COMING SPEND TEN DAYS RESERVE SIMPLE ROOM NEAR YOU
WILL ARRIVE TOMORROW THURSDAY ELEVEN THIRTY COCTEAU

From her mother's house in the rue Aumont, where she often worked with "wax in her ears like Ulysses," to deaden the sound of the constant air-raid sirens and airplanes, Valentine found Cocteau a room in the Hotel Dervaux, British military headquarters, and through a friend in the mayor's office obtained permission for him to spend his ten days in Boulogne, whose dangerous importance as one of the principal Channel ports put it out of bounds to ordinary visitors. "Rather than come to Paris, with its barracks and Ritzians, I am resting in Boulogne," he wrote to Etienne de Beaumont. "Sunny balcony, pyjamas, plush armchair . . . Main street climbs like a procession toward the house of the charming Valentine. On curving staircase Scotch giant, kilt hiked up, showing everything except the decent parts, polishing ox-blood boots, watched by bedazzled elderly chambermaid." He was struck by the beauty and the lively complexions of the British troops, thousands of whom were continually passing through Boulogne on their way from England to the front or to England on leave, giving the town the air of a strange, shifting dream. "The English," he said, "are the proof that marble gives a wrong idea of the color of Greek faces." The hotel maid "cared for him like a son," and Valentine and her mother allowed him to make an "ogre" of himself at the tea table and to pound their old piano so joyously that the ivories flew from the keys. To the Gleizes he wrote from Boulogne that the war made him feel alone and sad, "amid the spectacle of destruction — madmen using all their ingenuity to destroy the old fables, but trampling on the new — iconoclastic gorillas — a death factory." He was finishing *Le Cap de Bonne-Espérance*, he told them, *Secteur 131* was giving him great trouble, and he was preparing a "surprise": that last was clearly all that he was willing to tell them about *Parade*.

In Boulogne a reassuring letter reached him from Satie.

Erik Satie to Cocteau

June 8, 1916

Cher ami,

For heaven's sake stop worrying, don't be nervous. I am at work. Let me do it my own way. I warn you, you won't see the thing until *October*. Not a note before that. I tell you so under oath. Will it be all right if I mention that you are the author of the scenario? I need to. Madame Edwards is all for the project. I told her that she would have to wait until October. I want to do a good job — very much so. You *must* trust me. If you come to Paris, let me know. Greetings to Valentine Gross and yourself.

Satie had been flattering Misia. Writing to her with a request that she be a patroness of a Granados-Satie concert that had been arranged by "Matisse, Picasso and other worthies," and was to be given on May 30, he added: "What you told me at your house about the Russian Ballet has already had its effect. I'm working on a thing that I propose to show you soon — it is dedicated to you in its conception and its composition. All that, chère Madame, is giving me the greatest pleasure. You *are* a magician, aren't you?" Thus did Satie pretend to Misia that the new "thing" on which he was working had been directly inspired by words of hers — a wise precaution considering her suspiciousness of any work that she could not persuade herself had originated around her table or in her salon. The result was: "Madame Edwards is all for the project." But Madame Edwards was notoriously capable of being an Indian giver of her support: the collaborators knew they had to tread carefully. Cocteau let Satie tell her that he was the author of the scenario, and drafted a letter to her himself.

Cocteau to Misia Sert

[n.d.]

Chère Misia,

A letter from Erik Satie absolves me from my vow of silence. One evening in your house, by thrilling coincidence,

Satie asked me to collaborate with him at the very moment I was about to ask him the same. That little miracle happened in the presence of Valentine Gross, who thus learned of the matter. I kept the secret until I was sure that the work was well on the way, having suffered from being overhasty with Igor. This was also Satie's explicit wish. Moreover, though nothing is left of *David*, *David*'s failure surely served to make possible the birth of the new work — there are mysteries that are beyond human understanding. You will be the first to hear it, so I am telling you about it at once — dropping my incognito (*for you alone*) the moment Satie asks me. We won't take less than your "love" — mere "approval" would kill us poor Arcueil-Anjou minstrels. It is a very short work, which resembles the composer — everything goes on behind the eyeglasses.*

To Anna de Noailles he wrote from Boulogne, saying nothing about Valentine (wisely concealing from one beautiful woman artist that he was visiting another) but describing the city as one that "might be in China or on the moon," so strange was its heavily British wartime atmosphere: he called the Highlanders "the Royal Scots Peliades in their little skirts." "Invoke the god," he begged her, "be the sybil of the rue Scheffer, learn the date of the Peace, be an oracle of calm. A war isn't like cloth — it isn't good just because it lasts forever."

"How can I thank you?" he wrote Valentine from his tent, after rejoining his ambulance. "Stupid to thank a rose for its fragrance and the sky for its stars. You were born marvelous, as others are born ugly or bad. I inhale you and feel better."

His unit was more "suburban-minded" than ever: he was being

---

* It is not certain that this letter was ever sent. It is not among those which Misia prints in her memoirs. Two slightly different versions exist, both formerly among the papers of the late Valentine Gross Hugo, to whom Cocteau apparently submitted the drafts for approval. Each bears a postscript indicating that he was unwilling to divulge to Misia the name he had found for his work. In one draft, clearly the earlier, the postscript reads: "Since the title is not definite, I leave it vague"; in the other, "Since the title is not definite I leave the ? [a question mark] of the Maîtres de New-York" — perhaps a reference to the symbol of interrogation favored by Marcel Duchamp and the other beginning New York Dadaists. Valentine once told the present author that she herself had sent Misia a lying letter, composed by Cocteau, assuring her that it was at Misia's house rather than in her own that *Parade* had really been conceived. Perhaps that took the place of anything signed by Cocteau himself.

criticized, he says, for taking solitary walks with his pet nanny goat, his *"petite chèvre d'Églogue."* (Valentine was later told one of the supposed reasons for the objection: the goat's leash was of government-issue bandage gauze, which was in short supply.)

Then suddenly, in mid-June, the ambulances were called elsewhere — given less than twenty-four hours to move. "Leaving the sector," he wrote Valentine on June 15. "We're wanted at Headquarters. I am deeply sad to be leaving the sea that has you on its shore. Turmoil — preparations for move. Terribly depressing. Staying a few days at C[oxyde] to keep an eye on the showers. Incredible exodus, with me thinking only of the goat." And the next day, in a letter which tells also of a performance recently given behind the lines by a theatrical troupe headed by the beautiful star Cecile Sorel,* he tells Valentine: "Don't worry about me. The Marines, the dear Marines, have taken me in, have adopted me just the way I adopted their goat. I'm grazing and sleeping in their quarters. No news of the unit. *Not a word.* I wonder (since they left between 11 P.M. and midnight the night of the move) whether they aren't somewhere in the fourth dimension." What had happened was that preparations were being made for a push on the Somme, and mobile hospitals were being rushed there from quieter areas in the expectation — all too hideously fulfilled — of great casualties to come. Cocteau lived with his "dear Marines" not more than a week; then, summoned to join his unit, he left the Nieuport-Coxyde sector for good. He was to recall the move in his long poem about Sector 131:

> On me rappelle dans la Somme . . .
> C'est ce soir le 22 juin;
> La journée de l'année la plus longue.
> Elle traîne, elle s'attarde,
> Moi aussi, je m'attarde, je traîne.
> Nous n'osons pas nous dire adieu†

He went first to Amiens, to await further orders. "Very frightened — an agonizing wait," he wrote to Valentine from quarters in

---

* See Appendix IV.

† I'm called to the Somme . . . / This is the evening of June 22, / The longest day of the year. / It drags, it lingers, / I, too, linger and drag. / We do not dare say our farewells.

the Hotel de Commerce, and to Madeleine LeChevrel he called the coming battle "the great ball of France, to which we are all invited." By the first week in July he was helping care for the first wounded in the terrible battle of the Somme.

Cocteau's letters from the Somme (Secteur Postal 111) are few — he was there only for the first weeks of the campaign — but they differ in tone from any written earlier in the war: their intensity recalls his descriptions of the wounded in Rheims in 1914. The cannonading and the slaughter were so tremendous that it seemed impossible anyone should survive. "We'll all die," he wrote Madeleine LeChevrel. To Valentine on July 8: "Too dispirited to write. . . . We're living like rangers in a Western — hunting for the dead — horrible deliveries of wretches battered to pulp — blood flows — the very sheds are groaning." Under the shelling the landscape changed before one's eyes. "Whole hills collapse, one upon the other, the crops are cut down by low-flying planes — strange sight, breathtaking, magnificent, stupid." On July 11: "The huge tent is shifted to a new location every five minutes. Dreary pageant of filthy bedding, the front advances, leaving us behind. To see you — to see each other — to see Erik — to see, to *live*, and to *create!*"

But the prospect of seeing Erik Satie and of creating was suddenly threatened by a letter that arrived from Misia in the midst of the shelling, a letter whose text is not available but in which she must have referred very disagreeably indeed to *Parade*. She had written it after learning from Satie that Cocteau was the author of the scenario; and from a few savage words in a letter Cocteau sent Valentine about July 24 — "Poor blacks are dying here. Misia would stuff them and gild them" — and from his careful reply to Misia herself, which Misia prints in her memoirs, one senses how unpleasant and ominous must have been some of her references to the past and present:

Cocteau to Misia Sert

[n.d.]

. . . Satie is an angel (well disguised). . . . I wish you could be as excited about our collaboration as I was the day I told him what he should write. An Anjou evening, unforgettable in its richness, a marvelous, electrifying exchange. I can

see from his postcards that things are going the way I most
want them to. It is *his* drama — and the eternal drama between the audience and the stage — in a form as simple as a
popular print. You know how I love Igor, what a cult I have of
him, how distressed I was about the stain on the lovely snow at
Leysin, and that I may write a book about him. Above all, he
mustn't imagine that I am "grafting" any cuttings of *David*;
David was partly clear, partly confused — some of that came
from myself and some, so to speak, was the result of circumstances. I stumbled on Igor at a time when I was moving, without knowing it, toward Satie, and possibly Satie is at a turn of
the road that will lead me back to Igor. All in all, the Stra-
vinsky-Cocteau venture was awkward and full of misunderstanding. With Satie, all is happy and light. Dear Misia, I am
boring you. . . . The big guns are shooting out great flashes
of heat lightning — groups of wounded Negroes are pouring
in — there is a roar of engines. . . .

The *N.R.F.* set, too, had been trying to influence Satie against
Cocteau, thus further endangering the project. Picasso, who had
made no commitment, was the most uncertain element of all, yet in
some ways the most satisfactory: "I'm not counting on Picasso,"
Cocteau wrote to Valentine in that letter of July 24, "but he has
certainly given me more pleasure than he could ever cause me
pain."
     The next day, Cocteau wrote Valentine what was to be his last
letter from any war zone.

Cocteau to Valentine Gross
[postmark July 25, 1916]

Ma chère Valentine,
     One longs to write you friendship letters the way one writes
love letters — letters full of wisdom and vehemently lucid,
something to please Minerva and Plato and to vex Venus. My
image of you, so sweet, so substantial, stands out against the
ronde of the *Rite* like a ringlet of George Sand's hair un-
curling in a Chopin waltz. This to make you understand that
you are helping me, pursuing me, like a musical motif. . . .
I am "humming" you with my eyes and my mouth. Hard to

explain — delicious phenomenon. Bad letter yesterday. Tear
it up. A storm of shelling was building up. A night of bombs
dropping from the sky, with red flashes lighting the tent. Solitude among volcanoes. . . .

Love   ♡

Jean

Three days later he was in Paris, sending Valentine, the afternoon of July 29, a *pneumatique* from the post office in the rue
Boissy d'Anglas. He had already seen her, but only briefly: "I have
seen my angel again, with her *new* little wings. I am waiting impatiently for your telephone call. This morning I was too upset to get
in touch with you. . . . P.S. I left you so soon because I was
afraid I would miss my cousin, who was leaving that night."

He had quit the Somme abruptly, in mid-battle, apparently with
no chance to notify anyone. For some reason he had been given
leave: "I take advantage of being on leave to write you," an August
11 letter to Stravinsky begins. Had he broken down? During that
August and September he was to tell Valentine several times that
the experience of the Somme had shaken his health. "Me, very sick
and thin. The sum total of the Somme. *Sinister* total — dizzy
spells, headaches, etc." (August 31). "I'm paying for the war trau-
mas, ridding myself of immense fatigue and disgust. Tics, dizzi-
ness, toxic smells that cling to my hands" (September 4). "No one
would recognize me, with my lacklustre eyes and my poor hair all
destroyed by the Somme" (September 12). On August 11 he wrote
Stravinsky: "In a week I shall return to my post on the Somme,
where big guns camouflaged as if by Bakst or the Cubists are shaking all Picardy"; but on September 22, still in Paris, he wrote Valentine that he was having "all kinds of trouble about the army and
the Red Cross": apparently it was now that he was trying to "leave
the war." Strings must have been pulled, and by late November
things were, at least temporarily, satisfactorily arranged. On the
twenty-fourth of that month, without having left Paris, he was officially released from ambulance service and transferred to a desk in
the Paris offices of the Etat-Major. "The trenches in the north must
be beautiful under the snow," he wrote from Paris, to Stravinsky in
Switzerland, that winter. "My old comrades write me from their
warm dugouts. Here we are freezing for lack of coal. How I long to

rejoin them! But my rheumatism persists, and I spend boring days at the ministry."

In a way — with fewer discrepancies, that is, than one might expect — it bears out his statement about his "leaving the war" when he realized, one night in Nieuport, that he was enjoying it: "That disgusted me. As soon as I made that discovery, I arranged to leave, taking advantage of being sick." * Cocteau's frankness in this case has brought him castigation; yet of the many people who take pleasure in the instigation and prosecution of wars, few have the capacity to recognize it, as he did, for the perversion that it is and to renounce it. But something else may have played a role in his decision to "leave the war." Danger: the danger which now, thinking back on *David*, he feared as being graver than anything that might befall him on the Somme — the danger threatening the creation of *Parade* in Paris.

Parade, *"The greatest battle of the war"* (1916–1917)

Besides, it was an advantageous time for an artist who thought of himself as belonging to the avant-garde to be in Paris. With the war preoccupying so many probable anti-modernist carpers, and having its effect on all conventions, the opportunity was not to be neglected. "I was able to see how the war rid us of foolishness, which found enough to do elsewhere," Cocteau wrote later. "In Paris the field was free. We moved in." "The intellectuals were going in for patriotism, and suddenly the patriotism of *art* took on an extraordinary intensity, because patriotism pure and simple had in a way emptied the city of those skin-deep intellectuals. We were torn between Paris and the spectacle of the war, with its bombs and its fireworks, but of course our real front was in Paris, in Montparnasse." It was in this sense that he was to refer to *Parade* as "the greatest battle of the war" — a phrase that was to fan the hostility of patriots, and that even today rings callously on the ear.

---

* See Appendix V for other statements by Cocteau about his "leaving the war."

Parade sounds like a simple affair as one reads its synopsis in a theatre program:

> At Country Fairs it is usual for a dancer or acrobat to give a performance in front of the booth in order to attract people to the turnstiles. The same idea, brought up-to-date and treated with accentuated realism, underlies the Ballet "Parade."
>
> The scene represents a Sunday Fair in Paris. There is a traveling Theatre, and three Music Hall turns are employed as Parade. These are the Chinese conjuror, an American girl, and a pair of Acrobats.
>
> Three Managers are occupied in advertising the show. They tell each other that the crowd in front is confusing the outside performance with the show which is about to take place within, and they try, in the crudest fashion, to induce the public to come and see the entertainment within, but the crowd remains unconvinced. After the last performance the Managers make another effort, but the Theatre remains empty. The Chinaman, the Acrobats, and the American girl, seeing that the Managers have failed, make a last appeal on their own account. But it is too late.

Seurat and Rouault had both painted pictures of *parades;* and in *David,* with memories of *Petrushka,* Cocteau had thought to combine a *parade* with legend. But considering Cocteau's lifelong obsession with aspects of artistic creation, it can scarcely be doubted that the chief theme of *Parade* — that any performance seen by an audience is as nothing compared with the invisibles that artists are up to within (whether behind the scenes, within their own heads, wherever), invisibles concerning which the painfully indifferent public lacks any interest, let alone understanding — must have had its true origin in his own realization of the contrast between what his poetic imagination was constantly suggesting to him and his dissatisfaction with most of what he had so far been able actually to produce — as well as in his fascination with the backstage, onstage, and out-front spectacles of the Ballets Russes. Many an audience must have filed out of the theatre after seeing *Parade* with no realization whatever of having been exposed to any such intimations. Cocteau had no wish to make his ballet heavily didactic — on a page of a notebook (a present from Massine) which he used during the completion of *Parade* in Rome he has scribbled "Beware of ideas"; but the nature of the theme must have formed part of the importance of the work in his own eyes. Each performance of *Parade* was to last no more than twenty minutes, but he felt it a privilege to be devoting himself to the details of the then novel "realistic" sights and sounds of which it is composed (it is subtitled *"Ballet Réaliste"*). His spirits were now high, now low, and there were chicaneries and difficulties. "Still," he wrote to Valentine Gross on August 13, 1916, "it's a great thing to be in the thick of the dog fights of great art."

Two days before, he had written about *Parade* in a letter to Stravinsky: "I often speak of you, dear Igor, with Satie and Picasso. Picasso, sentimental mandolinist and fierce Picador; Satie, an old angel who conceals the fact that he is really only twenty and composes marvelous music while his friend Claude [Debussy] reproves the young and 'has enough of all these Russians'!!! Satie and I are collaborating on something for Serge, since Serge, despite the abyss that I feel divides us, is still the only impresario with genius. Our piece will be ready in October. May it distill all the involuntary emotion given off by circuses, music halls, carrousels, public balls, factories, seaports, the movies, etc. etc. It is very short, and develops in depth."

His first chore on arriving in Paris from the Somme at the end of July, 1916, was to try to pacify Misia. She had learned, alas, that far from having been inspired to *Parade* by words that she herself had uttered that spring, as Satie had flatteringly written her, Satie had been meeting Cocteau about the project since the previous October in the house of the beautiful and younger Valentine. The apartment of Valentine Gross, not that of Misia Sert, had been the cradle of *Parade*. Now, despite the precautionary letters that Cocteau had been writing, and continued to write, to Stravinsky, Misia and Diaghilev displayed with reference to "their" Satie the same resentment they had shown Cocteau in his attempt to capture "their" Stravinsky for *David*. Misia informed Cocteau that she and Diaghilev were going to have to "begin all over again with Satie," excluding Cocteau from their project. She let it be known that she and

Diaghilev planned to use, for a Satie ballet, no new music by him, but some of his older works; and it came to Satie's ears that she had been saying: "Satie is old — let him stay old — it's so good that way." It was not in Satie's nature to turn the other cheek, and he quickly threatened to return blow for blow, to break, whatever the outcome, with "Tante Trufaldin," * as he baptized Misia. Cocteau wrote in alarm to Valentine on July 30: "I feel terribly alone and anguished — I beg you to let me hear from you, exorcise the devil, see Satie, learn what is going on. If this thing fell through it would be the end of me." And again on August 5: "I'm frightfully depressed and confused. What to do? My only comfort is being in touch with you. Impossible to work. Help!" Satie wrote to Valentine on the eighth, heading the letter "Tuesday, 3:12 P.M.": "It's happened! I've broken with Tante Trufaldin. What a bitch! Yes. To Cocteau's tomorrow morning. Bonjour, chère amie. You — you're a good sort, good and straight. Get anywhere with boors like that? No." But the next day Cocteau informed Valentine: "Very good day's work with Satie. Erik-Trufaldin catastrophe not serious and very serious." Meanwhile, Valentine had left for Boulogne: "There were so many storms," she wrote later, "that from time to time I left to spend a few days with my mother at Boulogne-sur-Mer, where the war atmosphere relaxed me after all the Paris wrangling." For a time the Cocteau-Satie collaboration proceeded in that atmosphere of uncertainty concerning Diaghilev's intentions.

Continuing his courtship of Picasso, Cocteau relayed to Valentine in Boulogne some of his impressions of Montparnassians and others.

Cocteau to Valentine Gross

August 13, 1916

Ma chère Valentine,

Nothing very new except that Picasso keeps taking me to the [Café] Rotonde. I never stay more than a moment, despite the flattering welcome given me by the circle (perhaps I should say the cube). Gloves, cane and collar astonish these artists in shirtsleeves — they have always looked on them as the in-

* "Tante": Misia was the aunt of Valentine's friend Marie Godebska, known as Mimi Godebski. "Truffaldin" or "Truffaldino": a crafty, false, boastful valet in the Commedia dell' Arte. Misia was also called "Tante Brutus" (because she stabbed her friends?) and "Faiseuse d'Anges" (because she aborted so many people's projects?); José-Maria Sert was "Oncle Brutus."

signia of feeblemindedness. Too much café-sitting brings sterility. . . . Max Jacob performs in dancing pumps on a slack rope. A convent gardener slipping dirty books to the nuns. A kind of sweet, dirty jack of all trades.

May I never put on such blinkers. Misia is now inseparable from Apollinaris, who is writing poems in the form of *croix de guerre*. What is she up to with him at Maxim's? She has quite abandoned Saint-Leger Leger for him. Our good Satie, in Arcueil, is composing *marvels* for me and refuses to see Tante Brutus. A long letter to Igor S. in which I let him know that I am far from being a party to inept intrigues. To tell you the truth, Diaghilev — that Italian tenor — finds it clever to attribute to me all the blunders of the Quai Voltaire, all due to my influence, he says — and naïve Igor accuses me of treachery.

Still, it's a great thing to be in the thick of the dog fights of great art. These chicaneries fade away as time goes on, and what is left is a divine group breathing sweetness and light. Let us not forget that we are in a phase of Mars — in which the moon grows full, art is transformed, and the prospect is for thirty years of wars. Ouf! Paris is hot — letter from Gleizes at Barcelona — I am writing little war poems relating to the terrible *Secteur 131*, which refuses to be born.*

He wrote similarly to Albert Gleizes in Barcelona, saying "Apollinaire very tiresome with his Bolivar beard, his scar and his stupid war. . . . Picasso I love. People are trying to set us against each other, but I refuse to listen to the obtuse, to his fellow painters who are furious with him for stealing their inventions.† An invention, in painting! As though there could be inventions!"

On August 24, news that was crucial in the history of *Parade*

---

* Saint-Leger Leger was the original literary signature of Alexis Saint-Leger Leger, who was later to sign his works Saint-John Perse: he has said that Cocteau's words in this letter pertain only to Misia's "*relations amicales*," with no implications concerning her "*vie privée*." The "long letter to Igor S." is probably that printed on pages 109–110 of the present volume.

† "During the great period of Cubism," Cocteau later wrote, "the Montparnasse painters barricaded themselves in their studios, for fear that Picasso might carry away some seed and bring it to bloom in his own soil. In 1916 I was present at interminable confabulations outside half-open doors when he took me to see them. We used to have to wait until they locked up their latest pictures. They were just as mistrustful of each other. . . . I remember one week when everybody was whispering and wondering who had stolen Rivera's formula for painting trees by spotting green on black."

reached Valentine in Boulogne on a postcard signed jointly by Cocteau and Satie: "Picasso is doing *Parade* with us." And on the
thirty-first Cocteau wrote Valentine that "Picasso and Satie get on
like Misia and Serge. Picasso is moulting, undergoing a transformation — Saturday night we begin real work." All his life, Cocteau was to boast of having captured Picasso as a collaborator on
Parade. "In Montparnasse, in 1916, grass still grew between the
cobbles," he wrote nostalgically in 1949. "Vegetable sellers trun-
dled their barrows, people palavered in the middle of the streets. It
was in the middle of the street, between the Rotonde and the Dôme,
that I asked Picasso to do *Parade*." And: "What concerns me is
Picasso the theatrical designer. He became one thanks to me. The
artists around him couldn't believe that he would go along with me.
A dictatorship hung heavy over Montmartre and Montparnasse.
Cubism was going through its austere phase. Objects that could be
placed on a café table, and Spanish guitars, were the only pleasures allowed. To paint a stage set for a Russian ballet (the dedicated young painters knew nothing of Stravinsky) was a crime.
Monsieur Renan behind the scenes at the Comédie Française never
scandalized the Sorbonne more than Picasso scandalized the Café
la Rotonde in accepting my invitation."

Probably Satie had always disliked one of Cocteau's original
ideas for *Parade* — that "after each music-hall number an anonymous voice issuing from an amplifying orifice (a theatrical imitation of a circus megaphone, the mask of antiquity in modern guise)
was to sing a type phrase outlining the performer's activity so as to
open up the world of make-believe." When Cocteau had written to
Valentine from his sector on May 28 "Dune dune dune cave cave
cave cano cano canon Ratodromes" he was imitating or parodying
this aspect of his libretto. He was specific about it when he wrote
her on August 31: Satie had his "pockets full of music," he wrote,
"and what music! The Chinaman is a masterpiece. There is an
enormous silence, and then the box chants:

> They put out his eyes
> They put out his tongue

The Chinaman exits and the American girl enters to the sound of
typewriters." Such words were designed to "extend the characters"

— that is, to indicate some of the qualities that they would have demonstrated in the "real" spectacle, inside the fair booth, of which *Parade* is a mere sample and to which it is a come-on. Those words from behind the scenes about the Chinese magician, for instance, were an indication that in the "real" spectacle he was to be shown "capable of torturing missionaries"; other words from backstage would show the American girl "capable of going down on the *Titanic*, the Acrobat of being on close terms with the angels." Cocteau had in 1916, and to a certain extent was always to keep, a rather Perils-of-Pauline picture of the U.S.A. "The United States," he wrote later, in one of his expositions of *Parade*, "evokes a girl more interested in her health than in her beauty. She swims, boxes, dances, leaps onto moving trains — all without knowing that she is beautiful. It is we who admire her face, on the screen — enormous, like the face of a goddess." * Some of the words and sounds that were to have issued from the megaphone to accompany the appearance of the American girl will serve as a sample of that aspect of the libretto: "Cube tic tic tic tic on the hundredth floor an angel has made its nest at the dentist's tic tic tic Titanic toc toc the Titanic sinks brightly lit beneath the waves . . . ice-cream soda Pullman tic tic."

None of those words and sounds, suggested to Cocteau perhaps by the *"bruitisme"* ("noise-ism") of the Italian Futurists and their friends, who had been championed in Paris by the poet Pierre Albert-Birot in his magazine *Sic*, were to be heard in the first performances of *Parade*, much to Cocteau's regret. Trouble between Cocteau and his collaborators over the sound effects broke out early, and in fact it was Cocteau's own words to Valentine, so happily written on August 31 — "Picasso and Satie get on like Misia and Serge" — that heralded it. Picasso had known and liked Satie for some time; doubtless Satie's presence as composer of *Parade* played a role in inducing Picasso to collaborate; and the cordiality and sympathy between the composer and the painter quickly turned to the librettist's disadvantage.

* Perhaps Cocteau was with Paul Morand and Misia Sert the evening of December 27, 1916, when they saw, at the Alhambra music hall in Paris, a number consisting of "a contest between the champion California lady orange-packer and the champion orange-crate maker, staged by an impresario with a megaphone. 'It's the beginning of the invasion of the American style,' said Misia. 'Think of what's to come!' "

Cocteau to Valentine Gross

September 4, 1916

. . . . Make Satie understand, if you can cut through the aperitif fog, that I really do count for something in *Parade*, and that he and Picasso are not the only ones involved. I consider *Parade* a kind of renovation of the theatre, and not a simple "pretext" for music. It hurts me when he dances around Picasso screaming "It's you I'm following! *You* are my master!" (*sic*) and seems to be hearing for the first time, from Picasso's mouth, things that I have told him time and time again. Does he hear anything I say? Perhaps it's all an *acoustical* phenomenon. Besides, I probably exaggerate, the way sick people do. . . . The swan will quickly make Satie understand many an enigma and calm him in his inordinate hatred for the *Tante*. Sh! Burn this, for the work is going ahead, and that's the main thing. Picasso is inventing marvels, and Satie's American girl is almost done.

Erik Satie to Valentine Gross

Thursday — September 14, 1916

Chère et douce amie —

If you knew how sad I am! *Parade* is changing for the better, behind Cocteau's back! Picasso has ideas that I like better than our Jean's! How awful! And I am all for Picasso! And Cocteau doesn't know it! What am I to do? Picasso tells me to go ahead, following Jean's text, and he, Picasso, will work on another text, his own — which is dazzling! Prodigious! I'm half crazy, depressed! What am I to do? Now that I know Picasso's wonderful ideas, I am heartbroken to have to set to music the less wonderful ideas of our good Jean — oh! yes! less wonderful. What am I to do? What am I to do? Write and advise me. I am beside myself. . . .

Erik Satie to Valentine Gross

Wednesday, September 20, 1916

Chère amie,

It's settled. Cocteau knows everything. He and Picasso have come to terms. How lucky! Did I tell you that I got along well with Diaghilev? Still no money from him. The "Tante" is in Rhum — I mean Rome. . . .

Cocteau to Valentine Gross
[September 22, 1916]
. . . . You were probably worried about Satie — let me quickly set your mind at rest. Caught between Picasso and me, our good Socrates from Arcueil has lost his bearings — our different vocabularies make him imagine that one of us is talking white and the other black. Have decided with Picasso to lie to Satie so that he'll be able to go ahead without getting confused. . . .

Who was fooling whom? According to Douglas Cooper, who has discussed *Parade* with Picasso, it was Picasso who encouraged Satie to stand out against Cocteau's introduction of words, sounds and phrases; both men felt that such supplementary, literary descriptions would interfere not only with the music, but also with the choreography and the décor, all of which could and should be self-sufficient. For the time being, Cocteau apparently let himself be persuaded, or pretended to. Cocteau wrote later about those "household quarrels" between himself and Satie: "When Satie was sulky with me, played me the kind of tricks that gradually alienated all his friends, I would do some soul-searching and discover in myself some weed that accounted for his seeming caprice. When the weed was plucked out, I would see Satie return to his usual self." Despite the scenes and the back-stabbings, or perhaps propelled by them, the work progressed, and by October 6 Picasso was writing to Cocteau "Come to my place tomorrow afternoon at six and if you can we'll have dinner together later at Diaghilev's."

Diaghilev had come up briefly from Rome, where he was spending the winter, bringing with him Léonide Massine,* the dancer whom he was now promoting as a choreographer, as he had formerly promoted Nijinsky. The main body of the company was on tour in the United States under the disastrous leadership of Nijinsky, whose participation had been insisted on by Otto Kahn; in Rome a few of the dancers were rehearsing for the next season. It is not certain whether Diaghilev and Picasso had met before that eve-

* МЯСИН in Russian. The first western spelling and pronunciation of the name, "Miassine," were soon changed.

ning of October 7, 1916: in any case, that meeting was a great success. Cocteau, who had known Massine since the young Russian had first joined the company in Paris in 1914, wrote about the evening to Misia:

Cocteau to Misia Sert

[n.d.]

Chère Misia,

Come back soon — I'm impatient to hug you and to laugh and kiss away a thousand misunderstandings that have been exaggerated by distance and fatigue. Very good meeting with Serge and Miassine — the latter's fresh intelligence and general air I like very much. I have the impression that Serge likes our work and that he understood perfectly the seemingly very simple motivation I provided for the union of musician and painter. I stand between them, giving a hand to each. Thanks to him I am inventing new effects, and his sense of the theatre stimulates me to discover, in my field, things he suggests in his own. I am sure he will tell you about the *soirée Babel* where Madame Errazuriz shouted in Spanish with Picasso, Serge in Russian with Miassine, and Satie in Sauterne with me . . . Picasso is moving [to a new studio] — I'm helping him and so is Apollinaire, who asks about you . . . For the first time I feel myself in rapport with Serge — a very nice feeling.

On October 7, 1916, the date of the *"soirée Babel,"* Cocteau was visited for the first time by a young man who was to become a friend — Paul Morand, a diplomat a year older than himself who had been an attaché at the French embassy in London and was now, at the Quai d'Orsay, an aide to Philippe Berthelot, the Director of Political Affairs. Berthelot had recently founded the Maison de la Presse, a war-information office where Cocteau himself had vague duties. Morand, whose father, a well-known *littérateur*, had been director of the Ecole des Arts Décoratifs, was himself a *littérateur* and a man about town. In his *Journal d'un Attaché d'Ambassade* he has left this account of his visit:

Went to see Cocteau, rue d'Anjou. I found him in a dressing gown, surrounded by plaster masks; on his table were a pair of enormous tortoiseshell spectacles brought back from Germany by J-E Blanche, some glass prisms, Cubist drawings, Allied flags. Cocteau is writing the scenario of a ballet with Erik Satie and Picasso, which Diaghilev will produce in Rome. Satie comes in, looking like Socrates; his face is made up of two half-moons; he scratches his little goatee between every two words. He doesn't speak about his genius; his great concern is to look mischievous. One recognizes the semifailure, the man who was dwarfed by Debussy and who suffers from it. Satie is writing a *Socrate* for the Princesse de Polignac. He seemed to me very jealous of Stravinsky.

Morand, who had taken an apartment in the Palais-Royal, combined party-going and party-giving with long office hours; and until mid-1917, when he was transferred from Paris to the embassy in Rome, he and Cocteau saw much of each other. Throughout the autumn of 1916 Morand's journal shows him and Cocteau continuously at parties or otherwise on the town. On November 16, 1916, for example, recording a *"soirée chez la Princesse Eugène* [Violette] *Murat,"* Morand takes note of several artists: "Bakst, with his look of a professional soldier, sparse reddish hair, small ridiculously dapper military moustache, nearsighted, glasses, wearing his dinner jacket like a croupier, speaks with a ridiculous lisp. Stravinsky very much the dandy, mustard-yellow trousers, black jacket, blue shirt and blue collar, yellow shoes, clean-shaven, slicked-down blond hair, bad teeth, myopic, thick lips. Satie a faun, little beard, cracked laugh . . . Stravinsky plays *Petrushka* . . . Darius Milhaud plays Satie's 'Morceaux en forme de poire' . . ." A week later, after dinner in a restaurant, Morand and Cocteau went on to the Cirque Médrano: "Green gaslight, hypertrophic and chlorophyllous clowns, pink tights, acid smell of horse dung. Jean knows everybody, is madly amused by the rabbit hunt and the trapezists. He says 'I like clowns so much better than actors; they are so much more intelligent; Mme. Errazuriz claims it's because clowns sleep with their poodles.' " On November 26, Cocteau read poems by his six-year-old cousin, Françoise Durand-Viel, and others in the Salle Huyghens, a Montparnasse studio and art gallery, the scene of many an early avantgarde artistic happening, to an audience that included Morand,

Satie, Sert and Apollinaire; on the twenty-ninth he joined a lunch party at Morand's after lunching himself at the Norwegian legation. (He had just written one of the three prefaces to the catalogue of an exhibition of Cubist and other School of Paris pictures at Oslo, the other two being by Apollinaire and André Salmon.) On December 16 there opened what seems to have been the first exhibition of primitive Negro art in a European art gallery, at Paul Guillaume's. (In his journal Morand associates the sudden popularity of Negro art in Paris with the welcome arrival of Senegalese troops.) On December 31 Cocteau attended, along with Picasso, Max Jacob, Pierre Reverdy, Juan Gris, Blaise Cendrars, Gide and many others, the celebrated lunch banquet organized to honor Apollinaire on the appearance of his "novel," *Le Poète Assassiné,* a banquet that delighted Apollinaire by becoming a scuffle between Cubists, Dadaists and other factions.

Although Satie had attended some of those affairs, chiefly he had been working on his score for *Parade,* and had finally received an advance from Diaghilev. "Satie is buying an umbrella a day,* and Diaghilev has cabled me 500 francs for him," Cocteau had written Valentine Gross on October 17; and on the nineteenth Satie had reported to Cocteau on a postcard, "I have been working on our 'thing' tooth and nail. . . . The 'rag' is thriving — it fits well." On December 12 Satie sent Valentine a few manuscript bars of the prelude of *Parade,* apparently the last part of the score to be finished. "It is a fugal exposition, very restrained and solemn, and even rather dry, but short," he wrote her. "I like that sort of thing, slightly banal, pseudo-naïve — blah, in fact." Having told Misia the previous spring that the "thing" was dedicated to her in both its conception and its composition, he now wrote *"Hommage à Picasso"* in a bold hand above the bars of music. This Misia apparently never saw, for she always continued to believe herself the dedicatee, complacently reproducing in her memoirs a letter written to her by Satie about the time of the *"Hommage à Picasso"* inscription, in which the composer blandly says: "I'll come on Tuesday, shall I, dear lady? If so, not a word to the others about

---

* "After Satie's death, when it was finally possible to enter his room in Arcueil where no one had dared venture during his life, we found a hundred or so umbrellas . . . some of them still in wrapping paper." (Francis Poulenc, *Moi et Mes Amis,* p. 85.)

what I have prepared for you. . . . I want you to like it." (The printed orchestral score of *Parade* bears *no* dedication.)

On Christmas Day Cocteau was one of a group of friends who lunched at Misia's bedside in the Hotel Meurice where she had gone to recover from the grippe, and on the twenty-seventh he dined there with her and Morand. On the thirty-first, after sitting through the Apollinaire banquet, he attended Misia's all-night New Year's Eve party, where he got drunk and quarreled with an anti-Cubist guest. That same evening he shouted *"On les aura!"* (the patriots' war cry) in so ironic a fashion that Morand noted in his journal, about him and other guests who showed themselves sarcastically war-weary, *"Très mauvais esprit."* Misia seems now to have been tamed, as far as *Parade* was concerned: one hears of no further trouble of her making, at least directly, although Cocteau was to have his difficulties with Diaghilev. As Satie wrote to Cocteau a few days later, "My 'sister-in-law' [another of his names for Misia] is no longer dangerous, I think. What luck!"

Letter contracts between Diaghilev and the three collaborators were signed early in the New Year.* Cocteau wrote the news to Etienne de Beaumont, who was making a propaganda tour in Rumania and Russia with Philippe Berthelot: "Poor me, I'm writing articles — my ink flows like George Sand's. I'm ashamed, and console myself by putting some order into *Secteur 131*, which will come after *Le Cap de Bonne-Espérance* in the series of poems. . . . Diaghilev is buying Cubist pictures and will come to put on *Parade* in May. The war will be over and you'll give a marvelous ball on the Arc de Triomphe." In a letter to Gleizes Cocteau explained that Diaghilev's picture buying was for the purpose of forming a collection for Massine: he had already bought canvases by Picasso, Gris, Rivera, Metzinger, Zarraga, Lhote, Léger and Braque; and Cocteau, constituting himself a salesman, saw to it that one by Gleizes "joined its sister pictures." "I asked him a thousand francs (a higher price than anyone else except Picasso), impress-

---

* They will be found in full, though in English translation only, and with a commentary, in Richard Buckle's *In Search of Diaghilev*, (New York and London, 1956) pp. 93–94. Cocteau surrendered his portion of the advance, 3000 francs, to Satie, to be made up to him from future royalties. (Mr. Buckle thinks he can never have been repaid, as *Parade* was not often given.) Picasso seems to have come off the best, receiving 5000 francs, which Mr. Buckle calculates to have been the equivalent in purchasing power of a thousand English pounds in 1956, plus a thousand francs more if he went to Rome.

ing on him that you were a 'star,' the leader of the group. . . . He admires you and is thinking of you for stage sets." Part of that is improbable, but one sees why fellow artists could like Cocteau. "Where are you?" he ends. "In Havana? Very hard to imagine Havana — the smell of a cigar box, hard-to-read signatures on a stamp, and Negroes sweating like whales — probably quite inaccurate."

Diaghilev had decided that Massine would not only dance the part of the Chinese magician in *Parade*, but would also be the ballet's choreographer, and he asked the three collaborators to join him in Rome for rehearsals. Cocteau, hoping to enlist Massine's support for the reinclusion of the *"trompe-l'oreille"* elements that remained dear to his heart despite the united opposition of Satie and Picasso, sent him to Rome a notebook filled with words, sounds and phrases designed to "extend the character" of the Chinaman.

Léonide Massine to Cocteau

January 21 [1917]

Mon cher Cocteau,

I have just written a few words to Picasso, telling him how much and how impatiently I look forward to working with him. Not only with him, but with our dear Satie and you, as well. M. Diaghilev is delighted with the music and the general conception of the work, and I hope that we shall succeed in the realization of this project that is so dear to you, and to which I must now give an outer form worthy of our common effort. You may be sure that I shall do my best. I thank you very much for the presents and the good wishes. I am very touched, and greatly enjoy leafing through the extraordinary little book devoted to your Chinaman.

On February 1, Picasso wrote to Cocteau "I am working at our project almost every day — no one need worry," and on the eleventh Cocteau informed Valentine (who was in Cannes, deciding to break her engagement to a wealthy young man named Charles Stern): "Diaghilev is carrying us off in his cyclone — Picasso, Satie and me — an enormous pink rhinoceros taking us to Rome on his back. Satie is buying 'bags.' Will I really go? I wonder: Tante T. is in charge!!!" As it turned out, it was Cocteau who did go and

Satie who didn't, preferring not to leave familiar haunts. "We leave tomorrow without Satie," Cocteau wrote on February 15 to Valentine. "Impossible to take along that funny shuffling little bundle. When the Minister asked him, 'Do you know Rome, M. Satie?' he answered, 'By name — only by name.' " Of the departure from Paris for Rome on February 17, 1917, Cocteau later wrote that "Picasso laughed to see our painter friends grow smaller as the train pulled away. I refer only to the hundred percent Cubists." Douglas Cooper points out that this means not that a crowd of painters accompanied them to the station, but that Picasso felt a certain triumph at escaping from Montparnasse — where, as Cocteau put it, "the Cubist code prohibited any trip other than that between Montmartre and Montparnasse on the Nord-Sud métro." Picasso was probably thinking of some of the painters he was glad to leave behind that day when he said, later, to Francis Poulenc: "Long life to our followers! It's thanks to them that we look for something else!"

Gertrude Stein, in *The Autobiography of Alice B. Toklas,* has written of meeting Cocteau on the eve of the departure for Rome. "One day Picasso came in and with him and leaning on his shoulder was a slim elegant youth. 'It is Jean,' announced Pablo, 'Jean Cocteau and we are leaving for Italy' . . . He was very lively at the prospect of going to Rome." Almost half a century after that visit to Gertrude Stein, Cocteau recited his recollection of it, on television: "Picasso said to me, 'Well, since we're to make a wedding trip, we'll go and tell Gertrude Stein about it.' We called on Gertrude Stein, in the rue de Fleurus, and told her — 'Voilà — we're leaving on our wedding trip.' "

Perhaps it was hindsight that led Cocteau to speak of the trip to Rome as a wedding journey; or, if Picasso, in his liveliness at the prospect of going to Rome, did use the phrase, he spoke more truly than he knew; for among the dancers awaiting Diaghilev and his traveling companions in Rome was Olga Koklova, a Russian army officer's daughter, whom Picasso was to marry the next year. But Cocteau himself was in a particularly wifely mood on this wedding journey. He resumed his availability signals to Diaghilev: members of the company noticed the lipstick and rouge he donned before his conferences with the impresario. (As before, Diaghilev's degree of receptivity is not known: at present he had a willing, if not an eager, favorite in one of his leading dancers, and there was an Italian valet as understudy.) More curious was the form taken in Rome by Cocteau's wooing of Picasso. It was to be a lifelong wooing, unrequited, deriving its satisfaction from futility: at the age of seventy Cocteau was still to be addressing Picasso as *"Cher Magnifique,"* and now, in Rome, with Picasso immediately attaching himself to Olga, Cocteau expressed his adoration by imitation: he took up a Russian ballerina of his own. "You will love my little Shabelska," he wrote to Misia, "who dances the American girl and looks like Buster Brown's dog."

Lydia Lopokova has testified that Marie Shabelska was an excellent dancer; at that time she was seventeen years old, new to the company, recently arrived from revolutionary Russia by way of Holland and England, inexperienced in some of the ways of the world. When the elegant Cocteau began to pay attention to her she was innocently flattered; enlightenment was soon vouchsafed her, both by Cocteau and by her laughing colleagues, and she was willing to continue the "affair" as a game for the pleasure of her "lover's" company — in walks around Rome, over tables in the Campagna, at the movies. They made the joke rather elaborate. Discovery in "compromising" situations, rumpled sheets, bedaubment of the "lover's" face and shoulders with ballerina's makeup, as Picasso's were bedaubed by Olga's — it was all part of the grotesquerie. Picasso laughed with the rest at the tribute being paid him.

In these early and confused days of the Russian Revolution, most of the Diaghilev company sympathized with the new regime, welcoming the collapse of Czarism in its final holocaust of war and chaotic tyranny. Paul Morand says that Diaghilev himself had been offered the post of Minister of Fine Arts in Moscow, and as late as May 10, at the opening of the 1917 Paris season, Diaghilev was to have a red flag unfurled onstage at the Théâtre du Châtelet, to the scandal of French patriots embittered by Russia's defection from the war. Shabelska had been able to join the company without too much difficulty. In Rome the dancers' hotel was the Minerva, behind the Pantheon; Picasso and Cocteau visited it together to call on their ballerinas, but they themselves, along with Diaghilev, Massine and Bakst, lived (appropriately enough) at the Hotel de Russie, in the Piazza del Popolo (now occupied by RAI, Italian radio and television). In some lines of Cocteau's called "Rome," probably written down in one form or another while he was in the city, and later characterized by him as "notes, rather, put end to end," he included various Roman memories:

> La nuit, les coqs aboient sur le mont Palatin.
> J'ai volé un citron dans les jardins du pape.
> J'ai rêvé que le pape me poursuivait
> dans les couloirs du Vatican . . .*

He says that beneath the joke with Marie lay frustration — *"O je souffre, seul";* he remembers the films that he and Marie saw on the nights they spent "together" — *"le soir . . . Cinéma la dixième muse se lève dans toutes les rues."* And in three lines he sings the freshness of the young ballerina, reveals the duration of the "affair," and confesses that it was an act:

> Ma chère petite Marie
> ta chambre d'hôtel est un mois de Marie
> et une loge de théâtre.†

The ballets being rehearsed in Rome were Massine's first assignments as choreographer, and S. L. Grigoriev, long the *régisseur* of the company, has recorded that Massine quickly showed himself the master of "a new, distinctive style — complicated, mannered and dry." *Parade* was scheduled to be the third new ballet‡ to be given during the coming spring season in Paris (it would be the first Paris season since 1914), and conferences about it began immediately. Some of them were stormy: "Work progresses with fruitful disagreements," Cocteau wrote to Valentine. "Every collaboration is a more or less successful misunderstanding. *Parade* is beginning well (touch wood)." The disagreements seem to have

---

* At night roosters bark on the Palatine Hill. / I stole a lemon from the Pope's garden. / I dreamed that the Pope was chasing me down the halls of the Vatican . . .
† My dear little Marie, / Your hotel room is a month of Mary [i.e., the month of May] / and a theatre box.
‡ The others were *Les Contes Russes*, a suite of scenes and dances on themes from Russian folklore, and *Les Femmes de Bonne Humeur*, based on a comedy by Goldoni, with music by Scarlatti orchestrated and arranged by Vincenzo Tommasini and décor by Bakst.

been chiefly with Diaghilev, who, in admiration of both Massine and Picasso, encouraged them, far more often than Cocteau found tolerable, to impose their ideas on the ballet at the expense of Cocteau's. "I could give you a picture of myself spitting in Diaghilev's face in Rome, when he tried to cheat me out of my role as choreographer," he later reminisced. Massine says today that there was no spitting in anyone's face, that there was merely the normal explosive give and take of theatrical collaboration; but Cocteau complained angrily to Massine about Diaghilev's behavior. Massine, he believed, welcomed his ideas: "Massine is a Stradivarius . . . I think up every slightest gesture, and Massine executes it choreographically," he wrote Valentine; and to his mother: "You would laugh to see the dancer I have become: Massine wants me to show him every slightest detail, and I invent the roles, which he then immediately transforms into choreography"; but Massine's continuous courtesy may have been in part an arrangement between him and Diaghilev, to spare Massine the task of countering Cocteau's determination — which was to win out in the long run — that his ballet be performed as he wished.

Picasso, whom, of the various collaborators, and despite all tensions, Cocteau most often called "my collaborator," worked in a studio in Via Margutta. There, "a little box contained the model for *Parade* — the houses, the trees, the booth. On a table, looking out toward the Villa Medici, Picasso painted the Chinese magician, the managers, the American girl, the horse (of which Madame de Noailles later wrote that it would make a tree laugh), and the blue acrobats, later compared by Marcel Proust to the Dioscuri." "Picasso amazes me every day," he wrote Misia. "To live near him is a lesson in nobility and hard work." For both of them, life in Rome was chiefly work. "We snatch our meals between working and walking, and fall asleep exhausted," Cocteau wrote Valentine. They were dismayed by the Forum. "What a mess!" Cocteau wrote. "It's like a room after a burglary. Drawers, tables, furniture of all kinds smashed, clocks stopped at the moment of the crime, a candlestick, an empty bottle, dirty glasses . . . the safe opened . . . the treasure gone." But the night walks across old Rome from the Minerva to the Russie were unforgettable: "We would cross a city made of fountains, shadows and moonlight." * Otherwise, Cocteau

* See Appendix VI for an unpublished poem by Cocteau, "Rome, la nuit."

took in little of the city. "In Rome, in 1917, I didn't look at Rome. I had eyes only for my collaborator."

Rome was the scene of an echo of the sorry episode of Madame Cocteau and the customs inspector. Léon Bakst, Cocteau's friend and protector in the ballet company, was now fifty and beginning to feel himself left behind. The rich oriental style of his décors had in its day been modern, a break from Benois and even from Art Nouveau; but now, although it was still loved in the older ballets by the public (and by artists — including Picasso, a great admirer), Bakst saw that Diaghilev was looking elsewhere. After buying School of Paris pictures for Massine, and employing Picasso, he had brought to Rome two "new" Russian artists, Natalia Goncharova and her husband, M. F. Larionov, who had been assigned the décor of *Les Contes Russes;* and the Futurist Giacomo Balla was preparing a décor with lighting effects to accompany Stravinsky's new symphonic poem *Fireworks,* to make a "ballet without dancers," only changing lights. Bakst made a naïve concession to "modernism" in his architectural sets for *Les Femmes de Bonne Humeur* by tilting his houses slightly forward, but, as usual in such cases, the concession was spotted as such and disliked. Just at this moment, in Rome, when things were tense between Bakst and Diaghilev, Cocteau chose to send Misia a letter ridiculing Bakst. Shortly thereafter, Diaghilev was to drop Bakst in favor of a School of Paris painter, Derain, as designer of a new ballet, *La Boutique Fantasque.* Cocteau's letter was probably not the direct cause, but it is a reminder that for anyone teetering in a vulnerable spot, especially if Cocteau had in any way been associated with putting him there, Cocteau's proximity could be dangerous.

About Giacomo Balla and his Futurist colleagues Cocteau wrote to Misia: "We see little of the Futurists — too provincial and bragging. They have always wanted to travel at top speed, which keeps them from seeing the road and in effect reduces them to immobility. When they succeed, it's very pretty, very graceful, like a toy or a poster." That sounds like an echo of Picasso, who thought little of Futurist painting. "The Futurists pursue us like provincials wanting to learn the Paris styles," Cocteau wrote to Valentine. Does any of that indicate that he perceived the difference in quality between the Futurists at their best and Picasso at his, that he felt the mysterious, unequalled *grip* of the Cubism of Picasso and Braque and

Gris? His definition of Cubism, "the fall of the angles," is as noncommittal as it is delightful. Excellent draughtsman though he himself was, Cocteau never penetrated fully into the plastic arts.

What he does display, in his letters from Rome and in the notebook he kept there while working on *Parade,* is a shrewd obsession
with those aspects of Cubist painting that best lend themselves to
impressive stage effects. His preferences reflect his theatrical flair.
In the *Parade* notebook he wrote:

> For the Chinaman, look at Braque
> For the girl, Léger
> For the acrobat, Picasso

— indicating his choice of precisely the three Cubist painters
whose work was capable of producing stage magic, a quality that
could probably not be associated with the excellent Gleizes, Cocteau's "first" Cubist. That the chosen painter had to be a Cubist is
obvious: Cocteau was still working in obedience to Diaghilev's
"Astound me!" and in 1917 Cubism, though long practiced by
the original Cubists, was still shocking to everyone else. At various
times Cocteau undertook in his writings to give graver grounds for
his choice of Cubism for his "realistic ballet." He wrote in his notebook: "Make the dancing realistic like Cubism, which is realistic,
which always carefully plans the grouping of forms, and which
seeks to render relief, volume, the texture of objects." But it was
the "Astound me!" that underlay it all.

As for his subtitling *Parade* "*ballet réaliste,*" Cocteau wrote
later: "I have the habit, no doubt detestable, of using ordinary
words in a sense that I attribute to them, without explaining myself.
Thus I called *Parade* a 'realistic ballet' meaning by that 'truer than
true'; and to be understood I relied solely on the fact that the contrast between this ballet and other ballets, between the word 'realistic' and the unreality of the show, would be evident to the spectators." More simply, if *Parade* can be called "realistic" it is because
unlike the earlier sumptuous ballets whose libretti were based on
myth or folklore or fairy tales, Cocteau's ballet takes place in a
Paris street, with street-fair characters, and quite lacks any supernatural touches à la *Petrushka;* Satie's music includes "realistic" sounds — the clicking of typewriters, revolver shots; Mas-

sine's simple choreography shows the modern characters miming
their occupations — "managers" who are burlesques of advertising, a magician and a pair of acrobats, an American girl acting out
supposedly real aspects of American life. Picasso's Chinese costume suggests China, his acrobats' tights are painted in suggestive
swirls and stars, his American girl wears a middy jacket, his
French manager and American manager wear carapaces suggestive
of boulevards, skyscrapers, and so on. This "realism," so obvious
today, was obscured to the public in 1917 by Picasso's Cubist style,
which although ten years old was still "new." Picasso's influence on
the other collaborators was considerable: he was able to get across
to them certain effective devices of his own which they could adapt
in their media. Massine, for example, could profit from a remark
of Picasso's that Cocteau jotted down in his Rome notebook: "Picasso says: 'Don't be afraid to glue a piece of newspaper to the
canvas — i.e., to use a movement whose meaning cannot be misunderstood, and which, remaining untransposed, gives full value to
the other movements.' "

Cocteau remained in Italy until after Easter (which in 1917 fell
on April 8), watching the choreography of *Parade* come alive day
by day in a Roman basement dance studio in the Piazza Venezia
called the Cantina Taglioni. The dancers practiced steps that had
sometimes been agreed on in conference by the collaborators only
the evening before; among other innovations, Massine insisted on
the addition of a second acrobat, to make possible a *pas de deux*.
During March the main body of the Diaghilev company had
reached Rome from New York (without Nijinsky, who had botched
the American tour* and came no further than Spain); Stravinsky
arrived from Switzerland to conduct *The Firebird* and his new
Fireworks for a brief Roman season at the Teatro Costanzi (now
the Teatro dell' Opera), opening with a gala for the Italian Red

---

* Nijinsky's tendency to make himself invisible in New York, to the despair of the
company and the sponsors, inspired a jingle by Edward Ziegler, later assistant manager
of the Metropolitan Opera House:

> Oh Mr. Nijinsky
> Where have you binsky?
> And if you are here
> Why don't you appear
> And save the ballet from ruinsky?

Cross.* The new ballet, *Les Femmes de Bonne Humeur*, was also danced, the score conducted by Ernest Ansermet, who was rehearsing *Parade*. Picasso and Stravinsky, who now saw something of each other for the first time, felt a mutual attraction and spent much time in each other's company — a conjunction of major planets that seems to have left others somewhat on the outside. Cocteau's letters and poems speak of loneliness, homesickness and his mother: "Talk to *maman*," he wrote to Valentine Gross, upset after breaking her engagement to Charles Stern. "She is infallible in matters of honor and morality." In mid-March he traveled with the company to Naples, where they danced at the San Carlo Opera House. The beauty and brio of Naples and its bay enchanted him after the high tone of Rome — "The Pope is in Rome, God is in Naples," he told Paul Morand — and he celebrated the irrepressible city in some amusing lines:

> Le Vésuve est un
> trompe-l'oeil qui fume;
> la plus grande fabrique de nuages du monde.
>
> Pompéi ferme à quatre heures;
> Naples ne ferme jamais.
> SÉANCE ININTERROMPUE†

On April 30 the company played a one-night stand in Florence and then entrained for Paris. In a studio on the Buttes Chaumont Picasso and a team of theatrical decorators (one of them, an Italian, was named Carlo Socrate — Charles Socrates) painted a drop curtain, scenery and costumes for *Parade*, and its opening was scheduled for May 18.

It may have been due either to Picasso or to Misia or to Cocteau himself that the person asked to write a program note for *Parade*

---

* It was for this occasion that Stravinsky orchestrated "The Song of the Volga Boatmen," with which Diaghilev decided to open the performance, replacing the hitherto played Russian Imperial anthem — the Czar having abdicated after the February Revolution. Cocteau mentions this in his poem "Rome": *"le chant des bateliers de la Volga détrone / Boje Tzara Krani de neige et d'or."*

† Vesuvius is an / optical illusion belching smoke; / the biggest cloud factory in the world / Pompeii closes at four o'clock; / Naples never closes. / CONTINUOUS PERFORMANCE.

was Guillaume Apollinaire; and Apollinaire probably welcomed this chance to put his name before a theatre-going public since his own play, *Les Mamelles de Tirésias*, was about to be performed. (In a poem, "Zèbre," which Cocteau contributed, in turn, to Apollinaire's program, he had used the word *"rue"* as a verb ("to rear") instead of a noun ("street"); this brought him a reprimand from a "tribunal," as he called it, of Cubist painters and poets, by that time well into their "austere" or "analytical" phase.) After attending some of the Paris rehearsals of *Parade* (a drawing by Larionov shows him sitting in the theatre beside Diaghilev), Apollinaire wrote his note, which appeared first in the newspaper *Excelsior* for May 11, and then, a week later, in the ballet program itself.* That program note on *Parade* has become famous because in it the word *"surréaliste"* † is used for the first time; but although the note was probably excellent propaganda, at least in avant-garde circles, it struck Cocteau a blow. For in it, amid the greatest praise for Satie, Picasso and Massine, he found himself mentioned by Apollinaire only as the person who had called the spectacle a *"ballet réaliste."* His role as originator, as inventor, as *animateur*, as participant, was ignored. One can imagine his feelings.

The probable lack of sympathy for Cocteau on Apollinaire's part even before their meeting has already been mentioned, as well as Cocteau's feline references to the friendship that had sprung up between Apollinaire and Misia, and his words to Gleizes about Apollinaire's beard, scar, and "stupid war." (But sick jokes about the wounded were the fashion among the artists in Montparnasse, who regarded the war as an insane disaster, not to be palliated by "patriotism." Gertrude Stein quotes Picasso as saying "Won't it be awful when Braque and Derain and all the rest of them put their wooden legs up on a chair and tell about the fighting.") By the end of 1916 Cocteau was writing to Valentine that Apollinaire was put-

---

* Appendix VII is a translation of Apollinaire's text.

† Although the term "surrealism" has become famous in English, the proper translation of the French *"surréalisme"* would be "superrealism," just as *"surnaturalisme"* is translated as "supernaturalism."

Professor LeRoy C. Breunig suggests that Apollinaire, taking his cue from Cocteau's label *"ballet réaliste,"* invented the term *"sur-réaliste"* chiefly to stress the intensification of mere "realism" in the ballet's fusion of music, dance, painting, etc. The sense would be that of Jean-Louis Barrault's phrase "total theatre." If so, it was a modest beginning for a term that snowballed so tremendously. Bakst also contributed a note to the program of *Parade*, speaking generously of Picasso's décor.

ting on "a little campaign" against him. "Campaign" is too strong a word, one suspects: Cocteau, always insecure and nervous, tended to exaggerate indifference and dislike as he exaggerated courtesy and casual praise, and Apollinaire was not known for pettiness or jealousy. At the time, he was often in a sombre, distressed state brought on by the experiences in the trenches that had culminated in his head wound and his trepanation, and one can only say again that he doubtless found Cocteau, who had as yet published nothing that could interest him, little more than a clever, annoying dandy. Perhaps he knew that the dandy was writing an occasional poem that resembled his own; and it is at this time that he was failing to secure the publication of Cocteau's *Le Potomak* by the Mercure de France. Perhaps he had expressed wonderment that an artist of the calibre and character of Picasso, with whom he had shared earlier days of poverty in Montmartre, should take up with the worldling Cocteau. All that is "perhaps." But now the too brief mention of the original begetter of *Parade* was unquestionably a snub, and it has remained one of the more famous snubs in the annals of modern art. Apollinaire, whose influence among the artistic avant-garde had become considerable, was letting it be known that in his opinion Cocteau was no Satie, no Picasso, not even a Massine.

On May 18, the day of the first performance, an article by Cocteau, the best short exposition of *Parade* in existence, appeared in *Excelsior*. "Our wish," he said, "is that the public may consider *Parade* as a work which conceals poetry beneath the coarse outer skin of slapstick.* Laughter is natural to Frenchmen: it is important to keep this in mind and not be afraid to laugh even at this most difficult time. Laughter is too Latin a weapon to be neglected. *Parade* brings together Erik Satie's first orchestral score, Pablo Picasso's first stage décor, Massine's first Cubist choreography, and a poet's first attempt to express himself without words. We have worked so closely together that the contribution of each is in close

---

* In one of his writings on *Parade* Cocteau says that his original idea had not been "humoristique." Slapstick (in French, *guignol*) was the spirit in which Alfred Jarry had decided in 1896 to present his famous farce *Ubu Roi*, which was revived in 1908. Lincoln Kirstein points out that one of Picasso's sketches for a manager's costume (reproduced in Douglas Cooper, *Picasso Theatre*, Fig. 106) carries the letters "MERD," which might be part of the famous "*Merdre*," the "obscenity" that opens *Ubu Roi*. In the Picasso drawing, however, "MERD" might be read as an in-joke against Misia Sert, whose name also appears there and who in the eyes of the *Parade* collaborators was certainly an *emmerdeuse*.

union with the contributions of the others without impinging on them. . . . It was appropriate . . . to do justice for the first time to the true meaning of 'realism' in theatrical terms. What has hitherto been called 'realistic art' is in a way a pleonastic art, especially in the theatre, where 'realism' consists in admitting onto the stage real objects which lose their reality the moment they are placed in nonreal surroundings. The elements of *trompe-l'oeil* and *trompe-l'oreille* in *Parade* create reality — which alone has the power to move us, well disguised though it may be."

Cocteau's encouragement to laughter "even at this most difficult time" was a reference to the particular horror of the war in that May of 1917. The holocaust was now in its third year. Russia had defaulted, Allied morale was low. The first half of May was a period of all but incredible slaughter on the western front: each day thousands of Frenchmen and their allies perished in seemingly futile attacks against German lines along the river Aisne, and among the French troops there were mutinies against the incessant commands to commit almost certain suicide by going over the top in the face of machine-gun fire. A few months before, Paul Morand had recorded a lunch-table conversation in Paris that summed up the battlefield butcheries, stalemates, and painful advances. "Tristan Bernard says: 'Still, Mangin has advanced several kilometers.' Marie Scheikevitch exclaims, 'But he is a butcher!' 'Yes,' answers Tristan Bernard, 'but a traveling butcher. The others are stationary butchers.' "

On May 18, in Paris, a hundred and fifty miles from the slaughter, it was a motley audience that filled the Théâtre du Chatelet for the matinée premiere (it began at three forty-five) of *Parade*, advertised as being for the benefit of various war charities. There was the usual contingent of Diaghilev's artistically more or less enlightened society patrons and patronesses — the Princesse de Polignac, Misia Sert, the Etienne de Beaumonts, the Countesses Greffulhe and de Chévigné; for the first time in the history of the ballets there were numerous artists from Montmartre and Montparnasse, including Gino Severini and Juan Gris, to all of whom Diaghilev had sent complimentary tickets. Diaghilev also had as his guests a number of Russian soldiers, on leave from a Russian brigade fighting on the western front; and there were Poulenc and Auric, Pierre Albert-Birot, Ricardo Viñes, Firmin Gémier, Apollinaire, and a young

American named E. E. Cummings. But as in almost any large gathering there was a heavy preponderance of bourgeois.

There was unanimous applause for Picasso's romantic, tender, drop curtain, a huge, fairy-tale-like picture of a backstage party of harlequins and circus folk — "giant figures as fresh as bouquets," Cocteau had called them in *Excelsior*. But its sweetness was deceptive, and when it rose and the ballet proper began, the house divided. "Satie's music, so simple, so raw, so naïvely intricate, like a painting by the Douanier Rousseau, shocked everybody by its breeziness," Francis Poulenc has written. "For the first time — it has happened often enough since, God knows — the music hall was invading Art with a capital A. A one-step is danced in *Parade*! When *that* began the audience let loose with boos and applause. All Montparnasse, in the top gallery, shouted *'Vive Picasso!'* Auric, Roland Manuel, Tailleferre, Durey and many other musicians shouted *'Vive Satie!'* It was a real bedlam." Among the most sensational elements were the towering eleven-foot Cubist constructions encasing two of the managers (still another manager had been introduced, but through a series of accidents he had turned into a comic horse), which have been described as ambulant chunks of Cubist scenery. Other grotesqueries were the tapping of typewriters in the score, and the dance of the American girl. The latter has been described by Lydia Sokolova, who danced the part in later performances, after Marie Shabelska had left the company: "It was lucky that the short, white-pleated skirt and blazer which the American girl wore were easy to move in, because her entrance and exit were extremely difficult. These consisted of sixteen bars of music, and with each bar she had to jump with both feet straight out together in the front and almost touch her toes with her outstretched arms. This is hard enough to do on the same spot, but when it was a question of moving around a vast stage at full speed it was no mean feat. When it got to dancing ragtime in this part, whacking myself on the head and tripping myself up with the back foot in true Chaplin style, I began to enjoy myself."

Cocteau's beloved megaphone effects were not the only casualty at that first performance. He had insisted on the inclusion, in Satie's score, of what he called "bits of acoustical illusion" (*trompe-l'oreille*). Those included, in addition to the typewriter clicking, imitations of a dynamo, Morse code, sirens, an express train and an airplane, which he says he used "in the same spirit as the Cubist painters used optical illusion (*trompe-l'oeil*) — newspapers, painted-in frames, imitation wood." As a result of "mechanical difficulties due to wartime conditions," including a "breakdown of the compressed air," some of these went unheard or barely heard at the premiere. One wonders how and why. Satie had always been sardonic about those sound elements. "I composed a background to certain noises that Cocteau says he needs to point up his characters," was one of his venomous, mock-modest descriptions of his score for *Parade;* and one cannot help wondering whether here, as in other instances, there was something of a cabal.

Cocteau's feelings, when he had been experiencing the even then interminable-seeming war with his ambulance unit, that his ballet was more important than the senseless holocaust, the cynicism about the war heard around the Montparnasse café tables, Apollinaire's dedication to the *"esprit nouveau"* in the arts despite his own war wound — it was too much to expect that a bourgeois wartime public would go along with much of that. It was characteristic of French bourgeois to consider any startling novelties "un-French" and therefore deplorable; by presenting *Parade* to such a public, particularly at a moment of wartime anguish, Cocteau and the rest were "asking for it."

But what was it, exactly, that they got? Cocteau's accounts of the *scandale* of *Parade* are all so highly colored that one recognizes a recurrence of his need to identify with every aspect of the *Rite of Spring* and to obey Diaghilev's "Astound me." From the audience, he claims, came cries of *"Boches!"* and demands that the authors be sent to the front. "They wanted to kill us," he has said. "Women rushed at us armed with hatpins. We were saved by Apollinaire because his head was bandaged, he was in uniform and was therefore respected: he set himself in front of us like a rampart." "The piece lasted twenty minutes. After the curtain went down the audience was uproarious for fifteen, and finally fistfights broke out. I was crossing the theatre with Apollinaire to join Picasso and Satie, who were waiting for us in a box, when a large lady singer recognized me. 'There's one of them!' she cried — she meant the authors. And she lunged at me, brandishing a hatpin, trying to put my eyes out." He and Picasso, he said, were delighted to hear a gentleman declare to his wife: "If I had known it was going to be so

stupid I'd have brought the children." The most extreme of Cocteau's versions, perhaps supercharged for American consumption,
appeared in *Vanity Fair* for September, 1917: "I have heard the
cries of a bayonet charge in Flanders, but it was nothing compared
to what happened that night at the Châtelet Theatre."

There was certainly, as Poulenc testifies, a demonstration of
some intensity. The mildness of Paul Morand's report, in his diary,
"Much applause and a few boos," probably reflects a loyalty to his
friends the authors that is apparent again in his next, regretful
entry ten days later: "The authors of *Parade* are in despair. They
are withdrawing their ballet. Simone de Caillavet [later to become
Madame André Maurois] who, at twenty-two, is the critic for the
Gaulois, massacres the piece. Bidou in the *Débats*, doesn't praise it
either, but does not deny that it is interesting." (It was, of course,
Diaghilev, not the authors, who withdrew *Parade:* when a ballet
was badly received, Diaghilev usually took it off, but would often
revive it later if it was something he liked.) The reviews mentioned
by Morand were certainly condescending, and uninteresting to
quote at this distance (except, perhaps, for Mademoiselle de Caillavet's reproach that "the great republic who is France's friend deserves better than to be symbolized on the stage by an American girl
who is certainly epileptic"). Cocteau has said that the reviews of
Parade caused him to cancel his subscription to his press-clipping
service. "Insults spread like oil on blotting paper. Some came from
China and Africa." The most openly vituperative was that in *Le
Temps,* by Pierre Lalo, son of the composer Edouard Lalo. Jean
Poueigh, who declared in *Le Carnet de la Semaine* that Satie
lacked everything — inventiveness, wit, and professional skill —
received in his mail an open postcard from the composer: *"Monsieur et cher ami* — you're no more than an arse — an arse without music. Erik Satie." Poueigh sued Satie for libel, claiming that
because the postcard was open-faced it had brought him public hu-
miliation, having undoubtedly been read by his concierge. Satie
was sentenced to a week in prison and a thousand francs damages.
He appealed, and on November 27 lost his appeal. At the second
trial Cocteau was one of the witnesses for the defense, and was himself fined for "making physical threats against a lawyer during the
execution of his office" (he had raised his cane in a gesture of anger
against Poueigh's attorney). "Satie didn't take the matter seri-

ously," Cocteau reported in a letter to Misia. "And the other side
treated him like a crapulous old idiot — it was terrible. And *l'In-
tran* — never missing a chance to be ignoble!* What's to be done?
If only he could be kept out of prison — prison would discredit
him in the eyes of his pupils and of Arcueil. (Just now Sert telephoned. I've told him to arrange something.)"

But *Parade* was a success in that the writers, painters and musicians of the *esprit nouveau* adored it, and the composer Louis
Durey tells of many of them being present on June 6, three weeks
after its premiere, at a concert organized in its honor in the Salle
Huyghens. Poems by Max Jacob, Apollinaire, Cocteau, Blaise Cendrars and others were recited, musicians played a "Trio" by
Georges Auric, and Durey's "Carillons" for four hands, and Satie
and a young pianist named Juliette Meerowitch played a four-hand
arrangement of *Parade* itself. It was probably this success of *Parade* among artists that made it possible for Marcel Proust to write
to Cocteau: "I cannot tell you how delighted I am by the considerable stir made by your ballet. It would be almost an insult to you
and your collaborators to call it a 'success.' And yet, inexplicable
though it might seem, the success is real and very great. Even
though in this case the success is no more than a mere foretaste, a
propitious aura emanating from the future, it is not to be belittled."

Cocteau never forgave Diaghilev for having *Parade* performed so
"incompletely" in 1917, shorn of all his words, phrases and noises.
During the Ballet's spring season of 1920 at the Paris Opéra, Dia-
ghilev scheduled its revival, still in its "incomplete" form, which
Cocteau managed to prevent by a bit of maneuvering with Jacques
Rouché, the Opéra's director. Diaghilev is supposed to have said of
Parade "It is one of the best bottles in my cellar; I don't want to
have it shaken up too often"; and although six months after that
frustrated attempt he was to give it a fuller-scale production that
Cocteau would call a "triumph," it was not danced very often.† Nor

---

* On November 28 the newspaper *l'Intransigeant*, reporting the confirmation of
Satie's sentence, wrote sympathetically of "the old artist" and his "blameless personal
life" — adding, however, that for *Parade* Satie "had written what he called 'the
music.'"

† Douglas Cooper lists the revivals of *Parade* as follows: London, November, 1919;

did Cocteau care for the towering "carcasses" in which Picasso en-
cased the Managers. The Managers' *pas de deux*, he always said,
which had been delightful when rehearsed without the carcasses,
"lost all its lyric force" when danced in the cumbersome cardboard
costumes. "Our *Parade*," he wrote, referring to the 1917 performances, "was so far from what I would have wished, that I never went
to see it from out front. I made it a point to stay in the wings and
hold the signs beginning the number of each turn."

In the face of the persistent minimizing of his role in *Parade*,*
Cocteau always wrote warmly of the ballet, sometimes even grandiloquently, claiming on one occasion that it had "revived the tradition of Greek dance." For him, since he had conceived it and had
lived its evolution and execution in all its aspects — scenario,
score, décor and choreography — it was naturally more precious
than it was to the rest of the team which he had succeeded in getting
together. Douglas Cooper has remarked, on the transitoriness of a
theatrical spectacle: "What is there for the historian to examine,
analyse and comment on, in the way of factual evidence beyond the
artist's designs (if they still exist), an album of photographs, and
some visual memories?" Satie's delightful score is often heard;
Picasso's great drop curtain can be seen in the Musée National
d'Art Moderne in Paris, some of his costumes survive, and much of
the rest of his décor was photographed. Cocteau's work, which
underlies that of all the others, survives in its descendants.

For *Parade*, in addition to being delightful, is a great ancestor. It
was a true theatrical innovation, the first totally modern ballet, the

---

Paris, December, 1920 (Théâtre des Champs-Elysées) ; May, 1921, June, 1923 (Gaîté
Lyrique) ; June, 1924 (Théâtre Sarah-Bernhardt) ; London, July, 1926. More lately,
there was a performance in Brussels in 1962, which was filmed under the direction of
Massine, and one in Toulouse in 1966. To celebrate the ballet's fiftieth anniversary, the
New York City Ballet Company sought to revive it in 1967, but was balked by difficulties concerning rights to scenery, costumes, and other elements. About the 1962 Brussels
production, too, Massine has written "It was unfortunate that in spite of repeated applications to Picasso we were unable to obtain the sketches for the original settings and
costumes, and had to do them from copies."

* E.g., by Gide (see p. 232) and Satie (p. 261). There has been a tendency to follow
Apollinaire's lead. Cocteau's own description of the collaboration in *Excelsior* remains
fair. In a letter to Massine complaining of Diaghilev's attitude he wrote with some
heat: "I made Satie write every note of the score, I enlisted Picasso's collaboration, over-
coming all his principles (despite what he may be saying now), with you I have
collaborated cordially, joyously and loyally, orienting your superb work in a direction
that is dear to me. I ask nothing more."

first balletistic "metaphor of the everyday," in Lincoln Kirstein's phrase. (*Jeux*, the tennis-match ballet, had been rendered idyllic by Debussy's music.) After *Parade*, with its satirizing of advertising and other aspects of modern life, came countless other ballets on commonplace modern themes, with modern music and modern sets — music by Poulenc, by Auric, by Milhaud, décors by Picasso, by Braque, by Derain, by Marie Laurencin, by Chirico. Such ballets continue to have their premieres today. Five years after Diaghilev's command had been given in the Place de la Concorde, it had been obeyed: "In 1917," Cocteau wrote, "the afternoon of the premiere of *Parade*, I astounded him." And further satisfaction came in the approval of the other great man who had rejected *David:* when Stravinsky saw *Parade* he said that it gave him "the impression of freshness and real originality." One of the most limpid appreciations of *Parade*, and of Cocteau's underlying inventiveness, is that of Juan Gris: "I like *Parade* because it is unpretentious, gay and distinctly comic. Picasso's décor has lots of style and is simple, and Satie's music is elegant. It is not figurative, has no fairy-tale element, no lavish effects, no dramatic subject. It's a sort of musical joke in the best of taste and without high artistic pretentions. That's why it stands right out and is better than the other ballets. I even believe that it is an attempt to do something quite new in the theatre. It had quite a lot of success although a group was organized to boo it. The idea of course was to boo Cubism, but the unprejudiced people were nevertheless swung over, and it was the applause which prevailed." Serge Lifar has said: "Massine's felicitous touches in *Parade* and subsequent ballets go back directly to Cocteau, with their literary flavor and their circuslike stylization. It was the turn of literature to have its say in ballet — music and painting already having had theirs. Everything that is now current in ballet was invented by Cocteau for *Parade*, which he knew by heart, and every step of which he had suggested."

During the subsequent checkered relations between Diaghilev and Cocteau, Diaghilev sometimes consulted him about ballet collaborations in the new art world to which Cocteau had introduced him by the presentation of Picasso. Some of Diaghilev's older colleagues resented the change: "Diaghilev's chief advisors were now the 'new friends,' " Alexandre Benois writes at the close of his charming *Reminiscences of the Russian Ballet*, "[among them] Jean Cocteau, who up till 1914 had been considered by us as a sort of *enfant terrible*."

As for Picasso, in being commissioned by Diaghilev, thanks to Cocteau, to paint the huge drop curtain for *Parade*, and to design the sets and costumes, some of which were reproduced in color in the program, he had been given a one-man show of a magnitude hitherto vouchsafed to no artist of the School of Paris. Even before *Parade* he had left poverty behind: dealers and private collectors had been buying his work, but to Parisian "society" and the larger public he was little known. He seems to have had no one-man show in Paris since 1902. The display of his genius in *Parade* changed that. Early in 1918 Paul Guillaume held an exhibition of Picasso's work along with pictures by Matisse; on July 12, 1918 Picasso married Olga Koklova, with Cocteau, Max Jacob and Apollinaire as his witnesses; Madame Errazuriz invited the painter and his bride to spend the summer in her villa at Biarritz, and on their return they rented a bourgeois apartment in the rue La Boétie, among the picture galleries. Picasso was taken up both by society and by the dealer Paul Rosenberg, brother of the more pioneering Léonce; and helped by Rosenberg's salesmanship, by the accessible beauty of his temporarily more realistic painting, and by repeated commissions from Diaghilev, he rapidly became what he has been ever since — the most famous painter in the world.

It is natural for a Picasso, knowing in retrospect that he had been bound for fame in any case, to prefer not to keep in mind, let alone ever mention, the close connection between the great change in his fortunes and a ballet invented by someone else; but Cocteau, throughout the years of his own fame, just as naturally never forgot it. All his life his admiration for Picasso continued at a level of infatuation. In the words of one of his friends, "Picasso was a real sickness with him"; and the sickness was not diminished by his realization that all too often, over the years, Picasso's only reciprocation was tolerance — a tolerance that Cocteau was indiscreet enough to strain most particularly by painting, in later life, a series of murals that aped Picasso. One hears some cruel gibes by Picasso about Cocteau; but for Cocteau Picasso was always the revelation

Cocteau in 1916. Pencil drawing by Picasso.

Cocteau the Aviator, 1915.

Annunciation at Grasse, 1918. (Cocteau and Comtesse Edith de Beaumont.)

Cocteau (third from left) with his ambulance group. Region of Nieuport, 1916.

Cocteau near Nieuport, 1916. (*Génie* means "corps of army engineers" as well as "genius.")

Cocteau and Marie Shabelska
in Rome, 1917.
Drawing by Picasso.

AUTRE CONCILIABULE.

One of Cocteau's "atrocity" drawings from *Le Mot*, 1914–15.

Cocteau, 1916-17. Oil by Amedeo Modigliani.

he had been in 1915 and throughout "the greatest battle of the war."

Cock and Harlequin (1917–1918)

At ten o'clock in the evening of June 15, 1917, a group of Parisians began to gather in Paul Morand's apartment in the Palais-Royal. Earlier that evening Morand had dined with Misia Sert on her Quai Voltaire terrace, in a company that included José-Maria Sert and Madame Errazuriz. During the dinner Misia had spoken sharply of Jean Cocteau: "He needs to make himself liked by everybody at the same time — by Picasso, Madame de Chevigné, the Marines, etc. He's spoiling his best years getting himself liked, instead of trying to be disliked." On Cocteau's behalf, it could be said that he had lived up to Misia's idea of virtue by showing a certain pleasure in being loathed by members of his ambulance unit and in being lunged at, amid a hostile crowd at the premiere of *Parade,* by a large lady with a hatpin. But Misia would have dismissed those episodes as being cases of detestation merely by the dull, a state of affairs she surely considered natural, even essential. What she was referring to, in her shrewd if ill-natured way, was Cocteau's desire, becoming increasingly obvious, to "keep in" with all factions of the colorful: the aristocracy, the intellectuals, the heroes, and the exotics, including artists of all shapes and shades. (Not until the close of his life, however, was Cocteau touched by the attraction of the merely rich — a corruption to which talented people often succumb in early years; and he never developed a taste for what Misia was really urging on him — the demeaning petty rivalries of artistic cliques.)

Cocteau's name had naturally been on people's lips that evening because it was he whom Morand's ten-o'clock guests at the Palais-Royal were coming to listen to: he was to give a reading, his first, of his suite of war poems, *Le Cap de Bonne-Espérance,* and he himself had chosen the listeners. Morand, in his journal, describes them as they arrived: "Valentine Gross, with her wide-open eyes, her face painted like a doll's, her hair smoothly parted in the center; Edith de Beaumont, short hair à la Joan of Arc, ravishing, looking like Titian's *Man with a Glove;* Etienne de Beaumont, his hands crossed over his stomach; and then Porel and then Gautier-Vignal. When they had all assembled, Cocteau read. "Sultry," Morand noted. "Not a breath of air, not a sound; under a lamp, Cocteau opens a notebook in which words in his large, naïve handwriting run on and jostle one another in keeping with today's aesthetic. It is a long poem dedicated to Garros: the machine-gun rattle of images is hard to keep up with; then a lovely passage on hangars, another on the Marne, then at the end Garros' flight from Fréjus to Tunis. Those last two parts, the best in the poem, very concise, without metaphors, and with silences that are like airpockets."

Jacques Porel, who had been serving with the Second Cuirassiers and had not seen Cocteau since before the war, found him that night "very much himself, but strangely composed, having acquired a more serious idea of his gifts and his role." "The poem was beautiful," Porel says, "but I had the impression that he had imposed it on himself as a task. He read standing, with a new gravity that bothered me a little. I missed his old lightness, that delightful flyaway side of his that he is through with but which I was used to. We were all — not disappointed, but surprised. He pretended to be delighted. And then he talked, justified himself with persuasive eloquence, and we were won over again. Impossible to resist him. Our little group was unquestionably under his spell."

Porel was seeing the new Cocteau, the Cocteau who had begotten *Parade,* sparked a *scandale,* and astounded Diaghilev, as contrasted with the youth he had seen bring Misia a bouquet at lunch during the early days of the ballets. The end of the reading was probably not the end of the Cocteau monologue; that evening Cocteau was ceaselessly effervescent and much enjoyed. "After Cocteau," says Paul Morand, "with his piercing eyes, his speaking hands, his mimicry, everybody else's gestures seem clumsy: the next day, you remember nothing. The Grand Duchess Anastasia [mother-in-law of the German crown prince] used to say: 'He is priceless, that young M. Cocteau; unfortunately I forget everything he says. I'm going to bring a little notebook.'" Many of Cocteau's listeners have confessed, like Morand and the Grand Duchess, that as soon as his performance ceased, the remarks were forgotten — it was the impression of brilliance that remained.

That reading of *Le Cap de Bonne-Espérance* took place the evening of the day on which General Pershing, just arrived in Paris, had been cheered in the Chamber of Deputies. (A fortnight later, American infantry and marines parading up the rue de Rivoli on the Fourth of July were only mildly applauded, Morand records, the war by now having become so crushing a burden to the French as to deaden all enthusiasm: "The crowd, especially the women, weary, every spark gone, wanting only the quickest possible end to the war.") The reading was inserted into a prolonged bout of party-going, a social round of the kind that Cocteau indulged in whenever he was in Paris. Paul Morand's journal shows Cocteau at innumerable affairs. At a dinner given by Cécile Sorel a few days after the premiere of *Parade* the hostess welcomed Cocteau with an enthusiastic "Hail conqueror!" — but proceeded to seat him "next to Lalo, who had written two days before in his column in *Le Temps* that *Parade* was 'a bit of pretentious silliness.' " (At that dinner both Cécile Sorel and Coco Chanel — "who, decidedly, is becoming a 'personality,' " writes Morand — appeared with bobbed hair, the latest mode. Morand says: "Cocteau claims that this fashion was launched for charitable purposes — that all the cut hair is put together by Bailby [Léon Bailby, the newspaper editor] and sold for the benefit of the wounded.) There was a dinner at the Ritz given by Princesse Hélène Soutzo (a lovely Rumanian whom Morand was later to marry) with "the Princesse Eugène [Violette] Murat, Pierre de Polignac . . . Proust, Cocteau, l'Abbé Mugnier, Zuboff." At lunch at the Comtesse de Chevigné's, with the Princesse Soutzo, the Beaumonts and Cocteau, Cocteau had hay fever, and lamented " 'To think of every July being ruined for me until I'm fifty — my favorite month, etc.' From the way he talks about his colds you'd think they were railway accidents." Valentine Gross now also moved into an apartment in the Palais-Royal, and entertained, among many others, "Gautier-Vignal, Cocteau, Fargue, Porel, Jean Hugo and Charles Daudet. Ricardo Viñes plays Chopin and Granados deliciously." After another dinner at the Ritz, given by Hélène Soutzo with "the Etienne de Beaumonts, J. Reinach, Monzie, Porel, Cocteau, Proust," amidst experiments with hypnosis there was a "sudden darkness. Searchlights in the starry skies; from the direction of Le Bourget, something like rockets; one by one the French planes climb up. Sirens wail. 'Somebody's stepped on the Eiffel Tower's toe, and it's complaining,' says Cocteau." One day Cocteau, who had seen a film of the newly invented tanks, said: " 'It's like a safe falling from the top floor of a house, then standing on its hind legs like a dog, asking for a piece of sugar.' And he cries that tanks will be begetting children on locomotives." Morand makes no mention of Cocteau's friends from Montmartre and Montparnasse, whom Cocteau was doubtless seeing during those same social weeks: Juan Gris inscribed a charcoal still-life drawing to him in July. Until he set about destroying his reputation as a worldling, Cocteau was to alternate periods of such party-going with weeks or months of retreat.

He retreated now, in August, 1917, to Le Piqueÿ, a cluster of fishermen's cottages and a small hotel or two on the bay of Biscay in the Gironde, a Robinson Crusoe-ish spot that had been discovered by André Lhote. Here, where he knew only the Lhotes and Gino Severini, the Italian Futurist painter, who was at nearby Le Canon, he read Goethe's *Conversations with Eckermann, Treasure Island,* and *Kidnapped,* sunbathed on the dunes, paddled (he never learned to swim), and worked on both *Le Cap de Bonne-Espérance* and the second group of war poems, about Flanders, that he still referred to as *Secteur 131.* "I'm living in Uncle Tom's Cabin in a Negro village on the bay of Arcachon," he wrote to Gide. "The Lhotes have a cabin very close. Thank you for your letter, which is company in my solitude — a kind of Texas — a colonial charm about this deserted shore where I row and chase squirrels — my beard is growing — I walk barefoot on the brambles and hobnob with Uncle Tom." In letters to Valentine Gross, who was in Paris designing theatre costumes for the Vieux-Colombier and cutting wood blocks to illustrate an edition of the *Métamorphoses,* he shared his relish of the mentality of his fellow hotel guests, chiefly petty bourgeois who could not afford the hotels at the nearby flourishing summer resort of Arcachon: "Example — a lady at the next table to whom I said yesterday 'It's funny, with the sea so calm — you can't tell where that pole begins and where its reflection ends.' After studying the situation through binoculars she answered 'The pole begins just at the point where it emerges from the water.' Lhote's lady neighbor asked how I could be a poet, since one 'had to be dead to be a poet.' " Half naked, turning first red then "Negro color," with mail arriving only when the postman chose to come, he repeatedly pictured himself, in his letters, as living in "Texas," or "a corner of the Far West" (in Paris he and Valentine and others of what he called his "dear group" were fans of American Westerns), or in Uncle Tom's Cabin or in a bit of landscape out of Lamartine's *Graziella,* or even in Tahiti. He was glad to be distant from poor Satie, whose diatribes against French "justice," as he continued to fight in the courts against the confirmation of his sentence, were fatiguing even his most loyal friends such as Valentine: "Maman tells me that Satie is wearing you down. I can't blame you. A genius who demeans himself and exposes his admirers to ridicule is more dismaying than his stupid critic." By the end of the year he had finished the poem and was busy at something new. He wrote to Gleizes, in New York, from Grasse, where he was visiting friends.

Cocteau to Albert Gleizes
January 30, 1918

. . . . Your letter reaches me in Grasse. More and more I'm against Impressionist decadence — which doesn't keep me from recognizing the individual values within Impressionism and its unity of style. Yes — of course Renoir, but I say down with Renoir the way I say down with Wagner. I have finished *Le Cap.* I'm working on *Secteur 131* and on a little book about music. . . . Bring me back as many Negro ragtimes and as much great Russian-Jewish-American music as you can.*

What had happened since *Parade,* and especially since Cocteau's return from Le Piquey, was that he had been seeing something of a number of young composers who had gathered around Satie as disciples and whose music was being increasingly played at the happenings in the Salle Huyghens, amid the African sculpture in Paul Guillaume's gallery, and elsewhere. Two young musicians, particularly, Georges Auric and Francis Poulenc, barely out of their teens, were showing Cocteau that they enjoyed his company; they paid court to him much as they did to the composer they called master, seeking him out and asking permission to set his verse to

---

* Did he mean songwriters like Irving Berlin and (as he perhaps thought) George M. Cohan?

music. Satie did nothing to discourage his disciples in this alliance: despite his quarrels with Cocteau he had such respect for his promotional abilities that he was soon to ask him to prepare a prospectus for an "invention" of his own — *"la musique d'ameublement,"* background music, to be imbibed rather than listened to. Cocteau had received the further pleasant news that the Diaghilev company had performed *Parade* in Madrid before the king of Spain, and in Barcelona, and that during their visit to Rio de Janeiro they had been requested, at a party at the French Embassy, to dance parts of that ballet for the ambassador, Paul Claudel, and his secretary, the young composer Darius Milhaud. In the United States, too, there was interest in *Parade,* and *Vanity Fair* for September, 1917 printed an article about it by Cocteau himself. All this suggested to Cocteau the idea of writing a manifesto in favor of the new music and what it promised to engender among the young. French music should now sound simple even though it might be "intricately constructed"; it should contrast with the "Impressionist" music of Wagner, Debussy, Ravel and even some of Stravinsky; it should no longer be "music to be listened to with one's head in one's hands"; and it should be purely French. (The fact that Satie's mother was a Scot Cocteau dismissed with "Nothing germinates unmixed.") There was also the obvious parallel between Impressionist music and the Impressionist and Post-Impressionist painting that the Cubists had so rebelled against. "Work with three colors — too many colors make Impressionism (Picasso)": Cocteau had written that on one of the pages in his Roman *Parade* notebook. Such music and such painting might not be intrinsically bad, but they were bad for today, bad in the artistic scene if art was to flourish: lovely though they might be, they were as unwanted nowadays as the loveliest poppies and cornflowers in a wheatfield. In all that there was much to write about. Serious treatment of the subject might be thought to require musical knowledge as well as daring; Cocteau had plenty of the latter, and if he were to replace the former by flair, that would only give his "little book about music" a lighter tone — more in keeping with the music and the general artistic spirit that he was publicizing.

Shortly before this time there had appeared in Cocteau's life a young poet in uniform of whom little remains known except his name, Jean LeRoy, a few youthful poems, a few notes on poetry,

and a few letters sending kisses to Cocteau, but whose advent marks
the development in Cocteau's habits of attachment that has already
been mentioned. While continuing as always to idealize the "big
boys" (in the cases of Diaghilev and Picasso it was as though he
were constantly trying by various approaches to acquire for himself a magnitude identical with theirs), he began now, much as
women past their first bloom often take younger lovers, to play the
role of protector, much romanticized in his own mind, to appealing
younger artists in whom he also saw himself. Of these LeRoy was
the first. "Help LeRoy," the twenty-eight-year-old Cocteau im-
plored Valentine Gross when he had left Paris for Grasse at the end
of December. He felt no need to beg anyone to look after Auric or
Poulenc, young artists also, of approximately LeRoy's age: much
practical good though he might set about doing them, and himself
along with them, and homosexual though Poulenc was, neither of
them happened to be a candidate for sentimentalizing, whereas Le-
Roy, if one may judge from his several better-known successors,
must have differed from those musicians in ways that both expressed his own emotional needs and evoked Cocteau's. Furthermore, unlike Auric and Poulenc, LeRoy was at the front, living in
the mud of the trenches — mud so soupy, he wrote Cocteau, that
in it "frogs choked to death and rats drowned." He was a soldier
hero, and Cocteau himself was suffering from rheumatism and
"atrocious stomach cramps," which at times he attributed, in his
letters, to anguish about the war or to his experiences in the Somme.

Cocteau's ill health, which was always to be a major preoccupation, was unfortunately of the kind that seldom brings one
sympathy except from one's mother: he was constantly miserable,
constantly demanding attention and sympathy from doctors and
friends while remaining for much of his life, as friends sometimes
said, "the healthiest of us all." Particularly this winter of early
1918, which in Paris was the worst of the war, sombre and dreary,
with little food, less heat, and not much work for artists, it was
irritating to Valentine Gross, for example, with the prosecuted
Satie on her hands and her new fiancé, Jean Hugo (great-grandson
of the poet) at the front, to receive complaints about stomach
cramps and facial twitches and her lack of attentiveness in not re-
laying Paris gossip to the sufferer in his lonely, distant Riviera
"sanatorium," as he called it — the whole interspersed with re-

marks like "Here as I write you I have one cheek in the sun — 'like a peach,' as Byron puts it." Cocteau was well aware of conditions in Paris — "The little news I hear from Paris is appalling — Valentine with her kerosene and my mother on her iceberg," he wrote to Jean Hugo on January 15 — and yet he could write Valentine four days later: "Here impossible to imagine icebergs — window open tonight."

Especially since Valentine knew quite well what the invalid's "sanatorium" was. In Grasse Cocteau was a guest at the villa of the Francis de Croissets', and present also at the January house party were Edith and Etienne de Beaumont and Madame de Croisset's daughter by her first marriage, Marie-Laure Bischoffsheim, now a girl of fifteen. In later life Marie-Laure told of her girlhood friendship with Cocteau: "My grandmother, whose name was Laure de Sade . . . had a close woman friend with whom she used to make lint for bandages during the 1914 war and who was none other than the mother of Jean Cocteau. That was how I knew Jean. We saw each other every day. We talked. . . . Everything was chaste and pure. I looked like Raphael's self-portrait. . . . In short, I was Jean Cocteau's Lolita. I told my grandmother: 'When I'm fifteen years and three months old I'll marry Jean.' She made such an outcry that I abandoned the idea." Marie-Laure had seen a good deal of Cocteau at the rue d'Anjou while visiting her grandmother (who, in Proust's cork-lined room, was at the moment well on the way to becoming the Duchesse de Guermantes), and now the poet and his Lolita played on the terraces of Grasse. Such was the "sanatorium" where among lemon trees and fountains Cocteau worked on his poems and the book on music that he had mentioned to Gleizes. The war ground on. "This formless monster, which hops, flounders, tramples people in its clumsiness, eats them out of gluttony and vomits right and left, is certainly a glorious sight," Cocteau wrote bitterly to Jean Hugo. "What are the Americans saying?" * To both Valentine and to André Gide he sent prints of photographs he had taken with the Beaumonts in the villa gardens. With one of them he wrote to Gide: "Enclosed a miracle photo. I'm

---

* When Hugo's French regiment mutinied in May, 1917, he asked to go to another unit and was sent as liaison officer to the 1st American Division, which had just arrived at Gondrecourt, in Lorraine. There the chief of G3 (Operations) on General Sibert's staff was "young Colonel [George C.] Marshall."

the angel in the bathrobe and the Virgin is Mme. de Beaumont." It is the earliest, or one of the earliest, of Cocteau's montages — a charming Annunciation made from two negatives, showing a towel-draped Virgin, and an angel in what would now be called a terry-cloth robe holding in place a bath-towel wing. Later, when in his films Cocteau reached the height of his talent for montages, he often gave his images a touch of the comically outré: had the Grasse Annunciation photograph been made ten years later, he might have suppressed the photographer's silhouette, but scarcely the angel's spats.

Cocteau's "little book on music," a seventy-four page pamphlet that he called *Le Coq et l'Arlequin* (Cock and Harlequin), appeared in the spring of 1918. Its imprint was that of a new publishing house, "Les Editions de la Sirène," which Cocteau says he founded along with his fellow poet Blaise Cendrars, since "nobody wanted to publish the work of either of us." ("Nobody" included notably the *N.R.F.*, to which for some time Cocteau would vainly offer his manuscripts through Valentine.) Jean Hugo drew a siren with the form of a sea horse as an emblem for the new firm, and Marcel Proust wrote to Walter Berry: "I understand why Cocteau should have the Sirène, because he himself really looks like a siren, with his thin fish-bone nose and fascinating eyes. He looks like a sea horse, too." The pamphlet was illustrated with two "monograms" of a cock and a harlequin by Picasso, and with Picasso's portrait drawing of Cocteau, the "Ingres" drawing in uniform of which he had written to Valentine. Cocteau dedicated *Le Coq et l'Arlequin* to his new friend Georges Auric. Had he not already dedicated *Le Cap de Bonne-Espérance* (in manuscript) "to Garros, in captivity," he said in his preface, he would have dedicated the new book "To Garros, escaped from Germany";* Auric was a worthy substitute because he, too, had "escaped from Germany" in the sense that he was a musician who had turned against Wagner. The catchy, alliterative title contains half of Cocteau's

---

* Garros had escaped from the last of his German prisons in February, 1917 and was now training to return to combat flying. It was probably he who was responsible for Cocteau's writing the preface to an illustrated booklet on military aviation called *Dans le Ciel de la Patrie*, published by the "Société SPAD," Paris, "L'An de guerre 1918." In this preface, dated January 1, 1918, Cocteau calls airplanes "furious angels" — apparently his earliest printed mention of the winged spirits that were to become one of his great themes.

own name,* and he explains further that the cock he had in mind (clearly the *coq Gaulois,* one of the emblems of France) "cries '*Cocteau*' twice." Here he fell into onomatopoeic embarrassment, however. For it has been pointed out that while the French rendering of the cry of the rooster, "*cocorico,*" (our "cock-a-doodle-doo"), can, with some practice, be made to sound something like "*cocteau cocteau,*" more normal utterance of "*cocteau cocteau*" tends rather to resemble the cry of a hen who has just laid an egg — an image quite lacking the nobility that Cocteau had in mind.

But *Le Coq et l'Arlequin* is a clever egg for the pullet cock to have laid. Composed largely in aphorisms à la Nietzsche, in a quicksilver style that Cocteau now made his own and would henceforth use in all his "*poésie critique,*" the witty, lightly chauvinistic, anti-Wagner, pro-Satie tract abounds in attractive formulations that young people, especially, have always enjoyed:

Art is science made flesh.

The musician lets numbers out of their cage — the draftsman liberates geometry.

A work of art must satisfy all the Muses — this is what I call "test by nine." †

A YOUNG MAN MUST NOT INVEST IN GILT-EDGE SECURITIES.

TO BE DARING WITH TACT IS TO KNOW HOW FAR WE MAY GO TOO FAR.

Wagner, Stravinsky, and even Debussy are first-rate composers. Whoever goes near them is hard put to it to escape from their tentacles; Satie leaves a clear road open upon which everyone is free to leave his own imprint.

If you shave your head, don't leave a curl for Sundays.

MUSICAL BREAD is what we want.

In his demand for "purely French music," Cocteau continued anything but consistent, and *Le Coq et l'Arlequin* includes more

---

* In the *Figaro littéraire* for April 14, 1966, "Aristide," the author of the column "Usage et Grammaire," wrote: "Cocteau is a diminutive, a contraction of *coqueteau,* meaning 'little cock.'" When a correspondent wrote in suggesting that "Cocteau" might come rather from the Latin *coctor* (cook) — the term "*maître coq*" being used for a cook on a ship — "Aristide" expressed doubt (June 30, 1966). He suggested "*coctelien*" as the proper adjective for "cocteau." Cocteau once described his own name as being "the plural of 'cocktail'."

† "*Preuve par 9*" in French. The more technical English equivalent of this mathematical expression, "casting out nines," is not too useful as a translation.

than one word of welcome to the American jazz that Paris was now beginning to hear:

> The music-hall, the circus, American Negro bands — all this is as fertilizing to an artist as life itself.
> The kind of thing that sweeps away Impressionist music is, for example, an American dance that I saw at the Casino de Paris. The accompaniment was an American band with banjos and big nickel tubes. On the right of the little black-coated group there was a barman of sound effects in a gilt pergola full of bells, triangles, boards, and motorcycle horns. With these he mixed cocktails, adding from time to time a dash of cymbals, all the while rising from his seat, posturing and smiling vacuously. Mr. Pilcer, in tails, thin and rouged, and Mlle. Gaby Deslys, like a big ventriloquist's doll, with a porcelain complexion, corn-colored hair, and a gown with ostrich feathers, danced to this hurricane of rhythms and drumbeats a kind of domesticated cataclysm which left them completely drunk and dazzled under the streaming glare of six air-raid searchlights. The house stood and applauded, roused from its torpor by this extraordinary number, which is to the frenzy of Offenbach as a tank is to an 1870 *calèche*.

Such passages as those led Paul Souday to say in *Le Temps* that Cocteau's aesthetic "fluctuated between Cubism and vaudeville," and everyone saw that the book abounded in exaggerations and contradictions. But its wit, its sharpness, its capturing of the artistic mood of the moment made it a success, and the first edition was quickly sold out. The Princesse de Polignac speaks in her memoirs of the book's "great influence"; according to Arthur Honegger, "Cocteau, without being genuinely a musician, served as a guide to many young folk; he stood for the general sense of reaction against the prewar aesthetic . . . [and] gave the signal for music in the trenchant style"; and Louis Durey, the least well known of "Les Six" has written: "Cocteau's remarks, expressed with such originality and pungency, sometimes anticipated our own experiments and sometimes came after them — they were almost always in harmony with our work." Honegger points out, however, that well before Cocteau "a Strauss, a Stravinsky, a Schoenberg had already rebelled against Debussyism"; and more than one irritated composer and musician considered Cocteau's emphasis on the Satie "revolution" mere proof of the ignorance, or at best the partisanship, of a musical upstart. Two years later the book was to bring Cocteau a letter from Proust, who added to some typically phrased praise: "You contradict yourself sometimes, and that enchants me, because I like people to show their different faces. I contradict myself all the time. . . . What a pleasure to hear you mention Chardin, Ingres, Manet. Unfortunately I have never seen a Cézanne. Where can one see some? *Mille tendresses de votre Marcel.*"

In his magazine *Ecrits Nouveaux* for March, 1918, André Germain published a one-act "heroic farce" entitled *Cocteau Bourgeticide ou Apollinaire Sauvé*, which casts light on how Cocteau was regarded at that moment in certain Parisian artistic circles. Into a restaurant where the immensely respectable novelist and academician Paul Bourget is dining with two duchesses comes Apollinaire, dressed in Cubist costume and carrying two tin breasts from his *Les Mamelles de Tirésias*, "daubed in violent colors by Picasso." After an argument, Bourget indignantly strikes Apollinaire with one of the tin breasts, and a crowd of Apollinaire's disciples, "Cubists and Nunists," Cocteau among them, surges in and knocks Bourget to the ground:

> GUILLAUME APOLLINAIRE: One more symbolic gesture is required! Who will place his foot on the head of the prostrate dragon?
>
> UNANIMOUS VOICES: You, you, beloved leader!
>
> APOLLINAIRE (*recognizing Cocteau*): No — it shall be the youngest and the most innocent, the babe still at the breast, the suckling of the future, Jean Cocteau!
>
> THE FAT DUCHESS (*to Cocteau*): If you do that, remember that never again will you tango at my house with the Grand Duchess Anastasia!
>
> COCTEAU (*remembering that though he is Apollinaire's lieutenant, he has hitherto been adored by the salons and loved by various Academicians — caught in a cruel dilemma*): You wish to do me too much honor, Master.
>
> APOLLINAIRE: As leader, I order it.

(*Cocteau, despite a terrible look from the fat Duchess, gives a sign of assent, grasps with bad grace a wooden sword handed him by a rabid lady Nunist, and advances one charming little foot in the direction of the Academic front.*)

CHORUS OF NUNISTS AND CUBISTS (*to a melody by Erik Satie*): A solemn moment is at hand!

(*Cocteau, intoxicated by the singing, proceeds with supreme elegance to mime the decapitation of Bourget.*)

APOLLINAIRE (*exalted*): Astride the modern Goliath, dear child, you look like a young and radiant DAVID!

Thus did André Germain repeat, about Cocteau, Misia Sert's "He needs to make himself liked by everybody at the same time," indicating that his choice of "modernism" had been made hesitantly and under duress, but indicating also that at least in certain circles he was now recognized as a foe of academism and as Apollinaire's "lieutenant." That there were other circles, who did not so recognize him, will soon become apparent. A conservative's view of the Cocteau of this time is given by Jacques-Emile Blanche, eventually to be elected to the Académie des Beaux-Arts, who lamented to Paul Morand: "Cocteau has periods. He is cyclic. I remember the Anna de Noailles phase six years ago: Jean talked about her to us so much that we, who all loved her, couldn't bear to hear her name! Today it's the Picasso phase. I have seen friends of Picasso in Barcelona and know a good deal about him. He's a clever fellow at making use of people, for all his blunt air of a Montmartre bohemian. He has made use of Cocteau."

In the spring of 1918, after some time had passed without news of Jean LeRoy from the front, Cocteau became anxious, and wrote to Etienne de Beaumont, asking whether he knew anything, and adding, about his own brother, "Paul has been flying over Frankfurt — we can't sleep for thinking of it." News of the young poet came soon enough: on May 24 Cocteau wrote to Gide: "I write you because I am in pain. They have killed my friend Jean LeRoy, whom I adored and for whom I was everything. LeRoy had become in a way my 'pupil' — I was cultivating in him qualities that my own disorder has kept me from putting to the best use. He was young, handsome, good, brave, full of genius, simple — everything that Death loves . . ."

When Cocteau wrote, some years later, "I have lost my seven best friends," his count probably began with that loss in May, 1918 of Jean LeRoy. Etienne de Beaumont invited him to stay with him, for a time, in the house in the rue Duroc, and it was from there, on July 12, when the Germans were again close to Paris, this time at Château-Thierry, fifty miles away, that Cocteau went to be a witness, along with Apollinaire and Max Jacob, at the two ceremonies, civil and Orthodox, of Picasso's marriage to Olga Koklova. (Apollinaire himself had married in May, and on the arrival of Cocteau's wedding present, an Egyptian statuette, had sent him a letter and a poem of thanks, referring to the two of them as *"rois de la poésie"* and inviting Cocteau to call on him — at his office.) Cocteau wrote to Edith de Beaumont, who was at Grasse with Madame de Chevigné and Marie-Laure, of parties that he and Etienne were attending and giving — one evening their guests included (unless he was joking) Mistinguett, Anatole France and André Citroën the automobile king; and later, in mid-August, once again at Le Piqueÿ, he thanked Etienne for his consoling shelter and reproached him for waiting until he had left Paris to give, in his garden, a "great Negro fête" that he hears from everyone was marvelous. Apparently this musical garden party, which included a performance of Francis Poulenc's *Rhapsodie Nègre*, was the first private party in Paris to feature American jazz,* supplied on this occasion by American Negro soldiers. "Yes, everybody tells me about the gold and silver trombones of your Negroes in the rue Duroc," Cocteau wrote to Poulenc from his sunny beach. "I'm beginning to be dark enough to play in the band." The Duroc jazz may have been accompanied by other sounds, for during that summer the Germans were bombarding Paris with 42-cm. shells from their "Big Bertha." After a direct hit on the church of St.-Gervais on March 29, in which seventy-five people were killed, the Paris churches had been closed, and children were given First Communion in various hastily consecrated cellars, among them that of the Bon Marché department store, not far from the Beaumont garden.

---

* Paul Morand speaks in his journal of a party in London two years earlier — "a most amusing party with 'coons,' the first jazz of the period."

A few weeks later, with American troops adding their force to the attack, the German lines broke, German strength quickly ebbed both materially and morally, and the end of the war was in sight.

Satie won his contest in the courts: the critic Poueigh's demand for damages was in the end denied, and the composer's prison sentence was cancelled or suspended.*

On October 5, 1918 came the news that Roland Garros had failed to return from a mission. He had been much weakened by his years of German captivity, and his return to combat flying had been opposed by friends and colleagues. After an arduous period of retraining, he destroyed a German plane on October 2. A few days after October 5 his body was found amid the wreckage of his plane in the Ardennes. The cause of his crash remains unknown. So perished the second of Cocteau's "seven best friends."

And then, early in November, two days before the Armistice, Apollinaire died of influenza.

Cocteau to André Salmon
Saturday midnight, November 9, [1918]

Mon cher André,

Poor Apollinaire is dead. Picasso is too sad to write. He asks me to do it, and to attend to notices in the newspapers. I have no experience of such things — will you be so kind as to take care of it?

Apollinaire did not know he was dying — my doctor hoped to save him, but both his lungs were affected. It's very sad. He managed to stay alive until five o'clock by a miracle of energy. His face is calm and utterly young.

Je vous embrasse.

---

* Satie's letter to the Princesse de Polignac on this occasion has been preserved by her heirs:

Arcueil-Cachan, October 10, 1918

Chère et Bonne Princesse — I am writing to ask you a great favor. When I was sentenced, you very kindly gave me the sum of *eleven hundred francs.*

Of that sum, I paid out 211 francs 26 centimes. There remains 888 francs 74 centimes. This is what I have to ask you:

As a consequence of the misfortunes and peculiarities of the present war, I find myself destitute of *sols,* ducats, and other articles of that kind. The lack of such trinkets results in my being not too comfortable. Yes — and *Necessity* (that very strange animal), Chère Madame, makes me turn to you and prompts me to ask you to authorize me to use the 888 francs 74 centimes above-mentioned.

. . . May I dispose of this remainder? As an *advance?* . . .

Picasso is said to have received the news of Apollinaire's death while shaving before a mirror in the Hotel Lutétia, where he and Olga were living temporarily before moving to their new apartment in the rue La Boétie. Struck by his own mournful expression, he replaced razor by pencil, and the resulting superb example of graphic narcissism, apparently the last self-portrait Picasso ever drew, has been called, by professional Picasso-ans, a "farewell to youth," and, even more sentimentally, a "memorial to his friend Apollinaire." In 1911, when Apollinaire had been mistakenly jailed in connection with the theft of the Mona Lisa from the Louvre, the terrified Picasso had denied, before a judge, that he knew him. Apollinaire forgave that bit of panic, though it is improbable that he forgot it, and he considered Picasso his friend to the end. That momentary denial by Picasso, who was an indubitably close friend, stands in dramatic contrast with the immediate and continuous claims to close friendship made after Apollinaire's death by Cocteau, whose actual degree of friendship with Apollinaire the preceding pages make it possible to measure fairly accurately. When Cocteau spoke of the "seven best friends" whom he lost by death, he did not list their names, but everything indicates that he came quite quickly to think of Apollinaire as the third, after LeRoy and Garros.

In that letter announcing Apollinaire's death to André Salmon (who along with Picasso had been Apollinaire's friend for years — one of Apollinaire's better-known poems was written on the occasion of Salmon's marriage), Cocteau already presents himself as Apollinaire's intimate. But the scene at the deathbed is clarified by Cocteau himself in another of his writings — a tribute to Apollinaire that appeared, along with many others, in the February, 1919 issue of the magazine *Sic*. "When I became Apollinaire's friend, he was already fat and in poor health," one paragraph begins, "but I did once see him young, and that was on his deathbed. Picasso held a lamp, and saying to me 'Look — he's as he was when we first met,' he showed me an admirable face, in profile, lean and very young." Cocteau, one realizes, had come to the death chamber to accompany Picasso, whose terror of death was notorious; and the vague phrase "my doctor hoped to save him" is in essence proprietary. As Apollinaire's body lay in his apartment before his funeral on November 13, the great news of the Armistice broke on the world, and Paris was bedecked with flags. Many of Apollinaire's friends enjoyed fancying that it was in his honor that the city was *en fête,* but it was Cocteau who went the furthest. "We never thought for a second that it was for the Armistice that all the flags were flying," he has said, "but for the death of Apollinaire." On another occasion he wrote: "I should like to set down a few recollections of a man with whom, because he was considerate to the point of mania, I never had the slightest disagreement. This was Guillaume Apollinaire." On June 8, 1919, at a *"matinée poétique"* in Apollinaire's memory at Léonce Rosenberg's art gallery, L'Effort Moderne — an occasion which was to be momentous for Cocteau in other ways — he read a poem, "La Mort de Guillaume Apollinaire." * But most striking among Cocteau's many writings about Apollinaire, to one who remembers his fashionably callous language in the 1916 letter to Gleizes about Apollinaire's scar, is a passage in one of his later books commemorating that same scar: "I knew him in his horizon-blue uniform, his head shaved, one temple marked by a scar that was like a starfish. He wore a contrivance of leather and gauze that looked like a turban or a small helmet. It was as if that small helmet concealed a microphone, thanks to which he heard what others cannot hear, and was secretly in touch with an exquisite world. From that world came messages, which he transcribed."

Such was Cocteau's self-transformation, both immediately and over the years, with regard to Apollinaire. One begins to understand that it was natural enough, and understanding will continue to come. Apollinaire's death had removed from the scene the only person who was hero to all the rapidly multiplying factions of the *"esprit nouveau."* Cocteau had already been called, in print, Apollinaire's "lieutenant," and had not Apollinaire himself referred to the two of them as "kings of poetry"? *"Le roi est mort. Vive le roi!"* Certainly, especially for someone who in Misia's words needed "to make himself liked by everybody," it was better to think of oneself as successor to an intimate friend. And in fact in retrospect a posthumous intimacy has grown up between Cocteau and Apollinaire, despite the erratic nature of their connection during Apollinaire's lifetime and Cocteau's subsequent exaggeration of their friendship. In annals of the *"esprit nouveau"* the name of

* See Appendix VIII.

the one constantly finds itself in close proximity to that of the other, and literary history has made them closer companions than many a pair who in life were inseparable. Despite disparities of personality, background and production, they shared a singular conjunction of times and talents.

Meanwhile, Cocteau observed the Armistice in other ways. The dressmaker Paul Poiret gave a victory party, and Cocteau wrote later: "Do you remember, Derain, how the night of the Armistice Poiret put on fancy dress, metamorphosed himself, and was so inventive, mimed so marvelously, that when daybreak came we thought it was still only eleven, like the travelers in the German ballad held spellbound by the nightingale?" He wrote to Beaumont: "Yes, dear Etienne — peace touches me like grace, and I wear its dove on my shoulder amidst the monkeys and the wolves." On Christmas Eve he took refuge from some of the "monkeys and wolves" — or perhaps among some of them — at the Ritz, where he was a dinner guest, along with Proust, of Princesse Lucien (Marie) Murat. She and her party went on afterwards to the flat of a member of the Italian armistice delegation, where Cocteau "sang ditties of the 1900's" to the piano accompaniment of Frédéric de Madrazo. And Cocteau wrote a Christmas quatrain for his mother, one of the fortunate Frenchwomen whose two sons had survived four years of slaughter:

Noël 1918
Dix neuf cent dix neuf fait cesser
Ta guerre aux discordes cruelles
Un de tes fils ferme ses ailes
Et l'autre les sent repousser.*

One war was over, and with "growing wings" Cocteau could now continue to fight in the other war — the war of art in which he had already won two battles, the battles of *Parade* and *Le Coq et l'Arlequin.* August, 1914 had found him a frustrated poet of the salons and a balletomane among many. He entered 1919 a *coqueteau* of the roost, a young *chef d'école.* "I am trying to rise higher so as to be worthy of a following," he had written his mother from Coxyde

---

* Nineteen nineteen brings to a close / Your war with its cruel discords. / One of your sons folds his wings / And the other feels his grow again.

in 1916; and with his ballet and his book he had succeeded. What his following, his *école*, was, it would be hard to say. It did not have, and never would have, a definite name, like Dadaism or Surrealism, but his chieftainship went beyond merely being the champion of Satie and a handful of young musicians. It was, one can only say at this point, the school of certain segments of modern artistic, aesthetic youth. Just what it was, and was not, may become clear in the chronicle that follows of the continuing war of art.

5
Inventing the Twenties

THE artistic skirmishes in which Cocteau was now to participate, during the years immediately preceding and immediately following the end of the First World War, were not the aspect of the literary life that meant most to him. As he began to contend with the Dadaists and other factions he was unaware, as he had been just before the war, that drama was shortly to break on him. This time the drama was to be a personal one, and once he was in the grip of what proved to be his greatest attachment he felt himself largely above the battle. In the interim, the artistic wrangles involved him when he was trying to place his "new" work, at a time when it happened that his private life was not very intense. Chronologically, intellectually and emotionally, many of the skirmishes occupy what might from his point of view be called a prelude; but it was a "prelude" during which crucial developments were taking place in French artistic life.

Magazines as backdrop

The poet Apollinaire had always loved little magazines. It was chiefly little magazines that had been willing to publish his work, and in the years before the war he had founded more than one of his own. His last, *Les Soirées de Paris*, to which Cocteau had subscribed, had ended with its issue of August, 1914, and to read it is to be reminded of how brilliant a spectacle of the arts it was on which the curtain of war had come plunging down. Its twenty-seven issues had been filled with writing by Apollinaire himself, Max Jacob, Alfred Jarry and others of new and great quality, and with reproductions, sometimes in excellent color, of work by Picasso, Braque, Léger, Matisse, Marie Laurencin, Gleizes, Rousseau, Derain and Archipenko. Since the demise of *Les Soireés* there have been many admirable avant-garde magazines, but none has ever succeeded in being quite so spectacular in its revelations, for nowhere since the First World War has young artistic genius emerged in such profusion as in those years in Paris. Dadaism, Surrealism and the other postwar phenomena seldom produce the *frisson* that one feels in witnessing the birth of modern art in the earlier Fauvism, Cubism and Futurism that had made the first, prewar years of the century a time of genesis. Cocteau, detested by André Breton, the self-appointed high priest of the subsequent, postwar Paris avant-garde, ridiculed by Breton's cohorts, and belittled by intellectuals of the *N.R.F.* stamp who claimed that he was insufficiently serious in comparison with themselves and with the Breton-ists (actually they alternated between belittling him for his sense of fun and jeering at him whenever he did anything that *wasn't* funny) — Cocteau emerges from that artistic infighting of the late teens and early twenties immeasurably more of an artist than most of the other protagonists.

Among the new little magazines that sprang up before and after the wounded Apollinaire's return to the Paris literary scene in 1916, four were founded by his admirers. In January, 1916 the poet Pierre Albert-Birot brought out the first number of *Sic,** in which Apollinaire was to print much of his later poetry. *Sic* was at first sympathetic to the Italian Futurists and a group closely allied to them called the *"Bruitistes"* ("Noise-ists"), and later announced itself as the organ of "Nunism" (from the Greek ηγη, "now.") In March, 1917 another poet, Pierre Reverdy, an old friend of the Montmartre Cubists, launched his *Nord-Sud* (named after the Paris subway line — now called simply "No. 12" — that connects two artists' quarters, Montmartre and Montparnasse). In *Nord-Sud,* too, Apollinaire published late verse. In December, 1916, Apollinaire's friend the painter Francis Picabia had founded his *391,* a sequel to *291,* a monthly on which he had collaborated in New York, where he had spent some time with Marcel Duchamp and Gleizes. (*291* had been so named after Alfred Stieglitz's Photo-Secession Gallery at 291 Fifth Avenue.) And in March, 1919, after Apollinaire's death, three young poets, two of whom had been introduced to each other by Apollinaire, and all of whom had published

* The word *sic* is the Latin categorical affirmative; in addition, Albert-Birot thought of each of its letters as being "the initial of an essential word: *sound, idea, color.*"

in *Sic* and *Nord-Sud* — André Breton, Louis Aragon and Philippe Soupault — began their own magazine, *Littérature.*

Those four magazines are the chief protagonists in one of the bloodiest chapters of the history of literary feuding. *Sic* was in character the most naïve and amiable, like its founder, but it quickly lost distinction after the death of Apollinaire; *Nord-Sud,* like Reverdy, was the most austere, the most purely poetic; *391,* like Picabia, was by far the cleverest, most amusing, and least endowed with anything resembling a sense of responsibility; *Littérature,* taking its tone from Breton, was often brutal and disdainful, but well furnished in a literary way. Hot and cold insults, throat-cutting and back-stabbing among the editors and contributors, particularly in the cases of *391* and *Littérature,* alternated with spasmodic pretenses of solidarity and support; one magazine's editors or contributors might publish in another, only to feature in their own next issue blasts at their recent host or at members of their own ranks. From the founding of *Sic* in January, 1916 to the demise of *391* in October, 1924 (it was the longest lived because Picabia could finance it), all four magazines made it clear, whether by abuse or by various degrees of silence, that Cocteau was low on their list of admirations. Thus did Apollinaire's literary friends and self-appointed heirs prolong the snub administered by their master in the program note on *Parade.* For none of them was Cocteau Apollinaire's "lieutenant" or successor.

And in addition to the four, there was also the *Nouvelle Revue Française,* which resumed publication in June, 1919 after its wartime silence. So obsessed was the *N.R.F.* with charting, cataloguing and analyzing its own points of view that Cocteau described it as being "too busy adjusting its opera glasses to take in the show."

All the magazines were affected by Dada, that movement that has been called a "permanent revolt of the individual against art, morality and society," founded by the Rumanian-born Tristan Tzara and others in Zurich in 1916 and anticipated in New York, without the name, by Marcel Duchamp and Picabia. Its founders declared that the name Dada meant nothing, was meant to mean nothing; it declared itself to be an "inventory" of the ruins of art and society left by the great negative of the war; and its principal novelty was publicity, with Tzara as chief publicity agent. Perhaps the violence and vociferousness of Dada's stunts, meetings, manifestations and "congresses," all of them wilfully incoherent, did reflect the insane savagery of the war; perhaps the infantilism of the slogans Dada employed against religion, patriotism, politics and art itself were also a reflection of the years when millions had been reduced to primitive, infantile combat in the bare struggle to survive. Dada "artists" were particularly proud of their "Art is dead — let's kill it" stand, for so closely entwined with the heart-strings of putrid society was putrid "Art with a capital A" that they declared "It takes more courage to paint a moustache on the Mona Lisa [as Marcel Duchamp had done] than to insult a priest." *

It was *Sic*, in 1917, that first announced to France the Swiss birth of Dada; and that same year Picabia printed a poem by Tzara in *391*. In 1920 Picabia brought Tzara himself to Paris, associated l imself with some of Dada's harangues, and broke with the group tae next year. But Dada's great French-born champion was André Breton. He, his two associates Aragon and Soupault, and their magazine *Littérature* became as though mesmerized by Tzara and Dada, taking orders from Tzara like disciples — until Breton, too, rebelled, and founded Dada's successor, Surrealism, in 1922, carrying Aragon and Soupault with him.

Such vast convulsions have beset the world since the Twenties that one might be tempted to shrug off those Parisian aesthetic conflicts as trivial, were it not that the merest glance at a newspaper or magazine of today — prose style, poetry, journalistic techniques, subjects treated, kinds of entertainment announced, artwork — brings the realization that the extreme movements born, after the First World War, out of their prewar prototypes, are the ancestors of

---

* Madame Gleizes tells in her unpublished memoirs how the Dadaists seemed to the wife of a Cubist:

"Occasionally I attended the big public Dada demonstrations. Holding hands and forming a chain, like little girls in a round-dance, a dozen disillusioned young men (and there was certainly plenty to be disillusioned about) would move to the front of the stage and groan: "No art, no literature, no politics, no republic, no royalists, no philosophers, no nothing — *Dada, Dada, Dada.*" . . . Just as in 1913, when they first heard the rumblings of *The Rite of Spring*, the enraged audience would shout, stamp, whistle. In the wings, Tristan Tzara almost climbed the walls with joy: 'It's exactly like the Communist meetings in Berlin.'

"During intermission the audience would quiet down and wonder: were we, or were we not, supposed to understand? Jacques-Emile Blanche would perambulate in search of revelation. People would stop him and ask him what he thought of it all. Fearful of missing the bus, and equally fearful of compromising himself, he would look around in a worried way and say, 'Where is Cocteau? What does Cocteau say?' And Cocteau would be flitting from one group to another, saying things that were very funny but a bit obscure and that only added to the confusion."

many of today's commonplaces. Cocteau has said that "France between 1914 and 1924 presents the spectacle of an incredible literary revolution," and the new trends so violently expressed in those four Parisian magazines were significant parts of that revolution. It is no more separable from its antecedents than is any other revolution — far further back than Futurism and Cubism, the Romanticism of the 1830's is seen by some to be the "beginning" of it all — and it is blatantly still in progress, perhaps at a more feverish pace than ever. Nothing could sound more familiar to witnesses of the late 1960's; and Madame Gleizes' cool description of a Dada happening could be applied with a minimum of change to many a "love-in" (often a love-hate-in) of half a century later.

Along with Apollinaire's snub in the program note to *Parade*, Cocteau experienced another *esprit nouveau* misadventure back in that same May of 1917. *Sic*, which had never published anything by him (perhaps because of its allegiance to Apollinaire), now printed over his signature a thirteen-line poem, "Restaurant de Nuit," which at first glance looks innocent enough, obscure, fragmentary, and seemingly casual, like many a poem by Apollinaire himself.

Un poème de l'auteur du thème de *Parade*.
Restaurant de Nuit

Paris mes cinq cents louis ont filé dans ton fleuve
Ah n'entendez-vous pas
Un voyou moribond pollue son habit noir
Verte une fille nue piétine ton chapeau
Regardez-les danser implacablement ivres
Extatiques fantômes aux yeux hallucinés
Sifflez sifflez voici les âmes que je fus

Bactriane ô cité des idoles tes temples
Instincts marée profuse flot de feu
Rivalise donc enfin
O flamboiement atroce et doux de cette fête nocturne
Tandis que mon frère meurt asphyxié

Sinistre éveil d'une ère nouvelle

JEAN COCTEAU *

* Paris my five hundred gold pieces have disappeared into your river / Ah! don't you hear / A moribund guttersnipe polluting his black clothes / Green a naked girl is

But, as Cocteau reports it: "One morning in 1917 . . . Blaise Cendrars telephoned me to say that he had been reading in the magazine *Sic* a poem, signed with my name, that he was surprised not to have heard of and that was not in my style; he said he would read it to me over the telephone so that I might confirm that it was not by me. The poem was a fake." It was also a joke, a little dirty and a little sick: *"polluer"* has a special meaning, and whoever had signed Cocteau's name to lines about "a billow of fire," and a "flaming" and a brother who "dies suffocated" can scarcely have been unaware that Paul Cocteau was flying a combat plane over Germany, and that as Cocteau had written to Etienne de Beaumont his family "couldn't sleep for thinking of it." Furthermore it was a *Sic* joke on the editor: the first letters of the thirteen lines spelled "Pauvres Birots" (the "Poor Birots" being Pierre Albert-Birot himself and everyone associated with him).

The poem had been submitted to Albert-Birot in a handwriting that purported to be Cocteau's, accompanied by a note purportedly signed by Cocteau (actually the handwriting resembles Cocteau's not at all). In *Sic*'s next issue poor Birot printed his regrets, and Cocteau issued several disclaimers of his own, including a printed slip that declared "This kind of trick has its title to nobility: it was played on Charles Baudelaire. Even so it is a wretchedly low thing." He said later that Apollinaire, curiously enough, "made a great thing of the incident. He went from café to café, from Montparnasse to Montmartre, from one newspaper office to another, questioning, suspecting, accusing everybody except the culprit, who, much later, acknowledged that he was the author of the trick." The man who confessed to being the jokester was Theodore Fraenkel, a friend of André Breton, a Surrealist-minded doctor noted for his scalpel humor. (Fraenkel once wrote to Tristan Tzara when Tzara was sick: "Are you coughing? Spitting? J. Vaché died immediately after I asked him those same questions in writing — but the formula has often failed.") Given Fraenkel's mystificatory personality, doubt about his culpability in the matter of "Pauvres Birots" springs from the very fact that he confessed to it. There was

---

trampling on your hat / See them dancing implacably drunk / Ecstatic phantoms with hallucinated eyes / Whistle whistle here are the souls that I was / Bactriana oh city of idols your temples / Instincts profuse tide billow of fire / Vie then finally / O atrocious and sweet flaming of this nocturnal fête / While my brother dies suffocated / Sinister waking of a new era.

also, lurking somewhere close to the scene, a mysterious, never-identified "Alfreyd O. Montagne Ené de Piro" (the name is a supposed but unsolved anagram), who published several issues of a magazine called *Modernisme-Compréhension: Revue d'Art*, in which he gleefully lampooned Albert-Birot as an ignoramus for having been taken in by "Restaurant de Nuit." He belabored the point so much that, whoever he may have been, he has been suspected of being the poem's true author — as for the same reason one might suspect Apollinaire.

"Restaurant de Nuit" was a prelude to episodes more truly sinister: members of the various groups took to battering each other with their fists as "punishment" for heretical opinions. Breton once broke the arm of the critic Pierre de Massot by a furious blow from a cane, administered in public, on a stage; there were various other bloody encounters; and more than once Madame Cocteau picked up the telephone at night, when Jean was absent, to hear a sepulchral voice, the voice of some Dadaist or Surrealist wag, tell her that her son was dead.

Pierre Reverdy's *Nord-Sud* published one article by Cocteau — "La Collaboration de *Parade*," in its issue for June-July 1917, in which Cocteau gave his version of how *Parade* had come to be. From Reverdy's apostrophe to Cocteau in his little aesthetic credo, *Self-Defense*, in 1919 — "How did it happen that having started so late you are already ahead of the others?" — he seems, whether or not he liked *Parade* and *Le Coq et l'Arlequin*, to have marveled that Cocteau, whom he had previously thought of as "the youngest of the Rostands," should be capable of such manifestations of *l'esprit nouveau*. But Reverdy, an intensely serious man, of fanatical artistic, poetic and religious fervor, could not long continue relations with Cocteau. He was to play a role in Cocteau's brief period of active Catholicism, and was dismayed when that ended. As Reverdy grew increasingly unworldly, finally retiring to live with his wife close to the abbey of Solesmes, his adverse opinion of Cocteau hardened considerably.

The magazine *Littérature* aroused Cocteau's interest from the moment he heard of its being planned. Of its three founders, Aragon and Soupault were gifted and attractive, and Breton was intelligent, dynamic, sometimes uncanny in his insights. Through Aragon, Cocteau's name was included in the list of contributors to the first issue, but whatever he may have offered was not printed. Breton had banned him. Earlier, Tristan Tzara had written directly to Cocteau from Zurich, thinking him a possibly valuable adherent to Dada, and Cocteau had sent him several poems, which were printed in *Anthologie Dada* (1919); meanwhile Breton warned Tzara against Cocteau, and Tzara replied: "Cocteau has written me a letter (pseudo)-enthusiastic about Dada," and Breton later wrote of Cocteau to Tzara: "You don't know what he's really like. My opinion — completely disinterested, I swear — is that he is the most hateful being of our time. And I repeat, he never did anything against me, and I assure you that hatred is not my strong point."

One wonders whether Breton really knew himself so little. He was the most intense of haters — he made a career of hatred — and his hatred of Cocteau was almost maniacal. Cocteau realized it, and characterized it to André Germain as being "a mystical state." Maurice Barrès once wrote: "When someone born Dog meets someone born Cat, and both refrain from leaping at each other's throats, they have the gratifying sensation that they are demonstrating the utmost refinement of civilization." Breton disdained that aspect of civilization. Cocteau may never have done anything *against* Breton, but merely by being himself he did plenty *to* him. Marcel Duchamp has said that to Breton Cocteau's wit was the rag to the bull, and that Cocteau's precocity, his early social and literary successes (much though Cocteau himself now deplored or pretended to deplore their salon character) stirred Breton's envy and scorn. Breton was the son of a rural policeman; wanting him to rise to the professional class, his parents financed his medical studies, and they bitterly cut off his allowance when he rejected their ambitions and turned to literature. In his rebellion against "bourgeois despotism" — so it has been phrased by Adrienne Monnier, the avant-garde bookseller and friend of writers — and against a society that had sent him to war, Breton felt the need of particularly "violent novelty." For a time, to make ends meet, he worked as proofreader at the *N.R.F.*, where Proust had much to complain of in his "corrections" on *The Guermantes Way*. Georges Hugnet, a Surrealist whose hand was broken and ears almost torn off by a trio of former comrades after he had left the group and written against it, describes Breton as being awkward, either aggressive or obsequious, in the company of the well bred and well-to-do: Cocteau's conspicuous ease in every kind of company irritated him beyond endurance.

Cocteau's elegance in dress, too, brought down Breton's fury. Cocteau was always something of a dandy. Before the war he had become acquainted with Reginald Bridgeman, the elegant young private secretary of the British ambassador, Lord Bertie of Thame; later Bridgeman was in Paris again as private secretary to the new ambassador, Lord Derby. Cocteau enjoyed visiting at the Embassy, and adopted Bridgeman's style of dress. Mr. Bridgeman casts an amusing light on one detail of Cocteau's apparel. "Before the first World War," he says, "I followed a somewhat foppish style of dress, one of the features of which was a satin bow necktie modeled by my haberdasher on that worn by Baudelaire in one of the editions of *Les Fleurs du Mal*. The day I met Jean for the first time I was wearing this necktie, which he at once recognized, and he took to wearing that kind frequently. It was Baudelaire's elegance rather than mine that Jean was imitating." *

Some time after Cocteau's exclusion from *Littérature*, Breton, either to play a practical joke or in need of a prominent name, wrote to him, saying that he was willing to revise an unfavorable judgment that he had somewhere expressed on *Le Cap de Bonne-Espérance*, and asking him to collaborate on the magazine. Cocteau had the good sense to decline, and was able to write later of having been asked. In Breton's book *Les Pas Perdus* (1924) there is a contemptuous reference to "Monsieur Cocteau (I apologize that his name should ever come out of my pen)"; and in 1928, irritated at the amount of publicity Cocteau was receiving, Breton wrote to Picabia: "Those who dislike Jean Cocteau talk about him the most." No wonder that Robert Desnos, one of the Surrealists, writing to Picabia in 1924, marveled: "How can you believe Satie when he says that Breton and Cocteau are reconciled? That day, hell will freeze over."

Picabia and his magazine *391* constituted a different story. Cocteau enjoyed the company of the expansive artist, famous for his

* From Mr. Bridgeman comes another sartorial detail concerning Cocteau's circle. Bridgeman was invited to a number of Etienne de Beaumont's postwar costume balls, each of which had a theme — the court of Louis XIV, the French colonies, and so on. To the first ball, in 1919, one was invited to come, in Mr. Bridgeman's words, "leaving exposed that part of one's body that one considered the most interesting." Cecil Beaton, who attended later Beaumont balls, wonders whether that one may not have been a bore, saying "Even to that society the theme offered rather limited possibilities."

women and his racing cars (he is said to have owned a total of one hundred and twenty-seven automobiles), so talented and intelligent, sceptical and fantastic. Cocteau often came to the flat in Passy that Picabia shared with Germaine Everling, and with his mimicry and wit he was a welcome guest. Picabia was not particularly sectarian: he had a cool view of the Paris artistic scene. Cocteau himself was cool enough to participate, despite continued evidences of hostility by Breton, Tzara and others, in Dada happenings, and several times he offered poems to Picabia for publication in *391*. But they were refused in various brash and insulting ways, and in 1920 Cocteau wrote to Picabia protesting his friendship but announcing his "break" with Dada — the break of a connection that had existed but tenuously. Picabia printed the letter, with a sarcastic comment, not in *391* but in another of his publications, called *Cannibale*. Shortly thereafter, at a Dada manifestation in the Salle Gaveau a balloon inscribed "Jean Cocteau" was pierced by a dagger wielded by Philippe Soupault. After Picabia himself broke with Dada he did print an occasional contribution by Cocteau in *391*, along with gibes *at* Cocteau by Satie and others. Cocteau and Picabia continued to correspond in an amiable, mutually sceptical way for a number of years.

Sic, Nord-Sud, Littérature and *391* may have caused Cocteau annoyance: the *Nouvelle Revue Française* caused him rage and grief. At the *N.R.F.*, of course, there was André Gide. And between Gide and Cocteau relations that had never been very cordial, at least on Gide's side, took a turn for the worse in December, 1917. In that month there occurred an event which Gide later confessed to Cocteau was to poison him against him until close to the end of his life. Part of the story, an episode of homosexual jealousy, is told, under the protection of initials, in an entry in Gide's *Journal* for December 8, 1917:

"The day before yesterday, for the first time in my life, I experienced the pangs of jealousy. I tried to suppress them, but in vain. M. did not return until 10 P.M. I knew he was with C. I was beside myself. I felt myself capable of the worst. I measured the depth of my love by the degree of my suffering. For all that, the suffering did not last. Next morning, C., whom I went to see, completely restored my composure when he related, as he always did, everything that had happened that evening they spent together, down to the most trivial exchanges and gestures."

Cocteau was able to read those words in 1939, when Gide's *Journal* was published, containing additional anti-Cocteau remarks; and in 1949, two years before Gide's death, Gide revealed to Cocteau in a conversation the nature of the "worst" of which he had felt himself capable when the young man stayed out late. "I wanted to kill you," he told Cocteau.

Cocteau later wrote that "Gide asked me to take (let's call him Olivier) in hand. Olivier, his disciple, 'was getting bored among all the books.' I was to introduce him to the Cubists, to the new music, to the circus — he shared my love for big bands, acrobats and clowns. I did it, with some qualms. I knew Gide and his almost feminine jealousy. Now young Olivier thought it very amusing to irritate Gide, to keep singing my praises, swearing that he wouldn't leave me, that he knew my *Potomak* by heart." That was written by Cocteau only in 1953, after Gide's death: Gide was not present to reply, as he might have, that Cocteau could be very seductive indeed with an interesting young man when he wished to be — and Gide obviously suspected that with "Olivier" he had wished to be. But Cocteau lamented in writing in 1949, after hearing Gide's confession: "That is the very prototype of the dangerous visits one can be paid by young men. . . . Wanting at all costs to make himself interesting, to play a part, an idle young man goes from one older man to another, carrying stories that he has made up. Gradually doubt filters in. The fuse lights, grows shorter, and the friendship goes up in smoke. Men who could be reconciled in five minutes remain leagues apart. Victimized by mythomaniacs, it took Gide and me years to come together and recapture our old affection. Gide would like to swallow his words. It is too late. But what matter? What does not come from the heart amounts to nothing. And perhaps we love each other all the more for what happened."

During the two years that separated Gide's death from Cocteau's publication of Gide's double confession (that he had "wanted to kill" Cocteau and that it was the 1917 episode that was at the bottom of his lifelong hostility) and Cocteau's own phrase "it took Gide and me years to come together and recapture our old affection," Gide made no denial of any of it. It may all be true. The difficulty is, there is no trace of any pre-1917 "old affection," at least on Gide's part, and plenty of evidence that Gide's venom was the climax of years of rankling jealousy. Gide had a "fixation" on Cocteau: the graces he most desired were embodied in this troubling phenomenon. Few of Gide's letters to Cocteau are available; there had been the condescending 1912 review of *La Danse de Sophocle* in the *N.R.F.*, signed by Ghéon but in which Gide may have had a hand; in Gide's *Journal* there is little more, before 1917, than the 1914 hostile entry concerning Cocteau in the tearoom. Then came Gide's homicidal rage in December, 1917. In January, 1918, from Grasse, whence he sent Gide the "miracle photograph" of the Annunciation, Cocteau wrote to Valentine Gross, "Ah, if you could arrange the *Cap*-Gide matter before my return — how grateful I should be." That meant that Cocteau was still hoping, through Valentine and Gide, to have *Le Cap* published in the *N.R.F.*, which was to be revived in June — an indication, perhaps, that Cocteau truly did not realize to what extent Gide was enraged against him. In April, 1918, after the "Olivier" episode, Gide made a note in his *Journal* on a difference he had thought he had discovered between himself and Cocteau as artists: "Nothing is more alien to me than this worry about being modern that obviously influences Cocteau's every thought and action. This is not to say that he is wrong in thinking that art is alive only in its newest guise. However, only what will outlast its own generation is of interest to me." In the following month came an exchange of letters on the death of Jean LeRoy. Anything Gide did held for Cocteau an importance disproportionate to the act itself. Like Diaghilev, Gide was another of Cocteau's all-powerful older heroes-in-art.

The effect was explosive, therefore, when Gide finally showed his true feelings in an "Open Letter to Jean Cocteau" in the *N.R.F.* for June, 1919. Gide had attended at least two of Cocteau's readings of *Le Cap de Bonne-Espérance*, but despite Cocteau's appeals to Valentine the poem had not been accepted by the *N.R.F.* and had recently been published by the Sirène. The "Open Letter," which thus appeared in the very issue in which Cocteau had hoped to have *Le Cap*, begins with Gide's irritatingly praising the poem that his magazine had declined. And Gide then goes on from where the Ghéon or Ghéon-Gide review of *La Danse de Sophocle* had left off — to say that in *Le Coq et l'Arlequin* Cocteau had overreached himself, that only a few bright little passages, like the note about the Harry Pilcer–Gaby Deslys American dance, were within his range, and that in presuming to comment seriously on art and music he was deceiving himself as to the extent of his talent and was making himself ridiculous. Cocteau should confine himself to trivia. Furthermore, Gide suggested that if the audience and critics had been hostile to *Parade* (which, although he did not confess it, he had not seen), it might be less because they were stupid than because *Parade*'s theme — that the "true spectacle" was not the *parade* itself but something unseen to which the *parade* was inviting the public — was unsuitable for a work of art. Gide twisted the knife at the conclusion of the "Open Letter" by assuring Cocteau of his utterly friendly feelings, and reminding him that he himself had once said that "the worst fate that can befall a book is that no one should find fault with it."

When Cocteau, who had learned of the imminence of the "Open Letter," masochistically asked Gide (who sadistically complied) to be allowed to read it at Gide's house in Auteuil before publication, it apparently contained even more offensive remarks, later removed; and Gide has described Cocteau's reaction to the letter as hysterical, composed of "protestations, imprecations, flourishings of his sword cane, supplications, oaths on the heads of his parents." Gide's "Open Letter" could certainly have remained unwritten; by someone other than Cocteau it might have been passed over in silence — after all, *Parade* and *Le Coq et l'Arlequin* could look after themselves (and have always done so, as far as their reputation is concerned); but Cocteau was touched to the quick. The *N.R.F.* found the reply he composed too personal and scurrilous against Gide to print; Cocteau served the magazine with a writ in an attempt to force publication; failed, and published his answer, somewhat toned down, in *Ecrits Nouveaux* for August, 1919. Among his remarks was a description of Gide's house where he had read the "Open Letter": certain of its architectural features, he suggested, symbolized its owner — "The windows don't look out toward the front. Inside, halls and stairs crisscross — *contradict* one another." Gide now had a pretext for writing again, and he made the most of it: "It is not given to everyone to be original. M. Cocteau is not at his first imitation. What my 'Open Letter' reproached him for was not so much his assimilating the art of others as his claim to be a *chef d'école* and an inventor: not so much for following, as for pretending to precede. I tried, in the most courteous terms, to expose M. Cocteau's double personality — one his own and by far the more charming, the other borrowed but insistently claimed by him to be the real one. What he wants is to be talked about. Is he satisfied? I apologize for tiring the reader."

Cocteau had what revenge he could. Shortly after the exchange of "Open Letters," he wrote a sequence of light quatrains that recounted sailortown episodes reminiscent of some of his adolescent experiences in Marseilles, to be called *Escales* (Ports of Call) and published in a volume with illustrations by André Lhote. There was to be a special edition that would include a *"musée secret,"* a section consisting of a few poems and pictures of a more overtly erotic kind than the rest; and in Cocteau's autograph manuscript there is a partly legible note to Lhote regarding a drawing that was to show a sailor's whore practicing a simple form of contraception. His suggestion is amiable: "Make her look like Gide, low life, with her behind on a bidet."

When *Parade* was revived in December, 1920, Gide wrote in his *Journal:* "Saw *Parade.* Hard to say what is more striking, the pretentiousness or the poverty. Found Cocteau walking up and down in the wings, older, tense, uneasy. He is perfectly aware that the sets and costumes are by Picasso, and that the music is by Satie, but he wonders whether Picasso and Satie aren't by him."

André Germain has said of Gide and Cocteau "Both of them could be swishy and seductive in the extreme — our two great and admirable courtesans." Courtesans perhaps: certainly a pair of viperish ladies. About 1922, a kind of truce was reached between them, and a surface politeness was maintained until the "reconciliation" of 1949. Even before that resumption of "our old affection," it was remarkable how often Cocteau wrote to Gide, or tried to see him, displaying a longing to please him that was almost always frustrated and ended in resentment. He even dedicated, rather acerbically, a travel book to him.

Gide's accusation of non-originality was by no means the last that Cocteau-Fregoli was to receive, but it was probably the most unjust: he had invented the very idea of *Parade* (Gide admitted that by attacking it), and it would be hard to find a more personal little tract than the sparkling *Le Coq et l'Arlequin.* Not only jealousy of an attractive younger man who had paid attention to a beloved boy had directed Gide's pen in the "Open Letter": literary politics (a temporary taking-up of Breton and the Dadaists by the *N.R.F.*) and envy of lightness and flair must have counted for much. It was not, as between Cocteau and Breton, a case of Dog meets Cat — not quite: one can imagine that Gide may have had Cocteau in mind, in a partly literary context, when he made his famous remark about someone else: "*Je suis pédéraste, il est tapette.*" Gide's death in 1951 left Cocteau to have the last word. He had it more than once, and on several of these occasions he forgot any inhibitions due to "old affection." "Gide's *Journal* is a great hoax," he wrote Jean Genet. "He adopts the pose of frankness in order to lie with impunity." On another occasion: "He knew how to forget offending remarks — especially those that had come from his own pen." And in 1956, when he went to Oxford to receive the same honorary doctorate that Gide had been awarded there some years before, and the university, seeking to spare him the expense of buying a gown, offered him the use of one of its own, he declined with a shudder: "It might have been worn by Gide."

Such, in resumé, were a few aspects of the Paris literary scene that formed a backdrop to Cocteau's activities during the early 1920's. It was like a stage set splashed on by a motley crew of scene painters, against which Cocteau proceeded to perform, in his works, a poetic, intellectual, journalistic, aesthetic Fregoli ballet.

Le Cap de Bonne-Espérance (1919)

Not only in Paul Morand's apartment in June, 1917, but also on several other occasions Cocteau had read *Le Cap de Bonne-Espérance* from manuscript or page proof to friends and fellow artists — partly, no doubt, to give it advance advertising in literary circles, but also to hear it himself and hear the opinions of others.

Valentine Gross (now soon to become Madame Jean Hugo) held one of the readings in her flat, also in the Palais-Royal. "There were several people present connected with the *N.R.F.*," she later recalled, "people important to Jean, including Léon-Paul Fargue, Gaston Gallimard and Valéry Larbaud. Jean had invited Proust, but after we had waited an hour or so and Proust hadn't appeared, Jean began to read. In mid-reading the doorbell rang. There was no electricity that evening, and I took one of the lamps with me out into the hall. When I opened the door, there were three people I had never seen before — Proust, Marie Scheikevitch,* and Walter Berry, of the American Chamber of Commerce. Then Jean came rushing out from the drawing room behind me. He was furious, and cried: '*Va-t-en, Marcel! Tu gâtes ma lecture! Je ne peux pas recommencer!*' Proust answered, '*Calme-toi, Jean, je m'en vais.*' Madame Scheikevitch gave me such a look! '*Mais c'est abominable,*' I said to them. '*Entrez au moins pour un instant, vous venez de monter quatre escaliers.*' But Proust preferred to go. I escorted them down to Proust's automobile, and invited them to come again." †

On December 3, 1918 Cocteau again read *Le Cap* at Valentine's, to Misia Sert, Picasso, André Lhote, the actor Pierre Bertin, Jean Hugo, and André Breton, who was still in uniform as an auxiliary army doctor. "When the reading ended," Jean Hugo recalls, "André Breton's comment was to make a face. Cocteau, in an attempt to charm him, said good-naturedly, '*Trop sublime?*' — the '*sublime*' being clearly spoken in a tone of self-disparagement. But Breton said nothing." There was another reading, at the Beaumonts', the evening of Sunday, January 26, 1919, where the listeners included Harold Nicolson, now a diplomat in Paris for the Peace Conference; Nicolson found the *Cap* "not very convincing." Probably that was the reading at the conclusion of which Etienne de Beaumont rushed up to Cocteau and exclaimed, "*Mais vous êtes Voltaire!*" — at once the most extravagant and the subtlest of compliments, with its allusion to the young Voltaire's celebrated readings from his long poem *La Henriade* before its publication, and to the voltairean brilliance that had dazzled the Paris salons of two hundred years before. Cocteau, though he preferred to think of himself as Rousseau, and later even said that "poetry avoids Vol-

---

* Author of a volume of memoirs, *Souvenirs d'un Temps Disparu.* Once dubbed by Misia Sert "*la fille de Minos et Polichinelle.*"

† "Proust did come again," Valentine's account continued. "I had given a party to which I had invited him, and everyone had gone home. At four in the morning my doorbell rang, and it was his chauffeur. '*Monsieur s'excuse; si Mademoiselle pouvait le recevoir si tard. . . . Si non, Monsieur comprend parfaitement.*' I said 'Yes, of course,' and received Proust in my dressing gown."

taire the way electricity avoids silk," can that evening only have understood the allusions and been pleased. And Adrienne Monnier says that Cocteau tricked her into having a reading in her avant-garde bookshop in the rue de l'Odéon by telling her that Gide wanted it. Breton and Soupault attended, she says, "holding themselves very stiff and radiating hostility."

As *Le Potomak* is the earliest of Cocteau's prose that he was willing to have reprinted in later life and included in his "Complete Works," so *Le Cap de Bonne-Espérance* is the earliest poetry (much of it having been written before the little poems from Italy). Dedicated to Garros, it was transformed into an epitaph by Garros' death as it went to press: Cocteau said later that proofs of the poem were found in the cockpit of Garros' wrecked plane. "Seven years," he wrote in a preface that appeared only in the original edition, "separate it from my last [poetical] publications," and one senses his feeling that it was, rather, an entire age that had intervened. As *The Cape of Good Hope,* the poem can be found in complete English translation by Jean Hugo, corrected by Ezra Pound, in the Autumn, 1921 number (called the "Brancusi Number" because of its illustrations of Brancusi's sculptures) of *The Little Review,** the celebrated magazine that had been founded in Chicago in 1914 by Margaret Anderson and "jh" (Jane Heap). Four of its issues had recently been seized by the United States Post Office, and the Brancusi number contains the announcement: "As PROTEST against the suppression of the Little Review containing various installments of the 'ULYSSES' of JAMES JOYCE the following artists and writers of international reputation are collaborating in the autumn number of Little Review: BRANCUSI, JEAN COCTEAU, JEAN HUGO, GUY CHARLES CROS, PAUL MORAND, FRANCIS PICABIA, EZRA POUND." Pound is listed as "Collaborator" and Picabia (known to Margaret Anderson from his activities in New York) as "Foreign Editor." One can imagine how Breton and his cohorts received the news that with Pound's and Picabia's approval it was Cocteau who had been given precedence over them for trans-Atlantic publication.

Adrienne Monnier, always interesting on the subject of contemporary French poetry, has written: "Cocteau is never the first to

* Cocteau wrote to Gertrude Stein: "If the poem in the *Little Review* pleases you, lend me your copy so that I may correct the mistakes to be found on every page."

stand in the breach, but it is always he who hoists the flag — and after all that has to be done by someone. In composing the *Cap*, he probably wanted to hoist the flag of the 'Coup de dés.' In that poem Mallarmé first made use of the kind of typographical effects later taken up by Apollinaire, and especially by Reverdy starting with 'La Lucarne ovale . . .' Apollinaire had abolished punctuation. Reverdy restored it by means of judiciously arranged blank spaces in the text, so that each poem might have its own form, revelatory of 'a superior order.' Cocteau did not hesitate to write a long poem using this still unfamiliar technique and at the same time centering it on Roland Garros, who was more than well known — an aviator and a hero. One could not ask for better wings! . . . The fact is, the *Cap* was an interesting poem. As in everything that Cocteau writes, he achieved here many dazzling and even personal artifices and effects . . . There was even a *'lettriste'* passage, which would have been overwhelmingly novel if Pierre Albert-Birot had not been the first to employ the sound of letters in this way." *

Like *Le Coq et l'Arlequin, Le Cap* brought Cocteau a letter from Proust, this one written in polite denial of having stolen one of its images (apparently he had been told that Cocteau was making that complaint) and going on to distribute praise and questioning: did Cocteau perhaps display, in the poem, a certain overinsistence and lack of discrimination in his use of images? Proust exquisitely withdraws his hesitant questions immediately after putting them, but they are well asked, and the letter is one of those that most notably illustrate his critical acuteness. There is a feline touch at the end — a reference to his expulsion by Cocteau from the apartment of Valentine Gross: "It seems that one cannot possibly imagine what you are like when you read this poem. How can I not believe in fate when I count all its successive whims, some of them taking the most bizarre forms, that have prevented me from hearing you!"

* "A very comprehensive American college yell," is what the English critic F. S. Flint likened that passage to, writing in *The Chapbook* for October, 1919. He thought it showed the influence of Marinetti, and said also: "It reminds me of a poem by M. Pierre Albert-Birot in *Sic* for November, 1918, 'Poème à crier et à danser, L'AVION.' But M. Cocteau is a more serious poet."

Carte Blanche (1919)

Shortly after the appearance of *Le Cap*, the newspaper *Paris-Midi* asked Cocteau to write a weekly article on the Paris scene, giving him a free hand — "*carte blanche*." Using that phrase as his general title (the editors of *Littérature* had considered it and discarded it), he contributed a series of twenty short pieces between March and August — his first popular journalism apart from *Le Mot*. Max Jacob particularly admired his account of the victory celebration on July 14, 1919 — the parade of the Allied armies down the Champs-Elysées on the first Bastille Day since the Armistice: "Here is General Pershing, rigid on his pink horse. His troops halt, mark time, and are off again, like chorus girls. The Marines, entwined in their silver horns, play the latest fox-trot." (Darius Milhaud identifies the fox-trot as "Over There.")

But for the most part *Carte Blanche* consists of glimpses, afforded by Cocteau to the public, of the world of the arts in which he moved. "I have spoken rather broadly," he says, "in a rather picture-book, ABC-for-children style, in order to make an impression on the kind of reader who skims over the newspaper during lunch and perhaps puts it in his pocket in order to read the non-skimmable parts more carefully at home." The public, he said, knew of nothing between the Academy and popular "Boulevard" entertainment: he will enlighten it concerning the avant-garde. Public and critics still make no distinction between Futurists and Cubists: he will write about the painters he knows. The public tends to take its entertainment for granted: he will call attention to the *art* of Mistinguett, of Charlie Chaplin, of jazz. Film criticism is in its infancy: does the public realize that a fight scene in *Carmen of the Klondike* is "as memorable as the greatest books in the world"?* (The diary of Jean Hugo, who married Valentine Gross

---

* Cocteau's praise of *Carmen of the Klondike* is celebrated in film annals. In *Carte Blanche* he credits the film to Thomas H. Ince, whose pictures were much liked in France: actually its makers were people who had previously worked with Ince. (Information kindly supplied by George C. Pratt, Associate Curator of Motion Pictures, George Eastman House, Rochester, N. Y.)

that August 7, 1919 — Cocteau and Satie being Valentine's witnesses — tells of their going frequently to the movies, especially
American movies, with Cocteau. They saw William S. Hart in *Pour
Sauver sa Race* [*The Aryan*], Fanny Ward in *La Petite Tennessee*
[*Tennessee's Pardner*], and many another film with those actors
and with Douglas Fairbanks, Bessie Love and Priscilla Dean.)

Carte Blanche rolls a few logs: publications by the Sirène, a concert in the Salle Gaveau at which the score of *Parade* achieves respectability by being played along with pieces by Beethoven, Schubert, Schumann, César Franck, Fauré and Debussy; a performance
of Darius Milhaud's cantata *The Libation Bearers* (*Les Choëphores* — libretto by Claudel after Aeschylus) at which young
Milhaud, recently returned from Brazil, asks Cocteau to play the
drum. *Carte Blanche* is a delightful, valuable little commentary
on artistic Paris at the threshold of the twenties.

Le Boeuf sur le Toit (*the "Spectacle-Concert"*)
(1920)

"I have alternated 'clannish' articles with articles of general interest," Cocteau confessed as *Carte Blanche* came to an end; and in
fact two of the twenty numbers are devoted to one particular subclan, a group of six young composers — Georges Auric, Louis
Durey, Arthur Honegger, Darius Milhaud, Francis Poulenc and
Germaine Tailleferre. Of those, Auric was the closest to Cocteau,
and was included more often than the rest in the lunches, dinners, movie-going and other outings of a larger, partly intersecting, "clan," whose steadiest members were Cocteau, Jean and
Valentine Hugo, Paul Morand, Lucien Daudet, and a sixteen-year-
old poet named Raymond Radiguet whom Cocteau had seen at
Léonce Rosenberg's "*matinée poétique*" in memory of Apollinaire
and who had subsequently been sent to him by Max Jacob. As to the
composers, who were soon to be baptized "*Le Groupe des Six*"
(after the Russian "Five" — Balakirev, César Cui, Moussorgsky,
Rimsky-Korsakov, Borodin) by "a music critic in quest of a slogan," as Poulenc put it, Poulenc himself has written: "Never did

we have an aesthetic in common, and our music has always been dissimilar. Our tastes and distastes were different. Thus Honegger never liked Satie's music, and Schmitt, whom he admired, was the *bête noire* of Milhaud and myself. . . . Jean Cocteau, always attracted by every novelty, was not our theorist, as many have claimed, but our friend and our brilliant spokesman." Today Cocteau still speaks for the Six (and for himself in connection with them) : not an album of their music but carries one of his texts, and usually his portrait as well.

Most if not all of the Six set poems by Cocteau to music, but Milhaud's collaboration with him took a special form.

In the second issue of *Littérature* (April, 1919), which contained a barbed nonreview of *Le Coq et l'Arlequin* by Louis Aragon, there appeared an article called "Le Boeuf sur le Toit (Samba carnavalesque)" and signed "Jacaremirim." After describing the festivities of the carnival in Rio de Janeiro, the singing and dancing in the streets and in the Negro clubs where each night the ladies' costumes were of a different color, "Jacaremirim" tells of meeting Darius Milhaud there one night in a street full of dancers. "We walked away together," "Jacaremirim" says — and it was true, for the author "Jacaremirim" (a Brazilian Indian word meaning "little crocodile") was none other than Darius Milhaud himself — "and when I left him under the palms of his moonlight-drenched garden he said to me: 'I adore Brazil. How full of life and fantasy this music is! There is much to learn from these lively rhythms, these melodies that they play over and over again all night long, so impressive in their very monotony. Perhaps I shall write a ballet about the carnival in Rio that will be called 'Le Boeuf sur le Toit,' from the name of that samba ["O Boi No Telhado" — "The Steer on the Roof"]* the band was playing tonight as all the Negresses danced and danced in their blue dresses.' "

When that article appeared, Milhaud had been back in Paris for several months, and had already composed a score called *Le Boeuf sur le Toit*. In his memoirs he speaks of having intended the *Boeuf* to be something quite different from "a ballet about the carnival in Rio." "Still haunted by my memories of Brazil, I assembled a few

---

* According to Monsieur Michel Simon, a specialist in Brazilian folklore, as consulted by Senhor Josué Montello, Cultural Counselor of the Brazilian Embassy in Paris, there is no legend concerning "O Boi No Telhado": the title is merely a picturesque combination of words. My thanks to those two gentlemen.

popular melodies, tangoes, maxixes, sambas, and even a Portuguese fado, and transcribed them with a rondo-like theme recurring between each two of them. . . . I thought that the character of this music might make it suitable for an accompaniment to one of Charlie Chaplin's films. . . . Cocteau disapproved of that idea, and proposed that he should use my music for a show, which he would undertake to put on. Cocteau has a genius for improvisation. Hardly has he conceived the idea of a project when he immediately carries it out. To begin with, we needed some form of financial backing. Jean took the plan of the Comédie des Champs-Elysées to the Comte de Beaumont, who undertook to reserve in advance, at a high price, the boxes and the first rows of orchestra seats. A few days later, as if at the wave of a magic wand, the whole theatre was sold out, and the Shah of Persia even paid ten thousand francs for a front seat from which he could not see a thing, but was himself in full view of everyone. The expenses of the show being covered, all that remained to be done was to set to work."

In the past, Cocteau would have taken his project to Diaghilev, and had it been accepted it would have been executed in the usual way — by a choreographer, a designer and a cast of Diaghilev's choice. With *Le Boeuf sur le Toit,* there seems to have been no question of Diaghilev: with Diaghilev Cocteau had temporarily "broken" — probably because of the sound effects of *Parade.** Speaking of the "show" that he wrote as a scenario to Milhaud's music — he calls it a "farce" — he says that he had been wanting for some time to write what he considered a "true" farce, because he had so often seen the term "farce" improperly applied to *Parade.* He wanted to "arrange it in such a way that it would give an impression of confusion, of improvisation, but with nothing left to chance." When he heard Auric and Milhaud play a four-hand piano arrangement of the *Boeuf* — on one occasion Artur Rubin-

---

* "Jean is exhausted by the show that he is organizing at the Théâtre des Champs-Elysées with the Médrano clowns, *les fils Footit,* Darius Milhaud, Poulenc and Auric," Madame Cocteau wrote Valentine Hugo January 26, 1920. "The Russians are here — Jean goes seldom, because of Diaghilev, whom he detests and for good reason. Misia is very unhappy about it — she is hypnotized by that monster." (Madame Cocteau always wished that her son would stay out of the theatre. "Jean has better things to do than become a stage director," she had written to Valentine a little over a year before, when she saw him associating with "peculiar types from the Vieux-Colombier." "He suffered about Gémier-Médrano, he suffered from Diaghilev, he will suffer still more, considering how mad his projects are. I regret it but can do nothing. I am not listened to, and I suppose that is more or less as it should be.")

stein joined in to make it six hands — he "saw" his farce, and he tried to reconstruct what he "saw." Cocteau says nothing about the *Littérature* article, and perhaps it counted for nothing in his decision to write a scenario for the *Boeuf*: but is it not likely that it did count for something, that it provided an added incentive to action? The chance to seize, to take over, something introduced by the magazine that had snubbed him, and to transform it into a "show" with which his name would always be associated?*

The show that Cocteau quickly invented is a pantomime laid in a bar in a North American city during the then current Prohibition, *"le régime sec."* It included such coctelian features as a Negro boxer smoking a "cigar as long as a torpedo," a Negro dwarf, a decapitated policeman searching for his head, a red-haired woman dancing around the policeman on her hands "like the Salomé on Rouen cathedral," and a barman described by Cocteau as "all pink and white" and by Milhaud as "looking like Antinoüs," who tickles the policeman. The bar customers drink, flirt and dance, the policeman is eliminated and revived, the barman presents him with a bill two yards long: the actors move slowly, in deliberate disobedience to the quick music; they all wear "masks" larger than life (actually, artificial heads like those of carnival figures). Except for the presence of Negroes and the grotesque heads, the scene has nothing to do with the Latin-American carnival provenance of the tunes. The *Boeuf* is like a modern, "realist" dream. *"Parade* still had a literary content, a message," Cocteau has written. "Here I avoid subject and symbol. Nothing happens, or what does happen is so

---

* It must be said in outright defense of Cocteau that he was far from reciprocating the scorn shown him by *Littérature* and its editors, especially at this early point in its existence, before it had succumbed to Dada. (Later he referred to Dada, with its anti-art slogans, as a "suicide club.") He respected *Littérature*, along with the other magazines, as a manifestation of *l'esprit nouveau;* he had tried to join it, had had the good sense to decline its belated, probably treacherous invitation, and did not discourage his friends from contributing to it. Even with Dada he felt considerable sympathy although naturally resenting the treatment it accorded him. "Though I disapprove of Dadaism and isms in general, the excellence of certain Dada artists compels me to defend it against ignorant boors. There are no schools, only individuals." Everywhere amid the quarreling factions he seems genuinely to have sought art, not denying its existence even in someone so aggressively hostile to him as Breton, and trying to create his own art in his own way. He was constantly accused of having *no* way of his own, of borrowing from everyone. "It is instinctively, without noticing it, that M. Cocteau adapts himself to the taste of the day, the hour, the moment," was one of the kinder remarks made about him by the French Dadaists — who had, of course, themselves borrowed their very name, just as Breton was to take the name "surrealism" from Apollinaire, who had coined it for Cocteau's ballet.

crude, so ridiculous, that it is as though nothing happens. Look for no double meaning, no anachronisms, in the *Boeuf*. I repeat: it is an American farce, written by a Parisian who has never been in America."

Etienne de Beaumont financed the *Boeuf* as the first of two *"Spectacles-Concerts"* with which he hoped to interest the public in *l'esprit nouveau;* the second would be a *"Festival Erik Satie."* The Théâtre de Comédie des Champs-Elysées (a small hall on an upper floor of the Théâtre des Champs-Elysées) was rented for four performances; the Fratellini trio, Paul, François and Albert, the clowns from the Cirque Médrano with whom Cocteau had wanted to work in the days of the ill-fated Cocteau-Gleizes-Lhote *Midsummer Night's Dream*, were now engaged to play the barman and the two women, the remaining roles being confided to other performers from the Médrano; and Guy-Pierre Fauconnet agreed to do sets and costumes. A schedule was set up: the *"répétition générale"* for invited guests on Saturday, February 21, 1920; a high-priced performance, also a matinée, the following Monday for the benefit of a war charity, "l'Oeuvre de Mme. la Marquise de Noailles, 'Hôpitaux Militaires, Section des Régions Libérées' " (boxes to begin at 500 francs and single seats at 100); and a pair of ordinary public performances later. Since the *Boeuf* was short,* other novelties were billed: an overture by Poulenc; a fox-trot by Auric called "Adieu, New-York," interpreted by two clowns; Poulenc's "Cocardes," written to three poems by Cocteau and sung by Koubitsky, "accompanied," Milhaud recalls, "by violin, trumpet, clarinet, trombone and big drum"; a "musical intermission — American bar"; and Satie's "Trois Petites Pièces Montées." The *Boeuf* would close the program. The conductor was Vladimir Golschmann.

The enterprise was accompanied by dramas of various dimensions. In mid-preparation, Fauconnet died of a heart attack, and his work was taken over by Raoul Dufy; the oversized masks that Cocteau had ordered, and that he rather grandiloquently spoke of as being a "rejuvenation of the masks of antiquity," looked wrong: Picasso spotted the trouble — insufficient variety in size and

---

* As recorded by the Orchestre du Théâtre des Champs-Elysées, with Milhaud himself conducting, the score lasts fifteen minutes. It was probably less concentrated, or more repetitious, for the show.

design; responding to the invitation in the program to visit the "American bar" during intermission, the audience crowded in, expecting mixed drinks, only to find that the mixture was purely musical — a mandolin trio playing jazz.

Cocteau spoke later of a change — a typical, Fregolian quick change — that he claims to have sought in connection with the *Boeuf*: at its premiere, he said, he took pains to avoid any *scandale*. "A *scandale* is a very lively thing," he wrote, "but it disturbs the actors and musicians, and prevents the few serious members of an audience from grasping the thousand nuances of a work that has taken several months to prepare. I avoided it at the opening of the *Boeuf* by going in front of the curtain and saying a few words that put the audience on my side." The public liked the *Boeuf*, and came in increasing numbers: after the last performance Jean Hugo noted in his diary: "Full house, great success." The Shah of Persia was accompanied by a suite that included his foreign minister, Firouz Mirza ("Prince Turquoise"), of whom more will be heard. The show won the approval of the most exacting of the Paris drama critics, Maurice Boissard (Paul Léautaud) of the Mercure de France, who had enjoyed Cocteau's visits to the offices of the Mercure while *Le Potomak* was languishing there. He called it "a choppy, voluptuous fantasy with real charm," and said that, compared with the clown Footit, "with his litheness and lightness, his thin pale face, his agile and graceful silence," the conventional wares of such boulevard dramatists as André Rivoire and Eugène Brieux were as Caliban to Ariel.

Milhaud's memoirs imply that he came to have certain regrets about the use of his score for the farcical show. "Forgetting that I had written *The Libation Bearers*, the public and the critics decided that I was a writer of comic circus music, whereas I detest anything slapstick and in composing the *Boeuf* had wanted only to create a merry, unpretentious divertissement in memory of the Brazilian rhythms that I had found so seductive, certainly never laughable." Milhaud's "merry divertissement," the ancestor of countless subsequent concert pieces interspersed with Latin-American rhythms, is far pleasanter and certainly less pretentious than most of them, but his "theme that returns between the tunes like a rondo" is as circuslike and slapstick as his sambas are seductive, and that theme is heard so often (thirteen or more times during the fifteen minutes) that there is nothing inappropriate in Cocteau's having made his scenario a farce.

As in the case of *Parade,* Cocteau's role in the show *Le Boeuf sur le Toit* is prime: he had begotten it. It is the second of his transpositions of the everyday, his nonsublime, nonfolkloristic, nonexotic spectacles that were so greatly to influence ballet repertoire.

On July 12 the *Boeuf,* subtitled for the English public *The Nothing-Doing Bar,* and with an English cast, opened at the Coliseum in London, where it was successful enough to be held over for a second week. The programs show that the first week it was sandwiched between Ruth Draper and Grock, the French clown, and the second week between Kharum, a "Persian pianist," and Fred Duprez (Mr. Manhattan), "The Famous American Monologist." Cocteau went to London with Milhaud to give some supervision during rehearsals. His utter Parisianism, and his degree of dependence on his Parisian entourage and on his growing Parisian celebrity, are wonderfully evident in passages from letters he sent during his first taste of London to the young Raymond Radiguet, who had written some of the publicity for the Paris production.

Cocteau to Raymond Radiguet
Carlton Hotel, Pall Mall, London.
[n.d.]

Mon cher Raymond,

It's you who should be here, wearing a little cap, on your way to school and football. *I* have rheumatism in several places, and think that London looks like the Conciergerie, like the Galeries Lafayette, like the streets of Lyons or Brussels. The buses look like books by Cendrars. Firouz is a real Prince Turquoise, a black-browed angel.* Thanks to him my trip has been regal, and I have a little white automobile that darts in and out among the cabs or the sheep. In the city, naturally, I know nothing about the secrets of the place — artists, bars,

---

* Prince Firouz was in London on official Persian business. "This morning I attended a meeting of the League of Nations at St. James's Palace," Cocteau writes in one of his letters. "A game for nitwits. Poor Firouz — so aghast at it all that his eyebrows shot up to his hairline." Firouz was for a time the delight of the clan, and was even to play a role in the genesis of Raymond Radiguet's second novel, *Le Bal du Comte d'Orgel.* See Appendix IX for details concerning him, kindly supplied by Mr. Reginald Bridgeman.

films, etc. I'm too lazy to quit my incognito. I'll be back soon. Paris is better. *No doubt about it.*

Cocteau to Raymond Radiguet
Carlton Hotel, Pall Mall, London.
[n.d.]

Mon cher vénérable Boby Esq.,

Not a single word from any of you — I am alone with my fate, which greatly tires me and saddens me. You all promised absolutely that you'd write. The moment I leave [rue d'] Anjou, I'm as good as dead. I was able to talk with Maman on the telephone this morning despite the Channel and *enormous* layers of spleen (the London sickness, which does exist). "HUGO RUMBOLD PRESENTS COCTEAU'S GREAT PAR-ISIAN SUCCESS" — such is the *folie* one sees in gold let-ters at the entrance to the Coliseum. The apostrophe 's' makes me sneeze. Sunday, in the country, on a hill overlooking the Thames, five old Salvation Army ladies were playing a hymn on the trombone. When it began to rain they broke off and ran for it, tucking up their skirts, and resumed their playing under a tree. The trombone player at the Coliseum is a woman, too. I'd like to bring you back a top hat.

Another letter ends, "Without you all, my life is dreary." Ac-cording to Milhaud, Cocteau enjoyed overhearing, or being told of, a Cockney workman's expression of appreciation of *The Nothing-Doing Bar,* after a performance at the Coliseum: "You can't say it's funny, but it's fun because it's different." *

Le Coq. Enter Raymond Radiguet (1919–1920)

Vladimir Golschmann,† who conducted the orchestra at the *Boeuf sur le Toit* and the rest of the *"Spectacle-Concert,"* is one of

---

* That, at least, is how the remark might be put back into English from Milhaud's French: *"On peut pas dire que c'est rigolo; mais comme c'est différent, c'est rigolo."*

† Golschmann, just beginning his career, had met Cocteau and the musicians in his search for modern music to play at a series of ten "Concerts Golschmann" which a

many who have told of the pleasures of the Saturday night dinners that began about the time Cocteau was writing his *Carte Blanche* articles. Members of the clan, their guests, and their wives or women friends — the painters Valentine Hugo, Marie Laurencin, Irène Lagut, the pianist Marcelle Meyer — would meet at Cocteau's flat, or Lucien Daudet's, or Morand's, or the Hugos', or Milhaud's or Poulenc's; someone would mix cocktails, and dinner would follow at a flat or a restaurant. Ordering in a restaurant was simple: the *plat du jour* was usually accepted, and the conventional dessert was a *pot de crême au chocolat*. The bill was equally divided. Both Milhaud and Jean Hugo say that the earliest meetings took place at Milhaud's flat in Montmartre, moving on to the nearby restaurant Le Petit Bessonneau, and then to the Foire de Montmartre — the stretch of boulevard lined with fair booths between the Place Blanche and the Place Pigalle — or to the Cirque Médrano in the same quarter; but Hugo's diary lists also the restaurant Delmas in the Place de la Madeleine, a tearoom called Le Thé Butterfly in the rue St. Honoré, an establishment known as Chez René, which began in the rue Demours and later moved out to the suburb of Robinson and was run by a character with a prison in his past who went under the name "René de Amouretti." Also favored were the Montmartre restaurant of Madame Coconnier, whose son had been cook in Jean Hugo's officers' mess at the front, and a restaurant near the Bibliothèque Nationale named for its owner, one Gauclair, who owned a vineyard at La Rochecorbon in Touraine that supplied many a magnum for the clan. After dinner the group would go, if not to the Médrano or the street fair, to the Folies Bergère, or to an American film or an amusement park, Luna Park or Magic City, to watch the sideshows and the shooting galleries and have themselves photographed against comic back-

friend had subsidized. Cocteau asked him to conduct the *"Spectacle-Concert"* on the sudden illness of Félix Delgrange, the usual conductor for the Six. For Golschmann the *"Spectacle-Concert"* was a *porte-bonheur:* "Stravinsky attended one of the rehearsals or performances, and asked me to spend the summer with him and his family in Brittany. He auditioned me on the traps and many other instruments, and said little, but in September I was visited by Walter Nouvel, Diaghilev's *éminence grise:* Diaghilev wanted me to be one of the conductors with the Ballets Russes." Golschmann tells of the particular brilliance of the Saturday dinners during the period when Cocteau was writing *Carte Blanche:* he used the dinners as a kind of rehearsal for his articles, and his friends found his — and sometimes their — brightest remarks in *Paris-Midi* the following week.

grounds. The evening usually ended in somebody's flat, with music and poetry. Everyone agrees with Golschmann about the fun. In a description of the dinners that he included in a lecture at the Collège de France in 1923, Cocteau said that they were eventually abandoned chiefly because they became too institutionalized, too much of a duty: he himself, he said, had come to resent any defection, like his own grandfather at a family gathering. At one of the dinners, that of March 6, 1920, was born an important little publication. An entry in Jean Hugo's diary for that date reads: "Saturday dinner. Founding of the magazine *Le Coq*."

The four numbers of the broadsheet *Le Coq* (May, June, July-August-September, and November, 1920; Numbers Three and Four are called *Le Coq Parisien*) are one of Cocteau's answers to the magazines that snubbed him — his most direct answer, combating them with a form of warfare that was theirs rather than his. (Of course their continual sniping at him reveals their awareness that he was someone to reckon with.) *Le Coq* imitated Picabia's *391* in its folded format, fragmented text and variegated typography, and surpassed it in wit and high spirits; it was merrily anti-Dada, although in adopting Dada's methods of slogan and, occasionally, scurrility, it became itself anti-Dada Dada; it was put together chiefly by Cocteau himself and the now seventeen-year-old Raymond Radiguet, with contributions by all the members of the clan. The first number, printed on pink paper, openly proclaimed the group to be a "Mutual Admiration Society," a phrase that Morand had coined to describe the Saturday dinners. For Number One, Jean Hugo designed a cock, Roger de la Fresnaye contributed a drawing, Radiguet protested against a Frenchman's obligation to be intellectual — "Ever since 1789 they've been forcing me to think — it's given me a headache"; there was a dig at Stravinsky in the form of praise of a "rival" — "Arnold Schönberg, the six musicians hail you!" and there was Satie's thrust at Ravel: "Ravel refuses the Legion of Honor, but all his music accepts it." Against Dada, there was the jeering accusation that it was "too timid," and the simple reproduction, without comment, of a particularly fatuous Dada anti-art slogan attributed to Tzara: "The path of breathing ends in a tree from which India ink is extracted, and this always ends with a poem or a drawing."

With *Le Coq* there begins in earnest one of the most striking French stories of two artistic geniuses, analogous to the story of Verlaine and Rimbaud: for now Cocteau had an alter ego — Raymond Radiguet, the prodigious adolescent. The story has never been properly told: a brief introductory flashback is needed.

It was while Cocteau was writing his *Carte Blanche* articles that he and Radiguet had met, either at Max Jacob's, as Cocteau once said, or more probably in Jacob's presence at the Sunday *"matinée poétique"* in memory of Apollinaire in Léonce Rosenberg's art gallery, L'Effort Moderne, in the rue de la Baume on June 8, 1919 — the gathering at which Cocteau read his poem "Coupe à ta muse les cheveux." "Radiguet," says Jean Hugo in his diary for that day, "read a text by Apollinaire."

Born June 18, 1903, Raymond Radiguet was almost sixteen. His father, Maurice Radiguet, was an artist, making a modest living selling humorous drawings to Paris newspapers, as Jacques Villon and Juan Gris had done earlier. Raymond was the oldest of seven children, all living with their parents in the riverside suburb of Parc St. Maur. There Raymond had gone to school, and fished and boated on the Marne and from the nearby island in midstream called L'Ile d'Amour. André Salmon tells of first seeing Raymond when he was a boy in short trousers, delivering his father's drawings to the newspaper *L'Intransigeant,* where Salmon was an editor. He seemed to grow into an adolescent overnight, he showed Salmon drawings of his own, and poems, and Salmon introduced him to Max Jacob. He had always had what parents optimistically call an "independent spirit," and now he began to slip out of the suburbs on the last train to Paris, visit Max Jacob and other artists in Montmartre and Montparnasse (he became especially friendly with Juan Gris), and return home at dawn.

André Salmon says, "The day after they met, Raymond Radiguet was calling Max Jacob simply Max; two days later he was addressing him as *'tu'*. It is difficult to say exactly what Raymond Radiguet, a poet prodigy, could be given by Max Jacob." Among the things the boy was given by Jacob, who was as notorious for his pederasty as for his conversion from Judaism to Catholicism, was the address of 10 rue d' Anjou. "The first time he came to see me," Cocteau has said, "sent by Max Jacob, my mother's maid said 'There's a little boy with a cane.' And in fact he was carrying a little cane that he never put down all the time he was there and that looked odd held by him." "I sensed his star," Cocteau said later; and he immediately wrote to Max Jacob: "Radiguet is quite somebody. You were right as always." *

Salmon speaks of feeling from the beginning that Radiguet "promised to develop into someone quite cruel"; in a newspaper job that Salmon found for him his cool insolence "now spontaneous, now calculating" made veteran journalists "hesitate between hating him and admiring him." A woman of thirty or so, whom Salmon and many of his fellow journalists knew and liked, became infatuated with the boy; in the affair that followed, his extraordinary callousness to her made the older men who witnessed it "a little afraid of him." Jacques Porel calls Radiguet *"un étrange éphèbe"* and speaks of his *"beau visage lourd et obstiné"*; Stravinsky describes him as "silent . . . with something of the young bull in him"; Jean Hugo calls him "silent, sulky, arrogant, amazingly mature in his judgments, certainly not affectionate." Even in the descriptions of him by Cocteau, who now made him the successor, in the role of young lover, to Jean LeRoy, there is no pretense that the boy was what is commonly called "agreeable." At the Saturday dinners, Cocteau says, "Radiguet was like a young chess prodigy. Without opening his mouth, simply by the scorn conveyed by his nearsighted glance, his badly cut hair and his chapped lips, he beat us all. Remember: the very finest players were sitting around that table." And Cocteau quotes the boy's retort to a painter who remarked that a painting he was showing Radiguet and Cocteau was as yet unfinished: "It would be humane to finish it off."

The friendship developed rapidly. In his *Carte Blanche* article for June 30, 1919, three weeks after their first meeting, Cocteau called attention to the boy as "the youngest of our young poets," mentioning his poem "Dictée," about the painter Irène Lagut; and the next day, writing to confirm an appointment, he asked, "Did

* André Breton, who at the time of the Apollinaire *"matinée poétique"* had already published poems by Radiguet in *Littérature*, later told Valentine Hugo that he himself had introduced Radiguet to Cocteau that day. Everybody wanted to be part of the story of the marvelous boy, and quite a few people were. At only fourteen, he had submitted to Pierre Albert-Birot, for *Sic*, verses that he signed "raimon-rajky." Tzara had published some of his poems in the review *Dada* in Zurich and had mentioned him in a poem of his own in *391*. Cocteau always minimized the extent to which Radiguet, young as he was, had been "around" before they met.

you see that I spoke about you?" and signed himself "Your old
friend." The boy took Cocteau to Parc St. Maur and showed him
some of his haunts along the Marne; it was probably Cocteau who
took the sixteen-year-old to another fancy-dress victory party given
by Paul Poiret on that July 14. In his final number of *Carte
Blanche,* dated August 11, Cocteau told his readers that he was
about to "leave Babel to sunbathe in the mountains," and Jean
Hugo noted in his diary for that same day: "Cocteau and Louis
Durey left from the Gare d'Orsay for the Pyrenees (Hotel Bellevue, Ahusky, near Mauléon, Basses Pyrénées). Radiguet was with
us."

Ahusky was a remote Basque village accessible only by foot or
on muleback, consisting of a few houses, "a chapel made from an
old stable, a fronton that was simply an old wall," and known for
its mineral spring. "After a four-hour walk, very steep, in cloudy
heat, we reached the farm," Cocteau wrote Radiguet in his first letter. "Alone in the world up here; but the more tired, the more removed and alone I am the more energetic I become. Not a tree, not
a patch of shade. The shepherds sing Poulenc.* How I love my little room! Imagine a white box in the sky. I should have taken you
by the scruff of the neck at the station and made you come along."
With his second letter Cocteau enclosed a poem dedicated to Radiguet; in his third he calls him his "adopted son"; in his fourth he
says that the mountain air gives him strength, so that he "feels like
a love-sick Hercules"; in his fifth he laments "If only you-know-
who were here I'd be very happy"; in his sixth, "If I feel too lone-
some I kiss the mule on the nose." All in all, during the seven
weeks he was away from Paris he wrote Radiguet a score of charming, humorous, affectionate letters, reproachful when too few came
in return; some of them are arranged in semi-verse form, and one
is a fourteen-page "Pearl White film," a chronicle partly written in
trains, recounting his journey with Durey across southern France
from the Pyrenees to visit Darius Milhaud in Aix-en-Provence. He
was putting together a volume of his poems, and Radiguet was
doing the same, sending Cocteau some of them and a draft of a
preface. "I open your two letters and bits of paper fly out, like
butterflies from a magician's hat," Cocteau wrote. "They keep me

* During the stay at Ahusky, Louis Durey wrote several songs inspired by Basque
shepherds' airs, with words by Cocteau, notably "Prière," "Polka," and "Attelage."

company. Send more. I feel them through the envelope. I pin every
one of them on the walls of my cell." In advising him, Cocteau
pretended to be a schoolmaster, giving the poems grades. At other
times he assumed what he called a "family" air: "I beg you to be
careful and keep close to the shore. I'm giving real family-type
advice, but after all you're my adopted son." "Be a good boy and
wear large glasses," he wrote, for Radiguet was nearsighted and
had been neglecting his eyes, screwing his face into grimaces in
order to see. "The small kind are detestable. I recommend big
round ones — they'll make you look like a Chinese poet or a frog."
He asked him whether he was in touch with Irène Lagut, for he
knew that Irène had fallen in love with the boy and that he might be
responding a little; and knowing Raymond's tendency to spend
his time in artists' studios rather than stay home and write, he
urged him to remain at Parc St. Maur, "far from the dreary city
and the charcoal-dust of the Montmartre studios (except for Gris,
whose friendship for you takes the place of a fresh-air cure). Go
sit near the viaduct, cast out your line with a pen and a few words
— after an hour or two you'll fish out a poem." He himself, he
said, was leading "a cowlike existence. Try it at the Parc. Montmartre and Montparnasse spike the milk."

The intimacy had only begun, or was only beginning — Cocteau
still calls Radiguet *"vous"*: *"Après je vivrai sur le bord de la
Marne, en face l'Ile d'Amour et vous viendrez manger des fritures
avec moi* . . . Have you found the dream inn on the Marne for
me? Keep looking . . . My childhood is very close to me, thanks
to you, and I am soaking myself in it — I'm back with my celluloid
duck in the bathtub! . . . You are the Ile d'Amour . . . One is
always alone . . . you are and will be alone as I am alone. Yet
you are not really alone, because I grasp every one of your intentions, even the slightest, and enjoy a well-placed comma . . ."

In the section of the "Pearl White film" written in a train approaching Marseilles, there is an example, rare in Cocteau's letters, of a coctelian sexual joke, and a reminiscence of his own
Marseilles experiences: "I am writing this in a crowded corridor. I
have a fat lady on my left thigh and a sailor on my right thigh.
(Heads or tails?) . . . In Marseilles, I'll be walking with you.
It's marvelous there, like the fête de Montmartre." After the cross-
country train trip, so long, fatiguing and full of changes that he

called it "Around the World in Eighty Days," he and Durey arrived at Aix and put up at the Hotel des Thermes Sextius, where ancient Roman baths were (and are) still in use and where the proprietor sold antiques from the rooms occupied by his guests. There Cocteau finished the "Pearl White film" and mailed it to Radiguet: "I'm finishing these notes at Aix, in a hotel that's an antique shop and a Roman bath. I bathed in an unlighted cellar, groping my way, and Durey is writhing with frightful stomach cramps. Have seen Darius — in white ducks — very much a Darius elephant. He has just written a score for brasses and drums to a poem of mine. I'm to see him tomorrow in his garden, twenty minutes from our hotel.

I am

going

to

sleep

Jean."

In Aix (where he and the portly Milhaud apparently had some of their first discussions about the as yet unrealized "show" of *Le Boeuf sur le Toit*) there had been no letters awaiting him, and none arrived the first day or two. "Cher Monsieur," he wrote to Radiguet with reproachful formality, "Despite your silence I'm saying goodnight to you before going to bed. I saw Cézanne's little house, and picked a pear outside his window for Picasso's mantelpiece. The caretaker thought we had come to steal the fruit, and reviled me, not understanding that this pear tree bears still-lifes. . . . In the window of a bookshop, *Littérature*, with your name."

"I've had a little box of candied fruit sent to your brothers and sisters, and a pot of jam to you," he wrote on one of the following days, and the same letter contains the first indication that he sought literary judgment from the boy, as well as the other way round: "I am leaving my poems alone now. I need to get away from them to know what they're like. You are the only person who intimidates me, you stone-ager. But I think that *Vocabulaire* or *Poèmes* will be a *good* book." * He signed one letter "Your adoptive father," and on September 15 he sent one that was to have a sequel.

---

* *Poésies 1917–1920* would be the title for this volume. *Vocabulaire* was used for a later collection.

Cocteau to Raymond Radiguet

September 15, 1919

Mon cher petit,

I'll be back in Paris before next week. I'm telling *no one in the world* (except my mother) and will expect you at the Hotel M. at half-past two. (I'll telegraph you the date.) Promise me to be very prompt (not three o'clock) for certain reasons that I will explain to you. It is the only way to see you and talk without a thousand people and a whole shipwreck of suitcases. Will you please *reply* to this letter. (You never answer a single question.) Make this slight effort out of friendship for me. Let me know immediately whether everything is clear and whether I can send you the telegram the day I leave Aix . . . P.S. If anyone asks you when I'm getting back, don't tell.

But for all his eagerness to be reunited with Radiguet, Cocteau delayed his return to Paris by making a detour to the Villa Croisset in Grasse, his old "sanatorium," where he now stayed for ten days. The pleasures of *la vita in villa,* contrasting with life in Paris flats and hotels, country inns, and more or less bohemian surroundings, was always to have an appeal for him, especially when he could be with old friends like the three generations who were probably at the Villa Croisset that autumn — the elderly "Corporal Petrarch," the Francis de Croissets themselves, and Marie-Laure Bischoffsheim. Besides, after having gone "Around the World in Eighty Days" he had been dreading the train trip back to Paris, and the Croissets had an automobile. "I leave Wednesday," he finally wrote Radiguet on September 29. "Rather long trip — five days by auto, if the tires hold out."

Back in Paris in October, Cocteau devoted himself to supervising the preparation of Radiguet's volume of poetry and his own, and the publication of new editions of *Le Cap* and *Le Coq et l'Arlequin.* Then, in mid-November, he had to write a difficult letter.

People in Paris, perhaps around the newspapers, had apparently been calling Monsieur Maurice Radiguet's attention to the growing friendship between his son and the notorious Cocteau, and hinting that the boy sometimes spent the night with Cocteau at a hotel, probably the Hotel de Surène near the Madeleine, where Cocteau occasionally took a room for several days at a time to work and meet friends away from his mother's apartment. Somehow Monsieur Radiguet came upon Cocteau's letter of September 14 from Aix and a letter that Raymond had written to Cocteau but not sent.* Monsieur Radiguet was an affectionate father, protective, bourgeois but not unsophisticated; and the letters increased his alarm. He wrote to Cocteau, and Cocteau replied.

Cocteau to Monsieur Maurice Radiguet

Sunday, November 16, 1919

Monsieur,

I have just received your letter and must reply despite my regret at being unable to explain the inexplicable. It is possible that my friendship for your son and my deep admiration for his gifts (which are becoming increasingly apparent) are of an uncommon intensity, and that from the outside it is hard to make out how far my feelings go. His literary future is of primary consideration with me: he is a kind of prodigy. Scandal would spoil all this freshness. You cannot possibly believe for a second that I do not try to avoid that by all the means in my power.

I know nothing of the letter from Raymond which you mention. If he did not send it to me, it was probably something of a fantasy that he would have been embarrassed to have me see.

As to this hotel, your son has sometimes spent the night here if he missed the last train to Parc St. Maur, since I am never able to put anyone up at home.

The appointment at the Hotel M. was at the Hotel Meurice, where I was to stay on my return from Grasse, but where I did not stay. You must have found — I hope you did — a special delivery letter in which I asked Raymond to come to my house and not to the Meurice.

I hope you understand that meetings between us are unavoidable, since we constantly see the same artists and I am

* Perhaps a letter written apparently very early in the friendship, which includes the phrases: "I am writing to a delightful friend whom I love. This letter is for you — the most sealed of letters. I adore you. Till tomorrow at five sharp." This is now in the Cocteau archives at Milly-la-Forêt. If Cocteau tells the truth about it in his letter to Monsieur Radiguet, he saw it only some time after Monsieur Radiguet found it.

publishing his book, but that I respect his youth too much
to wish to harm him by giving the slightest false impression.

The original of that letter is written in so much fairer a hand
than most of Cocteau's letters that it can only have been copied
from one or more drafts, and one wonders whether it may have
been composed in collaboration with Raymond himself. The boy
loved his father and his family, but since when have parents not
been fair game for lovers? Whatever the circumstances of the Cocteau-Radiguet love may have been, the letter from Aix about the
appointment at the "Hotel M" had been couched in so imploring a
tone — it was even more intense than Cocteau's usual letters to absent friends — that explanation was certainly difficult, and Cocteau's answer to Monsieur Radiguet was probably the best he could
do. That Monsieur Radiguet, who must have wanted desperately to
be reassured, told Cocteau that his reply was not totally convincing,
is evident from Cocteau's next letter.

Cocteau to Monsieur Maurice Radiguet
November 27, 1919

Monsieur,

Your letter touches me deeply. Goodness and a father's love
can be read between the lines. I cannot resent your being incredulous, since the situation is incredible. Confidence in me is
the only thing.

Look at Raymond. The abnormal development of his brain
is interfering with the normal development of his body. He
stoops. He is pale, nearsighted, talks in a weak voice. Before
there can be any question of his taking a job, he must be made
well, his strength must be restored. My role is to urge him to
listen to you, yours to insist that he exercise, eat, sleep.

Without the slightest trouble, Raymond can write a short
article every week. My good friend Doucet will pay him 50 fr.
per article. He likes to say that his library of modern literature begins with Baudelaire and ends with your son.

Few boys of his age earn 50 fr. a week with their work. As
for invitations, François Victor Hugo* tells me that he tele-

* Half-brother of Jean Hugo.

phoned him, and I know that Raymond lunched on Monday with Lord Derby's secretary, Reginald Bridgeman, who finds him charming. That is all I know of.

If friends complain about no longer seeing him, I give his health as an excuse. He has had nosebleeds in public, so the excuse is very plausible.

Take care of him. Literary talent always implies a tendency to nervousness, and exhaustion would allow this tendency to grow unchecked. Raymond must weather the cape of a difficult age, which in his case is not like that of most boys.

I respect you, and love you through him.

It was true that the couturier Jacques Doucet, who was forming the collection of manuscripts and rare editions of modern French writers that was the nucleus of the present Bibliothèque Littéraire Jacques Doucet, had recently been convinced of Raymond's importance (André Breton was one of Doucet's advisors) and was buying some of his manuscripts (though not one a week); but Cocteau's vagueness about the boy's "invitations" is disingenuous. Raymond had other friends, including women friends, outside the clan, and of them he may not have told Cocteau everything; but from Jean Hugo's diary it is evident that Raymond was constantly with Cocteau's group, and for Cocteau to claim to know of only two of the boy's associates (each of them connected with an imposing name) was to be far from frank.

Monsieur Radiguet seems to have written no more to Cocteau for the moment. During that winter of 1919–1920 Raymond became a full-fledged member of the "Mutual Admiration Society," going everywhere with them and writing publicity articles for the "*Spectacle-Concert*," for the work of Satie, for the Six, and for Cocteau's new book of verse, *Poésies*, which appeared in May.* His own volume was published: *Les Joues en Feu*, with four drypoints by Jean Hugo. He was hailed by all factions of the literary avant-garde as the greatest young prodigy since Rimbaud, which he probably was (although perhaps not quite yet); and now he played his part in the founding of *Le Coq* and the writing of its four numbers. (When

---

* F. S. Flint, again in *The Chapbook* (November, 1920), wrote of *Poésies* that it showed Cocteau as belonging "to the right of the left wing, of which the Dadaists are the extreme tip." Cocteau himself wrote to the Gleizes' that the book expressed his "revulsion against super-Dadaism."

Cocteau was in London with Milhaud, his letters to Radiguet show him counting on the boy to prepare the June number and to have the proofs ready for him on his return.) Radiguet's verse and prose published in *Le Coq,* much of it witty, disillusioned comment on aesthetics and the artistic scene, made people say of him, now seventeen, that he had been "born forty years old."

During that first year of the friendship Radiguet seems to have behaved well with Cocteau (who was now thirty), won by the charm of the ever-young older man, by his accomplishments and by his milieu, which, since he adopted it as his own, he must have preferred to that of Breton and the other Dadaists, who had also been courting him by printing his poems. He could be forgetful of his manners, and Madame Cocteau was uneasy about his constant, untidy presence at 10 rue d'Anjou — he did much of his writing at Cocteau's desk — but as usual she accepted her son's opinions and said little. Cocteau was sometimes "governessy" (Reginald Bridgeman's word), and the boy sometimes rebellious, but things went well enough.

Cocteau credits Radiguet, who continued on good terms with the Dadaists and admired some of them as artists, but who himself preferred classical forms, with an important role in his own (Cocteau's) formulation of his aesthetic ideas in the first number of *Le Coq* — that first explicit statement of where he claimed to stand in the Paris world of art that Dada had turned into such a battleground. Since the grotesqueries of *Le Boeuf sur le Toit,* conservative critics, unaware of the cleavages within the avant-garde, had found it easy simply to call Cocteau a Dadaist; the misnomer irritated Breton; and Cocteau, delighted by both the misnomer and the irritation, took his cue from both.

"The articles that group me with the Dadaists amuse me greatly," he wrote in the first issue of *Le Coq,* "because I am the very model of an anti-Dadaist. The Dadaists know this very well, and if they sometimes ask me to collaborate with them it is to prove that their system is to have no system. If they stand at the extreme Left, I am at the extreme Right. The extreme Right used not to exist. Every Right is timid. I invented the *extreme* Right. . . . Extremes touch. I feel myself so far from the Left and from the Right, so close to the *extreme* Left, with which I close the circle, that people confuse one of us with the other. I constantly have to keep speci-

fying in a loud voice whether I am Right or Left, and this is tiring
— whereas, just over the wall, without raising my voice, I can talk
with Tzara and Picabia, my neighbors from the other end of the
world. . . .

"Critics always compare. The incomparable is outside their ken.
In the eyes of the critics a man in search of himself is on the wrong
track, and a man who finds himself is lost. Dada having become the
synonym of nothingness, nothing is more natural than that I should
be bracketed with it by eyes and ears that can no longer keep up
with me. Besides, these confusions are of no importance. But if I
ever had to be president of something, I would choose to preside
over an Anti-Modern League."

In taking this paradoxical, ironic stand against those who
claimed to be Apollinaire's heirs, Cocteau repeatedly evoked Apollinaire himself, whom he would scarcely have felt so free to claim
for his own had he been alive. He remembered (perhaps a little
conveniently) that Apollinaire had been "ill at ease in being the
most advanced point of his epoch. One day when we were walking
near the Ministry of Colonies where he worked, he told me of his
dissatisfactions. The modernism whose apostle he had become irritated him considerably. Sometimes he would curse the flood that
had come pouring out from a sluice which he himself had opened,
and claim that he had opened it as a joke." Since Apollinaire's
death, Cocteau had seen the world of modern art, Apollinaire's
flowering *esprit nouveau,* horridly covered by "a snowfall colder
than death" — the deadly snow of Dada. "The aim was to heap
abuse on literature and destroy it. This peculiar, blue-eyed suicide
attracted me. But the actual demolition was carried out by writers
gone mad." In writing *Le Cap,* he claimed, he had gone beyond Mallarmé and Rimbaud, and even beyond Cubism. "I felt myself
really alone. As a group, only the Dada Suicide Club seemed acceptable to me. But I did not feel myself suited to its tasks. Music
had already turned me to different tasks. I had just written *Le Coq
et l'Arlequin."* Thus he had come to the Six, to the clan, to Radiguet, and now to *Le Coq.* In short, the position he took, or claimed
to take, was this: since "modern" had come to mean "le Suicide-
Club Dada," the only way to express the *esprit nouveau* was to be
"anti-modern."

And so the subsequent numbers of *Le Coq* took as their theme variations of the slogan that had appeared in Number 1: "Return to poetry. Disappearance of the skyscraper. Reappearance of the rose."

The "disappearance of the skyscraper" part had also been expressed in the title, "Adieu New-York," of Auric's fox-trot played at the *"Spectacle- Concert,"* and it was heard again in a squib by Auric in *Le Coq No. 2.* Jazz, he said, had been a marvelous revelation; but although he had in the past been "moved to tears" by such American jazz pieces as "Hindustan" and "Indianola," it had now become necessary to "reinvent nationalism. Jazz woke us up: from now on let's stop our ears so as not to hear it." That did not mean that the clan clamped an embargo on American cultural goods. They continued to enjoy American films and to play and listen to American jazz. That part of the slogan was simply slogan. None of their anti-New York talk was aimed at the pre-Dada Dada that had been introduced there during the war by Picabia and Marcel Duchamp.

But the "reappearance of the rose" counted for more. Cocteau had a particular rose in mind. *Le Coq* was being printed by Cocteau's school friend and former partner on *Schéhérazade,* François Bernouard, now a master printer, apparently at Bernouard's own expense. From his establishment, "La Belle Edition," in the rue des Saints-Pères, Bernouard had printed Radiguet's *Les Joues en Feu,* with its Hugo illustrations. Bernouard's emblem, always appearing on his title pages, was a rose. And in "La Rose de François," a poem written in praise of Bernouard, and printed by Bernouard in a special edition, with a portrait of Cocteau by Marie Laurencin, Cocteau stepped aside from modern rhythms and wrote what amounted to a pastiche of Ronsard, the great poet of the Pléiade whose most celebrated ode begins: *"Mignonne, allons voir si la rose . . ."* * The association is so close that it may have begun

---

* Two stanzas from "La Rose de François":

> Voici le bouton, d'abord,
> Frisant son jeune prépuce,
> Ensuite, d'Amour l'astuce
> Le défrise, le détord,
> Et, peu à peu, cet étrange
> Adonis de sexe change.
>
> De ses doigts Amour rieur
> Ouvre un timide calice,

as an association of sounds — Bernouard, Ronsard, rose, François, France. The rose to reappear, the rose de Ronsard, the rose de François Bernouard, is the rose de France; and this part of the slogan, tinged with the chauvinism that was a factor in much anti-Dada (Dada was international: Apollinaire himself had declined Tzara's request for poems because of the latter's German associates), marks the return of Cocteau, at Radiguet's urging, toward the French classics. Some of Cocteau's best work, and all of Radiguet's best, were to come, and quite soon, from this embrace.

On December 9, 1920, just after *Le Coq* had ended with its November issue — François Bernouard was no longer able to finance it, and other support was not forthcoming — Francis Picabia, who had not yet broken with Dada, invited a large number of friends to the opening of an exhibition of his pictures at the Galerie de la Cible, in the rue Bonaparte. The guest list was motley, including, along with Breton, Tzara and the other Dadaists, a crowd of fashionable and artistic folk who detested, or in some cases feared, Dada; and Picabia took his greatest pleasure, perhaps, in announcing, in his invitation: "Parisian jazz, executed by Auric, Cocteau, Poulenc." Cocteau, whom Aragon had baptized *"le poète-orchestre,"* because of the amateur virtuosity he had acquired on a variety of instruments, wore a top hat that night, and with Auric and Poulenc at the piano he performed on the drum, the bass drum, castanets, drinking glasses, the mirliton and a klaxon. The numbers rendered by the combine included "Mon homme," "Adieu New-York," and some of Milhaud's sambas from the *Boeuf.* In the crowded rooms Tristan Tzara mounted a podium and recited a composition of his own entitled "Dada manifeste sur l'amour faible et l'amour amer" ("Dada has its say on love, weak and bitter"), consisting of six "chants," each ending with a variation on the theme *"Je me trouve très charmant."* This humorous Dada-in-a-dinner-jacket for the carriage trade was not at all to the taste of Breton, who glowered at the sight of Picabia himself in evening clothes and at the presence of Cocteau's trio supplying vigorous interludes between Tzara's "chants." Breton's only humor was *l'hu-*

Dont se chiffonne et se plisse
Fraîchement l'intérieur.
Mystère phanérogame:
C'est fini, la rose est femme.

mour noir, and that irreverent vernissage of Picabia's was one portent of the parting of their ways.

Quite willing so to associate with the Dadaists on his own terms, Cocteau enjoyed pretending, when Diaghilev revived *Parade* that same month, that he was generally recognized as their precursor. "The horse of *Parade* is to return to the stage of the Théâtre des Champs-Elysées," he announced in *Comoedia.* "When we first gave *Parade,* Dadaism was unknown. We had never heard it mentioned. Now the audience will certainly recognize Dada in our inoffensive horse. I love my friends Picabia and Tzara. If necessary, I lend them a hand, but *I am not a Dadaist.* That is still probably the best way to be one. No, *Parade* is neither Dadaist, nor Cubist, nor Futurist, nor of any school. PARADE IS PARADE, in other words, a big toy."

Apparently in this revival, staged December 21, unlike the attempted revival the previous spring, Diaghilev restored at least some of Cocteau's beloved sound effects. "Diaghilev is sweet as sugar and is letting me stage *Parade* as it always should have been staged," was the way Cocteau had announced the event to the Hugos in a letter dated November 27, and quite possibly that accounts for the acerbity — and, one must say, the silliness — with which Satie wrote to Valentine about it.

Erik Satie to Valentine Hugo
December 13, 1920

. . . *Parade* goes on the 21st of this month. Cocteau is repeating his tiresome antics of 1917. He is being such a nuisance to Picasso and me that I feel quite knocked out. It's a mania with him. *Parade* is his alone. That's all right with me. But why didn't he do the sets and the costumes and write the music, for this poor ballet?

Cocteau wrote the Hugos on December 23: "Let me tell you right away that *Parade* was a triumph. Why weren't you there?" And in a later account he said: "There were twelve curtain calls, and Satie, Picasso and I had to appear in a box and bow. The same people who wanted to murder us in 1917 stood up and applauded in 1920. What had intervened? What made those conceited theatregoers do a *volte-face* and admit their mistake so humbly? A lady gave me the explanation, in the way she congratulated my mother: 'Ah, madame,' she cried. 'How right they were to change it all!' "

Cocteau, laughing at the lady, did not pretend that it was the few changes made in *Parade,* much though those changes pleased him, that accounted for the different reception. What had chiefly changed was the *air de Paris* — that volatile substance that Marcel Duchamp had pretended so Dadaistically to seal up in a bottle and offer for sale. That, and the position of *Parade*'s authors. Cocteau, Satie, Picasso and Massine were all better known than they had been three years before: Cocteau had won considerable celebrity by *Parade* itself, by the *Boeuf,* by his volumes of verse and the continual proclamation of his opinions in *Le Coq et l'Arlequin, Carte Blanche,* and *Le Coq.* Satie might write that peevish letter to Valentine Hugo, and Gide might snarl secretly into his *Journal,** but from Proust came a letter in which he "compared the acrobats to the Dioscuri," Cocteau says, "and called the horse 'a great swan acting like a madman.' " And along with what other ballet had *Parade* been danced, this time? With *The Rite of Spring.* That Diaghilev should now choose to revive Stravinsky's revelation and *Parade* together was a definitive victory — a rewinning, more satis-fying even than the original engagement, of the "greatest battle of the war." Another satisfaction was the presence in the audience of "Monsieur Bébé," as Cocteau now commonly called Radiguet. "Secretly" (although most of their friends knew it), the boy had joined Cocteau for a few days at Le Piqueÿ early that autumn, and now he wrote an appreciation of *Parade* that appeared in the *Gaulois* on Christmas Day, thus associating himself with the work so close to Cocteau's heart.

Le Gaya and Les Mariés de la Tour Eiffel (*1921*)

Ever since the early 1900's — when Apollinaire and Picasso first met in an "English bar" near the Gare St. Lazare — bars have shared with cafés the affection of Paris painters and literati. Some-times a bar *is* a café, especially when it is called one, as for exam-

* See above, p. 232.

ple the little Basque bar, known for its good port, called the Café
Certà, in the Passage de l'Opéra, where Breton, Aragon and Soupault set up the Paris headquarters of Dada, and where they entertained Tzara, Marcel Duchamp, Man Ray, Max Ernst, Jean Arp
and many another. The Certà was distant from both Montmartre
and Montparnasse — one of its suitabilities, Louis Aragon said,
for Dada. A year or two later, Cocteau and his anti-Dada clan set
up their headquarters in a small bar that sold Spanish wine, called
the Gaya, not far from the Certà. The similarities of location and
product seem to have been coincidental: the Gaya was chosen because of its pianist.

"After *Le Coq et l'Arlequin*," says Cocteau, "we ran the risk of
being taken seriously, which is the beginning of death. One morning when I was depressed about it Darius Milhaud said to me,
'Would you like me to give you a bar?' It was the Gaya, in the rue
Duphot. It was always empty. Jean Wiener, who had studied at the
Conservatory with Darius, played American music there, marvelously. He had asked Milhaud to have me take over the bar as headquarters. I didn't hesitate a minute. The bar belonged to Louis
Moysès."

Louis Moysès' parents were the near-peasant owners of a small
café in the northern French town of Charleville, whose most famous son is Rimbaud; Moysès was to endear himself to Cocteau by
noticing a photograph of Rimbaud in Cocteau's room and asking
"Haven't I seen that fellow's picture somewhere before?" He was a
good-natured young man, unpretentious, accommodating, full of
songs and jokes and other hostly qualities, and coming to Paris
after the war was set up in business at the Gaya by a friend who was
one of the managers of the Hotel Meurice. The premises of the
Gaya were inconvenient — two rooms, one on each side of the
building entrance leading to apartments above; the bar was in one
room, a restaurant in the other, and customers could pass between
them only by crossing an interior court or by using the street.
Moysès was enchanted by his new regular customers, and decorated the walls with colored posters bearing their names. Word
quickly spread that the little place had been, or was about to be,
taken up by the clan, and on February 22, 1921, when Jean Hugo
first mentions it, he, Cocteau, Radiguet and Auric arrived there
after seeing a Sessue Hayakawa film to find Tzara and Picabia al-

ready on the scene, the latter making cocktails. Within a few days
Jean Hugo was recording: "*Saturday*, to the Gaya Bar, rue Duphot,
where we dine at ten in the midst of a crowd."

Milhaud says of Jean Wiener, his fellow student of composition at
the Conservatory, whom he thus found after the war piano-playing
at the Gaya to support his family, what anyone who has heard Wiener knows — that he "played syncopated music with ethereal ease;
his timbre was very delicate and his rhythm light." (Later Wiener
and Clément Doucet would tour the world as a celebrated two-piano
team, and Wiener would compose scores for French films and television.) Wiener's partner at the Gaya was an American, Vance
Lowry, according to Wiener a charming man who spoke excellent
French with an "endearing" American accent and played the banjo
(with his fingernails, using no plectrum) and the saxophone.
"Without any transition," says Milhaud, "those two would pass
from fashionable ragtime and fox-trots to the most celebrated
works of Bach . . . As the bar's customers invariably arrived
later than we did, and left before us, there was always part of the
evening when we were alone and free to make music to our hearts'
content." One of the music-makers was of course Cocteau. "I play
jazz very well and am proud of it," he says. "Along with drawing,
it is my *violon d'Ingres*. Jazz was a better intoxicant for me than
alcohol, which I cannot stand. With jazz, you feel yourself pushed
about by twenty arms; you are a god of noise . . . I played on an
instrument bought by Stravinsky — one that had had the honor of
serving in the orchestration of *Les Noces*. I played with Darius Milhaud, with Marcelle Meyer, Wiener, and a delightful Negro, a true
demon of harmony, named Vance. Paul Morand used to say to him,
'Vance, nighttime is the Negroes' daytime — keep playing' . . .
Those innocent pleasures launched the bar. It was a worthy successor to the cafés of Verlaine's day."

At the Gaya, everybody was enthusiastic about everybody. The
atmosphere can scarcely have been so relaxed at the Certà a few
blocks away, and one is glad to think of the half-playboy Picabia
and the sometimes droll Tzara (the two Dadaists who seem to have
been most capable of occasional frivolity of a nonpretentious kind)
coming in for cocktails. It was quickly rumored, especially among
the Dadaists, that Jean Cocteau had finally found his proper level,
as night-club manager. "I was forever lost, compromised," he

pretended to lament. "From the danger of being taken too seriously, after *Le Coq et l'Arlequin* and the other books, *nous étions sauvés!*"

Visiting Paris that winter of 1920–21 was the company of the Swedish Ballet, under the aegis of Rolf de Maré, a rich and accomplished young Swedish Diaghilev. Maré was interested in new works, and when Diaghilev declined to produce a ballet that Milhaud had written in Brazil to a libretto by Claudel, *L'Homme et Son Désir*, Maré took it on, and, in addition, asked for a ballet by Auric to a libretto by Cocteau. They both accepted, but somehow the score became a cooperative enterprise: Maré agreed that five of the Six should write separate numbers.* In and out of each other's houses Cocteau and the musicians worked through the winter, and just as the Gaya was beginning, on February 23, 1921, there took place in the Hugos' flat in the Palais-Royal (Jean Hugo was to do the costumes, Valentine assisting) a reading of Cocteau's "*tragicomédie*" to Maré and members of his troupe. It was called *La Noce*, or *La Noce Massacrée*, a title soon to change to *Les Mariés de la Tour Eiffel*, and the story concerned a petit-bourgeois wedding party and its misadventures one Fourteenth of July in the lower platform restaurant of the Eiffel Tower — an updating in more ways than one of Zola's famous wedding party in *L'Assommoir* and its hilarious visits to the Louvre and the Vendôme column. The script was apparently approved with enthusiasm: after the reading the clan attended the Swedish Ballet, sitting in the box of the choreographer, Jean Borlin, and then went on to the Gaya, where Cocteau beat the bass drum.

Cocteau had never been content to use the streets of Paris as mere passageways: to ignore the fascinations of Paris street life would be to waste opportunities; and François Hugo, for example, tells of Cocteau and his friends penetrating many a courtyard to use and abuse the "*privilège de la cour*," the hospitality customarily extended by concierges to pedestrians in need of a lavatory, and approaching as many good-looking *agents de police* as they dared to demand the "*privilège de la cape*," described by M. Hugo as a similar "customary tolerance" — the partial, momentary conceal-

---

* Louis Durey declined to participate, and he always felt later that Cocteau's line in a poem of *Plain-Chant* — "Auric, Milhaud, Poulenc, Tailleferre, Honegger" — (omitting Durey), was a kind of revenge.

ment, behind a policeman's outspread cape, of a gentleman pressed by the same need. Occasionally Cocteau would mime, in private or even in public, a pompous, gaga general of his own invention whom he had christened "le Général Clapier" — "General Hoare-house," one might say. "Watch out," Picasso would sometimes warn Cocteau when he was acting the General, "or you'll turn into him." "Le Général" became one of the characters in *Les Mariés de la Tour Eiffel.* Cocteau enjoyed attending the annual Paris *mi-carême* drag, and even in each other's houses the members of the clan liked to dress up; one evening Morand and Poulenc got themselves up as postcard bathing beauties — "the origin," Jean Hugo notes in his diary, "of the Trouville bathing beauty in *Les Mariés*" (both the character and Poulenc's polka named after her). The Eiffel Tower had been the subject of one of Cocteau's aesthetic reflections in both *Carte Blanche* and *Le Coq:* when the tower was built as a splendid decoration for the great industrial World's Fair of 1889 it was a veritable "Queen of the Machines," as he put it, and "did no work"; since then, grown dowdy and with a telegraphic station installed within it, it had become a mere "telegraph operator." "It would be built quite differently nowadays," Cocteau said. "It looks like one of those pathetic Lalique Art Nouveau pendants." Consequently the *Mariés* was costumed in 1890 style, and five ballerinas danced a "dance of the telegrams" to a *Telegram Waltz* composed by Germaine Tailleferre. A charming squib in *Le Coq,* signed only by a telephone number, Elysées 08–74 (it was Cocteau's), gave a variation of the Ganymede and Jupiter-eagle myth: "Ganymede married. His conduct seemed to have become exemplary. The entire wedding party betook itself to the Ile d'Amour in the Marne. He, still charming, with his tiny moustache and his evening clothes in broad daylight. The other ladies and gentlemen in high spirits. . . . Everything would have gone marvelously but for an unfortunate remark by the photographer: 'Don't move. Look straight into the camera. A bird is going to fly out.' Scarcely had he uttered those words when a bird did indeed fly out of the camera — and carried off the bridegroom . . ." The Eiffel Tower photographer in the *Mariés* is no less fatal a personage. Out of the camera with which he is to photograph the wedding party comes an ostrich, a bathing beauty, a baby (a very large one, symbolizing the importance of everybody's baby), a lion who eats the General but finds him unpalatable, and finally a dove of peace.

As in the *Boeuf*, the story of the *Mariés* is pantomimed by the dancers and the other participants, but in the *Mariés* there is also a commentary by two voices (at some of the performances Cocteau's was one of them) speaking through horns, like gramophones, as in the following sample:

SECOND PHONOGRAPH: You are wondering what has happened to the Ostrich Hunter and the Manager of the Eiffel Tower. The Hunter is going from one platform to another looking for the ostrich. The Manager is looking for the Hunter and is managing the Eiffel Tower. This is no sinecure. The Eiffel Tower is a world, like Notre Dame. She's the Notre Dame of the Left Bank.

FIRST PHONOGRAPH: She's the Queen of Paris.

SECOND PHONOGRAPH: She *was* the Queen of Paris. Now she's a telegraph operator.

FIRST PHONOGRAPH: One must live, as they say.

SECOND PHONOGRAPH: Don't move. Smile. Look at the lens. Watch the birdie.

(*A Trouville bathing beauty appears. She wears a bathing suit, carries a little fishnet and wears a basket on a shoulder strap. Colored lights. The wedding party gestures delight.*

FIRST PHONOGRAPH: Oh, what a pretty postcard!

Les Mariés de la Tour Eiffel reflects the high spirits and harmony that pervaded the Mutual Admiration Society. Those were happy days for the clan. "When I think of doing such a show today," Cocteau said in 1951, "I realize that it would be impossible. First of all it would be too costly; and there had to be something else — how shall I put it — we all had to live together a great deal, which isn't the way nowadays. People live together less, I think. At certain times in my life we were constantly with each other, talking, discussing the same things, trying out our work before presenting it. Now it is not like that — there is only solitude. And perhaps we used to put more of ourselves into that fun than goes into work that pretends to be serious but really is not. I mean that a poet owes it to himself to be a very serious man, and yet, out of politeness, to appear the opposite. I think that in this way we lent an air of fun to something that was perhaps more than fun."

The production was scheduled for June 18, 1921.

But for all its good humor and fun, the Mutual Admiration Society was unequally endowed artistically. Paul Morand, Valentine Hugo, the Six and others of the clan were all gifted, intelligent, elegant artists, regardless of the fluctuations of fashion — and, in the case of Morand, the political behavior — that have affected their reputations in various ways. But Cocteau, and certainly Raymond Radiguet, went beyond them. They could both contribute, along with the others, to making *Le Coq* one of the brightest little broadsheets ever published; and Cocteau could go further, and by masterminding *Parade*, the *Boeuf* and the *Mariés* cast a beam far into the future of the ballet and other forms of theatre.* With Cocteau and Radiguet, together, however, even that was far from the entire story. For Cocteau, Radiguet was a marvelous accident: as he heard the boy express his precocious opinions, he began to discover in himself capabilities hitherto unrealized. The discoveries were to be immensely fruitful, but they were not without their cost.

More and more frequently Raymond had been failing to take the last train back to Parc St. Maur. After a late party with the clan he might walk the several miles home, across the Bois de Vincennes — like Keats walking back from Hampstead — or he might sleep with the Hugos, or go to other friends, or take a room in a cheap hotel (he was usually without money or with very little). Cocteau often knew where he was, but not always. Now once again he had to answer a distressed and accusing letter from M. Maurice Radiguet, and this time his tone was sharper.

* Cocteau described his vision, in his preface to the printed text of the Mariés (1922): "Before our very eyes a new theatrical genre is being born in France — one that is not ballet properly speaking, and whose proper home is neither the Opéra nor the Opéra Comique nor any of the boulevard theatres. The new genre, on the fringe of all that, is an adumbration of the future. . . . It expresses the modern spirit, and is still a world unmapped, rich in discoveries, a revolution that opens the door wide to explorers. Our young people can experiment with new combinations of *féerie*, the dance, acrobatics, pantomime, drama, satire, orchestra, the spoken word. With limited funds at their disposal they will mount productions of a kind that official artists consider amateur theatricals, but which are nonetheless the plastic expression of poetry."

Cocteau to Monsieur Maurice Radiguet
November 3, 1920

Monsieur,

If I did not sense your genuine sadness I should have the right to be a little angry. You say to me, "I expect Raymond this very morning; tell him so." — whereas I believed him to be at the Parc and expected to see him at six o'clock at the Sirène. The day before yesterday, for the Princesse de Broglie's party, my mother and I dressed him in a dinner jacket and he said that you knew he would not be home.

DO something. Make him stay three days a week at the Parc. I am not his father.

Seeing him looking half-dead, I took him to my doctor, who made him look human again. Knowing that you wanted him to have a job, I got Laffitte to take him on at the Sirène from half-past two to six. Thus he has to come into the city every day, which is deplorable, for he is too weak to force himself to return to the Parc for dinner, and since I often dine out or alone with my mother he hangs about I don't know where. It would be better if he stayed at the Parc and finished his book, which Laffitte keeps asking for, and the articles he plans to write but never does.

Where can he be? He stopped in to see me last night with V. Huidobro, who was taking him home for dinner. He left there at eleven-thirty to take his train. Your note worries me enormously. He was to pose for Lipchitz and lunch there. I beg you not to hold me responsible, and to make Raymond stay at the Parc and work. The fact that he is not at the Parc this morning proves that he lies to me as he does to you. I have never known anyone at once so docile and so stubborn as Raymond. One should never leave him alone. *My life makes this role impossible.*

I cannot go to Lipchitz's, but if I see R. at the Sirène around six I will forcibly put him on a train — be sure of that.

In mid-January, 1921 the Jean Hugos returned to Paris and the clan after spending Christmas and New Year's in rooms above a beach bistro called Hotel Gilly et Jules at Carqueiranne, a Mediterranean fishing village that François Hugo had found near Toulon. "Radiguet has grown," Jean Hugo noted in his first new entry in his diary: the frightening boy had not yet reached full height. A few weeks later, at a Saturday dinner, "Radiguet was drunk." And on February 27, a few days after the reading of the *Mariés* to the Swedes, "Radiguet leaves for Carqueiranne." He left alone — "ran off," says Valentine Hugo, "for the first time, to be away from Jean Cocteau for a while." At Carqueiranne Radiguet began to write at once, and mailed some of his poems to the Hugos. Cocteau did not leave him alone for very long. Less than three weeks later, after working on the *Mariés* with the Hugos, the musicians and Irène Lagut, who was to do the scenery, and after attending the *mi-carême* drag with the Hugos and the Beaumonts, and a costume ball at the house of the dancer Caryathis (later Madame Jouhandeau), to which he came as Mercury, Auric as a chef and Lucien Daudet as the Spectre de la Rose (Daudet's rose petals kept coming off, and Max Jacob kept licking them back in place), he too went to Carqueiranne and lived with Radiguet at "Gilly et Jules." There he worked on his long poem about Nieuport and the Marines, *Secteur 131*, now about to be rechristened *Discours du Grand Sommeil*.

"To me, Radiguet is a marvel," he wrote to Valentine on March 24. "His poems are like peach-down, and they grow for him like violets, like wild strawberries. But the ones you know seem to me insignificant in comparison with the more recent ones." (Cocteau was showing himself a little jealous of Radiguet's attachment to the Hugos.) "His room is a beehive, a real honey factory. An infectious room. My enormous poem encourages Bébé to write longer ones, and his verse is helping my rather bare poem to blossom. We entertain ourselves by depicting Venus in every conceivable posture, and evenings we surprise each other by displaying the latest discoveries concerning her birth and metamorphoses." Radiguet's Carqueiranne poems are generally thought to be his best. Much of his verse has been overrated, but this is regular and classical and mellifluous. Almost all the poems are about Venus and her mother the sea: for him, he said, a "naïve inhabitant of the Ile-de-France," this first visit to the shores of the Mediterranean brought mythology alive "in all its nakedness."

Cocteau wrote of Radiguet to Valentine on the twenty-ninth:

"He has just finished 'The Misadventures of a Chaste Young Man' — 64 stanzas (65, M. Bébé calls out!) — obscene and very pretty. Thanks to me, Bébé has become obsessed with death in his poems, and thanks to him I have taken on an indecency mania. Bizarre exchange!" And in his letters to both Hugos he kept loading them and other friends with commissions concerning the *Mariés,* commissions that some of them thought he might more properly be attending to himself, in Paris. In his frequent assumption that others will assume distasteful tasks, his letters from Carqueiranne remind one of his note to Salmon on the death of Apollinaire. But alone with Radiguet he was in a kind of paradise, oblivious of many things.

While at Carqueiranne Cocteau received a reproachful letter from his mother, wringing from him a retort that developed into an impassioned manifesto.

Cocteau to Madame Cocteau
March 30, 1921

Ma chérie,

My pleasant stay here is quite shot to pieces. Your letter has come — the letter that I now know so well and that would inevitably arrive even were I to go as far as Texas for a little quiet.

When will you stop seeing me through the eyes of the cheap press?

To be specific:

1. The bar [Gaya]. A charming place, easy, where we can all meet without going to cafés like the artists of a generation ago. Lautrec himself tried to have something of the kind. Wiener and his Negro play very well indeed. Stravinsky has lent me his drum, and I play it as often as I can as relaxation — I love the instrument for various reasons, poetry not excluded.

2. The "hyenas" you speak of invent whatever they don't see — so what they say makes no difference.

3. Radiguet was supposed to leave. It was I who prevailed on him to stay. I admire and respect him, and nothing and *nobody* can change my opinion, for my own first rule is not to

commit the injustice that the pious practice every day of their lives. He has received from B. Faÿ, acting for *The Dial,* a thousand francs that makes it possible for him to stay on.

4. As for what you term my having "wasted a winter" — I wrote and prepared the *Mariés*: a mere nothing for you, perhaps, but for me something quite considerable. I brought off the triumph of *Parade*. I published *Escales* with Lhote — a book that I haven't even shown you, knowing that you would dislike it. I was given a commission by Diaghilev. I don't mention my bust by Lipchitz, or the poems I wrote for the volume I am finishing here, in addition to the *Discours* and a number of other activities that would fill *ten* winters for anybody else.

You pray a great deal. But watch out: one thing prayer does is to keep you from analyzing things and seeing them as they really are. Kindness and encouragement from you would help me more than a candle. But I've given up all hope of this, and "my heart is broken," as you would put it. . . .

"Pull yourself together," you say? That's a good one. Don't you realize yet that I spend my life disengaging myself from my instincts, keeping them under observation, sorting them as they emerge, and then taming them for my advantage? Such is the discipline that you never manage to understand, the discipline that is entirely of my own creation, like everything I do. NEVER AGAIN expect me to do anything in a conventional way. ONCE AND FOR ALL.

. . . . If some kind person should say to you, "Isn't your son the leader of a Negro jazz band?" answer: "Yes. We think it's the best job he's ever had, and he is resigned to it. As a matter of fact he's even beginning to like it. . . ."

Even so, any real challenge to his mother was unthinkable to him, and on the same day he is asking Valentine Hugo to intercede and placate Madame Cocteau on her own terms: "Get in touch with Maman and go see her. Only you are clever enough to reassure her about a lot of nonsense she is reproaching me with: the bar, Bébé's presence here, etc. She doesn't see that this child is a guardian angel for my work. She cannot understand that two weeks with him are a cure for a year at home."

At Carqueiranne there were visits from Roger de la Fresnaye, who did a portrait drawing of Radiguet, and from Juan Gris; and Cocteau and Radiguet returned to Paris together in mid-April. On May 4, 1921, at dinner at Jacques Porel's, Radiguet refused to leave when Cocteau wished to, and Cocteau walked out angrily alone. By June 18, at lunch in the restaurant Chez Francis in the Place de l'Alma with Jean Hugo (it was the day of the opening of the *Mariés,* and Radiguet's eighteenth birthday), Cocteau was so nervous that he "flew into a rage and knocked over the table."

That night, the gala preview of the *Mariés* at the Théâtre des Champs-Elysées was the scene of a Dada anti-Cocteau demonstration. The Dadaists were in a particularly belligerent mood because of a frustration they had just suffered in the same building. For the past few weeks a "Salon Dada" had been in progress in the Studio des Champs-Elysées (a small hall on the theatre's top floor). Temporarily rechristened the Galerie Montaigne, it had been filled by Dada artists with an assortment of readymades, sculpture and paintings, including works by Arp, Max Ernst and Man Ray — an exhibition important in the annals of Dada. The night of the seventeenth, the theatre itself was rented to Marinetti and other Italian Futurists for a *"concert bruitiste."* This was invaded by Tzara and other Dadaists, who began a demonstration, whereupon the management, which had already been annoyed by rowdy Dada demonstrations in the gallery upstairs, retaliated by locking the Dadaists out of their own exhibition, where a Dada matinée had been scheduled for the afternoon of the eighteenth. The Dadaists were doubly frustrated: by the lock-out, and by the certain prospect of making themselves ridiculous if, after all their self-proclaimed anarchism, they were to appeal to the law. That evening a number of them, infiltrating the smart invited audience of the Swedish Ballet, "kept standing up and sitting down at various points in the theatre, shouting 'Vive Dada!' with the result that the critics were unable to hear enough of the words or music to be able to write proper reviews." There were cheers, however, both at that and at the following performances; on June 22 Rolf de Maré entertained the collaborators and the company at lunch on the Eiffel Tower with *smörgasbord* and *akvavit;* and of the last performance, on June 25, Jean Hugo could write *"Succès."* All the musicians enjoyed the unanimous failure of the critics to recognize in Honegger's "Funeral March" (which certain critics pronounced the only "real music" in the score) a parody of the waltz from *Faust*.

The effects of the *Mariés* have been considerable. Diaghilev, after seeing it, commissioned from Poulenc an "atmospheric ballet, a kind of modern *Sylphides*": this brought about the birth of Poulenc's celebrated *Les Biches*, with décor by Marie Laurencin. Several ballets by Auric, and one by Milhaud with libretto by Cocteau and décor by Picasso, *Le Train Bleu*, were also to be produced by Diaghilev. It was a partial merger of the Ballets Russes with some of the Six and with the Mutual Admiration Society, which for a time enabled the aging impresario to prolong the youth of his enterprise. The playwrights of today's Theatre of the Absurd do not pretend to be unaware of the *Mariés*; and Jean Anouilh has written that his chance reading of it, when he was eighteen, caused "a mass of ice, transparent and impassable," that had been blocking his path, to "melt away," and determined his vocation in the poetic theatre. Cocteau himself said in his preface to the printed text that in the *Mariés* he had "perfected the formula" that he had experimented with in *Parade* and the *Boeuf*.

That summer of 1921, the Bar Gaya closed for the season on June 27, and the various members of the clan left for the country. "I like your prose as much as your poetry," Cocteau had written Radiguet from Aix in 1919; and from Grasse the same year, *"Mon Dieu,* what a good book you're going to write in prose." Those remarks were called forth by a number of the boy's early essays and stories (later published with others in his second printed volume, *Devoirs de Vacances*). He had been working on a novel, and now this summer Cocteau encouraged him to concentrate on it. They went first, with Auric and the Pierre Bertins, to Auvergne, found the Auvergnats "dirty, lying, lazy, harsh, thin-skinned, sarcastic, and smelling of sour milk," and moved on to Le Piquey. In Auvergne, Radiguet had "behaved badly" — in letters to Valentine, Cocteau is not specific, saying only "If Radiguet seems to continue to act badly, it is because he is awkward and is his age, for all his maturity" — but at Le Piquey he began to work. "Radiguet has already written 120 pages of a novel which in my opinion can be compared only to the *Confessions* or *La Princesse de Clèves*," Cocteau reported on August 29.

"Radiguet would arrive in the country saturated with alcohol, and immediately, without effort, would switch to water and milk: to that alternating diet we owe his books," Cocteau wrote later. And: "Raymond Radiguet was sure that he had the ability to produce wonders, and at the same time he remained a lazy, moody schoolboy. At Piqueÿ, on the bay of Arcachon, I had to lock him up to make him work; he would escape through the window, and if he had promised to write would quickly scribble anything, it didn't matter what, in an illegible hand. Then he would become the Chinese sage again, roll himself cigarettes, bend over his classroom notebooks until his face almost touched them, and look like a grind, a serious, conscientious author. Out of these contradictions, and out of the long intervals during which he lived a life of frightful disorder, came a masterpiece of French literature, *Le Diable au Corps*."

Cocteau, that summer, wrote poems and put together another collection of notes on art. Used as a lecture or parts of a lecture that he was invited to deliver in Geneva and Lausanne on December 8 and 9, 1921, they were dedicated to the university students of those two cities when they were published the next year under the title *Le Secret Professionnel.* So outstanding that they were praised even by Gide (who later, in his *Journal,* characteristically retracted his praise), they are devoted more to literature than to music or painting. Anti-Flaubert (that is, against what Cocteau considered the elaborate), pro-Stendhal, pro-Balzac, pro-Proust as a chronicler like Saint-Simon, written "in solitude," they breathe the closeness of the eighteen-year-old beside him on the beach, writing, "like a piece of homework," *Le Diable au Corps,* an extraordinarily strong, precocious *roman démeublé* — a "love" story stripped to the bone. Speaking later of the few poems he wrote this same summer, Radiguet said that it was Ronsard, Chénier, Malherbe, Lafontaine and Tristan Lhermite who had "told him what poetry was," and his novel is similarly classic in inspiration. It is the story of a child in an adult adventure, of an affair between a sixteen-year-old boy and the wife of a soldier fighting at the front (she dies after bearing the child's child), written with some of the eighteenth-century iciness of Choderlos de Laclos' *Les Liaisons Dangereuses*, which Radiguet had in mind as he worked.* To read it is to understand Cocteau's saying of Radiguet: "He was hard: it took a diamond to scratch his heart." Just as Cocteau's volume of notes written at Le Piqueÿ betrays the presence of Radiguet, so *Le Diable au Corps* is colored by the presence of Cocteau. Its style is often aphoristic, in Cocteau's manner; Cocteau said Radiguet wrote the way Beau Brummel dressed — "no tics, no patina, but a special gift: that of making the new look as though it had been seen before." (Radiguet had said to Cocteau one day — apparently with reference to Diaghilev's old command — "Elegance consists in *not* astounding.") Furthermore, Radiguet called his novel (written in the first person) "a false autobiography." In writing it he was recording, despite all its departures from factual autobiography, his own childish cruelty to a woman that had "almost frightened" André Salmon and his friends a few years before — a recital to which Cocteau could give encouragement that was not merely literary in its enthusiasm.

Le Diable au Corps was almost finished when Cocteau and Radiguet returned to Paris in the fall of 1921, and some time that winter the publisher Bernard Grasset accepted it on hearing Cocteau read its opening pages. (Grasset has described Radiguet sitting silently in his office during the reading, like "a big boy just introduced to his headmaster.") He gave Radiguet a contract and a drawing account of 1500 francs a month; the boy now lived no longer with his family but in the Hotel de Surène, and began again to drink heavily. After a brief affair with Beatrice Hastings, a bizarre Englishwoman who had been the mistress of Modigliani, Radiguet rose in new rebellion against Cocteau. This time it was as though he were defying his efforts to make him finish his book. Once again he ran away.

The episode, fragments of which have been told by various of Cocteau's friends, is most completely recounted by Nina Hamnett, in a paragraph that is probably at least an approximation of the circumstances:

---

* It has lately been pointed out that in a passage omitted from the novel's final text, the narrator asks a girl to let him call her Cécile, and informs the reader: "I was thinking of Cécile Volanges" (the young victim in *Les Liaisons Dangereuses*).

"Cocteau had told me that one evening, some days before the official opening,* he and some friends would be there. . . . We went to the rue Boissy d'Anglas about eleven o'clock. We found there Marie Beerbohm, Picasso, Madame Picasso, Marie Laurencin, Cocteau, Moïse [*sic*], Radiguet and Brancusi. They were drinking champagne and we joined them. . . . The evening was an enormous success and I left for Montparnasse with Brancusi and Radiguet, who had on a dinner jacket. Brancusi lived near Montparnasse and said that he would see me home. We arrived at the Dôme at five minutes to two, just in time to buy some cigarettes. Brancusi had an inspiration. He said to Radiguet and me, 'Let us go to Marseilles now.' I, being very stupid, said that I must go home. I did not really think that he meant it. . . . Brancusi and Radiguet, the latter still in his dinner jacket, took a train for Marseilles a few hours later, without baggage, just as they were. On the way to Marseilles they decided that, being once started, they might as well go on to Corsica. When they arrived at Marseilles Radiguet bought some clothes from a sailors' shop and they took the boat for Corsica. They remained there for two weeks. . . . Some nights after was the official opening of the Boeuf sur le Toit. . . . We dined at a restaurant near the Madeleine and went there about eleven-thirty. Cocteau, whom I had last seen at the unofficial opening, showed me a telegram which was from Corsica and from Brancusi and Radiguet. It said that they were having a splendid time and would return to Paris perhaps soon and perhaps not. Cocteau was much disturbed at the complete disappearance of Radiguet. We talked about it for a short time and came to the conclusion that he would be quite safe in Brancusi's care. They returned a few days later, having had a wonderful time with the peasants and the Corsican brandy."

Valentine and Jean Hugo tell of Cocteau's being nervous and upset concerning Radiguet's absence when he lunched alone with them on January 12, 1922. After lunch Ezra Pound arrived. Pound "read and sang his opera on François Villon to the three of us," Jean Hugo recalls. "He wanted me to do the decorations. Cocteau giggled all the time, as anything to do with the Middle Ages and

* Of the new night club in the rue Boissy d'Anglas, successor to the Gaya, called "Le Boeuf sur le Toit." The official opening was January 10, 1922. (See p. 281.)

Gregorian music seemed then quite ridiculous to him. Pound must have noticed he was being made fun of, and the décor was not mentioned again." Nor was Radiguet's flight to Corsica ever mentioned by Cocteau, or by any of Cocteau's friends to Cocteau. When the boy returned there was a brief coldness between him and his "adoptive father." When forgiveness came, it had been made in some ways easier, in some harder, by the fact that, as Cocteau and Nina Hamnett had agreed, Radiguet had indeed been "quite safe" in Brancusi's care: Brancusi's tastes were not such as to have put the boy in danger in that respect, though perhaps encouraging him to other types of infidelity. In all of Cocteau's many writings about artists, there is no word about Brancusi.

On January 31, at the Hugos', Cocteau read *Le Diable au Corps* to Picasso and Olga, Misia and Sert, the Beaumonts, Pierre de Lacretelle, the hosts, and Radiguet. Edith de Beaumont fell asleep; but the others, familiar though they were with Radiguet's precocity, were amazed by his accomplishment. Still, the book was not finished. Jean Hugo records in his diary for March 31, 1922: "To Fontainebleau with Auric to see Radiguet, who reads us the end of *Le Diable au Corps* (rewritten?) at the Hotel du Cadran. Back in Paris, visit Cocteau." But Cocteau gives a more complete account: "I had given Radiguet's manuscript to the Sirène. Suddenly I met Grasset. Grasset was looking for a new best-seller after publishing *Maria Chapdelaine*. . . . I showed him the manuscript and he was mad about it. Radiguet became his star dancer." (It is as though Cocteau were evoking Nijinsky.) ". . . Grasset gave a good deal of money to buy the rights, but Radiguet did not give the money to the Sirène. He bought himself a magnificent camel's-hair overcoat, a magnificent pigskin suitcase, and went off with a group of Americans to Fontainebleau, to write — supposedly — the end of his book. I was very sick — I had sciatica. I was in bed, and he brought back what resembled a piece of homework put together in a hurry by a bad pupil. I told him so. He had one of his cold rages and threw the pages into the fire, and the next day told me I was right. As soon as I was well I took him to Chantilly, where I locked him in a hotel room and he wrote the great conclusion to his book."

The novel was scheduled for publication only the March following (1923): Grasset was publicity minded, and wanted time for a campaign.

Meanwhile, parts of Cocteau's second long war poem, *Discours du Grand Sommeil*, appeared in the November issue of *Ecrits Nouveaux*, and it was now that the publication of *The Cape of Good Hope* in *The Little Review* in New York made his name known to a few Americans. In Paris he became acquainted with several American expatriates or visitors, among them Man Ray, whose photographs were exhibited in Philippe Soupault's bookshop in December, and Man Ray's assistant, Berenice Abbott. "Americans come to see me and I speak with them in sign-and-grimace language," he wrote to Valentine December 1, 1921. Both photographers made portraits of him, and in a prose poem, *Les Photographies de Bérénice*, he crowned Miss Abbott queen of the camera by invoking her famous homonym, the royal Bérénice of Racine.

But the most important American for Cocteau at this time was a young critic who wrote for *Vanity Fair* over the signature "Edmund Wilson, Jr." Wilson had recognized the *Mariés*, when he saw it at the Théâtre des Champs-Elysées, as a masterpiece of nonsense which nevertheless showed "a genuine gift for rendering certain aspects of life." He called on Cocteau. "I was struck — though I did not agree with him — by his saying that Flaubert was always getting ready to shoot but did not hit the target whereas Stendhal aimed and hit the mark again and again," Wilson has written of their conversation. "I later found this idea developed at the beginning of *Le Secret Professionnel*." Later Wilson wrote to Cocteau for photographs of his ballets, about which he was planning an article for *Vanity Fair*, and referred in his letter to some of Cocteau's aesthetic pronouncements.

Cocteau to Edmund Wilson, Jr.

10 rue d'Anjou
November 16, 1921

Dear Wilson,

You are mistaken. It is because of Stendhal, Balzac, etc. that I like neither A. France nor Flaubert. I am even considered here the only modern detractor of the skyscraper and the poster. The skyscraper is fine in its place, if it is useful — stupid if it is transported to the Place Vendôme. Similarly, posters are legitimate only under a certain kind of sun — a kind that does not shine here.

I have been able to assemble my articles and photographs and will send them all to you in a day or two. I will include my *Carte Blanche* articles, which will tell you (although *grosso modo*) what I think of "Americanism" in art.

Edmund Wilson quoted a phrase or two from that letter of Cocteau's, and other phrases from their conversations, in an entertaining article printed in *Vanity Fair* for February, 1922, "The Aesthetic Upheaval in France: The Influence of Jazz in Paris and Americanization of French Literature and Art," * which brought to many Americans their first news of French Dada, the artistic cult of the machine, etc. Despite Wilson's enthusiasm for the *Mariés*, however, it was not very popular when the Swedish Ballet performed it in Philadelphia and New York in 1923. "It never seemed as amusing here as in Paris," Wilson says, "— partly due, I think, to not having Cocteau's voice on the megaphone and the unfamiliarity of the audience with the bourgeois custom of having weddings on the Eiffel Tower. Don Stewart was allowed to do a clowning opening monologue that didn't improve the situation. [Cocteau] did not send me any more of his books after the failure of *Les Mariés* in New York." And Donald Ogden Stewart has "a painful recollection of coming out in front of the curtain in Philadelphia and laying a terrible egg in an attempt to make them 'love' the Swedes."

Several articles by and about Cocteau appeared in *Vanity Fair* during the early twenties. In the August, 1922 issue, in an article entitled "On the Swings and Roundabouts: The Intellectual Somersaults of the Parisian vs. the Londoner's Effort to Keep His Stuffed Figures Standing," Ezra Pound spoke of Cocteau's tapping with drumsticks on the piano at the Gaya; the article is illustrated by a drawing of Auric, captioned ". . . by Jean Cocteau, the poet and critic, who in his spare moments operates a cabaret and makes line drawings." Cocteau commented on this in a letter to Wilson written

* See Appendix X for excerpts.

August 7, 1922: "Auric is with me at Le Lavandou. . . . The last *V.F.* made us laugh, but do please ask Mr. Crowninshield to correct one of E. Pound's dangerous jokes. I have never managed the slightest bar. I went there the way Verlaine or Moréas went to their cafés — nothing more. If I sometimes played jazz there, it was for fun. . . . Tell Crowninshield that all the young men who see his magazine find it very alive — there is nothing like it in the world."

At this time the *canard* that Cocteau was the owner or manager of a bar was being circulated more assiduously than ever by the Dadaists and other foes. What had happened was that with Milhaud's and Cocteau's permission, Louis Moysès had given the name "Le Boeuf sur le Toit" to a new bar, larger successor to the Gaya, that he inaugurated the night of January 10, 1922, in the rue Boissy d'Anglas. The clan had attended the opening en masse — it was apparently directly from that party that Radiguet and Brancusi had set out for Corsica. The Gaya had been a success: the Boeuf was a sensation. Almost overnight it became an essential feature of the Pariscape, its legend snowballing to rival that of Maxim's or the Moulin Rouge, but with an up-to-the-minute aura. The Boeuf sur le Toit is part of the mythology of the period; it set the tone for one movement of the as yet unwritten musical suite that might have "The Twenties" as its title. "The Boeuf became not a bar at all, but a kind of club, the meeting place of all the best people in Paris, from all spheres of life," Cocteau said later, "— the prettiest women, poets, musicians, businessmen, publishers — everybody met everybody at the Boeuf." It gave its name to at least two books about the period, Maurice Sachs's *Au Temps du Boeuf sur le Toit* and Jacques Chastenet's *Quand le Boeuf Montait sur le Toit*, and it remained a magnet for years, in various locations, until it sank to a lower level of distinction in its present quarters in the rue du Colisée. (The present *patronne* is one of Louis Moysès' sisters.) Almost any history of the Twenties in France contains a passage on the Boeuf, the very cradle of café society.

Cocteau, the Boeuf's presiding genius, tells of being sick with grippe and jaundice in the nearby Hotel de Surène during one of the first months of the bar's success, and of being kept abreast of activities: "People, Joseph Kessel especially, would go and come between the bar and my room and tell me everything that was happening." From accounts of the Boeuf in countless books and conversations, one knows some of the details witnessed by Kessel and others then and later — Mary Reynolds drinking "desperately" beside Man Ray when Marcel Duchamp married, the Prince of Wales flanked by Princesse Violette Murat and Artur Rubinstein, Clément Doucet reading a detective story propped up on the music-rack as he played his flawless jazz. It all took place under the gaze of Picabia's painting of an enormous eye, *L'Oeil Cacodylate* (now in the Musée National d'Art Moderne).

Meanwhile, especially after the flight to Corsica, friends observed Cocteau and Radiguet. "We never tired of watching them," says Jacques Porel. "There was a touch of diabolical curiosity in this; we wanted to see how far Radiguet would carry his taste for liberty, how he would succeed in freeing himself from the tutelage of his mentor. We observed Radiguet-and-women, Radiguet-and-alcohol. A little more and we would have encouraged him. It was a dangerous game."

They both looked sick and dissipated when they left Paris for the Mediterranean in May, 1922.

The Best Time (1922)

But there are literary miracles as well as other kinds: the summer and fall of 1922 saw a phenomenal flowering. In Le Lavandou and the nearby village of Pramousquier, Radiguet wrote most of his second novel, *Le Bal du Comte d'Orgel*, and Cocteau produced *Plain-Chant* (a series that includes some of his finest poetry), *Antigone* (an adaptation from Sophocles), and two excellent short novels, *Le Grand Ecart* and *Thomas l'Imposteur*. All three of the books Cocteau wrote during those months would be published the next year, and *Antigone* would open in Paris early in the winter, on December 20, with music by Honegger, décor by Picasso, and costumes by Chanel. The novel by Radiguet would be published only posthumously.

Radiguet seems to have started work first.

Raymond Radiguet to Madame Cocteau
Le Lavandou
Sunday, May 28, [1922]

Madame,

I should have taken the liberty of writing to you before this, but my novel was using up all the ink in my inkwell. Jean helped me admirably as always, with this rather difficult work. Now I hope that my book will not displease you too much. I am happy to see Jean well again, after being such a worry to you and his friends. . . . From this distance I can no longer "realize" Paris at all, or how, when I was there, I could give myself over to so many foolish, even disastrous, things in a single day. . . . I don't know how to express my gratitude for your kindness this past winter, when I felt rather at loose ends away from my family. . . .

Cocteau has said that for *Le Bal du Comte d'Orgel* "Radiguet set up his easel in front of *La Princesse de Clèves*," that erotic, chaste chronicle of passion agonizingly suppressed which Madame de La Fayette (who had also lived in St. Maur), writing in the seventeenth century, set in an earlier French court; and he has said that the style of Radiguet's book recalls Madame de La Fayette's "regal elegance." That seems true enough, but the changes that Radiguet rang on the old story transform it into something that is his own, and of the Twenties. Radiguet had been watching Edith de Beaumont, the admirable, reserved, loving wife of an aristocrat in whose character frivolity played a great role, contrasting with her own cultivation and seriousness; he put aspects of her, as the Comtesse d'Orgel, in the place of Madame de La Fayette's infatuated but resistant princess, and he put himself, elevated in the social scale, as François de Séryeuse, in the place of the princess's suitor the Duc de Nemours. But whereas the Princesse de Clèves dies in a convent, after the heartbroken death of her loving husband to whom she has confessed her love for the duke, in Radiguet's book the Comtesse d'Orgel remains very much alive, and as the story closes is being directed by her ceremonially worldly husband, to whom she has confessed her love for François de Séryeuse, to invite him to the ball that the Orgels will soon give in their house.*

_____
* It has been well put that the Comte d'Orgel, "a purely social figure, with a passion

Radiguet had already attended one costume ball at the Beaumonts', on February 27, 1922, the "Bal des Jeux," to which he came with clay pipes and a cardboard target stuck on his evening dress, representing a shooting gallery in a fair. (With him were Valentine Hugo as a merry-go-round, Jean Hugo as a game of billiards, and Jean Godebski — Misia's nephew — as a house of cards.) The intrigue of the novel takes place in a landscape very much like that of the clan. There is an opening scene at the Cirque Médrano, and another that recalls a social event recorded by Jean Hugo in his diary for May 15, 1920, following the opening night of the Stravinsky-Pergolesi ballet *Pulcinella* at the Opéra, with décor by Picasso: "Russian ballet at the Opéra. *Contes Russes*, premiere of *Pulcinella, Soleil de nuit*. Afterwards, in a string of automobiles to Robinson, chez René (formerly of the rue Dumours). Supper given by Prince Firouz. Misia, Picasso and Olga, Stravinsky, Auric, Cocteau, Lucien Daudet . . . Sert, Poulenc, Radiguet. Stravinsky, drunk, throws mattresses from the bedrooms down into the dining room from an interior balcony." And Jean Hugo added later: "Evening described by Radiguet in *Le Bal du Comte d'Orgel*."

Among Radiguet's literary remarks, as reported by Cocteau, is one that Cocteau says contained the essential determinant of a great change in the direction of both of them: "We must write poems and novels like everybody else." Radiguet admired the great romantic poets "because they could sit down at a table and write a love poem," he told Jean Hugo, and doubtless he wished he could do the same; but in the remark to Cocteau the emphasis was on novels, for Radiguet declared that he was bent on making his name well known, and to the fulfillment of such an ambition it was novels that he felt best lent themselves. Also, for Cocteau and Radiguet to write novels "like everybody else" — "classical" novels — would be to write novels like *nobody* else — nobody else, that is, in the avant-garde, the only literary world regarded seriously by both of them, even though Radiguet, and Cocteau partly through his influence, disliked the forms in which the avant-gardists were at present expressing themselves. In those years no Dadaist except Philippe Soupault was

for fancy-dress parties, averts disaster by a sort of transcendent frivolity. *Le Diable au Corps* is a tragedy of emotion indulged; *Le Bal* is a comedy of emotion denied." (Francis Wyndham, in *The Sunday Times* [London], January 29, 1967.)

condescending to write anything recognizable as a novel: it was only later, when the group had split up, that they put themselves forward as Surrealist "novelists" — Aragon with his charming but static *Le Paysan de Paris* in 1926, and, in 1928, Breton with his "masterpiece," *Nadja,* which is perhaps a novel but certainly (in the words of Marie Bonaparte) "narcissistic overestimation of the self." For Cocteau and Radiguet, with their modern vision, to write novels in classical style in the early Twenties was to be newer than the new, as well as to produce works of literature that might be more valuable in themselves than the Dadaist effusions, however influential the latter. As Cocteau phrased it: "Radiguet arrived on the scene in the heyday of Cubism and Dadaism. . . . He taught us that it was wrong to drift with the current, and that only a seemingly conformist attitude could discomfit the aesthetes and prove truly anarchistic."

Thus while Radiguet was writing out, with "regal elegance," his fantasies of entering the life of the exquisite Madame de Beaumont, Cocteau, in a style that was equally classic but livelier and studded with his characteristic aphorisms, turned to portions of his own past and spun two chronicles: one, *Le Grand Ecart,** of his adolescence, when he was a disorganized student in the tutorial establishment of M. Dietz and "madly in love with Madeleine Carlier"; the other, *Thomas l'Imposteur,* of life among the Marines in the Flanders dunes, as seen through the eyes of a charming young social nobody, endowed with a fantasy that drives him to pass as a general's nephew, as Cocteau was to claim that he himself had passed as a false Marine.

Cocteau's two books had different fates when they were published. *Le Grand Ecart,* a serious though seldom solemn portrait of a sensitive, very Parisian adolescent (the opening pages are a beguiling revelation of how Cocteau, at thirty-two, liked to look back on himself at seventeen), attracted a large public, thanks in part no doubt to its ballet of students tumbling in and out of bed with each other's girl friends (they still called them mistresses), whom they sometimes found in bed with each other. The hero's emergent pederasty is suggested with skillful lightness, but apparently Cocteau was

---

* *Le Grand Ecart* is a catchy title in French, being a dance term meaning "the split" or "the splits." However, "*écart*" in itself means "separation," or "distance between," and Cocteau explained that he referred to the distance that exists between a woman of experience and a naïf young man.

not aware of how often the pederastic note is unintentionally sounded throughout the book. "Gide was incapable of admitting that I wasn't a blind follower of his religion," he once wrote; "he saw in Madeleine Carlier a man in woman's guise, like Proust's Albertine" — whereas Cocteau insists that for the character of Germaine he drew on a "realistic source," Madeleine Carlier herself, who had really been his mistress. But it is rather in countless smaller touches that the author's predominant sexual inclinations color this delightful novel. About *Le Grand Ecart* Cocteau wrote to his mother:

Cocteau to Madame Cocteau

Le Lavandou, July 19, 1922

Ma chérie,

My silence is due not to my cold . . . but to the novel that I am working on with full steam. Little matter whether it be liked or disliked — it gives me pleasure, whereas poetry is suffering and criticism a mere game. For the first time I am enjoying myself while writing — and I think that that's the essential. I am trying to do something at once funny and sad. You know that I've always been possessed by those two demons, laughter and melancholy. The hero is not me, but resembles me in certain respects. A rich, pure nature involved in the low life of a city and moving at its brink like a sleepwalker along the edge of a roof. A sensibility with vague desires is rebuffed at a certain point and reacts as though it were a question of eternal love. In brief, a *"Confession d'un enfant du siècle"* in very simple and lively form. I have written a complete draft. Now I must "retouch" every page, go over it until it is a "likeness," as I do with my portraits or caricatures. I, who swore never to write again! It is as though a runner swore never to sweat again. A mind runs and sweats — that's what a book is.

Je t'aime.

Jean

Concerning *Thomas l'Imposteur*, Cocteau wrote to his mother from Pramousquier on October 24, 1922 that "I call it a novelette even though it is longer than my novel. . . . It is the war seen as Waterloo was seen by Fabrice — the reverse of the coin, or the view from backstage. If I have succeeded, it is an enormous step in my work. If I have failed, it's a *mousse au chocolat*. Radiguet, a severe judge, thinks I have brought it off. Don't tell anyone that I'm working — people don't like to hear that. . . . If you wonder why I have taken so long to write "accessible" books, I will explain. At first I was not complicated enough. I had to *tighten* up before having the right to *loosen* up. One day the logic of my development will be understood."

Thomas, which is perhaps even fresher in its survival than *Le Grand Ecart,* had fewer readers, probably because it was still rather early for a novel set in the war zone, and because of the greater delicacy of the theme. The germ of the book is contained in an item in one of the issues of the wartime *Le Mot.** Cocteau — taking as his model, as he told his mother, *La Chartreuse de Parme* (for its love intrigue and the scenes of Fabrice on the field of Waterloo) — puts his hero into the two sectors of the war that he himself had known best, Champagne and Flanders, and he portrays imposture as a kind of poetry, requiring noteworthy feats of imagination. Even when Thomas is shot by an enemy patrol in no-man's-land, he pretends. " 'A bullet!' he told himself. 'I'm done for if I don't pretend to be dead.' But in him, fiction and reality were one. Guillaume Thomas *was* dead." Cocteau was particularly attached to *Thomas l'Imposteur* as an admirable illustration of the theme of the poet and his "lies." Gallant, outside society, dying in pursuit of his dream, his hero seemed to him the very essence of a poet; and Cocteau emphasized his affection for the book by giving part of Jean LeRoy's name — Roy — to one of its characters, a young Marine killed as he was about to go on leave. "Our characters are so little our property that I remember experiencing what Alexandre Dumas felt after the death of Porthos, and announcing the death of Thomas to Radiguet with the same sadness," he once wrote. "The terrible thing is that I would have been incapable of postponing it by a minute: I had to submit to his destiny rather than follow the graph of my story." As was to become usual in works by Cocteau, the homosexual aspect is prominent, and, one senses, in ways not entirely intentional. Ostensibly Thomas seeks death rather than reveal his imposture to the lovely girl enamored of him and to her mother; but in this case Gide was shrewd, if perhaps a little crude, in saying, as Cocteau reports, that he "approved *Thomas l'Impos-*

* See Appendix XI.

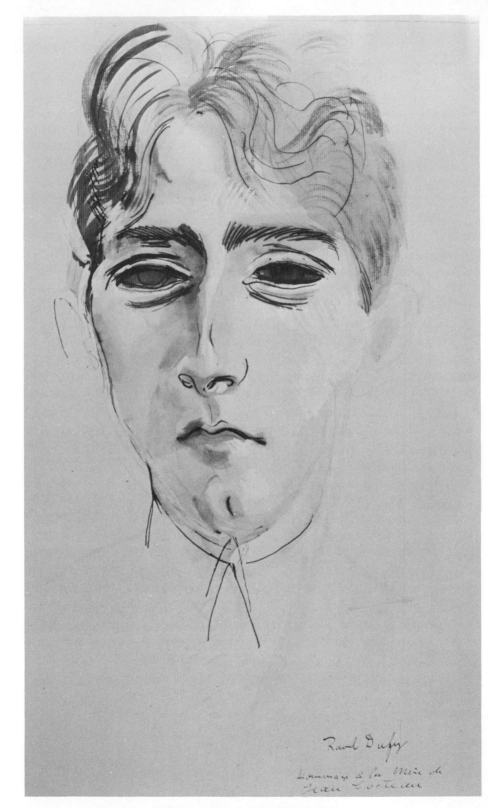

Cocteau. Drawing by Raoul Dufy.

Cocteau and "Les Six." Left to right: Francis Poulenc, Germaine Tailleferre, Louis Durey, Cocteau, Darius Milhaud, Arthur Honegger.

Valentine Gross Hugo.
Drawing by Cocteau.

Cocteau at one of the megaphones in *Les Mariés de la Tour Eiffel*.

Raymond Radiguet at fifteen.
Drawing by Cocteau.

Raymond Radiguet asleep.
Drawing by Cocteau.

teur unreservedly, because he saw in him one of his own mythological heroes."

Cocteau's two other productions of that summer and fall are also considerable works.

"At Pramousquier," he wrote later, "I had a visit from Philippe Legrand, with whom I played on the beach as a child. He had just been in Greece, and had brought back one of those shepherd's crooks that end in a goat's horn curved like Minerva's eyebrow. He gave it to me, and in the course of my long walks around Cap Nègre it gave me the idea of putting new dress on old Greek tragedy, adapting it to the rhythm of our own day. I began with *Antigone.*"

But whether or not a childhood friend brought Cocteau a Greek shepherd's crook during that summer he was spending with Radiguet at Pramousquier, it was not the cane that suggested to him the idea of adapting *Antigone:* he and Honegger had spoken of it as early as the previous February. Cocteau wanted to have something new on the Paris stage, and, in his present classical mood, something different from the *Mariés.* The theme of *Antigone* was attractive — disobedience to the establishment.* Cocteau's adaptation follows Sophocles closely, often speech by speech, the greatest cuts being in the choruses: it was something he could do quickly, and he accomplished the feat of preserving considerable nobility of language in his modernizing. He called his text "a pen drawing after a painting by an old master," and defended himself against detractors who might accuse him of disrespect for Sophocles by quoting Stravinsky's reply when accused of showing disrespect for Pergolesi's music in his score for *Pulcinella:* "You respect; *I* love." "I had seen *Antigone* earlier, at the Comédie Française," he wrote. "It was incredibly boring. The age of the actress playing Antigone

---

* Of course in Cocteau's mind "establishment" meant, at this moment, the dictatorial Breton and his avant-garde. The inevitable was befalling Breton: he was losing control of his cohorts in French Dada and lashing out at most of them as "traitors." Soon he, Aragon and Eluard would style themselves "Surrealists." Breton says, in his *Manifeste du Surréalisme*, that it was to honor Apollinaire, who had coined the term, that he adopted it for his "new" movement. One wonders again whether Cocteau didn't see to it that Breton was reminded of a fact amusing to everyone except Breton — that it was for a ballet by him, Cocteau, Breton's *bête noire*, that Apollinaire had invented the word. One night in June, 1923, after Cocteau's *Antigone* had completed a successful run, living Dada was to experience what might be called its final paroxysm — the spectacle called "Le Coeur à Barbe," at the Théâtre Michel, during which, on the stage, Breton became enraged and broke Pierre de Massot's arm with the blow of a cane, and Paul Eluard, after striking Tzara and René Crevel in the face, was himself manhandled.

made her walk to her tomb all too natural, and consequently anything but touching. Old men — quite obviously chorus-boys in
white beards — sang unintelligible words to music by Saint-Saëns.
That was a true *scandale*." His "contraction" of the play, as he
called it, he described as "an aerial photo of the Acropolis."

The poems that Cocteau wrote that summer and published in the
volume called *Plain-Chant* take a high place in the tradition of
French love poetry: so great is their beauty that they are easily
forgiven their closeness to sixteenth-century verse. It is doubtful
that Radiguet often repeated to Cocteau the *"Je vous adore"* in the
letter written shortly after they had met; in the poems of *Plain-
Chant* there exists nothing of what the French call a *"climat d'a-
mour,"* the mutuality of passion that pervades the poems of a Victor
Hugo for a Juliette Drouet; *Plain-Chant* is inspired not by reci-
procity, but by desire; the most beautiful of the poems speak of
Radiguet as asleep, or imagine him or the writer as being dead.
Throughout Cocteau's life sexual "fulfillment" was expressed in
verse only in minor, occasional, unpublished pieces of "erotica";
the desire poems of *Plain-Chant** are true erotic poetry, of a quality that reciprocal eroticism seems never to have inspired in Cocteau. One feels that even during that extraordinarily intense summer at Pramousquier "fulfillment" could, and may well, have been
provided by others, or otherwise: what was unique was the desire.
The same impression is conveyed by the beautiful series of drawings of the sleeping Radiguet that Cocteau made that summer: the
poetic quality of their very line far surpasses that of the "erotic"
drawings he was to make all his life.

It was either from Pramousquier, or shortly after their return to
Paris, that Cocteau wrote, on November 3, 1922, a letter to the
Abbé Mugnier, commenting in a rather special way on some of the
work of the summer just past. At lunch and dinner parties in Paris
he was constantly seeing this fashionable priest, so tolerant — so
fond — of the black-sheep worldlings who used and abused his
confessional. Cocteau sent him his books — "You know that I
never like to give birth to a book without having it baptized by

---

* Cocteau himself can be heard reading some of them on the disc "Jean Cocteau
Reading in French" (Caedmon TC 1083). Of course Breton and his colleagues disparaged these poems in classical style. "Needless to tell you," Cocteau wrote to Stravinsky on July 24, 1923, "our self-styled 'modernists' are pulling long faces about *Plain-
Chant*. I haven't done with them yet."

you"; the Abbé kept in touch with him, and to his occasional letters Cocteau would reply in a tone that he used when writing to no one else. Three years before, the summer of his early separation from Radiguet, he had written the Abbé from the Pyrenees: "Here I am finishing a book of poems. . . . We must learn the real world by *heart* and remake it above the clouds, on a level that is poetry. To describe, to depict, to deform, is no longer enough for me. Pray for my work, M. l'Abbé." Now the Abbé wrote him about rumors that had reached him concerning the new novels, *Le Grand Ecart* and *Thomas l'Imposteur:* perhaps he had heard of them from Auric, a practicing Catholic, who, along with the Jean Hugos and Pierre de Lacretelle, had been in Pramousquier. Cocteau's reply presents the first of the novels in a guise that some of its readers may find surprising.

Cocteau to Abbé Mugnier
November 3, 1922

. . . . I can see that you are pricking up your ears as a confessor, for you are saying to yourself that if a man like me, who is not of the "Have you read me?" type, opens his heart in a book, it must be because he shuns the confessional. I admit it. I need your forbearance. At least for the first of the books: take care to read it where you won't be seen. But once you have read it you will perhaps give me absolution, and you will agree that there is a world of difference between the thing portrayed and the portrayer . . . In brief, my intention, if any, was to show how a religious soul that lacks faith wastes its substance and suffers from contacts against which nothing shields it, indeed toward which it is irresistibly drawn. There is this sentence in it: "He did not limit his beliefs, he did not make them explicit. To do that would have strengthened his soul in the same way that to limit and make explicit one's tastes in art strengthens one's mind." For the book is actually an indictment of *formless faith* (there: I have put my finger on it!), which is my own sickness, as well as that of many others — especially the spiritually dead. *Readers will find only wickedness in the book. They will be wrong.* I felt I should forewarn you.

The other book, I think, merits no condemnation. In it I speak of the war without the boches, without the poilus, without the heroic aspect. (Of course this is the attitude that is most disapproved.) All this is due to a certain reserve on my part, though the surface appears utterly frivolous. You know that there is method in it. Ouf! I have opened the little grating between us after all!

Radiguet is about to finish a novel so beautiful that I am impatient for his earlier book to be published so that this one can appear. It will bewitch you.

Cocteau and Radiguet were back in Paris some time before the death of Marcel Proust on November 18, 1922.

In a passage in *La Fugitive* (*Albertine disparue*; *The Sweet Cheat Gone*) that was certainly composed after *Parade* and perhaps after the *Boeuf* and the *Mariés*, Proust, writing of his character Octave, of whom Cocteau the show-writer is one of the elements, indicates that at some time he had learned about the adolescent flight to Marseilles: "This young man produced certain sketches for the theatre, with settings and costumes designed by himself, which have effected in the art of today a revolution at least equal to that brought about by the Russian ballet. In fact, the best qualified critics regarded his work as something of capital importance, almost as works of genius, and for that matter I agree with them. . . . At school he had always been a dunce, and had even been expelled from the lycée (to annoy his parents, he had spent two months in the smart brothel in which M. de Charlus had hoped to surprise Morel)."

Relations between Proust and Cocteau had continued to fluctuate, though never violently — a few months before his death Proust had written to Gaston Gallimard of being annoyed by some words of Cocteau about the *N.R.F.* — but Proust's appreciation of Cocteau's genius never lapsed. It was Proust who most brilliantly characterized Cocteau's artistry when he addressed him, in one of his letters, as "You who enjoy representing the highest truths by a dazzling symbol that contains them all." Some time after the founding of the Editions de la Sirène, Cocteau had asked Proust whether he would allow that press to publish some of his work; and Proust, while regretting his inability to do so — he was then busy correcting the proofs and rewriting the final volumes of his great novel — took the occasion to express affection. "Since the last time we met," he wrote, "I have all at once begun to love you much more. You know what my feelings have always been, but there were light clouds, and I had to make an effort to recall the form of the star they veiled. It would be rather hard for me to tell you why our most recent meetings were for me like a practical and conclusive demonstration of what you really are. However, dear Jean, I will not elaborate on this, for nice though it is to say such things it is even nicer not to repeat them too often."

Cocteau's printed recollections of Proust after their earlier meetings are few, however, and are characterized by a curious vagueness — there is a puzzling little anecdote about Proust's offering him an emerald to pay for an overcoat — until the November day in 1922 when he was admitted to Proust's bedroom to see his corpse. In his account of that visit he included a now famous mention of the manuscript of *A la Recherche du Temps Perdu,* which he saw piled up on the mantelpiece beside the dead man: "That pile of paper on his left was still alive, like watches ticking on the wrists of dead soldiers." * There on his deathbed Proust was photographed by Man Ray, to whom Cocteau telephoned at the request, or with the permission, of Dr. Robert Proust.† On the twenty-first, Cocteau, Radiguet and one or two others slipped away from the long funeral procession and stopped off at the Boeuf sur le Toit before taking a taxi to the cemetery. "Radiguet . . . immediately ordered pancakes from Moysès and went off to telephone," says Maurice Martin du Gard in his Parisian chronicle *Les Mémorables.* M. Martin du Gard is not given to retailing irrelevancies, and if he tells of Radiguet making a telephone call while Cocteau sat with others in the Boeuf we can assume that the people present, perhaps noticing some reaction of Cocteau's, attributed significance to the detail. As Jacques Porel said, everyone was watching.

* Later, Cocteau was to express certain reservations about Proust as novelist. "There is no doubt that Proust perceived *real* time — the false perspectives that it affects, and our possibility of imposing new ones upon it. But Proust is too greedy, too obsessed with an eglantine, a hotel table, a particle, a dress, to really launch out on the open sea. Doubtless this is legitimate, since his real purpose is to go beyond realism." And in a letter to Max Jacob he wrote at length about Proust's "hypocrisy" with regard to Albertine and homosexuality.

† Probably with permission, for Man Ray says: "It was impressed upon me that the picture was not to be released to the press — just a print for the family, one for Cocteau, and a third, if I liked, for myself. Later on, the picture appeared in a smart magazine — bearing the name of another photographer. When I remonstrated with the editor, he promised to print a rectification in the next issue. When it appeared, it said simply that I claimed the work as mine." Who sent the photograph to the magazine?

The last year with Radiguet (1923)

Arthur Honegger wrote for *Antigone* what he himself called "a little score for oboe and harp" (later he was to use Cocteau's "rapid and violent text" as the libretto for a full-fledged "musical tragedy"), and the play opened at Charles Dullin's Théâtre de l'Atelier high up in Montmartre on December 20, 1922, along with Pirandello's *La Volupté de l'Honneur* (*Il Piacere dell' Onestà*). Dullin played the role of Creon, and, at least during the first part of the run, Cocteau himself spoke the words of the "chorus" from backstage through an opening in the backdrop. Dullin was famous for his rages, and it was probably after a stormy rehearsal that Radiguet remarked, "Now I understand why they used not to bury actors with other people." "I replied," Cocteau says, "that I liked those strange animals, those race horses, those thoroughbreds who may very well kick you the very moment you're giving them sugar."

The scenery was designed and painted by Picasso — a simple violet-blue backdrop whose undulations became rugosity when lit, and, in the center, painted masks of the men, women and children of the "chorus" clustered around the grilled opening. As Picasso worked, Cocteau says, Doric columns, their marble rendered in sanguine, emerged from his brush "so suddenly, so surprisingly, against the backdrop, that everybody applauded." "To costume my princesses," Cocteau says, "I wanted Mlle. Chanel, because she is our leading dressmaker and I cannot imagine Oedipus's daughters patronizing a 'little' dressmaker." (That remark has always enraged the humorless.) "I chose some heavy Scotch woolens, and Mlle. Chanel's designs were so masterly, so instinctively right, that an article in the *Correspondant* praised them for being historically accurate. Between us, they were admirably inaccurate." "Because he deserved such confidence, Cocteau was one of the rare authors whom Dullin allowed to interrupt his directing whenever he wished," one member of the cast has written. "Cocteau offered excellent suggestions, and if he had wanted to play all the roles himself I think he would have done them very well." Dullin himself wrote that "Cocteau was a charming companion. He set to work in the same spirit as the rest of us, spending his days in a white smock, like a young surgeon, painting the masks. . . . Many society people came to the performances because of Chanel, Picasso and Cocteau. Sophocles was only a pretext, and Pirandello a mere curtain-raiser."

Cocteau liked his Antigone, Genica Atanasiou, a young Greek dancer who spoke little French and whom he taught to enunciate each syllable. "Her name," he said, "means 'daughter of immortals': I chose her not for that, however, but for her quality of nobility, rare in actresses." Maurice Sachs, a young man who at this time adored Cocteau from afar and was soon to enter his life, has written of the excellence of the young woman and of the production in general: "Her Greek accent, which made the French language more sonorous than it really is, drove the author's words deep into our hearts. She wore a white mask, and the immobility of this plaster face made one feel that Sophocles' rebellious royal daughter, majestic, cruel, but just, had left the tomb where she had lain for millennia, to utter amidst the maelstrom of Paris the luminous words of her Greek truth that a French poet had restored to life. Certainly Sophocles did not need Cocteau to make himself understood, but we needed Cocteau in order to discover Sophocles."

Maurice Sachs tells also of the veritable cult of Cocteau among young men that began to grow up about this time: "Young men were so smitten by Cocteau's work and were so under his spell, that they found it quite natural to attend *Antigone* as a claque, in the same spirit in which they would have gone to Mass. . . . One heard tales of some of them scaling the lamp-posts in the rue d'Anjou to see Cocteau leave his house." That is the earliest of many accounts, spanning a generation, of the invasion of Cocteau's dwelling places by crowds of young men from Paris, from the provinces, and from abroad — a kind of voluntary slave market, or rather a perpetual troop of Narcissi, composed of all types, of all degrees of talent and non-talent. Cocteau on occasion picked and chose; however, those whose names became known through association with his had rarely come as such common invaders, but were rather introduced by friends or discovered more or less by chance at the beginnings of promising careers.

Antigone ran for about a hundred nights: among those who praised it was Ezra Pound, in his "Paris Letter" in *The Dial*. Cocteau says the success of his play was due to the good luck of having Pirandello on the same bill, and as he grew older he tended to increase, in interviews, the number of performances: by 1951, on radio, he was saying two hundred. The little Montmartre theatre attracted popular audiences, who were unfamiliar with Sophocles and listened respectfully: only the preview was marred by laughter from the fashionable, who greeted as coctelian quips lines that were straight Sophocles. On the third night, shortly after the curtain rose and Antigone spoke a line about Creon, "He attaches the greatest importance to the execution of his orders," somebody shouted from the balcony, "He's wrong!" "I recognized the voice," Cocteau said later. "It was the voice of one of our fellow fighters [it was Breton's], and I shouted back at him through the opening that we wouldn't proceed with the performance until the interruption ended and the troublemakers were removed. They were escorted out and the play continued. This is the sort of thing that happened in those days: everything was done *en famille*." Raymond Duncan came twice, clad in his usual peplum and each time leading a group of self-styled "traditionalists" in shouting, through miniature bull-horns, protests against the novelties of the production. André Gide attended the single performance that was given, for some reason, on January 15, 1923 at his friend Jacques Copeau's Théâtre du Vieux-Colombier, and wrote of the piece in his *Journal:* "Suffered unbearably from the ultra-modern sauce poured over this admirable play, which remains beautiful despite Cocteau rather than thanks to him. However, we can understand what he was trying to do, and he concocted it with consummate skill; but those who applaud him are those who until now have thought Sophocles a great bore, and who have never drunk *the true, the blushful Hippocrene*. Cocteau's play is not a bit *blushful*." * (Gide was himself to write a "modernized" classical Greek play, *Oedipe*, ten years later.) There was some laughter at the Vieux-Colombier performance, despite the supposedly high cultural level of the audience, and on January 20, after he had been reciting the choruses of *Antigone* for a month, Cocteau wrote to Valentine Hugo, who was vacationing with her husband in the south of France: "Same thoughts, same affection every day, but

* The italicized words of Keats are in English in Gide's text.

a life without paper or ink, without calm, without courage to write details. *Antigone* is going very well, despite the actors, who are 're-becoming themselves,' and the dirty costumes. . . . You will laugh at the following, which is one in the eye for Gide. We gave *Antigone* at the Vieux-Colombier and the audience snickered and laughed. Gide had the cheek to say that the laughter was at my expense, and I answered that it was because the *N.R.F.* had prepared the ground so well. At that point Gide said something sublime. 'Perhaps the audience is at fault,' he said. 'In my play *Saul* I wrote certain lines for laughs and there was no laughter at all.' See how I go on. . . ."

Probably it was too much to expect that critics and sophisticates would not be baffled by an artist who offered *Les Mariés de la Tour Eiffel* one year and *Antigone* the next: by now Cocteau's versatility — the poems in various styles, the farces and the tragedy, to say nothing of the two novels just announced, and the changing pronouncements about art — was making people "dizzy," as the critic Fernand Vanderem complained. W. H. Auden has commented on this aspect of Cocteau:

> Most artists devote themselves to one medium; whether their complete *oeuvre* is a single masterpiece, as in the case of Proust, or a succession of works, as in the case of Dickens, it is comparatively easy to grasp it as a whole. There, in a uniform edition, is a row of books, The Collected Works. There is nothing left out. Both the general reader and the critic have a manageable task.
>
> Now and then, however, an artist appears — Jean Cocteau is, in our time, the most striking example — who works in a number of media and whose productions in any one of them are so varied that it is very difficult to perceive any unity of pattern or development. . . . Both the public and the critics feel aggrieved. . . . His fellow artists who know how difficult it is to succeed in one medium are equally suspicious and jealous of a man who works in several.
>
> His attitude is always professional, that is, his first concern is for the nature of the medium and its hidden possibilities: his drawings are drawings, and not uncolored paintings, his

theatre is theatre, not reading matter in dialogue form, his films are films, not photographed stage effects. . . .

A person who is so open to the outside world, so little concerned with 'self-expression,' is naturally responsive to the present moment and liable, therefore, to incur the charge of wanting, at all costs, to be chic. To this one can only answer that to be 'timely' is not in itself a disgrace: Cocteau has never followed fashion though he has sometimes made it.

The lasting feeling that his work leaves is one of happiness; not, of course, in the sense that it excludes suffering, but because, in it, nothing is rejected, resented or regretted. Happiness is a surer sign of wisdom than we are apt to think, and perhaps Cocteau has more of it to offer than some others whose claims are louder and more solemn.

During the run of *Antigone,* and while Radiguet and Cocteau were proofreading their novels, Radiguet received from the War Department the summons to do his military service that he must have been expecting as his twentieth birthday approached. Cocteau swung into action, consulting his friend Dr. Capmas, the same who had "hoped to save" Apollinaire, as to how to approach politicians who might secure an exemption.

Cocteau to Valentine Hugo
Hotel du Grand Condé
Chantilly
February 6, 1923

Ma chère Valentine,

I'm here for a few days' rest. Listen carefully, for I'm going to ask you something very simple but very important. Jean *must write to A. Thomas* and say that Radiguet should have his physical examination at St. Maur on March 6.* Capmas tells us that a single word from Thomas to the head of the Board will save Radiguet. (Can you imagine the poor fellow in barracks?) Then Capmas will get in touch with the doctor, if he learns his name — but this wouldn't even be necessary, for an

---

* Albert Thomas, the statesman, head of the International Labour Office. He had been Jean Hugo's tutor and a witness at his marriage.

ex-deputy and Président du Conseil from St. Maur retains all
his influence and nobody will refuse him anything.

In writing him, Jean should speak of Radiguet as an intimate friend and say how disastrous it would be to draft someone who is *blind,* a *cardiac case,* etc. — someone who cannot
bear the slightest criticism, will go AWOL, etc. I know I can
count on you as on myself, but Jean doesn't like to write, and
I hope you will keep after him.

To Jean Hugo himself, Cocteau wrote on the fifteenth: "Radiguet
in barracks (sounds like the title of a film) would go AWOL if he
didn't fall sick first," but he was apparently confident that the boy
would soon be free and able to travel with him, for in the same
letter he asks about hotel rooms in Beaulieu-sur-Mer, where the
Hugos were staying. Jean Hugo thought that military service would
be good for Radiguet, and was opposed to Cocteau's idea of getting
him off (he has since thought that army service might have saved
his life). "I'm eager to see you in uniform," he wrote to Radiguet
on a postcard from Beaulieu. But Radiguet was somehow exempted,
and that April of 1923 he and Cocteau went traveling together —
not to Beaulieu, but to England, on an expedition that gave rise to
one of Cocteau's more curious legends about himself.

It was a holiday trip for Cocteau, apparently, after his declaiming through the hole in Picasso's *Antigone* backdrop, and perhaps
an exemption celebration for Radiguet. They crossed the Channel
and visited Reginald Bridgeman. Bridgeman had now left the diplomatic service, was engaged to be married, and was living in Pinner, near Harrow, in a charming house that he had inherited from a
remote great-uncle and to which he would soon be taking his bride.
Cocteau and Radiguet were his first house guests. Cocteau, writing
five years later in an essay on the painter Giorgio di Chirico, in
which there is much talk of dreams, chose to describe the trip to
England as follows:

"I had a mad craving for one of those crook-handled canes such
as our grandfathers carried, on which the crook, at right angles, is
part of the cane itself and not joined artificially. All I could find
were canes with handles that were joined or curved.

"One night I dreamed that I was visiting Harrow, and that in a
little shop with a crocodile in its window I found thirty of those

canes. They were standing in a large vase. An old man asked fifty francs for them. Each of the canes ended in a bell which the old man cut off.

"The next day I told my dream to Radiguet and suggested that we leave for Harrow. We left. We had forgotten to change any money, and arrived in London with empty pockets. At Victoria Station I found myself face to face with Reginald Bridgeman, a friend of mine who lives in the country in England and whom I had not told of our arrival. He carried us off and put us up. I told him about my dream and asked him where Harrow was. 'It's the next station to mine,' he said. 'We'll go there tomorrow. Harrow was my school. But your little shop doesn't exist, and besides tomorrow's Sunday and nothing will be open.'

"In Harrow, we lunched at the King's Head. After lunch we walked up the High Street, in ruins (it was being rebuilt). I see a shop, open, with a crocodile golf bag hanging in the window. I go in, find my thirty canes in the big vase, and pay the old man fifty francs. The bells were metal bands that had come loose and that he tightened by tapping them with a hammer."

Mr. Bridgeman's comment on that account throws into relief some of the elements that Cocteau had injected:

"Jean and Raymond came to stay with me in this house in April 1923. It was bitterly cold and Jean was saddened by the sight of the daffodils whose heads were abashed by the frost. My invitation to them to come may well have been in response to a letter from Jean saying that he wanted to come to England and visit Harrow. I certainly went to Victoria Station to meet them, having got this house ready for their reception, therefore the meeting on the platform was not fortuitous, but in their perplexity at realizing that they had run out of cash I may have appeared as a sort of deus ex machina. Jean probably told me of the dream, but I have only a hazy recollection of this and did not take the matter very seriously. We did have luncheon at the King's Head Inn in Harrow and walked afterwards up the High Street, which was 'up' for repairs. I vaguely remember his finding about three walking sticks standing in a jar in the corner of a nondescript little shop, and the ferrules of which he had dreamed as 'grelots' may have been hammered on to the sticks by the shopkeeper. I have no remembrance of a golf-stick bag in crocodile skin. Three sticks may easily have become thirty. . . . Radiguet would have been inclined to pooh-pooh the reality of dreams, but Jean believed in them and knew how to poetize them."

Today, when to many of us the significance of dreams seems not always a total mystery, that "dream after the event" of Cocteau's impresses us as being one of the earlier indications of the fund of naïveté existing in this most sophisticated — in many ways — of Parisians. "There is a little boy with a cane"; "At Pramousquier, Philippe Legrand, with whom I played on the beach as a child, brought one of those shepherd's crooks that end in a goat's horn"; "I find my thirty canes." "Each of the canes ended in a bell which the old man cut off." It was only a year after writing about the canes that Cocteau would be asking "Will some Freudian kindly tell me the meaning of a dream?" and seeking enlightenment concerning the recurrent, certainly more "genuine" dream about his father. Apparently canes did not suggest to him what they suggest, so tritely, to us, appearing in his writings as they do almost solely in connection with Radiguet, and, in the Harrow dream and narrative, so swollen from their original three.

From England Radiguet wrote charmingly to Valentine. "The day before yesterday we visited Oxford, that paradise without Eves. What an admirable city! Once again I see that the so-called lives of poets are the only truths. How like its poets Oxford is! It is really their property room. Deer, architecture both Gothic and Greek, lawns 'enameled' with Pre-Raphaelite flowers." Cocteau, on the other hand, in a lecture that he delivered at the Collège de France soon after his return to Paris, said: "I was bored by the cloisters and by the meadows with their Burne-Jones flowers. The marvelous thing in Oxford is its shops." Lightly said! But in Oxford Cocteau and Radiguet did patronize the shops: what they bought was several pairs of fancy knitted gloves. They presented a pair to Reginald Bridgeman; and in Paris, one night shortly thereafter, they were seen by Gilbert Seldes touching glove to glove as they separated: the bright striped Oxford gloves, Mr. Seldes says, "seemed to have a life of their own." Like the Harrow canes, the Oxford gloves illustrate more than merely the trip to England. It was about this time that Cocteau began to have his hands constantly photographed. Sometimes they were photographed alone, and they were even cast in bronze; but in almost all photographs of Cocteau from now on they are featured. They appear all the more fetishistic because of his habit of unbuttoning and turning back the cuffs of his jacket or shirt, the better to feature the beautiful hands. The hundred-times-repeated representation of that combination — hands in proximity to opened buttons — strikes us today as another strange bit of naïveté, apt to raise a snicker.

That spring, and for a few months more, Radiguet could buy all the gloves he liked. With the publication of *Le Diable au Corps* his talent was immediately recognized, and although patriots lamented the picture of a schoolboy cuckolding a soldier who was fighting for France, and Radiguet saw the novel treated in various newspaper articles as true autobiography, and himself described as a *"petit voyou"* — a rat — the book caught on at once. Grasset's publicity took forms unusual for those days. "For a week the movie newsreels showed Grasset, sitting nobly at his desk, majestically signing the first check for 100,000 francs ever presented by a French publisher to a twenty-year-old author and immortalized on film. . . . *Le Diable au Corps* was sold on street corners and in railroad stations: Radiguet became famous." Grasset exploited Radiguet as "the youngest of the French novelists," and it was the element of youth in this non-war novel laid in wartime (non-war because the "hero" was too young to fight) that was the great novelty. The most widely quoted sentence of the book was a shocking one on its opening page: "Those who are already resenting what I say must imagine what the war was for so many young boys: a four-year-long vacation."

Radiguet had written in *Le Coq:* "I speak of advertising — to my mind the only literature possible in a daily newspaper. . . . In publicity, more than anywhere else, I see the future of the sublime, so threatened in modern poetry." Cocteau later claimed that Grasset's publicity was really a kind of anti-publicity, dreamed up by Radiguet, who with his flair for the spirit of the age sensed that irritation of the public would bring the best results. "Before Radiguet, publicity was a very discreet affair, with the author pretending to be totally unaware of it. Radiguet was the first author courageous enough to take a long chance by launching a campaign that might have alienated immediate buyers, but thanks to which within two weeks his book was in the hands of readers who formerly might not have known about it for years."

Bernard Faÿ, a young French writer and professor, had during a visit to the United States been entrusted by Mrs. Frederick Keep, a Washington francophile, with seven thousand francs, to be given, as "Le Prix du Nouveau Monde," to a new French book that would "foster Franco-American friendship." Faÿ, who according to Cocteau had previously secured for Radiguet a grant of a thousand francs from the American magazine *The Dial,* formed a committee of seven, and from the moment he included Cocteau among its members the outcome was inevitable. "Jean was all over me with eagerness, niceness and compliments," he has written. "I felt then how easy it was for him to make himself liked; his extreme subtlety and alertness enabled him always to do precisely the right thing when he wanted to please, and — a more delicate matter — when he wanted to display a friend to advantage. . . . When he thought I was ready, he said, straight out: 'The prize must go to Radiguet . . . He deserves it.' I looked around to see whether I could find a book better adapted to the donor's wishes, but I found nothing, and surrendered. Then I saw Jean organize the operation with admirable care, precision and discretion." The only other candidate was Philippe Soupault's *Le Bon Apôtre,* a *roman à clef* describing the infighting among Apollinaire's "heirs." During the counting of the vote on May 15 (at lunch in a restaurant) Faÿ describes Cocteau as being "so nervous that he had difficulty controlling his voice and behavior." Radiguet won, four to three. Jean Hugo recorded in his diary: "Voted for Radiguet: Cocteau, Max Jacob, Jacques de Lacretelle and Bernard Faÿ. Voted for Soupault: Giraudoux, Morand and Valéry Larbaud." Max Jacob sent his vote from the Benedictine abbey of St. Benoît-sur-Loire, where he had begun a retreat that was to continue, with many interruptions, for twenty years, ending with his arrest by the German SS and his death in 1944. In letters to Cocteau, one of them beginning "You know my religious feelings and my fear of hell," he confessed to having seen only portions of the book and to being hesitant about voting for it lest it be "anti-religious and obscene," unworthy of being "supported by a Christian"; he would have preferred to be replaced on the jury, but Cocteau reassured him.

The entire committee of literary men had obviously interested itself little if at all in the abstraction of Franco-American unity (it is not apparent to what extent that could be fostered, at least among patriots or politicians of either country, by a story of adultery on the French home front while doughboys fought in Flanders fields), and although literary politics played its part in the vote — Valéry Larbaud, associated with the *N.R.F.*, would naturally vote against Cocteau's candidate, whereas Soupault's defeat was another slap at the Dadaists, now so soon to become Surrealists — the victory of *Le Diable au Corps* is a rare example, in the weird game of literary prizes, of an award going to what is indubitably a remarkable work of literature by a new writer. Paul Morand has written: "When I voted at the Prix du Nouveau Monde it was not *against* Radiguet, but *for* Soupault, a Surrealist who never had his chance, Radiguet being already well known, with a strong man (Grasset) behind him." Despite his adverse vote Morand dined at the Hugos' that victory night, along with Cocteau, Radiguet and two of Radiguet's brothers. Two weeks later Radiguet wrote a letter of thanks to Max Jacob, who was feeling neglected.

> *Raymond Radiguet to Max Jacob*
> Cayre's Hotel, 4 Bd. Raspail, Paris VII
> May 29, 1923

Mon cher Max,

. . . . How can I tell you of my gratitude? Not so much for your vote as for what I owe you in a literary way. You have been my master, and you still are. Forgive me if for a long time I have given no sign of life, but you know better than anyone the demon of Paris that makes us not forget our friends but act in such a way that they think we do. But silence does not matter in our case. I love you and admire you more than ever. Write me in care of Jean. . . .

On May 3, in the Collège de France lecture in which he spoke of Oxford, Cocteau had praised Radiguet and his novel (Radiguet is said to have been in the audience); and from now on, from Prize Day* until their departure for the summer two months later, Coc-

---

* It was a condition of the Prix du Nouveau Monde that the winner be translated into English and published in the United States. For some reason *Le Diable au Corps* made its transatlantic appearance only in 1932, translated by Kay Boyle, with a preface by Aldous Huxley. But it attracted little attention, and became known to Americans in any considerable numbers only when it arrived in film form in 1950, with Gérard Philipe and Micheline Presle.

teau and Radiguet, now a celebrity in his own right, went from party to party. Radiguet was doing a good deal of drinking — "A bottle of whiskey and a bottle of gin a day," according to Cocteau's probably exaggerated later account — and he had been introduced to opium smoking by a Madame de Warkowska, a lady unknown to the rest of the Cocteau set but sometimes seen, "a white face emerging from a black silk samurai cloak," Jean Hugo says, at the Boeuf sur le Toit, and whose attitude toward opium was expressed in her one recorded remark: *"L'opium? Pourquoi faire tant d'histoires? On a fumé à ma première communion, à Shangaï."* Radiguet kept repeating an injunction he said he had heard from Apollinaire: *"Il faut faire les choses"* — "You have to *do* things." At a dance hall, the Bal Bullier, he had picked up a pair of sisters, Bronya and Tilya Perlmutter, eastern European girls who belonged to the fauna of Montparnasse, and their names, especially Bronya's name, began to appear in Jean Hugo's diary as lively companions of the clan. On May 30 the Beaumonts gave their annual fancy-dress ball, this time the "Bal Louis XIV": there was a *grande entrée,* with the Comtesse de Castries borne in on a chair as "La Malade Imaginaire," after Molière's play; Jean Hugo recalls that Radiguet was one of her followers, "a patient, made up with spots, meaning measles." On June 1, the Swedish Ballet gave the *Mariés* again, with a new quadrille; on June 2 the clan was joined by Clive Bell at the Boeuf and went on to a concert by Jean Wiener; on the thirteenth there was the Russian ballet, with the premiere of Stravinsky's *Les Noces* (Auric played one of the four pianos called for by the score), and a party at the Boeuf afterwards — almost every evening seemed to begin or end (sometimes both) at the Boeuf; on the fourteenth everybody went to the Café Balzac in the rue des Ecoles after a lecture by Satie at the Collège de France on "The School of Arcueil," a group of four young musicians — Henri Cliquet-Pleyel, Roger Désormière, Maxime Jacob and Henri Sauguet — who had so baptized themselves with the name of Satie's suburb. On the seventeenth, at a party for Stravinsky given by an American couple, Sara and Gerald Murphy, in a barge restaurant on the Seine, Cocteau donned the barge captain's uniform and "went about carrying a lantern and putting his head in at portholes to announce *'On coule'* ('We're sinking')." On warm nights the friends would sometimes dine in the restaurant of the Parc

Montsouris: after dinner there on June 30, Jean Hugo records, "Radiguet disappears in the park, falls asleep — we find him at one A.M." The season ended on July 5:

> *July 5.* Milhaud's housewarming, Boulevard de Clichy. Cocteau, Satie . . . Radiguet, Cendrars, Brancusi, Stravinsky, Diaghilev, Misia, Sert, Cypa and Ida Godebski, Jacques and Anne-Marie Porel . . . Marie Laurencin . . . Poulenc, Honegger . . . Morand, Auric, P. Bertin, Marcelle Meyer, Survage. . . . A bird trainer (*oiseleur*) shows his performing birds.

What was to come, the terrible end of the story, is outlined in the following extracts from Jean Hugo's diary for the rest of 1923:

> *July 25. Arcachon.* Cocteau, Radiguet and Auric meet us at the station. A launch takes us to Le Piqueÿ, where we find François de Gouy, Russell Greeley and Bolette Natanson. Hotel Dourthe.
> *August. Piqueÿ.*
> *September 3.* Motorboat excursion to Moulleau. Saw d'Annunzio's villa.
>   *4.* Visit from André Lhote.
>   *13.* Leave Le Piqueÿ. Cocteau and Radiguet come with us as far as Bordeaux. Sightseeing in Bordeaux (cab). Dinner at the "Chapon Fin," spend the night there. Say goodbye to Cocteau and Radiguet.

Then, on December 12:

> *Montpellier.* Telegram from Milhaud announcing Radiguet's death during the night.

We can trace the course of the tragedy. After the Milhaud housewarming, Cocteau and Radiguet had left together for Le Piqueÿ: it was not to be another summer *à deux* — various friends were to join them — but they began it alone. *"Mon cher papa,"* Raymond wrote home early in July, making no mention of Cocteau (although his part in the boy's literary success had probably already begun to soften Monsieur Radiguet toward him), "I have been here since

Monday morning — I set to work immediately and am correcting *Le Bal du Comte d'Orgel,* which I think will be quite a long novel. There are parts that I expect to revise radically — there's a good deal to be done. So far, as you can imagine, I haven't moved about much. But Auric, Bolette Natanson, and then later Gouy d'Arcy, will be coming in a few days. I await Auric like the Messiah — he has a typewriter!" * That same day he wrote to his younger brother, René, asking him to find, in his bedroom in his parents' house, and to send him, "proofs of a book of poems, and the manuscript of those same poems" — for in addition to finishing his novel that summer he was writing a preface to a new, enlarged edition of his volume of verse, *Les Joues en Feu.* He also asked his brother to "sort the papers I left at the house." In the last pages of *Le Diable au Corps* he had already written of presentiments: "A disorderly man who has no idea that he is about to die suddenly puts everything around him in order. His life changes. He sorts his papers. He rises early, goes early to bed. He renounces his vices. His family and friends are overjoyed. No wonder his sudden death seems all the more unfair. 'Just when he was going to enjoy life!' " Cocteau says that during that summer of 1923 Radiguet did the same: "Radiguet was becoming regular, he slept, kept his papers in order, made clean copies. I was stupid enough to rejoice: what I had thought to be an unhealthy absence of order was really the complexity of a delicate mechanism." But Radiguet was also thinking of future work, making notes for a possible fictional biography of the fifteenth-century poet Charles d'Orléans. A diary that he began, in imitation of Jean Hugo — "August 16, 1923. Yesterday I saw Jean Hugo's journal, which he had been keeping every day for four years. It makes me jealous." — he abandoned after his third entry.

That summer Radiguet did not make his usual more or less complete shift from alcohol to "milk and water," but continued to drink chiefly alcohol, encouraged by Russell Greeley, a wealthy

---

* "I enjoyed [Milhaud's] bird party," Cocteau wrote Stravinsky on July 24, "but I was sorry to say goodbye to you. Here Auric turns his back on the sea and typewrites: Radiguet is dictating his novel to him. Auric and Poulenc tell me about your *Octet,* and I'm sick with jealousy. I'd like not to be working, but the trouble is, work likes me, so I must go on. Are you working?" Cocteau says that one day while they were working Auric and Radiguet were assaulted by the pet of a fellow guest: he sent Stravinsky a drawing captioned "This is the gentleman who owns the enormous parrot that bit the typists."

American homosexual, and Greeley's friend Comte François de
Gouy, both of them great drinkers, whom he had been seeing in
Paris and who now came to Le Piqueÿ. Jean Hugo says that Radiguet "picked de Gouy's brains" for *Le Bal du Comte d'Orgel:*
"What Radiguet got out of de Gouy was the idea that the really
good aristocratic families are those who, having made no 'misalli-
ances' and consequently having little or no money, live obscurely
in the provinces. Most of the brilliant 'aristocratic' names of today,
de Gouy told him, including the Beaumonts, whom de Gouy particularly detested, are held by families who came up in the last century." To that "idea" Radiguet gave flesh and blood in his character the Comtesse d'Orgel.

In an article called "After Thirty Years" that she wrote in 1953,
Valentine Hugo describes some death threats aimed at Radiguet
that had come through, the spring of 1923, during a few sessions of
table-tapping in the Hugos' Paris apartment; and she goes on to say
that the summer in Le Piqueÿ had something unhealthy about it
from the beginning, that the atmosphere contained "a lurking malaise, at once physical and moral." She insists that that is not mere
hindsight, and points to photographs of the group as evidence that
throughout the summer no one was quite well. But she says that they
all did a good deal of walking in the pine woods and beside the
marshes, and much delightful sitting in the sun, that *Le Bal du
Comte d'Orgel* was indeed typed on Auric's typewriter, that Auric
composed on a piano he had shipped from Arcachon, and that each
evening they gathered round a table covered with checkered oil
cloth, drawing, talking, reading, listening to him improvise "ravishing, ephemeral operas." Cocteau sent Stravinsky drawings of
Auric with his typewriter and his rented piano: "Auric plays *Les
Noces* every night," he wrote on one of them. It does not sound
ominous. Nor was there any hint of tragedy in a letter in mirror-
writing that Cocteau sent Stravinsky on the eve of the Hugos' departure, or in the farewells at Bordeaux:

Cocteau to Igor Stravinsky

September 1923

Mon cher Igor,

I must tell you that tomorrow I am going with the Hugos as
far as Bordeaux, to eat at the Chapon Fin. I'll be very sick and

will repent too late, like you. Auric told me about your menu at Biarritz and your visit to Madame Errazuriz. I write this mirror-wise because I have no typewriter.

                                                     Jean

P.S. All day long we sing *"Chez ma Nastasie la démarche est légèr-e. Sa pelisse est un drap d'or, Avec un col de castor."*

Cocteau to Valentine and Jean Hugo
[Le Piqueÿ, September 19, 1923]

I vaguely heard you leave, in a kind of half-dream. We had a 150-franc lunch and saw a film, *Les 5 gentlemen maudits* . . . It was very strange to come back to Piqueÿ — for me Bordeaux means the way back to Paris. *Mézugo*, it's too sad here without you — I enclose a piece of the table [cloth]. I'm cold, keep covering myself with the quilt — you took the sun away with you. . . . Radigo is working. . . .

The same to the same
[Le Piqueÿ, October 2, 1923]

Mes chéris,

After a few summer days the sky clouded over but without turning cold. Only the asphodels are in bloom, under the blue sky of your elegant paper — thank you. I'd like never to be apart from you — I'd like us to go on loving and boring each other until we're all gaga. I have finished the essay on Picasso (have done over the end). . . . I leave the 4th.

But — whether or not the others had suffered from the "malaise" described by Valentine — Radiguet and Valentine herself had both, without knowing it, contracted typhoid, probably from eating oysters; there was no diagnosis, and the fever, not yet reaching any height, had been making them mildly unwell.

Both cases of typhoid developed.

Valentine and Jean Hugo were in the Camargue, riding with a Provençal poet friend, Folcò de Baroncelli, Marquis de Javon, helping him drive some of his half-wild herd of black cows and bulls to villages in Languedoc for bull-teasing games. After several weeks, Valentine wrote to Cocteau, who was back in Paris, of feeling increasingly ill.

Cocteau to Valentine Hugo

November 23, 1923

Ma chère Valentine,

Such news you send us! We were thinking of you as escaping our disgusting weather; we understood your depriving us of yourself and Jean; but now we scold you. You must have Camargue fever. Flee the place at once! Come home fast!

Nothing to report. *Thomas* is the same — it's a book that makes friends for me, though the critics are being patronizing about it, etc. My dream would be to be rich enough and well enough never to write again and let others flounder in the mud. . . .

The god of friendship has punished you for never being in the city when we are. Your great loss for 1923 has been Barbette — a terrific act at the Casino de Paris. Barbette is a young American who performs on the trapeze dressed as a woman. Ten unforgettable minutes. A *theatrical* masterpiece. An angel, a flower, a bird. We all found him an absolute knockout. He left this morning at eight on a tour of European cities. I hope that he'll be back and that you will see him. The Gounod family accepts Satie-Poulenc but refuses Auric. It's always the way. Long live Gounod! Long live Auric! Long live refusals! *

Take care of yourself. Rise from your bed and flee Paludes.†
Hurry here — we love you. . . .

Stricken, finally, with a violent pain, Valentine was operated on for peritonitis in a Montpellier hospital on December 10 and at once began to mend.

In his letter to her from Paris, Cocteau had remained silent about Radiguet, who was behaving in a way that caused Cocteau later to write: "The winter in town was excruciating. What good did it do him that I supplicated him, changed my way of life to set him an example? Debts, alcohol, insomnia, heaps of dirty linen, moving

---

* Diaghilev had asked Satie to transform the spoken parts of Gounod's opera *Le Médecin Malgré Lui* into recitatives for voice and orchestra, and had asked Poulenc to do the same for Gounod's *La Colombe*. The permission of Gounod's heirs was sought and granted; what they refused Auric is not clear. The two Gounod operas were to have been given during a festival of French music scheduled by Diaghilev in Monte Carlo the following January.

† *"Paludes,"* Latin "swamps" (the Camargue); but *Paludes* is also the title of an early novel by Gide!

from hotel to hotel . . ." It was finally in the Hotel Foyot, opposite the Luxembourg, right across Paris, far from Cocteau, that Radiguet chose to go to live; and it was not Cocteau whom he allowed, from time to time, to live with him. "He had taken a fiancée," Cocteau says, "a girl who later became Mme. René Clair" — that is, Bronya Perlmutter. Georges Auric remembers Radiguet telling him, as the two of them were walking one night behind Cocteau and Bronya, that he intended to marry the girl — not because he loved her, but because he "refused to become a forty-year-old man called 'Madame Jean Cocteau.' " Everyone who saw Radiguet at this time speaks of his strange behavior. Grasset says of their leave-taking after what proved to be their last meeting that Radiguet "took off his scarf and gave it to me — 'as a keepsake,' he said." About the same time as Valentine Hugo's, Radiguet's typhoid, too, began to flare, but differently from hers. As he continued to revise *Le Bal du Comte d'Orgel* in his hotel room he was shaken by chills; Cocteau's Dr. Capmas diagnosed pneumonia, but someone dissatisfied and worried appealed to Mademoiselle Chanel, and she sent her doctor. Only then was Raymond's typhoid recognized — too late for him to be saved, weakened as he was by his excesses. He was taken to a hospital, where he died in the early morning of December 12, 1923.

Radiguet's mother had been sitting with him — she herself caught typhoid, in a mild form — but she was not with him the last night. The boy died alone. When Monsieur Maurice Radiguet arrived the morning of December 12 he was told by a nurse: "Your son is no longer in his room"; she led him to the chapel, and there he saw Raymond's dead body. A friend of the Hugos told them that from the expression on the boy's lifeless face she imagined that he had regained consciousness during the night, found himself alone, and been appalled by the realization that it was the end: "I have never seen a face so terrible, expressing such despair and frustration, as Raymond's the day he was 'laid out' in the hospital in the rue Piccini."

Cocteau, in the preface he was soon to write for *Le Bal du Comte d'Orgel,* speaks of a day shortly before the end: "These were his last words. 'Listen,' he said to me on December 9, 'listen to something terrible. In three days I am to be executed by God's firing squad.' As I held back my tears and made up some hopeful story, he went on, 'Your information is less good than mine. The order was given. I heard the order.' Later, he said: 'There is a color walking around, with people hidden in it.' I asked if I should send them away. He answered, 'You can't, because you don't see the color.' Then he sank. His lips moved, he spoke our names, looked with surprise at his mother, at his father, at his own hands." "He died without knowing it," Cocteau said. It is what we all want to believe, and do our best to believe, when we are directed by affection.

Cocteau did not spend Radiguet's last night with him, nor could he bear to see Radiguet dead, or to attend his funeral. "I did not want to see him on his deathbed. All the dead look alike, and they do not look like themselves. They are recumbent waxen figures, their faces hermetically closed. One longs to say to them: 'What have I done to you?' It is like a definitive break. I did not want to see Raymond Radiguet on his deathbed. I stayed at home. Besides — I was paralyzed — in shock." Cocteau took to his bed. His cousin Marianne Lecomte Singer, closer to him than his brother and sister, was called in by Madame Cocteau to soothe him, and found him "in a terrible state." Both women had deplored Radiguet's unsettling, exciting presence in Cocteau's life, although Madame Cocteau had always behaved impeccably. For Madame Singer, Radiguet was "bad. And bad for Jean. Talked to him insultingly. An *arriviste*. He used Jean. Not a friend." "What a bit of luck for Jean," was her feeling when she learned of the boy's death. Bourgeoise and affectionate, perhaps jealous, she saw it as the end of a thralldom.

Radiguet was not yet twenty-one: for all his precocity, his coffin was white — the coffin of a child. Nina Hamnett has described the funeral, at the church of St. Honoré d'Eylau:

It was foggy and raining. The church was filled with white flowers and near the altar was the raised platform, waiting for the coffin. The church was crowded with people. In the pew in front of us was the Negro band from the Boeuf sur le Toit. Picasso was there, Brancusi, and so many celebrated people that I cannot remember their names. Radiguet's death was a terrible shock to everyone. "Coco" Chanel . . . arranged the funeral. It was most wonderfully done. Cocteau was too ill to come. We waited some minutes for the arrival of the body, in its white coffin, covered with white flowers; it was carried up the aisle and placed on the platform. After a short service we walked round the coffin and shook the Holy Water over the coffin, the men walking one side and the women the other. We could hardly see, as Marie [Beerbohm] and I and everyone else's eyes in the church were filled with tears. We had to walk round the church and shake hands with the relatives. It was the most tragic sight that I have ever seen. Radiguet's sisters, the youngest being about six, stood in a row, their faces contorted with weeping. Marie and I burst into tears and went out into the street to see the procession start off. The hearse was covered in white and was drawn by two large white horses, like those in the war picture by Uccello in the National Gallery. They stood patiently and waited. The coffin was carried out with its white pall, and on it was one bunch of red roses. Many wreaths were carried out, and by the time the procession started the white hearse and a carriage following were covered with white flowers. We walked down the boulevard, following the procession, and waited and watched the hearse and the long train of mourners disappear into the distance on their way to Père Lachaise. It was not yet ten o'clock and still pouring with rain. Fortunately, in Paris, the cafés are open all the time, so we went to the Café Francis, which is near the theatre Champs-Elysées, drank some brandy, and sat silently gazing at the rain.

Eventually, Cocteau wrote to the Abbé Mugnier, and to Valentine.

Cocteau to Abbé Mugnier

[n.d]

. . . . The death of my poor boy has been the finishing blow for me. Death would be better than this half-death, for the only thing that impels me to go on living is my wish not to hurt Maman. Friends, religion, bring me no comfort; you know what I need, and it is not something to be had for the asking. . . . I suffer night and day. I shall never write again. . . .

Cocteau to Valentine Hugo
Monday
[December 18, 1923]

Ma chère Valentine,

Forgive me. I am trying, for Maman's sake, not to die, that's all. I love you. My only joy has been to know that you are well. *Je vous embrasse.*

Jean

P.S. Send me all the drawings of him that you have.

Valentine, I am sorry for you, but I beg you to tell yourself that apart from the disappearance of what one loves, NOTHING matters.

In the hospital room at Montpellier, when Milhaud's telegram arrived, Valentine has written, "We were in utter despair. Jean Hugo, his face buried in his arms on my bed, wept silently like an unhappy child. And I, unable to move, flat on my back, let my tears flow. . . . It was the first grief we shared - - my heart still aches to think of it."

Jean Hugo was once asked what he thought it was that had kept Cocteau from spending a last night with the boy he loved, and from attending his funeral service. "His grief. With Jean, his grief took precedence." Mademoiselle Chanel is harsher. "Cocteau came to me," is the way she remembered it during a recent conversation, "and told me that Radiguet was dying. 'Are you going to leave him alone?' I asked him. 'What can I do?' 'Spend the night with him.' But Cocteau was afraid. You know Radiguet's mother sat with him, and caught typhoid."

"He knew that in order to live on earth one must follow the fashion — and hearts are no longer worn," are the last words in Cocteau's novel *Le Grand Ecart*. Paris, as usual, wasn't slow to coin a quip: *"Le veuf sur le toit"* — "the widower on the roof" — was the smart way to refer to Cocteau.

6
Opium, Orpheus, and *The Blood of a Poet*

Roméo et Juliette, *the Drug, and the Sacraments* (*1924–1925*)

"**V**OILÀ — I suffered a great loss, and I ran away," Cocteau wrote on January 2, 1924 from Monte Carlo, apparently to a Paris editor. "Here my musician friends are looking after me. When will I ever write again? Forgive me: Radiguet was my son." As he put it later, "For me Radiguet's death was an operation without chloroform." It was about a fortnight after the "operation" that he went to Monte Carlo, to convalesce.

In Monte Carlo, presenting a festival of French music at the Casino, was the Diaghilev company (most of its members, like Stravinsky and other Russians who had remained abroad, now stateless as a result of the revolution, and cut off from all home connections and resources). Poulenc and Auric were there to attend rehearsals and premieres of their ballets, respectively *Les Biches* (décor by Marie Laurencin) and *Les Fâcheux* (décor by Braque): Cocteau had had a hand in both scenarios. Satie, to whom Poulenc and Auric had grown very close, was also in Monte Carlo, transforming into recitatives for voice and orchestra the spoken parts of Gounod's opera *Le Médecin Malgré Lui*. (Poulenc was doing the same with Gounod's *La Colombe*.) Also present was a musicologist, Louis Laloy. Laloy was an important journalist — music critic of the newspaper *Comoedia* — and Secretary-General of the Paris Opéra besides. He was detested by Satie.

A friend of Debussy and a lover of his music, Laloy had disliked the compositions of Satie and Les Six and had written a hostile review of the *"Spectacle-Concert"* that had included *Le Boeuf sur le Toit*. The anti-Debussy passages in *Le Coq et l'Arlequin* had hardened his heart against Cocteau, and of *Parade* he wrote disapprovingly that it "protested against the sublime." In Monte Carlo, however, something — whether an actual "oversweetening" in the recent music of Auric and Poulenc, as Satie was soon bitterly to claim, or deliberate flattery by the two composers for practical purposes — had won them Laloy's approval. Cocteau joined the icebreaking, addressing Laloy for the first time with the words: "It's not the sublime that I'm against, it's the false sublime." The four began to see much of each other, Satie "turning away" whenever their paths crossed. It took only a few days for the maniacal Satie to see his two disciples' frequenting of Laloy as "concessions," as treachery, as utter betrayal of the musical standards and principles of himself and Les Six. Abruptly, after "covering his friends with incredible abuse," he took the train to Paris, "standing up during the entire journey in the corridor of his sleeping car." It was his irrevocable break with Poulenc and Auric, and, of course, with Cocteau. In Paris he wrote a characteristic article, which appeared in the newspaper *Paris-Journal* on February 15, 1924:

THE RUSSIAN BALLETS AT MONTE CARLO
by Erik Satie
(Travel Notes)

The state of music? . . . Hm . . . Monte Carlo? . . . Gloriously oversweet . . . A mixture of sex, un-sex, and emetics . . .

Syrups of all kinds . . . Musical lemonade aplenty . . . Yes . . . *Les Biches* . . . *Les Fâcheux* . . . Gounod.

BUT:

Intensive work . . . Diaghilev? Always the same: conscientious, sympathetic . . . Yes.

Glimpsed the horrible Laloy (more disgusting than ever) . . . What an abomination . . . A real mole, so nearsighted; but sly as a monkey . . .

BUT:

He (Laloy) has written splendid articles . . . too splendid . . . on my friends Poulenc, Auric . . . His praise is compromising . . . Yes . . . So they succeeded in "getting" him? . . . At what price? . . . Hm . . .

BUT:

Cocteau triumphant . . . Yes . . . Maintains mysterious, dark alliance with said Laloy . . . Hm . . . Why? Strange idea, to "get" that gentleman . . . What's behind it all? . . . Why not leave him strictly alone? . . .

Schemes? . . . Perhaps . . . Tiny schemes (surely no more than that, I'm sure) . . . Yes . . .

BUT:

In short, success at the Casino . . . After all, aren't the audiences there sub-subtle, sub-urbane, sub-sophisticated? . . .

No wonder musical lemonade is in such demand . . . Gushing reviews in all languages . . . Brazen rewards for small, perpetual concessions . . . Applause from all parts of the house . . . Lollipop music. . . .

Such was the first of two dramas that unfolded that January in Monte Carlo.

The second is hinted at in Satie's mention of "emetics," and in a few words in Laloy's memoirs concerning his daily meetings with Poulenc, Auric and Cocteau in a hotel: "The floor waiters knew without being told that we wanted to be left undisturbed; if a visitor arrived unannounced he was asked to wait, and the evening mail was discreetly slipped in under the door." It was the floor waiters' sophisticated sense of smell that told them not to disturb the little group: seeping out under the door was the unmistakable odor of opium.

Laloy was a man of extraordinary cultivation and achievements, and a delightful writer. In addition to his work in music, he learned Greek and Russian (he was a Franco-Russian interpreter during the war), and studied Chinese at the Ecole des Langues Orientales. His Chinese readings led him to opium, and he published in 1913 a fascinating book called *Le Livre de la Fumée* (The Smoke Book), a history and manual of opium-smoking, its delights and its dangers, which became fashionable reading and has been credited with playing a role in the prevalence of opium-smoking in European postwar society. It is not known to what extent if any Poulenc and Auric had smoked before Monte Carlo (Auric became an habitual, controlled smoker); Cocteau had smoked little if at all;* but now he began. "After the death of Radiguet, whom I

* A recent book on Cocteau quotes a letter written to him in 1916 or 1917 by a Marine named Marrast, proposing an evening "around a little lamp." It also quotes a 1917

thought of as a son, my nervous suffering became so unbearable, so overwhelming, that Louis Laloy at Monte Carlo suggested that I relieve it this way. Opium is a living substance. It does not like to be forced. At first it made me sick. Only after fairly long trial did it help me." Satie's "emetics" were, in one sense, Cocteau's first opium pipes.

Laloy was a moderate smoker. "He had to be, poor chap — he didn't have much money," opium-smoking friends of his and Cocteau's have said. Laloy's book is full of counsels of moderation, and he combined opium-smoking with normal family and professional life: Cocteau's letters to him usually contain, along with occasional references to "cigarettes" and related matters, affectionate messages to Madame Laloy and the children. Laloy's combination of opium-smoking and domesticity was well known, and in a letter Cocteau wrote to Madame de Noailles in 1924 or 1925 after the signing of his brother Paul's marriage contract he tells of an awkward moment during the *"dîner de contrat"* with Paul's future in-laws, the Rageots. "Now let's all go out to Louis Laloy's in Bellevue and have a nice little smoking party," Monsieur Gaston Rageot jocularly proposed, as something preposterous. There was a silence, for one or two people at the table knew that that was precisely what Jean Cocteau was in the habit of doing once a week. "Certain people," Cocteau once wrote, "smoke only on Sunday. On Sunday they can't *not* smoke: smoking is part of their Sunday routine."

In Monte Carlo, after the nausea stopped, Cocteau was hooked. For the rest of his life he was to smoke opium, to write about his

letter from Valentine Hugo to Cocteau in which she says that she prefers not to "smoke pipes" with him at the Hotel Chantecler in Le Piquey — pipes which she is quoted as having later identified as opium pipes. Jean Hugo comments on that as follows: "I am sorry to contradict Valentine, but smoking opium at the Hotel Chantecler is not conceivable. The rooms were separated by ill-joined wooden boards; one could see between them, hear every sound from one room to another; the smoke and smell would have gone all over the house. The pipes, to my eyes, are the white Gambier clay pipes Apollinaire used to smoke, the pipes Picasso and Braque painted in their still lives, and that all of us — except Valentine, who never cared much for tobacco — smoked in those days. On the other hand, the Marrast letter is convincing. The little lamp cannot be anything else. I do not deny that Cocteau had tried opium before Radiguet's death. He may have smoked occasionally, as Apollinaire and Picasso did, as Radiguet did on his own, but no more than they can he be called *then* an opium smoker — no more than someone who, being occasionally offered a drink, drinks it, can be called a dipsomaniac." There seems no reason, therefore, to doubt on these grounds Cocteau's story that his serious smoking began with Laloy, in 1924.

addiction, and to undergo "cures," the first two of which were considerably publicized after their completion. A modern specialist in drug addiction has expressed the belief that there is no reason to doubt Cocteau's statement that he originally began to smoke as a flight from depression. "Addiction beginning at the age of thirty-four or thirty-five is not a search for excitement or pleasure, as in the very young." But with time Cocteau's addiction took on another aspect. As Stravinsky has put it, "the chief purpose of the drug-taking came to be book-making." The opium-smoking friends of Cocteau's and Laloy's mentioned above say that Cocteau always smoked less than he pretended, far less than many other people they knew, and that if his "cures" really took as long as he said they did, "He must have chosen to prolong his stays in the sanitariums for other reasons: remember, such institutions are nice quiet places to write books in." (As we shall see, the very excellence of some of the books is closely connected with the opium.) They point out, too, that Cocteau was of nervous temperament, usually agitated and active, seldom at rest: opium, in their opinion, "demands more respect than that" — a point which Cocteau himself was to make about the drug, contrasting leisurely Chinese smoking with Western hurry. Had he smoked with more "respect" his friends think — that is, in a setting of greater tranquillity — he could have dispensed with cures.

There was no drug-taking in the Diaghilev company: at least, none was countenanced by Diaghilev. Lydia Sokolova tells in her memoirs of his severity when he detected, that same January in Monte Carlo, that without realizing it she had sniffed a little cocaine. Massine had mortally offended Diaghilev in 1921 by marrying and leaving the company, and the choreographer was now Bronislava Nijinska, Nijinsky's sister. Two new male dancers, both handsome, were attracting attention. A particularly athletic young Anglo-Irishman named Patrick Kay (christened by the Russians Patrikeyev, then rechristened Anton Dolin — Antoine Doline when in France) was already Diaghilev's favorite, and was given a role in *Les Fâcheux;* and a nineteen-year-old Russian, Serge Lifar, was giving himself airs from his supposed obscurity in the *corps de ballet.* That was a dangerous game to play with Diaghilev, but Lifar, in addition to his dancing genius, had a sure talent for flirtation. One of the first manifestations of his flair for attracting Dia-

ghilev's notice was his flouting of a company rule forbidding dancers to be seen on the wrong side of the footlights. Whether or not he
had heard of Diaghilev's earlier jealousy and mistrust of Cocteau,
he sought him out. "My seat was next that of Cocteau, Auric, Treb-
nikov and others. Diaghilev came in. . . . 'I forbid you, once and
for all, to be seen in the body of the theatre. If you don't choose to
obey me, you're at liberty to leave the company and spend all your
nights in the front row with Jeanchick.' " Cocteau was doing some
publicity for the company and his friends, attending every performance and preparing articles on Poulenc and Auric and their
ballets; and he sought to appease Diaghilev by devising a ballet
around Dolin. The young Irishman, whose offstage exhibitionism
rivaled Lifar's, was forever doing handstands and turning cart-
wheels in the wings, and Cocteau proposed a beach ballet, with
Dolin impressing a bevy of bathing beauties of both sexes by his
antics on the sands. He called it *Le Train Bleu,* after the Paris-Rivi-
era express that brought vacationers to the Mediterranean; and
after he left Monte Carlo for Paris with Auric on January 26 Nijinska began its choreography. Diaghilev commissioned a score from
Milhaud and a décor from Henri Laurens.

Such was Cocteau's production, efficient but peripheral, during
the early weeks of his bereavement — his first attempts to master
a grief that would torment him for years. Louis Laloy wrote
warmly of him in Monte Carlo: "It is now a month since his friend
Radiguet died in the prime of youth. Like all noble souls he con-
trols his grief only for the sake of people he loves." The pieces on
the Poulenc and Auric ballets, written so soon after he had said "I
shall never write again" and "When will I ever write again?" and
first published in the *N.R.F.* for March 1, are not at all without
verve. Monte Carlo is sunny and pleasant, he says; "the white gin-
gerbread façades add zest to life"; and he regrets that the Casino
terrace lacks "a bust of Pascal, to whom we owe the game of rou-
lette." Back in Paris, there was immediate activity. Massine's three-
year marriage had foundered, his attempts to mount independent
productions had left him in debt, and the unforgiving Diaghilev
had refused his request to be taken back into the company. Now
Etienne de Beaumont, out of affection, was trying to refloat him,
and was organizing — really for his benefit, though not ostensibly
so — a series of programs for the month of May, to be called, after

the name of Apollinaire's prewar magazine, "Les Soirées de Paris." He invited Cocteau to contribute something — something in which there would *not* be a role for Massine, in order that the pro-Massine purpose of the Soirées be at least slightly disguised. Some time before, Cocteau had written a short "adaptation" of *Romeo and Juliet* in the manner of his *Antigone*, and now he began, with Jean Hugo, to prepare it for the Soirées.*

Four years earlier, on April 8, 1920, Cocteau and the Hugos, with Paul Morand, Lucien Daudet and others, had dined at the restaurant Les Vendanges de Bourgogne in the rue Saint-Antoine and had gone on to a street fair called the Foire du Trône in the east end of Paris. There among other sideshows they saw an act called "Miss Aérogyne, the Flying Woman." A woman wearing a light-catching tinsel bodice and white tights "flew" against a densely black background: she was strapped by a rhinestone-studded belt and braces (which left her legs free to kick and her arms and hands free to send kisses) to a peg or knob that moved along invisible rails; when she reached the end of the track, there was the sound of a clutch changing gear, and she turned upside down and "flew" back in the direction from which she had come. Dazzling lights directed at the spectators' faces kept them from seeing anything except the glittering "flyer." Cocteau wrote a poem about her the next day:

> . . . Aérogyne
> Elle ment avec son corps
> Mieux que l'esprit n'imagine
> Les mensonges du décor . . .†

---

* For a time there was a question of a five-act play in verse by Cocteau laid in the present day, called first *Bajazet* (like Racine's tragedy) and then *L'Impromptu de Montmartre* (after Molière's comedy *L'Impromptu de Versailles*). It was to open with a dog named Bajazet sitting up with a lump of sugar on his nose and with a "*tragédienne*" named Roxane (as in the Racine tragedy) addressing him with Racine's line: "*Ecoutez, Bajazet, je sens que je vous aime.*" During the brief period of its abortive gestation Cocteau considered adding to the cast a sea horse and a *vitrier* (an ambulant glazier, carrying his wares on a frame strapped to his back and extending out on each side, thus giving the impression of a pair of wings and causing Cocteau to think of him as an angel on earth — as the glazier Heurtebise was later to be in his play *Orphée*). Before it was abandoned, Jean Hugo made notes and sketches, including one of the glazier, later used for *Orphée*.

† Aérogyne! The lies she tells with her body / Thwart the mind's attempts to see through / The lies of the décor . . .

With Miss Aérogyne in mind — recalled to him, perhaps, by Romeo's words about Juliet hanging "upon the cheek of night / Like a rich jewel in an Ethiope's ear" — Hugo designed for the "excuse for a stage production" (so Cocteau modestly called his adaptation*) a set whose hangings and floor would be of black cloth with colored linear decorations, and for the actors black tights and black velvet dresses, doublets and short hose, painted with "embroidery" that would be picked out by lighting. As Cocteau put it: "With Jean and Valentine Hugo I had invented an entirely black set, in which only the colors of certain arabesques, costumes and props were visible. Red lights framing the stage kept the audience from seeing anything else." The speaker of the first-act prologue "flew," like Miss Aérogyne herself.

Choice of a cast kept Cocteau busy; on March 21 he had to return briefly to Monte Carlo for rehearsals of *Le Train Bleu* (costumes for that were to be by Chanel); and back in Paris again rehearsals for *Roméo* began. Unfortunately Massine's absence from the cast, strategic though it was, resulted in Beaumont's taking little interest in *Roméo*, and its rehearsals suffered from his neglect; he became inaccessible, and Cocteau had to write him, complaining that "Except for me, there is nobody to direct," and that there was a "total lack of discipline." Beaumont, made nervous by the thousand details of the enterprise — he had undertaken more than he realized — grew short-tempered. In more letters, Cocteau protested his affection, his "heartbreak" at the way things were going, and the fatigue that was making him "wish for death"; for a time he refused to attend rehearsals, promising only to play the role of Mercutio, which he had added to his directorial duties, at a single performance; but this he later extended.

Among the principals, Yvonne George (as Juliet's nurse) was also an opium addict; at the moment she was suffering from short supply, and during rehearsals kept weeping and blowing her nose. Andrée Pascal, as Juliet, was "rather below the mark," according to Jean Hugo, and "completely lacked feminine charm: *'Roméo et*

---

* English readers, especially, will not quarrel with Cocteau concerning his modesty in this case. The text of his *Roméo* is bare: the passage quoted above, for instance, appears in his French as *"un seul diamant orne l'oreille de la nuit, c'est elle."* The richness and poetry of the production were chiefly visual, provided by various staging devices of Cocteau's invention and, especially, by Jean Hugo, as can be seen in an edition of Cocteau's text illustrated by Hugo's designs. (Paris, Au Sans Pareil, 1926.)

Jules' was the quip that went around Paris." In fact the only display of feminine grace, Hugo recalls, was by "two charming English girls" who danced in a miniature ballet.* Mercutio's page was, appropriately enough, an eighteen-year-old whom Cocteau was employing in real life as part-time secretary and errand-boy — Maurice Ettinghausen, who preferred to be known as Maurice Sachs. (Sachs was the family name of his mother, whom he had recently helped flee to England to escape prosecution for passing a bad check.) For this, his only stage appearance, he took yet another name: the Paris telephone exchange "Saxe" had recently been changed to "Ségur," and as "Ségur" Maurice Sachs, who will be heard of again, is listed in *Roméo*'s cast. Throughout rehearsals the rank and file caused trouble, failing to follow Cocteau's wish that their movements be slow and stylized — "I had worked out a very interesting way of walking for all the young men of Verona" † — to harmonize with the musical accompaniment, a medley of old English airs that he had commissioned from the young composer Roger Désormière, Beaumont's conductor for the Soirées. But after the preview, on June 2, Jean Hugo could again write in his diary, "Success"; his murky décor and glowing costumes were appreciated. Yvonne George's intelligence enabled her to carry off the nurse's role well, and Cocteau's performance as Mercutio was praised. To die onstage, in full view of the public, night after night — there were about ten performances of *Roméo* in all — gave him a macabre thrill: "What a blinding nightmare were those shows at the Cigale! Even during a performance that gives the impression of calm, backstage is like a sinking ship. Madness and jit-

---

* Three women dancers or actresses with English-sounding names are listed in the program — Miss Joyce Myers, "Hawkins," and "Hewitt": impossible to know which of them were the two graces. The latter had as one of their male partners the talented twenty-one-year-old English dancer Rupert Doone (born Ernest Reginald Woodfield). Doone and Cocteau were lovers at the time, and when Doone's difficult personality began to annoy the rest of the company Cocteau vainly pled with Beaumont against his dismissal, admitting that he was a *"terrible raseur"* but praising his dancing and calling him a poor fellow who "clings to my coat-tails like a stray dog." In 1929 Doone was hired by Diaghilev as *premier danseur*, but that phase of his career was cut short by Diaghilev's death the same year. Later he was one of the founders of the Group Theatre. (See Robert Medley, program notes to "Rupert Doone Remembered by his Friends," Morley College, June 23, 1966.) Doone told Medley that his intimacy with Cocteau ended because of his stubborn refusal to join Cocteau in smoking opium.

† A stage direction reads: "All the elegant young men of Verona have a certain aggressive way of walking, one hand always on the hilt of their sword. Only Romeo does not follow this fashion, and moves as though sleepwalking."

ters pervade the crowded half-darkness where the crew of actors, stagehands and dressers silently move about. I was playing the part of Mercutio. Only a corridor separated my dressing room from the stage. I could hear the sound of the bagpipes that accompanied certain passages. It upset me. I was weeping tears of exhaustion, asleep on my feet. The other actors pushed me onstage like a dumb animal. My dresser talked about 'before M. Jean dies,' or 'after M. Jean dies' — and it is true, I never played the duel scene without hoping that my pantomime would deceive Death and induce it to take me. In short, two months of working night and day, my grief, all kinds of pills, turned me into an insect, Jean Hugo's costume being my outer shell. Had I been cut in two like a wasp, I would have gone on living, moving my painted ruff and my legs. For I am tough. One has to be, to stand such things." The performances scheduled for June 21 and 22 were cancelled on Cocteau's insistence because from the beginning Beaumont "had not allowed sufficient rehearsals" — Cocteau wrote to the newspapers threatening legal action if the play went on — but matters were patched up, and there were two final performances on the twenty-seventh and twenty-eighth.

(The sideshows sparked by the tension between Cocteau and Beaumont were not the only unscheduled attractions accompanying the season of the Soirées. On June 14, at the opening performance of Satie's ballet *Mercure*, danced by Massine against a décor by Picasso, Diaghilev displayed agitation, feeling that there was a threat to the Russian ballet in this independent creation by two of his former collaborators; and that same night the theatre was invaded by demonstrating Surrealists, who admired Picasso but deplored his collaborating with a "bourgeois" like Beaumont. Another evening, according to Bernard Faÿ, Beaumont found no one in the theatre except his mother and a few of her friends in a box: receipts had been meager, and to encourage her son Madame de Beaumont had bought up the entire house — but being sometimes vague had forgotten to distribute the tickets.)

On June 20 *Le Train Bleu* opened at the Champs-Elysées. The décor by Laurens had proved disappointing, and Diaghilev had called on Picasso to repeat the success of his great front curtain for *Parade*. His *Train Bleu* curtain, showing two monumental women clad in white tunics running ecstatically hand in hand along a beach

against blue sky and sea, was so handsome that Diaghilev thereafter used it as the official front cloth for the Russian Ballet.* Balletomanes greatly appreciated Nijinska's choreography, "ingeni-
ously based on movements characteristic of various games"; Cocteau, in his depressed mood, found it "silly, slight, and without
novelty." (*Le Train Bleu* was, as it turned out, his last work for
Diaghilev.) Meanwhile, on June 1, the first of two installments of
Radiguet's novel *Le Bal du Comte d'Orgel* appeared in the *N.R.F.*,
where to Cocteau's indignation Jacques Rivière saw fit to preface it
with disparaging remarks about *Le Diable au Corps* and the opinion that nothing in Radiguet's work gave promise of his becoming,
had he lived, one of the *"grands explorateurs du coeur humain."*
Some time this year the *N.R.F.* published a collected volume of
Cocteau's poetry, including the previously refused *Cap de Bonne-
Espérance*. It was this year, 1924, too, that Cocteau published, in
an edition of 625 copies, his well-known large volume of *Dessins*
(dated 1923, but the printer had spoiled the first impressions of
the plates, and the work had had to be done over), containing more
than a hundred of his early line drawings — portraits of Madame
de Noailles, of Picasso, of Radiguet, of Jean Hugo, of himself and
others, and, in a series called *"Souvenirs du Ballet Russe,"* two
particularly witty drawings — that of Stravinsky playing the *Rite*
while strange shapes listen, and that of Stravinsky in a top hat
stooping to speak to Picasso in a bowler. The volume is dedicated
to Picasso: "Poets do not draw. They untie the knots in handwriting
and then retie them differently. That is why I take the liberty of
dedicating to you a few strokes that I have made on blotters, table-
cloths and the backs of envelopes. Had you not suggested it, I
would never have dared bring them together here." The cheerful
tone given the book by the early drawings contrasts with the sombre-
ness of this moment of publication; justly, it has always been
Cocteau's best-liked portfolio.

By the end of the season, having thus kept himself at least somewhat distracted from his grief during the first six months following
Radiguet's death, beginning to realize that the quantity of opium he
had been smoking was too much for him, little though it might be

* The huge curtain, actually executed from a Picasso sketch, supposedly in twenty-
four hours, by Prince Schervachidze, Diaghilev's scene painter, but inscribed by Picasso himself to Diaghilev (supposedly in sign of approval), was sold at auction in
London in 1968 to the British Arts Council for £69,000 ($165,600).

for others, tormented by the quarrel with Beaumont (a few years later he would affectionately dedicate a printed edition of *Roméo et Juliette* to Beaumont and his wife), overwhelmed by malaise, Cocteau went south to join Auric in a villa at Villefranche-sur-Mer — a villa whose name, "Le Calme," Auric later said, seemed a mockery in more ways than one as Cocteau alternated, during the months that followed, between prostration and agitation. From there he wrote to the Hugos.

> *Cocteau to Valentine and Jean Hugo*
> Villa Le Calme
> Villefranche sur mer
> [postmark August 7 (?), 1924]

Mes amis chéris,

I am thinking of you. I would be happy to be near you. I am suffering — suffering in the sun, and this is atrocious. I keep to myself as much as possible because Auric dislikes the sight of suffering. But with you I would suffer openly. I would weep, and that would relieve me a little.

I am smoking less and less. I have reduced the doses to the point where they do me good. I think that I shall be able to stop earlier than I had expected. I am already burned quite black, but my outer blackness is in keeping with the blackness within. Raymond's book seems to be asserting itself slowly but surely. I had a letter from Romain Rolland — he thinks *Le Bal* a masterpiece. *Je vous embrasse. Ecrivez — ayez pitié.*

He wrote to Gide: "Here I am trying to live, or, rather, I am trying to teach the death within me how to live. It is all hideously painful. Your affection comforts me." (Perhaps Gide's motive in sending Cocteau some words of "affection" at this time, if he did so, was to palliate a little the effect of another bit of Gidean behavior of which Cocteau had recently become aware and which even Gide himself may have realized was gross and gratuitous: Gide chose this moment to republish, implacably, five years after the original event, in a volume called *Incidences*, the "Open Letter to Jean Cocteau.") To Poulenc, who had sent him snapshots of Raymond: "The photos broke my heart. I feel the hurt as keenly as the first day. I am dragging out a meaningless life." "All I could look forward to was a desert, memories," he later wrote about that summer in Ville-franche. Memories and concern for the posterity of Raymond's book led him to write to the boy's father:

Cocteau to Monsieur Maurice Radiguet
Le Calme
Villefranche sur mer, A.M.
August 1924

Mon cher ami,

You must have been very happy, as I was, about the articles on *Le Bal*, and especially the one by Massis. They give me courage, here in this villa "Le Calme," where my calm is more like death than anything else. I have not been able to recover my balance — will I ever? And must I? Perhaps my true role on earth was to help bring to birth your son's masterpieces. Give me news of Mme. Radiguet and all the family. . . .

And to Raymond's younger brother:

Cocteau to René Radiguet
Villefranche sur mer
Sept. 1924

Mon cher René,

Your card gives me pleasure — a very sad kind of pleas-ure, like the kind your dear little tearful face gives me each time I kiss you and have the illusion of hugging my own poor child. I am trying to live without Raymond, but it won't work. Give me news of your family — of Paul and the little girls. My love to all, especially to you, who were Raymond's fa-vorite. You realize, don't you, that every day your brother's fame is growing in height and depth?

Cocteau later described, in terms that an authority on addiction has called strikingly realistic, some of the darker aspects of those first months of smoking: "Sleep was my refuge. The prospect of waking kept me from sleeping properly and determined my dreams. In the morning I could no longer face resuming life. Real-ity and dream overlapped, making an unsightly blob. I got up, shaved, dressed with people in my room, and let myself be dragged anywhere. Oh, those mornings! It was like being thrown back into dirty water and made to swim. In this state one cannot bear to read a newspaper: such evidence of general activity and those who write about it is murderous. My flight into opium is Freud's 'flight into sickness.'

"If the awakening is painful, one smokes in the morning, and if it is difficult to smoke at home one *eats* opium. Eating makes things worse: one would have to smoke twelve pipes to undo the effects of one little ball, because by eating one absorbs the morphine and the dross. Then the trouble begins — waves of sweat, chills, yawns, running nose, choking fits, a lump in the solar plexus. I confess that at the time I didn't realize the cause of those symptoms. I was seeking suicide and taking massive doses."

Those last words go rather far: the wish for death was certainly strong in Cocteau at this time, but even now it was less strong than its opposite; and the search for suicide was less resolute than the search for something else. He rented a room in a Villefranche hotel called the Welcome, sat at a table, stared at himself in the door-mirror of the wardrobe, drew himself over and over again, and festooned thirty of the drawings with captions. "I was alone," he wrote in a preface. "I was looking for various ways of resolving the same face; and since Edouard Champion had long been asking me for a manuscript to be reproduced in facsimile, and since I have stopped writing, I added a few notes in the margin to give him a surprise." He called the portfolio — Champion published it in a small facsimile edition — *Le Mystère de Jean l'Oiseleur, Monologues.* (A *oiseleur* is a bird-catcher, or, like the one who entertained Milhaud's housewarming guests in June, 1923, a bird-tamer.)* The birds that Jean the Bird-catcher caught are, in the notes, fleeting thoughts plucked out of the confusion existing within and around him, and tamed in prose; but in the series of self-portraits, such as so many artists have delighted in making, one sees that already some of the effects of the opium, even though he was smoking too much, were the opposite of injurious: the drawings are quite equal

---

* In this self-baptism Cocteau associated himself, as usual, with others. He says in one of the "monologues" that Apollinaire considered that "Cubism had its source in Paolo di Dono" (called "Uccello" — "bird" — from his particular skill in depicting winged creatures), who "died in solitude"; and that Apollinaire had called Picasso "the Benin bird," "from a bronze and copper bird from Benin that stood on the poet's worktable."

in quality, and in certain aspects superior, to their sunnier predecessors in the volume *Dessins* of the year before. The name "Jean
the Bird-catcher" holds, of course, an old association. At the end of
his preface to the volume Cocteau says, "As for whatever relationship may exist between the words and the faces, whatever confessions and poetry may be expressed in the lines, they must be interpreted as signs of the illness that for nearly twelve years now has
forced me to strain my will to the utmost." Twelve years before was
1912, the year of Diaghilev's command that had ended the recurrent dream about poor Georges Cocteau as parrot: the dream was
over, but there was no escape from the bird.

Now occurred one of the most bizarre episodes of Cocteau's career — his "return to the sacraments."

Auric had been acquainted since the age of fifteen with Jacques
Maritain, a neo-Thomist philosopher and professor at the Institute
Catholique, who in 1919, in a work called *Art et Scholastique*, had
quoted several of Cocteau's aphorisms from *Le Coq et l'Arlequin*.
The Cocteau pamphlet had been given to Maritain by a young
friend and disciple named Charles Henrion, who soon thereafter
became a Catholic priest proselytizing among the tribes of the Sahara, following in the footsteps of the martyred missionary Père de
Foucauld. Jacques Maritain was handsome, with a Christ-like appearance; he and his wife, Raïssa, both of them converts to Catholicism, were themselves great proselytizers, combining, along with
considerable cultivation and charm, the insistence that sometimes
accompanies religious idealism. The story of the so-called "lack of
pressure" which, according to Raïssa in her autobiography, *Les
Grandes Amitiés*, preceded the "embracing of the true faith" by her
Russian Jewish parents, makes painful reading for agnostics.* The
Maritains' house in suburban Meudon, whence Maritain commuted
to his philosophy classes, contained a chapel where by permission
of church authorities Mass could be said. Auric had read *Le Cap de
Bonne-Espérance* to the Maritains, and sometime, apparently during or shortly after Cocteau's nightly dying onstage in *Roméo et
Juliette*, Auric had taken him to Meudon. "Yes, Death had you by
the throat, Mercutio!" Maritain wrote later, recalling the visit; and

---

* Cocteau later described Raïssa as being *"fragile comme un fil de la Vierge et
robuste comme une lame d'acier"* ("Frail as gossamer and strong as a steel blade").

Cocteau later spoke of it, or of his next meeting with the Maritains, as a moving occasion that brought back his childhood (of which the sacraments had of course been a part): "Yes, my dear Jacques, dining with you for the first time at Meudon I recognized the odor of Maisons-Laffitte where I was born, the same chairs, the same plates that I used obsessively to turn so that their blue design was beside the bottom of my glass."

Perhaps at this time Cocteau, amid his opium fumes, was already thinking of a return to his childhood religion. In his case there was no question of "conversion." Like many Frenchmen he tended to ignore, except on ceremonial occasions, the church in which he had been baptized, but he had never broken with it. He had kept on good terms with the Abbé Mugnier (not a difficult task for a worldling); and his words to the Abbé after Radiguet's death — "You know what I need, and it is not something to be had for the asking" — could be interpreted as an invitation to begin revivalist proceedings. But whatever the Abbé may have replied, he was apparently shrewd enough to see that even — or particularly — at this moment of intense emotion, exhortation of Cocteau could well be a dangerous undertaking. Max Jacob, on the other hand, had for years been baldly urging Cocteau to practice his religion. Jacob seems to have hoped that the hostility shown Cocteau by the Surrealists, who were self-proclaimed atheists, might lever him back into the church. On various occasions Cocteau had written Jacob that he had gone so far as to light candles before a church altar at a moment of depression, and lamented his lack of faith: "I envy you. It is excruciating, *excruciating*, to be an unbeliever with a spirit that is deeply religious." On Radiguet's death Jacob had sent to Monsieur Maurice Radiguet a "Christian" letter containing, among other phrases supposedly designed to comfort the grieving father, "I can't tell you how sorry I am that you are not deeply Christian! Alas! I pray God that he may bestow his grace upon you. It is such a comfort to offer one's sorrows to God and to hope to see again those whom one has lost." To Cocteau he wrote a long letter advising him to take Communion "the way one goes to a doctor." "What!" Cocteau wrote him. "You advise me to swallow the Host like an aspirin tablet?" And Jacob answered, "The Host *should* be taken like aspirin."

Maritain, orthodox, traditionalist, but much interested in modern artists, especially in their power for "good" (i.e., their ability to deliver clearly legible "spiritual" messages: among his later particular enthusiasms were Rouault and Chagall), recognized the power of Radiguet's writing, and when he read the posthumous novel in the *N.R.F.* he was impressed by the boy's admiring portrayal of the Comtesse d'Orgel, a woman loyal to traditional virtues. He was aware of the opinion of Gide and others on the *N.R.F.* that it was their group alone which recognized and championed French classicism in literature in its most modern forms, and since that group tended to be agnostic and politically Left, Maritain felt that their claim should be challenged. He wrote a strategic letter to the Catholic literary journalist Henri Massis: "I have just read the Radiguet in the *N.R.F.* In my opinion it is really good and important. Wouldn't this be a good time to write something about him? This would seem to me very desirable simply in itself. Moreover I know that Cocteau and his friends are eager for something like that, and it would be very opportune." (One senses the alertness of the proselytizer.) "This is the moment, I should think, to welcome this whole movement and keep it from being taken over by the *N.R.F.*, which is really not sympathetic to it." Massis immediately wrote an article on Radiguet and his two novels, for the August 15, 1924 issue of the *Revue Universelle*, which he had founded with the royalist Jacques Bainville. The article was in part a *riposte* to the strictures that Rivière had included in his preface to the first installment of *Le Bal du Comte d'Orgel*, and ended as follows:

"It assimilates, selects and distills the best of Proust, Gide, and, even more closely, Cocteau and Morand. It is by this modernity that *Le Bal* will win the young and influence them. But it contains something more enduring. Other adolescents may have more genius, more 'originality,' may have revealed something more peculiar, a fulguration that was only in themselves. Radiguet has achieved something more difficult. At one stroke he has attained the simplicity that is the secret of the very greatest."

Cocteau wrote at once to Massis from "Le Calme": "I read your article through my tears. . . . Maritain will tell you of my distress. For five years I renounced *myself*, trying through Radiguet to carry out an experiment that I could never have accomplished alone with my own fouled instruments. (Still, in *Thomas* I did hit the target. *La Princesse de Clèves* and *Thomas* were the books Ra-

diguet loved best in the world.) We wrote *Le Bal* and *Thomas* on
the same table: we were trying to create something 'invisible,'
'heavenly.' I am suffering. I am left behind, in a state of complete
exhaustion, amid the rubble of what was once a workshop for cutting crystal." And he wrote to Maritain: "Out of all the youth, I
chose Radiguet, to make him my masterpiece. Imagine his death,
and me alone, half-mad amidst the rubble of a crystal-cutting
workshop. Here I am trying to live, with little success. Auric is
helping me. Alas, what can he do? I live in a nightmare, in another
world inaccessible even to friendship. Probably, instead of giving
in I ought to raise my hands to heaven. I am ashamed not to have
the strength to do so."

That went further than his earlier words to the Abbé.

Cocteau stayed at Villefranche, smoking steadily and drawing
himself in the mirror, until November. He went to London with the
Diaghilev company for the opening there of *Le Train Bleu* on November 22, returned to Paris on December 17, and called on Maritain almost immediately. "When I next saw you, in December,"
Maritain later wrote, "you came to talk about God."

It was during the following January and February, 1925, that
Cocteau, in addition to his daily smoking and his frequent conversations with Maritain, went once a week to Bellevue to smoke in a
domestic atmosphere with Louis Laloy. One wonders whether he
ever went from the Meudon talks "about God" directly to the Bellevue *fumerie:* the two suburbs are but a few miles apart. Jean
Hugo's diary shows Cocteau frequenting other Paris opiomanes and
seeing something of Picasso: perhaps it was during these weeks that
Picasso remarked that the odor of opium is the "least stupid" smell
in the world. On February 27 Cocteau spoke to the members of a
long-established lecture group in Paris called the Université des
Annales, composed chiefly of cultivated ladies of all ages; the talk,
called *La Jeunesse et le Scandale* and peppered with anecdotes
concerning artists and *scandales* he had known, is still brilliant
and charming to read; and when it was printed, as were all the
lectures in the series, in the Annales' own publication, a special
footnote announced that the interruptions of "approval, surprise
and delight" had been far too numerous to be indicated on the
printed page. One can imagine the delight of the ladies when Coc-

teau, at his most charming, took leave of them with a graceful: "I hope that as you return home each of you will take along with you the image of me less as a thinker than as the dancer I really am." Who would have thought that two weeks later he would be undergoing a cure, of the kind now called "cold turkey"?

The possibility of a return to the sacraments was probably not the main reason for Cocteau's decision to undergo an opium cure. Although the drug did not prevent him from delivering a brilliant lecture, it was making him impotent, it was frequently making him sick, and he was beginning to hold it responsible for his not writing. However, there was clearly a feeling that *should* there be a return to the sacraments, decency forbade that the Host and opium be mingled; and Max Jacob and Maritain, as well as Cocteau's doctors, participated in the arrangements for the cure. Shortly before entering the hospital Cocteau wrote to Etienne de Beaumont.

Cocteau to Comte Etienne de Beaumont
10 rue d'Anjou
February 1925

Mon cher Etienne,

I am very touched by your invitation, but I am in a pitiable state and cannot "go out." . . . Radiguet's death literally killed me. I did *Roméo* as though in a dream, and every day has deepened the hole into which I have been sinking. Pity me, dear Etienne — I know your great heart. Never will I forget Edith's tears at the time of the death of Jean Leftoy. . . .

In mid-March he allowed himself to be "locked up" in the Thermes Urbains — "The Urban Baths" — a private hospital at 15 rue Chateaubriand. An advertisement for this establishment can be found as far back as 1917 among the perfumers' and dressmakers' and jewelers' announcements in the Russian Ballet's souvenir program for *Parade*, where it calls itself *"La plus importante clinique médicale de Paris."* Cocteau was to stay there about six weeks. Perhaps he told his mother what he is known to have told her on the occasion of a later cure — that he was under treatment for "a liver complaint": on March 21 his brother Paul was married at a full-dress ceremony in the church of Saint-Honoré d'Eylau (the scene of Radiguet's funeral), and Jean's non-appearance at the church and at the reception that followed, given jointly by the two families, must have called for some such explanation.

Abstinence, aided by cathartics and enemas, was at that time the only cure for addiction, although additional touches seem to have been provided by Cocteau's doctors. "I spare you the diary of a 'cure,' " he wrote to Maritain, "showers, electric baths, nerves on edge, jerking legs that want to walk on the ceiling and stretch out across the street to the building opposite." Festoons of electrodes appear in several of a series of more or less Surrealist drawings that he made during the cure and published the next year in a volume called *Maison de Santé.* "Trying hard not to write," he says in a preface, "I drew. Otherwise my right hand would grow frantic from four o'clock to midnight. In this way I kept myself occupied and at the same time provided a young intern with data on my symptoms. It would be a mistake to look in these pictures for the slightest trace of delirium." The drawings are much concerned with eyes (featuring the pinpoint pupils of addicts) and with veins (suggesting that Cocteau was not unfamiliar with the needle); phallic symbols so proliferate as almost to give the cure itself the guise of a masochistic homosexual experience. Apparently it was an "easy" cure as cures go, but the drawings well express some of the physical and mental distress attendant on any withdrawal. As he put it in a letter to Max Jacob, "I had no idea what a drama this cure was to be. What they do is extract a veritable Chinese tree from your system." According to Jacques Maritain, Cocteau had smuggled into the hospital "a little box with a supply of pills — enough to escape from the pains of the withdrawal," but he made no use of them. Maritain wrote him often, Jacob everyday. (Jacob's letters are particularly rich and considerate.) He also received daily letters from Maurice Sachs, who continued to fill offstage the pageboy role he had played in *Roméo,* and from a still more recent acquaintance, a handsome youth named Jean Bourgoint. The doctors said "no visitors," but Cocteau charmed his nurse, Madame Jacquelin, and she made an occasional exception toward the end. The Hugos lived just opposite, at 17 rue Chateaubriand, and to emphasize their nearness and the continuity of things Valentine sent him a fanciful view of the hospital from her window, done in gouache.

Cocteau to Valentine and Jean Hugo

[n.d.]

Mézugos,

I love you and kiss you. I think of you every minute of the day. What decided me to come here was the knowledge that you would be close by, and I was right. Your proximity is a comfort to me during the very bad times, and there are plenty of those. Has Maurice told you that withdrawal was completed three days ago?

The same to the same

[n.d.]

Mézugos,

The picture of the Thermes is a masterpiece — a rose in the black of the night. Mme. Jacquelin has triumphantly thumb-tacked it to the wall . . . I am dying of loneliness. This suffering without suffering is atrocious. In my legs there is a queue of ten thousand people standing waiting for the opening of ticket windows that don't open. Keep sending me little surprises. The gouache transformed a day that was *very bad.*

Other letters to Valentine from the hospital show intensified anxiety about other friends' affection. "Auric hasn't yet answered the following letter I wrote him ten days ago: 'Deeply depressed without word from you.' Nor have the Laloys written. Many things are becoming clear, thanks to my stay here." "Please discover for me the real reason for Auric's silence despite my two letters. Work and laziness aren't enough, you will admit. . . . Very very depressed because of the Laloys' silence." "Here I am being cared for, but my friends are killing me. The pusillanimity of Auric and Ganda-rillas is *killing* me. Laloy does not answer my letters. . . . I am being *killed* by my friends, who are impeding my recovery. You who love me like a sister — I charge you to tell them, to telephone to the Laloys, etc. I will never forget that Maurice Sachs, Jean Bourgoint and Max Jacob have written me every day. Auric is a *monster.*" He dismissed Valentine's suggestion that the hospital might be withholding or opening some of his mail, and asked her to reassure herself on that score: "I *implore* you to come in, and ask downstairs for Mme. Jacquelin."

The various crises passed; the cure ended the last week in April
— earlier than it should have, Cocteau always thought, because the
hospital building was scheduled for demolition. The doctors sent
him to spend a fortnight in a quiet hotel at Versailles, and on May
11 Jean Hugo wrote in his diary: "Dinner at Mme. Cocteau's. Cocteau returned from Versailles this afternoon. Maurice Sachs comes
in after dinner."

The aesthetic, comfortably brought-up but penniless Maurice
was now working as desk-clerk in a hotel run by friends. Before
Roméo, he had been Cocteau's fan from the time of *Antigone,* and
had haunted the bar of the Boeuf; the *N.R.F.* collected volume of
Cocteau's *Poésies* was his "Bible"; his "head was on fire" when a
friend brought him to 10 rue d'Anjou and introduced him to Cocteau; and in his own room, "almost entirely papered with photographs of Cocteau," there was "one particular portrait that I
prayed to every day." The hysterical, dark-haired Maurice was not
handsome, being somewhat puffy-faced and pudgy, but his charm is
said by all to have been considerable, qualifying him to become
one of Cocteau's "children": there was a group of young men whom
Cocteau called his *"gosses,"* his *"enfants"* or his *"jeunes."* The
other leading "child," Jean Bourgoint, was nineteen, blue-eyed,
tall, large-limbed, a "Greek god," bound by twin-like ties to an
equally beautiful sister, Jeanne, who sometimes worked as a mannequin for the dressmaker Madeleine Vionnet and with whom he
lived, at home, in a strange kind of isolation *à deux* (they slept in
the same bedroom) despite the presence of a worldly though im-
poverished widowed mother and a brother who, although really
Jeanne's twin, was unsympathetic to both of them. Jeanne, somewhat crazy, had once been married for a year to a dim man of
business, quickly expelled by the spiritual twins. Like Maurice
Sachs, Jean Bourgoint was penniless and poorly employed; he was
lazy, drew a little, and had a natural, untutored literary style and a
complete lack of practicality; people took him up for his beauty,
his remarkable sweetness, and his homosexual possibilities. Cocteau was at once struck by those qualities: meeting him in a friend's
house shortly before entering the hospital, he gave him "his first
whiff of opium in a kiss."

Cocteau has been accused of trying to "ruin" Jean Bourgoint,
that whiff of opium being the first step in the process, and of simi-

larly "ruining" other youngsters. Lists have been made of Cocteau's "victims," with Bourgoint close to the top. It would be more accurate to say that among the innumerable charming young men who made themselves available to Cocteau were a number with a bent for one kind or another of self-destruction, like Radiguet (although Radiguet was the only genius among them) and, as it turned out, Maurice Sachs; that bent Cocteau seems to have recognized, and he seems often to have been willing, at some level of his consciousness, to further the process. But Bourgoint belonged to another category — that of parasites: he was a beautiful, sunny, candid "silly," a simpleton, slothful, greedy and charming — Glenway Wescott has called him "one of God's fools" — with no ambition whatever, either for glory or ruin: as will be seen, the parasite, far from being a victim, eventually achieved a remarkable salvation.

There were other "children," but Sachs and Bourgoint were the most in view, and both were to be radically affected by their intimacy with Cocteau. Both were doubtless in Cocteau's thoughts when he wrote to Max Jacob on April 3: "Phenomena of withdrawal: Sexual comeback (!) – memory — remembering of telephone numbers — poetry — it takes time." But when he left the hospital the last week in April, it was to discover that while he could still make practical use of the infatuated Maurice, it was as though he were seeing the equally infatuated Bourgoint with new eyes: the Greek god had turned into a too big, too clumsy, not very bright young mortal who no longer held sexual appeal and who threatened to become an embarrassment. Bourgoint hadn't the means to procure opium regularly, but since that first whiff he had been smoking when he could: Cocteau sensed some of his strange qualities, recognized a certain responsibility for him, and for some years was to alternate uneasily between enabling him to smoke and trying to procure him an independence.

Scarcely out of the hospital, Cocteau suddenly found himself hurtled back to the sacraments.

The background, in Paris that June of 1925, was the International Exposition of Decorative Arts, with pavilions lining both banks of the Seine between the Pont Alexandre III and the Pont de l'Alma, Lalique's glass fountains playing, and a hundred exhibitions by painters and other artists in galleries throughout the city.

Both the Russian and the Swedish ballets performed, the Revue Nègre was the rage (it introduced Josephine Baker), and Cocteau had an exhibition of his own, at the Galerie Briant-Robert in the rue d'Argenteuil, chiefly of drawings and stage designs. Among the quieter activities of the summer was the planning, by Maritain, Massis and others, of a literary series to be called *Le Roseau d'Or* (The Golden Reed), after the name of an already existing Catholic magazine of which Maritain was editor. Cocteau was invited to contribute a volume, and on June 15, the day his exhibition opened, he dined at Meudon with some of the others to discuss the project. What happened has been described by Cocteau, by Maritain, and by Raïssa. The dinner was animated; Cocteau, "cured," was in excellent form though physically wobbly. He was to leave at ten: an automobile was to call for him and take him to the Russian Ballet — probably in time to see a preview performance of Auric's *Les Matelots*, with choreography by Massine, who was once again with the company, and with Lifar as chief dancer. But the automobile was late. That day, Maritain had had a telegram from Père Charles Henrion, back in France from the Sahara for part of the summer, to say that he would be coming to Meudon; and before Cocteau's automobile arrived the missionary appeared, a tall, tanned figure in a white burnous. Embroidered on the breast of his robe was the melodramatic device invented by Père Foucauld to rivet the eyes of the infidel — a crimson cross above a blood-red heart.

"Jacques, was that your trap? Had you been lying in wait for just that moment?" Cocteau wrote later. "A heart entered, a red heart surmounted by a red cross, in the middle of a white shape that glided in, bent over us, spoke, shook hands. The heart hypnotized me, diverted me from the face, beheaded the burnous. The heart was the white shape's real face: it was as though Charles were holding his head on his breast, like the martyrs. No wonder the sunburned head was like a mirror-image of the heart, a mirage in all that African light. . . . Let me come to the most important point — the man's easy grace: compared with it I felt my best to be mere stagey charm. He smiled, told stories, exchanged recollections with Massis. I, stupid, 'groggy,' as boxers say, was gazing as through a thick windowpane at the white shape moving against the sky. I suppose that your wife and your guests must have realized what was going on: room, books, friends — nothing existed any longer. It was at that moment, Maritain, that you gave me a push. A push from your athletic soul. Everyone saw that I was losing my footing. No one came to my aid, because they knew that to help me, at that moment, would be my ruin. . . . A priest gave me the same shock as Stravinsky and Picasso."

"He is handsome," Raïssa wrote of Père Charles in her diary. ". . . . the entire company is impressed. I see Jean Cocteau standing silent beside the window, *caught*. Clearly this is God's answer to our prayers, to our anxiety; for several weeks we were wondering to what priest we should send Cocteau, for the time had come — and we could think of none."

And Maritain wrote, addressing Cocteau: "God was hurrying you. . . . If there was a plot, the angels were responsible. . . . As soon as Charles entered . . . we knew he had come only for you."

"The auto arrives at ten-thirty, half an hour after Charles," Raïssa noted on the sixteenth. "When I see Cocteau out I ask him to attend the Mass that Charles is to say in our chapel the nineteenth, feast of the Sacred Heart. Cocteau replies evasively. But I am confident. The moment Charles came in Cocteau saw — I cannot doubt it — the sign of his destiny in a human heart. The heart with which he signs his letters has all at once become *the heart of Jesus*.

"*Same day, Tuesday, June 16*. Reverdy came to see us for the first time. We speak of Cocteau, of Charles. Reverdy thinks we must wait no longer, that Cocteau must make his confession to Charles and take communion with us on the nineteenth. Vera [Raïssa's sister, also a convert] immediately telephones to the Bishop's office in Versailles and asks that Charles, without being consulted, be authorized to hear confession in our house. This is granted. We tell Charles, who protests strongly, resists, but in the end cannot refuse the task we pitilessly impose on him.

"*Wednesday, June 17*. Jacques went to see Cocteau, to encourage him to make his confession to Charles immediately. Delicate, difficult mission.* Cocteau promised to come tomorrow to *talk* with Charles, nothing more.

"*Thursday, June 18*. Jacques called for Jean at his house and

---

* In annotating his wife's diary, Jacques Maritain has interpolated here: "Reverdy was present, and vigorously urged Cocteau. 'How can you understand anything without the sacraments? They are the earphones! Take the earphones!'"

brought him here about four o'clock. Cocteau had a long talk with Charles in the salon. . . . Finally we heard Charles and Cocteau go up to the chapel. Then Charles called Jacques. Jean made his confession, saw Jacques, and left, deeply shaken.

"Friday, June 19, feast of the Sacred Heart. Charles said Mass in our chapel. Cocteau took Communion with us. . . . Maman attended Mass as usual. One more example for her. *Misericordias Domini."*

Cocteau had returned to the fold.

Why had he done it? Raïssa's phrase, that once Père Henrion entered the room Cocteau was "caught," describes only the final, histrionic step of the process. His own words — "A priest gave me the same shock as Stravinsky and Picasso" — reveal how immediately the dynamism of the missionary had made itself apparent: it was an artist, almost an angel in costume, that had appeared. Both the missionary and the differently impressive Maritain were older than Cocteau: for a moment he was back among his older artist-heroes. Furthermore, Cocteau was enfeebled — "groggy" — vulnerable; one senses the intensity with which the others in the room displayed their conviction that the angel had appeared for him; and neither Raïssa nor Maritain hides the relentless — in their own word the "pitiless" — speed with which they brought the matter to a climax.

But before the grogginess was the opium cure, before the cure was the opium, and before the opium was Radiguet's death; and Radiguet's death had shattered the picture of himself that Cocteau had been building up for several years — of himself as at once the protector and the protégé of the prodigy, as one who after a series of attempts at attachment had at last found someone who was truly a hitherto missing part of himself, with whom he could accomplish great artistic things — whether vicariously or directly made little difference. Supported by Radiguet, he had done better work than ever in the face of the antagonism of the Dadaists and Surrealists, with whom in so many ways he felt himself in sympathy and by whom he had a wish, though by no means a total wish, to be accepted; and Radiguet's work seems to have given him the kind of satisfaction that an artist usually feels in his own — a state of affairs that might well not have continued had Radiguet lived. In his own language — his mentions of his various "moultings" —

Cocteau had frequently confessed that he thought of himself as "a changed man"; he was accustomed to conversions; his self-image had been anything but stable and continuous; his self-doubts were fundamental, welling up from the deep sources of his sexual guilt. For a time the merger with the amazing Radiguet had eased all that. Then came what can truly be called death and destruction: Radiguet's death brought the destruction of a precarious equilibrium; without him life was unbearable. Opium partially restored the balance: as Cocteau said later, "I preferred an artificial equilibrium to no equilibrium at all." But the artificial equilibrium began to show cracks and dangers: "Beware the shadow of the silence produced by your pipe," he was soon writing in a verse "to be inscribed on a bamboo," and in another verse he invented the pun-word *"artifi-ciel,"* reminiscent of Baudelaire's "artificial paradises" of hashish; his writing had been reduced to the brief notes on Jean the Bird-catcher's drawings. Radiguet's support was gone; opium was imperfect, bringing with it what seemed to be (but probably were not) new sicknesses, new depressions; his friends were tirelessly reminding him of his childhood religion, which was at once authority, refuge and absolution. Conversion was in the air. Jacques Copeau, of the *N.R.F.* and the Théâtre du Vieux-Colombier, had been converted; and Pierre Reverdy, and Gide's old companion Henri Ghéon; Gide himself was said to be on the way. Into the room glided a new mentor in white robes with a blood-red heart . . .

One cannot help wondering whether Cocteau — who, despite his frequent denial of intelligence ("Intelligence is not my strong point," he wrote), seems to have been by far the most intelligent member of the cast of the sacramental drama — ever for a moment ceased, as the drama unfolded, to think of himself as being on a stage: as being reborn there as he had died onstage nightly in *Roméo.* If he was dramatizing himself, he was doing it, of course, with all the "sincerity" of the most dedicated *artiste.*

Maritain wrote him ecstatically, enclosing a "relic from Lisieux": "What a great friend of God you can be, my dear Jean! Keep your heart for him alone." Père Henrion sent the news to Paul Claudel: Claudel wrote at once to Cocteau to express "the immense joy I experience in your conversion, which occurred at the very moment I was in Avila gazing at the radiant face of our sister

Theresa. . . . How glad your mother must be. . . . I embrace you fraternally *in X°* [*in Christo*]." And Claudel wrote to Jacques Copeau: "I have seen Cocteau. He is utterly transformed: there is a light on his face." Jean Hugo noted in his diary on July 13: "Cocteau comes to rue Chateaubriand and tells us of his plans for Catholic activity." Maurice Sachs, fired by Cocteau's talk of God and the church, was sent by Cocteau to Meudon; after a single hour of conversation Maritain passed him on to a priest for instruction; six weeks later, on August 29, the eighteen-year-old who had so recently been praying to Cocteau's photograph was baptized in the Maritains' chapel, renouncing, as the baptismal certificate puts it, "the errors of the Jews." Raïssa (who expressed some well-founded doubt about Maurice in her diary) was his godmother; Cocteau was his godfather — but in absentia.

On August 1, after persuading the still-infatuated Bourgoint, too, to join the Maritain circle for instruction (he said later that to ease his own conscience he wanted the boy "saved" — from what he did not specify), Cocteau had left Paris for Villefranche. There he installed himself again in the hotel where he had stared so long and profitably into the mirror — the Welcome. It was, and is, a quayside inn, quiet enough, but in those days becoming riotous whenever its bar and bedrooms accommodated sailors from visiting warships and the prostitutes who flocked to Villefranche to meet them from the brothels of Nice and Marseilles. There, after a few weeks, he would begin a *Letter to Jacques Maritain,* a pamphlet celebrating the joys of an artist's disintoxication and his return to the sacraments — an edifying document designed to bring other artists into the fold, away from the atheistic Surrealists: this was one of his "plans for Catholic activity." As it turned out, it was touch and go as to which would reach its end first — his composition of the pamphlet celebrating his abstinence from opium, or the abstinence itself. He said later that his abstinence lasted five months. If that is precise, then he was smoking again even before finishing the *Letter.* Even in the *Letter* itself he does not condemn opium outright, saying "I do not regret the experience." But he adds: "Opium resembles religion to the extent that an illusionist resembles Jesus." The equivocal situation which developed over the next months, and which apparently became known to the Maritains rather later than to others, has been sadly commented on by

Raïssa: "At the moment when the poet's soul, purified by the sacraments, was full of love for God, Charles had given him a precious last word of advice — 'Remain free.' Cocteau has not always obeyed this in the sense in which it was intended."

But before beginning the *Letter*, Cocteau plunged, at the Hotel Welcome, into a new period of creation, one of the most fruitful of his life. He drew illustrations for a new edition of *Thomas l'Imposteur*. He had brought with him some poems written before and during his cure, and now he wrote others: the result was to be the volume *Opéra*, probably the best known, certainly along with *Plain-Chant* the finest, and unquestionably the most essentially coctelian, of his collections of verse. And at the Welcome he wrote the scripts of two dramas. One was his play *Orphée*, now less well known than the film he made from it twenty years later. He had planned, he said, to write a play about the Virgin and her inexplicable pregnancy, but "The plot lent itself to such misinterpretations that I gave it up," and it became, instead — we shall see how, in part — a play about Orpheus and the inexplicable birth of poems. The other was a libretto — again based on a Greek myth, that of Oedipus, for an oratorio by Stravinsky, which he knew from the beginning would never be sung in the words he was writing, but only in Latin translation.

The fact is that opium, especially in playing an important role in the creation of a certain poem, one of Cocteau's finest, a poem which in turn led directly to the creation of the play *Orphée*, was showing itself, despite all its disadvantages, to be, at this high point of his career, far more useful to the artist Cocteau than the sacraments.

L'Ange Heurtebise, Orphée, Oedipus Rex
(*1925–1926*)

Some time the previous spring, in the midst of his addiction, Cocteau had been invited to lunch by Picasso, in Picasso's flat in the rue la Boétie. "When heavily drugged," he wrote later, "I would sometimes fall into a sleep that seemed interminable but turned out to have lasted half a second." (He is describing a state called "hypnogogic hallucination," between waking and sleeping, with strong feelings of reality.) "In the elevator I imagined that I was growing larger alongside something terrible — I don't know what — that was going to last forever. A voice was calling to me: 'My name is on the plate!' A jolt woke me, and I read on the brass door-plate: HEURTEBISE ELEVATOR." * During lunch the conversation touched on miracles, with Picasso characteristically remarking that "Everything is a miracle: it's a miracle not to melt in the bathtub, like a lump of sugar." After forgetting the episode in the elevator, that night Cocteau woke abruptly; "the next day I staggered about, half sunk in a swamp of dreams, horribly disturbed. An angel was dwelling within me, without my suspecting it; to make me aware of i's presence it took the name 'Heurtebise,' which little by little became an obsession." The cry, "My name is on the plate!" came through as a message: Cocteau knew that it was his anguish, or whatever it was he was full of, naming itself. There were several more days of torment: "My crises followed one another more rapidly, and became a single crisis comparable to pre-delivery pains. A monstrous delivery, however. . . . Imagine parthenogenesis, a couple made up of a single body that gives birth. Finally, one night when I was thinking of suicide, the expulsion began, in the rue d'Anjou. It took seven days, during which the newcomer behaved with amazing cheek, forcing me to write against my will." The newborn was a poem, *L'Ange Heurtebise.* He finished it before entering the hospital, and it was published in a magazine, *Les Feuilles libres,* in its issue for May-June. The next time Cocteau called on Picasso, he looked at the door-plate in the elevator. "On it was the name OTIS-PIFRE; the elevator had changed its make." We, and perhaps Cocteau too, are left to wonder whether it had ever been called Heurtebise.

Such is Cocteau's account of the genesis of a remarkable poem, obscure in details of its fantasy, ingenious in technique — some think over-ingenious in its wordplay — defiant of translation, but certainly one of the most striking evocations ever written of the in-

---

* "Heurtebise" is a not uncommon name in France, both as a family name and the name of country properties, usually in exposed situations — something like "Wuthering Heights" or "Windybank." *"Heurte"* suggests a kind of buffer; *"bise"* a wind.

visible, mysterious guest, the "angel," who swoops out of the unknown to rape or otherwise enter the artist, remains quiet within
him for a time, then suddenly awakes, causes excruciating suffering, and finally, if all goes well, expels itself and astonishes the
wracked artist by the visible form it has assumed. *L'Ange Heurtebise* can thus be read, if one wishes, as a description of the painful
process by which it was itself created. More deeply, it is a beautiful
and spiritual fantasy of passive love.

The angel is a figure that Cocteau had liked to use from the time
he introduced it into his wartime preface to an airplane company's
brochure and then, with a kind of profligate inevitability, into the
aerial *Cap de Bonne-Espérance*, where Garros' plane is made (not
too skillfully, in this early poem) to personify the Annunciation in
being both an angel and a "pregnant Virgin," and where shells, too,
are angels spitting deadly gas. Cocteau says he derived from a certain Madame Bessonet-Fabre the information that in Hebrew
"angel" and "angle" are synonyms; and on that identity he constructed, here and there throughout his works, clever bits of wordplay, especially in reference to Cubism. Unfortunately it would
seem either that he misunderstood Madame Bessonet-Fabre or that
she misinformed him: Hebrew scholars find no connection between
the two words in their language. Gabriel was one of Cocteau's favorite angels: the Annunciation is the theme of several early
poems, as well as of the "miracle photograph" made at Grasse in
1918: the poet constantly participates in the announcement of his
own pregnancy. Gradually, in his work, the angel image gathers
force and intensity. In *Plain-Chant*, the beautiful poems of desire
for Radiguet, Radiguet himself is the angel, the "soldier of the nine
sisters," who "takes" the poet, mingles with him, and is more precious than the resulting poem:

> Tu m'empoignes par la main.
>
> Ange de glace . . .
> Ton gantelet me tourmente.
>
> Le coeur indifférent à ce que je serai,
>   Aux gloires du poème,
> Je vivrai, libre enfin, par toi seule serré,
>   En te serrant de même,

> Alors profondément devenus à nous deux
> Une seule machine
> A maints têtes et bras, ainsi que sont les dieux,
> Dans les temples de Chine.*

Writing of Radiguet in a postscript to a small facsimile edition of two of the boy's notebooks published in March, 1925, Cocteau said, "I knew he would die quickly. . . . I respect his angelic exit." In *L'Ange Heurtebise,* the angel resembles Radiguet even to having *"joues en feu"* (flaming cheeks), the very title of one of Radiguet's books. The imagery is even more strongly sexual and pederastic:

> L'ange Heurtebise, d'une brutalité
> Incroyable saute sur moi.   De grâce
> Ne saute pas si fort,
> Garçon bestial, fleur de haute
> Stature.
> Je m'en suis alité. En voilà
> Des façons . . .
>
> Cheveux d'ange Heurtebise, lourd
> Sceptre mâle . . .†

Homosexual desire; possession by the one desired; and at the same time identification with him; hands and gloves — all those familiar themes, the constant elements of Cocteau's narcissism and verse, had been heightened by opium to such a point that the emergent poem, "at once inspired, and formal as a chess game," was, he considered, a perfect work of art. "If someone could prove that I would be signing my death sentence if I didn't burn *L'Ange Heurtebise,* I might burn it," he wrote later. "But if someone proved to me that I would be signing my death sentence if I didn't

* You grip me by the hand, / Angel of ice / Your gauntlet torments me. / With my heart indifferent to what I shall be, / To the glories of the poem, / I shall live, free at last, held tight by you alone, / And holding you just as close, / Then, having become, in essence, the two of us, / A single machine / With many heads and arms like the gods / In the temples of China. (Note the feminine *e* on *seule* — one of Cocteau's equivalents of Proust's Albertine.)

† L'Ange Heurtebise, with incredible / Brutality leaps on me. I pray you / Don't leap so hard, / Bestial boy, flower of high / Stature. / It has put me to bed. What / Manners you have! / The hair of l'Ange Heurtebise, heavy / male sceptre.

add or subtract one syllable, I still could not touch it. I would refuse, and die." And: "I have written only one poem in my life with luck favoring me to the very end: it is *L'Ange Heurtebise*."

The reader who has followed Cocteau's history this far must already have perceived the absence of a certain familiar element from the foregoing analysis (partly Cocteau's own) of the genesis of *L'Ange Heurtebise:* apart from Radiguet, who is here in a special role, the ever-changing but ever-present "someone else" who has hovered in the background of his other works has not in this case been mentioned. Not that the inevitable "someone else" necessarily diminishes the coctelianism of a work by Cocteau, any more than Cocteau's own presence in the work of younger writers like Anouilh and Ionesco diminishes their accomplishment. Everything that Cocteau created bears his unmistakable mark, but as one of the ingredients to be assimilated in his creative process he needed someone else's distinct and definite artistic presence, and preferably personal presence as well. To recall a few, Madame de Noailles had been a presence both artistic and personal in the early poetry; the ballet *Schéhérazade* loomed close behind *Le Dieu Bleu;* Stravinsky's personal presence was exaggerated, but in *Parade* he is present with *Petrushka* and the *scandale* of the *Rite;* the Futurists were there too; we have examined the myth of Apollinaire, described the infatuation with Picasso, and chronicled the real presence of Radiguet; Sophocles and Shakespeare, too, are in the list. Although *L'Ange Heurtebise* is the purest and most concentrated Cocteau, no more than the rest does it lack the essential ingredient of outside influence. This time Cocteau himself has provided not direct information but a characteristic clue.

Following closely on *L'Ange Heurtebise,* Cocteau's play *Orphée,* written now during the summer of 1925, presents the angel Heurtebise again, as a character in the cast. We have already noticed several fictions put forward by Cocteau after the death of Rainer Maria Rilke concerning Rilke himself and Cocteau's *Orphée —* that Rilke had seen it performed in Berlin, that Rilke was translating it when he died, that in a telegram to Madame Klossowska about Cocteau and myth Rilke said that he "loved" Cocteau (whereas what he had actually expressed was "admiration"). Now it becomes clear why Cocteau felt obliged to invent that myth of personal closeness to Rilke. He had been following Rilke's work, he once said, since Blaise Cendrars revealed it to him in 1916 (one doesn't know how much of it he actually read); just before Cocteau's *L'Ange Heurtebise*, Rilke published in rapid succession a striking pair of masterpieces: the *Duino Elegies*, perhaps his most famous work, which contain swarms of angels, and the series of fifty-five *Sonnets to Orpheus* — both volumes dated 1923. In Cocteau's mind the myth of the personal closeness must have served to provide a kind of blessing to the closeness with which his pair of masterpieces followed after Rilke's on the same subject. Opium, inducing a half-dream state in the elevator, might be said in the absence of a better word to have *fertilized* Rilke's angels for Cocteau, producing *L'Ange Heurtebise*, and it must have been in large part his awareness of the intense relevance of that poem to himself that induced him to follow it with a direct sequel — to avoid the peripheral myth of "the Virgin and her inexplicable pregnancy" and to write, more directly, of "Orpheus and the inexplicable birth of poems."

The play *Orphée* was finished at Villefranche in September, 1925. Cocteau read it first to Stravinsky, who was living at nearby Montboron on the outskirts of Nice. The second reading would be to Jean Hugo, in Paris, in December; and the play would be produced, with décor by Hugo, the following June.

Concerning the oratorio, *Oedipus Rex*, Igor Stravinsky has among his papers an orange folder, containing over fifty letters, telegrams and other documents, labeled:

OEDIPUS REX
Irritating and futile correspondence with J. Cocteau*
on the subject of the first performance of *Oedipus*, in
which many people wanted to have their say, and which
considerably frayed my nerves.
I. Stravinsky
* and many others.

Those of the documents which originated with the composer himself, including a letter agreement with Cocteau, dated "Nice, October 11, 1925," in which he proposes that Cocteau compose a text on a theme from antique tragedy for translation into Latin, have been published by Mr. Stravinsky and Robert Craft. Many of the rest are in Cocteau's hand, and all but one or two of these relate, as Stravinsky says, not to the writing of the work but to the confusions and chicaneries in Paris preceding the first performance at the Théâtre Sarah-Bernhardt on May 30, 1927.

It was because he liked Cocteau's version of *Antigone*, Stravinsky says, that he asked him to write the *Oedipus Rex* libretto. They had met by chance the previous summer in a sleeping car (Cocteau characteristically calls it a "reconciliation"), and following that meeting Cocteau sent to Stravinsky in Montboron a few of the "Jean l'Oiseleur" self-portrait drawings he was doing in the Hotel Welcome in Villefranche. He used the drawings as letter paper, scribbling messages to Stravinsky around his face. One of Stravinsky's requests in the October, 1925 letter agreement was the following: "I should like these lines to bear witness to the promise we exchange to keep our collaboration secret, not merely for its duration, but even after the piece is finished: i.e., never to mention it in any form whatever (books, letters, articles, interviews, speeches.)" The reason for the secrecy was Stravinsky's wish to prepare the work as a surprise for Diaghilev on the twentieth anniversary of the impresario's first theatrical activity, which would occur during the summer of 1927; and for a time the habitually indiscreet Cocteau seems to have observed the composer's wish with surprising fidelity — there exist very few remarks by him about this collaboration. He set quickly to work. Stravinsky has said that "Cocteau's first libretto draft was full of ideas. The second was still full of ideas. I didn't want ideas. I wanted *words*" — recalling a similar remark by Mallarmé to Degas about the fabrication of sonnets. Elsewhere he has said that he told Cocteau that what he wanted was "not an action drama, but a 'still-life,' and that the libretto must be conventional," and that Cocteau's first draft was "a music drama told in horribly meretricious prose." However, by October 28, when Cocteau left Villefranche for Paris, he was able to take with him a text that Stravinsky had approved, to be given to a translator.

Along with it he took *Orphée*. There was a question of *Orphée*'s being produced by the repertory company headed by the famous acting couple Georges and Ludmilla Pitoëff, but Cocteau's friend the actor Marcel Herrand had also asked to produce it, making difficulties. "The second half of vacation is sad," Cocteau had writ-

ten to Valentine on September 9, 1925, "but at the end is the sun of
our reunion. Especially since we must see each other for work on
Orphée. I am very vexed about Herrand. 1. He is in Canada.
2. He would deprive me of Madame Pitoëff. 3. How can he produce my play? 3. [*sic*]. If he consents to play with the Pitoëffs, he
will play the part of Heurtebise, which I wrote for the film actor
Haziza, who would be marvelous in the role. *Zut.* You see the problems. Tomorrow night I read my play to Igor S." *

There was also the *Letter to Jacques Maritain,* to show to Maritain himself. It had been arranged that the *Letter,* and a *Reply to
Jean Cocteau,* to be written by Maritain, would be publicized simultaneously, like twin political pamphlets.

On Christmas Eve, 1925, after completing most of his business
in Paris, Cocteau took Communion, apparently at Meudon, with
Maurice Sachs and Jean Bourgoint. As Jacques Maritain was to put
it, somewhat violently, in his *Reply:* "The Lord is generous. His
grace explodes like a grenade, making many victims at once. He
did not want you to return to his house alone. Two baptisms . . .
one vocation to the priesthood . . . followed upon your encounter with Jesus. (Six months later, it was between your two godsons
that I saw you take Communion on Christmas Eve.)"

The "vocation" was Sachs's. Soon after being confirmed by the
bishop of Versailles on September 13, he had written to Cocteau in
Villefranche of his wish to become a priest, and a week after the
Christmas Eve Communion, on January 2, 1926, he was to enter the
Carmelite Seminary in Paris. "Poor Sachs is buying his soutane,"
Cocteau wrote to Max Jacob. "I haven't at all concealed from him
what I think of the world of the clergy, but the *anger* of the Jews,
free-thinkers and Protestants close to his family is driving him to
the seminary." ("When we learned that you were at the 'Seminary,' we thought it must be a new night club," Sachs says one of
his friends wrote him; and Jean Wiener tells of almost losing control of his automobile in sheer amazement when, on his return to
Paris from a South American tour, he was suddenly hailed in the
Place St. Sulpice by a figure in a soutane and recognized the semi-

* The letter continues: "He is kindly helping me with the musical side, which I am
organizing myself. . . ." As staged, the play *Orphée* was accompanied by no music.
Stravinsky "believes that there was a question of incidental music for it, but cannot
remember what it was to have been."

narian as Sachs — whom he had last seen with a carnation in his buttonhole among opium fumes at 10 rue d'Anjou.)

Bourgoint, communicating at that Midnight Mass, was on leave from barracks in Nîmes, where he was doing his military service and whence he had come to Paris to spend Christmas with his mother and sister. After his baptism in the presence of the Maritains, he had spent part of September and October with Cocteau at Villefranche, where they paddled together about the bay in a tiny boat baptized by Cocteau the "Heurtebise"; he began his military service November 1. The army sent him first to Metz, in the north. "Poor Jean leaves for Metz this morning in this cold," Cocteau wrote, after his return to Paris, to Glenway Wescott at the Welcome. (Wescott had arrived at the hotel in mid-September with Monroe Wheeler, and the four men had become acquainted, with a special affection developing between Wescott and Bourgoint.) "He wanted Oran," Cocteau went on. "I asked for Oran, and now suddenly I'm afraid that my request will be granted and that Abd el-Krim will start up the war again." Bourgoint was wretched at Metz. "We're dying of cold," he wrote Wescott, "we have only ten minutes to wash, and the rest of the day we wash the horses. Without the Blessed Virgin I'd cry all night." It was Cocteau's influence that had caused him to be transferred from Metz not to Oran, but to Nimes. On New Year's Eve, two days before Sachs entered the seminary, Bourgoint was back in the Nîmes barracks, writing to Wescott about "heavy Catalan peasants dancing lightly to the sound of guitars." In Nîmes, too, his work was washing horses, but the provençal sun made life easier.

In Cocteau's case, that Christmas Eve communion between his two godsons resembled, in a way, that other Christmas Eve, exactly ten years before, when from behind the front lines in Flanders he had sent out contrasting Christmas messages — "silence of Bethlehem, smell of the manger" to the Abbé Mugnier, and "Senegalese sharpshooters do the belly dance" to André Gide. For as he knelt to receive the sacrament, he must just have smoked his evening opium pipes (he wrote that he usually smoked three at eleven o'clock); and Maritain was now reading with unsuspecting delight the *Letter* in which the opium-smoking communicant had so recently written disparagingly of opium that it "resembles religion to the extent that an illusionist resembles Jesus."

On New Year's Day, 1926, Cocteau returned to Villefranche for the rest of the winter. "I am happy," he wrote Jean Hugo from the Welcome on January 16. "Yesterday I saw the Pitoëffs and all is settled about our collaboration. I beg you to see them the moment you are back. They will be expecting you — they want you for the maquette. Chanel is attending to the costumes." He found Stravinsky, himself just returned from a concert tour of Germany and Switzerland, eagerly awaiting the Latin text of *Oedipus Rex*. The translator to whom they had confided the task in Paris (probably on Maritain's recommendation) was a twenty-year-old seminarian named Jean Daniélou (later a celebrated Jesuit theologian and now a cardinal), and on January 8 Cocteau wrote to him. "I await — we await — your first text with the greatest impatience. Stravinsky calls it 'waiting for the proofs,' as though my French were coming back from the photographer." The letter and the text must have crossed each other in the mail, for the first bar of Stravinsky's score is marked "January 11, 1926." Cocteau now drafted, for the oratorio, a prologue and several brief narrations to introduce the separate scenes — texts that were to remain in French and to be recited by a "speaker." These, too, required consultation with the composer, and Cocteau wrote later of "returning from Stravinsky's along the Montboron road, my ears still dazzled by the golden, annular, chiseled music of *Oedipus Rex*." Elsewhere he attributes one of those adjectives to Stravinsky himself, saying that the composer told him he wanted the music to be "in tight ringlets, like Zeus's beard." "I say nothing about what you let me hear," he wrote Stravinsky after one visit to him at Montboron. "This would require a vocabulary of the kind that embarrasses you and me. To such delights it is possible to react only with one's face, one's gaze, and silence. I have been saved from my shadows only through my work with you — and God." (With Stravinsky, Cocteau seemed doomed always to strike the wrong note. The composer found the language of that letter "stagey" and displeasing: he was on the eve of his own return to the sacraments, those of the Russian Orthodox Church — a return that would be considerably less publicized than Cocteau's.)

The language might be stagey, but the shadows were real enough: all the palliatives that he had been feeding himself since the death of Radiguet — work, "children," opium, cure, sacraments, escapes to Villefranche, Stravinsky — were not saving him from depression.

There were echoes from the seminary. The director had quickly recognized Sachs to be a somewhat special case. It was discovered that his decision to renounce the world's vanities had not included the payment of a number of debts, and it was suggested to his friends, including Maritain, that it would be well to satisfy the creditors who were beginning to knock at the seminary door. Also, although beginning seminarians customarily wore civil garb, the director reluctantly granted Maurice's request, seconded by Maritain, that he be allowed to wear a soutane. "I was trying to build an impassable barrier between temptation and myself," Sachs wrote later, "a black fence that would keep out the human beast for good. . . . When, after kissing it (as is the custom before dressing), I put it on for the first time, it gave me a pleasure that was not altogether pious. Black makes one look taller and slimmer; in black one thinks oneself handsome. . . . and, recalling that even as a child I dreamed of being a girl, it is easy to imagine what strange longings, unknown even to myself, were gratified when I would take the folds of my gown in both hands, like a young woman, to climb the stairs." And once in his soutane, Maurice says, "I dreamed only of converting the world and persuading Cocteau to enter a monastery — something that in my astonishing naïveté I believed was possible and even impending."

In Villefranche there were sounds and other elements out of harmony with Stravinsky's Zeus-like music. Glenway Wescott, spending the winter at the Welcome writing his novel *The Grandmothers*, told in letters to friends of a gradually swelling chorus of American voices in the hotel — those of navy wives assembling to await their husbands' arrival on the destroyer *Pittsburgh;* and by the time the ship reached the bay, early in January, other sounds were added. "We are living in a brothel," Wescott wrote; and Cocteau told friends about his throbbing "hotel-brothel," full of carousing sailors fighting, whoring, and belly-dancing in the bar: the sailors in their tight revealing suits added to the atmosphere a special carnality dear to homosexuals.* (When the *Pittsburgh* left, with its band playing the "Marseillaise" in a sad, slow tempo, it trained its

---

* "I wonder why young men should be put in such costumes except to excite desire." (Julien Green, *Terre Lointaine*, p. 25.)

searchlights on the weeping girls waving from the windows of the hotel.) Bourgoint came on forty-eight-hour leave, ecstatic to be away from peasants and horse dung, eager to smoke a few pipes, depressed when the time came to leave. Bourgoint was still calf-like and lovelorn; and Cocteau, who at this time tended to extol chastity without mentioning that his own had its source in a return of opium-induced impotence, encouraged the consolation offered the boy by Wescott but showed signs of jealousy if it seemed to be going too far.* Wescott, Wisconsin-born and in French eyes puritanical and with unshaded negative-positive views, startled Cocteau by reproaching him for hypocrisy in simultaneously smoking and correcting the proofs of the very *Letter* in which he associated, in dramatic terms, his abandonment of opium with his return to the sacraments. Stravinsky, too, saw what was taking place, but said nothing, either of the piety or the smoking, both of them in his eyes equally "stagey." Cocteau was conducting a correspondence with Max Jacob in which he was beginning to hint that his inability to achieve "perfection" (i.e., sinlessness) was making him wonder whether the effort was worthwhile; Jacob confessed frankly that his own chief reason for living at his abbey was his inability to live in Paris without sinning, and that, in any case, God considered sin normal for mankind. "Just try to go to Mass on Sunday," he advised Cocteau. "That will do you good." Cocteau's sinning was at this moment his smoking. He was smoking "prudently": "I never went beyond ten pipes a day. I smoked three at nine in the morning, four at five in the afternoon, three at eleven o'clock. In this way I thought to reduce the risk of intoxication." But for some people ten pipes can be quite a lot. He himself was impressed by the confusion in which he lived, and wrote friends of feeling a "horrible loneli-

---

* Bourgoint himself, at this time and for twenty confused years to come, presents a picture of ambivalence that would be farcical were it not, in his case, so touching. He wrote to Wescott begging him for pin-up pictures of movie stars to keep him company in his barracks — "That marvelous bunch, Gloria [Swanson], Charles Ray, Bessie Love — maybe you know somebody who knows them" (after his death signed photographs of Gloria Swanson and others were found among the possessions he had left with a friend); and at the same time he was already dreaming of entering a monastery. "Glenway mon chéri . . . Last week I was at Solesmnes in a marvelous monastery. There I discovered what peace and purity are, and I'll be homesick for them all my life." On "Tuesday of Passion Week" Sachs wrote Bourgoint from the seminary advising him to think things over carefully. Bourgoint's possible vocation, and his own, Sachs wrote, were the greatest proof of the state of grace in which Cocteau, their common protector, was living; life among monks would be hard; their peace is made up of many "thorns in the flesh."

ness." "At that time I was once again entirely alone," he said later, on a disc. "The great spells of solitude and the great spells of communion which followed one another . . . made for the mysterious beauty of that period." Sachs and Bourgoint had joined him in the sacraments, but neither of them was a child to replace Radiguet. Neither of them could do him honor, as Radiguet had done. They were a pair of disappointments. It was even unlikely that he himself could be of real use to either of them. For the time being, he could only accept from Villefranche what compensations it offered. As Max Jacob wrote him, "Keep telling yourself that you are in the sun, that you are happy."

In March he delivered to Stravinsky a dossier consisting of parts of the Latin text copied out in his own hand, and the French narrative sections, together with ideas for sets and costumes to guide Stravinsky's son Theodore, who was hoping to be the designer of the production. Then he returned to Paris. He wrote Stravinsky from there.

Cocteau to Igor Stravinsky

10 rue d'Anjou
May 1, 1926

Cher Igor,

I feel very depressed and exiled away from our work. Ask Theodore to write me how things are going, and, if there are new drawings, to send me the sketch. Paris exhausts me. *Orphée* will open in late May or early June — more fatigue in store. The letter to Maritain and Maritain's reply will be out Monday. Your copy will be mailed to you. I hope with all my heart that you will like my letter and that you will find in it further proofs of my boundless admiration and affection.

Nobody in the world suspects the existence of *Oedipus*. What is curious is that the Comédie Française, too, has asked me for an *Oedipus*. I will do theirs after ours is performed.

The coincidence that the Comédie Française should suddenly, out of the blue, without having the slightest suspicion that Cocteau had been doing an *Oedipus Rex* for Stravinsky, ask him to do an *Oedipus Rex* for them, is too much for us to swallow — as it was too much for Stravinsky. Once again he said nothing, but he was — and remained — certain that Cocteau had not kept the secret.

Cocteau claimed later that he had written his *Letter to Jacques Maritain* as a "bomb," to shatter the pretty, painted, plaster-saint aspects of French Catholicism and to "restore to the Church virtues that it had lost." What happened, he said, was that the Church, and Maritain himself in his *Reply*, "de-fused" the bomb by ignoring its content and simply smothering it under effusive welcomes to Cocteau as a prodigal son. The *Letter* was useless, he said — "a sword stroke in the water." Today, with the Church in confusion and Maritain an anti-ecumenicalist, the pale *Reply* has lost whatever little interest it may have had, and Cocteau's *Letter* is striking chiefly in its passages of "autobiography," many of them particularly mythical. "For thirteen years I have not gone into society, I am a man of solitude and simple pleasures"; "Every night at Villefranche I sit alone on the quay"; "I do everything to avoid public places"; "I decline to write articles or give lectures." Such was the picture that Cocteau enjoyed painting of himself at the moment. The *Letter* contains references to his "adversaries" the Surrealists; in it (before Breton's flirtation with Communism) he praises the Russian people for their revolution — "I consider the Russian revolution the only significant result of the war. I absolutely refuse to criticize a people that changes its skin"; and his manifestations of religiosity consist chiefly of a few slogans: "Art for art's sake, art for the crowd are equally absurd. I propose art for God"; "I should adopt your [Maritain's] motto — 'I am an ass who is bearing the Lord.' . . . May I, while praising him, retain my own ways, remain free as Charles Henrion advises, and not be afraid of putting my foot in it." The greatest value of the *Letter* lies in its particularly clear revelation of Cocteau's confusion, as illustrated in his attitudes toward opium: outright defense of opium when properly smoked;* relegation of opium to the role of mere "illusionist" in comparison with Jesus; simultaneity of that relegation and Cocteau's own return to the drug — and at the same time continuing with the sacraments. The chief reaction to the *Letter*, apart

---

* The *Letter* contains a eulogy of Louis Laloy: "I point to Laloy as one of those minds which are religious despite all appearances, one of those thinking hearts beloved by heaven."

from pious expressions of joy in Catholic magazines,* was a renewed outpouring of scorn by the Surrealists. Other people, too,
who belonged to no particular literary group and who had admired
Cocteau as a free poetic spirit, deplored his "scuttling back to the
church." "He knew of nowhere else to go but to the traditional de-
pository of spiritual comfort," wrote the English novelist Mary
Butts. "Was it ignorance or fear that did not allow him to look into
his own heart?"

Some of those persons were doubtless among the audiences at the
play *Orphée,* which opened at the Théâtre des Arts on June 15,
1926† and ran for a fortnight (the Pitoëffs eschewed long commercial engagements), and there they must have been further displeased. For although *Orphée* has many aspects, not all of which
can even then have been apparent to everyone, those aware of the
Surrealist-Catholic conflict saw that Cocteau had portrayed his Orpheus as a Surrealist poet who had been taking his inspiration from
the devil (the tapping horse in the play) and who at the end was
converted, addressing himself to God in a prayer that delighted
Maritain: "We thank You for having saved me, because I adored
poetry and poetry is You." That was by no means *all* there was to
Orphée, and the Catholic activist aspect of the play has evaporated
into history, but it was sufficient to antagonize more than only the
Surrealists who came to the Théâtre des Arts.

Cocteau spoke of the play as containing many "miracles" (their
enactment onstage caused unkind critics to speak of "tricks"), and
said that this "miraculous" character derived from Picasso's remark at lunch the day of the message in the elevator — that
"Everything is a miracle: it's a miracle not to melt in the bathtub,
like a lump of sugar." In *Orphée* Heurtebise reveals his angelic
nature by remaining at one moment suspended in the air; he calls
mirrors "the doors through which Death comes and goes," and
through a mirror on the stage Death does come and go, and through
it Orpheus passes into and out from the underworld. The mirrors

---

* For example, in *La Semaine Religieuse de Paris,* August 21, 1926: "Let us greet a
prodigal brother who has returned to his father's house. His guide has been the angel
of suffering and death. Welcome to him! His soul is that of a child — only the hearts
of children can understand him."

† On the same bill with the short *Orphée* were Marcel Achard's *Et dzim la la* and
Pierre Chaumière's one-act *Séquence.* Whatever those plays may have been like, there
was apparently a feeling on the part of dramatists that the Pitoëffs tended to compose
ill-assorted programs.

belong to Cocteau's autobiography. In the Hotel Welcome, perhaps in the same room in which he wrote *Orphée*, he had stared into a mirror for hours at a time, the year before, seeking an answer to his own "mystery," which included the mystery of Radiguet's advent and disappearance. The great mirrors in Etienne de Beaumont's ballroom had always impressed him as being "gates of death," for, reflected in them, the brilliant guests at the Beaumont balls had grown older each year, and from them some, like Radiguet, were constantly disappearing. The tribunal of female bacchantes which condemns and eventually beheads Orpheus for using "an injurious word" had its origin in the "tribunal" of Cubists that censured Cocteau, in 1917, for his "misuse" of the word *"rue"*; and the diabolical tapping horse recalls the table-tapping at Valentine Hugo's that had brought prophecies of Radiguet's death.

Cocteau's specific direction that Death, modern death in rubber gloves, be played by a "very beautiful young woman," his portrayal of Eurydice as a saccharine housewife with whom Orpheus's life had become "rotten," and the fact that the initials of the words prophesying her return from the other world — *"Madame Eurydice reviendra des enfers"* — spell an exasperated comment, the "injurious word" for which Orpheus is beheaded by the female furies — all those are sometimes considered by homosexuals as double entendres, to be fully savored by themselves alone, and that may have been true at the time; but today there is nothing private about that aspect of Cocteau's *Orphée*. The play is now recognizable by all as a homosexual's imaginative deformation of a legend which, in its previous versions by Virgil and Ovid, Shelley and Rilke, Poliziano, Lope de Vega and Calderón, Glück, Rameau, Offenbach and many another, had already been presented in any way its author wished. The most extreme homosexual touch concerning Cocteau's *Orphée* is his claim that the "very beautiful young woman" cast as Death had in fact been inspired by a man — by the strange beauty of the American female-impersonator trapeze-artist Barbette, of whose dazzling act at the Casino de Paris he had written to Valentine Hugo in 1923.

Cocteau had quickly become a friend and admirer of Barbette. To announce Barbette's coming to Brussels on tour he had written to Paul Collaer, a Belgian music critic: "Next week . . . you'll

see a music-hall act called 'Barbette' that has been keeping us en-
thralled for a fortnight. The young American who does this wire
and trapeze act is a great actor, an angel, and he has become the
friend of all of us. Go and see him, be nice to him as he deserves,
and tell everybody that he is no mere acrobat in women's clothes,
nor just a graceful daredevil, but one of the most beautiful things
in the theatre. Stravinsky, Auric, poets, painters and I myself have
seen no comparable display of artistry on the stage since Nijinsky." And to another Belgian friend he wrote, "Don't miss Barbette. . . . Call on him and tell him I sent you. You won't be wasting your time. He's both a great acrobat and a discriminating
reader, in close touch with contemporary writing." In Barbette Cocteau found the perfect illustration of the comparison he had made
in 1916, in one of his letters to Etienne de Beaumont from Flanders, between a tightrope dancer's skilled, perilous performance
and the painful creativity of a poet; and now, about the time of
Orphée, he published in the *N.R.F.* an essay, "Le Numéro Barbette."

    In the *N.R.F.* essay Cocteau tells of having a sandwich and a
hard-boiled egg with Barbette one evening, arriving with him at his
dressing room at eight o'clock (although his act would begin only
at eleven), and watching the conscientiousness of his preparations
— "a conscientiousness unknown to French actors, and characteristic of clowns, Annamite mimes, and the Cambodian dancing girls
who are sewn each night into their golden costumes." As Barbette
stripped and began to strap on a leather girdle, some chorus girls
pushed open the door and gave little screams at the sight; all the
conventional decencies were observed — they withdrew, and Barbette threw on a bathrobe before going to the door to talk to them.
Then came the making-up, and Barbette remained a young man, a
"drôle de jeune diable," even in his completed makeup that was
"precious as a brand-new box of pastels, his chin enameled with
something white and shiny, his body unreal as though coated with
plaster." It was only when he held some hairpins between his teeth
and began to adjust his blond wig that he began to "imitate every
last gesture of a woman arranging her hair." Then, as he stood up,
began to walk in a certain way and put on his rings, there was a
transformation: "Jekyll is Hyde," says Cocteau. "Yes, Hyde! Because now I find myself frightened. I look away, put out my ciga-

rette, remove my hat. The door opens again; it is the girls, now not at all embarrassed; they come and go quite at home, sit down, powder themselves, talk about clothes."

Barbette could slip in and out of his woman's role at will, and even before the curtain went up he revealed his genius for quick, back-and-forth transformations — one of the elements that made his act seem to take place "in the streets of dream," as Cocteau put it. His maid came in, helped him on with his dress, curled the feathers on his hat; they all left the dressing room; and on the stairs leading down to stage level "Barbette is once again a boy, dressed up for a joke, tripping on his skirt, and longing to slide down the banister. He is still a man as he walks about the stage inspecting his equipment, does leg exercises, grimaces at the spot-lights, hoists himself on to wires, clambers up ladders. The moment the question of danger is settled, he is a woman again — a society woman, giving her salon a last-minute inspection before the ball, patting cushions, moving vases and lamps."

Then, watching from out front, Cocteau describes what the spec-tators saw: "The curtain goes up on a functional décor — a wire stretched between two supports, a trapeze and hanging rings. In the back, a sofa covered with a white bearskin." On the sofa, between the wire and the trapeze parts of the act, Barbette was to do a little striptease as he removed his long evening gown — "a scabrous little scene," Cocteau calls it, "a real masterpiece of pantomime, summing up in parody all the women he has ever studied, becom-ing himself *the* woman — so much so as to eclipse the prettiest girls who precede and follow him on the program." And here Cocteau begins to talk of Barbette's act, and of other theatrical examples, as parables of the artifice, the "lie," that all art is. "Don't forget," he says, "we are in the magic light of the theatre, in this trick-factory where truth has no currency, where anything natural has no value, where the short are made tall and the tall short, where the only things that convince us are card tricks and sleights of hand of a difficulty unsuspected by the audience. . . . Thanks to Barbette I understand that it was not merely for reasons of 'decency' that great nations and great civilizations gave women's roles to men. He brings to mind François Fratellini, explaining to me, when I was exhausting myself trying in vain to get something out of an English clown engaged for the role of the bookmaker in 'Le Boeuf sur le

Toit,' that an Englishman would never make a convincing Englishman; and Réjane's remark: 'When I play a mother, for example, I have to forget that I myself have a son. At other times, in order to put myself across the footlights I have to imagine that I am a man.' Such detachment, such labor!" Cocteau exclaims. "There's nothing like a lesson from a technician."

Cocteau compares the cumulative effect of Barbette's perfect disguise and elegant stage entrance — an effect achieved through just such labor — to a cloud of dust thrown in the eyes of the public. Bursting on the audience as a "ravishing creature," "he throws his dust with such force that from then on he is free to concentrate on his wire work, in which his masculine movements will help him instead of giving him away": thanks to the "dust," the audience will see him not as a man, which in his acrobatics he obviously is, but as "one of those Amazons who look so dazzling in the advertising pages of American magazines." Then comes the interlude on the sofa, the striptease and the "scabrous little scene" — another bit of dust, for once again he is going to need complete freedom of movement as he swings out from the stage over the audience on his trapeze, hangs from one foot, pretends to fall, half the time staring upside down at the spectators, "with the face of a crazy angel." In none of those gyrations does he *really* look very feminine; but the greater part of the audience continues to think of him as such. The reason for Barbette's popularity, Cocteau thought, was that he "appeals to the instinct of many audiences in one, and people vote for him for opposite reasons. He is liked by those who see him as a woman and by those who sense the man in him — not to mention those stirred by the supernatural sex of beauty."

But perhaps Barbette displayed the subtlest artistry of all, Cocteau thinks, in the masterly close of his act — once again a model, in its meticulous attention to detail, for practitioners of any art form, who well know the difficulty of strengthening their effects through to the very end, of remaining at high tension while unwinding. "Imagine what a letdown it would be for some of us, if at the end of that unforgettable lie Barbette were simply to remove his wig. You will tell me that after the fifth curtain call he does just that, and that the letdown does take place. There is even a murmur from the audience, and some people are embarrassed and some blush. True. For, after having succeeded as an acrobat in causing some people almost to faint, he now has to have his success as an actor. But watch his last tour de force: simply to rebecome a man, to run the reel backwards, is not enough. The truth itself must be translated, if it is to convince us as forcibly as did the lie. That is why Barbette, the moment he has snatched off his wig, *plays the part of a man*. He rolls his shoulders, stretches his hands, swells his muscles, parodies a golfer's sporty walk. And after the fifteenth or so curtain call he gives a mischievous wink, shifts from foot to foot, mimes a bit of apology and does a shuffling little street-urchin dance — all of it to erase the fabulous, dying swan impression left by the act." And Cocteau, addressing himself to his fellow poets, sums it all up in two remarks: "Barbette's effect is instinctively calculated: we must transpose it into our own domain and use it deliberately." And: "How does a poet become a classic? By rising above everything. Barbette apes poetry, and this is his fascination. For his acrobatics are not really perilous. His affectations ought to be unbearable to us. The principle of his act embarrasses us. What is left, then? That thing he has created, going through its contortions under the spotlight."

After publishing that essay Cocteau wrote about Barbette several times more, once after watching his act from behind the scenes at the Médrano Circus in the company of other performers. "With Barbette, the acrobat is a pretext," he wrote on this occasion. "No wonder his triumph is a dead letter for the circus people. It affronts them. 'What! My wife could do as well as that! My son . . . My daughter . . .' So? The electric card trick escapes them. Wrapped in their bathrobes, they watch from outside the ring, near the stables. They listen round-eyed to the curtain calls for the androgyne."

Cocteau's various writings on Barbette, especially the article in the *N.R.F.*, constitute a classic in the literature of aesthetics, on the nature of art.

It was at the time of *Orphée*, with its Catholic activism and its homosexual overtones, that Cocteau was forced to recognize a change in his life that he must have sensed earlier: Valentine Hugo, the one "very beautiful young woman" with whom he had been on terms of what seemed to him perfect friendship, was cooling towards him. In August he wrote her: "It hurt me terribly to feel that you were withdrawing your friendship; to feel that it was returning filled me with *incredible* joy. . . . The mysterious coldness never for a single moment changed my heart: I had kept expecting to awake from a bad dream." And in October he wrote to Jean Hugo: "I sent Valentine a letter written from a full heart, but have had no answer." What had happened was that Valentine had been, in Jean Hugo's words, "going over to the Surrealists." The Catholic, anti-Surrealist aspect of *Orphée* displeased her, and when, by a mistake, she and Jean Hugo were sent no seats for the preview, she was glad to have a reason for not going, and glad that her absence should be noticed. (The Hugos went the next day, in a less conspicuous audience, and Valentine still had sufficient detachment, and loyalty to Cocteau, to tell Count Kessler that *Orphée* was a "masterpiece.") "Cocteau felt her disapproval," Jean Hugo says, "and, as he always did when he felt hostility, made a move toward her and gave her two vases his uncle the ambassador had brought back from Persia." Valentine avoided the offense of returning the vases, but sold them shortly afterwards.

One wonders whether Cocteau's homosexuality played a role in Valentine's change of feeling. Jean Hugo says that "if so, the reaction would have been unconscious," and that homosexuality "certainly was not among the things that Valentine, publicly or privately, held against Cocteau." Valentine was a charmer, but not in the most softly feminine way; by nature she was forceful, and was never known, among the poets and painters and musicians who were her friends, to give way for a moment to weakness or defeat. Even Misia Sert, with her drive and her thousand irons in the fire, was — as the story of her love for Sert shows — more vulnerable than the handsome, superb Valentine. But Jean Hugo says that Valentine's "esteem for Cocteau's character" had begun to decline some time before — "as far back as 1923"; and certainly the aspects of Cocteau's personality that might cumulatively have been most abrasive to anyone, and especially to any woman, were attributes of homosexuality. Furthermore, Valentine's new friends the Surrealists were of generally, though not completely, anti-homosexual orientation, whereas Cocteau was becoming increasingly the prince of homosexuals. After the *Orphée* difference subsided, Jean Hugo says, there was a certain degree of reconcilation between Valentine and Cocteau; and Cocteau assumed, or pre-

tended to assume, that there would be a restoration of the old intimacy.

Thanks to *Orphée*, Cocteau became more than ever a figure of
glamorous attraction among his fellow homosexuals, and more than
ever he was courted by the young among them. At the time of *Antigone*, youths had been said to climb the lamp-posts of the rue
d'Anjou; now, 10 rue d'Anjou itself was invaded. Jean Bourgoint
had been in Paris for a time, sent there from Nîmes by ministerial
order (obtained by Cocteau) to be operated on for appendicitis;
apparently he did some convalescent resting and entertaining in the
Cocteau apartment. After his departure Cocteau wrote to Max
Jacob: "I long for Villefranche. 10 rue d'Anjou is bedlam again.
The return to barracks quieted things a little, but what a strange lot,
our disciples! The suicide variety, or, 'Give me back my photographs!' or, 'I'm giving up literature.' You know the types." Self-
recommendation to Cocteau by photograph was common among
youth both French and foreign, and it continued to the end of his
days. "Yes, I sent him my picture, with a flirtatious note," one good-
looking young American has said, "and it brought me a flirtatious
note back. I didn't go so far as to send my *nude* photograph, as
—— did to —— ." A visit to Cocteau's room in his mother's
apartment, and a description of his regular use of it as a *fumerie*,
occupy a page or two in numerous memoirs of the period: one of
the best, less well known than some, is in Maurice Sachs's posthumously published novel, *Chronique Joyeuse et Scandaleuse*.* The
invasion of Cocteau's room by youths from hither and yon, resulting in the disappearance of some of his possessions, especially inscribed books, was chronicled by Cocteau himself in a letter to the
publisher Roland Saucier, printed in 1926 in an edition of twenty-
five copies under the title *Lettre-Plainte*.†

For all its fantasy and originality, *Orphée* was closer to the
usual forms of literary drama than the earlier, freewheeling spectacles — *Parade*, the *Boeuf* and the *Mariés;* and it brought Cocteau
more serious consideration from the conventional theatre world of
Paris and from the Comédie Française. He wrote later: "Of my
plays, it is the one most often performed in universities in all coun-

* See Appendix XII.
† See Appendix XIII.

tries. It was also often played in the stalags — incidentally, the prisoners staged it very well." Today the play is overshadowed by Cocteau's film of the same name: the resources of cinema permitted him twenty years later to achieve a richer rendering of the myth.

Another effect of the play *Orphée* is foreshadowed in passages from Cocteau's stage directions: "Clothes should be contemporary with any production. Orpheus and Eurydice should be dressed for the country, as simply and inconspicuously as possible. Death is a very beautiful young woman in a bright pink evening gown and fur coat. Coiffure, dress, coat, shoes, gestures, general deportment all up to the minute." The simple country clothes as cut by Chanel were no less smart than her elegant evening gown, and they launched a vogue for informal dress that has "taken us where we are today" — just as the leather jackets of the motorcyclists in the film *Orphée* were to foretell another vogue. Much of it was suggested to Cocteau, people of the time say, by the demeanor of Jean and Jeanne Bourgoint, whose beauty was enhanced by the informal clothes they habitually and unaffectedly wore: the handsome Jean, walking about Paris in tennis clothes and sneakers, would have been surprised to learn that he was a prophetic fashion plate.

Hoping to ease the various pains and distresses that never seemed to leave him, Cocteau put himself that spring into the hands of a fashionable Hindu practitioner of whom Madame Gleizes has written in her memoirs. "At his institute in the rue de Bénouville, Varma-Yoghi treated half of Paris. He massaged Bergson, Cocteau, a number of professors at the medical school. In many instances his treatments were unquestionably successful. Varma-Yoghi had the greatest contempt for our Western science and for our philosophy as well. When he had Bergson at his mercy, stretched out on his torture table, he would sermonize him. 'A fine philosopher you are,' he would say. 'Look at the state you're in. Where does your philosophy get you?' I don't know what kind of sermons he preached to Cocteau, but he always spoke of him with dismay, repeating: 'Ah! The poor boy! The poor boy!' "

The "poor boy" stayed in Paris a few weeks after *Orphée* ended its first run on June 30, and then sought Villefranche. It was a different summer from the last. The Welcome had been "discovered," especially by painters — Leonid Berman, Christian Bérard,

Georges Hugnet and Francis Rose among them. It was possible to live quietly, but that was not the common taste. Francis Rose's seventeenth birthday party was the occasion for a riotous party that included his mother, Lady Rose (who was a medium), her pugnacious friend Captain Williams, and Isadora Duncan in her Greek tunic and the dance pupils she had brought with her from her studio in Nice. The odor of opium pervaded the hotel; Bérard and Cocteau quickly became friends and smoked together. "Life was not a series of parties, but one constant long party," Glenway Wescott has said, "impromptu dressing-up, processions, fireworks. Cocteau wore beautiful pajamas and dressing gowns; he held levées; friends [he called them his '*escadrille*,' his 'squadron'] crowded into his room; he would talk with them as he shaved, interrupt shaving and conversation to dash off a letter or add a few words to a manuscript or make a drawing; in a few seconds a portrait head would be done; it might be discarded as inadequate and another begun immediately, or it might be glanced at narrow-eyed, approved, and kept or given; he wrote poems faster than his hand could move; there was a constant flow of verse." There was a girl named Marie-Louise Robinet-Duris but nicknamed "Robinet d'Urine"; Man Ray brought his mistress Kiki de Montparnasse, who was not the soul of tranquillity; as battleships steamed in and out, the corps of prostitutes waxed and waned; Monsieur Georges Isarlo, a now venerable Paris art historian, tells of driving to Villefranche from Monte Carlo with a diamond merchant's wife in search of atmosphere and finding Cocteau beating the drum with a sailor's jazz band in the Welcome bar. Bourgoint, still in barracks at Nîmes, came on leave as before. Cocteau not only drew, but made "constructions" out of pipe cleaners and plaster, for an exhibition to be held in Paris in December, to be called *"Poésie Plastique — Objets, Dessins."* * Bérard painted for him a gouache of a

---

* Gino Severini has written of this exhibition that some of the objects were adaptations of "the *collages* that had been done by Picasso and other Montmartre artists." In the catalogue Cocteau wrote, among other aphorisms, "A farmer has just found in his field the arms of the Venus de Milo. To whom do they belong? To the farmer, or to the Venus de Milo?" According to Severini, those words infuriated Picasso, who took them as not at all a lighthearted quip, but as a deliberate reference to his recent still lifes that included classical heads, plaster arms, etc. "Picasso . . . was enraged by Cocteau's words," Severini says, "and he broke with him, refusing for ten years to have him in his house. For Picasso, Cocteau became one of the tribe of *emmerdeurs.*

poet looking with alarm at two women seated on his bed: it would be on the cover of the volume *Opéra*. The last poems for that collection were written this summer — "the first that I consider as expressing my essence, poems which contain all the paraphernalia that I will one day be reproached for using. . . . It is not mere bric-a-brac; I have paid a high price for the right to shelter this motley host of phantoms within myself and set them free at will." And he said that the poems in *Opéra* (the volume includes *L'Ange Heurtebise*) display "the celebrated deformations due to opium — slowness, indolence, dreams of passivity. *Opéra*," he said, "is the work of an opium addict."

In the midst of it all, Maurice Sachs's vocation collapsed. Allowed to leave the seminary to vacation with his grandmother, Maurice accompanied her to what she remembered from her wedding journey as a "quiet spot on the Mediterranean": it turned out to be Juan-les-Pins, which had recently undergone some changes. (That is how Maurice tells the tale: others, who saw no grandmother with him, think the choice of resort was made by him in full knowledge.) On the beach were Rebecca West with her small son Anthony, the novelist G. B. Stern, Picasso, Marie Laurencin, the Etienne de Beaumonts, and other members of not-too-quiet international society, including a handsome American minor named Tom Pinkerton who was there with his mother and at the sight of whom Maurice's heart melted in his soutane. Clad in the soutane, he strolled hand in hand with the boy on the beach; in his infatuation he let the boy borrow the soutane and wear it as a beach-robe; Mrs. Pinkerton had hysterics, wrote to the bishop of Nice, and threatened to sue no one knew quite whom; the Côte d'Azur laughed; Sachs fled. He made a retreat at Solesmes, but in cell, church and

---

Perhaps Cocteau's art objects in this exhibition were the first Paris vulgarization of *papiers-collés*."

Severini seems to be alone in suggesting that the cause of the long coolness between Picasso and Cocteau was the latter's quip in that December, 1926 catalogue. Douglas Cooper, for example, says: "I don't think Picasso would have been cross on that account. . . . There is no doubt that Cocteau was alienated from Picasso by the Surrealists." In a letter to Max Jacob dated February 2, 1926, Cocteau writes of not having seen Picasso since certain "Spanish incidents," which he does not identify. "We telephoned each other at Christmas," he writes, "but something remains of those *crimes de coeur*." Elsewhere, Cocteau writes resentfully to Jacob about Picasso's denigration of Christian Bérard as a painter.

refectory could think only of Tom. Cocteau had not laughed, but
had written to Maritain. At the seminary, the director decided: "A
good Christian is better than a bad priest. Do your military service
— it will give you time to think things over." Sachs abandoned
soutane and seminary. "I hoped you would do what you have done
(or are doing) and would do it soon," Glenway Wescott wrote him.
". . . . What has happened . . . shows clearly that you have not
a vocation — not a religious reason for doing that religious thing.
. . . Those who care about your life must hope that this present
situation (your relation to Tom) will prove to be as blessed and
satisfactory as the other was hopeless and untenable." But the "relation to Tom" was as illusory as the vocation: Sachs entered the
army (he was put to work guarding latrines), and the affair died
away.

On September 14, in Isadora Duncan's dance studio at 343,
Promenade des Anglais, in Nice, at five P.M., there was held a
*"Récital Jean Cocteau, avec le concours d'Isadora Duncan, de
l'auteur et de Marcel Herrand."* For the program cover Cocteau
made a neoclassic drawing inscribed "Mysteria-Nice"; the studio
was decked with flowers; Isadora danced by candlelight, "baring
her breasts," while Cocteau read from *Orphée* and from his latest
poems; Marcel Herrand, the Heurtebise of *Orphée,* read the poem
L'Ange Heurtebise, and he and Cocteau recited their phonograph
narrations from *Les Mariés de la Tour Eiffel.* After that, most
people left the Welcome, but Cocteau stayed on through October.
He wrote to Wescott about opium and Maurice Sachs: "As for o,
you are right to fear it — I fear it even more than you. But since
the devil has put explosives into my hands, I try to trick him by
manipulating them cleverly with the help of my angel. What I hold
against Maurice is, that with the devil having tricked us by putting
him into a soutane, he didn't outsmart the devil by continuing to
wear it. I have had a painful letter from him; he is undergoing the
tortures of love (*sic*) — his frankness is disarming." The frantic
summer had been a kind of desperate dance; and now, almost alone
at Villefranche, he wrote to Jean Hugo, in that letter lamenting the
lack of word from Valentine: "Without the two or three people on
earth who matter to me, I am alone in the dark, and afraid." To T.
S. Eliot in London he wrote concerning a review of *Orphée* by Bon-
amy Dobree that had appeared in *The New Criterion* for October:

Poster by Marie Laurencin for Comte Etienne de Beaumont's
"Les Soirées de Paris," 1924.

Jean Desbordes.

Barbette.

Valentine Gross Hugo at one of Comte Etienne de Beaumont's costume balls.

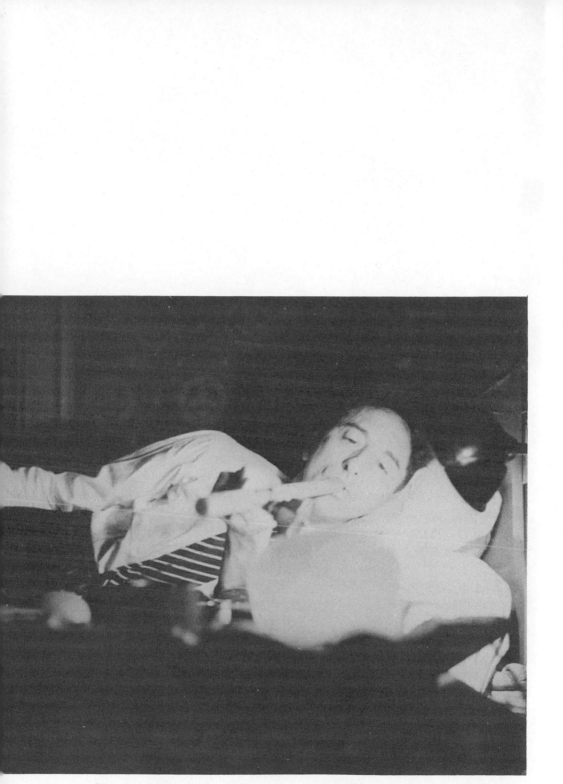

The inevitable photograph of Cocteau smoking opium.

Marcel Khill and the shadow of Cocteau.

Cocteau to T. S. Eliot

Nov. 1926

Villefranche sur mer, A.M.

Mon cher Eliot,

Of my tremendous effort, of the long agony, the emergency surgery that my work is, *nothing* is seen or even glimpsed. Coming from close to you, this hurts me particularly. . . . There is not a single symbol in *Orphée.* Twelve dramatic years are projected, hidden, in it.*

And he wrote to Germaine Picabia.

Cocteau to Germaine Picabia

November 1, 1926

Chère Germaine,

. . . . All Paris is a dive, a cabinet minister's waiting room, a department store. Vulgarity, careerism, politics, etc. . . . Breton preaches. Aragon lives at the Boeuf sur le Toit with Nancy Cunard, etc. I salute Francis as a free man who is never absurd. I myself have made many mistakes, but I have never done anything dirty. . . .

In December, three years after Radiguet's death — it was as though a conventional period of mourning had been observed — Cocteau announced the appearance of a new "son," Jean Desbordes.

Jean Desbordes, Opium, La Voix Humaine, Les Enfants Terribles *(1926–1929)*

The atrocious death inflicted on Jean Desbordes by the Gestapo and the French militia, which will be recounted in its place, and in

---

* Mr. Dobree has written, about his review of *Orphée:* "On rereading my effusion it seems to me generous and fairly understanding. . . . In sending me [Cocteau's] letter Eliot wrote to me, 'Don't worry over Cocteau! There is no pleasing people like that, & I have too much experience offending people to care. I shall write and rebuke him and point out the English view of such matters.' Beautifully reassuring." ("T. S. Eliot: A Personal Reminiscence," in *T. S. Eliot: The Man and His Work,* edited by Allen Tate, Delacorte Press, New York, 1966.) Mr. Dobree's review was, in fact, only fairly understanding; Mr. Eliot's remarks are indeed beautifully reassuring — to the reviewer.

which he achieved an ultimate heroism, makes it difficult to speak objectively of this young man of whose entry into his life Cocteau wrote a friend, "A miracle has happened in heaven — Raymond has come back in another guise." In respect to literary merit, Desbordes was far from being another Radiguet. His letters to Cocteau, preserved by Cocteau's heir, are by order of *his* heir (his sister) uncommunicable, and people differ widely in their estimate of him. He was a soft-spoken youth of twenty when he appeared on the scene, short, slight, unremarkable in appearance, "like a little clerk," Glenway Wescott has said. Except for Cocteau, those who had known Radiguet were not impressed by Desbordes. "Desbordes was kind, emotional, a mawkish lover of animals; honest, nothing of an opportunist, immature, like a boy of fourteen, not at all effeminate," says Jean Hugo. "His words were always of admiration, never of criticism, with a complete lack of intelligence or fantasy or personality. But his heroic death proves that we somewhat misjudged him." His position as an ambitious young writer profiting from an older writer's infatuation naturally laid him open to suspicions: some felt that his gentleness overlay a particularly steely determination (his final behavior under torture might corroborate this), and that on his side his relation with Cocteau was based entirely on his burning ambition to achieve fame as a writer. The third "Jean" among Cocteau's "children," he was called "Jean-Jean" to distinguish him from Jean Bourgoint and from Cocteau himself; and the name Desbordes, close to *"déborder"* ("overflow") — a word he often used — is peculiarly appropriate to the gushy effusiveness of his writings, which Cocteau found so fresh and admirable.

He seems to have been a "born" writer (not always a guarantee of quality!), and as a boy in the country, living with his mother and sisters, he wrote constantly. *Le Grand Ecart* — a copy was left behind in the Desbordes house by a visitor — was the great revelation, and soon he was one of the youths writing to Cocteau from the provinces. Apparently they met somewhere earlier than Cocteau says; but on Christmas Day, 1926, when Cocteau places the meeting, Desbordes was in Paris, wearing "the most charming uniform in the world," doing his "military" service as a land-based sailor in the Naval Ministry in the Place de la Concorde. "He brought me a manuscript," Cocteau says, "a typewritten mass of formless utterances. There would be sudden dream passages in which he would speak of another world, soar in air, walk on water. My decision was quickly made. I would devote myself to teaching him how to provoke such spells of dreaming rather than leave them to chance, and to become aware of his talent without losing his freshness. I will never forget how uneasy this innocent boy's starry gaze made me feel as I gave my first advice. I had very quick results." Is that Cocteau's way of saying that he taught Desbordes to smoke? Or only that he "helped him with his writing"? In fact he did both; together they smoked, and together they worked over Desbordes' prose, accumulating sufficient short pieecs to make a volume.

Meanwhile, the printed text of *Orphée* was published, and Cocteau wrote to Etienne de Beaumont.

Cocteau to Etienne de Beaumont

March 1927

Cher Etienne,

I have been putting myself on a regime of rest and silence, the way you sometimes do — a housecleaning of the mind and heart. I cannot tell you how touched I was by your letter, and to know that you like *Orphée* in book form. I was afraid that away from the footlights all that would remain of it would be like the remnants of submarine plants found on the sand, or what is left of dreams on waking. . . . During work being done at 10 rue d'Anjou, I am staying at the Hotel de la Madeleine, but always lunch and dine with Maman,*

Dullin revived *Antigone* that spring, and Cocteau wrote of it to Stravinsky: "This afternoon I shall see to the lighting for the revival of *Antigone*, but the light will lack something without all of you in the theatre." He wrote similarly to Anna de Noailles, who was living in an increasingly morbid preoccupation with death, and who, at fifty-one, was exhibiting pastels at the Galerie Bernheim

---

* Central heating was being installed at 10 rue d'Anjou. "I think I shall live in this hotel," Cocteau wrote Max Jacob from the Hotel de la Madeleine. "I have discovered that what I was looking for at Villefranche was less the south than a hotel room — a marvelous abstract thing where sleep, waking, breakfast, and all the rest are restored to their original significance and are no longer distorted as when seen through the thick layer of the memories that fill my room at home. The walls of 10 rue d'Anjou stare at me and devour me." From now on he was to spend increasing amounts of time away from his mother's flat, until in 1931 he moved completely out of it.

and had published a volume of verse called *L'Honneur de Souffrir,*
dedicated "To my friends who have left me, but whom I do not
leave." Cocteau's letter, inviting her to the rehearsal of *Antigone,*
contains purplish passages that echo those he had sent her fifteen
years before: *"Ma chère Soeur,* For more than a year I have been
trying to solve the problem of masks in the theatre, and I am bringing back *Antigone* to test the results of my work. What I must tell
you is that every day as I listen to the flow of sublime lines that
never flag, it is your face that I imagine behind Antigone's mask,
your hands beneath her cloak. . . . Saturday at two-thirty I rehearse my lighting. With you in the theatre, *Antigone* will have the
light it needs. There will be four or five friends, and you — no one
else."

Preparations for *Oedipus Rex* were under way at the same time,
and since it was thought that it would be given in the form of a
spectacle, with the ballet company participating, Diaghilev, although still not allowed to hear the music, had to be told of the
"surprise" (which he had undoubtedly been told of already).
Diaghilev's involvement made inevitable that of the still inseparable Misia; and Misia proved to be as indefatigable a
troublemaker concerning *Oedipus Rex* in 1927 as she had been ten
years before concerning *Parade.* (When Chanel, whose participation was desired, returned to Paris after a visit to London, Misia's
greeting was: "Everybody's waiting for you, dear — you hold the
purse strings.") For the spectacle, Cocteau urged Theodore Stravinsky's designs and his own on Diaghilev, and wrote constantly to
the composer in Nice, reporting every latest bit of news concerning
Misia, Chanel (who eventually did not finance the production) and
the Princesse de Polignac (who did). It was that buzz of Paris
gossip and intrigue as conveyed in Cocteau's letters that led Stravinsky eventually to inscribe his *Oedipus Rex* dossier as "irritating
and futile." What it caused him to do at the moment was abruptly
to detach himself from production plans and put everything in the
hands of Diaghilev. Chiefly for financial reasons, Diaghilev decided with equal abruptness that there should be no spectacle,
simply three concert-form performances, the cost of which could be
covered by the Princesse de Polignac's best offer of approximately
two thousand dollars. Apparently the brusqueness with which
Diaghilev — or, more probably, Misia — announced the decision

to Cocteau was extreme, and Cocteau's reaction is conveyed most openly by Jean Bourgoint (who had been released from the army on May 4 and was now idling in Paris): "Jean is having a lot of trouble because of Diaghilev's malice," he wrote Glenway Wescott shortly before the premiere. "Stravinsky's cowardice is the last straw. *Les sales Russes!*" Cocteau had written to Stravinsky, "I will be the Speaker if Diaghilev asks me. If he wants an actor, I will try to find one." Cocteau was not asked to do anything. It was "certainly to spite Cocteau," Stravinsky has said — probably it was an echo of old feuds — that Diaghilev "deliberately" engaged "a very handsome, very young man" to recite the French prologues. Cocteau wrote to Stravinsky courteously, but with distortions that reveal his anger: "I find the oratorio form very noble and very abstract. But the entire balance depends on the Speaker. See to it that I am allowed to rehearse the actor when you rehearse the orchestra. Diaghilev is capable of doing anything to ensure that the work be a failure, even though it was composed as a cantata in his honor."

"I was late in finishing the score," Stravinsky has written about *Oedipus Rex*, "so late that the singers hardly had learned the notes before the piano preview performance, which took place at Edmond de Polignac's a few days before the public one. At the Polignac soirée I accompanied the singers myself, and from the reactions of the guests I foresaw that *Oedipus* was not likely to succeed with the Parisian ballet audience. But my austere vocal concert [the premiere was May 30], following a very colorful ballet, was an even greater failure than I had anticipated. The audience was hardly more than polite, and the Sganarelles of the press were a lot less than that: 'The man who composed *Petrushka* now gives us this Handelian pastiche. . . . A lot of badly dressed people sang badly. . . . The music for Creon is a Meyerbeerian march,' etc. Performances were rare in the next two decades, but since then they have been more and more frequent." There had been considerable anticipation about the premiere, but despite Stravinsky's conducting the performance seems really to have been mediocre — Nicholas Nabokov remembers that both chorus and soloists sang badly — and in the inner circle enthusiasm was dampened by Diaghilev's freely expressed dislike of his anniversary present. He called it "unsuitable," and *"un cadeau très macabre."* "Everybody knows I dislike sleeping with women," he told Nabokov, "and that includes

old hags like Jocasta, even if she should happen to be my mother";
and when the public's coolness became evident he said, "What
should I do now, tear my eyes out?" Glenway Wescott, who attended the premiere, wrote to George Platt Lynes that "the Stravinsky production was a famous fiasco, thanks to a row which makes
the causes of the last war seem simple. The music seemed glorious,
in so far as one could tell"; and he wrote in *Good-bye Wisconsin* of
"the first night of the *Oedipus* oratorio, when all magnificent-
looking Paris had listened as if to a poorly performed revival of
Handel or Rossini."

On which side of the footlights was Cocteau, that first night? He
who even in the freshness of his grief for Radiguet had been driven
to mount the stage and play Mercutio, had been silenced by Diaghilev in connection with this oratorio whose libretto he had written,
and made to listen to someone else recite the only lines remaining
in the language in which he had written them. Little wonder that in
the future he was to seize every opportunity to make the "Speaker"
of *Oedipus Rex* one of his most notable roles — in a 1952 Paris
production with masks designed by himself (the performance
which, of all performances, most pleased Stravinsky visually);
later in London; and permanently, in the splendid recording by the
Cologne Radio Symphony Orchestra and Chorus.*

Perhaps it was to palliate Diaghilev's snub that the Pitoëffs, reviving *Orphée* for a short second run, asked Cocteau himself to
take one of the parts — to play his own angel. Bourgoint had announced the event in a letter to Wescott: "Jean put on *Antigone* —
perfectly beautiful. I can't imagine anything more beautiful in the
theatre. Perhaps *Orphée* will make me change my mind, with Jean
playing Heurtebise. *Vive Lindbergh!*" There was no question of
not accepting, but in letters to friends who had written him in admiration of the Orphée text, Cocteau expressed dissatisfaction with
his own performance and perhaps with the play itself: he was
discouraged, he said, by his "lack of subtlety, of mystery."

Increasingly infatuated with Desbordes, he was still loved by his

---

* (Columbia ML 4644, with printed English translation of Cocteau's French by
E. E. Cummings.) One critic has written: "Is it that only Cocteau, speaking his original French, could bring to it [the Speaker's part] that peculiar blend of suavity and
commitment? I shall never forget his '*Adieu, Oedipe; on t'aimait*': it went to the heart
as the music always does, the commentary almost never." (Alan Blyth, *The Times*,
London, February 6, 1970.)

two earlier "children." Sachs sent letters from his barracks in the French-occupied Ruhr. Bourgoint was charming, lazy and disorganized, living at home, working in a Left Bank art gallery. Cocteau saw him occasionally. "Jean scratches his huge and beautiful body as he lies on beds digesting bags of sweets and boxes of candied fruit," he wrote to Wescott. "I suppose he will keep his job with [the Galerie] Pierre. It requires little work and leaves time for him to devour books and all kinds of food." Jean Bourgoint had reason for distress in the hostile, defiant behavior being displayed by his sister Jeanne, who had fallen under the sway of the obese, wealthy Princesse Violette Murat, lesbian and opiomane — Jean called her "the monster." Desbordes, who had been released early from military service through Cocteau's influence, was continuing to write short pieces, among them several eulogies of Cocteau.* "Fashionable people are all alike," Cocteau had written in one of his letters to Stravinsky that spring, reporting on the chicanery surrounding the preparations for *Oedipus Rex.* "I see no one any more except Maritain and a few very young poets. I feel all the better for it." But Cocteau was now seeing Maritain much less; and Desbordes, in one of the pieces he was writing under Cocteau's influence, praised Cocteau's *Letter* but not Maritain's *Reply*, and spoke of God in quite un-Maritain terms.

Cocteau and Desbordes spent part of the summer in Chantilly and then motored south, visiting Gertrude Stein in Belley. On September 14, in Nice, Isadora Duncan met her famous death by strangulation when the flowing red scarf she was wearing caught in the wheel of her automobile. Cocteau, who had known her since she had first danced publicly in Paris, wrote to Wescott: "Isadora's end is *perfect* — a kind of horror that leaves one calm." Nineteen twenty-seven, Cocteau's first year with Desbordes and his first year in over a decade that was barren of artistic accomplishment, ended with his giving another lecture at the Université des Annales, this one consisting chiefly of his reading *Orphée* and another short play called *Oedipe Roi*, similar in form to his *Antigone*. This *Oedipe*, now

---

* One of these, written after Desbordes had seen Cocteau in *Orphée* from backstage, provides a glimpse of the behavior of both the audience and Cocteau himself during a performance: "People laughed at the horse with human legs and at his name, 'Horse.' They laughed at Orpheus and his anger, at death in a red dress, at the length of that dress, at the angelic angel with glass wings. You could hear the audience stir at each word it liked, and fall silent the moment the angel's angry tone made them understand that it wasn't funny."

read for the first time, was, he announced, "taken from my draft for the Latin text of an oratorio in collaboration with Stravinsky, *Oedipus Rex*." As printed in his "Complete Works," it is called "a free adaptation after Sophocles," and dated "Villefranche-sur-Mer, October 27, 1925": clearly he had been determined from the outset to salvage what French he could from the latinizing. The reader will recall that the Comédie Française "happened" to ask him for a French *Oedipus* just when he had been preparing in "secrecy" the *Oedipus* to be latinized for Stravinsky, and that Stravinsky had little or no credence in the "coincidence." Had Cocteau shown them this *Oedipe*? Only now, in 1927, did he publicly reveal its existence. It was not destined to be performed by the Comédie Française, but ten years after its first reading at the Université des Annales it would be given a production in Paris in which one member of its three-man chorus would be a young actor, hitherto unknown to Cocteau, named Jean Marais.

A biography of Cocteau is not a biography of Gabrielle Chanel, but there are points at which the one could temporarily become the other or from which the two could for a stretch run parallel. Chanel's costumes for Cocteau's productions, with the resultant influence on fashion as seen particularly in *Le Train Bleu* and *Orphée;* the camaraderie that grew up between them and included bursts of affectionate generosity on Chanel's part, as exemplified especially in her sending her doctor to Radiguet and paying for his funeral — there could be a number of such chapters. The year 1928 could be a chapter in itself. Since that night at the Ritz in 1917 when Paul Morand noted that she was "definitely becoming a 'personality,' " Chanel had not only become the most famous couturier in the world, but, as Maurice Sachs put it, "She in a way inaugurated the reign of the couturiers. She held court and open table, and dispensed privileges and pensions that Bernard Grasset called 'the pensions of the Grande Mademoiselle.' " At this time she was living in an immense *hôtel particulier* in the Faubourg St. Honoré, whose garden ran back to the Avenue Gabriel. According to Sachs (who was now free after his eighteen months of military service), she commissioned him on Cocteau's recommendation to assemble a library for her, giving Sachs ample funds for the purpose, funds which he misused. Cocteau himself she asked to be her house guest. "Jean is now living in a palace," Bourgoint wrote Wescott. "From his bed he can see the trees of the Champs-Elysées and the obelisk, at the foot of a big garden"; and Jean Hugo's journal for 1928 makes frequent mention of brilliant dinner parties at Chanel's with Cocteau and Desbordes among the guests. Mademoiselle Chanel's responses to questions concerning the non-dressmaking aspects of her career can best be described as irregular: perhaps some future Chanel biographer will describe the episode of her sheltering Cocteau that spring and early summer. Nowadays she speaks of him in terms that vary with the day. One day: "He was charming — very well mannered — so nice that one forgave him everything. Very little money — I could put him up, pay for his cures." Another day: "Cocteau? An insect! An *amusing* insect, if you will." *

How many of his cures she paid for is not known: perhaps she had taken care of the bills from the Thermes Urbains and the doctors in 1925; and now, in 1928, a young American, Wesson Bull, who spent part of the autumn at the Hotel Welcome in Villefranche, happened to learn of her new participation: "One day I went through the Welcome lobby while Cocteau was on the telephone. (There were none in the bedrooms.) He was speaking in a pleading voice, apparently almost in tears. Later it was explained to me that he had been begging Mlle. Coco Chanel to allow him to go on smoking longer than had been agreed. (He was overdue at a *maison de santé* for a cure.) And Mlle. Chanel had said *no!*" "Cocteau and Desbordes spent most of the day in their room smoking opium heavily," Mr. Bull says. "One always knew when, since its particular and unmistakable 'fumes' filled the corridors. (I remember wondering how it was possible to smoke so openly in a public hotel without trouble from authority — but there never was any to my knowledge.) . . . They wore their hair alike, longish

* In a recent article in an American magazine Mademoiselle Chanel is quoted as calling Cocteau "a snobbish little pederast who did nothing all his life but steal from people." In the same article she is also quoted as saying that "Fashion must be beautiful first, and ugly afterward. Art must be ugly first, then beautiful afterward." The article fails to mention that the second quotation comes from a eulogy of Chanel by none other than Cocteau himself, which appeared during the Fifties in *Harper's Bazaar*. Cocteau in his early works frequently recurs to this theme of the strangeness of new beauty in art, and has often been quoted by other writers. See, for example, Harold Acton, in his novel *Peonies and Ponies* (1941): "New beauty, as Jean Cocteau had said, cannot have a beautiful air: it should not seem or appear to be beautiful on new acquaintance."

and unparted, rather silky as if always just washed and dried. Once they put in appearance with brilliant scarlet gums and tongues, quite startling in effect. It was some kind of mouthwash Cocteau had discovered and used doubtless in order to 'astonish': it was never referred to."

Cocteau was now writing his *Livre Blanc,* whose quality of extreme voyeurism reflects his opium-induced sexual impotence. He had not been faithful to his resolve to smoke prudently. As with most addicts, the propensity to increase the dose was irresistible, and he became another illustration of the doctors' adage: "If you need it that badly, you can't use it in moderation." One of the reasons he later gave for undergoing his second cure was: "It is impossible to imagine the effort I had to make to break through the walls by which opium had completely separated me from the world, in order to help with *J'Adore.*"

J'Adore was Desbordes' first book, out that autumn, a collection of short effusions for which Cocteau wrote a fulsome blurb, printed by Grasset along with the author's picture in his sailor suit. The title expresses the worship Desbordes claims to accord everything in the world: the book has sometimes been lent the unmerited dignity of being called "pantheistic." "My heart is full of love, my limbs are filled with sap and live in a perpetual springtime," one passage reads. "I come everywhere, in gardens and on my own body; it is a carnal prayer. I have ceased to experience silence. When I think of nothing, I listen to love rising. I sense my sex at the lightest touch of a hand. . . . I take love from everything. I can sense every drop of sperm in the air, and I never fail to transform it. Everything fertilizes me." Another: "I declare that the Holy Sacrament which is a loving presence exists in affection. I declare that when this miraculous affection brings together two beings, to the point of causing them to die for each other, the Divine presence is no longer in the church, but in the lovers' soul. . . . Jacques Maritain murmurs that human love is a disfigured, violated love, grace betrayed. Love is royal. It reigns over the many Versailles of the heart. It stops Satan as fire stops wild beasts."

Maritain's reaction to sentiments of that kind caused Cocteau to write to Wescott, "Maritain thinks that Jean is a devil in disguise. He is mistaken. Jean is a love. . . ." One sympathizes with Maritain, who wrote sardonically in *Le Roseau d'Or:* "They adore, do they! God and the genitals (and the printed page)."* For *J'Adore*, in its sexual élan, is the most self-indulgent, the most inanely masturbatory of books; purely in terms of language and imagery, its repeated featuring of hands — in close proximity to mentions of sperm, the genitals, and masturbation — is such as to make Cocteau's photographs with unbuttoned cuffs, and his talk of Harrow canes and Oxford gloves, seem the ultimate in conscious reserve and control.† Cocteau's own literary product that sinks closest to the level of *J'Adore* is *Le Livre Blanc*, the book he pretended never to admit was his, in which he clumsily grafted elements from Maurice Sachs's conversion adventures onto a chronicle of sex and voyeurism — a combination that must have further revolted poor Maritain. To picture the pair of lovers simultaneously writing *J'Adore* and *Le Livre Blanc* is to realize how distant Cocteau was, at this moment of Desbordes' first ascendance, from the summer of five years before on the beach at Le Lavandou and Pramousquier when Radiguet was writing *Le Bal du Comte d'Orgel* and Cocteau *Le Grand Ecart*, *Thomas l'Imposteur*, *Antigone* and *Plain-Chant*.

In addition to *Le Livre Blanc*, Cocteau was writing an essay in praise of the painter Giorgio di Chirico, called *Le Mystère Laïc*, and these two books, plus his sponsoring of *J'Adore*, mark his first artistic stumbling. But along with them he had composed a moving one-act dramatic monologue that was destined for great success; and almost immediately afterward would come a fascinating diary, a masterly novel, and a masterpiece in a new medium — film; nor would these be his last works of excellence. From now on he was to fluctuate. The sponsoring of *J'Adore* revealed that the need to associate himself with a "son" was now so strong as to blur his percep-

* Maritain's mention of *J'Adore* in *Le Roseau d'Or* reads in full as follows: "I have just received the final page proofs of a book with a preface by Jean Cocteau in which he makes himself a laughing stock by celebrating the author as an Adam before the fall and by urging the young to embrace a new religion of love — a religion which proclaims all love to be pure. The dying echo of Les Charmettes. They adore, do they! God and the genitals (and the printed page). I know how puerile this is, but it is a betrayal of Christ perpetrated with the most horrible lack of awareness. I also know what tragic suffering dwells in Cocteau's heart, and I wish I could be silent. But to suffer the profanation of the Gospels, the confusion of raving sensuality with religion — that is impossible."

† One of the masturbation fantasies, which takes place beside a tree — "I touch the tree and the branch stands up" — aroused the resentment of Serge Lifar. "I told Cocteau about making love to a willow tree, in Russia," he once said indignantly, "and a few months later I found the story signed 'Jean Desbordes'!"

tion of what the son's intrinsic value might be, and *Le Mystère Laïc* betrayed an equally glaring lack of plastic vision. The resulting flaw was from now on to show itself frequently. It was to produce a number of banalities, some of them appearing simultaneously with his greatest works. This contrast — inexplicable, but perhaps even necessary to the artist — was to be characteristic of the later Cocteau.

Chirico's early, intense, dreamlike paintings had been admired by the Surrealists, but in 1928 Breton had just dismissed his late work in his volume *Le Surréalisme et la Peinture*. In one of his self-defenses against the charge of always flowing with the current, Cocteau spoke proudly of having written *Le Mystère Laïc* "when it was considered the moment to drop Chirico" — a reference to Breton; but Breton had not dropped Chirico, only his later work; and certainly Chirico's later, heavy-handed stylizations of antiquity are sadly inferior to his early pictures. James Thrall Soby's contrast between Chirico and Picasso, pointing out that Chirico "lacked the insolence and wit which permitted Picasso to treat antiquity as a fascinating charade, capable of infinite and often irreverent interpretation," could be made equally well between Chirico and Cocteau: Chirico's neoclassical canvases lack the verve of *Orphée*. Although Cocteau's defense is on the surface a mere doctrinaire rebuttal of Breton, strangely enough there seems to be a relation between this defense of indefensible painting and the onset of fluctuation in the quality of Cocteau's own drawing. Already on the 1926 program cover for his recital at Isadora Duncan's studio in Nice, his drawing is reminiscent of the new Chirico; and from now on there are all too many Orpheuses with lyres and chitons and other neoclassic paraphernalia. Cocteau's earlier drawings — the witty caricatures in *Dessins*, the series of searching self-portraits done in the mirror at the Welcome — are, like Chirico's early paintings, on a different level from most of his later work. In 1934 he was to write an inferior verse text to accompany a series of lamentable Chirico lithographs. Like all Cocteau's essays, *Le Mystère Laïc* has its attractions — the story of the dream of the Harrow canes is there, and it contains the most celebrated of all his quips: "Victor Hugo was a madman who thought he was Victor Hugo." But it is badly defaced by doctrinaire, almost philistine sneers at Redon and Freud — to say nothing of a dismissal of the Impressionists *en bloc* — and is in general not a happy work. Along with *Le Livre Blanc* it is the first indication that Cocteau's pen could not always be depended on, as in the earlier days, to flow dazzlingly in any one of the constantly changing channels of his predilection.

But now once again, as with *L'Ange Heurtebise* and *Orphée,* came the unexpected.

On December 16, 1928 Cocteau entered a clinic in suburban Saint-Cloud. This cure, or at least his stay in the hospital, lasted over three months — far longer than medically necessary, and long enough to inspire his friends' quite appropriate remark that "clinics are nice quiet places to write books in." In a letter to Anna de Noailles, asking her to write to the rue d'Anjou, whence his mail was brought to him at the hospital, he said "Maman does not know" — an extraordinary fact if true. "Believe it or not," he wrote to Monroe Wheeler, "I have taken my courage in both hands, and send you this letter from a clinic. I am under treatment. I didn't want to give Jean [Desbordes] a bad example." (But the bad example had already been given: Desbordes, himself now an addict, about this same time underwent home withdrawal under the care of his sister near Fontainebleau.) After the first week in Saint-Cloud, Cocteau began to keep a notebook, later published under the title *Opium.* ("You are the first patient I have ever seen write after the first week," his nurse marveled: but how many Cocteaus had she known?) Like the notebook of any writer of consequence, whether intended for publication or not — one thinks of the jottings of Flaubert, Hawthorne, Henry James — it is a fascinating document and has been widely translated. There are passages that have brought particular praise from doctors, such as "I should like this account to be placed alongside medical pamphlets and the literature of opium. May it serve as a guide to beginners who do not realize that in the very slowness of opium there lurks the most dangerous form of speed." In that salutary warning that any drug "gets you there before you know it," Cocteau's use of the word *"vitesse"* ("speed" — now in English the common nickname of methamphetamine) is another of his uncanny anticipations of usages to come, like so many casual touches in his early spectacles, in *Or-phée*, in the swinging aspects of his way of life. Decorated though *Opium* is with coctelian exaggerations, fantasies, coincidences and other self-projections, doctors find it sound in its medical observations: even an improbable entry like "I am writing these lines after twelve days and twelve nights without sleep" casts light on the tendency of patients in post-withdrawal depression not to know that they have slept — they dream that they are awake. There are sharp details concerning the importance of the personality of nurse, physician and psychiatrist for a patient in isolation. The dramatic, tortured-looking drawings accompanying the text resembled those that Cocteau made during his first cure; entire figures are sometimes composed of phallic, tubelike shapes that one realizes have one of their origins in opium pipes. Doctors say that some of the drawings are clearly adapted from anatomical illustrations in medical books, and that the prevalent sureness of line rules out the degree of psychotic hallucination under which Cocteau implicitly suggested all were done.

During the first month of withdrawal, purges and sudations he had no visitors. Among his correspondents was Gertrude Stein, to whom he wrote thanks for her kindness; Princess Bibesco sent him her just published *Au Bal avec Marcel Proust*, which perhaps inspired him to write the section in *Opium* called "Nous Deux Marcel: Notes sur Proust." (Those pages marked, he said, the "return of memory" as his intoxication diminished.) There are also paragraphs in praise of Raymond Roussel, the eccentric author of *Impressions of Africa* and *Locus Solus*, inspired by Roussel's presence as patient in the same clinic: Cocteau could look down into Roussel's room from his own. After five weeks he wrote: "Regain healthy appearance and strength in my legs." Friends began to come — Desbordes, Bérard, Max Jacob, Paul Morand, Maurice Sachs; on February 21 the Hugos, and Marcel Jouhandeau and the dancer Caryathis, who announced their engagement. To Gabriel Astruc, who wanted to come on business, Cocteau wrote suggesting that he not come Sunday afternoon, for then he often had visits from *"jeunesse."* On February 28 Gide came. On March 19 Cocteau made his "first outing in an automobile," to the Comédie Française — not to a performance, but to a meeting of the Reading

Committee. Some time before entering the hospital he had written and sent in a one-act monologue that he had entitled *La Voix Humaine* (The Human Voice), and now he had been invited to read it to the committee of actors and administrators who accepted or rejected new plays. In *Opium* he jotted down details of his reading that afternoon: "Dark little room, full of portraits of Racine, Molière, Rachel. Green baize tabletop. Lamp as in an examining magistrate's office. [He meant that the lamp was turned full on him: was the comparison inspired by memories of the confrontations with "police, magistrate, and mayor" following "youthful indiscretions" when he was nineteen or twenty?] The members of the committee listen in poses reminiscent of some famous painting, 'Z—— reading X——.'" After the reading, which brought immediate acceptance of *La Voix Humaine* for production by the Comédie Française, he drove back to Saint-Cloud.

There was no medical reason for his remaining. In fact Mademoiselle Chanel, who had been paying the very large bills, had recently returned from a trip, heard about his daily entertaining at the clinic, visited him, found him well, and suggested to him that he move out — "*quitter,*" as a French biographer elegantly puts it, "*la villégiature coûteuse.*" But he obtained a few weeks' grace: something was going on.

Cocteau says that it began with a visit to the clinic from Jacques Chardonne, a partner in the publishing house of Stock, which had issued *Le Grand Ecart* six years before. Like most publishers, Chardonne wanted "another novel." "He scolded me: 'The thought of having to write a masterpiece is giving you writer's cramp. You're paralyzed at the sight of a blank sheet of paper. So begin any old way. Write: "One winter evening . . ."' So I wrote: 'The Cité Monthiers is wedged in between the rue d'Amsterdam and . . .'" Such is Cocteau's account of the writing of the famous opening of *Les Enfants Terribles:* as usual, one can only say that it *may* have been that way. "My unconscious self . . . kindly allowed me to become its scribe, and dictated my book to me," he once said of the novel; and in *Opium* he said that it was written in the hospital in seventeen days. In 1935 he wrote that "A great force was raging in me, dictating eighteen pages every day"; on television in 1963 the story was different: "I wrote seven pages a day. I think that I once said that I wrote seventeen, but that was a bit of bragga-docio. I wrote seven pages a day, no more. And in the middle of the book, when Elisabeth marries the young American, I wanted to say things that interested me about America. I wanted to take a per-sonal hand in it, I wanted to 'take off,' and the mechanism promptly broke down. I had to wait two weeks before it started up again." *

His concentration impressed his nurse — "She told Raymond Roussel (who occupied a nearby room), and he repeated it to me: 'When my patient is writing, he looks like someone you wouldn't want to meet in a dark wood' " — and the writing of *Les Enfants Terribles* was clearly one of those blessed creative acts that take place quickly with great drive. He wrote to Gide: "The real benefit of my treatment: work has laid hands on me. I am producing a book that I have been wanting to write since 1912. It is emerging without a struggle. It gives me its orders and is a hard taskmaster: I'll have done several months' work in nineteen days."

The writing of *Les Enfants Terribles* partakes both of the pre-opium fertility of the summer of 1922 and the unexpected, post-cure onrush of *Orphée* (issuing out of the narcoticized *Ange Heurtebise*) in 1925: the uncanny atmosphere of the novel is closer to that of the play than to the limpidity of the earlier books, and Cocteau, in one of the last entries in *Opium*, his novel finished, wrote well and prophetically of the drug and his work:

"Now that I am cured I feel emptied, disheartened, sick. I'm adrift. The day after tomorrow I leave the clinic. Leave it for what? Three weeks ago I felt something like elation, I asked M. about altitudes, about little hotels in the snow. I was about to emerge. But in fact it was a book that was about to emerge. It is a book that 'is coming out,' is about to be released, as publishers say — it is not me. I could die, and it wouldn't care. The work that is exploiting me needed opium; it needed my giving up opium. . . . I was won-dering — will I go back to smoking or won't I? Useless to pretend

---

* For some reason, Cocteau all his life kept mentioning precise figures in connection with *Les Enfants Terribles*. He wrote in 1962: "I have often told how I was stopped in the writing of *Les Enfants Terribles* at the Clinique de Saint-Cloud — in batches of seventeen pages each — by having presumed to drop my role as medium and replace it with certain personal ideas; the mysterious force that was dictating the book to me turned its back on me and silently withdrew. I had to wait, rebuked, until after seven-teen days the rhythm consented to start up again."

nonchalance, dear poet. I'll smoke again if my work so decides —
and if opium so decides."

Les Enfants Terribles is a novel of genius, weirdly prophetic in
its forecasting of today's era of alienated youth. Its brother-and-
sister pair of leading characters, Paul and Elisabeth, inspired by
Jean and Jeanne Bourgoint, are among Cocteau's most striking
literary inventions. No characters like them had appeared in
fiction before, and Cocteau embodied in them qualities which,
while always present in young people, were at the time this influential novel was written just beginning to grow into a wave that has
since become tidal. In this book, which, as Cocteau says, "opens
with a white ball [a snowball] and closes with a black one [a bul-
let]," he brews together, in the tenebrous atmosphere that opium
had made his, various pungent ingredients gathered over forty
years: a bloody snowball fight in the Cité Monthiers (an alley
where he had played as a schoolboy); the bully "Dargelos" and his
erotic magnetism; the angelic simplicity of Jean Bourgoint and his
room-sharing twinship with the beautiful delinquent Jeanne; their
room, as cluttered as Cocteau's own in the rue d'Anjou, and another
room, large, bare, mysterious, resembling a greenhouse, like one
into which he had looked from his hospital window; a revolver shot
and blood that go back to the rue La Bruyère in 1898 and to Venice
ten years later. To Gertrude Stein he wrote that he had been
"carrying the book" since 1913. She had asked him whether Jean
Bourgoint was the "original" of Paul, and he replied that though he
had not tried for a "resemblance," "no doubt certain impressions
of our Jean provided a foundation. As I see it, a novel should be a
roman à clef only for us, the authors." For Elisabeth, he said, "I
'saw' Greta Garbo at eighteen." Also to Roland Caillaud, who in
1931 was Greta Garbo's neighbor in California, he wrote: "Tell
Madame Garbo that I had her in mind when I wrote about Elisabeth. I even put in an exact description of her features at the end,
when Elisabeth takes up the revolver."

On its publication in 1930, *Les Enfants Terribles* became one of
those books that are adopted as a kind of *vade mecum* by the young.
Today Frenchmen and non-Frenchmen of middle age and over still
speak of its extraordinary effect of revealing to them hitherto unsuspected depths of their adolescent selves, inspiring them with

feelings of proud youthful exclusivity. Cocteau came to know that
he had invented a youth that would come to fullest flower only
later. After the Second World War he wrote that he had been surprised by the popularity of the strange book, and that the popularity
had already come in two waves. "The book's success made me
realize that many young people of both sexes found themselves
mirrored in Paul and Elisabeth. That was the first wave. The second
wave was made up of young people who tried to imitate the strange
agoraphobia of the room in which my heroes were avoiding the
'plural' that was waging a fierce war against the 'singular.' "

In the meantime, following withdrawal, there came what Cocteau
called "the worst moment," all the worse for his having clung so
long to his hospital: "It is hard to live without opium when you
have experienced it, because once you have experienced opium it is
hard to take this earth seriously. And unless one is a saint, it is hard
to live without taking the earth seriously. After the cure comes the
worst moment, the greatest danger. Health, but with a great hole in
it, and immense depression. The doctors loyally hand you over to
suicide." He moved out of the clinic to the small Hotel St. Germain-
des-Prés in the rue Bonaparte. "Those little hotel rooms where I
have been camping for so many years," he added to the notes of
Opium. "Rooms for making love in, where I have been practicing
friendship without respite — an occupation a thousand times more
exhausting than lovemaking. When I left Saint-Cloud I kept telling
myself 'It's April. I'm strong. I have a book that I didn't expect.
Any room in any hotel will do.' Well, my hanged-man's room in the
rue Bonaparte became truly a room to hang oneself in. I had forgotten that opium transfigures the world, and that without opium a
sinister room remains sinister."

At this moment he was for some reason particularly short of
funds. Gabriel Astruc asked him on behalf of Philippe de Rothschild, whose father, Baron Henri de Rothschild, had refurbished for
him the Théâtre Pigalle in Montmartre, for permission to name a
bar that was to open in the building "Le Bar de Thomas l'Imposteur" (Moysès having made a success not only of "Le Boeuf sur le
Toit" but of another bar with a coctelian name, "Le Grand Ecart,"
in Montmartre); and Cocteau replied from the Welcome, whither
he had escaped with Desbordes from the suicidal room in the rue
Bonaparte.

Cocteau to Gabriel Astruc
Hôtel Welcome
Villefranche-sur-Mer, A.M.
May 1929

Très cher Gabriel,

Think of Thomas, the snow, his death, and you will understand that it is not possible to associate him with drink-
peddling. Besides, I'm broke and trying to find the wherewithal to pay my Villefranche hotel bill. This poverty is the
result of my having always followed a straight line. Why spoil
the picture and encourage people to go on saying that I am
growing rich from bars?

But I don't like to refuse you and scold you, and I would
like to do Philippe de R. a favor. So tell him that he can have
"Le Bar des Mariés de la Tour Eiffel," and that no one else
will have my permission to use that name. But please tell
everybody that I'm not a barman . . . In return, Ph. de R.
could perfectly well put on midnight performances of *Oedipe*
for a couple of weeks. Chanel would do the costumes gratis.

Astruc promptly offered to send him money, but there is no record as to whether Cocteau accepted. *Oedipe* was never performed at
the Pigalle, which proved to be an unpopular, unlucky theatre. Its
bar, eventually baptized "Les Enfants Terribles," also failed to
catch on.

During the summer and autumn *Les Enfants Terribles* (the
novel) enjoyed a generally triumphant press, including a nine-
page consecration as a masterpiece by Albert Thibaudet in the
N.R.F.; the shower of praise was interspersed with numerous
scenes of jealousy and reconciliation with Desbordes, who was in-
dulging in escapades with companions of both sexes. (His vehicle,
in the literal sense, was the Citroën bought by Cocteau with his
earnings from *Oedipus* and from Moysès, and which Desbordes
eventually drove into a wall and demolished.) "I came back to a
thousand personal unpleasantnesses, and in addition I have to rehearse Bovy," Cocteau wrote to Astruc in October or November.
"Bovy" was the actress Berthe Bovy, who had been chosen for the
solo role in *La Voix Humaine*.

Of all Cocteau's works for the stage, it is probably *La Voix*

Humaine that has been most widely performed, and certainly it is the most immediately accessible, the most directly human and moving. It is a one-act monologue, spoken into a telephone by a woman in despair; her lover of many years, with whom she is still infatuated, is to be married the next day to someone else; this is their farewell. The lover pretends to be alone, telephoning from his own house; it becomes obvious that he is lying, that he is with his bride-to-be; his deceit is motivated partly by cowardice, partly by unbearable kindness; his inexorableness, the bleak horror of the mistress's anguish, are searingly conveyed — the depth of feeling displayed is rare in Cocteau, and suggests inspiration from personal experience of a similar kind, perhaps the memory of some renegade adventure of Radiguet's. The drama is heightened by consummate use of the maddening idiosyncracies of the telephone — wrong numbers, unanswered rings, cuttings-off, overheard music. It has had a triumphant worldwide career of bravura solo performances by many actresses — among them, in addition to Berthe Bovy at the Comédie Française, Anna Magnani (in Italian, on film), Ingrid Bergman (in English, on disc and on television), Jo Ann Sayers (in French on a New York stage), Lillebil Ibsen (in Norwegian, on a stage in Oslo). "Very moving," Ingrid Bergman has said of it, "and the most difficult thing to do, as you are alone throughout with a mute telephone for inspiration." Francis Poulenc later gave it a vocal and orchestral score, to which it has been sung in French by Denise Duval at the Opéra Comique in Paris, at La Piccola Scala in Milan, and on a disc. It has a high professional finish, and very early in its run at the Comédie Française it was clearly seen to be bound for extraordinary success: Tristan Bernard wrote of it that it "rolled along like a gold piece."

Its first preview, however, or *"répétition intime,"* at the Comédie Française the afternoon of February 15, 1930, was the occasion of a grotesque episode. Berthe Bovy, beautiful and agonized in the nightgown and negligee designed for her by Christian Bérard, had just begun her tormented monologue, when suddenly, in the words of Cocteau's latest French biographers, "someone in a box began to wave a newspaper to attract attention and cries were heard — 'Obscene! Enough! Enough! It's Desbordes on the other end of the line!' Bovy was bewildered and became confused. Others in the audience shouted back. Cocteau, from his seat, called for silence. The film director Eisenstein had been sent two tickets; he had come with Paul Eluard, who had kept on his hat and shouted the first insults. One of Cocteau's partisans snatched off Eluard's hat, another burned him on the neck with a cigarette; a fight was about to break out. Cocteau intervened. Eluard was ejected. Gradually order was restored. The *scandale* had its conclusion after the performance, in the administrator's office, where Eluard and Cocteau exchanged words. The episode did not prevent the two men from meeting on a friendly basis later."

The poet Paul Eluard, in his combination of artistic and personal sensibility with aberrations that included hard-line hooliganism, was a Surrealist mutation of Cocteau and *his* strange mosaic of traits; and his gesture was ostensibly just another Surrealist cutting-down of Cocteau. That this dandy and pederast, far from falling by the wayside as they had decreed, should have moved brilliantly to the forefront enraged them; and they branded him more contemptible than ever for having openly "joined the establishment" with production of his play at the state-controlled Comédie Française, the "Maison de Molière." But the French biographers make no mention of what was for Cocteau the heart of the matter. What makes Eluard's irruption — apparently the last Surrealist disturbance at a Cocteau production — dramatic and even touching in Cocteau's biography is the fact that at that moment it was Eluard, among the Surrealists, whom Valentine Hugo had made her particular friend (she and Jean Hugo had by this time separated). Whether or not Valentine had known in advance of Eluard's intention to cause a disturbance, his abuse can only have seemed to Cocteau as emanating from close to her, his "sister" since 1916. Five days after the event he wrote her.

Cocteau to Valentine Hugo

February 20, 1930

Très chère Valentine,

I very much hope that you don't think I am "avoiding" you out of some ridiculous vanity, but this play cost me so much effort, so much toil, represents in my eyes a turning-point so invisible and so difficult, I have staked so much on it, that, loving you, respecting you, believing you, I am afraid of being discouraged at a moment when I need every ounce of my

courage. I understand perfectly that you may dislike both the
play and the actress, and that my present perspective differs
from yours — but anything you say carries so much weight
with me both intellectually and emotionally that I have forbidden myself to step outside my own domain, lest I see it in
another light. . . .

It has been said that the inspiration of *La Voix Humaine*, which
thus marked another step in the alienation of Valentine Hugo from
Cocteau, may have been the telephone conversation of a couple in
disagreement,* one end of which Cocteau overheard and wrote
about in a letter to Max Jacob: "They kept losing the connection,
hanging up, and trying again. Georges kept groaning 'Hello
Hello!' into a dead mouthpiece." That may have suggested the
frame, but the peculiar power and poetry of this monologue can
only be the fruit of personal suffering. Cocteau is not a writer from
whom one usually expects direct evocation of human tragedy —
rather, his power lies in his ability to reveal, by strange fantasies,
paradoxes, dislocations and juxtapositions, innumerable facets of
experience both emotional and intellectual. (One recalls Proust's
"representing the highest truths by a dazzling symbol.") *La Voix
Humaine* is a masterly exception. Perhaps it was his transcription
of it into heterosexual terms that accounts for what might be considered its flaws: the degree of acceptance and "understanding" im-
puted by Cocteau to his abandoned woman is scarcely plausible in
the heterosexual context he portrays — he himself seems to have
realized this, and inserted the observation that people in general
cannot be expected to understand; and the lack of any suggestion
that the devoted lover might have married his mistress rather than
turn to someone else hints at the greater disorder, the lesser motivation, of many homosexual relations.

* Possibly Prince and Princess Georges Ghika. The princess was the former cour-
tesan Liane de Pougy. "Liane reproaches Georges for his loose living," Cocteau writes
in the same letter.

The Blood of a Poet (*1929–1932*)

On February 10, 1923, at Grasse, the lady who later described herself as having been Cocteau's "Lolita," the twenty-one-year-old heiress Marie-Laure Bischoffsheim (granddaughter of Laure de Sade — Comtesse de Chevigné — Duchesse de Guermantes — "Corporal Petrarch"), had been married to the Vicomte Charles de Noailles, of a branch of the family different from that married into by Anna, née de Brancovan, the poetess. Cocteau was not present, being at the time busy every evening in Montmartre as the chorus of *Antigone,* but the wedding reception at the Villa Croisset (his old "sanatorium") was attended by a throng of guests both titled and untitled (the elderly American painter Mary Cassatt was among them), and the young people proceeded within the next few years to divide their time among their several houses — the splendid Bischoffsheim town house on the Place des Etats-Unis in Paris, a chateau near Fontainebleau, and a villa called Saint-Bernard at Hyères on the Mediterranean, close to Edith Wharton's Sainte-Claire. The young vicomtesse, who had had her portrait drawn by Picasso, enjoyed avant-garde artistic activities, carrying her more traditional-minded husband along in her wake; and on July 10, 1929, Jean Hugo records, after a dinner in their Paris house at which the guests included Cocteau, Madame de Chevigné, Poulenc, the Jean Hugos and the Etienne de Beaumonts, there was a showing of *Un Chien Andalou,* the film which Salvador Dali and Luis Buñuel had made the year before and which had not yet been shown publicly, although there had been private screenings at the Théâtre du Vieux-Colombier. *Un Chien Andalou* is still an impressive film, and must then have been sensational, with its nightmare images of a wounded hand crawling with ants, an eyeball slashed by a razor blade, a bloody calf on a piano. It is sometimes called "the first Surrealist film," but it would be more accurate to say that it was among the films adopted by the Surrealists as precursors of their movement, as they had adopted Chirico's early paintings. Dali and Buñuel formally joined the Surrealists after making *Un Chien Andalou.*

At the end of the year, Cocteau was one of the guests at a New Year's houseparty at the Noailles' villa in Hyères. It was probably there that he learned of the death, on Christmas Eve, of Jeanne Bourgoint. Always erratic, the girl had lately been the subject of ever-increasing gossip: there were stories of a male lover's suicide, slaps and insults from the "monster" Princesse Violette Murat, an abortion, alcohol, narcotics, cures in an Arcachon clinic, wooing by a worthy, dull, unbearable man. The elegant mannequin, the casually smart young woman, had become a slut, seldom dressing or bathing, sleeping in dirty sheets. That Christmas Eve, Jean Bourgoint and Georges Geffroy (today a well-known Parisian designer and decorator) had been visiting a friend; in the antique velvet of their host's Régence sofa, Bourgoint, lolling and awkward as usual, had burned a hole with his cigarette; the host had made an "observation," and Geffroy, offended for the embarrassed Bourgoint, had taken him away; they parted at the door of the Bourgoints' house in the rue Hippolyte-Lebas. An hour later Geffroy was wakened by the ringing of his doorbell; it was Bourgoint, in tears: his mother had found Jeanne unconscious in bed, and the girl had been rushed to the Hôpital Lariboisière in an ambulance. Together Geffroy and Bourgoint went to the hospital: Jeanne was already dead, of barbiturate poisoning. Such was the cruel end of one of the "originals" of Cocteau's *enfants terribles.*

After that, we next hear of Cocteau when Bernard Berenson, the historian of Italian Renaissance painting, who was visiting Edith Wharton in her Château-Sainte-Claire, was invited to lunch with Mrs. Wharton at Saint-Bernard. Cocteau began to praise Picasso's painting, and displayed a Cubistic collage, which Berenson declared repulsive; whereupon the entire Noailles houseparty so sharply ridiculed Berenson's blindness to Picasso and to modern art in general that he went away feeling depressed and out of things, although unswerving in his poor opinion of the picture he had been shown. Actually, the "Picasso" had been concocted by Cocteau himself out of newspaper, nails and sacking the night before. If the episode can be thought of as anything more than a pointless undergraduate rag, it perhaps rebounds on Cocteau himself, as illustrating a certain lack of confidence in the very art he championed.

Among the house guests at Saint-Bernard was Auric, who declared that he would like some day to write a score for an animated cartoon. The idea amused Marie-Laure de Noailles, and Cocteau was asked whether he would write a scenario, which would then be given to a draughtsman to execute. For a time he considered doing this. The project was in the air just at the time he wrote Valentine Hugo following Eluard's demonstration at *La Voix Humaine,* and after Valentine answered him about that he wrote her again.

Cocteau to Valentine Hugo

[n.d.]

Ma chère petite Valentine,

You know that between you and me things are at a very high level, and that inattentive people who rush to conclusions are incapable of grasping subtle nuances. The main thing is to know what is possible and what is impossible, and to act accordingly. My letter, which you took as it was meant, would have been interpreted by others as offensive. I kiss you affectionately and would like to see you. Auric and the Noailles want to meet me at Fourques to discuss our project of animated cartoons. I have agreed, on the condition that I would consult you, and that I would not go to Fourques if you had any objection. Would you please telephone me and tell me whether you approve?*

Auric arrived at Fourques on February 10. About April 15 Cocteau and Desbordes joined him there, and it was apparently then that the idea of an animated cartoon was abandoned and the making of a real film with a Cocteau scenario and an Auric score was decided upon. "The technical side of the film was put in charge of a young man called Michel J. Arnaud," says one of the persons con-

---

* Mas de Fourques ("Fourques Farm") is the name of a property in the south of France, at Lunel in the Hérault, which Jean Hugo had inherited from his grandmother in 1929, and to which he had moved after separating from Valentine. Cocteau is politely asking Valentine whether she would be offended if he went to visit "the other side." He was unaware, or chose to be unaware, of how indifferent Valentine was to him at this time.

cerned, who wishes to remain anonymous, and, with Arnaud, Charles de Noailles "settled all the expenses of the film." The Noailles allotted a million francs for the Cocteau-Auric picture, and the same amount to Dali and Buñuel for a successor to *Un Chien Andalou.*

Cocteau immediately embarked on the new project — a film that was to concern the birth of poetry and to be called *La Vie d'un Poète* (The Life of a Poet), a title later changed to *Le Sang d'un Poète* (The Blood of a Poet). He was, as it turned out, to be associated with the making of many films over the years, but he never forgot the freedom he enjoyed when making his first: "I was completely free only with *The Blood of a Poet,*" he said later, "because it was privately commissioned and because I didn't know anything about the art of film. I invented it for myself as I went along, and used it like a draughtsman dipping his finger for the first time in India ink and smudging a sheet of paper with it. Originally Charles de Noailles commissioned me to make an animated cartoon, but I soon realized that a cartoon would require a technique and a team non-existent at that time in France. Therefore I suggested making a film as free as a cartoon, by choosing faces and locations that would give me the freedom enjoyed by a draughtsman who invents his own world. Moreover, I was frequently helped by chance (or at least by what is commonly called chance but never is for one who lets himself be hypnotized by a task), including even the petty vexations of the studio, where everybody thought I was mad. Once, for example, as I was nearly at the end of *The Blood of a Poet,* the sweepers were told to clean up the studio just as we had started on our last shots. But as I was about to protest, my cameraman (Périnal) asked me to do nothing of the kind: he had just realized what beautiful pictures he would be able to take through the dust raised by the sweepers in the light of the arc lamps.

"Another example: as I didn't know any film technicians, I sent out postcards to all the cameramen in Paris, giving them an appointment for seven o'clock the next morning. I decided to take the one who came first. It happened to be Pèrinal, thanks to whom many pictures in *The Blood of a Poet* can vie with the loveliest shots of our time. Unfortunately, in those days a silver salt was used in film printing, which was done at a pace impossible today. This is why cinematic art is so fragile. A very old copy of *The*

Blood of a Poet is as bright and shows as much contrast as any modern American film, whereas more recent copies look like old copies and weaken the whole effect of the film."

The "story" can be thought of, once again, as the conception of a poem (like the conception of *L'Ange Heurtebise* in Picasso's elevator) — the representation, by means of images, of a few moments in a poet's life, a speck of time whose brevity is illustrated by the opening and closing shots of a tall chimney during the few moments of its fall. Like *Orphée*, it is an attempt to tell "where poems come from," and in this new medium, with the freedom of fabrication for which he so eloquently expresses his gratitude, Cocteau reached the high point of his entire career. There has never been another film like *The Blood of a Poet*. It is not, to use the term in a doctrinaire way, a Surrealist film (the Surrealists typically branded it as a poor imitation of one): dreams and unlikely juxtapositions are not its chief matter, although they play their roles in a poet's inspiration. Cocteau said that he tried to film *poetry*, as deep-sea explorers photograph submarine life; he called the picture "a realistic documentary of unreal happenings." It is an allegory of a poem's origin in assorted realities and unrealities (in so far as those can be differentiated); and despite certain crudities and benefiting from others, it achieves the status of a poem itself. Cocteau professed scepticism concerning attempts to interpret the picture.* "The film offers, of course, immeasurable surfaces for interpretation. People often look at me with incredulity when I truthfully tell them that I could not possibly confirm or reject their interpretations, because they are entirely a matter of individual comprehension and appreciation, exactly as may be the case with most of Aesop's fables." "I am a cabinetmaker," he said. "I fashion a table: it's up to you to make it turn and talk." Cocteau also denied that the film contained any symbolism, and he displayed characteristic false naïveté in pretending to see no phallic content.

For all his decrying of interpretations, he provided one of his own:

"A film of this kind cannot be put into words. I might try to give you my personal interpretation. I might tell you: the poet's solitude

* Nevertheless, there have been several interesting interpretations, e.g., in English, C. G. Wallis, "*The Blood of a Poet*," *Kenyon Review*, Winter, 1944, and John Peale Bishop, "A Film of Jean Cocteau," in *Collected Essays* (1948). A third, sensitive, unpublished, was spoken by the American poet Richard Thoma in Hollywood in 1945.

is so great, what he creates he lives so intensely, that the mouth of one of his creations lives in his hand like a wound, and that he loves this mouth, that he loves himself, in short that he wakes up in the morning with this mouth beside him like someone he met by chance and brought home and tried to get rid of, and that he does rid himself of it by passing it on to a dead statue — and then this statue comes to life — and it takes revenge and involves him in ghastly adventures. I might tell you that the snowball fight is the poet's childhood, and that when he plays cards with his Fame, with his Fate, he cheats because he draws upon his childhood instead of upon himself. I might go on to say that after attempting to achieve earthly fame, he becomes mortally bored with the idea of immortality — that idea that is aroused in us at the sight of illustrious tombs. And I would be right to tell you all this, but I would also be wrong, for it would all be a text written after seeing the pictures. . . . I repeat that while I was working I thought of nothing, and this is why you must expose yourself to the film just as you do to Auric's noble music that accompanies it, and to any music. The same music can serve as vehicle for very different emotions or memories; and if each of us finds in this film a meaning that is right for him, then I think I have achieved my aim."

The filming and recording — Cocteau himself spoke the narrative portions — extended from April to September, 1930. Cocteau has described aspects of it in the preface and postscript accompanying the published scenario; Jean Desbordes played a small role; and a few reminiscences are provided by Lee Miller, the beautiful American girl who, having come to Paris to study photography, found herself being photographed in the film as the poet's "Fame," or "Fate":

"One night Cocteau stopped at the table where I was sitting with Man Ray at the Boeuf sur le Toit. 'Do you know anybody who wants to be tested tomorrow?' *I* did, and told Man so when Cocteau had moved on. Man disliked the idea, but told Cocteau anyway. The tests were marvelous: I fitted Cocteau's idea of a face. The script was constantly altered. Féral Benga, the black jazz dancer who played the angel, sprained his ankle and had to be a limping angel — Cocteau liked it better that way, but people have read all kinds of things into it. The star on Enrique Rivero's back was put there by Cocteau to cover a scar — he'd been shot by his mistress's husband. After nineteen retakes of the card-playing scene Rivero tore up the cards so there wouldn't be a twentieth — there was a party he wanted to go to. The chandelier was delivered in 3822 pieces, each wrapped in tissue paper, the very day the shooting was to begin. The studio was lined with mattresses to keep out sound — the mattresses were full of fleas and bedbugs that kept falling out. My 'armor' — when I was the statue — didn't fit very well: they plastered the joints with butter and flour that turned rancid and stank. They covered me with Nujol to make the costume cling: it cooked under the lights. The 'bull' (really an ox) was supplied by an abattoir and had only one horn: time and money were running out, so Cocteau made a second horn himself. A *bouvier* had to be called in to handle the animal — no one else could make it follow instructions. The little girl in the 'flying lesson,' or 'stealing lesson,' was a find from around the corner: Cocteau had a kind of Cophetua complex, you know. The Noailles came in and out, not interfering, just enjoying themselves."

The Noailles' enjoyment turned to dismay when they saw the film at its first screening in their projection room. To amuse them Cocteau had invited them and a few of their friends (Prince and Princesse de Faucigny-Lucinge, Lady Abdy, André Raval, Arturo Lopez-Wilshaw), all in evening dress and the ladies in tiaras, to be filmed as the occupants of one of a pair of theatre boxes that had been constructed in the studio, and to chat, laugh, and, at a given signal, applaud. The aftermath can be recounted in Cocteau's own words: "A very strange thing happened to me. In the Cité Monthiers set, for the scene of the card game, with the snow, the death of the boy and the arrival of the black angel, two theatre boxes were put in the place of two windows. In them sit society people who chat and watch the show, and I had asked some society people to play themselves. When they saw the film, they were shocked to find themselves laughing at a suicide. They asked me to remake the scenes, and I did so, using extras and the famous acrobat Barbette.* In the cinema, you shoot little bits at a time; people

---

* Watching the film today, one sees Barbette, then twenty-six, as the blond young woman in evening dress in the front row of the left-hand box. For an encounter with Barbette, see Appendix XIV.

don't realize that. They were delighted to chat and laugh, and they didn't know what they were laughing at. And when they saw what they were laughing at, they were shocked."

Though finished in September, 1930, *The Blood of a Poet* was not shown publicly until more than a year later. The need to re-make the scene of the theatre boxes accounted for only a small part of the delay: there was more to the story than that. The Noailles' dismay at finding themselves applauding a suicide in *The Blood of a Poet* was as nothing compared with the anguish caused them by the second of their sponsored films, the Dali-Buñuel *L'Age d'Or*. It issued from its creators a Surrealist masterpiece, but the Spanish savagery of its anti-clericalism and anti-militarism, deliberately shocking and aggressive, provoked riots in the small Montmartre theatre, Studio 28, where it was shown in November and December, 1930; ultra-Rightist hooligans shouted, tossed stink bombs, attacked spectators, threw ink on the screen, slashed Surrealist paintings hanging in the lobby of the theatre. The Rightist press demanded the withdrawal of the film, and the censor complied, banning it and ordering the police to confiscate the reels, "out of con-cern for protecting family, country, and religion." The Surrealists retorted with a pamphlet signed by Aragon, Breton, Dali, Tzara and others. As sponsors of the unspeakable film, the Noailles were suspected of sharing the Surrealists' atheism; they were rebuked by friends like the Beaumonts who for all their artistic associations had always remained *bien pensants,* and there was talk of their being threatened with excommunication from the Catholic Church. The story usually heard is that thanks to influential connections this disaster was averted, but that Charles de Noailles found himself expelled from his club, the famous Jockey (for a Noailles a severe penalty); and apparently the license required for the public show-ing of *The Blood of a Poet* was not forthcoming. "I have made a film with my blood both visible and invisible, the blood of my body and that of my soul," Cocteau wrote to Anna de Noailles from Tou-lon in January, 1931. "This film is held up for the time being, perhaps forever, because of a vicious cabal directed against your nephew Charles and his wife."

The savage anti-Church images of *L'Age d'Or* continue to keep it from many a screen even today; but *The Blood of a Poet,* after a few weeks of semi-private showings, was finally given a gala public opening at the Théâtre du Vieux-Colombier on January 20, 1932, complete with an introductory address by Cocteau; and though reviews were naturally "mixed," and a chorus of scorn arose from the Surrealists, the film then and there began the career that has kept it more or less steadily available to the successive waves of enthusiastic youth who have attained movie-going age since its debut.

In the tradition of Voltaire presenting his royalties from his plays to the actors of the Comédie Française who had performed them so well, Charles de Noailles, *grand seigneur,* presented all rights to both films to their authors.

A curious detail connected with *The Blood of a Poet* is Cocteau's often repeated statement that he had not seen *Un Chien Andalou* before making it, despite Jean Hugo's journal entry placing him at dinner at the Noailles' the night the film was shown — July 10, 1929, months before *The Blood of a Poet* was begun. Hugo considers it "most unlikely" that Cocteau should have left before the screening. Two of Cocteau's images in his film — the appearance of an open mouth in the palm of a hand, and the wiping-off of the mouth from a canvas — recall the Dali-Buñuel open wound in the palm of a hand and the wiping-off of a smile; and both films are notably bloody. On the proof sheets of his book *Opium,* Cocteau added *Un Chien Andalou,* which by then he had seen, to the list of the three other "great" films he knew — *Sherlock Holmes, Jr.* (with Buster Keaton), Charlie Chaplin's *The Gold Rush,* and Eisenstein's *Potemkin,* all of them films that had been adopted as precursors by the Surrealists. "Hollywood was becoming a deluxe garage," Cocteau wrote, "and its films were more and more like sumptuous makes of automobiles. With *Un Chien Andalou* we were back at the bicycle." It is possible that he had not seen that film before making his own; but here Cocteau is protesting not only too much but quite unnecessarily: whether or not he had seen *Un Chien Andalou, The Blood of a Poet* is utterly his own.

By the time *The Blood of a Poet* was publicly shown, *L'Age d'Or* had been adopted by Breton and the other Surrealists as one of the glories of their movement — it was their martyr film; and shortly after the public premiere of his own film on January 20 Cocteau, finding in the newspaper *Figaro* an article in which it was praised while *L'Age d'Or* was denounced, wrote a letter to Valentine Hugo.

Cocteau to Valentine Hugo

[Early 1932]

Très chère Valentine,

  This morning I found . . . an article, and what an article, by M. Bodin on *L'Age d'Or* and on my film. I would be grateful if you would tell Breton (although he already knows my attitude) how ashamed I am to receive ridiculous praise alongside ignoble stupidities about Studio 28. Since I expressed my admiration for *L'Age d'Or* in an article in *Figaro* two weeks ago, I have thought it unnecessary to reply. Besides, is there a way to reply properly in such cases?

  He had directed the letter to Valentine because by this time her *"passage dans le Surréalisme,"* as she was to call it later, had reached its peak: she had become the mistress of André Breton. The letter was delivered to her in an envelope that had no need of a stamp, for in the fall of 1931 Cocteau, while keeping his room in his mother's apartment, had rented a flat of his own for the first time, and the flat he had chosen was at 9 rue Vignon, the building in which Valentine was now living alone. Cocteau had only to leave the letter with the concierge or slip it under Valentine's door. In a letter he had sent her in 1916, from his ambulance unit, he had written: "Ma chère Valentine, we should live next to one another, deriving comfort from seeing each other's shoes outside the door, as old George Sand used to say." Years later, Valentine wrote a commentary in the margin of a photocopy of that letter: "Oh no! No! He moved into my building in the rue Vignon, on the same floor,* just opposite my door, because the Surrealists he wanted to see visited me there, especially André Breton. Result: I had to refuse to let him in. It was a catastrophe." And elsewhere she said, "When I became Breton's mistress it was a terrible blow to Cocteau. I chose the Surrealists, and could not honestly continue with him."
  Cocteau was always to treasure the memory of his years of friendship with Valentine; he continued to send her affectionate let-

---

* Actually one or two floors below.

ters until his death in 1963; and she, too, especially in her later life when her circumstances were less bright, would write affectionately, though they rarely met, and at the end she was wont to tax him, rather generally, with "ingratitude." (She outlived him by five years.) That letter to her expressing his admiration for *L'Age d'Or* is like a summary of some of the leading coctelian traits: his affection, his dependence and desire to "belong" and to be recognized, his own remarkable talent, his generosity toward the accomplishment of others, his great sensitivity and insensitivity. It seems unlikely that Breton, with his own artistic perceptions, could have failed to appreciate *The Blood of a Poet*; but as Great Dictator he could not afford to admit it. He had been indiscreet enough at one moment in the early Twenties to invite, in writing, Cocteau's collaboration; Cocteau had declined (perhaps, as suggested earlier, wishing to accept but fearing a trick); and although Cocteau later became friendly with a number of Surrealists or ex-Surrealists, Breton always remained adamant.

It is ironic that it should have been Cocteau's greatest accomplishment that shut against him the door of the woman to whom he had been closest since *Parade*. We have quoted earlier the words of another woman who knew him well (it was Marie-Laure de Noailles): "You will not find that women speak well of Cocteau — they do not have very good memories of him." There are exceptions to that; and Valentine Hugo, in her later years, after Cocteau's death, recalled him with subtler shadings. She often dwelt on his shortcomings of character, suggesting that it was he who had ended their friendship; but despite her long association with the Surrealists she never belittled Cocteau as an artist, and she made no secret of the great role he had played in her youth.

Cocteau's triumphant creation of *The Blood of a Poet*, and the loss of Valentine Hugo, his "sister," came within ten years after the earlier novels and poems written with Radiguet and the loss of that "son"; and they form the closing scenes of the long first act — the act whose episodes and interludes we have been following — by far the major act — of Cocteau's career both artistic and personal.

Other events of various magnitudes also mark the break that came at this point in his life. Diaghilev's death in Venice in August, 1929, with Serge Lifar and Boris Kochno (Diaghilev's secre-

tary) exploding in jealous rage over his deathbed and fighting
"like mad dogs" as Misia Sert looked on, then accompanying his
body with Misia in a gondola across the lagoon to the island cemetery of San Michele, was in itself the end of an era. "Of course the
entire Russian Ballet and Diaghilev were eaten from within as
though by termites, and this death epitomizes the whole thing,"
Cocteau wrote to Valentine on hearing the story. "But it brings back
so many memories! It was at a ballet rehearsal that you and I first
met — you were wearing a beautiful green dress." In later life,
although he was to pay Diaghilev many a tribute, he tended to belittle the role of the ballets in his own development. It was then that
he would say "The Russian ballets were a kind of fireworks." He
felt that they had contributed little if anything to his great discovery, the discovery that poetry was "a great solitude — a struggle
against extraneous temptations and charms."

And the financial collapse on Wall Street in October, that great
crash with which the Twenties ended, changed the aspect of
everything. Madame Gleizes, in her memoirs, recounts "an incredible scene" that she witnessed one Sunday afternoon in 1930 or
1931 in the salon of the Comtesse Greffulhe, rue d'Astorg, the very
room in which more than twenty years earlier Diaghilev had had
his first encounter with Parisian society:

> Sixty or so people were chatting pleasantly around iced
> drinks and cakes. Suddenly the hum of voices stopped and a
> deathly silence fell as all eyes stared hungrily at a gentleman
> who had just come in. There was absolutely nothing extraordi-
> nary about his appearance to account for the attention he re-
> ceived. Albert Gleizes and I, ignorant of what went on behind
> the scenes in the world of finance, looked at him with surprise.
> The gentleman walked straight up to Madame Greffulhe and
> they exchanged the customary greetings. Then, immediately,
> before he could sit down or even take more than a few steps,
> he was surrounded, practically submerged, by people who
> crowded around him, gesticulating, talking, trying to mo-
> nopolize him. It was Madame Anna de Noailles who won.
> Armed with a cup, she planted herself in front of him and then
> backed slowly away, step by step, all the while fixing him with
> her huge, beautiful eyes and saying, "Monsieur Loewenstein,

iced chocolate! Monsieur Loewenstein, iced chocolate!" He followed her, as though spellbound, and they sat down together in a distant corner.

All eyes were on them, and Madame Greffulhe seemed very amused. I asked her who this personage was. She told me that he was a very important businessman who had done extraordinary things with matches and was now doing the same with other commodities. She added, rather cynically, "They're all looking for tips on the market." Soon Madame de Noailles, looking radiant, reemerged with the great financier. Glancing around at the company, which he saw was ready to stampede him again, he proffered these words of counsel: "Sell your shirts! Buy shares in holding companies!" A manservant who was just handing me a glass of orangeade gave a start despite his training and almost drenched me. All the other servants who were passing around with trays had also heard. A few minutes later everybody in the pantry knew that it was imperative to buy shares in holding companies, and all the chauffeurs waiting in the two courtyards and the rue d'Astorg knew it too — and next day all the salespeople in the big Félix Potin grocery at the corner of the Boulevard Malesherbes, and all the concierges and storekeepers and other servants in the neighborhood, were also buying holding company shares — which in fact rose considerably.

The poetess of Cocteau's youth, who in her fifties could still charm a financier, was to die in 1933, and Cocteau would write a eulogy beginning "I have just lost a sister" — words that were equally applicable to the still-living Valentine Hugo. For the ten years between the crash and the new war, and then during that war, he would be able, with the help of opium when he could get it, to escape more or less successfully from what he and everybody else came, at first gradually and then suddenly, to see was a new order of things — some characteristics of which, especially among young people, he himself had strangely foretold. From Toulon, where he vacationed and smoked in 1931 with Jean Desbordes and Christian Bérard, he wrote to Richard Thoma: "Here there isn't the faintest shadow of the *crise*." "*Crise*" is the usual French term for the 1929 financial crash and its aftermath, and possibly that was what Cocteau was referring to. Or he may have meant the various changes in his own life. In any case, his words were a whistling in the dark. The various *crises* did indeed cast shadows, lengthening shadows, and the second act of Cocteau's two-act career was to be essentially an act of recapitulation. But the recapitulation was to contain marvels of its own — cinematic marvels, chiefly, which Cocteau was particularly suited to realize, with his inventiveness and his singular gift for divining truth by means of the fantastic. Cocteau's second act was at its brightest on film.

7
Cocteau, Jean Marais, and the Tenth Muse

The Thirties: A lesser decade

E DITH WHARTON's rhapsodic words about the youthful Jean Cocteau recalling Wordsworth's "Bliss was it in that dawn to be
alive" were written in 1933 or 1934, a year or two after the first
public showings of *The Blood of a Poet*, and her rhapsody is immediately followed by lament over Cocteau as he had become. "Every
subject touched on — and in his company they were countless —
was lit up by his young enthusiasm," she says; and then: "It is one
of the regrets of later years to have watched the fading of that light.
Life in general, and Parisian life in particular, is the cause of
many such effacements — or defacements; but in Cocteau's case
the pity is particularly great because his gifts were so many, and
his fervors so genuine. For many years I saw a great deal of him;
he came often to the rue de Varenne, and to many of my friends'
houses; but I never enjoyed his talk as much as in the leafy quiet of
Offranville."

"The leafy quiet of Offranville" was Jacques-Emile Blanche's
country house in Normandy before the First World War, and
clearly Mrs. Wharton felt that her once young friend had been
losing his "light" from the moment he first read Gertrude Stein and
met his first Cubist — neither of whom, one suspects, ever came to
the rue de Varenne. Mrs. Wharton was talented and intelligent, but
she was a *grande dame* of the old school, whose very way of speaking French was characterized by her friend Paul Bourget as *"un
peu Louis Quatorze"*; in her Château-Sainte-Claire at Hyères she
was often made uncomfortable by the modernistic antics of her
neighbors the Charles de Noailles at Saint-Bernard; and if, to her,
Cocteau's twenty years of achievement after 1913 seemed a fading
light, then *The Blood of a Poet* must have represented near eclipse.

After making *The Blood of a Poet* Cocteau let ten years go by
without further exploring the medium that had shown itself so particularly appropriate to his genius — fifteen, before making an-

other film of his own. When asked why, in later life, he replied: "Because I didn't think of it as working in a new medium. For me it was like anything else — I didn't keep telling myself 'I've made a film.' It was just something I'd done, like a poem." But the delay in exploiting the new field is only one aspect of what can be called Cocteau's *dimness* during the 1930's. It is a peculiarly coctelian kind of dimness: between *The Blood of a Poet* and the outbreak of the Second World War he wrote a series of plays that made his popular reputation, a volume of memoirs, a chronicle of a trip around the world, a sequel to *Le Potomak*, and more besides; nevertheless, something was lacking. The fact is that though Mrs. Wharton had not hit *the* mark, she had hit *a* mark: just when she was writing her sad words about Cocteau he had entered his period of least genial productivity.

His decade of the Thirties opened with an adventure as bizarre as the return to the sacraments five years before. To a private showing of *The Blood of a Poet* Serge Lifar brought a beautiful young woman with whom Cocteau seems almost instantly, amid clouds of opium, to have decided to "fall in love" and beget a son. (From now on he was frequently to say that he longed for a son of his own, and to speak of his frustration in this regard as the reason for his continuing "adoption" — there was never a legal adoption — of young men.) The beauty was a Princess by birth, worldly and elegant, married to a gifted husband much in view; she was a café-society favorite, cinema-struck, later to have a brief film career of her own. Today her "refusal" to discuss her relations with Cocteau, while charmingly incomplete, does seem to include the preference that her name not be given. In these pages let her be simply the Princess that she was, and the reader will interpret her remarks as he chooses. "There was a group of us," she has said, "who went to the movies almost every day. It was the thing to do, a form of competition: 'How many times have *you* seen *Shanghai Express?*' — that sort of thing. And we began a game of 'reporting to Jean.' His flat in the rue Vignon was a kind of shrine, with a Chinese boy, a tray of opium and pipes; lots of us smoked along with him. Sometimes there was something stronger than opium — would it have been cocaine? Jean never let me try that, though I'm sure I'd have adored it. I was mad about Jean's wit and charm, but for him the affair with me was purely physical. He wanted a son, but he was only as

Cocteau (center rear) at the Palais de Justice, Paris. (From the newspaper *Le Franc-Tireur*, January 23, 1947. One of the few unposed photographs of Cocteau.)

Cocteau and W. H. Auden at Oxford, 1956.

Jean Bourgoint in the 1920's,
and as Brother Pascal
in December 1965, two
months before his death.

Jean Marais between two "attendants"
at one of Comte Etienne de Beaumont's costume balls.

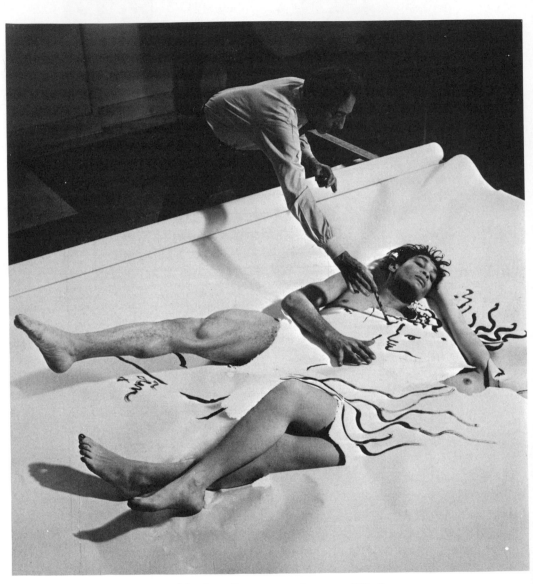

"The Poet Bringing an Image to Life."
Cocteau with Leo Coleman and a model.

Cocteau at the Villa Santo Sospir.

potent with me as one can be who is completely homosexual and full of opium. It was all shameful and disgraceful. There was no love. I didn't inspire a single one of his poems — I had no good effect at all on his writing: everyone knows that that was the least productive period of his life. There was much gossip, and my husband asked for a divorce. Finally I went to Switzerland to think things over, because Jean was always with Jean Desbordes and then I saw him getting interested in a handsome Algerian. He said he wanted to marry me, but I doubt that he would have gone through with it."

"Shameful and disgraceful" are the Princess's words: it was certainly grotesque. Did the Princess know, one wonders, of the role of the photographs in the affair? A frame displaying her photograph stood near Cocteau's bed; hidden within was a second photograph, representing, in the words of one who prefers to remain anonymous, *"un jeune homme assez souple et assez bien pourvu pour pratiquer sur lui-même ce que les médecins appelent laidement la* fellatio." That second photograph was like a talisman — analogous, one might say, to the little phallic horns of coral carried by Neapolitans against the evil eye — to counteract the dangers of the first. For a year or more Cocteau dramatized the affair with the Princess in letters and talk, and then he announced to friends that it was terminating in a new cure in a clinic — a more appropriate end than he seems to have realized for the anomalous little episode. "The worst is over," he wrote to Richard Thoma. "I love, I am loved in return, we are being parted. Without Jean Desbordes' sublime friendship I'd be dead." And he went into detail to correct the rumors that seemed to him the gravest:

Cocteau to Richard Thoma

9 rue Vignon
June 1932

For God's sake, dear Richard, don't believe that. Throughout this turmoil Jeanjean has been an angel of patience and tact. I fell desperately in love with ——, who completely reciprocated. Her husband was in America. After his second trip, since I hate the usual Parisian way of doing things I insisted that she tell him. At first he was "sublime," which I detest — it meant that he was the one to be sorry for. Then he refused to

let his wife go. I therefore decided that they should live together until the day when he would realize the stupidity of
such a relationship and would give her her freedom. Jeanjean,
who for me has always been a son, is for her a brother — in
fact he resembles her brother who was killed during the revolution. That's the story. I detest confusion and worship the
truth. This is, I assure you, the first time I have put anything
about this drama in writing, but I couldn't stand your thinking
that the Jean-Jeanjean relationship could be vulnerable to any
kind of threat from the outside. . . .

The same to the same

Clinique Salem
[February 1933]

Cher Richard,

Many strange things have been happening to me, and the
end is the strangest of all — a new cure. My work demands it,
and so do my responsibilities. . . .

Cocteau had told friends that the Princess's visit to Switzerland
was for the purpose of terminating a pregnancy for which he was
responsible; Paris laughed at him, saying that "there had always
been an opium tray between them"; and it has never been clear
whether the Princess's own quick denial of Cocteau's charge referred to both its parts or only to the second. In the acute misogyny
of his later years Cocteau was wont to refer to women as "those
killers of poets' children." "I *almost* made a little Hapsburg," he
was in the habit of lamenting — using, instead of "Hapsburg," the
name of the lady's equally illustrious family. How much was
opium fantasy or cruder mythomania on Cocteau's part will probably always continue unclear. And the entire episode could be dismissed as gossip not worth the recounting, did it not have a certain
relevance. It constitutes a kind of gloss on Mrs. Wharton's remarks
about Parisian life causing Cocteau's light to fade. It is just the
kind of Parisian episode, which, reaching her fastidious ears in the
rue de Varenne, would reinforce her in that opinion; whereas what
it really illustrates is how close together, in an artist's life, can
come the disciplined creation of a masterpiece, like *The Blood of a
Poet,* and the wildest confusion of living. It shows how mistaken are

the sometimes well-meaning commentators (and among them were friends dazzled by his presence) who say of Cocteau that "it was his life, not his work, that was his masterpiece." Out of his life, so often derailed, came the work that makes the life worth recounting.

Valentine Hugo's withdrawal of her friendship left Cocteau the poorer. Under conditions of no risk he had always enjoyed the company of women; in addition to the Comtesse de Noailles and Valentine, Irène Lagut and Marie Laurencin had been his affectionate correspondents: as Jacques Porel put it, women "formed part of the décor of his life." For years he had been accustomed to Valentine's presence even when they were apart, to a constant interchange with a beautiful woman artist of strong and fascinatingly enigmatic personality, and perhaps it was in part her forbidding him her door that had made him immediately attempt closeness with the Princess. But both the new kind of closeness and the new kind of woman were a mistake: writing about the Princess a few years later he called her "Princess Fafner," after the legendary Norse ogre, and in the film *Orphée*, the poet's death itself is not only a beautiful woman, as in the play, but is called "the Princess." Thus did he continue to associate her with his deepening misogyny.

Meanwhile he had his other intimates. He was close to the talented Christian Bérard, who, largely under the spell of opium and society, was changing from a promising painter into a fashion artist and stage designer. Jean Desbordes married in 1937; a literary and personal disappointment, he had despite Cocteau's letter to Thoma been displaced by the Algerian whose advent had made the Princess decide to "think things over." This was Marcel Khill, born Khelloui, the son of an Algerian soldier and a Norman peasant, enticed by Cocteau away from his discoverer, a French naval officer who had plucked him from a road gang and had been keeping him in his house in Toulon, in Arab costume, to help with opium pipes and other details. Cocteau dazzled Khill by putting him into the cast of one of his plays, took him around the world with him in 1936, and enjoyed with him what was apparently the most sensual relationship of his life. Henry Wibbels, Maurice Sachs's American lover of this time, has said that in speaking of Khill Cocteau tended to display uncharacteristic effeminacy in voice and manner. " 'He's a brute, you know; he slaughters me,' " Wibbels describes Cocteau as saying with a shivering gesture. " 'He's really too wild, but he's got under my skin: what can I do? He kills me.' " Wibbels had been introduced to Cocteau by Sachs, who had brought him to Paris from the United States. (Sachs had gone to the States to be an art dealer just at the time of the Wall Street crash, had married the daughter of a West Coast Protestant minister, and left her for Wibbels.) Wibbels tells of seeing Cocteau beginning to "clear out" his room in his mother's apartment at 10 rue d'Anjou:* this was the occasion of Cocteau's turning the housecleaning over to Sachs, and of Sachs's selling many more of Cocteau's letters and other documents than he should have, and pocketing most of the money paid for them by the buyer.†

It is Wibbels who in his account of his first visit to Cocteau with Sachs reveals most clearly Cocteau's way, or one of his ways, of charming and showing favor to a young aesthete:

> *"Voici,"* said Cocteau, *"une lettre de Marcel Proust."*
>
> "I was just telling Jean," said Maurice, "that you have read all Proust, in translation, and . . ."
>
> "Yes," I said stupidly, and smiled to make up for my lack of French.
>
> Jean handed me the fold of crisp *pur fil* white stock. I held it with all the respect I genuinely felt. It was an invitation for Cocteau to take tea with him the following Tuesday, and signed *"A toi, Marcel."*

* See Bibliography, Sachs, III. At this time Cocteau was abandoning his flat under Valentine Hugo's at 9 rue Vignon. For several years he was now to live in hotels, among them the Hotel de Castille in the rue Cambon adjoining Mademoiselle Chanel's dressmaking establishment, and the Hotel Vouillemont in the rue Boissy d'Anglas. The latter (now no longer a hotel) was owned by a Sicilian named Delle Donne, whose children, Marie and Robert Delle Donne, had induced him to hire their friend Maurice Sachs as reception clerk. When Cocteau proposed moving into the hotel, all the Delle Donne family was alarmed, fearing that his smoking would attract the police; but he assured them that he was "cured," and the children obtained their father's reluctant consent. Soon, however, opium fumes began to filter out from under Cocteau's door, there was at least one police visit, and Cocteau was made unwelcome by Monsieur Delle Donne. According to Marie Delle Donne (Baronne Wasmer), Cocteau shared an occasional pipe with his hotel maid, as a kind of tip; she became unfit for work, saying in a kind of ecstasy, "All I want to do is smoke opium with Monsieur Cocteau." Marie and Robert Delle Donne had many artistic homosexuals among their friends. Barbette speaks warmly of their kindness and hospitality. (In 1938, after the advent of Jean Marais, Cocteau rented an apartment again, with Marais, at 9 Place de la Madeleine, and in 1940 he took, again with Marais, a small apartment at 36 rue Montpensier, in the Palais-Royal. Cf. p. 439.)

† See Appendix XIII.

After reading it several times I attempted to give it back, but Cocteau lifted his ten fingers like a fence between us and said, "For you. *Je vous l'offre.* For you." His accent in English was almost Chinese, and he smiled. How good he was, how surprisingly generous! I turned to Maurice. "Yes, I am sure Jean wants you to have it." I felt like a schoolgirl making my thanks, but I got through the poor disclaimers and still came away with my precious relic. . . . Before we were quite out the door he dug his fingers into my shoulder, very hard. . . .

As for Jean Bourgoint, whom Cocteau now saw seldom, in 1932 he had just been dropped by his most recent lover, a rich Egyptian named Félix Rollo; on the verge of suicide, he was rescued by Jean Hugo and taken to Fourques, where he was to remain, with interruptions, for fifteen years, and where he will be heard of again.

Cocteau's fullest stage version of the Oedipus legend, the play *La Machine Infernale,* produced by Louis Jouvet, with Jean-Pierre Aumont and Jouvet himself in the cast and Cocteau as narrator, opened at the Théâtre Louis Jouvet (as the Comédie des Champs-Elysées had been temporarily renamed) on April 10, 1934 — that is, about a year after he had disintoxicated himself from the spell of the Princess; and it introduces the paradoxical spectacle of Cocteau's final attainment of wide popular theatrical success with a series of plays that call for no extended discussion here. For the present portrait of Cocteau, the importance of the plays of the 1930's lies far less in their texts than in the fact that it was their success that would later facilitate his reentry into films, where he would again reach the heights of *The Blood of a Poet.* Intrinsically the plays are but an interlude, and in the minds of those for whom Cocteau's *raison d'être* is his poetry — his poetry in any field — a rather arid interlude.

For the large public *La Machine Infernale* was still esoteric, played as it was in a small theatre often associated with the avant-garde, with "strange" sets and costumes by Bérard and with characters bearing legendary names. The success came from Cocteau's crisp "modern" dialogue and startling confrontations: Raïssa Maritain was shaken to the point of writing in her journal that "Cocteau is certainly the only tragic writer of our time." Apparently Cocteau's technique and the production were so effective as to conceal what seems so apparent now — that despite lofty pretentions, a high old legend had been reduced fairly close to the level of modern situation-comedy; and to the "richness" of its treatment one tends now to prefer Cocteau's early *Antigone,* so often belittled for bareness. The next play, *Les Chevaliers de la Table Ronde,* a similar treatment of the Galahad story, was less liked, but the third, *Les Parents Terribles,* which Cocteau specifically says he wrote "to reach the public at large," was his greatest popular stage success. In it he was hailed for "out-Bernsteining Bernstein," which is French for "Welcome to Broadway"; his technique had become so perfect and the cast was so good (we shall hear more about the cast later, in the discussion of the film) that the dissection of the story by one or two all but incredulous critics, including Paul Léautaud, fell on deaf ears. Then came *Les Monstres Sacrés* and *La Machine à Ecrire,* plays so tawdry that anyone could see that Cocteau's heart wasn't in them. "Can it be that Jean Cocteau is losing his imagination with age?" Paul Léautaud wondered; and Eric Bentley wrote: "Jean Cocteau seems to me to have become a lost soul. What is disturbing is the awful vacuity of these pieces." * But they brought Cocteau a degree of "importance" far beyond anything ever previously accorded him by the many. In the days of *Le Coq et l'Arlequin* he had gaily cried that to be taken seriously was "the beginning of death": now he was putting himself in need of resurrection.

The Thirties were also a period of coctelian journalism. As a celebrity he was constantly asked for articles, and two of his books of these years were born as newspaper serials. Both are light and graceful. The brighter is the series of memoirs of his early years, *Portraits-Souvenir,* which has been drawn on, with attempts at discretion, in the present volume. Cocteau wrote some of the pieces at the Hotel Vouillemont, and Henry Wibbels, who was living there with Maurice Sachs in a room down the hall from Cocteau's, says that Cocteau "constantly risked being late with copy," which included a number of drawings for illustrations. "One day he asked me to stay with him long enough to see him through the drawing of a sufficient number of sketches to finish the series at once; other-

* Readers seeking further discussion of these plays can find it in Bentley, Fergusson, and especially Oxenhandler.

wise, he said, 'I'll run away from myself and never finish the astra-khan!' " Wibbels had to be told that "astrakhan" meant "persian lamb," much used for muffs, hats, and trimmings on dresses and coats at the turn of the century. "His sleeves were always neatly folded back when he drew with rather broad-nibbed pens and India ink," Wibbels says. "He drew fairly rapidly, using his whole fore-arm as much as hand and fingers. Sometimes he stood at the table, and the clean deliberation of his gestures reminded me of a sur-geon using a scalpel, or, when it came to the 'astrakhan' — a scribble of small circles — like a pastrycook decorating a wedding cake. He rarely went over a line (and his art in general was pre-dominantly linear) but if it was unsatisfactory discarded the drawing at once."

About the other journalistic series, the reportage of a neo-Jules Verne exploit published under the title *Mon Premier Voyage* (*Tour du Monde en 80 jours*), Cocteau was apologetic, saying that it was the first writing for many years that he had done "awake" — almost everything since *Le Potomak* having been done "asleep." (It was his way of distinguishing, the reader may recall, between works done from inner compulsion and those done delib-erately. *Portraits-Souvenir*, he said, was done half-sleeping, half-waking.) According to Cocteau, it was Marcel Khill, fired by the reminiscences in *Portraits-Souvenir* of the thrilling old stage ver-sion of *Around the World in Eighty Days* that Cocteau had seen as a child, who suggested a reenactment of the trip. The newspaper *Paris-Soir* accepted the idea. It sounded easy of fulfillment, thanks to the increases in the speed of transportation achieved over the sixty years since Verne had published his book in 1876, but investiga-tion revealed that "those famous eighty days came true only later — they were one of Jules Verne's dreams, like his phonographs, his airplanes, his submarines, his deep-sea divers. Eveybody believed in them because masterpieces are always convincing." Actually, Cocteau says, in 1936 Phileas Fogg's itinerary would require, at a minimum, even profiting from air travel within the United States, precisely eighty days. The volume is the account of how they "just made it." Crossing the Pacific, Charlie Chaplin, whom Cocteau had never met before, was on the same ship (neither could speak the other's language, and their separate accounts of their shipboard companionship — Chaplin's is in his autobiography — are scarcely to be reconciled); in New York there was just time for the essentials — Harlem, Minsky's Burlesque, and Coney Island. Marcel Khill, the valet Passepartout to Cocteau's Phileas Fogg, seems to have provided valiant services as travel companion — services that were not, however, to prevent his being eclipsed as closest friend, beginning the next year, by Jean Marais, now about to enter the scene. André Gide accepted Cocteau's dedication of the volume: "My dear André: You once reproached me for being too tense, for not letting myself go, and you quoted as an example of the way I sometimes *could* let myself go a note in *Le Coq et l'Arlequin* in which I described the first jazz. . . . After these travel notes, which I hereby offer you as proof of my devotion, you will never again be able to reproach me for not letting myself go." By accepting it, Gide seems to have taken the ironic language at face value: for "devotion" read "implacable memory."

Another group of articles, which appeared in various newspapers and have never been fully reprinted, recounts Cocteau's brief career as manager of a prizefighter, the Negro bantamweight Panama Al Brown. The son of an American construction worker in Panama, Brown had lost his world's title to the Spaniard Balthazar Sangchili in Valencia in 1935 — Brown had been carousing before the match, but claimed also to have been poisoned — and Marcel Khill, finding him a drugged and demoralized performer in a Paris night club two years later, brought Cocteau to see him. Various considerations — probably a combination of novelty, the grace of movement for which Brown is still remembered, Brown's willingness to reciprocate Cocteau's attentions, and perhaps a certain relief on Cocteau's part at discovering an "outside interest" that he could share with the somewhat limited Khill — determined Cocteau to make Brown into a new Cocteau spectacle, a sports-world *Boeuf sur le Toit* or *Mariés de la Tour Eiffel*. With moral support that included Cocteau's newspaper stories, with financial backing by Mademoiselle Chanel, and after drug withdrawal and serious training, Brown succeeded in regaining his form, and — to shorten a tale that was a sports sensation — won back his title from Sangchili in a match at the Palais des Sports in Paris on March 4, 1938. After one more match he retired from the ring, and for a time the Médranos featured him in their circus in a shadow-boxing dance act to a jazz accompaniment by Negro musicians. (Coached by Cocteau, Brown entered the circus ring clad in the long dressing gown he had worn the night of his famous fight, then dropped it to reveal an elegant all-white tail-suit.) Later he took the number on tour with the Cirque Amar. Brown's courage and persistence were extraordinary (for Mademoiselle Chanel he remains one of the few people of "value" close to Cocteau in the Thirties), but in so far as it concerns Cocteau there is something *retardataire* about the Al Brown story. One can prefer it to the plays, but it is rather too neo-Twenties, too much an imitation of a genre that had earlier been fresh and fun.

Despite the cure in 1933 and another in 1936, Cocteau's slavery to opium continued now to be at its worst: he was smoking a large number of pipes and was several times summoned before police courts. Something over a dozen poems, printed in the volume *Allégories* in 1941, make up almost his total published verse of the decade, and the quality is not of the highest. For all his celebrating *"la poésie de la boxe"* in his articles on Al Brown, the non-poetical aspect of his 1930's is all pervasive; that is why one prefers to chronicle the decade but briefly, and one can only speculate on the role played by opium in the absence of poetry, as well as in the concomitant falsity of the affair with the Princess, the emptiness of the plays, and the overindulgence in journalism. (For opium Cocteau needed money, and to get it at this time he not only wrote his articles, but sold more of his possessions, including his portrait by Marie Laurencin and a plaster cast of his hands.) The affair with the Princess can be thought of as a kind of opium dream; its mythomania was outside the realm of art; in it he displayed indifference to his artistic qualities and flouted his innermost nature; his moral gaucherie was pronounced. Cocteau is not the only artist-addict to respond in those ways to overindulgence: one thinks of Crabbe and Coleridge. And as we shall see, it was to be after several years of association with Jean Marais, who resolutely opposed all drugging, and after the suspension of drug supplies by the war, that Coctelian poetry would revive in new form.

The young actor Jean Marais entered Cocteau's life in 1937, when the poet was testing the pupils of a Paris acting school who were to put on, at last, the short play *Oedipe-Roi* that he had drawn out of his libretto for Stravinsky's *Oedipus Rex*. Twenty-four, astonishingly handsome, "an Antinoüs sprung from the people," blond, with "all the characteristics of those blue-eyed hyperboreans mentioned in Greek mythology," the impecunious Marais, born in Cherbourg, had for some years been playing in Paris the well-known role of obscure, struggling young actor. He and Cocteau quickly became intimates, and friends of Cocteau remember a brief period when his usual company was the full trio of black Al Brown, the swarthy Marcel Khill, and the Apollonian Marais. At the first night of *Les Chevaliers de la Table Ronde*, October 14, 1937, when Jean Marais followed what is now the printed stage direction — "He tears open his tunic and displays his bare breast" — le Tout-Paris knew that Jean Cocteau had a new friend, and the Parisian stage a new *jeune premier* (imposed by Cocteau), of exceptional beauty. Perhaps Cocteau himself still knew little more than that: the principal reviews did not mention Marais, and only gradually would it become apparent to the public that the young man was a hard-working and versatile actor, and, perhaps, to Cocteau that in him he had acquired his most valuable friend since Radiguet. Marais' devotion to Cocteau was to become very great; and today to an extent that is impressive and gratifying, loyalty banishes from his conversation anything that might blur his repeated reminder: "You know, I owe Cocteau everything."

In 1939, after playing for some time in *Les Parents Terribles*, Marais fell ill, and Cocteau took him to convalesce at Le Piquey, a place that had its meaning, for he had last been there with Radiguet in 1923. On the way and while there Cocteau for the first time in almost a decade "fell asleep," he says, and wrote *La Fin du Potomak*. It was a bad sleep, producing many pages of sequel that quite lack the confused but beguiling young freshness of *Le Potomak* itself, as it had been sparked off by Gertrude Stein and Stravinsky so many years before; but at the end a few lines of poetry emerge:

> La mort aimait l'enfant qui finissait un livre.
> Toujours il travaillait et dormait à demi.
> Depuis qu'il a cessé de vivre,
> Le bonheur est mon ennemi.
>
> Mort ne soyez donc pas habile,
> Allez, allez votre chemin:

Vous voyez, je reste immobile
Et même je vous tends la main.

Voulez-vous que je vous aide?
Peut-être serait-ce mieux.
Mort, êtes-vous belle ou laide?
De vous je suis curieux.

Ai-je une minute à vivre?
Ce pas est-il votre pas?
Qu'importe, je laisse un livre
Que vous ne me prendrez pas.*

The new presence of Marais had briefly evoked Radiguet, his
classicism, and his death, as well as the dormant muse.

But the times were anything but conducive to the rapid sloughing
off of a bad decade, and Cocteau was to wait several years more
before his gift was revitalized.

A Further Delay: The Second World War
of Jean Cocteau

On the outbreak of war in September, 1939, Jean Marais was
mobilized, and Cocteau — whose immediate question on learning
of the declaration of hostilities is said to have been "How will I get
my opium?" — moved temporarily into a room in the Hotel de
Beaujolais, overlooking the gardens of the Palais-Royal. Christian
Bérard and Boris Kochno were living there: perhaps the trio
thought of pooling opium resources.

In the Hotel de Beaujolais, Cocteau suffered a great shock on the
morning of May 10, 1940. That was the morning the world awoke

---

* Death loved the child who was finishing a book. / He was always half-working,
half-asleep. / Since he has ceased to live, / Happiness is my enemy.

Death, be not clever, / Do as you will: / You see, I am waiting, standing still, /
Even extending my hand.

Do you want me to help you? / Perhaps that would be better. / Death, are you
lovely, or ugly? / About you I am curious.

Have I a minute left to live? / Is that your step I hear? / What matter? I leave behind a book / That you will not take from me.

to the news that during the night German armies had invaded simultaneously Belgium, Holland and Luxembourg and were sweeping on toward France, with air bombardment clearing their way. But the friend who found Cocteau half-prostrate, that day, crying "I've been assassinated by the Fifth Column!" quickly learned that the cause of his anguish was not the blitzkrieg. It was the proofs, which he had just seen, of a hostile article about him that was to appear in the June number of the *N.R.F.*, that magazine with which Gide was still so closely associated.

The author was Claude Mauriac, the son of François Mauriac the novelist. Cocteau and the older Mauriac had been friends and more than friends for a time in their youth; Cocteau had known Claude as a boy, had recently been aware that the young man was beginning a literary career by writing about him, and had encouraged him to do so, even allowing Mauriac to watch him work and make notes on his conversation. That had been a dangerous thing to do, for father and son were close, and the older Mauriac, who had turned fervently to the Church after sowing his few wild oatlets, had long been displeased by Cocteau's post-Maritain career. Now, to his consternation, Cocteau read the younger man's judgment that he, Cocteau, was except for the poems to Radiguet in *Plain-Chant* little more than a punster, trickster and publicity-hound. There had been further reason to be apprehensive about young Mauriac: Cocteau must have known that he had been frequenting not only his own father, but Gide himself. Today we know from Claude Mauriac's later-published volume, *Conversations with André Gide*, to what extent Gide had helped him formulate some of the opinions concerning Cocteau that Cocteau now found in the proofs. Unfavorably as young Mauriac looked on Cocteau, Gide had pretended to think him a Cocteau partisan in granting Cocteau any feelings whatever: "It seems to me that you have given in to the pleasure of creating the Jean Cocteau of your dreams," he told the young man. "The real Cocteau does not suffer." "Mauriac must be arrested!" Cocteau cried wildly that morning of the German blitzkrieg: he was in one of his periods of heaviest drugging, and there could be no question as to order of importance between the overwhelming private betrayal and mere public catastrophe.

The Gide-Mauriac article had come at a particularly bad private moment. Cocteau's innate guilt feelings, which were usually inflamed by some recent indiscretion or extravagance, always impeded him from summoning up a restorative sense of his own authenticity in the face of attack, and this time he knew that he had openly proclaimed that with *Les Parents Terribles* he had aimed "to reach the public at large." Everything was further exacerbated by the absence of Marais, the present Other on whom he was always so dependent, and who would have provided consolation. It is scarcely too much to say that Cocteau's departure from Paris a few weeks later, when so large a part of the city's population fled southward away from the threat of German destruction — it was the great exodus, *"Le cortège, les cris, la foule et le soleil,"* as Aragon was soon to write — was as much a flight from the wound of the article as from the approaching armies.

In Perpignan, where he stayed with friends, he was soothed by the arrival of Marais, demobilized in that same region after the French collapse and the Pétain armistice; but Cocteau had been drugging continuously, with both opium and cocaine, and his letters reveal the extreme vitrifaction of sensibility characteristic of the confirmed addict. In the face of the national and international tragedy a number of desperately grief-stricken Frenchmen had chosen oblivion, and among the suicides was that of the country's greatest brain surgeon, the sixty-four-year-old Dr. Thierry de Martel de Janville. In the First World War Dr. Martel had been severely wounded and his son of seventeen had been killed, and his self-destruction amid the new cataclysm was regarded throughout France as a stunning scene from an apocalypse; but in July, 1940 Cocteau wrote thus about it to Christian Bérard: "Except for the situation pertaining to 'health,' I find these days exciting. Too bad Martel was so lacking in curiosity." ("Health" — *"santé"* — was Cocteau's code word for "opium"; Bérard's was *"hygiène."*) For Cocteau the appeal of novelty, almost any novelty, had always been irresistible; but beyond that, in callously deploring the doctor's "lack of curiosity" he was exposing one of the roots of his own nature — the great curiosity that had fed his art. At this terrible moment he could write to Roger Stéphane, "As for me, you know I relish these great climaxes." It quickly became apparent that the greatest of the novelties to be savored was the spectacle of Occupied Paris, full of German uniforms. At the end of the summer the Paris theatres began to reopen, and in September Cocteau wrote from

Perpignan to Georgette Leblanc, who had asked him to preface a book, "I must quickly return to Paris, where they are reviving *Les Parents Terribles*. . . . Miracles are happening everywhere, and I am intensely curious about this unreal Paris." He was incapable, that summer, of taking in the enormity of the disaster, of sensing the intensity of the conqueror's evil, the magnitude of its triumph and the scope of its implications. "Life will be hard [in Paris]," he wrote Roger Stéphane in July. "I shall return after trying here to restore my balance, and I assure you that our hearts will not be as heavy as they have been these last weeks. . . . It was a losing game. I knew it, and didn't want to say it. May it have served some purpose. The attitude of the English will probably result in our adopting the old policy of B. and C. I have always favored that policy, even though I knew that France was not imaginative enough to adopt it, and that she would first have to drink the bitter draught to the end." *

In his repellent detachment, Cocteau expresses something of the tragedy of France in 1940. Like Cocteau, other Frenchmen had exhausted in the charnel house of the First World War their reserves of national pride, of confidence in those who led them, even of proper horror and indignation over their own fate. What was left, in Cocteau's case, was an intense desire to see what would come next; for others, there was only impotent degradation.

In the fall, Cocteau and Jean Marais returned to Paris and settled into the new apartment in the Palais-Royal that Cocteau was to keep for the rest of his life.

The Occupation of Paris by the Germans from 1940 to 1944 was a period so macabre as to defy description even by those who were there, and to baffle understanding by those who were not. It was possible, it has been said, to avoid "collaboration" with the conquerors in only one way — by refusing any activity that required licensing. But almost any activity did require licensing, and no license was given without German approval. To refuse to ask for a license meant, for artists, no publication of books, no production of plays, no showing of films, no concerts, no exhibitions. One be-

---

* "The old policy of B. and C.," whomever those initials may stand for, is clearly the policy of Franco-German entente, which had implied, since 1933, cooperation with the Nazi regime.

came a "collaborator" merely by legally exercising one's profession. The courageous French writers who eschewed publication under those conditions did not include Cocteau. Cocteau had no hesitation about seeking German-approved authorization to produce his plays; he saw Germans constantly, though not in his own home; in 1944 he published a volume of poems he said he had written in German — "I spoke German in my childhood because I had a German governess. . . . A poet must always express himself, whatever the language. . . . French, English, German or Russian is but a thin coating." However, so difficult was avoidance of contact with the Occupiers that his fellow Parisians regarded him with comparative indulgence except in a solitary, specific instance — the publicity article he published in the newspaper *Comoedia* in May, 1943, for a Paris exhibition by the German Arno Breker, Hitler's favorite sculptor. In return for that service he claimed to have obtained, through Breker's intervention, the exemption of French film employees from having to work in Germany. After the Liberation he was either exonerated by one of the Conseils d'Epuration, the tribunals that judged suspected collaborators, or was not even summoned — the stories differ. He is said to have kept an "Occupation Journal," still in manuscript, which may some day be published and cast more light on his activities. During the four-year period he displayed his usual ambivalences in heightened form, his usual affinity for paradox, his usual insecurity concerning his "position"; and despite the official clearance he emerged from the Occupation more seared by inward guilt than ever before. It was inevitable that that should be so: mere existence alongside the disciples of Hitler begot guilt in many an innocent Frenchman trying simply to live quietly during the Occupation; among active Resistants themselves, bloody deeds took their psychological toll; Cocteau's ambivalence made him the more vulnerable.

It was in the fall of 1940 that Jean Marais began to show the full scale of his value to Cocteau: back in Paris he persuaded him to forestall the coming shortage of drugs by undergoing a new cure without delay and by refusing to smoke even if opportunity should offer. Cocteau apparently stuck to his promise throughout the rest of the war, and the result was all to the good: it enabled him to begin life under the Occupation with an act of courage.

In 1938, in Paris, *Les Parents Terribles*, absurdly accused of immorality in its portrayal of a supposedly incestuous relationship, had been expelled from the city-owned Théâtre des Ambassadeurs. (Thanks in part to the publicity sparked by the charge, it had gone on to success in another theatre, where its run had been interrupted by the outbreak of war.) After the 1940 armistice the Vichy government had at once begun to foster an intensely moralistic attitude, accusing many elements in prewar French society of a decadence that had "caused the defeat" — this in conjunction with the now official anti-Semitism that was part of its cooperation with the conquerors. Just before the blitzkrieg Cocteau had published an anti-racist article in a newspaper which was one of those now quickly suppressed by the new regime; and that, his homosexuality, and the supposed incest theme of *Les Parents Terribles*, all made him a target. Even before his return to Paris the more violent Vichyite journalists had begun to revile him. "Believe it or not, those worthies have decided that Gide and I are to blame for everything," he wrote Georgette Leblanc from Perpignan. "I am astonished that they should erase those twenty admirable years when poetry was made flesh and dwelt among us. . . . They go so far as to say that *Les Parents Terribles* is responsible for the defeat." "I dread purification pyres," he wrote to Roger Stéphane. "They're burning indiscriminately — daubs and Leonardos." And: "I suppose that the 'Newfrance,' alerted by Claude Mauriac, will burn me as a sorcerer." In the face of the attacks, in December, 1940, Cocteau published, in one of the few newspapers still willing occasionally to stand against the current, an article entitled "Adresse aux jeunes écrivains: Les Territoires de l'Esprit," in which he praised Gide (who had left Paris and was living in as-yet-unoccupied Nice), decried the fashionable condemnation of pre-1940 writing, and spoke of *Parade* and of the "war of art" in which he and other young writers and painters had taken Paris by storm during and after the earlier war. It ended:

> 1940! Attention! There is a tremendous task to be performed: to defend, against your unworthy fellow countrymen, the domains of the spirit, to employ your violence on their behalf, to enlarge them continually. No one stands in your way. Do not say: "It is too hard: I'll go into hiding." Say: "I must do the impossible. I declare my position."

What do you risk? I wonder. The ire of those who attack
Gide? If so, you owe it to him.

Think, write, love, destroy. Launch little magazines. Produce plays. Trample on us, if possible. Take the word of a
specialist in the ways of fate and its mysteries. Seize your opportunity while there is time. It is here, now.

He had a considerable response, and in January he wrote a sequel, beginning: "What I find admirable is the tone of the letters I
receive. Never an insult of the kind now so fashionable. No mud-
slinging. Dignity, nobility, magnificent impatience to begin."

The publication of those pieces at that time refutes the charge
sometimes made that Cocteau's only claim to having resisted the
Vichy regime lay in his having been attacked by it: in fact his
voice, in those articles, was among the few to be raised in protest.
But the increasing severity of the Occupiers and the fullness of
Vichy's cooperation soon put an end to any such freedom of speech.
Both Cocteau's latest play, *La Machine à Ecrire,* and the revived
Les Parents Terribles (which was once again temporarily withdrawn) were the occasion for further personal attacks in the newspapers; stink bombs exploded in the theatres, and hoodlums filled
the aisles and climbed onto the stage, shouting obscenities at Cocteau and Marais as a couple. On one occasion Marais risked arrest
for both of them by thrashing a critic who had been particularly
poisonous in personal vilification, and it is the opinion of Cocteau's
latest French biographers that had Cocteau replied at all openly to
the racist and sexual insults that poured down on him he would
have been arrested as a self-confessed criminal.

Against the continuous strafing Cocteau sought what support he
could find; and it is now that one begins to hear of his acquain-
tanceships among Germans — artistic, sympathetic Germans who
would agree that the Vichyites were at times overzealous and who
could, by conveying a few words to Occupant overlords, see to it
that the vassals were restrained. Much was made, by the more in-
gratiating Germans and Germanophile French, of the fellowship of
artists and its obliteration of national lines. There was Ernst
Jünger, author of the German best-selling novel *On the Marble
Cliffs,* full of mystical heroism and evil, which has been interpreted
as an allegory of the rise of Nazism (one has the impression on

reading it that allegory has taken over to such an extent as to hide actuality from the author himself). Jünger was a cultivated nationalist who seems to have regarded Jews* and Hitler with similar distaste while doing his duty as an occupying German officer in uniform, and he writes in his journal of spending evenings with Cocteau in the houses of various Vichyite Parisians, including Paul Morand (who was later to be Vichy's ambassador to Rumania). Jünger describes Cocteau as "sympathetic, yet tormented like one living in a hell of his own — but a comfortable hell," and tells of hearing him read parts of his new play, in verse — *Renaud et Armide*, whose characters are taken from Tasso's *Jerusalem Liberated*.

One evening in the 1920's, at the Boeuf sur le Toit, someone had introduced to Cocteau a young German sculptor named Arno Breker, who had a studio in Paris; but nothing came of the meeting. In 1933 Breker returned to Germany, where his mastery of the style of heroic realism won him the friendship and patronage of the Führer. He was commissioned to create a veritable portrait gallery in bronze of the leaders of the Third Reich, as well as a pair of gigantic figures, "Torchbearer" and "Swordbearer," to stand forever on either side of the entrance to the new Chancellery building in Berlin, and other heroic bronzes; the catalogues of his exhibitions were appropriately prefaced not by art critics or historians but by Reichsministers and Gauleiters. Now he appeared in Paris, sent to circulate among French artists as part of an official Nazi-Vichy cultural interchange (Derain, Vlaminck and Despiau accepted invitations to tour Germany). The fulsome "Salute to Arno Breker" written on the occasion of his 1943 Paris exhibition is generally considered to be Cocteau's "low point of the war," morally and politically speaking. It may not be that, if it was really recompensed, as he claimed, by the exemption of the French cinema workers from labor in Germany; but it was certainly his most depressing wartime action from the artistic point of view, a confirmation of the insensitivities revealed in his essays on Chirico, a further foretaste of the portentousness that would characterize much of his own later plastic work. Had André Gide not been so

---

* Jünger, apparently priding himself on his broad-mindedness, remarked in his journal (in 1946!) : "Many things can be said about the Jews, but not that they are ungrateful." (*Sic.*)

immune to the plastic arts, and had his advice to Cocteau about remaining a *prince frivole* been made with reference to those arts rather than to literature, it would have had more validity: Cocteau's late, ambitious wall decorations were to be a lamentably far cry from the skillful fun of the early drawings, and the admiration for Breker — that it was sincere is attested by Cocteau's posing to Breker after the war for his own bust — partakes of the spirit of the playwriting of the 1930's. Cocteau seems to have had a certain acquaintance with Otto Abetz, the German ambassador, and Serge Lifar says that he was "protected" by Bernard Radermacher, the artistic, "francophile" personal representative of Goebbels.

It was the strangely assorted company of a few Germans like Jünger and Breker, of close friends, and of some of the French youth who had responded to his printed articles, that Cocteau chiefly kept in the "unreal Paris" (it was all too real) of the Occupation years — the Paris where churches and theatres were crowded "because," as someone has said, "there was no dancing"; where the suicide of the French fleet at Toulon in November, 1942 was both mourned and celebrated by a display of miniature warships with flags at half-mast in a show window of Le Nain Bleu, the toy shop in the rue St. Honoré; where customers of a restaurant or café would sometimes suddenly hear a few bars of the forbidden "Marseillaise" or another French military march inserted by the orchestra between innocuous tunes; where the fate of anyone with "Jewish blood" could vary from the full protection that some German caprice or reason of policy accorded a rare Marie-Laure de Noailles, to the more usual deportation and death; where Darius Milhaud and many another escaped that fate only by fleeing to America, while Etienne de Beaumont intrigued (in vain) for the post of Director of the Opéra, Bernard Faÿ took the place of the deported Julien Cain as director of the Bibliothèque Nationale, and Auric could write in his column of music criticism in the *N.R.F.*, now Vichy-oriented under the editorship of Drieu La Rochelle, that "the 1941–42 season has been brilliant"; the Paris where uniformed Germans offered their seats in the subway to old ladies and beat with their pistols on the doors of suspects in the early hours of the morning; where, as Jean-Paul Sartre wrote: "When . . . women went to Gestapo headquarters on the Avenue Foch or the rue des Saussaies to find out what had happened to their men, they were received with courtesy. And when they returned from these visits they would sometimes have kind words to report. Yet people who lived on the Avenue Foch or the rue des Saussaies near the headquarters heard screams of pain and terror all day and late into the night. There was not a single person in Paris without a friend or relative who had been arrested or deported or shot" — the Paris of fear, famine, cold, the black market, high living, brilliant *premières* and *vernissages,* and — above all — complete uncertainty as to just who was up to just what.

Amid it all, Cocteau clung to Marais, who was busy enlarging his experience as an actor. He played in Cocteau's pieces, in French classics — Racine's *Andromaque* and *Britannicus* and Molière's *L'Avare,* entering for a time the Comédie Française — and he began to appear in films, a *Carmen* in Italy, and in 1943 *L'Eternel Retour,* of which more will be heard. Marais continued to be harassed by Vichyites, but was refused admission to an actors' Resistance group because, as Louis Jourdan, one of the members, put it, "Cocteau talks too much." After the Liberation he rejoined the French army, serving for a time under General Leclerc. In January, 1943, Madame Cocteau died in a Paris convent, where she had spent her last, wandering-minded years in the care of nuns. The previous year Cocteau had become acquainted with the homosexual thief Jean Genet, who had written, while in prison, a powerful poem addressed to a guillotined friend, *Le Condamné à Mort,* and a novel, *Notre-Dame des Fleurs;* when Genet was arrested again, for stealing a volume of Verlaine from a bookshop, Cocteau had him defended by the celebrated lawyer Maurice Garçon, testified on his behalf, and rejoiced in his acquittal; from then on Genet avoided jail, and gradually attained his worldwide literary fame. The association with Genet brought Cocteau more insults in the press, and one day, failing to remove his hat as the tricolor was borne past in a parade of French volunteers about to leave to serve with the Germany army on the eastern front, he was recognized by the usual Vichyite hoodlums and beaten.

Too frequently, considering what it most often was, came news of others. More than a year after the event Cocteau learned that Marcel Khill had been killed while serving with the French army in Alsace, a few hours *after* the signing of the Pétain armistice, whose proclamation had in his sector been fatally delayed. For Maurice

Sachs, it was the fellowship of pederasts, rather than of artists, that
obliterated national lines. After disposing of all his grandmother's
possessions when the old lady fled from Paris to Vichy — "She's
playing bridge in the provinces, so I sold everything" — he was
befriended by a German officer and lived with him in the rue de
Rivoli: there are Parisians who remember Sachs's private horse-
cab standing conspicuously before their house in that otherwise
empty street. (Cocteau had not prosecuted him following the affair
of the sold documents, and his reward was to learn that Maurice,
like Claude Mauriac, had written pages excoriating him — for
"heartlessness." In 1941 Maurice wrote him, expressing regret for
those pages, and saying they would never be published; actually he
had already sold them to Gallimard.) Things went badly between
Sachs and his German friend; for a time he played the black market with Violette Leduc, and then escaped deportation by volunteer-
ing for work in Germany, where for a time he operated a crane in
Hamburg. Seeing possibilities in his charm and his knowledge of
several languages, the Gestapo invited him to leave the crane and
circulate freely in the city, which swarmed with foreign workers,
reporting to headquarters anything interesting that he might hear.
This he willingly did — throughout the war he seems to have lived
in an almost continuous state of sado-masochistic ecstasy — and
succeeded in betraying a number of confidants to the Gestapo. But
he overreached himself, invented accusations that he could not substantiate, and was sent to a Gestapo prison outside the town, where
he was given drug and other privileges in return for reporting the
conversation of his fellow inmates. When his prison was evacuated
before the Allied advance, guards took him and others on a forced
march toward Kiel; anyone who stumbled was eliminated; Sachs
did not reach Kiel — he lies in a grave in Holstein, a bullet hole in
the back of his skull. Raïssa Maritain, his godmother, who was still
writing him affectionately in 1939, never learned of his fate: "God
have pity on him, dead or alive," she wrote in her journal in 1947.
In February, 1944, Max Jacob, now sixty-eight, whose brother, sister and brother-in-law had already been deported and exterminated
in German camps, was arrested by the Gestapo in his retreat at St.
Benoît-sur-Loire; in the train taking him to prison he wrote a note
to Cocteau, and managed to have it delivered:

Max Jacob to Cocteau

[February 1944]

Cher Jean,

I am writing this in a train, profiting from the leniency of our guards. We shall soon be at Drancy. That is all I have to say. Sacha [Guitry], when he was told about my sister, said "If it were Max himself I could do something." Well, this time it is myself.

Je t'embrasse.

Max

Cocteau wrote and signed a petition to Otto Abetz, and obtained several more signatures, but with no known result: Jacob died of pneumonia in Drancy prison.

Then, in July, 1944, little more than a month before the Liberation of Paris, came the tragedy that for Cocteau was to be the most haunting of the war.

Jean Desbordes was working for the Polish underground, sometimes flying back and forth between Paris and the London headquarters of the Polish government in exile. In the spring of 1944 his friend Georges Geffroy — he who had accompanied the distraught Jean Bourgoint to the hospital after Jeanne Bourgoint's suicide on Christmas Eve, 1929, and one of Barbette's favorite Parisians — was advised to leave Paris for a time, as his intimacy with Desbordes was making him suspect; and when he left the city he asked his cousin, a physician, Dr. Charles Berlioz, to occupy his flat at 248 rue de Rivoli, lest it be requisitioned during his absence. Dr. Berlioz was glad to accept: he had been living with his parents, and the move would give him greater independence of action for the work he was doing with a Resistance group. Geffroy's maid, Rose, also lived in the flat.

On June 24 Jean Desbordes rang the bell of the flat. He told Dr. Berlioz, who had met him only once before, with Geffroy at a literary party, that disrupted train service was making it difficult for him to commute to "his work in Paris" from suburban St. Ouen, where he and his wife lived, and he asked whether Dr. Berlioz would allow him to live for a time in the flat. The doctor made him welcome, and Desbordes moved in. The two men saw almost nothing of each other, each being busy in his own way, but each sensed that the other was doing Resistance work.

On Wednesday, July 5, Dr. Berlioz, returning in the evening, saw from the street that the flat was brightly lit, and when he opened the door on the landing he found himself faced by four men in uniform, all holding submachine guns. In a panic he turned and ran, but was quickly caught on the stairs, dragged up, and beaten. The most brutal of the four gunmen, one who wore the uniform of the Vichy militia (the most savage of all groups of collaborators), accused the doctor of knowing "Duroc," and when he denied it he was beaten again. "Duroc," he was told, had been arrested that afternoon in the Café Colibri in the Place de la Madeleine and was at that very moment being "questioned"; he, too, would be "questioned" unless he admitted belonging to the same Resistance unit as "Duroc." Insisting that he knew nothing — in fact he did know nothing of "Duroc," and he was never asked about his own Resistance activities — he was handcuffed and taken, along with Rose, down to the street and into a police car.

Rose was dropped off with one of the men at the Place Beauvau (probably to be taken to Gestapo headquarters in the nearby rue des Saussaies), and the doctor was driven to an apartment house at 180 rue de la Pompe, another notorious Gestapo torture center. Upstairs, in a richly furnished salon and dining room, he found Germans and Frenchmen, some in uniform and some not, chatting and drinking champagne as at a party. As they looked on (others who suffered at 180 rue de la Pompe have told of German officers playing Mozart on the grand piano in the salon as the torture orgies progressed), he was repeatedly questioned and struck. Then he was taken to a lower floor. There, on a stretcher, his face "white as marble" beneath blood and bruises, his body covered up to the neck, he saw Jean Desbordes. His eyes were closed; he was breathing heavily: the doctor recognized that he was in coma, near death.

"That is Duroc, do you know him?"

"Yes."

"Who is he?"

"Jean Desbordes, a literary man."

"*Il est kaput.*"

Forbidden to give any help, Dr. Berlioz was taken upstairs

again; having to vomit, he was shown into a bathroom splattered with fresh blood — Desbordes' place of torture.

After further questioning — the greatest brutality continued to be shown by the Frenchman (who was later identified and shot) — the doctor was taken to Fresnes prison, and after three weeks transferred to a prison camp at Royalieu near Compiègne. There he met Poles who knew Desbordes: he had been employed by them, they said, as a paid worker. Dr. Berlioz eventually escaped from a train that was to have taken him across the Rhine — the Germans were by now careless, unnerved by the Allied advance — and after walking from his place of escape to the country house of relatives, he bicycled to Paris. Desbordes' wife did not, and his sister did, wish to be told the details of his end. Geffroy, back in Paris, took his cousin to see Cocteau. But Cocteau, that day, was nervous. It was very soon after the Liberation; he was about to attend a meeting of the FFI, the resistant French Forces of the Interior, and as his position had not yet been regularized he was uncertain as to how he would be received. He preferred that Geffroy and the doctor postpone their story. A year later, at a memorial service for Desbordes, Cocteau still asked no questions.

But from someone — perhaps Desbordes' sister, who on learning of her brother's arrest and not knowing that he was already dead, had obtained from Cocteau a useless letter of appeal to Otto Abetz — Cocteau heard a version of the facts. To Harold Acton and other members of the Allied forces who came to Paris after the Liberation he spoke again and again of the torture and death of Desbordes. He was obsessed with what he had been told, or said he had been told, about Desbordes' eyes. "They tore them out," he kept saying. "They tore out his eyes!" But Dr. Berlioz, who had seen the dying Desbordes, by that time certainly past further torturing, knows that his eyes were closed.

Gossip has not been kind to Desbordes. It is often said that he married his wife, a pharmacist, solely to have a sure supply of drugs; and that because of wartime scarcities and high prices it was for drugs that he needed his wages from the Poles. Such are some of the tales: whether or not there is truth in them, Desbordes' end was heroic, for the Poles in the prison camp told Dr. Berlioz that whatever he may have told his torturers, it was nothing that led to anyone's capture. So has Desbordes achieved immortality.

He may have achieved a kind of distinction in another way, as well. His first book of autobiographical musings, *J'Adore,* so extravagantly praised by Cocteau, and the two novels that followed, *Les Tragédiens* and *Les Forcenés,* reveal no genius. His last published work was one of scholarship, a study of Sade and sadism, *Le Vrai Visage du Marquis de Sade,* in which he arranges and discusses quite capably various newly found documents, some of which he says were lent him by members of the Sade family: that could mean that Marie-Laure de Noailles had been generous to him. But his most interesting work is a short two-act play, which he wrote in 1933 and which Cocteau took to the Comédie Française, read to the Committee, and had accepted. Published under the coctelian title *La Mue,* it was retitled *L'Age Ingrat* when it was finally performed in 1938, its distinguished cast of three consisting of Jean Weber, Berthe Bovy and Madeleine Renaud. *L'Age Ingrat* is expertly written, so expertly as to stand out among Desbordes' works and make one suspect that Cocteau may have had a considerable hand in it. It concerns a post-adolescent who has spent a night or two away from home without explanation, in order to dramatize to his doting, hysterically possessive mother and his more understanding sister the fact that he is a man, with a life of his own to lead. The theme is close to that of *Les Parents Terribles,* which Cocteau wrote the year Desbordes' piece was performed, which we have seen to be successful and controversial on the stage, and which Cocteau was later to turn into a film that has become famous. Perhaps a fraction of the fame should be credited to Desbordes. Cocteau never spoke of Desbordes' play in connection with his own play or film: it was always said that the idea for *Les Parents Terribles,* which Cocteau wrote for Jean Marais, came from Marais' love-and-conflict troubles with his own mother. If Cocteau did owe an unacknowledged debt to *L'Age Ingrat,* the thought of it may have played a role in the obsessive guilt he displayed after the Liberation concerning Desbordes' end.

However, the very fact of survival, in the face of such deaths as those of Marcel Khill, Max Jacob, Maurice Sachs and Jean Desbordes, and with the special strains of war and Occupation added to all the rest, would have been enough to bring acute dis-ease to anyone, let alone Cocteau. The night the church bells of Paris proclaimed the Liberation, he heard, over the radio, a message to

France spoken by Jacques Maritain. (He, too, because of Raïssa's Jewish parentage, had had to flee.) By the time of the memorial service for Desbordes, in 1945, Cocteau had long since been assured that no official blame was attached to him. He attended parties at the British Embassy, where long ago he had visited Reginald Bridgeman and which now in post-Liberation days was the smartest place in Paris; but at those parties he was not one of the shameless Parisian ex-Germanophiles to whom Duff Cooper and Lady Diana Cooper were now and again officially or unofficially urged to show a little less favor; he wrote a Liberation poem, "25 Août 1944," which appeared in the first issue of *Les Nouvelles Littéraires* to be printed after Liberation, and for *Vogue* an article in praise of Lady Diana. The false ex-Resistants who proliferated in liberated Paris reminded him of his hero Thomas l'Imposteur: "Many young mythomaniacs panicked, changed their appearance, took false names, and ended up as heroes in their own eyes." He himself was making many drawings of Marianne in a Liberty Cap, wearing the tricolor rosette of the FFI, and one of them was diffused around the world in millions of miniature copies, having been adopted by the Fourth French Republic as its twenty-centime stamp.

But the survival and the exculpation exacted their price. He began to suffer from a tormenting skin ailment, and his old friend Harold Nicolson writes cruelly of him in his diaries as looking in 1945 like "an aged cockatoo," excusing himself for not having joined the Resistance — "not very dignified." And new attacks in books came quickly. Claude Mauriac's *Jean Cocteau, ou La Vérité du Mensonge*, of which his article in 1940 had been made up of excerpts, appeared in 1945, and the next year Maurice Sachs's posthumous *Le Sabbat*. It was high time for the Tenth Muse to come to the rescue.

The Great Cocteau Film Festival

It begins rather modestly, the career of Cocteau the *cinéaste*, after the long delay following *The Blood of a Poet*. One French writer on film put it this way: "He realized that if he was to reemploy 'that incomparable vehicle of poetry' [as he called the cinema], and wanted to repeat the achievement of *The Blood of a Poet*, he would have to proceed differently: he would have to spend some time with professionals, acquaint himself with the work of good artisans. But what is admirable is that Cocteau neither saw nor remembered the mechanical aspects, and preserved his own internal mechanisms intact. He did not learn the trade, but rather discovered that he had always known it." What he did was to write dialogue for one director, and scenario for another, before making his own second film; and even after making it he sometimes worked with other directors. Nevertheless his most remarkable films were those he directed himself. He was unique among film makers in bringing to the cinema a sensibility that had already achieved full expression in other media, and even after his return to the cinema in the 1940's he was never only a film maker.

Much as Cocteau the artist had in earlier days derived greater benefit from the vice of opium than from the sacraments, so during the trauma and oppressiveness of the war and the Occupation he was at least more alive poetically than he had been in the stagnant though "successful" Thirties. The hundred and twenty stanzas of his visionary wartime poem "Léone" may not strike us as his most compelling verse, but they brought a salute from Ezra Pound: "I have just read 'Léone,' you have saved France!" His verse play staged during the Occupation, *Renaud et Armide*, lovely in its opening, and then faltering, echoes that first night at the Diaghilev ballet when he saw *Le Pavillon d'Armide* danced by Nijinsky and Pavlova; its story of bewitchment and awakening, with its clear reference to his own recent emergence from heavy drugging, announces, along with "Léone," that he was beginning to awaken from the spell that had muted him throughout the previous decade.

And just as it was Jean Marais who had persuaded him to disintoxicate, so it was Marais who now led him, a *"poète en mal de poésie,"* to utilize once more the "incomparable vehicle" of the film.

What Marais wanted above all was to be not merely an actor, but a film star. In his autobiography, *Mes Quatre Vérités*, he tells of being taken as a small boy in his native Cherbourg, wearing "a blue velvet suit with a hideous collar of Irish lace," his ears scorched from the curling iron his mother had used on his hair, to see Pearl

White in *Les Mystères de New-York,** and of the determination, then kindled and never lost, to triumph on the screen. After his early stage successes he made one or two non-Cocteau films in Occupied Paris, causing no great sensation. Then in 1942 he went for nine months to Italy, where *cinéastes* were less harassed by wartime shortages than in France, to be Don José to Viviane Romance's Carmen in a spoken version of the Mérimée story.

LE BARON FANTÔME. It was obvious to Cocteau that if he was to continue to share Marais' life he would willy-nilly be involved with cinema, and it was when Marais was in Italy that he began, at fifty-three, what can only be called, despite *The Blood of a Poet,* his apprenticeship. After a few preliminaries he undertook the not very exalted task of writing dialogue for a Grade-B scenario entitled *Le Baron Fantôme,* to be directed by Serge de Poligny — a story designed to distract Occupied Frenchmen from their miseries for an hour or two and involving a ghost baron's ruined chateau, hidden treasure, a love story, and various other weakly related elements, the cast in costumes of the Romantic 1830's. Cocteau must have recognized that such material could be properly transfigured only by a director who was a master of fantasy, and it was probably his realization that Poligny was not such a one that made him decide to make his dialogue as amusing as possible. Here and there amid the flat stretches one has the feeling that as one smiles one is sharing the dialogue-writer's own wry amusement at the situations he has undertaken to grapple with; and sometimes one senses that the most expert of the actors, the excellent Gabrielle Dorziat, is similarly conveying, with the greatest finesse, a certain incredulity at finding herself where she is. With his love of "transformations" and disappearing acts, Cocteau enjoyed a distraction of his own in the midst of the Occupation grimness: he had himself made up à la Grand Guignol and played the role of the Phantom Baron of the title, who crumbles splendidly into dust before our eyes.

L'ETERNEL RETOUR. Next, the illustrious wartime film apprentice tried his hand at scenario-*cum*-dialogue; and it was to call Marais

---

* The title given in France to the serial *The Exploits of Elaine.* (Not, as is sometimes said, to *The Perils of Pauline.*)

home that Cocteau and the producer André Paulvé kept him informed, in letters sent to Rome during the protracted making of
Carmen, about the role that was awaiting him in Paris — that of a
present-day Tristan, in a modern-dress adaptation by Cocteau of
Tristan and Isolde to be directed by Jean Delannoy. Cocteau said
that his title, *L'Eternel Retour,* borrowed from Nietzsche, meant
that "the old myths can be reborn without their heroes knowing it."
Marais returned as soon as he could escape from the looming danger of being held by contract in Italy to make *The Girl of the
Golden West* as his second film there, and he brought with him a
certain pullover sweater that was to become famous. "When I
bought it in Italy I had the picture in mind," he wrote later. "It
had a Jacquard pattern with a mediaeval look about it. People
wrote me from all over France asking for a photograph of it or for
the stitch." It possessed the double virtue of subtly alluding to the
mediaeval Tristan's coat of mail — so, at least, it was pointed out
in publicity stories — and of creating a fashion in men's haber-
dashery. The Isolde of the film, played by Madeleine Sologne (Cocteau had wanted Michèle Morgan, who was absent in America, and
whom Madeleine Sologne so resembles), launched a similar vogue
for modern woman: dressed in white, her blond hair parted and
falling straight and long, she continues today to be found in a million counterparts. In *L'Eternel Retour,* Marais and Sologne were
like the Jean and Jeanne Bourgoint who were behind the stage *Orphée* of almost twenty years before, imposing on the young a new
look envisioned by Cocteau.

Perhaps that transformation of Tristan and Isolde into the glam-
our-couple of the year was inevitable, given the combination of the
tragic myth and film. W. H. Auden thinks so. "Its pure artifice ren-
ders opera the ideal dramatic medium for a tragic myth," he has
written. "I once went in the same week to a performance of *Tristan
und Isolde* and a showing of *L'Eternel Retour,* Jean Cocteau's
movie version of the same story. During the former, two souls,
weighing over two hundred pounds apiece, were transfigured by a
transcendent power; in the latter, a handsome boy met a beautiful
girl and they had an affair. This loss of value was not due to any
lack of skill on Cocteau's part but to the nature of the cinema. . . .
Had he used a fat middle-aged couple the effect would have been
ridiculous, because the snatches of language which are all the

movie permits have not sufficient power to transcend their physical appearance. Yet if the lovers are young and beautiful, the cause of their love looks 'natural,' a consequence of their beauty, and the whole meaning of the myth is gone." The realism in *L'Eternel Retour* is at odds with the legend (and, incidentally, also with itself: "Lanvin gowns in bistros," as one French critic puts it); Cocteau's parallelism between modern scenario and myth is heavier-handed than in *Orphée*. The direction is often obtrusive, and the décor, which could have helped, is of an uncouth aestheticism. Fantasy is freest in Roger Hubert's photography, especially in the images of garden, mist and sea (the "sea" was the Lake of Geneva, access to the Brittany coast of the myth being forbidden by the Occupiers), and in a few of Cocteau's details, especially his casting of the unforgettably malevolent dwarf Piéral. As in *Le Baron Fantôme*, one of the most unlikely presences is that of an excellent actress of realistic roles — this time Yvonne de Bray. (It was probably loyalty and concern for their wartime needs that made Cocteau recruit, for these early films made during the Occupation, Mademoiselle Dorziat and Madame de Bray, for whom he had written the two chief female roles in *Les Parents Terribles*.)

But *L'Eternel Retour* was a critical and popular success. For all its flaws it is of a different metal from *Le Baron Fantôme;* it has a poetic atmosphere, and held a considerable power of enchantment for war-weary audiences. Marais modestly attributes some of his personal triumph in this, his first film role of consequence, to his pullover and to his dog Moulouk (whose acting in the film is indeed irresistible); but the idolizing he experienced was the result rather of the film makers' skillful revelation of his young charm and especially their exploitation of his extraordinarily handsome physique, which both he and Cocteau now foresaw might be a hindrance to his growth as an actor. (The note of his physical beauty being a *disadvantage* was skillfully struck in publicity.) Marais was never thought of as Tristan or even as Patrice (the modern Tristan's name in the film), but always as Jean Marais. While the film was being shown in Paris, he wrote, "Girls spent the night on my stairs, stood in crowds in the rue Montpensier and in the Palais-Royal garden. We were watched every second. When I went out they would come with me, take the métro with me, leave it when I did, walk home with me, and wait until I went out again. In the garden they sat in chairs, in rows, as though it were a theatre: my window was the stage. . . . Once in a while one of them would ring my bell and ask for an autograph or for a few kind words. Sometimes I would lose my temper and shout at them to go away, insult them. Jean Cocteau scolded me, telling me it was part of the profession I had chosen. I had asked for it and I was getting it. Gradually I learned to be more patient. But I remember one night when Cocteau and I were leaving a theatre where I was appearing in one of his plays: there was a jostling crowd threatening me with fifty fountain pens, and suddenly amid the tumult I heard a voice: 'Look! There's the author! He's connected with the play, too!' I was ashamed, furious — Cocteau calmed me with a smile."

Cocteau was always proud of *L'Eternel Retour*, and he had reason to value the way its popularity set the stage for his and Marais' joint triumph on the screen, now so soon to come; but speaking with an interviewer at the moment of its success he was frank about the differences between it and *The Blood of a Poet*.

QUESTION: Are you in favor of films like *The Blood of a Poet*, "avant-garde" films? Aren't you dismayed by the success of *L'Eternel Retour*?

ANSWER: There is a great difference between a poem and a stage play. Each has its own kind of originality. I made *The Blood of a Poet* for fifty people. I made *L'Eternel Retour* hoping to bridge the eternal gulf — to build a bridge that would bring together film connoisseurs and the public at large. For me each new work is a problem to be solved. Your puzzlement about *L'Eternel Retour* seems to prove that this problem *is* solved. It makes me very proud, and I attribute most of the success to the irresistible, never-fading charm of the legend.

The Blood of a Poet, [he repeated to the interviewer] was a visual poem for fifty film connoisseurs. Only slowly, and abroad, did it become a screen "classic." At that time the movies were the movies — they weren't the Louvre. I made *The Blood of a Poet* alone, like Méliès. I invented a technique. That is probably why that technique remains alive. It has nothing to do with "advances," which other advances render unfashionable.

BEAUTY AND THE BEAST. In the pages of reflection and reminiscence that he wrote in 1947 and called *La Difficulté d'Etre* (The Difficulty of Being), the most serious and rewarding of his prose volumes of recapitulation in being at once the most poetic and the least embroidered, Cocteau wrote that he had long been haunted by two projects — "that of a film that would plunge me into a lustral bath of childhood, and a book of the kind I'd have liked to carry around with me when I was very young and very alone. I made the film — *Beauty and the Beast*. I am writing the book: it is this one."

Beauty and the Beast, the first film of Cocteau's own since *The Blood of a Poet*, and his finest poem since then, is by general consent one of the most enchanting pictures ever made, and its production was one of those undertakings that with a kind of general benevolence shed lustre on all its participants. It brought new accolades to Madame Leprince de Beaumont, the eighteenth-century author of the fairy tale. Jean Marais had suggested the film: for him, his face masked by the fur and the fangs of the Beast, his body padded and swathed in velvet, his hands made into claws, it was his triumph of acting over physique. Lovely Josette Day played Beauty, the good country girl, with an intelligence and a dancer's grace that Cocteau praised without reserve; and she, the actresses who play her wicked sisters, and the rest of the cast are outstanding in the way they speak, move, wear their clothes, and form tableaux à la Vermeer and Le Nain. The Gustave Doré sumptuousness of Christian Bérard's costumes and décor is reminiscent not in style, but in spirit and success, of Bakst's lavishness in ballet. In Bérard, Cocteau had found a new fellow master of fantasy, an anti-modern, neo-baroque successor to the Picasso of *Parade;* and the high style of his famous perspective of human arms emerging from draperies to grasp lighted candelabra that materialize in the air, the moving eyes of his dusky, smoke-breathing caryatids, his pair of Louis XIV marble busts of Turks, lend fantastic cinema a nobility that had been previously hinted at — one can only mention the earlier film again — in *The Blood of a Poet*. Henri Alekan gave the photography the tone Cocteau wanted, the "soft gleam of hand-polished old silver," particularly exquisite in the swaying, sheer white curtains, in Beauty's tear that turns into a pearl. The most haunting feature is Marais' beast mask, a remarkable creation, so appealingly beastlike as to be more "becoming" than his lover's-postcard transfiguration as Prince Charming at the end of the film. In his autobiography Marais talks about it:

"For my mask we went to Pontet, an elderly gentleman, a real genius, one of those men who make you realize that one can be passionately in love with one's work whatever it may be. He devoted a great deal of thought to how the mask could be given the look of my own face and not interfere with its mobility. He made a cast and worked on it endlessly. I often went to see him with Moulouk, and the dog taught us things: the unevenness and shagginess and spottiness of the fur that make it seem so alive are due to Moulouk. M. Pontet made my mask like a wig, hair on a webbing base, but in three parts — one down to the eyes, a second as far as the upper lip and the third to the base of the neck. . . . It took me five hours to make up — that meant thirteen hours a day in the studio. Because of the fangs attached to my teeth, all I could eat was mush, and that by the spoonful. Between takes I scarcely dared open my mouth lest the makeup become unglued: no one understood what I said, and that exasperated me." "In my opinion," wrote Cocteau, "one must have Marais' passion for his work and his devotion to his dog, to persevere as he did in deserting the human race for the animal race."

The idea of the film was hard to sell to a producer, and although it became a professional and commercial undertaking, with well-paid stars, jealous unions, watchful insurance companies and budgeted financing by Gaumont, *Beauty and the Beast* nevertheless represented a triumph over primary difficulties. Like most of the combatant countries, France emerged from the war stripped; Cocteau himself was receiving food packages from Jean-Pierre Aumont in California, and when he fell ill he was treated with American penicillin; everything was in short supply. Old cameras jammed, old lenses developed flaws, no two batches of film were alike, electric current failed or was bureaucratically cut off; there was small choice of fabrics for costumes; sheets without patches were sought everywhere for the farmyard laundry scene; the curtains of Beauty's bed were stolen from the set. There were the usual coctelian coincidences and contradictions. In the manor outside Tours used as Beauty's house was found a disc of Cocteau reading his poems; as a setting the place was perfect — but it was near a military airfield, and though the good will of the commanding colonel was secured, he proved forgetful or a poor disciplinarian, and training flights constantly interfered with sound-recording. The Château de Raray near Senlis, used for exterior shots of the Beast's castle, had "the most bizarre park in France," with a fantastic sculptured stone procession of hunting dogs silhouetted against the sky atop a high parapet; that made it, too, an appropriate setting — but there in the north rain was incessant. (And local children, come to watch the filming, ran off terrified as the Beast emerged from bushes.) Just when the carcass of a deer was needed, the Paris wholesale game markets went on strike. Most of the cast was accident-prone. Cocteau, scourged by his post-Occupation eczema, so disfigured that for a time he wore "a veil made of black paper, fastened to the brim of his hat with clothespins, with holes for his eyes and mouth," developed jaundice, and filming was interrupted while he was hospitalized in the Institut Pasteur. The journal he kept during the filming, the predecessor of many later blow-by-blow accounts of the making of movies, and unique in being the work of the artist-moviemaker himself, swarms with the names of doctors. (The maddening irritation of the skin disease was one of the reasons Cocteau returned to opium for a time in 1946–47. On January 23, 1947 the newspaper *Franc-Tireur* published his photograph — one of his few unposed pictures — amid a group of addicts summoned to the Palais de Justice. In later years Cocteau seems to have smoked with moderation when at all.)

Before beginning the filming of the "lustral bath of childhood," Cocteau gave himself a different lustral bath. "I am living with you, near you, around you, as you can imagine," he was impelled to write, after their long silence, to Valentine Hugo from Le Piqueÿ, where he now once again took Jean Marais for a short stay. "Even though the coast is changing, filling up with ugly houses, there are still enough plank walks, fishnets and pines to relive our dream. Alas, it is no longer possible to walk to the ocean over the dunes — there are mines everywhere." It was another evocation of Radiguet, as though to bless the work.

The filming of *Beauty and the Beast* brought Cocteau an enchantment reminiscent of his days with the Diaghilev troupe, the sensation of being part of a hard-working family of sacred monsters; moving from manor to chateau to Paris film studio they were like mountebanks; Cocteau's journal celebrates the camaraderie and good will of the company — the actors' professional tolerance of each other's *crises de nerfs,* their busy shuttling between the film studio and the legitimate theatres where some of them were simultaneously appearing in plays, the combination of familiarity and respect shown by the grips, their never failing improvisation when rescue was needed, the studio sweepers' praise after the first rushes, the Vouvray wine with the picnic meals, cast and crew playing cards during rests, Marais hilariously plunging clothed into a fountain one midnight, celebrating with the people of Tours the first anniversary of their Liberation. "I wonder," Cocteau wrote, "whether these days of hard work aren't the most delicious of my life. Full of friendship, affectionate disagreement, laughter, profiting from every moment." The breakup was sentimental. "We shall be working tonight. The last night. I know nothing sadder than the end of a film, the dissolution of a team that has developed ties of affection."

After cutting, after the synchronization of Auric's music — Auric was the only veteran of *The Blood of a Poet* to collaborate on *Beauty and the Beast,* — the first showing of the film for an audience of any size was for the technicians in the Joinville studio. The invitation was written on the studio blackboard; schedules were changed to leave everyone free. "The welcome the picture received from that audience of workers was unforgettable. It was my greatest reward. Whatever happens, nothing will ever equal the grace of that ceremony organized very simply by a little village of workmen whose trade is the packaging of dreams." That night the journal ends: "Afterward, at ten, I had dinner at the Palais-Royal with Bérard, Boris, Auric, Jean Marais, Claude Ibéria [the editor of the film], and we promised each other to work together always. May fate never separate us."

Close to the end of the journal, Cocteau wrote several passages on France and the cinema:

If other countries ask France, "What are your weapons?" she can answer, "I have none. I have a secret weapon." If she is asked what that is, she will answer that secret weapons are kept secret. If she is forced to tell, she risks nothing, since her weapon is inimitable. It is her tradition of anarchy.

In France, every time an attempt is made to organize, to adopt systems, the individual rebels and slips in between the gears of the mechanism. One result of this is that crooks easily get the upper hand, but another is the formation of under-ground élites — a vast hidden force with a spirit of contra-diction that is the very basis of the spirit of creation — beyond the reach of the official élites. For centuries this has been the French rhythm, and yet Frenchmen continue to believe that France is decadent! . . .

The film industry is dead set against "change," "the unfore-seen," "anarchy." Last week [Gabriel] Pascal saw my film. "France is at present the only country where such a work is possible," he said. Whether my film is liked or not is some-thing else again. I was able to bring it to completion thanks to a free producer's spirit of risk, thanks to the cooperation of my colleagues, thanks to the resourcefulness of the crew, thanks to that tradition of anarchy that still makes it possible, here in France, for chance to intrude amidst all the order.

It is absurd, he says, to say that "the cinema is not art." It is not an art only where it is kept from being one; and it will become one when those film makers stop merely excreting film, and instead of remaining mere "silkworms," use their brains and imagination and become true "makers of silk."

For all the camaraderie, he had been aware, as he worked, of "the inevitable solitude of poets." "The grips love me, would go through fire and water for me, but in the end I have to work alone. . . . There is nothing more glorious than to write a poem with people, faces, hands, lights, objects, arranging them all as one likes." The language of his poem is simple, his additions to Mad-ame Leprince de Beaumont always remain in the realm of fairy tale. The film has never needed explication, but one French writer has spoken of the Beast's marvelous pavilion that is one of Coc-teau's inventions: "This pavilion contains the Beast's most precious treasure, the basis, the very source, of his power. There can be no doubt that this treasure is the treasure of childhood. If jealously preserved, it can enrich our interior worlds and thus become an inexhaustible source of poetry. Who seeks to violate it pays for the sacrilege with his life: this profanation in the film is the equivalent of the theft of the Ace of Hearts in . . . *The Blood of a Poet.*"

During the making of *Beauty and the Beast* Cocteau signed a contract with a Swiss publisher for the printing of an edition of his so-called "Complete Works," and he received a copy of the second book to be written about him — the study by Roger Lannes that even today continues to be reprinted in the series "Poètes d'Aujourd'hui" although it does not extend beyond 1945. Cocteau and Lannes were friends; and the study, which is eulogistic to the point of sycophancy, as well as factually inaccurate, was probably conceived as a riposte to Claude Mauriac's attack.

Those first two studies of Cocteau immediately set the two contrasting tones that were to characterize much of the future writing about him. Denigration was answered by adulation; later the order was sometimes reversed. Interest in Cocteau's work or in his personality often triggered salvos of critical abuse. Sometimes, as in Mauriac, there is an unmistakable echo of Gide; or latter-day partisans of Dada and Surrealism parrot their leader, Breton. In the field of abuse, there are few instances in literature comparable to the writings about Cocteau: so magnetic is his fascination that hostile critics have devoted years of their lives to proving that he has no artistic existence. Such attacks range from wild obsession to calculated capitalization on Cocteau's drawing power. When, as is always the case, the detractors find themselves obliged to point out "exceptions" in his work, the faintness of their reluctant praise stands in amusing contrast to the strength of the admiration, even dedication, implied in the energy and scope of the attack.

This compulsion to abuse Cocteau at length and in detail recalls W. H. Auden's lines in his "Letter to Lord Byron":

> By looking into your poetic style
> And love-life on the chance that both were vile,
> Several have earned a decent livelihood,
> Whose lives were uncreative but were good.

One American lady of letters has harangued the present author, and others, on a number of separate occasions with her Pavlovian

— and sole — response to the phenomenon of Cocteau; which is to draw up either orally or on paper a list of those whom Cocteau in various ways "destroyed." Perhaps single-minded ladies compiled similar, even lengthier, lists about Lord Byron in his time.

Cocteau is one of those few artists — and in this he resembles Proust — whose flavor is so pervasive that those who merely know his name believe themselves familiar with his works. Acquaintance with a single book, a single film, will sometimes bring authoritative pronouncements on all his vast production. In a way this is a favorable condition for both an artist and his public: from here the way is open to true knowledge and appreciation.

THE EAGLE HAS TWO HEADS. Cocteau's housekeeper at 36 rue Montpensier during the last decades of his life, Madeleine Bourret, has spoken of his increasingly misogynistic habit of talk — "Yes, yes, she's very nice, but she's a woman, and that means she's an actress" — and examples of misogyny proliferated in his works. "A devil can disguise himself as a woman if he likes," says his character Olivier in *Renaud et Armide*. "More than one woman I've known is a devil and has told me so." And in a ballet scenario of 1946, *Le Jeune Homme et la Mort*, Cocteau repeated his casting, as in the play *Orphée*, of Death as a lovely young woman.* (The literalness of this scenario, with its hanging rope and a death's-head, makes one enjoy by contrast the airy remark of the much younger Cocteau, when he was taken by Princess Bibesco and Marie Bonaparte to call on a fashionable doctor whom he found pretentious and whose study contained a complete skeleton: "We all live with a skeleton, but most of us have it *inside*.") Now in a new play, *The*

* Another aspect of Cocteau's misogyny, the queenly note he could strike in remarks about women, is illustrated by his comment on the appearance of a not-quite-young-enough actress in a screen test for one of his films — "Voltaire, toward the end of his days." One of his favorite bits of praise was the comment of a studio handyman on *Beauty and the Beast*: "That's a story — not the kind of drivel our wives keep talking." His book on Jean Marais contains a remarkable passage on feminine feelings: "Jean Marais would like a son, and he would like to have that son by a woman willing to be used for that purpose only, but he has always felt that any woman might come to resent that and take his son away from him." And there is a *lettera buffa* about a once handsome young boy of Villefranche: "The president of the fishermen's union is none other than the lad who used to clean my boat. He has three daughters and two sons, all of whom would turn the head of Casanova or Oscar Wilde. This entire radiant progeny gives the impression of having issued from his [*sic*] great belly. He himself was what poor Wilde used to call a young God."

Eagle Has Two Heads, which began its career in the fall of 1946 with the London production of an adaptation by Ronald Duncan,* quickly followed by Cocteau's own production in Paris with Edwige Feuillère and Jean Marais, Cocteau portrays another aggressive woman, this time a nineteenth-century queen, who is a young poet's destroyer (even though it is he, dying from self-administered poison — *her* poison — who murders her); and the next year he made the excellent film of the same name, splendidly acted by much the same cast. Each of the two, the play and the film, is notable for a significant "first": on the stage, Tony, the queen's deaf-mute servant, was played by Georges Aminel, who twenty years later was to become the first Negro ever engaged by the Comédie Française; and the film marked the first screen appearance of a new young man in Cocteau's life, the last of his "adopted sons," Edouard Dermit (known as "Doudou," as Jean Marais was "Jeannot").

The public aspects of Edouard Dermit — as an actor (he appeared in four of Cocteau's films) and as a painter (Cocteau encouraged him to paint and exhibit) — can in principle be as freely discussed as anyone else's, but here one is inhibited by a sense of indebtedness: Dermit is Cocteau's legal heir, and only his formal permission has made possible some of the foregoing pages. In any case, there have been no Dermit screen appearances, and few Dermit paintings, since Cocteau's death; like Jean Marais, Dermit can say that he owes Cocteau everything, but in his case the portion of the "everything" represented by a career is far less than Marais', due in part to his more passive nature. For Cocteau's last fifteen years Dermit was willing to be his inseparable companion — in the Paris apartment, in the house at Milly-la-Forêt bought jointly in

---

* Duncan says he invented the English title, adapting it from a phrase near the end of Act II, *"l'aigle à deux têtes"* ("the two-headed eagle"). With the accent dropped, the meaning becomes "the eagle has two heads." Cocteau, who had considered several other titles, adopted, without the dropping of the accent, his own phrase that had inspired Duncan. "With this," Duncan says, "he gave the impression that I had mistranslated the title. . . . He enjoyed telling his friends in Paris this." Quite possible, though Duncan often shows himself quick to find offense. Cocteau disliked Duncan's adaptation. In 1955 he wrote to Rosamond Lehmann, who was translating *Les Enfants Terribles,* urging her not to fall into Duncan's "errors" — "your genius as a novelist is opposed to that."

While on the subject of translation, it might be noted that when Stanislas in this play reads aloud, in French, lines from *Hamlet,* the translation used by Cocteau is *not* the version that had recently been published by Gide.

1947 by Cocteau and Jean Marais and later ceded by Marais completely to Cocteau, and in the Villa Santo Sospir at St. Jean Cap Ferrat, where, beginning in 1950, they were the guests of Madame Francine Weisweiller for over a decade. When legal adoption proved impossible, permission was secured from Cocteau's family that Dermit be named residuary legatee; and today, married, the father of two children, he lives chiefly at Milly, much of his time taken up by consultation with advisors concerning the legal and literary complexities of his inheritance.

In *The Eagle Has Two Heads* Dermit made his debut as an extra — a waltzing guardsman given a bit more screen footage than the rest. (His debut in Cocteau's life had been as gardener at Milly, a refugee from the iron mines of the Ardennes.) As director, Cocteau elicited from the principals a bravura style that suits the story and the Graustarkian setting of the castle of "Krantz"; an atmosphere of sensuality is achieved — the very feminine screen personality of Edwige Feuillère kindles in Marais a rare semblance of man-woman response; but essentially the film is a thriller, and the poetry with which Cocteau once again filled his work is the poetry of Romantic melodrama, in the spirit of Victor Hugo's *Hernani* or *Ruy Blas*.

RUY BLAS. From *Ruy Blas* itself, Victor Hugo's swashbuckling five-act Romantic drama in verse, Cocteau had made a screen play for Jean Marais just before the filming of *The Eagle Has Two Heads;* and in the film *Ruy Blas* the Marais whose first screen ambitions had been inspired by Pearl White made himself the French Douglas Fairbanks of the 1940's, with plenty of wall scaling and chandelier swinging to prepare himself for the spectacular fall down a flight of stairs with which he closes the *Eagle*. In *Ruy Blas* and the *Eagle* his roles are somewhat similar — in each he is a sensitive young man of the people who bears a startling resemblance to an exalted personage and is in love with a queen — and with these two pictures his fame became worldwide: "Jean Marais Clubs" were organized as far away as Tokyo, where he was known as "the most beautiful western man."

Cocteau's screen treatment of *Ruy Blas* for the director Pierre Billon brought protests from many admirers of the original play, and especially from Victor Hugo's great-grandson, Cocteau's old friend Jean Hugo, who had now remarried and was living at Fourques. He has written of the episode as follows:

"Cocteau had asked me to design the clothes and decorations: I had refused before reading the scenario, as I didn't want to work any more for the stage. I would have been very embarrassed later if I had accepted. Jean Cocteau did not admire Victor Hugo as a poet, and still less as a playwright. He had always admitted it to me openly. He had a kind of admiration for the man, which he expressed in his famous 'Victor Hugo was a madman who thought he was Victor Hugo.' All he saw in *Ruy Blas* was an opportunity for Jean Marais to act two parts in the same play. . . . He said and wrote that the plot of *Ruy Blas* was utter nonsense. He changed the play entirely, centering it on the likeness of Ruy Blas and Don César de Bazan. I have never seen the film, but I have read the scenario: it is intolerable for anyone who likes the play. Lovers of Victor Hugo's work were shocked still more than Shakespeare's admirers were by Cocteau's *Roméo et Juliette*. In *Roméo* he had cut all the famous lines but respected the plot, whereas in *Ruy Blas* both poetry and plot were suppressed or changed. . . . We could not but put in a protest: our family lawyer wrote an official letter: it was all we could do."

In writing to Jean Hugo, Cocteau called the changes he was making mere "simplifications required by the cinema"; Jean Hugo replied that the introduction into the scenario of "the horrid word *sensationnel,*" to take but one example, was not imposed by any consideration: it is the familiar quarrel about the "vulgarization" of a classic. Cocteau wrote frankly to Hugo that he was doing much of his screen work for money — "Next week Rossellini begins *La Voix Humaine* with Anna Magnani, the actress of *Open City*. After *Ruy Blas* I have to make *The Eagle Has Two Heads*. This schedule appalls me, but I must pay for this house, where some day or other I hope to find peace. My dream is to see you there" — but the fact is that his new vein of poetry was these days very strong, and anything connected with him in the realm of film took on a touch of magic, whether the *Eagle* directed by himself, or the smoldering Magnani-Rossellini *Voce Humana* (modernized for a dial telephone!), or films for which he wrote merely a narration, like *Les Noces de Sable,* in which he tells a Moroccan love legend as the film unrolls amid a Saharan landscape, or the Italian "art short" *La Leggenda di Sant' Orsola,* for which he wrote a commentary on the Carpaccio St. Ursula series in the Accademia in Venice. All of those, and more, done in 1947 and 1948, helped to pay for the house at Milly.

One of the "simplifications" to which Cocteau subjected Victor Hugo's *Ruy Blas* was not "imposed" by the cinema, but was rather the exploitation of one of the cinema's best-known possibilities — the playing of two characters, who confront each other, by the same actor. As Jean Hugo says, that was the *raison d'être* of the film; but it was also the realization of what had probably been an unattainable wish of Victor Hugo. In the play, Don César, the nobleman-turned-bandit, and Ruy Blas, the modest secretary, are cast to resemble each other as closely as possible,* and Hugo's regretful recognition of the stage limitations of resemblance is evident in some wistful lines. "We looked so alike we were taken for brothers," Ruy Blas says to Don César; and of Ruy Blas masquerading as the other a courtier remarks "Very changed! I'd have scarcely recognized him," to which Hugo quickly provides the explanatory reply "Ten years away!" Although the incompleteness of the resemblance adds some tension, might not Victor Hugo himself have admitted that a double portrayal by a single gifted actor provides the possibility of greater drama, perhaps even more poetry, than utilitarian lines of dialogue?

Cocteau said of *Ruy Blas* that "It was a question of making a 'Western,' a cloak-and-dagger film." In it, he said, he "did not commit himself personally," and — any film being a portrait of its director — *"Ruy Blas,* little understood by the famous elite but much liked by the public at large, expressed the charm and malice of Pierre Billon." The costumes, especially those of the men, black with white ruffs, are excellent in the photographs, and splendidly worn; some of the group scenes are patterned after canvases by El Greco — about whom Cocteau, fascinated by a sketch owned by José-Maria Sert, had recently written an essay. The Spain portrayed in the film, Cocteau said, was intended to be to the real Spain what the Romantic restorations of Viollet-le-Duc were to the real Middle Ages.

* As though Marais were to have played opposite Jean-Pierre Aumont, to whom, as he himself says in his autobiography, he had "a certain resemblance."

The Blood of a Poet.
Barbette (front row, center) and extras.

The Blood of a Poet.
The Black Angel (Féral Benga).

Beauty and the Beast.
Josette Day and Jean Marais.

Beauty and the Beast.
Jean Marais in his Beast Mask.

Orphée. Maria Casarès and Jean Marais.

LES PARENTS TERRIBLES. This is generally considered by connoisseurs Cocteau's greatest technical accomplishment in cinema, the sole admitted flaw being Jean Marais' somewhat too mature look for his part. (When the play first opened in 1938 he had been twenty-five and looked about twenty-two, the stage age of the son whose love for a girl outrages and eventually "kills" his mother.)

Cocteau had long been an admirer of two staunch French actresses, neither of them a beauty, but each with memorable appearance, strong stage personality and considerable skill, and old enough to be cast as the mother and the aunt of Jean Marais in *Les Parents Terribles*. These ladies were Yvonne de Bray and Gabrielle Dorziat: he says he wrote the play "for" them and Marais; he always retained a fidelity to both actresses, finding them parts in several of his films. With those three in the play was the excellent actor Marcel André (Beauty's father in *Beauty and the Beast*); the role of the young girl, weak and improbable, was given to various actresses. The four principals formed a tightly unified team, a true small company; Cocteau, and they themselves, took great pride in each performance and in the play's success, and they all liked the film for reproducing the stage play exactly.

"I wanted three things," Cocteau has said of the film. "First, to record the performances of incomparable actors; second, mingle with them myself and look them full in the face instead of seeing them at a distance on a stage. I wanted to put my eye to the keyhole and surprise them with a telescopic lense." The economy of the transfer from stage to screen, the picture's compression and concentration, Cocteau's success in making the spectator feel that he himself is mingling with the actors, the confinement of the action to a few closely relevant interior sets, the absence of exterior shots that would have brought air into a story essentially airless, the use of the camera to achieve close-up candid portraits and telling still-lifes impossible of projection from a stage — all that has brought the picture great celebrity. Of all Cocteau's plays it was the most "naturalistic" (though, as has been said, the weaknesses of the story have been pointed out by critics); and even those who feel that Cocteau's own *raison d'être* diminishes in direct proportion to his withdrawal from what for want of a better term is called poetic fantasy, and who find the phrase "the poetry of naturalism" not too convincing when applied to the theatre, must admire his tact and technique in excluding from the strange values displayed in the tale any of those disheartening shafts of sweetness and light so often introduced by self-indulgent writers to show that their own hearts, at least, are in the right place.

Some of Marais' feelings for his own mother were transferred to Yvonne de Bray, his mother in *Les Parents Terribles;* between the two actors there was such a degree of affection offstage as well as on that Marais brought his autobiography to a close with Madame de Bray's death. Their performance of one of the scenes on the first night of a later revival of the play inspired him to write as follows: "I had never forgotten our rehearsals in her room, and now I saw it all come to life again on the stage of this great theatre. I saw the transfiguration of her face as I came in, I flung myself on the bed beside her, I kissed her, caressed her, she overflowed with words of maternal love that went far beyond the text; that carried me away; I said whatever came into my head, anything. . . . I felt that I was playing this young man ten times better than ten years before: surely I owed it to her." His real mother, Marais says, came to nourish a hatred for Yvonne de Bray, and gave way to jealous outbursts even after the actress's death. Madame Marais was known to all as *"une mère excessive,"* and the tone and quality of her real-life behavior faithfully reproduce, and are reproduced by, the tone and quality of *Les Parents Terribles.*

The making of that picture about a family that Cocteau likened to a lot of disorderly gypsies living in a caravan culminated in an incident celebrated in film annals and recounted by Marais: "One extraordinary detail. In the final scene, Josette Day [the young girl in the film] and I are at the foot of the bed in which Yvonne de Bray has just died. The camera, which had been in for a close-up, moves away, further and further away on its dolly, gradually taking in the entire room, the entire apartment, of the *Parents Terribles.* With this scene the words 'The End' were to appear on the screen. The next day, during the rushes, we saw that the dolly tracks had not been firmly fastened to the floor; the image was shaky from the moment the dolly shot started. We all — producers, cameramen, actors — looked at each other in dismay: we were going to have to remake the scene. 'No,' said Cocteau. 'We will not do it over. I'll add a few words. I'll say: "And the gypsy caravan continued on its way." ' And actually the shaking did give the im-

pression that the entire scene was taking place inside a wagon jogging along a rough country road. Anyone else would have done it
over. Cocteau transformed the technical accident into a poetic *trou-
vaille*. For me, that is genius."

LES ENFANTS TERRIBLES. The novel that "begins with a white
ball and ends with a black one," and that had taken youth by storm,
was given its screen treatment by Cocteau himself but directed by J.-
P. Melville, in a style that Cocteau considered close to his own. It
was shot in Melville's own flat, in the lobby of a gloomy newspaper
building, in the hall of a town house belonging to a cousin of the
star, in a theatre. The film critic Pauline Kael has called it "almost voluptuous in its evocation of temperament and atmosphere,"
and said that "Dismissed as 'arty' and 'embalmed' by many critics,
this film is 'embalmed' in the memory of those of us who think it
one of the most exciting films of our time."

Nicole Stéphane's brilliance in the role of Elizabeth points up
by contrast a strange defect in the casting of two other parts. We
have seen how since his schooldays Cocteau had been haunted by
the type of handsome young bully to whom in *Les Enfants Terribles* and elsewhere he gave the name Dargelos — a name (borne
in life by an uninteresting schoolmate) whose sound somehow
held for Cocteau the rugged, sensual glamour of his "ideal." His
early drawings of "Dargelos" are striking prefigurations of Jean
Marais: in this respect, Marais' appearance in his life must have
been a recognition of a preconceived physical type. To a certain
degree this was true also of Dermit, and Cocteau spotted many another, lesser "Dargelos" over the years. No woman gave him this
experience of recognition until, after making drawings of his character Elisabeth in *Les Enfants Terribles*, he saw Nicole Stéphane
in Melville's film *Le Silence de la Mer*. Cocteau told her that she
and Dermit (who is also in *Les Enfants Terribles*) had "been" his
characters, and the drawings he had made for the story, "even before they were born." The harsh masculinity of Dargelos was ill
conveyed in the film by Melville's all but incredible casting of a
young woman, Renée Cosima, in the two roles of Dargelos and
Agathe, who in the story are said to resemble each other: Cocteau
always regretted that mistake. Otherwise, he said, "Were I to write

the book now, I would be influenced by the characters the actors have created."

In January, 1949, following the release in Paris of the film *Les Parents Terribles,* Cocteau flew to New York for a three-week visit. *The Blood of a Poet* had long been a favorite of New York film buffs, and he was asked to speak at a New York preview of the film *The Eagle Has Two Heads.* (A poor American production of that play, adapted from Ronald Duncan's English adaptation and starring Tallulah Bankhead and Helmut Dantine had done badly on Broadway.) Parisian to the highest degree, his excellent manners a cloak, sometimes transparent, worn over his artist's egotism and his insecurities, uninterested in speaking with Americans or understanding their speech, Cocteau was not at all one of those Frenchmen, so numerous in the history of the relations between the two countries, who easily conceive an empathy for American ways. He was willing to charm his New York listeners with his speech at the film premiere (partially translated from the stage by Jean-Pierre Aumont), and he visited the boxer Al Brown, now sick and poor, in Harlem; but in general he chose, during his visit, and afterwards in a hastily written *Letter to Americans,* to play rather crudely the condescending and scolding European. Lincoln Kirstein, who met him at the house of friends, recalls that "Cocteau was a model of ill grace and exquisite rudeness, impatience and boredom. . . . I was idiotic enough to try to ask why he never made a film of *Père Goriot,* with Jean Marais as Vautrin . . . and I was annihilated." There was a difference of opinion between him and *Life* magazine, concerning some photographs made by Philippe Halsman. "*Life* photographed me quietly sitting in a chair, and when the pictures were developed I saw myself flying, my feet to the ceiling, holding out my hand toward Leo Coleman in the nude," was one of Cocteau's versions of the episode. Actually, photographs show him posing with Coleman (the young Negro dancer who had been appearing in Gian Carlo Menotti's *The Medium*) and others in scenes that could have been conceived only by himself. Another of his versions is funnier. After a number of bizarre pictures had been taken, he says, the *Life* editor "asked an astonishing question: 'What do you suppose a man in a Massachusetts barbershop will make of these photographs? Aren't you afraid they'll puzzle him?' They brought up the grave problem of text, asking me how they could explain the inexplicable. I suggested saying that they had taken normal photographs, but that the camera had played a trick on them. That the public must not blame them, that . . . it had become dangerous to entrust man's image to a machine. Perhaps they could interest Rolleiflex in some advertising. For example: ROLLEIFLEX THINKS." The most coctelian of the scenes, conceived, Mr. Halsman says, as showing "the poet bringing an image to life," remained unpublished by the magazine because one of the model's nipples was in view — twenty years too early for the mass media.

A week after his return to Paris he received a cable from the dean and provost of Harvard, inviting him to come to America again, this time as Charles Eliot Norton Professor of Poetry for the following academic year; he would be in residence for seven months and deliver six public lectures in French — Harvard suggested the cinema as subject and $14,000 as salary. Cocteau sent a cable of regret: "TRAVAIL EMPECHE ACCEPTER GRAND HONNEUR DE CE POSTE FIDELEMENT COCTEAU." Ubiquitous though he could be, it is difficult to think of Cocteau spending seven months in either of the two Cambridges; and in any case there was indeed work that prevented acceptance — the project of a film to be made from his play *Orphée,* or, at least, on the same subject. There was a delay, however. During March, April and May he accompanied a repertory company that included the cast of his *Parents Terribles* on a tour of the Near East that seems to have been an official or semiofficial French cultural mission. They acted several of his own plays, and pieces by Racine, Feydeau, Sartre and Anouilh. Once again he kept a journal, published under the Arab title *Maalesh.* Work on *Orphée* began during the summer, after he finished an adaptation for the French stage of Tennessee Williams's *A Streetcar Named Desire,* working from a literal translation of the American text.

ORPHÉE. One of Cocteau's self-imposed tasks of film-making apprenticeship before undertaking *Beauty and the Beast* had been the writing of dialogue for a "psychological" film whose scenario had been adapted to the present-day Paris scene by the director Robert Bresson from an episode in Diderot's novel *Jacques le Fataliste,* about a man who unknowingly marries a prostitute. The filmed adaptation, *Les Dames du Bois de Boulogne,* has an inadequate theme (the bride of a twentieth-century businessman turns out shockingly to have been a *dancer!*), but several members of the cast are excellent. Especially powerful is the star, the dark-haired young Maria Casarès; and Cocteau now remembered her grim, businesslike beauty in the picture, and her skill at portraying quiet, total ruthlessness, when choosing the actress to create the striking role of the "Princess," who is Orpheus's own death, "a satellite of Death itself," for his new film. Madame Casarès has told about working with Cocteau:

> Here was a writer, a man of the theatre, a film director, offering me a fictional character and asking me to give it life. We talked, and he never argued. He asked questions, seemed to be seeking information. Cocteau all but gives you the impression that *you* are giving the cues, and yet there is nobody more precise than he, nobody more aware of what he wants. But: he knows that he is dealing with human beings. He respects and loves actors the way actors, in turn, love the characters they create. And once he has chosen his actors he makes use of them as they are, and not as he wishes they might be, to arrive at the desired end. This makes it fascinating to work with him. I wasn't well while we were making *Orphée,* I had serious worries, I was playing Death; but I have never lived a film role as I lived that one.

In letters to Mary Hoeck, an Englishwoman who had approached him in 1948 about translating his verse, who did translate several poems and plays, and with whom he maintained a correspondence for the rest of his life, Cocteau wrote of *Orphée:* "Its moral is that the poet should be personally committed rather than be a follower of causes and parties. I think that this film is worthy of you and of our friendship. It is much less a film than it is myself — a kind of projection of the things that are important to me." For the Cocteau of 1949, the hostility shown the poet Orpheus by his eventual assassins in the film had a wider reference than the allusions to the Surrealists and Dadaists which it carried over from the play of the 1920's. He had just found himself excluded from Gaëtan Picon's

1949 anthology, *Panorama de la Nouvelle Littérature Française*
on the ground that as the *"grand couturier des lettres françaises"*
he belonged to "a 1920 climate that has nothing to do with us
today"; and when the film opens with its confrontation of two generations of poets at the "Café des Artistes," there is no doubt that
Orpheus, a celebrity despised by young moderns, is one of Cocteau's fears concerning himself at sixty. (He was to have another
confirmation at the opening of a revival of Stravinsky's *Oedipus
Rex*, in 1952, when he was booed for his narration.) His retort to
the snub in the *Panorama* was perfect and powerful — the film
Orphée itself.*

Orphée is one of the triumphant examples of the use of the resources of film to intensify and extend fantasy beyond its possibilities of realization on a stage. The momentary suspension of Heurtebise the glazier in mid-air and the single mirror door of the Pitoëff
production of 1926 are mild marvels compared with the windswept
no-man's-land sequences of the picture, the double actors, twin
rooms and multiple mirrors. Another comparison — that with *The
Blood of a Poet* — illustrates Cocteau's development as exploiter
of cinematic resources. Although that earlier film about poetry
remains, in its artistry and the strength of its strange appeal, at
least the equal of the later, *Orphée* is more expert and less epi-
sodic. As Cocteau himself said, *"Orphée* orchestrates, twenty years
later, the theme that in *The Blood of a Poet* I played clumsily with
one finger." In its combination of intellect with imagination of genius, in its mystery, it becomes almost legendary itself in its recounting of the legend.

Cocteau has described many of the technical devices employed
in the filming of *Orphée*. For his imagination, everything served as
material. Whether or not he himself had been called before one of
the Conseils d'Epuration in Paris in the days following Liberation,
the examinations of the prisoners in *Orphée* summon up such ses-

---

* The anthologist himself failed to hear the message, and in a new edition of the
Panorama printed ten years later retained the same references to the "outdated" Cocteau: it is now the anthology that has the outdated air.
  In connection with the film, it has been pointed out that the vogue for the younger
poet Cégeste (played by Edouard Dermit) and the decline of Orphée (Jean Marais) is
analogous to the roles of the two men in Cocteau's intimate life: since the "adoption"
of Dermit, Marais had been gradually withdrawing. (A third young man, Paul Morihien, who had also been one of the household and who had acted as Cocteau's secretary, withdrew at this same time.)

sions in all their grimness. In the magazine *Paris-Match* he saw a photograph of General Giraud's funeral procession preceded by two motorcycle policemen: hence the pair of helmeted, dark-goggled, gauntleted, leather-jacketed riders so intensely realized in the film, the roar of their motors so modern and terrifying a herald of onrushing death, to be copied in innumerable film sequences in the future. (The Orphean trio of motorcycles and Rolls-Royce opens a highly praised and popular American "mod" film being shown as these words are written.) German bombs had destroyed the French military academy at St. Cyr near Versailles: that no-man's-land made by the war became "The Zone," the no-man's-land between life and death that lay beyond Orpheus's mirrors — but for certain scenes ruins had to be constructed, in a studio. The teenage "existentialist" proto-beatniks, swarming in 1949 in the cafés and *caves* of St. Germain-des-Prés, were apt to speak of Cocteau and his contemporaries as he was spoken of in the *Panorama;* Juliette Greco, in full celebrity as a singer, was the idol, the muse, of St. Germain-des-Prés; her enlistment by Cocteau in the cast of the film, along with some of her band, as the girl leader of Orpheus's enemies, brought St. Germain-des-Prés to Cocteau and gave the beatnik image an early currency that is unchanged today. Cocteau changed the position, in the musical score, of some of the themes from Glück's *Orpheus and Eurydice* that Auric had inserted: the new positions were less logical, but they produced, he thought, a "syncopation," a greater effect by reference. Orpheus's pursuit of the Princess through city streets is a montage of several short sequences filmed in widely separate sections of Paris, each chosen for its value as an image. One of the film's "mirrors" was a 300-kilo tub of liquid mercury; another existed not at all, and Marais, striking "it," beat his fists against mere empty air — sound was added later.

For all the beauty of the photography, the last scenes of *Orphée* (though not the stunning very last scene) seem overlong, and Cocteau persisted in once more giving the role of Eurydice its irritating, misogynistic inanity of the play. But it is a magic film, Cocteau's greatest poem of recapitulation. Diaghilev's command, "Astound me!" is echoed by an elderly gentleman at the "Café des Artistes"; the name Heurtebise reappears, given this time not to a glazier angel but to a recently dead young man serving as the Prin-

cess's chauffeur, whereas an anonymous young glazier, also recently dead, makes a brief appearance in no-man's-land; the
talking horse has become a radio operator transmitting cryptic
messages (Cocteau says his inspiration was British broadcasts to
France during the Occupation); the operator's earphones are reminiscent of Apollinaire's First World War headband, of which Cocteau had said that it seemed to conceal a microphone bringing
messages from "an exquisite world"; in fact one of the mysterious
messages in the film, *"L'oiseau chante avec ses doigts"* ("The bird
sings with its fingers"), is, according to Cocteau, a line that Apollinaire had once sent him in a letter. (The earphones also recall Pierre Reverdy's image, at the moment of Cocteau's "conversion," concerning the crucial importance of the sacraments: "They
are the earphones! Take the earphones!") Those and other elements from the past take their places as though naturally in this
great transformation of the play.

"On the last day of our work in the studio," Cocteau has been
quoted as saying, "I was rather depressed, and remarked that
Orphée would probably not appeal to the public. Whereupon our
clapper boy exclaimed: 'But Monsieur! Everybody has some of his
near ones among the dead!' I gladly took his remark as *vox populi.*" When the film opened, in a large cinema on the Champs-
Elysées, its quality was immediately recognized, and its novelty
attracted crowds. Among other commentaries it brought an article
by Claude Mauriac (the same Claude Mauriac who had written the
earlier attack), hailing Cocteau as a *"grand cinéaste"* and *"grand
écrivain français."* Cocteau had thought it well to prepare in
advance for the inevitable question "But what does it mean?" and
some of the publicity for the film contained coctelian "explanation":

Realism in the unreal is a trap set from minute to minute.
One is constantly told "This is possible," or "That is impossible," but how much do we understand of the mechanism of
fate? It is this mysterious mechanism that I try to render
plastic. Why is Orpheus's Death dressed in such or such a
style? Why does she travel in a Rolls-Royce, why does Heurtebise appear and disappear at will in certain circumstances,
while in others he abides by human rules? It is the eternal

"why" that haunts all thinkers, from Pascal to the most minor poet. . . . I wanted to touch on the most serious problems with a light hand, and without philosophizing in a void.

I have always liked the dusk of evening, that half-light in which enigmas flourish, and have always thought that moving pictures could exploit it marvelously, provided that what is called "the marvelous" be featured as little as possible. The closer one approaches to mystery, the more important it becomes to remain a realist. Automobile radios, code messages, short-wave broadcasts, power failures — such elements, familiar to all, make it possible for me to keep things down to earth.

No one would believe in a famous poet whose name has been invented by an author. What I needed was a singer, the singer of singers. He of Thrace. And his adventure is so beautiful that it would be foolish to seek another. It is the fabric on which I embroider.

And Cocteau proceeded to proclaim an aesthetic that critics are constantly thinking they discover in him and brandish accusingly:

"I do nothing but follow the rhythm of fables, which are always transformed by the teller. . . . I always advise the copying of a model. It is impossible to copy exactly; new blood is always infused, and it is by that that we can judge the poet."

Orphée won the First Prize at the International Film Festival in Venice; but whether it had won prizes or not Cocteau had consolidated with it his great decade of poetry on film. All the films exist; many of them are constantly shown, and the rest are in the archives. He had made film his own, and his inimitable use of language accounts for much of his success. "It is probably true," he said, "that an author's text is the very foundation of a spoken film, but no more than the foundation. The real syntax of a film remains silent, wordless. Its style is visual. It is that 'writing' — the mechanism of the photographing of the scenes and the rhythm with which they are put together — that is the hallmark of the film-maker's language."

"Cocteau has taken his place in the front rank of our directors," say the authors of the principal French history of the film. "Critics have not always understood what is original and fruitful in his pictures. They have been unfair to him, and too often denied him the praise to which he is entitled. . . . He found his way back to himself — that is, back to *The Blood of a Poet* — after exploring the realm of myth and legend, from which he carried away perfumes and treasure, like the caravans of old."

The Epitaph of an Enfant Terrible

It is often said that poets should die young, but no lover of poetry or film or history can wish that Cocteau had disappeared before making *Orphée* at sixty. It and the other films are a double good fortune. Not only does one enjoy seeing the old themes treated with the fantastic resources of the cinema, but as one looks back on Cocteau's earlier poems, novels and spectacles, one realizes that the films have illuminated what he was up to from the beginning.

The painter Degas is said to have rebuked his fellow artist Whistler, whose work he admired: "Mr. Whistler, you behave as though you had no talent at all"; and Cocteau's creative life, too, was accompanied by showmanship that is often irritating. The magnitude of his talent was constantly called on to withstand his exhibitionism and posturing. His career was marked by interruptions of which the decade of the 1930's was the most arid; it was marred by moral gaucherie as in the episode of the Princess and in aspects of his life under the Occupation; and gravest of all, it was limited by the incomplete opening of his heart, so crippled by early circumstances. But there have been few artists whose fantasy was as iridescent, whose invention as fecund, whose artistic curiosity as insatiable. Now one tone prevails, now another, and one recognizes his particular rainbow.

It would be a happy state of affairs if the artist were always, in his private life, a "noble soul." Certainly that is the persistent public wish: nor is this wish misdirected, for the artistic vision often comprehends a large and profound view of man's fate. But that great vision may perfectly well derive from a contorted temperament. What is essential is to perceive vision and temperament as an inseparable whole: whatever the temperament may be, regretting its adverse effects, but rejoicing in its beneficial ones. In Cocteau's case it is particularly apparent that his genius was fed not only by his wit and imagination, but also by those very characteristics that marred his private — and all too public — life. His art was in this respect a marvelous reverse of the coin.

For ten years after *Orphée*, Cocteau again made no films — he blamed the commercialism of the cinema and the dependence of film makers on financial backers — and then in the last years of his life he made one that would have been better left unmade. In the meantime, much the way he had enjoyed speaking during the winter of 1917–18 about his "sanatorium" (the Villa Croisset at Grasse, where he lived with friends beside the Mediterranean amid terraces and lemon trees), he found a similar Mediterranean pleasure house in which, as we shall see, it pleased him to say over the next decade he lived "the life of a monk."

In 1947 Jean Bourgoint, the survivor of the original pair of *enfants terribles*, rescued by Jean Hugo in 1932 when he had been on the verge of suicide after being dropped by his Egyptian lover, had been living for most of the intervening fifteen years as Hugo's guest at the Mas de Fourques. Soon after his arrival he had been guided in opium withdrawal by the local doctor, who prescribed laudanum and hard physical work, and though he occasionally relapsed during trips to Paris to see his mother, or when addicts like Christian Bérard brought opium to Fourques or sent him their dross through the mail, he was usually without it and lived quietly, helping on the farm, planting, watering, felling and rooting out trees, carting heavy loads, picking and shelling the year's crop of almonds. He did some sculpture, and, Jean Hugo says, "an enormous amount of talking, a considerable amount of reading: all Balzac several times over, Dickens, Gobineau, Stendhal, Baudelaire over and over again, Dostoevsky, Leskov, Jünger, Thomas Mann, and then back to Racine, etc. . . . and endless newspapers from the first line to the last. He no longer read Saint-Simon or Proust, only opened them occasionally: he knew them by heart." Hugo had become a fervent Catholic, and Bourgoint went to Mass with him and once spent a few weeks of prayer and hard labor in a retreat at the nearby Cistercian monastery of Aiguebelle. On one of his visits to Paris he asked Father Charles Henrion whether he would hear his confession every morning: the priest refused, perhaps as a way of telling

Bourgoint that the compulsion to homosexual promiscuity that plagued him in the city called for a different kind of control. He had no money. "His father, a *huissier,* had left his mother, and then died, leaving debts," Jean Hugo has written. "His mother lived on some very small pension. He had no need of money. Here, he was occasionally given a few francs for cigarettes and newspapers. I once brought him a pair of clogs. But he usually went barefoot." In 1939 he was mobilized into an artillery regiment and after the Armistice returned to Fourques for most of the rest of the war. The year 1944 he spent in Paris, nursing his now invalid mother, leading "a more meritorious life than at Fourques," says Jean Hugo. "He looked after her night and day, and walked miles through Paris to get her food that friends might have to spare." What followed next can be told in Jean Hugo's notes:

1945. J.B. comes back to Fourques at an uncertain date. His mother is ill in Paris. He puts off indefinitely going to see her. She is taken to a good clinic on some charity arrangement settled by some of his friends. The nurse turned against her and managed to have her thrown out and shut up in the lunatic asylum of Ste. Anne; she realized where she was, went off her head and died. J.B. went back too late and felt guilty about it until the end of his life. This was the real turning point of his vocation, as he himself later said.

1946. September, October. J.B. at Fourques, rather badly drugged.

November. A fire started at Fourques, near the kitchen; the flames were reaching the library when the wind turned and the fire went out. It produced a kind of moral shock. Father W——, O.P. was here. J.B. spoke to him. The Fr. took him back with him to the Dominican convent at Toulouse where he stayed a few days. Came back changed.

December. Fourques. Mass every morning.

1947. January to March. Fourques. The same.

April to November. Dominican convent at Saint-Maximin. Helps in the kitchen garden, is sent to markets shopping. Feels too free, too tempted.

November 17. Comes back to Fourques with Fr.

W——, a complete wreck, all willpower collapsed.

December. Fr. W—— is staying here, convalescent. J.B. attends daily Mass in the chapel, but is in complete moral dissolution. Fr. W—— speaks to him firmly and packs him off to Citeaux. He leaves Fourques on Dec. 22.

At the Trappist monastery of Citeaux in Burgundy Jean Bourgoint was admitted as a lay brother. He was given the name Brother Pascal, and was put to work milking cows. He remained there seventeen years, his work changed to laundering when mechanized milking was introduced on the monastery's model farm. Visitors found him bearded, cheerful, studying theology and the rule of St. Benedict, reflective, in his forties finally less a child. As one writer has said, "It would be easy to see the monk's cell as a new version of the famous room of the *enfants terribles* as described by Cocteau, and religion as a new drug, a new game, a different kind of escape," and the cows make one think of the horse-washing in the Nîmes barracks from which he used to escape to visit Cocteau at Villefranche; but as it turned out, Citeaux was only a station on the way to what would be at once the grimmest and the noblest period of the life of the ex-*enfant terrible*.

In the latter part of 1949 some of the scenes of the film *Les Enfants Terribles* were being made in the Paris house of a cousin by marriage of Nicole Stéphane (born Rothschild), a pretty young woman named Madame Alec Weisweiller (born Francine Worms). Lavishly provided for by her husband since their informal separation, with a villa on the Côte d'Azur as well as the house in Paris, Madame Weisweiller had urged Cocteau and the director, J.-P. Melville, to call on her for financial help should the completion of the film require it; and Cocteau, who was to her as to so many others a figure of glamour, his celebrity now worldwide, wrote her at the end of the year on the stationery of Melville Productions, 18 rue d'Enghien.

Cocteau to Madame Alec Weisweiller
Friday, December 30, 1949

May I call you "my dear friend"?

I am writing you without telling Jean-Pierre, and this is

why. I know that you have guaranteed the proper completion of the film. It so happens that because of the holidays Melville has been unable to get from Gaumont the pay for our crew (five hundred thousand francs). Knowing you as I do, I think that you would be displeased with him if stoppage of the work brought us a reproach from Gaumont. Since you were so good as to ask me to let you know if we ran into any trouble, I feel it my double duty to write you despite Melville, who would prefer to suffer an unnecessary disaster rather than turn to you. This seems to me so crazy and involved that I am taking it on myself to disregard it.

From the bottom of my heart,
Jean Cocteau

It is a crucial letter. Madame Weisweiller's immediate testimony of financial generosity, and her evident satisfaction at being associated with Jean Cocteau, transformed the remainder of Cocteau's life. In May, 1950 he went with Edouard Dermit to spend a few days at her Villa Santo Sospir at St. Jean Cap Ferrat, on the Mediterranean near Villefranche. Apparently that first visit was in the nature of an experiment, which quickly proved a success on both sides. In the hostess's words, "They arrived with small valises 'for a weekend.' They stayed for months."

The first months were interrupted by several trips — one to the Venice Film Festival for the triumph of *Orphée* — and by the end of the summer all character of "visit" had been lost: the original "weekend" was to become a residence, broken by much coming and going, that lasted more than ten years. Cocteau always kept his small flat in the Palais-Royal and the house in Milly; but even in Paris, after that summer, he spent much of his time as Madame Weisweiller's guest in her house on the Place des Etats-Unis, and until almost the end of his life Santo Sospir was his principal and favorite home. "Francine, Jean and Doudou" formed a trio that for years was constantly photographed, a design for living that was the joy of gossip writers. One read about their three identical triple-banded rings; how at Francine's expense Doudou's family was brought down from the mines of the North and set up as flower growers in nearby Biot; how Doudou's sister Emilienne became the schoolmate and companion of Francine's daughter Carole; how

Jean designed the décor for Carole's coming-out party in Paris. Amid the luxury of the villa, the servants, the garden with the Mediterranean at its foot, the yacht called *Orphée II*, the travels to Italy, to Spain, to Greece, to Belgium, to Switzerland, to Germany, to Austria, to Poland, to Baalbek, between appearances on the juries of film festivals, to the accompaniment of a publicity that seems to have become his breath of life, between hair dyeings, permanent waves and face-liftings (he had had his first *"nettoyage de la peau"* in 1935), Cocteau's production and activities continued unchecked, perhaps more voluminous and varied than ever; but in few of the many bottles is the wine of the best, and no detailed inventory is called for. It is as though he himself knew that with *Orphée* the splendid recapitulation had been made, but as though that knowledge was unconscious: certainly it was never admitted.

In a letter to Mary Hoeck written soon after his arrival at the villa he tells of his newest activity.

Cocteau to Mary Hoeck

May 1950

Ma très bonne Marie,

Forgive my silence — it is due to the abrupt transition from my usual life of work to the life of leisure I lead in Francine's house. It is a bath of laziness and flowers, but since I cannot stay quiet and my hands haven't the knack of hanging idle, I have decorated all the walls, one after the other, with the help of an old Italian from nearby who is skillful at fresco. . . .

Cocteau's soft-toned wall decorations in the Villa Santo Sospir are charming, there are some pretty mosaics in the garden; up the coast at Eze there are other restrained Cocteau touches in the outdoor theatre of a youth center, and his stylized frescoes of plants in the chapel at Milly-la-Forêt have their admirers; but for the most part, although he always retained a skill at catching a likeness in a line drawing, the wall decorations, paintings, and tapestries of his last decade display what can most politely be called an immense absence of tact — not to mention talent. They culminated in a grotesque commission, given him by the mayor of Menton (who claims to see nothing inappropriate in the choice of artist) to decorate the *Salle des Mariages* in the Menton city hall: the result of that provocation is the explosion in paint of a homosexual amateur muralist's unconscious, of some of whose implications one hopes the couples united in their presence may always continue unaware. The lack of artistry in the public murals and their inclusion of many neo-Picassian elements are the more discomfiting in view of Cocteau's continued hero worship of Picasso, his proximity to him on the Côte d'Azur, his eagerness to see him whenever possible, and the pain caused him by Picasso's indifference. Picasso, who had chosen to see little of Cocteau following the "Poésie Plastique" exhibition of 1926, had now, after his generation-long series of liaisons, embarked on a second marriage and a new period of embourgeoisement comparable to that in which his friendship with Cocteau had first flourished; and especially following the death of his close friend Paul Eluard, one of the Surrealists who had remained cold to Cocteau, Picasso was once again willing to see, from time to time, his old friend the inventor of *Parade*. But it was a condescending willingness, and kind friends can scarcely have failed to repeat to Cocteau some of Picasso's gibes — "Don't shake hands with Cocteau: one never knows what disease the Germans left behind"; "Cocteau is the tail of my comet." Cocteau's compulsive persistence in painting murals, each of which could be counted on to exacerbate the sarcasm of his idol still further, resembles the masochistic homosexual fantasies of his early opium cures.

The first of the public undertakings was the decoration of the Romanesque fishermen's Chapelle de St. Pierre that had stood for centuries on the quay at Villefranche. Opposite is the Hotel Welcome, scene of the antics and the poetry of the Twenties. The small chapel had long been disaffected and used as a storage shed by the local fishermen, and Cocteau's successful application to the municipality to be allowed to refurbish it and have it returned to ecclesiastical use brought their active opposition: his ladders were stolen, and a night watch had to be set to prevent destruction of the work. (The hostility vanished when tourists began to pay admission fees and buy postcards: all proceeds go to a Fishermen's Benevolent Fund.) Geraldine Chaplin tells of being invited with her parents for a "private visit" to the chapel while Cocteau was still working on it: on arrival they discovered the place swarming with photographers and reporters whom Cocteau had alerted, and there were many flashes amid the sacred scenes.

A little later, while he was still living in his "monastery" of Santo Sospir and coming each day to put the finishing touches on the chapel, Cocteau wrote to his old *enfant terrible*, whom he had seen occasionally at Fourques but never since Bourgoint had entered his — somewhat different — monastery in Burgundy. The letter bears no salutation: perhaps he was unsure of what form to use.

> *Cocteau to Jean Bourgoint (Brother Pascal)*
>> St. Jean Cap Ferrat, A.M.
>> Sunday, January 20, 1957
>
> On the scaffoldings of my little Romanesque chapel *across the street from the Welcome,* I think of you. I often ask your advice, and I am guided by your answers. *Do you know it?* No longer ago than yesterday we were sitting side by side on a plank under the vault. A line from you would give me courage in my undertaking.
>
> *Je t'embrasse.*
>
>> Jean

In 1960, after learning of the death of Raïssa Maritain, he wrote again:

> *The same to the same*
>> Santo Sospir
>> Christmas 1960
>
> *Mon Jean,*
>
> It is of you that I have been thinking since hearing of Jacques' tragic loss. . . . I hope that your prayers may help me to follow your example and take refuge in resignation. Very little is needed for me to become an inhabitant of those high solitudes where I so often meet and talk with you. . . .

By the time Cocteau wrote that second note he had had two serious illnesses, a heart attack and a hemorrhage, each of which had almost killed him. When he writes about death in these years it is much more apparent than in the past that he is thinking of his own, and he speaks more specifically than before about the Christian religion and about the Church. In 1945–46 he had written

"La Crucifixion," the finest of his late verse poems, and now in 1959–61 came "Le Requiem." His turning wall painter was of course another of his *"transformations de Fregoli,"* but although countless painters in France were painting in churches and chapels in the years following the war, it is scarcely meaningless that he should have chosen to decorate two chapels, each close to one of the places in which death would most probably find him — Villefranche and Milly. Julien Green, visiting him after his second heart attack in 1963, found an image of the Virgin hanging over his bed and a crucifix on the table beside him.

But the notes to Brother Pascal indicate a concern for more than the apparatus of orthodoxy. They are more than mere rhetoric: one senses his realization that he was writing to someone who had always appreciated his — Cocteau's — authenticity, perhaps even the fragility of it, and who was finally, after a long and curious voyage, finding an authenticity of his own. Amid the thousand activities of his last years Cocteau must have had many an intimation of the most intense solitude — it is evident if only in "Le Requiem" — many a moment of realization that if there were others who knew where his poetry lay they were not always his present companions.

Many of the people alive today who say they were "friends of Cocteau's," who display letters from him and offer anecdotes, knew him only during his last, declining decade, and their accounts tell of his encouragement of younger artists or his jealous mistreatment of them; of his unaffectedness or of his arrogance and overcalculated pronouncements, of his financial stinginess or of bank notes obtained by him from Madame Weisweiller (he was never wealthy himself) for friends in need, of his chilling self-absorption or of his sympathetic company. It is as it always was: a picture less of Cocteau as chameleon than of the endless variety of responses he provoked. Of his newer friends, many frequented him for his wit and celebrity and for their own aggrandizement, and then, if there were disagreements, deplored the shortcomings that were always clearly there from the beginning. But there were a few young men of rare quality who admired Cocteau's genius, relished the details of his long activity, sought out the friends of his past (many of whom felt alienated by the publicity of his present), and preserved and transmitted Cocteau's story. Chief among them was Pierre

Georgel (himself to become a distinguished scholar), Cocteau's close friend and literary aide-de-camp during his last years, who later organized and catalogued the retrospective exhibition "Jean Cocteau et son temps," at the Musée Jacquemart-André in 1965; and there was Jacques Perry, less close to Cocteau, but invaluable as the recorder of his spoken memoirs.

What role did some of the prewar friends whom we have met play in the last part of his life? Jean Hugo he visited from time to time at Fourques; with Valentine Hugo there was a revival of correspondence on the illness and death of her mother, the lady in whose house at Boulogne-sur-Mer, when that town was crowded with British troops, he had spent so much of his leave in 1916. When the pious François Mauriac violently attacked his last play, *Bacchus,* as blasphemy, Cocteau's old friends must have recognized him less in the play than in his retort that he "now preferred not to go to heaven, since that would apparently entail running into Mauriac"; and in 1964 they doubtless concurred in the printed reminder by Roger Peyrefitte (in his turn another of Mauriac's targets) that, had Cocteau chosen, he might have referred, in his reply, to still extant early Mauriac letters addressed to him — which for the sake of Mauriac's present peace of mind and reputation were better not released. His announcement of his candidacy for the French Academy they can only have recognized as yet another *"transformation de Fregoli";* as he paid the required visits to the Academicians his charm operated with its usual efficacy, melting the reserve of the crustiest generals and dukes; his acceptance speech on October 20, 1955, skating lightly over unsavory aspects of his predecessor, Jérome Tharaud, echoed the moral gaucherie of the years of Occupation; and the satisfaction he took in the various forms of social precedence accorded in France to a member of the Academy — he was capable of insisting on them — evokes his proximity as a child to the diplomatic, official world of his mother's brother, Georges Lecomte. He was received into the Royal Belgian Academy the same day as Princess Marthe Bibesco, who had known him since before the flights with Garros, to succeed to the place left vacant by Colette, his neighbor in the Palais-Royal, whose husband, Maurice Goudeket, had been one of his classmates at the Lycée Condorcet when they were both twelve or thirteen. Reginald Bridgeman, listening in 1956 at his radio in the same house at Pinner where Cocteau had visited him with Radiguet in 1923, to Cocteau's Oxford speech on the occasion of his honorary doctorate, suddenly heard himself referred to as having long ago impressed Cocteau, by the purity of his acquired French, with the need to defend the elegance of that language; and he heard Cocteau end his speech with the words "Gentlemen, the Queen!" and heard the audience's laughter that was at first hesitant then full. Peggy Guggenheim, for whose London gallery, Guggenheim Jeune, in 1938, Cocteau had made, on a bed sheet, a drawing of nudes complete with pinned-on fig leaves that the police had ordered displayed only in a back room, now in Venice introduced him to an artist-glassmaker, Egidio Costantini, whose furnace, threatened with closing, he adopted, christened "La Fucina degli Angeli," and saved both by direct subsidy and by supplying it with designs — one of several tributes to the city where as a child with his mother he had experienced his "first bitter taste of being alone amidst crowds" and where later he had met Vyvyan Wilde and written verses on a Wildean suicide. Reconciled with Louis Aragon, who had been expelled by André Breton from the ranks of the Surrealists, he signed at his urging an appeal in favor of Spanish refugees and as a result found himself expelled from Franco's Spain (but when an official apology was forthcoming he returned); Aragon supported him in a ludicrous election to succeed Paul Fort as "Prince of Poets," thus incurring Breton's increased wrath; and together the reconciled poets recorded — it is not clear why — a long and tedious dialogue on the subject of the pictures from the destroyed museum in Dresden. Unfortunate also is Cocteau's film adaptation of the seventeenth-century novel *La Princesse de Clèves*, Radiguet's model for *Le Bal du Comte d'Orgel:* even his memories and admiration were insufficient to enliven this belated venture.

But friends must have found it a coctelian detail that in London, for the bombed and rebuilt French church in Soho, Notre-Dame de France, which Cocteau decorated, the French prostitutes of the neighborhood contributed a carpet that was blue, the color of the Virgin. And that the support of one or another segment of youth was never far away was shown again when the young director François Truffaut contributed the prize money he had won for his film *The Four Hundred Blows* toward the making of Cocteau's last completed picture, the mawkish *Testament d'Orphée*, a regrettable item in his film legacy.*

It is on that note of youth, perhaps, that a biography of Cocteau can most fittingly draw to a close, for he himself is one whose proper reputation is in a way still young, still to be made: he is now emerging as a first portrayer, on levels from the lightest to the most macabre, of the convulsions that characterize contemporary life. It is only as this process progressively reveals itself that Cocteau's prophetic genius is coming to fulfillment, entering into the first stages of its true perspective, and continuing to elucidate for us the disorders of new generations. His greatest films entitle him, in the words of Pauline Kael, to be called "the true celebrity and progenitor of the new wave," and we have seen how the films were an extension and distillation of his life and poetry.

The paradox of Cocteau can be given another illustration in the words and behavior of one of his greatest idols, who always had much that was severe to say about him. In Paris, in May, 1963, says Robert Craft, Igor Stravinsky's companion and assistant, "A journalist calls asking I.S. to record a get-well message to Cocteau, as Braque and Picasso have already done. I.S. refuses, however, and so firmly that parts of the telephone fly off as he cradles the receiver. Then, at lunch, with all ears to him, he says that *'Cocteau ne peut pas mourir sans faire réclame.'* . . . Nevertheless . . . only two weeks ago the news of Cocteau's heart attack (or the thought of the subtraction and the narrowing circle) deeply upset him. Then, when a few days ago he heard that Cocteau had begun to recover, little signs of annoyance began to appear, as though having already written off an account he disliked reopening the books. . . . I have heard only sharp remarks about him in all my fifteen years with I.S., in any case ('talented, yes,' preluding the devastation) and the last time the two were together, in Paris a year ago, I.S. jibbed at keeping the appointment." When Cocteau did die, on October 11, 1963, at Milly, amid extraordinary *réclame* that was due to a coincidence — he had just been interviewed by a throng of reporters on the death of Edith Piaf that same morning — Craft

* Left unfinished at his death was his commentary, adapted in part from his volume *Maalesh*, for a beautiful documentary film about the ruins of ancient Egypt, *Égypte Ô Égypte*, a cinematic poem in color by Jacques Brissot. It has since been edited and exhibited, with Cocteau's spoken narrative.

observed Stravinsky again when he heard the news, and saw the ambivalence repeat itself: he had seen the elderly composer experience the news of the deaths of many friends, he said, but seldom had he seen him so disturbed as by the disappearance of Cocteau. Stravinsky wept.

One of Cocteau's fellow Academicians delivered a conventional funeral address at Milly, and a year later an anniversary address was given in the chapel there by another Academician — René Clair, who had long been the husband of Bronya Perlmutter, Radiguet's last friend. On this occasion Cocteau's bust was unveiled in the chapel — a bronze effigy by none other than Arno Breker, who went unmentioned in René Clair's awkward, perhaps embarrassed, little speech.

Shortly after Cocteau's death, a childhood friend of Jean Bourgoint's, who had been a witness from the beginning of how Cocteau had courted Bourgoint, "ruined" him, done his best to drop him, and been all but out of touch with him for years, and with whom Bourgoint had left all his possessions, his "estate," when he entered the monastery, wrote him that she and her brother supposed Cocteau's death could touch him but little; and she had a long letter in reply. An indulgent letter — magnanimous might be a better word; but one that must impress us with its insight and nobility.

Jean Bourgoint (Brother Pascal) to
Madame Jeannette Kandaouroff

[1963]

. . . I want to correct your mistake concerning Cocteau's death, which — quite the opposite of what you think — touched me profoundly: he was my oldest friend (you and Gaëtan being citizens of the paradise gardens of childhood, which somehow transcend the logical order of time). One thing I should like to clear up at once is the word *Satan*, which you think you remember and which I do not remember having used concerning him. Isn't there confusion here? Didn't I speak of *Lucifer*, bright name of "the most beautiful of the Angels" before his fall? (In fact, don't you have a magnificent photograph of him, part of my "estate," signed by him with that name?) However, it is possible that at some time (but in this case I should like to know just when) I may have spoken to you about him with irritation (never with resentment), in connection with one or another of the humiliating defeats that have composed the fabric of my life from as far back as I can recall (and which still do). The fact is that for someone like myself, whose soul was neither well-tempered from birth (and the breed of born heroes is rather rare, don't you agree?) nor precociously formed, to live in Jean's orbit and within range of his radioactivity was not without danger for a young boy. But it was in the manner of a star that Jean was dangerous. His death, which even today I am unable fully to "take in," has at least made it possible for me to sort out carefully a mass of memories, of "ideas," of impressions. Subjectively speaking, so far as I am concerned I endorse wholeheartedly Gaëtan's verdict, which finds more good than bad in the balance sheet of L'Oiseleur, and I would add that if the good was really part of himself, the bad on the contrary came only from me, from my weakness, as was the case with many another of those around him. (Take opium, for example. In Jean's life opium is one episode among others. He let himself be dominated by it episodically only in so far as it was compatible with his poetic mission.) And looking at things objectively, not only do I find a great deal of good in that balance sheet, but I find *only* good. A great poet is always an incalculable benefit to humanity, not only for his contemporaries but for the human race as such. But above and beyond that extraordinary radioactivity with which Jean illuminated our half-century (and the future), beyond it and perhaps at the source of his influence as "beacon," which has been so extraordinarily effective in the realm of the beautiful and of human sensitivity to the beautiful, I truly think that there is an activity of another order (although it too is part of his "poetic mission") : I mean he had not only the genius of language and of images, he had also that of friendship. For people as for things, Jean was a kind of "universal brother." He had that *gentillesse royale* which perpetually amazed not only his friends, but whoever came near him; none of them ever forgot it, and the effect was repeated at each meeting. And the reason why his generosity of self most deeply merited the gratitude of those who benefited from it, was that he himself needed it in order to *be* himself in his relations with others, with the world. It is not difficult to foresee that his purely poetic work, his image as a great poet, will as a result of his very disappearance undergo a kind of transfiguration and will be able to assume its true stature. On this plane, destiny and the public have already begun, I think, to do him justice. But besides all those heaven-sent gifts that sparkled in him, he had humble and beautiful qualities as a man unsuspected by many of those who considered themselves his friends, and which historians (there will be plenty of those) will probably know nothing of. To begin with, that royal generosity not only of his gifts but of himself was accompanied by good humor, boundless optimism even at the moments of greatest suffering, a courage to live — and to live the most unforeseeable requirements of his "mission" as Poet-Proteus, as it was put by Bresson (who, by the way, seems to know only his plays and films, and none of the rest of his work). Jean was of an exquisite temperance. He was — this will surprise you — profoundly chaste. Just as he smoked his opium chastely, like the Chinese sages, so in his loves he was of a delicacy and temperance of heart seldom found in the commonalty of men, and seldom even in poets. Finally, his generosity in living the unique role he maintained for so long, in a period difficult for the world of the intelligence, his so scrupulous exactitude with regard to his duty as a poet, were founded on an authentic strength of soul that was sensed by plain people, no doubt, more immediately than by the intellectuals who surrounded him. "He was good!" I see in the press clippings that have been sent me that his gardener, his servants, the good people of Milly, all agreed with the Curé of St. Blaise-aux-Simples in so testifying about him. In various senses, in the best senses of the word, and in his very own way, Jean was eminently *"social"* (in the very lofty meaning that the word has in Bergson's *Two Sources*), and it is also and perhaps especially in this sense that one can, in my opinion, apply to him the words of Oscar Wilde: "I put my talent into my works and my genius into my life." And that is why I understand Maritain, who writes me that despite his immense grief at Jean's death it is with a "feeling of joy" that he prays for him — and that is why I have confidence in God concern-

ing him. The rare letters I have had from him these last years
— although in them he avoids mentioning God by his Names
— all strengthen me in that confidence. It is for all these reasons, too, that I am glad to know that Gaëtan was at the cemetery in Milly the day of the burial, and that I am grateful to
him for having been "deeply moved."

By the time he wrote that letter, Brother Pascal had already told
his superiors at Citeaux that he felt his life there was insufficiently
useful, and had said that he felt himself "called toward the blacks,
to whom we certainly owe a debt." A year or so after Cocteau's
death he succeeded in having himself transferred to Africa, to the
parish of Notre-Dame de Granselve in the North Cameroons. Nor
was that active enough, and in 1965 he was sent to Mokolo, "the
poorest village in the world," he called it, "a village of lepers."
There he tended lepers and other patients and established a workshop for the fashioning of orthopedic shoes for those who had lep-
rosy of the feet. Soon he was found to have cancer; he died in a
nearby hospital on March 11, 1966, and is buried behind the lep-
rosarium.

Such was the end of the second of the *enfants terribles*. He had
written Cocteau's most eloquent epitaph.

Orphée. Final scene.

Appendices

APPENDIX I (For Chapter 4, p. 122)

PORTIONS OF COCTEAU'S MILITARY DOSSIER

Ministère des ARMEES

—

Etat-Major de l'Armée de TERRE

—

Bureau Central d'Archives
administratives militaires

—

EXTRAIT DES SERVICES

—

Le Colonel J. BARBE, Commandant le Bureau Central d'Archives
Administratives Militaires, certifie que des dossiers, pièces ou documentation en sa possession, il a été extrait ce qui suit, concernant:

Nom: COCTEAU

prénoms: Clément, Eugène, Jean, Maurice,

Né le 5 Juillet 1889 à MAISONS LAFFITTE (Seine & Oise)

inscrit au registre matricule du Bureau de recrutement de VER-
SAILLES sous le N° 5598, classe 1909 — Exempté en 1910 —

Classé Service Auxiliaire par le Conseil de Révision de la SEINE dans
sa séance du 26 Novembre 1914

Appelé à l'activité le .... 4 Mars 1915

et affecté au 13° Régiment d'Artillerie de campagne

Passé à la 22° Section de Commis Ouvriers le .... 18 Mars 1915

Placé en sursis au Titre de la Société Française de

Secours aux blessés, rue François Ier à Paris, le .. 13 Novembre 1915

Sursis prolongé jusqu'au .... 30 Décembre 1916

Passé à la 20ème Section de Secrétaires d'Etat-Major

le 24 Novembre 1916

Réformé Temporaire N°1 par la 2ème Commission

de Réforme de la SEINE, le .... 31 Juillet 1917

Réformé N°2 par la 6° Commission Spéciale de Réforme

de la SEINE le .... 3 Juillet 1918

Pour Extrait

A Pau, le 28 Juin 1967

APPENDIX II (For Chapter 4, p. 130)

Quand Nous Serons "Ceux de la Guerre"

Je n'oublierai jamais Vareddes
Le lendemain de la bataille;
Les arbres aux larges entrailles,
Les chevaux morts aux jambes raides.

Le fade musc de la gangrène
Rampait tout le long du village . . .
On voyait, derrière un grillage,
Un chien maigre aux yeux de hyène.

Dans une demeure sans porte,
On entendait un bruit de ruche
Autour d'un fauteuil de peluche,
Où la paysanne était morte.

Des casques, des sacs, des bouteilles,
Et un piano mécanique,
Voilà, les étranges reliques
Des héroïsmes de la veille.

Est-il possible que renaisse
Vareddes pareille à naguère,
Quand nous serons ceux de la guerre,
Quand nous n'aurons plus de jeunesse?

Quand on voudrait que l'aube monte,
Et que recommence la route;
Et être celui qui écoute,
Au lieu de celui qui raconte.

(*Le Mot*, No. 6, January 16, 1915)

Cocteau perhaps considered this poem too traditional and "simple" to add lustre to his fame. If so, his opinion is not without its irony when his poem is compared with a celebrated poem that is also very beautiful, and not dissimilar, "Les Lilas et les Roses," written twenty-five years later, during another war, in 1940, by Louis Aragon, who was for many years his Dadaist and Surrealist "enemy," until their reconciliation in their later years.

Les Lilas et les Roses

O mois des floraisons mois des métamorphoses
Mai qui fût sans nuage et Juin poignardé
Je n'oublierai jamais les lilas ni les roses
Ni ceux que le Printemps dans ses plis a gardés

Je n'oublierai jamais l'illusion tragique
Le cortège les cris la foule et le soleil
Les chars chargés d'amour les dons de la Belgique
L'air qui tremble et la route à ce bourdon d'abeilles
Le triomphe imprudent qui prime la querelle
Le sang qui préfigure en carmin le baiser
Et ceux qui vont mourir debout dans les tourelles
Entourés de lilas par un peuple grisé

Je n'oublierai jamais les jardins de la France
Semblables aux missels des siècles disparus
Ni le trouble des soirs l'énigme du silence
Les roses tout le long des chemins parcourus
Le démenti des fleurs au vent de la panique
Aux soldats qui passaient sur l'aile de la peur
Aux vélos délirants aux canons ironiques
Aux pitoyables accoutrements des faux campeurs

Mais je ne sais pourquoi ce tourbillon d'images
Me ramène toujours au même point d'arrêt
A Sainte-Marthe   Un général   De noirs ramages
Une villa normande au bord de la forêt
Tout se tait l'ennemi dans l'ombre se repose
On nous dit ce soir que Paris s'est rendu
Je n'oublierai jamais les lilas ni les roses
Et ni les deux amours que nous avons perdus

Bouquets du premier jour lilas lilas des Flandres
Douceur de l'ombre dont la mort farde les joues et vous
Et vous bouquets de la retraite roses tendres
Couleurs de l'incendie au loin roses d'Anjou

APPENDIX III (For Chapter 4, p. 145)

BERNARD FAŸ: *LES PRECIEUX*

Bernard Faÿ, in his memoirs, *Les Précieux* (p. 32), tells of a scandal involving Cocteau and North African troops:

"[Cocteau's] 'profuse kindness' to one of the Goumiers [Arabs] had aroused the jealousy, then the fury, of a Goumier sergeant. The poor poet came close to being hacked to pieces by the Moroccans or standing court-martial. Beaumont got him out of it by means of cries of indignation, presents, smiles, useful contacts, and the abrupt recall of the sector, 'since there was no more fighting in Flanders.' "

That something untoward may have occurred is indicated in a passage in an undated letter from Cocteau to Etienne de Beaumont: "I am sorry to have shocked a General Staff that I have never seen. Quick, a shell, and the world will be purged of my ridiculousness." Perhaps Cocteau's transfer after his April, 1916 leave to a new sector, where there were no North Africans, was connected with such an episode. But there is no evidence of a Beaumont ambulance section having been recalled; and Faÿ further clouds his narrative by placing the episode late in 1914 or early 1915, whereas it is clear from Cocteau's letters that he began his service among the Africans only a year later.

Faÿ also portrays Etienne de Beaumont and Cocteau scandalizing a group of British officers, including Sir Douglas Haig, in the dining room of an inn in northern France, by appearing in pyjamas and ankle bracelets. That episode, too, he places a year before there is any evidence of Cocteau's working with the Beaumont ambulances. Cocteau's one reference to being on leave in "April, 1915" (see p. 146) is almost certainly a misprint.

APPENDIX IV (For Chapter 4, p. 156)

A TROUPE OF ACTORS VISITS THE FRONT

The June, 1916 visit to Sector 129 by a group of *artistes* that included Cécile Sorel is clearly the basis of a well-known episode in Cocteau's novel, *Thomas l'Imposteur*. He describes it as follows in a letter of June 15 (unpublished) to Valentine Gross:

"Mad visit by Sorel in felt hat and cloak. I organized for her an unforgettable reception — a French Acomedy [*sic*] show [*spectacle de l'Acomédie Fr.*] — at Camp Bador. Royal flush for a Taube — all the brass and, as it should be, poilus in the back. An amazing 'Marseillaise' sung by hams male and female wearing caps with red pompoms and carrying rifles decked with flowers. Why wasn't it *you,* wearing Gabriel's* helmet, whom I escorted afterward through the 'hollowed-out city'? Cécile, alas, was a bit like a captain of the territorials. Best of all (in the sweep-you-off-your-feet category) was the General standing up and reading the extraordinary Russian communiqué† — the entire audience rose to its feet, ecstatic, and out burst the Russian Imperial hymn. Then, like haystacks catching fire one from the other, *all* the Allied anthems, one after the other. (Out of this world.)"

* Probably General Jean-Gabriel Rouquerol, commandant of the sector.
† Probably the announcement of the Russian summer, 1916 offensive.

APPENDIX V (For Chapter 4, p. 160)

COCTEAU "LEAVES THE WAR"

As Cocteau's letters show, he stayed with his "dear Marines," who "adopted" him, for a week in June, 1916, then proceeded to Amiens, toward the battle of the Somme. Previously he had written little about the Marines, apart from lamenting to Valentine Gross on May 16: "Where are the Zouaves and the Marines, so careless with their money and so prodigal with their hearts?" There exists a photograph of Cocteau with two princes, Xavier and Sixte de Bourbon-Parme, who were apparently among the Marines' officers.* In his novel, *Thomas l'Imposteur*, he portrays Marines with hero-worshipping admiration.

Certain of Cocteau's purportedly factual, "autobiographical" writings and broadcasts concerning himself and the Marines are closer to the fictional picture in *Thomas l'Imposteur* than to the chronology attested by his letters with their postmarks. For example, interviewed on French radio by André Fraigneau in 1951, Cocteau declared:

"I shouldn't have taken part in that war of 1914, because my health forbade it. I went fraudulently, with Red Cross convoys. And then I slipped into Belgium, at Coxyde-Ville. I slipped into Coxyde-Bains among the Marines, and was forgotten. The Marines adopted me, I wore their uniform and ended by believing that I was a Marine.

"One day the Admiral proposed me for the *croix de guerre;* and the cat was out of the bag! I left Coxyde-Bains between two policemen, and the two policemen went with me to Coxyde-Ville where I was living in a cellar. I told them that I would just get my things; I slipped out through an airshaft and walked in the opposite direction.

"The automobile of General Elie Boissel, the commandant of the sector, came along just at that moment, and in the auto was Louis Gillet, who was an old friend of mine and the General's Chief of Staff. He stopped the car and asked me what I was doing on that road. In return I asked him where he was going: he was going to Dunkirk. "So am I." "Good." I got in. Then I asked Gillet to have the car go past the Marines' quarters; and the Marines, who had just seen me taken away by two gendarmes and were

* Georgel catalogue, No. 154.

sad about it because I was their mascot, now saw me go by again in the commandant's car. Those who weren't killed, for example Combescure who became an admiral, still talk about it. . . . The policemen saved me, because all my comrades were killed the next day, at St.-Georges." (Cocteau, EF, 14–15)

Twelve years later, in the television interview with Roger Stéphane, Cocteau told the story as follows:

"Etienne de Beaumont had me included in a Red Cross unit at the front. And so I reached the front. There was a young daredevil there who cheated at cards — he charmed everybody, but had to be discharged, and I was sent to take his place. The men in this unit, French and North Africans, thought that I had had the other fellow sent away in order to unsurp his place, so I was sent out every day on missions of certain death, across a wood that was called the *Bois triangulaire*. I have always wondered that I got back alive. And then they thought they would play a trick on me by leaving me all alone to guard the equipment, when they went to the Somme . . . The second day, the Marine captain came to see me and said — "Listen — you're not going to stay here guarding a showerbath! I'm taking you with me." So he took me to Coxyde-Bains. There was Coxyde-Ville, where our Red Cross unit was stationed, and Coxyde-Bains, with the quarters of the Marines, who were fighting at St.-Georges, on the Yser. Little by little I became a sham Marine — they disguised me as a Marine. I became a bit their mascot. Everybody was so taken in that the Admiral proposed me for the *croix de guerre,* and the result was that I was caught like a rat! Two gendarmes were sent to get me, and I went off between them.

"That bad luck was perhaps good luck, since almost all my comrades were killed at St.-Georges. . . . I was miraculously saved by those two gendarmes, who took me to Coxyde-Ville. I asked them to wait for me on the road, saying I was going to get my things; I went into our house and slipped out by an airshaft behind, on another road. At that moment there came along the automobile of the General who commanded the sector; and Colonel Gillet, who was an old friend of mine and his Chief of Staff, said to me, "Where are you going?" I said "I'm going to Dunkirk." So I got into the car and said to him, "Listen — do something for me — have the car go past the Marines' encampment, that's all I ask." One of the rare survivors, who is now an admiral, was talking to me about it just the other day. The Marines, who were in tears because I'd been taken away, saw me drive through the camp in the commandant's car with its gold-embroidered flag. I saluted them right and left, and was on my way . . . I returned to Paris. Philippe Berthelot just barely saved me from court-martial and stuck me in an office where I was bored to death, and finally liberated me from that office since I was only an auxiliary." (Cocteau, ES, 98–100)

In offering, as fact, those two fabulous versions, neither of which mentions his own presence on the Somme, Cocteau seems to have been inspired by the irresistible delightfulness of his own fiction in *Thomas l'Imposteur*, which he himself once characterized as *"réalité fabuleuse."* One may mention, perhaps, that in the official history of the Marine Batallion at St. Georges-Zuydcoote* there is no record, that summer, of the annihilation of a group of Marines, as reported by Cocteau on both radio and television. The Hotel Dervaux (British Headquarters) in Boulogne-sur-Mer, where Cocteau had spent ten days in June, was destroyed sometime after Cocteau's departure. Was it that event, perhaps, that inspired him to exterminate the Marines?

* *Archives du Service Historique de le Marine. Historique du Bataillon de Fusiliers-marins, 1916.* Cote: Série F. Carton 1. Dossier 1715.

Rome, la Nuit

Et qui me prouve que vous n'êtes
Pas un ange déguisé
Pas un voleur de diamants?

Quelquefois la folle malice
Des étoiles les change en fleurs
Sur votre pommier, nuit d'Avril
Pour mieux déjouer la police

Le diamant, où est-il?
Répondez-nous jeune impie.

Pies et anges sont des voleurs
Ils empruntent le nom de Pie
Aux papes, pour en abuser.

Sur le pont du Château Saint-Ange
En robe pie, anges charmants
Combinent un mauvais coup
Car, baigneuses, vos rivières
S'attachent derrière le cou.

Lorsqu' à Pâques volent les cloches
Comme montgolfières de neige
Les uns se mettant du voyage
D'autres, craignant qu'on les rattrape,
Changent le chiffre de leur âge.
D'autres deviennent les amants
Des duchesses. Leur beauté
Fait d'autres prendre pour étoiles
Qu' entretiennent des Cardinaux.
D'autres se laissent mettre en cage.

Ils sautillent et bavardent
Pour détourner l'attention.

Bagues, diadèmes, broches,
Fruits de notre arbre frivole,
Partent de cette manière
Aux quatre points cardinaux
Enrichir le ciel d'été
A l'abri de tout soupçon.

Alors que faire? Ouvrir les malles?
Sortir de force le pape
Du Vatican pour tendre un piège?
Rien à faire. Les anges volent.

(This unpublished poem by Cocteau is printed with the kind permission of the owner of the manuscript, Mr. William Crawford.)

"PARADE"

BY GUILLAUME APOLLINAIRE

Definitions of *Parade* are bursting out everywhere, like the lilac branches of this delayed spring. . . .

It is a stage poem that the innovating composer Erik Satie has set to astonishingly expressive music, so clean-cut and so simple that it mirrors the marvelously lucid spirit of France itself.

The Cubist painter Picasso and that most daring of choreographers, Léonide Massine, have staged it, thus consummating for the first time this union of painting and dance — of plastic and mime — which heralds the advent of a more complete art.

Let no one cry paradox. The ancients, in whose life music held such a prominent place, were absolutely ignorant of harmony — whereas modern music is almost nothing but harmony.

This new union — for up until now stage sets and costumes on the one hand and choreography on the other were only superficially linked — has given rise in *Parade* to a kind of super-realism ["*sur-réalisme*"]. This I see as the starting point of a succession of manifestations of the *"esprit nouveau"*: now that it has had an opportunity to reveal itself, it will not fail to seduce the elite, and it hopes to change arts and manners from top to bottom, to the joy of all. For it is only natural to wish that arts and manners should attain at least the level of scientific and industrial progress.

Breaking with the tradition dear to those who not so long ago in Russia were curiously dubbed "balletomanes," Massine has taken good care not to fall into pantomime. He has produced a complete novelty, one so marvelously seductive, of a truth so lyrical, so human, so joyous, that it might well be capable of illuminating (if this were worthwhile) the frightful black sun of Dürer's *Melancolia* — this thing that Jean Cocteau calls a "realistic ballet." Picasso's Cubist sets and costumes bear witness to the realism of his art.

This realism, or this Cubism, whichever you prefer, is what has most deeply stirred the arts during the last ten years.

The sets and costumes of *Parade* clearly disclose his concern to extract from an object all the aesthetic emotion it is capable of arousing. Frequent attempts have been made to reduce painting to its own rigorously pictorial elements. There is hardly anything but painting in most of the Dutch school, in Chardin and the Impressionists.

Picasso goes a good deal farther than any of them. Those who see him in *Parade* will experience a surprise that will soon turn into admiration. His main purpose is to render reality. However, the motif is no longer reproduced, but merely represented; or, more accurately, it is suggested by a combination of analysis and synthesis bearing upon all its visible elements — and, if possible, something more, namely an integral schematization that might be intended to reconcile contradictions, and sometimes deliberately renounces the rendering of the obvious outward appearance of the object. Massine has adapted himself in a surprising way to the Picassian discipline. He has identified himself with it, and art has been enriched by adorable inventions like the realistic steps of the horse in *Parade* whose forelegs are supplied by one dancer and the hind legs by another.

The fantastic constructions which stand for those gigantic, astonishing characters the Managers, far from hampering Massine's imagination, have enabled it, if one may say so, to function with greater freedom.

In short, *Parade* will upset the ideas of quite a number of spectators. They will be surprised, to be sure, but in the pleasantest way, and fascinated; and they will learn how graceful modern movement can be — something they had never suspected. A magnificent music-hall Chinaman will give free rein to the flights of their imagination, and the American girl, by turning the crank of an imaginary automobile, will express the magic of their everyday life, while the acrobat in blue and white tights celebrates its silent rites with exquisite and amazing agility.

APPENDIX VIII (For Chapter 4, p. 213)

La Mort de Guillaume Apollinaire

Coupe à ta muse les cheveux
Picasso, peintre aux doigts de fée;
Les objets te suivent, Orphée,
Jusqu'à la forme que tu veux.

Mais il est mort, celui qui change
Les mots de forme de couleurs;
Picasso, ta muse est en pleurs.

Guillaume Apollinaire
Amateur de tulipes,
Vous fumez votre pipe
Le petit doigt en l'air.

Vous racontez aux anges
Par exemple que les nègres sont d'anciens Bretons
Ou que Cléopatre a inventé les oranges.
Ils vous écoutent bouche bée.

Vous parlez, vous riez dans votre main d'abbé,
Vous n'avez plus mal à la tête.
Vous êtes mort un samedi;
Rousseau vous attendait devant le paradis
Avec des oeillets du poète.

Le Dimanche déjà vous fondiez "l'éternisme"
(Nouvelle école)
Dans un article de journal;
Etoiles, faux-cols, prismes.
Aussi les gens du ciel aiment beaucoup
Déjeuner et se promener avec vous.

(Printed in *Vient de Paraître*, No. 24, November 15, 1923. Not reprinted
in the "Complete Works.")

APPENDIX IX (For Chapter 5, p. 244)

PRINCE FIROUZ (FIROUZ MIRZA)

Mr. Reginald Bridgeman kindly writes as follows:

"Firouz means turquoise in Persian and Mirza means prince. . . . He was the eldest son of Farman Farma, a very wealthy Persian aristocrat, who may have been related to the Kajah dynasty, and was at one time Governor of the Province of Fars. After the Russian revolution of 1917, the Bolsheviks renounced the Czarist Government's privileges in Persia and the virtual control of the Northern Zone. . . . Persia had been partitioned into three zones by the Anglo-Russian Agreement of 1907, the northern Russian, the central neutral, and the southern British. The British Government of Lloyd George, of which Lord Curzon was Foreign Secretary and Winston Churchill Minister of War, thought the opportunity favourable to extend its control of Persia by means of an Anglo-Persian Agreement the draft of which was negotiated in London with Firouz Mirza, who in consideration of lavish personal bribery undertook to persuade the Persian Government to accept it. Had the Agreement been accepted, Persia would have been reduced to semi-colonial status comparable to that of Egypt at that time. The government set up after the Coup d'Etat of 1921 rejected it.

"Firouz was bright and intelligent, with a good measure of aristocratic panache, his pockets always full of bank-notes, owning a dazzling motorcar, staying in Paris at the Hotel Meurice, giving almost nightly supper parties at the Restaurant Larue in the Rue Royale, frequently inviting Jean [Cocteau]. I understood that he had been killed out hunting in 1921. I never heard that he had been murdered." (Other accounts speak of Firouz's "murder" during the 1921 coup d'état.)

APPENDIX X (For Chapter 5, p. 280)

From "The Aesthetic Upheaval in France: The Influence of Jazz in Paris and Americanization of French Literature and Art," *Vanity Fair*, February, 1922. By Edmund Wilson, Jr.:

". . . [Cocteau] is in love with all the droll and homely aspects of the Parisian world — the music halls, the revues, and the bals musettes, the Eiffel Tower with its photographer and its post-cards of beautiful bathers, the popular fairs with their side-shows and their jingling merry-go-round tunes. Cocteau has protested repeatedly that he wants to make something *real;* and it is true that, for all his nonsense, he does make something real. When he turns a bourgeois wedding into a side-splitting harlequinade, we none the less get the feeling of a vivid reaction to life, of a bodying forth of objects which the artist has seen and felt. It is precisely this seriousness about his art which, in the last analysis, differentiates Cocteau from an Englishman producing the same sort of thing. The Frenchman theorizes about his art; he formulates an aesthetic doctrine; he relates his own contribution to the body of art of the world. . . . One scarcely knows which to admire the more, the classic-mindedness of a public which requires to have such simple, if fantastic, spectacles explained to it, or the artistic seriousness of a writer who takes a charming harlequinade as a pretext for laying down aesthetic principles in the manner of Aristotle. . . . It is a great pity that someone will not undertake to produce this ballet over here — or even to get Cocteau over to write a new ballet for America. His fine gift for nonsense and burlesque (though it seems to me he sometimes makes blunders, as is natural in a man of a race which has no tradition of nonsense) should be better appreciated by us, I think, than by the audiences of his own country, who either try to take his absurdities seriously or regard them as *mauvaises plaisanteries*. And he would bring to our comic stage something which it sadly lacks: a serious artistic interest in the possibilities of burlesque and a daring imagination to deal with the rich materials of the review."

APPENDIX XI (For Chapter 5, p. 287)

AN ANECDOTE FROM *LE MOT* (May 1, 1915)

. . . . Young T. de C. . . . appeared one day at Dr. B.'s auxiliary mobile hospital, suddenly, like a flower blooming out of nowhere. Unbelievably young, two wounds in his left leg, two life-saving medals on his military tunic, a Saint-Cyr cap over one ear, he said he was waiting for orders from Colonel de M. . . . who was still prone after a terrible amputation. Since his chief left him to his own devices, he made himself generally useful, helping the nurses, greasing the automobiles, and going as orderly with the automobile convoys that Dr. B. had been authorized to send to the front. Young T. de C. became everybody's favorite. He would boast modestly of being the nephew of the famous General de C. . . . : "It's not because I'm the general's nephew . . ." he would say, or, "My uncle is one of those men who . . ." — and that echo of glory, plus his adolescence, his medals, and his wounds, inspired affection and respect in men and women alike. He became a kind of Fanfan la Tulipe.

When he recounted his campaigns and the sublime deaths of his cousins, his eyes would fill with fire and tears. Everyone adored him.

One fine day, alas! everything was turned upside down. C. . . . was not his own name, but the name of the town where our young mythomaniac was born. No more general, no more colonel, no more Saint-Cyr epaulettes, medals, wounds. . . . *Presto chango!* And the jokester vanished. . . .

Three months later we were in the hospital in the Grand Palais and heard an orchestra playing. Gabriel Astruc was at the door. "I'm giving a concert for the patients," he said, "in the great hall, and do you know who's the master of ceremonies? The nephew of General C. . . , *mon cher*. Only nineteen, two bullets in his arm and two medals on his chest."

The story will probably be continued. . . .

APPENDIX XII (For Chapter 6, p. 370)

FROM MAURICE SACHS's NOVEL, *CHRONIQUE JOYEUSE ET SCANDALEUSE**

NOTE: *In this novel by Sachs the character based on Cocteau is called both "Jean Duvant" and "Sanqueur" — "Heartless." (In his best-known work,* Le Sabbat, *Sachs wrote that Cocteau was "without a heart" — an opinion that he subsequently withdrew in a letter to Cocteau.)*

He lived in a typical late nineteenth-century building, with a spacious staircase and large landings. An elderly houseman opened the door, we entered a dark, luxurious, bourgeois anteroom and then passed through another door. . . .

The bedroom gave on a court and was quiet. In one corner, a brass bed with a thick quilt. The mirror and mantelpiece were covered with papers, addresses, photographs, street-fair bric-a-brac, postcards, dried flowers, pictures of all kinds — amidst all this, a fine Persian head. It would be impossible to give a complete list of all the strange objects that cluttered this room. Clay pipes, a blue glass pipe, crystal triangles, portraits of Duvant by Picasso, by Marie Laurencin, by Jean Hugo, two caricatures by Jean Cocteau, boxes with tropical butterflies, books, fabrics. . . .

Nimbly, he drew out from under his bed a tray holding various objects; he stretched out on one side, lit a small lamp, and began to fish with a short silver stick in a little box of sticky black liquid; then he held a drop of the liquid over the flame, which thickened it, and did the same thing repeatedly until the black ball was the size of a pea; he flattened it to a triangular shape and inserted its point into the narrow opening of the bowl of a long bamboo and amber pipe; then, inhaling deeply, he breathed in all the smoke from the little ball of opium, held it for a moment, and exhaled it in a great blue cloud. What particularly struck the newcomer was how freely, here, right in his family's house, he performed these rites that most people indulge in only with the deepest secrecy, and how very naturally he asked his guest: "Would you like a pipe?"

NOTE: *No comment by Madame Cocteau on her son's smoking has been printed, though probably references to the subject exist in unpublished family letters. Other prominent objects in Cocteau's room were busts of both him and Radiguet by Lipchitz, and numerous "sculptures" made by Cocteau himself out of pipe cleaners, plastic, and other materials.*

APPENDIX XIII

(For Chapter 3, p. 111, Chapter 6, p. 370, and Chapter 7, p. 429)

FROM *LETTRE-PLAINTE*

BY JEAN COCTEAU

You know that I detest disorder. . . . The fact is, I detest myself. I *am* disorder. . . .

Every morning, this room — this room in which I sleep, force myself to work, and escape from as often as possible — is open to any comer. Sometimes when I go out I leave in it people who do not know each other (friendships have been formed here). And sometimes young people of a new race, poetry fetishists, wait for me here while I take my bath.

I accuse no one (books are not stolen, they are just "borrowed" or "filched"), but from my room books simply fly away. Where are my treasures, my first editions, my volumes of the poets with long inscriptions in their own hand, my Apollinaire adorned with a Calligramme in the form of my profile? One of those lost treasures has just reappeared — a pretty story, as you will see.

Marcel Proust used to send me books that were veritable letters. You know the kind of inscription I mean. He would fill the margins with what amounted to a correspondence. In the volume I refer to now, he asked me why our mutual friend* whom he made the Duchesse de Guermantes stubbornly refused to read him, and he begged me to convince her that she should. He also let me know that the episode of Saint-Loup walking on the banquettes "is you, dear Jean, at Larue." † He added these lines:

> Tel un sylphe au plafond, tel sur la neige un ski
> Jean saute sur la table auprès de Nijinski.
> C'était dans le salon purpurin de Larue
> Dont l'or, d'un goût douteux, jamais ne se voila.
> La barbe d'un docteur blandisseuse et drue

* Madame de Chevigné.

† But as George D. Painter points out (I, 367 and II, 162), a similar exploit at Larue's by Proust's friend Comte Bertrand de Fenelon ("Bertrand de Réveillon"), had been described in *Jean Santeuil* many years before "Saint-Loup" was thought of.

Affirmait : Ma présence est peut-être incongrue
Mais il n'en reste qu'un je serai celui-là ;
Et mon coeur succombait aux coups d'Indiana . . .

. . . . Well, that volume has just been sold at auction. Now it belongs
to a collector. Everybody will be at liberty to assume that I disposed of it
myself.

That, my dear friend, is what is really distressing — the theft of books.
A hand that hesitates to take a necktie does not hesitate to take a book.
Sometimes this disappearance of my entire library makes my work more
difficult. It is bad enough when books disappear once and for all, like a
notebook given me by Madame de Noailles which contained the drafts of
the principal poems of *Les Eblouissements*. Such a theft was at least perpetrated out of love. But books that reappear at auction! This letter is to
warn everyone who owns books inscribed to me that I never dispose of
books sent to me by their authors — not even after erasing the inscription,
a current practice that I consider the worst of all.

The collection of Monsieur Henri Lefèbvre contains many flyleaves torn
from books, all bearing authors' inscriptions to Cocteau. This devastation
and sale were apparently perpetrated by Maurice Sachs when Cocteau in-
judiciously asked Sachs to sell some of his possessions at the time he was
clearing out of his room in his mother's apartment in the rue d'Anjou; Sachs
seems to have sold a good deal more than he should have, and pocketed
most of the money. After Cocteau discovered the fraud, he wrote to Monsieur Lefèbvre that he would not prosecute Sachs. (He said more than once
that he "preferred thieves to the police.") Cocteau speaks of the episode on
the *disque Perry*. It is not clear what became of the *"centaine de lettres de
Marcel,"* which Cocteau says also disappeared *"par un abus de confiance."*
(See *Bulletin de la Société des Amis de Marcel Proust*, 1963.)

APPENDIX XIV (For Chapter 6, p. 409)

A VISIT TO BARBETTE, 1966

In his various writings on Barbette, Cocteau several times speaks of his being Texas-born, and a few years ago, learning that he was living in the United States, I sought him out and found him in Austin.

I had been told that most people flying to Austin from New York are apt to be en route to conferences with either legislators or professors (Austin being both the state capital and the seat of the state university), and that my mission to talk with a gentleman who had rocked the international vaudeville world in the 1920's and 1930's with the trapeze act he did disguised as a girl, to the music of Wagner and Rimsky-Korsakov, would not be considered by his fellow Texans a sufficiently serious reason for visiting their state. I suspected at the time that my informant was not entirely correct, and my suspicion has since been confirmed. In Texas there are quite a few vaudeville buffs who are respectfully knowledgeable about the career of Barbette, and Cocteau's *N.R.F.* essay on him has made his name, at least, known to a certain number of professors and students of literature in Texan universities as well as in others. But it seemed to be generally unknown that Barbette had returned to the state and was living in Austin.

The person who had finally found him for me was an Austin professor who had never heard of him before, a Hellenist and Latinist I had once known in Tuscany, named Paolo Vivante. I had obtained Barbette's Austin address through friends of mine who spend the winters in Florida, near Sarasota. Someone had told me that Barbette was now associated with a circus, and although Ringling Brothers and Barnum and Bailey Combined Shows moved its winter quarters some time ago from Sarasota to Venice (Florida), I knew that quite a few retired circus people continue to live in Sarasota, and my friends learned about Austin from one of them. But when I wrote to Barbette in Austin (my friends' informant said that he used the name Barbette as a last name, and that his first name was Vander) he didn't answer, and fearing he might not be there I asked Vivante to drive over from the university and inquire. He found him there — "a very nice, delicate man," he wrote me, "rather reticent, and wondering whether or not to encourage you to come down"; and a few days later came a note from Barbette himself consenting to see me.

He was standing beside Vivante at the Austin airport when I arrived, one spring evening (I learned later that he had been nervous while waiting, and had remarked to Vivante "I feel this is the arrival of the literary FBI"), and I was at once struck by his careful grooming. Almost everyone else within sight was dressed with the utmost casualness — there was scarcely a necktie to be seen; but Barbette was wearing a dark, well-cut suit, white shirt, striped tie, and a narrow-brimmed brown straw hat. When he took his hat off, his sandy hair was impeccably brushed. He was spare and very erect, with thin, almost pinched features. He looked like a very trim, older-man fashion model — less than his age, which I knew to be a bit over sixty; but when he moved he seemed older. His gestures and his gait, which at first struck me as mincing, I saw were not that, but curiously careful — stiff and a bit jerky: I had heard something about his career having ended with an accident, and assumed I was seeing the result. Also noticeable were his irregular teeth and a white scar near his mouth. His first words after greeting me were about Vivante: "What a particularly elegant ambassador you sent me!" That startled me, for Vivante, classicist though he is, had adopted what was apparently the accepted local style of dress in a big way, and had come to the airport wearing a rusty black T-shirt, blue jeans and sneakers; the contrast between his appearance and Barbette's was striking. But Barbette set me right, and in a way that revealed his grasp of the authentic. "The most complete gentlemanly refinement I've met with in anyone since the Vicomte Charles de Noailles," he said. The French title rang out oddly in the Austin airport. Vivante, looking a bit abashed at the tribute to his manners, suggested that we find my suitcase and get into his car. We did so, and at the Stephen F. Austin Hotel, after I checked in, we sat down in the coffee shop.

Before long Barbette was reminiscing about the remake of the scene in *The Blood of a Poet.* "Cocteau told me that I was substituting for the Vicomtesse de Noailles, whom I knew," he said, "but neither he nor she nor anybody else told me why. Sitting in the box I tried to imagine myself a descendant of the Marquis de Sade, of the Comtesse de Chevigné (in other words the Duchesse de Guermantes), and of a long line of rich bankers, all of which the Vicomtesse was. For a boy from Round Rock, Texas, that demanded a lot of concentration — at least as much as working on the wire." Famous though Barbette was as an acrobat at that time, he told me that he was as naïve about movie making as the others had been, and that he shared some of their scruples. "I didn't see the film until a couple of years later," he told me, "and when I did I was absolutely dismayed. Chanel told me afterwards that before recruiting the extras and me Cocteau had suggested that the ladies in the box be a few of her mannequins, but knowing the story she refused to lend girls — only dresses. The dress I wear in that scene is a beauty, but of course I was used to great dresses: in my act I always made my entrance in an evening gown. I went in for lamés and paillettes, with trimmings of feathers and lace — showy things for the stage, but always beautifully made."

By the time that scene in *The Blood of a Poet* was filmed, Barbette — who was born Vander Clyde, at Round Rock, a few miles from Austin, on December 19, 1904 — was quite Parisianized. He had done his earliest practicing on a permanently stretched galvanized iron clothesline in his mother's backyard in Round Rock. "My mother was a milliner by trade and famous in the neighborhood for the drawn work and embroidery she'd learned from Mexicans," he said. "She was very artistic, and admired culture. The first time she took me to the circus in Austin, I knew I'd be a performer, and from then on I'd work in the fields during the cotton-picking season to earn money in order to go to the circus as often as possible. My mother told me I couldn't leave home till I finished high school, and that encouraged me to 'double-up' — I was quick in class: I graduated at fourteen. The chief subject I regretted not going on with was Latin — I'd had only two years of it. I read *The Billboard* magazine and went to San Antonio in answer to an ad I'd seen in it, inserted by one of the 'Alfaretta Sisters, World-Famous Aerial Queens.' The other sister had died, and this one — in private life she was the wife of a blackface comedian billed as 'Happy Doc Holland, the Destroyer of Gloom' — needed a new partner for a double trapeze and swinging ring act. In the circus there's a long tradition of boys dressing as girls, and especially in a wire act women's clothes make everything more impressive — the plunging and gyrating are more dramatic in a woman — and Alfaretta asked me if I'd mind dressing as a girl. I didn't; and that's how it began. From Alfaretta I went into 'Erford's Whirling Sensation,' a revolving apparatus with three people: we hung by our teeth and did our opening number wearing big butterfly wings."

After that, Barbette said, he began to develop his own single act, which he designed not as just an imitation of a woman's trapeze act, but rather as an exercise in mystification and a play on masculine-feminine contrast, using trapeze and wire as, quite literally, his "vehicles." This Cocteau was to see as a parallel to the poet's use of words; and in fact poetry had played a role in Barbette's concept of his act. "I'd always read a lot of Shakespeare," he told me, "and thinking that those marvelous heroines of his were played by men and boys made me feel that I could turn my specialty into something unique. I wanted an act that would be a thing of beauty — of course it would have to be a strange beauty." As part of the strangeness he sought a name with a feminine sound that could also be a family name — hence Barbette. His act caught on quickly all over the United States — chiefly, he thinks, because of its surprise element, his revelation, at the end, of his masculinity, which to him was always only one part of the whole; and the William Morris Agency sent him to England and then to Paris in the fall of 1923.

"Paris was *the* experience," he told me. "As soon as I got to my little Hotel Moderne near the Place de la République, even before opening at the Alhambra music hall, I felt that I'd found my city. And at the theatre I could tell that the audiences appreciated all the little refinements I'd worked so hard on. As soon as I finished at the Alhambra, the producer Léon Volterra put me into his revue at the Casino de Paris, and there the most wonderful people began to come around to my dressing room. It was an American society woman, Helen Gwynne, who first took me up. She introduced me to her friends, most of them wealthy expatriates — the Harry Lehrs, the Berry Walls, the Elisha Dyers — and to Princess Violette Murat. Soon I was being invited out by Violette's French friends — Cocteau, Radiguet, the Noailles, Georges Geffroy (You know Georges Geffroy, the great decorator? He invented the modern Empire style), writers and painters and composers, people who sensed from seeing my act that we were artists together. The name of Volterra's revue was *'Il n'y a que Paris'* — *'There's Only Paris'* — and that's how I felt. The magazine *La Nouvelle Revue Française* printed a fine revue of my act by a French intellectual named Drieu La Rochelle. He said that the interest lay not in the acrobatics, but in the beauty of the performer. He loved the difference between the way I looked and the 'fat, muscular, graceless females,' as he called them, whom one usually sees. But of course the most perceptive was Cocteau. He saw even more in the act than I had realized was there myself."

I showed Barbette the passages in Cocteau's letters praising him, and he said, "The French paid me the supreme compliment of thinking I was somehow too good to be true. One journalist walked unannounced into my hotel room one day, obviously hoping to find something unimaginable. I was lying naked on my bed at the moment, my face smeared with a blackish skin-bleaching cream. 'Two-sexed on the stage and two-colored at home,' he wrote in his account of the visit, and he expressed amazement at seeing on my bedside table Joyce's *Ulysses,* Cocteau's *Le Grand Ecart,* and a book by Havelock Ellis. In another way, my lucky choice of name made French people think of me as one of themselves from the beginning."

After that first season, Barbette returned to Paris almost every year, playing at the Alhambra, at the Empire, at the Moulin Rouge, at the Médrano Circus. "Of course Paris was the best place, but there were other amusing cities, like Berlin, Hamburg, Copenhagen, Warsaw, Madrid, Barcelona, and when I appeared there friends I'd made in Paris would often come and we'd do the sights together." As he prospered he traveled with "twenty-eight trunks, a maid, and a maid to help the maid." Except at Médrano, where it was impossible to keep other performers from watching, he allowed only two people to look on from backstage during his act — his maid in one wing, and the stage manager in the other. "I would tolerate nobody else," he said. "I was well known to be a martinet."

I could believe that, especially as I'd noticed several little severities to which Barbette had subjected our waitress in the coffee shop — the harsh rejection of a smudgy plate, a biting sarcasm when the coffee arrived too early. Luckily, she was a good-natured girl, who seemed to find such fastidiousness comical: she tipped me a wink when Barbette gave an exaggerated start and said *"Please!"* as she put down some spoons rather noisily. "Since those years in Paris I've never been able to readjust to crudity," Barbette said. "I'm living temporarily with my sister here in Austin before joining a big show a few months from now. I'll not be a performer, of course, but a trainer, trying to give young present-day acrobats some faint idea of what a refined act can be. I have to say that apart from my family everything about Austin offends me. And I know I'll be lucky if in return for my very handsome salary I succeed in persuading a few young trapezists just not to chew gum during their act. Imagine!"

It sounded prim, and I noticed a quizzical look on the face of Vivante, by whose Tuscan parents, I well knew, all the refinements — including the moral and intellectual refinement that led them into exile from Mussolini, and the refinement of non-snobbery — were taken so for granted as never to be mentioned. But I knew what Barbette was thinking of, and I recalled some of the tributes Cocteau paid him in his famous essay on his act — tributes to the flair and supreme professionalism that had enabled him to make what might have been a mere stunt — and a distasteful stunt at that — into an *"extraordinaire leçon de métier théâtral,"* a work of art. "He walked tightrope high above the audiences without falling," Cocteau said, "— above incongruity, death, bad taste, indecency, indignation."

The day after our talk in the coffee shop I saw Barbette again, and this time his conversation consisted chiefly of anecdotes. Two of them, which I thought quite funny, turned, once again, on his favorite subject — refinement. His friend Princess Violette Murat, although ugly and obese, retained her "natural elegance," he said, even when being absurd — sniffing cocaine in her New York hotel room as she reproached her sister-in-law, Princesse Hélène Murat, who had just returned from a Harlem nightclub, for leading an "unhealthy life." Whereas Madame Aline, the severely black-clad proprietress or manageress of a Marseilles brothel once visited for its blue films by Barbette, Cocteau and Cocteau's friend Maurice Rostand, displayed her brand of refinement when replying to Cocteau's request for a homosexual film: "Ah, Monsieur, we do have a film of that kind, and everybody asks for it, but unfortunately it is being repaired. *Je suis désolée*." Barbette's imitation of Madame Aline's intonation, especially of the word "*dé-so-lée*," and of her accompanying gesture of regret and apology — fingers of both hands joined under her chin — was a marvelous bit of mimicry; I could see what his "scabrous little scene" on the sofa, as Cocteau called it, might have been like. (During the running of the only blue films available at "Chez Aline," Barbette said, Maurice Rostand fell asleep and snored, and Cocteau kept up a commentary on the defects of the acting.) Barbette was amusing, too, in his description of the panicking of Barnum and Bailey's troupe of elephants, all of them clad in pink tutus, at a rehearsal of an act called "The Elephant Ballet," directed by Balanchine: the stampeding was either caused by, or comically coincided with, the first performance by the circus band of Stravinsky's *Circus Polka*, which had been specially commissioned for the "ballet."

During the last hour I spent with Barbette he spoke about the end of his performing career. The scar on his face, he told me, came from early falls and from an accident in Paris that was "not serious." One night in 1929, at the Moulin Rouge, someone must have been running behind the backdrop curtain; it billowed just as Barbette was about to plunge; the billow distracted him, and he fell, and had to cancel the rest of the engagement. But later, in 1938, at Loew's State in New York, when he was sweating heavily after his act, he caught a chill in a backstage draft. When he awoke the next morning he could hardly move: it was as though he had been "turned to stone" overnight, in the position in which he had slept; and at the Post-Graduate Hospital he was found to have pneumonia along with a sudden crippling affliction of the bones and joints. The latter required surgery for rehabilitation: he spent eighteen months in the hospital and had to learn to walk again. Property he had bought in Texas had to be sold. Since then he has been a trainer of performers — including performers in two acts of his own devising which travel across the country.

Before we parted, Barbette gave me a list of people — most of them titled or otherwise distinguished — whom I should see in Paris. I did see some of them later, and found that he was very well remembered indeed, in quite a variety of circles. In a Paris library I found a collection of reviews of his act by French magazine and newspaper critics: they all praised it for its beauty and delicacy, and their articles, marked by much discrimination, were of a higher level than one usually finds in reviews of popular entertainment. The poet Paul Valéry, I discovered, after seeing Barbette's act, wondered whether there wasn't a Greek myth called "Hercules turned into a swallow." And the afternoon of December 19, 1930, at a *"Vendredi littéraire"* at the Lido on the Champs-Elysées — a party organized to promote a book by one of Barbette's admirers, the critic Gustave Fréjaville,* about those Shakespearian boy actors of women's roles whose example had influenced Barbette in his original conception of his act — Barbette appeared "With the authorization of M. and Mme. Médrano" and recited, in English, the epilogue to *As You Like It*. Shakespeare wrote it to be spoken by the boy actor who played Rosalind, and it ends: "If I were a woman, I would kiss as many of you as had beards that pleased me, complexions that liked me, and breaths that I defied not: and, I am sure, as many as have good beards, or good faces, or sweet breaths, will, for my kind offer, when I make curtsy, bid me farewell." Dressed demurely in white, Barbette "comported himself," one of the reviews said, "with an air of chaste simplicity that freed his performance from the slightest hint of bad taste. He was most enthusiastically applauded."

Barbette and I said good-bye on the sidewalk outside the Stephen F. Austin Hotel, and as he moved away with his curious, careful, stiff walk I felt that it was as though a part of the best years of Cocteau himself were vanishing. It is seldom, I suspect, that one can watch a poet's inspiration (for Cocteau, Barbette was a strange inspiration, perhaps, but an indubitable one) walking away, in flesh and blood, bearing the wounds of his devotion to his art, along a Texas sidewalk.

F.S.

* Gustave Fréjaville, *Les Travestis de Shakespeare* (Paris, Editions Seheur, 1930). It contains several photographs of Barbette *en travesti*.

Bibliography

MOST, but not all, of the following books and other documents are referred to in the Notes. (Letters quoted in the text, however, are not referred to in the Notes if they are listed in the Bibliography.) Certain other items, not in the Bibliography, are referred to only in the Notes or footnotes. French publishers are in Paris unless otherwise noted.

JEAN COCTEAU

OC   *Oeuvres Complètes*, 11 vols. (Marguerat, Lausanne, 1946–51). Works included in this set of "Complete Works," which is far from complete, are listed in the notes by their name, volume, and usually page. Other works by Cocteau are listed separately, as follows:

BB   *La Belle et la Bête, Journal d'un film* (Editions du Rocher, Monaco, 1958).

BR   *De la Brouille* (Editions Dynamo, Pierre Aelberts, Liège, n.d.).

C   *Le Coq*, Nos. I–IV, May–November 1920. (All four numbers reprinted in smaller facsimile in *L'Approdo Musicale, q.v.*).

CA   *Cahiers Jean Cocteau I* (Gallimard, 1969).

CN   *La Comtesse de Noailles, Oui et Non* (Librairie Académique Perrin, 1963).

CO   *Le Cordon Ombilical* (Plon, 1962).

D'E   *La Difficulté d'Etre* (Editions du Rocher, Monaco, 1947).

DEM   *Démarche d'un Poète* (*Der Lebensweg eines dichters*) (F. Bruckmann, München, 1953).

DIAG   On Diaghilev, in catalogue of Diaghilev exhibition, Paris, 1939.

DP   *Disque Perry*. (Autobiographical monologue recorded privately, under direction of M. Jacques Perry, 1958. Unpublished. Material used with kind permission of M. Perry.)

DU   "Lettre à Picasso," in *Du* (1961).

EC   *Entretiens autour du Cinématographe, Recueillis par André Fraigneau* (Editions André Bonne, 1951). English translation by Vera Traill: *Cocteau on the Film* (Roy Publishers, New York, and Dennis Dobson, London, 1954).

EF   *Entretiens avec André Fraigneau* (Bibliothèque 10–18, 1965).

ES   *Entretiens avec Roger Stéphane* (Editions Tallandier, 1964).

HMF   *Les Heures de Milly-la-Forêt, Mai–Juin, 1966. Sous le Signe de l'Amitié Satie-Cocteau.* (Catalogue of documents referring to Satie and Cocteau.)

JI   *Journal d'un Inconnu* (Grasset, 1953).

JM   *Jean Marais* (Calmann-Lévy, 1950).

LA   *Lettre aux Américains* (Grasset, 1949).

LB   *Le Livre Blanc* (Paul Morihien, n.d.).

LP   *Lettre-Plainte* (R. Saucier, 1926).

M   *Maalesh, Journal d'une Tournée de théâtre* (Gallimard, 1949).

LE MOT   *Le Mot* (twenty issues, 1914–15).

NTP   *Nouveau Théâtre de Poche* (Gallimard, 1960).

O   *Le Mystère de Jean l'Oiseleur, monologues* (Champion, 1925).

PA   *Les Poèmes Allemands* (Krimpeer, La Haye, 1944).

PC   *Poésie Critique*. 2 vols. (Gallimard, 1959–60).

R   *Radiguet, Deux Cahiers Manuscrits, Reproduits en facsimile* (1925).

RE   *Le Requiem* (Gallimard, 1962).
SP   *Le Sang d'un Poète* (Editions du Rocher, Monaco, 1957). English translation by
       Lily Pons: *The Blood of a Poet* (Bodley Press, New York, 1949).
TM   "Le Théâtre et la Mode," in *Masques, Revue Internationale*, Année 1, No. 1
       (Mars 1945).
VV   "Venise vue par un enfant," in *Revue Hebdomadaire*, Mai 1913.

(Two journals by Cocteau are said to exist and to be scheduled for full or partial
publication in France: one kept during the German Occupation, and another, called
Le Passé Défini, begun in 1950.)

Letters to Gabriel Astruc. Chiefly unpublished. Courtesy Mlle. Lucienne Astruc.
Letters to Comte Etienne de Beaumont and Comtesse Edith de Beaumont. Unpublished.
       With related papers. Courtesy Comte Henri de Beaumont.
Letters to Jean Bourgoint (Brother Pascal). Unpublished. Courtesy Mme. Jeannette
       Kandaouroff and Jean Hugo.
Letters to André Gide. Fonds Gide de la Bibliothèque Littéraire Jacques Doucet de
       l'Université de Paris.
Letters to Albert and Juliette Gleizes. Bibliothèque Littéraire Jacques Doucet de
       l'Université de Paris.
Letters to Jean Hugo, to Valentine Hugo, or to both. Chiefly unpublished. Courtesy
       Jean Hugo and the late Valentine Hugo.
Letters to Max Jacob. Chiefly unpublished (a few passages quoted in Kihm, II).
       Bibliothèque Royale de Belgique.
Letters to Louis Laloy. Unpublished. Courtesy M. Vincent Laloy. (Archives du Domaine
       de Rahon, par Chaussin, Jura, Série E.)
Letters to Georgette Leblanc. Unpublished. Manuscript Division, Syracuse University
       Library.
Letters to Madeleine LeChevrel. Unpublished. University of Florida Libraries.
Letters to Comtesse Anna de Noailles. Unpublished. Courtesy Comte Anne-Jules de
       Noailles.
Letters to Raymond Radiguet, to M. Maurice Radiguet, to René Radiguet, etc. Partially
       unpublished. With related documents. Courtesy M. René Radiguet and Signora
       Liliana delli Ponti Garuti.
Letters to Gertrude Stein. Chiefly unpublished. Beinecke Rare Book and Manuscript
       Library, Yale University.
Letters to Roger Stéphane. Unpublished. Courtesy M. Stéphane.
Letters to Igor Stravinsky. Unpublished. Courtesy Mr. Stravinsky.
Letter-Drawings to Igor Stravinsky. Unpublished. Collection of the author.
Letters to Richard Thoma. Unpublished. Courtesy Mr. Thoma.
Letter to Mme. Alec Weisweiller. Unpublished. Courtesy Mme. Weisweiller.
Letters to Glenway Wescott. Unpublished. Courtesy Mr. Wescott.
Letters to Monroe Wheeler. Unpublished. Courtesy Mr. Wheeler.
Letters to Edmund Wilson. Unpublished. Beinecke Rare Book and Manuscript Library,
       Yale University.

OTHER WORKS

Acton, Harold. *Memoirs of an Aesthete* (Methuen, London, 1948).
Adéma, Marcel. *Guillaume Apollinaire, le mal-aimé* (Plon, 1952).
Alexandre, Arsène. *L'Art Décoratif de Léon Bakst* (with "Notes sur les Ballets" by
       Cocteau) (Maurice de Brunoff, 1912).
Anouilh, Jean. "Cadeau de Jean Cocteau," in *La Voix des poètes* (Avril-Mai-Juin
       1960); reprinted in *Points et Contrepoints* (No. 58, Octobre 1961); reprinted

also in *Théâtre*, No. 365–366, 1 Oct.–15 Oct., 1966, "Spécial Cocteau." With the disc of *Les Mariés de la Tour Eiffel* (Disques Adès 15501).

Apollinaire, Guillaume. *Chroniques d'Art* (1902–1918), Textes réunis, avec préface et notes, par L.-C. Breunig (Gallimard, 1960).

L'Approdo Musicale, No. 19–20, 1965, "Il Gruppo dei Sei." Published by ERI, Edizioni Rai, Radio-Televisione Italiana, Roma. Certain articles from this interesting double issue concerning Les Six are listed separately in this bibliography, under authors' names. (And see under Cocteau, C [*Le Coq*].)

Aragon, Louis. *Le Crève-coeur* (Gallimard, 1941).

Arnaud, Lucien. *Charles Dullin* (L'Arche Editeur, 1952).

Astruc, Gabriel. *Le Pavillon des Fantômes* (Grasset, 1929).

Bardèche, Maurice et Brasilach, Robert. *Histoire du Cinéma*. 2 vols. (Le Livre de Poche, 1964, 1966).

Barrès, Maurice. *Le Jardin de Bérénice* (Le Livre de Poche).

Benois, Alexandre. *Reminiscences of the Russian Ballet* (Putnam, London, 1941).

Bentley, Eric. (I) *The Playwright as Thinker* (Reynal & Hitchcock, New York, 1946).
(II) *In Search of Theatre* (Vintage Books, Inc., New York, 1953; Dennis Dobson, London, 1954).

Bibesco, Princesse Marthe (I) "Jean Cocteau et son Etoile," in *Revue Générale Belge* (Décembre 1963).
(II) "Requiem pour Jean," in *Les Nouvelles Littéraires* 17 Octobre, 1963).
(III) *La Duchesse de Guermantes, Laure de Sade, Comtesse de Chevigné* (1951).

Blanche, Jacques-Emile. *Cahiers d'un Artiste. Deuxième Série, Novembre 1914–Juin 1915* (N.R.F. Paris, 1916).

Borgal, Clément. *Cocteau, Dieu, la Mort, la Poésie* (Centurion, 1958).

Bourgoint, Jean (Brother Pascal). Letters to Glenway Wescott (courtesy Mr. Wescott); letter to Mme. Jeannette Kandaouroff (courtesy Mme. Kandaouroff).

Breton, André. *Les Pas Perdus* (Gallimard, 1925).

Breunig, LeRoy C. "Le Sur-réalisme," in *Guillaume Apollinaire, 1965. La Revue des Lettres modernes*, No. 123–126, 25–27. And see under Apollinaire.

Brown, Frederick. *An Impersonation of Angels: A Biography of Jean Cocteau* (Viking Press, New York, 1968, and Longmans, Green, London, 1969).

Buckle, Richard. (I) Catalogue, "The Diaghilev Exhibition" (Edinburgh, 1954).
(II) Introduction to Catalogue: "Costumes and Curtains from Diaghilev and de Basil Ballets" (Sotheby and Co., London; sale of 17 July, 1967).

Butler, E. M. *Rainer-Maria Rilke* (Cambridge University Press, 1941).

Chanel, Pierre. Catalogue, "*Exposition Jean Cocteau*." Musée de Lunéville, 27 Juillet–6 Octobre, 1968.

Chastenet, Jacques. *Quand le Boeuf Montait sur le Toit* (Fayard, 1958).

Churchill, Randolph S. *Winston S. Churchill, Vol. 2: Young Statesman (1901–1914.)* English edition subtitled *The Young Politician*. (Houghton Mifflin, Boston, and Heinemann, London, 1967.)

Collaer, Paul. "I 'Sei': studio dell' evoluzione della musica francese dal 1917 al 1924," in *L'Approdo Musicale* (*q.v.*), 11–78.

Cooper, Douglas. *Picasso Theatre* (Editions Cercle d'Art, 1967; Weidenfeld & Nicolson, London, and Abrams, New York, 1968). And see under Gris.

Coquiot, Gustave. *Rodin à l'Hôtel Biron et à Meudon* (Ollendorff, 1917).

Crosland, Margaret. *Jean Cocteau: A biography* (Peter Nevill, London, 1955: Knopf, New York, 1956).

Deharme, Lise. *Les Années Perdues, Journal (1939–1949)* (Plon, 1961).

Delarue, Jacques. *Trafics et Crimes sous l'Occupation* (Fayard, 1968).

Desbordes, Jean. (I) *J'Adore* (Grasset, 1928).
(II) *Les Tragédiens* (Grasset, 1931).
(III) *La Mue* (Stock, 1936).
(IV) *Les Forcenés* (Gallimard, 1937).

(V) *Le Vrai Visage du Marquis de Sade* (Editions de la Nouvelle Revue Critique, 1939).

Dullin, Charles. *Ce Sont les Dieux Qu'il Nous Faut* (Gallimard, 1969).

Duncan, Isadora. *My Life* (Boni & Liveright, New York, 1927: Gollancz, London, 1928).

Faÿ, Bernard. *Les Précieux* (Librairie Académique Perrin, 1966).

Fergusson, Francis. *The Idea of a Theatre* (Princeton University Press, 1949).

Fermigier, André. *Jean Cocteau entre Picasso et Radiguet* (Hermann, 1967).

Fifield, William. "Jean Cocteau, an Interview" ("The Art of Fiction," XXXIV), in *The Paris Review*, No. 32, Summer-Fall, 1964, 13–37.

Follain, Jean. *Pierre Albert-Birot* (Poètes d'Aujourd'hui) (Pierre Séghers, 1967).

Garros, Roland. *Mémoires, Présentées par Jacques Quellennec* (Hachette, 1966).

Garuti, Liliana Delli Ponti. *Raymond Radiguet, gli Inediti* (Ugo Guanda, Parma, 1967).

Geist, Sidney. *Brancusi, A Study of the Sculpture* (Grossman, New York, and Studio Vista, Ltd., London, 1968).

Georgel, Pierre. (I) *Jean Cocteau et Son Temps, 1889–1963.* (Catalogue of Cocteau exhibition at Musée Jacquemart-André, Paris, 1965).
(II) "L'Introspection dans l'Oeuvre de Jean Cocteau." Mémoire présenté pour le Diplôme d'Etudes Supérieures des Lettres Modernes à la Faculté des Lettres de Paris (1963–1964). Unpublished. Courtesy M. Georgel.

Germain, André. (I) *Les Clés de Proust, Suivi de Portraits* (Editions Sun, 1953).
(II) *Les Fous de 1900* (La Palatine, Paris-Genève, 1954).

Gide, André. *Journal, 1889–1939* (Gallimard, La Pléiade, 1951).

Gilson, René. *Jean Cocteau* (*Cinéma d'Aujourd'hui*) (Pierre Séghers, 1964). In English, *Jean Cocteau, An Investigation into His Films and Philosophy*, translation by Ciba Vaughan (Crown, New York, 1968).

Gleizes, Juliette Roche. "Mémoires." Unpublished. Courtesy Madame Gleizes.

Grigoriev, S. L. *The Diaghilev Ballet, 1909–1929* (Constable, London, 1953; Penguin Books, 1960).

Gris, Juan. *Letters of Juan Gris (1913–1927)*, translated and edited by Douglas Cooper (privately printed, London, 1956).

Hamnett, Nina. *Laughing Torso* (R. Long & R. R. Smith, New York, and Constable, London, 1932).

Haskell, Arnold L. (in collaboration with Walter Nouvel). *Diaghileff, His Artistic and Private Life* (Simon & Schuster, New York, and Gollancz, London, 1935).

Hayter, Alethea. *Opium and the Romantic Imagination* (Faber, London, 1968).

Holland, Vyvyan. *Son of Oscar Wilde* (Dutton, New York, and Rupert Hart-Davis, London, 1954).

Honegger, Arthur. *I Am a Composer* (Faber, London, 1966).

Hugo, Jean. Extracts from unpublished diaries, and from correspondence with F. S. Courtesy M. Hugo.

Jacob, Max. (I) *Choix de Lettres de Max Jacob à Jean Cocteau, 1919–1944* (Morihien, 1949).
(II) *Correspondance.* Editée par François Garnier. Tome I, 1876–1921 (Editions de Paris, 1953); Tome II, 1921–1924 (1955).
(III) Unpublished letters to Cocteau. Collection of M. Henri Lefèbvre. Courtesy M. Lefèbvre.

Jullian, Philippe. *Prince of Aesthetes: Count Robert de Montesquiou 1855–1921*, translated by John Haylock and Francis King (Viking Press, New York, 1968). English edition called *Robert de Montesquiou* (Secker & Warburg, 1967).

Jünger, Ernst. *Journal de Guerre et d'Occupation, 1939–1948* (Julliard, 1965).

Kael, Pauline. (I) *I Lost It at the Movies* (Atlantic-Little Brown, Boston, 1965).
(II) *Kiss Kiss Bang Bang* (Atlantic-Little Brown, Boston, 1968).

Kihm, Jean-Jacques. (I) *Cocteau* (Gallimard, 1960).

(II) (co-authors Elizabeth Sprigge and Henri C. Béhar) *Jean Cocteau, l'Homme et les Miroirs* (Table Ronde, 1968).

Kochno, Boris (in collaboration with Maria Luz). *Le Ballet* (Hachette, 1954).

Krier, Yves. "Un homme de 14 ans, ou la croisée des chemins de Radiguet," in *La Parisienne*, Décembre 1953, 1673–75.

Laloy, Louis. *La Musique Retrouvée* (Plon, 1928).

La Rochefoucauld, Edmée de. *Anna de Noailles* (Editions Universitaires, 1956).

Léautaud, Paul. *Le Théâtre de Maurice Boissard*. 2 vols. (Gallimard, 1958).

Leduc, Violette. *La Bâtarde* (Farrar, Straus & Giroux, New York, and Peter Owen, London, 1965).

Lieven, Prince Peter. *The Birth of Ballets-Russes* (George Allen & Unwin, London, 1936).

Lifar, Serge. (I) *Serge Diaghilev, His Life, His Work, His Legend* (Putnam, London, 1939; Putnam, New York, 1940).

(II) *Serge de Diaghilev, Sa Vie, Son Oeuvre, Sa Légende*. Préface par Jean-Louis Vaudoyer, de l'Académie Française. (Editions du Rocher, Monaco, 1954).

(III) *Ma Vie* (Julliard, 1965).

Lune, Armand. "L'Adolescenza Creatrice di Darius Milhaud," in *L'Approdo Musicale* (*q.v.*), 92–103.

Marais, Jean. *Mes Quatres Vérités* (Editions de Paris, 1957).

Mariano, Nicky. *Forty Years with Berenson* (Knopf, New York, and Hamish Hamilton, London, 1966).

Maritain, Jacques. *Réponse à Jean Cocteau* (Stock, 1928).

Maritain, Raïssa. (I) *Les Grandes Amitiés* (Desclée de Brouwer, 1949).

(II) *Journal de Raïssa, publié par Jacques Maritain* (Desclée de Brouwer, 1965).

Martin du Gard, Maurice. *Les Mémorables (1918–1923)* (Flammarion, 1957).

Martin du Gard, Roger. *Devenir*, in *Oeuvres Complètes*, Vol. I (Gallimard, La Pléiade, 1955).

Massine, Léonide. *My Life in Ballet* (St. Martin's Press, New York, and Macmillan, London, 1968).

Massis, Henri. (I) "Raymond Radiguet," in *La Revue Universelle*, 15 Août, 1924, 488–95.

(II) *De Radiguet à Maritain, Hommage à Cocteau* (Editions Dynamo, Pierre Aelberts, Liège, 1963).

Mauriac, Claude. (I) *Jean Cocteau, ou La Vérité du Mensonge* (Odette Lieutier, 1945).

(II) *Conversations with André Gide* (Braziller, New York, 1965).

Milhaud, Darius. *Notes Without Music* (Dennis Dobson, London, 1952; Knopf, New York, 1953).

Monnier, Adrienne. *Rue de l'Odéon* (Albin Michel, 1960).

Morand, Paul. *Journal d'un Attaché d'Ambassade* (Gallimard 1963).

Myers, Rollo. *Erik Satie* (D. Dobson, London, 1948; Dover Publications, New York, 1968).

Nicolson, Harold. (I) *Peacemaking, 1919* (Houghton Mifflin, Boston, and Constable, London, 1933).

(II) *Diaries and Letters* (Atheneum, New York, and Collins, London, 1967).

Nijinsky, Vaslav. *The Diary of Vaslav Nijinsky*, edited by Romola Nijinsky (Gollancz, London, 1937).

Noailles, Marie-Laure de. "J'étais la Lolita de Jean Cocteau," in *Figaro Littéraire*, 16 Juin, 1966.

Oxenhandler, Neal. *Scandal & Parade: The Theatre of Jean Cocteau* (Rutgers University Press, New Brunswick, New Jersey, 1957).

Painter, George D. *Proust: The Later Years* (Atlantic-Little Brown, Boston, and Chatto, London, 1965). (In England now called *Marcel Proust*, Vol. 2.)

Peyrefitte, Roger. "Jean Cocteau," in *Arts*, No. 999, 31 Mars au 6 Avril, 1965, 2–4.

Polignac, Princesse Edmond de. Memoirs in *Horizon*, No. 68, August, 1945.

Porel, Jacques. *Fils de Réjane: Souvenirs*. 2 vols. (Plon, 1951–52).

Poulenc, Francis. (I) *Moi et Mes Amis* (La Palatine, Paris-Genève, 1963).

   (II) *Correspondance 1915–1963, réunie par Hélène de Wendel*, Préface de Darius Milhaud (Editions du Seuil, 1967).

Proust, Marcel. (I) *Remembrance of Things Past* (various editions in England and the U.S.)

   (II) Walter A. Strauss: "Twelve Unpublished Letters of Marcel Proust," in *Harvard University Bulletin*, Vol. VII, No. 2, Spring 1953.

Radiguet, Raymond. *Oeuvres Complètes* (Club des Libraires de France, 1959).

Ray, Man. *Self-Portrait* (Atlantic-Little Brown, Boston, 1963).

Reverdy, Pierre. (I) *Self-Defense: Critique-Esthétique* (Imprimerie Littéraire, 1919).

   (II) *Le Voleur de Talan*. Appendice par Maurice Saillet. (Flammarion, 1967).

Rey, Robert. "Chez l'adolescent prodige," in *Les Nouvelles Littéraires*, 17 Octobre, 1963.

Rilke, Ranier-Maria (I) *Die Aufzeichnungen des Malte Laurids Brigge*, translated into English as *The Journal of My Other Self*, by M. D. Herter Norton (Norton, New York, 1930).

   (II) *Ranier-Maria Rilke et Merline*, Correspondence 1920–1926 (Max Niehaus, Zurich).

Robbins, Daniel. Catalogue, "Albert Gleizes 1881–1953, A Retrospective Exhibition" (The Solomon R. Guggenheim Museum, New York, 1964).

Robert, Frédéric. *Louis Durey, l'Aîné des "Six"* (Les Editeurs Français Réunis, 1968).

Rostand, Maurice. *Confessions d'un Demi-Siècle* (Jeune Parque, 1948).

Sachs, Maurice. (I) *La Décade de l'Illusion* (Gallimard, 1932).

   (II) *Alias* (Gallimard, 1935).

   (III) *Au Temps du Boeuf sur le Toit* (Editions de la Nouvelle Revue Critique, 1939).

   (IV) *Le Sabbat* (Gallimard, 1946).

   (V) *La Chasse à Courre* (Gallimard, 1949).

   (VI) *Chronique Joyeuse et Scandaleuse* (Corréa, 1950).

   (VII) *Derrière Cinq Barreaux* (Gallimard, 1952).

   (VIII) *Lettres* (Le Bélier, 1968).

Salmon, André. *Souvenirs sans Fin*. 3 vols. (Gallimard, 1955–61).

Sanouillet, Michel. (I) *Dada à Paris* (Pauvert, 1965).

   (II) *391, Revue Publiée de 1917 à 1924 par Francis Picabia. Réedition Intégrale*, I (Le Terrain Vague, 1960).

   (III) *Francis Picabia et 391*, Tome II (Eric Losfeld, 1966).

Sartre, Jean-Paul. (I) *Saint-Genet, Comédien et Martyr* (Gallimard, 1952).

   (II) "The Parisians and the Germans," in *Playboy*, January 1966.

Scheikévitch, Marie. *Souvenirs d'un Temps Disparu* (Plon, 1935).

Sert, Misia. *Misia and the Muses, The Memoirs of Misia Sert* (John Day, New York, 1953). (Translation by Moura Budberg from the French *Misia*, Gallimard, 1952). Published in England under the title *Two or Three Muses* (Museum Press, 1953).

Severini, Gino. *Tempo de "l'Effort Moderne"; La Vita di un Pittore*, Vol. 2. A Cura di Piero Pacini (Firenze, 1968).

Soby, James Thrall. *The Early Chirico* (Dodd, Mead, New York, 1941).

Sokolova, Lydia. *Dancing for Diaghilev, The Memoirs of Lydia Sokolova*, edited by Richard Buckle (Murray, London, 1960).

Stein, Gertrude. (I) *The Autobiography of Alice B. Toklas* (Harcourt Brace, New York, and John Lane, London, 1933).

   (II) *Everybody's Autobiography* (Random House, New York, 1937; Heinemann, London, 1938).

Stravinsky, Igor. (I) *An Autobiography* (Steuer, New York, 1958).

   (II) "On Music and Other Matters," in *New York Review of Books*, March 14, 1968.

   (III) Postcards to Cocteau. Unpublished. Collection of M. Henri Lefèbvre. Courtesy of Mr. Stravinsky and M. Lefèbvre.

Stravinsky, Igor and Robert Craft.

(I) *Conversations with Igor Stravinsky* (Doubleday, New York, and Faber, London, 1959).

(II) *Memories and Commentaries* (Doubleday, New York, and Faber, London, 1960).

(III) *Dialogues and a Diary* (Doubleday, New York, 1963; Faber, London, 1963).

(IV) *Themes and Episodes* (Knopf, New York, 1966).

Vlad, Roman. *Stravinsky* (Oxford University Press, 1960).

Wharton, Edith. *A Backward Glance* (Century-Appleton, New York, and Appleton-Century, London, 1934).

White, Eric Walter. *Stravinsky* (University of California Press, and Faber, London, 1966).

Notes

PAGE references to Anglo-American books are usually to American editions. Roman numerals following an author's name refer to an author's various works as numbered in the Bibliography.

CHAPTER ONE

3	*young enthusiasm:* Wharton, 285. The passage reads: "Except Bay Lodge I have known no other," etc. Bay Lodge was a Massachusetts friend of Mrs. Wharton's.
3	*his memoirs:* Rostand, 122.
4	*invisibility:* JI, 13.
5	*blows:* JI, 20.
6	*the truth: Opéra,* OC, IV, 152.
7	*the world:* D'E, 25.
7	*horses:* Seymour de Vaulchier, conversation.
8	*dabbling:* D'E, 25.
8	*marry:* DP.
8	*eyeglasses: Portraits-Souvenir,* OC, XI, 59–60.
8	*Tuesdays: Opium,* OC, X, 149.
8	*ten:* DEM, 8.
9	*suicide:* Marais, 62.
9	*suicide today:* ES, 44.
9	*novels and plays:* ES, 44 and Madame Singer, conversation.
9	*seeing nothing: Opium,* OC, X, 148–149.
10	*smile: Opium,* OC, X, 138–139.
12	*a monster:* the story was told to various people, including the young Jacques Barzun. A blunted version is in Crosland, 12–13.
12	*in a dream: Portraits-Souvenir,* OC, XI, 73.
13	*sperm:* LB, 19–20.
13	*stranger still: "Sexual Digest,* Octobre, 1949, No. 7." (So quoted in Kihm, I, 174.)
13	*jeunesse lointaine:* Roger Peyrefitte, "Jean Cocteau," in *Arts,* No. 999, March 31–April 6, 1965, 2–4.
14	*vamps: Opéra,* OC, IV, 98.
14	*loved by them:* Sartre, 84n.
14	*theatre-itis:* DP.
14	*without cause: Éloge des Pléiades,* OC, X, 238.
15	*usual stages:* VV.
15	*after another:* DP.
15	*mast:* ES, 65.
15	*existed: Éloge des Pléiades,* OC, X, 238.
16	*where we were:* ES, 65.
16	*opium-smoking:* Jean Denoël, conversation.
16	*ecstasy: Opium,* OC, X, 100.
16	*his own feet:* ES, 65.
16	*Le Fantôme de Marseille:* OC, I, 289 and OC, VIII, 411.
17	*merchandise:* LB, 51.

18   *very carefully:* LB, 55–56.
18   *passive:* Paul Morand (conversation and correspondence), and others.
18   *my real school:* ES, 65–66.
18   *two gendarmes:* ES, 65.
18   *set me free:* ES, 66.
19   *twenty-year-old intelligence:* Roland Caillaud, conversation.
19   *Nicolson:* Glenway Wescott, conversation.
19   *Jeanne Reynette: Portraits-Souvenir,* OC, XI, 93.
19   *Christiane Mancini: Portraits-Souvenir,* OC, XI, 93.
20   *Cocteau documents:* Chanel, Pierre.
20   *an idiot:* DP.
21   *comic-opera Nero: Portraits-Souvenir,* OC, XI, 93.
21   *menagerie: Portraits-Souvenir,* OC, XI, 92.
21   *taken in:* Léautaud, I, 220; II, 26, 79.
22   *in tears: Portraits-Souvenir,* OC, XI, 94.
22   *évanescente:* Mme. Simone, conversation.
22   *bourrrrgeoise:* Mlle. Gabrielle Chanel, conversation.
22   *resemble:* JI, 35–36.
23   *respective doors: Portraits-Souvenir,* OC, XI, 97–98.
23   *let live: Portraits-Souvenir,* OC, XI, 98.
23   *wings of fame:* DP.
27   *hidden strength: Portraits-Souvenir,* OC, XI, 98.
27   *unforgettable to me: Portraits-Souvenir,* OC, XI, 98.
28   *existence might be:* DP.
28   *Cocteau's indication:* Martin du Gard, R., 66 *passim.*
29   *my poems:* Fifield.
29   *tangle: Opium,* OC, X, 150.
29   *sursaut:* CO, 7.

CHAPTER TWO

34   *motorboat:* Holland, 171–172.
34   *to be smart:* Germain, I, 186.
36   *seven best friends: Lettre à Jacques Maritain,* OC, IX.
36   *Help me!:* letter partly printed in catalogue of *Vente de la Collection Léon Muller,* Versailles, March 31, 1968.
36   *can't go out!:* letter in collection of Mme. Simone André-Maurois, in Georgel, I, 30.
38   *disreputable hotel: Portraits-Souvenir,* OC, XI, 108 *et seq.*
39   *filth:* Coquiot, 16–18. Other material about Rodin, Rilke and the Hôtel Biron comes from Rilke, Combe, Butler.
41   *led him:* Rey.
42   *seashore:* Rilke, II, 592.
42   *his death:* DEM, 11–12.
43   *as she did:* Rostand, 26 and *passim.*
45   *April sun: Portraits-Souvenir,* OC, XI, 105.
46   *devoted to poets:* ibid.
47   *fever of 104:* Georgel, I, 29–30.
49   *wept at the sight: Portraits-Souvenir,* OC, XI, 139.
51   *Montesquiou:* Jullian, 244–245.
51   *January:* Scheikevitch, 89.
52   *Laure de Sade:* Painter, *passim.*
52   *all that was best: Opium,* OC, X, 229.
52n   *Maisons-Laffitte:* Seymour de Vaulchier, conversation.
53   *face powder:* Bibesco, III.
53   *Antigone:* La Rochefoucauld, 26 and *passim.*

53   *Luxor:* Nicolson, I.
57   *while she drank:* CN, 20.
57   *Acropole de la pensée:* Bibesco, I.
57   *and listen:* Comte Anne-Jules de Noailles, conversation.
58   *Anna-mâle:* Bibesco, I.

CHAPTER THREE

65   *memoirs:* Benois, 373 and *passim.*
65   *repetitious:* Haskell, 141, 166 and *passim.*
65   *recovered from:* Kochno, 126–127 and *passim.*
65   *stockings:* Duncan, 184.
66   *galoshes manufacturer:* Lieven, 76–77, 200 and *passim.*
66n *too early:* Bibesco, I.
67   *Greffulhe:* Astruc, *passim;* and Astruc papers in the Library and Museum of the Performing Arts (The New York Public Library at Lincoln Center).
67   *and others:* Grigoriev, *passim.*
69   *member of the troupe:* TM.
69   *Nile:* D'E, 72.
69   *opera glass:* TM.
69   *four walls:* Valentine Hugo, conversation.
70n *C'est une femme:* Sir Osbert Sitwell, conversation.
71   *describes it:* Morand, 55.
71   *irresistible:* Porel, I, 348.
72   *with colors:* D'E, 47.
72   *and weakness:* TM.
73   *have allowed:* Igor Stravinsky, conversation.
74   *to Astruc:* Bakst's letter to Astruc (unpublished), recommending Cocteau, is in the possession of Mr. Richard Buckle, who kindly sent me a transcript.
75   *all in capitals:* Astruc papers (see note for *Greffulhe,* above).
75   *Harold Acton:* Acton, 113.
76   *at that time:* Stravinsky and Craft, II, 77.
76   *please circulate:* Astruc papers.
76   *non-ballet friends:* e.g., Madeleine LeChevrel (letters Cocteau-LeChevrel).
76   *William Shakespeare:* Astruc papers.
77   *not very good:* Buckle, I.
77   *early aesthetic:* Georgel, I, 35.
77n *1911:* Sokolova, 36–37.
77n *world of art:* Buckle, II.
78   *in profile:* Kochno, 174, 177.
78   *saw dancing: Portraits-Souvenir,* OC, XI, 107.
79   *avant-garde:* Morand, 79.
79   *au ventre:* Cocteau-Astruc, n.d.
79   *his face:* D'E, 69–70.
79   *moody: ibid.*
79   *perfume:* Alexandre, 26.
79   *Flaubert: ibid.*
80   *Diaghilev gave in: Portraits-Souvenir,* OC, XI, 107.
80   *and so on:* Stravinsky and Craft, II, 40n.
82   *marvels:* DIAG.
83   *introducing himself:* Stravinsky and Craft, III, 44.
83   *famous:* White, 18.
84   *Rite of Spring:* DP.
84   *Monte Carlo: Igor Stravinsky et le Ballet Russe,* OC, IX, 42. "Mr. Stravinsky [who was living in Beaulieu at the time], says that he does remember talking about *Petrushka* to Cocteau at Monte Carlo but he doubts it was

in the Salon de Jeu. However, he says that this was not the first time he met Cocteau, and that in any case he did not finish *Petrushka* in Beaulieu but in Rome." (Robert Craft, correspondence.)

84   *the Rite: ibid.*

85   *childhood:* White, 172.

85   *prehistoric ballet:* Vlad, 13.

85   *witnessed: La Jeunesse et le Scandale*, OC, IX, 325.

87   *artists alone: Le Sacre du Printemps*, OC, IX, 43–48.

87   *contradiction:* DP.

89   *Leysin: Le Sacre du Printemps*, OC, IX, 48–49.

89   *Venice:* Stravinsky and Craft, I.

89   *Rite scandal:* Igor Stravinsky, correspondence.

90   *Volga:* LE MOT, March 13, 1915.

90   *external sounds: Lettre à Jacques Maritain*, OC, IX, 293.

90   *modern tragedy:* Cocteau–Anna de Noailles, August, 1913.

90n   *vipère sans queue:* Mme. Gleizes, conversation.

90n   *chocolate cake:* Romaine Brooks Goddard, conversation.

91   *jellyfish:* my thanks to Mr. Ernst Kirstener, American Museum of Natural History.

91   *owes its name:* "Potomac" means "something brought." (The Indian village that gave the river its name was the principal residence of a wero-wance, or powerful headman, to which the tribes along the river and its vicinity brought tribute.) Frederick W. Hodge, ed., *Handbook of American Indians North of Mexico*, Vol. II (Washington, Government Printing Office, 1910. Smithsonian Institution, Bureau of American Ethnology Bulletin 30). Kindness of the Library of Congress.

92   *intelligence:* LE MOT, March 27, 1915.

92   *kind of preface:* Bibliothèque Nationale. Correspondance d'Alfred Mortier et Aurel. Unpublished. ALS from Cocteau, Le Lavandou, Var, June 26, 1922. Probably to Mme. Aurel.

92   *proof of confidence: Le Potomak, Prospectus, 1916*. OC, II, 16.

93   *Cocteau's friends:* Gertrude Stein, who apparently never read *Le Potomak*, thought that Cocteau had quoted from her *Portrait of Mabel Dodge*. She says in *The Autobiography of Alice B. Toklas* (p. 250): "Lipchitz had told Gertrude Stein a thing which she did not know, that Cocteau in his Potomak had spoken of and quoted The Portrait of Mabel Dodge. She was naturally very pleased as Cocteau was the first French writer to speak of her work."

      Mr. Donald Gallup, of the Yale University Library, has kindly furnished a photograph of the relevant page of the manuscript of *Tender Buttons*. Mr. Gallup has written: "I don't see how Cocteau could possibly have seen *Tender Buttons* in 1913 since it just didn't exist at that time. Furthermore the reference in *Potomak* to the passage's appearing in the middle of a blank page . . . seems to imply that Cocteau had seen the manuscript. I doubt that Gertrude would have allowed this out of her hands but it is barely possible that Blanche was allowed to borrow it. . . ." (Donald Gallup, correspondence.)

93   *as he used:* Paul Léautaud, *Entretiens avec Robert Mallet* (Paris, 1951), 116.

93   *Vanderem: Le Miroir des Lettres*, February 1, 1920, quoted in Georgel, II.

94   *and a text: Le Sacre du Printemps*, OC, IX, 49.

103   *indeed biblical:* collection of M. Henri Lefèbvre.

111   *from memory: Bulletin de la Société des Amis de Marcel Proust*, 1963. *[1908?]:* CA, 64–65.

112   *Jeunes Filles en fleurs:* JI, 126.

113   *listen to it:* PC, I, 126.

117   *ne se rencontre pas:* Kihm, II, 75 (glossing a passage in *Le Potomak*, OC, II, 154).

CHAPTER FOUR·

121   *world:* Churchill, 489.
121   *twenty million others:* estimate by Barbara Tuchman, correspondence.
121   *much to his taste:* Germain, I, 184–185.
122   *being sick: Opium,* OC, X, 94–95.
123   *if necessary:* Cocteau-LeChevrel, August 24, 1914.
124   *clumsy, dull, morose:* Gide, 473.
126   *best in yourself: Visites à Maurice Barrès,* OC, IX, 143.
126   *favorable verdict:* Bibesco, II.
126   *Chasseur Alpin, please:* Bibesco, I.
127   *above enemy lines:* Bibesco, I.
127   *his career:* Garros, *passim.*
128   *she speaks:* Bibesco, I.
128   *ghastly nightmare:* LE MOT, May 1, 1915.
128   *propeller: Lettre à Jacques Maritain,* OC, IX, 293.
129   *interest aviators:* ES, EF.
130n   *grow young:* Bibesco, I.
131   *its opposite:* cf. Collaer, 20.
131   *ambulance uniform:* The oil is in the collection of Mrs. Siegfried Ullman, Palm Beach, Florida. The gouache is in the collection of Mme. Gleizes. See Robbins, especially p. 75, Nos. 101 and 102.
131n   *Edith Wharton:* postcard, Berry to Cocteau (1920), collection M. Henri Lefèbvre.
131n   *rue des Saints-Pères:* ES.
132   *wonderful project:* Astruc, 112–113.
132n   *I'm coming:* Mme. Gleizes, conversation.
133   *green dress:* Cocteau-Valentine Hugo, summer, 1929.
133   *annals of ballet:* see, for example, Robert Siohan, *Stravinsky* (Paris, 1959), 49; and rear cover of *Les Ballets Russes de Serge de Diaghilev, 1909–1929* (Exhibition at Strasbourg, 1969).
133n   *not opened one:* D'E, 26–27.
134   *an engagement party and passim:* Valentine Hugo, conversation.
135n   *Wien-Leipzig:* Robbins, p. 75, Nos. 101 and 102. And Kihm, II, 91, n. 1.
136   *came to nothing:* Astruc, 113.
137   *encounter for me:* EF, 21.
138   *Götterdämmerung:* Picasso, OC, IX, 251.
138   *in 1923:* DU; and Cooper, 19, n. 19 and *passim.*
138   *deluxe: Igor Stravinsky et le Ballet Russe,* OC, IX, 47 (quoted in Fermigier, 12).
138   *in the stars:* DU.
139   *history of* Parade: Fermigier, 12–13.
140   *said of her:* Comte Henri de Beaumont, Valentine Hugo, Jean Hugo.
141   *Beaumont's plan:* Faÿ, 32–33.
143   *to the other: Thomas l'Imposteur,* OC, I, 149.
144   *smell of the manger:* Bibesco, II.
144   *in the game:* "Both in and out of the game and watching and wondering at it" (*Song of Myself,* IV, 14) translated by Bazalgette (1909) as "*A la fois mêlé au jeu et hors du jeu, l'observant et s'émerveillant.*" My thanks to Professor Roger M. Asselineau.
146n   *Three acrobatic numbers:* quoted in Kihm, II, 75.
147   *Bravo:* HMF, No. 31.
147   *a famous one:* now the property of M. Jean Marais.

148   *subscriber:* courtesy of John H. Field.
148n   *letter . . . to Bakst in Rome:* courtesy of Mme. Gilberte Cournand; printed also in *La Revue des Lettres Modernes,* Nos. 183–188, 1968 (4).
150   *Lipchitz, Stravinsky:* DP.
150n   *"detested" him:* Anon.: "Cocteau par Modigliani . . ." in *Arts,* November 27–December 3, 1963.
154   *Valentine Gross and yourself:* HMF, No. 13.
154   *aren't you?:* Sert, 117.
158   *roar of engines:* Sert, 142.
160   *we moved in:* D'E, 48.
160   *in Montparnasse:* DP.
161   *too late:* His Majesty's Theatre, London, July 15, 1926.
162   *notebook:* kindly sent me in photocopy by M. Edouard Dermit.
164n   *vie privée:* Mme. Alexis Léger, correspondence.
164n   *green on black:* D'E, 240–241.
165   *to do* Parade: M, 32.
165   *my invitation:* Picasso, OC, IX, 244–245.
166   *angels: La Collaboration de "Parade,"* OC, IX, 53.
166   *goddess: Carte Blanche,* OC, IX, 126.
166n   *to come:* Morand, 117.
168   *usual self: L'Exemple d'Erik Satie,* OC, IX, 69.
168   *at Diaghilev's:* unpublished. Courtesy of William S. Lieberman.
169   *nice feeling:* unpublished. Collection F.S.
170   *jealous of Stravinsky:* Morand, 28 and *passim.*
171   *André Salmon:* Apollinaire (Breunig), 482.
171   *fits well:* HMF, No. 19.
173   *your Chinaman:* unpublished. Courtesy of William S. Lieberman.
174   *hundred-percent Cubists: Picasso,* OC, IX, 245.
174   *something else:* Poulenc, I, 82.
174   *wedding trip:* ES, 79.
175   *paid him:* Maria Shabelska Yakofleff, conversation.
175   *from the war:* Morand, 209.
176   *end to end: Poésies* ("Le Voyage en Italie"), OC, III, 122–124.
177   *choreographer:* BR, 7.
177   *says today:* Léonide Massine, conversation.
177   *choreography:* CA, 41.
177   *Dioscuri:* Picasso, OC, IX, 246.
177   *treasure gone: Des Beaux-Arts considerés comme un assassinat,* OC, X, 227.
177   *moonlight: Le Mystère Laïc,* OC, X, 83.
178   *collaborator: ibid.*
178   *La Boutique Fantasque:* Grigoriev, 154.
179   *spectators: Le Secret Professionel,* OC, IX, 170.
180n   *ruinsky:* courtesy Mrs. Suzanne Ziegler Gleaves.
181   *ININTERROMPUE: Poésies* ("Le Voyage en Italie"), OC, III, 126–127.
181   *Carlo Socrate:* Douglas Cooper, correspondence; and *Les Ballets Russes de Serge de Diaghilev, 1909–1929* (Exhibition at Strasbourg, 1969), 308.
182   *about the fighting:* Stein, II.
182n   *tremendously:* Breunig.
184   *butchers:* Morand, 154.
185   *bedlam:* Poulenc, I, 88–89.
186   *imitation wood: La Collaboration de "Parade,"* OC, IX, 53–54.
186   *compressed air: ibid.*
186   *his characters: ibid.*
186   *like a rampart:* EF, 23.
186   *my eyes out: La Jeunesse et le Scandale,* OC, IX, 323–324.
187   *children:* EF, 23.

187	*interesting:* Morand, 250.
187	*attorney: Opium,* OC, X, 97; and see HMF, No. 98 (letter from Louis Durey to Cocteau, November 28, 1917).
188	Parade *itself:* Robert, 27.
188	*belittled:* CA, 70–71 (but see note for page 262).
188	*too often:* Myers, 105.
188n	*revivals:* Cooper, 28n.
189	*each turn: Le Coq et l'Arlequin,* OC, IX, 30.
189	*visual memories:* Cooper, 27.
189n	*copies:* Massine, 275.
189n	*nothing more:* Cocteau to Massine, n.d. Courtesy William S. Lieberman.
190	*astounded him:* D'E, 50.
190	*originality:* Stravinsky, I, 93.
190	*prevailed:* Cris, 49.
190	*suggested:* Lifar, II, 268–269.
198	*spell:* Porel, I, 349.
200	*Le Canon:* Severini, 39.
202	*listened to:* HMF, No. 36.
202	*Barcelona:* Grigoriev, 132.
202	*Milhaud:* Milhaud, 79.
204	*abandoned the idea:* Noailles.
204n	*Marshall:* Jean Hugo, correspondence.
205	*sea horse, too:* Proust, *Correspondance générale,* V, 80 (quoted in Proust, II).
206	*in mind:* André Fermigier, correspondence.
206n	*as a translation:* courtesy Prof. Torsten Norvig.
207	*calèche: Le Coq et l'Arlequin,* OC, IX, 13 *et seq.* Also Jean Cocteau, *A Call to Order,* translated from the French by Rollo H. Myers (London, 1926).
207	*great influence:* Polignac.
207	*trenchant style:* Honegger, 104.
208	*Debussyism:* Robert, 30.
208	*Marcel:* Proust, II.
209	*use of Cocteau:* Morand, 246.
210	*in the band:* Poulenc, II, 18.
211	*Cocteau to André Salmon:* Adéma, 253–255.
211n	*an advance?:* unpublished. Courtesy M. Alain Ollivier.
213	*death of Apollinaire:* DP.
213	*This was Guillaume Apollinaire:* D'E, 169.
213	*transcribed: ibid,* 169–170.
214	*nightingale: Portraits-Souvenir,* OC, XI, 141.
214	*repousser:* Georgel, I, No. 163.
215	*in 1916:* CA, 41.

CHAPTER FIVE

220n	*sound, idea, color:* Follain, 12.
221	*the show:* C, I.
221	*society:* Chastenet, 85.
223	*literary revolution: Portraits-Souvenir,* OC, XI, 142.
224	*fake:* D'E, 175.
224	*trick: ibid.*
224	*confessed:* Prof. Michel Sanouillet, correspondence.
224	*failed:* Sanouillet, I, 91, n. 2.
225	*true author:* courtesy of Mme. Pierre Albert-Birot.
225	*the others:* Reverdy, I (quoted in Reverdy, II, 170–171).

226   *about Dada:* quoted in Sanouillet, I, 479.
226   *strong point:* quoted in Sanouillet, I, 105.
226   *mystical state:* Germain, II, 260.
226   *civilization:* Barrès, 371.
226   *scorn:* Marcel Duchamp, conversation.
226   *violent novelty:* Monnier, 97.
226   Guermantes Way: Sanouillet, I, 559.
227   *endurance:* Georges Hugnet, conversation.
227   *imitating:* Reginald Bridgeman, conversation and correspondence.
227   *asked:* Sanouillet, I, 105, n. 2; and Prof. Michel Sanouillet, correspondence.
227   *my pen:* Breton, 135.
227   *the most:* quoted in Sanouillet, I, 531.
227   *freeze over: ibid*, 551.
229   *by heart:* JI, 111.
229   *happened:* M, 26–27.
231   *parents: Ecrits Nouveaux,* October 1919, 70–72.
232   *reader: ibid.*
232   *bidet:* courtesy of The Times Bookshop, London.
232   *courtesans:* Germain, II, 262.
232   *travel book: Mon Premier Voyage.* Cf. p. 433 of present volume.
233   *own pen:* JI, 111.
233   *Gide:* Sir Isaiah Berlin, conversation.
234   *convincing:* Nicolson, I, 249.
234n   *Polichinelle:* Morand, 114.
235   *hostility:* Monnier, 107–108.
236   *this way:* Monnier, 105–106.
236   *hearing you:* Proust, II.
239   *little crocodile:* Lune, 103. "Jacaremirim — come il cocodrillo viene chia-mato in sabir, dialetto negro-indio di Rio." The Consulate General of Brazil in New York confirms that "jacaremirim" is an Indian word mean-ing "little crocodile," but adds: "The word 'sabir' does not exist as far as we know. . . . To our knowledge, there is no Negro-Indian dialect."
240   *set to work:* Milhaud, 101.
240   *chance:* Georgel, I, No. 271.
241   *"saw": D'un Ordre Considéré comme une Anarchie,* OC, IX, 216.
241n   *only individuals:* C, I.
241n   *the moment:* as quoted in Sanouillet, I, 105*n.*
242   *in America:* quoted in Georgel, I, No. 271.
242   *later:* Beaumont papers.
242   *antiquity:* quoted in Georgel, I, No. 272.
243   *design:* JI, 223.
243   *jazz:* Louis Laloy in *Comoedia,* February 23, 1920.
243   *my side: La Jeunesse et le Scandale,* OC, IX, 326.
243   *Ariel:* Léautaud, II, 121.
243   *never laughable:* Milhaud, 104 (translation sometimes slightly altered here and elsewhere).
244   *letters:* Certain Cocteau-Radiguet letters, or parts of them, have been printed in Goetsch (*q.v.*), in Garuti (*q.v.*), and in *Le Vieux Saint-Maur, Bulletin de la Société Historique et Archéologique de Saint-Maur-des-Fossés, et des Localités Avoisinantes* (Nos. 22 et 23, Automne 1957). Un-published letters and related documents as in Bibliography.
245   *Golschmann:* Vladimir Golschmann, conversation and correspondence.
248   *Salmon:* Salmon, II, 41–47.
248   *dawn:* Krier.
249   *held by him: D'un Ordre Considéré comme une Anarchie,* OC, IX, 457.
249   *as always:* Radiguet papers.

249	*around that table: Lettre à Jacques Maritain*, OC, IX, 276.
249	*finish it off: Raymond Radiguet*, OC, X, 268.
250	*Poiret:* Paul Morand, "Paris Letter," *The Dial*, May, 1924, p. 451.
250n	*Attelage:* Robert, 41.
251	*a little:* Garuti, 225, n. 3.
254n	*five sharp:* printed in *Empreintes*, No. 7–8 (May-June-July 1950), 104–105; and in Radiguet, II, 317–320.
258	*joke: D'un Ordre considéré comme une Anarchie*, OC, IX, 211.
258	*death: ibid*, 212.
258	*Le Coq et l'Arlequin: ibid.*
260	*"chants":* Sanouillet, I, 230–233.
261	*toy: Comoedia*, December 21, 1920; partially quoted in Sanouillet, I, 60.
262	*change it all: La Jeunesse et le Scandale*, OC, IX, 324.
262	*madman: Opium*, OC, X, 117. CA contains two letters of praise and congratulation from Proust about *Parade* (pp. 70–72). It is not entirely clear which performance or performances they refer to, and neither mentions the Dioscuri.
263	*for Dada:* Sanouillet, I, 179.
263	*Moysès: D'un Ordre Considéré comme une Anarchie*, OC, IX, 212.
263	*street:* Herbert Jacoby, conversation.
264	*rhythm light:* Milhaud, 125.
264	*Verlaine's day: D'un Ordre Considéré comme une Anarchie*, OC, IX, 212.
264	*compromised: ibid*, 212–213.
265	*sauvés: ibid*, 213.
265n	*revenge:* Robert, 48*n*.
266	*turn into him:* François Victor-Hugo and Jean Hugo, conversation and correspondence.
266	*telegraph operator: Carte Blanche*, OC, IX, 125. One could make a pedantic correction of Cocteau by quoting the following: "Le 10 Septembre 1889: inauguration du bureau télégraphique de la troisième plateforme de la Tour — 8 employés et 4 facteurs." (*La Tour Eiffel, Présentée par Le Corbusier*, Texte de C. Cordat, Paris, 1955.)
266	*bridegroom:* also in *Poésies*, OC, III, 171–172.
268	*fun:* EF, 33–34.
268n	*expression of poetry:* OC, VII, 16–17. Reprinted in *Théâtre*, No. 365–366, Oct. 1–Oct. 15, 1966. (See Bibliography, Anouilh.)
270	*back in place.* François Victor-Hugo, conversation.
271	*March 30, 1921:* CA, 45–47.
273	*proper reviews:* Sanouillet, I, 285.
274	*poetic theatre:* Anouilh.
275	*wrote later: Lettre à Jacques Maritain*, OC, IX, 301.
275	*Le Diable au Corps:* Raymond Radiguet, OC, X, 267.
275	*1921:* Cocteau to Valentine and Jean Hugo, December 1, 1921; and see *La Revue de Belles-Lettres* (Genève), No. 1–2, 1969, "Mémorial Jean Cocteau," 11–30.
275	*homework: D'un Ordre Considéré comme une Anarchie*, OC, IX, 219.
275	*what poetry was:* Radiguet, I, 16.
276	*Les Liaisons Dangereuses: ibid*, 484.
276	*heart: Lettre à Jacques Maritain*, OC, IX, 276.
276	*before: Des Beaux-Arts Considérés comme un Assassinat*, OC, X, 190.
277	*brandy:* Hamnett, 195–197.
278	*about Brancusi:* confirmed by Sidney Geist (*q.v.* in Bibliography).
278	*his book:* ES, 92.
279	*December:* Sanouillet, I, 298.
279	*Racine:* in *Opéra*, OC, IV, 158.
280	*the Swedes:* Donald Ogden Stewart, correspondence.

281   *Boeuf:* ES, 91.
282   *married:* Ray, 237.
282   *Rubinstein:* Chastenet, 104.
282   *jazz:* Sachs, II, 178–179.
282   *sick and dissipated:* photograph in Radiguet, II.
284   *everybody else: Souvenir,* OC, XI, 458; JI, 23n.
285   *anarchistic: Souvenir,* OC, XI, 457–458.
285   *Carlier:* CO, 24.
285n   *naïf young man:* Pierre Lagarde, "Philéas Fogg No. 2: Jean Cocteau
        devant soi-même et devant le monde," in *Les Nouvelles Littéraires,* January
        30, 1937.
286   *July 19, 1922:* CA, 47–48.
286   *October 24, 1922:* CA, 48–49.
287   *my story: ibid,* 18.
292   *Antigone: ibid,* 25.
292   *old master: Le Jeunesse et le Scandale,* OC, IX, 320.
292   *I love: Lettre à Jacques Maritain,* OC, IX, 277.
293   *scandale: La Jeunesse et le Scandale,* OC, IX, 320.
293   *Acropolis:* O, 19.
294   *baptized by you:* Bibesco, II.
294   *M. l'Abbé: ibid.*
294   *Cocteau to Abbé Mugnier: ibid.*
295   *Morel:* Proust, I, Vol. 2, 806–807.
295   *them all:* CA, 74.
296   *too often:* CA, 75–76.
296   *soldiers:* PC, I, 132.
296   *Les Mémorables:* Martin du Gard, M., 264.
296n   *realism:* JI, 168–169.
296n   *Man Ray says:* Ray, 177.
297   *musical tragedy:* Honegger, 104.
297   *sugar:* JM, 16.
297   *applauded:* Picasso, OC, IX, 248.
297   *inaccurate: La Jeunesse et le Scandale,* OC, IX, 320.
298   *very well:* Arnaud, 58.
298   *curtain-raiser:* Dullin, 276–277.
298   *actresses: La Jeunesse et le Scandale,* OC, IX, 320.
298   *discover Sophocles:* Sachs, II, 32.
298   *house:* Sachs, II, 236 and *n.*
299   *en famille:* EF, 48. For another version of the episode see *La Revue de
        Belles-Lettres* (Genève), No. 1–2, 1969, pp. 46–47.
299   *Raymond Duncan:* Arnaud, 60–61.
301   *more solemn:* "Jean Cocteau," *Flair,* February 1950, 101–102. Courtesy
        W. H. Auden.
303   *hammer: Le Mystère Laïc,* OC, X, 36–37.
304   *poetize them:* Mr. Reginald Bridgeman, correspondence.
304   *shops: D'un Ordre Considéré comme une Anarchie,* OC, IX, 210–211.
304   *their own:* Mr. Gilbert Seldes, conversation.
305   *famous:* Fay, 58, 273.
305   *for years: Une Entrevue sur la Critique avec Maurice Rouzaud,* OC, IX,
        352.
306   *behavior:* Fay, 244 *et seq.,* 275.
306   *reassured him:* Jacob, II, 142–144.
307   *behind him:* M. Paul Morand, correspondence.
307   *audience:* Kihm, II, 151–152.
308   *later account:* ES, 92.
308   *do things:* Jean Hugo, correspondence.

308	*clan:* A story by Djuna Barnes, "The Little Girl Continues," in *This Quarter*, Vol. 1, No. II, 1925, is said to be based on Radiguet's acquaintance with the Perlmutter sisters. Indicated in *Being Geniuses Together*, by Kay Boyle and Robert McAlmon (New York, 1968), 126*n*.
308	*sinking:* Calvin Tomkins, "Living Well is the Best Revenge," *The New Yorker*, July 28, 1962.
311	*"After Thirty Years":* in *La Parisienne*, December 1953, 1679–1688.
314	*to hotel: Lettre à Jacques Maritain*, OC, IX, 275.
314	*Clair:* ES, 92.
314	*keepsake:* Goesch, 54–55. From a letter from Bernard Grasset to Cocteau, printed in *Concordia*, December 11, 1943.
314	*mild form:* M. René Radiguet, conversation.
314	*rue Piccini:* Valentine Hugo, in *La Parisienne*, as above.
315	*in shock:* ES, 93–94.
315	*boy's death:* Mme. Singer, conversation.
316	*rain:* Hamnett, 299–302.
316	*never write again:* Bibesco, II.
317	*to think of it:* Valentine Hugo, in *La Parisienne*, as above.
317	*caught typhoid:* Mlle. Gabrielle Chanel, conversation.

CHAPTER SIX

321	*son:* unpublished. Courtesy M. H. Matarasso.
321	*chloroform: Lettre à Jacques Maritain*, OC, IX, 277.
322	*false sublime:* Laloy, 278.
322	*sleeping car:* Collaer.
323	*under the door:* Laloy, 278.
323n	*recent book:* Kihm, II, 105.
324	*help me:* D'E, 45.
324	*routine: Opium*, OC, X, 84.
325	*very young:* Dr. Henry Brill.
325	*cocaine:* Sokolova, 219.
326	*Jeanchik:* Lifar, I, 265–266.
326	*loves:* Laloy, 277–278.
327	*disguised* and *passim:* Jean Hugo, conversation and correspondence.
327	*décor:* in *Vocabulaire*, OC, III, 190.
328	*anything else:* JI, 222.
328n	*c'est elle:* noted also by Oxenhandler, *q.v.*, 54–57, for an interesting discussion of *Roméo et Juliette*.
329	*Verona: ibid.*
330	*such things: Lettre à Jacques Maritain*, OC, IX, 277–278.
330	*collaborators:* Cooper, 59.
331	*sans novelty:* Cocteau to Gautier-Vignal, as quoted in Kihm, II, 159.
332	*agitation:* Georges Auric, conversation.
332	*meaningless life:* Poulenc, II, 60.
333	*memories: Lettre à Jacques Maritain*, OC, IX, 278.
344	*doses: ibid*, 282.
335	*Foucauld:* J. Maritain, 10.
335	*Mercutio:* J. Maritain, 12.
335n	*d'acier:* ES, 74.
336	*glass:* in this section, the constant references to the *Lettre à Jacques Maritain*, in OC, IX, will be given simply as *Lettre à J.M.*
336	*lost:* unpublished. Courtesy of M. René Radiguet.
336	*aspirin: Lettre à J.M.*
337	*sympathetic to it:* Massis, II.
338	*crystal: ibid.*

338	*to do so:* J. Maritain, 13.
338	*about God: ibid.*
338	*printed page: Revue des Annales,* No. 18, September 1, 1926.
339	*really am:* OC, IX, 309–341.
339	*ceremony: Comoedia,* March 22, 1925. Courtesy of Jean Hugo.
340	*opposite: Lettre à J.M.*
340	*no use of them:* J. Maritain, 17.
342	*on fire:* Sachs, IV, 115.
342	*every day: ibid,* 139–140.
342	*both of them* and *passim:* Mme. Kandaouroff, Glenway Wescott, both in conversation.
342	*a kiss:* Jean Hugo, as quoted in Kihm, II, 166.
344	*stage designs:* Jean Hugo, diary.
345	*and Picasso: Lettre à J.M.*
345	*none:* R. Maritain, II, 167.
345	*for you:* J. Maritain, 17.
346	*Domini:* R. Maritain, II, 167–168.
347	*at all: Opium,* OC, X, 55.
347	*artifi-ciel:* inscriptions on a drawing in the Museum of Modern Art, New York (1968). Courtesy of William S. Lieberman.
347	*for him alone:* Chanel, Pierre, No. 85.
348	*in Christo: ibid,* No. 86.
348	*his face: Cahiers Paul Claudel,* Vol. III, quoted in Claude Mauriac, Claudel, Copeau et l'Histoire Parallèle des Ames," in *Figaro,* April 18, 1966.
348	*Jews:* Sachs, IV, 163.
349	*intended:* R. Maritain, I, 437.
349	*gave it up:* JI, 48.
350	*ELEVATOR: Opium,* OC, X, 70.
350	*my will:* JI, 51.
350n	*Heurtebise:* my thanks to Norbert Guterman and Jacques Barzun for translation suggestions.
351	*their language:* my thanks to the New York Public Library, Hebrew Division; and to Dr. Sidney B. Hoenig, Yeshiva University.
352	*exit:* R.
353	*and die: Opium,* OC, X, 142–143.
353	"L'Ange Heurtebise": *Secrets de Beauté,* OC, X, 350.
354	*Stravinsky:* JI, 54.
354	*December: ibid,* and Jean Hugo.
355	*Craft:* Stravinsky and Craft, III.
355	*reconciliation:* JI, 53.
356	*Christmas Eve:* J. Maritain, 18.
356	*wrote him:* Sachs, IV, 175.
356n	*have been:* Robert Craft to FS, February 17, 1969.
357	*rue d'Anjou:* Jean Wiener, conversation.
358	*photographer:* Georgel, I, No. 372.
358	*chiseled music: Portraits-Souvenir,* OC, XI, 84.
358	*beard:* JI, 54.
359	*stairs:* Sachs, IV, 183–184.
359	*impending: ibid,* 199.
360	*do you good:* Jacob, I, 24.
360	*intoxication: Opium,* OC, X, 55.
360n	*in the flesh:* the photographs of film stars and the letter from Maurice Sachs were included in the sale of "Dessins, aquarelles et souvenirs provenant de la Collection Jean Bourgoint vendus au profit de la Léproserie de Mokolo" at the Hôtel Drouot, Paris, November 4, 1966. Nos. 24 and 168.

361	*that period:* DP.
361	*are happy:* Jacob, I, 24.
362	*in the water:* PC, II, 21.
363	*own heart?:* Robert H. Byington and Glen E. Morgan, "Mary Butts," in *Art and Literature,* No. 7, Winter, 1965, 173–174.
363n	*understand him:* quoted in Georgel, II, 196.
363n	*programs:* Kihm, II, 179, 199.
364	*disappearing:* Comte Henri de Beaumont, conversation.
371	*very well:* ES, 51–52.
372	*flow of verse* and *passim:* Glenway Wescott, conversation.
372	*Welcome bar:* M. Georges Isarlo, conversation.
372n	*Severini:* Severini, 244–245.
373	*at will:* EF, 71–72.
373	*addict: Opium,* OC, X, 81.
373	*the tale:* Sachs, IV, 203.
374	*untenable:* unpublished. Courtesy Glenway Wescott.
374	*baring her breasts:* letter from Marie-Louise Robinet-Duris to Jean Bourgoint, in sale of the Bourgoint Collection; No. 19, incorrectly catalogued as being from Cocteau. Mistake discovered by Pierre Georgel, confirmed by Jean Hugo; correct identification by Glenway Wescott.
381	*hidden, in it:* courtesy of The Houghton Library, Harvard University.
381	*dirty:* Sanouillet, I, 542.
382	*guise:* to Bernard Fay, as quoted in Kihm, II, 188–189.
382	*uncommunicable:* Pierre Chanel, correspondence.
383	*quick results:* preface to *J'Adore.*
384	*purse strings:* in letter Cocteau-Stravinsky, spring 1927.
385	*French prologues:* Stravinsky and Craft, III, 25.
385	*frequent: ibid.*
386	*eyes out?:* Nicholas Nabokov, conversation.
387	*Antigone: Autour d'"Orphée" et d'"Oedipe,"* OC, IX, 342–345.
387n	*wasn't funny:* Desbordes, I, 117.
388	*Grande Mademoiselle:* Sachs, IV, 293.
389	*if you will:* Mlle. Gabrielle Chanel, conversation.
389n	*recent article.* Hubert Saal, "Kate and Coco," *Newsweek,* November 10, 1969.
390	*referred to:* Wesson Bull, correspondence.
390	*J'Adore: Opium,* OC, X, 130.
391n	*signed 'Jean Desbordes':* Serge Lifar, conversation.
392	*drop Chirico: Une Entrevue sur la Critique,* OC, IX, 354.
392	*interpretation:* Soby, 84.
393	*Fontainebleau:* Kihm, II, 197n.
393	*first week: Opium,* OC, X, 47–168, *passim.*
395	*coûteuse:* Kihm, II, 197.
395	*Cocteau's account:* in *Opium.*
395	*every day:* Georgel, I, No. 403.
396	*started up again:* ES, 21.
396	*dark wood: ibid,* 20.
396n	*start up again:* CO, 18.
397	*revolver:* unpublished. Courtesy of M. Roland Caillaud.
398	*'singular':* CO, 34.
398	*sinister: Opium,* OC, X, 74.
399	*accepted:* Gabriel Astruc to Cocteau, "Samedi 27 Avril 1929." Either the Cocteau letter or the Astruc is misdated. Courtesy of Mlle. Lucienne Astruc.
399	*catch on:* Herbert Jacoby has described the Pigalle as "a 'cold' theatre, a dud from the start, like the Ziegfeld in New York." (Conversation.)
400	*for inspiration:* Miss Ingrid Bergman, correspondence.

401   *basis later:* Kihm, II, 203, quoting Maurice Martin du Gard, *Les Mémorables*, II, and "ocular testimony, particularly that of Lee Miller."

402   *dead mouthpiece:* quoted in Kihm, II, 199.

403   *among them: Excelsior*, February 11, 1923.

405   *championed:* Jean Hugo, December 30, 1929; Mariano, 176–177.

407   *of the film:* EC, 14–16. The translation used here is, with a few changes, the excellent one by Vera Traill in *Cocteau on the Film* (Roy Publishers, New York, 1954), partially reprinted in *Film: An Anthology*, edited by Daniel Talbot (University of California Press, 1966), 218–219.

407   *unreal happenings: Le Sang d'un Poète*, OC, X, 323.

407   *Aesop's fables:* Francis Koval, "Interview with Cocteau," in *Sight and Sound*, Vol. 19 (New Series), August 1950, 229 *et seq.*

407   *turn and talk: Secrets de Beauté*, OC, X, 359.

408   *my aim:* SP, 112–113.

408   *published scenario: idem, passim.*

409   *enjoying themselves:* Lady Penrose (Lee Miller), conversation, London, February 2, 1967.

410   *shocked:* ES, 162.

410   *religion:* René Micha, "L'Age d'Or Aujourd'hui," in *N.R.F.*, April 1, 1967, 937–945.

415   *a sister: Mais Qui Peut Comprendre? Personne*, OC, X, 329.

CHAPTER SEVEN

420   *like a poem:* EF, 92.

428   *décor of his life:* Porel, I, 352.

429   *He kills me* and *passim:* Henry Wibbels, correspondence.

430   *our time:* R. Maritain, II, 216.

431   *at large: Madame de Bray et Madame Dorziat dans "Les Parents Terribles,"* OC, XI, 403.

431   *Léautaud wondered:* Léautaud, II, 347.

432   *convincing: Visites à Maurice Barrès*, OC, IX, 150.

433   *implacable memory:* Cocteau-Gide, October 1936, asking Gide to read the dedication before printing.

433   *Al Brown:* Cocteau's articles appeared in *L'Auto, Ce Soir, Neuf*. See also Georges Peeters, "Al Brown, l'énigme de la force," in *Sport-Digest* (Paris), No. 7, 1949, 103–118; "The Poet and the Boxer" (chiefly extracts and quotations from Peeters' book, *Monstres Sacrés du Ring*, Paris, 1959) with preface by Robert Cantwell, in *Sports Illustrated* (March 2, 1964), 62–72. Also Anon. (Maurice Goudeket), "Al Brown Accuse," in *Confessions* (Paris, January 7, 1937).

434   *Coleridge:* Hayter, *passim.*

435   *people:* Jünger, 131.

435   *mythology:* JM, 29.

437   *friend:* Roger Stéphane, conversation.

437   *not suffer:* Mauriac, II, 91.

438   *curiosity:* unpublished. Courtesy Jean Hugo.

440   *coating: Le Sang d'un Poète*, OC, X, 271.

440   *Germany:* Kihm, II, 277.

441   *new regime:* Kihm, II, 268n.

442   *impatience to begin:* in *La Gerbe*, December 5, 1940 and January 2, 1941. Reproduced in Kihm, II, 420–423.

442   *criminal:* Kihm, II, 273.

443   Jerusalem Liberated: Jünger, *passim.*

444   *Goebbels:* Lifar, III, 225.

444   *no dancing:* Jacques Hébertot, conversation.

444   *St. Honoré:* Deharme, 133.
444   *Opéra:* Lifar, III, 243–244.
445   *shot:* Sartre, II.
445   *too much:* Jean Marais, conversation.
445   *nuns:* JI, 35.
446   *wrote him:* letter in *Biblio,* October 1955.
446   *skull: passim;* Sachs, VII, 7–11; Yvon Belaval, conversation; *Le Figaro,* October 28, 1968, p. 13, Anon., "Maurice Sachs était-il l'agent de la Gestapo 117?" (quoting the *Suddeutscher Zeitung*).
447   *Drancy prison:* Pierre Lagarde, *Max Jacob, Mystique et Martyr* (Paris, 1944), *passim;* Kihm, II, 285.
447   *of the war:* Georges Geffroy, Dr. Charles Berlioz, Harold Acton, conversation; Delarue, 125 *et seq.;* Kihm, II, 286.
451   *Liberation:* Kihm, II, 290.
451   *Lady Diana: Vogue* (French), Hiver 1945–1946.
451   *own eyes:* D'E, 97.
451   *not very dignified:* Nicolson.
452   *always known it:* Gilson, 19.
452   *saved France:* Cocteau to Mary Hoeck, January 15, 1950.
452   *Irish lace:* Marais, 91.
454   *knowing it: L'Equipe de l'Eternel Retour,* OC, XI, 442.
454   *second film there:* JM, 45.
454   *stitch:* Marais, 134 135.
455   *gone:* W. H. Auden, *The Dyer's Hand* (New York, 1962), 469.
455   *puts it:* Bardèche & Brasillach, II, 155.
456   *smile:* Marais, 136–137.
456   *unfashionable: L'Eternel Retour,* OC, X, 342–344.
457   *this one:* D'E, 233–234.
458   *exasperated me:* Marais, 175–176.
458   *animal race:* EC, 89.
459   *mouth:* Marais, 176.
460   *Liberation:* BB, 42 and *passim.*
461   *order: ibid,* 236–238.
461   *silk: ibid,* 229.
462   The Blood of a Poet: Borgal, 178–179.
462   *"Letter to Lord Byron":* copyright, courtesy Random House, Inc.
463   *inside:* Bibesco, II, 50.
463n *end of his days:* Marais, 77.
463n *young God:* Cocteau-Milorad, quoted in Kihm, II, 363.
464n *Paris this:* Duncan, R., 150.
464n *opposed to that:* letter in catalogue of Charles Hamilton, April, 1967.
466   *could do:* Jean Hugo, correspondence.
467   *essay: Le Mythe du Greco,* OC, X, 305.
467n *a certain resemblance:* Marais, 38.
475   *owed it to her:* Marais, 182–183.
476   *our time:* Kael, II, 262.
476   *were born:* Nicole Stéphane, conversation; Cocteau's inscription in her copy of *Soixante Dessins pour Les Enfants Terribles* (Paris, 1935).
477   *nude:* M, 219.
478   *ROLLEIFLEX THINKS:* LA, 20–21; in *Flair,* February 1920, 101–102.
478   *FIDELEMENT COCTEAU:* Harry Levin, correspondence.
479   *that one:* Maria Casarès, "La Comédienne face à la camera," in *Théâtre d'Aujourd'hui.* (Date of issue not given; reproduced in French and English in *World Theatre,* Vol. 8, No. 1, Spring 1959, 51–52.)

480   *one finger:* EC, 39.
480   *filming of* Orphée: *ibid, passim.*
480n   *same time:* Kihm, II, 308.
481   Paris-Match: Kihm, II, 321.
482   vox populi: Francis Koval, "Interview with Cocteau," in *Sight and Sound,* Vol. 19 (New Series), August 1950, 229 *et seq.*
483   *judge the poet:* Publicity folder (in English) distributed by Discina International Film Corporation, New York. Original French not available. A few changes made in the translation.
483   *film-maker's language:* quoted by Claude Mauriac in "Jean Cocteau et le Cinématographe," in *Empreintes,* May-June-July 1950, 55.
484   *of old:* BB, 250–252.
487   *escape:* Denise Van Moppès, "Des Drogues au Lépreux, Mort d'un Enfant Terrible," in *Le Monde,* June 22, 1966.
490   *Geraldine Chaplin:* conversation.
494   *Virgin:* M. René L. Varin, conversation.
495   *Pauline Kael:* Kael, I, 132.
495   *Robert Craft:* Stravinsky and Craft, IV, 244; Robert Craft, conversation.
499   *debt:* Van Moppès, *op. cit.*

Acknowledgments

ALTHOUGH whenever possible my references to Cocteau's works are to their texts as printed in the *Oeuvres Complètes*, let me thank the following publishers for their permission to quote from texts by Cocteau that they originally issued and of which they hold the copyright:

Gallimard: *Les Mariés de la Tour Eiffel; Poésie 1916–1923; Le Fantôme de Marseille; Mon Premier Voyage; La Fin du Potomak; Poésie Critique; Thomas l'Imposteur, Cahiers Jean Cocteau I.*

Stock: *Lettre à Jacques Maritain; Le Rappel à l'Ordre; Opium; L'Ange Heurtebise.*

Grasset: *Journal d'un Inconnu; Lettre aux Américains;* preface to Raymond Radiguet, *Le Bal du Comte d'Orgel; Portraits-Souvenir.* (In connection with the last named, Peter Owen, Ltd., of London, has asked me to mention the existence of an English translation, entitled *My Contemporaries,* published by them in the British Commonwealth and by the Chilton Publishing Company in the United States.)

Editions du Rocher: *La Difficulté d'Etre; Le Sang d'un Poète.*

Librairie des Quatre Chemins: *Le Mystère Laïc.*

Editions André Bonne: *Entretiens autour du Cinématographe* (ed. André Fraigneau).

Plon: *Le Cordon Ombilical.*

Editions Tallandier: *Entretiens avec Roger Stéphane.*

I also thank the following publishers and individuals for permission to quote from the following works, of which they hold the copyright:

Gallimard: Guillaume Apollinaire, *Chroniques d'Art* (ed. Breunig); Maurice Sachs, *La Décade de l'Illusion;* André Gide, *Journal;* Paul Morand, *Journal d'un Attaché d'Ambassade;* J.-E. Blanche, *Cahiers d'un Artiste.*

Gallimard with Louis Aragon: Louis Aragon, *Les Lilas et les Roses.*

Révue Générale Belge: Princesse Marthe Bibesco, "Jean Cocteau et son Etoile" (Décembre 1963).

Plon: Jacques Porel, *Fils de Réjane.*

Jeune Parque: Maurice Rostand, *Confessions d'un Demi-Siècle.*

Grasset: Gabriel Astruc, *Le Pavillon des Fantômes.*

Librairie Académique Perrin: Bernard Faÿ, *Les Précieux.*

Albin Michel: Adrienne Monnier, *Rue de l'Odéon.*

Desclée de Brouwer: Raïssa Maritain, *Le Journal de Raïssa.*

Index

(*This index was prepared by Georgina Johnston.*)